HOLOCAUST LITERATURE

HOLOCAUST LITERATURE

AN ENCYCLOPEDIA OF WRITERS AND THEIR WORK

Volume II
Lerner to Zychlinsky
Index

S. Lillian Kremer
Editor

Routledge
New York London

Editorial Staff
Project Editor: Laura Smid
Production Editor: Jeanne Shu
Production Manager: Anthony Mancini, Jr.
Production Director: Dennis Teston
Director of Development Reference: Kate Aker
Publishing Director: Sylvia Miller

Published in 2003 by
Routledge
29 West 35 Street
New York, NY 10001-2299
www.routledge.ny.com

Published in Great Britain by
Routledge
11 New Fetter Lane
London EC4P 4EE
www.routledge.uk.com

Routledge is an imprint of Taylor & Francis Books, Inc.

10 9 8 7 6 5 4 3 2 1

Printed on acid-free, 250-year-life paper

Manufactured in the United States of America

Acknowledgements on page 1451.

Library of Congress Cataloging-in-Publication Data
Holocaust literature : an encyclopedia of writers and their work / S. Lillian Kremer, editor.
v. cm.
Contents: Vol. 1. A-L—vol. 2. M-Z.
ISBN 0-415-92985-7 (set : alk. paper)—ISBN 0-415-92983-0 (vol. 1 : alk. paper)—
ISBN 0-415-92984-9 (vol. 2 : alk. paper)
1. Holocaust, Jewish (1939–1945), in literature—Encyclopedias. 2. Holocaust, Jewish
(1939–1945)—Bio-bibliography. I. Kremer, S. Lillian, 1939-

PN56.H55 H66 2002
809'.93358—dc21

2002023694

CONTENTS

MOTTI LERNER

(1949–)

MICHAEL TAUB

MOTTI LERNER WAS born on 16 September 1949 in Zichron Yaacov, Israel, into a family of secular, left-wing Zionists. He studied theater at the Hebrew University in Jerusalem, in London, and in the United States. His major works include *Kastner* (1985), *Waiting for Messiah* (1987), *Exile in Jerusalem* (1990), *In the Dark* (1992), *Temporary Kingship* (1993), and *Pollard* (1995). Lerner has also written scripts for several successful television programs. Lerner was neither a first- nor a second-generation Holocaust survivor. His parents, Arie and Dvora, came to Palestine long before the war in Europe. Lerner married and he and his wife had three children.

Israel (Rezso) Kastner

The play *Kastner* is a critical examination of the controversial Holocaust-era negotiations between Hungarian Jews and the Nazis. In 1943, Zionist organizations in Hungary established a "rescue committee" to save and aid thousands of refugees fleeing Nazi-occupied areas of Eastern and Central Europe. Otto Komoly, the head of the Hungarian Zionist organizations, was elected to head this committee. Joel Brand and Dr. Rudolph "Rezso" Kastner served as his deputies.

With the German invasion of Hungary in March 1944, Adolph Eichmann, head of Section 4-B of the Reich security main office (Jewish Affairs), arrived in Budapest to oversee the deportation from Hungary of Eastern Europe's last sizable Jewish community. The 'rescue committee' responded on three separate fronts, negotiating with the Hungarian government (Komoly), with the Germans (Kastner), and with neutral governments such as Sweden and Switzerland (Moshe Kraus). Through Dieter Wisliceny, Eichmann's deputy, the Germans offered to spare Jewish lives in return for dollars and military material. Until the middle of May the rescue committee had transferred partial sums of money out of a total $2 million the Germans had demanded to save the entire Jewish population of Hungary.

As transports to Auschwitz were pulling out of Budapest's train station, by some estimates carrying between 10,000 to 12,000 deportees a day, Joel Brand and Israel Kastner continued their rescue efforts. Brand traveled to Istanbul to meet with Jewish leaders and arrange a deal involving trading Jews for military trucks. On 30 June 1944 a train with 1,684 people whom Kastner did manage to save left for Switzerland. Several times in 1944 Kastner had traveled to various European capitals (with a German passport), to negotiate "blood for money" arrangements with various German, Jewish, and other officials.

In the famous Nuremberg trials of Nazi leaders after the war, Kastner served as a witness for the defense at the trial of Kurt Becher, a German officer with whom he had successfully negotiated the release of some Hungarian Jews. Kastner's wartime activities became the subject of a trial in Israel, where he lived after the war, worked for the government, and was active in Mapai, a left-wing political party. In January 1954 Malkiel Grunwald, a member of a rival, right-wing organization, filed a lawsuit against Kastner, charging that he collaborated with the Nazis, that he rescued mainly friends and wealthy Jews, that he colluded with the Nazis in repressing the truth about Auschwitz, thus practically eliminating any possible resistance to what was to unfold in Hungary—the extermination of 70 percent of its Jewish population (Dawidowicz, pp. 515–517).

In June 1955 the Israeli courts concluded that "Kastner had sold his soul to the Devil," but that he committed no crime. On 4 March 1957 three members of a right-wing political organization shot Kastner in front of his Tel Aviv home. He died eleven days later. The following year, the Israeli Supreme Court declared that

"Kastner did not collaborate with the Nazis." The historian Yehuda Bauer asserted in 1985 that Kastner was right to believe that his approach—negotiating with Eichmann, pressing for concessions, delaying transports, rejecting armed resistance—was the only one that under the circumstances had any chance of producing any positive results.

The Political Aftermath

A great deal has happened between Kastner's trial and Motti Lerner's 1985 stage interpretation of the events. Only four years after Kastner's death, in 1961, Israel and the world revisited the *Shoah* horrors as the Eichmann trial unfolded in Jerusalem. Once again, as in the earlier Nuremberg trials, the key issues centered on responsibility for the atrocities committed. The most chilling line, and one that everyone who watched or listened to the trial remembers, was Eichmann's reply to the prosecution's charges of genocide: "I only followed orders."

While Eichmann's guilt was easy to ascertain, the situation of some surviving Jewish officials, mainly members of the *Judenrat* (the Jewish councils), was much more problematic. Was their work with the Germans in the ghettos an act of cooperation for the sake of the common good, or was it collaboration with the enemy? Did these officials (some appointed by the Germans) help the Nazis carry out their murderous designs in order to save their own skins? Did their involvement actually diminish suffering and slow down the Nazi death machine? In Israel, some of these difficult, and often controversial, questions were tackled by Ben Zion Tomer's 1963 play *Yaldey Hatzel* (*Children of the Shadows*). Except for Tomer's moderately popular play, the Israeli national narrative during the early decades of statehood featured the enemy (Germans and their helpers) on one side and Jewish victims on the other, as prominence was given to armed Jewish resistance—the Warsaw Ghetto Uprising, the Jewish partisans, and Hanna Senesh's martyrdom.

Lerner's play, based on Kastner's activities during the *Shoah*, reflects not only an artistic interpretation of his role in the Hungarian rescue efforts, but the dynamics of contemporary Israeli-Palestinian tensions. The 1967 Six Day War ushered in several years of national euphoria. However, the occupation of a large Palestinian population in Gaza and the West Bank gradually began to chip away at the Israeli self-image of a morally upright people engaged in a constant struggle for survival, protecting itself against external mortal dangers. A gradual change from an unblamable people to a self-doubting one was reflected in literature and drama. Israeli Holocaust drama of the 1980s has in large part been shaped by a series of traumatic events that took place a few years earlier: the disastrous 1973 Yom Kippur War, the controversial Lebanon invasion of 1982 (Israel's "Vietnam"), and the Intifada, the uprising of Palestinians on the West Bank and Gaza in the mid 1980s (Taub, 1997, p. 133). The accumulated effect of these events has been, among others, the loss of confidence in military power, a reexamination of claims of moral superiority in the Palestinian crisis, and a reevaluation of the *Shoah* and the events leading up to the formation of the state in 1948.

This, then, is the political background against which Lerner's 1985 play *Kastner* is to be understood. In earlier decades, as the state was forging an identity, it was necessary, perhaps even desirable, to "make national heroes out of brave soldiers like the leaders of the Warsaw Ghetto Uprising rather than of morally ambiguous ghetto leaders like Jacob Gens (in Vilna), and negotiators like Kastner in Budapest" (Michael Taub, quoted in Abramson, p. 167). In 1985, however, the new realities in Israel had prepared the ground for a reevaluation of hitherto controversial or much maligned figures ("collaborators") like Kastner. The topic of "collaboration" and the *Judenrat*, plays about heroes who never held a gun in their hand, imperfect heroes, became popular on the Israeli stage within a short span of seven years (1984–1991). Lerner's *Kastner* shared the spotlight with three other plays on the same subject, namely Joshua Sobol's well-known Vilna ghetto trilogy *Ghetto* (1984), *Adam* (1990), and *Underground* (1991).

As Dan Laor points out, Lerner's play about Kastner is the culmination of several other, earlier works about this prominent Hungarian Jew. In 1982 Israeli television commissioned Yehuda Kaveh to produce a documentary about Kastner, and in 1984, David Levine, then director of Habima, Israel's National Theater, collaborated on a trial drama named *Reszo*, "which challenged the previously accepted notion about Kastner and called for his rehabilitation" (Laor, 1998, pp. 103–104). But it was Lerner's 1985 drama, and the subsequent television series (1994), that drew the most attention to Kastner, his actions during the Holocaust, his trial in the 1950s, and his reputation as a "Nazi collaborator."

Kastner

Lerner's protagonist is an ambitious man, an activist determined to save as many lives as possible. He works tirelessly to convince Jewish leaders that resistance to the Nazis means suicide, all along pressing Eichmann and his deputies to spare lives in return for money and the promise of legal assistance if and when the Nazis face the wrath of the Allies' courts. While it is true that Kastner enjoys the night life, extramarital affairs, and dining in fine restaurants with Eichmann's deputies, in the end what counts is the fact that his actions, including fraternizing with the devil, result in the rescue of 1,684 people. It is not clear how many thousands more escape death as a result of his efforts. While some in the *Judenrat* question his work, Kastner believes that when lives are involved all else is immaterial. In short, Lerner's hero is obsessed with saving lives. He is a flawed individual. He confronts the Germans head on and the Germans tolerate his chutzpa because they believe he can be of use to them, especially in helping them quell rumors about a mass deportation to Auschwitz. While no one disputes Kastner's role in saving hundreds of lives, the historical figure was far from the elegant, eloquent, worldly, lady killer presented in this particular stage version. Kastner's reliance on Eichmann's word (his promise to spare a certain number of Jews) may seem naïve in retrospect; however, in the context of the times—the Russians fast approaching Hungary and divisions within the highest German ranks as to the wisdom of a "Final Solution" with the end in sight—there is no doubt that his assessment of the situation was valid.

In one of the play's typical dramatic exchanges with Freudiger (of the *Judenrat*), Kastner reacts to the charges of immorality in dealing with the devil: "I am the one who is contaminated with his (the devil's) slime when I come to offer you things in his name. I am doing all that, not you! But when he offers to release Jews, I'm willing to do business with him, even for a single Jew. And when he offers me a chance to save a million Jews, who am I to say 'no more deals with the devil'? You, who are supposed to be the leaders of these Jews, who gives you the right to say a thing like that?" (*Kastner*, p. 250). It is through such exchanges that the viewer becomes familiar with the various antagonists and their views on how best to deal with the Germans and the Hungarian fascists.

As the play indicates, this Jewish leader puts life before anything else. Lerner's subtext suggests that while true that heroic, armed resistance helps preserve Jewish pride and that morally pure fighters who died "*al kidush hashem*" (sanctifying God's name) must be honored, in the final analysis, one must consider how many Jews live because of heroic actions and how many because of the less-than-honorable actions of Kastner and others like him. In the political environment of 1985 Israel, Lerner's challenge to conventional narratives' glorifying only the fighters of the resistance resonated with the viewing public. In an Israel torn by a controversial Vietnam-like war in Lebanon, a Palestinian uprising in the making, and deep divisions over the fate of the occupied territories, Kastner's call for pragmatism and respect for human life over idealism and nationalism found many listening with great interest.

Reactions to *Kastner*

The Israeli public had mixed reactions to Lerner's play. The more liberal among them delighted in Lerner's rehabilitation of this rather controversial figure in Israeli society. Kastner's family was equally pleased with the play's sanctioning of Kastner's actions. Some reviews pointed to the implicit parallel between Kastner's dealing with the devil and Israel's need to deal with its own devil for the sake of peace, namely the PLO leadership. Many on the right side of the political spectrum denounced Lerner and voiced displeasure with what they felt was a disgraceful glorification of the activities of a self-serving collaborator. Theater critics praised the importance of the play for historical reasons and for daring to revisit some of the more controversial issues related to the *Shoah*. They were almost unanimous in criticizing Lerner's didactic tone, the play's excessive length, and its lack of sufficient tension and drama. The play is written in realistic style like a documentary, with scenes rapidly following each other and is reminiscent of Brecht's "Epic Theater" style of the 1930s. The issues raised in *Kastner* were hotly debated across the pages of Israel's newspapers, featuring famous historians, survivors, Kastner's children, and others. If nothing else it surely rehabilitated Kastner in the eyes of most Israelis, who were taught that collaborators were "cowards" and "traitors."

Bibliography

Primary Sources

Kastner. 1985.
Waiting for Messiah. 1987.
Chevley Mashiach (*Messiah's Pain*). 1988.
Elsa (Exile in Jerusalem). 1990.
In the Dark. 1992.
Temporary Kingship. 1993.
Star (*Autumn*). 1993.
Pollard. 1995.
Kastner. Translated by Imre Goldstein. In *Israeli Holocaust Drama*, Edited by Michael Taub. Syracuse, N.Y.: Syracuse University Press, 1996.

Secondary Sources

Abramson, Glenda. *Drama and Ideology in Modern Israel*. Cambridge: Cambridge University Press, 1998.

Bauer, Yehuda. "Yoter Malach mi Shed" (More of an Angel than a Devil). *Davar* (1 August 1985).

Ben Zvi, Linda, ed. *Theater in Israel*. Ann Arbor: University of Michigan Press, 1996.

Dawidowicz, Lucy. *The War Against the Jews: 1933–1945*. New York: Bantam Books, 1981.

Elon, Amos. *Timetable: A Novel About One Man's Mission to Rescue Hungary's Jews*. New York: Doubleday, 1980.

Feingold, Ben Ami. *Hashoa Be-Drama Haivrit. The Holocaust in Hebrew Drama*. Tel Aviv: Hakibutz Hameuchad, 1989. Details in novelistic fashion Bran's mission to Istanbul to meet with Western Jewish leaders and discuss Eichmann's proposal to exchange lives for military vehicles.

Isser, Edward. *Stages of Annihilation: Theatrical Representations of the Holocaust*. Madison, N.J.: Fairleigh Dickinson University Press, 1997.

Laor, Dan. "Theatrical Interpretations of the *Shoah*: Image and Counter-Image." In *Staging the Holocaust*. Edited by Claude Schumacher. Cambridge: Cambridge University Press, 1998.

Skloot, Robert. *The Darkness We Carry: The Drama of the Holocaust*. Madison: University of Wisconsin Press, 1988.

Sobol, Joshua. *Ghetto*. Tel Aviv, Israel: Or Am, 1984. Adapted by Jack Viertel. In *Plays of the Holocaust*. Edited by Elinor Fuchs. New York: Theater Communications Group, 1987.

———. *Adam*. Tel Aviv, Israel: Or Am, 1989. Trans. Ron Jenkins. In *Israeli Holocaust Drama*.

———. *Bemartef* (Underground). Tel Aviv, Israel: Or Am, 1991. Adapted by Ron Jenkins. *Theater* (Summer–Fall 1991).

Taub, Michael. "The Challenge to Popular Myth and Conventions in Recent Israeli Drama." *Modern Judaism* 17 (1997): 133.

———, ed. *Modern Israeli Drama*. Portsmouth, U.K.: Heinemann Press, 1993.

Tomer, Ben Tzion. *Yaldei Ha-tzel. Children of the Shadows*. Tel Aviv, Israel: Amikam, 1963. In *Israeli Holocaust Drama*. Edited by Michael Taub. Syracuse, N.Y.: Syracuse University Press, 1996.

PRIMO LEVI
(1919–1987)

ROBERT S. C. GORDON

PRIMO LEVI'S WORKS of testimony, narrative, poetry, and essays about his time in Auschwitz are among the most widely read and lauded of all writing on the Holocaust. Perhaps no other survivor wrote of these unbearable events with such accessible economy, elegant wit, and humane power over such a long period of time. And if he started as one of many survivors who turned to writing in the immediate aftermath of the outrage they had endured, only to be ignored by most around them, the literary quality of his work has meant that he has increasingly come to be regarded as one of the essential voices of twentieth-century literature.

In an oeuvre forged over four decades—between 1946 and his death in 1987—Levi demonstrated an extraordinary capacity to confront, with directness and persistence, the complexities of human cruelty and human suffering he had learned firsthand in Auschwitz. His readers consistently found in him a sane, if troubled, voice to guide them through the quagmire of moral and historical dilemmas posed by the Final Solution. They also found in him a builder of bridges between the horrors of the camps and the fragile values of the liberal, modern, secular world to which he belonged, and which had been pushed so close to annihilation by National Socialism. Through him, many readers—Jewish and non-Jewish alike—could see themselves living and thinking through the events he described. This won him not only praise, but also an intense, even intimate engagement with his readers. At his death—presumed by almost everyone who knew him, including his close family, to have been by suicide—many wrote of a sense of bereavement, of the loss of a friend or companion as much as of a great writer.

Life

Primo Levi was born on 31 July 1919 on the Corso Re Umberto, in Turin, northwest Italy, in the apartment where he was to live his entire life, except for the period immediately before, during, and immediately after Auschwitz. He was the first child of Cesare Levi and Ester (née Luzzati). His sister, Anna Maria, was born two years later. The family belonged to the small and largely assimilated Jewish community of Turin, with roots back into the Sephardic communities of Spain and southern France that had moved into Piedmont in the sixteenth century (Levi describes some of his eccentric extended family in the "Argon" section of *The Periodic Table*).

Levi attended the Liceo Massimo d'Azeglio, a school once famous as a seedbed of liberal antifascist views, although somewhat tamed by the time of Levi's arrival in 1934. His father, an electrical engineer, had been close to the positivist circles of the city's intelligentsia (which included the criminologist Cesare Lombroso), and Primo followed him in his voracious, eclectic reading and in his rejection of the humanist education on offer at the *liceo*. He also acquired a taste for mountaineering as another way out of the stultifying school curriculum. He opted to study chemistry at Turin University. Despite the obstacles set in his path by the antisemitic 1938 Race Laws—modeled on the Nuremberg Laws but in certain respects even more repressive—he managed to graduate in 1941 in the physics faculty. In the same year, his father died.

Levi then spent a period working in Milan and frequenting a lively group of friends, but with the fall of fascism in July 1943 and Italy's armistice with the Allies in September, everything changed. He joined the armed resistance against the rump Fascists and the Nazi occupiers of northern Italy, but he was betrayed and captured almost immediately. Preferring to declare himself a Jew rather than to risk execution as a partisan, he was sent from the Valle d'Aosta to a holding camp at Fossoli where, in February 1944, he was deported to Auschwitz. On arrival there he was selected as fit to work and sent to the satellite camp Auschwitz III-

Monowitz, where he remained until liberation by the Red Army in January 1945, having been left behind by the evacuating Germans to die of scarlet fever. His first book, *Se questo è un uomo* (*If This Is a Man*, also published as *Survival in Auschwitz*, 1947)—perhaps the greatest single work of Holocaust testimony—is an account of his eleven months in the camp. He reached Turin again in October 1945 after a long, halting journey home described in *La tregua* (*The Truce*, 1963).

On his return, he immediately began writing stories and poems about his time in Auschwitz. With the doctor and fellow deportee Leonardo De Benedetti, he completed a medical report on the sanitary conditions in Monowitz that they had drafted for the Russians while in the holding camps at Katowice. The paper appeared in a prestigious medical journal, *Minerva medica*, in 1946, and is significant as Levi's first piece of published work. Several of his stories were published at the time in small journals, and they gradually came together to form a book, published as *Se questo è un uomo* in 1947 by a small, short-lived publishing house, De Silva, run by a well-known antifascist activist Franco Antonicelli. This book had been rejected by several more prestigious publishers, including Einaudi in Turin, where the writers Natalia Ginzburg and Cesare Pavese were editorial consultants. It was praised by a small number of reviewers (including the young Italo Calvino) and won a certain reputation within Turin, but had little wider impact.

Levi meanwhile started a career as an industrial chemist and manager, mostly in a paint factory outside Turin, where he worked for thirty years. He also settled into domestic life with his wife, Lucia (née Morpurgo), whom he married in 1947. They had a daughter, Lisa, in 1948 and a son, Renzo, in 1957. Levi stopped writing with regularity, although he continued to conceive and sketch out stories and poems throughout this phase of apparent silence. He traveled occasionally for work, and, from the mid-1950s onwards, spoke constantly in public about his Holocaust experiences and about his books. His life was to remain remarkably stable from the late 1940s onward.

In 1955, with interest in the Holocaust growing, Einaudi reconsidered their original verdict and offered Levi a contract for a second edition of *Se questo è un uomo*. He made a small but significant number of changes, polishing the style and adding several new sequences. After a delay, the book was republished in 1958 and was well received. The 1958 edition, the one read today (with certain additions), was the foundation for Levi's extraordinary subsequent reputation. It was almost immediately translated into English, appearing in 1959–1960 in Britain in the powerful version of the young British historian Stuart Woolf, who worked with Levi on the translation in a series of visits to his apartment on the Corso Re Umberto. In Italy, this and other books (beginning with *La tregua*) were soon adopted as set texts in high schools, of immense importance in explaining the depth of contact between Levi and Italian readers over the following decades, despite the slightly faint praise of the literary elite. The success of *Se questo è un uomo* and the encouragement of friends persuaded Levi to write more assiduously, and in 1963 he completed and published *La tregua*, which won a literary prize and launched him into a career as a writer *per se* for the first time. In 1966 and 1971 respectively, he published two collections of science-fantasy stories, *Storie naturali* (*Natural Histories*; initially under a pseudonym, Damiano Malabaila, as he feared alienating readers who expected only solemn, Holocaust-related work from him) and *Vizio di forma* (*Formal Defect*).

In 1975 he published *Il sistema periodico* (*The Periodic Table*), an autobiography loosely structured around the chemical elements. Each chapter centers on a real, fictional, or metaphorical encounter with an element at a certain time of Levi's life. His next work, *La chiave a stella* (*The Wrench*, 1978), was, by contrast, very local in its style and theme (although not in geographical setting): it consisted of stories of an industrial rigger, Libertino Faussone, who, in an odd mixture of Piedmontese dialect and technical jargon, tells of his epic and intimate struggles with bridges, dams, and the like. And yet, as several interviews show, Levi saw *The Wrench* as closely related to *The Periodic Table*, and incorporated his most cherished values into both books.

The Wrench, set in an unnamed Soviet town (in reality based on Togliattigrad, which Levi had visited for work), also stands as a farewell meditation on his working career: as he was composing it he was also going into retirement to become, finally, a full-time writer. His only full-fledged work of fiction, *Se non ora, quando?* (*If Not Now, When?*), the story of a Jewish partisan band in World War II, followed in 1982, winning two prestigious prizes but also some criticism for its "over-researched" reconstruction of the Ashkenazic culture of Eastern Europe.

By the 1980s, Levi already had a devoted but relatively small following abroad, but when *The Periodic Table* was translated in the mid–1980s, it was hailed in America especially—Saul Bellow called it "a necessary book"—and it was responsible for propelling Levi's international reputation to new levels. All his work was rapidly translated in the following years, and he made a number of trips abroad, including to America and Britain. Back in Italy, his fame and his retirement facilitated a stream of publications of collected and new essays, stories, poems, and articles. The year 1981 saw *Lilít e altri racconti*, containing essays, camp stories, and science-fiction stories, and *La ricerca delle radici* (*The Search for Roots*), a fascinating annotated anthology of his favorite and formative books. He was more a public figure now, writing for the Turin newspaper *La Stampa* and turning out prefaces to a whole series of important books and exhibitions about the Holocaust (including work by Yitzhak Katzenelson, Leon Poliakov, Edith Bruck, Hermann Langbein, Rudolf Höss and the television series *Holocaust*), an activity that made him a key figure in encouraging the translation and dissemination of Holocaust-related material in Italy. Between 1983 and 1985 translations of Kafka's *The Trial* and two books by Claude Lévi-Strauss appeared. His collected poems appeared in 1984 under the Coleridgean title *Ad ora incerta* (At an Uncertain Hour) and in the following year came his most characteristically eclectic and curious volume of essays, *L'altrui mestiere* (*Other People's Trades*). More of his articles for *La Stampa* were collected for the 1986 volume *Racconti e saggi* (Stories and essays).

A year before his death, he drew together his reflections on Auschwitz in his most considered, but also most troubled book, *I sommersi e i salvati* (*The Drowned and the Saved*). These essays, prepared over a period of several years, revisit many of the moral and historical questions raised by the Holocaust that had concerned him for so long, and are models in humane, ethical meditation. At the same time, they contain moments of genuine anguish, anger, and ambivalence. Indeed, the acceleration in publishing and growth in public profile in the 1980s was by no means without pressures and anxieties for Levi. He was vexed by periods of writer's block, frustrated by the distortions in his reception abroad (especially in America, where he felt he was being lionized but also absorbed into a conception of the European Jewish writer that he knew he did not fit, only then to be criticized for not fitting it), and deeply concerned by pernicious negationist and "revisionist" accounts of the Holocaust appearing in France and Germany. He was also increasingly disillusioned with speaking to the young: he felt they no longer understood why what he had to say was important. Finally, he was depressed by his own state of health and that of his aging mother and mother-in-law. Nevertheless, he remained active, talking, writing, and planning future work (including a new novel, tentatively entitled *Il doppio legame* (The Double Bind), until his presumed suicide on 11 April 1987 at the age of sixty-seven.

If This Is a Man

If This Is a Man was written by a young man of twenty-seven, struggling to come to terms with his deportation and his survival. He was unsure of the future and strangely alienated from those around him at home, who had lived through equally dramatic but profoundly different experiences of war and civil war during his absence. He immediately felt the impulse to tell stories to family, friends, and strangers, and to write them down (as he had at Monowitz, where he scribbled notes even though he knew they would be lost and could easily cost him his life). His resonant lifelong identification with Coleridge's Ancient Mariner, forced to tell his "ghastly tale" to all who pass before him, begins here. During 1946 and 1947, however, as he told and retold the stories that were to become *If This Is a Man*, there occurred in his relation to his writing a change that was to be fundamental to his future oeuvre, a move from catharsis and memorial to articulate reflection and a careful search for understanding. He describes the process in *The Periodic Table*:

> [At first] what I had seen and suffered burnt within me; I felt nearer to the dead than the living and guilty simply for being a man, because men had built Auschwitz and Auschwitz had swallowed up millions of human beings . . . I thought I could cleanse myself by telling the story . . . [Gradually, however] the writing itself turned into something different, no longer a painful journey of convalescence, no longer a way of begging for compassion and friendly faces from my solitude, but rather a lucid work of construction. I was like the chemist who weighs and separates, measures and judges by certain indices, and works hard to answer questions why (Opere, i, 870, 872–873) translated by Robert S. C. Gordon).

Clearheaded analysis never quite eliminates the anger and pain in Levi, however, pace too many descriptions of him as the epitome of the calm, rational eye. Both sides run throughout his work and through *If This Is a Man* in particular. This and other internal conflicts led Levi more than once to compare himself to the figure of a centaur. The book's two prefatory texts—its poem-epigraph and preface—neatly illustrate the split. In the former—a paraphrase of the *Shema* prayer—Levi's anger is Mosaic, auguring those who do not heed him "that your house might crumble, / that illness might impede you / that your children might turn their faces from you." (*Opere*, i, 3) In the latter, by contrast, he offers his work modestly as "a set of materials for the calm study of certain aspects of the human mind."

The main body of *If This Is a Man* comprises seventeen chapters. It does not offer a detailed, sequential chronicle of events in the camp. Chapters are instead episodic and largely self-contained (one of Levi's instinctive talents was for the resonant closing off of a chapter or episode). They are shaped principally around either sketches of people he encountered or around meditations on fear, humiliation, violence, shame, happiness, survival, and the like. In neither case is Levi's testimony notably introspective; indeed, his other-centered style of storytelling is one of his most distinctive characteristics. Thus "A Good Day" relates a rare set of circumstances that led to Levi's work group having time to rest and eat, and in moving through those precious hours of calm, the chapter turns into an ironic meditation on the nature of happiness and freedom (". . . for a few hours, then, we can be unhappy, just like free men"). The chapter that gave Levi the title of his last book, "The Drowned and the Saved," uses a series of character vignettes to pose the tricky moral-ethological question whether certain character types were predisposed to survive or not.

The timeless quality of the book is no accident: By dulling or localizing the sense of narrative sequence or suspense, the book takes a turn toward a range of ethical, psychological, political (in a loose sense), or anthropological issues that are veiled behind that phrase from the preface, "a calm study of certain aspects of the human mind" (*Opere*, i, 5). But timelessness was also an essential and alienating reality of camp life itself: the sense of repetitiveness and stasis engendered by a system of oppression where every day brought the same struggle for food and rest, the same crushing work, the same fear of random assault, and a regimentation bordering on the absurd. This is perhaps best encapsulated in a passage from "The Events of the Summer": "[H]ours, days, months spilled out sluggishly from the future into the past, always too slowly, a valueless and superfluous material, of which we sought to rid ourselves as soon as possible. . . . For us, history had stopped" (*Opere*, i, 113).

Despite all this, Levi crafts a loose sense of progress through the months and the seasons in *If This Is a Man*. The first three chapters—"The Journey," "On the Bottom," and "Initiation" (the latter added for the 1958 edition)—are transitional, taking us on the terrible physical and psychological journey from Italy to the camps, by way of the cattle trucks, the rituals of selection and initiation, the continual and total bewilderment of Levi and his companions, through to an ambivalent first lesson in moral survival given by the Austrian officer Steinlauf:

> that precisely because the Lager was a great machine to reduce us to beasts, we must not become beasts; that even in this place one can survive, and therefore one must want to survive, to tell the story, to bear witness; and that to survive we must force ourselves to save at least the skeleton, the scaffolding, the form of civilisation (*Opere*, i, 35).

It is a moving moment, but also one that Levi questions, seeing in Steinlauf's noble stance at least a hint of the Teutonic rigidity of pure principle that, in perverted form, subtended the *Lager* itself. This nuanced self-positioning and openness to doubt is characteristic of Levi's mode of inquiry throughout his work.

If the first three chapters frame *If This Is a Man* at one end, it is framed at the close by its two final chapters, "The Last One" and "The Story of Ten Days." The former, with its story of the hanging of the last resister in the camp in front of the massed ranks of prisoners, including Primo and his close companion Alberto, is self-consciously eschatological, as its title suggests. It marks the nearing collapse of the Nazi regime, but also the darkest depths of abjection felt by Levi and his fellows, stripped of all will to resist. Immediately following, "The Story of Ten Days" describes in diary form the days of appalling limbo—"the world of death and phantoms,"—between the Germans' departure and the arrival of the Red Army, when Levi and a small number of sick inmates are left behind to die rather than forced, like thousands of others, onto the death marches toward Germany. The sequence is terrifying and grotesque, as Levi and his companions are forced to choose between sharing what little food they have among themselves or dying by sharing it with the many clamoring at their ward door. Thus "the work of bestial degradation" (*Opere*, i, 168) continues with a sort of awful momentum even after the Germans have gone. At the same time, infinitesimal signs of rebirth take on momentous symbolic significance: after Levi and his French friends manage to construct a makeshift stove, for example, he comments exultantly (and ironically), "we were broken by tiredness, but we seemed to have finally accomplished something useful—perhaps like God after the first day of creation" (*Opere*, i, 157).

The layered combination of stasis and sequence in *If This Is a Man* also points to fundamental features of Levi's attitude toward the Holocaust and the task of his testimonial work. In particular it works to strengthen a thread running through much of the book: its focus on sites or moments of fragile reprieve, when a residual human consciousness resurfaces, when Levi and his fellows see themselves. This applies not only to the chapters at the beginning and end of the book, but also to the passages on dreams (a dream is a reprieve, a moment of rest, but also often one of excruciating, tantalizing suffering); to the chapter on the camp hospital ("Ka Be"), hardly a place of caring, but just tranquil enough for feelings of shame and memories of home to resurface; to the chapters set in the Buna chemical laboratory, where encountering some local girls only serves to remind Levi how physically repugnant he now is, and how unthinkingly guilty of passive collaboration most "on the outside" are.

No other writer has mapped these strange, temporary, or metaphorical nonplaces—"gray zones" neither wholly within nor wholly outside the camp system, where he is both victim and observer at once—with more acuity than Levi. In such "no man's lands" between "there" and "here," his vision of the sense and the nonsense of the concentration camps is at its sharpest. It is a pattern repeated later in his work also, reaching a zenith in perhaps the very darkest page he ever wrote, at the end of *The Truce*, when he describes his occasional fear that nothing, not even his refound family, friends, and home, is wholly outside the *Lager*, that in an instant, all could be revealed as another tantalizing dream, that "nothing is true outside the Lager" (*Opere*, i, 395).

Describing and redescribing the moments of partial reprieve and transition pulls Levi toward certain key themes that mark out his unique contribution to the literature of the Holocaust. Three of these, key themes in *If This Is a Man*, are of special and sustained importance for his oeuvre as a whole: language, friendship, and culture.

The fascination with language—idiom, translation, symbols, and so forth, is perhaps the dominant pure intellectual pleasure of Levi's career after chemistry. In *If This Is a Man*, language plays a role of immense importance, in part for the very practical reason that Levi, as an Italian, was one of very few Jewish inmates of Auschwitz not to speak Yiddish, even if he was fortunate to have a smattering of scientific German. The risk of neither understanding fellow prisoners nor German guards heightened his sensitivity to the life-or-death importance of language and communication, to the strange Babel of languages in the camps, which merged to form jargons unique to that place and time, degrading other languages and displacing communication onto other "signs of meaning," such as punches, kicks, and blows. It also sensitized Levi from an early stage to the obstacles he would meet in using language afterward to represent Auschwitz, a defining problem of writing on the notion of testimony as it later developed: "Then for the first time we realised that our language has no words to express this offence, the demolition of a man" (*Opere*, i, 20).

Parallel to his focus on language is Levi's running concern with human relations, with the reciprocity and humane acknowledgment of friendship, even in the violently hostile, systematically divisive universe of the concentration camps. Levi's friendships with Alberto, his camp "twin," and with the Italian laborer Lorenzo, whose selfless favors help him survive, are the strongest human links running through the book, and the strongest links to a continued sense of human worth. They are also indicative of another element of careful ethical (perhaps even political) positioning by Levi, who chooses such bonds of companionship, of the local and contingent, over either the atomized isolation or the indistinct massification that were encouraged by the Nazi system at one and the same time. Of course, Levi has no illusions about the capacity of friendship to challenge violence: Alberto disappears on the death march after Auschwitz's evacuation; Lorenzo, as a later essay reveals, returns to Italy a broken man.

Finally, *If This Is a Man* shows Levi as, in at least two ways, an analyst of culture and its role in the camps. First, as critics like Marco Belpoliti have consistently pointed out, Levi in all his writings is instinctively an "anthropologist," interested in human behavior, rituals, perceptions, and symbols, and what happens when these are torn away:

> consider how much value and meaning there is in the smallest of our everyday habits, in the hundred objects that even the humblest beggar owns: a handkerchief, an old letter, the photo of a loved one. . . . And now imagine a man who, along with his dearest, is deprived of his home, his habits, his clothes, in short of literally everything he possesses: he will be a shell of a man . . . (*Opere*, i, 20).

Levi was also drawn to culture in the narrower, "higher" sense, as the most famous episode of all in *If This Is a Man* testifies. In the chapter "The Canto of Ulysses," as Levi slowly carries some soup with his French companion Jean (another rare, brief moment of respite), he takes up the crazy project of reciting from memory and translating into French the great Ulysses canto of Dante's *Divine Comedy* (*Inferno* XXVI). The evocation of the canto, the school-learned verses, Ulysses' speech urging his men on to "virtue and knowledge" in the face of adversity, the landscape that reminds Levi of his home, the delirium of exhaustion and fear, and the human contact with Jean, all come together in a heady sequence in which Levi thinks he intuits for an instant "the very reason for our fate, for our being here today . . ." (*Opere*, ii, III). It is typical of Levi that this oblique episode, in itself strangely detached from the horrendous place and time in which it occurs, should produce the moment of highest clarity about the Holocaust and the human condition anywhere in his work.

From *If This Is a Man* to *The Drowned and the Saved*

In *The Drowned and the Saved*, published in 1986, Levi looks back at *If This Is a Man* and describes it as "a nomadic animal which has for forty years now left behind it a long and intricate trail," suggesting that his later work might be read as what Alberto Cavaglion has called an extended series of glosses on that first book (*Opere*, ii, 1124). This is not to say that his work is repetitive (although one of the tasks of any survivor-witness is to find ways of repeating him– or herself). Levi shapes his testimony into many forms over the forty years of his literary and public career, including essays, poems, short stories, science fiction, fiction, autobiography, journalism, occasional writings, legal depositions, interviews, lectures and discussions at schools and public meetings. His style changes also over the decades, perhaps most notably in the thinning out of what several critics have identified as the rather formal, antiquated rhetorical touches in *If This Is a Man*, which include doses of Old Testament and Dantesque calques, in favor of a growing lightness and rhythmic fluidity of style. But there are also strong lines of continuity from first to last.

There is, first of all, a thin line of evolution that connects the writing and substance of *If This Is a Man* to that of *The Drowned and the Saved*. As noted above, the title of the latter derives from the former (indeed, it was Levi's title for his first book until Franco Antonicelli intervened). As also noted, there is a prehistory to *If This Is a Man*, in the medical report for *Minerva medica* and in the poems Levi wrote in 1946–1947, eight of which would appear in his collected poems, *Ad ora incerta*, in 1984. The medical report is a sort of "degree zero" of Levi's clinical, analytical writing style, which he later liked to compare to a weekly factory report. The poetry, by contrast, shows a more intense, emotive, angry Levi, as in "Shemà." This use of poetry as an escape valve for anger, even sarcasm, continued in his later occasional bursts of verse writing, as in a 1960 poem "Per Adolf Eichmann": Oh son of death, we do not wish you death. / May you live longer than anyone ever lived, / May you live sleepless five million nights.

In the mid–1950s, Levi rewrote parts of *If This Is a Man*, adding several important passages. The book was adapted for radio in 1964 and for the stage in 1966, with his collaboration. In 1961 and 1979, he wrote important prefaces for the German editions of the book, and in doing so, as he confessed later in *The Drowned and the Saved*, realized that his ideal audience, the reader he had subconsciously intended as he wrote the book, was a German, one of those who had stood by in so-called ignorance. In 1973, he wrote an introduction and explanatory notes for a school edition of the book. In 1976, he added a lengthy appendix, in which he selected and answered the most common questions he had been asked over the years. This appendix became an integral part of later editions of the book, and is also the seedbed of the essays that over the following decade would coalesce into *The Drowned and the Saved*. This direct line to *The Drowned and the Saved* is paralleled by another line of work in the intervening years that took Levi's testimonial concerns in indirect and often more literary directions. There are four key moments in this line: *The Truce*, parts of *The Periodic Table*, the Holocaust-related short stories in collections of the 1980s, and *If Not Now, When?*

The Truce describes, with exuberant, picaresque energy, always underpinned by the raw memory of the *Lager*, Levi's meandering journey home after liberation. Although parts of it were already among the stories he had sketched out in the 1940s, most of it was written at a distance of a decade and more from the events it relates, and the book is more stylish, more literarily achieved, and more varied as a result. For all its lightness, however, *The Truce* shows Levi extending several of the techniques, motifs, and concerns already on display in *If This Is a Man*. First, the overarching conceit of the title image—the journey home as a truce, a pause between two realities: the camps and the everyday world—leads directly back to the spaces of transition so characteristic of *If This Is a Man*. In this transitional, contingent phase, the most acute moral reflections and intense human interactions seem to emerge from chance encounters and events. The capacity of Levi and others in *The Truce* (especially his two cunning, tricky companions Cesare the Roman and Mordo Nahum the Greek) to exploit the vagaries of fortune to their advantage brings out and develops a further thread already hinted at in the first book whose preface began with the bold irony: "It was my good fortune to be deported to Auschwitz in February 1944 . . ." (*Opere*, i, 5). In the camps, the random arrival of death was so overwhelming that maneuvering for advantage and "organizing" (as camp jargon had it) all too often proved futile. *The Truce* also displays, greatly extended, Levi's penchant for the character vignette: the book is packed full of comic, vital, often caricatural presences. Levi's contacts with the characters he describes also echo his faith in friendship and human contact, here often glossed as a sort of commerce—the exchange of trust, goods, or human warmth for mutual advantage. Those same contacts also extend his fascination with language and communication, as shown in one of the book's comic set pieces, in which Levi and Cesare are forced to mime a chicken in order to ask for food from some local peasants.

In the chaos of colliding groups, nationalities, and rules of law in postwar Eastern Europe; in the long months stuck in holding camps or traveling east by train in order to go west—the sheer pointless disorder of it all works to rekindle a sense of life in Levi, after Auschwitz. But the book ends on a terrifying note of pessimism that underscores the closed, temporary pattern implied by the book's title, *The Truce* (a nuance lost in the other English title of the book, *The Reawakening*).

The Periodic Table has only two chapters directly related to Levi's time in the camps, although several of the early chapters include delicate and rich portraits of moments in his early life in Fascist Italy that, retrospectively, seem to foreshadow his later experiences (most eloquently, the chapter "Iron," on his mountaineering with his friend Sandro, who was driven by "an obscure need to prepare himself (and me) for an iron future which was getting nearer day by day") (*Opere*, i, 778). "Cerium," the only story set in the camps, expands on a moment of *If This Is a Man* to tell the full story of how Primo and Alberto used their chemistry and cunning, respectively, to manufacture cigarette lighters using cerium found in Levi's laboratory workplace. "Vanadium," set many years after the war, tells of Levi's chance contact through work correspondence with one of the German supervisors of that camp laboratory, Müller. Müller wants a form of absolution from Levi, and a meeting. Levi cannot give the former and is deeply troubled by the prospect of the latter. The German dies suddenly, before the meeting can take place.

"Cerium" is one of a kind with the dozen or so *Lager* stories in *Lilít* and another handful of stories and essays in *Racconti e saggi*. In this vein, Levi seems to project the lighter tone and adventurous qualities of *The Truce* back into the world of the concentration camp. He also develops a self-conscious interest in Yiddish culture and humor, giving hints of his reading of Isaac Bashevis Singer and Sholem Aleichem; this interest would bear fruit in his only work of pure fiction, *If Not Now, When?*

If Not Now, When? is a tragicomic, broad-canvas historical novel of the Jewish resistance to Nazism in Eastern Europe. It centers on Mendel, a wearied hero whose village has been destroyed and wife killed. He joins up with the taciturn and enigmatic Russian Leonid, and they in turn join first a Russian partisan group and then—the true heroes of the piece—a motley Jewish partisan group, led by the violin-playing, Chagallian figure Gedale. As a map in the book shows, Mendel's travels crisscross the same terrain traveled by Levi in *The Truce*. And indeed, Mendel's character and responses make of him a sort of Levi without a home to go to (a contrast that serves to underline the importance of the motif of home in Levi). In interviews about the book, Levi spoke of his unease at attempting the novel form so late in his career, but also of how compelling he found the independent lives of the characters he had created. Mendel and his friends end up in Italy, waiting for passage to Israel, and the novel closes (perhaps too neatly) as the atomic bomb explodes at Hiroshima.

The Drowned and the Saved brings together the two strands of Levi's testimony discussed thus far: direct extensions of *If This Is a Man* and the freer adaptations of Levi's testimonial concerns in other literary forms and registers. It is a book of essays, but it retains the strong episodic, narrative texture of his other work. At certain points, it explodes into an anger that recalls moments of his poetry. Indeed, some have seen the tensions between the essay form (none of his earlier works contained essays of the substantial historical-moral kind attempted here) and Levi's more natural narrative impulse as signs of how problematic the practice of testimony had become for Levi decades after the Event.

There are eight essays in the book, as well as a preface and conclusion. The core themes of the essays are, respectively: memory and its deceptions in both the guilty and the innocent; the "gray zone" of moral ambiguity that lies between the simple stereotypes of victim and oppressor—a notion since taken up by many writers on Fascism and Nazism; shame, especially the paradoxical shame of the survivor; communication; Nazi violence, defined resonantly as "useless," by which Levi means something between redundant in its excess and solipsistic in its generation of further violence and nothing else in what he calls a "genealogy of violence" (*Opere*, i, 778); the benefits and dangers of being an intellectual in Auschwitz (this chapter is an extended response to the work of Jean Améry); stereotypes—their uses but also the dangers of applying them to complex and extreme situations such as the *Lager*; and, the role and responsibilities of German civilians, related in a powerful sequence of letters exchanged between Levi and German readers of *If This Is a Man*.

Crucial to the immense and subtle impact of the book is the delicate balance Levi strikes between the personal and the analytical, the individual case and the general assessment, guilt and innocence. Subtending all these ambiguous and complex "gray zones" is the ambiguous position of the survivor generally, which Levi captures with intensity:

> Let me repeat, we the survivors are not the true witnesses. This is an uncomfortable thought, one that I have only gradually come to realise reading other people's memoirs and rereading my own after many years. We are a small, anomalous minority: those who managed, through some form of prevarication or trickery or luck, not to touch bottom. None of those who did so, none of those who looked at the Gorgon's head, came back to tell the tale, or they came back struck dumb; but it is they, the "Musulmänner," the drowned, the genuine witnesses, whose evidence could have had some wider meaning. They are the rule, we are the exception (*Opere*, ii, 1055–1056).

Many, if not all, the essays in *The Drowned and the Saved* seem to pick up on this ambiguity and to be rooted in a personal and general sense of uncertainty and the limits of the survivor's position: the uncertainty of memory, the ambiguity of responsibility, the weaknesses of our ways of understanding, the almost insurmountable difficulties of communicating in the camps but also afterwards with, say, the German readers. At the same time, as a matter of principle, Levi refuses to take this sense of uncertainty and limitation to mean that it is impossibile to understand or express the realities of the Final Solution: "Except in cases of pathological incapacity we can and must communicate. . . . To deny that we can communicate is false: we always can. To refuse to communicate is [morally] wrong" (*Opere*, ii, 1059–1060). As Bryan Cheyette has forcefully argued, far from supporting the common notion that to deal with the Holocaust is to try to deal with the ineffable, Levi's uncertainty can be read as the basis of an ethical sensitivity that is perhaps the key characteristic allowing him to bridge the gap between the horror of Auschwitz and the examination of it here and now.

Beyond Testimony

Levi's achievements in Holocaust literature can be fully appreciated only when his testimonial writing is set alongside the several dimensions of his work that go beyond testimony. Even when writing directly about Auschwitz, he approaches his task in ways that embrace larger questions about human nature and human society. Conversely, he also works in other fields, where there are only oblique or distant echoes of his Holocaust concerns. The quality of the interplay between these complementary dimensions is one of the sources of his acute and original insights, offering new lenses through which to see and interpret the Holocaust and also suggesting lines of connection between it and those other fields, in a way that defies attempts to hold the Holocaust inaccessible or radically "other." Levi's work in these other areas deserves and has increasingly received recognition in its own right. Undoubtedly the most significant of them is his science.

Levi's science implies not only his chemistry, but also a broad, eclectic mix of disciplines and technologies that fascinated him. These provided him not only with themes, but also with values, heuristic tools, even stylistic models for his writing. This bridging of literary and scientific culture places him firmly in a rich Italian tradition that stretches back to Dante, Leonardo da Vinci, and Galileo and forward again to Levi's contemporary and friend, Italo Calvino.

There are several sides to science in Levi's work. *The Periodic Table*, for example, is among other things a self-conscious attempt to write a vivid history of his profession as a working chemist, in the vein of, say, Cellini's autobiography of his life as an artist. In his science-fiction stories (*Storie Naturali*, *Vizio di forma*, parts of *Lilít* and *Racconti e saggi*) he deliberately chooses an apparently minor literary genre to work through a mass of moral quandaries, several of which connect closely with the moral questions in his Holocaust writing (the excesses and the "errors of perspective" of science; system and rule as opposed to disorder and improvisation; memory, selfhood, and the machine; responsibility and responsiveness; the interconnectedness of matter). His flawed fantasy technologies and the societies that produce them always stand in relation to our everyday world in ways somehow similar to the position of that other flawed, perverted society, the concentration camp world (David Rousset's *univers concentrationnaire*). A handful of these stories have even tighter links to Levi's Holocaust work, by dint of either close textual echoes or settings in or around Nazi Germany. Their political aspects—in the loose sense of an examination of the workings of power, violence, and control—echo his acute analyses of the hierarchies and networks within the camps. Finally, in several articles and essays (in *L'altrui mestiere* and *Racconti e saggi*), Levi reveals an abiding commitment to monitoring the achievements and excesses of science in the real world, from the moon landings to Hiroshima, and he used the history of science's excesses to explain aspects of the Holocaust on occasion.

Levi's science is above all an applied science, as his working chemistry was; in it the need for control, responsibility and acknowledgment of ambiguity and limits is at its greatest. Other applied sciences—that is, certain social sciences—provide him with an almost endless set of complex images and inspiration for his writing: these include linguistics or semiotics (at work in *If This Is a Man* and *The Drowned and the Saved*, and repeatedly also the source of essays and stories); and behavioral sciences, especially those whose natural, animate or inanimate models and metaphors are used to study humans, in a characteristically Levian mix that the Italian writer Daniele Del Giudice has dubbed "anthropochemicozoology."

This emphasis on working science can also be seen in the mechanical engineering of Faussone, the hero of *The Wrench*. Both *The Wrench* and *The Periodic Table* are largely made up of problem-solving adventures from within their respective professions, and both invest heavily in the moral value of individual, intelligent, useful work, a bulwark against the "useless violence" and the *Arbeit macht frei* of Auschwitz. In this respect they are truly complementary to Levi's Holocaust writing. Indeed, both books allude to his Holocaust stories in similar, oblique ways: "That I, a chemist, . . . have lived another, different season has been narrated elsewhere" (From *The Periodic Table*, Opere, i, 860); "on other evenings I told [Faussone] all my own stories" (From *The Wrench*, Opere, i, 989). The clear implication is that the two areas of his writing are best read hand in hand.

One final aspect of Levi's work can be seen as an epitome of the delicate relationship he established between his Holocaust writing and his other work, and thereby between the Holocaust and our ordinary world: that is, his irony, humor, curiosity, even playfulness. Inevitably, these qualities emerge with most exuberance in his picaresque writing (*The Truce* and *If Not Now, When?*) and in his non-Holocaust work (his poems and dialogues about animals; *The Search for Roots*; *Other People's Trades*). But it is there also, in the form of a pregnant irony and multiplicity of perspective, a sensitivity to absurdity and contradiction, even at the darkest moments of *If This Is a Man*. His humor, like all the aspects of his writing, is ethically weighted and calibrated, open to challenging, doubting, and testing—in Auschwitz and after Auschwitz, for survivor and reader alike; which perhaps represents the defining dynamics of this extraordinary body of work.

Bibliography

Primary Sources

Se questo è un uomo (*If This Is a Man*, also known as *Survival in Auschwitz*). 1947; 2nd edition 1958.

La tregua (*The Truce*, also known as *The Reawakening*). 1963.

Storie naturali (Natural Histories, partly in English in *The Sixth Day*). 1966

Vizio di forma (Formal Defect, partly in English in *The Sixth Day*). 1971.

Il sistema periodico (*The Periodic Table*). 1975.

La chiave a stella (*The Wrench*, also known as *The Monkey Wrench*). 1978.

Lilít e altri racconti (Lilith and Other Stories, partly in English as *Moments of Reprieve*). 1981.

La ricerca della radici (*The Search for Roots*). 1981.

Se non ora, quando? (*If Not Now, When?*). 1982.

Ad ora incerta (At an Uncertain Hour, in English as *Collected Poems*). 1984.

L'altrui mestiere (*Other People's Trades*). 1985.

I sommersi e i salvati (*The Drowned and the Saved*). 1986.

Racconti e saggi (Stories and Essays, partly in English as *The Mirror Maker*). 1986.

All of the above and several hundred pages of further miscellaneous writings are to be found in Primo Levi, *Opere*, vols. i-ii, edited by Marco Belpoliti (Turin: Einaudi, 1997). Selections of the miscellany are to be found in Primo Levi, *L'assimetria e la vita* (Turin: Einaudi, 2002).

Secondary Sources

Agamben, Giorgio. *Remnants of Auschwitz*. New York: Zone Books, 2000.

Angier, Carole. *The Double Bond: Primo Levi, A Biography*. London: Viking, 2002.

Anissimov, Myriam. *Primo Levi: Tragedy of an Optimist*. London: Aurum Press, 1998.

Belpoliti, Marco, ed. *Primo Levi*. Milan: Marcos y Marcos, 1997. [in Italian].

Belpoliti, Marco. *Primo Levi*. Milan: Bruno Mondadori, 1998. [in Italian].

Bernstein, Michel André. "A Yes or a No." *The New Republic*, 27 Sept. 1999.

Cavaglion, Alberto. *Primo Levi e "Se questo è un uomo."* Turin: Loescher, 1993. [in Italian].

Cheyette, Bryan. "The Ethical Uncertainty of Primo Levi." In Bryan Cheyette and Laura Marcus, eds. *Modernity, Culture and "the Jew."* Cambridge, England: Polity, 1998, pp. 268–81.

Cicioni, Mirna. *Primo Levi: Bridges of Knowledge*. Oxford: Berg, 1995.

Ferrero, Ernesto, ed. *Primo Levi: un'antologia della critica*. Turin: Einaudi, 1997. [in Italian].

Gambetta, Diego. "Primo Levi's Last Moments." *Boston Review* (Summer 1999): 25–29.

Gilman, Sander. "To Quote Primo Levi: 'If You Don't Speak Yiddish, You're Not a Jew.' " In *Inscribing the Other*. Lincoln: University of Nebraska Press, 1991, pp. 293–316.

Gordon, Robert. *Primo Levi's Ordinary Virtues: From Testimony to Ethics*. Oxford: Oxford University Press, 2001.

Gunzberg, Lynn M. "Down among the Dead Men: Levi and Dante in Hell." *Modern Language Studies* 16 (1986): 10–28.

Langer, Lawrence. "Legacy in Gray: The Ordeal of Primo Levi." In *Preempting the Holocaust*. New Haven: Yale University Press, 1998, pp. 23–42.

Murawski, John. "In Order to Tell: Primo Levi and the Subversion of Literary Language." *Prose Studies* 14 (1991): 81–96.

Ozick, Cynthia. "The Suicide Note." *The New Republic* 21 March 1988.

Patruno, Nicholas. *Understanding Primo Levi*. Columbia: University of South Carolina Press, 1995.

Rudolf, Antony. *At an Uncertain Hour: Primo Levi's War against Oblivion*. London: Menard Press, 1990.

Sodi, Risa. *A Dante of Our Time: Primo Levi and Auschwitz*. New York: Peter Lang, 1990.

Tarrow, Susan, ed. *Reason and Light: Essays on Primo Levi*. Ithaca: Center for International Studies, 1990.

Thomson, Ian. *Primo Levi*. London: Hutchinson, 2002.

Todorov, Tzvetan. *Facing the Extreme: Moral Life in the Concentration Camps*. New York: Metropolitan Books, 1996.

Woolf, Judith. *The Memory of the Offence: Primo Levi's "If This Is a Man."* Market Harborough, England: University Texts, 1996.

Interviews

Camon, Ferdinando. *Conversations with Primo Levi*. Marlboro, Vt.: Marlboro Press, 1989.

Levi, Primo. *The Voice of Memory. Interviews 1961–87*. Edited by Marco Belpoliti and Robert Gordon. New York: New Press, 2001.

Levi, Primo, and Tullio Regge. *Conversations*. London: I.B. Tauris, 1989.

EMMANUEL LEVINAS

(1906–1995)

SUSAN E. SHAPIRO

EMMANUEL LEVINAS WAS born in Kovno (Kaunus), Lithuania, on 12 January 1906, but after emigrating to France he celebrated his birthday using the Western calendar on December 30. His father, Yehiel Levinas, a bookseller, and his mother, Devora Gurvitchy, moved the family to the Ukraine at the beginning of World War I, returning to Lithuania after the Russian Revolution in 1917. Levinas left for France in 1923 to study at the University of Strasbourg where he met Charles Blondel and Maurice Halbwachs and befriended Maurice Blanchot. From 1928 to 1929 he studied at the University of Freiberg in Germany with philosophers Edmund Husserl and Martin Heidegger. The influence of both on his thought is evident in his 1930 doctoral thesis (*The Theory of Intuition in Husserl's Phenomenology*) and thinking thereafter, even when their thought is critiqued and reversed. In 1930 Levinas was naturalized as a French citizen and in 1932 he married his wife, Raisa, a musician originally from Vienna, Austria. They had two children, Simone (Hansel) and Michael.

In 1939 Levinas served as a translator of Russian and German in the French army; in 1940 he was captured by the Nazis. Because he was a French officer, Levinas was interned as a prisoner of war in Germany, where he was subjected to forced labor instead of being sent to a concentration camp as a Jew. While Levinas was imprisoned in Germany, his wife and daughter—aided by Blanchot—were hidden in a French monastery for the duration of the war. Levinas's entire family in Lithuania, however, died in the *Shoah*.

After receiving his Ph.D. in 1930, Levinas taught in Paris at the Alliance Israelite Universelle until he was captured by the Nazis in 1940. In 1946 he became the director of the Alliance, and held this position until 1961. After the war, Levinas also studied the Talmud with the mysterious Mr. Chouchani (as did Elie Wiesel). Levinas's Talmudic readings, first delivered orally at the Colloque des Intellectuels Juifs de Langue Francaise, were greatly influenced by his studies with Mr. Chouchani. Levinas took his first academic position in the French university system in 1961 at the University of Poitiers. He then taught at the Nanterre branch of the University of Paris beginning in 1967 and, finally, at the Sorbonne from 1973 until his retirement in 1976, after which he continued to direct a seminar until 1980. Levinas was productive until the end of his life in December 1995.

The Holocaust and Philosophy: Levinas's Books

The dedication to Emmanuel Levinas's major work in philosophy, *Otherwise Than Being or Beyond Essence* (1974), reads: "To the memory of those who were closest among the six million assassinated by the National Socialists, and of the millions on millions of all confessions and all nations, victims of the same hatred of the other man, the same anti-semitism" (Otherwise than Being or Beyond Essence, translated by Alphonso Lingis, The Hague: Martinus Nijhoff, 1981). In Hebrew, at the bottom of the page, is a personal memorial, a virtual tombstone, to the memory of the souls of his parents, his two brothers, and his mother-in-law and father-in-law, all of whom died in the *Shoah*. Written in accord with the Jewish tradition, it uses their Hebrew names and those of their fathers and concludes with the acronym appearing on Jewish tombstones, that signifies: "Let her soul be bound within the bonds of life." This double dedication raises the question not only of the relationship between Levinas's philosophical and Jewish writings—a distinction Levinas purposely drew and consistently held—but also between his ethics and his response specifically to the *Shoah*.

None of Levinas's books focus on the Holocaust as such, and only a few of his essays are about or explicitly refer to the *Shoah* in a sustained manner. The scattered references and muted treatment of the Holocaust throughout his writings, however, testify to more than a view of the *Shoah* as an instance or example of genocide. Rather, as is made clear in his essay "Useless Suffering" and evident elsewhere in his work, the *Shoah* is paradigmatic for Levinas of a certain hatred that produces violence and suffering. Indeed, despite the overall dearth of explicit references to the *Shoah* in his philosophy, Levinas's ethics may be legitimately considered a post-Holocaust response, one that seeks to get at the roots of hatred within Western thought so as to reverse its deadly logic.

The root of the "hatred of the other man" is found, Levinas suggests, in the foundations of Western thought, specifically in its logic of identity and identification grounded in the ontological priority of the self and its unquestioned task or right to preserve itself in being. This logic is lodged in one of the primary gestures of what Levinas terms "Greek" (as opposed to "Hebrew") thought in which ontology is regarded as first philosophy. The consequences of this priority given to ontology and its centering around the self is that *any* ethics that follows ontology will necessarily also begin with the priority of the self's persistence in being. What the *Shoah* paradigmatically makes evident—but which has always been the case—is that ethics, not ontology, should be/is first philosophy. Levinas argues that the first questions to be asked are those centered around the self's ("my") obligation to the other person(s), especially the responsibility to preserve the other person in being. It is not my, but the other person's mortality that commands my ethical attention. [This concern results in one of Levinas's major critiques of Heidegger, evident as early as his 1934 essay "Reflections on the Philosophy of Hitlerism" and his first book, *Existence and Existents* (1947), written primarily during his internment by the Nazis, a fact that may well have been part of his notion, developed in this text, of the *il ya*, which describes being in rather horrifying and claustrophobic terms.] Ethics as first philosophy reverses the priority in being of self and other. "My" obligation is to preserve the persistence of the other in being rather than myself. This primary obligation of the self to the other, Levinas argues, is not possible if ontology is first philosophy.

The term that orients the self to the other in Levinas's first major philosophical work, *Totality and Infinity* (1961), is the "face." This term signifies the distinctive, even unique, humanity of the other person; it is an ethical optics—seeing the color of someone's eyes is *not* seeing their "face." It is in seeing the "face" of the other person that the self is displaced from its priority and is instead oriented by the self's ("my") inescapable and infinite responsibility to the other person. In Levinas's later writings, these terms for the obligation of self to other become intensified and more extreme. For example, in *Otherwise Than Being*, Levinas refers to the self as "persecuted," as "hostage" to and, even, as a "substitution" for (suffering on behalf of) the other. This extreme form of responsibility may be considered a response to the effacing—indeed the destruction of the "face" of the other by the Nazis, their collaborators, and bystanders during the *Shoah*. The totalizing logic of identity and identification embedded in the treatment of ontology as first philosophy results, Levinas proposes, in hatred and violence to the other person, indeed, in genocide. For, if the self has ethical obligations only to other selves—to others who are regarded as in the same category as the self—those others who are not regarded as a member of this category are excluded from any ethical obligation. As the promulgation of the 1935 Nuremberg laws demonstrates (defining Jews as noncitizens, reversing and undoing the terms of the emancipation), the logic of identity and identification, which forms the basis of the modern nation-state, is vulnerable to such monstrous reversals. The other person, as a nonself, may even come to fall outside the "social contract" altogether. Thus, Levinas shifts the basis of philosophy from ontology (and the logic of identity founded in the self) to ethics (and an infinite obligation to the other person(s) founded on her or his very alterity). Some interpreters of Levinas find this reversal too extreme. However, this shifting and his use of "excessive" ethical terms and positions may be read as intervention into institutionalized logics that regularly produce violence and injustice, precisely so as to displace, alter, and even reverse these logics. Considered in this context, these terms take on a more effective and performative character. Levinas's uncompromising critiques of ideology and the state may also similarly be understood as interventions into discourses, logics, and practices that, as such, are most difficult to otherwise critique or displace.

The Holocaust and Judaism: Levinas's Essays

Levinas explicitly treats the *Shoah* in only a few of his essays, including "Useless Suffering" (in *Entre Nous* [Between Us], 1991), "Loving the Torah More Than God" (in *Difficile liberté* [*Difficult Freedom*], 1963), "Nameless" (in *Noms propre* [Proper Names], 1976), "Reflections on the Philosophy of Hitlerism" (in *Esprit*, 1934; *Critical Inquiry*, 1990), and "Damages Due to Fire" (in *Nine Talmudic Readings*, 1990), the first two of which have been the most influential.

"Useless Suffering" takes up the problem of post-Holocaust theodicy. Among these events is the Holocaust of

> the Jewish people when the reign of Hitler seems to me the paradigm of gratuitous human suffering, in which evil appears in its diabolical horror . . . The disproportion between suffering and every theodicy was shown at Auschwitz with a glaring, obvious clarity. Its possibility puts into question the multimillennial traditional faith (*Entre Nous*, Columbia University Press, 1998, p. 97).

Agreeing with Emil Fackenheim, whom he quotes, Levinas argues that traditional Christian and Jewish explanations for suffering that justify it either in terms of original sin or as a punishment for sin are not only theologically untenable, but immoral.

> But does not this end of theodicy, which imposes itself in the face of this century's inordinate trial, at the same time and in a more general way reveal the unjustifiable character of suffering in the other, the outrage it would be for me to justify my neighbor's suffering? (p. 98).

It is, Levinas notes, the sin of Job's "friends" to attempt to find a reason for Job's suffering. As in Job's case, the search for reasons to explain and thereby justify the suffering of those caught in the *Shoah*, further inflicts violence on its victims. "Pain in its undiluted malignity, suffering for nothing. It renders impossible and odious every proposal and every thought that would explain it by the sins of those who have suffered or are dead" (p. 98).

According to Levinas, however, it is still legitimate to ask after one's own sinfulness when one suffers, and to suffer on behalf of the other's suffering. The suffering of the other person is "useless" and meaningless. My suffering on behalf of the other—my compassion for the other—may be meaningful, as the

> suffering for the useless suffering of the other, the just suffering in me for the unjustifiable suffering of the other. . . . In this perspective there is a radical difference between *the suffering in the other*, where it is unforgivable to *me*, solicits me and calls me, and suffering *in me*, my own experience of suffering, whose constitutional or congenital uselessness can take on a meaning, the only one of which suffering is capable, in becoming a suffering for suffering . . . of someone else (p. 94).

According to Levinas, the suffering of one for the other offers an ethic after theodicy in which humans take on the "medicative" work formerly assigned to God.

> Must not humanity now in a faith more difficult than before in a faith without theodicy continue to live our sacred history; a history that now demands even more from the resources of the *I* in each one of us, and from its suffering inspired by the suffering of the other, from its compassion which is a non-useless suffering (or love), which is no longer suffering "for nothing," and immediately has meaning? (p. 100).

Levinas characteristically moves in "Useless Suffering" from theodicy as a logic of totality that seeks to preserve its coherence by blaming the other for her or his suffering, to an infinite compassion for the other person. This same move is made in "Loving the Torah More Than God" in which Torah (as the locus of obligation to the other person[s]) is adhered to even when one must reject a notion of God that preserves theodicy. "What can this suffering of innocents mean? Is it not proof of a world without God, where only man measures Good and Evil? The simplest and most common answer would be atheism" (*Difficult Freedom*, Johns Hopkins University Press, 1990, p. 143). Even so, he asks why the character Yossel still believes in God. (In the fictional and anonymous text Levinas is interpreting in this essay, "Yossel, son of Yossel, Rakover, from Tarnapol, speaks to God.")

> The certainty of God is something Yossel, Son of Yossel experiences with a new force, beneath an empty sky. For if he is so alone, it is in order to take upon his shoulders the whole of God's responsibilities. The path that leads to the one God must be walked in part without God. True monotheism is duty bound to answer the legitimate demands of atheism. The adult's God is revealed precisely through the void of the child's heaven. . . . The God who hides His face is not, I believe, a theological abstraction or a poetic image. It is the moment in which the just individual can find no help. No institution would protect him. The consolation of divine presence to be found in infantile religious feeling is equally denied him, and the individual can prevail only through his conscience, which necessarily involves suffering. . . . This condition reveals a God Who renounces all manifestation, and appeals instead to the full maturity of the responsible man (p. 143).

Again, along the same lines, Levinas reads the conclusion to the book of Job not as providing a theodicy from within the whirlwind, but as a question, "Where were you?" posed to the self in regard to its obligation to the other person(s). It is the question that parallels the phrase through which the self signifies his or her obligation to the other: "*Hinenni*, Here I am."

In Levinas's philosophy generally, then, this explicitly post-Holocaust move is tantamount to the claim that ethics is first philosophy. Levinas regards the Holocaust as a paradigmatic challenge to ethics, a challenge, however, that persists after the *Shoah* and indeed precedes it. The theological or religious responses Levinas makes in his essays, thus, clear the ground for his philosophical ethics. Levinas consistently treats the problem of the suffering of the other person throughout his writings; the Holocaust is the paradigm both of this suffering and of the moral response to it.

Bibliography

Primary Sources

Théorie de l'intuition dans la phenomenologie de Husserl (*The Theory of Intuition in Husserl's Phenomenology*). 1930, 1970, 1973.

De L'évasion. 1935, 1982.
De l'existence à l'existant (*Existence and Existents*). 1947, 1978, 1988.
En découvrant l'existence avec Husserl et Heidegger (*Discovering Existence with Husser and Heidegger*). 1949, 1967, 1974, 1988.
Totalité et infini: Essai sur l'extériorité (*Totality and Infinity*). 1961, 1969, 1971.
Difficile liberté: Essais sur le judaïsme (*Difficult Liberty: Essays on Judaism*). 1963, 1976, 1990.
Quatre lectures talmudiques (*Four Talmudic Lectures*). 1968.
Humanisme de l'autre home. 1972.
Autrement qu'être ou au-delà de l'essence (*Otherwise Than Being or Beyond Essence*). 1974, 1981.
Sur Maurice Blanchot (*On Maurice Blanchot*). 1975.
Noms propres (*Proper Names*). 1976, 1996.
Du sacré au saint: Cinq nouvelles lectures talmudiques. 1977.
De Dieu qui vient à l'idée (*Of God Who Comes to Mind*). 1982, 1992, 1996, 1998.
L'Au-delà du verset: Lectures et discourse talmudiques. 1982.
Éthique et infini, dialogues with Philippe Nemo (*Ethics and Infinity*). 1982, 1985.
Transcendance et intelligibilité. 1984.
Hors sujet (*Outside the Subject*). 1987, 1993.
A l'heure des nations. 1988.
La Mort et le temps. 1991.
Entre nous: Essais sur le penser-à-l'autre (*Entre Nous: Thinking of the Other*). 1991, 1998.
Dieu, la mort et le temps (*God, Death, and Time*). 1993, 2000.
Liberté et commandement. 1994.
Les Imprévus de l'histoire. 1994.
Altérite et Transcendence (*Alterity and Transcendence*). 1995, 1999.
Nouvelles lectures talmudiques (*New Talmudic Readings*). 1996, 1999.
Time and the Other. 1947, 1988.
Nine Talmudic Readings. 1968, 1977. Translated by Annette Aronowicz (Bloomington: Indiana University Press, 1990).
Beyond the Verse: Talmudic Readings and Lectures. 1982, 1994.
Collected Philosophical Papers. 1987.
The Levinas Reader (edited by Seán Hand). 1989.
Emmanuel Levinas: Basic Writings (edited by Robert Bernasconi, Simon Critchley and Adriaan Peperzak). 1996.
"Useless Suffering." In *Entre Nouse*. New York: Columbia U Press, 1998.
"Loving the Torah more than God." In *Difficult Freedom*. Baltimore: Johns Hopkins U Press, 1996.
"Nameless." In *Proper Names*. Stanford: Stanford U Press, 1996.
"Reflections on the Philosophy of Hitlerism." *Critical Inquiry* 17, no. 1 (autumn 1990).
"Damages Due to Fire." In *Nine Talmudic Readings*. Bloomington: Indiana U Press, 1990.

Secondary Sources

Chanter, Tina. "Neither Materialism nor Idealism: Levinas's Third Way." In *Postmodernism and the Holocaust*. Edited by Alan Milchman and Alan Rosenberg. Amsterdam: Editions Rodopi B.V., 1994, pp. 137–154.
Cohen, Richard A. "What Good Is the Holocaust? On Suffering and Evil." In *Ethics, Exegesis and Philosophy*. Cambridge: University of Cambridge Press, 2001, pp. 266–282.
Gibbs, Robert. "Unjustifiable Suffering." In *Suffering Religion*. Edited by Robert Gibbs and Elliot R. Wolfson. London and New York: Routledge, 2002, pp. 13–36.
Goodhart, Sandor. "The End from the Beginning: Evil and Accusation in the Book of Job." In *Sacrificing Commentary: Reading the End of Literature*. Baltimore: The Johns Hopkins University Press, 1996, pp. 168–213.
———. "Writing on Fire: The Holocaust, Witness, and Responsibility." In *Sacrificing Commentary: Reading the End of Literature*. Baltimore: The Johns Hopkins University Press, 1996, pp. 215–243.
Grob, Leonard. "Emmanuel Levinas and the Primacy of Ethics in Post-Holocaust Philosophy." (Responses and critiques by Peter J. Haas, David H. Hirsch, David Patterson, Didier Pollefeyt, and John K. Roth). In *Ethics after the Holocaust: Perspectives, Critiques, and Responses*. Edited by David H. Hirsch. St. Paul, Minn.: Paragon House, 1999, pp. 1–333.
Handelman, Susan A. "The Holocaust: To Love the Torah More Than God." In *Fragments of Redemption: Jewish Thought and Literary Theory in Benjamin, Scholem, and Levinas*. Bloomington: Indiana University Press, 1991, pp. 275–278.
———. "The Witness and the Holocaust." In *Fragments of Redemption: Jewish Thought and Literary Theory in Benjamin, Scholem, and Levinas*. Bloomington: Indiana University Press, 1991, pp. 271–275.
Hatley, James. "Transcendence of the Face." In *Suffering Witness: The Quandary of Responsibility after the Irreparable*. New York: State University of New York Press, 2000, pp. 73–103.
Llewelyn, John. "sELection." In *Postmodernism and the Holocaust*. Edited by Alan Milchman and Alan Rosenberg. Amsterdam: Editions Rodopi B.V., 1994, pp. 189–204.
Manning, Robert John Scheffler. "Serious Ideas Rooted in Blood: Emmanuel Levinas's Analysis of the Philosophy of Hitlerism." In *Postmodernism and the Holocaust*. Edited by Alan Milchman and Alan Rosenberg. Amsterdam: 1994, pp. 125–136.
Miller, Helmut. "The Same Hatred of the Other Man, the Same Anti-Semitism." In *Postmodernism and the Holocaust*. Edited by Alan Milchman and Alan Rosenberg. Amsterdam: Editions Rodopi B.V., 1994, pp. 167–188.
Mole, Gary D. "Auschwitz and Limits of Dis-course." In *Lévinas, Blanchot, Jabès: Figures of Estrangement*. Gainesville: University Press of Florida, 1997, pp. 131–76.
Peukert, Helmut. "Unconditional Responsibility for the Other: The Holocaust and the Thinking of Emmanuel Levinas." In *Postmodernism and the Holocaust*. Edited by Alan Milchman and Alan Rosenberg. Amsterdam: 1994, pp. 155–166.
Watson, James R. "Levinas's Substitutions and Arendt's Concept of the Political: Becoming the Plurality Who We Are." In *Postmodernism and the Holocaust*. Edited by Alan Milchman and Alan Rosenberg. Amsterdam: 1994, pp. 113–124.
Wright, Tamara. "Post-Holocaust Judaism." In *The Twilight of Jewish Philosophy: Emmanuel Levinas' Ethical Hermeneutics*. New York: Routledge, 1999.
Wyschogrod, Edith. "Self, Language, and Community." In *Spirit in Ashes: Hegel, Heidegger, and Man-Made Mass Death*. New Haven: Yale University Press, 1985, pp. 201–211.

Interview

Is It Righteous To Be?: Interviews with Emmanuel Levinas. Edited by Jill Robins. Stanford: Stanford University Press, 2001.

ITAMAR LEVY

(1956–)

DVIR ABRAMOVICH

IN DIFFERENT WAYS, Itamar Levy's controversial book *Agadat ha'agamim ha'atsuvim* (Legend of the Sad Lakes) uncomfortably pushed the parameters of post-Auschwitz aesthetic representations, in essence redefining, or perhaps resisting, generic boundaries. To be sure, Levy utilized a novelist's license in his strategies of narration to create a complex chamber for reflections about the nature of Nazism and the damaged self of the second generation. His strategies sometimes pressed aside narratological constraints and conventional categories of exactitude and faithfulness to the historical record. The author's choice of a revised palette of approaches, of refuting the mimetic trend to choose the fantastic as a thematic and structural element, can be said to be driven by the realization that "to establish an order of reality in which the unimaginable becomes imaginatively acceptable exceeds the capacities of an art devoted entirely to verisimilitude; some quality of the fantastic, whether stylistic or descriptive, becomes an essential ingredient" (Langer, p. 43). Interestingly, Levy is not the son of Holocaust survivors, which indicates that the consuming passion to relate to the catastrophe affects all the generation born after the war, not only those whose lives were directly marked by their survivor parents. It has been argued that Levy offers his readers an intellectual game, tacitly acknowledging that his tale is a fairy tale. However, the thematic premise of fairy tales, more often than not, is scented with a happy texture and happy ending. Yet the primary narrative of this story is freighted with pathos and beautifully wrought tragic passages. The author's point is that it is incumbent upon the spectator to choose whether this is a fable, to suspend disbelief of the fantastic style, or to choose to see the fantastic as real since the literary material is based on actual events. In this context, Batya Gur observes that the entire story is written as if on the verge of a dream (p. 8B).

In content, style, and structure, *Agadat ha'agamim ha'atsuvim* presents a reality in which the constituent ingredients of the real world have been reversed with no fastening line to the ground or a kinship to the realistic. It is a stage, as Avraham Balaban correctly asserts, where nothing is stable or indisputable, where the expressionistic plot is denuded of the anchor of real time or space (Balaban, p. 9). Formally, the novel consists of a welter of shifting styles, braiding idiomatic Hebrew with Agnonesque speech as well as a myriad of erotic and violent situations mounted unremittingly on top of one another. Amplifying its amalgam conformation of jerky styles, techniques, and tones is the novel's truly polyphonic makeup, with six narrators who combine to tell the story of the Nazi regime and the inferno of the camps. The blurring of identities makes it, at times, difficult to ascertain the identity of the speakers, adding to the novel's jarring distortion of plot and narration. At the peak of the book's colorful innovation, which intermingles the trivial and the terrible, readers encounter a talking parrot who discourses on Nazi historiography with Arnon, Nazi pets who frequent a lake to talk among themselves, and a cow whose milk offers horrific accounts of the treatment of the Jews in Europe.

The story opens in Tel Aviv in February 1988, with the arrest of Yochanan Greenberg, accused of being the SS officer Obersturmführer Joachim Kron. Not only did the Nazi criminal of Dachau choose to hide in the land of his victims, it is claimed, he even had a son, Arnon, with a Jewish camp inmate whom he married after the war. The devastating chain of events begins when Baruch Feine, a Holocaust survivor who, in the camps, served as the Jewish plaything to the alleged Nazi officer, recognizes Greenberg's neck as they are traveling on a bus. Having had to watch the beastly criminal rape members of his family and friends in the camps, Baruch, in revulsion, had turned and focused on Kron's neck, perfectly memorizing it.

Kron/Greenberg is covertly arrested and placed in complete isolation in Acre prison. During his trial, his wife dies, although her voice is not muffled—she freely narrates her and the Jewish community's inferno throughout the book.

Faced with the accumulating evidence and a personal crisis, Arnon sets out to prove his father's innocence by traveling to Munich where he hopes he can find exculpating proof. The trip to Germany, however, backfires as he uncovers conclusive confirmation that his father is the Nazi Satan. Visiting a cemetery, where his Nazi father is allegedly buried, Arnon discovers the grave is empty. The gravesite was created by a cadre of aging ex-Nazis, of which his father was an active participant, to conceal the fact that Kron was still alive. Although Arnon does not present his father with the condemnatory facts he has unearthed, his father confesses to the charges through a letter he sends to his son and dead wife (which he signs "Heil Hitler") and commits suicide in his cell.

The possibility that Arnon is the offspring to a Nazi monster brings about a simultaneous outburst of fury and doubt as well as the desire to reclaim the foundations of his previous identity that has disintegrated. At first, he leaves his pregnant wife, Einav, and moves to a run-down hotel, as he cannot stand the thought of siring a Nazi offspring. Then, understandably, he feels bound to trace his family's history in an attempt to recover and reclaim his crushed sense of being. The fantastic, irrational nature of the discovery forces the author to employ a spectrum of different narratorial styles, mirroring the agony and anguish that Arnon feels, which partly enables Arnon to configure some emotional constancy into his shattered existence. The young man is forced to confront Nazism headon, as he considers the possibility that he, the son of a Nazi officer, may have inherited the evil poison transmitted by his father. Arnon's wife believes the wrecked legacy will be passed on to the third generation, her unborn child (whom she thinks of as the heir to survivors and destroyers). On her way to meet Kron's lawyer, she recites a poem for her baby, firmly placing it in the whirlwind of an imminent *Shoah*, "My Child / Hide in my belly / Do not lift your eyes to the danger / Your mother / Is warning you / My Child / Hide in my cellars / Learn your height so you can adjust to the low walls / Prepare your eyes for the darkness / My Child" (*Agadat ha'agamim ha'atsuvim*, Tel Aviv: Keter, 1989, p. 72).

Struggling with the psychological reality and growing alienation from the defilement of his heritage, Arnon sets out to learn about his and his family's origins. At one point, he asks himself, "Am I the hunted or the hunter . . . Am I a Jew or a Nazi" (Levy, p. 54). Moreover, the pervasive analogy between Jew and Nazi promoted in the book is reinforced when, after being attacked by Odessa members in a graveyard, Arnon, bloodied and bruised, decides to accept his fate—he decides to become like the same dark animal that attacked him. This motif is heightened by Lana, a German woman who sleeps with Arnon, whom she calls "My Little Nazi" because he smells of Aryan blood like her father, and by Arnon's dead mother, who affirms the son's divided self, in the following narration:

> In his outward appearance my son is split between the good and the bad. His right eye is quiet, his left is raging. One ear is flat, the other stands out. My son's face is divided. Half is like me, half is like his father. His actions too, are divided. Because despite the accusations, the threats and the charges, he cares for his father, but on the other hand he leaves his wife Einav and avoids her temptations (Levy, p. 60).

Toward the end of the story, Arnon's father underlines the deep connection his son has with Nazism, how his German roots are an integral component of his psyche and identity. Raised in a household devoid of love, Arnon was brought up on the Nazi code and ethos, leafing through newspaper cuttings dedicated to the Führer and listening to German bedtime stories that his father secretly read to the young boy. The following passage reflects the loss of identity central in the book:

> You are not a Jew, Arnon, because the Jews are not a race, but fragments of a nation. Whereas you are a German, member of the purest race. Your name, too, is not Jewish. Your real name is Rudolph Kron. I saw you growing up strong and noble. . . . When the verdict is given it will be your verdict too. . . . You are the son of a Nazi (Levy, p. 114).

In the end, the boundary between victim and killer is crossed, as the raging fury leads Arnon to kidnap and murder an old Nazi SS officer.

In the novel's most stirring monologue, Arnon conveys the internal cry of pain shared by all survivor children:

> Why don't I write about my feelings one to one? Why don't I listen to my heart like I have been told to do? Why do I evade, close gates, build walls, forget and remember and suppress and ask and erase the blue numbers that float and appear on my left skin? Why do I ignore the smells, and the sounds and the colors? Why do I insist on listing you by your names and professions but never tell about the sorrow, the suffering and the pain? . . . How do I tell about the fear of trains I inherited? Why don't I mention my childhood battles against the Nazis? I only browse the truth? . . . What do I blame myself for? What haven't I done yet? Against whom haven't I taken vengeance yet?

Why don't I tell about my work? Why don't I write poems about the Holocaust? Why don't I record my dreams? Why do I pray? Why do, night after night, I close the shutters around me? Why do I leave the light on my porch? Who am I afraid of? Am I a "second generation"? Why do I travel around the world seeking meetings with other survivor children? . . . Don't know how to feel. Don't know how to cry. Don't know how to scream. Don't know how to explain. . . . Do I store food? Do I throw away bread? Am I in dream therapy? Nightmare therapy? How am I affected by knocks on the door? Or by the sharp ring of the phone? Am I sad on Holocaust Day? . . . Does everyone have a mother with a number on her arm? Who's asking? Who's crying? Who's lonely? Who hates? Who eats white meat? Who's afraid of dogs? Who am I named after? Is it my grandfather who was murdered by the Nazis? Is it after my uncle who was murdered by the Nazis? Is it after my grandmother who was murdered by the Nazis? (Levy, pp. 53–54)

The accusation that in some ways Levy's narrative borders on the sensational and voyeuristic is partly validated in two detailed, elongated, generatively imagined torture and humiliation passages. The first deals with the Nazis' response to his grandfather's refusal to cooperate in the construction of a death camp:

Because Grandfather Greenshpan refused to build their city of death and insisted on charging them two Zlotties as a passage tax, the Nazis began torturing him. They whipped his back and hands. They forced him to clean the street's pavements with sulphuric acid that burned his wounds. They threatened his life if he wouldn't sing "Heil Hitler" for them as he cleaned. Afterwards, they shaved his beard with their knives, tearing pieces of flesh together with the hair. They ordered him to lay tefilin, and in the end they covered him with gasoline and threw him into the burning synagogue of Plotzk. Since he came out unharmed, and since he had no smell of ashes on his skin, they accused him of separatism, i.e. Communism, and they continued to torture him. They forced him to bend his knees again and again, for six straight hours under the blazing sun and under a shower of blows. They shoved needles under his fingers, hit him with an electrical shock, gave him a postcard and forced him to scribble a message to his loved ones: "I have arrived safely. I am healthy. I am happy and feeling well." They crushed his testicles and welded his fingers together. They ordered him to carry stones from here to there for no reason, to dig holes and cover them up again. They competed against each other taking aim and practising at the tip of his nose and his earlobes. All the while his anguished eyes scanned the camp around him. . . . Since all of their deeds did not help and the Jew continued to refuse and mock, the Nazis adopted new tactics. They tied his limbs to a "seesaw" device that stretched and dismembered his body. They put starved rats into his trousers and shot at bottles placed on his head. In the end, they dragged him to the forest and there, just for fun, for they had long forgotten what they wanted from him, they shot him in the neck, back, stomach, temples, mouth and heart. God had made a miracle, for my grandfather, and although he was dead he did not allow blood to flow out of his body but created a miraculous blood that dripped only from the wounds of his pants and the cut in his shirt. His upper skin and lower skin remained smooth and clean (Levy, pp. 20–21).

In the second passage, Arnon wonders about the particulars and extent of his father's brutal deeds:

Did you send their organs for medical testing? Did you use Zyklon B against them? Did you hang them by their wrists with their arms tied behind their back? Did you inject gasoline into their blood? Did you pour frozen water over their skin? Did you enjoy seeing this and that standing and watching their wife and sons walking to their death? Did you force them to wipe the streets with their tallith, burn their holy books and dance around the bonfires? Did you force them to stand in front of the hanged corpses of their families and sing "I will never forget my concentration camp, the Eden of the Jews"? Did you insert wooden beams under the fingers of the one standing in front of you and light them? . . . Did you throw children off speeding carriage cars? Did you throw live, suffering kids into a burning fire? . . . Did you kill people with your bare hands? Did you step over their bodies and shoot those still alive? Did you order the hanging of your naked prisoners on the camp's trees? Did you unleash your dogs onto their private parts? . . . Did you strangle your victims with ten fingers? Is it true you drowned their heads in buckets of water? Is it true you forced them to bend and eat horse faeces? Why did you skin your victims and decorate the lamps in your office with it? (Levy, pp. 23–24, 55).

It should come as no surprise that the extensive and graphic passages of the torture and degradation of Jews provoked a heated debate among several commentators. Avner Holtzman's moral reservations, for example, rested on the overly detailed descriptions of the dreadful humiliation and death of Jews peppered throughout the book. Of the horrific passages, Holtzman wrote, "Perhaps the tangible descriptions are part of the desire to shock and astonish, but the result achieved is the opposite. The impression is of a simplistic, incautious use of materials which wiser authors understood were not to be touched, realising that it is better to present the horror in small doses indirectly and by allusion" (Holtzman, p. 28). In a later article, he added this caveat, with Levy in mind, "It is good that young and talented Israeli authors have the need to write about the Holocaust. However, this is a subject that—perhaps the only one—that imposes restrictions on anyone who deals with it, since playing with explosives, with all its attendant attraction and adventure, carries within it great danger to insensitive hands" (Holtzman, p. 120). Yigal Schwartz, countering Holtzman, believes that Levy's text performs a trustingly moral duty. He begins by contending that Levy did not try to understand, imagine or concretize the *Shoah*. Rather, says Schwartz, Levy attempted to look at the catalog of texts that have previously touched upon the Holocaust (Schwartz, p. 122). According to Schwartz, this is a novel protesting the failures of the Holocaust corpus, an indictment against those works that instead of opening a window for the young generation, so as to allow it to connect with the world over there, have erected an impenetrable textual wall that prevents any cognitive or emotional engagement. Levy's objective, thus, was to rally against the failings of the earlier models, which Schwartz labels with the neologism of "actualisation to the point of absurdity" (Schwartz, p. 123). This creative route suggests that the Holocaust can be understood only through synecdoche that focuses the story of one person in a specific situation, and will explicate the fate of an entire community in an extended territory. Levy rebuts this method through his description of Grandfather Greenshpan's torture, cited earlier. It is abundantly evident, Schwartz observes, that Levy condenses the entire Holocaust experience on Grandfather Greenshpan to signal to the reader that there exists no one man, real or imagined, whose story can reflect the black fate of the six million Jews. After all, no human being could withstand such inflictions, especially one as frail and old as the victim. Schwartz concludes his vehement defense of Levy by stating that through his novel, the author remonstrates against the fossilized and decayed state of the Israeli literary and cultural consciousness as regards the Holocaust (Schwartz, p. 125). Balaban concurs: "There are those who will say this is a postmodern work. However, beyond these labels, this is an extraordinary novel about the Holocaust, its past and present victims . . . about the ways fiction can confront the Holocaust" (Balaban, p. 9B).

Biography

Itamar Levy was born in 1956, in Tel Aviv, Israel. He studied theater at Tel Aviv University and published his first story in 1978. Levy is also a dramatist and writes radio scripts. He has worked as a journalist as well.

Bibliography

Primary Sources

Zelig Maints Ve-Ga'aguav El Ha Mavet (Zelig Maints and His Longings for Death). 1985.

Agadat ha'agamim ha'atsuvim (The Legend of the Sad Lakes). 1989.

Otiot Hashemesh, otiot Ha-Yareah (Letters of the Sun, Letters of the Moon). 1991.

Etiudim Le-Morgana (Morgana Morgana). 1996.

Secondary Sources

Balaban, Avraham. "Ledaber agnonit otentit." *Haaretz*, 23 March 1990, p. 9.

Gur, Batya. "Review." *Haaretz*, 3 November 1989, p. 8B.

Holtzman, Avner. "Hatziyat Gvul." *Efes Shtaim* no. 1 (1992): 119–120.

Kotz, Miriam. "Sipur shemadbikim lo safam." *Yediot Ahrnonot*, 11 November 1989, p. 14.

Langer, Lawrence. *The Holocaust and the Literary Imagination*. New Haven, Conn.: Yale University Press, 1975.

Morahg. Gilead. "Breaking Silence: Israel's Fantastic Fiction of the Holocaust." In *The Boom in Israeli Fiction*. Edited by Alan Mintz. Hanover, N.H.: University Press of New England, 1997.

Schwartz, Yigal. "Mesima musarit Be'hekhlet." *Efes Shtaim* no. 1 (1992): 121–125.

SAVYON LIEBRECHT

(1948–)

LEON I. YUDKIN

SAVYON LIEBRECHT WAS born in Germany to Holocaust survivors and immigrated to Israel as an infant. Her parents had met in Europe as displaced persons. Like many Holocaust survivors, they tried, under cover of silence, to shelter their children from the horrors they had experienced. Of her parents' actual experience, Liebrecht claims:

> I know almost nothing about their past. They kept total silence in our home about their Holocaust experiences. To this day, I don't know how many brothers and sisters my parents had. I don't know their names, I don't know what happened to them during the war, and I don't know in which concentration camps my father was held. But I do know that he went through several ("The Influence of the Holocaust on My Work," Yudkin, ed. 1993, p. 125).

Liebrecht's background, albeit considerably shrouded in silence and mystery, constitutes a considerable layer of her writing and thrust of her work. For although she grew up ostensibly as a Sabra (native-born Israeli), the unspoken underside of her existence has assumed major importance, sometimes explicitly, and more often, implicitly.

The Holocaust in Liebrecht's Work

Of the significance of the Holocaust to her writing, Liebrecht observes:

> The influence of the Holocaust on my work cannot be separated from the influence of the Holocaust on my life. The very subjects which trouble you and inspire you and haunt you as a person, are those which are—in all sorts of disguises—going to reveal themselves in your work. And since the Holocaust is the event which, more than any other, has left its marks on my life, it has become a subject in my work ("Influence," p. 125).

Like so many narrative writers in Israel (such as Aharon Appelfeld, Amos Oz, Abraham B. Yehoshua, Amalia Kahana-Carmon), Liebrecht wrote short stories before going into longer fiction. She then branched out into television drama, and, more recently, a novel. Her first work appeared in print relatively late; the first volume, *Tapuhim min hamidbar (Apples from the Desert)*, came out in book form first in 1987, with many prints successively following its huge success, before republication in 1992. Since then she has become increasingly prolific. She has written about those who have suffered from comparative inaudibility in Israeli society in general, and from within Israeli fiction in particular; women in a male-dominated environment, Arabs in an Jewish-dominated economy, and Holocaust survivors within a context that has attempted to supercede the dreadful events of the past, and, in some respects, to act as though they had not occurred. Liebrecht studied philosophy and literature at Tel Aviv University and received the Prime Minister's Prize for Literature.

Much of Liebrecht's writing is born out of a creative response to silence and the suppression of the significant. The tension in her writing reveals the pain Liebrecht experienced as a child of *Shoah* survivors, one "born into the Holocaust to parents who were broken, who had lost everything—including their language, their cultural background, and their optimism" ("Influence," p. 129). She has said that the typical behavior pattern of survivors is either total silence in regard to the traumatic events, or obsessive repetition in the form of constant verbal reliving of the scene. Her characters embody either or both of these behaviors, sometimes on the part of one person whose responses are triggered by a specific event to which that person obsessively returns, and from which his/her bearings are taken. In other cases, various of her characters evince the opposite reactions.

Liebrecht's writing reflects the influence of the doyenne of Israeli women short story writers, Amalia Kahana-Carmon, with its short exclamatory sentences, the introspective interspersed with the retrospective, and the attempt on the part of the narrator to grasp the fleeting emotional moment of a distant feeling, now seeking recapture. Much of Liebrecht narrative suggests the limits imposed on reaching out to another person in attempted communication and, thus, of reaching out successfully and meaningfully to the reader. Experience may be an essentially private mode, first person in sense as well as in grammar, and therefore misconstrued when the attempt is made to put into language what has been boxed into feelings. Often told by a female narrator, Liebrecht's stories are shaped by the underlying emotional conflict of the characters' history and involve preservation of memory.

From the vantage point of the grown child of Holocaust survivors, Liebrecht's stories often engage unresolved Holocaust dilemmas—the inherited aftermath of the Holocaust, the outcome of the horror rather than the horror of the camp universe. A recurrent theme, obsessive revisitation of the past, is recorded in such stories as "Haalbum shel ima" (Mother's Photo Album), when a young physician reflects that there seems to be no record of "the bad days" in a photo album from his childhood. In his hospital, however, when he inspects his schizophrenic mother's medical record, he chooses to attach to the record a particular photograph that tells him of a shared and distant past and reminds him of his mother's insistence on preserving the album. The war years in Poland shattered her life, both directly and indirectly. Having married, she seemingly began a new life after the war, but her husband later left her when he discovered that his first wife, whom he had assumed dead, had, in fact, survived the *Shoah*. The invasion of the present by the past constantly recurs and complicates communication between individuals who cannot access each other's experience.

Memory Suppressed

Liebrecht has dealt in her fiction with the effects of the suppression of traumatic memory, specifically in relation to the horrors of the Holocaust and the Second World War. Of the silence that pervades the survivor's home she writes:

> The silence in the homes of Holocaust survivors is unique. It is a silence that covers pain and dark secrets, and it takes time until the child who grows up in such a home understands that this secret is not a personal one but a national, or even a universal, one. . . . [H]e grows up believing that there is something terribly wrong with him and his family. Homes of Holocaust survivors are quiet homes: parents don't speak about the past; they don't speak about their thoughts; they don't speak about their feelings. In a way, the children in such homes are compelled to develop alternative ways of expression ("Influence," p. 126).

The process is two way; there are those who bear the memory, and there is the environment of others who might well wish to reject any such suggestion of that other world.

In the story "Hagigat haerusin shel hayuta" (Hayuta's Engagement Party) in the volume *Tapuhim min hamidbar*, it is the grandfather, Mendel, who is said by the "objective" narrator to bring disgrace on the family. The principal focus of consciousness is Bella, Hayuta's mother, daughter of Mendel, who acts as a shuttle between the two generations. On one hand, she is to some extent sympathetic to her father, to his history, and to his efforts in the past to nurture the granddaughter; while on the other, she dreads her daughter's fear of disruption and her insistent demand for a smooth passage. She also feels she has to be accepted by the socially superior family into which her daughter is marrying, and does not want to be seen as a pariah. The daughter first wants to exclude her father from the celebration, a radical affront that seems to go too far beyond the spirit of compromise. Mendel's behavior had radically altered: "Up until six years ago he never said a word about what happened to him in the war . . . A secret door to the memories of the war—what had been shrouded in blissful oblivion for decades—suddenly burst open forcefully. It all started on the eve of Rosh Hashanah" (*Tapuhim min hamidbar*, Jerusalem: Ketar, 1992, p. 122). But lately Mendel seems more and more drawn into spoken reminiscences of the horrors of the past, and these are particularly triggered by the sight of abundance of food and luxury. Joyous family and holiday celebrations are the catalyst for the survivor's voice, for it is these occasions that spark barely submerged memories of the relatives murdered in the Holocaust, although for Bella, the death camp tales are "a key to the riddle that haunted her all those years" (p. 125). The compromise arrived at is that Mendel should attend the engagement party, but only on the assurance that he remain relatively silent. At the party, all seems to be going well until the moment when he again seems to be at the point of raising the past. The family's abrupt intervention ensures not only the interruption of the speech, but also the final moments of Mendel. His collapse denies him the moment of final release. It seems that the two realities cannot be sustained together. We have an observation about memory, suppression, suffering, and also subterfuge and pretense. Generations deny each other, even when they have derived their own sustenance from the rejected source. The younger generation's disinterest in the survivor generation's story is evocative of the conspiracy of silence of a disinterested world while the SS killers and their accomplices were busy at work and an immediate postwar imposition of silence on the survivors.

Another such story is "Kritah" (Cutting), from *Susim al kvish geheh* (Horses on the Highway). Here, the third-person narrator tells of the grandmother, Henya, vigorously, almost violently, cutting off her granddaughter's hair for fear of lice, which have been spotted by the schoolteacher. Although we soon discover that this act of "cutting" is an acting out of repetition compulsion learned in the camp, the reaction of Henya's son, and then, more hysterically, of the daughter-in-law, categorizes Henya's activity as delegitimized madness. Children, the younger woman insists, should hear of Cinderella, not of Auschwitz. The story ends, not with the pursuit of the episode, but with a flashback to the source incident and suppressed memory. The grandmother's current behavior is overpowered by memory of adopted camp behavior, when cutting lice-ridden hair affected survival ("Influence," p. 128). Again, the two levels cannot be accommodated together: the *soi-disant* comfort of the reconstructed Israeli life, with the protected children, and the not-so-distant history of the older generation. Commenting on this story, Liebrecht states that it is fitting that the rebellious voice belongs to the daughter-in-law, an in-law; the child of survivors could not have uttered such words.

Communication with the Past

The title story of the volume *Sinit ani medaberet elekha* (I'm Speaking Chinese to You) relates the private world of the individual and its effect on others. The principal character, an elegant woman, is searching for a suitable apartment, but the apartment that she is actually interested in belies her present affluence. She is in search of the apartment of her childhood, site of a vivid childhood memory of her mother's frigidity and refusal of her father's advances, and her father's ensuing frustration. During such intense encounters, the daughter overheard her mother tell her father "I'm speaking Chinese to you," a cryptic comment on his failure to comprehend the true intent of her words. The elegant woman has returned to the scene of her childhood unhappiness to excise the initial fear, reencountering it in order to reverse its implications. Aware of her mother's concentration camp past but unaware of how that past destroyed her ability to experience physical pleasure, and unwilling to cause her mother additional pain by her own open rebellion, she is free after her mother's death to rebel—to rescue her life from her mother's obsession. What had been a venue of repression, sexual fear, and inhibition, now turns into a place of eroticized freedom. She seduces the real estate agent, who is puzzled, overwhelmed, and excited by the approaches of this lovely woman. With the satisfactory culmination of this act, the devils of the past can be expelled. The woman is released from her past and from those fears. Sex is normalized, the ceiling "stains" that she recognizes from her past can be seen in proportion, the mother can be seen for what she is, and her own life can resume its appropriate path. The story brings together layers of time, which are also layers of life, and the past interplays with the present. Only one brief image of the parents' connection, "bound together by war," and the daughter's memory of the father's words recalling his wife's beauty—"Even after the war, when sometimes I couldn't tell a woman from a man, only she, with her grey eyes—like a butterfly"—suggest that her parents' lack of communication and mother's sexual aversion are bound to Holocaust trauma (*Sinit ani medaberet elekha*, Jerusalem: Ketar, 1992, p. 18).

Much of Liebrecht's work presents the reader with several layers of reality. The reader is confronted with one surface that is the apparent reality. This is the picture as immediately viewed; the version, for example, that the real estate agent of the story observes when the client enters his office in all her finery and control. The other layer bubbles beneath and can, in fact, be decisive in the shaping of this woman's destiny and ultimate fulfillment. The parties to this are her two selves, that of the present and that of the past, including her mother as she remembers her; her father as recalled in his romantic infatuation, despite all the obstacles he must overcome in relation to her mother; the realtor, who actually does come into his own in his capacity as "agent," that is, as the instrument for the implementation of her will; and finally, the apartment. The apartment had taken on mythical proportions as a source of dread and sin (the stains), and also as a source of fascination and introduction to adult secrets. Now, it can be seen in another light, and restored to what is seen by the agent—a rather inferior and dilapidated construction not worthy of her consideration. He is an instrument of her attempted return to normalcy; however, she tries to reassure him that he is more than just a means to an end.

The Suppression of Women

One of the repeated themes in Liebrecht's stories is the position of women vis-à-vis men. This also intercuts with the recurrent Holocaust theme, where it acquires its most extreme expression. The settings are various and broadly imagined, from "Westernized" scenarios in contemporary Israel, where the woman is still very often the junior partner in a relationship with a man; to a totally patriarchal Arab society, in which the female barely exists as an independent entity; to the ultimate subjugation and sadism to which women were subjected under the Nazis.

An example of the first is the story "A Married Woman" ("Eshet ish," in *Tapuhim min hamidbar*), in which the newly divorced Hannah must face the rebuke of her adolescent daughter for not adopting a stronger line with her playboy husband. Hannah defends him as being weak and subject to the ministrations of artful women. As so often in the author's narratives, the past intersects with the present, flashbacks of their first meeting in Warsaw intercut the current sadness. "Mercy" ("Hesed," in *Sinit ani medaberet elekha*) presents the highly complex scenario of Clarissa, a Jewish woman who had been raised as Christian in a convent during the *Shoah* and, following her postwar emigration to Israel, converted to Islam to marry an Arab. Her present plight is that her daughter has run away and will no doubt be trapped by her vengeful son-in-law. She is left with the daughter's illegitimate baby, whom she, the loving grandmother, now cradles and drowns, protecting the infant from masculine cruelty by exercising her own form of power. In "Morning in the Park Among the Nannies" ("Boqer bagan im hametaplim," in *Sinit ani medaberet elekha*), horrific memories invade a present moment of a woman among caregivers tending the needs of infants in a play center. She imagines a conversation with a young woman whom she remembers as a beautiful favorite and later victim of German officers. When she finally addresses the young woman, whom she had assumed to be the mother of the child she was tending, she finds it is someone else's child and the young woman is just another nanny. Readers may have difficulty disentangling fact from fiction and reality from fantasy in this story.

A Man, a Woman and a Man

The movement out of the short story form represents not only a shift of genre, but also the broadening of a search. A major theme of Liebrecht's writing is the difficulty of communication. From the vantage point of an individual, a woman, the "other" is seen as at least potentially, if not actually, hostile. But communication is essential for human life, and in its ultimate expression, it is love. This is the theme of the novel *A Man, a Woman and a Man* (1998). A chance meeting takes place between a woman visiting her mother in an old age home, and a man, Saul, similarly attending to his helpless father. The woman sympathizes not only with her own mother and the man's father, in an even worse state, but with the condition that befalls all. Her husband, to whom she confides these anxieties, has no time for her concerns. A familiar theme emerges: the woman, Hamutal, feels excluded in her own environment—here, by her husband and daughter. The horror of aging links the two principals in the novel, and the attachment between them develops naturally and gradually, but the plot is also advanced by the element of fantasy and through the agency of related dreams (Hamutal's work as an editor revolves around a periodical issue devoted to nightmares). Both project themselves into the skin of their parents, seeing themselves in their situations, mindless and helpless, terrorized.

The novel focuses on relationships: Hamutal's obsession with her mother's decline may suggest a type of revenge for earlier inattention. Further questioned is the underlying and persistent nature of post-Holocaust trauma, and the adult's ability to reinterpret childhood impressions of a traumatized parent. This trauma was typically, as in the novel, suppressed by the mother, who did not verbalize the events to the daughter, but rather redirected them in her insistence on discipline and ambition. This resulted in distancing and lack of love, or even failure of basic communication between the two generations. The novel climaxes with the death of Saul's father and his own emotional distancing from Hamutal; it continues with his return to Chicago, and finally with the death of Hamutal's mother, followed by a reunion with her husband and children. The nurse at the home advises her to "return to life" and surrender the unwholesome preoccupations that have led her on difficult and painful paths.

The Nature of the Story

A popular Israeli writer, Liebrecht is perceived by many as an author who writes her generation's preoccupations. Beryl Lieff Benderly's view is representative of critical opinion that argues:

> She recognizes young Israelis' need to encapsulate a hideous past in monuments and ritual commemorations that

> permit them to carry their own and their children's lives into a future that demands all their energy and attention. But she also knows why the survivors need to validate that past, give it some human meaning, to express to descendants who have never known hunger or mass murder how that inexpressible reality felt (p. X03).

Similarly, Harvey Grossinger, author of *The Quarry*, which addresses similar themes, praises Liebrecht for describing the core of "these riveting stories . . . highly charged though understated explorations of the aftershocks of the Holocaust, specifically as they surface and resurface in the quotidian lives of the survivors' offspring and grandchildren" (p. 19).

There is considerable exposition in Liebrecht's stories. We, usually through the intervention of the omniscient narrator, know all that is going on, and it is translatable into consciously formulated language in the minds of the chief protagonists. We are told of situations that project conflict, extension, development, and potential resolution. The sources of conflict might well relate to generalized stances and divisions in society. There is a colonialist situation in regard to Jews and Arabs in Israel, where the Jews play out the role of the colonizers, and the Arabs the colonized. There is a situation of religious tension as between the secular and the observant, the former of whom might be the Westerners (Ashkenazim) and the latter, Easterners (Sefardim). And there is a sexual tension as between men and women, where it is often the latter who are more aware of the explosive implications of the erotic, electrical charge between male and female.

In Liebrecht's writings, the plasticity, the terseness, and the unexpected turn, based on psychological observation and the analysis of interpersonal relationships, emerge brilliantly in the brief narratives. As we saw in her later volume of short stories, the author again deals with relationships, with assumptions made by individuals regarding others, and with sudden revisions. A new attachment becomes possible when the past is confronted. The point made by a Liebrecht story is to uncover what had hitherto been hidden. Just as in life, individuals only discover facets of their personality unexpectedly, or perhaps through analysis or introspection; so fictional devices can lead to revelation. This, of course, is a source of narrative tension, and one of the enduringly appealing aspects of narrative fiction.

The Liebrecht story is often marked by the unexpected twist, but the narrative turn is not arbitrary or conventional. Rather it is based on a fictive life taking over the plot and directing it in a manner that illuminates character and then life in general on a deeper level. By the end of such a story we know more about the person involved, the life already lived, and the potential for further development. Liebrecht likes to provide a "rounded" end to her stories; the characters can be allowed a new impetus in life when their past lives have been confronted. The Holocaust, an aspect of the past very much alive in the present, Israel's class divisions, the tension between Arab and Jew, and the unequal balance between male and female act as catalysts for some of the most remarkable and arresting contemporary Hebrew fiction.

Bibliography

Primary Sources

Tapuhim min hamidbar (Apples from the Desert). 1987.

Susim al kvish geheh (Horses on the Highway). 1988.

Sinit ani medaberet elekha (I'm Speaking Chinese to You). 1992.

Tsarikhs of lesipur ahavah (On Love Stories and Other Endings). 1995.

Ish Veishah Veish (A Man, a Woman and a Man). 1998.

"The Influence of the Holocaust on My Work." In *Hebrew Literature in the Wake of the Holocaust*. Edited and with an introduction by Leon I. Yudkin. Rutherford, N. J.: Fairleigh Dickinson University Press, 1993.

Secondary Sources

Benderly, Beryl Lieff. "This Year in Jerusalem." Review of *Apples from the Desert. The Washington Post*, July 19, 1998, p. X03.

Cohen, Leslie. "Liebrecht's Women." *The Jerusalem Post*, May 7, 1999, p. 13B.

Glazer, Miriyam. "Introduction to Savyon Liebrecht's ' "It's Greek to You," She Said to Him.' " In *Dreaming the Actual: Contemporary Fiction and Poetry by Israeli Women Writers*. New York: State University of New York Press, 2000.

Grossinger, Harvey. "Short Stories of Long Struggles in Israel." Review of *Apples from the Desert. Houston Chronicle* 2 Star Edition, January 17, 1999, p. 19.

Mesher, David. "The Malamud Factor: Recent Jewish Short Fiction." *Judaism* 49 (winter 2000): 120.

Ruta, Suzanne. "Bridges in the Sand." Review of *Apples from the Desert. New York Times Book Review*, September 13, 1998, p. 36.

Yudkin, Leon I. *Hebrew Literature in the Wake of the Holocaust*. Rutherford, N.J.: Fairleigh Dickinson University Press, 1993.

———. "Holocaust Trauma in the Second Generation: The Hebrew Fiction of David Grossman and Savyon Liebrecht." In *Breaking Crystal: Writing and Memory After Auschwitz*, 170–181. Edited by Efraim Sicher. Urbana: University of Illinois Press, 1998.

Jakov Lind

(1927–)

PETER STENBERG

Jakov Lind was born in Vienna in the middle of the deceptive lull between the First and Second World Wars. At the time of his youth, during the 1930s, there were still millions of mainly Yiddish-speaking Orthodox Jews living in the countries that had been carved out of the eastern parts of the former Austro-Hungarian Empire, especially in Galicia in reestablished Poland and in the western part of the Soviet Union. This population was destined to take the brunt of the killing during the systematic attempt by the Nazis and their allies to eliminate the Jews of Europe during the first half of the 1940s. As a result, there is today virtually nothing left of the Jewish religion and culture in that vast area of Eastern Europe, where it had been prominent for half a millennium. However, in the preceding half century, the erosion of that world had already begun, as a significant proportion of the East European Orthodox Jews had either begun to assimilate into western European languages and cultures or had actually emigrated to the great cities that were the gateways to western Europe and North America.

These immigrants were faced with the same problems that most immigrants must learn to cope with —foreign languages, alien cultural traditions, and a different way of life—but in addition to these challenges, the new Jewish residents of Vienna, Berlin, and New York had to determine to what extent they felt obligated to continue to follow the religious practices that tended to identify them as permanent outsiders, if not pariahs, in a very Christian world. In novels such as Joseph Roth's *Hiob* (Job), readers can follow a generation clash as the children of Jewish emigrants from Eastern Europe to the urban West (in this case New York) look with increasing skepticism on the strict religious laws observed by their parents and make many compromises in their attempts to become an accepted part of a completely different culture. Thus the practical solution to what was, in effect, an economic problem—for instance the demand by employers that Saturday be considered a normal working day—often led to the abandonment of old traditions by the new generation.

As a consequence, much of the traditional East European Jewish world was in the process of becoming secularized by the 1920s. Thus, the children of Jewish immigrants in western Europe and North America often dropped their parents' native languages and traditions and could not imagine that they would live the same kind of lives as their parents had. Lind's biography displays, in a very clear way, this trend toward secularization in second-generation Jews of Vienna between the two wars. The generation of his parents, Simon and Rosa Landwirth (their son changed his name to Lind after the war), mirrored the great demographic, religious, and cultural metamorphosis that was transforming Central and Eastern Europe in the decades surrounding the turn of the century.

Family Background

In *Counting My Steps* (1969), the first of the three autobiographical works Lind wrote in English between 1969 and 1991 (the other two, dealing with his life upon returning to Europe from Israel after the war, are *Numbers*, 1972, and *Crossing. The Discovery of Two Islands*, 1991), he presents a rather paradoxical portrait of the world of his parents and of his love/hate relationship to Vienna. His father, who had left home at age eleven, was an immigrant from southern Poland and been involved with various marginal business ventures in Vienna before marrying into a relatively wealthy Jewish family from the Bukovina in 1921. By the 1930s, when Lind was growing up, his father, "half Luftmensch and half duke" (*Counting My Steps*, London: Macmillan, 1969, p. 32), was an unsuccessful traveling salesman, trying to raise a family on virtually no income, and was at least partially responsible for his own bad luck. It is surely no coincidence that Lind has written that he considers Arthur Miller, the author of *The Death of a Salesman*, to be one of the greatest of all dramatists. On page 87 of *Counting My Steps* Lind writes, "The Nazis romanticism had transformed life into kitsch and the small insignificant man into a tragic hero. The milkman and the travelling salesman (his father's profession) had a face for the first time . . . They had expected to run around this town forever. And battle forever making a living. All this was superfluous now . . . the small man became the new tragic hero. Arthur Miller sang their swan song when he mourned the Death of a Salesman and because of this one play I count Miller among the greatest playwrights of all time."

The biography of Lind's mother, Rosa Birnbaum Landwirth, also culminates in the futile attempt of an East European Jew to find a foothold in western Europe in the face of the uncertainties of life for a Jew back home. Sent to Vienna after the war by a family unhappy with her unmarried status and fearful of the approaching Cossacks, Rosa met her future husband through a marriage broker and settled into married life with a man considered by her religious family to be an unreliable, assimilated playboy. Like her husband, she is also portrayed by her son as an oddly sympathetic figure, who was too distracted, or too weak, to deal, in any kind of effective manner, with the rise of the antisemitic Austrian fascists and the increasing threat of the Brown Shirts.

In *Counting My Steps*, Lind describes a childhood played out against the background of the naïve Jewish-Viennese petit bourgeois at the very edge of the abyss. While the antisemites were beginning to display their muscle in an increasingly open and threatening manner, Lind's mother was attempting to convince her skeptical son of the importance of God and of Lind's marks in the Jewish high school that he had entered in 1937. Meanwhile, his often absent father continued to sit in the café, making phantom business deals while complaining about the orthodox *Ostjuden* (East European Jews), who were becoming increasingly evident in Vienna. "My father loathed the Orthodox Jews . . . despised the righteous and the respectable, called them all hypocrites" (*Counting My Steps*, p. 33).

Early Life and War Experiences

The Landwirth's third child and only son, Jakov, was born on 10 February 1927 in Vienna, the grand capital city of the no-longer-so-grand First Austrian Republic, the German-language state that was all that was left of the once all-powerful Austro-Hungarian Empire. The Republic would cease to exist with the annexation of Austria by Nazi Germany in March 1938. The threat to the Jewish population of Vienna, which had become very concrete in the wake of the *Anschluss* (annexation of Austria by Germany), convinced Jakov's parents to put their eleven-year-old son, along with his younger sister, on a train to the Hook of Holland in December 1938 and to place their children's fate into the hands of a Dutch Zionist organization. Soon thereafter, the parents managed to arrange for their own passage to Palestine, where they lost everything they owned upon arrival when their ship, which had been refused entry into Palestine, was blown up by the Haganah, the defense force of the Jewish settlers in Palestine. Almost a decade would pass before Jakov would see his father again, find out that his mother had died of cancer in Tel Aviv in 1941, and discover that his father was hopelessly employed as a cobbler's assistant on a kibbutz. During this decade, Jakov undertook one of the strangest odysseys of any Jew who managed to survive the Holocaust.

At first, the urban centers of Holland must have appeared to offer a secure alternative to the terror that was overwhelming the Viennese Jews as the Austrian Nazis took full advantage of the free reign they had received to finally allow their antisemitism to run amok. Jakov stayed with a prosperous Jewish family in Amsterdam, continued his schooling, and lived under relatively normal conditions as he was not yet threatened by the Dutch Nazis. Unfortunately, the expansionary ambitions of Nazi Germany would soon catch up with Jakov in Amsterdam as they had in Vienna, and, with the occupation of the Netherlands in May 1940, the thirteen-year-old Austrian lost his firm foundation. He landed in a kind of Zionist agricultural youth camp that was meant to prepare him for emigration to Palestine, but he soon found himself left on his own when the camp was closed by the Dutch Nazis in 1943. He attempted to disappear into the nebulous underworld of illegal and threatened refugees in urban Holland and to somehow find a method of survival there.

In 1943, having managed to avoid the search operations of the Gestapo in the Netherlands for three years, the now sixteen-year-old Jakov took on the first of several false identities he would eventually use. This one was based on a forged Dutch passport made out to Jan Gerrit Overbeek. He used it to sign on as a worker on a Rhine barge and sail to Germany: "Inside the lion's mouth I would not have to fear the animal's teeth and claws" (*Counting My Steps*, p. 116). Concluding that he had a better chance of survival as a native German speaker in Germany with a forged Aryan Dutch passport than as a native German speaker in the Netherlands with no passport, he became a minor cog in the wheel of the machine that would have gladly murdered the entire Landwirth family. (He explained his native German language skills by fabricating an Austrian mother, which of course in reality he actually had.) As a vigorous and hard-working Dutch teenager playing the waterways of Germany in the service of Nazi industry, Jan Gerrit Overbeek fulfilled all the expectations of his fellow workers and their superiors, sharing their concerns for the increasingly pessimistic course of the war and even complaining that his comrades were not as antisemitic as they should be.

In 1944, when the Nazi world was being reduced to rubble in a debacle that was dangerous even for the few Jews who had managed to survive on German soil, Jakov found himself at The Institute for Metallurgical Research of the Imperial Ministry of Air Traffic (*Das Metallurgische Forschungsinstitut des Reichsluftfahrt-Ministeriums*), an obscure organization whose very name lends itself to the kind of grotesque satire he would soon be writing. There he served as a favored assistant of the director, a Prussian officer. This bizarre charade in which an Austrian Jew outwits an imminent death threat by masquerading as a young, hard-working antisemitic Dutchman, in retrospect, must have seemed to Jakov to have offered an excellent paradigm for the absurdities of life for a European Jew during World War II. His own life offered the kind of biographical material that he would be able to draw upon when he began to consider how an author could transform such a surrealistically disfigured world into fiction.

Years in Palestine and Israel and the Return to Europe

With yet another forged passport, this time under the name of Jakov Chaklan, Jakov made his way via Holland to Marseilles, where he illegally boarded one of the overcrowded, rusty ships that were transferring the traumatized, surviving Jews of Europe to the Promised Land. There they were met by one more threatening scenario—the British blockade in defense of the immigration quota of their protectorate in Palestine, which had helped turn the Middle East into yet another war zone, this time between Jews, Arabs, and Great Britain. Arriving in Palestine in the summer of 1945, Jakov was ready to make his final metamorphosis into Jakov Lind, the real Jewish teenager from Vienna who had made it through the European war in much better physical shape than most of his fellow refugees and who was ready to take on any job he could find—actor, construction worker, beach photographer, fruit picker, airport controller, hospital attendant, and fledgling author. He soon met another future iconoclastic novelist, Edgar Hilsenrath, in the unemployment office in the coastal city of Netanya, Palestine. Healthy and smiling, Lind had himself photographed with his future wife, Ida, and Hilsenrath, as they walked jauntily down a street in Tel Aviv in 1947. It is a scenario that speaks volumes about the difference between being twenty at the end of the Holocaust, as the trio in the photo, and being the parents of a twenty-year-old, as were their parents, who were dead or permanently injured. Lind remained in Palestine/Israel long enough to write his first literary text, *Das Tagebuch des Hanan Edgar Malinek* (The Diary of Hanan Edgar Malinek), which appeared in Hebrew translation as a newspaper serial. He was also there to witness the birth of Israel but was convinced that this was not where he wanted to stay permanently. Ida was pregnant when the couple returned to Europe; their marriage dissolved soon after.

Like many other European Jews who often took on great risks to reach what they hoped was going to be their promised land, Lind finally felt defeated by the strangeness of the world of the Middle East. Its climate, topography, and languages were all alien to him. There were also the political uncertainties dictated by a dominant Jewish presence with which he felt little or no affinity. After five years, he returned to Austria before moving on to the somewhat alienating security of Great Britain. He attempted to reintegrate himself into the cultural scene in what might normally have been his home city, Vienna, but it now had almost none of the Jewish input that had been so central to its makeup when he had grown up there only twenty years before. Once again, as in Israel, Lind found himself in the position of having to take on whatever jobs, or other money-making opportunities, that were available. He spent some time working as a journalist and also studying theater direction, on a fellowship, at the Max Reinhardt Theater Institute.

Despite the fact that in Vienna Lind succeeded in coming into contact with the important writer H. C. Artmann and his circle of friends, he could no longer feel at home in Austria and went back to the Netherlands, where he spent a year studying political science in Amsterdam. There he also failed to find a satisfactory postwar place in his former refuge and moved on via Copenhagen and Paris to London, where he began work as a literary and film agent. There he settled down in what was his principal city of residence after 1954. He also had lengthy stays in the United States and at a summer house in Mallorca. Like Hilsenrath in New York, he attempted to become a successful German-language author in an English-speaking country that had little interest in anything written in German.

Literary Works and Importance in Holocaust Literature

In 1962, Lind made a startling and controversial literary debut when the prominent German publishing house, Luchterhand, published seven short stories by the totally unknown and unpublished author. The collection was named after the longest and most remarkable of the included tales, *Eine Seele aus Holz (Soul of Wood)*. For exactly one page in this story, Lind depicts the train journey that ended at the station whose very name best conveys the fact that most of the European Jews had been murdered en masse. He tells the tale of Mr. and Mrs. Barth, a Jewish couple from Vienna, who board a train they assume is headed for their birthplace of Odessa. They end up instead in a Polish city they have never heard of. Lind needs only this one page to cover this terrain: "Of course they didn't make it to Odessa. In the Polish city of Auschwitz they were met by uniformed officers and on the same day burned" (Neuwied, Germany: Luchterhand, 1962, p. 7). This closing sentence of this opening page of *Soul of Wood* was a calculated provocation to fiction writers, suggesting that they should not bother to continue to tell this tale in a complex literary manner and that they should either come up with some other strategy or limit themselves to one page of supposedly objective factual reconstruction. Lind then continues on the next page with the presentation of a life that illustrates his own alternative literary strategy.

This story is about the Barth's son, Anton, who is left in the care of strangers, like Lind, by parents who were busy trying to make their own escape. Paying off dubious potential caretakers and boarding the train that goes straight to Auschwitz, the Barths leave their son in the care of totally unreliable strangers. The biographical relationship between Anton and Lind seems clear enough, but Lind has no intention of telling the story of his own adventures in a roman á clef. Unlike Lind, Anton is not only psychologically handicapped by this parental abandonment, he is also so physically handicapped that he is totally dependent on the one-legged Hermann Wohlbrecht. Wohlbrecht doesn't simply take the boy's money and run; he first assuages his guilty conscience by arranging for the transport of Anton, in a box, to a mountain hut, where it is assumed that without direct intervention he will soon die. Instead, Anton comes into contact with an animalistic visionary world where he experiences a level of existence that had been completely closed to him in the world of humans. When the tide of the war changes, multiple phony rescuers realize that they would be in a much better position if they could claim that they had hidden a Jew and saved him from the fate of his parents, so they rush to the mountain hut and fight to the death over the right to claim to have been on the side of the victims.

This story is a particularly bitter and sarcastic commentary on postwar heroes. It reflects the fate of a writer living in English exile, who was alive only because he had depended on nobody but himself to work out a plan to survive the killers. It is also a radically different way of using the Holocaust as literary material. Lind's depiction does not seem to be limited to the catastrophe of the Holocaust; rather it leaves the impression that is the apocalyptic presentation of a world gone berserk, at one and the same time an autobiography; a parody of the most famous fictional character of postwar German literature, Oskar Matzerath, the dwarf in *The Tin Drum*; a satire of the hypocrisy of Austrians; and a travesty of bloodthirsty Nazis, their fellow-travelers, and pathetic phony rescuers.

For the most part, Lind's stories from his "German" period offer startling, macabre, and sometimes grotesquely humorous tales about "those who didn't have the papers for life and so prepared themselves for death" (Lind, *Seeleans Holz*, p. 7). Immediately, the alert reader who is familiar with Lind's biography realizes that this is also a comment on a real historical situation. Lind always managed to secure the papers for life. Usually only tangentially related to identifiable stories of Holocaust victims, the most successful of his often metaphorical tales, full of vicious perversion and crazed visions, also manage to articulate the dimensions of the calamity he is ultimately attempting to convey. In the second story in *Soul of Wood*, "Night Journey," and in the last one, "Resurrection," Lind once again uses claustrophobically enclosed spaces—the locked compartment of the night train from Nice to Paris and an underground chamber/hiding place in Holland—to fuse together a bizarre authorial vision with an all-too-real historical locale—the cattle car trains to Auschwitz and the tiny refuges of hidden Jews.

However, Lind's train compartment is completely different from the suffocating jammed cattle cars to Auschwitz. His only companion turns out to be a cannibal from St. Pölten, who carries a tool-box full of cutting and boring equipment, so that, as he explains, he can dismember his planned meal after Lind falls asleep. The ensuing conversation and meditation have a Hitchcock-like bizarre humor that at first may seem to be alien to a story about the Holocaust.

> Everybody has to die. Is the way you go about it so important? You can get run over, you can get shot by mistake, you can have a heart attack when you reach the right age or you can die of lung cancer, which is common these days. We all have to go some day. Why not get eaten by a lunatic on the night train from Nice to Paris? . . . Here is a lunatic. He wants to eat me up . . . But at least he wants something. What do I want. To not eat somebody up. Is that so great? (p. 85).

In "Resurrection," a Jew, who is so proud of the fact that he has converted to Christianity that he has a crucifix hanging on the wall of his miniscule underground hiding chamber, has a "real" Jew with tuberculosis forced upon him by his paid keepers. They too are on the road to Auschwitz but spend their final days in discussions about the will to live and the proposed answers to the inevitable failure of that will in the teachings of Christianity and Judaism, dialogues that sound straight out of absurd theater. The conversations are disturbingly funny because both the participants and the readers are well aware of the fact that the fanatic defender of Christianity won't have a chance if the "real" Christians actually find him, which, of course, they do. In such a world, only one crazy conclusion seems to make any sense: "When you think about it, Goldschmied thought to himself, it's better to talk to an idiot than to a wall" (p. 139). Lind's conclusions almost always seem closer to Woody Allen than to Elie Wiesel, but in the best of them his readers are not allowed the luxury of forgetting that they are also reading about the individuals who would meet their cannibals on the ramp at Auschwitz.

Many readers felt that the author of this grotesque caricature of society was actually suggesting that this disaster really resulted from an outbreak of a sickness called humanity. Thus the Holocaust was not so much the product of a particular historical event as the apocalyptic eruption of a latent disease that had been jolted into life by the rise to power of a violent group of always available killers who had been invited to destroy the normal defense mechanisms of the social body. The fact that this mutant group was led into power by an Austrian antisemite who had spent his apprentice years in Vienna must have made the story even more piquant and personal to Lind. However, that did little to affect the feeling that this was a universal, nightmarish vision of a society permanently teetering on the edge of a nihilistic fall into chaos, in which the corrupt, the ruthless, and the insane held power, and only the amoral had a chance of survival. Nothing like this had ever been written about the Holocaust, in any language, and the critics took notice, for the most part, in a very positive way. Generous excerpts were reprinted in the Munich-based newspaper *Süddeutsche Zeitung*; it was immediately translated into English and became something of a cult book of the 1960s in both English and German.

Suddenly, a young author had appeared who lived in London but wrote in German and had delivered a fictional account of the most destructive of all wars. This was a book that had none of the melancholic, tragic sadness that characterized the works that had set the standards in this area, such as *The Diary of Anne Frank*. Instead, Lind proposed a different way of portraying an insane and murderous time, a method not based on an attempted historical reconstruction of terror that many people considered to be beyond words but on an apocalyptic, often incomprehensibly bizarre, and chaotic vision of a world gone so off course that only an abstract, distorted expressionism, which ranged on surrealism, could be used to picture it in words.

In 1963, Lind's second book, the short novel *Landschaft in Beton* (*Landscape in Concrete*) followed immediately on the success of *Soul of Wood*. Its motto, "There is a plague called man," can be considered a summary of the apocalyptic, brutal, and sometimes uncontrolled bestial visions with which Lind attempts to convey the horror of World War II. This time, it is the macabre story of the gigantic Gauthier Bachmann, a pathologically unstable and violent German sergeant who claims to have lost his battalion in the swamps of Eastern Europe and to have spent months searching for it. Significantly, Bachmann is not searching for Jews, who play virtually no role in the novel, but for any situation that would allow his violent visions to become real. Considered mentally unstable even by semi-crazed Nazi officers, Bachmann wanders from the Ardenne to northern Norway in search of the appropriate killing fields. Like *Soul of Wood*, *Landcape in Concrete* was translated quickly into English and received very positive reviews, but German critical reaction was much more divided this time, with a fair bit of speculation that the explosive anarchy of Lind's apocalyptic imagery could not bear the weight of a full-length novel or, for that matter, of much repetition.

In 1966, Lind published the last of his German-language works of fiction, *Eine bessere Welt* (it appeared in a successful dramatic version in English under the title *Ergo*), and in Germany the trend toward negative criticism of Lind's way of writing about the war became dominant. Feeling that the doors were being closed on him as a German writer, Lind made the decision to switch to English and has written only in this language ever since. While critical reaction to the German translation of the first volume of his autobiography was very positive, the second was met with increasing disinterest, and the third was only translated into German six years after its English publication. German literary critics have also not paid much attention to his subsequent English works of fiction.

English critics, as well, seem to have found his works dealing with the war to be his most interesting literary texts, although his two English novels have their critical defenders. His subsequent English-language works after the autobiographical trilogy include a journalistic account about his return to Israel, *Journey to Jerusalem* (1972); a utopian novel, *Travels to the Enu* (1982); and a letter-novel, *The Inventor* (1987). While there are certainly important critics who consider Lind to be a much underrated English writer, it would be an exaggeration to claim that his switch to English has resulted in a reputation and list of publications that triumphantly confirm the promise of his German works. In fact, Lind simply hasn't published enough in the last quarter-century to capture and hold the attention of the literary world and has dedicated much of his creative energies during this period to a quite successful second career as a painter.

German-Jewish Authors After the Holocaust

When the war ended and the remnants of European Jewry had to make decisions about where they should now live and what they should do next, those German-Jewish authors who had been adults when the war began were faced with the difficult problem concerning the future of their literary careers. Most of them had continued to write in German in exile (Anna Seghers in Mexico; Nelly Sachs in Sweden; Elias Canetti in Great Britain; Friedrich Torberg, Lion Feuchtwanger, Hermann Broch, Hans Sahl, and many others in the United States; Alfred Döblin and Manes Sperber in France; Else Lasker-Schüler, Arnold Zweig, and others in Israel) with little or no critical, popular, or financial response. Some of them would eventually master a new language well enough to write essays in it, but it was a different matter to write fiction in a language one had learned as an adult.

Where should an author live if the only literary language he could really use was spoken almost exclusively in a society that had made every attempt to murder him and his family? After the war, more German-speaking Jews lived in Zürich than anywhere else in Europe, but it was very difficult to get a residence permit for Switzerland. East Germany was a possibility only for those who supported the political system, such as Anna Seghers, Stefan Heym, or Stephan Hermlin, all born in the first fifteen years of the century and far more dedicated to socialist ideals than to their Jewish backgrounds. Most German-Jewish writers felt that they didn't want to live in the DDR, were not interested in returning to their birthplaces in what had become West Germany or the Second Austrian Republic, and were not allowed to settle permanently in Switzerland.

The situation was different for a native German-speaker who had somehow survived the Holocaust as an adolescent. This young adult could imagine starting a new life in what would very likely be a new language. The biographic and literary career of Lind offer an excellent example of this. By the time he was twenty he had spent a considerable length of time in Austria, the Netherlands, Germany, and the Middle East, had no identifiable homeland, and was living in an occupied protectorate (Palestine) that was about to become an independent country (Israel) in 1948, where German was precisely the wrong language for a writer. In the attempt to find some kind of firm foundation for the rest of his life, he would eventually change his name, his place of residence, and even his literary language.

Like many other survivors, he would find it impossible afterward to call any place home, and, long after the end of the war, he still carried the passport of the country that had once violently rejected him.

> Why not? I don't represent any country . . . I could have had a British passport long ago. I lived there for 36 years and was even married to an English citizen. But I have a connection to Austria through mentality, humor and language. These finer things have remained with me. I feel completely Viennese, I don't know if that makes me an Austrian. . . . If you have to analyze it, you would see that I'm not an Englishman, even though I write in English. And certainly not an American. When you live between many languages and cultures, and I also have Dutch and Hebrew, when you roam around the world in many languages, it doesn't make your life any easier. In the end you have to find yourself.
>
> Your voice (*Der Standard*, Vienna, 4 July 1990, pp. 13–14).

Fifteen years after the end of the Holocaust, a young Lind transformed this story of complete social, religious, and personal disorientation into apocalyptic, visionary fiction, describing a world so out of kilter that it would never be the same. "If I'm sick, then so is all of Germany, all of Europe, the whole world" (*Landschaft in Beton*, Neuwied, Germany: Luchterhand, 1963, p. 86), the clinically insane Gauthier Bachmann speculates. When his creator provided a madman with such meditations, he was also securing for himself a permanent place in any discussion of the literature of the Holocaust.

Bibliography

Primary Sources

Das Tagebuch des Hanan Edgar Malinek. 1949. Published under the pseudonym Jakov Landwirth.
Eine Seele aus Holz (*Soul of Wood*). 1962.
Landschaft in Beton (*Landscape in Concrete*). 1963.
Die Heiden (The Heathens). 1965.
Anna Laub (Anna Laub). 1965.
Das Sterben der Silberfüchse (The Dying of the Silver Foxes). 1965.
Eine bessere Welt (*Ergo*). 1966.
Angst und Hunger Zwei Hörspiele (Fear and Hunger Two Radio Plays). 1968.
Counting My Steps. 1969.
Numbers, a Further Autobiography. 1972.
The Trip to Jerusalem. 1973.
Travels to the Enu. The Story of a Shipwreck. 1982.
The Stove. Short Stories. 1983.
The Inventor. 1987.
Crossing: The Discovery of Two Islands. 1991.

Secondary Sources

Koopmann, Helmut. "Wenn Gott zu müde ist, weitermachen." *Frankfurter Allgemeine Zeitung*, April 9, 1988.

Kraft, Thomas. "Einer der auszog das Gruseln zu lernen." *die tageszeitung* December 13, 1997, p. 16.

Langer, Lawrence. "Blessed Are the Lunatics" In *The Holocaust and the Literary Imagination*, 205–249. New Haven Conn.: Yale University Press, 1975.

Reich-Ranicki, Marcel. "Jakov Linds Selbstporträt." In *Über Ruhestörer. Juden in der deutschen Literatur*, 81–86. Munich: Piper, 1973.

Sahl, Hans. "Das absurde Schicksal des Schriftstellers Jakov Lind," *Die Welt*, January 8, 1970, p. 6.

Stenberg, Peter. "Edgar Hilsenrath and Jakov Lind meet at the employment office in Netanya, Palestine, discuss literature and contemplate their recent past." In *Yale Companion to Jewish Writing and Thought in German Culture, 1096–1996*, 642–647. Edited by Sander Gilman and Jack Zipes. New Haven and London: Yale University Press, 1997.

Strümpel, Jan. "Jakov Lind." In *Metzler Lexikon der deutschjüdischen Literatur*, 388–390. Weimar, Stuttgart: Metzler, 2000.

Veichtlbauer, Judith, and Stephan Steiner. "Jakov Lind." In *Kritisches Lexikon zur Aeutsch Sprachigen Gegenwartsliteratur*, 1995.

Interviews

Interview by Michael Cerha. In *Der Standard*, Vienna July 4, 1990.

"Fragebogen." *Frankfurter Allgemeine Magazin*, August 8, 1997.

ARNOST LUSTIG

(1926–)

JOSHUA L. CHARLSON

"TO WRITE OF Auschwitz-Birkenau as it was—no one will do," Arnost Lustig has written ("Auschwitz-Birkenau"; translated by Josef Lustig, *Yale Review* 71:3, spring 1982, p. 393). Yet the challenge of writing about the death camps, the concentration camps, and the experience of the Holocaust has been the singular focus of this Czech author's productive literary career. Born in Prague on 21 December 1926 to Emil and Therese Lustig, Arnost Lustig endured the terror of the Nazi occupation during his formative teenage years. His family spent several years in the so-called model ghetto of Theresienstadt (Terezin)—one of the most frequent settings of his stories—and Lustig later was a prisoner in Auschwitz and Buchenwald. He survived by escaping from a train of prisoners, a dramatic event recounted in fictionalized form in his autobiographical novel *Darkness Casts No Shadow* (1958). He returned to Prague to join the anti-Nazi paramilitary rebels, and he remained there following the defeat of the Germans.

The writing career of Arnost Lustig began immediately after the war, when he found himself "exploding with experiences which I could never tell to anyone," because of his interlocutors' disbelief at the truth of the Holocaust (Trucks, p. 70). Yet after writing his first novel at eighteen and having it accepted by a publisher, Lustig decided he was not satisfied with its quality and withdrew it. Instead, he returned to school to get the formal education he had been denied, earning a master's degree from the Prague College of Political and Social Sciences, and began a career in journalism. It was not until more than ten years later that Lustig would publish his first collection of stories, *Night and Hope* (1957).

Lustig became a well-regarded author in Czechoslovakia in the 1960s, associated with a group of acclaimed postwar writers that included Vaclav Havel, Milan Kundera, Ivan Klima, and Josef Skvorecky. Like his compatriots, Lustig produced work that challenged the normative Communist-era aesthetic expectations. He also made important contributions to the New Wave of Czech cinema through screenplays based on his fiction. Like many of his fellow Czech authors, Lustig left his homeland for a permanent exile following the Soviet invasion of 1968. Since 1970 he has lived in the United States, teaching writing at American University in Washington, D.C.

A somewhat puzzling aspect of Lustig's career is that despite his prolific pen and the critical respect accorded him in both the Czech Republic and the United States, his work is not widely known in either the broader literary community or the tighter circle of Holocaust studies. Few of the major studies of Holocaust literature, for instance, give his work even passing mention, much less expansive treatment. Lawrence Langer's 1986 comment that Lustig is "not well-enough known for his contributions to Holocaust literature" holds true today (Langer, p. 10). Why this should be the case is unclear. Some possibilities suggest themselves, however: the elliptical, fragmentary narrative style of much of his work, which may alienate some readers; the emphasis in his career on short stories, which tend to attract less notice than novels and memoirs; and the lack of major English-language publishers or a consistent set of in-print translations. This last deficiency has been partially remedied over the past five years by the work of Northwestern University Press, which has undertaken a major effort to republish much of Lustig's work in its Jewish Lives series.

Major Themes and Motifs

The imagination of Arnost Lustig has an impressive range. The narrators deployed in his fiction range from young boys to teenage girls to middle-aged Nazi bureaucrats; his stories may take place in a concentration camp, in Prague in the chaotic closing days of World War II, or in the deceptive calm of postwar Europe. Yet certain major themes, and the literary forms in which he conveys them, resound throughout his work.

The ethical locus of Lustig's writing is the question of conscience: what defines it, whether it can exist in a world of usually unmitigated evil. Conscience is both an explicit and implicit subject in Lustig's fiction. The narrator of *The Unloved: From the Diary of Perla S.* (1979) recalls Hitler's notion that conscience is "a mere Jewish invention that cripples the character" and wonders herself whether "If I were a German, would I do without a conscience?" (Evanston, Ill.: Northwestern University Press, 1996, pp. 42–43). Yet conscience persists, often emerging in strange and unexpected ways; it frequently serves to differentiate those who maintain their integrity and hope under the duress of Nazi terror from those who do not. As Manny in *Darkness Casts No Shadow* says, "Conscience is like your heart—you can't carve off a piece and expect the rest to function like before" (in *Children of the Holocaust*, Evanston, Ill.: Northwestern University Press, 1995, p. 462). In "Moral Education," one of the most powerful stories from *Night and Hope*, a boy eager to earn a place in the clique of older boys with whom he has bunked in the ghetto concocts a robbery plan, during which he strikes down a young mother. Overcome by guilt, he forsakes his share of the take, telling himself over and over that "I am not going to get anything out of it" (in *Children of the Holocaust*, 1995, p. 114). Nor is conscience solely an attribute of the victims for Lustig; in "Rose Street," Werner Binde, the driver for Herz, a high-ranking officer in Theresienstadt, brings a tin of sardines to a woman whom he has witnessed being beaten by the officer. Yet the act of compassion is a gesture of mixed intentions that Binde cannot even himself understand.

Conscience is but one component of the larger struggle by Lustig's characters to maintain their identity and dignity in circumstances that act to deny them both. As Jonathan Brent writes, Lustig strives "to win for each of his characters a stubborn, inviolable identity" (p. iii). Protagonists in his stories are often referred to by nicknames, pronouns, physical traits ("the girl with the scar"), or generic epithets ("the old man"), as if to indicate the difficulty of sustaining their identities as individuals. If the maintaining of conscience is one strategy for survival, physical resistance is no less important in Lustig's universe. Whether it is braving certain death to steal a loaf of bread ("The Second Round") or reacting violently against victimizers, as in *A Prayer for Katerina Horovitzova* (1964), the physical cruelties of Nazi oppression are never far from the consciousness of Lustig's characters, nor is the need to escape and resist pain, hunger, and death. Many of the stories feel shaped by bodily limitations, reading less as fully unfolded expositions of plot than as intense moments of action compressed by time and narrative perspective. Yet it is often the decision to refrain from acts of vengeance or retribution—the emergence of conscience—that redeems a character. Manny of *Darkness* is far from alone in Lustig's writing when he ponders the meaning of his own restraint: "[The determination to kill] was always stronger than you were, but as long as you lived, you could try to resist it" (in *Children of the Holocaust*, 1995, p. 495).

What Jonathan Brent has labeled the "deathly dialectic" of Lustig's writing derives from this repeated polarity between characters who carry the burden of their consciences, who are able to seek out the individual human in the person before them, and those who view Jews only in the light of abstractions like ideology, nationalism, and antisemitism. At rare moments the two perspectives do produce some kind of meaningful convergence, but more often they end in violence, humiliation, or simply silence. This last is epitomized in "Beginning and End," in which Jiri, a young Jewish prisoner, tries to solve the mystery of a soldier guarding their transport who seems to have smiled toward them in a friendly manner. Later, after an Allied bomb has shattered the camp and Jiri has been recruited to help bury German bodies, he discovers the now dead soldier and realizes that "it wasn't a smile and it wasn't a grimace of grief; it wasn't anything at all" ("*Night and Hope*" in *Children of the Holocaust*, 1995, p. 301).

The conceptual dialecticism of the stories is echoed in one of Lustig's most distinctive aesthetic traits: rapidly shifting narrative perspectives, often from multiple viewpoints. This technique can have a dizzying, disorienting effect on a reader, reflecting both the external conditions in which the characters live and their internal confusion and isolation. Indeed, it is not simply the use of many narrative perspectives that produces a sense of disorientation; rather, it is the fact that the various characters so often fail to communicate even when they are together, "locked into themselves in a world that is madder than their own madness," as David Lynn writes (p. 164). In two of the stories from *Indecent Dreams* (1988), for example, a man and woman spend a night together while contemplating concealed intentions quite at odds with one another, with violent consequences.

The subjects who provide the divergent perspectives in Lustig's stories are often children, reflecting his own experience of the Holocaust as a teenager. These children are rarely innocents; they are fully attuned to the grim pragmatism required to survive in a ghetto or concentration camp. Indeed, the very term "child" is misleading when referring to such characters: Lustig's children, who range from preadolescent boys to teenage girls on the edge of womanhood, are prematurely wise and jaded. Yet while it is true that children play a defining role in his work—particularly in his earlier stories—they do not by any means constitute the whole of his characterizations. Rather, children are emblematic of a type of character to whom Lustig is drawn—the outsider, isolated even among those already shunned by the dominant group. The elderly, prostitutes, orphans—in their capacity to live with some degree of hope and integrity, these and other victimized misfits give the lie to the Nazis' efforts to eradicate the lives and spirits of the Jews. "Winter's rough. It's worst for children and animals and old folks. . . . Winter's antisemitic," says Thomas (nicknamed Ugly) in "The White Rabbit" ("Diamonds of the Night," in *Children of the Holocaust*, p. 234). Thomas steals a rabbit from an officer's yard, at great risk to himself, as a gift to a female friend who has already been transported East—a quixotic endeavor that in its mix of hopeful action in the face of desperate circumstances captures the central and constant ambivalence of Lustig's writing.

Short Fiction

Short fiction is arguably the most important genre for Arnost Lustig, the form most responsive to his aesthetic and thematic concerns. *Night and Hope* and *Diamonds of the Night* (1958), the two early collections of short stories now paired in one volume in *Children of the Holocaust*—along with the novella *Darkness Casts No Shadow*—share much in terms of style and subject. Both feature protagonists who are children or elderly, and almost always male; the stories employ a hard-edged, naturalistic form of realism that is often distorted or intensified by Lustig's deep narratorial penetration into his characters' psyches. Each collection also traces a general arc from grim tales, set in environments of such unrelieved oppression that time is collapsed into the present moment, to stories of tempered hope that take place on the brink of liberation or in its immediate aftermath. One rarely gets a higher-level analysis of the workings of the Nazi extermination process or the mind-set of the victim in these stories, as one finds in Tadeusz Borowski or Primo Levi, for example; what one most often encounters instead is a view of the constricted daily existence of individuals trapped in the physical and psychological imprisonment of Nazi-occupied Europe.

"The Return," the opening story of *Night and Hope*, establishes several themes crucial to Lustig's early short fiction. One is the loss or confusion of identity that occurs in the Holocaust. Hynek Tausig, who has obtained the identity card of one Alfred Janota, struggles with the stress of making himself into a Gentile: "He must convince himself in the first place that he no longer had anything in common with Hynek Tausig" (in *Children of the Holocaust*, p. 6). The false identity is untenable, however; succumbing to his loneliness and escalating paranoia, Tausig joins a transport to Theresienstadt and is "born anew this moment" (p. 28). But the story changes course once again when, in the end, Tausig attempts to flee the ghetto. This reversal points to a second emblematic theme of the story: the irrepressible desire for freedom. Tausig is an admittedly weak man, "a mouse" (p. 36). But his rejuvenated identity compels him to escape, as characters are similarly motivated to devise strategies of resistance and survival in stories such as "Blue Flames," "The Lemon," "The Second Round," and "Michael and the Other Boy with the Dagger."

Lustig expands his palette in later collections, using a broader array of character types and plot situations, though his standard preoccupations remain. In *Street of Lost Brothers* (1973), for example, "First Before the Gates" virtuosically examines the minds of both gentile bystanders and a German perpetrator. The story triangulates between Maria Kubarska, a Czech washerwoman who has taken an interest in the prayer book of her departed Jewish neighbor; her grandson, who is fascinated with the displays of power by the occupying Germans; and Captain Johann Wolfram von und zu Wulkow, the highly cultured Wehrmacht leader whose inability to see people or events through the lens of anything other than the ideology of the Third Reich leads him to make an example of the boy and his grandmother. Other stories bear similarities to Lustig's early work; one particularly chilling example is "Night" (taking the title of Elie Wiesel's best-known work) in which a father and son are sent on a labor detail to bury the dead of Lidice, a town all of whose male inhabitants were murdered by the Nazis in the wake of the 1942 assassination of SS leader Reinhard Heydrich. The story is characteristically understated, yet reveals in its attention to detail a frightening initiation into Nazi violence and its potential to rupture even the blood relationship between father and son.

Indecent Dreams represents an even sharper departure from Lustig's early writing. Composed of three novellas, the collection takes a mise-en-scène familiar from several earlier stories—Prague in the closing days of the war—but each tale is narrated, unexpectedly, by a non-Jewish woman. The stories form a cohesive set, to the point that some critics have found the collection repetitive. Each features a disaffected bystander who, given an opportunity, participates in an act of retribution against the Germans. In "Blue Day," Inge Linge, a German prostitute, receives as a visitor a German military judge in hiding, whom she later betrays to the Czech rebel forces. But her apparently courageous action follows from ambiguous and mixed motives, including resentment at her own treatment by fellow Germans and guilt over her attitude toward an elderly Jewish neighbor who was transported East. In "Girl with a Scar," the adolescent protagonist is boarded at a Nazi reeducation school for orphans; her own parents have been killed as political enemies of the Reich. When she discovers that a soldier who has taken an unseemly interest in her was involved in the indiscriminate sweep of arrests that took her parents, she overcomes her fear and attraction to take vengeance. Both stories make a connection between violence and the erotic, a theme also found in those of Lustig's novels that focus on women. While the stories in this collection, like some of his novels, can shade toward melodrama, they are of a piece with his entire body of work in their refusal to settle for reductive answers to questions of ethical and moral responsibility.

Novels

Although most commonly recognized as a novel, the powerful, autobiographical *Darkness Casts No Shadow* is more properly thought of in relation to Lustig's short fiction. A novella-length work that originally appeared in the same volume as *Diamonds of the Night*, it strongly echoes, in subject, tone, characters, and intensity, his early short stories, only in more extended fashion. Based on wartime experience (and written in a two-week burst), *Darkness* chronicles the escape of Manny and Danny from a train transporting prisoners, which has been shot up by an Allied plane. The breathtaking drama of their escape is punctuated by flashbacks to the horrors they have left behind. Manny and Danny are doubles, as their names suggest, and their struggle to remain as one throughout their escape embodies the challenges to both individual identity and comradeship that reverberate in all of Lustig's writing. The pair prove that they have not lost their conscience, both by their faithfulness to each other and by their decision not to kill a woman from whom they take food. The novella's obscure ending has puzzled many readers: some believe the boys escape one final time, while others are sure they are murdered. The author has said that he wanted the ending to be ambiguous.

Lustig's three other novels that have been translated into English—*Dita Saxova* (1969), *A Prayer for Katerina Horovitzova*, and *The Unloved: The Diary of Perla S.*—all feature women as their protagonists. Lustig has accounted for this by speaking of his respect for women in general, particularly for the women he saw suffering at Auschwitz. Still, the choice invites scrutiny. For Dita, Katerina, and Perla, sexuality is double-edged: it turns them into objects of male desire in potentially dangerous ways but also can be used to build their own power and security. None of these novels describes daily life in a concentration or death camp, as many of the stories focused on men do. Nevertheless, the events and consequences of the *Shoah* are never far from the central consciousness of each work.

Dita Saxova chronicles the trials of the title character in postwar Prague as she attempts to contend with memories of the past and her murdered family, while making a romantic and professional life for herself in the present. The novel has a drifting quality, consonant with Dita's own wanderings, but critics have taken issue with the pacing and plot development. Likewise, they have questioned the proliferation of clichéd utterances that issue from the characters' mouths, failing to realize that such speech is the author's device for accentuating the futility of language after the Holocaust. Lustig here persuasively reveals the difficulty for survivors of piecing their lives back together; Dita's escalating sense of exile from both her inner self and the place and people with whom she feels at home leads her down a self-destructive path.

Better received both critically and popularly—in Czechoslovakia and the West—is *Katerina Horovitzova*, which was nominated for the National Book Award in 1974. Yet the novel is in many ways Lustig's most anomalous. Although Sidra Ezrahi classifies the book as "documentary art (p. 48)," it has a clearly mythical quality to it. Indeed, Lustig has called *Katerina* "a legend," and in that respect it is a departure from the unadorned realism most typical of his work (Trucks, p. 72). The novel is based on an actual rebellion by a group of prisoners heading for the gas chambers in Auschwitz, which resulted in the death of SS Sergeant Major Josef Schillinger (an event also related by Tadeusz Borowski in his story "Lieutenant Schillinger"). The instigator of the resistance is elevated in Lustig's retelling to a saintlike figure whose innocent attempt to purchase her family's freedom unwittingly plays into the plans of the manipulative Friedrich Brenske, commandant of the camp's "secret division"; it is only once the full truth of her fate has sunk in that she conceives her plan of rebellion. *Katerina* has strong elements of melodrama, and certain aspects of the plot seem far-fetched, in particular the device of twenty American men who are shuttled as pawns in a fraudulent prisoner exchange. Yet these apparent flaws serve to advance the allegorical and mythical purposes of the novel: to underscore, via the example of the deceived Americans, how ordinary Jews could have been led to the gas chambers, and at the same time to acknowledge and valorize the spirit of resistance.

Violent resistance also serves as a climactic event in *The Unloved: The Diary of Perla S.*, which received the Jewish National Book Award. This novel as a whole, however, is a more subtle and realistic rendering of life during the Holocaust. Written from the perspective of a teenage Jewish prostitute in Terezin, the novel adeptly plays on the form of the diary, a genre often considered among the most authentic in its testamentary function. Perla's relationships with two key figures—one a powerful member of the Judenrat, the other a Luftwaffe pilot—provide her with inside knowledge of the fate of the Jews, a gradually dawning revelation that gives her story its poignancy and dramatic tension. The novel is fraught with ethical questions: should Perla have intervened somehow when she learned a friend was about to be transported to Poland? Is the Jewish self-governing body complicit in the genocidal activities of the Nazis? Do the favors Perla earns for her work make her ethically culpable when, for instance, another person is sent in her place? Perla's diary is ultimately a self-destructing document. First everyone with whom she is close disappears, and finally Perla has her own number called. Her killing of the Luftwaffe officer provides a moment of visceral satisfaction, but it does not offer any consolation to counter the narrative of genocide.

Film

Although literary fiction is Lustig's chief means of expression, his significant contributions to Holocaust film also deserve mention. Lustig has written screenplays for three of his novels that became Czech movies. The most highly regarded is *Diamonds of the Night* (1963), an adaptation of *Darkness Casts No Shadow*. Directed by Jan Nemec, this hallmark film of the Czech New Wave combines abstract, metaphorical visuals with cinéma vérité style to create a "modernist, nonlinear narrative" that is nevertheless a "trenchant, unsentimental" account of the harrowing escape of the two boys from a train (Liebman and Quart, p. 50). The movie submerges most of the specific Jewish identification of the novella, probably to conform with the demands of state censors. The ending, however, brilliantly captures the ambiguousness of the original text's conclusion by actually presenting two different versions: one in which the boys are shot dead, another in which they escape again.

Transport from Paradise (1963), directed by Zbynek Brynych, cobbles together stories from *Night and Hope* to form a semicohesive narrative of a day in the life of Theresienstadt. The film effectively strives for a documentarylike effect, even weaving in archival Nazi film. Lustig's characteristic concerns regarding ethical behavior and collaboration versus resistance are present, but the coherence and force of the individual short stories is diffused and fragmented by the film's attempt to create a more comprehensive narrative out of them. *Dita Saxova* (1967), which under the direction of Antonin Moskalyk styles itself in the mode of Michelangelo Antonioni, seems to inherit some of the problems of the novel itself. The overt luminousness of Dita, which is accented in the film's visual effects, is at odds with the underlying pain and even nihilism that results from her past. In the novel this tension is partially resolved via authorial irony, but in the movie the two sides to Dita simply seem incompatible.

Conclusion

Well into his seventh decade, Arnost Lustig continues to write with precision and insight on the *Shoah*. In recent years, he has devoted much energy to revised translations of his work, commenting that he is "not rewriting. I am completing" (Trucks, p. 72). His stories and novels present distinctive views of the fate of Czech Jews in the Holocaust, the day-to-day life of prisoners in Theresienstadt, and the particular challenges faced by children. Even more crucially, Lustig frames the Holocaust as a series of ethical choices. His characters are faced with the gravest of conditions, and death is almost always the outcome of resistance, yet many of them do hold on to their conscience and integrity. Night and hope coexist in Lustig's universe; the darkness can never be vanquished entirely, but neither can hope be eradicated, so long as some choose to assert their individuality and their obligation to others in need.

Bibliography

Primary Sources

Noc a nadeje (*Night and Hope*). 1957.
Demanty noci (*Diamonds of the Night*). 1958.

Tma nemá stîn (*Darkness Casts No Shadow*). 1958.
První stanice stesí (First Stop of Happiness). 1961.
Nikoho neponizis (Thou Shall Humiliate No One). 1963.
Modlitba pro Katerinu Horovitzvou (*A Prayer for Katerina Horovitzova*). 1964.
Bílé brízy na podzim (*White Birches in Autumn*). 1966.
Horka vune mandli (Burnt Smell of Almonds). 1968.
Dita Saxová (*Dita Saxova*). 1969.
Milácek (*Darling*). 1969.
Ulice ztracenych bratri (*Street of Lost Brothers*). 1973.
Z deniku sedmnactilete Perly Sch. (*The Unloved: From the Diary of Perla S.*). 1979.
"Auschwitz-Birkenau." Translated by Josef Lustig. 1982.
Indecent Dreams. 1988.
Children of the Holocaust. 1995.
The House of Returned Echoes. 2001.
Lovely Green Eyes. 2002.

Screenplays

Diamonds of the Night, 1963. Directed by Jan Nemec.
Transport from Paradise, 1963. Directed by Zbynek Brynych.
Dita Saxova, 1967. Directed by Antonin Moskalyk.

Secondary Sources

Brent, Jonathan. "Arnost Lustig's Deathly Dialectic." Introduction to *Night and Hope*. Evanston, Ill.: Northwestern University Press, 1985: i–xi.

Ezrahi, Sidra DeKoven. *By Words Alone: The Holocaust in Literature*. Chicago: University of Chicago Press, 1980.

Haman, Ales. "Man in a Violent World: The Fiction of Arnost Lustig." *Czechoslovak and Central European Journal* 11, no. 1 (summer 1992): 73–80.

Kaplan, Johanna. "Savage Boulevard, Easy Streets." *New York Times Book Review*, 19 June 1988: 24. Review of *Indecent Dreams*.

Langer, Lawrence. "Paying the Price of Survival." *Washington Post Book World*, 12 January 1986: 10. Review of *The Unloved: From The Diary of Perla S.*

Liebman, Stuart, and Leonard Quart. "Czech Films of the Holocaust." *Cineaste* 22, no. 11 (winter 1996): 49–51.

Lynn, David H. "The Lost Brother." *Kenyon Review* 14, no. 3 (summer 1992): 161–165. Review of *Street of Lost Brothers*.

Patterson, David. *The Shriek of Silence: A Phenomenology of the Holocaust Novel*. Lexington, University Press of Kentucky, 1992.

Pawel, Ernst. "In the Camps." *New York Times Book Review*, 18 March 1979: 21.

Rothberg, Abraham. "Chant for the Dead." *Southwest Review* 59, no. 1 (winter 1974): 87–89. Review of *A Prayer for Katerina Horovitzova*.

Townsend, Charles E. Review of *Dita Saxova*. *Slavic Review* 54, no. 2 (summer 1995): 458–459.

Interview

Trucks, Rob. "A Conversation with Arnost Lustig." *New England Review* 20, no. 14 (fall 1999): 68–76.

JEAN-FRANÇOIS LYOTARD

(1924–1998)

JONATHAN JUDAKEN

THE FRENCH PHILOSOPHER Jean-François Lyotard considered the Holocaust an event of such magnitude that it necessitated a rethinking of ethics, aesthetics, and politics. As a leading theorist of postmodernism, his numerous discussions of Jews and Judaism, antisemitism and the *Shoah* have shaped the way philosophers, literary critics, and historians talk and think about Auschwitz and its centrality to the meaning of the postmodern age.

Biography

Born 10 August 1924 in Versailles (Seine-et Oise) to Jean-Pierre Lyotard and Madeleine Cavalli, from an early age Jean-François Lyotard expressed an interest in culture. He considered becoming a Dominican monk, a painter, a historian, or a novelist. After studying at the lycées Buffon and Louis-le-Grand, he pursued advanced degrees in philosophy at the Faculté des lettres de Paris. He passed the *agrégation* in 1950 and then began to teach first at a lycée in Constantine, the capital of the French department of East Algeria, and then in La Flèche in the metropole until 1959. From 1954 to 1966, Lyotard served on the editorial committee of the journal *Socialisme ou barbarie* and then the newspaper *Pouvoir ouvrier*, both sectarian, avant-garde mediums for elaborating a marxist critique of Stalinism. His first articles, later published together as *La guerre des algériens* (The Algerian War, 1989), opposed the French colonial regime in Algeria. He taught at the Sorbonne's Nanterre campus, the site of the beginnings of the student revolts that led to the national uprisings in May and June 1968, which he energetically supported. He completed his *docteur ès lettres* in 1971 and also taught at the University of Paris at Vincennes and Saint-Denis, a post which he held until his official retirement in 1989. He was one of the founders of the International College of Philosophy, serving as its second director, and he continued to teach in various international institutions until his death of a second bout with cancer on 21 April 1998.

Lyotard's first published book, *La phénoménologie* (Phenomenology, 1954) is still considered a classic introduction to the subject. Becoming fascinated with psychoanalysis after he attended Jacques Lacan's seminars, in the mid–1960s he began to reevaluate Marxism. Intrigued with Lacan's critique of ego-psychology and his structuralist remapping of the unconscious via linguistics, Lyotard eventually published works in the late 1960s and early 1970s that challenged the Freudian and Lacanian emphasis on the Oedipus complex. Like many of his contemporaries in France in the 1970s, he contributed to the revival of Friedrich Nietzsche and the attention to the will to power at work in truth claims. When he began to articulate his postmodern critique in the late 1970s and early 1980s, he demonstrated a profound interest in the work of Emmanuel Levinas and more generally in Judaism as providing a critical perspective from which to deconstruct and reevaluate the history of Western thought. Lyotard's own intellectual route (Marxism, phenomenology, decolonization, psychoanalysis, May 1968, Nietzsche, deconstruction) is thus a quintessential example of the aggregate of influences acting on postmodern thought.

Postmodernism and "The Jewish Question"

Lyotard's oeuvre aims at a critique of totalizing and totalitarian thinking. He articulates this critique of totality most clearly in *La condition postmoderne* (The Postmodern Condition, 1979), the book that gave the term "postmodern" its philosophical foundation and that remains the ur-text for the modern-postmodern debate. Lyotard argues that the postmodern condition is constituted by a crisis of legitimation derived from the incredulity toward metanarratives in contemporary society. By metanarratives, Lyotard means narrations that claim to provide a universal story according to which all other claims can be evaluated, like science, Marxism, or psychoanalysis. The postmodern is characterized by a lack of consensus upon a metanarrative that provides a basis for a universal explanation or a universal law that can resolve political disputes.

Although the crystallizations of Lyotard's insights about the postmodern condition are concomitant with his ever-more-frequent references to Jews and Judaism, themes related to "the Jewish Question" and to the significance of the *Shoah* have a long history in his work, starting with his first published text, a review of Karl Jaspers's *Die Schuldfrage* (The Question of German Guilt, 1947) just after World War II. In the 1960s and 1970s he developed this interest via psychoanalysis in general and his reading of Sigmund Freud's *Moses and Monotheism* in particular. In "Jewish Oedipus" (1970) and "Figure Foreclosed" (1984), Lyotard linked the problems in psychoanalysis and philosophy he was considering by drawing a parallel between the unconscious and the figure of "the Jew" in Western culture. He later extended these insights, arguing that "the Jew" signified an incomprehensible, unidentifiable alterity that the European tradition has consistently excluded, repressed, or otherwise forgotten. His philosophical magnum opus *Le différend* (*The Differend*, 1983), Lyotard's concept for a dispute that can no longer be resolved with reference to a common *metanarrative*, threaded its philosophical questions around the event of the *Shoah*. In the context of "the Heidegger affair," which erupted in France in 1987 and concerned the problematic influence of Martin Heidegger on contemporary French thought given his role as a Nazi sympathizer, Lyotard published *Heidegger and "the Jews"* (1988). He argued in "Europe, the Jews, and the Book" (1990), that the disinterring and vicious violation of a Jewish body at a cemetery in Carpentras, France, in 1990 was only the latest in a long series of attempts in the West to erase the differend dividing Jews and Europe. In *Un trait d'union* (*The Hyphen: Between Jews and Christianity*, 1993), Lyotard traced its origins to the hyphen, the *trait d'union*, which marks the differend in the so-called Judeo-Christian tradition. Through a reading of Paul's Epistles, Lyotard explores the *trait d'union* as an effort to erase the differend between Jewish and Christian conceptions of time, memory and history, election, revelation and redemption, justice, ethics, knowledge, and language.

Lyotard's analysis of antisemitism, as woven into his postmodern theory, thus encompassed a critique of the whole Greco-Roman-Christian-Enlightenment tradition, using the figure of "the Jew" to demonstrate the West's incapacity to remain open to heterogeneity and cultural difference. By the 1980s "Auschwitz" came to function metonymically to indicate a series of philosophical questions about history and reference, ethics, and politics that registered the break between modernity and the postmodern. " 'Auschwitz' can be taken as a paradigmatic name for the tragic 'incompletion' of modernity," Lyotard stipulates, insisting that "it is the crime opening postmodernity. . . . How could the grand narratives of legitimation still have credibility in these circumstances?" ("Apostil on Narratives" in *The Postmodern Explained: Correspondence 1982–1985*, translated and edited by Julian Pefanis and Morgan Thomas, Minneapolis: University of Minnesota Press, 1992, p. 19).

Auschwitz and the Differend

The Differend, Lyotard's philosophical masterwork, is a series of "notices" or sketches of thought, preserving the exploratory process in thinking, judging, and reading he sought to encourage. It opens with an extended discussion of Auschwitz, which Lyotard (like Hannah Arendt) considered an event of such magnitude that it shatters the criteria of judgment about it since "even the authority of the tribunal that was supposed to establish the crime . . . was exterminated" (*The Differend: Phrases in Dispute*, translated by Georges Van Den Abbeele, Minneapolis: University of Minnesota Press, 1992, p. 56). There is a differend that separates the experience of victims and perpetrators. As for Alain Finkielkraut, Auschwitz signals irreparable rupture and infinite loss without the possibility of reconciliation for victims. Even though the event represents an indeterminate situation where one cannot appeal to a universal law or agreed-upon criteria, Lyotard nevertheless insists that Auschwitz demands judgment.

Auschwitz is therefore not a mere historical event, but a limit experience, what Lyotard calls "a sign of history": an event that cannot be expressed in previous idioms. His analysis takes as its point of departure the final section of Theodor Adorno's *Negative Dialectics* (1966), where Adorno meditates on metaphysics and what is entailed in thinking "after Auschwitz." Adorno's basic project in *Negative Dialectics* was to demonstrate the totalitarian nature of "identity thinking"—thinking that demands a final reconciliation between subject and object, thinking absolutely, thought determined to stand universally and transhistorically; in short, any thought that defines itself as "the final solution." For Adorno, Auschwitz is a sign that represents the final culmination and death of the logic of identity thinking, a sign demanding that thought not repeat the logic of Auschwitz. However, to construe a determined meaning to Auschwitz, for example, to fix its significance in terms of the equation "Auschwitz equals identity thinking" repeats the logic of identity thinking. Auschwitz is a sign, then, for the impossibility of encapsulating its significance. Taking Adorno's ruminations on thinking "after Auschwitz" as a model, Lyotard argues that Auschwitz names an event that can be felt, that radically disturbs us, but that cannot be cognitively apprehended or expressed. Every historical representation situates Auschwitz within the continuum of history, thus intimating the comparability of the *Shoah* with other historical events. He concurs with Claude Lanzmann, the director of the famous documentary *Shoah*, in insisting that efforts to re-present Auschwitz "as it really was" banalize it and mask its abhorrence. The monstrosity of Auschwitz is sublime in the sense that we are awed by something but the referent of that awe cannot be represented.

Lyotard thus raises the question of the adequacy of any witness to Auschwitz and the general problems of testifying to trauma. Rather than dismiss Holocaust deniers like Robert Faurrison off-hand, Lyotard probes the limits of historical representation that constitute their lever in demands for a "revisionist" approach to the Holocaust. Even as the deniers' work is an effort to continue the Final Solution by silencing all testimony about it from survivors, they have a point when they claim that there are no witnesses to the gas chambers since every true witness was exterminated in the process. What continues to burn about Auschwitz is that the process of destruction attempted to destroy even the memory of the *Shoah*, to eliminate even the traces of the devastation. Faurisson claims to challenge the accuracy of witnessing to the *Shoah* on historical grounds alone, whereas Lyotard sought to reveal that there is always more than merely historical knowledge in survivor testimony. There is thus a differend between every representation of Auschwitz and the suffering of the victims. The task of thinkers, writers, and artists becomes not to represent Auschwitz, which is impossible, but to bear witness to this impossibility. Lyotard also urges thinkers, writers, novelists, and artists to bear witness to other differends, to other "signs of history" (the title of the last chapter of *Le différend*). The task of postmodern philosophy and art as Lyotard sees it is to represent the limits of representation and to express the differend between representation and the unrepresentable. Auschwitz is a model of the exigency to communicate this incommunicability and the need to judge where universal criteria do not exist.

Heidegger and "the Jews"

Heidegger and "the Jews," Lyotard's intervention into the Heidegger Affair, extends his reflections on "the Jewish Question" and his examination of the relation between history and memory in any account of the Holocaust. His basic thesis is that all thinking, and therefore all remembering, forgets. There are lacunae and limits to all thought. Specifically, Lyotard is critical of Heidegger's philosophy, which was centrally concerned with the forgetfulness of the West in its failure to think Being because his thought itself forgets, evident in Heidegger's silence on the *Shoah*. Heidegger's role in the Nazi Party and, more perniciously, the fact that he made almost no comment about the Holocaust in the postwar period, implicated Heidegger in the Nazi Final Solution—the effort to eliminate European Jewry without trace or memory. The "Final Solution" was a politics of absolute forgetting that resulted in a politics of extermination. Since for Lyotard, there are two modes to the politics of forgetting—effacement and representation—the question is how one remembers this forgetting, and more generally how one remembers the limits of thought—the unrepresentable, the unthinkable in thought—which Lyotard names in this work "the Jews."

He argues that there is a double obligation on any history or monument to the memory of "the Jews": (1) we must remember that in memorializing we forget; this forgetting results in effacement and (2) in remembering "the Forgotten," we must also recognize that no history, literary work, or other memorialization of the Holocaust is capable of representing the shock of the past "as it really was." As David Carroll suggests, the obligation in remembering the *Shoah* should thus *not* be phrased as "never forget" but rather "never forget that in all memory there is 'the Forgotten' " ("Memorial for the *Différend*," p. 24). Every history, every memorialization that wishes to remain sensitized to the memory of the victims of the Holocaust, must negotiate this double bind of history and memory.

Lyotard has justifiably been criticized for appropriating and allegorizing "the Jews" to serve a philosophical function in his thought, valorizing images of "the Jew" pivotal to their historical exclusion and thus reinforcing a hypothesized, abstract image of Jews and Judaism that denies Jewish history and forgets Jewish tradition. Several critics argue that Lyotard's rebaptizing the critical constructs in his philosophy—trauma, *écriture*, alterity, nomadism, the un(re)presentable, *Nachträglichkeit* (deferred action), not-forgetting-that-there-is-the Forgotten—"the Jews" erases the particularity of the Jewish past, and in a Pauline gesture spiritualizes the embodied experiences of Jews and Judaism within European history. Speaking of postmodern approaches more broadly, Max Silverman warns that "employing an ethnic allegory to characterize the tension between order and disorder, reason and resistance to reason, the self-constituted self and the heterogeneous self, Europe and its other(s), this postmodern theory would appear to overlap uncomfortably with the ethnic allegory employed frequently in the age of modernity" (p. 199). Lyotard's importance to Holocaust literature is nevertheless his reminder that those who meditate on these events must be sensitive to the complexities of language, identity, and the often paradoxical relationship of history and memory ruptured by the radical negativity of Auschwitz. He thus reminds us of our duty to remember the Forgotten, forcing us to recall that we will never come to terms with this remembering.

Bibliography

Primary Sources

"La Culpabilité Allemande" ("German Guilt"). 1948.
La phénoménologie: Que sais-je? (*Phenomenology*). 1954.
"Oedipe juif" ("Jewish Oedipus"). 1970.
Discours, figure (Discourse, Figure). 1971.
Des dispositifs pulsionnels (Affective Systems). 1973.
"Discussion" (Discussion). 1973.
"Notes sur le retour et le Kapital" (Notes on "the Return" and *Capital*). 1973.
Economie libidinale (*Libidinal Economy*). 1974.
Le mur du Pacifique (*Pacific Wall*). 1975.
Instructions païennes (Pagan Instructions). 1977.
Rudiments païens (Pagan Rudiments). 1977.
Les transformateurs Duchamp (Duchamp Transformations). 1977.
Au juste: Conversations with Thébaud (*Just Gaming*). 1979.
La condition postmoderne: Rapport sur le savoir (*The Postmodern Condition: A Report on Knowledge*). 1979.
"Logique de Lévinas" ("*Levinas' Logic*"). 1980.
"Discussions; ou, phraser 'après Auschwitz' " ("*Discussions; or, Phrasing 'After Auschwitz'* " 1981.
Le différend (*The Differend: Phrases in Dispute*). 1983.
"Figure forclose" ("*Figure Foreclosed*"). 1984.
Tombeau de l'intellectuel et autres papiers (*Tomb of the Intellectual*). 1984.
La faculté de juger (The Faculty of Judgment). 1985.
Les immatériaux (The Immaterial). 1985.
L'enthousiasme: La critique kantienne de l'histoire (Enthusiasm: The Kantian Critique of History). 1986.
Le postmoderne expliqué aux enfants: Correspondance 1982–1985 (*The Postmodern Explained*). 1986.
Heidegger et "les juifs" (*Heidegger and "the Jews"*). 1988.
L'inhumain: Causeries sur le temps (*The Inhuman: Reflections on Time*). 1988.
Peregrinations: Law, Form, Event. 1988.
La guerre des algériens: Écrits 1956–1963. 1989.
Benjamin, Andrew, ed. *The Lyotard Reader*. Cambridge, Mass.: Blackwell, 1989.
"L'Europe, les juifs et le livre" ("*Europe, the Jews, and the Book*"). 1990.
Political Writings. Translated by Bill Readings and Kevin Paul. Minneapolis: University of Minnesota Press, 1990.
Leçons sur l'analytique du sublime: Kant, Critique de la faculté de juger (*Lessons on the Analytic of the Sublime*). 1991.
Lectures d'enfance (Lectures on Childhood). 1991.
Moralités postmodernes (Postmodern Moralities). 1993.
Un trait d'union (*The Hyphen: Between Judaism and Christianity*). 1993.
La chambre sourde: L'antiésthetique de Malraux (The Muted Room: The Anti-Aesthetic of Malraux). 1998.
La Confession d'Augustin (The *Confession* of St. Augustine). 1998.
Signé Malraux: Biographie (*Signed, Malraux*). 1999.
Misère de la philosophie (The Misery of Philosophy). 2000.

Secondary Sources

L'arc 64 (1976). Special issue on Lyotard.
L'esprit créateur (1991). "Passages, Genres, Differends: Jean-François Lyotard," *L'esprit créateur* v. 31, no. 1. Special issue on Lyotard.
Bellamy, Elizabeth J. *Affective Genealogies: Psychoanalysis, Postmodernism, and the "Jewish Question" after Auschwitz*. Lincoln and London: University of Nebraska Press, 1997.
Benjamin, Andrew, ed. *Judging Lyotard*. London and New York: Routledge, 1992.
Bennington, Geoffrey, *Lyotard: Writing the Event*. New York: Columbia University Press, 1988.
———. "Lyotard and 'the Jews.' " In *Modernity, Culture, and "the Jew."* Edited by Bryan Cheyette and Laura Marcus. Oxford: Polity Press, 1998, pp. 188–205.
Carroll, David. *Paraesthetics: Foucault, Lyotard, Derrida*. London and New York: Methuen, 1987.
———. "The Memory of Devastation and the Responsibilities of Thought: 'And Let's Not Talk about That.' " Foreword to *Heidegger and "the Jews."* Minneapolis: University of Minnesota Press, 1990.
———. "Memorial for the *Différend*: In Memory of Jean-François Lyotard." *Parallax* 6, no. 4 (2000): 3–27.
Diacritics 14, no. 3 (1984). Special issue on Lyotard.
Jameson, Fredric. Foreword to *The Postmodern Condition: A Report on Knowledge*. Minneapolis: University of Minnesota Press, 1984.
Jay, Martin. "The Ethics of Blindness and the Postmodern Sublime: Levinas and Lyotard." In *Downcast Eyes: The Denigration of Vision in Twentieth-Century French Thought*. Berkeley: University of California Press, 1993.
Judaken, Jonathan. "Bearing Witness to the *Différend*: Jean-François Lyotard, the Postmodern Intellectual, and 'the Jews.' " In *Studies in Contemporary Jewry: An Annual*, v. 16. *Jews and Gender: The Challenge to Hierarchy*. Edited by Jonathan Frankel. New York: Oxford University Press, 2000, pp. 245–264.
LaCapra, Dominick. "Historicizing the Holocaust." In *Representing the Holocaust: History, Theory, Trauma*. Ithaca, N.Y., and London: Cornell University Press, 1994.

Pefanis, Julian. *Heterology and the Postmodern: Bataille, Baudrillard, and Lyotard*. Durham, N.C.: Duke University Press, 1991.

Readings, Bill. *Introducing Lyotard: Art and Politics*. London and New York: Routledge, 1991.

Rorty, Richard. "Habermas and Lyotard on Post-Modernity." *Praxis international* 4, no. 1. Reprinted in *Habermas and Modernity*. Edited by R. Bernstein. London: Polity Press, 1985.

Silverman, Max. "Re-Figuring 'the Jew' in France." In *Modernity, Culture, and the Jew*. Cambridge, U.K.: Polity Press, 1998, pp. 197–207.

Weber, Sam. "Literature: Just Making It." Afterword to *Just Gaming* (English translation of Lyotard's *Au juste*). Translated by W. Godzich. Minneapolis: University of Minnesota Press, 1985.

Weingrad, Michael. "Jews (in Theory): Representation of Judaism, Anti-Semitism, and the Holocaust in Postmodern French Thought." *Judaism* (winter 1996): 79–98.

Yeghiayan, Eddie. "Checklist of Writings by and about Jean-François Lyotard: A Selected Bibliography." In *Peregrinations: Law, Form, Event*. New York: Columbia University Press, 1988.

BERNARD MALAMUD

(1914–1986)

EILEEN H. WATTS

BERNARD MALAMUD WAS born on 26 April 1914 in Brooklyn, New York. The older son of Russian immigrant grocers Max and Bertha (née Fidelman) Malamud, Bernard attended Erasmus Hall High School in New York City; the City College of New York, graduating in 1936 with a B.A. in English; and Columbia University, where he earned an M.A. in 1942. In 1932 Malamud gained his first literary recognition when his story "Life—From Behind a Counter" was awarded the Richard Young First Prize Term Essay by *Scholastic Magazine*.

In 1939 and 1940 Malamud taught English at Lafayette High School in Brooklyn and tutored immigrants in English, many of whom were refugees who had escaped Hitler's death camps. From 1940 to 1948 Malamud taught evening high school English classes at Erasmus Hall. During this span, his stories were published in *Threshold, American Preface, New Threshold, Assembly*, and *Harper's Bazaar*. Malamud married Ann de Chiara in 1945; their son, Paul, was born in 1947 and their daughter, Janna, in 1952. The family moved to Corvallis, Oregon, in 1949, where Malamud taught at Oregon State University until 1961, when he moved to Bennington, Vermont, teaching at Bennington College for the remainder of his career.

In the 1950s Malamud's stories appeared in *Partisan Review, Harper's Bazaar*, and *Commentary*. The *Partisan Review*–Rockefeller grant financed Malamud's sabbatical in Rome and his European travels. His novel *The Assistant* won the Daroff Memorial Award; *The Magic Barrel* garnered the Rosenthal Foundation Award of the National Institute of Arts and Letters and the National Book Award. The 1959 Ford Foundation Fellowship Grant allowed Malamud to write *A New Life*.

Malamud traveled extensively in the early 1960s to research his novels, visiting England and Italy in 1963, when *Idiots First* appeared, and France, Spain, and the Soviet Union in 1965 in preparation for *The Fixer*, which was published in 1966. Malamud visited Israel in 1968, and in 1969 published *Pictures of Fidelman: An Exhibition*, which received the O. Henry Short Story Award. *The Tenants* appeared in 1971, *Rembrandt's Hat* (also an O. Henry Award winner) in 1973, *Dubin's Lives* in 1979, and *God's Grace* in 1981. The self-selected *The Stories of Bernard Malamud* was published in 1983, and in 1984 Bennington College published Malamud's lecture "Long Work, Short Life." *The People and Uncollected Stories* was published in 1989, and *Bernard Malamud, The Complete Stories* appeared in 1997, both with introductions by Robert Giroux.

Malamud was awarded a multitude of prizes and honors. The more prominent of these are election to the National Institute of Arts and Letters of the American Academy in 1964, the National Book Award and the Pulitzer Prize for *The Fixer* (1966), and membership in the American Academy of Arts and Sciences (1967). Malamud served as president of P.E.N. American Center (1979–1981); held membership in the American Academy–Institute of Arts and Letters in 1980; and won the Brandeis University Creative Arts Award in Fiction (1981), the American Academy of Arts and Letters' Gold Medal for Fiction (1983), and the International Award for Fiction of the Mondello (Sicily) Prize (1985). Between 1951 and 1984 eight Malamud stories were selected for the annual *Best American Short Stories* volumes. Posthumous honors include Farrar, Straus and Giroux's establishment of a literary award in his name, under P.E.N.'s auspices.

Malamud's Interest in the Holocaust

Malamud articulated his interest in the Holocaust in several interviews. In 1958, he explained to Joseph Wershba of the *New York Post*, "The suffering of the Jews is a distinct thing for me. I for one believe that not enough has been made of the tragedy of the destruction of 6,000,000 Jews. . . . Somebody has to cry—even if it's only a writer, 20 years later" (Lasher, 1991, pp. 5–6). In a 1966 interview with Phyllis Meras, he expanded on his earlier statement: "With me, the effects of Hitler have had some bearing. Hitler made me aware of the Jewish life of the past and the values the Jewish people tried to uphold" (p. 18), and on receiving the National Book Award for *The Fixer*, Malamud revealed that the novel indeed drew its inspiration from the Nazi Holocaust. Even though, as he told Leslie and Joyce Field, "*The Fixer* is largely an invention, . . . in it I was able to relate feelingfully to the situation of the Jews in Czarist Russia partly because of what I knew about the fate of the Jews in Germany" (pp. 37–38). With more specificity, Malamud later described his intent in *The Fixer* as "shaping the whole to suggest the quality of the afflictions of the Jews under Hitler" (Cheuse and Delbanco, 1996, p. 89). Finally, Malamud wrote in his autobiographical entry for *World Authors 1950–1970*, "The rise of totalitarianism, the Second World War, and the situation of the Jews in Europe helped me to come to what I wanted to say as a writer" (Wakeman, 1975, p. 917).

Despite not addressing the Holocaust directly in his fiction, Malamud was profoundly affected by it. Indeed, the importance of Malamud's work to Holocaust writing lies in its realistic reflection of how survivors, refugees, and Jews who were not physically affected by the Holocaust continue to be affected by it. Nonetheless, he has been criticized and vilified for approaching, but stepping back from, the Holocaust, or dealing with it indirectly. To Joel Salzberg, a well-known Malamud biographer, Malamud insisted that he "was compelled to think about [the Holocaust] as a man rather than a writer," and that "someone like Elie Wiesel who had first-hand knowledge of the experience is in a better position to write about it than [he]" (Lasher, 1991, p. 129).

Responding to the Holocaust as a man who is a writer, Malamud created Jewish characters who carry their history on their backs—and in their hearts. Malamud's talking animals may be fantastical, but their pasts are steeped in Jewish history and its defining flashpoint, the Holocaust. It is a fixed element of their identities. Malamud's status as a Holocaust writer derives from his ability to translate his "feelingfulness" for the six million who perished into Jewish characters who live in the Holocaust's indelible shadow.

Holocaust Representations in Short Stories

Malamud's representations of the Holocaust vary widely. From Oskar Gassner, "The German Refugee" who escapes Hitler's ovens only to commit suicide, and Isabella del Dongo of "The Lady of the Lake," a Buchenwald survivor whose suffering means something to her, to the talking animals of "Talking Horse" and "The Jewbird," he created allegories of Jewish persecution and identity issues. In four other short stories, Hitler is actually mentioned. "The First Seven Years" and "The Loan" both mention "Hitler's incinerators"; "The Mourners" and "Take Pity" contain Hitler's name. Throughout, however, the paradigmatic themes in these works involve piteous suffering by a lonely, displaced Jew who, having fled one pogrom or another, emerges as a teacher or savior. Those who escaped to America endure lives of poverty, endless hard work, unrelenting sorrow, and misery. For Malamud's characters, there is effectively no escape from Hitler's reach, yet in exile, they become teachers of morality.

In "The German Refugee," for example, Oskar Gassner, an accomplished German literary critic and journalist, leaves his gentile wife behind, one month before *Kristallnacht* (Crystal Night—night of November 9, 1938 in which Jewish businesses were attacked and over 200 synagogues were burned), and emigrates to New York City, where he is invited to give a lecture on "The Literature of the Weimar Republic." Knowing no English, he is tutored by Martin Goldberg, the narrator, and lectures successfully. But the dislocations are too much; English is too difficult, German too loathsome, and Oskar cannot express himself. He feels soulless, with no identity. "For this and alzo whatever elze I have lozt I thank the Nazis," he cries. Even Martin's attempts to use Walt Whitman's poetry to teach Oskar English remind him only that Whitman's *brudermensch*, brotherhood, "does not live long on German earth" (*The Stories of Bernard Malamud*, Penguin USA, 1984, p. 105). After receiving his mother-in-law's letter describing his wife's conversion to Judaism and subsequent slaughter by Nazis, Oskar asphyxiates himself via his oven, finishing Hitler's job. Thus, he teaches Goldberg the real sufferings of refugees and the meaning of loyalty and love.

In contrast to Oskar's refugee experience, Isabella del Dongo, of "The Lady of the Lake," who had, with her family, survived Buchenwald, bears numbers tattooed on her chest. Originally named del Seta, her father is a caretaker of an Italian estate. Meanwhile, in New York City, Henry Freeman, born Levin, travels to Italy, changes his name, and falls in love with Isabella. Throughout their courtship, she asks Freeman three times whether he is Jewish. He, assuming she is Gentile, answers repeatedly no, and when he proposes, she declines, revealing her tattooed chest. "Buchenwald," she says. "The Fascists sent us there. The Nazis did it. . . . I can't marry you. We are Jews. My past is meaningful to me. I treasure what I suffered for" (*The Magic Barrel*, Pocket Books, 1972, p. 123). But as Freeman appears to reluctantly admit he is Jewish, she vanishes. Neither Isabella, who assumes an Italian surname, nor Levin, who assumes a non-Jewish surname, is forthcoming about either's true identity. For Isabella, the fear of revealing her Jewishness derives from the torture of Buchenwald; for Levin, of desire for the Gentile-appearing Isabella. Ironically, the identity that had condemned so many to death would here have engendered marriage. Because Isabella and Freeman deny their origins, matrimony eludes them. Thus, identity and happiness are, again, casualties of the Holocaust, and the cautious Isabella has taught the duplicitous Freeman what it means to be a Jew.

Opposing pulls of Jewish identity are further explored in "Talking Horse," an animal allegory that also bears the Holocaust's weight and imprint. Set in a circus, this is the tale of Goldberg, a trainer, and Abramowitz, his talking horse. A wild success, their act consists of Goldberg's supplying answers and Abramowitz, appropriate questions, while Goldberg mercilessly beats him. Obviously Jewish, the horse wonders about his identity. Is he a man inside a horse, or a horse who can talk? After pleading repeatedly for freedom from the abusive Goldberg, they fight furiously, and Goldberg literally pulls off the animal's head, to reveal a centaur, half man, half horse, who, at the story's end, canters freely away. This allegory of arbitrary, unjust cruelty and unbearable suffering relieved only by release of forced identity corresponds with Jewry's tragic situation in Nazi Germany, where racial laws determine national status. Jews were damned whether they converted to Christianity or remained Jewish. Under the Nuremberg Laws, a Jew who converted was still a Jew, still executed. Similarly, no matter how well Abramowitz obeys Goldberg, the horse is still threatened, whipped, flayed.

Identity and assimilation are further dramatized in Abramowitz's dream of two men fighting in a stone pit, "one thin [wearing a multi-colored hat]. . . , the other a fat stranger wearing a huge black crown" (*The Stories of Bernard Malamud*, p. 331) that weighs him down. While this is a rough version of Daniel in the lion's den, the heavy, black crown suggests a Hasid; the multicolored hat signifies secularity or assimilation. This dream represents the wrestling match occurring in Abramowitz's soul, and resonates with the Jew's pull between living traditionally and being shut out of the host society, or assimilating and being treated miserably. Abramowitz's cry to the audience, "Here I am in this horse," evokes Abraham's and Moses's answer to G-d's call, "Here I am." The Jewish man inside the horse embodies the opposing claims on the Diaspora Jew's identity, which, when compromised, places the Jew at the mercy of the trainer/oppressor. Lest we miss this, Goldberg taps in Morse code on the horse's head, "In the beginning was the word," the opening sentence of "The Gospel according to Saint John." Assimilation is a form of imprisonment (p. 335).

The horse shifts from a symbol of assimilation to imprisonment, mirroring the trajectory of German Jews, who went from prominent citizens to concentration camp prisoners. Thus, Abramowitz implores the circus audience, "Free a fellow man," and Goldberg responds, "Nobody is going to believe you." We recall that nobody believed reports of Hitler's genocide in the early 1940s. Abramowitz's cry, "*Gevalt*. Get me out of here! I am one of you," is met with the cruel irony of the band's playing "The Star Spangled Banner," Malamud's rebuke of the United States for its silence in response to the genocide of European Jewry. The circus metaphor captures the absurdity of an "audience" that watched and did nothing (p. 345).

"The Jewbird" positions Schwartz, an old, Yiddish-speaking "Jewbird," in Harry Cohen's top-floor apartment's kitchen window. In return for sanctuary and food, Schwartz tutors and teaches violin to Cohen's young but not-too-bright son, Maury. Sadly, Schwartz's kindness is repaid with pitiless abuse; he is tortured by the family cat and finally hurled out of the top story window into the snow, in a perverted enactment of *schlucken kaporis*, a Yom Kippur custom in which one's sins are symbolically transferred to a chicken that has been swung around one's head three times and then donated to the poor.

Schwartz's exclamations of "*gevalt*, a pogrom" and Yiddish-accented "anti-Semeets" also evoke the programmatic extinction of Jews, who, like Schwartz, valued education, succeeded in the arts, contributed significantly to society, and were scapegoats for that society's failings. As Germany blamed the Jews, so Cohen blames Schwartz—for Maury's zero in arithmetic. Cohen calls Schwartz "A number one troublemaker," and even accuses him of wanting to sleep with Cohen's wife, Edie (p. 145). Unjust accusation and denial of murder, echoes of the Holocaust, continue to reverberate when Edie asks Cohen where the bird is, and Cohen replies, "I threw him out and he flew away. Good riddance." The narrator's next words are "Nobody said no," echoing the fact that nobody said no to the extermination of six million Schwartzes. However, Malamud has Maury weep upon finding the dead bird. " 'Who did this to you, Mr. Schwartz?' he cries. 'Anti-Semeets,' Edie said later." In Maury's tears lie the Jewbird's lesson—compassion (p. 154).

The Assistant: A Metaphor for the Holocaust

The Assistant's evocations of the Holocaust are far more subtle than *The Fixer*'s, consisting of a matrix of conditions and events that resonate with the Holocaust's. Morris Bober, a poor grocery store owner, takes on as an assistant Frank Alpine, who had robbed Morris's store. During the course of their relationship, Frank is humanized and sensitized to Judaism. After Morris's death, Frank takes his place behind the counter and converts to Judaism. Michael Brown has detailed the novel's Holocaust allegory, observing that a German, Italian, and a Pole catalyze the failure of Morris's business; that is, the Axis powers and fellow victims combine to destroy the Jew. In addition, Morris's neighborhood contains but three Jewish families, one of which is destroyed in a fire. Thus one third of the neighborhood's Jewish population is burned, just as the Nazis incinerated one-third of the global Jewish population. Morris's life is riddled with poverty, disease, and hopelessness. Like the victims in the camps, he is in his own horrific world from which there is no escape. Finally, Morris contracts pneumonia from shoveling snow, and like Oskar Gassner, dies, as many of the six million had.

The Fixer, A Holocaust Novel

A world silent at the persecution of a single Jew, Mendel Beilis, is the historical scaffolding of *The Fixer*, Malamud's most apparent Holocaust novel. Falsely imprisoned on blood libel charges (these were medieval charges that Jews killed Christian children to use their blood in making unleavened bread during Passover), Yakov Bok, a poor, hapless handyman, spends years in a Russian prison awaiting trial. Enduring progressively harsh privation and indignities, Yakov realizes that "Being born a Jew meant being vulnerable to history" and that "there's no such thing as an unpolitical man, especially a Jew. You can't be one without the other. . . . You can't sit still and see yourself destroyed" (*The Fixer*, Pocket Books, 1986, p. 305). Too late, Yakov Bok teaches himself what it means to be a Jew in an antisemitic world, a pawn in a game of political exploitation of antisemitism. His lawyers useless, his case internationally known, Yakov is led to trial and certain doom.

As Alvin Rosenfeld has noted, *The Fixer* evokes the Holocaust from a standpoint in history that anticipates it, by setting the novel at the end of the czarist era. In addition to portraying the suffering of one unjustly imprisoned Jew, whose name connotes "Israel the Scapegoat," the novel gives us a glimpse of "the political manipulation of antisemitism on a mass scale" (Rosenfeld, 1980, pp. 66–67). Malamud's 1966 text, set in 1911, casts a post-Holocaust shadow on pre-Holocaust antisemitism, linking Russian pogroms to Hitler's genocide. Bok's years of torture in prison are analogous to Nazi death camp conditions. As S. Lillian Kremer has written, "[Yakov] endures extremities of weather without proper clothing, sleeps on a vermin-infested mattress, eats foul food garnished with roaches . . . is brutalized, beaten, starved, poisoned, and subjected to daily body searches" (Kremer, 1989, p. 98). Like the Holocaust's victims, Yakov is imprisoned in a Kafkaesque world of irrational forces, adumbrated by the boatman's antisemitic superstitions dating to medieval Europe. While rowing Yakov across the Dneiper River, he describes how Jewish corpses would be piled up and burned; jewels, silver, and furs returned to the poor. References to wiping out Jews, Jews hiding in attics or cellars, killing young and old, burning bodies, and stealing money and valuables from corpses all evoke the Holocaust (*The Fixer*, p. 23). Yakov is redeemed, however, to the extent that he refuses to confess to the murder, choosing instead to sacrifice himself for his fellow Jews. His redemption is not religious but political.

Consequences of the Holocaust in *God's Grace*

In *God's Grace*, Malamud's allegory of apocalyptic nuclear devastation, the consequences of historical holocausts are rehearsed to dramatize how humankind has failed God. The surviving man, Calvin Cohn, attempts in vain to rebuild civilization by teaching humanity and religion to apes, particularly Buz, a talking chimp. To Cohn, Noah's Flood, Sodom and Gomorrah, and the Holocaust—"the Jewish one [he] lectured on in class"—are all Holocausts (*God's Grace*, Avon Books, 1982, p. 236). The wreckage that is Jewish history provides a framework for Malamud's indictment of humanity and religion, as Cohn notes that Christianity had not prevented the Holocaust, thus placing its moral responsibility squarely on Christian shoulders. But, Cohn argues, God did not prevent the Nazi Holocaust either. Moreover, Cohn sees a progression from Russian pogrom to German Holocaust to nuclear devastation. *God's Grace* is Malamud's most Judaic novel, drawing on Talmudic theology, ritual, and liturgy, all of which will vanish with Cohn's demise, the Final Solution realized. It is ironic then, when Buz "schechts" Cohn, slitting his throat according to Jewish law, George, the gorilla, wearing a yarmulka, recites the Sh'ma and begins "a long Kaddish for Calvin Cohn" (p. 258). So ends the novel; Judaism is left to be practiced by animals in an Eden sans Adam. The optimistic coupling of Christian and Jew represented by Calvin Cohn's name suggests brotherhood, but it too is destroyed. God's grace appears to lie in destroying man, for history has proven him incapable of any human grace.

Critical response to Malamud's Holocaust fiction has generally polarized into two camps. Among those who see Malamud's characters as representing a post-Holocaust sensibility and struggle to come to grips with its legacy are Sanford Pinsker (1969), Michael Brown (1980), Dorothy Seidman Bilik (1981), Alan Berger (1985), and S. Lillian Kremer (1989). Among those who view Malamud's oblique treatment of the Holocaust as a retreat from moral responsibility are Leslie Field (1977) and Lawrence Langer (1995). More broad-based critical attention to Malamud's Holocaust-related fiction has burgeoned recently and promises to continue.

Bibliography

Primary Sources

The Natural. 1952.
The Assistant. 1957.
The Magic Barrel. 1958.
A New Life. 1961.
Idiots First. 1963.
The Fixer. 1966.
A Malamud Reader. 1967.
Pictures of Fidelman: An Exhibition. 1969.
The Tenants. 1971.
Rembrandt's Hat. 1973.
Dubin's Lives. 1973.
God's Grace. 1982.
The Stories of Bernard Malamud. 1983.
The People and Uncollected Stories. Edited and introduced by Robert Giroux. 1989.
Bernard Malamud, The Complete Stories. 1997.

Secondary Sources

Abramson, Edward A. "Bernard Malamud and the Jews: An Ambiguous Relationship." *The Yearbook of English Studies* 24 (1994): 146–156.

——— *Bernard Malamud Revisited*. New York: Twayne, 1993.

Alter, Robert. "Jewishness as Metaphor." *After the Tradition: Essays on Modern Jewish Writing*. New York: Dutton, 1969. Reprinted in *Bernard Malamud and the Critics*. Edited by Leslie and Joyce Field. New York: New York University Press, 1970.

———. "Confronting the Holocaust." *After the Tradition: Essays on Modern Jewish Writing*. New York: Dutton, 1969, pp. 163–180.

Berger, Alan L. *Crisis and Covenant: The Holocaust in American Jewish Fiction*. Albany: State University of New York Press, 1985.

Bilik, Dorothy Seidman. "Malamud's Secular Saints and Comic Jobs." *Immigrant Survivors: Post-Holocaust Consciousness in Recent Jewish American Fiction*. Middletown, Conn.: Wesleyan University Press, 1981.

Brown, Michael. "Metaphor for Holocaust and Holocaust as Metaphor: *The Assistant* and *The Fixer* of Bernard Malamud Reexamined." *Judaism* 29, no. 4 (fall 1980): 479–488.

Cheuse, Alan, and Nicholas Delbanco. *Talking Horse: Bernard Malamud on Life and Work*. New York: Columbia University Press, 1996.

Field, Leslie A., and Joyce W. Field, eds. "An Interview with Bernard Malamud." *Bernard Malamud: A Collection of Critical Essays*. Edited by Leslie A. Field and Joyce W. Field. Englewood Cliffs, N.J.: Prentice-Hall, 1975, pp. 8–17.

———. "Bernard Malamud and the Marginal Jew." *The Fiction of Bernard Malamud*. Edited by Richard Astro and Jackson J. Benson. Corvallis: Oregon State University Press, 1977, pp. 97–116.

Kremer, S. Lillian. "Seekers and Survivors: The Holocaust-Haunted Literature of Bernard Malamud." *Witness through the Imagination: Jewish American Holocaust Literature*. Detroit: Wayne State University Press, 1989, pp. 81–102.

Langer, Lawrence L. "Malamud's Jews and the Holocaust Experience." Edited by Joel Salzberg. *Critical Essays on Bernard Malamud*. New York: G. K. Hall, 1987, pp. 115–124. Reprinted in Langer, *Admitting the Holocaust*. New York: Oxford University Press, 1995, pp. 145–155.

Lasher, Lawrence. *Conversations with Bernard Malamud*. Jackson: University Press of Mississippi, 1991.

Pinsker, Sanford. "The Achievement of Bernard Malamud." *Midwest Quarterly* 10, no. 4 (July 1969): 379–389.

Rosenfeld, Alvin H. "Imagination in Extremis." *A Double Dying: Reflections on Holocaust Literature*. Bloomington: Indiana University Press, 1980, pp. 62–81.

Wakeman, John, ed. *World Authors, 1959–1970: A Companion Volume to Twentieth Century Authors*. "Bernard Malamud." New York: H. W. Wilson, 1975, pp. 917–920.

Watts, Eileen H. "Not True Although Truth: The Holocaust's Legacy in Three Malamud Stories, 'The German Refugee,' 'Man in the Drawer,' and 'The Lady of the Lake.' "*The Magic Worlds of Bernard Malamud*. Edited by Evelyn Avery. Albany: State University of New York Press, 2001.

———. "The Holocaust and Repetition in Kafka's *The Trial* and Malamud's *The Fixer*." *Modern Jewish Studies Annual* (2002): 100–128.

———. "Jewish Self-Hatred in Malamud's 'The Jewbird.' " *MELUS (Multi-Ethnic Literature of the United States)* 21, no. 2 (summer 1996): 157–163.

ELIAS WOLF MANDEL
(1922–1992)

MICHAEL GREENSTEIN

MANDEL WAS BORN on 3 December 1922 in Estevan, Saskatchewan, to Charles and Eva who had emigrated from Ukraine. The family moved to Regina where Mandel went to school before going to Europe for military service during World War II. After returning from Europe he resumed his studies at the University of Saskatchewan where he received his B.A. and M.A. in English in 1949 and 1950 respectively. He married Miriam Minovitch in 1949, moved to Toronto to complete his Ph.D. at the University of Toronto, and taught at York University and the University of Alberta.

A prolific poet, essayist, and anthologist, Mandel won the Governor General's Award for poetry in 1967 for *An Idiot Joy* (1967), and in 1982 was appointed a fellow of the Royal Society of Canada. He died in Toronto in 1992.

Language in Mandel's Poetry

Mandel's poetry mediates between his Jewish and Canadian roots in a postmodern aesthetic that comes to terms with the Holocaust. "For Elie Wiesel" (in *Stony Plain*) uses a number of postmodern techniques in its fragmentation, shifting of line spacing, and elimination of capital letters and punctuation. The visual effect of the poem is almost that of an epitaph inscribed on a gravestone. The opening phrase, "bear witness:", stamps the words on the page, carves them on stone: the single colon is the only punctuation in the entire poem. It serves to introduce or reintroduce history by re-inscribing what Wiesel (and Mandel after him) did; they not only bear witness to the Holocaust and poetically instruct others to do so, but they are also "bare" witnesses, stripping language to minimalist levels.

> bear witness: live it all
> again content though source
> be pitch and sewer
> boneyard
> skull place Golgotha (*Stony Plain*, Erin, Ont.: Press Porcépic, 1973, p. 63)

This first stanza makes death come alive again in a grotesque resurrection where pitch black makes it impossible to bear witness. The sewer is stagnant, frozen into history's boneyard.

In the second stanza the poet imagines that the "jew / is only the german's / bad dream." The poem ends with the second-person pronoun "you"—at once reader, Mandel, and Wiesel.

> you
> pass through camps
> at the world's end
> beyond the horizon's barbed wire
> close to the
> endless oven (p. 63)

Endless suffering carries through generations, while sibilance throughout the poem underscores the sounds and silence of the Holocaust. In this brief testimony, Eli Mandel identifies with Elie Wiesel.

Mandel's Longest Poem

The long title, "On the 25th Anniversary of the Liberation of Auschwitz: Memorial Services, Toronto, January 25, 1970 YMHA Bloor & Spadina," gives the occasion for Mandel's longest, most detailed Holocaust poem (in *Stony Plain*). This poem has been published in different versions, and Mandel has written a long essay describing the process of its composition and revision. Indeed, the poem emphasizes process over product, that is, the ongoing process of writing the impossible, working through negatives and indirection as a response to Theodor Adorno's "no poetry after Auschwitz." Mandel highlights the impossibility of representing such experiences in postmodern free verse, which collapses time and space in a collage of his prewar childhood on the prairies and his postwar reflections from Toronto.

The opening line, "the name is hard," refers to the harsh sound of the German word "Auschwitz," but also to the difficulty of pronouncing a word with its excruciatingly painful associations. Mandel captures both the silence and the scream of the German sound by mouthing it on the page—a synesthesia where all sense and senses dissolve and are denied meaning.

the gut guttural throat
y scream yell ing open
voice mouth growl
and sweat (*Stony Plain*, p. 66)

The stuttering poet breaks down language into syllables for his primal scream, which in turn breaks down the distance between victim and survivor. Like a camera that changes focus, the poet distances himself even as he brings himself closer to the Holocaust in this paradoxical poem.

Mandel quotes Jerzy Kosinski's famous lines, "the only way out of Auschwitz / is through the chimneys," before going on to describe the context or occasion for this memorial service. The breakdown of language reflects the emotional breakdown of past and present; "out of" the opening "gut" to the repeated historical way out of Auschwitz. Language remains not only at a minimalist level, but also a subminimal level of syllabic stuttering:

of course
that's second hand that's told
again Sigmund Sherwood (Sobolewski)
twisting himself into that sentence
before us on the platform
the poem
shaping itself late in the after
noon later than it would be: (p. 66)

The spaces between the words are almost as important as the words themselves, for they suggest breathing spaces in the stuttering voice, spasmodic expression, random thoughts, the gap and gasp of historical representation. The Polish-Jewish speaker with his double identity (Sherwood and Sobolewski) twists himself into the sentence even as Mandel twists syntax and scatters words across the page somewhere between shape and shapelessness. The colon, the end-line pause in the poem, acts as a transition between past and present.

The next stanza shifts from the speaker on the platform to another synesthetic context of hysteria:

Pendericki's "Wrath of God"
moaning electronic Polish theatric
the screen silent
framed by the name
looking away from / pretending not there
no name no not name no (p. 66)

Postmodern music contrasts cacophonously with silence, and the poet resorts to a series of negatives to reflect his own absence and the overall aesthetic of absence both during the Holocaust and in the post-Holocaust world. The opening "hard name" culminates in "no name"—the impossibility of naming Auschwitz. Mandel's paradoxical no-naming succeeds in writing (no) poetry after Auschwitz.

Although the word "Auschwitz" in Gothic lettering dominates the hall, the hall becomes a parody of Mandel's childhood auditoriums on the prairies—the Orpheum in Estevan, the Capitol in Regina. That innocent and not-so-innocent western childhood game of killing cowboys highlights the distance between Europe and North America. Mandel describes the procession of Polish legionnaires, and confuses what is depicted on the screen and what surrounds him:

so the procession, the poem gradual
ly insistent beginning to shape itself
with the others
walked with them
into the YMHA Bloor & Spadina (p. 67)

The procession and the process of poetry go hand in hand, from line to line and words broken down into syllables:

thinking apocalypse shame degradation
thinking bones and bodies melting
thickening thinning melting bones and bodies
thinking not mine / must speak clearly
the poet's words / Yevtyshenko at Bab:-Yar (p. 67)

The present participle in these lines indicates an ongoing process of the shaping of a poem, the creative process coming to terms with the destructive process: the "th" thickens the stuttering of thick and thin—the staccato of tattooed bodies. Yet Mandel must find the impossible words for the occasion, much as Yevtyshenko rendered the massacre at Babi-Yar. There are precedents for this unprecedented event in history.

Diagonals slant the occasion between different realities and mark off the poet from the performance at different stages of composition. The next stanza continues the stuttering mode of connectedness and disconnectedness between past and present:

there this January snow
heavy wet the wind heavy wet
the street grey white slush melted concrete
bones and bodies melting slush
saw (p. 67)

Weather conditions further link Toronto's 1970 winter to the Polish winters twenty-five years earlier with Auschwitz's unbearable conditions. Mandel's tortured and belabored language imitates the horrific conditions of the camps. The heaviness of the walk reflects the hardships of history, while the repetition of "melting" contrasts with the frozen state and combines all bodies dead and alive.

The marchers in uniform re-create history so that the line blurs between pictures on the screen and the procession in the hall, "SLIDES" appears in the middle of the page opposite "GOTHIC" to highlight the staccato and stuttering of representation. Identity is both affirmed and taken away: "this is mother / this is father." In contrast to the staccato are the "running" and "waving" images of arms and hands that create blur and fragmentation. Identity becomes further complicated: "the poem becoming the body"; that is, Mandel re-creates the past experience by defamiliarizing the present in such a way as to indicate the total disorientation of life at Auschwitz. The words empty until they form part of mouths and oven, while the black leather of Nazi uniforms melts into the victims' phylacteries (black leather straps wrapped around the left arm of religious Jews during morning prayers).

After the melting bodies, "the poem flickers, fades / the four Yarzeit [memorial] candles guttering." These guttering candles toward the poem's conclusion recall the "gut guttural" of the opening: history stammers between the generations. Mandel's "words drift" like "smoke from chimneys and ovens," and by the end of the poem

we drift away
to ourselves
to the late Sunday Times
the wet snow
the city

a body melting (p. 69)

In between drifting words and bodies, Mandel recalls his "western" boyhood cheering the cowboys who shot "the dark men," "me jewboy yelling." Mandel's childhood before the war seems so remote from Europe's killing theater.

For Mandel the poem was never complete, for its unending process carries over to his essay, "Auschwitz and Poetry" (in *The Family Romance*), devoted to the poem's composition. Written fourteen years after the poem, the essay deals not only with the poem but with Mandel's entire life. The essay is both a footnote and a continuation of the poem; it is "occasioned as randomly and as obsessively as the poem itself" (p. 3). Part of the paradox is that the work—poem and essay—is occasional yet lifelong, momentary yet historical. The obsessive occasion goes to the heart of Mandel's "unease," and provides "exorcism and liberation"—Mandel's liberated self identified with the liberation of Auschwitz. His theoretical frame contextualizes the "unsayable poem" with its "not-language." This negative language meshes with the random time frame of 1970, 1984, and August 1946 when Mandel returns to Saskatchewan from Europe to sort out his "sense of things" (p. 4).

To deal with a sense of alienation or remoteness, Mandel relies on paradoxical inversion, a special language of negativity, derealization, disorientation, fragmentation, and displacement. The camps hit home as he substitutes the graves of the war dead in Europe for his father's grave on the prairies. When he sees survivors in camp uniforms on 25 January 1970 he has the uncanny sense that it is his own past he is entering. Toronto, 1970; Europe, 1944; Estevan, 1930;—with such time frames, Mandel realizes that his poem would be a camp poem by not being a camp poem.

Bibliography

Primary Sources

Trio. 1954.
Fuseli Poems. 1960.
Black and Secret Man. 1964.
An Idiot Joy. 1967.
Crusoe. 1973.
Stony Plain. 1973.
Out of Place. 1977.
Dreaming Backwards: Selected Poems. 1981.
Life Sentence. 1981.
The Family Romance. 1986.

Critical Works

Criticism: The Silent-Speaking Words. 1966.
Irving Layton. 1969, 1981.
Another Time. 1977.

Secondary Sources

Beddoes, Julie, ed. *Essays on Canadian Writing*. Eli Mandel Issue (45–46): 1991–1992.
Cooley, Dennis. "Eli Mandel and His Works." *Canadian Writers and Their Works*. Toronto: ECW Press, 1992, pp. 187–277.
Stubbs, Andrew. *Myths, Origins, Magic: A Study of Form in Eli Mandel's Writing*. Winnipeg: Turnstone, 1993.

EMILY MANN
(1952–)

EDWARD ISSER

EMILY MANN WAS born on 12 April 1952 in Boston, Massachusetts, to Arthur Mann, a historian, and Sylvia B. Blut, a remedial reading specialist. She graduated from Radcliffe in 1974 and received a master of fine arts degree from the University of Minnesota in 1976. Upon completing her graduate work, Mann became a directing fellow at the Guthrie Theater in Minneapolis and was an associate director for the company in 1978 and 1979. She also served as resident director at the Brooklyn Academy of Music Theatre Company in 1981–1982. In 1990 she became artistic director of the McCarter Theatre Center for the Performing Arts in Princeton, New Jersey. Mann has been the recipient of numerous fellowships and awards including a Guggenheim Fellowship (1983); the Rosamond Gilder Award (1983), an artists' grant from the National Endowment for the Arts (in 1984 and 1986); a McKnight Fellowship (1985), a Helen Hayes Award (1986); and the Dramatists Guild Award (1986). She was a Great American Play Contest co-winner in 1985 and has won six Obie Awards for various productions in New York City. In 1994, the McCarter Theatre, under her stewardship, received a Tony Award as outstanding regional theater.

Oral History

An award-winning playwright and director, whose work has been produced on Broadway and across the United States (as well as internationally), Emily Mann is best known for documentary theater work that investigates social issues. A Jewish-American woman who identifies strongly with her ethnic background, Mann has created two theater pieces that address the issues of the *Shoah*.

Mann asserts that she first became interested—almost obsessed—with the Holocaust because of the work of her father, Arthur Mann, who was appointed the head of the American Jewish Committee's oral history project. Parts of Professor Mann's duties were to record the memories of Holocaust survivors. In 1968, when Emily Mann was in high school, her father allowed the teenager to listen to a number of tapes. One tape in particular—that of a Czechoslovakian female survivor who was being interviewed by her daughter—deeply impacted the precocious teenager. The mother spoke in a thick Czech accent and had a European perspective. The survivor's daughter was completely Americanized both in speech and outlook. Mann was interested as much in the separation between mother and daughter as she was in the actual narrative of the survivor: "both of them reaching toward each other across a language barrier, as well as an experiential barrier. It was extraordinary" (Savran, p. 82).

Mann thought her father should make the tapes available to the public, and when he could not, she determined to conduct her own interviews. She is now famous for her "theater of testimony," in which she conducts voluminous interviews, from which she distills dramatic documentary theater. This creative model has resulted in pieces covering diverse subject matter, including *Still Life* (1979), which explores the experiences of a Vietnam veteran; *The Execution of Justice* (1986), which looks at the murders committed by Dan White in San Francisco; *Greensboro: A Requiem* (1997), which examines the mass killing of black protestors marching against the Ku Klux Klan; and her most acclaimed piece, *Having Our Say* (1996), which recounts the experiences of two elderly African American women (the Delany sisters).

Annulla

Mann's first documentary work—her first "theater of testimony"—chronicles the experiences of a Holocaust survivor named Annulla Allen. While still an undergraduate at Radcliffe, Mann traveled to England, where she met this feisty survivor. A few years later, while working at the Guthrie Theater in Minneapolis, she was able to mount and direct a one-character show titled *Annulla: Autobiography of a Survivor.* In 1984–1985 Mann revised the play, by adding her own reactions to Annulla's story, and retitled the work *Annulla: An Autobiography*. This version of the play premiered at the Repertory Theatre of St. Louis and was later mounted at various regional theaters.

Mann uses a series of alienation devices in *Annulla: An Autobiography* that allow the audience to engage the biography of the protagonist on a level that transcends a purely emotional or visceral reaction. First, Mann uses a process of triple separation that creates and acknowledges the distance between the audience and the subject matter. A woman is placed on a stage that is intended to represent a London flat in 1974. This woman then proceeds to recount events from thirty years earlier, while another woman, who is a disembodied voice temporally situated ten years later, comments ironically upon the exposition. Thus a character in 1974 recalls events from 1940 and is interrupted by someone in 1985.

Annulla Allen is a tough, highly opinionated old lady who is educated and articulate. Fluent in seven languages and extremely political, she offers witty, entertaining, and often acerbic Jewish-feminist interpretations of events during the first half of the twentieth century. Annulla manages to survive the Holocaust by posing as a gentile and slipping off to England. But before she escapes, she has the effrontery to go to Dachau to demand (successfully) the release of her husband from the concentration camp there. Now a widow (in 1974), Annulla cares for her ailing sister and tries futilely to write the great epic novel that will lay out her political and social agenda. Annulla believes fervently that the woes of the twentieth century are due directly to male domination of political and social institutions. It is Annulla's contention that if women seized political control there would be no more violence, war, death camps, or nuclear confrontation.

Annulla's experiences in German-occupied Austria during the late 1930s are chilling. Living in Vienna at the time of the *Anschluss* (German annexation of Austria) in 1938, Annulla and her husband are swept up in the rapidly deteriorating situation. After the *Kristallnacht* (anti-Jewish riots) of November 1938, her husband is seized and sent to Dachau. Annulla—a resident alien from the Ostland (present-day Estonia, Latvia, Lithuania, and Belarus)—is left alone with her young son. Annulla arranges for her child to find refuge in Sweden with a charitable organization. On the verge of a nervous breakdown, she travels to Dachau and presents herself as a gentile woman looking for her husband:

> It was the worst day of my life. You see, I was so indifferent to what would happen to me. One day, some man from the Gestapo came to see me and said, "If I am going to buy your house, I will give you so-and-so marks for it. You have to sell it to me." I said "But my husband is in Dachau." And he said, "Well, you'll have to get his signature." So I went to Dachau. I took a train from Munich to Dachau, spent the night in a hotel . . . can you imagine, a Jewish woman in Dachau in 1938 and I took a room in a hotel! The cheek! . . . And do you know, he came out on the thirty-first of December? Yes, you see they were moved by the many steps I had taken. They couldn't understand. They asked me why do you not leave this Jewish husband? They asked me in Vienna, they asked me in Munich—I did not say it was because I was also Jewish. I said, "Because I love him" (*Annulla,* collected in *Fruitful and Multiplying,* edited by Ellen Schiff, New York. Mentor, 1996, p. 198).

In April 1939, Annulla's husband manages to acquire an exit visa to England. Aware of the ever-increasing danger, Annulla desperately seeks a means to emigrate, but is stymied. Finally she makes a daring escape whose method is little more than boundless chutzpah. Still disguised as an Aryan, without identity papers or a passport, Annulla bluffs her way out of Germany and into England.

Emily Mann clearly adores Annulla and paints a vivid and endearing picture of her, but the playwright is far too sophisticated to produce a simplistic valentine. Mann—using the voice of the disembodied speaker—corrects and challenges a number of Annulla's assertions. First, we learn that Annulla is a bit off on the facts now and then—her memory is clearly slipping. Second, a number of Annulla's assertions are undermined by her own behavior. Annulla is not particularly nurturing and loving either to her own children or to her ailing sister—thus her personal actions undercut her political assertions regarding the inherent superiority of a matriarchal society. Third, Annulla—for all her talk of feminist empowerment—allows herself to occupy stereotypical roles throughout her life—putting her husband, her children, and now her sister before her own autonomy. Finally, the disembodied voice of the speaker (Emily Mann) directly challenges the mainstay of Annulla's thesis that women are morally superior to men.

All of these corrections, realignments, challenges, and disembodied insights serve to alienate the action, thereby creating a critical frame for the audience, but also ironically to make Annulla even more human and charming. Annulla emerges as a real flesh-and-blood person full of contradictions, neurosis, and irritating habits—just like everybody in the audience! The final result is not the story of the Holocaust, but quite simply a story of the Holocaust, and the audience is forced to choose what specifically to believe—what points of view to agree with—and, ultimately, what to make of the entire theatrical experience. The play is a sophisticated exercise in Brechtian storytelling full of alienation and contradiction that challenges the audience to think critically.

Meshugah

Twenty years after her first foray into representing the Holocaust, Emily Mann returned to the topic by writing a stage adaptation of Isaac Bashevis Singer's novel *Meshugah*. Her dramatic adaptation follows the original work closely and captures faithfully the essence of the source material.

Meshugah poses a series of questions and offers a set of challenges without providing simple answers or solutions. The central issue of the play revolves around Aaron Greidinger's obsessive attraction to a young survivor and the unfolding mystery surrounding her life during the war. As the narrator attempts to make sense of Miriam's experience, he finds himself passing judgment on her actions. Miriam survived the horror by committing a series of morally questionable acts. But Greidinger, who escaped the catastrophe and knows only secondhand the grim realities of that period, realizes that he has no right to judge the survivor. Emily Mann's adaptation of Singer's novel uses the confusion and discomfort of Aaron Greidinger to illustrate the impossibility of such sweeping judgments and implicitly forces the audience to question its own moral certitude in such matters.

Meshugah is a powerful example of survivor Holocaust drama—plays that represent events which transpire after the historical occurrence. The protagonists are haunted, pursued, or obsessed by aspects of the Holocaust that intrude into their contemporary lives. These plays are temporally and spatially distanced from the event. This separation of time and space is bridged by modes of exposition that describe the unbearable in lieu of enactment. The flashback, the dream sequence, the vivid memory, the discovered document, and the courtroom testimony provide a picture of a past that impacts upon the present. In *Meshugah*, however, Singer, and by extension Emily Mann, avoid such simplistic devices. The audience is given only a fractured, shifting narrative that never allows us to know what actually happened during the war. For most of the play, Miriam is our only source of information, and her story changes constantly, leaving us off balance and confused. Even after the startling and chilling revelation that occurs toward the end of the piece, the narrator—and the audience—is left without certainty as to what actually occurred, or what will happen from here. Will Aaron Greidinger desert Miriam, or will he help to heal her shattered soul? Will we in the audience continue to pass simplistic moral judgments, or will we accept the inherent craziness in ourselves, in those we love, and in the world around us? And the play's overarching question, it seems, is to ask, will the Jewish people move forward or continue to be victims of their collective past?

Bibliography

Primary Sources

Still Life: A Documentary. 1979.
Nights and Days. Adaptation of a play by Pierre Laville. 1984.
Annulla: An Autobiography. 1985.
Execution of Justice. 1986.
Betsey Brown. With Ntozake Shange and Baikida Carroll. 1989.
Having Our Say: The Delany Sisters' First 100 Years. 1996.
Greensboro: A Requiem. 1997.

Secondary Sources

Bienen, Leigh Buchanan. "Emily Mann." In *Speaking on Stage*. Edited by Philip Kolin and Colby Kellman. Tuscaloosa: University of Alabama Press, 1996.

Bigsby, Christopher. *Contemporary American Playwrights*. Cambridge: Cambridge University Press, 2000.

Burke, Sally. *American Feminist Playwrights*. New York: Twayne, 1996.

Daniels, Rebecca. *Women Stage Directors Speak: Exploring the Influence of Gender in Their Work*. Jefferson, N.C.: McFarland, 1996.

Dawson, Gary Fisher. "Documentary Theatre in the United States: An Historical Survey and Analysis of Its Content, Form, and Stagecraft." In *Contributions in Drama and Theatre Studies*. Westport, Conn: Greenwood Press, 1999.

Istel, John. "Emily Mann: Searching for Survivors." *American Theatre*, 13 February 1996, pp. 44–45.

———" You, the Jury." *Village Voice*, 12 March 1996, p. 72.

Mann, Emily. "In Conversation." *Theater Topics* 10, no. 1 (2000): 1–16.

Salz-Bernstein, Melissa. "Playwright's Forum: Emily Mann: Having Her Say." *American Drama* 6, no. 2 (spring 1997): 81–85.

Interviews

Betsko, Kathleen, and Rachel Koenig. *Interviews with Contemporary Women Playwrights*. New York: Beech Tree, 1987.

Savran, David. *In Their Own Words: Contemporary American Playwrights*. New York: Theatre Communications Group, 1988.

Shteir, R. "I Became an Optimist: An Interview with Emily Mann." *Theater* 22, no. 1 (winter 1991): 20–26.

Thomas Mann
(1875–1955)

MARK H. GELBER

In order to understand Thomas Mann's relationship to the Holocaust, some preliminary contextualizations of the topic are in order. First, his personal relations to individual Jews and Jewish issues, especially to antisemitism and Zionism, should be considered, especially in terms of possible attitudinal changes in face of the rise of Nazism and the Holocaust. Second, the background and possible significance of Thomas Mann's incorporation of Jewish literary characters into his work until 1933 need to be taken into account and then contrasted to his work after the Holocaust. Third, his opinions concerning Nazism and his activities related to Jewry during the Nazi period and afterward should also be remembered. Last, in light of having established the appropriate context for a literary analysis, his major literary work, the novel *Doktor Faustus*, may be assessed from the point of view of writing during and after the Holocaust. This novel was written, in one sense at least, as a serious attempt to comprehend the tragedy of German civilization, which led to World War II and the Holocaust. Mann's voluminous correspondence and diaries, especially those which date from the Nazi period, and following it, need to be scrutinized as well in this framework.

As a matter of fact, the three different contextualizations listed above—his early attitutes to Jews and Jewish issues, his Jewish literary characters, and his activities during the Nazi period—are all relatively complicated issues. Mann's relationship to Jews and Jewish issues has regularly been called ambivalent, but there are certain parameters to each topic that may be sketched briefly. He was acutely aware of the Jewish background of a particular person or issue he considered, and he incorporated this dimension into his assessment of things and into his literary work. Concerning individual Jews Mann tended to discern consistently between positive and negative Jewish types. His discriminations along these lines usually tended to be very personal, although he saw these types as contributing positively or negatively to culture at large. He categorized as positive Jewish types those Jews who appreciated and lauded his literary accomplishments and those who tended to view the world, especially the world of literature and art, in ways similar to his own. These included, for example, the literary and cultural critic Samuel Lublinski, who was one of the first important observers to praise unstintingly Mann's first major novel, *Buddenbrooks*. Mann was ever grateful to Lublinski, because he encouraged him at a fateful, early moment of his literary career. Samuel Fischer, Mann's publisher, with whom he maintained an exemplary and positive relationship over many years, also fits in this category.

Mann, however, perceived his Jewish detractors and those critical of his literary production, including Alfred Kerr and Theodor Lessing, both of whom were influential writers in the first part of the twentieth century, to be representative of negative Jewish types, who were a baneful influence on cultural development in general. Furthermore, in the first decade of the century, Mann married Katja Pringsheim, who came from a well-known, highly assimilated Jewish family in Munich, with branches of the family resident in Berlin and elsewhere. Despite the high degree of assimilation characteristic of the Pringsheims and other family members of Jewish descent, Mann was quite sensitive to the fact that his wife and children were racially Jewish. At the beginning of the century, he expressed pleasure with this racialist fact, since it may have seemed to promise cultural enrichment as well as genetic diversity in his family life. Later on, the racist laws of Nazi Germany, when they came into effect in the 1930s, certainly applied to Katja, their children, and to her larger family.

Although Mann toyed at first with the idea of a possible accommodation with Nazism, even searching for the good in Nazi Germany, he very soon abandoned this track. Since he was abroad on a lecture tour at the time of the Reichstag fire and the implementation of the emergency measures that rapidly led to a Nazi takeover of power and Hitler's ruthless dictatorship, Mann never returned to reside in Germany again. He eventually became one of the most outspoken public critics of Nazi Germany from his domiciles in exile in Europe, and from the United States, while he eventually became an American citizen. During the years in exile, he sought to present an image of himself as the true German. He claimed to represent, even while living at a distance from German soil, all that was positive in the German spirit, which had been corrupted in the meantime by Nazism.

In terms of Jewish issues, it is fair to characterize the early Mann as politically conservative, but with a certain dual perspective concerning antisemitism and Zionism. Thus, despite the strong impact of Arthur Schopenhauer, Friedrich Nietzsche, Richard Wagner, Paul de Lagarde, and others who articulated antisemitic and quasi-antisemitic views and who have been cited as exerting a seminal impact on his intellectual development, he was fairly content with the prospect of Jewish assimilation as a condition for full integration into the fabric of German society. At the same time, he saw the Jews generally as a positive fermenting agent in European culture, which overall added a potent and creative dimension to cultural development. Thus, for Mann, Zionism would be a negative phenomenon to the extent that this Jewish fermenting factor would be commensurately missing in Europe, if masses of Jews were to abandon the continent in favor of Zion. Mann visited Palestine shortly after he won the Nobel Prize for Literature in 1929. Although he took ill during the trip, he was able to observe at first hand the Zionist accomplishments in the land, which he appreciated and commented on positively in subsequent interviews. At the same time, he expressed his concern for the resident Arab population, in face of more reactionary Zionist revisionist attitudes and actions.

In his fiction through the Nazi period, Mann tended to include relatively negative minor Jewish characters. These figures are in general either physically ugly or repulsive, parvenu types, or morally defective. In only one fictive work, *Wälsungenblut* (Blood of the Walsungs, 1905), which he referred to in his correspondence as his "Judennovelle" (his Jewish novella) did the Jewish issue take center stage. Mann conceived the work as a literary travesty of Wagner's *Walküre*, incorporating autobiographical material related specifically to the Pringsheim family, and written with supreme ironic discretion, as far as the Jewish content is concerned. The words "Jew" and Jewish" do not appear at all in this story about incest, decadence, and racial revenge in an assimilated, highly cultured, German-Jewish household in Berlin. There was something of a scandal concerning the publication of the work, owing to objections about the use of Yiddishisms in the original ending. Although Mann altered the ending and deleted the potentially offensive Yiddish expressions for the sake of publishing the work, it did not appear at the time in print. Pirated versions did circulate however, and many years later Mann did publish the work with the revised ending. As late as 1940, Mann defended the story in his correspondence, claiming that the work should not be thought of in terms of the present conditions in Nazi Germany. Rather, the work was written at the beginning of the century, "when antisemitism was rare in Germany," and when "a Jewish setting had no particular significance for a story." The view that Mann defended here was part of a long-standing, so-called "enlightened" European view that Jews, like any other particular ethnic or religious or national group, are proper subjects for satirical treatment in fiction, and are in no way exempt from critical or humorous examinations by non-Jewish artists and intellectuals.

After the Nazi takeover and following his decision not to return to Nazi Germany, Mann tried at first to keep a low public profile, while expressing privately his dislike of certain aspects of the Nazi regime and its antidemocratic policies. Eventually, this posturing proved to be short-lived. In 1936, Mann was stripped of his German citizenship on the grounds that he ostensibly appeared at demonstrations of international organizations, mostly under Jewish influence, whose hostility to Germany was well-known. Later, after he moved to the United States, Mann became an outspoken critic of Nazi Germany. He attempted to present his critical voice in public lectures and interviews, and on radio broadcasts, in the name of a true German humanist spirit in exile, since Nazism had corrupted or silenced that spirit in Germany. Mann worked closely with humanitarian groups who attempted to find shelter, refuge, and employment for displaced Central European writers and intellectuals, many of whom were Jewish. In this overall effort he forged new partnerships with Jewish personalities and organizations in the United States.

In the midst of the war, Mann embarked on an ambitious literary project focusing on the Faust theme, which eventually was published as "Doctor Faustus: The Life of the German Composer Adrian Leverkühn." Mann began writing the work as Nazi Germany was being defeated and as he began to learn about the Nazi atrocities and attempted genocide of the Jewish people. Judging from his diaries and correspondence, it is fair to say that he was revolted by what he read regarding the Nazi massacres of Jews. Still, his major novel about the Nazi period and the German path to the Third Reich tends to view Nazism as an aberrant stream of German culture, with which various German factions made their peace. Nevertheless, that particular path was doomed and it led ultimately to the physical destruction of Germany. What is most problematic from the point of view of the Holocaust and its impact on Mann's literary work is that a series of negative Jewish characters is presented in "Doctor Faustus," although a few minor, positive references to Jews or to a minor Jewish figure do also appear. This literary development runs parallel to Mann's idea that certain anti-liberal or reactionary circles, either with Jewish members in them or Jewish in their own right, accorded well with Nazism and in a sense may have helped prepare the way for Nazism in Germany owing to their own proto-fascism. "Doctor Faustus" has been called an example of literary antisemitism, but it is a minor example by any account, because the Jewish issue occupies a relatively minor space in the massive work's literary economy. When Mann was challenged regarding the negative Jewish characters, he attempted to relativize the issue by claiming that most of the figures in the work were negatively drawn, whether they were of Jewish origin or not. In face of the destruction of German Jewry, Mann failed here to provide a convincing literary depiction of positive Jewish types, which would have amounted to an unambiguous anti-Nazi position in fiction, following the Holocaust.

Although Mann avoided further explicit literary treatment of the Nazi era and the Jewish issues related to it, he may have been encouraged to adopt a more positive public stance on Zionist aspirations, in wake of the Holocaust. Although he had serious reservations before the war, and even during it, about the ultimate Zionist goal of founding a Jewish State in Palestine, after the Holocaust Mann was outspoken in his support for the establishment of a Jewish State. He never altered his public position in this regard again, despite a certain amount of pressure to do so.

Bibliography

Primary Sources

Gesammelte Werke. 13 Bde (Collected Works, 13 Vols.). 1974.

Diaries 1918–1939. Translated by Richard and Clara Winston. 1982.

Letters 1889–1955. Translated by Richard and Clara Winston. 1971.

Secondary Sources

Berendsohn, Walter. *Thomas Mann: Kuenstler und Kaempfer in bewegter Zeit*. Luebeck: Schmidt-Roemhild, 1965.

Elsaghe, Yahiya. "Die Juedinnen in Thomas Manns Erzaehlwerk." *Monatshefte*, 93 (3): 159–176.

Gelber, Mark H. "Indifferentism, Anti-Semitism, the Holocaust and Zionism." In *Tel Aviver Jahrbuch fuer deutsche Geschichte*, 1991, pp. 327–337.

———. "Thomas Mann and Anti-Semitism." *Patterns of Prejudice* 17 (4): 31–40.

———. "Thomas Mann and Zionism." *German Life and Letters* 37 (2): 118–124.

Hamilton, Nigel. *The Brothers Mann*. New Haven: Yale University Press, 1979.

Prater, Donald. *Thomas Mann: A Life*. Oxford: Oxford University Press, 1995.

Thiede, Rolf. *Stereotypen vom Juden: Die fruehen Schriften von Heinrich und Thomas Mann*. Berlin: Metropol, 1998.

Winston, Richard. *Thomas Mann. The Making of an Artist 1875–1911*. London: Constable, 1982.

DONALD MARGULIES

(1954–)

STEVEN DEDALUS BURCH

AFTER RECEIVING THE 2000 Pulitzer Prize for playwriting, one of the United States's finest dramatists, Donald Margulies, emerged as a major chronicler of late twentieth-century Jewish American existence. He was born to Bob and Charlene Margulies on September 2, 1954 and raised near Coney Island, Brooklyn. As a child, Margulies was often taken to Broadway theater productions, and later, while studying at the State University of New York at Purchase, he decided to try playwriting. Toward this goal he requested a tutorial with Julius Novick, a professor of literature and drama studies and a renowned critic for the *Village Voice*. Novick was impressed with Margulies's first play with its individual vision of American Jewish life that was to be found in many of his later plays. In 1983, the Jewish Repertory Theater in New York staged *Gifted Children*, Margulies's first full-length produced play. Margulies's *Found a Peanut* was produced by Joseph Papp at the Public Theatre in 1984, and in 1985 his next play, *What's Wrong with This Picture?* marked the beginning of his long association with the Manhattan Theatre Club.

Plays

While Margulies's work largely focuses on the social and personal pressures of contemporary Jewish American life, the impact of the Holocaust on his characters, and on American Jewry in general, becomes most visible in *The Model Apartment* (1985). An inference to this subject may be found in his 1984 *Found a Peanut*, in which a group of preteen Jewish children is disrupted by Gentile bullies, and in two later plays, *The Loman Family Picnic* (1989), and *Sight Unseen* (1991), the subject of the Holocaust is peripherally approached.

The Loman Family Picnic presents a lower-middle-class Jewish family as it ascends the Protestant American assimilation ladder. The play's title makes reference to Arthur Miller's *Death of a Salesman*, but Margulies's play pointedly underlines themes that are only implicitly acknowledged in Miller's. Unlike the Loman family in Miller's play, with their overriding concern for paying for their house, Margulies's Loman family spends money it can never recoup to pay for their son Stewie's bar mitzvah. In the end, Margulies's Lomans arrive at an even more profound emptiness in their lives.

Doris, the boy's mother, opens the *The Loman Family Picnic* by sharing her dreams of upward mobility with the audience and confides that, though highly intelligent, her sons have not been brought up to display their superiority. Quoting from the play, published by Theatre Communications Group in 1995, she says: "I raised my boys to stand out but not too much, you know? otherwise people won't like you anymore. Look what happened to the Jews in Europe. Better you should have friends and be popular, than be showy and alone" (*Sight Unseen and Other Plays*, p. 200). At the start of the play's second act, in a fantasy version of the bar mitzvah, Doris conjures up dead relatives, including Uncle Izzy from the concentration camp and Cousin Rivka from the Triangle Factory fire. The play, though, does not address the Holocaust directly, except as one of many historical conditions that inform Jewish life in America.

Sight Unseen, also published in *Sight Unseen and Other Plays*, in its tale of an artist's recent celebrity during his first European exhibition, presents a riveting showdown between the painter Jonathan and a German interviewer, Grete, in which she scathingly comments on Jonathan's most notorious painting, which features a black man making love to a white woman in a vandalized Jewish cemetery. When he attempts to counter her interpretation of the painting as a rape, Grete responds by dismissing Jonathan's view of himself as a disruptive artist outside the mainstream, asserting that "the artist, like the Jew, prefers to see himself as alien from the mainstream culture. For the Jewish *artist* to acknowledge that the *contrary* is true, that he is *not* alien, but rather, *assimilated* into that mainstream culture . . ." (*Sight Unseen and Other Plays*, Theatre Communications Group, 1995, p. 316). Interrupting her antisemitic critique, Jonathan immediately takes greater offense at being categorized as a Jewish painter and emphasizes, "I'm an *American* painter. *American* is the adjective, not *Jewish, American*" (p. 316). This passionate and well-received drama continues one thematic line from *The Loman Family Picnic*, that of a perceived loss of Jewish identity, an identity that is partially informed by the Holocaust and the Diaspora and codified by traditional enemies, a loss that appears to be pandemic in late twentieth-century assimilated American life.

Unlike Margulies's other plays, *The Model Apartment* directly and disturbingly confronts the Holocaust's legacy among the survivors, their descendants, and even the acquaintances of those descendants, stressing the psychological damage they suffered and the father's retreat into fantasy and silence. Much of this legacy is in the recovery of memory that is both personal and collective. In his Introduction to the second volume of *The Theatre of the Holocaust* published by the University of Wisconsin Press, Robert Skloot invokes the public image of Anne Frank (as does Margulies in this play) to ask incisively: "What ethical place can be occupied by audiences whose familiarity with history is *inevitably* biased or partial, and therefore in some absolute sense, *always* mistaken?" (p. 11). This question seems to strike at the very heart of Margulies's profoundly upsetting "comedy." In the course of its often scabrous depiction of a monumentally dysfunctional family, the play continues to force its audience to choke on their own laughter as they confront their culturally preconditioned responses to the survivors of the Holocaust and their families, and to the real—and imagined—ghosts of its victims, in this case Max's daughter Deborah and Lola's camp friend, Anne Frank.

The Model Apartment opens with the arrival in the middle of the night of Max and Lola at a model condominium showcase apartment in Florida. They have purchased a new condominium apartment only to discover on their arrival that it has not been completed, necessitating their spending the next couple of days at the development's showcase apartment. As they fumble around the apartment and discover that most of its appliances are only for show and have no practical function, the audience quickly learns that they have left New York City to begin their new life of retirement. But the audience also learns that they have fled their only child, their grown daughter, Debby.

Later that night, however, Debby arrives, a grotesquely obese woman-child in her thirties, who is both disturbed and disturbing. Much later that night Debby's lover Neil, a fifteen-year-old, mildly retarded African American youth, breaks into the apartment searching for her. For the remainder of the night, Debby consciously disrupts the sanctuary to which her parents have fled, and the audience discovers that the parents have kept their move a secret from their profoundly needy daughter. A fifth character also "joins" them by silently flitting through the shadows of the darkened apartment as Max sleeps. It is the ghost of his first daughter, Deborah, who died in infancy along with Max's first wife in a concentration camp while Max spent the war hiding in the woods. In Max's dreams, Deborah is an adult, having somehow survived, and she soothingly converses with him, offering Max emotional and spiritual succor from the monstrosity of his everyday life.

At the play's core is the fragile attempt, wildly and frighteningly comic, by each member of this dysfunctional family to seek and claim a refuge from their overwhelmingly sad present-day existence. For the remainder of the evening, Debby subjects her parents to yet another display of her gluttonous needs for food, sex, and affection, as her arrival triggers an all-out, continuing assault on Max's wall of silence regarding his guilt over the trauma of surviving.

Max and Lola are initially escaping from a daughter who engorges on the trash of a disposable culture. Debby's physical and emotional monstrosity is the ultimate and final grotesque distortion of Max and Lola's identities as European Jews. But Debby, alone, does not account for their pathetic flight to a Florida condo. Max and Lola's discomfort in the model apartment provides possible echoes of Max and Lola's existence in the ghettoes and camps, where a numbing passivity and acquiescence toward authority had taken hold of their daily living. That the apartment's refrigerator is only a prop, like the shower heads at Auschwitz, is a discomforting reminder of this couple's inability to assert their agency by rejecting their circumstances. Max and Lola, at least initially, want only to shut their eyes and blot out the world around them. It is a measure of the play's sadness that, in the end, Lola's absence in the final scene suggests that she cannot shut out the world that contains her disturbed and needy daughter and that Max, who has finally freed himself from his real family, has found refuge only in the imagined conversations with the ghost of his dead daughter.

Told in fifteen short scenes, *The Model Apartment* displays the anguish and the anger that this cataclysmic event has had upon a child of Holocaust survivors. In scene one, Max and Lola are distraught by the ersatz refrigerator and television, yet grumpily make their adjustment to the temporary inconveniences, unwilling to complain, touch, or alter anything in the apartment. By scene four Debby arrives and proceeds to wreak her emotional havoc with devastating precision. In a near Joycean stream-of-consciousness reverie, Debby energetically delivers an aria of historical and pop cultural references and juxtapositions, from singer Connie Francis's rape trial to Howard Johnson's restaurant and motel chain being a front for the Nazis, before she moves on to pizza and lovemaking with her boyfriend, Neil. She concludes by accusing her parents of running out without telling her they were moving to Florida. By scene six, as Lola attempts to accommodate her daughter's physical and emotional needs, Max finds his only refuge in sleep, as he conjures, for the first time in the play, the ghost of his first daughter, Deborah, a gentle and elusive presence who slips around the darkened room as her father lovingly hums a Yiddish lullaby to her.

Scene seven brings more of Debby's stream-of-consciousness chatter as she verbally juggles late twentieth-century American pop cultural images—Beefsteak Charlie's, *Hogan's Heroes'* Kommandant Klink, Miss America, Hollywood—with a comically grotesque fantasy of a beauty contest and summer camp outing in the concentration camp. Later, as Debby and Max sleep, Lola awakens from a dream/memory of abandoning her own mother in the concentration camp at Belsen, by not acknowledging to the Nazi camp guards her connection to the older woman.

In scene nine, Neil crashes into the apartment looking for Debby, and they immediately begin fornicating in the room in front of her horrified parents. While examining the apartment, Neil accidentally snaps off a fake candle from the apartment's dining table display, antagonizing Max, who wants to be accommodating to the condo company and not to disturb anything that does not belong to him or Lola. Trying to alleviate the tension between her husband and the stranger, Lola engages Neil in conversation about his family, discovering that he is homeless but that he had grown up in the same section of Brooklyn where Max and Lola first lived after the war. This connection to her past prods Lola to remember her time at Bergen-Belsen and to equate Neil's present homelessness with her youthful misery. In one of the play's most dazzling sequences, Lola describes her friendship at Bergen-Belsen with another teenager, Anne Frank, and Lola's encouragement of Anne to write another diary of her experiences in the camp. Lola weeps at the memory of Anne dying in her arms and of the Nazis' destruction of the second diary in which Lola was the heroine:

> The Heroine. Well, it was *her* book, true, but I was there, on every single page. "Lola did *this*," or "Lola said *this* today." "Lola gives me the strength to go on." "Lola has such courage." Can you imagine? *Me*, Lola, I gave Anne Frank the will to live may she rest in peace. (*Sight Unseen and Other Plays*, p. 182).

After lamenting that if this diary, her story, had not been destroyed it would have given hope to millions, and that she, Lola, could have inspired others through her example of triumphing against suffering, Lola finishes this sad, ridiculous, mesmerizing story only to have Neil respond with "Who?" (p. 183).

The play reaches its almost unbearable crescendo of comic horror when Max decides that they must escape from Debby, as Lola grows weary from this battle between husband and daughter. When Max tells Debby that he and Lola are leaving, Debby begins to frantically rearrange the furniture in an attempt to create more space in the cramped apartment. Then she confronts Max with her fears that he does not love or like her and that she is too fat. This leads to an implosion of all the cultural references that she has carried with her, from Josef Mengele to Maximilian Schell in *Judgment at Nuremberg*, as she tearfully explains:

> They're all inside me. All of them. Anne Frank. The Six Million. Bubbie and Zaydie and Hitler and Deborah. When my stomach talks, it's *them* talking.Telling me they're hungry. I eat for them so they won't be hungry. Sometimes I don't know what I'm saying 'cause it's *them* talking (p. 189).

This startling speech ends with Debby bewailing that she can never be Deborah to Max, that she's sorry that she was not exterminated like Deborah was. Then she angrily accuses Max of letting all the dead people inside her room. The scene ends as she attempts to strangle Max.

In Ellen S. Fine's essay regarding collective memory and absent memory, she writes that the latter comes from the "feeling of exclusion both from experience and from knowledge about the experience" (p. 187), including the regret, traumatic and emblematic in Debby's case, for not having been there in the camp. But this regret can also apply to Max, who had spent those years hiding in the forest as his first wife and beloved daughter perished in the camps. Fine contends that the memory of the survivors casts a shadow on the next generation, a "hovering presence that will not go away" (p. 187), and that this presence yokes the survivors to those who were not then alive.

Trussed up and waiting for the ambulance to arrive and take her to a psychiatric hospital, Debby sits gagged as Max lovingly strokes her hair and explains that all he wants is peace and that they must part forever. Lola, however, realizes that she can neither abandon her daughter nor can she join Max. In the play's moving final scene the audience is presented with a final ambiguous image in the play, that of Max asleep in a chaise lounge, dressed in a cabana suit, and listening to an opera on a Walkman as Deborah enters and brings Max up to date on all he has missed since the war. She concludes with a description of a seder Max missed, and of her being continually hungry at the feast: "but my eyes are closing, they're closing, and I don't want to fall asleep and miss the feast, I don't want to miss the feast" (p. 195).

Commentary

In *Stages of Annihilation: Theatrical Representations of the Holocaust*, Edward Isser subclassifies Holocaust drama into three major groupings: ghetto and martyr drama, survivor drama, and death camp drama. Logically placing *The Model Apartment* into the second category, Isser submits that this second category is the most common of Holocaust theatrical reenactments, for it presents haunted or obsessed protagonists for whom the trauma continues to intrude on their contemporary lives. More recently, new survivor drama adds another element to the Holocaust's lasting legacy: alienation between the generations (pp. 23–24). This legacy, in Margulies's drama, is, in part, one of profound longing for an escape not only from a memory that is unsustainable but from a culture and a world that cannot restore dignity to the victims.

Lola's struggle becomes perhaps more profound, at least more life embracing, as she potentially severs her connection with the present (Max) in order to remain with the deeply troubled future (Debby). Even her compulsive need in retelling her (perhaps imagined) connection to Anne Frank (and in Debby's echoing and prodding of the story, it has clearly become a ritualistic retelling in the life of Lola and her family), Lola continues to seek meaning of and closure with her own suffering as she laments the loss of Anne's second diary in which Lola was the book's heroine: "I could've given people hope" (p. 182).

While generally acclaimed, *The Model Apartment* has, not surprisingly, alienated some audiences and critics, such as Laurie Winer of the *Los Angeles Times*, who, reviewing a 1997 production at the La Jolla Playhouse, faults the play as "stubbornly problematic" and a "deeply disturbing comedy [which] rings hollow in a futureless setting" (p. 1). Part of the problem, for some, is what Winer decries as the play's hopelessness. Faulting what he perceives as the incessant need in the American theater and cinema for heroic narratives with hopeful and uplifting endings, Lawrence Langer writes of this dichotomy that "Holocaust writing itself serves two masters: a clear intellectual perception of how Nazism shrank the area of dignified choice and reduced the options for human gestures; and the instinct to have victims survive heroically even within these less-than-human alternatives" (p. 223). But such heroic survival of the meaningless cruelty of the Holocaust, Langer claims, only falsifies the experience of those who suffered and perished. *The Model Apartment* bravely refuses to sentimentalize the victims of the Holocaust. That said, however, Margulies's grotesque comedy remains a difficult and frequently painful portrait at odds with a need to sanctify the sufferers.

Skloot calls *The Model Apartment* "an adult cartoon" (p. 26), and rightly concludes that the play is a failed "search for meaning and love in a post-Holocaust world" (p. 28). All four of the play's characters skate quite perilously close to the thin ice of trivializing the enormity of the pain and loss of all who have suffered. Max, Lola, Debby, and Neil are the human detritus of the late twentieth century and none of them finds either meaning or justification for their sufferings. Only Max, through abandoning all ties to the real, human world of his earthly family, appears in the final scene to be able to release himself from his trauma. Or does he? How deep is this freedom from history that he is finally experiencing? Margulies wisely concludes his story here, leaving any further resolution up to the audience, challenging them to accept that the price everyone must pay for the Holocaust is that there will never be any resolution.

The Model Apartment was nominated for a Pulitzer Prize. Of Margulies's more recent plays, *Sight Unseen* received an Obie Award in 1992, the Dramatists Guild/Hull-Warriner Award, and was a Pulitzer Finalist, as was *Collected Stories* in 1997. Both plays have been extremely popular in the United States, receiving multiple productions in regional theaters. Margulies's most recent full-length play, *Dinner with Friends*, received the 2000 Pulitzer Prize for drama.

Margulies joined New Dramatists in 1990 and was elected to the Dramatists Guild Council in 1993. He has received grants from the National Endowment for the Arts, the John Simon Guggenheim Foundation, New York Foundation for the Arts, and Creative Artists Public Service (CAPS), while his plays have premiered at the Manhattan Theatre Club, South Coast

Repertory, Actors Theatre of Louisville, and the Los Angeles Theatre Center.

Bibliography

Primary Sources

Luna Park. 1982.
Gifted Children. 1983.
Found a Peanut. 1984.
The Model Apartment. 1985.
Zimmer. 1987.
What's Wrong with This Picture? 1988.
The Loman Family Picnic. 1989.
Sight Unseen. 1991.
Pitching to the Star. 1992.
Sight Unseen and Other Plays. 1995.
July 7, 1994. 1995.
Collected Stories. 1997.
Dinner with Friends. 1998.
Backstory: "Misadventure." 2000.

Secondary Sources

Coen, Stephanie. "Donald Margulies." *American Theatre* (July 1994): 46.

Feingold, Michael. "Donald Margulies, or What's an American Playwright?" In *Sight Unseen and Other Plays*. By Donald Margulies. New York: Theatre Communications Group. 1995.

Fine, Ellen S. "Transmission of Memory: The Post-Holocaust Generation in the Diaspora." In *Breaking Crystal: Writing and Memory after Auschwitz*. Edited by Efraim Sicher. Urbana, Ill.: University of Illinois Press. 1998.

Isser, Edward R. *Stages of Annihilation: Theatrical Representation of the Holocaust*. Madison: Fairleigh Dickinson University Press. 1997.

Kremer, S. Lillian. *Witness through the Imagination: Jewish-American Holocaust Literature*. Detroit, Mich.: Wayne State University Press. 1989.

Langer, Lawrence L. "The Americanization of the Holocaust on Stage and Screen." In *From Hester Street to Hollywood*. Edited by Sarah Blacher Cohen. Bloomington, Ind.: Indiana University Press. 1983.

Safdie, Oren. "Donald Margulies." In *Contemporary Jewish-American Dramatists and Poets*. Edited by Joel Shatky and Michael Taub. Westport, Conn.: Greenwood Press. 1999.

Skloot, Robert. "Introduction." In *The Theatre of the Holocaust: Vol. Two*. Madison, Wisc.: The University of Wisconsin-Madison Press. 1999.

Interview

Arkatov, Janice. "Playwright Explores Emotional Legacies." *Los Angeles Times* (11 Nov. 1988): 24.

Review

Winer, Laurie. "Review of *The Model Apartment*," by Donald Margulies, *Los Angeles Times*, 29 July 1997: 1.

JADWIGA MAURER
(1932–)

THEODOSIA ROBERTSON

JADWIGA MAURER WAS born in Kielce, Poland. Hidden as a child in Slovakia, she reunited with her family at the end of World War II. Several years later, she and her family left for Munich. She received her doctorate in 1956 from the University of Munich and in the same year she emigrated to the United States, where she became professor of Polish literature at the University of Kansas at Lawrence.

Jadwiga Maurer is both a scholar and the author of two collections of short stories published in Polish in London: *Liga ocalałych* (League of the Saved, 1970) and *Podróż do wybrzeże Dalmacji* (Journey to the Dalmatian Coast, 1982). Her stories have been published in journals in Poland and abroad, and in English in the United States. She has given a number of interviews to the Polish press. Since the 1980s, her reputation has grown in Poland. Her scholarly study, *Z matki obcej . . . Szkice o powiazaniach Mickiewicza ze światem Żydów* (From a Foreign Mother . . . Essays on the Connections between Mickiewicz and the Jewish World, 1990; 2nd ed., 1992), treats the relation of the nineteenth-century Polish Romantic poet, Adam Mickiewicz, to the Jewish world of his time.

Fiction and Narration

Rooted in the daily realities of life and human relations from wartime to the present, Jadwiga Maurer's stories treat the contradictions of Occupation life, the practicalities of organizing escape out of Poland, life hidden in a convent, and the strangeness of survivors' existence in Europe and America. While the voice of the narrator in her leisurely, conversational prose provides cohesiveness to the fiction, the narrator is not completely identifiable with the author. Maurer herself has said that she is not responsible for her narrator; in other words, her narrator is also a fictional character.

Maurer's wartime stories do not recount the horror of Holocaust experiences, but focus upon the feelings and reactions of characters for whom danger is deathly close. Her narrator remembers when, as a child, one went without explanation to stay overnight, or for a walk with a stranger; it was understood what was happening ("Polska idealna" [An Ideal Poland]). She notes the paradoxes of daily life in the Kazimierz district of occupied Krakow: the cool darkness of churches that soothes a Jewish schoolgirl, worn Pilsudskite (Polish nationalist) slogans within sight of Nazi governor Hans Frank's headquarters, and the effect of Polish literature upon an antisemitic schoolteacher.

The narrator is also a hidden child. In "Biskup" (The Bishop), she describes the routine of convent school life in occupied Slovakia, adding observations about those who care for her. Survival requires being exactly like the other girls; the narrator is so successful that, she says, "I was once a saint." Only the sounds from nearby tracks penetrate the safety of the school. Express passenger trains hurtle toward the Tatra mountain resorts, while transports of Hungarian Jews sealed in cattle cars lumber toward the extermination camps in Poland. The school is inspected by Slovak police, and she observes the nuns' anxiety as the battle front approaches. A chance encounter reveals to her that without his ceremonial garb, the bishop is ordinary; the Catholic road to holiness is not for her. Years later, reading about the bishop's arrest, she writes on his behalf. Only a hidden child could have preserved this experience.

The narrator spends the first postwar year in Sopot on the Baltic coast, in former German territory. The times are open and fluid; she is back in school, but in the wrong class. Everyone is in some kind of uniform, or its remnants; men routinely carry a pistol. Listening to the stories adults tell, she muses:

> I see before me a labyrinth of forest things. All the confusion of betrayals, extortion, threats, and sentences. No

chronicler will ever note them down, no one will ever learn about the reasons for this or that ignoble act. The corporal has no idea that I know, that I also lived through it even though I was not with the partisans ("Ojczyzna" [Fatherland]). *Podróż na wybrzeże Dalmacji,* London: Oficyna Poetów: Malarzy, 1982, p. 102).

Her family emigrates, but the narrator's focus is people, not travel or locale ("Miejsce którego nie było na mapie" [A Place Not on the Map]). She describes her confreres at the University in Munich, not yet divided into the successes and failures of normal life. A vague hope buoys the "league of the saved": former POWs, widows of German soldiers, young Jewish men just out of concentration camps, and even twins who survived Auschwitz ("Podwójny życie" [A Double Life]). The narrator's spare enumeration of various Holocaust experiences binds the disparate group together. In these "blessed, beautiful UNRRA [United Nations Relief and Rehabilitation Agency] times" they exist suspended in space and time at their long table in the last Jewish student dining hall, like the representatives of Old Poland in Adam Mickiewicz's epic poem, *Pan Tadeusz,* at the last banquet of an idealized Polish kingdom ("Polska idealna" [An Ideal Poland]).

The narrator assists weaker survivors, even conspiring to fool the more successful ones who "think that we live in the past . . . it's impossible to explain [to them] that we have discarded illusions and live with reality" ("Spisek" [Conspiracy]. *Liga ocalałych*, London: Naktadem Polskiej Fundacji Kulturalnej, 1970, p. 177). She also becomes the chronicler of the remnant of her parents' cohort: aging Jewish couples in Munich and their desultory lives, the women's bracelets concealing camp number tattoos. They live on a *gleijt* or "safe conduct" enabling them to survive when they were meant to die ("Był sobie dziad i baba" [There Once Was a Grandfather and Grandmother]). As she says, "I don't want to be immodest, but other than I the undersigned, they have had no chronicler" (*Liga ocalałych*, p. 212). As with Tadeusz Borowski's narrator, Tadek, fate has rendered Jadwiga Maurer's narrator the accidental "historian/chronicler of places not on the map and events not recorded by history" ("Miejsce Ktcrego nie było na mapie," *Liga ocalałych*, p. 123).

The narrator refers to the Germans' "blunt talk" immediately after the war and notes that their sense of guilt developed only later, with postwar prosperity, because (again echoing Borowski) "ultimately, conscience is a luxury" ("Pełnoletność" [Maturity]). Upper-class Germans observe her as a Jewish specimen, while German colleagues at the Institute seem suspiciously enthusiastic about her possible trip to America. Her Munich concierge anticipates falling heir to her flat. Germans seem oblivious to these painful situations, which Maurer's narrator matter-of-factly records.

The Mature Narrator

Visiting in America, the narrator encounters survivors and understands those who are unable to make a new life, as in the case of camp veterans who are now forever students ("Spisek"). While she notes the bizarre customs of America, it remains the one place left to go, at least "for us" (Jews). She perceives its benefits for permanently scarred survivors like Zygmunt. Wandering around America, he encounters the gum-chewing, curler-bedecked Jean, and finds someone who is impressed with his romantic past life—partisans, camps, and deprivations. He is not a failure in her eyes ("Zygmunt"). Other survivors manage by embracing America's shallow affluence, by showing off their comforts to their fellow-survivor, the narrator. She does not condemn them, but admires all appropriately; "what harm does it do?" she asks ("Antyojczyzna" [Anti-Fatherland]). Ironically, she eventually comes to live in America as well.

Increasingly, the narrator discovers her own solitude: "Now, at least, I am waiting for no one and not worried about what to wear—just grab something from the closet . . . happy that I am alone and not burdened with the company of another." The death of her parents' generation is a turning point. Emerging from the "generation of children forbidden to speak," she takes her place in the "front lines." She receives the torch of memory with sorrow and a sense of liberation from parental control over the past ("Q i pensjonarka" [Q and the Schoolgirl], *Tygodnik powszechny* 21 [24 May 1998]: p. 9). In the opening and closing stories of the volume *Podróż na wybrzeże Dalmacji* (Journey to the Dalmatian Coast), an older narrator addresses the reader more directly. Time and space have loosened the links among the "saved." In "Area Code 415" the numbers in a telephone book trigger a séance; their cabalistic magic allows an intrusion into another person's life. Other unexpected "connections" occur: of the narrator's memory with history, in unexpected encounters with other survivors, and in mystical connections among Jews—with whom, she says, one speaks "a bit as if to someone in the same family." "Podróż na wybrzeże Dalmacji" ironically contrasts the narrator's Midwest university town with the exotic Dalmatian coast. A visiting Polish professor prating antisemitic prejudices turns out to be Jewish, a child raised in a wartime orphanage. Two women Auschwitz survivors are condemned to their memories, and eventually they are unable to talk to others at all. A visit to the district where poet Langston Hughes grew up prompts the narrator to reflect on another accident of history: looks. Hughes's black skin condemned him to a struggle with prejudice. Jewish features sentenced her to another fate. In each case, factors beyond individual control determine a life story.

Recent Fiction

Several stories of the 1990s deal with the survivor-narrator's reflections on time. Waking in her parents' apartment in "Żebrak" (The Beggar), she sees

> the expanse of my own life and the life of my parents sealed up within these silent walls, scattered throughout desk drawers and photos. I step into the past, but the future no longer holds any mystery. I already know every "how it will turn out" and "how it will be." That young person and my present self interact with one another in this apartment ("The Beggar." *Periphery* 3 (1/2): p. 122).

Loneliness intensifies, as the narrator loses those who complained about her as "an intractable child, warped by the war, mainly because [she] no longer [makes] appointments with the hairdresser." ("The Beggar," p. 123). "Władek" (1993) honors a member of the secret organization *Żegota* [a cryptonym for the Council for Aid to Jews]. The child who was rescued by being taken to the Slovak convent now rescues Władek's story from oblivion. In "Q i pensjonarka" (Q and the Schoolgirl), now free from those who had controlled her past story, she invents an interlocutor—"Q." The narrator insists upon her recollection, asserting control over the past, as was done to her. As she tells her story, she merges the wartime with the present into one whole made from two worlds: the other world—the real world in which the Jews had been put to death—and the survivor's unexpected afterlife.

Jadwiga Maurer's fiction subtly traces an individual survivor's experience, without pathos or drama. Instead, the perceptive and ironic narrating voice tries to make sense of experience by conversing with the reader. At the close of "Q and the Schoolgirl," the adult narrator recalls the words of Father Superior in the convent where she was hidden. Rumored to have prayed for a German victory, he nevertheless aided a Jewish child, and enjoined her, the budding chronicler, to *Ciesz się życiem*! or, "be happy with life." The Polish phrase echoes the Hebrew expression *L'Chaim*! ("to life!"). Maurer's narrator seems to have accepted his injunction to appreciate life and along with it, to accept the paradoxes and mysteries of survival.

Bibliography

Primary Sources

Fiction

"Życie na niby: szkoła" (Pretend Life: School). 1965.

"Życie na niby: spacery z Baśką" (Pretend Life: Strolls with Baśka). 1965.

Liga Ocalałych (League of the Saved). 1970.

Podróż na wybrzeże Dalmacji (Journey to the Dalmatian Coast). 1982.

"Władek" (Wladek). 1993.

"Enklawy" (Enclaves). 1994.

"Żebrak" (The Beggar). 1997.

"Kazimierz" (Kazimierz).

"Q i pensjonarka" (Q and the Schoolgirl). 1998.

Nonfiction

Z matki obcej . . . Szkice o powiązaniach Mickiewicza ze światem Żydów (From a Foreign Mother . . . Essays on the Connections between Mickiewicz and the Jewish World). 1990. 2d ed., 1992.

Interviews

"Poza etniczne opłotki (rozmowa z Jadwiga Maurer)" [Beyond Ethnic Barriers. A Conversation with Jadwiga Maurer] by Ryszard Wasita. *Literatura na świecie* (Literature in the World) [Warsaw] 1–2 (1994): 322–344.

"Biale plamy w biografii Mickiewicza." z professor Jadwiga Maurer rozmawia Andrzej Józef Dąbrowski. [Blank Spots in Mickiewicz's Biography. Andrzej Józef Dąbrowski Talks with Jadwiga Maurer]. *Przegląd Polski* [New York], 16 March 1995.

Interview series (on symbolism in the works of Adam Mickiewicz) by A. Cholodecki for *The Polish Morning Show*. Broadcast, WRN [Chicago]. 16, 17, 18 November 1995, 9 January 1996. 60 minutes.

"Conversations with Prominent Poles Abroad: Jadwiga Maurer." Interview by Andrzej Zulawski. Broadcast on the First Program of Polish National Television, Sunday, 21 January 1996. 30 minutes.

Secondary Sources

Frajlich-Zając, Anna. " 'Z matki obcej . . .' ", *2b* [Chicago], v. 3–4 (1994): 81–83.

"Maurer, Jadwiga." In *Mały Słownik Piszary Polskich na Obczyźnie*. 1939–1980. [Small Dictionary of Polish Writers in Emigration. 1939–1980]. Warsaw: Wydawnictwo Interpress, 1992.

GERDA MAYER
(1927–)

PETER LAWSON

> I am on a raft and they are in a choppy sea. I am eleven, possibly just turned twelve, and they cry out to me—though in the politest possible way—"If you should happen to have a lifeline or lifebelt on the raft, if it is not too inconvenient . . ." It is a forlorn hope. Their heads bob on the surface and the waves grow higher and higher ("Prague Winter," *Writers' Awards 2001*, pp. 88–89).

Thus the poet Gerda Mayer reflects on her childhood relationship, as a Holocaust refugee, to her parents stranded in Nazi Europe. Together with Czechoslovakia's Jews, they were facing insurmountable odds. Nazism would soon defeat their attempts to survive.

Biographical Information

Mayer (*née* Stein) was born on 9 June 1927, daughter of Arnold Stein, proprietor of a small dress shop, and Erna (*née* Eisenberger), who operated a knitwear business. The family made its home in Karlsbad, Czechoslovakia.

In September 1938, shortly before Hitler invaded the German-speaking Sudeten in which Karlsbad was situated, the Steins fled the town. Mayer explains the situation:

> The German Jews were, in a way, fortunate. They had been the first to experience Hitler. They had been able to take stock and many had had the chance to emigrate. By the time Austria was annexed, emigration had become more difficult. A great many Austrian Jews had taken the easy way out and had "emigrated" to Prague. By the time the Sudeten district, the German part of Czechoslovakia, was taken, there was an enormous number of Jews in Prague, seeking desperately for an exit ("Prague Winter," *Writers' Awards 2001*, p. 6).

Mayer's poem "The Emigration Game—Winter 1938/39" (*Bernini's Cat*, 1999) addresses the futile efforts of her mother to obtain visas for the family: "In vain / From consulate to consulate her steps / Inscribe petitions" (p. 96). Early in 1939, her parents contacted Trevor Chadwick, an Englishman who, together with Nicholas Winton, was arranging *Kindertransporte* (children's transports) from Prague to Britain. Chadwick's mother, Muriel, generously guaranteed to support Mayer until she was 18. The poet expresses her gratitude in a book dedicated "to the memory of Muriel Chadwick and her son Trevor Chadwick to whom I owe my preservation" (*A Heartache of Grass*, 1988).

On 14 March 1939, Mayer arrived by plane in England, vividly noting the civic and environmental contrasts with her former home: "It was English daffodils instead of the snow and slush of Prague. It was pretty shells on the Swanage sands. It was also the day that Hitler marched into Prague" ("Flight to England"). Mayer relates her refugee experiences as one of the (anonymous) contributors to fellow *Kindertransport* poet Karen Gershon's *We Came as Children* (1966), a collective autobiography of youngsters whose parents sent them to safety in Britain.

Like other *Kinder* who escaped Nazi-occupied Europe, Mayer was convinced that she would see her parents after the war. However, a letter from Mayer's mother hints at their desperate plight. Erna wrote: " 'Under no circumstance do I want you to bother your benefactors who have already done so much for you; but if you should meet someone who strikes you as particularly kind . . .' " ("Prague Winter," *Writers' Award 2001*, p. 88). Mayer's parents shared the fate of most European Jews. In 1939, Arnold was sent to the concentration camp at Nisko, Poland, from which he escaped, fleeing to Russian-occupied Lemberg (Lwow). His final correspondence was penned in June 1940. It is possible that he died in one of the many Russian camps. Erna Stein was deported from Prague to Theresienstadt on 24 October 1942, and from there to Auschwitz on 20 January 1943. Neither survived the war. Johanna, Mayer's half-sister from Erna's previous marriage to the Roman Catholic Hans Travnicek, did survive, working for a bank in Prague.

From 1940 to 1942 Mayer attended an English boarding school in Swanage, Dorset; and from 1942 to 1944, a refugee boarding school in Haslemere, Surrey. While finding the latter "heavenly" (*private correspondence*, 21 June 2001), she experienced ridicule at the former as a perceived German: "I especially resented being called a German," she writes, "[and] I was furious when I was nicknamed 'Girder' at school" (Gershon, p. 90). Despite the psychological pain of dislocation, Mayer refused to dwell on her personal sorrows as a refugee. "I disapprove of the refugee whinge," she explains. "It not only insults the people and nation who saved us; it insults the memory of those who perished in the camps" (*private correspondence*, 21 June 2001). Mayer's scholastic success was confirmed when she passed the school certificate exam at 17, after which she joined her guardian, Muriel Chadwick, at Stratford-upon-Avon.

Briefly intending to make *aliyah* (emigration to Israel), Mayer trained for kibbutz life from 1945 to 1946, in a *hachsharah* in Worcestershire and Surrey, but in May 1946, opted for secretarial work in London. She married Adolf Mayer on 3 September 1949. In 1963 Mayer completed a degree in English, German, and the history of art at Bedford College, University of London. Her first collection of poems, *Oddments*, was published in 1970.

Poetry

Whimsical yet pessimistic, colloquial while imbued with a fairy-tale unreality, Mayer's poems convey a unique sense of poise between domestic security and fear (Watson, p. 66). Although some of Mayer's poetry is aimed specifically at children, other collections feature what Peter Porter describes as "children's rhymes for grown-ups" (p. 33). Such poems juxtapose, in the lilt of nursery rhymes, the tentatively self-assured perspectives of children with adult knowledge of the murder of innocents in the Holocaust.

Mayer's poem "On Reading Karen Gershon's 'Poems on Jewish Themes' " gives a sense of her emotional balancing act:

Karen, you have ventured down
Into the pit of desolation;
I balance on its lip and clown,
Afraid of the stench; unwilling to call
On the bored pity of those decent English;
(It was not their funeral). Afraid
NOT to appal (*Bernini's Cat*, p. 75).

To be sure, Mayer does not shy away from the horrors of the Holocaust ("the pit of desolation" is more than a metaphor, with its "stench" of dead bodies). Yet the poet cannot resist entertaining an audience, presumably consisting of "those decent English." Her final line, with its uppercase "NOT," resonates like the circus drum of a "clown," or the punch line of some appalling joke: "Afraid / NOT to appal." The poem's balance is precisely between fear of the unspeakable ("Afraid"; "I balance on the lip") and a "decent" reticence ("unwilling to call"): voiced through humor.

Other poems of grim, dark humor include "The Agnostic's Prayer" and "Carve Me Up When I Die." In the former, Mayer ironically addresses "God to whom I'm still inclined to/Say my prayers":

Thank you for your grace and favour,
though the memory's remote.
Keep my cat safe, keep my neighbour's,
keep them from each other's throat. (*Bernini's Cat*, p. 38).

"Carve Me Up When I Die" is darker still, as the poet imagines the relief of her corpse upon its macabre dissection:

Bury my tongue and my ears
well away from each other:
so that my ears
need not be afflicted
by the tale of my life (*Bernini*'s *Cat*, p. 75).

Thus, the violence of the Holocaust ("the tale of my life") is buried with the speaker's body. A pun emphasizes the poem's humor: the corpse's hands "shall be/ bone idle." Accompanying such ghastly playfulness is a deep sorrow, as the poet urges her readers to preserve just her feet: "Send them back into childhood: / Bury them in the garden there" (p. 75).

Mayer deploys childhood as the benchmark of value by which she judges the Holocaust. From the perspective of children, all living adults are implicated in the atrocities of recent history. As Elaine Feinstein remarks: "For all the humour, her [Mayer's] pessimism is deep" (p. 74).

Betty Parvin has compared Mayer's tone with that of Sylvia Plath (p. 34). However, whereas Plath appropriates Holocaust imagery to express private psychic pain, as in "Lady Lazarus" and "Daddy" (*Ariel*), Mayer writes about the Holocaust itself. Unlike Plath, Mayer does not use the *Shoah* as an analogy; Mayer's trauma results from a family destroyed by the Final Solution. She writes in "They Went":

My father went hiking without passport or visa and was
intercepted

My sister went mad my mother
went into that Chamber trusting
  in God
God picked the bones clean they lie
without imprint or name dear
  mother (*Bernini's Cat*, p. 20).

To be sure, Mayer does resemble Plath in her frequent deployment of "nursery rhyme and rhythms" (Feinstein, p. 74); for example, in "Grandfather's House" (*Bernini*'s *Cat*, p. 91):

Grandfather's house rose up so tall,
Its steps were like a waterfall
It had a deep stairwell, as I recall.

And down the banisters slid my mother,
And her sisters, and her brother,
And many a child, many another.

The banisters wobbled and down fell all.
Down, down, down, and beyond recall.
And so I was not born at all.

Better it is not to have been,
Than to have seen what I have seen.
So deck their graves with meadow-green.

Here the poet "was not born at all," and so avoided seeing her mother, aunts, and uncles murdered in the *Shoah*. Well, not quite—Mayer has, in fact, seen the horrors. She has seen too much.

Reading Mayer frequently feels like reading William Blake's *Songs of Experience* (1794). Take, for example, "Children with Candles" (*Bernini's Cat*, p. 90):

The children are the candles white,
Their voices are the flickering light.

The children are the candles pale,
Their sweet song wavers in the gale.

Storm, abate! Wind, turn about!
Or you will blow their voices out.

Here, as in Blake's poems, the vulnerability of innocence ("candles white"; "flickering light") is juxtaposed with brutal experience ("blow their voices out"). Blake's romantic faith in social amelioration has, however, been superseded by Mayer's post-Holocaust apprehension that innocence is likely to be repaid with destruction.

"Children with Candles" is helpfully read in tandem with "Commemorating the Maccabees" (*A Heartache of Grass*, p. 42), which reveals that the historically specific children are Mayer's cousins ("Hans nine, Susi eleven like me") singing to celebrate Chanukah in "that bleak Prague winter of nineteenthirtyeight." The childishly concatenated date ("nineteenthirtyeight") points to the poem's dialectic between innocent childhood perceptions and tragically informed adult retrospection ("that bleak Prague winter"). Moreover, the celebration of Chanukah in that time and place is darkly ironic. The festival commemorates a victory of the Jewish army led by Judah the Maccabee in the second century B.C.E. In 1946 Mayer learned that "Susi and Hansi and their widowed mother had all gone into the gas chamber together [at Auschwitz]" ("Prague Winter," p. 19).

Bibliography

Primary Sources

Poetry

Oddments. 1970.
Gerda Mayer's Library Folder. 1972.
Treble Poets 2 (with Florence Elon and Daniel Halpern). 1975.
The Knockabout Show. 1978.
Monkey on the Analyst's Couch. 1980.
The Candy-Floss Tree. 1984.
March Postman. 1985.
A Heartache of Grass. 1988.
Time Watching. 1995.
Bernini's Cat: New and Selected Poems. 1999.

Other

"Flight to England." *Poetry Review* 88, no. 4 (winter 1998–1999): 25–27.
"Prague Winter" (extracts). In *Writers' Awards 2001*. Bath: Waterstone's/Arts Council of England, 2001, pp. 83–89.
"Prague Winter" (extracts). In *New Writing 10*. Edited by Penelope Lively and George Szirtes. London: Picador/The British Council, 2001, pp. 150–153.

Secondary Sources

Bax, Martin. *Ambit* 89 (1982): 95.
Feinstein, Elaine. "Sparkling Mildew and Doubt." *The Jewish Quarterly* 43, no. 1 (spring 1996): 74.
"Gerda Mayer." In *Contemporary Poets*. Edited by Tracy Chevalier. Chicago: St. James Press, 1996, pp. 702–703.
Gershon, Karen, ed. *We Came as Children*. London: Papermac, 1989.
Hofmann, Michael. "The Logic of Recurring Dreams." *Quarto* 17 (May 1981): 16.
Jacobs, A. C. "Refugees Turned English Poets." *The Jewish Quarterly* 36, no. 3 (autumn 1989): 64.
Kops, Bernard. "Microscope." *Jewish Chronicle*. 28 October 1988, p. 32.
Lucas, John. "The World We Wake Up To." *New Statesman & Society* (7 April 1989): 39–40.
Parvin, Betty. *Outposts* 132 (spring 1982): 34.
Plath, Sylvia. *Ariel*. London: Faber, 1965.
Porter, Peter. "The Muse in the North East." *Observer Review*, 15 March 1981, 33.
Stevenson, Anne. "Waiting for the Apeman." *The Listener* (3 June 1976): 716–717.
Sullivan, Mary. *British Book News*, October 1975, 739.
Thrilling, Isobel. *Other Poetry* 25 (1989): 45.
Watson, Maureen. *Iron* 57 (February–May 1989): 66.

Archives

The complete manuscripts of Mayer's autobiographical "Prague Winter" and "Names Calling" are available on request from the poet at: 12 Margaret Avenue, Chingford, London E4 7NP.

PHILIP MECHANICUS
(1889–1944)

DICK VAN GALEN LAST

PHILIP MECHANICUS WAS born in Amsterdam on 17 April 1889, the oldest of seven sons of a poor Jewish family. His father, Elias Mechanicus, was an alcoholic ragman, and his mother, Sarah Gobes, who lost three of her sons at a very young age, suffered from depression and needed the support of Philip to raise her five surviving sons. The social problems that the Mechanicus family confronted were not exceptions in the old, densely populated *Jodenbuurt*, the Jewish Quarter, with its unsanitary housing conditions. Like so many other sons of the Jewish proletariat, Philip was educated through home study and training given by the Social Democrat Party (SDAP), and by reading everything he could lay his hands on. As a twelve-year-old, he started his career working the lowest level jobs at newspaper companies, eventually becoming a journalist at the age of seventeen at the socialist daily *Het Volk*.

In 1910, at the age of twenty-one, he was invited to write for the Indonesian newspaper the *Sumatra-Post* in Medan. In 1916 he became deputy editor in chief of *De Locomotief* in Semarang, Java. It was in the mountains of Java that he caught typhus, and thereafter his character changed. He became more irritable, said his first wife, Esther Wessel. Many people who knew him said that Mechanicus was handsome and liked to wear expensive suits. People who worked with him recalled that he could be arrogant and quite difficult to deal with. He was a good father to his daughters, despite the fact that he was married several times.

In 1919 he returned to the Netherlands, and the following year he became a reporter on foreign affairs for the liberal daily newspaper *Algemeen Handelsblad*, for which, in 1936, he became chief of the editorial staff for foreign affairs. He built a solid reputation through his coverage of the Soviet Union, which he visited in 1929, 1931, 1932, and 1934. His reports were published with the titles *Russische Reisbeelden* (Russian Travel Images) and *Van sikkel en hamer* (Of Sickle and Hammer), in which he became gradually more critical of the Soviet system to the point where he was no longer given visas to visit the so-called Worker's Paradise.

In 1933 Mechanicus traveled to Palestine, where he commented on the growing animosity between the Jews and the Arabs and the friction within the Jewish community between German Jews and other Jews, an antipathy that he would encounter again in the Westerbork concentration camp. In 1933 a collection of his articles was published as *Een volk bouwt zijn huis* (A Nation Is Being Built Up). He was not a Zionist because he did not see any future for the Jews in a Palestine surrounded by jealous neighbors. He foresaw that violence would result from the problematic cohabitation of Jews and Palestinians.

Mechanicus was no less visionary about the Nazis. He belonged to the small group of people who had no illusions about the Nazis' intentions. On 20 June 1938, he wrote: "It becomes more and more clear that the German national-socialists are aiming for the total destruction of the Jews in the Third Reich. Their ultimate goal is that within a few years there will be no Jews left in Germany" (quoted in Broersma, *Buigen onder de storm*, p. 87). After the German invasion of the Netherlands in May 1940, he continued working for newspaper *Algemeen Handelsbad*, using a pseudonym until his inevitable dismissal in July 1941. His proud attitude becomes evident from what he told a friend at the beginning of the German occupation: "Why should I go into hiding, *I* am not wrong, *they* are wrong" (Broersma, p. 83).

On 25 September 1942, a Dutch police officer arrested Mechanicus while he was walking in Amsterdam without the obligatory yellow badge—something that all Jews in Holland were required to wear on their clothes in public after May 1942. He was imprisoned and, on October 25, deported to Amersfoort, the police camp notorious for its sadistic regime, where many

Jews, including Mechanicus, were maltreated. On November 7 he was sent to Westerbork, the transit camp where he would stay for seventeen months (November 1942–March 1944) and of which he became the most famous chronicler. In March 1944 he was sent to Bergen-Belsen. On 9 October 1944 Mechanicus was transported to Auschwitz. Shortly after his arrival at Auschwitz-Birkenau he was shot in the crematorium, probably on 15 October 1944.

In dépôt

In *In dépôt* Mechanicus compared the Jews in Westerbork with "merchandises, which are temporarily stocked in dépôt, in anticipation of their transportation to elsewhere" (English edition, *Waiting for Death*: *A Diary*, London: Calder and Boyars, 1968, p. 71). This diary was recorded in several notebooks from 28 May 1943 to 28 February 1944. Unfortunately the first two notebooks did not survive the war, and neither did his notebooks from Bergen-Belsen. The surviving diary was literally a chronicle in which Mechanicus wrote down his observations as they occurred. "I feel like as if I am an official reporter giving an account of a shipwreck," wrote Mechanicus on 29 May 1943. Especially under the regime of Obersturmführer Gemmeker (1942–1945), this German camp worked as a well-oiled part of the destruction machinery of the Nazis. Westerbork had become a *Polizeiliches Durchgangslager* (Police Transit Camp) in July 1942, when the German administration took over command of the camp that had served, since 1939, as a camp for Jewish refugees from Germany. Westerbork was the gateway to death for more than 100,000 Jews. "All roads lead through Westerbork," SS-Hauptsturmführer Ferdinand Hugo Aus der Fünten once remarked to some Jews who had come to plead a postponement of deportation. In fact, the efficiency of the camp in organizing the regular transit of specified numbers of Jews to the East is remarkable.

In advance of the arrival of the SS, the German Jewish inhabitants had organized their own "management" of the camp. Mechanicus gave a clear account of their position and power in his diaries: "the German Jews have undeniably abused their position of supremacy and continue to do so" (Mechanicus, p. 33). Jacob Boas, himself born in Westerbork, argues that three or more years of camp life and the view that they had been abandoned, both by the Dutch government and their co-religionists, made the German Jews even more ill-disposed toward their Dutch counterparts and even more enthusiastic to exploit their new positions of power.

Like other diarists, Mechanicus also felt he had "a duty to continue writing" even if for no other reason than to inform "those who want to have an idea of what has happened here." His diary and that of Etty Hillesum are the most important sources of information on Westerbork. Their diaries make this microcosm and its inhabitants stand out in a stark and unforgiving light. However, while Etty Hillesum records her own impressions and reflections, Mechanicus merely observes and notes down events and other people's responses to them. Mechanicus was a man of facts, and his very precise descriptions are often characterized by thorough reflections and balanced conclusions. He walked around Westerbork as a very observant reporter, a "special reporter" as he called himself, but conscious of the fact that he was also an inhabitant of this microcosmos. It is only at the end that his record becomes more emotional. On 1 February 1944, after he witnessed another transport, he could not restrain himself anymore: "Where are you, you thousands and tens of thousands who have been carried away from one place to another—what has been your fate? You are silent because they will not let you speak. We stand here breathless with agitation and disgust and indignation—the emotions awakened in us by each successive transport." And the following day he wrote: "Where have all the familiar faces gone? How bare it has become, how thin the ranks are!" (Mechanicus, p. 240).

He also reported on the mood in the camp, on the tensions between the different groups, on the cabaret shows, the schools, the love affairs, and the rumors. He noticed nobility and vulgarity, greed and humanity, tenderness and brutality, tender love and coarse eroticism. Mechanicus characterized the atmosphere in Westerbork as that of an artificial movie city. Because he was ill, he was discharged from the duties of the camp discipline and yet he was able to walk around the camp with his notebook. "I belong to the happy few in the camp who do nothing at all, but I am not ashamed of that. After all, most of the work is done on behalf of the *Wehrmacht*, and I do not have a calling for that" (30 October 1943). Westerbork reminded him of his experiences in Soviet Russia: "In a way it is here like communist society, people have to line up for everything." In fact the camp could be compared to a big enterprise; the hospital that is often featured in Mechanicus's book contained 1,725 beds, 120 doctors, and more than 1,000 employees. On his rounds through the hospital wards, Mechanicus came across the strangest of scenes: a nine-month-old baby with "a criminal record," because of having been abandoned by her parents, which made her an S-case (*S* for *straf*, or punishment).

Central in all the testimonies about Westerbork is the transport, or train: the train that divides the week (before Tuesday morning 11 A.M. and after), the train that divides the camp, and the train that divides people. Between 15 July 1942 and 17 September 1944, the day of the last transport, 107,000 Jews were transported. Only 5,000 would survive. Mechanicus wrote: "The transports are as loathsome as ever. The wagons used were originally intended for carrying horses. The deportees no longer lie on straw, but on the bare floor (Mechanicus, p. 25). Mechanicus witnessed the departure of many of his friends and members of his family. People that had to leave on the Tuesday morning train were told that they were going to work camps in Poland, but some realized that the reality was much more sinister—it was only in September 1943 that a Dutch underground newspaper used the term *gas chamber* for the first time. Mechanicus also mentions several cases of suicide in 1943: "Early this morning two men in my hut tried to commit suicide. Unsuccessfully. One of them cut his jugular vein and the knife was wrenched out of the hand of the other man before he could harm himself. The house physician did an excellent job. A mood of depression and great emotion" (Mechanicus, p. 68).

Etty Hillesum (1914–1943) praised Mechanicus in a letter from Westerbork as "a stylish, strong person" and she cited in another letter what he had said about the impact of the camp on his view of life: "I became more easy going in this camp, all people have become quite equal, they are all like grass under the wind, they all bend under the hurricane" (quoted in Hillesum, p. 291). It was her observations and letters from Westerbork that would subsequently become a best-seller, while *In dépôt* passed almost unnoticed, which is probably due to its early (1964) date of publication. Another reason for this relative neglect may be the cool, detached way in which Mechanicus described camp life, most unlike the emotional outbursts of Hillesum's writings.

Nevertheless, *In dépôt* was the first camp diary to reach a wide audience, and it was used by several historians (Herzberg, Presser, de Jong, and Moore), who integrated Mechanicus's testimony into their historical narrative. The persecution of the Jews in Holland is very well documented. However, it was only in 1993 that the first biography of Mechanicus was published: *"Buigen onder de Storm" Levensschets van Philip Mechanicus 1889–1944* (Bending under the Storm). Earlier in 1987 one of Mechanicus's three daughters, Ruth Mechanicus, published the letters that her father wrote in Westerbork to a pupil and to his ex-wife, whom he divorced in 1927 as *Ik woon, zoals je weet, drie hoog* (I Live, As You Know, on the Third Floor. Letters from Westerbork). In one of the last letters to his daughter Ruth, Mechanicus wrote on 9 March 1944: "The birds are tweeting and singing again" (*"Ik woon, zoals je weet, drie hoog,"* p. 72) *In dépôt*, together with Etty Hillesum's letters and the diaries of David Koker (1921–1945), still stands as one of the most important Dutch autobiographical documents of World War II. It has been reprinted several times and has been translated into English and German.

Bibliography

Primary Sources

Van sikkel en hamer (Of Sickle and Hammer). 1932.

Een Volk bouwt zijn huis. Palestijnsche reisschetsen (A Nation Is Being Built Up: Palestinian Travel Sketches). 1933.

In dépôt. Dagboek uit Westerbork (A Year of Fear: A Jewish Prisoner Waits for Auschwitz). 1964.

"Ik woon, zoals je weet, drie hoog." Brieven uit Westerbork (I Live, As You Know, on the Third Floor. Letters from Westerbork). 1987.

Secondary Sources

Boas, Jacob. *Boulevard des Misères. The Story of Transit Camp Westerbork*. Hamden, Conn.: Archon Books, 1985.

Broersma, Koert. "Als een officieel reporter. De dagoekafschriften van Philip Mechanicus." In *Westerbork Cahiers 1*, 66–80. Hooghalen, Netherlands: Herinneringscentrum Kamp Westerbork, 1993.

——— *"Buigen onder de storm" Levensschets van Philip Mechanicus 1889–1944*. Amsterdam: Van Gennep, Herinneringscentrum Kamp Westerbork, 1993.

de Jong, L. *Het Koninkrijk der Nederlanden in de Tweede Wereldoorlog 8: gevangenen en gedeporteerden*. The Hague: Staatsuitgeverij, 1978.

Galen Last, Dick van, and Rolf Wolfswinkel. *Anne Frank and After; Dutch Holocaust Literature in Historical Perspective*. Amsterdam: Amsterdam University Press, 1996.

Herzberg, Abel. *Kroniek der Jodenvervolging 1940–1945*. Amsterdam: Querido, 1978.

Hillesum, Etty. *An Interrupted Life: The Diaries, 1941–1943 and Letters from Westerbork*. New York: Henry Holt, 1996.

Laqueur, Renata. *Schreiben im KZ. Tagebücher 1940–1945*. Bremen: Donat, 1992, pp. 130–133.

Moore, Bob. *Victims and Survivors: The Nazi Persecution of the Jews in the Netherlands 1940–1945*. London: Arnold, 1997.

Presser, Jacob. *Ondergang. De vervolging en verdelging van het Nederlandse jodendom 1940–1945*. The Hague: Staatsuitgeverij, 1965.

Archives

The notebooks of Mechanicus can be found in the NIOD, the Netherlands State Institute for War Documentation, Amsterdam.

VLADKA MEED

(1922–)

ROCHELLE G. SAIDEL

VLADKA MEED, OR Feigele Peltel-Miedzyrzecki, the daughter of Jewish parents Shlomo and Hanna Peltel, was born in Warsaw. As a teenager during the Holocaust, she was active in the Zukunft youth organization of the Bund political movement, and served in the resistance by passing as a Christian outside the Warsaw ghetto. The title of her only book, *On Both Sides of the Wall* (1999), refers to her daily life inside and outside the ghetto. More a personal, historical record than a memoir, her account begins with the deportations in Warsaw on 22 July 1942. The original version ends with the general uprising in Warsaw two years later, followed by a short section on her return to Warsaw after the Soviet Army liberated the city in January 1945.

On Both Sides of the Wall

Meed's account was written soon after the end of World War II, and her detailed recollections of people and events give the book a feeling of immediacy. It was first published in Yiddish by the Educational Committee of the Workmen's Circle in New York in 1948. The book was based on twenty-seven articles she had written in Yiddish for *The Forward*, the newspaper associated with the Workmen's Circle. The newspaper published these articles about her experiences in Warsaw during 1946 and 1947, starting soon after her arrival in New York. When the book was first published in Yiddish, the prominent writers of Yiddish literature in New York honored her with a reception. She believed that they saw in her writing a connection to the world they had come from years before (Saidel interview).

Since then, Meed's book has also been published in English, Hebrew, Spanish, Japanese, and German. The first English edition was issued by *Beit Lohamei Hagetaot* (Ghetto Fighters' House) and Hakibbutz Hameuchad Publishers in Israel in 1972. A 1993 English edition was reprinted in 1999 and published by the United States Holocaust Memorial Museum. In advance praise of this edition, Elie Wiesel wrote: "Vladka's book is not 'just another work,' or merely an autobiography of the Holocaust. It is written with inspiration, with exaltation. Every sentence rings true, every scene burns itself into the reader's memory."

The 1993 edition has an epilogue, "33 Years Later," which recounts Meed's first return visit with her husband to Poland. Recalling their visit to Treblinka, she wrote:

> We looked and looked at the big graveyard and, suddenly, I felt as if the stones had come to life, turned into Jews, men and women, the elderly, Jews with sacks, with children. Among them, I saw my own family, my mother, brother, and sister, my friends, and neighbors. They filled the vast, empty field of Treblinka, and my heart wanted to cry out, to reassure them that while they were in a hostile Poland that has remained almost devoid of Jews, they are not alone, that they are with us in our hearts and souls, and in the memories of our people (p. 269).

With the exception of the epilogue, Meed's reportage of the events she witnessed is rather factual and unemotional, although the subject matter is gripping. For example, she reports the murder of a woman as follows:

> On the corner of Gesia and Zamenhof I caught sight of an old woman walking all alone. How had she gotten there? Probably she had been left alone in the house, and was now seeking a hiding place. I anxiously watched her halting steps. She was conspicuous in the deserted street. A young German in an automobile called to her to halt but she went on, unheeding; perhaps she was deaf. The automobile came to a stop. The young German, pistol in hand, got out, walked up to the old woman and almost casually fired two bullets into her. She collapsed, bleeding

profusely. The German calmly returned to his car and drove away.

The incident had passed like a flash. The Ukrainians did not permit us to go near the dead woman. We passed by the corpse in silence (p. 67).

In another factual passage, Meed reported on the deportation of renowned educator Janusz Korczak and the orphans in his charge, an incident which has since been recounted poignantly and emotionally by others. She wrote:

At Gesia 13, from the window in the hiding place, I saw the march of the orphanage of Janusz Korczak. The children went silently, carrying blankets, walking hand-in-hand, surrounded by German soldiers and led by Dr. Korczak, a stooped, aging man. The noted educator, who had maintained his home and school for orphans of the ghetto against the greatest odds, was now accompanying his wards to their deaths. That day, the Germans "liquidated" the ghetto's remaining children's institutions (pp. 51–52).

Looking back, in a 2001 interview with Rochelle Saidel, on the writing of the memoir, Meed said she would approach the book differently if she were to write it again, but "with the same thoughts but different feelings." "At that time I thought, 'who would be interested in people's feelings from a world destroyed?' " she explained. "I limited myself in expressing feelings. I survived. I should cry? Here in the [United] States I learned that the individual means a lot, and people are very interested in personal things, everyday life." If she were to write her book again, she said, "I would write with more emotional input, but I considered my feelings not important compared to what took place." She agrees that her book is more a narrative of events in Warsaw than a memoir; it explains how things changed when the deportations started and offers objective descriptions rather than meditating on the situation. Her story is told in a matter-of-fact way, and she is opposed to the idea of using "literary language" regarding the Holocaust.

In addition to offering more feelings, perhaps Meed would change her book in another way if she were writing it today. Although she was associated with the Bundists in Warsaw, she later became an ardent Zionist, as Yitzhak "Antek" Zuckerman, a commander of the Jewish Fighting Organization (*Zydowska Organizacja Bojowa*, or ZOB), pointed out in his own memoir. The Bund, an abbreviation for the General Jewish Workers' Union, was a strong Jewish socialist-democratic party, founded in 1897. The organization was opposed to Zionism and advocated Yiddish language and culture and secular Jewish nationalism in the Diaspora.

"Not all Bundists, in the ghetto and later, stuck to their Bundist positions," Zuckerman wrote. "I published the Hebrew edition of Wladka [Meed]'s book (*On Both Sides of the Wall*), written in 1947–1948 in the United States, from a Bundist perspective. When we were about to publish the book in Hebrew [*Beit Lohamei Hagetaot*, Israel, 1968], she asked me to put some changes in it. I wanted to know what changes. She had a Bundist education and was now 'pro-*Eretz* Israel.' I saw that she wanted to change her perspective and I couldn't agree. I had to convince her that the basic value of the book was her authentic view of the 1940s, when she was still a Bundist. I told her she could write about the changes in her worldview, but that was another book, since now she was an active Zionist. During the Yom Kippur War, she wanted to come to Israel and help in hospitals or something" (Zuckerman, p. 462).

Life

Meed was a teenager living in Warsaw when the Nazi invasion of Poland began. She had graduated from the Yiddish *Folkshul*, a secular school. Although her father was extremely knowledgeable about Judaism, he became a liberal Jew and a socialist. The *Folkshul* was private, with all subjects taught in Yiddish, and Polish taught only as a second language. Her younger sister Henia, however, went to a Polish public school and spoke with her in Polish. Therefore, she was able to speak Polish fluently.

Meed was a member of the Jewish underground from its first days, as part of the Zukunft youth organization. She took the name Vladka when she was given an assignment outside the ghetto, on the "Aryan" side of Warsaw. Her father died of pneumonia in the ghetto, and her mother, sister, and younger brother Chaim were deported to Treblinka and murdered there.

Because of her typically "Aryan" appearance, fluency in Polish, and resourcefulness, she was a successful underground courier. She not only smuggled weapons across the wall to the Jewish fighting organization the ZOB, but also helped Jewish children escape from the ghetto and find shelter in the homes of Christians. In addition, she visited and assisted Jews who were in hiding in the city, and established contact with those still surviving in the labor camps and the partisans in the forest. All of these accomplishments are modestly described in her book. ZOB commander Zuckerman described her as having "demonstrated supreme devotion" (Zuckerman, p. 462).

Vladka Meed met Benjamin Miedzyrzecki, later known as Ben Meed, in the underground in Warsaw. They married soon after the end of World War II and arrived in New York City on 24 May 1946 on a military vessel, the second ship bringing survivors from Europe. Soon afterward, leaders of the Jewish Labor Committee and the International Rescue Committee realized that she was an effective speaker, and sent her to give lectures. She spoke as a witness, describing what she had seen and how she had participated in the resistance. Her purpose was to give people in the United States a sense of what had really happened to the Jews of Europe, she said. Their daughter, now Dr. Anna Scherzer, was born in 1948, and their son, Dr. Steven Meed, in 1951.

Continued Involvement

Meed has, since her earliest days in the United States, lectured on her experiences during the Holocaust. Although she did not write other books, along with her husband she has been extremely active in Holocaust education and memorialization. As vice president of the Jewish Labor Committee for many years, she ran the Yiddish Cultural and Welfare Department. She was responsible for production of a filmstrip, which later became a video, about her role in the resistance. Titled *Warsaw Ghetto: Holocaust and Resistance*, it is introduced by Elie Wiesel and narrated by Theodore Bikel. She also coordinated an exhibit on the Warsaw Ghetto Uprising for the Jewish Labor Committee. For ten years she was that organization's Yiddish-language commentator on a weekly program on WEVD, the Yiddish radio station in New York.

Meed was also one of the leaders of an effort to create a Holocaust memorial in Battery Park in lower Manhattan in the 1960s (Saidel, pp. 66–79). Although the project ultimately did not succeed, she was instrumental in having the renowned artist Louis Kahn design a memorial sculpture for the site. She was the chairperson of cultural events for the World Gathering of Jewish Holocaust Survivors, held in Jerusalem in 1981, as well as the group's second meeting in Washington, D.C., in 1983. She initiated in 1985 and still directs the annual American Teachers' Seminars on the Holocaust and Jewish Resistance, which take place in Poland and Israel. She is also the coordinator of the biennial Alumni Teachers Conferences, cosponsored by the United States Holocaust Memorial Museum in Washington, D.C.

She has been the recipient of many awards, including the 1973 award of the Warsaw Ghetto Resistance Organization (WAGRO), the 1989 *Morim* (Teachers) Award of the Jewish Teachers' Association, the 1993 Hadassah Henrietta Szold Award, and the 1995 Elie Wiesel Remembrance Award. She received a Doctor of Humane Letters *Honoris Causa* from Hebrew Union College in 1998, as well as a similar degree from Bar Ilan University in Israel.

Bibliography

Primary Sources

On Both Sides of the Wall. 1948, 1972, 1993, 1999.

"Jewish Resistance Perspective: The Warsaw Ghetto." In *In Answer: The Holocaust: Is the Story True? Why Did the World Community Not Respond? What Are the Lessons*, 65–75. Edited by Franklin H. Littell, Irene G. Shur, and Claude R. Foster, Jr. West Chester, Penn.: Sylvan, 1988.

Secondary Sources

Saidel, Rochelle. *Never Too Late to Remember: The Politics Behind New York City's Holocaust Museum.* New York: Holmes & Meier, 1996, pp. 58–60, 67–69, 71, 73, 76–81.

Zuckerman, Yitzhak. "Antek." In *A Surplus of Memory: Chronicle of the Warsaw Ghetto Uprising*, 462–463 and passim. Berkeley: University of California Press, 1993.

Interviews

Meed, Vladka. Interview by Rochelle G. Saidel. New York, 8 May 2001.

Meed, Vladka. Video taped interview by Linda Kuzmack. 19 June 1991. Archives of the United States Holocaust Memorial Museum, Washington, D.C. Call number RG = 50. 030–0153.

AHARON MEGGED

(1920–)

STANLEY NASH

AHARON MEGGED IS unique among Hebrew authors of the Palmach, or 1948 generation, in his preoccupation with the *Shoah* and with such collateral concerns as the intentional disassociation by nativist Israelis from their Diaspora "roots" and from Yiddish language and culture. Megged's earliest writings in the 1940s—when he lived for twelve years on Kibbutz Sedot Yam—betray a heightened sense of guilt over the failure of the Yishuv, or pre-state Jewish Palestine, to come to the aid of the victims of the European Holocaust, save for the heroic deeds of a few, such as Megged's fellow kibbutz member Hannah Senesh. From the early 1950s one discerns Megged's singular perception that Hebrew culture in Israel has triumphed on the ruins of, and at the expense of, the decimated Yiddish-speaking population. In the process, the values of folk warmth and intimacy associated with Yiddish have been lost. His celebrated short story "Yad va-shem" ("The Name," in *Yisra'el Haverim*, 1955) dates from this period, as do his essays "A Forgotten Heritage" and "Our Old and New Culture." "Yad va-shem" dramatizes the psychological cost incurred by a Sabra, or native-born Israeli, couple when they refuse their grandfather's request to perpetuate the memory of a grandson, Mendele, who was killed by the Nazis. They refuse to name their newborn child after Mendele, claiming that the name is *galuti* (tainted by the ethos of the Diaspora) and that they have no connection with "all of that."

Megged's own parents were staunch Hebraists in Poland, before they and Aharon, at age five and one-half, immigrated to Palestine in 1926. His warm feelings toward Yiddish stem from the time Megged's grandparents arrived, shortly before World War II, and from his acquaintance with the artist Yosl Bergner and Bergner's father, the Yiddish writer Melekh Ravich. Megged was also probably in rebellion against his mother's zealous anti-Yiddish and antireligious attitudes. Throughout the 1950s and 1960s, Megged, as a journalist and editor, wrote about the search for faith and roots and, at the same time, about the Holocaust and related topics. These included his antipathy toward the renewal of friendly relations with Germany; the acceptance of German reparations by Israel; and the introduction of German culture into Israel.

Holocaust Influence

Megged's two plays, *Hannah Senesh* (1958) and *The High Season* (1965)—or *Job*, as it was called in an earlier version—reflect the intensity of his involvement with the Holocaust in the 1950s and 1960s. *Hannah Senesh* emerged out of Megged's ten-year personal commitment to the project; his several attempts, including a radio skit; and his pursuit of documentation through his acquaintance with Hannah's mother. The play's action focused on scenes in the Hungarian jail and courtroom. In the opinion of various critics, it depicted Hannah as "a Jewish Joan of Arc" speaking in an overly didactic Zionist and "anti-Diaspora" tone. A good deal of formative Zionist rhetoric had leveled a harsh critique against the Jewish Diaspora's alleged ethos of passivity, bookishness, capitalism, and religiosity. *Hannah Senesh* did not, therefore, command a theatrical response in Israel equal to that of *The Diary of Anne Frank*.

Beginning in the 1960s a goodly number of Megged's works focus on the complex and difficult German-Israeli relationship after the Holocaust. *The High Season* is an allegorical play that satirizes a modern-day Job who blithely accepts German reparations and is prepared to hide from the horrors of the past that well up and destroy him. While the play reads well, it was not a theatrical success. A scene in Megged's novel *Fortunes of a Fool* (1959) also caricatures an Israeli couple ogling a German Volkswagen, and his novels *On Trees and Stones* (1973), *Heinz and His Son and the Evil Spirit* (1975), and *The Bat* (1979) all deal with the Holocaust tangentially. The first two novels deal with unresolved problems of guilt and anger. The third chronicles the bizarre case of a maverick Israeli right-wing extremist who seeks refuge from the Nazis by becoming a monk, and then acts to save Jews during the war. Most directly, Megged's important short story "The Visit of Mrs. Hilda Hoffer" (1976) provides a summary statement on Megged's enduring ambivalences toward the new Germany. The finest efforts at a meeting of minds between an Israeli theologian, Kurt Levy, and the well-meaning German woman, Hilda Hoffer, reach an awkward and distressing impasse. Hilda envisions establishing a permanent center in Israel to further German-Israeli relations. Levy elaborates on the "deep rift" between their views:

> Essentially you propose changing the idea [of reconciliation, of *Wiedergutmachung*] into *a church*. . . . I know: you don't intend this. But this will be the result! . . . You say that "human responsibility" obligates you, as a Geman woman, to do something, on your part, as a collective body, towards us, as a collective body, while I *do not acknowledge* collective responsibility of this sort. I acknowledge personal responsibility! Personal alone! . . . For here is where I see the source of the evil, in the reduction to mass experience [*himmun*] of morality, in the collectivizing of morality! In the two poles, both of them together, that of the guilty party and that of the one who suffers! The builders of the pyramids, the taskmasters and overseers of Pharaoh, and the slaves of the Israelites—*all of them together* erected gigantic monuments over the grave of morality! . . . This is the tragedy of mankind! (in *Ma'aseh megunneh*, Tel Aviv: Am Oved, 1986, pp. 99–100).

Megged's Holocaust-related novels of the 1970s enjoyed a modicum of success and critical attention, although by this time Megged was beginning to suffer from the collective disregard in Israel for authors identified with the Palmach, or 1948 literary generation.

Foigelman

After two powerful personal experiences, Megged wrote his magnum opus on the impact of the *Shoah* on Israeli culture, the novel *Foigelman* (1986). Megged had written a documentary volume entitled *The Story of Selvino's Children: Journey to the Promised Land* (1984). This required conducting interviews with individuals who had survived the *Shoah* as children in a host of frightening and inspiring ways and who had spent time in a rehabilitation center in Italy whose activities were conducted under Zionist auspices. The second experience was Megged's pilgrimage with his family to his birthplace in Poland and to the sites of Nazi atrocities.

Foigelman recounts the ambivalent friendship between a Sabra researcher of the Ukrainian pogroms of the 1920s, Tzvi Arbel, and a Paris-based Yiddish poet, Shmuel Foigelman. Arbel is both drawn to and repelled by Foigelman, but his sense of guilt and obligation to the annihilated Jewry of Europe leads him to become more and more involved with Foigelman. The same obsessiveness that Megged details in his article "I Was Not There" (1986) leads Arbel to become the go-between for Foigelman in having the poet's works translated into Hebrew. This project was Arbel's suggestion to Foigelman in the latter's quest to find a place, a "nest," for himself in Israel. The idea of translating Yiddish into Hebrew also carried out one of the contentions made by Megged as a journalist in the 1950s and 1960s—that Hebrew literature had the moral and cultural obligation to salvage the remnants of Yiddish literature, not only as a testimonial but also as a means of enriching itself by restoring its links to a rich centuries-old culture.

The novel contains a host of complex psychological and cultural conflicts. Arbel's wife, Nora, a woman of German-Jewish (hence anti-Yiddish) ancestry and scientific background exhibits an extremely negative reaction to Foigelman. Arbel is exposed to the anti-Jewish influence of his Israel-centered archaeologist father. Foigelman is plagued by ambivalences toward much of Israeli culture and toward the worldwide "industry" of Holocaust studies; Foigelman's actress wife, Hinda/Henrietta, after a few drinks, confesses her dislike of the surfeit of *yiddishkeit* from which she earns her glory and livelihood.

Arbel's own guilt-ridden, and not always wholehearted, actions in helping Foigelman with large sums of money and considerable tedium lead to the failure of Arbel's marriage and Nora's suicide. After the fateful and costly venture that brought them together, Foigelman and Arbel are both devastated by the failure of Foigelman's work in translation to attract critical attention.

The most enthusiastic response to *Foigelman* came from critics on the right of the political spectrum, such as Hillel Weiss, who viewed it as representing the "Ongoing *Shoah*" of Jewish existence. Others gave Megged credit for a valiant and serious effort, but still focused on its literary liabilities in areas such as character portrayal. Gershon Shaked, in a balanced appraisal, sees *Foigelman* as Megged's most successful psychological dramatic novel, but he finds that even in this novel Megged's strength is not in the unique psychological portrait of his characters but rather in "the relationship between the various social personae of his characters . . . and what is revealed when one tries to tear off the mask from their faces" (p. 303).

It was perhaps the negative reaction to melodramatic aspects of the novel that impelled the authors of the stage version of *Foigelman* (1991) to produce it as a macabre play with some grotesque and comic features. In fact, Megged's later novel *Until the Evening* (2001) continues the more grotesque Kafkaesque approach to Holocaust-related themes that was successful in late-twentieth-century Israeli literature. Although *Foigelman* was a best-seller in Israel and has been translated into French and German, some Israeli critics will probably favor Megged's reversion to a measure of surrealism.

The protagonist of *Until the Evening*, a Sabra, has developed a sense of inferiority vis-à-vis his wife, a Holocaust survivor. Unlike the way he felt about the "power-balance" in their relationship when they first met, when he was a native-born insider and she a newly arrived immigrant, this Megged antihero "says to [himself]":

> In complete contrast to what I felt then, the opposite is the case, she is on the inside and I am on the outside, I stand outside the precincts of her world, which is the true and profound world, and I will never penetrate the depths of her psyche, because I will never experience what she experienced there, beyond the impenetrable black curtain, in the heart of darkness (*'Ad ha-'erev*, Tel Aviv: Zmora-Bitan, 2001, p. 52).

In relating details of his life to a Yiddish-speaking man who helped him in a moment of trouble, Megged's protagonist invents for himself the false biography of a Holocaust survivor. This groping for a false persona only intensifies the troubles and guilt that beset this antihero, one in a long series of curiously marginal types that have afforded Megged a prism through which to comment on a wide variety of cultural and political phenomena in Israel, not the least of which is the Holocaust and its offshoots.

Bibliography

Primary Sources

Ru'ah yammim (Spirit of the Seas). 1950. Short stories.
Harheq ba-'Aravah (Far Away in the Aravah Desert). 1951. Play.
Hedvah va-Ani (Hedvah and I). 1953. Novel.
"Ha-Seneh ha-bo'er." 1954. A play about Hannah Senesh.
Yisra'el Haverim. 1955, 1963. Short stories. Includes "Moto shel Mendel Efrat" (1953) and "Yad va-shem" (1955).
Hannah Senesh. 1989. Play.
Miqreh ha-kesil (*Fortunes of a Fool*). 1959, 1962.
Ha-Berihah. 1962. Novellas.
Bereshit (*The First Sin*). 1962, 1983. Play.
Mi-sipure ha-yom ha-sheni. 1965. Short stories.
Ha-hai 'al ha-met (*The Living on the Dead*). 1965, 1970.
"Ish Yehudi!" ("A Jewish Man") 1966, 1968. Short story.
Ha-'Onah ha-bo'eret. 1967. Play.
Ha-hayyim ha-qesarim (*The Short Life*). 1972, 1980. Novel.
Hasot ha-yom. 1973. Anthology.
'Al 'Esim va-avanim. 1973. Novel.
Mahberot Evyatar. 1973, 1982. Novel.
Ha-'atalef. 1975. Novel.
"Biqqur ha-geveret Hilda Hoffer" ("The Visit of Mrs. Hilda Hoffer"). 1976, 1978. Novella.
Mass'a be-av. 1980. Novel.
Ashahel (*Asahel*). 1978, 1982. Novel.
Mass'a ha-yeladim el ha-Aretz ha-Muvtahat: Parshat yalde Selvino (*The Story of Selvino's Children: Journey to the Promised Land*). 1984, 2000. Documentary account.
Ha-gamal ha-me'ofef ve-dabbeshet ha-zahav (*The Flying Camel and the Golden Hump*). 1982, 1986. Novel.
Ezor ha-ra'ash. 1985. Articles on culture and politics.
Ma'aseh megunneh. 1986. Three novellas.
Shulhan ha-ketivah. 1989.
Yom ha-or shel 'Anat. 1992. Novel.
Ga'agu'im le-Olga. 1994. Novel.
'Avel. 1996. Novel.
Duda'im min ha-Aretz ha-qedoshah. 1998. Novel.
Persephone zokheret. 2000. Novel.
'Ad ha-'erev. 2001. Novel.

Secondary Sources

Abramson, Glenda. *Drama and Ideology in Modern Israel*. Cambridge: Cambridge University Press, 1998.
"Aharon Megged, 1920– ." In *Contemporary Autobiography Series*, vol. 13: 141–159.
Avishai, Mordechai. "On Trees and Stones." *Hebrew Book Review* (spring 1974): 4–6.
———. "*The Bat*, by Aharon Megged." *Modern Hebrew Literature* (1976): 51.
Ben-Simon, Daniel. "Ke-Esh ha-Bo'eret be-'Asmotav." *Davar, Devar ha-shavu'a* (16 October 1987): 13–14.
Brenner, Rachel Feldhay. "Between Identity and Anonymity: Art and History in Aharon Megged's *Foigelman*." *AJS Review* 20, no. 2 (1995): 359–377.
Cohen, Yisrael. *Pirqe Aharon Megged*. Tel Aviv: 'Eqed, 1976.
Feinberg, Anat. "Fathers and Sons: Aharon Megged's *Journey in the Month of Av*." *Modern Hebrew Literature* (winter 1981/82).
———. "An Interview with Aharon Megged." *Modern Hebrew Literature* (spring/summer 1983): 47–52.
———. "An Interview with Aharon Megged." *Modern Hebrew Literature* (fall/winter 1988): 47–49.
Feingold, Ben-'Ammi. *Ha-Shoah ba-dramah ha-'Ivrit*. Tel Aviv: Ha-Kibbutz ha-Me'uchad, 1989.
Fuchs, Esther. *Encounters with Israeli Authors*. Marblehead, Mass: Micah Publications, 1982.
Giniewski, Paul. "Arabs and Other Problems—A Conversation with Aharon Megged." *Midstream* 45, no. 3 (1999): 29–32.
Green, Jeffrey M. "The Professor and the Poet." *Modern Hebrew Literature* (fall/winter 1988): 85–87.
Kohansky, Mendel, "Latter-Day Job." *Jerusalem Post*, 20 January 1967.
Megged, Eyal. "Hosi'u 'al Kullanu Hozeh." *Ma'ariv*, 25 August 1991.

Nash, Stanley. "Livte ha-Perat be-Sippure Megged." *Ha-Do'ar*, 30 January 1987, 16–18.

———. "Conscience and Confession in Aharon Megged's Fiction." *Midstream* 34, no. 7 (October 1988): 37–40.

———. "Perspectives on Aharon Megged's 'Yad va-Shem'—A Generation Later." *Journal of Judaism and Aging* 4, no. 4 (summer 1990): 227–233. The entire issue of this journal is dedicated to Megged's story.

———. "Parshanut le-Shire Bialik be-Tsel ha-Sho'ah." *Hadoar* 71, no. 13 (1 May 1992): 19–20.

———. "Ha-Sho'ah ve-Hashlekhotehah bi-Yesirat Aharon Megged: Ha-Derekh el *Foigelman* ve-Aharav." *Bitzaron* 11, no. 49–51 (September 1991–June 1992): 194–196.

———. "Fiction and Publicistics in the Work of Aharon Megged." In *Through Those Near to Me: Essays in Honor of Jerome R. Malino*. Danbury, Conn.: The United Jewish Center, 1998, pp. 267–284.

———. "Patterns of Failed Return in Aharon Megged's Work: Revisiting the Jewish-Christian Nexus." *Modern Judaism* 19, no. 3 (October 1999): 278–292.

———. "Authors and Women as Antiheroes in Aharon Megged's Later Works." Forthcoming in *Modern Judaism*.

Shaked, Gershon. "He-Hakham 'al ha-Kesil (Aharon Megged)." In *Ha-Sipporet ha-'Ivrit 1880–1980*. Tel Aviv: Hakibbutz Hameuchad, 1993, pp. 290–316.

Shoham, Uri. " 'Atalef Shahor 'al gabbe Sus Lavan ('al *Ha-'Atalef* me'et Aharon Megged)." In *Ben Historiyyah le-Sifrut*. Edited by Michal Oren. Tel-Aviv University, 1983, 169–206. Also in Uri Shoham, *Gibbor Dorenu ba-Aretz*. Tel-Aviv University, 1986, pp. 67–105.

Weiss, Hillel. "*Shoah* Holekhet ve-Nimshekhet." *Nequdah* 117 (16 January 1988): 40, 42. Reprinted in idem., *'Alilah: Sifrut ha-Killayon ha-Yisre'elit*. Bet-El: Sifriyyat Bet El, 1992, pp. 114–118.

Zehavi, Alex. "The Tragedy of Immigrant Society." *Modern Hebrew Literature* 3, nos. 1–2 (summer 1977): 81–85.

Zusman, Ezra. "Hannah Senesh be-ha-Bimah." *Davar* (6 June 1958); also in his *Ahare ha-Bekhorah—Biqqorot Te'atron* (on *Hannah Senesh*). Tel-Aviv: 'Am 'Oved, 1981, pp. 43–45.

ISCHA MEIJER
(1943–1995)

PASCALE R. BOS

ISCHA MEIJER WAS born in Amsterdam, the Netherlands. The son of Jaap Meijer, a well-known historian of Dutch Jewry of Orthodox background, and Liesje Voet, a middle-class daughter of a labor organizer, Meijer was raised in a household rife with religious and class tension. More than these conflicts, however, it was the family's war experiences and the war's effects on the Dutch Jewish community that would come to determine Meijer's life and writing.

"The Boy Who Had to Heal All Wounds": Ischa Meijer's Settling of Accounts

Born in February of 1943, as the Dutch Jewish community found itself in the most critical period of Nazi deportations, Meijer was defiantly named Israel Chaim, "the Jewish people live." His parents made arrangements to put him into hiding, but he was given up, and, barely a year old, wound up deported with his parents from Westerbork to Bergen-Belsen. Although all three survived, the camp experience destroyed his parents emotionally. Ischa, however, remembered little of the entire experience, for he had been so young. More determined than ever to live a Jewish life, the family resettled in Amsterdam amid the remnants of the Jewish community. Their return to the Netherlands was filled with disillusionment, for they were not welcomed back, and friends responded to their stories with disbelief. Among these severely traumatized Jews, Ischa would receive, as he later called it, "an excellent intellectual education," but also an upbringing devoid of love and emotional connections. His parents, having lost everything, were unwilling or unable to form new and lasting emotional attachments. Weighed down by their traumatic camp experiences, they became emotionally unapproachable and extremely distrustful, even of their own son. Perhaps it was necessary to shut him out, Meijer later concluded in his *Brief aan mijn moeder* (Letter to my mother, 1974), because his presence served to remind them of the past, while they had hoped to forget it, considering it too shameful.

The parents' inability to foster any positive bond with Ischa or with his siblings, who were born after the war, worsened as he got older, and led to an eventual nearly complete estrangement. His parents' distrust, fear, and anger would come to affect all of Ischa's future relationships, and figures centrally in his work. Judged to be a "failure" by his parents, but feeling sorry for their suffering, he felt torn between loyalty toward them and the "outside" world.

At age 18, Meijer set out for the rest of his life to prove his parents wrong, working for the next thirty years in a manic pace on an extremely wide variety of literary, theater, and media projects. He started working as a journalist, first as a theater critic, and next as a reporter for a national weekly magazine, for which he conducted in-depth interviews of well-known Dutch public figures. Eventually, he started writing autobiographically about his childhood.

Best known is his work *Brief aan mijn moeder*, which deals with his childhood and the effects of the war on his family. *Rabbijn in de tropen* (Rabbi in the tropics, 1977) features a Holocaust survivor who thinks he is the Messiah and who works as a rabbi in a tropical colony; it is loosely based on Meijer's family's short-lived 1950s experience of emigration to the Dutch colony of Surinam. *Hoeren* (Prostitutes, 1980) presents a ruthless personal portrait of Meijer's fascination with prostitutes and his inability to relate to women. Meijer's themes remained remarkably constant, his literary as well as his journalistic work focusing as much on the intricate details of his personal life (the life of a Jewish survivor in postwar Dutch culture) as it did on broader cultural and political issues tied to the legacy of World War II in the Netherlands.

When in the 1980s and 1990s Meijer did one-man theater shows and a weekly television talk show, and wrote and directed for the theater, his interest in both the personal aspects of the wartime past and the larger political ramifications of these events remained central. His answers were never simple. Equally adept at shining light on the hypocrisy of the Dutch, who cared little for the Jews during the war but who like to see themselves after the fact in a heroic resistance role, and on the Jewish community itself, which, he felt, romanticized the prewar past and supported Israel too unconditionally, he managed to provoke Jews and non-Jews alike. He was particularly critical of Jewish martyrdom and self-righteous anger. Jews, he suggested repeatedly, were certainly not better or worse than the Nazis, they just happened to have been victims. From the Dutch, he expected respect for that legacy, and he thus made it a point to highlight continued antisemitism whenever it showed itself, but he also expected a realistic attitude toward surviving Jews and the State of Israel. He wished to see Jews neither vilified nor put on a pedestal.

From 1991 on, Meijer wrote a daily column, titled *De Dikke Man* (The Fat Man), for an Amsterdam newspaper. These short stories about the daily adventures around town of the Dikke Man, a barely concealed self-portrait, had a light, often comic, tone, but were also deeply personal, and were often tied to Meijer's favorite themes. When his parents both passed away in 1993, the columns became a vehicle for Meijer to examine once more his relationship with them and the effects of the Holocaust. The series became a great success, and was published in book form in several volumes.

In 1995, Meijer died unexpectedly from a heart attack.

Approaching the Unapproachable: Parents and the Past

Both Meijer's "letter" to his mother and the pieces he wrote after his parents died shed a surprising light on the dynamics between these Holocaust survivors and their survivor son. "Letter" was written after an intensive eight-year psychoanalytic treatment. The text is set up as a letter in which Meijer speaks to his mother in formal address (*u*), and alternates between Meijer's observations and quotes that represent his mother's voice. Together, they give the effect of a belated dialogue. Ischa searches for answers for their strained relationship, seeking to make sense of it, both through the insight he has gained from psychoanalysis and through his own understanding of the effects of war trauma, about which little or nothing was known to a lay audience in 1974. Wasn't the fact that no one ever spoke of the war, some argued, a sign that it really did not play a role in their lives? So many decades later, of course, the silence is seen as indicative of the degree of trauma survivors experienced, rather than as an absence of trauma.

Brief, then, represents the attempt of the adult child of survivors to come to terms with the child he once was and with relationships with both parents that never moved beyond the extremely strained dynamics of the postwar period. In analyzing his mother (and in the process, indirectly, his father), the son comes to understand who his parents were, or had become after surviving the camps, and he attempts to see their relationship in that light. He conceives of his mother, belatedly, as a deeply depressed woman, severely affected by her war experiences. As his parents had not wanted to seem vulnerable, this had led to severely "cramped behavior" and a "complete inability to surrender to any form of essential mourning" (*Brief aan mijn moeder*, Amsterdam, Bert Bakker, 1979, p. 22). Observations of other family members, as recorded in *Brief*, at once corroborate and complicate Meijer's observations: an uncle describes his mother in 1946 as "a woman turned wild through the life in the camps whom no one could manage, no longer used to any human contact, not capable of any adjustment, desperate" (p. 25). Ischa, in contrast, remembers her as an "absurdly controlled woman, cool and collected, untouchable" (p. 25). It is precisely this contrast which he now sees as typical of trauma, and this insight helps him in coming to terms with her distant and antagonistic behavior toward him.

In pushing away the need to mourn the loss and the trauma of the camp experience, Meijer's parents in fact ended by distancing themselves from everyone except each other. Ischa and his siblings were seen as intruders into the lives of their parents, a threat to their vulnerable equilibrium. The effects of this absence of trust and love on Ischa were dramatic and lasting, the text suggests: "Love and destruction have long remained synonymous for me" (p. 54). Meijer's psychoanalysis and this book, then, represent the attempt to fight against this upbringing, to "talk back" to his parents, his mother in particular, and finally to break free. Here he portrays his parents as victims of the Nazis, their own background, and their poor marriage, but he also suggests how they became abusive in their relationship to him, in their attempts to degrade, insult, and destroy him. He comes to see himself as "a victim of war victims."

Interestingly, Meijer's later writing on his parents, in particular the stories and poems in *Een jongetje dat alles goed zou maken* (*A Boy Who Would Make Everything Right*, a selection of Meijer material from 1972 to 1995, published posthumously by Prometheus, Amsterdam, in 1996), is marked by a somewhat milder tone. He never fully reconciles himself with them, but he sees much of the family dynamics in light of the fact that the parents were wholly unable to leave their war experiences behind. "There has never been space for postwar life in our family," Meijer concludes. He now writes not only of his parents' continued distrust of their (non-Jewish) environment, but also describes many instances of postwar antisemitism that seem to confirm their worries. In a moving poem, he writes of the longing to come home to his parents, and the role he was meant to play as a second generation child but never could:

> I am standing still in the door post
> In order to come home.
> And so easy it is
> to come to this difficult conclusion:
> That I am no longer a child; that I long
> for someone who was never able to exist;
> a boy who would heal all wounds—
> and time that stood still and allowed him to be (p. 39).

Reception

While all of Meijer's journalistic and literary work was autobiographical to a certain degree, it is with *Brief* that he made his mark. At the time of publication, however, critics were not sure of what to make of either the work or Meijer. Was this a Dutch *Portnoy's Complaint*? Hardly. The text was too serious, not funny at all. Over time, Meijer's literature, in particular *Brief*, came to be seen as "second-generation literature before the term was coined," even though, technically speaking, Meijer is himself a survivor as well as a child of survivors. In fact *Brief aan mijn moeder* has often been called the "first book of second-generation literature" in the Netherlands. The text has been highly influential with younger Dutch Jewish readers and authors, and has seen several reprints since 1990. The work of one of the Netherlands' most successful younger second-generation authors of the late 1990s, Arnon Grunberg, seems strongly indebted to Meijer.

Bibliography

Primary Sources

Brief aan mijn moeder (Letter to my mother). 1974.
Interviews. 1974.
Rabbijn in de tropen (Rabbi in the tropics). 1977.
Ischa Meijer's Weekboek (Ischa Meijer's Weekly Notes). 1979.
Hoeren (Prostitutes). 1980.
De handzame Ischa (The handy Ischa). 1986.
Interviewen voor beginners (Interviewing for beginners). 1987.
Ons dorp, de schoonheid en het leven (Our village, the beauty and the life). 1988.
De Dikke Man (The Fat Man). 1991.
Och, zei de Dikke Man (Oh Well, said the fat man). 1991.
Enkeltje heimwee (One-way ticket homesickness). 1992.
Mijn lieve ouders (My dear parents). 1993.
Spitsuur in de hel (Traffic jam in Hell). 1994.
De Dikke Man voor altijd (The fat man forever more). 1995.
Een jongetje dat alles goed zou maken (A Boy Who Would Make Everything Right). 1996.

Secondary Sources

Cornelissen, Igor. *Een Joodse dwarsligger: Jaap Meijer 1912–1993*. Amsterdam: De Kan, 1995.
Palmen, Connie. *I.M.* Amsterdam: Prometheus, 1998.
Palmen, Connie, and Rob Grootendorst, ed. *Zing, m'n jongen, Zing! De radioteksten Voor Cor Galisen Ischa Meijer*. Amsterdam: Prometheus, 1997.

ALBERT MEMMI

(1920–)

JULIETTE DICKSTEIN

BORN IN TUNIS, Tunisia, the novelist and critic Albert Memmi is professor emeritus of sociology at the University of Paris, Nanterre and also at the École des hautes études commerciales. He is an officer of the Legion of Honor and an officer of the Palmes académiques. His writing has received numerous awards and prizes, most notably the Prix de Carthage, the Prix Fénéon, the Prix Simba, and the Grand Prix littéraire du Maghreb. Memmi is recognized internationally as one of the most important critical voices of our times. His study of the condition of colonialism, *Portrait du colonisé, précédé du portrait du colonisateur* (*The Colonizer and the Colonized*), to which Jean-Paul Sartre had written the introduction, launched his literary career in 1957 and established him as a staunch defender of the rights of the oppressed. Memmi has written six novels and numerous sociological studies on subjects such as racism, dependence, Jewish identity, Jewish literature, and the relationship between Jews and Arabs. He also has published a collection of poetry, and has edited literary anthologies devoted to writers of the Maghreb. In 1979, Memmi's autobiographical 1953 novel *La statue de sel* (*The Pillar of Salt*) was made into a film by the Israeli director Haim Shiran.

In his introduction to *The Pillar of Salt*, Albert Camus wrote, "Here is a French writer from Tunisia who is neither French nor Tunisian. . . . The first pogrom where the Arabs massacred the Jews demonstrated this to him. His culture is French. . . . Nevertheless, Vichy France delivered him to the Germans, and Free France, the day he wanted to fight for her, asked him to change the Jewish resonance of his last name" (*La statue de sel*, Paris: Gallimard, 1966). Indeed, Memmi has devoted much of his scholarly career to exploring questions of identity and to theorizing on experiences of colonialism, racism, and antisemitism he endured as a child and young adult.

Memmi's father, François, was of Italian Jewish origin, and his mother, Marguerite Sarfati, was of Berber Jewish descent. Memmi grew up in poverty in the Jewish quarter of Tunis. In 1946, he married a Frenchwoman, Germaine Dubach. This mixed marriage motivated him to study and to want to understand better the relationship between "Occident" and "Orient." "I discovered that the couple is not an isolated entity," he writes in his preface to *The Colonizer and the Colonized*. "[O]n the contrary, the whole world is within the couple" (*The Colonizer and the Colonized*; translated by Howard Greenfield, Boston: Beacon Press, 1991, p. vii). *The Colonizer and the Colonized* is an "inventory of conditions of colonized people [Memmi undertook] in order to understand [himself] and to identify [his] place in the society of other men" (p. viii). "I was Tunisian," he states, "therefore colonized. I discovered that few aspects of my life and my personality were untouched by this fact."

Tunisia, a French protectorate since 1883, won independence in 1956. Memmi identified strongly with the postwar anticolonial struggle and national ambitions of his Tunisian compatriots, and the portrait he depicts of the colonial situation is one that appeals to many oppressed peoples. "My compatriots were aspiring to become a nation: in a world essentially composed of nations, or of oppressed minorities, what could be more just?" (*Portrait d'un juif*, Paris: Gallimard, 1962, p. 12). That the young nation-state should declare Islam its official religion seemed reasonable to him. In July 1956, however, when the Suez crisis erupted, Memmi, as well as all other Tunisian Jews, quickly understood that they were going to be violently rejected as citizens by the postcolonial Arab world. When the newspaper for which he worked, and had helped found, ran on its front page the headline, "Whoever Spills Egyptian Blood Also Spills Our Blood," Memmi finally accepted that Arab nationalists had no place for the Jews with whom they had shared a home for so many years.

The Tunisian Jews not only were associated with the State of Israel and the Zionist cause, but were also much more assimilated into French culture than the Arabs. Indeed, French law enabled North African Jews to become French citizens without too much difficulty. To make matters more complicated, certain Jews had even taken the side of the colonialists, as was the case during the revolt in Algeria. As a result of their "allegiances" to Israel and to France, Jews were considered traitors by Muslim Tunisians who were engaged simultaneously in liberation struggles against the French and the project of nation building within the Arab world.

In *Portrait of a Jew*, Memmi moves away from a sweeping analysis of the condition of colonialism and oppression to a more specific yet far-reaching description of Jewish identity and experiences of antisemitism in the Arab world and in Europe. *Portrait of a Jew* is a massive undertaking, part personal exploration, part sociological study of the condition of the Jew throughout history. Memmi not only lays bare the antisemitic apparatus put into place by different nations and different groups throughout time, but also attempts to debunk vulgar stereotypes of Jews: "When a Jew has a big nose, it's as if he wears a so-called permanent Jewish sign in the middle of his face. . . . This poor nose, which would have nothing to do with being Jewish if it were on another person's face, finds itself inflated with all the supposed Jewishness of its possessor" (p. 142).

In addition to demystifying certain universal prejudices against Jews, Memmi undertook *Portrait of a Jew* in order to better understand his identity: "I am searching to understand who I am as a Jew," he states in the introduction to his four-hundred-page study. As an African Jew with a French education who is married to a French Christian woman, Memmi has struggled to understand his place: "With what country, what corner of the earth do I belong?" (p. 237). Such questions, concerning notions of national and religious identity, are the driving force of this book. Memmi explores in depth the awakening of Jewish consciousness in response to experiences of persecution and violence, and analyzes intensely the relationship of Jews to the world around them: "The religious condition of people being what it is, the nation being what it is, the Jew finds himself, in a certain sense, *outside the national community*" (p. 232). To a large extent, Memmi was prompted to undertake this project by a sense of deep disappointment with Europe—above all, with democratic and egalitarian France, which had been the first European country to grant citizenship to its Jews, in 1791, but which also brought forth antisemitic legislation and practices during World War II.

During the first two years of World War II, the Vichy authorities ruled Tunisia, and Jews were subject to laws that restricted their personal and professional lives. During the German occupation of Tunisia (November 1942 –May 1943), they suffered deportations, forced labor, and slaughter. *The Pillar of Salt*, which chronicles the coming of age of a young Jewish Tunisian boy, Alexandre Mordekhai Benillouche, records Memmi's own experience in a German work camp, from which he managed to escape. Approximately five thousand Jews were put into work camps in over thirty locations across Tunisia; with the declining military situation of the Germans, many prisoners escaped. The Germans surrendered to the Allies in early May 1943. At this time, according to the *Encyclopedia of the Holocaust*, only sixteen hundred Jews were being held in the camps.

Two chapters of *The Pillar of Salt* focus on Memmi's camp experience and subsequent escape. While his descriptions bring to our attention a much overlooked aspect of the Holocaust, the fate of the North African, especially Tunisian Jews (Tunisia was the only North African country to be occupied by the Germans), his portrayal of daily life in the camp mostly concerns the complexity of the relationships among the different groups of Tunisian Jews being held: religious and secular, educated and uneducated, working class and bourgeois.

Indeed, the narrator's—Benillouche's—relationship to the other inmates is marked by a strange mixture of suspicion and respect; he feels unsure of his purpose in the camp, because for health reasons he had not been deported but at first had been placed in an office providing services to the newly organized community. Benillouche himself asks to join the workers in the camp. "How could I stay there," he says, "while all the young Jews were being beaten, humiliated, and killed in the camps?" (p. 305). His fellow detainees cannot understand why someone with his education would volunteer, since all the intellectuals and bourgeois have been able to finagle their way out of the camp: "What innocence, what passion, and what assurance did I have at my disposal? I thought I was going to be taken in by the others simply because I went towards them, and because I had the desire and the goodwill" (p. 311).

The narrator's commitment to the camp is based on a complicated altruistic need to help and to provide solace; complicated, because Benillouche soon realizes that his desire is based on his own need, not that of the others. Moreover, he struggles with the fact that his intellectual pursuits make him quite different from the rest of the group, a member of the working class who has received a "bourgeois" education: "It was in the camp, during my daily life with them, that I realized the extent of my distance, how high school and my studies had made a communal life with my people impossible for me" (p. 309).

Nonetheless, the group asks him to provide them with religious offices, and for a short period of time, he is made the camp "rabbi." Despite his French education and the gap in scientific knowledge that exists between him and them, and despite the fact that he can't speak the Judeo-Arab dialect very well, the narrator is able to give his brethren some kind of encouragement.

In the pages that follow, Memmi describes his and his fellow inmates' escape, under the leadership of an Italian lieutenant, just before the German defeat. The inmates, who are being transferred from one location to the next, manage to capitalize on the general German confusion, and make their way back to Tunis. Once home, the narrator lies low until the Allies invade.

The Pillar of Salt, like Memmi's other works of fiction and nonfiction, brings to the fore questions of the consequences of traumatic history for the formation of group and individual identity:

> In order to explain who I am, I would need an intelligent audience and time: I am culturally French but Tunisian. . . . I am Tunisian but Jewish, that is to say, politically and socially excluded. I speak the language of the country with a particular accent, badly in tune with the passions that move the Moslems; I am Jewish, yet I have broken away from the Jewish religion and the ghetto. . . . (p. 364).

As a French-educated Tunisian Jew, Memmi finds himself betwixt and between hosts of contradictory historical experiences. He is, however, first and foremost a writer who searches for social justice in a world afflicted with poverty, discrimination, and prejudice. His works, which have been read and studied for almost half a century, continue to shed light on the appalling injustices of colonialism and the particular plight of the Jews not only during World War II, but throughout history.

Bibliography

Primary Sources

La statue de sel (*The Pillar of Salt*). 1953.
Agar. 1955.
Portrait du colonisé précédé du portrait d'un colonisateur (*The Colonizer and the Colonized*). 1957.
Portrait d'un juif (*Portrait of a Jew*). 1962.
Anthologie des écrivains maghrébins d'expression française (Anthology of Francophone Writers from the Maghreb). 1964.
La libération du juif (*Liberation of the Jew*). 1966.
L'homme dominé (*Dominated Man : Notes Towards a Portrait*). 1968
Anthologie des écrivains francais du Maghreb (Anthology of French Writers from the Maghreb). 1969.
Le scorpion, ou la confession imaginaire (*The Scorpion; Or, The Imaginary Confession*). 1969.
Juifs et Arabes (*Jews and Arabs*). 1974.
Le Désert, ou la vie et les aventures de Jubaïr Ouali El-Mammi. 1977.
La Dépendance: esquisse pour un portrait du dépendent (*Dependence*). 1979.
Le Racisme: déscription, définition, traitement (*Racism*). 1982.
Ce que je crois (What I Believe). 1985.
Le Mirliton du ciel (The Mirliton of the Heavens). 1985.
Anthologie du roman maghrébin (Anthology of the Maghrebin Novel). 1987.
Le Pharaon (The Pharoah). 1988.
Bonheurs: 52 semaines (Happiness: 52 Weeks). 1992.
Le Juif et l'Autre (The Jew and the Other). 1996.
L'Exercise du bonheur (The Exercise of Happiness). 1998.
Le Buveur et L'Amoureux (The Drinker and the Lover). 1998.
Le nomade immobile (The Immobile Nomad). 2000.

Secondary Sources

Dayan-Rosenman, Anny. "Albert Memmi: l'exil, le désert, l'écriture." *Pardes 21* (1995): 183–195.
Dejeux, Jean. "Littérature maghrébine d'expression française : le regard sur soi-même : qui suis-je?" *Présence francophone* (Spring 1972): 57–77.
Dugas, Guy. *Littérature judéo-maghrébine d'expression française*. Philadelphia: CELFAN, 1988.
Gaugeard, Jean. "Albert Memmi ou la longue marche à l'authenticité juive." *Les Lettres françaises*. Sept–Oct. 1966.
Khatibi, Abdelkébir. *Le roman maghrébin d'expression arabe et française depuis 1945*. Paris: EPHE, 1965.
Klein, Judith. La Littérature judéo-maghrébine de langue française. *Présence francophone* (1990): 115–129.
Marx-Scouras, Danielle. "Reconciling Language and History in Maghrebine Literary Criticism." *The Maghreb Review* (May–August 1984): 58–66.
Roumani, Judith. "Responses to North African Independence in the Novels of Dib, Memmi and Koskas : The End of Muslim-Jewish Symbiosis." *Middle East Review* (Winter 1988): 3–39.
———. *Albert Memmi*. Philadelphia: CELFAN, 1987.
Sartre, Jean-Paul. (Préface au 'Portrait du colonisé' d'Albert Memmi.). *Les Temps modernes* (July–August 1957): 289–293.
Schneider, Judith Morganroth. "Albert Memmi and Alain Finkielkraut: Two Discourses on French Jewish Identity." *Romanic Review* (January 1990): 130–136.

Works and Essays on Jews in North Africa

Bar on, Bat-Ami, and Edith Shaked. "The Jews in Islam-Tunisia." Presentation at the 19th International Congress of Historical Sciences, University of Oslo, Norway. August 2000. Online.
Chouraqui, André. *Between East and West: A History of the Jews in North Africa*. New York: Atheneum, 1973.
Laskier, Michael. *North African Jewry in the 20th Century: The Jews of Morocco, Tunisia and Algeria*. New York: NYU Press, 1997.
Lewis, Bernard. *The Jews in Islam*. Princeton: Princeton University Press, 1987.

ANNE MICHAELS

(1958–)

STEVE McCULLOUGH

ANNE MICHAELS IS a gifted and celebrated Canadian poet and novelist. She was born in 1958 in Toronto, where she continues to live and write. She earned a B.A. in English literature from the University of Toronto in 1980 and taught creative writing there for several years. Her debut collection of verse, *The Weight of Oranges*, was awarded the Commonwealth Writer's Prize for the Americas. Her second book, *Miner's Pond*, received the Canadian Author's Association Award. She has been most highly recognized, however, for her first novel, *Fugitive Pieces*, which was on the national best-seller lists for more than two years and won many literary awards, including Canada's Trillium Award, the Chapters / *Books in Canada* First Novel Award, and the United Kingdom's Orange Prize. Michaels has since published a third volume of poetry (*The Skin Divers*, 1999) and is writing a second novel.

Michaels is the daughter of Rosalind and Isaiah Michaels; he is a Russian immigrant, and she is a third-generation Torontonian. Michaels has identified these varied parental relationships with home and history as pivotal to her writing; both the loss and dislocation associated with emigration and the profusion of narrative associated with established family residence play important roles in her work, which notably foregrounds issues of memory, identity, history, and language.

Poetry

Michaels's poetry does not often address the Holocaust, but it consistently foregrounds issues of language as key to both experienced and historical time. She addresses the links between language and suffering in her long poem "What the Light Teaches," which is about the experiences of writers under Joseph Stalin but also attends to the horrors of the Nazi genocide. In this extended meditation on oppression, language is seen to salvage, for history, experiences it cannot wholly convey: "Truth is why words fail. / We can only reveal by outline, / by circling absence. / But that's why language / can remember truth when it's not spoken" (*The Weight of Oranges/Miner's Pond*, p. 116). The experienced moment is lost in expression, but language nevertheless retains its traces. Not only a means by which people attempt to represent the past, language itself is changed in such commemoration: "Language remembers. / Out of obscurity, a word takes its place / in history. Even a word so simple / it's translatable: number. Oven" (*The Weight of Oranges/ Miner's Pond*, p. 113). Language and the past are thus inextricably entwined inasmuch as each always resonates in the other. In Michaels's poems, language is repeatedly used in creative acts of memory giving rise to selfhood, rather than in mimetic historical presentation. Despite the loss of directly referential truth in such representation, the memorial function of language allows survivors access to the past and so permits them to re-create their selves: "what we save saves us" (*The Weight of Oranges/Miner's Pond*, p. 113).

Michaels's poetry also addresses the experiences of later generations grappling with historical representations of violently traumatic history. Her poem "Lake of Two Rivers," for example, includes reference to a reader's sudden identification with Holocaust victims: "When I was twenty-five I drowned in the River Neman, / fell through when I read that bone-black from the ovens / was discarded there" (*The Weight of Oranges/Miner's Pond*, p. 9). The intensity of this experience is explicitly textual and stands witness to the capacity of language to convey the past in a manner that tranforms the reader in a moment of unanticipated recognition and identification. Such moments of textual memory are both familiar and alien because although they come to belong to the readers, they cannot be anticipated. The same poem states, "We do not descend, but rise from our histories /. . ./ A name, a word, triggers the dilatation" (*The Weight of Oranges/Miner's Pond*, p. 8). The past, then, arises before the reader as that which will have been, and it so arises because language has the capacity to retain the traces of past lives that, in reading or hearing, become one's own. Such recognition is always mournful, however, inasmuch as it is a presence of absence, a recognition of loss. Michaels's poem "The Hooded Hawk" states, "History is the love that enters us / through death; its discipline / is grief" (*Skin Divers*, p. 44). Language thus simultaneously relegates history to the past and invites it to take a ghostly place in the present; it permits lost past experience a present place as the experience of mourning this loss. Therefore language has a primarily affective relation with time, whose passage is experienced through emotional and physical feelings of loss and recovery more than by means of cognitive retention and comprehension.

Fugitive Pieces

Michaels conceived of *Fugitive Pieces* in 1980, but it took six years of research and a further ten years of writing and revising before the novel was published in 1996. *Fugitive Pieces* has been published to popular and critical acclaim in twenty-five countries and in every major European language. It foregrounds themes of memory, writing, and the personal and interpersonal experiences of Holocaust survival. It does so by focusing on the character of Jakob Beer, who as a child escapes the violence of his family's fate and is haunted both by their loss and by his lack of comprehension of what happened to them. A child survivor in hiding, he is directly traumatized by the impact of the Nazi genocide, yet did not directly witness that violence. He is thus emblematic of both the difficulty survivors face in testifying to their experiences and the difficulty others face in attempting to read or to listen to and comprehend Holocaust experiences.

Part I of *Fugitive Pieces* takes the form of retrospective narration written by Jakob, whose unexpected death in a car crash is announced before the presentation of his posthumously discovered memoir begins. When he is only seven years old, Jakob narrowly escapes the raid in which his parents are murdered and his sister Bella is deported. He survives the attack by hiding in a place that his sister had outgrown and so could not share. Wedged inside a wall, he is able to hear—but not to see—the deaths of his mother and father. Jakob flees the house and escapes into the Polish countryside, eventually to stumble upon the archaeological dig at Biskupin, where he encounters and is rescued by Athos Roussos, a Greek man of letters, geographer, scholar, and specialist in archaeological preservation of damaged wood. Athos smuggles Jakob back to Greece. This encounter saves Athos as well, as the Nazi invaders, unable to tolerate the existence of an ancient non-Aryan civilization, destroy the site and deport all those working there. Athos devotes many years to writing *Bearing False Witness*, a book documenting this and other Nazi attempts to eradicate ideologically untenable scientific facts. In parallel, Jakob engages in a lifelong attempt to mourn the destruction of his family and come to terms with his tortured memories of them.

These parallel tasks link self-transformation and epistemology, and poetry and science are entwined in dense metaphorical and thematic collusion throughout the novel. Jakob recalls, "Athos was an expert in buried and abandoned places. His cosmology became mine. I grew into it naturally. In this way, our tasks became the same" (*Fugitive Pieces*, Toronto: McClellard & Stewart, 1996, p. 49). In the study of geology, Jacob finds the passage of millennia simultaneously and miraculously present in physical form: "I was transfixed by the way time buckled, met itself in pleats and folds" (p. 30). Correspondingly, the effects of memory are often experienced by Jakob in relation to objects and in bodily terms. A common relationship with time draws empirical physicality and ineffable personal memory together, and Michaels deploys the phenomena of radiation and carbon dating as symbols to link the evanescence of time with the concrete methodology of science. Two chapter titles—"The Gradual Instant" and "Vertical Time"—reflect this attention to the historical materialism of geology, in which the past has literal weight and spatial coexistence, and the paradoxical notion that the past is sought in the present yet has given rise to the present. In both cases, the pastness of the past is found "now," in an instant itself always falling into the past. Michaels insists on this complex vision of time in her consideration of the still more problematic physical and mental effects of obsession with intransigent and paralyzing Holocaust memory.

Hidden and housed by Athos, Beer learns a new language, Greek, and is raised in his new godfather's world of poetry and scientific curiosity. In this refuge he is haunted by the aural memories of the deaths of his parents and by the spectral presence of his sister Bella, whom he is convinced inhabits this new world with him, experiencing what he experiences and seeing what he sees. Jakob is tortured by the notion that his obsession with his murdered family is hurtful to them, that his incessant remembering ties them to a world of suffering from which they deserve the release of his forgetting.

After the war, Athos accepts a faculty position at the new department of geography at the University of Toronto, and Jakob learns yet another new language, English, in which he ultimately comes to grapple with his past. The role of the witness, a term carrying overtly visual implications and a theme that pervades Holocaust writing, is here rendered especially problematic. In the writing of Holocaust survivors, inability to attest to the reality of the horror is usually associated with the inadequacy of language and the sense that conveying the facts of the matter—were it possible—would nevertheless fail to convey their experiential nature and so their essential quality. Michaels's protagonist, however, suffers a still more categorical inability to testify; regardless of the communicative sufficiency or insufficiency of words, Jakob literally did not see the events that haunt him. Moreover, he is incessantly haunted by the sounds he heard, the invisible experiences that both demand and escape his capacity to portray them.

Jakob passes from the uncontrollable grip of horrifying memory to a desire to record this past in terms that do it justice. His life in Canada and the new language he learns offer him this opportunity. "And later, when I began to write down the events of my childhood in a language foreign to their happening, it was a revelation. English could protect me; an alphabet without memory" (p. 101). He can at first find only silence when he tries to write, but the inadequacy of this response leads him to writing that wrenches language apart: "I wanted a line in a poem to be the hollow ney of the dervish orchestra whose plaintive wail is a call to God. But all I achieved was awkward shrieking" (p. 112). Jakob eventually pits his imagination against the demanding silence of his memories and imagines Bella's fate, following her with his words into the gas chambers where he imagines she perished. "I want to remain close to Bella. To do so, I blaspheme by imagining" (p. 167). His response to the annihilating and dehumanizing Nazi language of destruction is an assertion of his continued love for the dead in the face of the monstrous crime of their murder. *Fugitive Pieces* thus demands faith in words; a faith not in their capacity to simply convey external referentia but in their capacity to take effect, to effect transformation. The lyrical and metaphoric style of this novel affirms this thematic insistence on the healing power of language. Beginning with the fragmented and discontinuous narration of Jakob's flight and discovery, the narrative becomes progressively more coherent in form as his life proceeds toward the realization that, in language, memories of suffering can be transformed from a negative burden into a positive force.

His imagining is an act of release that separates him from his traumatic identification with the dead, rather than an attempt to simply give them voice. As he asserts, some silences are impenetrable, some differences absolute: "no one could bear the responsibility of forgiveness on behalf of the dead. No act of violence is ever resolved. When the one who can forgive can no longer speak, there is only silence" (pp. 160–161). By writing into this silence in a manner that does not seek to fill or replace it, Jakob is able to distinguish himself from the victims yet bear witness to their loss. Ethical relationships are at the heart of this memory-work of language: "History is amoral: events occurred. But memory is moral; what we consciously remember is what our conscience remembers. History is the *Totenbuch*, The Book of the Dead, kept by the administrators of the camps. Memory is the *Memorbucher*, the names of those to be mourned, read aloud in the synagogue" (p. 138). This and other references situate Jakob's effort firmly in Jewish traditions of remembering. "It's Hebrew tradition that forefathers are referred to as 'we,' not 'they.' . . . This encourages empathy and a responsibility to the past, but more important, it collapses time. The Jew is forever leaving Egypt. A good way to teach ethics" (p. 159).

This focus on identifying with epic generational history points to the necessity of romantic love for Jakob's return to himself. Jakob at first regards desire as dangerous, as he is afraid of demands to explain himself, his unorthodox life with Athos, or his past. It is his second wife, Michaela, with whom he is finally able to exchange stories and so find a hope for peace. This relationship of mutual listening and commemoration completes his coming to terms with language, silence, memory, and history, and he is finally able not only fully to inhabit the present, but to forge tentative links with a hoped-for future. Emblematic of this possible future is Jakob and Michaela's decision, should they have a child, to name a son Bela or a daughter Bella. Michaels thus presents reproductive generational hope as uniting the past and the present in the form of a desired child who will embody individual reconciliation with traumatic collective history.

Part II both interrupts and takes up the themes and events of Part I by shifting the narrative voice to a new narrator and protagonist, a young professor of literature named Ben. Ben is the child of Holocaust survivors and has been named only "ben" (son of) in the hope that this will render him less vulnerable to the persecution his parents continuously expect. Michaels presents in Ben's familial experiences many of the characteristics of second-generation children who grew up in homes explicitly shadowed by Holocaust violence. Ben's parents were insistent that he know as much as possible about the horror of the past, yet keep from him knowledge of the existence of his brother and sister, who died in the genocide. His education about the Holocaust is insistent yet impersonal, and these experiences of silence and betrayal make problematic the surviving generation's hope of renewal in a child. Ben is thus presented as vicariously subject to the traumatic weight of history and so repeats much of Jakob's personal trajectory; this similarity is emphasized in the four chapter titles of Part II that repeat, in order, four of the seven chapter titles of Part I. Michaels thus takes up the ongoing presence of the past in the continued effects of the Holocaust on the second generation, who are not, then, the anticipated recuperation of the past, but must themselves negotiate the demands of unassimilable history.

After Jakob and Michaela die childless, Ben takes up the task of traveling to Greece to seek out Jakob's final writings. In Part II *Fugitive Pieces* shifts from concerns with the possibility of writing as a reconciling act of memory to the possibility of its fulfillment in reading. Ben lives in the house where Jakob retired to write and explores with a sacramental reverence the space where Jakob and Michaela lived. This domestic archaeology impresses on him the spatial presence of past time. Rooms and possessions are seen to offer mute testimony to the presence of their lost inhabitants: "Every room emanated absence yet was drenched with your presence" (p. 265). Ben is first able to experience the material historicity of the present much as Jakob found in geography the "gradual instant" of history. Symbolically and tragically, Ben discovers a note left by Michaela for Jakob indicating that she was pregnant when they died. Ben is thus positioned by happenstance as both a surrogate heir to Jakob and Michaela's familial memory and as a privileged reader who takes up the continuing memory work that Jakob began in his memoirs. Ben, having read the memoirs he finds, is able to return to Canada filled with a sense of the necessity of reconciliation, of love, and of forgiving that which it is possible to forgive.

Fugitive Pieces inspired popular and academic debates over the role of literary beauty in the portrayal of the Holocaust. Most reviewers praised the lyricism of Michaels's novel while embracing its transformative narrative of self-recovery through reflection and love. Critics of the novel accuse its lyrical bent of homogenizing the characters, rendering them as mere projections of the central consciousness of Jakob, a centrality that is, in turn, problematically determined by his all-pervasive identity as traumatized survivor. This disproportion is linked by Adrienne Kertzer to an ethical question about aesthetics: Although Jakob and Ben are overwhelmingly determined by the violent history of the Holocaust, *Fugitive Pieces* conspicuously avoids portraying this physical suffering, thus implying that beauty and redemption are made possible only by this elision. Michaels, on her part, has been unequivocal over her intent to write a story of recovery and hope: "I didn't want to leave the reader in a dark place" (WordsWorth interview). *Fugitive Pieces* ultimately addresses the problems attendant on coming to terms with the Holocaust as a mediated and distanced event, one that for most people must be understood as intimately related to the language by which they come into contact with it. "Language itself is redemptive in the book, so it makes sense that the language of the book is intense because of the intensity of experience to be conveyed to the reader" (WordsWorth interview). It is in this linguistic sphere that Michaels locates both the possibility of reconciliation with the past and a hope that the experience of loss is not itself lost in language.

Bibliography

Primary Sources

The Weight of Oranges. 1986.
Miner's Pond. 1991.
Fugitive Pieces. 1996.
Skin Divers. 1999.

Secondary Sources

Cook, Méira. "At the Membrane of Language and Silence: Metaphor and Memory in *Fugitive Pieces.*" *Canadian Literature* 164 (spring 2000): 12–35.

Hillger, Annick. " 'Afterbirth of Earth': Messianic Materialism in Anne Michaels' *Fugitive Pieces*." *Canadian Literature* 160 (spring 1999): 28–45.

Kertzer, Adrienne. "*Fugitive Pieces*: Listening as a Holocaust Survivor's Child." *English Studies in Canada* 26, no. 22 (June 2000): 193–217.

Interviews

Fetherling, Douglas. "Narrative Moves: An Interview with Anne Michaels." *Prairie Fire* 17, no. 33 (autumn 1996): 236–241.

WordsWorth interview with Anne Michaels. http://cg.wordsworth.com/www/present/michaels/"Peter Oliva interviews Anne Michaels." http://www.pages.ab.ca/michaels.html

ARTHUR MILLER
(1915–)

NORMAN J. FEDDER

ARTHUR MILLER WAS born 17 October 1915 in New York City to parents of Polish-Jewish origin, Isadore and Augusta. Miller graduated from the University of Michigan in 1938. He has resided for most of his adult life in rural Connecticut.

If ever any Jews should have melted into the proverbial pot, it was our family," Miller recalled of his youth. He saw himself as "no sallow Talmud reader but Frank Merriwell or Tom Swift, heroic models of athletic verve and military courage." More significantly, his father's "refusal to attribute naturally superior virtues to all Jews and antisemitism to all gentiles" set up in him, "if not a faith in, then an expectation of universal emotions and ideas" devoid of ethnic boundaries. But the Holocaust, as it would turn out, made a massive onslaught on his "fortress of denial" (*Timebends* New York: Grove Press, 1987, p. 62).

That "watershed of our history," as he calls it, looms large in Miller's work. It threads through his autobiography, *Timebends;* it pervades his novel, *Focus*; it dominates his plays *After the Fall, Incident at Vichy, Playing for Time,* and *Broken Glass*. Miller also finds "an echo of the theme" in his play, *The Creation of the World and Other Business,* "where the dilemma for God himself is his inability to determine his responsibility for the indifference to murder in the minds of his most gratifyingly successful creatures" *(Arthur Miller's Collected Plays*, vol. 2. New York, Viking, 1981, p. 2).

Focus

Focus (1945) has been called the "first American novel of the Holocaust" (Mesher, p. 469). Its subject is antisemitism in New York at the close of World War II; but, as Miller notes in his "Introduction" to *Focus* (Syracuse University Press, 1997), it also reflects his "Hitler-begotten sensitivity" at the time: "Whatever the actual level of hostility to Jews that I was witnessing, it was vastly exacerbated in my mind by the threatening existence of Nazism . . ." In the novel, Miller observes, he depicts this hostility as a warning that the "conjunction between mere private prejudice and public calamity" (pp. v–vii) that occurred in Germany could not happen here (the United States).

Middle-aged and unmarried, the novel's hero, Lawrence Newman, resides with his paralyzed mother in a drab Queens neighborhood and has little to live for but his position as a personnel manager in a large Manhattan firm. He takes particular pride in his facility at recognizing and rejecting Jewish applicants and is thrilled to find his bias affirmed by antisemitic graffiti on subway pillars and swastikas on Jewish gravestones. But one day, his Jew-spotting "focus" fails him, and he hires a new typist who turns out to be "not our type of person" (p. 17). So his boss insists that he get himself a pair of eyeglasses, which, ironically, make him resemble the very people he despises. It isn't long before he is told it is intolerable to have a Semitic-looking face in so visible a job, and is demoted. Finding this blow to his ego unbearable, he quits. But in his search for like employment, he is subject to the same kind of treatment he had previously meted out and winds up with a menial job in a firm that will "hire anybody" (p. 82). His interviewer turns out to be Gertrude Hart, whom Newman recently mistook for a Jew and didn't hire but whose sensuality aroused him. This and their common experience of rejection eventuate in marriage.

The discrimination worsens. The couple is refused accommodations at restricted hotels and ostracized in their neighborhood. Gertrude, who has no use for Jews, is outraged that Newman and she should be taken for Jews; and, to counter this calumny, she would like her husband to take an active role in their persecution. She urges him to join the local Christian Front and banish from the neighborhood Finkelstein, who owns the corner candy store. But, as much as Newman shares the Front's hatreds, he shrinks from their methods, going so far as to resist their attempts to disrupt the storekeeper's business. This makes Newman a prime target for Front vandalism. Try as he does to convince them that he is not Jewish, Newman finds garbage thrown on his lawn, and a threatening note in his newspaper.

These actions unwillingly bring him in closer touch with Finkelstein, who is determined to stand his ground against the proto-Nazis. The storekeeper rejects his father's ghetto mentality that Jews are fated to victimization, prepares for armed resistance to his persecutors (with baseball bats he has bought for the purpose), and meets head-on Newman's moral myopia. Finkelstein asks Newman just why he wants him off the street. "It's not what *you've* done," he tells the storekeeper, "it's what others of your people have done" (p. 168). "In other words," concludes Finkelstein, "when you look at me you don't see me" (p. 168).

But Gertrude prevails on her husband to prove his ethnic purity by attending a Front rally. This backfires when, failing to applaud the speech of the movement's leader, Newman is branded a Jew and ejected from the hall. Not long after, he and Gertrude find themselves at a theater watching a movie about Nazis taking Jewish prisoners to the gallows. The latter are accompanied by a rabbi and a priest. The rabbi affirms they are innocent and "must not be killed merely because they are Jews," while the priest proclaims "it is not Christian to murder" them (pp. 200–201). This can't help but affect Newman's growing distance from his former convictions.

The novel ends as Newman comes to "see" Finkelstein at last and joins him in fighting off the punks who attack them. When Gertrude tries to bring her husband back to the fold, he angrily rejects her and leaves to report the crime. The policeman, taking Newman for a Jew, inquires: "How many of you people live there?" (p. 217). Newman could correct the man, he feels, but "the officer had assumed he was, and it seemed now that to make the denial was to repudiate and soil his own cleansing fury of a few moments ago" (p. 217). He replies: "There are the Finkelsteins on the corner . . ." (p. 217). The policeman interrupts him: "Just them and yourself?" "Yes. Just them and myself," Newman says (p. 217).

Focus has been taken to task for credibility of both plot and viewpoint. Benjamin Nelson in *Arthur Miller: Portrait of a Playwright*, echoing other critics, faulted the use of the eyeglasses to generate the action. To represent the absurdity of looks as the basis for prejudice, it may well be valid; but it seems unlikely Newman's putting the eyeglasses on could so totally change the way he is perceived. The novel is also replete, Nelson comments, with coincidences that belie credulity—such as the woman he refuses a job becoming the person who later hires and marries him. David Mesher objects to the author's conception of Nazi antisemitism. Attacking the Jews, Miller has Finkelstein say, is merely a strategy to dominate the mass of Germans. Mesher criticizes Miller for misreading Hitler's genocide, which was decidedly more than a means of attaining power; it was an ultimate goal. At the same time, Ladislaus Lob has favorably compared *Focus* with Max Frisch's play, *Andorra*, in which a gentile is also tragically mistaken for a Jew; and Miller has been praised by Mesher and Nelson for being one of the very few writers of his generation to attempt to deal with the subject, and to do so, for the most part, with accuracy and effectiveness.

"Universalistic" Interpretation

In his 1958 critique of the Holocaust play, *The Diary of Anne Frank*, Miller wrote that "with all its truth" it lacked "the over-vision beyond its characters and their problems, which could have illuminated not merely the cruelty of Nazis but something even more terrible . . . that we should see the bestiality in our own hearts, so that we should know how we are brothers not only to these victims but to the Nazis" (*The Theater Essays of Arthur Miller,* p. 187). In early 1964, Miller was brought in proximity to the horror he had only known from a distance: he visited the concentration camp at Mauthausen, Austria. After this, he felt compelled to observe and report on the Nazi war-crimes trials in Frankfort, Germany. The question of the trials, he wrote, "spreads out beyond the defendants . . . into the heart of every man. It is his own complicity with murder, even the murders he did not perform himself with his own hands. The murders, however, from which he profited if only by having survived" ("How the Nazi Trials Search the Hearts of All Germans," *Herald Tribune*, March 15, 1964, p. 24). For these opinions, which permeate his work, Miller has been called "perhaps the foremost spokesman for a universalistic . . . interpretation of the Holocaust" (Isser, p. 62).

After the Fall

Miller's interpretation is amply evident in the play he wrote upon his return from the trials. *After the Fall* (1964) dramatizes the inner struggle of Quentin, a lawyer in mid-career, to come to terms with his betrayal of the people in his life and their betrayal of one another; but the Holocaust, Miller noted, is "at the center of the play's theme" (*Collected Plays*, vol. 2, p. 2): the dominant setpiece is "the blasted stone tower of a German concentration camp" (*After the Fall*, p. 1).

Quentin's visit to the camp, early in the play, sets its subject and tone—his identity with the place as both victim and victimizer: "Why do I *know* something here?" Quentin asks: "Why do I feel an understanding with this slaughterhouse?" (pp. 15–16). The tower in this camp is evoked, from that point on, at every moment of betrayal. For example, when he's accused by his first wife, Louise, of his indifference to her and every woman, Quentin denies the accusation, yet he cannot help but "believe she's right" (p. 30). The image of the tower makes "something in [him] bow its head like an accomplice" (p. 30). The tower is seen three times more, illuminating the cycle of betrayal set off by Quentin's colleague Mickey's subpoena by the red-baiting "Committee": when Quentin learns that Mickey will be fired from the firm if he does not testify; when Mickey reveals he is going to implicate Lou and condemn their old professor for hypocrisy, and when Quentin admits his "joy" that Lou killed himself and therefore he will not have to defend him. With his eye on the tower, Quentin cries: "This is not some crazy aberration of human nature to me" (p. 59). He "can easily see the perfectly normal" camp workers "laying the pipes to run the blood out of this mansion; good fathers, devoted sons, grateful that someone else will die, not they, and how can one understand that, if one is innocent?" (p. 59) Finally, following his climactic encounter with his second wife, Maggie, which culminates in her suicide, Quentin "*turns toward the tower . . . as toward a terrible God*" and draws the play to its closure: "Who can be innocent again on this mountain of skulls? I tell you what I know! My brothers died here—*He looks from the tower down at the fallen Maggie*— but my brothers built this place; our hearts have cut these stones!" (p. 113). Its dreadful reality together with his own have taught him "that we are very dangerous!" (p. 113).

The matter of Quentin's life so resembles Miller's that *After the Fall* has been deplored as embarrassingly confessional—the subject of particular condemnation being its negative portrait of Maggie/Marilyn Monroe. Moreover, the structure was considered discursive, the secondary characters undeveloped, and the dialogue inflated. For Leonard Moss, Miller's equating Quentin's faults with those of the Nazis was especially specious: His treatment of others may be callous; he comes close to manhandling Maggie; he attempts, in his mind, to kill his mother; and he accuses himself of being a potential murderer, but this can hardly be equated with the cruelty of even a run-of-the-mill storm trooper. On the other hand, the play has been praised by Norman Nadel and Nelson for its powerful rendering of the turmoil of the mind as it plumbs the depths of its confusion and pain toward growing awareness and healing.

Incident at Vichy

Incident at Vichy (1964) has its roots in a story, told to Miller by a friend, of a Jewish psychoanalyst who was picked up by the Nazis in Vichy, France. A Gentile that the psychoanalyst did not know enabled him to escape by taking his place in the line of suspects. The Gentile in this story merged in Miller's mind with an Austrian prince of his acquaintance, who had opposed the Nazis and was punished for it. Miller developed this concept into the play set in 1942 at a French Nazi collaborationist detention center. In the play, a group of men with non-Aryan features has been rounded up to determine (by inspection of their papers and penises) if they are Jews (or Gypsies) and thus candidates for deportation and extermination. In charge are a zealous German professor of "racial anthropology" and a dubious major, aided by the ruthless Vichy police. There are six French Jews (Lebeau, a painter; Bayard, an electrician; Monceau, an actor; Leduc, a psychiatrist; a waiter; and a boy) and one East European, ultra-orthodox "Old Jew," together with three Gentiles: a Gypsy, a French businessman (Marchand), and an Austrian prince (Von Berg). The play mounts in tension as they wait to be examined, and each, in his own way, confronts the impending doom.

Marchand is convinced it is merely "a document check" (p. 4). And for him, as a Gentile, it turns out to be just that. Monceau considers the others' fears "hysterical" since "Germans are still *people*" (p. 19) and refuses to help Leduc overpower even the one guard. He blames Leduc and his like for giving "Jews a reputation for subversion, and this Talmudic analysis, and this everlasting, niggling discontent" (p. 52). Bayard doesn't doubt the fate that awaits him; but he tries to face it by dreaming of "the day when the working class is master of the world," ignoring Von Berg's claim that "ninety-nine per cent of the Nazis" are from that class (pp. 32–33). Lebeau has no recourse but desperation. Despite himself, he cannot help but feel the Jews are guilty of something after years and years of hearing "such terrible things about us" (p. 50). He is especially perturbed that he and his parents didn't leave France before it was too late because his mother "had this brass bed, and carpets, and draperies and all kinds of junk"(p. 50). When the turn of the waiter comes, he tries to run away and must be thrown into the office. Lebeau and the boy volunteer to help Leduc take on the guard, but Leduc rejects both as too weak for the task. Von Berg is persuaded by the boy to take a valuable ring to his destitute mother when the prince is released; after which the youngster unsuccessfully tries to escape. The major, who has reluctantly been assigned to this duty, finds it all "inconceivable" (p. 53); yet he scornfully rejects Leduc's appeal that he risk his life to save him. The major represses his feelings of decency with drink and hides behind a mask of misanthropy. The Gypsy and Old Jew are disdained by the rest for their otherness. When their time comes, the Gypsy reluctantly parts with the pot he's been fixing, and the Old Jew, who prays silently throughout, refuses to relinquish his large bundle, as if it were his soul. When the professor attempts to pull it from him, it rips open and blows out a "*white cloud of feathers*" (p. 64).

Von Berg would like to think Nazism is "an outburst of vulgarity" (p. 23). How can "people with respect for art go about hounding Jews?" (p. 24). But he is forced to admit that he knows "many cultivated people who . . . did become Nazis" (p. 24). Yet he still maintains: "There are people who would find it easier to die than stain one finger with this murder" (p. 65). Leduc begs to differ: "Each man has his Jew," he declares, "it is the other. And the Jews have their Jews. And now, now above all, you must see that you have yours—the man whose death leaves you relieved that you are not him, despite your decency" (p. 66). The prince emphatically denies that he had "something to do with this monstrousness!" (p. 66). He would rather have put a pistol to his head. Then Leduc informs him that Baron Kessler, the cousin he so admires, is the Nazi who helped remove all the Jewish doctors from Leduc's medical school. The psychiatrist concludes,

> And that is why your thoughts of suicide do not move me. It's not your guilt I want, it's your responsibility—that might have helped. Yes, if you had understood that Baron Kessler was in part . . . in some small and frightful part—doing your will. You might have done something then, with your standing, and your name and your decency, aside from shooting yourself! (p. 68).

Von Berg responds to Leduc's indictment by doing "something" now. In the play's final moments he gives the psychiatrist his pass (and the boy's ring) and allows him to escape.

Incident at Vichy has been disparaged by Robert Brustein and Dennis Welland as contrived, didactic, static, and overloaded with improbable coincidences. Edward Isser declares it historically inaccurate: In 1942, Isser notes, Vichy/Nazi agreements protected all native-born French citizens, and only the foreign Old Jew would have been subject to deportation. Philip Rahv takes issue with Miller's universalistic theme: Leduc's charge that people are all as "full of murder" (p. 65) as the Nazis. For Rahv, this is to absolve the Nazis of all guilt. If everyone is to blame for the Holocaust then no one is. Nelson argues, however, that by "complicity" with evil Miller does not mean "equality." All people aren't Nazis, to be sure, but they all have that potential in them, and when by their indifference they allow such depravity, they cannot claim innocence. Leduc should not be conflated with his author since the prince, by his sacrifice, refutes the psychiatrist. More concerned with artistic truth than historical detail, Nelson found the play quite convincing and well constructed: each dialectical encounter moves the action forward, decreasing the possibilities of escape and increasing the impending horror—building to a climax that is both compelling and conclusive.

Playing for Time

It took another sixteen years before Miller was to write another play about the Holocaust. In 1980 he adapted for television *Playing for Time* (*Collected Plays*, vol. 2), the memoir of the French Jewish singer Fania Fenelon, a survivor of Auschwitz. In his teleplay with the same title (he also wrote a stage version), Miller is generally true to the original, while condensing and sharpening plot, character, and language for dramatic purposes. Yet he does take the liberty to draw from the story his familiar motifs that he enlarges and emphasizes: Fania's disgust that to stay alive she must serve the Nazis and be despised by the other prisoners for doing so, her despair that she and her persecutors "are the same species" (p. 483), and her humanity in the face of it—doing all she can for those in need around her, refusing to retreat into tribal chauvinism or moral degeneracy.

Fania's survival in Auschwitz is dependent on her musical talent. She is there because her boyfriend is in the Resistance and her father is Jewish. A Parisian singer of note, she is recruited for the camp's female orchestra, which has been created to accompany the prisoners on their way to work and to give concerts for the officers. She later becomes the group's orchestrator. Her abhorrence for the task and her compassionate persona come up against the artistic perfectionism and authoritarian methods of the German Jewish conductor, Alma Rose, niece of the renowned composer

Gustav Mahler. But in the end, Fania thanks Alma who "probably saved us all" (p. 512). Ironically, Rose saves all but herself. She is poisoned by the jealous Frau Schmidt, head of the clothing depot.

Frau Schmidt's lethal doings are right in line with those of the camp's band of butchers: Mengele's consigning the Jews to slaughter with the point of a finger, Mandel's beating prisoners at will and sending to death the Polish boy she temporarily favored, the guards assaulting the steady stream of people being marched into the gas chambers, the unrelieved cruelty of the *blockawas* and *kapos* (inmate overseers). Yet "the ultimate horror" is that these monsters are human: Mengele is a connoisseur of music who is "totally—moved" by Fania's singing (p. 481); Mandel is "beautiful and human. . . . And that is what's so hopeless about this whole thing" (p. 483). "I mean," Fania concludes, "we know a little something about the human race that we didn't know before. And it's not good news" (p. 516).

Nonetheless, Fania does her part to promote the welfare, and raise the spirits, of her fellow sufferers. She risks her life by refusing to join the orchestra unless her friend, Marianne, is also invited; she shares her food with her gluttonous companion and "anyone who wants it" (p. 473). She would even "try to teach" the savage *Blockawas* a lesson in human kindness (p. 473). She defies Alma's rigidity while at the same time serving as her confidant. She does likewise for all who come within her contact; she washes the clothes of a woman recovering from typhus, supports the feelings of two others confused by their mutual attraction, and becomes the person to whom everyone tells their troubles. She is someone they all can trust. Maybe that is because, as Elzvieta comments, Fania has "no ideology"; she is "satisfied just to be a person" (p. 503). Indeed Fania has no use for the narrowness of some of the camp's inmates: "I am sick of the Zionists-and-the-Marxists; the Jews-and-the-Gentiles; the Easterners-and-the-Westerners; the Germans-and-the-non-Germans; the French-and-the-non-French. I am sick of it, sick of it, sick of it! I am a woman, not a tribe!" (p. 492).

There are inmates, like Polish Elzvieta and Jewish Mala, who emulate Fania in reaching out to others, but more of the inmates are completely self-absorbed, like Marianne. While Fania responds to her degradation by growing in humanity, Marianne degenerates, exchanging her body for bread and sausages, becoming increasingly coarse and belligerent. Although she owes her life to Fania, Marianne falsely accuses Fania of deserting her, and, finally, having been appointed a *kapo*, Marianne mercilessly beats her benefactor.

Fania's will to live is encouraged by a fellow prisoner, Shmuel, a character Miller created. Shmuel seems to speak for some otherworldly presence who has picked her to bear witness to this nadir of civilization. One can hardly imagine that the playwright is implying that his atheist heroine has been divinely delivered, but maintaining her values in defiance of her doom may well be regarded as something transcendent.

Apart from the controversy over Palestinian Liberation Organization (PLO) partisan, Vanessa Redgrave, portraying Fania, *Playing for Time* was widely watched and well received. Susan Abbotson in "Revisiting the Holocaust for 1980's Television," admired it as a telling lesson of the ultimate in human depravity and the will to survive it. There were critics who had reservations: While ranking the play among Miller's best achievements, Jack Kroll writes that it loses its dramatic build toward the middle. Tom Shales is equally laudatory but thinks that some of the characters are underwritten and the figure of Shmuel is gratuitous. Isser complains that Miller's Fania, unlike the real Fenelon, parrots the playwright's universalistic views and has decidedly more courage, as evidenced by her interceding for the orchestra with Dr. Mengele and asking for extra rations from Frau Mandel. It is true that his Fania's notion of kinship with the Nazis is vintage Miller, but a case could be made that she is a good deal like her real-life model. Her invective against tribalism is taken directly from the memoir *Playing for Time* by Fania Fenelon in which she also risks her life for Marianne ("Clara" in the original), and though her other acts of courage are different in the play, they compare well with such deeds in the memoir. When requesting the kind of pencils she wants from the kommandant, she daringly hands him one stamped "Made in England," according to her memoir. (p. 95).

Broken Glass

The Holocaust as a subject for drama persisted well into Miller's later years with his writing of *Broken Glass* (1994) in his seventies. The play is set in 1938 while the Nazis were ravaging through Germany, burning synagogues, vandalizing Jewish shops and homes, rounding up Jewish men for incarceration, destroying Jewish property, and assaulting and killing Jews in what came to be known as *Kristallnacht*, the night of the broken glass. Like the death camp evoked in the imagery of *After the Fall*, *Kristallnacht* atrocities haunt the background and extend the meaning of the play's domestic American conflict.

Sylvia Gellburg in *Broken Glass* is a middle-aged Jewish woman obsessed with *Kristallnacht*. Her sister, Harriet, and brother-in-law, Murray, cannot understand what business it is of hers to be interested in Germany. But Sylvia is horrified by the pictures in the newspaper of the Nazis "making old men crawl around and clean the sidewalks with toothbrushes" (p. 33). Something must be done, she hysterically cries, "before they murder us all!" (p. 105). Her obsession with Jewish victimization in Germany appears to be at least partly why she suddenly becomes paralyzed from the waist down for no apparent physical reason. Her psychosomatic symptoms are compounded by her feeling of victimization by her husband, Phillip, whom she subconsciously identifies with the Nazis in a dream. She is fearful of him because of his negative attitudes toward Jews and his repressive treatment of her. She can never forgive Phillip for refusing to let her pursue her career as a bookkeeper, and her hatred of him has, in turn, made him impotent and violent.

Phillip is a classic self-hating Jew trying to "disappear into the Goyim" (p. 123). Indifferent to the rise of the Nazis, he blames *Kristallnacht*, in part, on the snootiness of the German Jews. Ultrasensitive to being misnamed Goldberg, not Gellburg, proud to be the only Jew who ever worked for his WASP bank and set foot on his boss's yacht, boastful that his son is a graduate of West Point who might well become "the first Jewish General" (p. 37), he is at frenetic odds with his ethnic identity: "There are some days when I feel like going and sitting in the Schul with the old men . . . and be a full-time Jew the rest of my life. . . . And other times . . . yes, I could almost kill them. They infuriate me. I am ashamed of them and that I look like them" (p. 127).

The play takes its shape from the attempt of their doctor, Harry Hyman, to cure Sylvia and counsel Phillip. In due course, Hyman is able to get them to reveal the bitter truths of their relationship. The doctor is himself no model husband. In contrast to Phillip, he has a history of womanizing; and his approach to treating Sylvia has sexual overtones, which she encourages. Hyman carries his Judaism lightly. Married to a Gentile, an uncharacteristically Jewish horseman, he belittles Sylvia's foreboding about the Nazis. Having taken his medical degree in Germany, he assures her that it is impossible for the Germans to "suddenly change into thugs like this. This will all pass. . . ." (p. 101). Hyman has little patience with Phillip's lament that the Jews are uniquely victimized. Everybody thinks they're persecuted, the doctor maintains: "The poor by the rich, the rich by the poor, the black by the white, the white by the black, the men by the women, the women by the men, the Catholics by the Protestants, the Protestants by the Catholics—and of course all of them by the Jews." When Phillip retorts, "So you mean there's no Hitler?" Hyman writes off the Führer as "the perfect example of the persecuted man! I've heard him—he kvetches like an elephant was standing on his pecker!" (pp. 127–128).

The doctor's prescription for Sylvia and Phillip is that they resume their sex life, which proves to be impossible. Confronting their marital difficulties, however, leads the two to the verge of self-knowledge and reconciliation. Phillip finally realizes that his personal life is impacted by the historic. Furious with what he perceives to be his boss's antisemitic accusations, he quits his lifetime job. This precipitates a heart attack and final scene with his wife. The broken glass of their shattered marriage conjoins with that of *Kristallnacht* as he confesses that fear underlay his abuse of Sylvia: fear of being a Jew in a gentile world, of Germany, of "what could happen to us here" (p. 131). He doesn't "want that anymore" (p. 131). He implores her to forgive him and regain her mobility. In this he succeeds: unsteadily, she rises and absolves him of blame. But as she desperately struggles to reach him, "*Phillip falls back dead*" (p. 132).

Broken Glass has received mixed reviews. Linda Winer found fault with Miller's relating Sylvia's paralysis to *Kristallnacht*—as if the Nazis wouldn't have concerned her if Sylvia had a good job and sex life (p. 132). Miller was criticized for promoting his Holocaust theories through Hyman. Furthermore, the ending was ridiculed by Brustein in his "Separated by a Common Playwright" for its melodrama. Abbotson, however, wrote at length in his "Issues of Identity in *Broken Glass*" on the strengths of the play. Hyman for her, far from being Miller's spokesman, is as much a multidimensional character as Phillip and Sylvia; the doctor's reaction to *Kristallnacht* is as limited as theirs. The conflict is best described as the failure of all three characters to attain a proper balance between individual and social identity. The play has been lauded by Kinereth Meyer and Benjamin Nelson ("Arthur Miller") for its bold exploration of the Jewish condition in the shadow of the greatest threat to its survival.

Conclusion

During a trip to Italy in his mid-thirties, Miller encountered a group of concentration camp survivors awaiting passage to Palestine. To his distress, his attempts to communicate with them as fellow Jews failed:

> Their mistrust was like acid in my face; I was talking to burnt wood, charred iron, bone with eyes. In coming years I would wonder why it never occurred to me to throw in my lot with them when they were the product of precisely the catastrophe I had in various ways given my writing life to try to prevent. To this day, thinking of them there . . . I feel myself disembodied, detached, ashamed of my stupidity, my failure to recognize myself in them (*Timebends*, p. 167).

In these five absorbing works, one might well contend, he has more than made up for his self-defined failure.

Bibliography

Primary Sources

Plays

The Man Who Had All the Luck. 1944.
All My Sons. 1947.
Death of a Salesman. 1949.
An Enemy of the People. 1951 (adaptation of the play by Henrik Ibsen).
The Crucible. 1953.
A View from the Bridge with a Memory of Two Mondays. 1955.
A View from the Bridge. 1957.
After the Fall. 1964.
Incident at Vichy. 1964.
The Price. 1968.
The Creation of the World and Other Business. 1973. (*Up from Paradise*—musical version. 1984).
Two Way Mirror (*Some Kind of Love Story* and *Elegy for a Lady*). 1984.
Playing for Time. 1985 (adaptation of the memoir by Fania Fenelon—stage version).
Danger: Memory! (*Clara* and *I Can't Remember Anything*). 1986.
Two Plays (*The Archbishop's Ceiling* and *The American Clock*). 1989.
The Ride Down Mt. Morgan. 1992.
The Last Yankee. 1994.
Broken Glass. 1994.
Mr. Peters' Connections. 1998.

Screenplays

The Misfits. 1961.
Playing for Time. 1981 (adaptation of the memoir by Fania Fenelon).

Novel

Focus. 1945 (with an "Introduction by the Author." 1997).

Stories

I Don't Need You Anymore and Other Stories. 1967.

Reportage

Situation Normal. 1944.
"How the Nazi Trials Search the Hearts of All Germans." 1964.

Memoir

Salesman in Beijing. 1984.

Autobiography

Timebends: A Life. 1987.

Collections

Arthur Miller's Collected Plays. 1957.
Arthur Miller's Collected Plays. (Vol. 2) 1981.
The Portable Arthur Miller. 1971.
The Theater Essays of Arthur Miller. 1996.

Archives

No Villain. 1936.
They Too Arise (Revision of "No Villain"). 1937.
Honors at Dawn. 1937.

Secondary Sources

Abbotson, Susan C. W. "Issues of Identity in *Broken Glass*: A Humanist Response to a Postmodern World." *The Journal of American Drama and Theatre* 11, no. 1 (1999): 67–80.

———. "Re-Visiting the Holocaust for 1980's Television: Arthur Miller's *Playing for Time*." *American Drama* 8, no. 2 (1999): 61–78.

Antler, Joyce. " 'Three Thousand Miles Away': The Holocaust in Recent Works for the American Theater." In *The Americanization of the Holocaust*. Edited by Helene Flanzbaum. Baltimore: The Johns Hopkins University Press, 1999 125–141.

Brater, Enoch. "Ethics and Ethnicity in the Plays of Arthur Miller." In *From Hester Street to Hollywood*. Edited by Sarah Blacher Cohen. Bloomington: Indiana University Press, 1983, 123–136.

Brustein, Robert. "Arthur Miller's Mea Culpa." *The New Republic* 150. (8 February 1964): 26–28.

———. "Muddy Track at Lincoln Center." *The New Republic* 151. (26 December 1964): 26–27.

———. "Separated by a Common Playwright." *The New Republic* 210. (30 May 1994): 29–31.

Fenelon, Fania, with Marcelle Routier. *Playing for Time*. Translated by Judith Landry. New York: Atheneum, 1977.

Isser, Edward R. "Arthur Miller and the Holocaust." In *Stages of Annihilation: Theatrical Representations of the Holocaust*. Madison, Teaneck, N.J.: Fairleigh Dickinson University Press, 1997.

Kroll, Jack. "The Activist Actress" (Vanessa Redgrave and Arthur Miller's *Playing for Time*). *Newsweek* 96, (29 September 1980): 52–58.

Langer, Lawrence. "The Americanization of the Holocaust on Stage and Screen." In *From Hester Street to Hollywood*. Edited by Sarah Blacher Cohen. Bloomington: Indiana University Press, 1983, pp. 213–230.

Lob, Ladislaus. "Insanity in the Darkness: Anti-Semitic Stereotypes and Jewish Identity in Max Frisch's *Andorra* and Arthur Miller's *Focus*." *Modern Language Review* 92, no. 3 (1997): 545–558.

Mesher, David. "Arthur Miller's *Focus*: The First American Novel of the Holocaust?" *Judaism* 29, no. 4 (1980): 469–478.

Meyer, Kinereth. " 'A Jew Can Have a Jewish Face': Arthur Miller, Autobiography, and the Holocaust." *Prooftexts: A Journal of Jewish Literary History* 18, no. 3 (1998): 239–258.

Moss, Leonard. *Arthur Miller*. Boston: Twayne, 1980.

Nadel, Norman. "Miller Play One of Inward Vision." *New York World Telegram* and *The Sun*, January 24, 1964, in *New York Theatre Critics' Review* 25 (1964): 375.

Nelson, Benjamin. *Arthur Miller: Portrait of a Playwright*. New York: David McKay, 1970.

———. "Arthur Miller." In *Contemporary Jewish-American Dramatists and Poets: A Bio-Critical Sourcebook*. Edited by Joel Shatzky and Michael Taub. Westport, Conn.: Greenwood, 1999, 141–158.

"*Playing for Time* Draws Large Audience." *The New York Times*, (2 October 1980), Section C, 24.

Rahv, Philip. "Arthur Miller and the Fallacy of Profundity." *New York Review of Books* 3. (14 January 1965), 3–4.

Shales, Tom. "The Scar That Binds—*Playing for Time:* Redgrave's Triumph." *The Washington Post*, (30 September 1980), B1, B7.

Simon, John. "Review of *After the Fall*." *Hudson Review* 17 (1964). In *Critical Essays on Arthur Miller*. Edited by James J. Martine. Boston: G. K. Hall & Company, 1979, pp. 119–121.

Skloot, Robert. *The Darkness We Carry*: *The Drama of the Holocaust*. Madison, Wisc.: University of Wisconsin Press, 1988.

Welland, Dennis. *Miller the Playwright*. London and New York: Methuen, 1979.

Winer, Linda. "Arthur Miller's Morality Soaper." *New York Newsday*, April 25, 1994. In *New York Theatre Critics' Reviews* 55 (1994): 131–132.

Liana Millu

(1913–)

JUDITH KELLY

Liana Millu was born in Pisa in 1913. The Italianized surname, which is of Turkish derivation (Millul), is sometimes used in articles (see Spadi), although the author's immediate forebears were all of Italian origin. After leaving school Millu became a trainee journalist in Milan, an unusual occupation for a woman at that time. Following the imposition of the Fascist Racial Laws in 1938 she found that she was not permitted to enroll as a student at the University of Pisa. In her interview with Suzanne Branciforte she describes how she joined a partisan group based in Genoa, but explains that the group was betrayed by an infiltrator, and she herself was arrested in Venice in 1944. At that time northern Italy was under Nazi occupation. She was sent first to Fossoli internment camp near Modena, and later deported to Auschwitz once her Jewish identity became known. The other members of the partisan group, who were not Jewish, were sent to Mauthausen. Millu spent five months in Birkenau and was then sent to Ravensbrück.

Millu's testimonial writing was little known in Italy until the 1980s, when her documentary account of the deportations from Liguria to the death camps was published, followed shortly by the third reprinting of the account she had written in the few months following her return from the death camps, *Il fumo di Birkenau* (*Smoke over Birkenau*). Originally published in 1947 by a small Milanese publisher, and republished by Mondadori in the 1970s, it was not until the 1986 republication that it caught the public's attention. The text has recently been translated into German, having previously appeared in French, Norwegian, and Dutch. The American translation was the winner of the 1991 PEN Renato Poggioli Award for translation.

Millu was one of the few survivors in a position to recall the nature of women's experience of the death camps. In her interview with Milvia Spadi she indicates that women inmates retained a more optimistic outlook because of their pragmatic approach during their ordeal, but that many of them, after their return home, faced the additional burden of having their testimony denied or held to be unreliable because of the very fact that they had survived.

Millu attributes the fact that she was sent to Ravensbrück as one of the turns of fate that led to her survival because she was deported to Ravensbrück in October 1944, just as the severe Polish winter was approaching; she feared that she would not have survived in Birkenau. In addition, she had just contracted scabies, which would have led to her immediate removal to the gas chamber in Birkenau, but was treated medically in Ravensbrück (Branciforte, pp. 292–293).

In the immediate postwar period, Millu found herself without a home to return to or relatives to welcome her back. In addition, she had no paid employment and was unable to find work as a journalist. In her interview with Spadi, Millu recalls this period as a low point in her life, even worse than the period spent in the death camp because she had been stripped of hope (Spadi, p. 77). She settled in Genoa and became a teacher and writer.

In recent years Millu has attended conferences of survivors in Italy, as well as spending much time visiting schools and talking to young people about her experience.

Literary Output

Liana Millu's best-known work is *Il fumo di Birkenau* (*Smoke over Birkenau*), which gives an insight into conditions in the women's section in Auschwitz. This is not a chronological narrative, but rather comprises six chapters in which the author describes episodes relating to individuals encountered in the camp. The narrator herself is not the main focus of the stories, but provides the observing eye. The preface to the text was penned by Primo Levi, who writes that the condition of the women in Auschwitz-Birkenau was worse than that of the men, not only because of the heavy, degrading work they performed, but because the chimneys of the crematoria were at the center of the women's camp.

Millu tells Branciforte that she entered the women's camp, rather than being sent to the gas chamber, because a girl from Bologna whom she had met in Fossoli internment camp asked Millu to join her queue of people. They both entered the camp, whereas those behind them in the queue were turned around and sent to their death because the camp administration was unable to deal with the number of people arriving at that time (Branciforte, p. 292).

The extent of the women's ordeal is evoked by subtle references, such as the surprise and painful nostalgia created at the sight of chairs which, to prisoners who were only accustomed to sitting on the ground, conjured up thoughts of home and a former way of life.

In the first chapter, young Liana is assigned to a work detail where she reencounters seventeen-year-old Lily Marlene, thus nicknamed because of the song she constantly sings to herself while working. Having had her cards read by Madame Louise, who warns her to beware of a woman who intends her harm and predicts a change and a long journey, Lily finds the prediction is true when her jealous Kapo indicates to Mengele that Lily is no use for work, and her number is listed for the final journey to the gas chamber. Millu does not dwell upon the nature of Lily's eventual death, but rather evokes the tragedy of the young woman's fate through the description of her passivity when confronted by the Nazi selection process, as contrasted with her former vivacity, even in this place of death.

Millu recalls in her interview with Branciforte that Mia, the Kapo of "Lily Marlene," a German political prisoner, effectively saved her life at a later period by allowing Millu to rejoin her work detail (Branciforte, p. 298).

The other five chapters in *Il fumo di Birkenau* recount the suffering of other women prisoners in these inhumane conditions. There is Maria, who manages to hide the signs of her maturing pregnancy with the help of the women in her block, but who dies after having given birth, alone in filth, because her friends must attend roll call. There is also Bruna, who fears that her teenage son is to be sent to the gas chamber and calls out to him across the electric fence to which they both rush, their meeting ending in a fatal final embrace. Liana meets Zina in the infirmary, and is present at her death after a savage beating resulting from an attempt to aid the escape of a Russian compatriot, Ivan, who reminds her of the beloved husband who has almost certainly died in the camp. There is the terrible story of the Dutch sisters, Lotti who becomes an inmate of the camp's brothel in order to survive, and Gustine who subsequently disowns her sister. Finally, there is the tale of Lise, who wants to survive so that she can return to her husband and knows that to do so she may have to barter her body for extra food rations.

A parallel can be drawn between the early literary output of both Liana Millu and that of Primo Levi, insofar as both *Il fumo di Birkenau* and *Se questo è un uomo* (*If This Is a Man / Survival in Auschwitz*) are accounts that testify to the atrocity of Auschwitz, whereas both *I ponti di Schwerin* (The Bridges of Schwerin) and *La Tregua* (*The Truce / The Reawakening*) are stories of the individual's survival and the epic journey of return from the death camp. Both are accounts grounded firmly in biographical experience, but in which some details are altered or fictionalized. In the case of *I ponti di Schwerin*, fictionalized aspects predominate, and while Millu may draw upon memory to help weave her tale, it should not be read as autobiographical in nature.

The journey of the protagonist of *I ponti di Schwerin*, Elmina, a former Resistance fighter, is recounted from the point of her departure from the concentration camp to her return home in 1946. The tale is not only an account of her physical journey from Schwerin, the German city near Hamburg, which was the geographical location from which survivors traveled either to the East or to the West, but it is also a tale of her personal journey of psychological readaptation to the world outside the Nazi concentration camp. This is not a tale of a happy homecoming, and the bridges that she must cross are both physical and spiritual in nature. Memories of her life before deportation interweave with her experiences in this postliberation period. She remembers the man who saved her from suicide in her younger days, only to exploit her vulnerability and leave her pregnant; this episode can be compared to that of her rape by the unknown fellow survivor. The general theme of the novel might be understood as that of the countless bridges that must be crossed in the course of a lifetime.

In *Il fumo di Birkenau* there are some episodes and leitmotifs in common with those encountered in Primo Levi's testimony, such as the happiness Liana experiences when given the task of fetching the soup, as described in "Scheiss egal," which is a faint echo of Levi's transcendent moment while recalling Dante's canto of Ulysses for Pikolo while they both go to collect the soup ration. There are also more direct references to Dante's *Inferno*, just as in Levi's account: the grey, still, timeless nature of the camp, as described in "Lily Marlene"; the unchanging nature of the experience, as mentioned in "Scheiss egal"; and, in an additional parallel with the Ulysses episode in Levi's *Se questo è un uomo* Liana attempts to recall long passages of poetry, including canto VII of Dante's *Inferno* in which the hoarders and spendthrifts roll large rocks around, in order to divert her mind from the weight of the heavy stones she must carry in "L'ardua sentenza" (Hard Labor).

In the final paragraph of his preface to *Il fumo di Birkenau*, Primo Levi refers to the aura of sad lyricism of Millu's testimony as "mai inquinata dalla collera o dal lamento scomposto" ("never polluted by anger or by unseemly lament") (Florence: La Giuntina, 1998, p. 8) which echoes comments by many critics about the restraint shown in Levi's own testimony. The strength of Millu's testimony resides in its measured tones, rather than in angry denunciation.

Bibliography

Primary Sources

Il fumo di Birkenau (*Smoke over Birkenau*). 1947.

I ponti di Schwerin (*The Bridges of Schwerin*). 1978.

Dalla Liguria ai campi di sterminio (From Liguria to the Extermination Camps). 1980.

La camicia di Josepha (Josepha's Shirt). 1988.

"Guardare in un fondo dove strisciano serpenti" ("To Look into the Depths Where Serpents Crawl"). In *Il ritorno dai Lager* (The Return from the Concentration Camps). Edited by Alberto Cavaglion. Milan: FrancoAngeli, 1993, pp. 53–57.

Testimony in *"Meditate che questo è stato": Testimonianze di reduci dai campi di sterminio* ("Consider That This Has Been": Testimonies of Extermination Camp Returnees). Edited by Marco Abbina, et al. Federazione Giovanile Ebraica d'Italia (Jewish Youth Federation of Italy). Florence: La Giuntina, 1996, pp. 75–81.

Dopo il fumo. Sono il n. A5384 di Auschwitz Birkenau (After the Smoke. I Am Number A5384 in Auschwitz Birkenau). 1999.

Secondary Sources

Druker, Jonathan. "Jewish Novel: On the Holocaust and After." In *The Feminist Encyclopedia of Italian Literature*. Edited by Rinalda Russell. Westport, Conn. and London: Greenwood Press, 1997, pp. 165–168.

Interviews

Branciforte, Suzanne. "Writer's Desktop. Intervista con la storia: Una conversazione con Liana Millu" (Writer's Desktop. Interview with History: A Conversation with Liana Millu). *The Italianist*, no. 18 (1988): 289–304.

Spadi, Milvia. "La normalità del reduce." In *Le parole di un uomo. Incontro con Primo Levi* ("The Normality of the Returnee." In A Man's Words. A Meeting with Primo Levi). Rome: Di Renzo, 1997, pp. 33–38.

"About the Author." Smoke over Birkenau. Translated by Lynne Sharon Schwartz. Philadelphia, New York, Jerusalem: The Jewish Publication Society, 1991, pp. 199–202.

Czesław Miłosz

(1911–)

MONIKA ADAMCZYK-GARBOWSKA

Czesław Miłosz, the Nobel Prize recipient of 1980, was one of the first Polish gentile poets to respond to the destruction of the Jews taking place in front of their very eyes. Two of his poems, written in Warsaw after the failure of the ghetto uprising in spring 1943, are among the most often quoted and discussed poems on the Holocaust. The first one, "Campo dei Fiori" (often referred to as "Campo di Fiori"), was originally included in an underground anthology *Z otchłani* (From the Abyss) published in April 1944 in Warsaw by the Jewish National Committee. The poem was brought to the editors by the Polish Jewish writer Adolf Rudnicki, and was initially received by them rather critically as being too pessimistic. The other poem, "Biedny chrześcijanin patrzy na getto" (A poor Christian looks at the ghetto), was rejected for similar reasons, and additionally on the grounds that it could be unfavorably received by the Polish reader.

Two Significant Poems

"Campo dei Fiori" is a reflective philosophical poem with a subtle moralizing message in which the Christian martyr of sixteenth-century Rome is juxtaposed with the contemporary Jewish victims of the Nazi terror. Drawing a parallel between the two martyrdoms could be misleading, and one could argue that there is very little in common between the individual death of a Christian freethinker and the mass death of a whole people sentenced to annihilation by a mad ideology. However, the point of the parallel is not so much the comparison of Giordano Bruno to the Jews, as the similar responses of the crowds, in both cases indifferent to the respective tragedies. Supposedly Miłosz himself was not particularly happy with "Campo dei Fiori." A contemporary reader may voice reservations that the poem is too clear and obvious in its message and, considering the tragic context, perhaps too regular and aesthetically pleasing because of its slow-paced rhythm and soft imagery.

"Campo dei Fiori" is internationally known while "Biedny chrześcijanin patrzy na getto" made the greatest impact in Poland itself, although not when it was first written but more than forty years after its creation by means of an article written by the esteemed critic Jan Błoński for the Cracow-based Catholic weekly *Tygodnik Powszechny*. This can be, to some extent, explained by the political situation in Poland and the fact that for many years Miłosz was banned there. The article made such an impact in the country and abroad that commentators, while addressing the issue of Polish-Jewish relations, sometimes refer to pre-Błoński and post-Błoński times. The title of the article, "Poor Poles Look at the Ghetto," is a paraphrase of the semi-ironic title of the poem, which was first published in 1945 (together with the reprinted "Campo dei Fiori") in the first collection of poetry by Miłosz after the war. It is more intense than "Campo dei Fiori" and uses surrealist images. The opening scene is that of total, apocalyptic destruction of a city, accompanied by the tearing of all material substance, of trampling and breaking, of sizzling fire leading to the collapse of everything. Bees and ants move industriously among human remains, "building around the honeycomb of lungs" and "white bone" (*Polin* 2 [1987], pp. 334–335). After that terrifying, feverish image, we have a short pause—a depiction of silence, a wasteland "with one leafless tree" (pp. 334–335). It is in this wasteland that an ominous figure appears, that of the guardian mole who, equipped with a little red lantern, makes his way among the bodies, touches them, counts and identifies the ashes. The narrator of the poem, who describes himself as "a Jew of the New Testament," expresses his fear of the guardian mole who resembles a biblical prophet and may include the "poor Christian" among the uncircumcised "helpers of death" (pp. 334–335).

The most frequent reading of this poem is as a manifestation of the sense of guilt and bad conscience of Polish Christians for not helping enough or being indifferent to the plight of the Jews in the Warsaw ghetto in particular, and Jewish victims of the Nazis in general. Nevertheless, in his reading, Błoński refers to Miłosz himself, reminding us that the poet declined to answer who actually was represented by the guardian mole and claimed that he had written it "spontaneously." Błoński says that if we accept this explanation,

> the poem would be a direct expression of the terror which speaks through images, as is often the case in dreams and also in art. It makes tangible something which is not fully comprehended that was and perhaps still is, in other people's as much as in the poet's own psyche, but in an obscure, blurred, muffled shape. When we read such a poem, we understand ourselves better, since that which had been evading us until now is made palpable (p. 327).

The critic applies his interpretation to Polish Jewish relations during the war and after, up to the present time. Traditionally poets, the most outstanding among them being called the national bards, have played a very important role in Poland, often appealing to the conscience of the people. While Romantic poets such as Adam Mickiewicz or Juliusz Słowacki performed such a role at the time of the partitions of the Polish-Lithuanian Commonwealth in the late eighteenth century and later during the periods of political oppression, Miłosz can be treated as a moralist of today. To paraphrase his words from another poem, "Dedication," poetry "does not save nations or people," but can be at least heard by those who listen (*Selected Poems*, New York: The Seabury Press, 1973, p. 45).

While "Poor Christian" gave vent to various more or less sophisticated interpretations, there has been a tendency to read "Campo dei Fiori" almost literally as a description of a concrete scene, perhaps because its message is so obvious and because there was really a merry-go-round (also mentioned by a number of other writers) near the walls of the Warsaw ghetto in April 1943 just before Easter. Gradually the merry-go-round has grown to the rank of a compelling symbol, but as Błoński notes, Miłosz himself wondered

> whether there really was such a street in Warsaw. It existed and, in another sense, it did not. It did exist because there were indeed merry-go-rounds in the vicinity of the ghetto. It didn't because in other parts of town, at other moments Warsaw was quite different. It was not my intention to make accusations (pp. 322–323).

Apart from this explanation of a historical and ideological nature, Miłosz also looked self-critically at his own poem considering it as too journalistic.

Other Works

Soon after the war, Miłosz referred to the Jewish tragedy in the poem "Child of Europe" (1946) where he addressed "the child of Europe" as among others "inheritor of synagogues filled with the wailing of a wronged people" and alluded to the situation of those who survived and whose very fact of survival makes them indirectly "helpers of death" (*Collected Poems 1931–1987*, New York: The Ecco Press, 1986, p. 86). In some of his later poetry Miłosz also refers to the destruction of the Jews, as in *Traktat poetycki* (*Treatise on Poetry*, 1956) in which he included powerful images of a dying Jew pushed into a clay-pit and of Jewish maidens whose names slowly fade and freeze in the air.

In one of his essays, "Ruins and Poetry," Miłosz talks about the Holocaust and its representation in art. He states that "probably in no language other than Polish are there so many terrifying poems, documents of the Holocaust" but "with few exceptions, these are poems that survived and whose authors did not" (*The Witness of Poetry*, Cambridge, Mass.: Harvard University Press, 1985, pp. 83–84). Miłosz does not mention any names here but this category may include Władysław Szlengel or Krzysztof Kamil Baczyński. He also refers to postwar poetry on the Holocaust and states that in most cases "the subject is beyond the authors' capabilities and rises up before them like a wall. The poems are considered good primarily because they move us with their noble intentions" (*The Witness of Poetry*, p. 84). His doubt concerning "whether certain zones of reality can ever be the subject of poems or novels" makes one think of Theodor Adorno's words about the impossibility of writing poetry with the awareness of what happened during the war (p. 84).

Miłosz's position is very characteristic of a group of Polish gentile poets and writers who together can be called witnesses, direct or vicarious, in contrast to Polish Jewish artists, the victims and survivors. The most characteristic feature of gentile witnesses is that even if they try to express their empathy with Jews, the question as to what extent Christians passed the test in humane behavior while forced to witness the destruction of the people to whom they had earlier harbored ambivalent if not hostile feelings frequently surfaces.

Works in General

From the formal point of view Miłosz's poems on the Holocaust can be placed in the wider context of his poetry in general: that is, catastrophic, ironic, with a moral message; poetry of social protest and penetrating visions. What especially predestined him to take a stand so early might have been, apart from his sensitivity as a poet, his upbringing in eastern Poland, where various ethnic groups (Poles, Jews, Lithuanians, and others) had coexisted in a fairly tolerant atmosphere, as well as his leftist views and aversion to Fascism and extreme nationalism. Born in Szetejnie (present-day Lithuania), he attended a high school in Wilno (Vilnius) where he later studied at the King Stefan Batory University. It was in Wilno that he made his debut as a poet in a student periodical in 1930 and where he cofounded the Zagary poetic group. After the war he was in diplomatic service with the Communist government, but in 1951 he decided to seek political asylum, which led him, via France, to the United States where he taught Slavic literatures at the University of California, Berkeley.

Considering how extremely prolific Miłosz has been as a poet, essayist, prose writer, critic, and translator (from Hebrew among other languages), one might voice an argument that Jewish themes with a focus on the Holocaust constitute barely a fraction of his writings. The artist's seeming restraint, however, may be somewhat in agreement with his belief that "next to the atrocious facts, the very idea of literature seems indecent" ("Ruins and Poetry," in *The Witness of Poetry*, p. 84).

Bibliography

Primary Sources

Ocalenie (*Rescue*). 1945.
Zdobycie władzy (*The Seizure of Power*). 1953.
Śuiatio dzienne (Daylight). 1953.
Zniewolony umysl (*The Captive Mind*). 1953.
Dolina Issy (*The Issa Valley*). 1955.
Traktat poetycki (*Treatise on Poetry*). 1957.
Gucio zaczarowany (The enchanted Gucio). 1965.
Wiersze (Poems). 1967.
Rodzinna Europa (*Native Realm: A Search for Self-Definition*). 1968.
Widzenia nad Zatoka San Francisco (*Visions from San Francisco Bay*). 1969.
Selected Poems. 1973.
Utwory poetyckie (Poems). 1976.
Emperor of the Earth. Modes of Eccentric Vision. 1977.
Ziemia Ulro (*The Land of Ulro*). 1977.
Bells in Winter. 1978.
Gdzie wschodzi słońce i kedy zapada (Where the sun rises and where it sets). 1980.
Nobel Lecture. 1980.
Człowiek wśród skorpionów (Man among scorpions). 1982.
The Witness of Poetry. 1983.
Osobmy zeszyt (*The Separate Notebooks*). 1984.
Ogród nauk (The Garden of Knowledge). 1986.
Collected Poems, 1931–1987. 1988.
Rok myśliwego (*A Year of the Hunter*). 1990.
Zaczynajâc od moich ulic (*Beginning with My Streets: Essays and Recollections*). 1990.
Provinces. 1991.
The Unattainable Earth. 1992.
Wyprawa w dwudziestolecie (A journey into the twenty years between the wars). 1992.
Wypisy z ksiâg użytecznych (Extracts from useful books). 1994.
Facing the River. 1995.
Piesek przydrożny (*Road-Side Dog*). 1997.
Życie na wyspach (A life on the isles). 1997.
Abecadio Mitosza (*Mitosz's ABC's*). 1997.
Inne Abe sadto (A Different ABC). 1998.
To (This). 2000.
New and Collected Poems 1931–2001. 2001.
To Begin Where I Am: The Selected Essays. 2001.
Druga przestrzeń (Another dimension). 2002.

Secondary Sources

Adamczyk-Garbowska, Monika. "A New Generation of Voices in Polish Holocaust Literature." *Prooftexts: A Journal of Jewish Literary History* 3 (1989): 273–287.
Błoński, Jan. "The Poor Poles Look at the Ghetto" (Appendix with "Campo dei Fiori," "A Poor Christian Looks at the Ghetto," and "Dedication"). *Polin: A Journal of Polish-Jewish Studies* 2 (1987) 321–336.
Davie, Donald. *Czeslaw Milosz and the Insufficiency of Lyric*. Cambridge: Harvard University Press, 1986.
Fiut, Aleksander. *The Eternal Moment. The Poetry of Czeslaw Milosz*. Berkeley: University of California Press, 1990.
Gömöri, George. *Polish and Hungarian Poets of the Holocaust*. The Polish Studies Center, Bloomington, Ind.: Indiana University Press, 1986.
Gross, Natan. *Poeci i Szoa*. Sosnowiec: Offmax, 1993.
Maciejewska, Irena. *Mêczêństwo i zagłada Żydów w zapisach literatury polskiej*. Warszawa: Krajowa Agencja Wydawnicza, 1988.
Milanczówna, Elzbieta. " 'Campo di Fiori' i rzeczywistość." *Odra* 10 (1996): 28–30.
Vendler, Helen, " 'A Lament in Three Voices.' " *The New York Review of Books* 9 (31 May 2001): 27–31.

MARGA MINCO

(1920–)

JOHAN P. SNAPPER

THE LITERARY TREATMENT of the Jewish persecution in the Netherlands runs the gamut from Nazi propaganda and preparation for the Final Solution, the collaboration and resistance of the Dutch citizenry, the diaries of Anne Frank and Etty Hillesum, the paradoxical role of the Jewish Council, the perplexing activities on the part of the SS and the Jewish overseers at the notorious transit camp Westerbork, the plight of returning and surviving Holocaust victims, and the burdensome guilt shared by the children of the war, including the offspring of murdered Jews and the traitors who facilitated the atrocities in the first place. Dutch literature is replete with moving accounts and continuing evaluations of the Holocaust. By and large these works fill the reader with horror, bafflement, and awe. It is little wonder, for whereas the *Shoah* claimed the lives of two out of every three Jews in Europe, the ratio in the Netherlands was three out of four, the highest percentage on the mainland.

In apparent contrast to the historic magnitude of the Holocaust in Holland, and the emotional undertones that accompany the literary treatment of it in most works, stands the sober, minimalist prose of writer Marga Minco.

Life

Marga Minco was born in the city of Breda in the southern part of the Netherlands in 1920. She was the daughter of orthodox Jewish parents, but, along with her brother and sister, never identified with Judaism, at least as a child; but, to use her own words, the war gradually turned her into a true Jew. The only survivor of her family—her parents and brother perished in Sobibor, her sister in Auschwitz—she settled in Amsterdam after the war and had two daughters with the poet Bert Voeten, who died in December 1992.

Minco's oeuvre includes five novels, four of which have been translated into more than a dozen languages, including English. They are *Bitter Herbs* (1957), *An Empty House* (1966), *The Fall* (1983), and *The Glass Bridge* (1986). All of them, in addition to her 1997 work, *Nagelaten dagen* (The Remaining Days), deal directly or indirectly with the Holocaust as experienced in the Netherlands. Her remaining work consists of some thirty stories, sixteen of which deal with the Holocaust; most of them are available in numerous languages. She has also written a number of children's stories as well as radio and television plays.

Role in Dutch Literature

The role of Marga Minco is something of an enigma in Dutch literature. On one hand, she is one of Holland's best known and most interviewed writers; several of her works number among the all-time Dutch best sellers. Her novels, especially *Bitter Herbs*, are required reading in all secondary Dutch curricula, where she is among the students' favorites, it is often joked, because her novels are "so nice and thin." She is also Holland's most translated writer after Anne Frank. On the other hand, with few exceptions, higher education has, until recently, paid scant attention to her works, and the rest of the world is largely ignorant of their existence.

Perhaps Minco herself has contributed to this irony, as she labeled the work that first put her on the literary map, *Bitter Herbs*, "a little chronicle." The modifier "little" implies not only that the novel is brief, but that it represents a relatively small selection of recollections that she has savored from the war years. Inasmuch as it grapples with one of history's greatest catastrophes, the irony is clear.

Bitter Herbs

When Minco finished *Bitter Herbs*, she was thirty-six years old. The historical period covered in the book took place when the author was between twenty and twenty-five, while the narrator's age ranges from fourteen to eighteen. Minco consciously portrayed the narrator as a child in order to underscore the guilelessness of a child contrasted with the blame of the adult world. Indeed, that is precisely the effect she creates and for which critics globally have praised her. Gerrit Kouwenaar, arguably Holland's greatest living poet, who has known Minco since the end of the war, is impressed by the authenticity inherent in the "smallness" of *Bitter Herbs*.

> It is precisely the unmistakable "smallness" which characterizes this chronicle in virtually every respect, that makes the book for me so oppressively true. The naiveté and the incomprehension that the writer and her family members manifest in the face of their fate, are in fact still present in the writer herself. And this is, I believe, precisely the stamp of this book's authenticity, the reason why these stories that just barely seem to touch the unfolding [tragedy] behind them, thereby do so all the more convincingly (Kouwenaar, p. 27; translation is mine).

The German critic Gabriele Wohmann characterizes the narrator's voice as the unsentimental voice of a child, whose simplicity achieves a powerful effect, which can only fill the non-Jewish reader with deep shame (p. 32). The Englishman Storm Jameson puts a more psychological spin on it. He contrasts the child's detachment with the emotional impact on the reader: "The story would be as unbearable as it is ordinary . . . if it were not for the clear cool voice in which she tells it, like a child talking, with a child's dreadful acceptance of cruelty and treachery. A voice to which we shut our ears at our peril" (p. 36).

The stories in *Bitter Herbs* chronicle an extensive and frightful range of events, observations, and reflections, including the invasion by the Germans and the mass evacuation of the narrator's home town; the increasing denial of human rights for Jews; the arrival of the dreaded yellow stars they were forced to wear; the day the family was officially photographed (for posterity); the arrest of the narrator's only sister; the summons to the labor camp; the evacuation of the parents to the Amsterdam ghetto; and the neighbors' eagerness to take the family's possessions for ostensible "safekeeping." Poignant are the accounts of the narrator's joining her parents in the "*Judenviertel*," the strange Sabbath celebration in the ghetto, the purging of a Jewish retirement home, the arrest of her parents and her own escape. The narratives include a sensitive reflection on family and strangers on the Night of Passover; the role of the Resistance, and the narrator's visits to her guilt-laden surviving uncle after the war. All these recollections are recorded objectively. Indeed, the narrator leaves it to the reader to place them in their proper historic context and evaluate them.

Use of Irony

Instead of imbuing the stories with emotion, Minco creates much of the punch of her prose through irony, which breaks the illusion of reality, a process in which the artificiality of art is deliberately articulated, in some of her children's stories, in the form of humorous postscripts, in which she provides editorial comments on the plot. She also uses an "irony of fate"—a reversal of expectations.

Irony turns Minco's relatively simple prose into a perceptive exposé of Dutch society (including her fellow Jews), as well as the Germans and collaborators, before, during, and after the war. Probably the first example of such irony is also her most pervasive, running like a dark thread throughout her prose: a persistent sense of optimism on the part of Dutch Jews that sharply contrasts with the reality to which the reader is privy. Minco's fictional personages, who often closely resemble the writer's own family members, are in denial, pretending that life is still normal, that the fate of the German and Polish Jews would never befall them, and that conditions are never as bad as the rumors have it. Minco paints her characters as if they willingly substitute a persistent fantasy for what they must have known to be the truth.

A case in point is the very first chapter of *Bitter Herbs*, where Minco describes the outbreak of the war by mentioning that the entire city of Breda, a Dutch military garrison, had to evacuate because the Germans were coming. Thousands of residents fled in the direction of the Belgian border, while bullets were fired from both sides of the road on which they made their escape. Their cue to return to their homes, however, came from the German soldiers driving along the road—precisely those from whom they fled in the first place! When they returned, the narrator's father reassured everyone that no harm would come to the family and that their daughter Bettie would be even safer because she lived in Amsterdam. The irony is heightened by the fact that the reader, aided by historical hindsight, knows better. After all, Amsterdam was the focal point of the Nazi raids on Dutch Jews.

An even more vivid example of the irony of fate is the scene in the story "Stars," where irony emanates from the baffling conduct of the whole family. The father comes home with a package of yellow stars of David with the word "Jew" printed on it. There is no expression of sorrow, disgust, or anger in his voice; rather, he pretends to bring them all presents with the compliments of their generous German friends, who gave him as many stars as he wanted. The family in turn reacts as if they were the beneficiaries of a special fashion prize. They eagerly sew the insignias on their outer clothing. The narrator, who compares the stars to "little windmills that could begin to turn any moment" is elated; marking this day a festive occasion, "just like the queen's birthday"—the Dutch national holiday—she exults in an expression of ultimate irony. (Extending the irony is the fact that Queen Wilhelmina had already fled to London.) The chapter ends with a further ironic gnarl when the narrator's brother Dave decides not to wear the stars until the next day, because he—unlike them—wants to be "normal" a little longer: "No," he says, "if I can, I'd like to be ordinary, for today." When he leaves, the rest of the star-bedecked family considers him the odd one for not wearing the compulsory star: "When he opened the garden gate and walked down the road, the five of us gaped after him as if there was something very extraordinary about him" (p. 17). Such subtle ironic understatement distinguishes Minco as an astute observer of human tragedy.

The finest example of romantic irony is provided by the story "The Day My Sister Married" (1970), where Minco turns up her use of irony a notch or two. One of the principal themes of the story is the collective delusion of normalcy. Since their forced evacuation from their own home, the Minco family has been living temporarily with the narrator's brother Dave and his wife, Lotte. This was to be the place where Bettie would be married. It is May 1942, shortly after all Dutch Jews were required to wear the yellow stars. Nevertheless, it was "a beautiful month to get married," according to a neighbor. Although most of the relatives were afraid to attend, it was important for those who did to pretend that things were the way they would have been in the good old days. The house—always a potent motif in Minco's works—had to look as "normal" as possible, especially for Minco's mother:

> "I had the strong feeling," the narrator says, "that she wanted to pretend as if nothing had changed, as if she would have a house full of guests. She would again walk through the rooms and imagine how it had always been: furniture put aside, long rows of chairs, tables shoved together, everywhere vases with flowers" (p. 83).

But the irony of this story does not fully come into focus through the family's behavior. Each one, after all, was quite aware that they were somehow creating a fantasy of normalcy. The wedding served the purpose of play therapy, as if this were a last performance before the final curtain would fall. Even the normally sober Bettie, the bride, agreed to play along: "Did you really think that we would have gotten married with such a hullabaloo under normal circumstances? No way!" (p. 87).

Where then does Minco provide the ironic twist in a story in which the fable itself consists of so many twists between reality and pretense? The answer lies in a game that takes place within the narrator herself, which trumps the game the others are playing. Whereas the family turns its back on reality and devises a game of make-believe in order to be able to participate in the spectacle, the narrator's game consists of deliberately juggling fantasy and reality. Unfortunately the family's game of pretense is short lived and becomes a foil to tragic inevitability. This is seen in the beautiful and unusual bridal bouquet of Japanese flowers (that look like little stars), which loses most of its blossoms on the wedding day. The wedding, with its promise of living happily ever after is a fairy tale. The wedding ceremony itself reminds the narrator of a popular but ambiguous game that Dutch children like to play: "*In Holland staat een huis*" (There is a house in Holland). In this children's game participants recite a song with a number of stanzas: a man chooses a wife, then the wife a child, then the child a doll, and so forth. And in the last verse all participants joyfully set fire to the house. The wedding, too, is an innocent and merry game, but without a happy ending. It turns deadly. Within a single paragraph, in which Minco once again demonstrates the power of her minimalist prose, she weaves play and reality into one brilliant artistic and ironic tapestry:

> It was as if we wanted to screen the bride and groom from the outside world through the circle we formed. I thought of the game we children used to play: "There is a house in Holland." The master chooses a wife, my sister, of course. Together they are standing in the circle and we continue reciting the words of the game, about the child and the maid and the servant and all the things that are chosen after that, till finally the house is burned down. The face of my sister was hidden under the veil, through which I could not see her reactions. . . . And after that I had no more opportunity to discuss it with her. Three weeks later, in the first pogrom in Amsterdam-South she and Hans were taken from their home and carried off. (*Breda. Een herinnering in proza en een zeefdruk*, p. 90).

In Minco's work "being in denial" is not exclusively a Jewish proclivity but a tendency among much of the Dutch population, albeit with different motivations. The story "Homeward Journey" ("Thuisreis") (1992) is a case in point. It is an autobiographical account of Minco's memorable return to Breda after the war, a recollection of time and place, replete with familiar memories. At the conclusion of the visit, the narrator meets an old neighbor whose postwar portrayal involves an ironic mirror image of Minco's fictional family during the war. However, where the Jews are portrayed in an innocent, perhaps desperate denial, by claiming that everything was really quite "normal," the non-Jewish neighbor is pictured as being in calloused denial, unwilling to acknowledge the disappearance of his former Jewish neighbors. Once again Minco's subtle irony functions as a pungent indictment of her fellow Dutchmen. The story ends with the passage: "Somewhere a door opened and out came an old neighbor, who shook my hand and asked how I was and my family. I said I was fine and that I found the street quite changed. Oh no, I was wrong. He smiled. 'Everything is still the same. Everybody is still living here' " (*Breda, Een herinnering, in proza en een zeefdruk*, translation by Johan P. Snapper, 1992).

Symbolism and Titles

The titles of many of Minco's stories have a symbolic function. They usually consist of a noun or pronoun that captures the essence of the story in a single image or leitmotif, reminiscent of the Dutch *Dingsymbool* (literally, a "thing symbol"), similar to the central image that nineteenth-century German critic Paul Heyse considered essential to the novella. Although Minco uses one such dominant image, it is less obtrusive than Heyse would require. Her implementation of this image comes closer to a German tradition, that of the *Dinggedicht* (literally "thing poem"), often associated with the poetry of Rainer Maria Rilke (e.g., "The Panther"). Nearly every story in *Bitter Herbs* is entitled with a concrete symbol, such as "The Little Bottle," "The Girl," "The Men," "The Crossroad," and "The Tram Stop." While most of these titles capture some of the irony that inevitably characterizes the particular story, some of them are explicitly ironic.

A fine example of titular irony is the story "Cloister Drive" ("Kloosterlaan"), which is the actual name of a street in Breda. Here, long before the war, Minco recalls jeering Catholic children with their antisemitic epithets, accusing their Jewish playmates of having crucified Christ, of whom the narrator had never heard. Catholic parents also forbade their children to set foot in Jewish houses. Through this title, Minco links the distant antisemitism in Germany with that from deep within the local community. She actually has her father admit, inadvertently, that the problem was not only of recent vintage, but dated back to his own childhood. Thus Minco shows that while the Jews were aware of the subtle antisemitic sentiments on the part of the Dutch population, they were in denial as far as the blatant persecution by the Nazis was concerned. Beyond that, there is an implied specific indictment of the Christian community. In a collective sense "Cloister Drive," with its specific Catholic flavor, is now a metonymy for all the other treacherous streets in Minco's work.

Often Minco uses titular irony by making the titles ambiguous. In the story "Storing," which can be translated as both "static" and "disturbance," the narrator and a woman at whose house she was once briefly in hiding—a thoroughly disagreeable person—are about to be interviewed on radio. However, static makes it impossible to proceed, much to the relief of the narrator, who was clearly "disturbed" not by the "static," but by the self-righteous woman. Even more frequently, Minco uses titles for her narratives that are implicitly false, and denote the opposite of what the story suggests. Such is the case in the beautiful story "Bitter Herbs," with its reference to Passover, but also in stories like "Homecoming" ("Thuiskomst") and "The Return" ("Terugkeer," 1965), where the narrator or the main personages find that the surviving Jews could never really go home again.

In the case of "The Return," a story about a husband and wife who spent the war years in hiding, Minco's irony reaches much further. After the war the couple returns, only to find that strangers are now living in their home, their friends are gone, their children will never return because they were killed in concentration camps, and that their beloved synagogue has been converted into a paper factory. Notwithstanding these horrendous obstacles, Mr. and Mrs. Goldstijn try to find a new life, a future in spite of a broken past, but their path toward recovery runs into a deadly roadblock.

In one of Minco's most ironic *tours de force*, "The Return" refers not merely to the return of two straggling Jewish refugees, nor to the children who won't be returning, but also to the return of the enemy, who seems to have the last word after all. As changed as the Goldstijns's life has become, the enemy has come back in stubbornly unaltered form. Like an echo of the old Nazis who first uprooted the family more than ten years earlier, a new neighbor has moved in. Deep into the night, the hissing sounds of the hated Horst Wessel song, "*die Fahne hoch, die Reihen fest geschlossen, S.A. marschiert*," the party song of the German National Socialists, haunt them once more. The fact that this takes place shortly after Mr. Goldstijn has begun to accept the present, and at precisely the point when he has resolved to establish friendly relations with the whistling newcomer (who keeps them awake at night), represents yet another twist to the ironic ending of the story:

> The whistling sounded muffled, almost hissing, as if it was not supposed to be heard by anyone. Why would that man whistle the Horst Wessel song in the middle of the night? He felt himself becoming warm, sweat appeared on his forehead, in his neck, on his back. Did he whistle it because it had accidentally entered his mind? But who would remember this particular song? He could be no older than his mid-thirties. An ex-Nazi, only recently released? (*The Other Side*, p. 80).

The ignominious rallying cry of yesteryear emanating from the shed below takes on a prophetic dimension. The past that Goldstijn has been struggling with for years has caught up with him. While Goldstijn looks at his watch to see what time it is, Minco reiterates that the horrible past, permanently carved on the streets with their returning travelers and on the houses with their displaced inhabitants lives on in the present. No matter what Goldstijn's watch says, the hands of Minco's clock show that the past and present are in collusion, and that in a profound sense it is both earlier and, therefore, also later than it seems. In the final analysis, "The Return" represents her most explicitly pessimistic and ironic view of history.

Marga Minco is undoubtedly one of Holland's least philosophical major writers, and a minimalist in every sense of the word. But her simple prose is so imbued with irony that it veils a powerful impact. Two of Minco's most pervasive and dominant leitmotifs, the images of domesticity and travel, represented respectively by such pregnant emblems as the empty house and the hazardous road, serve as ironic metaphors. Some of Minco's works deal explicitly with one or the other (the novels *An Empty House* and *The Glass Bridge*), or both, such as the story "Homecoming"; nearly all the other stories do so implicitly. Even in her children's stories, the theme of leaving and returning home—or not—is prominent, but this is not immediately evident because Minco hides these themes behind objects that function metonymically or as a synecdoche. In Minco's prose these concrete images have a wider application and are, in effect, ironic metaphors of Hitler's Final Solution.

Because much of the travel in Minco's oeuvre is on foot, it is little wonder that she places particular emphasis on the feet. Nowhere is this more striking than in *Bitter Herbs*, especially in the moving chapter "In the Basement." The narrator and her parents are sitting below street level behind grated windows in the Jewish ghetto of Amsterdam, looking at the feet of passers-by on the sidewalk and the street. While the narrator does not explicitly say so, a raid seems to be in the making. In the image of the oppressive boots of the enemy, contrasted with the scurrying but reluctant shoes of his doomed victims, and alluding to the "road" these innocent feet will be forced to travel, Minco emblematizes the Holocaust in a nutshell:

> At first, nobody passed. But after a few minutes we saw big, black boots appear, jackboots, which made a loud clicking noise as they walked. They came from the house to the right of us, and they went obliquely past our window to the edge of the pavement, where a car or a truck was standing.
>
> We also saw ordinary shoes, walking along beside the boots. Men's brown shoes, a pair of pumps worn at the heels, and sports shoes. Two pairs of black boots stepped to the vehicle slowly, as if they had something heavy to carry.
>
> "There are a lot of people living in the house next door," Father whispered. "It's a convalescent home, and there are quite a few sick folk among them."
>
> A couple of beige-colored child's boots stopped in front of our window. The toes were turned slightly inwards, and the lace of one little boot was slightly darker than the lace of the other. "That's little Lizzie," my mother said softly. "She grows so fast. Those boots are much too small for her already." The child raised one foot, and the other boot jumped to and fro in front of our window as if she was playing hopscotch. Until a pair of black boots came up. . . . They were well polished and had straight heels. . . . The boots started to move, and we watched first the left one moving off, then the right one, then the left one, then the right one, away from the window, on to the left.
>
> At the house to the left of ours we heard the bell ring. (*Bitter Herbs*, 53f.)

This jarring image of shoes embarking on their last journey is worth a thousand words and as powerful as the piles of shoes—thousands of them—in the Holocaust museums in Washington and elsewhere.

Finally, an equally poignant leitmotif of Marga Minco's prose is that of the rucksack, required of all Jewish deportees to the Dutch transit camp Westerbork and beyond. It symbolizes not only the Jews en route to their merciless end, but also their homelessness. Thus Minco's characters, always on the run, must carry their home, or what is left of it, on their backs, like turtles and snails. The novel *An Empty House* develops this tragic process, in which a disenfranchised young hitchhiker is en route from her underground address to recently liberated Amsterdam. Her family and her home have been destroyed; all she has left is the contents of her backpack. Try as she may, the guilt-laden woman is unable to adjust to life without her loved ones, so she finally joins them in death, by jumping out of a speeding train and leaving behind the proverbial rucksack, signifying all she had and did not have. The emblematic irony lies in the ambiguity of the rucksack, once associated with freedom and vacation travel; now the synecdoche of the hunted and dispossessed.

The principal characters of *An Empty House* are two young women whom fate seems to have hurled together through a series of remarkable coincidences. They are totally different in looks and temperament, but they come from similar families, all of whom have perished in a concentration camp. One, deeply depressed, has spent most of the war in hiding. Minco calls her "Yona," the female equivalent of "Jonah in the whale," she says marking her as the quintessential "underdiver" (*onderduiker*), as the Dutch refer to people in hiding during the war. Even her aspirations after the war are devoted to the past (she works for a Jewish war and remembrance foundation).

The other, in many ways her alter ego, is Sepha, the narrator of the story. More attractive and energetic than Yona, she seeks to counter her own grief by indulging in pleasure, but also by looking for security in the form of a house for herself and her husband in the hope of starting a new life for their fragile marriage. Yet, ironically, what binds the two women is what they no longer have: their family homes in Amsterdam, even as empty houses. What is left to them are ruins of buildings—the only things standing are the walls, or simply the walls facing the street. On separate occasions, both Sepha and Yona cannot resist placing their hands through the mail slot in one of these grotesque façades, and reacting with horror at the wind-propelled emptiness emerging from the hole in the single deceptive wall.

Much of Minco's prose deals with two women yoked together by coincidence or fate. Often the other woman is the narrator's martyred older sister, about whom she usually writes in the form of childhood recollections. Sometimes these accounts also appear in the present tense, as if Bettie were still alive, as in Minco's published dreams. In *Nagelaten dagen* (1997) (The Remaining Days) Minco adds a future dimension to this sibling bond by means of a cherished memory book she had made for and presented to Bettie on the occasion of her wedding more than fifty years ago. The story deals with the scrapbook's miraculous odyssey from Amsterdam to Jerusalem to Santa Barbara, California, where the narrator traveled to retrieve it from an uncooperative last "owner" and take it home with her. Bettie was home at last.

In *The Glass Bridge* the close relationship between two women is that of the narrator and a deceased non-Jewish Flemish woman, whom she did not know, but whose identity she had formally assumed. After the war the narrator travels to Belgium to learn about the benefactress's true identity and learn of her life and tragic demise. In the process of discovery, she senses a true bond with the stranger and can once again reclaim her own name.

For Minco's characters, nothing will ever be over. This is one reason why, in *An Empty House*, all recollections and flashbacks are written in the present tense, instead of the narrative past. Things are only over when they are terminated naturally. The Jewish houses did not die a natural death any more than the people who lived in them. Consequently, they remain unresolved issues that continue to be part of the lives of the survivors.

Such examples of the irony of fate present themselves to the discerning reader who must often read between the lines to complete Minco's deceptively simple narratives. If the rucksacks (or suitcase, in Sepha's case) of the two wandering women in *An Empty House* function as a kind of mobile home, which is later destined to be abandoned, never is the rucksack a more ironic image than when it is worn by those who have no inkling that it marks them as being doomed. In a subtle passage in the chapter "Lepel Street" *(Bitter Herbs)* we witness a tragedy in the making. At the point of being arrested herself, the narrator spots a little boy coming through a nearby door: "He had a rucksack in one hand, and a piece of bread and treacle in the other. A brown smear ran down over his chin. From beyond an open door I heard heavy footsteps. . . ." When the soldier finally lets her go—she lived on a different street and her turn would come later—the narrator looks again at the boy and soberly observes: "The little boy in the doorway had finished his bread and treacle, and was tying the rucksack on his back" (*Bitter Herbs*, p. 69).

Conclusions

In the final analysis, the force of Minco's prose lies not so much in what she reports, but what she leaves out. By assuming the persona of an innocent child or a rather naïve but very observant adult, the narrator conjures up suggestions that are paradoxically empowered through her diminutive images. It may on one hand have been the only way the author could handle her very personal loss, but it is, on the other hand, an inventive exposé of the baffling contradictions of people and cultures that regress toward a dismal future. In Minco's treatment of the Holocaust the homes are mostly empty or inhabited by strangers and the roads seem to lead nowhere. Her streets are void of happy wayfarers; filled only with the memories of the doomed that died next to the doomed who survived. It is hard to say who is better off.

Bibliography

Primary Sources

Het bittere kruid. Een kleine kroniek (*Bitter Herbs*: *A Little Chronicle*). 1957.

Een leeg huis (*An Empty House*). 1966.

"Terugkeer." In *Verzamelde verhalen 1951–1981*. ("The Return." In *The Other Side*) 1982.

"De dag dat mijn zuster trouwde." In *Verzamelde verhalen 1951–1981* ("The Day My Sister Married." In *The Other Side*). 1982.

De val (*The Fall*). 1983.

De glazen brug (*The Glass Bridge*). *1983*.

"Thuisreis." In *Breda; Een herinnering in proza en een zeefdruk* (van Jaap de Vries) (Homeward Journey. In Breda: A Recollection in Prose and in Silk Screen by Jaap de Vries). 1992.

"Storing." (Static). In *Tirade* no. 38, p. 353 (July/August): 1994.

Nagelaten dagen (The Remaining Days). 1997.

Secondary Sources

Jameson, Storm. "A Child's Voice." In *Over Marga Minco: beschouwingen en interviews*. Edited by Dirk Kroon. The Hague: BZZTÔH, 1982, pp. 35–36.

Kouwenaar, Gerrit. 1982. "Zuivere kroniek van de jodenvervolging." In *Over Marga Minco: beschouwingen en interviews*. Edited by Dirk Kroon. The Hague: BZZTÔH, 1982, pp. 27–28.

Mijn, Aad van der. "In mijn dromen reis ik veel." In *Over Marga Minco: beschouwingen en interviews*. Edited by Dirk Kroon. The Hague: BZZTÔH, 1982, p. 148.

Snapper, Johan P. *Post-War Dutch Literature: A Harp Full of Nails*. Amsterdam: Delta, 1971.

———. "The Work of Marga Minco: A Wrangle of Time and Space." In *The Low Countries and Beyond*. Edited by Robert S. Kirsner. Lanham: University Press of America, 1992.

———. "Ut Pictura Poesis: The Pen and Brush of Marga Minco." In *Studies in Netherlandic Culture and Literature*. Edited by Martinus A. Bakker and Beverly H. Morrison. Lanham: University Press of America, 1994.

———. "Marga Minco's 'The Return.' " In: *Women Writing in Dutch*. Edited by Kristiaan Aercke. New York: Garland, 1994.

———. *De wegen van Marga Minco*. Amsterdam: Bert Bakker, 1999.

Taylor, Jolanda Vanderwal. "Bitter Herbs, Empty Houses, Traps, and False Identities: The (Post)-War World of Marga Minco." *Canadian Journal of Netherlandic Studies* 11, no. 2 (1990): 8–14.

———. *A Family Occupation: Children of the War and the Memory of World War II in Dutch Literature of the 1980s*. Amsterdam: Amsterdam University Press, 1997.

Wohmann, Gabriele. "So war es." In *Over Marga Minco: beschouwingen en interviews*. Edited by Dirk Kroon. The Hague: BZZTÔH, 1982, pp. 31–34.

Rivka Miriam
(1952–)

ERIC ZAKIM

LIKE OTHER SECOND-GENERATION Hebrew poets, Rivka Miriam's search for meaning within an idiom heavily laden with her family's experiences in the Holocaust becomes an intense inward expression of the poet herself. In Miriam's poetry, which dominates an artistic corpus that spans many literary genres and artistic media, Rivka Miriam articulates and wrestles with that "inherited fear" that characterizes much of a second generation's response to the physical destruction of their families and the psychological burden borne by its surviving remnants who are their parents. As a second-generation poet, Miriam's work thus resonates with the poetry of other Israelis of survivor families, poets like Oded Peled and Esther Fuchs, each of whom turns to the poetic medium to engage their own relation and position within the series of generations that has emerged out of the destruction of European Jewry.

Rivka Miriam cannot be classified strictly as a "Holocaust" poet or writer, and not just because she never writes thematically about the camps or any of the events that make up the history of the Holocaust. It isn't even that the psychological journey inscribed in her writing—like that, say, of Oded Peled—focuses intensely on a second-generation experience and the poet's relationship to her family, especially to her parents. Rather, the inheritance from the Holocaust that Miriam's work manifests explodes beyond the Holocaust itself, and her identity as an authorial voice emerges from the broader inheritance and the particular experience of being a woman in a Jewish world. For Miriam, these two features of her particular world—the Jewish tradition and a feminine identity—might fall within the shadows of the Holocaust, but the spectral resonance of that experience does not overtake and infect the entirety of her writing. Indeed, one is hard-pressed to find the Holocaust at all in her work, except in the sense that, as a Jewish experience, it must be subsumed within the context of a much larger history and a much larger personal identity.

Inheritances

Born Rivka Rochman in Jerusalem, Israel, on 2 October 1952, Rivka Miriam is the daughter of survivors, her father the Yiddish writer Leib Rochman. But the feminist legacies within the Jewish tradition more clearly define her writerly proclivities and allegiances. Her name, adopted from two strong biblical women, announces a feminine identity that is at once of the tradition but distinct from the patro-centric dominance of male authority. Rivka Miriam's name connects her personally to the experience of Jewish history and becomes emblematic of (and perhaps as well a key semiotic guide to) the relationship she is striving to build among the elements that make up her writing: a sense of personal identity as a woman, the Jewish tradition, and the past experiences of her own family. The name ties her both to the tradition in its abstract textual form and to the personal history of her family, that was destroyed in Europe: "I feel close to the preceding Jewish generations. I feel love for them, I feel I am their continuation, part of the chain. . . . I very much loved the grandmothers I never knew. I carry their name. Rivka is the name of my paternal grandmother and Miriam that of my father's sister. They both perished together at Treblinka" (Tsingel, p. 157 [Hebrew]; Sicher, p. 164 [English]).

Rivka Miriam, by naming herself and dropping the patrilinear designation of the family name, links directly to these women of the past. Unlike Zionist poets of a previous generation who clung to the name of the mother by highlighting familial connection (Yochevet *Bat*-Miriam, for instance, who mediates her own identity through the self-designation *daughter* of Miriam),

Rivka Miriam assumes the identity of her foremothers within an empathy we might call typical of a second-generation "post-memory" of those who perished in the Holocaust: a "post-memory" that recreates and re-experiences what the previous generation felt. In this way, when Miriam invokes the tradition poetically, the same ambiguity of identity reappears, and what seems so ephemerally metaphoric within a grand religious tradition (the name of the modern person, which is also the name of the foremother) resonates with the closeness of personal experience. Thus, Miriam writes in a poem from 1988: "I, of the heavy stone mothers / Call Abraham, Isaac, and Jacob to settle in my bosom" ("Poems of Stone Mothers," *Poems of Stone Mothers*, Sifriat Poalim, 1988, p. 19).

These lines from *Poems of Stone Mothers* redound with the ambivalent role of the modern Jewish woman within the tradition. As part of that tradition, Miriam's speaker takes into herself all the mothers of that history, and comforts the patriarchs through her role as nurturer. However, subversion exists in these lines as well, and a sadness too; the "heavy stone mothers" take on a primacy, a place prior to the men of that tradition, but a place that has lost its function, as Miriam laments, "Because of so much stone, I'm no longer suitable for today's babies" (p. 19). Bound up within the speaker, an identity emerges that is at once singular and plural, her own and that of the entire lineage of mothers who came before. More than a mere political reference to those women, Miriam's lines build an identity bound to the experiences of those foremothers. Bereft of that ability to nurture babies, the modern woman carries within her the entire tradition, including what comes from the experience of the Holocaust.

Internalizing the Holocaust as a Woman

The inability to suckle, the heaviness of Miriam's speaker, the weight of this contemporary stone mother: these themes return consistently throughout Miriam's poetry, which carries a sense of historical responsibility and the burden of reliving and reexperiencing what the previous generations have suffered. As Miriam herself explains of her writing: "I started writing at a very early age. . . . I felt . . . as if I was going with them to the gas chambers. As if I experienced it" (Sicher, p. 158). Perhaps the extent of the empathy Miriam feels toward that experience explains the lack of thematic reference to the Holocaust in her writing, as if the naming of that experience through linguistic signifiers would only serve to reify a separation between the language of representation and the experience of the event itself. Instead, a poem such as "I Will Never Be Like the Mother in the Picture" from the volume *Ets naga be'ets* (Tree Reached to Tree, 1978) articulates both the experiential imperative of second-generation poetry and the ambivalence that language and writing embody for the representation of that experience. From the beginning of that poem:

> I will never be like the mother in the picture
> Who suckles a baby from a white breast
> As he gropes for her face.
> My children will suckle ashes from within me (Tel Aviv: Dvir, 1978, p. 63).

If this is a poem about the Holocaust—how can we know for certain without direct thematic reference?—then the Holocaust exists within the body of the woman who is the speaker. It is internalized and passed on through physical, bodily experience.

These lines, like most of Miriam's writings, raise serious generic questions about Holocaust writing. Without thematic reference, what ties these lines to the Holocaust, except for a totalizing—and reductionist—view of modern Jewish experience, whose logic would then require all of this poetry to be designated "Holocaust" poetry? If we cannot discern and distinguish the Holocaust referentially, then everything risks becoming the Holocaust in a writing of personal experience that transcends the borders of history and immediacy. In that sense, Miriam's writing might be the inversion of Theodor Adorno's accusation against post-Holocaust culture where poetry becomes impossible after Auschwitz. Instead, in the experiential type of second-generation poetry Miriam writes, it isn't that poetry becomes impossible after the Holocaust, but that everything becomes Holocaust poetry.

Miriam, however, takes this argument one step further and extends the goals of poetry to be the entire Jewish tradition and even humanity in general. She never allows the Holocaust to become the telos of an intertextual language that constantly refers beyond the immediate articulation of the speaker or prose narrator. Her writing, caught ever between the person and the tradition, synthesizing the experiences of the two into a single unity, subsumes even the Holocaust within that dialectic. Between the search for identity as a modern woman and the historical inheritance of the tradition, the Holocaust casts a shadow in Miriam's writing but does not control the modern fate of the Jew.

Beyond Poetry

Rivka Miriam's first book of poems, *My Yellow Dress*, was published in 1966 when she was fourteen years old. Already there we can see the beginnings of her treatment of the themes—women, tradition, and the Holocaust—that would come to characterize her later writing as well. At fourteen, though, the folds in the layers of each of these themes are less subtle, and the Holocaust pokes out more as a referential marker than in later poems. For instance, the poem from which the book takes its title is dedicated "to grandmother," and from that dedication we begin to understand the yellow dress, a *kutonet* in Hebrew. *Kutonet* designates not a woman's dress, but instead acts as an intertextual trigger opening multiple associations with Joseph's multicolored vestment in Genesis, his *kutonet passim*, a striped vestment. Once that intertextual space is opened, the striped dress easily elides as well with the striped pajama of the concentration camp inmate, not because of explicit reference, but because of the impossibility of avoiding the reference. That is how Miriam's internalized experience of the Holocaust makes itself felt:

> She looks at me
> With compassion
> She was given a dress
> Yellow
> She walked along the way
> Imprinting her step—
> With them (Tel Aviv: Eked, 1966, p. 38).

The march is menacing; the enjambed "yellow" of the vestment forces us to confuse it with the yellow star the Nazis made Jews sew onto their clothing, an icon that appears as the title and theme of another poem in this early collection. Yet the reference is not unambiguous, despite how we might want to read the dedication and the march and the yellow *kutonet*. Each of these things can also be contextualized differently and take on other meanings. There is little tendency in any of Miriam's writing to confine language within a singular meaning.

At fourteen, Miriam reveals a path she will follow in coming years, where she will make the connections more refined and more subtle; what remains constant is a reliance on the connections and interactions among the main conceptual elements that drive all meaning in her work: religious tradition, women's identity, and the experience of history. In this, the Holocaust is ever-present and yet absent, always reasserting itself but never easily, consistently filtered through a complex intertextual world tied to a broad tradition of artistic creation, religious philosophy, and personal identity. Thus, Miriam does not confine herself to poetic expression, and in addition to several volumes of poems, she writes prose and paints as well. All of Miriam's activities as a creative artist and intellectual point to a view of the world as an all-encompassing experience whose threads intersect and interact, and that is the way that we too must understand the oblique and yet intense engagement in her work with the Holocaust.

Bibliography

Primary Sources

Poetry

Kutonati hatsehuba (My Yellow Dress). 1966.
Tavati bakhalonot (I Drowned in the Windows). 1969.
Kisa'ot bamidbar (Seats in the Desert). 1973.
Ets naga be'ets (Tree Reached to Tree). 1978.
Hakolot likeratam (The Sounds Towards Them). 1982.
Mishirei imot ha'even (Poems of Stone Mothers). 1988.
Makom, namer (Place, Tiger). 1994.
Mi-karov hayah ha-mizrah (Nearby Was the East). 1996.

Anthologies That Contain Poems by Rivkah Miriam

Kaufman, S., G. Hasan-Rookem, and T. Hess, eds. *The Defiant Muse: Hebrew Feminist Poems*. New York: Feminist Press, 1999.

Prose

Rak ha'esh vehamayim (Only Fire and Water). 1989.
Nafal Davar (Something Fell). 1996.
Nakh hayehudi (Resting Jew). 2000.

Children's Books

Me'ever lagiv'ot ha'akharonot (Beyond the Last Hills). 1991.

Secondary Sources

Sicher, Efraim, ed. *Breaking Crystal: Writing and Memory after Auschwitz*. Urbana: University of Illinois Press, 1998.

Yaoz, Hanna. *Hashoah beshirat dor-hamedina* (The Holocaust in the Poetry of the Statehood Generation). Tel Aviv: Eked, 1984.

Interviews

The Holocaust, Creation, and Israel (videorecording). Beachwood, Ohio: Beachwood Studios, 1987.

Tsingel, Shoshana. *Masa el tokh atsmanu* (Journey into Ourselves). Tel Aviv: Elisar, 1985.

ANNA MITGUTSCH

(1948–)

MICHAEL OSSAR

ANNA MITGUTSCH WAS born on 2 October 1948 in Linz, Austria. After graduating from a gymnasium in 1967, she began the study of German and English literature at the University of Salzburg, in the course of which she worked on a kibbutz in Israel (born a Roman Catholic, she converted to Judaism, according to Brigitte Schwens-Harrant). In 1970–1971 she taught in Yorkshire and Norwich in England. She finished her dissertation in 1974, and after teaching briefly in a gymnasium in Linz and at the Institute for American Studies of the University of Innsbruck, she went to England, where she was a lecturer at the German institutes of the universities of Hull (1971–1973) and East Anglia (1975–1978). The next year she spent teaching in Seoul, South Korea, followed by stays at various U.S. colleges and universities in New York and Boston (Amherst College, Sarah Lawrence College, Simmons College, Tufts University, Emmanuel College). In 1985 she returned to Austria, where she taught at the universities of Salzburg and Innsbruck. Since 1985 she has been a contributor to the *Oberösterreichischen Kulturbericht*, since 1986 for the *Standard*, and since 1987 for *Literatur und Kritik*. From 1987 to 1992 she served as a member of the editorial team of the Upper Austrian literary magazine *Die Rampe*. Since 1986 she has been a member of the Graz Writers Association. In 1996 Mitgutsch was writer-in-residence at Lafayette College; in 1997 she held the same position at Oberlin College and at Allegheny College. In the aftermath of the formation of an Austrian government that included the right-wing Freedom Party of Jörg Haider, Mitgutsch resigned from the Austrian PEN Club in April 2000. When she spoke against the Freedom Party at a demonstration in Linz, she was attacked by the president of her own Linz Jewish community, who was concerned that she might provoke an antisemitic backlash. She currently lives as a freelance writer in Leonding near Linz. She has won numerous literary prizes, including that of the city of Hanau (1985), the Cultural Prize of the State of Upper Austria (1986), the Claassen-Rose Prize (1986), the prize of the city of Bozen (1990), the Anton-Wildgans Prize (1992), and the prize of the Austrian Federal Ministry of Literature and Art (1995).

Mitgutsch's first novel, *Die Züchtigung* (*Three Daughters*, 1987), published in 1985, was the first in a series of works dealing with problems of self-definition, integration into often hostile or indifferent societies, and solipsism, most of them seen from a woman's perspective. It is a novel about mother-daughter relationships. Born on a farm in Upper Austria and raised in a brutal and loveless environment, Marie sees her only escape in marriage to Friedl, a day laborer. Both feel themselves as outsiders and are worn down by the depredations of postwar poverty and shortages. Marie eventually capitulates, placing all her hopes in her daughter, Vera, who is made to serve as a substitute for Marie's failure of a husband and whom she maims psychologically through daily floggings with a carpet beater. Despite the restrained language, Mitgutsch succeeds in making clear the relationship between brutality in private and in public life in Austria during and after World War II and its role in sexual repression and authoritarian child rearing (a brutality which, she implies, is both a cause and an expression of fascism). Particularly interesting in the context of Holocaust literature are the descriptions of how the villagers, men and women, react to the *Anschluss* and the subsequent Gestapo roundups, to the revelations about the concentration camps, and to the release of the surviving prisoners after the war.

Mitgutsch's second novel, *Das andere Gesicht* (*The Other Face*), published in 1986, is about two women who are unhappy in different ways—one an outsider, a pariah, depressed and inarticulate, seeking a sense of belonging, and the other a woman dominated by reason and apparently well integrated into society but pervaded by a sense of emptiness and unable to make demands on life or to snatch happiness from it. Her third novel, *Ausgrenzung* (*Jakob*, 1991), published in 1989, has no proximate connection with the Holocaust (apart from isolated episodes such as the one where an irritated woman in a train compartment remarks that under the Third Reich, Jakob would have been "euthanized"), yet it is clear that its description of the same brutal, loveless, unfeeling society we know from the two earlier novels continues Mitgutsch's project of showing in the abstract how outsiders could be marginalized and destroyed, much as Max Frisch provides a case study of antisemitism in the abstract in his *Andorra*. She leaves it to the reader to connect this kind of society with recent German history. *In fremden Städten* (*In Foreign Cities*, 1995), which appeared in 1992, is even more pessimistic than *Ausgrenzung* in its account of an American woman who marries an Austrian, moves to Innsbruck, and comes to feel ever more acutely that she is neither an Austrian nor an American, that she is at home in neither place and in neither language, that she is losing her grasp on her personality and her great source of hope, her writing talent. The penultimate novel, *Abschied von Jerusalem* (*Lover, Traitor: A Jerusalem Story*, 1997), which appeared in 1995, tells of an Austrian woman of partly Jewish origins, Hildegard, who changes her name to Dvorah, works for a time in a kibbutz, and makes several later trips to Israel. Twenty years after her first trip, she travels to Israel again, weighing the idea of moving there. Reluctant to leave Jerusalem, she delays her departure and falls in love with a Palestinian much younger than she who pretends to be an Armenian. Later, she reads of his death in a shooting during the *intifada* and realizes that he has exploited her for political ends. Mitgutsch weaves memories of Dvorah's Austrian homeland into her thoughts: the deportation of Jews from Vienna in 1941, the attitudes of the people in her hometown toward the Nazis—mordant memories reminiscent of similar passages in *Die Züchtigung*. The jungle of borders, of lines of demarcation, both visible and invisible, both within and without, presents Dvorah with a chaos of realities and competing possibilities for self-definition and identity, among which she is ultimately unable to choose.

A la Recherche du temps perdu: *Haus der Kindheit*

In her study of the relationship between Austrians and Jews after World War II, *Unzugehörig* (*Not Belonging*, 1989), Ruth Beckermann describes the third part of Alfred Hrdlicka's controversial "Monument Against Fascism and War." It depicts Orpheus on his way to the underworld, "where he apparently becomes acquainted with war and concentration camps, but still enchants the hellish dog Cerberus and Hades himself with his music. The latter gives him Eurydice as his wife with the sole condition that Orpheus not look back until they have again emerged into the light of the sun. Orpheus, however, looks back at his wife—and loses her forever. He who looks back instead of peering into the future is punished. All's well that ends well. Orpheus returns to the Second Republic" (Vienna: Löcker Verlag, 1989, p. 12).

Beckermann interprets the myth of Orpheus and Eurydice as the appropriate metaphor for the way that Austria has decided to deal with its past, the comforting conviction that by all rights its illustrious intellectual and artistic contributions to civilization have earned it the right to refrain from examining its past and that any look backward will lead to punishment and sorrow. What Anna Mitgutsch shows in *Haus der Kindheit* is the powerful claim that memory exerts, that Orpheus must look back, willy-nilly, a point she also makes elsewhere in her writing. For example, she begins her essay "The Autobiographical 'I' in Literary Texts" in *Altes Land, neues Land. Verfolgung, Exil, biografisches Schreiben* with the statement, "At the beginning of all writing is memory, and memory is a subjective personal process. It is the foundation of our personality. Loss of memory means a disintegration of the personality" (Vienna: Verlag ZIRKULAR der Dokumentationsstelle für neuere österreichische Literatur, 1999). Later on in the same essay she writes:

> There are those texts, which have marked the memory of our feelings most deeply, which indeed require our entire life so far lived as the condition of their credibility. They would have neither justification nor sense without the knowledge won from the experience that things were thus and not otherwise. There is an intensity of language and representation, a strength of conviction, that cannot be achieved in any other way. Here too, authenticity is at stake, and it is difficult to simulate it without the background of experience. It comes from injury, from pain, from irreparable harm. It demands a simplicity, an exactness, a directness that all seem incredible in the free play of imagination and would disturb us. Such texts have an aura of necessity about them. They are experienced by the reader as authentic, and he will understand them as autobiographical texts because he senses that here the author . . . is wrestling with an experience with which he/she has not been able to cope. This strong impression of authenticity is not only (in any case, not primarily) evoked by the external, narrated plot, for the plot can be more easily manipulated than the psychic experience that manifests itself in it. In it are embedded moods and emotional reactions, and these manifest themselves in unmistakable images that combine and intensify experiences. In this

> intensification the experiences lose their private nature, and in its realization through being read the original autobiographical "I," which became a fictional "I" through the literary process, now, through the effect of recognition, . . . becomes the "I" of the reader (pp. 12–13).

Haus der Kindheit is very much a novel in which the protagonist, Max Berman, is drawn forward and in a sense guided by memories that in their progressive intensification ultimately cause the fictional, autobiographical "I" to transcend fiction and merge with the "I" of the reader. It is the perfect realization of the process Mitgutsch described in her lecture, one year before the publication of her novel (on which she worked for about fifteen years). *Haus der Kindheit* is a bildungsroman, a novel of education, in which the fate of young Max is guided and determined by his particular interaction with his memories and demons, just as Wilhelm Meister's fate is guided in the archetypal bildungsroman by a secret society, the Turmgesellschaft, which watches over him and from time to time intervenes in his life.

Haus der Kindheit, a book in which photographs play a crucial role, begins with the description of one that has a magic, incantatory power:

> The photo had stood on the commode as long as Max could remember. It transformed every apartment they occupied into another place of exile. Unlike all the other objects they unpacked after every new move, its significance reached far into the past, and like an oath it obliged one to keep a promise. In the middle of their lives it pointed to a present which was painfully missing (Munich: Luchterhand, 2000, p. 7).

The photo depicts the house on the river in a small Austrian city, H, that Max's parents left behind when they fled to New York in 1928 when Max was five. His grandfather, his aunt, and her husband remain behind in this "house of his childhood" until they are deported and murdered and the house is "aryanized." Max and his two brothers, Viktor and Ben, fight their way through various rough New York neighborhoods as their mother, Mira, abandoned by Max's father Saul, moves them into increasingly shabby apartments. While Ben dies in a mental institution (there is no suggestion that his illness is directly related to the Holocaust; his schizophrenia seems to be organic in origin) and Mira withdraws more and more from an America that she can never see as a possible home, Max becomes a gifted and much sought-after interior architect. But the only house that really interests him is the one in the photo; the goal of his life is to move back into the house that had been stolen from his parents. He sees it with his own eyes for the first time in 1945 as a soldier in the U.S. army, and when his mother dies in 1974 he returns, now fifty-one years old, to demand restitution of his property. Mitgutsch describes in totally believable detail the great variety of bureaucratic hindrances and chicanery the local authorities contrive to put in his way, a description intended to be typical of the Austrian method of evading dealing with the question of reparations. Most telling is the depiction of the history of the house—its "aryanization" and its assignment to an SA family, whose right to live there is prolonged by laws protecting renters from eviction. Finally Max follows the advice of the leader of the small Jewish community of H (similar to the one to which Mitgutsch herself belongs), Arthur Spitzer, who later becomes his closest friend, to engage a lawyer. Eighteen years pass before Max is finally able to move into his family's house. Like St. Francis after his "conversion" restoring the church of St. Damian, the urbane architect of the first part of the book takes leave of his many love affairs and the excitement of New York and devotes himself in the second part to the renovation of his childhood home, the synagogue, and the Jewish community of H. He decides to write (with the help of Thomas, a sympathetic Christian archivist and historian) a chronicle of the history of the Jews of H to recover the suppressed "invisible" history of the city beginning in 1306–seven hundred years of pogroms that recur at approximately twenty-year intervals, plundering, murder, and unrequited love. Mitgutsch states in an interview that about 80 percent of Max's chronicle (which he eventually gives to Spitzer's daughter and never publishes) derives from the actual history of the Jews of Linz. The Christian reaction to the reestablishment of the tiny Jewish community is revealed in a series of self-conscious ceremonial events honoring Spitzer and Max, some of them staged by Thomas, which emphasize simultaneously the force of political pressure for publicly visible acts of reconciliation, the ambivalence of many Austrians, but also the goodwill of others. Finally, in 1993 Nadja, a woman he met on his second visit to H in 1974 and subsequently brought to New York, trained as a photographer, and had an affair with, visits him on her way to Poland and Ukraine. In one of the most moving passages in the novel, Max and Nadja realize that their chance for happiness is irretrievably gone, and Nadja continues her trip, stopping, at Max's request, at the cemetery where his ancestors are buried. Shortly thereafter, she is murdered by her male companion, Bogdan, in an argument over where to spend the night.

Earlier, when Max is honored by the city of H on his seventieth birthday (the mayor, in a well-meaning though tactless act symbolic of the difficulty of reconciliation, hangs a cross around his neck), a journalist asks whether he thinks antisemitism will ever return to H. Max answers with a question: "You mean, under what conditions it might assume violent forms again?" (p. 231). The function of Nadja's death in the economy of the novel is not simply to provide a reason for Max to leave H (the concept of "home" means people and language, Mitgutsch says in an interview); it also serves metaphorically to recall to the reader's mind Max's answer to the journalist. A brutality so violent that it can lead to murder and so senseless that it can be provoked by a dispute about who is to decide where to spend the night erupts without warning and, Mitgutsch implies, could erupt again at any moment.

Nadja's photos survive for Max to see, and shortly thereafter, his friend Spitzer and his erstwhile lover Nadja dead, Max returns to a New York that has suprisingly revealed itself as his true home: "He felt a wave of warmth well up within himself, and the closer he got to New York, the stronger it became" (p. 333). "We always look for what we have lost at the wrong place," Thomas tells Max when he hears of his plans, echoing the words of Fitzgerald's narrator, Nick, in *The Great Gatsby*: "[h]e had come a long way to this blue lawn, and his dream must have seemed so close that he could hardly fail to grasp it. He did not know that it was already behind him, somewhere back in that vast obscurity behind the city, where the dark fields of the republic rolled on under the night. . . . So we beat on, boats against the current, borne back ceaselessly into the past" (p. 182). In an unpublished interview with Simone Hamm, Mitgutsch analyzes the ending for us: "Max arrives at the insight of where he is at home, and that this experience with this Austrian provincial town was an illusion. . . . In Max there is much of myself. I too somehow have the feeling that the Austrian provincial town is not a place I can live." Max's insight that the photo of the house (the dust jacket of the novel shows a detail from Egon Schiele's painting, *Tote Stadt* [Dead City]), is ultimately a token of his mother's memory and not his own can be taken to be a private insight and not a statement about the reemergent Austrian Jewish community. In fact, despite the feelings voiced in her interview, Anna Mitgutsch lives part of the year in Boston and part in Linz, where she belongs to a small community very like the one described in *Haus der Kindheit*.

Through Nadja's penetrating and magically acute eyes, her lens, Max has glimpsed an invisible reality. Shortly before her death, Bogdan complains to Nadja as she photographs a beautiful and desolate landscape, "I don't see what there is to photograph here." And the narrator tells us: "More clearly than the prefabricated houses of modern suburbs, more palpably than the scattered cows and horses on green meadows, the German tanks stood before her eyes and the columns of those torn from their everyday lives and on their way to death" (p. 319). Nadja, who had entered Max's life as a messenger (from Spitzer, summoning him to a burial service), an angel, leaves it as a messenger as well–both of the memories of Max's ancestors and their fates, and of the possibility of future brutality.

Bibliography

Primary Sources

Die Züchtigung (*Three Daughters*). 1985.
Das andere Gesicht (*The Other Face*). 1986.
Three Daughters. 1987.
Ausgrenzung (*Jakob*). 1989.
Jakob. 1991.
In fremden Städten: (*In Foreign Cities*). 1992.
Abschied von Jerusalem (*Lover, Traitor: A Jerusalem Story*). 1995.
Lover, Traitor: A Jerusalem Story. 1997.
Erinnern und Erfinden: Grazer Poetik-Vorlesungen (Remembering and Inventing: Graz Lectures on Poetry). 1999.
Haus der Kindheit (House of Childhood). 2000.
On Poets and Poetry Second Series. Salzburg Studies in English Literature. With Joseph L. Schneider and Anita Weinzinger. Salzburg: Institut für Anglistik und Amerikanistik, University of Salzburg, 1980.
The Image of the Female in D. H. Lawrence's Poetry. With James Hogg. Salzburg Studies in English Literature. Salzburg, Institut für Anglistik und Amerikanistik, University of Salzburg, 1981.
Mitgutsch, Anna, and Lowell A. Bangerter. *In Foreign Cities*. Translated by Lowell A. Bangerter. Studies in Austrian Literature, Culture, and Thought. Riverside, Calif.: Ariadne Press, 1995.

Secondary Sources

Beckermann, Ruth. *Unzugehörig: Österreicher und Juden nach 1945*. Vienna: Löcker Verlag, 1989.
Fitzgerald, F. Scott. *The Great Gatsby*. New York: Scribner's, 1953.
Gauss, Karl Markus. "Photographierte Sehnsucht: Anna Mitgutschs grosser 'Haus der Kindheit' " (Longing Photographed: Anna Mitgutsch's Great Novel 'House of Childhood'). *Neue Zürcher Zeitung* 126 (31 May 2000).
Gerhardt, Ilse. "Von der Passion des Verlustes" (On the Passion of Loss). *Kärntner Woche*, 5–11 April 2000.
Grünefeld, Hans-Dieter. "Zugehörigheit als innerer Wert" (Belonging as an Inner Value). *Buchkultur. Das internationale Buchmagazin* 66 (June-July 2000).
Hackl, Erich. "Ahnung von einem Zuhause" (Sense of a Home). *Literatur und Kritik*, May 2000.
Hagn, Julia. "H. wie Hitlerstaat. Anna Mitgutsch über ihren neuen" (H. as in Hitlerland. Anna Mitgutsch on Her New Novel). *Münchner Merkur*, 10 May 2000.
Hamm, Simone. "Anna Mitgutsch: Haus der Kindheit" (Anna Mitgutsch: House of Childhood). Radio program segment, 2000.
Henning, Peter. "Berührend unsentimental. Erinnern. Anna Mitgutschs einer Suche" (Touchingly Unsentimental. Remembering. Anna Mitgutsch's Novel of a Search). *Profil* 31 (6 March 2000).
Hinck, Walter. "Im verlorenen Paradies. Heimkehrversuch: Anna Mitgutschs 'Haus der Kindheit'" (In Paradise Lost. At-

tempt to Return Home. Anna Mitgutsch's Novel 'House of Childhood'). *Frankfurter Allgemeine Zeitung* 99 (28 April 2000).

Hinderer, Walter, Claudia Holly, Heinz Lunzer, Ursula Seeber, editors. *Altes Land, neues Land. Verfolgung, Exil, biografisches Schreiben* (Old country, new country. Pursuit, exile, biographic letter). Vienna: Verlag ZIRKULAR der Dokumentationsstelle für neuere österreichische Literatur, 1999.

juko. "Angekommen (Arrived)." *Berliner Zeitung*, 29–30 April 2000.

Karl, Maria. "Geschichte hautnah. Der neue, grosse von Anna Mitgutsch" (Skin-close to History. The Great New Novel by Anna Mitgutsch). *Neues Volksblatt Linz*, 8 June 2000.

Kompatcher, Brigette. "Haus der Kindheit" (House of Childhood). *Neue Vorarlberger Tageszeitung*, 5 April 2000.

Kosbach, Julia. "Ein Leben in fremden Erinnerungen. Luchterhand präsentiert Anna Mitgutschs neuen 'Haus der Kindheit' " (A Life in Foreign Memories. Luchterhand Publishes Anna, Migutch's New Novel "Haus der Kindheit"). *Deutsche Bücher* 1 (1989): 1–19.

Lässer, Bruno. "Die Gnade der später Angekommenen. 'Haus der Kindheit' von Mitgutsch" (The Luck of Those Who Arrived Late. 'House of Childhood' by Mitgutsch). *Vorarlberger Nachrichten*, 1913, 14 May 2000.

Leipprand, Eva. "Die Sehnsucht des Heimatlosen" (The Longing of the Homeless Man). *Süddeutsche Zeitung*, 22–23 July 2000.

Presser, Ellen. "Auf der Suche nach der verweigerten Vergangenheit" (The Search for the Denied Past). *Allgemeine Jüdische Wochenzeitung* 17 (17 August 2000).

Reinhardt, Maria. "Exemplarisches Wiedersehen. In ihrem 'Haus der Kindheit' beschreibt Anna Mitgutsch die Frustrationen vieler zurückgekehrter Emigranten" (Exemplary Reunion. In Her Novel 'House of Childhood' Anna Mitgutsch Describes the Frustrations of Many Returned Emigrants). *Die Furche* 18 (May 2000).

Scheller, Wolf. "Suche nach der Vergangenheit" (In Search of the Past). *Kieler Nachrichten*, 25 July 2000.

Schmidt, Bettina. "Eine fremde Heimat" (Foreign Homeland). *Sächsische Zeitung*, 8–9 April 2000.

Schwens-Harrant, Brigitte. "Lebenslange Heimkehr" (A Lifelong Return Home). *Schriftzeichen* 2 (July 2000).

Sperl, Ingeborg. "Zögerliche Heimkehr, übliche Schwierigkeiten" (A Hesitating Return Home, Usual Difficulties). *Der Standard*, 19 February 2000.

Strempfl, Heimo. "Gibt es nicht immerhin die Möglichkeit von Liebe oder gar Glück? Die Romane der Waltraud Anna Mitgutsch" (Is there not after all the Possibility of Love or even Happiness? The Novels of Waltraud Anna Mitgutsch). *ide. Informationen zur Didaktik* 2 (1993): 83–91

Tauber, Reinhold. "Vom Wandern zwischen den Welten" (On Wandering Between Worlds). *OÖ Nachrichten* 56 (8 March 2000).

PATRICK MODIANO

(1945–)

SAMUEL KHALIFA

PATRICK MODIANO WAS born on 30 July 1945 in Boulogne-Billancourt, France, to a Jewish father, Albert Modiano, from Thessalonica and a Christian Belgian mother, Ivisa Colpeyn. His mother had arrived in Paris in 1942 to become an actress, and she "spent the war in Paris working for a German film company" (Nettelbeck and Hueston, pp. 102–103). With a father away on business trips and a mother away on tour, Patrick's life centered around school. Finishing high school in 1964, he undertook art studies at the Sorbonne for a year before devoting himself entirely to his writing. Nostalgia for his adventurous youth is prevalent throughout his work, as is the memory of the tragic death of his younger brother Rudy (1947–1957), to whom he dedicated all his early works.

At the age of twenty-three and with the support of Raymond Queneau (the poet, novelist, and French essayist), Modiano published his first novel, *La place de l'Etoile* (The Place of the Star, 1968), and received the Fénéon and Roger Nimier awards. Since then, Modiano's works have garnered many awards: the Prix de la Plume de Diamant for *La ronde de nuit* (*Night Rounds*, 1969), the Grand Prix for the novel for *Les boulevards de ceinture* (*Ring Roads*, 1972), the Prix des Libraires for *Villa triste* (*Villa Triste*, 1977), and, in 1978, the Prix Goncourt for *Rue des boutiques obscures* (*Missing Person*, 1978). He was awarded the Grand Prix for literature by the French Academy for his entire work in the year 2000.

Career

Modiano's exploration of the past centers on the German occupation of France and the collaboration of the Vichy government. Modiano's interest in the Vichy regime can be traced to the quest for his own identity and, above all, the traumatizing confrontation with the memory of his father, who remained in Paris during the Occupation using the alias Henri Lagroua. His arrest in a 1942 roundup and his quick release inspired several variants in the narrative—this can be seen in novels such as *La ronde de nuit* (Night Rounds), *Dora Bruder* (The Search Warrant) and *Livret de Famille*—and represents a crucial chapter of Modiano's family history. The "venomous odor of the Occupation" (*Livret de famille* [Family Record Book], Paris: Gallimard, 1977, p. 169), which was linked to some of his father's shady acquaintances, had a lasting effect on Modiano, whose curiosity about this period stems from his inability to understand his father's wartime role coupled with a post-*Shoah* feeling of guilt. In a 1996 interview with Louis Vidal, the fifty-year-old Modiano was still talking about the "mass grave" that was his birthplace.

The Vichy government and the Nazi occupation of France encapsulate a singular captivating force in Patrick Modiano's personal history and literary achievement, inspiring not only an exploratory fantasy world but also a larger project and literary aesthetic. Among the narratives published by the novelist, *La place de l'Etoile*, *La ronde de nuit*, *Les boulevards de ceinture*, and his 1997 novel *Dora Bruder* center around the Années Noires (the Occupation). The highly parodic and experimental *La place de l'Etoile* recounts the adventures of Raphaël Schlemilovitch, a young Jew who yearns to be a Frenchman and a novelist. This existential concern is spelled out early as the "Jewish joke," which stands as an epigraph to the novel: "In June 1942, a German officer walks toward a young man and says to him: 'Pardon me, sir, can you tell me where to find the Place de l'Etoile?' The young man points to the left of his breast" (Paris: Gallimard, 1975).

La Place de l'Etoile

By means of this "anecdote," Modiano cynically exposes the identity crisis that plagued thousands of

French Jews under the Occupation—how can a Jew be French? The four parts of the novel correspond to the stages of Raphaël Schlemilovitch's erratic quest as the archetypal Jew. In antisemitic 1940s France, the hero-narrator explores the initial hiatus between his Jewish being and his French nationality: the potential for friendship and assimilation he finds when he joins the French Parisian intellectuals is followed by rejection and his realization of the impossibility of assuming a French identity as long as the Jewish question is not resolved. At the end of his quest, Schlemilovitch is symbolically brought back to Paris under the Occupation and is executed in front of the notorious headquarters of the French Gestapo, 93 rue Lauriston. All the while, the narrative scheme of *La place de l'Etoile* introduces relations and family history in a kind of dizzying maelstrom, jostling the laws of logic so as best to come to terms with the weight of the past, the collaboration between the Thessalonian Jew Albert Modiano and the black-market dignitaries of the Occupation. Albert Modiano passes the four years of the Occupation in total illegality without leaving Paris. In 1942, he is taken in a roundup and is driven to a depot of the French police, where he succeeds in escaping at the last minute due to his faithful relations in the Parisian Gestapo. Albert Modiano's shady past is suggested to us in the background of most of his son's work, and can be seen in more detail in *Livret de famille*.

According to Juliette Dickstein,

> *La place* represents Modiano's most experimental, difficult and angriest work. [. . .] By pantomiming different identities from a French Jewish collaborator à la Maurice Sachs to French Jewish writer à la Marcel Proust, the narrator/protagonist, Raphaël Schlemilovitch, explores his identity as a French Jewish writer and vents his anger not only at French society and culture but also, and most poignantly, at his father, who has ties to collaborators and scheming black-marketeers . . . (pp. 146, 151).

La ronde de nuit

With *La ronde de nuit*, Modiano tackles once again the ontological problem broached in *La place de l'Etoile*. The third-person narrator, a double agent, is torn between his desire to rejoin the French Gestapo agents and his calling as a member of the Resistance. The hero lets himself be engulfed at the beginning of the Occupation in a secret police agency that becomes the headquarters of an annex of the French Gestapo and an active black market center. When he is called upon to infiltrate the Resistance, he becomes caught in his duplicity, betraying the Resistance and simultaneously endeavoring to kill the head of the Gestapo. He misses him and flees; the novel finishes with a long manhunt. The Jewish question, the main theme of *La place de l'Etoile*, is singularly absent from *La ronde de nuit*, a novel in which history and fiction overlap and dissolve into one another and fictional characters are modeled on historic figures.

Like *La place de l'Etoile, La ronde de nuit* provides a hallucinatory re-creation of the cosmopolitan microcosm that gravitates around the Gestapo offices. *La ronde de nuit* and *La place de l'Etoile* introduce the shady microcosms of 93 rue Lauriston and 3 Square Cimarosa, ancient jails still used for torture. Throughout *La place*, the glare of the interrogation chambers and the sound of beatings is prevalent at rue de Lauriston. In *La ronde de nuit*, the services of Square Cimarosa (an agency of the French Gestapo) mercilessly track down the personnel of Resistance networks and English liaison officers. Rather than dramatizing them, the narrator merely alludes to the brutal arrests carried out by the French Gestapo:

> Some nights I was woken up by the cries of pain and the comings and goings on the ground floor. You could make out the voice of Khédive—and that of Philibert. I was looking out from the window. Two or three shady figures were being pushed into two cars parked in front of the hotel (*La ronde de nuit*, Paris: Gallimard, 1976, p. 79).

This atmosphere of moral abjection is established early in the novel by descriptions of orgiastic parties where a medley of classless people indulge in scenes of debauchery: "All those faces that you gaze at one last time before night envelops them" (p. 24). The refrains of Johnny Hess (a French singer from the 1940s) and indecent moans mingle with the whimpering of the tortured:

> There came a yell, then another, and another, piercing ones . . . "It's the guy they found," whispers old Khedive, "the pamphlet man! He's getting a looking-after, he'll end up giving in, my dear."
>
> "You want to see him?—to Khedive's health!" yells Lionel de Zieff.
>
> "To the inspector Philibert's," adds Paulo Hayakawa while stroking the baroness's nape. There came a yell, then another, and a lengthy drawn-out cry (p. 37).

Les boulevards de ceinture

The theme of moral decay and corruption during the Occupation persists in Modiano's next novel, *Les boulevards de ceinture*, which explores the quest for the father, a quest intimately linked to the question of Jewish identity. At the beginning of the narrative, the discovery of an old picture inspires the narrator to embark upon an imaginary voyage of initiation in the Paris of the Années Noires. The narrator finds his father living under the assumed name of Baron Deyckecaire, among the circle of collaborationist journalists. Entering this gruesome microcosm in order to build a relationship with his father, the narrator discovers an enigmatic and spineless creature who does not recognize him. The father embodies the image of the shamefaced Jew, someone unsettled and slightly burlesque, a designated victim who smiles back when he is humiliated. The relationship between father and son is based on a process of mutual recognition. The father, a Jew without fatherland, endeavors to create a French identity through his son, and his son, knowing his father to be in danger among a group of collaborators, undertakes to protect him and even to rehabilitate him despite his cowardice. By introducing us to the world of collaborators, Modiano delves into the troubled waters of the Occupation. Behind the characters of Jean Muraille, a newspaper director; of Muraille's daughter Annie, a second-rate actress; or of the Count de Marcheret, a former Legionnaire, can be divined the real-life characters of Jean Luchaire, president of the daily Parisian press and director of the *Nouveaux temps*; of his niece Corinne, an actress notorious for her decadent life; and Guy de Voisins, a militiaman. The collaborationist journalists in the novel, Georges Lestandi and François Gerbère, represent the historical figures Jean Lestandi de Villani, the animator of the Cercle du grand pavois, and Eugène Gerbère, the owner of Editions Théophraste-Renaudot. These figures are exposed as being personally as well as politically corrupt. Political treason and collaboration are thus linked to personal immorality exercised as thievery and sexual debauchery.

Dora Bruder

Dora Bruder is the first-person narrative of an investigation about an adolescent Jewish girl before her deportation to Auschwitz. The narrator's investigation is triggered by his discovery of an archive document, a classified ad in the 31 December 1941 *Paris-Soir*: "We are looking for a young girl, Dora Bruder, 15 years old, 1,55 m, slim face, grey-brown eyes, wearing a grey coat, a dark red sweater, a dark blue skirt and hat, and brown casual shoes" (*Dora Bruder*, Paris: Gallimard, 1997, p. 9). From this description and hypothetical clues, the narrator discovers fragments of the young girl's existence: her date and place of birth, the hotel room on boulevard Ornano where she lived with her parents, her school, the religious institution where she was a boarder, the episode when she ran away in December 1941, the concern her parents helplessly felt while they hid walled up inside their rented room, and the statement made to the police by her father at the local police station. Historically contextualized by the investigator, this event takes on a tragic dimension. In this novel, "French responsibility in the deportation of the Jews and the extent of individuals' distress are no longer camouflaged. . . . The main contrast [from Modiano's earlier novels] resides in the narrator's tone, in his determination to stand up and affirm his position, expose his feelings about the atrocities of the deportation. . . . He is no longer an alter ego of the author; he claims authorship," write Martine Guyot-Bender and William Vanderwolk (pp. 184–185). The novel emphasizes the legal and administrative measures taken by the French state against the Jews and shows the spiral in which the Bruders are caught, as the capital is placed under curfew and ransacked and German rulings are enforced, including anti-Jewish decrees such as the imposition of the yellow star. Ernest Bruder, the father, is arrested without any known motive on March 1942; Dora is arrested on 19 June for failing to wear her yellow star. Both are sent to the Drancy camp before being deported to Auschwitz on 18 September of the same year. Cécile Bruder, the mother, leaves for the death camps five months after her daughter and husband. Throughout its telling, the story makes clear the direct responsibility of the French in the roundup of Jews for deportation.

For Modiano, *Dora Bruder* stands as a breaking point both literary and biographical. Modiano wrote *Dora Bruder* after reading Serge Klarsfeld's *Mémorial des enfants juifs déportés de France* (*French Children of the Holocaust: a memorial*), a book that freed him to drop the artifice of absolute fiction and consider appropriating his own memories for the purpose of creating literature, thus providing readers with direct access to his own process of remembrance. He now recognized the validity of literature in handling historical fact, re-creating emotional impact, and preserving the memory of the individual caught in the political actions of states. The text's alternation between research and speculation about Dora's evanescent fate enables Modiano to explore his own personal history and his relationship with his father. He specifies the circumstances of their estrangement when depicting a violent family argument. *Dora Bruder* is the only text where Modiano mentions his father's death and their failed reconciliation when his father was sent to the hospital. The novel shows the influence of writers important to Modiano including Friedo Lampe, Gilbert Lecomte-Gilbert, and Jean Genet. The text also retraces the genesis of *La place de l'Etoile* and explains how the title was borrowed randomly from a book by Robert Desnos, who died at the Terezin camp in 1945, the year of Modiano's birth.

Addressing the Vichy Past

Although some readers have criticized what they see as a taste for nostalgia in Modiano's work, his fundamental preoccupation is the issue of identity and memory for a French Jewish novelist. In France, the memory of the *Shoah* is a painful legacy with which a whole generation of Jewish writers must come to terms, despite the horror or the shame. In the postwar years, a whole generation is confronted with a double problem: how to assume the memory of the disaster with extermination camps and how to distance oneself with regard to a victimaire dialectic, the shame and the fault to have been appointed as a scapegoat-emissary. More than the imposed silence, it is about the ache stemming from the aftermath of the war together with the weight of the guilt of a stigmatized identity. In their works, Pierre Goldman and Georges Perec or Alain Finkielkraut convey the same feeling of being overwhelmed by the mutilation of their origins. For Modiano, the attraction for the Occupation stands out at first from the biographic register. The period of the Occupation conceals zones of shadows, which veil to the teenager, then to the adult, the precise circumstances of sound "to be for the world." This pathological curiosity results from the impossibility in which the writer is to be able to understand and justify his origin. It is an obsession of the unknown and an uncontrollable sense of guilt which taps Modiano: "I am a product of the Occupation, the time when one could simultaneously be a trafficker of black market, a gestapiste of the Lauriston street and a pursued man. It is in this time when I met my father, a cosmopolitan Jew, and my mother, a comedian of Flemish origin, in the pre-war cinema" (Pudlowski, p. 5).

For Modiano the question of Judaism is expressed in different terms. Since Modiano's mother was not Jewish and his father was an assimilated Jew, he defines himself as being cosmopolitan although he still proclaims a Jewish identity. He knew he was of Jewish descent from a very young age, and along with this knowledge he had the experience of coming across antisemitic books in his father's library—Lucien Rebatet's *Décombres*, Robert Brasillach's *Notre avant-guerre*, and Céline's pamphlets. As he learned more about the widespread expression of hatred toward people like his father during the period of the Occupation, he came to feel a Jew at heart. "I am not a Zionist but I feel for the Jews in adversity" (Jaudel, p. 37), he has said. For Modiano, the question of Jewish identity points to a larger identity crisis. His approach is not to offer a nostalgic celebration of a culture unknown to him, but rather to show the difficulties of the French-Judaic cross-culture. Modiano seems to remain scarred by memory of the Années Noires, if one considers the many figures of Nazi executioners, antisemitic hysterics, and cynical opportunists who appear throughout his fiction. In fact, he remains a prisoner of memories that are not his own but that he has made his.

Since the late 1960s, Patrick Modiano has been delving into the Vichy past, novel after novel, but not under any pretension of some realistic or historic restaging. He remains keenly aware that history is now suspect, notably as demonstrated by the way the French state has tried to minimize the extent of French collaboration during the Occupation. In the wake of the war, General Charles de Gaulle offered the country under reconstruction a watered-down and reassuring gloss of its wartime history. The charismatic general succeeded in foisting upon the nation a glorious revisionist legend of a country united in its resistance against Nazism, which remained unshaken for over twenty years. By denying its hand in the Nazi extermination policy, France remained in the grip of what Henri Rousso calls "the re-acting of the fault" (p. 93).

The generation born after World War II, however, feeling that justice had been denied and guilt unacknowledged, had an urge to uncover the past and search for the truth of France's response to the German occupation. The events of May 1968, by questioning the de Gaulle myth, led to a shift in the prevalent values. May 1968, at first, is marked by students' movements in revolt against the consumer society and the government in place since the postwar years. In general, it reveals a deep crisis occurring in French society, in its values and its renewal. This societal crisis opened the floodgates for an enlightened reading of the Occupation, although somewhat belatedly, and a spate of history books, essays, novels, and films ensued. As a writer of this second generation, Patrick Modiano was the first in France to tackle head-on his country's guilt-ridden and alienating obsession with denial, by exposing twenty-five years of official revisionist presentation of Vichy France in his 1968 novel *La place de l'Etoile*.

Modiano has also been part of the crucial role French film has played in exposing Vichy policies. In their documentary film *Le chagrin et la pitié* (*The Sorrow and the Pity*, 1971), Marcel Ophüls and Alain de Sedouy overturned the 1940s position by challenging the resistance myth. One year later an influential book by the American historian Robert Paxton disclosed the moral and political responsibilities of the Vichy regime in the deportation of Jews. In 1974 Modiano helped write the screenplay for *Lucien Lacombe*, a film produced by Louis Malle about the destiny of a young French peasant who works as a collaborator for the Gestapo. Directly influenced by *The Sorrow and the Pity, Lucien Lacombe* is a psychological analysis of a social misfit who joins the Gestapo as an opportunity to terrorize the bourgeois. In fact, however, the target of his terrorizing is two Jews from Paris. André-Pierre Colombat called the film "a milestone in the evolution of representation of the Holocaust in French cinema."

In later novels, Modiano exhumed the archives of the Années Noires, compiling details from which to tell the story of the obliterated promises (*Une jeunesse*, 1981), the shattered hopes (*Dora Bruder*, 1997), and the unspoken distress (*Chien de printemps*, 1993) of French Jews under the Occupation. *Dora Bruder* provides an oblique self-portrait of the artist as a vigilant yet circumspect "researcher" of the abyssal past: "under that thick layer of amnesia you could feel something, now and again, a muffled far-away echoing, not that it would have been possible to explain it precisely. It is like being on the edge of a magnetic field, without any pendulum for detecting the waves" (p. 133).

Modiano scatters clues about—historical, cultural, or toponymic sparks based on archival research and his own memories—which radiate through the text and the reader's fantasy world. Disjointed and resolutely vacant, the form of Modiano's novels reflects the legacy of the Années Noires for a whole generation of people—a scrappy and erratic memory "which must not at any cost be reconstructed, the truth filtering through the gaps" (Rousso, p. 152). As a second-generation writer, one who has a memory of the Holocaust without the experience, Modiano invites us to reflect on ways of coming to terms with memory, and above all to question the role of literature in representing memory of Vichy collaboration in France.

Bibliography

Primary Sources

La place de l'étoile. (The Place of the Star). 1968.
La ronde de nuit. (*Night Rounds*). 1969.
Les boulevards de ceinture. (Ring Roads). 1972.
Villa Triste. (*Villa Triste*). 1975.
Livret de famille. (Family Record Book). 1977.
Rue des Boutiques obscures. (*Missing Person*). 1978.
Une jeunesse. (A Youth). 1981.
Quartier perdu. (*A Trace of Malice*). 1984.
Remise de peine. (The Postponement of Punishment). 1988.
Voyage de noces. (*Honeymoon*). 1990.
Fleurs de ruine. (Flowers of Ruin). 1991.
Un cirque passe. (A Circus passes). 1992.
Chien de printemps (Dog of Springtime). 1993.
Du plus loin de l'oubli. 1996.
Dora Bruder. (*The Search Warrant*). 1997.

Secondary Sources

Delarue, Jacques. "La bande Bonny-Lafont." In *Résistants et collaborateurs: Les Français dans les années noires*. Edited by François Bédarida. Paris: L'histoire, 1985. Pp. 62–69.

Dickstein, Juliette. "Inventing French Memory: The Legacy of the Occupation in the Works of Patrick Modiano: 1968–1988." In *Paradigms of Memory: The Occupation and Other Hi/stories in the Novels of Patrick Modiano*. Edited by Martine Guyot-Bender and William Vanderwolk. New York: Peter Lang, 1998.

Guyot-Bender, Martine, and William Vanderwolk. "*A Suivre* . . . A Conclusion." In their *Paradigms of Memory: The Occupation and Other Hi/stories in the Novels of Patrick Modiano*. New York: Peter Lang, 1998.

Kaspi, André. *Les Juifs pendant l'Occupation*. Paris: Le seuil, 1991.

Khalifa, Samuel. "The Mirror of Memory: Patrick Modiano's *La place de l'Etoile* and *Dora Bruder*." In *The Holocaust and the Text: Speaking the Unspeakable*. Edited by Andrew Leak and George Paizis. New York: Macmillan, 2000. Pp. 159–173.

Nettelbeck, Colin D., and Penelope A. Hueston. *Patrick Modiano: Pièces d'identité*. Paris: Lettres Modernes, 1986.

Ory, Pascal. *Les Collaborateurs 1940–1945*. Paris: Le seuil, 1976.

———. "Comme de l'an quarante: Dix ans de *rétro satanas*." *Le débat*, no. 16 (November 1981): 109–117.

Paxton, Robert. *Vichy France: Old Guard and New Order 1940–1944*. New York: Columbia University Press, 1972.

Rousso, Henri. *Le syndrome de Vichy de 1944 à nos jours*: Paris: Le seuil, 1990.

Salgas, Jean-Pierre. *Le roman français contemporain, 1960–1990*. Paris: Ministère des affaires étrangères, ADPF, 1990.

Interviews and Archives

Interview with Marie-Françoise Leclère. *Elle*, 8 December 1969.

Interview with Victor Malka. *Les nouvelles littéraires*, no. 2353 (30 October 1972).

Interview with Françoise Jaudel. *L'arche* (October–November 1972).

Interview with Dominique Jamet. *Lire* (October 1975).

Interview with Gilles Pudlowski. *Les nouvelles littéraires*, no. 2774 (12 February 1981).

Interview with Louis. Vidal *Figaro Literary Supplement*, 4 January 1996.

KADYA MOLODOWSKY

(1894–1975)

KATHRYN HELLERSTEIN

ONE OF THE most prolific and respected Yiddish poets of the twentieth century, Kadya Molodowsky was born in Bereze Kartuska, in the Pale of Settlement (White Russia), on 10 May 1894. She was one of four children of Itke Kaplan Molodowsky, a small-business woman, and Isaac Molodowsky, a *kheder* (traditional Jewish primary school) teacher of Hebrew and Gemara. Like her younger brother, but unlike her older and younger sisters, Kadya was educated in Hebrew and Aramaic by her father, in Yiddish by her paternal grandmother, and in Russian by private tutors. She passed the high school graduation exams in the regional city of Libave in 1911 at age seventeen and obtained a teaching certificate at age eighteen. Buffeted by the political forces of World War I and the Bolshevik Revolution, Molodowsky studied, first in Warsaw and then in Odessa, to become qualified as an elementary school teacher of Hebrew between 1913 and 1917. Her mentor was the Hebrew revivalist educator Yehiel Halperin.

Life Before World War II

In Kiev in 1920, Molodowsky published her first poem and met her future husband, Simche Lev. They married in 1921 and settled in Warsaw, Poland, where they lived until 1935, except for some months in 1923 when they worked in a Joint Distribution Committee children's home in Brest-Litovsk. In Warsaw, Molodowsky taught Yiddish in the elementary school of the Central Yiddish Schools Organization and Hebrew in a Jewish community evening school for working girls. An active member of the Yiddish Writers' Union at Tlomtaske Street 13 in Warsaw, Molodowsky published the first four of her seven major books of poems: *Kheshvndike nekht* (Nights of Heshvan, 1927), *Mayselekh* (Tales, children's poems, around 1930), *Dzshike gas* (Dzshike street, 1933), and *Freydke* (1935). These poems, depicting the struggles of a young woman coming to terms with modernity, Jewish tradition, and socialism, established Molodowsky's reputation among Yiddish writers in Europe and in America.

In 1935, Molodowsky immigrated to the United States, living first with her sisters and father in Philadelphia, but soon settling in New York City. Her husband joined her there in 1938. In these years, Molodowsky gave poetry readings and lectures throughout the United States and Canada. Her fifth book, poems of exile, *In land fun mayn gebeyn* (In the country of my bones), was published in Chicago in 1937. In 1938, she published another book of children's poems, *Afn barg* (On the mountain), a play, *Ale fentster tsu der zun: Shpil in elef bilder* (All windows facing the sun: A play in eleven images), published in Warsaw in 1938, and in 1942, a novel, *Fun lublin biz nyu-york: Togbukh fun rivke zilberg* (From Lublin to New York: diary of Rivke Zilberg). During this period, Molodowsky wrote a column for the Yiddish daily *Forverts* (Forward) under a pseudonym (Rivke Zilberg) and cofounded and edited the first run of the literary journal *Svive* (Surroundings).

The War Years and After

Although she continued writing poems during World War II, it was not until the war ended and the extent of the Holocaust became known that Molodowsky published her sixth book of poems, *Der melekh dovid aleyn iz geblibn* (Only King David remained, 1946), which Molodowsky called *khurbn lider*, or "poems of the Destruction." Only nineteen years later did Molodowsky publish her seventh and last collection of poems, *Likht fun dornboym* (Light of the thorn bush), published in Buenos Aires in 1965—poems richly allusive to classical Hebrew sources. Yet Molodowsky wrote prolifically during these years in other genres.

In 1945 Molodowsky published another book of children's poems, *Yidishe kinder* (Jewish children), and the leading poets of Jewish Palestine translated her children's poems into Hebrew in a volume titled *Pitḥu et hasha'ar* (Open the gate), published in Tel Aviv. Over the next few years she published a book-length narrative poem (*Donna Gracias Mendes*, 1948), two plays, and a chapbook of poems titled *In yerushalayim kumen malokhim* (In Jerusalem, angels come, 1952). In 1957 she published a collection of essays on Zionism titled *Af di vegn fun tsion* (On the roads of Zion) and a volume of short stories titled *A shtub mit zibn fentster* (A house with seven windows). All of these prose works are infused with Molodowsky's awareness of the loss of Europe's Jewry in the Holocaust and her hopes for the regeneration of Jewish life and culture in Israel. In 1960 Molodowsky revived the quarterly literary journal *Svive* (Surroundings) that she had published for seven issues in 1943 and 1944. In *Svive* from 1965 to 1974 Molodowsky serialized her autobiography, *Mayn elter zeydns yerushe* (my great-grandfather's legacy). In 1962 she edited an anthology, *Lider fun khurbn* (Poems of the Holocaust), which includes, in the first half, poems by Yiddish poets who were "drowned near Kenigsberg . . . starved in the Ghetto . . . murdered in Maidanek" (*Lider fun Khurbn*, Tel Aviv: Farlag I. C. Peretz, 1962, p. 9), whom Molodowsky calls *kdoyshim*, martyrs—Leyb Ofeskin, Hirsh Glik, Mordkhe Gebirtig, Ida Grodzianovski, Hershele, Yitskhok Katzenelson, Leye Rudnitski, and others. The second half of the anthology collects poems written in the subsequent decades by those who survived in Europe—Avraham Sutskever, Rivke Basman, Rokhl Korn, Chaim Grade, Reyzl Zshikhlinski—or who witnessed from America, Australia, or Eretz Yisroel—Jacob Glatstein, Berish Weinstein, A. Leyeles, H. Leyvik, Gabriel Preil, Melekh Ravitsh. Joining together the poems of the dead and the living, in this anthology Molodowsky gives voice to the suffering, the mourning, and the strength of Jews to rebuild Jewish life in Israel, "as if once again the Pillar of Fire [from the book of Exodus] were to lead us through the desert of despair" (p. 13).

From 1949 through 1952, Molodowsky and her husband Simche Lev lived in Tel Aviv, Israel, where Molodowsky edited the Yiddish journal *Heym* (Home), published by the Pioneer Women Organization. At this time, she began writing a novel, *Baym toyer: Roman fun dem lebn in yisroel* (At the gate: novel about life in Israel, 1967). Molodowsky and Lev returned to New York in 1952, where they lived until Lev's death in 1974. In 1971, Kadya Molodowsky was awarded the Itzik Manger Prize in Israel, the highest award in Yiddish literature. She died in Philadelphia on 23, March 1975.

Holocaust Poems: Witnessing from America

Although Molodowsky lived in America during World War II and did not experience firsthand the Nazi destruction of European Jewry, she wrote some of the strongest and most memorable Yiddish poems commemorating the Jews and their culture destroyed in the Holocaust. Her best-known poem, "Eyl Khanun" ("Merciful God"), written in 1945, opens the book *Der melekh dovid aleyn iz geblibn*. Molodowsky writes this poem, indeed, this whole collection of poems, within the tradition of Jewish lamentation extending from the Bible to modern writers in Hebrew and Yiddish. These Jewish poems, written in the direst of historical moments, from the destruction of the Temple through pogroms, are protestations that at once deny and reaffirm the speaker's connection to the deity. Even more directly than the fiction of Isaac Bashevis Singer and Eli Wiesel or the poems of Jacob Glatstein and Uri Tzvi Greenberg, Molodowsky's prayer challenges the fundamental premise of Judaism—God's Covenant with the Jewish people:

Merciful God,
Choose another people,
Elect another.
We are tired of death and dying,
We have no more prayers.
. . . . . .
We have no more blood
To be a sacrifice.
Our house has become a desert.
The earth is insufficient for our graves,
No more laments for us,
No more dirges
In the old, holy books.
Merciful God,
Sanctify another country,
Another mountain.
We have strewn all the fields and every stone
With ash, with holy ash.
With the aged,
With the youthful,
And with babies, we have paid
For every letter of your Ten Commandments (Translated by Kathryn Hellerstein, in *Paper Bridges: Selected Poems of Kadya Molodowsky*, Detroit: Wayne State University Press, 1999, p. 353).

Molodowsky responds to the Nazi destruction of Europe's Jews with a poetic annihilation. Her poem transforms God's promise to the biblical patriarchs of the chosen people into a curse upon the enemies of the Jews. The poet evokes the Holocaust with the imagery of the "holy ash" covering the sacred mountains of Jewish law and worship, Sinai and Zion, too high a price to pay for the "chosen" status. Even as the poem rebukes God, however, in the tradition of sacred parody, it simultaneously confirms the poet's yearning to believe in a God who will listen to her words.

Poems written during the war in *Der melekh dovid aleyn iz geblibn* express the anxiety of a Jew in America, awaiting news from family and friends in Europe. Molodowsky describes such moments in her autobiography, but her poem "Briv fun geto" (Letters from the Ghetto, 1941) embodies these emotions most powerfully, as the poem's speaker receives postcards from family and friends in the Warsaw ghetto. These censored missives consist of "Three lines on a card, nothing more," yet their silences speak of the writers' suffering: "the white blankness pleads for mercy on the paper" (*Paper Bridges*, p. 361) and lead the poet to call for God to avenge the innocents. In "Tsu a kinds portret" (To a child's portrait), she imagines a baby girl in the ghetto, perhaps her brother's daughter, who, she later learned, perished there:

> I'm frightened by the large ball near your hands,
> It reminds me of a globe—
> A world that mourns, a world that burns,
> I'm frightened by the fire that is so close
> To your small hands (*Paper Bridges*, p. 367).

In "*Gezegenung*" (Leavetaking) written in 1943, Molodowsky describes how hard it is to write a poem in Yiddish when she intuits that the language itself is being destroyed with its speakers:

> Burned through,
> The last thread swings away,
> Letters crumble,
> And words pale.
> . . . . . .
> I've forgotten my alphabet in sorrow (*Paper Bridges*, p. 377).

Molodowsky evokes the loss of the Yiddish language here, when the poet forgets the very alphabet she needs to write her poems, as a trope for the loss of Europe's Jews. The imagery of fire in both these poems alludes to the Nazi burning of Jewish books and Torah scrolls on *Kristallnacht* (9 November 1938) but also suggests that the poet had some premonition before 1945 of the fires destroying Jews themselves in the concentration camp crematoria.

Mourning with Poison

Poems composed at the end of the war mourn loss through tarnished and distorted Jewish imagery. In "Toyter shabes" (Dead Sabbath), Molodowsky's speaker describes her experience of the Sabbath, once she knows that the Jewish communities are gone:

> Doors swing on silenced hinges.
> Iron and rust are light.
> All has lost its heft after millions of deaths.
> A dead Sabbath rests . . . (*Paper Bridges*, p. 397).

The speaker experiences the sharpest anguish when among the ghosts she encounters her brother, who has perished. She describes her pain when she recognizes his image among the passing shadows, "I grow small, stunted/And jammed up against the floating pain—/Are you, my brother, you?" (p. 397). She cannot escape from the guilt and pain of survival, from the unholy silence of this "dead Sabbath."

The destruction of Europe's Jews has polluted prayers and sacred texts. When Molodowsky prays, she asks for death, as in "A tfile" (A Prayer):

> I arise at dawn and my prayer
> Is poison.
> I ask that the Deluge shall come again,
> Raising the surge of the ocean
> Higher than towers and rooftops.
> The rescuing Ark shall not float (*Paper Bridges*, p. 413).

Awakening to her losses, the speaker wants the entire world to be destroyed by God, in a second flood in which, unlike the Covenantal story in Genesis, there will be no Noah and no Ark to rescue a remnant of humankind.

The Poet's Burden

In 1945 it must have seemed to Molodowsky that the Yiddish poet who had lived out the Holocaust was writing for an audience that no longer existed. Speaking for the dead, this poet bore a tremendous burden. Yet she continued writing. In New York, in the war years, Molodowsky, the author of children's poems for her young pupils in Warsaw in the 1930s, wrote a child-like poem, "Baynakhtike gest" (Night visitors), which carries a terrible message of abandonment and guilt. When a bird, a cat, and a little goat—characters from Molodowsky's earlier children's poems—come knocking on the speaker's door in the middle of the night, she welcomes them with food, drink, and rest. But when a person comes, asking for help, she "slammed the door shut, turned the lock, threw the bolt" (*Paper Bridges*, p. 397). When the person, a Jew seeking refuge, stands on the other side of the door and sobs, the poem's speaker puts her face in her hands and is surrounded by the night as dark as blindness. This lack of response to a person in need expresses the guilt and anguish of a Jew safe in America during the Holocaust.

Even when she discards a half-finished poem fraught with problems, Molodowsky's poet-speaker feels guilty of throwing away a human life, as in "Khad Gadya" (One Kid). The poem's character, a tall gray man with a pipe, thrown away with the poem, refuses to disappear. He persists in her imagination, like a *khad gadya*, the goat of the repetitive Passover song whose death begins a chain of divine retribution. In the end, when she looks into the mirror, the poet sees her own image replaced by that of the character, her victim.

The Poet's Affirmation

In Molodowsky's *khurbn lider*, biblical singers and musicians suggest the predicament of the Jewish poet writing in the aftermath of the Holocaust. "The fife-player of Sodom," whose "body is burn layered upon burn," sings to God from a "throne on the mountain of ash," asking, "Why have you elected me / To sing this Hallelujah for You?" (p. 401). He persists in his questions: why must he sing God's praises when "Death is engraved upon my forehead,"

When the Tigris and the Euphrates and the Vistula
Flow red
From my open wound,
From my anguished death
That is never dead? (*Paper Bridges*, p. 403).

Like this last musician surviving God's destruction of Sodom, the city of pagan sinners, King David, the author of the Psalms, is the only survivor of the Jews:

The nation was cut down—
Wound and death.
The roads bestrewn,
The houses burned.
Only King David remained,
He with his crown in his hands (*Paper Bridges*, p. 407).

Yet the despairing King David and the man who blows the shofar, or ram's horn, beneath "A sky without stars, Primordial darkness lost in darkness," where "There is no congregation, No quorum at all" (*Paper Bridges*, p. 369), reaffirm that Jewish tradition will continue through its remnants, even after such complete destruction.

Years later, this theme persists in Molodowsky's poetry, only somewhat resolved. In "Ikh bin a vider-kol" (I am an echo, 1960), the poet declares,

I am an echo
Of a vanished symphony.
My voice is a marvel,
Whether it's prayer or blasphemy (p. 481).

A phantom fiddler appears to the poet and performs ritual melodies. The actual fiddler, long since deceased, leaves only an echo, uttering,

Here I am, here I am,
You don't need what is real.
My voice will reach you.
Here I am, here I am,
Take along my echo
To the walls of Jericho.
Soon I will play
By the walls of Jericho (*Paper Bridges*, p. 481).

The Yiddish poet of 1960 in America echoes the vanished orchestra of the destroyed Yiddish-speaking world of Europe. Instead of despairing, however, Molodowsky finds a kind of messianic promise in the image of the shtetl fiddler returning like Joshua with his ram's horn to the Promised Land.

Bibliography

Primary Sources

Kheshvndike nekht: Lider (Nights of Heshvan: Poems). 1927.
Mayselekh (Tales). Circa 1930.
Dzshike gas (Dzshike street). 1933.
Freydke. 1935.
In land fun mayn gebeyn (In the country of my bones). 1937.
Afn barg (On the mountain). 1938.
Ale fentster tsu der zun: Shpil in elef bilder (All windows facing the sun: A play in eleven images). 1938.
Fun lublin biz nyu-york: Togbukh fun rivke zilberg (From Lublin to New York: Diary of Rivke Zilberg). 1942.
Yidishe kinder (Jewish children) 1945.
Pitḥu et hasha'ar (Open the gate). 1945.
Der melekh dovid aleyn iz geblibn (Only King David remained). 1946.
Donna Gracias Mendes. 1948.
Nokhn got fun midbar: drame (After the God of the desert: drama). 1949.
Heym (Home). Journal edited in Israel, June 1950–October 1952.
In yerushalayim kumen malokhim (In Jerusalem, angels come). 1952.
A hoyz oyf grand strit (A house on Grand Street). 1953.
Af di vegn fun tsion (On the roads of Zion). 1957.
A shtub mit zibn fentster (A house with seven windows). 1957.
Lider fun khurbn: Antologye (Poems from the Holocaust: Anthology). Edited by Kadya Molodowsky. 1962.
Likht fun dornboym (Light of the thorn bush). 1965.
Mayn elter zeydns yerushe (My great-grandfather's legacy. Serialized autobiography in *Svive*). 1965–1974.

Baym toyer: Roman fun dem lebn in yisroel (At the gate: Novel about life in Israel). 1967.

Martsepanes: Mayselekhun lider far kinder (Marzipans: Tales and poems for children). 1970.

Shirei Yirushalayim (Poems of Jerusalem). Translated into Hebrew by Mordehai Saber. 1971.

Svive (Surroundings). Journal edited 1943–1944, 1960–1974.

Secondary Sources

Hellerstein, Kathryn. " 'A Word for My Blood': A Reading of Kadya Molodowsky's 'Froyen-lider' (Vilna, 1927)," *AJS Review* 13, nos. 1–2 (1988): 47–79.

———."In Exile in the Mother Tongue: Yiddish and the Woman Poet." In *Borders, Boundaries, and Frames: Essays in Cultural Criticism and Cultural Studies (Essays from the English Institute)*, 64–106. Edited by Mae G. Henderson. New York: Routledge, 1995.

———. "A Yiddish Poet's Response to the *Khurbn:* Kadya Molodowsky in America," In *Freedom and Responsibility: Exploring the Dilemmas of Jewish Continuity*. Edited by Rela M. Geffen and Marsha B. Edelman, 233–249. New York: KTAV, 1998.

———, trans. and ed. *Paper Bridges: Selected Poems of Kadya Molodowsky*. Detroit: Wayne State University Press, 1999.

Klepfisz, Irena. "*Di mames, dos loshn*/The Mothers, the Language: Feminism, *Yidishkayt*, and the Politics of Memory." *Bridges* 4, no. 1 (winter/spring 1994): 12–47.

Zucker, Sheva. "Kadya Molodowsky's 'Froyen-Lider' " *Yiddish* 9, no. 2 (1994): 44–51.

Archives

Molodowsky's papers can be found in the archives at the YIVO Institute for Jewish Research in New York, New York.

HARRY KURT VICTOR MULISCH

(1927–)

DICK VAN GALEN LAST

HARRY KURT VICTOR Mulisch was born on 29 July 1927 in Haarlem, the Netherlands, the only son of Karl Victor Kurt Mulisch and Alice Schwarz. His father, an officer in the Austrian Army during World War I, had emigrated to Holland after the war. In 1936, his parents divorced, and the young Harry stayed with his father in Haarlem, where he went to school. He was to leave high school prematurely in 1944. During the German occupation, his father was one of the three directors of the Lippmann, Rosenthal and Company banking firm, the bank commonly referred to as the "robbery bank." It misused the name of a famous Jewish banking company and was in fact the focal point of the forced collection of Jewish assets. In that function, the elder Mulisch was able to keep his Jewish ex-wife and his son out of German hands. Later, Mulisch recalled his war years in Haarlem:

> I was Jewish too, I had a yellow card with the number of Jewish grandparents. If you had three or four Jewish grandparents you were arrested and killed, if you had two or one as I had, then you were half-Jewish and they did not bother you for the time being. If there were razzias in Haarlem and they captured Jews then they were done for, while non-Jews had to go to Germany to work. I was with my yellow card German enough not to be gassed and too Jewish to be allowed to work in a German factory: "weiter gehen" it was and thus I escaped. A completely surrealistic situation (interview *Haagse Post,* 8 February 1986).

After the war, Mulisch's father was imprisoned for three years for collaboration with the Nazis. His mother, whose own mother and grandmother were gassed in the extermination camp Sobibor, emigrated to the United States. This biographical background, his father being an Austrian Nazi and his mother being of Jewish descent, goes far in explaining Mulisch's witticism quoted in his autobiography, *Mijn getijdenboek* (Amsterdam: De Bezige Bij, 1975): "I didn't 'live' the Second World War that much. I am the Second World War." The function of the war as a guiding principle and consistent thread in his work can be seen from his early books, such as *Het stenen bruidsbed* (*The Stone Bridal Bed*, 1959), which deals with the bombardment of Dresden by the Allied Air Force in February 1945, to his most recent novels, such as *Siegfried* (2001), about Siegfried the so-called son of Hitler and Eva Braun.

From 1949 on, Harry Mulisch was a fulltime writer who took great interest in science. In 1951, he established his literary reputation with the novel *Archibald Strohalm*, for which he received the Reina Prinsen Geerligs award in 1951. The novel is named after a famous resistance fighter. In the Dutch literary world, Mulisch is linked with Willem Frederik Hermans and Gerard Reve as the most important writer of the postwar generation. Mulisch considered his two colleagues too Dutch, whereas he believed himself to be a cosmopolitan adventurer. His books have been translated into many languages and were widely praised, even more so abroad than in his own country. Although he has won almost every literary award that exists in Holland, some critics, as well as some sections of his public audience, have remained unimpressed. That may be due in part to the philosophical ambitions of many of his novels, a phenomenon quite unfamiliar to the pragmatic mentality in Holland, where his self-confidence and his dandy-like outlook are taken for arrogance and vanity. "I believe in myself so I believe in God," Mulisch once said. When a *Wall Street Journal* critic wrote in his review of *The Discovery of Heaven* that Mulisch belonged in the ranks of Homer, Dante, Milton, Walter Scott, Umberto Eco, and Steven Spielberg, Mulisch's characteristic reaction was: "It is almost too flattering!"

The year before Hannah Arendt published her report of the Eichmann trial, *Eichmann in Jerusalem A Report on the Banality of Evil* (1963), Harry Mulisch published his book *De zaak 40/61. Een reportage* (Case

40/61: A Coverage) in which he came to similar conclusions as Hannah Arendt. While Arendt's book gave birth to great controversy, Mulisch's book passed unnoticed, even although Hannah Arendt praised it in the reprints of her own book: "the Dutch correspondent Harry Mulisch . . . is almost the only writer on the subject to put the person of the defendant at the center of his report and whose evaluation of Eichmann coincides with my own on some essential points" (*Eichmann in Jerusalem*, New York: Penguin, 1978, p. 282). Mulisch's book can be considered an attempt to demythologize Evil. Eichmann, the Nazi official responsible for the deportation of tens of thousands of Jews, is described as a perfectly normal man, representative of the bureaucratic ethos. If Albert Schweitzer had commanded him to transport sick Negroes to Lambarene, he would have done it as efficiently as he gassed or shot Jews. In Mulisch's view, ideology or antisemitism played no role whatsoever for *Schreibtischmörder* (bureaucratic murderers) such as Eichmann. Eichmann, Mulisch wrote, was a robot, a machine without a will of his own, just like Norman Corinth, the American pilot of the Bomber Command that bombed Dresden in *Het Stenen Bruidsbed (The Stone Bridal Bed)*, who, ten years later, wanders through the remaining ruins and wonders who had caused all the destruction. In the literary imagination of Mulisch, the *Schreibtischmörder* of the Nazis and the Allied pilot are only pawns in a universe inhabitated by people without souls.

Eichmann cured Mulisch from his "noncommittal indignation" and made him realize that only when society changes, can people change too. The Cuban Revolution embodied for him a new morale. "Cuba was for me the branch of heaven, just as Auschwitz was a branch of the hell" (Heumakers, p. 148). Mulisch always had a very manicheistic view of good and evil, and never renounced his leftist sympathies. This uncritical engagement posed problems for all those who liked his literary work but for whom the disenchantment that followed the illusions of the 1960s did not pass unnoticed. Mulisch also distinguished himself from his older peers, Reve and Hermans, because of his optimism. Their vision of the world, wrote Mulisch, was formed through the 1930s when they were adolescents witnessing unemployment, boredom, and fear that would lead to a total catastrophe; whereas Mulisch grew up during the war, when the hope for liberation was the determining factor.

Fascism is for Mulisch the absolute evil. He denies that Hitler was part of "history"; the fascist is still alive in himself and in others. Evil fascinates Mulisch, in whose work art and literature are always closely related with death. As the personification of death and evil, Hitler was to haunt Mulisch, who unmasks Hitler in his last work *Siegfried* (Amsterdam: De Bezige Bij, 2001) as a man without a face, as the personification of "the nullifying Nothing" (p. 158). "At the end of the twentieth century it was my ambition to say something definite about Hitler," he said in a interview. For "*die Endlösung der Hitlerfrage*" ("The Final Solution of the Hitler Question,"*Siegfried*, p. 42) Mulisch did not try to understand Hitler psychologically but philosophically and theologically: "you must dare to think as ruthlessly about Hitler as he himself acted." Yet another example of Mulisch's love for paradoxes and absurdities was *De toekomst van gisteren* (The Future of Yesterday, 1972). This book is about a novel he had wanted to write, a novel about a world in which Hitler had won the war. Mulisch uses a protagonist who writes amid all the horrors about an imaginary world in which Hitler has lost the war. Apart from the journalistic passages in which he described his visits to Hitler's architect Albert Speer and to Bayreuth, *De toekomst van gisteren* is in the first instance a report on a creative process that has failed. Mulisch writes: "It is the major quality and internal consequence of my novel, that it is not here—that it destroyed itself. In that sense it is a masterpiece." To the critics who reproached him for his Hegelian juggling with negations that could discourage the readers, he answered he could not care less: "A novel is not communication with the public, but with that novel and thus with myself" (interview *NRC-Handelsblad* 2 February 2001).

It is impossible to do justice to his many-sided oeuvre; since he started writing, Mulisch has published one or more books every year, including novels, dramas, operas, essays, short stories, and several books of poetry. His most popular novel, *De aanslag* (*The Assault*, 1982), had more than twenty-five reprints. Although its point of departure is the liquidation by the Dutch resistance of a fascist police officer in Haarlem, it is far from just being a novel about the war and, in fact, spans the years 1945 to 1985. In this work, Mulisch raises, among others, the question of transgenerational guilt, of the impact and morality of armed resistance, and of the cooperation of many Dutch police officers with the persecution of the Jews in Holland. Mulisch here anticipates recent research by Dutch historians who confirm the active involvement of Dutch authorities (police, civil servants, and railway personnel). This form of collaboration contributed, according to Eichmann, to "such a smooth running of the transports that it was a pleasure to behold" (transcript of W. Sassen interview, Bundes Archive, Unterlagen Servatius, Germany). It also gives a clear image of the chaos in the Netherlands during the last year of the war, the daily misery people were confronted with, and the moral dilemmas that this situation produced.

Mulisch characterizes the stiuation as incomprehensible, unchangable, and insolvable. The novel perfectly reflects the author's strong conviction that the war is a point of reference, because it has re-calibrated the standards for human decency. With reference to *De aanslag*, critics have noticed that Mulisch is capable of coping with richer and more mature subject matters inversely proportional to a simpler narrative structure. His best friend and grandmaster Jan Hein Donner read this book "as an attempt to reconcile the irreconcilable . . . the adventure of the mind who takes offence at the absurdities of life and above all at the great absurdity of the time, that we have to live from backwards to forwards, to the future" (*NRC-Handelsblad*, 19 October 1985). This best-seller, with its many hidden meanings, was made into a film with the same title, which won an Academy Award as best foreign movie in 1986.

Bibliography

Primary Sources

Het stenen bruidsbed (*The Stone Bridal Bed*). 1959.
De zaak 40/61. Een reportage (The Eichmann Case: A Coverage). 1962.
De verteller (The Narrator). 1970.
De toekomst van gisteren (The Future of Yesterday). 1972.
Mijn getijdenboek (My Book of Hours). 1975.
De compositie van de wereld (The Composition of the World). 1980.
De Aanslag (*The Assault*). 1982.
De ontdekking van de hemel (*The Discovery of Heaven: A Novel*). 1992.
Het theater, de brief en de waarheid (The Theatre, the Letter and the Truth). 2000.
Siegfried. 2001.

Secondary Sources

Arendt, Hannah. *Eichmann in Jerusalem:The Bauality of Evil*. New York: Penguin, 1978.
Coming to terms with the Second World War in Contemporary Literature and Art. München: Verlag Silke Schreiber, 2000.
Donner, J. H. *Mulisch, naar ik veronderstel*. Amsterdam: De Bezige Bij, 1971.
Galen Last, Dick van, and Rolf Wolfswinkel. *Anne Frank and After. Dutch Holocaust Literature in Historical Perspective*. Amsterdam: Amsterdam University Press, 1996.
Heumakers, Arnold. *Schoten in de concertzaal*. Amsterdam: Arbeiderspers, 1993.
Meijer, Reinder P. *Literature of the Low Countries. A Short History of Dutch Literature in the Netherlands and Belgium*. Assen: Van Gorcum, 1971.
"Mulisch, Harry." In *Merriam-Webster's Encyclopedia of Literature*. Springfield, Mass.: Merriam-Webster Inc. Pulishers, 1995.
Rossem, M. van. "Eichmann in Jeruzalem. Een discussie over de banaliteit van het kwaad." In *Geschiedenis & cultuur. Achttien opstellen*. Den Haag: SDU, 1990, pp. 139–148.
de Rover, Frans C. de. *De weg van het lachen: over het oeuvre van Harry Mulisch*. Amsterdam: De Bezige Bij, 1987.
——— *Over De aanslag van Harry Mulisch*. Amsterdam: De Arbeiderspers, 1985.
Schmitz-Küller, Helbertijn *Over het stenen bruidsbed van Harry Mulisch*. Amsterdam: De Arbeiderspers, 1983.
Vinson, James, and Daniel Kirkpatrick eds. *Contemporary Foreign Language Writers*. London: St. James Press, 1984.

ZOFIA NAŁKOWSKA

(1884–1954)

MONIKA ADAMCZYK-GARBOWSKI

ZOFIA NAŁKOWSKA IS A major Polish novelist, short story writer, playwright, and essayist. She was born in Warsaw and grew up in the very cultured atmosphere of a literary and artistic world, as her father, Wacław Nałkowski, was a prominent scholar and journalist. She attended a boarding school for girls but was mainly self-educated, well read in such subjects as philosophy, psychology, the natural sciences, and literature, and fluent in four languages. Nałkoswska spent most of her life in Warsaw but also lived in Kiecle, near Vilnias, and in Grodno. She was very active in the social and political life of the country before and after World War II. In 1937 she became the first woman to be chosen as a member of the Polish Academy of Literature.

Nałkowska's early, modernistic novels, such as *Kobiety* (Women, 1906) and *Ksiaze* (The Prince, 1907), reflect a version of feminism inspired by the philosophical works of Friedrich Nietzsche, Arthur Schopenhauer, and Henri Bergson, and the aesthetic ideas of Oscar Wilde. In the later period Nałkowska leans toward social issues and traditional realism, such as in *Granica* (Boundary Lines, 1935). Quite different from all of these works is *Niecierpliwi* (The Impatient, 1939), innovative in form and concerned with the existential dilemmas of human life and various attitudes toward evil, suffering, and death. Her postwar collection of short stories, *Medaliony* (Medallions, 1946), describes German atrocities as reported by eyewitnesses she interviewed. Nałkowska left a detailed and fascinating diary, *Dzienniki* (Diaries, 1979–2000), that covers almost her entire life. There she refers a number of times to the impact the Holocaust, especially the burning of the Warsaw ghetto, and the war in general, had on her. As Diana Kuprel notes:

> This change, which can be charted in the *Diaries*, involved a developing consciousness of her obligation as a writer to bear witness to what was around her and to fix in words all that was being wiped off the earth to prevent it from vanishing without a trace (p. 180).

The *Medallions* Collection

Medallions consists of documentary prose based on reports and recollections from the survivors of the Nazi genocide during World War II, visits to the scenes of the crimes, and witnesses' testimonies. The writer collected materials for her stories in 1945 while working for the High Commission for the Investigation of Nazi Crimes. The cycle consists of eight pieces (first published in 1945 in periodicals). They describe, among other things, a German scientific institute where soap was produced out of human fat ("Professor Spanner"), the plight of women prisoners transported in sealed wagons to concentration camps, including Ravensbrück ("The Hole"), and various forms of extermination of the Jewish people ("The Cemetery Lady," "By the Railway Track," "Dwojra Zielona"), as well as the gassing of children in a death camp ("Adults and Children at Auschwitz").

In "The Hole" we listen to the testimony of a woman who went through a number of camps. She tells of horrible pseudomedical experiments on women, beatings, and unbearable hunger and cold, and of women going mad during transports in sealed boxcars. She remembers that once a curious German officer, alerted by the women's howling, ordered the car to be opened during a stop in spite of the fact that it was prohibited; what he saw visibly frightened him. The conversation in which Nałkowska lets her interlocutor speak with minimal intrusions on her part ends with the woman's attempt at rationalizing all her terrible experiences: "You see, madame, you see! Even the German was frightened when he saw us. Why is it so incomprehensible, then, that the women couldn't withstand it?"

(Evanston, Ill.: Northwestern University Press, 2000, p. 16).

In "Dwojra Zielona" we meet a Jewish survivor who asks herself aloud why the will to live did not leave her for a moment in spite of the fact that her relatives perished, and she lost an eye and suffered various atrocities. She realizes that she wanted to live to give testimony, to "let the world know," as she was afraid that "there won't be a single Jew left on the face of this earth" (p. 32). She also mentions that when she and her fellow prisoners were liberated by the Soviets, they did not even have the strength to feel any joy, the feeling that recurs in a number of memoirs, such as that of Halina Birenbaum.

In "The Man Is Strong" we learn the story of a Jew who was forced by the Nazis to bury thc corpses of gassed Jews, including the victims of the Chelmno death camp. When he saw the dead bodies of his wife and children he begged the Germans to kill him. However, they did not let him die: "One German said, 'The man is strong. He can still work hard.' And he beat me with a cudgel until I got up" (p. 43).

"The Cemetery Lady," which takes place during the liquidation of the Warsaw ghetto, is perhaps the most personal of all pieces, as it has its prototype in the writer's *Diaries* (especially in the entries from 28 April and 7 May 1943, where there are some reflections and images that were later used in the story). During the war, Nałkowska lived in Warsaw, and took care of her ailing mother, supporting herself by running a little cigarette store with her sister. After her mother's death she would often visit her grave. In the story the narrator contrasts a Roman Catholic cemetery, quiet, green, fragrant with spring blossoms, with the situation in which "[p]eople disappear in every manner, under every possible pretext and [o]rdinary, private death, next to the immensity of collective death, seems rather improper. Yet to live is an even greater impropriety" (p. 16). What makes the scene even more horrific is that the cemetery borders on the ghetto wall and the events of spring 1943 are seen from the narrator's perspective and that of one of the female caretakers, who comments in a quavering and muffled voice on the events observed behind the wall. This device serves as an authenticating strategy of witnessing rather than fictionalizing:

> We all live right by the wall, you see, so we can hear what goes on there. Now we all know. They shoot people in the streets. Burn them in their homes. And at night such shrieks and cries. No one can eat or sleep. We can't stand it. You think it's pleasant listening to all that? (p. 20).

The caretaker reports terrible scenes of mothers wrapping their babies in soft things, throwing them out on the pavement and afterwards jumping out themselves. But in spite of compassion revealed by her tearful face and trembling voice, the cemetery lady tries to give an ideological justification to what is happening, which reverberates with Nazi propaganda:

> "They're human beings after all, so you have to feel sorry for them," she explained. "But they despise us more than they do the Germans . . . If the Germans lose the war, the Jews will kill us all . . . You don't believe me? Listen, even the Germans say so . . ." (p. 20).

In "By the Railway Track" a Jewish woman who escapes with a group of others from the sealed train heading for a death camp is wounded by a bullet and is lying near the railway track. Villagers come but they are afraid to help her because offering help or shelter means risking certain death. She asks a young man to buy her some vodka and cigarettes and he agrees to do that. Then an old peasant woman brings her some milk and bread hidden in her shawl and hurriedly disappears looking from a safe distance to see if the woman drank it. Finally two policemen approach the site and the Jewish woman asks them to shoot her, but after deliberating the matter they decide not to carry out her request and leave. Finally the young man volunteers to shoot the bullet. "Why he shot her isn't clear," says the man who tells the narrator the story. "I couldn't understand it (p. 27). Of all people he really seemed to feel sorry for her." (The last sentence is Monika Adamczyk-Garbowska's translation.)

The above is a very characteristic ending for the whole collection, for what is left unsaid is very important in Nałkowska's stories. The conclusion to the last piece, "The Adults and Children in Auschwitz," which is considered a summary, an "attempt to comprehend the enormous scale of the expedited deaths and war actions that took place on Polish soil" (p. 45), is even more striking as it concerns the testimony of a witness who once asked two young children in Auschwitz "sitting in the sand and poking at something with a stick" what they were doing, to which they responded, "We're playing at burning Jews" (p. 49).

All in all, the horrifying register of crimes, mass murder, and martyrdom is presented by Nałkowska in a concise and restrained manner. While limiting her own commentary to a minimum, the writer gives voice to simple people, the witnesses and participants in the events. Their austere, terse, often clumsy reports not only constitute an accusation and testimony to the martyrdom of the helpless victims, but also show how the targets of the Nazi terror became infected with the poisonous ideology, the apathy and mental dementia in the face of crimes, the loss of a sense of human solidarity, and the degeneration of basic ethical instincts. The cycle, with its famous motto "People dealt this fate to people," quickly became a classic in Poland equal to Tadeusz Borowski's stories and was translated into German, Italian, Czech, Slovak, Serbo-Croatian, Slavonic, Romanian, Hungarian, Vietnamese, Esperanto, and only recently English.

Bibliography

Primary Sources

Kobiety (Women). 1906.
Książę (The Prince). 1907.
Rówieśnice (Peers). 1909.
Narcyza. 1910.
Węże i róże (Snakes and Roses). 1915.
Koteczka, czyli Białe tulipany (Kitty, or White Tulips). 1909.
Lustra (Mirrors). 1913.
Moje zwierzęta (My Animals). 1915.
Tajemnice krwi (Secrets of Blood). 1917.
Hrabia Emil (Count Emil). 1920.
Charaktery (Personal Portraits). 1922.
Romans Teresy Hennert (Teresa Hennert's Love Affair). 1924.
Dom nad łakami (The House over the Meadows). 1925.
Choucas. 1927.
Niedobra miłość (Bad Love). 1928.
Dom kobiet (Women's Home). 1930.
Ściany świata (The Walls of the World). 1931.
Dzień jego powrotu (The Day of His Return). 1931.
Między zwierzętami (Among Animals). 1934.
Granica (Boundary Line). 1935.
Niecierpliwi (The Impatient). 1939.
Medaliony. 1946. (*Medallions*) 2000.
Charaktery dawne i ostatnie (Personal Portraits—Old and New). 1948.
Węzły życia (Bonds of Life). 1948–1954.
Mój ojciec (My Father). 1953.
Widzenie bliskie i dalekie (A Close and Distant Vision). 1957.
Dzienniki czasu wojny (Wartime Diaries). 1970.
Dzienniki (Diaries). 1979–2000.

Secondary Sources

Adamczyk-Garbowska, Monika. "A New Generation of Voices in Polish Holocaust Literature." *Prooftexts* 3 (1989): 273–287.
Kuprel, Diana. "Paper Epitaphs of a Holocaust Memorial: Zofia Nałkowska's *Medallions*." *Polin: Studies in Polish Jewry* 13 (2000): 179–187.
Wójcik, Włodzimierz. *Zofia Nałkowska*. Warszawa: Wieolza Powszechna, 1973.
Zaworska, Helena. *Medaliony Zofii Nałkowskiej*. Warszawa: PZWS, 1969.

HUGH NISSENSON

(1933–)

VICTORIA AARONS

HUGH NISSENSON, WHOSE first stories were published in the early 1960s in *Harper's* and *Commentary*, has been described by the critic Robert Alter as "the only genuinely religious writer in the whole American Jewish group" (Alter, p. 75). To be sure, American Jewish fiction in the postwar years, its position established by the initiating triumvirate of Bernard Malamud, Saul Bellow, and Philip Roth, was defined by a kind of self-conscious secularism. For Malamud, this self-conscious secularism took the form of an ethics of communal suffering, while for Roth it defined itself in the ironies of the self-defeating hold on Jewish identity, and for Bellow, it took on a rhetoric of masculinist intellectual posturing. Indeed, in this context, when Malamud, Bellow, and Roth were being canonized as the architects of American Jewish literature, writers for whom the God of the covenant was at best antiquated, and at worst a willfully naïve regression, Hugh Nissenson's short stories would seem to punctuate a return to an overt religious polemic, a discourse of belief with which even his characters must contend.

Nissenson's first collection of short stories *A Pile of Stones* (1965) received the prestigious Edward Lewis Wallant Prize. In the epigraph to this collection, Nissenson cites the following line from *Genesis*, "Let me go, for the day breaketh" (32:27), a line that gives closure to Jacob's nocturnal wrestling with the adversary. But also, and more significant for Nissenson, this passage is the prelude to Jacob's invitation to participate in the covenant, for his antagonist, whether angel or man, represents, however ambiguously or portently, the will of God who, at this defining moment, renames Jacob as Israel, "for you have striven with God and men, and won out" (32:29–30). Jacob, appropriately, and not surprisingly, recognizing the personal and historical importance of his confrontation with the adversary, interprets the struggle as a divine intervention, one that offers the protection of the covenant that he has equivocally entered: "I have seen God face to face and I came out alive" (32:31–32).

Nissenson and the Holocaust

This covenantal guarantee of survival for Nissenson's contemporary "Jacobs," the host of characters who people his fiction, is not, by any means, so assured. In Nissenson's fiction, especially in his Holocaust literature, the short stories and journal pieces that directly or indirectly contend with the aftermath of the catastrophic events of the *Shoah*, the very nature of the covenant, and the implied relationship between human beings and God, become the recurrent and constant source of contention. The epigraph to *A Pile of Stones* sets the stage for the kind of crisis of conscience and struggle with faith that haunt the narratives, not only in this collection but also in *Notes from the Frontier* (1968), Nissenson's nonfiction account of his experiences in Israel, as well as in his second collection of stories, *In the Reign of Peace* (1972), and in *The Elephant and My Jewish Problem* (1988), a volume that contains both fiction and nonfiction entries. In these works, diverse pieces that reflect an ongoing dialogue in which Jewish history is viewed, at least in part, through the mythic lens of biblical narrative, readers find, as stated in the journalistic narrative "Israel During the Eichmann Trial," a return to "old stories," ancient antagonisms, betrayals, and ambiguities that bring to life the metaphorical figure of Jacob, envisioned as contemporary Israel, to "be true to itself and wrestle again with God" (Nissenson, in *The Elephant and My Jewish Problem*, New York: Harper and Row, 1988, p. 60). And wrestle with God, with the various voices and manifestations of divine license, censure, and procurement, he does. In a conversation with the interviewer Diane Cole, published in *Jewish Profiles*,

Nissenson, with no little ironic acuity, recollects a disappointingly thwarted question put to the rabbi at the time of his bar mitzvah: "How can you believe in God after the murder of the six million?" (Cole, p. 220).

Reading Hugh Nissenson's fiction is akin to entering into an ongoing debate, a quarrel long since initiated, in which the covenantal relationship and expectations—those both of God and human beings—are called into question. His writing also portrays the conditions and limitations of belief that preoccupy his characters and become the central tension of the narratives, both fictional and journalistic. The uninterrupted debates are played out on three central landscapes of historical and psychic trauma: America, Eastern Europe, and Israel. Nissenson's short stories and journalistic pieces span a period of time in Jewish history during which, in the aftermath of the Holocaust, Jews once again find themselves in the diaspora, relocating in America and Israel and leaving behind the battered remains of Europe.

America, for Nissenson, would seem to be the locus for the tension between secular and religious law, as well as for a reassessment and reaffirmation of the covenant through the distanced lens of the *Shoah*. The religious ambiguity, especially among Jewish immigrants, whose lives were defined in Europe by a secular, "enlightened" ethos, becomes in America, as is seen in a story such as Nissenson's "The Law," an urgency to reinvent the covenant for future generations. Nissenson's journalistic pieces, in which the author speaks in the first person, making himself a central character and spokesman in the discussion, spans a period from the Adolf Eichmann trial in Israel in 1961 to the Klaus Barbie trial in Lyon in 1987. Nissenson's travels to Israel as a reporter of the Eichmann trial seem to be an emotional journey in which no amount of exposure and condemnation of the accused can hope to expiate the crimes of the Nazis or compensate for a loss so searing that its images of murdered children in the concluding piece in *The Elephant and My Jewish Problem*, "The Pit: A Journal," can ever be expunged. In fact, in a kind of drumbeat of despair, Nissenson juxtaposes the tragic unfolding of the life of a young boy deported from Izieu by sealed boxcar to his death in Auschwitz with the author's own, as it were, "untouched" life and the life of his child. As Nissenson reveals, in *Jewish Profiles*, witnessing the Eichmann trial was a turning point that upended his religious sensibilities and an event from which he "never recovered. . . . It was the determining factor in my eventual loss of faith. It was impossible to believe there could be a God, given such terrible evil" (Cole, p. 220).

Nissenson and Israel

When the journals and short stories, such as "The Well," "The Blessing," and "Lamentations," take the author to Israel, Jewish survival, as seen through the kaleidoscopic and fractured lens of religious Jewish history, law, and myth, is opposed to the realities of living in a secular and precarious world under siege. Here Nissenson offsets Zionist fervor against an acute sense of loss. In stories such as "The Groom on Zlota Street" and "The Prisoner" (both in *A Pile of Stones*), Nissenson returns to a time, before the Holocaust, that serves as the foreshadowing of persecution. Nissenson's father, Charles, who lived in Warsaw until as a child he immigrated to America, may well be the source of these stories. In fact, his father's early years on New York City's Lower East Side, working initially in a sweatshop and later as a traveling salesman, before marrying Harriette Dolch, born of Polish parents from Lvov, may have formed the basis of Hugh Nissenson's literary reconstructions of America for the Jewish immigrant. Nissenson himself, born in Brooklyn in 1933 in the middle of the Great Depression and educated at Swarthmore and Stanford, received no formal religious training but nonetheless grew up, as his fiction shows, with a sense of the importance of biblical stories. As a Jew growing up in America in the 1930s and 1940s, Nissenson developed attitudes informed by two central events: the Holocaust and the establishment of Israel as the Jewish homeland.

At the heart of Nissenson's Holocaust narratives is the failure of the covenant for a generation of post-Holocaust Jews. Nissenson typically presents the problem of faith in unsentimental and complex terms, whether to retreat from an absolute conception of the divine or to embrace it. For some of his characters, the Holocaust is part of a historical and religious continuum, part of a Jobian design beyond the reach of human imagination. However, like Job's found vision, the Holocaust is nonetheless undeniable "proof" of God. For others, the Holocaust simply reaffirms the absence of God and the dangerous naïveté of belief that stifles human will and creates impossible conditions of passivity, blind acceptance, and self-denial, an all too willing acceptance of suffering, "degradation," as one of his characters so bluntly puts it in "The Blessing," in *The Elephant and My Jewish Problem* (Nissenson, p. 7).

But Nissenson's unambiguous, terse prose displays a starkness that directly confronts those issues of faith and religious conviction in the face of the atrocities of the Holocaust and raises the question of the possibility of belief in a covenantal God after the Holocaust. The twin compasses of negation and affirmation are expressed as mirroring images of one another. For example, in "The Pit: A Journal," Nissenson's journalistic narrative of his 1987 journey to France for the Klaus Barbie trial, the problem of faith shows itself clearly in oppositional terms. The author finds little comfort in the explanation of the Holocaust given to him by a Jesuit priest, who joined the Resistance during the war, and for whom the Holocaust simply confirms "the human condition since Adam and Eve. The world awaits its Redeemer. Nothing about the war—not even the murder of children—shakes my faith." To such an avowal, Nissenson can only reply, "It cost me mine" (Nissenson, *The Elephant and My Jewish Problem*, p. 206). Nissenson here, as elsewhere, refuses to sentimentalize the loss of faith, seeing in its denial despair rather than relief. And, finally, his characters find redemption in neither.

In the short story "The Blessing" (collected in both *A Pile of Stones* and in *The Elephant and My Jewish Problem*), which takes place in Israel, a man's helpless and incapacitating grief over the loss of his young son to cancer is constructed as a direct parallel to the suffering of his wife's aunt, the only member of her immediate family to have survived the death camps. His suffering and grief can only be compared to the absolute measure of suffering as defined by the *Shoah*. The suffering of the central character, Yitshaak, as well as his son's suffering and death are defined by their proximity to the events of the Holocaust. And while the suffering of the individual in the face of cancer is by no means viewed as comparable to the collective suffering of the victims of the Holocaust, this catastrophic event in Jewish history is for Nissenson the scale by which all individual suffering is finally measured and articulated. As Nissenson has put it in *Jewish Profiles*, "it's very dangerous to be a Jew, because you seem to be the victim. . . . Jews suffer history. If history happens, the Jews get it" (Cole, p. 220). The very language of his character's desolation over the death of his son is the language of the Holocaust, his son, "innocent," "condemned to suffer," so that his aunt's immediate response to the news of his death is the "involuntary . . . traditional invocation" of the Hebrew prayer, "Blessed art Thou O Lord our God who art the true judge in Israel" (Nissenson, *The Elephant and My Jewish Problem*, pp. 5–6). But Yitshaak cannot accept the terms of the covenant, cannot come to terms with a God whose arbitrary and unspeakable injustice would allow his son to die. While his aunt's faith "had survived three and a half years in Belsen," the father cannot be consoled by the belief in one who would so judge (Nissenson, p. 6). His aunt's expression of faith connects her to a community of sufferers in which she is able to find hope for the future. In the camps, wanting to "Curse Him and have done with it," she ultimately finds shelter in belief (Nissenson, p. 9). But Yitshaak, believing himself betrayed and abandoned by a covenant whose demands were "monstrously humiliating," wants nothing to do with God, or with the rabbi, or with religious ritual (Nissenson, p. 7). He cannot bring himself to attend his son's funeral and pray over his grave. But Yitshaak's negation of the covenant, to "curse Him and have done with it," brings him no victory. For, at the story's close, Yitshaak, freed from the unwanted and treacherous encumbrances of the covenant, casts himself out in his grief so completely that even nature seems to align itself with God in an "eternal order" from which, in his self-imposed isolation, he is barred (Nissenson, p. 10).

Although Nissenson places his narratives at a considerable remove from the actual sites of deportations and death camps, the countless atrocities of the Nazis and the suffering of their Jewish victims continually shape the dramatic action and dialogue in virtually all of his writing. The aftermath of the *Shoah* is the recurring stage on which events of a still recent Jewish past are indelibly imprinted on the lives of his characters, events that are the measure by which present suffering is articulated. When the black swastika imprinted on the back of a deck of cards becomes no more than child's play, in "The Elephant and My Jewish Problem: A Journal," the title story of his third collection of selected stories and journalistic pieces, readers are reminded, as they generally are in Nissenson's work, that the events of the Holocaust cannot, must not, be viewed as part of an aberrant past. Rather, while the scenes of his narratives take place well after the *Shoah*, the legacy of the past haunts the present as an inheritance that creates an ominous undercurrent throughout his stories. The past and "the future, too . . . are one and the same," as the rabbi avows, in the story "Forcing the End" (in *The Elephant and My Jewish Problem*, p. 147). Memory, seemingly for Nissenson as well as for his characters, "alone remains inexhaustible" ("The Throne of God," in *The Elephant and My Jewish Problem*, p. 138).

If there is any redemption to be had, then it is in Israel, in the newly developing state, where some form of reparation and renewal may be found. Israel is an important site for Nissenson, a dramatic landscape upon which the argument about the role of God in Israel's history and the complicity or absence of God during the Holocaust is played out in newly historical ways. For Nissenson, Israel's role in an ongoing drama of struggle and self-definition would seem to be patterned on the evolving, transformative contours of the covenant and its potential relevance to contemporary Jewish life. Nissenson's Israel is a landscape upon which he grafts the contemporary struggle for survival against a mythic covenant and the historical reality of the *Shoah*. Israel is the site of ancient dramas replayed in the shape of the Eichmann trial, the 1948 War for Independence, Syrian terrorism, and the threat of destruction. Israel is the terrain on which the temple is once again being rebuilt. Interestingly enough, the reappropriation of Israel, while couched in the very fabric of the covenant tradition, is conceived of, in Nissenson's terms, through communal redemption, where the idol of manufacture is not the golden calf but a reification of faith in the land.

In many ways, Israel, for Nissenson, would seem to be fraught with biblical resonance and symbolism: the reconstruction of the temple and the assemblage of a consanguineous community working in its own interests. Israel, thus, is a complex, paradoxical locus of both possibility and erasure. At once, Israel would seem to militate against redemption, appearing as a land where armed guards keep sentinel with loaded Uzis, watchful of terrorists outfitted with remote-controlled explosive devices ready to self-detonate. But Israel is also the locus of reparation, of a reconceptualization of the covenant in human terms of toil and commitment. Appropriately, Israel is, for Nissenson, the theater where ancient antagonisms and skepticism are embattled. "In the Reign of Peace," for example, a debate takes place between a secularist and a religious Jew, both workers on a kibbutz in northern Israel. In the dialogue that follows, the basic antagonisms surrounding God, the coming of the Messiah, adherence to the covenant, and observance of Jewish Law become the dialectic upon which the dramatic action of the story centers. When Chaim, a religious Jew, asks his interlocutor, the narrator, whether he believes in God and in the Messiah, the answer is unswervingly negative. But when asked whether the narrator believes in redemption, the response is far less deterministic. No longer on sure footing, not quite able to abjure completely, the narrator responds, falteringly, by yielding that, "yes . . . I suppose, in a way, that I do. I believe that one day everyone will live like this . . . sharing everything . . . what more would you want?" (Nissenson, *The Elephant and My Jewish Problem*, p. 163). Perhaps the answer to this question, for Nissenson, is in the intersection of Israel and America, the juncture of memory and maturation, unhampered by the weight of "my Jewish problem."

Bibliography

Primary Sources

A Pile of Stones. 1965.
Notes from the Frontier. 1968.
In the Reign of Peace. 1972.
My Own Ground. 1976.
The Tree of Life. 1985.
The Elephant and My Jewish Problem. 1988.

Secondary Sources

Alter, Robert. "Sentimentalizing the Jews." *Commentary* (September 1965): 71–75.

Bell, Pearl. "Idylls of the Tribe." Review of *My Own Ground. New Leader* (12 April 1976): 19.

Berger, Alan L. "American Jewish Fiction." *Modern Judaism* 10 (1990): 221–241.

———. "Judaism as a Religious Value System." In *Crisis and Covenant: The Holocaust in American Jewish Fiction*. Edited by Alan L. Berger. Albany: State University of New York Press, 1985.

Berkove, Lawrence I. "American Midrashim: Hugh Nissenson's Stories." *Critique* 20, no. 1 (1978): 75–82.

Cole, Diane. "Hugh Nissenson." In *Jewish Profiles: Great Jewish Personalities and Institutions of the Twentieth Century*. Edited by Murray Polner. Northvale, N.J.: Jason Aronson, Inc., 1991.

———. "Review of *The Tree of Life*." *Present Tense* 13 (1985): 57–58.

Fisch, Harold. "High Adventure and Spiritual Quest." Review of *In the Reign of Peace*. *Midstream* (January 1973): 71–72.

Fremont-Smith, Eliot. "Ohio Death Trip." Review of *The Tree of Life*. *Village Voice* (22 October 1985): 45.

Furman, Andrew. "Hugh Nissenson." In *Contemporary Jewish American Novelists*. Edited by Joel Shatzky and Michael Taub. Westport, Conn.: Greenwood, 1997.

———. "Hugh Nissenson's Israel: In Search of a Viable Israeli Ethos." *Studies in American Jewish Literature* 13 (1994): 59–71.

Goldman, Liela H. "Hugh Nissenson." In *Dictionary of Literary Biography: Twentieth-Century American-Jewish Fiction Writers*. Vol. 28. Edited by Daniel Walden. Detroit: Gale, 1984.

Lehmann-Haupt, Christopher. Review of *The Tree of Life*. *New York Times* (14 October 1985): C20.

Lester, Margot. "The Price of Redemption." *The Jewish Quarterly* (Autumn 1976): 48–50.

Mano, D. Keith. "The Genuine Article." *National Review* (9 July 1976): 737–738.

Ozick, Cynthia. Review of *In the Reign of Peace*. *New York Times Book Review* (19 March 1972): 4, 22.

Rosenfeld, Alvin H. "Israel and the Idea of Redemption in the Fiction of Hugh Nissenson." *Midstream* 26 (April 1980): 54–56.

Shaw, Peter. Review of *My Own Ground*. *New Republic* (10 April 1976): 29.

Wisse, Ruth R. "American Jewish Writing, Act II." *Commentary* (June 1976): 40–45.

Interviews

Cole, Diane. "A Conversation with Hugh Nissenson." *National Jewish Monthly* 92 (September 1977): 8–16.

Kurzweil, Arthur. "An Atheist and His Demonic God: An Interview with Hugh Nissenson." *Response* 11 (Winter 1978–79): 17–23.

Sara Nomberg-Przytyk

(1915–1996)

SHARON LEDER

SARA NOMBERG-PRZYTYK—teacher, journalist, memoirist—ranks high among the survivors of the Holocaust who have written literary accounts of their lives in Auschwitz and of the impact of Nazi rule in the ghettos. Nomberg-Przytyk is a Polish survivor of both the Białystok ghetto and the death camp at Auschwitz.

Her major work, *Auschwitz: True Tales from a Grotesque Land*—written in Polish (1966) and translated into English by Roslyn Hirsch (1985)—is a fictionalized memoir. Its unique contribution to the literature of atrocity is its penetrating psychological examination of what happens to human character in a death camp where the Nazi system has totally eroded moral values. The forty interlocking vignettes also provide details and insight into lesser-known aspects of camp existence—the underground hierarchy of Communist victims, women's bonding behaviors that deflect the effects of dehumanization, the survival strategies employed by female inmate physicians and their staff, the cruelty of Nazi doctors, and instances of active resistance. Nomberg-Przytyk writes in an unpretentious, straightforward style, amplifying her memories with various fictional devices, including dialogue, flashback, and complexity of character. While much Holocaust literature employs a tone of lamentation, Nomberg-Przytyk favors a truth-telling mode characterized by simplicity of diction, directness of observation, and emotional restraint.

Columny Samsona (The Pillars of Samson) is Nomberg-Przytyk's fictionalized memoir of her experiences in the Białystok ghetto from 1941 to 1943. Published in Lublin in 1966, it has not yet been published in English translation. (Many sections of the text were translated into English specifically for this article by Norbert Kamlot.)

Biographical Background

Sara Nomberg was born on 10 September 1915 in Lublin, Poland. She was brought up in the Hasidic atmosphere of a Jewish section of the city. Many of her relatives were rabbis. Her grandfather was a well-known Talmudist who became the principal of a Warsaw yeshiva and subsequently a rabbi outside of Lublin.

As a youngster, Sara knew poverty. She witnessed other Jewish children dying of malnutrition and saw Jewish women grow prematurely old. She herself was often sent home from school for not having the necessary tuition. In an interview with translator Roslyn Hirsch, she said she was introduced to injustice when cards were attached to her school record indicating that "Sara Nomberg is not allowed to attend classes" (Hirsch, p. x). Experiencing the hostility of neighboring Polish children, Sara began early to wonder about the causes of antisemitism. She recalled being on a picnic with her Jewish friends when nearby village youths called out, "Jews, scabs," and began to pelt them with stones (p. xi).

Eventually, she attended *gymnasium* in Lublin, then the University in Warsaw. Actively identifying as a Communist, she was arrested for her politics in 1934. Upon release, she returned to Lublin. In 1939, when Germany invaded Poland, Nomberg fled east to Białystok, which was then under Russian control. She became a teacher and developed a wide circle of acquaintances. But when the Germans reoccupied the city in the summer of 1941, and Białystok was made *Judenrein* (free of Jews), she joined the Jewish anti-Hitler volunteer army and attempted to travel to Warsaw. After reaching Slonim, however, she realized there were more options available to her in Białystok and therefore returned to that city.

Nomberg lived in the ghetto from 1941 to August 1943. After the Białystok ghetto uprising, she was transported to Stutthof concentration camp on the Baltic Sea, three hundred miles north of Auschwitz. The first two chapters of *Auschwitz: True Tales from a Grotesque Land* detail the alienation she experiences in Stutthof, where Jewish inmates are kept in a block separated from others. After almost two months, she was transported to Auschwitz. Carol Rittner and John K. Roth speculate that Nomberg was among the one thousand prisoners, male and female, transported to Auschwitz from Stutthof on 12 January 1944, as documented by researcher Danuta Czech in her *Auschwitz Chronicle 1939–1945* (translated by Barbara Harshav, Martha Humphreys, and Steven Shearier, New York: Holt, 1990). Sara remarks that she became a *Zugang* (new arrival) in Auschwitz on 13 January 1944. She was on the forced march from Auschwitz to Ravensbrück approximately one year later.

Liberated in late April 1945, Nomberg returned to Poland with the goal of helping to establish a socialist state. She married Andrzej Przytyk, a magistrate, in 1946, started a family, and worked as a journalist in Lublin. During this period, she also wrote her two memoirs, eventually publishing *Columny Samsona* in 1966. Although *Auschwitz* was accepted for publication by the same publisher, Communist Poland's antisemitism affected their plans. After Israel's victory in the 1967 Six Day War, the publisher told Nomberg-Przytyk that if she wanted the memoir published, she would have to remove all references to Jews. She argued, in response, that any narrative about Auschwitz would of necessity have to include Jews. But she also added that she had actually written about all the inmates she encountered "regardless of nationality, race, religion, or political persuasion" (Hirsch, p. xii). She withdrew the manuscript and took it with her to Israel where she emigrated in 1968. There, her friends in the Lublin Society deposited the typescript in the archives at Yad Vashem, Israel's national authority for commemorating the memory of the Holocaust. Later, in 1975, Nomberg-Przytyk left Israel to join the elder of her two sons in Canada.

Eli Pfefferkorn, a researcher and analyst for the U.S. Holocaust Memorial Council in Washington, D.C., discovered the manuscript of *Auschwitz: True Tales from a Grotesque Land* in Israel and presented it to Roslyn Hirsch for translation into English. Pfefferkorn and David Hirsch edited the translated manuscript, and wrote an afterword for it. Nomberg-Przytyk was living with her son on a small farm near Montreal when Roslyn Hirsch interviewed her before the translated memoir was published in 1985.

Auschwitz: True Tales from a Grotesque Land

Sara, the first-person narrator of *Auschwitz*, is Nomberg-Przytyk herself, the survivor looking back from a vantage point of two decades after her experience in the camps. Initially so isolated and depressed in Auschwitz that she contemplates suicide, Sara feels her mood lift when representatives of the Communist underground, directed by Orli Reichart, draw her into their network. Orli Reichart was a German Communist first imprisoned by the Nazis in 1933 when she was just eighteen years old; when Reichart reached Auschwitz, she rose in the prisoner hierarchy to become director of the entire area surrounding Sara's block. Orli arranges for Sara, as a fellow Communist, to be appointed as a clerk in the Auschwitz infirmary for female Jewish inmates.

From this position of relative privilege, Sara observes most keenly the complexities of character in a full spectrum of individuals, from top-ranking Nazis like Doctors Josef Mengele and Hans Wilhelm Koenig to German antifascists like Orli Reichart. All her character studies are concerned with the question of how one holds onto one's humanity and, at the same time, manages to survive in the midst of moral degradation. More specifically, she examines the degree to which victims either maintain allegiance to fellow inmates or ingratiate themselves with the SS in order to gain privileges and survive longer.

Orli Reichart's behavior represents one kind of response German victims with privilege exhibited. While Reichart was an antifascist and member of the resistance, she nevertheless curried favor with the SS and often justified her cruelty toward other victims with absurd, Nazilike rationalizations. Nomberg-Przytyk devotes no fewer than eleven chapters to the examination of Reichart's character. In the first of these vignettes, "What Kind of a Person Was Orli Reichart?" Sara says, "I must admit that even today I often think about her" (Chapel Hill, N.C.: University of North Carolina Press, 1985, p. 41).

About Reichart Nomberg-Przytyk draws no final conclusions. Rather, she presents a complex portrait, employing the skills of a fiction writer to show Orli "in a variety of situations" and how "in each situation she was a different person" (ibid.):

> On one occasion she would be defiant to the authorities; on another she would be cruel to the prisoners. At one moment she was filled with compassion for human suffering; at another, without blinking an eye, she made sure that not even one of the victims sentenced to the gas chamber would escape.

In the end, it is the reader, not the narrator, who decides how to evaluate Orli's role in the camp. Particularly telling is how Orli and other inmate functionaries deal with decisions surrounding the fate of fellow inmates. Working as staff members in the camp infirmary, Sara and her colleagues—the doctor, the nurse, and the other clerks—are privy to knowledge about the fate of the victims that the victims themselves do not have. How should the staff treat patients who come to them for counsel and care? Should they provide them with knowledge of their imminent deaths or let them go to their deaths unaware? Is there a better, more ethical way to die?

In the short vignette "The Price of Life," Sara lays out the questions about death that "flowed through" the "minds continuously" of the hospital staff:

> When death is inevitable is there any point in fighting for life? Is there really such a thing as a meaningful death? Is it better for a human being to face death, knowing that he is about to die, or is it better when death comes upon him suddenly, snuffing him out before he realizes what is happening? (p. 98).

These were, she says, no mere "academic questions. The way you answered these questions determined the way you behaved toward other people, including those who were condemned to death" (ibid.).

Sara herself must decide whether to tell Esther, an acquaintance who hid with her in the Białystok ghetto and is now pregnant in Auschwitz, that if she gives birth in the camp hospital, Dr. Mengele will kill her along with her newborn. "For the first minute," Sara says, "I really did not know what to tell her. Could I extinguish the happiness that emanated from her whole body? . . . Maybe I should let her live through her great love for her first baby and let the worst come later" (pp. 68–69).

The reader wonders: What will Sara decide? Instead of revealing immediately how Sara handles the situation, Nomberg-Przytyk employs the flashback technique to build dramatic tension. She has Sara remember exactly how and when she first learned of Mengele's policy of killing Jewish women together with their children. The flashback details the way female inmate physicians resist Mengele's sadism by secretly killing newborns in an effort to at least save the mothers' lives. The narrative then continues with Sara and the other functionaries deciding to tell Esther the difficult news. This sharing of knowledge with the victims is consistent with the view expressed in a later chapter, "The Price of Life," by Magda, a Slovak girl who has become Sara's "camp daughter": " 'Every human being has the right to a conscious death. . . . Let them suffer, but let them die like human beings. Our responsibility is to tell them about it' " (p. 99).

It would not have been possible for the female inmates to keep respect for one another's humanity alive without the bonding behaviors they developed to sustain a sense of community in the camps. Sara illustrates these relationships, often between older and younger women, in several vignettes. She describes the special relationship of protection and caring that exists in Stutthof between the *blokowa* (block supervisor) Ania, a Jewish woman from Białystok, and Liza, a prisoner ten years younger than she. Toward Liza, Ania displays "maternal affection": "Ania fed her and dressed her; she did all the hard work for her. . . . Only in the camp was it possible to find such affection among women" (p. 4). About her own "camp daughter" Magda, the eighteen-year-old whom Sara meets in the Auschwitz infirmary in February 1944, Sara says, "She was wonderful—very brave and also a happy girl. . . . Together we lived through many good and bad moments in Auschwitz, and for a short time in Ravensbrück" (p. 39).

The coterie of female Communists who work on the hospital blocks are therefore shocked and angered by Orli Reichart when she acts most like the SS by inflicting indiscriminate cruelty on victims and rationalizing her behavior. Because "Mengele had a weakness for Orli," she is in many instances "able to decide who could be helped and who could be sacrificed" (pp. 44–45). She is sorely criticized for appropriating that power with smugness and lack of compassion for her "sisters." In "Erika's Red Triangle," a German Communist inmate not only resents Orli for not intervening when her "dear friend," a Jewish woman recovering from pneumonia, is sent by Mengele to the gas; it is the way Orli uses her influence to "save some and push others into the car of death" that rankles most, since it imitates the unpredictable and random torture of the SS (pp. 48–50). In "A Plate of Soup," Orli pummels starving female prisoners who steal from large cans of soup before they reach their destination. Sonia, a nurse, witnesses the incident and realizes the starving women's "hunger was too strong a stimulus to be resisted" (p. 46). Orli, on the other hand, attempts to rationalize her violence by saying: " 'That's how you have to talk to people . . . no other way. These people deserve no better' " (p. 47). Her comrades condemn Orli mainly for her adoption of immoral attitudes toward other human beings, for succumbing to Nazi "logic."

Sara, whose life, after all, has been saved through Orli's orchestration, presents her in a positive as well as a negative light. At significant moments, Orli steps in to help Sara retrieve sensitivity to human life. When Sara says, "After eight months in Auschwitz, I could look at the dead with indifference" (p. 115), it is Orli who watches an arriving transport with Sara and forces her out of her complacency (pp. 116–117). At the New Year celebration held in Auschwitz in 1945, before the forced march to evacuate ahead of the approaching

Russians, there is a tender scene in which Sara and Orli even exchange gifts (pp. 123–126).

Nomberg-Przytyk's memoir also documents many acts of individual and organized resistance. There is, for example, the story of the beautiful Parisian dancer in the July 1944 transport of five hundred people to Auschwitz ("Revenge of a Dancer," pp. 107–109). Arriving in the middle of the night in a Pullman filled with men, women, and children, the dancer refuses to strip naked as demanded by an SS man, grabs his pistol, and uses it to shoot as many SS as she can before using the last bullet on herself. There is, as well, the successful plot on the part of the underground to blow up a crematorium in Auschwitz. Nomberg-Przytyk presents this event in personal terms, revealing the behind-the-scenes story of the characters, a married couple named Lisette and Karol, whose activities are responsible for this act of organized resistance ("Morituri te Salutant," pp. 58–62).

In January 1945, Sara is on the forced march out of Auschwitz. Following a series of fortunate circumstances that save her from total exhaustion and starvation ("The Bewitched Sleigh," pp. 127–131; "The Camp Blanket," pp. 132–136), she arrives at Ravensbrück, only to be transported again after just a few weeks to a military airport at Rostock. The SS evacuate the camp at Rostock ten days before the Germans surrender on 9 May 1945.

After liberation, Sara attempts to return to Lublin to help Poland build a socialist state. The memoir ends on a dissonant note, however, as she overhears Polish passengers on the train to Lublin speaking vehemently against the existence of a Communist Poland. In Lublin, Sara is immediately confronted with an Easter celebration and pictures posted of the "Holy Family," reminders of Poland's deep attachment to its Christian religious traditions.

Columny Samsona (The Pillars of Samson)

Like *Auschwitz*, *Columny Samsona* is a series of short vignettes organized in chronological fashion, the stories tracing Sara's experience in the Białystok ghetto up to the time of its liquidation. The memoir opens with the German takeover of Białystok from the Russians in June 1941. Nomberg abandons her position teaching elementary school there and attempts to escape. In the forests and countryside, she learns the Germans have already taken over another town where she taught, Slonim. She travels there and witnesses Jews suffering—workers under the Germans being whipped, refugees in the synagogue sick and starving.

As in *Auschwitz*, Nomberg-Przytyk is concerned with how these conditions affect human character. At this early point, some Jews recognize already how German occupation inflames incipient Polish antisemitism. In her escape from Białystok, Sara encounters a Jewish family—a father and two daughters—who out of fear no longer have any contact with their non-Jewish neighbors (pp. 11–15). Other Jews, like an influential family Sara meets in Slonim, fool themselves into thinking their situation will improve under the Germans (pp. 15–20).

After contemplating an escape to Warsaw with friends who possess forged identification, Sara decides instead to return to Białystok, where Jews are just beginning to settle into the ghetto. In the Anti-Fascist Club in Białystok, Sara connects with members of the Communist Party, many of whom she knew before the war. The club's main business is planning armed resistance against deportation to the camps, despite the different factions in the ghetto for whom resistance and dying honorably are not high priorities. Mothers with children and the elderly want life under any circumstances; others who believe not everything is lost prefer not to aggravate the Germans (pp. 29–33).

In an act of courage and resistance unknown to the *Judenrat* (Jewish Council), Sara organizes and teaches a class of seventh-grade students in the ghetto with their parents' permission. She documents as well the disappearance of the Jewish men of Białystok, whom the Germans either kill or deport to camps; the employment of Jewish women in the industrial plants set up for the German war machine; and the move on the part of many in the ghetto to arrange emergency hiding places. News about ghetto life travels by word of mouth, mainly through Jewish policemen; it includes warnings about Jewish collaborators who inform German authorities about hiding places, as well as acknowledgments of the acts of defiance by those Jews killed by Germans for opposing the deportations to Treblinka (pp. 114–115).

In one vignette, Sara highlights the "February Akcia" (organized raid), the killing by the Germans of nine hundred people in the ghetto, and the deportation of no fewer than ten thousand (pp. 127–129). At the time, Sara is in an industrial plant with other workers who are prepared to use assorted implements in their own defense—iron bars, hammers, shears. Sara herself is prepared with a makeshift combustible bottle, like a bomb. Fortunately, the workers' lives are spared (pp. 114–115).

In another vignette, the Anti-Fascist Club organizes the killing of Jewish collaborators. In the aftermath of the "akcias," Sara wonders if her students will think it worth their effort to continue their studies. She is surprised that all those who remain alive return to her class (pp. 123–125). The Gestapo now must deal with the Jews' growing awareness of the deceptions being imposed on them.

Reception

In his review in the *New York Times* (15 September 1985), David Stern was impressed with the psychological insights Nomberg-Przytyk applied to her studies of Mengele. He called *Auschwitz: True Tales from a Grotesque Land* a "remarkable memoir": "Mrs. Nomberg-Przytyk's . . . portrait of the evil doctor is characteristic of the extraordinary gifts of observation and memory she brings to this account of years of imprisonment in Auschwitz." Stern adds that "her unusual attention to the details of human character that emerged under the cruel and extreme conditions of the death camp sets 'Auschwitz' apart from the many important and moving books written by other survivors."

Stern also credits Nomberg-Przytyk's ability to present the ambiguities of human character with a level of complexity commensurate with the paradoxes of death camp existence: "The story is . . . a disturbing commentary on the difficulty of making a simple summary judgment on people's conduct in the camps."

The attention Nomberg-Przytyk gives to details of character is precisely what drew Roslyn Hirsch to translate the memoir. In her "Translator's Foreward," Hirsch writes, "What struck me about this manuscript was the author's ability to make the characters in the camp emerge as unique individuals, even against the backdrop of camp depersonalization and imminent extermination" (p. ix).

Feminist Holocaust scholars have found in the memoir a confirmation of the bonding behaviors used by women to support their daily survival. Myrna Goldenberg writes:

> In Sara Nomberg-Przytyk's memoir *Auschwitz: True Tales from a Grotesque Land,* we trace the movement of a woman from isolation, depression, and detachment into a community of women prisoners who, like her, were politically active Communists before the war. They gave her practical and moral support. . . . The persistent theme of this memoir is the need for connectedness. We are left with the implicit admonition to develop and nurture relationships, to care for one another, and to take responsibility for one another, for in loneliness, there is no protection against violence and despair (Goldenberg, pp. 328–329).

Critics acknowledge that Sara Nomberg-Przytyk has made a significant contribution to our understanding of the impact of Nazism on its victims. Readers will be enlightened by her honest treatment of what was required to survive this modern inferno.

Bibliography

Primary Sources

Columny Samsona (The Pillars of Samson). 1966.
Auschwitz: True Tales from a Grotesque Land. 1985.

Secondary Sources

Goldenberg, Myrna. "The Burden of Gender." In *Women in the Holocaust.* Edited by Dalia Ofer and Lenore J. Weitzman. New Haven: Yale University Press, 1998: 327–339.
Hirsch, Roslyn. "Translator's Foreward." *Auschwitz: True Tales from a Grotesque Land* by Sara Nomberg-Przytyk. Edited by Eli Pfefferkorn and David H. Hirsch. Chapel Hill: University of North Carolina Press, 1985: ix–xii.
Horowitz, Sara R. "Women in Holocaust Literature: Engendering Trauma Memory." In *Women in the Holocaust*: 364–77.
Pfefferkorn, Eli, and David Hirsch. "Editors' Afterword." *Auschwitz: True Tales from a Grotesque Land*: 163–181.
Rittner, Carol, and John K. Roth, eds. "Sara Nomberg-Przytyk" and "The Camp Blanket." In *Different Voices: Women and the Holocaust.* New York: Paragon House, 1993: 143–148.
Schmitt, Hans A. "Hitler: Obsession Without End." *The Sewanee Review*, vol. 96, no. 1 (winter 1988): 158–168.
Stern, David. "Death-Camp Memoir." *New York Times Book Review*, 15 September 1985.

JONA OBERSKI

(1938–)

DICK VAN GALEN LAST

JONA OBERSKI WAS born on 20 March 1938 in Amsterdam. He was the only child of Siegfried Oberski and Margaretha Foerder, who were German-Jewish emigrants. In 1943 the family was deported to Bergen-Belsen. Jona's parents did not survive the death camps, but Jona returned to Amsterdam and grew up with foster parents. From 1956 to 1964 he studied mathematics and physics at the University of Amsterdam, where he received a doctorate in physics and later made his career as a professor in that field. He married and the couple had three children.

In 1978, after he assisted the Dutch poet Judith Herzberg at a poetry workshop, she advised him to write about his wartime experiences. The result was the publication of his novella *Kinderjaren* (*Childhood*, 1978). This little book that makes the Holocaust palpable was translated and published in fifteen countries, including the United States and Japan, and has been reprinted twenty-four times in the Netherlands. Famous authors such as Harold Pinter, Heinrich Böll, Chaim Potok, Alan Sillitoe, and Isaac Bashevis Singer praised the book. Pinter's accolade on the jacket describes Oberski's tale—of Bergen-Belsen from the viewpoint of a young Dutch Jewish boy—as "shattering." It is, Pinter says, "a terrible perspective. The tone of voice never veers away from simple, terse description, but contains a world of bewilderment and agony" (*Kinderjaren* 's-Gravenhage: BZZTÔH, 1978, p. 104).

Childhood

The elements of Oberski's story are both affecting and familiar. A small boy without a name endures the ever more frightening sequence of anti-Jewish measures perpetrated by the Nazis. First comes the decree that Jews must wear the Yellow Star: "Look," his mother says, "now you've got a pretty star, just like daddy." "I thought the star was pretty," the boy thinks, "but I'd rather not have had it" (*Childhood*, Toronto: Lester and Orpen Dennys, 1984, p. 24. All quotations are from this edition.). Images of the deportation follow: the suitcases hurriedly stuffed, the transit camp Westerbork, the crowded freight car of the train, the family's fleeting hope that they are on their way to Palestine. At the center of the book is Bergen-Belsen, where the boy has a hard time understanding the laws of survival, for example, when he and other children have to clean out the cooking pots with their fingers, or when he must keep still as his parents make love secretly for the last time. After he watches his sick father die, the boy later looks for the body of his father in the "bone house":

> I went in and stepped over the first bodies. I climbed up on the pile and looked into the topmost bundled sheet. All I could see was an arm. I started to unwrap the sheet. . . . I pulled out the arm. The hand was like my father's. I tugged at the sheet until I could see the face. The face was black with beard. I climbed down the off pile and saw a body to the side. It wasn't getting much light. I looked at the face. The eyes were black. The cheeks were thin. The beard was short like my father's. The nose was like his, too. I looked at the hands. They were like my father's. But the body wasn't at all like my father's (pp. 78–79).

The Jewish deportees at Bergen-Belsen are next taken by train to Tröbitz, where the young protagonist and many other Dutch Jews would ultimately be liberated by the Russian army. Some of them, including the boy's mother, who was severely psychologically damaged, died shortly after liberation from disease or plain exhaustion. The slim volume ends as the boy begins life again with his foster parents in Amsterdam. Although many things in this narrative are not told, but rather implied, Oberski gives a vivid description of how difficult it was for the young boy to adjust to his new life with his foster parents, who brought him back from darkness to life: "My mouth filled with vomit. I almost suffocated. It came splashing out on the floor. It spattered her legs. She says: 'Now look what you've done. Just clean it up. You're not a baby any more.' She gave me a cloth. I started wiping it up" (p. 123). A reader may guess that this scene is in many respects autobiographical, especially in light of the book's dedication to Oberski's foster parents, "who had quite a time with me."

Oberski's story differs from Anne Frank's in that *The Diary of Anne Frank* is an actual document; Oberski's memoir is a literary artifact (the subtitle of the English edition is *A Novella*). Oberski admits that he used his experiences to make fiction, unlike, for example, Binjamin Wilkomirski, whose so-called memoir *Fragments: Memories of a Wartime Childhood*, originally published in German in 1995 and quickly translated in twelve languages, was exposed as a fraud in 1999. Both Wilkomirski—his real name was Bruno Grosjean, a Swiss clarinettist who never left Switzerland during the war—and Oberski wrote slim volumes on colossal cruelty, but written from the unmediated point of view of a child. Whether Oberski's account of his childhood as a Dutch Jewish boy in the Nazi concentration camp Bergen-Belsen is literally accurate is almost beside the point. Literary fiction gave Oberski more room (and techniques) than strictly documentary realism would have. The factual story of Bergen-Belsen takes up a relatively small place in the book, although the camp remains at the heart of the novel. More important is the way Oberski has been able to see the experience, after more than thirty years, through the prism of the small child that he once was. He writes the short, declarative sentences that we associate with childhood. Effectively, he contrasts this naïve narration with the horror that develops around him and thus connects the big events of the Holocaust with the world of a small boy who is four years old at the beginning and almost eight at the end of the book. The boy is too young to name his feelings; how he feels can be concluded from his sensory perceptions: "The air in my nose was cold. It was cold under the blankets too. I cuddled up to my mother and her warm breath blew into my nose" (p. 9). This guilelessness that speaks from *Childhood* presents the suffering of persecution more effectively than can be achieved by direct description. The events, seen through the eyes of a child, are restored to their completely incomprehensible horrendousness.

Critical Response

Confronted with critics who read *Childhood* as an autobiographical document, Oberski protested that the story must be considered fiction, "because what does one remember of one's childhood years?" (*Algemeen Dagblad*, 24 February 1995). Oberski elucidates his point of view in his second novel, *De ongenode gast* (The Uninvited Guest, 1995), in which the protagonist is the writer of a book called *Child in the War* (a clear allusion to *Childhood*), who gives lectures on his book ("Seldom had somebody read his interviews, seldom somebody posed him a new question"). Questioned by the audience about whether *Child in the War* expressed what he himself had experienced, the protagonist answers:

> I wanted to express what those circumstances meant to a child. The facts about the war are well-known, I did not need to repeat them. . . . some of the themes in my book are based upon my own experience, others I might have made up. . . . Every memory is transformed and distorted and that is also good. The book contains fantasy and yet it is still true (p. 78).

Oberski's approach to describing his wartime experience reminds one of the process used by the Polish American author Louis Begley, writer of the pseudo-autobiographical novel *Wartime Lies*, who pleads for the creation of an *artistic* truth to supplement what he considered to be an incomplete *historical* truth.

The stream of testimonies and novels about the experience of the concentration camps was yet to come when Oberski wrote *Childhood*. In the Netherlands, interest in the victims essentially began only in the 1980s. The public's understanding about Nazism and the murder of the Jews has come not so much from historians as from writers of fiction, filmmakers, playwrights, and televison producers. In this respect, Oberski was one of the first to have an enormous impact. The Italian movie director Robert Faenza made *Childhood* into a film in an Italian-French coproduction, *Jonah Who Lived in the Whale* (1994), a film that also influenced Wilkomirksi. In the 1990s, Oberski continued to write. *De ongenode gast* was followed in 1997 by *De eigenaar van niemandsland* (The Owner of No-Man's Land). Although his last novels were not regarded as convincing as *Childhood*, it becomes clear that World War II is, as he once said, the basis of his work.

Bibliography

Primary Sources

Kinderjaren (Childhood). 1978.

"*Ik van voor een oorlog*" (Me From Before a War). *De Tweede Ronde* 5, no. 4 (winter 1984): 17–23.

De ongenode gast (The Uninvited Guest). 1995.

De eigenaar van niemandsland (The Owner of No-Man's Land). 1997.

Secondary Sources

Galen Last, Dick van, and Rolf Wolfswinkel. *Anne Frank and After: Dutch Holocaust Literature in Historical Perspective*. Amsterdam: Amsterdam University Press, 1996.

JACQUELINE OSHEROW

(1956–)

SANFORD PINSKER

THE POET JACQUELINE Osherow was born in Philadelphia, Pennsylvania, on 15 August 1956. The daughter of Aaron (an attorney) and Evelyn Hilda (an elementary schoolteacher), she is the author of four collections of verse. Many of her poems are informed by Jewish history and the Jewish experience. As she is a poet of twentieth-century witness, the Holocaust plays a key role in her imaginative meditations. Sometimes these speculations are oblique, even buried. Consider, for example, "Ch'vil Schreiben a Poem auf Yiddish," partly a playful boast (she imagines writing a poem "so Yiddish" that it will be impossible to translate—even if she cannot speak the language), partly a somber recognition that her poem exists "in no realm at all"—that is, "unless the dead can manage to dream dreams." Thus, Osherow makes a veiled reference to the world of Yiddish-speaking Jews that was destroyed by the Holocaust, and can no longer speak.

Her study with the poet Robert Lowell while she was a student at Radcliffe College (1974–1978) introduced her to poetic forms such as the sonnet, blank verse, and especially terza rima, the tercet stanza of Dante's *Divine Comedy*. Quite rarely used in English poetry, this form appears not only in her poetry set in Italy (for example, "One Last Terza Rima / Italian Train"), but also in a wide variety of other settings. Other abiding influences include poets such as Emily Dickinson, Rainer Maria Rilke (see especially "Letter to Rainer Maria Rilke," with its haunting juxtapositions of Judaic and Christian images), and Paul Celan ("My Cousin Abe, Paul Antschel and Paul Celan" serves to honor not only the memory of Paul Celan, whose difficult, knotty work represents the quintessence of Holocaust poetry, but also the ways in which Holocaust transmission is braided through the generations).

Looking for Angels in New York

Osherow's first collection, *Looking for Angels in New York* (1988), put poems that had originally appeared in such prestigious venues as *The New Yorker*, *Times Literary Supplement*, and *The Georgia Review* between hard covers. As she declares in a poem on the death of Andrei Tarkovsky, "New York is not an easy place to dream. / There is always too much interference / From the movie theaters, from the dreamers / dreaming down the hall . . . " But dream Osherow does, because what she longs to see is "the dreams behind the pictures, nostalgia, the very dreams / I have no courage to see." The Holocaust becomes a significant part of this ongoing nightmarish dream. Not surprisingly, the poem in question is titled "Nostalgia," and it effectively introduces the difficulty that lay behind her project as a poet, the difficulty in recording honestly what looking for angels involves in the post-Holocaust world, a time when angelic aid is desperately needed.

Conversations with Survivors

Osherow's second book, *Conversations with Survivors* (1994), best exemplifies her commitment to witnessing. She includes a wide variety of subjects, from Rilke to Motown singer David Ruffin to Chilean coup victim Victor Jara. But it is the title poem that most directly addresses the difficult problem of American writers musing about the Holocaust. Because Osherow was born more than a decade after World War II ended, her perspective differs from that of an earlier generation. She seems not to be as worried as they often were about the claims of territory or the necessity of being a firsthand witness, nor does she apparently suffer the pangs of survivor guilt endured by an older generation of Jewish-American poets an ocean away from the cataclysm. For her, the Holocaust is linked to other subjects that have been too easily forgotten as the bloodiest century in human history came to an end, but with this important proviso: The Holocaust requires a willful act of reconstructive memory.

The collection's title poem explores the life of Fany, a Holocaust survivor, by concentrating on a highly unlikely but defining detail: the beautiful hats she fashions with material brought to her by SS women. Whatever they pick over from the piles outside the crematoria—"bijoux, dangling cherries, nesting birds"—are eventually turned into something akin to works of art. With "a crown from this, a feather from that, a brim," and the needles and thread the SS provide, Fany keeps their women elegant. She is also something of a beautician, so that "when she did their make-up and their hair / The lipsticks, brushes, hairpins, shadows, combs / The cigarettes they gave her outstripped gold / With the essentialist black marketers / Of Auschwitz." Thus does Fany engineer her survival.

Osherow's long poem moves from life in the concentration camp to life in America, where Fany spends the last four decades of her life. In the camp, Fany hustles a potato and turns it into soup that makes her and her sister "first delirious, then sick." The camp is a place of unspeakable horror where she learns how to "organize / To find stray undamaged seconds at Auschwitz / and piece them into minutes, hours days."

The poem is a flinty, rigorous unsentimental portrait of a survivor, one that brings her back to three-dimensional life. Take, for example, the detail in which Osherow's narrative tells us that Fany's husband, Sam, once won a couple of thousand dollars in the Pennsylvania Lottery by playing "the number still tattooed on Fany's arm / (his own wouldn't work; it lacks a digit)." No doubt some would prefer that Osherow be more pietistic, less given to pointing out that, in her final years, Fany owned "Two side-by-side refrigerators / (One in the Kitchen, one in the basement) / And a floor-to-ceiling freezer all crammed full." To be sure, Fany does not represent all Holocaust survivors, nor is she meant to, but the life that Osherow's poem patiently, meticulously unfolds, gives a portrait of one direction that life after the Holocaust can take. It is an act of empathy as well as one of witness. In truth, the two are virtually the same because Fany never forgets her days at Auschwitz, and in learning about them, Osherow learns what survivorhood requires, and what it means. The characters, unflinchingly etched, give witness to what the Holocaust meant—and the behaviors it changed. Osherow is also a witness as she gives significance to the arc of Fany's story. As Osherow puts it in the book's preface, "For my generation—those born in the aftermath of war—the horror is a fact of life. Indeed, it defined the world for us."

Among Osherow's finest poems paying homage to fellow poets are two raising crucial questions about literary transmission of the Holocaust, mourning the dead, and evoking the European cultures in which Jews dreamed and died. In "Letter to Rainer Maria Rilke," Osherow addresses the great German lyric poet in the magnificent city of his birth, Prague, a city that welcomed and persecuted Jews, a city whose architecture speaks dramatically and graphically of a former Jewish presence. She evokes the great gothic clock with its Hebrew letters marking the hours and the statue of Christ on the landmark Karluv Bridge, with Hebrew inscription "Holy, Holy, Holy, the Lord of Hosts" at its base, graphic reminders of the absence of Jews. The contemporary poet, responding to an age the older poet did not experience, speaks of their separation in time and poetic temperament. She identifies the wall separating them as "the wholesale devastation / Of a continent that fed on dreams / And the century you had the doubtful honor / Of gracing as its greatest lyric poet / In the final guiltless hour of your native / Language." She invokes *Shoah* imagery to show how she is constrained by its impact: "for those of us / Who, just like you, would rather speak of angels / There's a lasting streak of ash upon the tongue." The Holocaust specificity is achieved with juxtaposition of Hitler's orders not to burn the Prague synagogues, which he intended to spare for a new role as museums of an extinguished people, and a synagogue that is now a Holocaust memorial and whose walls are inscribed with the names of Prague's murdered Jews. Would Rilke have written elegies for the murdered Jews of Europe, Osherow wonders, had he lived to witness their destruction? And if so, she asks, "what could you have made of the destruction? / . . . Who, if you cried out, would ever hear?" For the poet who is compelled to write of the *Shoah*, the responsibility is immense, for "You cannot even make a catalogue / Of the atrocities. The list is burned. / The necessary words have been forbidden." Yet, she will not be deterred for, she insists, "We need a poetry that lets them in." Absence is a constant presence in this poem, from the absent readers of Hebrew to the unmentioned architectural site of Terezin / Theresienstadt, near Prague, where Czech Jews were incarcerated until those who managed to survive the harsh conditions were deported to the death camps of Poland.

In contrast to the absence of Holocaust geography in "Letter to Rainer Maria Rilke," in "Ponar," the poet names the killing field outside Vilna, the city where thousands of Jews from the Vilna ghetto were slaughtered in mass executions. The American poet imagines for the victims an afterlife mirroring the learning, piety, and political passion of their prewar lives. In her imagined vision, the victims rise from the forests of Ponar and return "to the twenty-seven libraries / And sixty study halls of the Vilna synagogue / To run the gamut of their youth organizations / From right-wing Zionism to left-wing Zionism."

With a Moon in Transit

In Osherow's third book, *With a Moon in Transit* (1996), meditations on the Holocaust continue to persist. We feel its presence in poems such as "Brief Encounter with a Hero, Name Unknown," "Song for the Music in the Warsaw Ghetto," and especially "My Cousin Abe, Paul Antschel and Paul Celan," where the specificity of Transnistria plays an important role. Here she takes Celan's query, "Where did the way lead when it led nowhere?" as her epigraph and remembers those, who with Celan and her cousin survived the Holocaust, and remembers their family history and Jewish collective life. From her earlier speculation on what Rilke might have written, Osherow thus turns her attention in other poems to those who did write about the *Shoah*. The Yiddish poet Jacob Glatstein, who wrote "Dead Men Don't Praise God" in theological Holocaust protest, also receives the young American poet's homage. As with "Conversations with Survivors," "Brief Encounter with a Hero, Name Unknown" uses a tiny detail—in this case, gold thread sewn into a dress—to launch a series of hypotheses about a woman who may have killed her SS guards just as she was about to be gassed. The poem operates on a series of "Maybe's" as the poem's speaker embroiders the gold thread into a tapestry of imagined details: "Maybe you'd seen a Western dubbed in Polish / Or Yiddish or Czech or whatever it was you spoke." Perhaps it was a "hokey John Wayne flourish" that provided the inspiration for her to take out four SS guards. Or "maybe" she was "an unexceptional girl / Who'd gone crazy on the claustrophobic ride." Or, again, "Maybe you had had a lover's quarrel" and had been contemplating suicide. Whatever the motive or set of circumstances, what this hero, "name unknown," did is truly remarkable: she "grabbed hold of Schillinger's own gun / And killed three other guards along with him." This, the speaker learns from her father-in-law. In the final analysis, "maybe it was simple recklessness," but if so, it was recklessness of a heroic cast, one that allowed life to triumph over the inevitability of death.

But haunting as "Brief Encounter . . ." is, it lacks the deeper resonance of "Song for the Music in the Warsaw Ghetto" because here the repeated word "pity" is set against the songs of lament once sung by the waters of Babylon after the destruction of the biblical temple. As Osherow's would-be psalmist puts it, after the Holocaust, "Where shall we weep? By which waters? / Pity the song bereft of words." Osherow, of course, means to supply "words" to those bereft of words because they were systematically murdered, just as her fantasized poem in Yiddish means to bring back the cadences of a language whose east European speakers were silenced.

Dead Men's Praise

Osherow's fourth book, *Dead Men's Praise* (1999), however, provides us with a psalm that once again draws from conversations with her father-in-law, a Holocaust survivor. "Psalm 37 at Auschwitz" is a stunning achievement, not only because it defies the conventional wisdom about what subjects are, or are not, possible for a poet of Osherow's generation, but also because it raises sharp questions about how a young scholar, raised to know the psalms by heart, would use or not use that knowledge as the shadows of death approached. Unlikely, the speaker concedes, but still wonders if one of the religiously trained, just one of them, might have mumbled the words "*Just a little longer and there will be no wicked one*." One feels intimations of that sentiment throughout Osherow's canon—how "the endless business of creation . . . Require(s) our participation" and how memory is a necessary act of witness.

Bibliography

Primary Sources

Looking for Angels in New York. 1988.
Conversations with Survivors. 1994.
With a Moon in Transit. 1996.
Dead Men's Praise. 1999.

ALICIA OSTRIKER

(1937–)

DONNA KROLIK HOLLENBERG

ONE OF AMERICA'S finest poets and literary critics, Alicia Ostriker is attuned to "convergences of the political, the erotic, and the spiritual" in her own poetry and in the works of others (*Dancing at the Devil's Party*, Ann Arbor: University of Michigan Press, 2000, p. x). Like William Blake, the subject of her first critical study, she believes that the true poet is "necessarily the partisan of energy, rebellion, and desire" and she opposes hierarchies of authority and rule that, under the guise of reason and law, wield power ruthlessly (*Dancing*, p. 2). Ostriker came of age during the flowering of the women's liberation movement in the late 1960s, and throughout her career her work has been preoccupied with the radical insight that women's supposedly "personal" experiences—motherhood, and even sexuality—are shaped in large part by the male-dominated institutions in which they occur; that is, that the personal is political. In such important books of feminist literary criticism as *Writing Like a Woman* (1983) and *Stealing the Language: The Emergence of Women's Poetry in America* (1986), as well as in her nine books of poetry, Ostriker explores central issues of the women's poetry movement, such as the quest for autonomous self-definition, the expression of desire and anger, and the practice of revisionist mythmaking as a means of exploring and attempting to transform the self and culture. Since the 1980s, Ostriker has made her experience of Judaism a focus of her work. In such works as *Feminist Revision and the Bible* (1993) and *The Nakedness of the Fathers: Biblical Visions and Revisions* (1994), as well as in many poems, she has written as a feminist Jew as well as a Jewish feminist, analyzing and reacting against gender assymetries in Jewish spiritual and liturgical traditions and exploring the implications these assymetries have for our conception of God. In this endeavor she is part of the rich tradition of Jewish writers who challenge God, who call him to account for the ongoing evil in the world. Her writing about the Holocaust is undertaken in this spirit of Holocaust-wrought theological crisis.

Life

Born in Brooklyn on 11 November 1937, Alicia Suskin Ostriker was a "Depression baby" whose parents, David and Beatrice Linnick Suskin, both earned degrees in English from Brooklyn College. Her father was a committed union man who worked for the New York City Department of Parks; her mother wrote poetry, tutored students in English and math, and later became a folk-dance teacher. Although descended from Russian Jews on both sides, Ostriker received little in the way of a formal Jewish education. In one autobiographical essay, she describes herself as a "third generation Jewish atheist socialist raised to believe that religion was the opiate of the people" ("Back to the Garden," in *People of the Book: Thirty Scholars Reflect on Their Jewish Identity*, edited by Rubin Dorsky et al., Madison: University of Wisconsin Press, 1996, p. 66). Yet the idea of God always had meaning for her, and she remembers praying, after her grandfather died when she was nine, that he would get into heaven even though he was a nonbeliever. In fact, it was from her grandfather, when she was a small child, that she first heard the phrase "the Jews of Europe." His emotional refusal to vote for Roosevelt because "no president will save the Jews of Europe" left an inchoate but indelible impression upon her of "global grief" (*The Nakedness of the Fathers*, New Brunswick, N.J.: Rutgers University Press, 1994, p. 221). In her family the destruction of the Jews was understood as "one terrible example of the evil of human hatred in the world and the moral for Jews was that we must always be on the side of whatever would alleviate human suffering" (letter to D. Hollenberg, 18 June 2001).

Alicla studied at Brandeis University and, after graduating in 1959, earned a Ph.D. in English literature in 1964 from the University of Wisconsin. In 1965 she joined the faculty of Rutgers University where in 1982 she was named Distinguished Professor, having won many awards for her work, including grants from the National Endowment for the Arts and the Rockefeller and Guggenheim Foundations.

Ostriker is the mother of three grown children; she resides with her husband, Jeremiah P. Ostriker, an astrophysicist, in Princeton, New Jersey. Her husband, whom she married in 1958, also played a role in her spiritual development. Of German Jewish descent, he was raised as a Reconstructionist Jew and it was at his suggestion, when they were in college, that she read the Bible. She immediately experienced "a sustained shock of recognition," feeling that the stories "belonged to [her], were [hers], were [herself]" ("Garden," p. 67). Her husband shared her European background, with its mixed legacy of survivor guilt and gratitude for the gift of life. As she put it, "my husband repeats what his father told him and his brothers: In the old country, you would be soap now" (*Nakedness*, p. 221). So pronounced were these feelings that during her first pregnancy she found herself thinking again about World War II and coming to the "absurd" conclusion that "the only thing one can do for the dead is to bring new life into the world" whether it be children or poems (*Nakedness*, p. 237). As she wrote in "Once More Out of Darkness," the title poem of her second book, "Whoever has died, I make this child for you" (*The Little Space*, Pittsburgh, Penn.: Pittsburgh University Press, p. 7).

Studies in Hebrew and the Bible

Despite her strong self-identification as a Jew, Ostriker was not affiliated with a Jewish religious institution until her son, at age eleven, surprised his parents by wanting to have a bar mitzvah. The preparation for this, in 1982, involved them in sabbath services at Princeton Hillel, where Ostriker found herself enjoying, in particular, the discussion and debate about the weekly Torah portion. This was the beginning of many years of Bible study and of the study of Hebrew language, culminating in the books of feminist biblical criticism, in many poems, in graduate seminars on "The Bible and the Feminist Imagination," and in workshops at the Havurah Institute on women's *midrash*. This commitment to study should not suggest an adherence to normative Judaism, however. Rather, Ostriker adopted a heretical approach, reading the Bible as "a poet, a critic, a feminist" ("Back to the Garden," p. 68). Her view of God and organized religion is personal, honest, passionate, and sometimes even humorous, as in "Everywoman Her Own Theology," where she welcomes the sacred into her kitchen, where it might "bump its chest against mine," even as she critiques the hypocrisy and cruelty of such religious reformers as Martin Luther, who hated "Jews and peasants" (*The Little Space*, pp. 98, 97).

Perhaps the greatest obstacle to belief in God for Ostriker is the ongoing fact of human evil, of which the Holocaust, indeed all genocide, is the most powerful example. To her, such evil spoils the dream of divine justice. Some of her most passionate poetry and prose reflect these feelings and thoughts. For example, in the fifth part of her poetic sequence "A Meditation in Seven Days," she includes two epigraphs—the first from Elie Wiesel's *The Gates of the Forest*, in which he angrily intends to "convict God for murder," and the second the Book of Genesis 27:38, in which the weeping Esau pleads for a blessing from Isaac—both of which resonate with her own anger and sorrow. In the body of the poem she poses an intensifying series of rhetorical questions that probe the meaning of traditional conceptions of God, heaven, and paradise in the face of the ashes of the death camps. These questions substitute for more traditional forms of prayer, but they nevertheless express deep spiritual longing:

> Does the unanswered prayer
> Corrode the tissue of heaven
>
> Doesn't it rust the wings
> Of the heavenly host, shouldn't it
>
> Untune their music, doesn't it become
> Acid splashed in the face of the king
>
> Smoke, and the charred bone bits suspended in it
> Sifting inevitably upward
>
> Spoiling paradise
> Spoiling even the dream of paradise (*The Little Space*, p. 147).

In the Book of Job, part of her innovative larger project, *The Nakedness of the Fathers* (1994), she meditates on the concept of divine justice, retelling Jewish scripture in commentary, poetry, fantasy, and memoir. She retells the familiar story, listing Job's afflictions, including the deaths of his children. She describes the folkloric happy ending, with God replacing Job's children with a new set. She then considers Job's unnamed wife, whose voice is barely heard. How can she, or any woman, accept the pointless killings or the eventual replacements, as an adequate state of affairs, she asks.

As Enid Dame has written, "Ostriker's Ms. Job is a grim realist ('Curse God and die,' she advises her husband.) Yet, for all her grim wisdom, she is a bystander in this story; she cannot 'curse God' herself" (p. 44). Ostriker identifies with this character, stating that she, too, has no illusions about the casual brutality of this world. Thoughts about the plight of Job's wife lead her to a series of autobiographical memories that conclude with the realization that "without rage, love is helpless" (*Nakedness*, p. 238). She concludes that women are not yet angry enough, that perhaps when they demand justice, God will respond. In fact, one outcome of Ostriker's revisionist thinking is the reclamation of the Shechinah, or female aspect of God. The book concludes with a powerful poem in which male and female aspects of the deity merge. "In response to the Holocaust we need not only grieve and remember," Ostriker has said. "We need also to do something much harder: re-imagine God" (letter to D. Hollenberg, 11 March 2001).

Meditations on the Holocaust

More obliquely, Holocaust-wrought theological crisis also informs Ostriker's more recent poetics and her view of the function of art. Belief in the necessity of facing historical horror is the main theme of poems about the Holocaust that include "The Eighth and Thirteenth," "Anselm Kiefer," and "Holocaust." Perhaps out of a need to reach beyond language, two of these are about fellow artists, or art, in other media. The numbers in the title of the first poem refer to two symphonies by Dmitri Shostakovich about the atrocities of World War II: "Music about the worst/Horror history offers," Ostriker writes (*The Little Space*, p. 178). Part of the composer's "War Triptych," Shostakovitch's Eighth Symphony memorializes the siege of Leningrad; his Thirteenth contains a setting for Yevtushenko's poem "Babi Yar" about the thousands of Jews massacred outside of Kiev in 1941, whose traces were later covered up by Soviet authorities. In composing these works, Shostakovitch remembers these horrors and protests against them, a view of art's dual social function that Ostriker shares. She incorporates Shostakovich's voice into the poem—"Art destroys silence"—as well as that of the Russian poet, Marina Tsvetaeva—"All poets are Jews" (*The Little Space*, p. 180). Together with these others Ostriker makes a claim for art that transforms pathos into ethos. As I have written elsewhere, "She substitutes an ethic of human relationship within history for one that mystifies the divine," preferring the clash of discordant music to the implied complacency of old harmonies (Hollenberg, p. 29). We see a similar example of this aesthetic in "Anselm Kiefer," a poem about the non-Jewish postwar German painter who has immersed himself in this legacy of historical trauma, repeatedly taking as his subject Germany's now absent Other, the Jew. (For example, a number of Kiefer's paintings are inspired by Paul Celan's poetic evocation of the death camps, "Fugue of Death.") Considering a characteristic Kiefer landscape, in which "the pale sky/Receives a faint, almost imperceptible stain" from this ignominious past, Ostriker admires the imaginative courage of this artistic project, Kiefer's determination to go where "it is opaque and truly entangling," to risk becoming "lost//As if swept away by history" (*The Little Space*, p. 224).

This kind of courage, an expression of the morally responsible human subject, is Ostriker's own objective in the poems above and in "Holocaust," a more direct meditation on this painful topic. In this poem Ostriker's worldview is Blakean in its edgy awareness of deep-seated paradox. Her epigraph reminds us that the word is from the Greek, "*holocaustus*, burnt offering," and it includes a full definition of the word "fire," ranging from "a rapid, persistent chemical reaction that releases heat and light" through "intensity, as of feeling. Ardor: Enthusiasm . . . Liveliness and vivacity of imagination" to "torment, trial, or tribulation," and "the discharge of firearms" (*The Little Space*, p. 225). In the body of the poem, Ostriker deftly and ironically encompasses the full range of these meanings in images and allusions to conflicting manifestations of this troubling "primal urge" (p. 225). These include, on the destructive side, repeated occurrences of "burning people" en masse in genocide and war, of burning individual "heretics, witches, fanatics," and of lynching. On the constructive side there are allusions to the potentially life-giving internal fires of religious fervor and fulfilled sexual desire. The poem opens with a parody of Auden's "Musée de Beaux Arts," and its tone progresses from dry irony to fierce sarcasm, aided by sardonic apostrophes: "Oh Jericho, ah Carthage,/ Oh Hiroshima" (p. 225). The feeling climaxes when the speaker connects the obsessive human sacrifices of war ("the fiery patriotic mind") with masturbation and unfulfilled sexuality ("Men stroking themselves/ Eyes half shut, women aroused") and then it overflows. In the last half of the poem, she addresses a "you" that includes readers, drawing us with her into the flames. Just as she is implicated in the paradoxes and disastrous perversions she confronts, so are we: "You draw close enough to set / Two hard fires ablaze in your two eyes / And they never go out—" (*The Little Space*, p. 226).

Are these the fires of hatred or of desire, "Satan's toys" or "God's flames"? Ostriker implies that they are both, and she invokes the power of our imaginations to make us experience this dangerous connection. We see the necessity of choice. In fact, this poem is a good example of the "poetics of postmodern witness," a phrase Ostriker has used to describe the vulnerable personal engagement characteristic of some late-twentieth-century poetry by others that, like her own, wrestles with the impress of catastrophe and ruin and resists it ("Beyond Confession," *American Poetry Review* 30, no. 2 [March–April 19] 35).

Ostriker's feminist scholarship is highly regarded and influential. Ostriker's poetry, although it also has been favorably reviewed, has not yet received extensive critical analysis. The criticism that does exist focuses broadly on the relationship between poetry and politics in her work (Cook), explores her expression of the anxieties and conflicts in close relationships (Heller), and compares her with H. D., a major poetic forerunner (Hollenberg). Maeera Shreiber has provided a useful overview of Jewish themes in Ostriker's work, but she does not address her work about the Holocaust. This will likely change now that we have a wide-ranging collection of Ostriker's work, *The Little Space*. In its broad humanity and unflinching courage, Ostriker's poetry provides an important ethical and political model for the reader.

Bibliography

Poetry

Songs. 1969.
Once More out of Darkness and Other Poems. 1974.
A Dream of Springtime: Poems 1970–1978. 1979.
The Mother-Child Papers. 1980.
A Woman Under the Surface: Poems and Prose Poems. 1982.
Green Age. 1989.
The Imaginary Lover. 1989.
The Crack in Everything. 1996.
The Little Space: Poems Selected and New, 1968–1998. 1998.

Selected Prose

Vision and Verse in William Blake. 1965.
Writing Like a Woman. 1983.
Stealing the Language: The Emergence of Women's Poetry in America. 1986.
Feminist Revision and the Bible. 1993.
The Nakedness of the Fathers: Biblical Visions and Revisions. 1994.
"Back to the Garden: Reading the Bible As a Feminist." 1996.
Dancing at the Devil's Party: Essays on Poetry, Politics, and the Erotic. 2000.
"Beyond Confession: The Poetics of Postmodern Witness." 2001.

Secondary Sources

Cook, Pamela. "Secrets and Manifestos: Alicia Ostriker's Poetry and Politics." *Borderlands* 2 (spring 1993): 80–86.
Dame, Enid. Review of *The Nakedness of the Fathers: Biblical Visions and Revisions. Belles Lettres* 10, no. 2 (spring 1995): 44–46.
Heller, Ruth. "Exploring the Depths of Relationships in Alicia Ostriker's Poetry." *Literature and Psychology* 38, nos. 1–2 (1992): 71–83.
Hollenberg, Donna Krolik. "Motherhood/Morality/Momentum: Alicia Ostriker and H.D." In *H. D. and Poets After*. Edited by Donna Krolik Hollenberg. Iowa City: University of Iowa Press, 2000.
Shreiber, Maeera. "Alicia Ostriker." In *Jewish American Women Writers: A Bio-Bibliographical and Critical Sourcebook*. Edited by Ann R. Shapiro. Westport, Conn.: Greenwood Press, 1994.
Williams, Amy. "Alicia Ostriker." In *American Poets Since World War II*, 5th series. Edited by Joseph Conte. Detroit: Gale, 1996.

AMOS OZ
(1939–)

ERIC ZAKIM

AMOS OZ, THE Israeli novelist and political commentator, presents something of a challenge for a reading of his work that looks critically through the prism of the Holocaust. Over the course of some dozen novels and several books of social and literary commentary, Oz mentions the Holocaust only briefly, and when he does his engagement with the Holocaust is oblique, always somehow displaced from the main focus of attention. And yet Oz makes a significant contribution to Holocaust literature because of the way he places it in and among the lives of his Israeli characters. In Oz's work, the Holocaust stands at the juncture of history and individuality, where the pressures of society bear on the individual psyche. Thus, when Oz does write about the Holocaust, he denies its deterministic value for the Jewish people as a whole and instead takes up the challenge the Holocaust offers to the individual survivor, to the survivor-society of Israel which must grapple with forging a quotidian reality within the context of a life harmed by evil in the world. In Oz's writing, we are aware of a haunting presence of historical tragedy, especially in his narratives of early Israeli statehood. The Holocaust hovers as a feeling in the background of this world, leaving us, the readers, to ferret out its meaning among the myriad shards of personal existence Oz depicts.

The Statehood Generation

Oz was born to Fania and Yehudah Arieh Klausner in 1939 in Palestine, and that fact begins to define his intense engagement with Israel—a reality he has always known, unlike any previous generation of Hebrew writers. It also explains a certain estrangement in his work from the determinism of a Jewish past in Europe. The two important settings in Oz's fiction—the sites of major contestation between society and the individual—emanate from Oz's youth, which was spent first in Jerusalem within his family of German intellectuals and then, from age fourteen, on his own on Kibbutz Hulda. These two formative experiences—more so than his education at Hebrew University and Oxford University—provide the significant topographies in his fiction and set up a critical opposition between the Israeliness of kibbutz life and the European origins that pervade his depictions of Jerusalem.

Oz belongs to a generation of writers known as the Statehood Generation, a group that matured as writers only after the foundation of the State of Israel. The Statehood Generation challenged the collective national aesthetics of the previous Palmach Generation, and sought to give expression to an everyday individualism in Israeli life. In their language they worked to shed the complex historical layers of Hebrew and present ideas in the simplicity and intimacy of quotidian speech. Within this context, Oz emerged in the early 1960s alongside novelist A. B. Yehoshua; together they explored in prose the everyday experience of individuals, focusing to varying degrees on the inner lives of characters negotiating a world dominated by social and political structures oftentimes inimical to individual existence.

Early Works

Oz's first literary ventures begin exploring the two worlds of kibbutz and Jerusalem, but within the comfortable hermeticism of a self-sufficient society. His early volume of stories, *Where the Jackals Howl* (1965), and his first novel, *Elsewhere Perhaps* (1966), only hint at the interpenetrations to come when Israel is set against the world beyond. Of the two, *Elsewhere Perhaps* more successfully begins to disrupt a co-

cooned Israel, not just by extending earlier criticisms of kibbutz society, but by introducing the problematic element of Germany into the scene. The Holocaust is never mentioned, but postwar Germany stands in the novel as an off-stage ghost, the site of repressed Jewish anxiety and desire. Eva Harish, wife of the protagonist, David, runs off with her cousin/lover back to Germany before the novel begins in a confusing search for origin. Just as life seems to return to normal in the middle of the story, her cousin/lover's partner, Zechariah Siegfried Berger, brother of another kibbutz member, invades the scene. He comes to seduce Noga, David and Eva's daughter, and entice her to return with him to her mother in Germany. The relations are complex and largely allegorical (as the names themselves). Germany never appears as such but remains always in the murky background, a place of seduction tinged with evil. Israel and the kibbutz completely fill the world of this novel, but because of that, Germany attains a larger, violating presence, the id-like attraction of something dark, evil, and seductively mysterious.

Oz's second novel, *My Michael* (1968), alternately takes up Jerusalem as the site of personal isolation and suffering, traversing the fault lines of an Israeli reality that impinges on the lives of Hannah Gonen and her husband, Michael. Here, Oz demonstrates his interest in the historical layers that Jerusalem brings to the fore, but Michael's studies as a geologist, implying the prehistoric layers of inanimate rock, echo his emotionless relationship to Hannah and also, perhaps, a significant gap in depicting the city. The intervening lacuna—a modern history somewhere between geology and present psychological suffering—ignores the Holocaust and prefigures the type of silence that will haunt Oz's writings of Jerusalem from the 1970s. *My Michael* does resonate with Yehuda Amichai's own novelistic depiction of Jerusalem from 1963, *Not of This Place, Not of This Time*, but there the theme of archaeology mines *all* the layers of the past, forgetting nothing, most especially the layer of the Holocaust.

Touch the Water, Touch the Wind

Oz's first novel of the 1970s, *Touch the Water, Touch the Wind* (1973), is his sole work to depict Europe during the Holocaust; it is also his most antireal novel. In it, the Holocaust emerges primarily as a psychic disturbance, a severe scar on the inner life of the protagonist, Pomeranz, who survives Nazi Poland through a series of antireal escapes, living "there in a state of pure spirit, lacking all physical needs" (translation by Nicholas de Lange, New York: Harcourt Brace Jovanovich, 1974, p. 14). Pomeranz gets through the war and spends most of the novel in Israel, first in Tiberias and then on a kibbutz, where he gains fame through his mathematical research on the problems of time and infinity. The narrative depends extensively on a serious encounter with philosophy and mathematics, avoiding a solipsistic reflection on the inner sufferings of a survivor. Rather, the novel shows how social discourse intrudes into and reflects upon inner life. In this, the Holocaust becomes an important prism through which to observe the intersections of intellectual thought and personal trauma.

The novel's depiction of real and antireal also echoes and becomes a critique of Israel itself, perhaps a comment on the popular Israeli slogan, "from Holocaust to resurrection." Once in Israel, Pomeranz leads an ostensibly normal life, now "grounded," so to speak, after levitating to escape the Nazis. But this existence, conveyed to us through a narrative style likewise based on realistic portrayal, stands against the interior space of Pomeranz's thoughts and research. Exterior existence, we might conclude, has returned to normal in Israel, but that gives little consolation to a mind still caught up in the mechanisms of the Holocaust. The words that greet Pomeranz's decision on Israel at war's end exude an irony only fully realized at the end of the novel: "Promised Land: *There to live in liberty, there to flourish, pure and free, there our hopes shall be fulfilled*—thought through action may be stilled. Death to the nightmares, *look the light in the eye*, make a new start in the blue brightness of summer. Settle. Down" (p. 37). "Down" arrives at the end of the book when the earth opens up and swallows Pomeranz and his love, Stefa, now together after years of separation after the war. But if earthiness finally allows rest for this *luftmensch*, then we are reminded, as the Six-Day War rages in the background, that the price of reality is always difficult.

Jerusalem and History

Oz never again depicts Europe in the grip of war, or even the desperate attempts of some other Pomeranz trying to survive the Nazi scourge, but the themes of history and suffering recur throughout the 1970s. Oz's other writings of this decade tease out the idea of the Holocaust in a more subtle way, almost in an approach-avoidance that reflects a political impasse caused generally by the Holocaust in Israeli society. In these works, Oz seems caught between an Israeli labor-establishment disdain of any unheroic mention of the Holocaust and a revisionist politics all too eager to exploit a national identity of victimization. Oz treads a middle ground that takes history into account but refuses it a deterministic function. In a telling invective addressed to Menachem Begin in 1982 and the problems of the Lebanon war, Oz writes, "There are times, when, like many Jews, I feel sorry I didn't kill Hitler with my own hand. . . . There is not, and there never will be, any healing for the open wound. Tens of thousands of dead Arabs will not heal that wound. But, Mr. Begin, Adolf Hitler . . . is dead and burned to ashes" (*Slopes of Lebanon*, translation by Maurice Goldberg-Bartura, New York: Vintage Books, 1992, p. 27). Oz's pronouncement, while less weighty than Friedrich Nietzsche's eulogy for god, reflects similar sentiments by claiming that Israeli reality does not gain national significance solely through the political and historical legacy of the Holocaust.

In that spirit, Oz's novellas "Crusade," in the volume *Unto Death*, and "The Hill of Evil Counsel," in the volume bearing that name perform a delicate balance of naming historical Jewish tragedy without naming the Holocaust specifically. "Crusade," from 1971, tells the tale of a group of medieval Christian crusaders making their way to Jerusalem. This is Oz's *Heart of Darkness*, an allegorical tale of Jewish suffering and trauma that descends into an increasingly antireal morass of violence. But the story, it is important to point out, does not focus on genocidal slaughter as a theme (violence remains an individual task: by individuals against individuals), nor does violence remain the sole property of Jews. Suffering abounds and this novella shows the general human capacity for evil. The crusaders never make it to Jerusalem. Escape from the mechanism of horror can only come, as in *Touch the Water, Touch the Wind*, with an escape from the world of form and flesh: "Shedding their bodies, they made their way, growing ever purer, into the heart of the music . . . and yet farther, leaving behind their loathsome flesh and streaming onward, a jet of whiteness on a white canvas, an abstract purpose, a fleeting vapor, perhaps peace" (*Unto Death*, translated by Nicholas de Lange, New York: Harcourt Brace Jovanovich, 1975, p. 81). The overtones of Ecclesiastes in the abandonment of the flesh mark a continuation for Oz of the flight into abstraction when dealing with the trauma of violence, a trauma that cannot be realistically rendered.

"The Hill of Evil Counsel," however, does arrive in Jerusalem and at realism, but jettisons the direct depiction of Holocaust suffering. The novella (translated by Nicholas de Lange, New York: Harcourt Brace Jovanovich, 1978) takes place in 1947 Jerusalem, the eve of statehood. Oz does not mention the Holocaust but human suffering is the theme, and the world of the story is populated with liminal figures that resonate with Holocaust origin. These are characters far different from the kibbutz members of earlier novels, or the young Israelis of *My Michael*. Instead, this is a diasporic world, like Y. H. Brenner's Jerusalem in his 1919 novel, *Breakdown and Bereavement*, but without Brenner's invective. Oz presents a Jerusalem of incomplete and wounded figures, isolated in their inner suffering even if thrust together in the artificial closeness of community. Thus, the novel acts less as an inheritor of Brenner than as a foreshadowing of David Grossman's *See Under: Love* (1986). Grossman picks up on the isolated individual remnants of a postwar Jerusalem, on the fragmented human survivors with their sexual deviance and their refusal to talk about "over there." Oz himself hides the pain of his characters, not allowing the Holocaust to take over and, in fact, confusing the intertextual resonance of the story by claiming prewar Palestinian pasts for all his characters. Yet the signals all seem to point toward a Holocaust reading despite the refusal to acknowledge a Holocaust genealogy for the story. " 'All gone!' " cries the mother with "desperate pathos," the mother who will eventually succumb to her own anxieties and run away with the British officer. "Dead and done for! Lost!" (*Hill of Evil Counsel*, p. 24) she screams suddenly upon listening to her son recite a story she had written in Polish before the war.

The character's paroxysm is Oz's reaction as well, a clue to understanding his political exclamation to Menachem Begin. What "The Hill of Evil Counsel" accomplishes—and what the antireal flights in *Touch the Wind, Touch the Water* and "Crusade" could not—is expressed in the ambiguity of the exclamation: a frightful, haunting memory of pain, yes, but one that must be left behind. "The Hill of Evil Counsel" stays within a realistic portrayal of aftermath, a portrayal of an Israel that stands at the center of Oz's novelistic and political concerns. But the Holocaust stands there too, a silent specter, an intertextual and contextual reminder that this country, even while moving beyond this tragic legacy, can never truly break from it.

Panther in the Basement

This simple dialectical logic returns in one of Oz's more recent novels, *Panther in the Basement* (1994), which now brings back postwar, pre-state Jerusalem. This novel seems to answer both Oz's "Hill of Evil Counsel" and Grossman's *See Under: Love* (and, of course, the growing popular awareness in Israel of the country's Holocaust past). While Grossman follows his child protagonist's perspective through a linguistic world of literality, Oz allows his protagonist to understand the complexities of meaning in the world, and Proffy, as opposed to Grossman's Momik, flows through a world where the Holocaust exists in the social and cultural reminders around him, without continuously recreating itself in the nightmare of repression that constitutes Momik's world. The past exists in Oz's novel as an explicit Holocaust trace, but the story is about the present and about getting from the present to the future. This is the lesson of the intervening years in which Oz experimented with characters whose struggles were individual: in *A Perfect Peace, Black Box, To Know a Woman Fima*. Those were all novels about adults. For Oz, the child takes us back into a public space and returns us to history, not because adults can shield themselves against the effects of politics and society, but because children more explicitly form themselves in relation to the anxieties and repressions surrounding them. The Holocaust emerges from this: a legacy of the mind, a brand that is part of the culture we take in around us.

Bibliography

Primary Sources

Fiction

Artsot hatan (*Where the Jackals Howl*). 1965.
Makom aher (*Elsewhere Perhaps*). 1966.
Mikhael sheli (*My Michael*). 1968.
Ad mavet (*Unto Death*). 1971.
Laga'at bamayim laga'at baruah (*Touch the Water, Touch the Wind*). 1973.
Har ha'etsah hara'ah (*The Hill of Evil Counsel*). 1976.
Memukah mekhonah (*A Perfect Peace*). 1982.
Kufsah shekhorah (*Black Box*). 1987.
Lada'at Isha (*To Know a Woman*). 1989.
Hamatsov hashelishi (*Fima*). 1991.
Panter bamartef (*Panther in the Basement*). 1994.

Nonfiction

Be'or hatakhelet ha'azah (*In This Blazing Light*). 1979.
Mimordot halevanon (*The Slopes of Lebanon*). 1987.

Secondary Sources

Balaban, Avraham. *Between God and Beast: An Examination of Amos Oz's Prose*. University Park: The Pennsylvania State University Press, 1993.

Schacham, Chaya. "Novellas Under This Blazing Light: Transformations in the Novella Writing of Amos Oz." *Orbis Litterarum: International Review of Literary Studies* 53, no. 5 (1998): 318–335.

Interview

Cohen, Joseph. "Amos Oz." In his *Voices of Israel*. Albany: State University of New York Press, 1990.

Archive

An Amos Oz Archive exists at Ben-Gurion University of the Negev, Beersheva, Israel. http://www.bgu.ac.il/aranne/Amos_oz/ENTER.HTM.

CYNTHIA OZICK

(1928–)

S. LILLIAN KREMER

ONE OF AMERICA'S most accomplished writers, Cynthia Ozick wrestles with the moral dilemma of writing about the Holocaust. Although she claims she would prefer not to write about the Holocaust in fiction because documentary work should suffice, the subject enters her work "unbidden, unsummoned" (Interview, 28 December 1986). Pertinent to her commitment to literature that she characterizes as "centrally Jewish in its concerns" ("Toward a New Yiddish," *Art & Ardor: Essays*, New York: Alfred A. Knopf, 1983, p. 174) is her interrogation of the Holocaust as the orienting event of the twentieth century, the relationship between the Holocaust and historic antisemitism, Holocaust transformation and Jewish self-definition, survivor syndrome and mission, post-Holocaust Jewish identity and Judaic values, and the problematics of Holocaust transmission. Although she prefers not "to tamper or invent, or imagine" the Holocaust (*Paris Review*, 1987, p. 185) it is central to her fiction.

Biography

Born in New York City in 1928 to William and Celia Regelson Ozick, Russian-Jewish immigrants who spoke openly of Russian and German anti-Jewish fury, the nascent writer was aware of violence that Jews endured. Her own youth was marred by taunts of public school classmates calling her a "Christ-killer" when she refused to sing Christmas carols during school assemblies, by the radio broadcasts of Father Charles E. Coughlin preaching antisemitism during the Depression of the 1930s, and by World War II and the Holocaust, when she became aware that her parents refused to sell popular Bayer aspirin in their drugstore in protest of Nazi aggression. Complementing this sensitivity to the brutal aspects of Jewish history was Ozick's immersion in the bright aspects of Jewish family life, recalled in adult memories, of her encouraging and resilient mother, who was an avid reader and wrote and painted; her father, a Talmudic rationalist and devotee of Yiddish literature; and an uncle Abraham Regelson, who was a reputed Yiddish poet.

Following academic success as an undergraduate at New York University, where she was graduated cum laude and Phi Beta Kappa in 1949, she received an M.A. at Ohio State University. Although she did not pursue a doctorate, she continued to study literature in Lionel Trilling's classes at Columbia University and embarked on a program of self-directed Jewish education. Celebrated as a superb stylist, Ozick has had her work translated and published in Sweden, Finland, Germany, France, Spain, Italy, and Israel. Her literary talent has been widely acknowledged with many awards, including a MacArthur Fellowship, a Guggenheim Fellowship, a National Endowment for the Arts Fellowship, the Edward Lewis Wallant Award, the Straus Living Award from the American Academy and Institute of Arts and Letters, the Jewish Book Council Award, the Memorial Foundation for Jewish Culture Award, the Koret Jewish Book Award, the Lamnan Foundation Award for Fiction, and the National Book Critics Circle Award. Five of her stories have been selected for republication in *Best American Short Stories* and three have won first prize in the O. Henry Prize Stories competition. She has been nominated for the National Book Award and the PEN/Faulkner Award.

Trust

Ozick's first published novel, *Trust* (1966), is a coming-of-age saga, mapping the education of an unnamed gentile woman. The protagonist's quest for a father dramatizes western civilization's Greek/Hebrew dichotomy in a contrapuntal structure juxtaposing the artistic and sensual lures of the Greek nature god Pan and the moral imperatives of the Hebrew prophet Moses. Rather than cloister, cathedral, and castle, which the young girl's mother intended to be her aesthetic introduction to European culture, she discovers, albeit indirectly, concentration camp, death camp, and crematorium. Countering the Hellenic and Christian influences of the young woman's biological father and of her first stepfather is the Jewish influence of her second stepfather, Enoch Vand, through whose dramatic and meditative role Ozick introduces the Holocaust as an enduring benchmark of radical evil and Judaic ethics as an abiding moral touchstone.

Reaction to the Holocaust as a criterion by which Ozick registers characters' moral standing is introduced in *Trust* and recurs in her later fiction. Allegra Vand and her daughter, "Pleasure seekers among the displaced" (*Trust*, New York: The New American Library, 1966, p. 62), stand aloof from the Holocaust tragedy while Enoch Vand becomes obsessed with the catastrophe. As an investigator for the Office of Strategic Services, Vand must record the Holocaust toll, cataloging the dead and the venues of their demise. Vand chants an unremitting dirge citing victims' names and the camps where they perished. He is moral foil to his wife, who escapes Holocaust reality in the myth, fantasy, and romance of castle and cathedral architecture and blames refugees of the Nazi occupation for their misfortunes. Her daughter, who sporadically shows sympathy for the plight of the victims, asserts that Holocaust history will endure in her memory, but dishonors that sentiment when she joins Allegra to advocate Holocaust amnesia. Of Enoch's incantation of the murdered in

> Dachau, Belsen, Auschwitz, Buchenwald, the order varying, Auschwitz, Buchenwald, Belsen, Dachau, now and then an alternation in the tick and swing, Belsen, Maidanek, Auschwitz, Chelm[n]o, Dachau, Treblinka, Buchenwald, Mauthausen, Sobibor—tollings like the chorus of some unidentifiable opera [she] . . . could remember the music but not the import (pp. 75–76).

She misinterprets commemoration as vengeful, urging the Jew to forgive, to be merciful, to be Christian. Holocaust grief remains the Jew's exclusive province expressed in biblical, liturgical, and folkloric allusion. The polarity of Holocaust sensitivity/insensitivity initiated in *Trust*'s husband/wife and father/daughter dichotomies is charged with the Jewish/Christian polarity that emerges throughout Ozick's oeuvre in prose redolent with Hebraic and Christian images and diction.

The Holocaust crucible accounts for Vand's metamorphosis from political to religious activism, from pre-Holocaust Communist to post-Holocaust observant Jew. In his evolution from apostate to believer, Vand is the literary patriarch of Ozick's prodigal Jews who return to Judaism either through their own Holocaust witness or through the guidance of a survivor. By insisting on bearing Holocaust witness and strengthening his commitment to Judaism, Vand (Yiddish for wall), allegorically named for the ghetto wall and the Wailing Wall, seeks to reinvigorate the Jewish people and rebuild Judaism as a viable response to the catastrophe.

More than most American writers, Ozick engages the theological implications of the Holocaust. Progressing thematically from human to divine culpability in the manner of Elie Wiesel and I. B. Singer, whose religious characters challenge the silent, passive God for betraying covenantal justice during the Holocaust, Ozick's Vand struggles with divine abdication of the biblical intercessionary role. Following intense study of Judaic sacred texts under the guidance of a *Shoah* survivor, he embraces the view of the mystical sages who argued that God is not absent from history, but is self-concealed, commanding greater human engagement in the redemptive process, a validation of the Judaic conviction in humanity's restorative task of helping to free the hidden God. Thus, Vand honors the victims by commitment to the religion that shaped the identities of pious and learned Jews of Europe.

Short Fiction

The ramifications of Holocaust-incurred cultural loss and political reckoning grow ever wider in Ozick's short story collections that function as transitions to the narratives of the later period that foreground the *Shoah*. "Envy; or, Yiddish in America" and "The Suitcase," collected in *The Pagan Rabbi and Other Stories* (1971), emphasize the moral burden of the Holocaust, its meaning in history, and its significance to nonwitnessing Jews. Ozick conceived "Envy" as an elegy for Yiddish and its murdered speakers. The story's antagonists, an obscure Yiddish poet, Edelshtein, and a celebrated Yiddish storyteller, Yankel Ostrover, write in a language whose audience has been systematically annihilated. Although much of "Envy" addresses one writer's jealousy of another's ability to attract a translator and gain an audience, it is also a lament for lost European Jewry and its language, which "died a sudden and definite death, in a given decade, on a given piece of soil" ("Envy," New York: Alfred A. Knopf,

1971, p. 24). Despondent that his rival's work is the only "survivor," "As if hidden in a Dutch attic like that child" (p. 51), Edelshtein argues for regeneration of the language that nourished Jews for centuries. The collection's second Holocaust story, "The Suitcase," counterpoints Jewish Holocaust sensitivity with German Holocaust amnesia, a drama of Holocaust antagonism between an elderly German and his son's Jewish mistress. Each strips away an assimilated American veneer to respond passionately to Holocaust history. Gottfried Hencke, a pilot for the Kaiser in World War I, no longer considers himself German and disdains the preservation of Holocaust memory. Genevieve Levin challenges his negation by exploiting every opportunity to address German culpability. Eventually, Hencke erupts in a self-damning speech festering with the poison of Nazi antisemitism. As in *Trust*, in these short fictions Ozick eschews foregrounding the Holocaust or rendering its universe through direct plotline development and graphic settings. Instead, she presents a meditation on the philosophic implications of the *Shoah* for those who were spared physical encounter but whose sensibilities are profoundly engaged or altered.

In marked contrast to her earliest Holocaust works, which focus exclusively on indirect witnesses, the second phase of Ozick's writing introduces the perspective of the Holocaust victim. Post-Holocaust Diaspora Jewish identity is the subject of "Bloodshed" (1970) and "A Mercenary" (1974), collected in *Bloodshed and Three Novellas* (1976). These narratives are studies of diametrically opposed responses to antisemitic victimization: Jewish self-hatred versus strengthened Jewish self-definition and communal association. "Bloodshed" is illustrative of a pattern in American Holocaust literature that casts the Holocaust survivor in the role of spiritual or moral guide to the spiritually perplexed. The protagonist, a secular American Jew, comes to scorn the observant religious of a Hasidic community of Holocaust survivors and their children and emerges from their service reconciled to Hasidism. Initially wary that the faithful will try to impose their ways on him, Bleilip has nevertheless come to this community of pious Jews because "He supposed they had a certain knowledge the unscathed could not guess at" ("Bloodshed," *Bloodshed and Three Novellas*, New York: Alfred A. Knopf, 1976, p. 59). Alan Berger observes that "Ozick combines the figures of rebbe and survivor as links with authentic Judaism. Survivors are bridges between American Jews and the vanished world of Eastern European piety, testifying to the Holocaust's centrality even for the American nonwitness" (Berger, 1985, p. 51). Ozick turns the tale on the skeptic, making him the subject of a Hasidic exemplum, commentary revealing the theological and human implications of the Holocaust that result in his openness to the possibility of spiritual restoration.

Stanislav Lushinski of "A Mercenary," born into a European society that annihilated Jews, sheds his Jewish identity to become an African. Along the road of transformation from pre-*Shoah* Polish Jew to post-Holocaust African, Lushinski survives Polish antisemitism, Russian purges, and the Nazi genocide. This self-denying Jew lives the first six years of his life in a sea of Polish Jew-hatred as the son of assimilated blond parents who took comfort in their Polish appearance and despaired only of their adored son's dark "gypsy" look. Like Jerzy Kosinski's child-fugitive in *The Painted Bird*, the helpless young Lushinski learns to think of himself as prey as Poles hired to protect him instead bait, beat, and finally hang him by his wrists to hold him for arrest by the Germans. So psychologically scarred is this victim that the remainder of his life is spent concealing his Jewish identity to assume the persona of his oppressor. The adult mercenary diplomat is the caricature of Jean Paul Sartre's externally defined Jew, his identity designated by his antagonist rather than shaped by his own civilization. Encouraged by European antisemitism to perceive himself only as victim, Lushinski is bereft of the religion, language, and culture that constitute an authentic, self-defining Jewish person.

Lushinski's character is an early portrait of post-Holocaust Jewish schizophrenia. His self-image is so distorted by the antisemite's lens that he executes his diplomatic role as the "Paid Mouthpiece" of a small African nation in the United Nations General Assembly, where he promulgates his adopted nation's anti-Zionist position. Having survived a continent where death was the penalty for Jewish identity, Lushinski privately condemns the Nazis yet physically aligns himself with the rhetoric of postwar Jewish opponents. Anti-Zionist mercenary though Lushinski is in public life, this self-reconstructed Jew privately acknowledges Holocaust truth. He insists his lover, whose identity is also in question, read *The Destruction*, a documentary account of the Holocaust, to learn the data—the tables and figures, the train schedules, the numbers of trains. Just as the white European cannot metamorphose into a black African, he will not erase history and therefore contests his lover's universalist argument that denies the particularity of Jewish loss by subsuming it under other national losses. His insistence on factual Holocaust reading for his mistress suggests greater connection to the history and people he outwardly rejects and is consistent with Ozick's increasingly complex treatment of Holocaust issues and the emerging dominant question of post-Holocaust Jewish identity.

Ozick's deft psychological analysis is matched by her political probe. Situating the self-hating post-Holocaust Jew in the United Nations, where he casts anti-Israel votes, reflects Ozick's political position, allowing her to expose the lie of United Nations neutrality, when in fact, it consistently demonstrates its anti-Israel perspective at the behest of forty voting Muslim nations. The post-Holocaust political consciousness that governs the text heralds the alarm that Jews continue to be the subject of genocidal intent; only the geographical venue has shifted in the post-Holocaust world from Europe to the Middle East.

The title story of the 1982 collection, *Levitation: Five Fictions*, returns to the theme of Holocaust sensitivity as a touchstone of authentic Jewish identity. As literary descendants of *Trust*'s Enoch and Allegra Vand, the Feingolds in this story are divided on the significance of historic Jewish martyrology and the Holocaust. Jim Feingold reads widely in Jewish history, writes about medieval Jewry, and is working on a novel about a fourteenth-century survivor of a Spanish massacre in which his relatives were among the six thousand Jewish victims. Lucy Feingold, who reads only Jane Austen's *Emma* and writes poetry, has developed an affinity for biblical Hebrews and converted to Judaism, but she lacks the collective memory and communal feeling of the story's other Jewish characters. During a party the Feingolds are hosting in an effort to boost their standing among literary luminaries, Lucy balks at the recitation by a Holocaust survivor of the horrors he witnessed. As the refugee speaks of a mass killing of families falling like sacks into a ravine, limbs all tangled, Lucy concludes that it is possible to become jaded by atrocity, to be bored by accounts of mass shootings and murder by gas, and she recasts the survivor's testimony Christologically to respond sympathetically, visualizing "a hillside with multitudes of crosses, and bodies dropping down from big bloody nails" (*Levitation*, p. 14). The heightened engagement of the Jews in attendance at the party, listening to the story and responding differently from Lucy, culminates in the sort of "floating" characteristic to the depictions of people and objects in paintings by Chagall: "The room rose like an ark on waters" (*Levitations*, p. 15). However, as a Christian, Lucy remains earthbound, responsive only to the crucifixion.

The Shawl

During the 1980s, the Holocaust moved from the background to the foreground of Ozick's fiction with a parallel shift from indirect to direct representation. The 1980s texts are set in the Holocaust era and landscape and develop variations of Holocaust survivorship. "The Shawl" (1980) marks the sole instance in which Ozick locates her fiction within the concentration camp universe. The story opens *in medias res*, focusing on two young women and an infant on a death march en route from one concentration camp to another and dwells on the choiceless choices of the Nazi universe. Rosa Lublin, a young mother carrying her infant concealed beneath her shawl confronts the dilemma of whether to entrust her child to a stranger or to conspire to preserve its life in her own vulnerable setting, a decision fraught with danger for mother and child since the penalty for stepping out of the line of march is death. Throughout her magnificently compressed narrative Ozick refrains from writing mimetic camp descriptions. Instead, she deftly introduces poetic images conveying the horror of "a place without pity," a place characterized by "bad wind with pieces of black in it" an "ash-stippled wind," a place of "stink mixed with a bitter fatty floating smoke that greased Rosa's skin" (*The Shawl* New York: Alfred A. Knopf, 1989, p. 9). The central symbol of the story and its novella sequel *Rosa* (1983), collected under the title *The Shawl* (1989), is the shawl that assumes magical properties in the short story, serving as the infant Magda's daily source of shelter, nourishment, and concealment. Looking for the shawl that her fourteen-year-old aunt, Stella, has usurped to warm her own frozen body, Magda toddles into the roll call square crying, uttering her first sounds since Rosa's breasts dried. In the climactic scene, as Magda reaches toward mother and the retrieved shawl, a German guard sweeps the infant up and tosses her on to the electrified fence. The witnessing mother crams the shawl into her own mouth to mute her grief, once again affirming the life-preserving properties of the shawl.

The power of the short story derives from metaphor and from dramatic and poetic concentration. *Rosa* (1983) is discursive, encompassing Rosa's pre-Holocaust history and the psychological burden of post-Holocaust survival. Beyond verbal echoes from the story to confirm the character constructs of the novella, key images and tropes—shawl, fence, and electricity—reverberate to link the two narratives and suggest the Holocaust's pervasive intrusion in the survivor's psyche. In the novella, images of electricity and shawl revive memories of the child and its brutal murder. The shawl, once a life-sustaining symbol, is the novella's most powerful objective correlative for Holocaust loss.

Rosa, one of literature's finest representations of survivor syndrome, portrays the title character at fifty-eight, nearly four decades after the events recounted in "The Shawl," and explores the protagonist's prewar life as well as her wounded postwar psyche. Here, Ozick delineates Rosa's transformation from promising young woman to aging victim who suffers the long-term effects of concentration camp deprivation and the loss of a child while maintaining her relationship with Stella, whom she continues to blame for Magda's death. The passage of time and distance from the site of her trauma has not been conducive to healing. Rosa is increasingly tormented by the loss of Magda and by public indifference to Holocaust witness. Assessing her life by the Holocaust, the survivor identifies three stages of experience: "The life before, the life during, the life after" (*Rosa*, p. 58). For Rosa, "before is a dream. After is a joke. Only during stays. And to call it a life is a lie" (*Rosa*, p. 58). Rosa's survival is bitter—the hell of lost family, lost aspirations, lost language, the hell of persistent memory and failed communication with those who evade her testimony, and the agony of those who would exploit her history. Her only solace is imagining lives for her deceased daughter. Holocaust imagery pursues Rosa in Miami, whose oppressive setting serves as metaphoric extension of Rosa's state of mind. Just as a disconnected telephone attests to the lodger's alienation from others, a starvation diet and slovenly appearance suggest replication of her Holocaust ordeal. Signifying her unresolved attachment to a loved one lost in environments where normal grief and mourning were forbidden are Rosa's postwar letters addressed to her dead child and Rosa's frenzied house cleaning and personal grooming in anticipation of delivery of a package containing Magda's shawl.

As a superb example of the literary representations of survivor post-traumatic stress, Rosa is an exemplar of symptoms psychiatrists associate with survivor syndrome: paranoia, suspicion, emotional isolation, and distance. Her invention of mature, prosperous adult lives for Magda accords with psychiatric theory that survivors indulge in various forms of denial, idealization, and walling off when they are unable to complete the process of mourning. In contrast to Stella, who is reportably adjusting to postwar life, embracing English, and pursuing an education, a career, and social relationships, Rosa remains strongly fixated on the past, stubbornly attached to Polish, using syntactically misstructured and fragmented English emblematic of the Holocaust-wrought rupture she endured. Antithetical survivors, Stella and Rosa perceive one another as mentally ill. For Rosa, the shawl is a holy emblem of her child; for Stella, it is Rosa's "trauma," "fetish," "idol." Rosa's traumatized personality is also conveyed by contrast with Mr. Persky, an immigrant who left Europe before the conflagration, who sought asylum from nongenocidal Polish antisemitism and a better standard of living and who is socially engaged, trusting, and at ease with his peers.

A believer in *t'shuva* (redemption), Ozick celebrates the idea that we can change ourselves, that we can change what appears to be our "fate." Therein lies hope for Rosa. Coupled with her insistence on appropriate Holocaust transmission, the first stirring of restoration is Rosa's decision to share a portion of her Holocaust history with Persky, the sort of Jew her parents had maligned, whom she had earlier misjudged, and whose *Shoah* interest she had rejected. Emblematic of her new interest in communication are her order to reconnect her telephone, her plan to return to live with Stella, and her acceptance of Persky. More certain signs that healing is underway are Rosa's muted interest in the shawl when it finally arrives, and her acknowledgment that the living, thriving Magda is a figment of her imagination. Emphasis on Magda's expected return juxtaposed with Rosa's reception of Persky suggests that although the Holocaust will remain a crucial influence in her life, trauma will be tempered by voluntary community with fellow Jews, leading her toward becoming a more effective Holocaust witness.

Morally sensitive to the possibility that fiction may corrupt or trivialize the Holocaust, Ozick weaves the theme of Holocaust transmission and misappropriation into the survivor's story. She lavishes the best of her sharp satire on Dr. Tree, a bogus pseudo-intellectual reminiscent of contemporary Holocaust deniers who seeks cooperation for his project "to observe survivor syndroming within the natural setting" (*Rosa*, p. 38). He is, in fact, an exploiter of Holocaust tragedy, an academic who misappropriates Jewish suffering. Rosa condemns his intent to capitalize on the Holocaust and resents his arrogant claim that he is writing the definitive work on the topic. Unwilling to be a partner to Holocaust misappropriation, Rosa denies the academic her cooperation. This act of defiance, motivated by her insistence on authentic and appropriate Holocaust transmission, is a step toward Rosa's recovery and heralds her return to Jewish community.

Drama

Ozick's unpublished play, *The Shawl*, which appeared originally under the title *Blue Light*, a reference to the blue lights of Warsaw, is neither a dramatized adaptation of the original collection nor a sequel but incorporates matter from the short story and the novella to denounce Holocaust denial. Set in 1979, the year the revisionist, pseudo-academic Institute for Historical Research held its first meeting, the play opens with the stage in total darkness, "electricity coursing through dangerous wires and the piercing sound of MAGDA'S CRY. Ma . . . ma!" (p. 1). This work dramatizes a Holocaust denier's attempted seduction of Stella and Rosa, his manipulation of Rosa into signing a document indicating that what happened to Magda was misrepresented, a document intended to bolster revisionist characterization of the Holocaust as a Zionist fabrication. Like Milton's Satan, Globalis captivates his victims with charm in the guise of personas they crave—for Stella, a lover and for Rosa, an attentive confidant. Progressing beyond the portrait of the pseudo-scholar of the novella who brought the insensitivity and arrogance of a self-aggrandizing academic to a subject demanding humility, in the play Ozick addresses the sinister realm of the intentional deceit of Holocaust deniers and revisionists, a dangerous movement making headway among the antisemites and historically illiterate who are easily hoodwinked.

Among changes Ozick made for the dramatic form is a shift and elaboration in Rosa's *Shoah* testimony. Instead of confining her witness to letters written to Magda, Rosa now reveals her ghetto and camp experiences to the living, speaking graphically of her camp brothel experience, of women suffering in long roll calls, of ill-clad women standing for hours in the cold, hungry, sick, smelling the stench from the crematoria, their eyes burning from the smoke. Stella's dramatic manner conforms to Rosa's delineation of her in the novella: a woman suppressing Holocaust memory to devote her energies to recovery and renewal. When she comprehends that Globalis exploited her to gain access to Rosa, however, she bitterly concedes that, like Rosa, she is "A piece of human . . . refuse! [who] has not forgotten anything" (p. 60). Finally, the woman who accused Rosa of making a relic or fetish of the shawl in the novella demands that Rosa show it to the denier, "Tell him what was in it! Get the shawl and show him!" (p. 67). Rosa is too weak to respond with anything other than bewilderment to the denier's trickery that has resulted in her signature testifying to her delusionary status and renouncing her Holocaust testimony, when, in fact, she thought she was signing a statement acknowledging Magda's death. Ozick gives Stella the speech that exposes revisionist motivation, identifying Globalis as a Nazi "from the kingdom of lies. . . . exploiter . . . persecutor . . . rapist! . . . you say it never happened, and you rejoice that it did. You want to undo it and you want to do it! You want to take human beings and turn them into nothing! . . . You want to turn the crimes against us into nothing! You want it to happen again" (p. 69). Although the play concludes with the women's reconciliation, the closing scenes nevertheless confirm the disturbing reality that has pervaded the drama's dark mood. Although Holocaust denial has been debunked by Stella, and the older generation of Jewish hotel guests has recognized Globalis for what he is, an ominous undercurrent persists in the voice of a young gentile hotel receptionist who agrees to disseminate the denier's pamphlets at her college. The play ends with the return of Magda's spirit, Stella's emphatic iteration of the continued presence of Holocaust memory, and her bonding with Rosa in the perpetuation of memory. As the curtain descends, the survivors are cradled in each other's arms, while the "humming sound of an electric sizzle" and Magda's cry wash over the audience. The victim's voice prevails as a haunting presence drowning out the distortions and lies of Holocaust revisionists.

The Cannibal Galaxy

Published the same year as *Rosa*, Ozick's second novel, *The Cannibal Galaxy*, is evidence of her continuing preoccupation with survivorship and renewed interest in thematically complex Holocaust representation. Paralleling the protagonists' decidedly different Holocaust experiences, one taking the brunt of the concentration camp universe and the other surviving the war in hiding or by escape, is their pre- and postwar Jewish identification. These two texts illustrate the author's expansive thinking about the effects of antisemitism on assimilated Jews of decidedly different cultural / political environments of eastern and western Europe. They also illustrate the delineation of the Nazi universe in each sphere and the representation of contrasting modes of survival rendered as survivor syndrome and survivor mission. Joseph Brill and Hester Lilt are authentic, self-defining Jews whose Holocaust experience not only failed to distance them from Judaism and the Jewish community but strengthened those bonds. In contrast to Rosa's exclusive Polish education, Ozick endows Brill with both Judaic and secular education. The son of Russian-Jewish parents who immigrated to France, where they continued to honor their ethnic / religious heritage, Brill excelled in traditional Jewish studies and in secular studies at the Sorbonne. Unlike the Lublins' aversion to Jewish neighborhoods and the sounds of Yiddish, Brill's family lives in a Jewish working-class neighborhood of Paris, where Joseph savors his neighbors' Yiddish dialects. Whereas Rosa Lublin's acculturation at the expense of Judaism fails her and accounts to some degree for her postwar cultural paralysis, Brill's strong prewar Jewish identity and continued study of Jewish canonical texts during Holocaust concealment explains his emergence from the *Shoah* as a dedicated Jew and accounts for his decision to redirect his career from astronomy to education. An even stronger foil to Rosa is Hester Lilt, who escaped Nazi Europe in a children's transport. Although Ozick neither dramatizes nor details Lilt's Holocaust experience, we understand that she suffered the loss of her family. Ozick's interest is clearly in this character's survivorship, which is predicated on devotion to Judaic scholarship and the midrashic narrative mode and to her political affirmation of Israel as contributing factors to post-Holocaust Jewish renaissance. Even the characters' names suggest their antithetical identities: Lublin is emblematic of the acculturation and annihilation of Polish Jewry; Hester is a variation of the Hebrew Esther, the heroine responsible for the survival of Persian Jewry when it was threatened with genocide.

Shifting the narrative from postwar America to prewar and Holocaust era France in a contrapuntal structure of alternate flashbacks and flash-forwards, Ozick relates Brill's postwar attitudes to his formative Holocaust experiences, taking the opportunity to dramatize the Vichy government's enthusiastic collaboration with Germany's genocidal goals. Ozick prefaces the novel's major Holocaust representation with the burning of a Parisian rabbi's library, an effective evocation of German *Kristallnacht* book burnings. The novel's primary *Shoah* scene is the infamous July 1942 French arrest of 28,000 Parisian Jews. Comparison of Ozick's account with those of historians reveals her attention to details of the methodical approach and ferocity of the action that herded civilian French Jews into captivity on French soil before their deportation to the death camps of the East,

> penned up without food or toilets, . . . under a devouring sun, squatting or sprawling among the faint and dying, day after day, . . . until the terrible delusive relief of the coming of the trucks—and then . . . hiatus in Drancy, and again the loading into boxcars, and again the unloading, the undressing, the run to the false showers (*Cannibal Galaxy*, p. 25).

Supplementing her realistic portrayal of the roundup and detention in the enclosed Velodrome d'Hiver sports arena prior to confinement in the transit camp at Drancy and the deportation to Auschwitz is her mythic allusion to the bestiality of the centaurs to convey the criminal behavior of collaborationist French gendarmes, detectives, bailiffs, and students from the police academy, accompanied by hundreds of political sympathizers identified by their blue shirts and armbands bearing the initials "PPF."

Ozick expresses outrage at European persecution of its Jewish populations across the centuries. She reminds us again that the Holocaust is an aberration only in degree. Her writing places the Holocaust within the historic context of perennial antisemitism. Brill's education in French antisemitism is initiated in childhood, advanced in the university, and completed in the Holocaust. Ozick evokes the Crusader slaughter of medieval Jews, the Enlightenment-era antisemitism of Voltaire, and the modern era's conspiratorial Dreyfus case. This catalogue is characteristic of Ozick's historicity, and the Voltaire and Dreyfus references clearly signify Vichy betrayal as a continuation of traditional French antisemitism.

The Messiah of Stockholm

In her most recent Holocaust work, Ozick combines historic and imagined representation. *The Messiah of Stockholm* (1987) is an atypical postmodern approach to the *Shoah*. As in several previous works, the Holocaust enters the fiction indirectly but now is presented in a highly experimental fusion of real and surreal. Alluding to the murder of Bruno Schulz, a Polish-Jewish writer, callously shot by the Nazis on the streets of a provincial Polish town, the novel speculates on the discovery of his final manuscript, entering the realm of fantasy through Lars Andemening, who imagines himself the surviving son of the novelist. The story of Schulz's death is told through incremental repetition. Each iteration adds detail and intensity to the crime, making it the pivotal Holocaustal event of the novel and a symbolic commemoration of all the people and their contributions to civilization aborted by the *Shoah*. Discussion of Schulz's work unrelentingly reverts to discussion of the shooting. In the end, Lars grieves, not so much for the manuscript, but for man, a man in a black coat who tried to save the book and was last seen hurrying toward the chimneys. The invented character's quest for the imagined surviving text is a redemptive memorial mission—an imagined mission of rescue and preservation.

Although the characters do not speak of their Jewish origins and each has a Swedish name, they are obsessed with the era during which unparalleled efforts were made to bring an end to Jewish history. Orphaned in World War II, Lars Andemening is a Polish refugee raised by a Swedish foster family. His obsession with his foreign identity caused him to leave their home. As his Swedish name suggests, Andemening looks inward to find meaning. He assumes the perspective of his spiritual father's murdered eye and adopts the emblematic name, Lazarus Baruch, a fusion of Jewish and Christian names signifying a blessed resurrection. A literary critic for a Swedish daily newspaper, Lars shares, with many of Ozick's characters, an exemplary dedication to literature. His interest lies in the writing of east and central European writers, thus, his choice and obsession with Bruno Schulz, whose voice and vision he believes he shares.

The novel's fusion of *Shoah* reality and fantasy is amplified by Andemening's association with a book dealer who joins his quest. Heidi Eklund alternately plays Lars's doppelgänger and foil, eventually becoming his "fellow collector," despite her skepticism that the manuscript will be recovered. The plot is complicated by the appearance of a counter-claimant to Schulz's paternity and manuscript, a woman calling herself Adela, the name of the maid in Schulz's *Street of Crocodiles*. She begs Lars to translate a manuscript that she claims is the authentic *Messiah*. The passage Ozick creates for *The Messiah* sequence is essentially Holocaustal and Schulzian in its tone and language and draws upon her own review of *Street of Crocodiles*. The juxtaposition of Schulzian diction and tone with Ozick's mimetic realism forcefully conveys the fragmentation and disruption the Holocaust wrought in the lives of ordinary people. Fearful that he would be authenticating a forgery, Lars concludes that the text perished in the camps and takes it upon himself to burn the counterfeit. Whether these flames signify the destruction of a false manuscript or not, they recall the Holocaust flames that turned Jewish life and art to ash. Given Ozick's passion for literature and Jewish history, and her coalition of those interests with the circumstances of the murder of Bruno Schulz, the novel is a lament for the murdered generation and the loss of its contribution to civilization. Bruno Schulz's Holocaust history, coupled with allusion to Nelly Sachs's Holocaust poems, *O Chimneys*, maps the novel's progress from loss of an extraordinarily gifted artist to the collective loss of European Jewry. Ozick's fiction, particularly those novels that evoke or foreground the *Shoah*, exhibit historic and moral vision complementing the extraordinary aesthetic sensibilities that have garnered Ozick near universal critical acclaim. She is a novelist whose subject matter and literary style fuse as a profound voice in contemporary literature.

Essays

As a prolific essayist, Ozick writes primarily about literature, but also about Jewish culture and history and personal reflections. Two essays in her most recent collection, *Quarrel & Quandary*, address the question of art's relation to the *Shoah* as expressed in Holocaust literature and drama. In "Who Owns Anne Frank?" she asserts that the adaptations of the *Diary of a Young Girl* have usurped and misappropriated the original, that the *Diary* has been "Bowdlerized, transmuted, traduced, reduced; it has been infantilized, Americanized; homogenized, sentimentalized, falsified, kitschified, and, in fact, blatantly and arrogantly denied" (New York: Alfred P. Knopf, 2000, p. 77). In "The Rights of History and the Rights of the Imagination," Ozick faults William Styron's choice of a Polish Auschwitz protagonist instead of a Jew in *Sophie's Choice* and Bernhard Schlink's presentation of a former Nazi as an illiterate in *The Reader* when, in fact, the Germany that perpetrated the *Shoah* was highly cultured. Following a lengthy argument in support of artistic freedom of invention and acknowledgment that "the aims of the imagination are not the aims of history," she concludes that the novelist's intention must be considered, and herein enter her concerns:

> when a novel comes to us with the claim that it is directed consciously toward history, that the divide between history and the imagination is being purposefully bridged, that the bridging is the very point, and that the design of the novel is to put human flesh on historical notation, then the argument for fictional autonomy collapses, and the rights of history can begin to urge their own force. . . . Here a suspicion emerges: that Sophie in Styron's novel was not conceived as a free fictional happenstance, but as an inscribed symbolic figure, perhaps intended to displace a more commonly perceived symbolic figure—Anne Frank, . . . and that the unlettered woman in Schlink's novel is the product, conscious or not, of a desire to divert from the culpability of a normally educated population in a nation famed for *Kultur* (p. 116).

For Ozick, a writer's attempt to link the Final Solution, "the annihilation of all traces of Jewish civilization," with other Nazi persecutions is "to dilute and to obscure, and ultimately to expunge, the real nature of the Holocaust" (p. 118).

Critical Response

Critics concur that Judaic thought, identity, and history are among Ozick's major thematic concerns. There is broad critical acclaim for her stylistic virtuosity, intellectual rigor, and imaginative range. Representative of the praise Ozick receives as a stylist is the assessment of A. Alvarez, who views her writing as "intricate and immaculate." He praises her "ear and precision and gift for the disturbing image . . . combined with the storyteller's sense of timing and flow, the effortless shift between the colloquial and the allusive" (p. 22). Sanford Pinsker assesses Ozick as the writer whose fiction "has radically changed the way we define Jewish-American writing, and . . . the way Jewish-American writing defines itself" (138). Hardly a critic writes of Ozick without paying tribute to the lyricism of her prose, the richness of her imagery and imagination, the range and brilliance of her intelligence and her moral authority. Alan Berger suggests that Ozick offers "a tough-minded and uncompromising portrayal of Judaism. One in which confronting the Holocaust is the litmus test of Jewish authenticity. . . . She steadfastly contends that the Holocaust touches the lives of all Jews, those who were there and those who were not" (Berger, p. 58). Elaine Kauvar speaks for many regarding Ozick's significant place and purpose in literary history: "She strives . . . to uphold tradition in art and to connect the individual talent, as a life and a personality, to that tradition" (Kauvar, p. 240). Victor Strandberg, whose subject is the tension of the Greek and Hebraic influences in Ozick's art, attests to the values so many critics admire: "Her variety and consistent mastery of style; her . . . original and unforgettably individualized characters; her vivid dramatization . . . of significant themes and issues; her absorbing command of narrative structure; her penetrating and independent intellect undergirding all she writes" (Strandberg, p. 191). Ozick's "distinctive liturgical style makes her a major voice in contemporary Jewish American literature and contributes to her growing stature in world literature" (Kremer, *Witness*, p. 278). Her "beautiful, dazzling, resplendent [prose] is a memorial in the finest sense, in the tradition of the great elegies" (Kremer, *Women's Holocaust Writing*, p. 174).

Bibliography

Primary Sources

Novels

Trust: A Novel. 1966.
The Cannibal Galaxy. 1983.
The Messiah of Stockholm. 1987.
The Shawl. 1989.
The Puttermesser Papers. 1997.

Poems

Epodes: First Poems. 1992.

Plays

The Shawl. 1994.

Collections of Stories

The Pagan Rabbi and Other Stories. 1971.
Bloodshed and Three Novellas. 1976.
Levitation: Five Fictions. 1982.
A Cynthia Ozick Reader. 1996.

Collections of Essays

Art & Ardor: Essays. 1983.
Metaphor & Memory: Essays. 1989.
What Henry James Knew: And Other Essays on Writers. 1993.
The Portrait of the Artist as a Bad Character: And Other Essays on Writing. 1994.
Fame & Folly: Essays. 1996.
Quarrel & Quandary: Essays. 2000.

Selected Uncollected Fiction

"The Sense of Europe." *Prairie Schooner* 30 (June 1956): 126–138. From unpublished novel *Mercy, Pity, Peace and Love*.
"Stone." *Botteghe Oscure* 20 (Autumn 1957): 388–414.
"The Laughter of Akiva." *New Yorker* 56 (10 November 1980): 50–60.
"At Fumicaro." *New Yorker* 60 (6 August 1984): 32–58.

Selected Uncollected Nonfiction

"Geoffrey, James, or Stephen." *Midstream* 3 (Winter 1957): 7–76.
"We Ignoble Savages." *Evergreen Review* 3 (November-December 1959): 48–62.
"The Jamesian Parable: *The Sacred Fount*." *Bucknell Review* 11 (May 1963): 55–70.
"The Evasive Jewish Story." *Midstream* 12.2 (February 1966): 78–80.
"Full Stomachs and Empty Rites." *Congress Bi-Weekly* (23 January 1967): 17–19.
"The Uses of Legend: Elie Wiesel as *Tsaddik*." Review of *Legends of Our Time* by Elie Wiesel. *Congress Bi-Weekly* (9 June 1969): 16–20.
"24 Years in the Life of Lyuba Bershadskaya." *New York Times Sunday Magazine* (14 March 1971): 27–29 (under the pseudonym Trudie Vocse).
"Four Questions of the Rabbis." *Reconstructionist* (18 February 1972): 20–23.
"A Bintel Brief for Jacob Glatstein." *Jewish Heritage* 14 (September 1972): 58–60.
"Germany Even Without Munich." *Sh'ma* (13 October 1972): 150–152.
"Holiness and Its Discontents." *Response* 15 (Fall 1972): 87–93.
"If You Can Read This, You Are Too Far Out." *Esquire* 79 (January 1973): 74, 78.
"Israel: Of Myth and Data." *Congress Bi-Weekly* (15 June 1973): 4–8.
"All the World Wants the Jews Dead." *Esquire* 82 (November 1974): 103–107.
"A Liberal's Auschwitz." *Confrontation* 10 (Spring 1975): 125–129.
"Hadrian and Hebrew." *Moment* 1.3 (September 1975): 77–79.
"A Response to Josephine Knopp's 'The Jewish Stories of Cynthia Ozick.' " *Studies in American Jewish Literature* 1 (1975): 49–50.
"Hanging the Ghetto Dog." *New York Times Book Review* (21 March 1976): 48–57.
"Notes Towards a Meditation on Forgiveness." *The Sunflower*. Simon Wiesenthal. New York: Schocken Books, 1976, pp. 183–190.
"How to Profit More from the Teachings of Clara Schacht than from All the Wisdom of Aristotle, Montaigne, Emerson, Cicero, et al." *Esquire* 87 (May 1977): 92ff.
"Passage to the New World." *Ms.* 6 (August 1977): 70–72, 87.

"On Living in the Gentile World." *Modern Jewish Thought.* Edited by Nahum N. Glatzer. New York: Schocker Books, 1977, pp. 167–174.

"Letter to a Palestinian Military Spokesman." *The New York Times* (16 March 1978): A23.

"What Has Mysticism To Do with Judaism?" *Sh'ma* (17 February 1978): 69–71.

"Notes Toward Finding the Right Question (A Vindication of the Rights of Jewish Women)." *Forum* 35 (Spring-Summer 1979): 37–60.

"Carter and the Jews: An American Political Dilemma." *New Leader* (30 June 1980): 3–23.

"On Jewish Dreaming." Talk at the University at Albany, SUNY. 19 November 1980.

"Torah as Feminism, Feminism as Torah." *Congress Monthly* (September-October 1984): 7–10.

"The Role an Author Plays in Jewish Communal Life." *The Jewish Week* (11 July 1986): 19.

Remarks. "Writing and the Holocaust." Conference, State University of New York at Albany. 7 April 1987.

"Reflections on Hanukkah." *New York Times Book Review* (15 November 1987). 44–45, 59–62.

"The Young Self and the Old Writer." Special issue of *Studies in American Jewish Literature* 6 (Fall 1987): 164–167.

"Rushdie in the Louvre." *New Yorker* (13 December 1993).

"The American Academy in the Twenties." *New Criterion* (September 1994).

"The Writer as Playwright." *Washington Post Book Review* (January 1995).

Interviews

Grossman, Edward. "Trust the Teller." *Jerusalem Post Magazine* (19 September 1986): 6–7.

Kaganoff, Peggy. "PW Interviews Cynthia Ozick." *Publisher's Weekly* (27 March 1987): 33–34.

Kauvar, Elaine M. "An Interview with Cynthia Ozick." *Contemporary Literature* 26 (Winter 1985): 376–401.

———. "An Interview with Cynthia Ozick." *Contemporary Literature* 34 (Fall 1993): 358–394.

Materassi, Mario. "Imagination Unbound: An Interview with Ozick." *Salmagundi* 94–95 (Spring-Summer 1992): 85–113.

Moyers, Bill. "Heritage Conversation with Cynthia Ozick." Transcript, WNET-TV, New York, 3 April 1986.

Ottenberg, Eve. "The Rich Visions of Cynthia Ozick." *New York Times Magazine* 47 (10 April 1983): 62–66.

Rainwater, Catherine, and William J. Scheick. "An Interview with Cynthia Ozick." *Texas Studies in Language and Literature* 25 (Summer 1983): 255–265.

Teicholz, Tom. "Cynthia Ozick: The Art of Fiction XCV." *The Paris Review* 29 (1987): 155–190.

Secondary Sources

Bibliographies

Chenoweth, Mary J. "Bibliographical Essay: Cynthia Ozick." Special issue of *Studies in American Jewish Literature* 6 (Fall 1987): 147–163.

Currier, Susan, and Daniel J. Cahill. "A Bibliography of the Writings of Cynthia Ozick." *Texas Studies in Literature and Language* 25 (Summer 1983): 313–321.

Lowin, Joseph. *Bibliography. Cynthia Ozick.* Boston: Twayne, 1988. 177–183.

Books

Bloom, Harold, ed. *Cynthia Ozick: Modern Critical Views.* New York: Chelsea House, 1986.

Cohen, Sarah Blacher. *Cynthia Ozick's Comic Art: From Levity to Liturgy.* Bloomington: Indiana University Press, 1996.

Friedman, Lawrence S. *Understanding Cynthia Ozick.* Columbia: University of South Carolina Press, 1991.

Kauvar, Elaine M. *Cynthia Ozick's Fiction: Tradition and Invention.* Bloomington: Indiana University Press, 1993.

Kielsky, Vera Emuna. *Inevitable Exiles: Cynthia Ozick's View of the Precariousness of Jewish Existence in a Gentile Society.* Frankfurt: Peter Lang, 1989.

Lowin, Joseph. *Cynthia Ozick.* Boston: Twayne Publishers, 1988.

Pinsker, Sanford. *The Uncompromising Fiction of Cynthia Ozick.* Columbia: University of Missouri Press, 1987.

Strandberg, Victor. *Greek Mind, Jewish Soul: The Conflicted Art of Cynthia Ozick.* Madison: University of Wisconsin Press, 1994.

Walden, Daniel, ed. *The World of Cynthia Ozick.* Special issue of *Studies in American Jewish Literature* 6 (Fall 1987). Kent, Ohio: Kent State University Press, 1987.

Articles and Book Chapters

Alkana, Joseph. " 'Do We Not Know the Meaning of Aesthetic Gratification?': Cynthia Ozick's *The Shawl*, the Akedah, and the Ethics of Holocaust Literary Representation." *Modern Fiction Studies* 43.4 (Winter 1997): 963–990.

Alvarez, A. "Flushed with Ideas." Review of *Levitation: Five Fictions. New York Review of Books* (13 May 1982): 22–23.

Berger, Alan. "Cynthia Ozick: Judaism as a Religious Value System." *Crisis and Covenant: The Holocaust in American Jewish Fiction.* Albany: State University of New York Press, 1985, pp. 49–59.

———. "Cynthia Ozick: Judaism as a Secular Value System." *Crisis and Covenant: The Holocaust in American Jewish Fiction.* Albany: State University of New York Press, 1985, pp. 120–137.

Cole, Diane. *Dictionary of Literary Biography.* Vol. 28. *Twentieth-Century American-Jewish Fiction Writers.* Edited by Daniel Walden. Detroit: Gale Research Co., 1984, pp. 213–225.

Finkelstein, Norman. "The Struggle for Historicity: Cynthia Ozick." *The Ritual of New Creation: Jewish Tradition and Contemporary Literature.* Albany: State University of New York Press, 1992, pp. 63–68.

Furman, Andrew. "American Short Stories of the Holocaust." *The Columbia Companion to the Twentieth-Century American Short Story.* New York: Columbia University Press, 2001.

Gordon, Andrew. "Cynthia Ozick's 'The Shawl' and the Transitional Object." *Literature and Psychology* 40.1–2 (Spring-Summer 1994): 1–10.

Gottfried, Amy. "Fragmented Art and the Liturgical Community of the Dead in Cynthia Ozick's *The Shawl.*" *Studies in Jewish American Literature* 13 (1994): 39–51.

Horvath, Rita. "Stella and Rosa." *AnaChronist* 19–21 (1996): 257–265.

Klingenstein, Susanne. "Destructive Intimacy: The *Shoah* Between Mother and Daughter in Fictions by Cynthia Ozick, Norma Rosen, and Rebecca Goldstein." *Studies in Jewish American Literature* 11.2 (Fall 1992): 162–173.

Kremer, S. Lillian. "Cynthia Ozick." *Jewish American Women Writers: A Bio-Bibliographical and Critical Sourcebook.* Edited by Ann R. Shapiro, Sara R. Horowitz, Ellen Schiff, and Miriyam Glazer. Westport, Conn.: Greenwood Press, 1994, pp. 265–277.

———. "Cynthia Ozick." *Women's Holocaust Writing: Memory and Imagination*. Lincoln: University of Nebraska Press, 1999, pp. 149–175.

———. "The Dybbuk of All the Lost Dead: Cynthia Ozick's Holocaust Fiction." *Witness through the Imagination: Jewish American Holocaust Literature*. Detroit: Wayne State University Press, 1989, pp. 218–278.

———. "The Holocaust and the Witnessing Imagination." *Violence, Silence, and Anger: Women's Writing as Transgression*. Edited by Dierdre Lashgari. Charlottesville: University Press of Virginia, 1995, pp. 231–246.

Langer, Lawrence L. *Preempting the Holocaust*. New Haven, Conn.: Yale University Press, 1998.

Lehmann, Sophia. " 'And here [their] troubles began': The Legacy of the Holocaust in the Writing of Cynthia Ozick, Art Spiegelman, and Philip Roth." *CLIO: A Journal of Literature, History, and the Philosophy of History* 28.1 (1998): 29–52.

Lowin, Joseph. "Cynthia Ozick, Rewriting Herself: The Road from 'The Shawl' to 'Rosa.' " *Since Flannery O' Connor: Essays on the Contemporary American Short Story*. Edited by Loren Logsdon and Charles W. Mayer. Macomb: Western Illinois University Press, 1987.

Mathe, Sylvie. "Voix de l'emotion, voix de l'indicible: 'The Shawl' de Cynthia Ozick." *Voix et langages Aux Etats-Unis*. Actes du Colloque des 20, 21, 22 mars 1992. Groupe de Recherche et d'Etudes Nord Americaines; Ricard Serge (pref.). Provence, France: Pubs. De l'Univ. de Provence, 1992, pp. 11–41.

Rochman, Hazel, and Darlene Z. Campbell. *Bearing Witness: Stories of the Holocaust*. New York: Orchard Books, 1995.

Rosenberg, Meisha. "Cynthia Ozick's Post-Holocaust Fiction: Narration and Morality in the Midrashic Mode." *Journal of the Short Story in English/Les Cahiers de la Nouvelle* 32 (1999): 112–127.

Scrafford, Barbara. "Nature's Silent Scream: A Commentary on Cynthia Ozick's 'The Shawl.' " *CRITIQUE: Studies in Contemporary Fiction* 31.1 (Fall 1989): 11–16.

Sokoloff, Naomi B. *Imagining the Child in Modern Jewish Fiction*. Baltimore, Md.: Johns Hopkins University Press, 1992.

Walden, Daniel, ed. *The Changing Mosaic: From Cahan to Malamud, Roth and Ozick*. Albany: State University of New York Press, 1993.

Wirth-Nesher, Hana. "The Languages of Memory: Cynthia Ozick's *The Shawl*." *Multilingual America: Transnationalism, Ethnicity, and the Languages of American Literature*. New York: New York University Press, 1998, pp. 313–326.

DAN PAGIS

(1930–1986)

RANEN OMER-SHERMAN

TOGETHER WITH AHARON Appelfeld and Paul Celan, Dan Pagis completes the famous troika of post-Holocaust writers born in the polyglot and culturally rich environment of the Bukovina area of Romania (formerly Austria, now divided between Romania and Ukraine). Born in 1930, Pagis had already experienced severe disorientation and loss even before the Holocaust, with the emigration of his father to Palestine in 1934, the early death of his mother not long after, and his own deportation at the age of eleven. Years later it emerged that, after his mother's death, Pagis's family in Bukovina had been convinced that his father would be unable to support him. Because of this belief, Pagis's family did not send him to Palestine and he thus remained among those Jews who were swept away by Nazism. As a result, unlike Appelfeld and Celan, who were fortunate enough to escape the camps, Pagis was incarcerated by the Germans for three years and spent his early adolescence in concentration camps in Transnistria (a term coined by the Romanian fascists to designate a territory of about 16,000 square miles designed for the extermination of Jews deported from Romania).

Palestine

In 1946 Pagis went to Palestine, where he was reunited with his father (though reportedly years of estrangement followed) and taught school on a kibbutz. Whereas Celan remained adrift in a language of his own making, perhaps unsure until the end of a destination or audience, Pagis had to cope with the challenge of addressing a clearly defined audience of Israelis who, though engaged in a collective act of repatriation, were perhaps somewhat ambivalent in their response to the presence of Holocaust survivors. Pagis's lyrics struggle with the ambiguity and tension of "homecoming," yet by the end of his life, he was one of Israel's most popular poets, whose radical skepticism reconnected the Israeli imagination to the ever-disruptive past. Though he remained in Israel, his poetry enacts a disturbing questioning of the significance of homecoming.

Jewish Scholarship

Perhaps what most astonishes about Pagis is that in the space of four years after his arrival in Palestine at the age of nineteen, he was publishing poetry and scholarly works in Hebrew, a language he had only recently acquired as a sixteen-year-old immigrant. Settling in Jerusalem in 1956, he received a Ph.D. from the Hebrew University and soon emerged as one of the most important scholars of the aesthetics of medieval and Renaissance Hebrew literature, also teaching at the Jewish Theological Seminary, Harvard University, and the University of California at Berkeley. By arguing for the strong individuality of the Hebrew-Spanish poets, Pagis challenged those who read them as merely formulaic and conventional, thus changing the nature of Hebrew scholarship. Though fascinated with Yehuda Halevi, a medieval Iberian poet, and other literary treasures of the Jewish past, Pagis's own richly colloquial poetry always remains as much in dialogue (if at times deconstructive) with the present-day conventions, codes, and clichés of Israeli culture as it is with its ancient origins. Together with Yehuda Amichai, Pagis has been widely credited with enabling modern Hebrew poetry to find a more natural, colloquial voice.

Dan Pagis died on July 29, 1986. His major collections of poetry, drawing from the Holocaust, biblical texts, and Jewish mysticism, include *The Shadow Dial* (1959), *Late Leisure* (1964), *Transformation* (1970), *Twelve Faces* (1981), *Double Exposure* (1983), and

Last Poems (1987). His scholarly works on medieval Hebrew literature include studies of the Hebrew poetry of Spain and Italy, as well as individual studies of figures such as Levi Ibn Altabban. Pagis also produced a critically acclaimed critical edition of the collected verse of David Vogel (1891–1944), a Jewish Russian poet and novelist who perished in the Holocaust and whose verse, like Pagis's, became an active, if idiosyncratic, influence in Israeli letters.

Critical Reception

As literary critic Lawrence L. Langer argues, Pagis's lyrics "leave to his readers the challenge of filling in the Holocaust referents" (*Art from the Ashes: A Holocaust Anthology*, Oxford: Oxford University Press, 1995, p. 584). But that claim may also be another way of suggesting that his poems of exile and return are more open-ended than the work of some of his contemporaries such as Nelly Sachs. Like Sachs and other secular Central European poets, a cosmopolitan or "universal" view of the Jewish victim gradually emerges. For readers and translators, Pagis is generally perceived as a poet who presents the Holocaust in its wider universal implications rather than as merely the historical culmination of Jewish catastrophes.

Though writing in Hebrew in Israel, Pagis presents no less a "cosmopolitan" perspective than Celan did reimagining the German language throughout his Paris sojourn. At times, the only concrete connections in Pagis's work are those that the conscientious reader creates. Hence, in the translator Stephen Mitchell's luminous rendition of the fragmentary qualities of "Written in Pencil in the Sealed Railway-Car" (*'Katuv b'iparon bakaron hehatum'*), humanity's sense of progress is undermined as the ominous beginnings of human history glare through present history like a murderous palimpsest:

here in this carload
i am eve
with abel my son
if you see my other son
cain son of Adam
tell him that i (*The Selected Poetry of Dan Pagis*, translated by Stephen Mitchell, Berkeley: University of California Press, 1989, p. 29).

Here is the classic exhibit of Pagis's incomparable genius for conveying horror through sheer allusion, without shrillness or hysteria. Cain is both "son of Adam" and *ben adam*, a twentieth-century human being fully capable of unleashing atrocity. Pagis's most famous poem is a text that presupposes a community of readers who will struggle to complete its "failure" of transmission. Accordingly, in Hebrew, the "you" addressed is the second person plural, "im tiru . . . tagidu," forming an imperative that demands the moral participation of both male and female witnesses. Hence this profoundly incomplete poem requires the intervention of a reader who has been ethically summoned to respond linguistically. In its sheer fragmentariness it is difficult to think of this poem as a "work" or a "text." Instead, it is a place we are urgently summoned to. The burden of freedom in this post-Auschwitz universe means being exposed to this closed space of exile. As Sidra Ezrahi, one of Pagis's most instructive critics, remarks, "lack of closure here is the absolute refusal of art as triumph over mortality" (p. 162). So it is fitting that Pagis's lines, composing one of the shortest lyrics in the modern Hebrew language, were carved onto an actual railway car, part of the Transport Memorial at Yad Vashem (1995), to serve as a textual meditation on the foreboding surface on which they are inscribed. And yet it is clear that Pagis's disturbing paean to deathly silence cannot be easily confined within national or conventional commemorative narratives, transcending any efforts to contain them. Ezrahi rightly notes that the manifest capacity of these lines to remain "disruptive, unassimiliable, even after being 'safely' embedded in commemorative public space reflects the poem's resistance to the sanctities and proprieties of ritualized speech" ("Reclaiming a Plot in Radautz," p. 162).

In Pagis's "The Roll Call," the poet addresses the deathly hermeneutics of the concentration camp, the erasure of ordinary individuality:

He stands, stamps a little in his boots,
rubs his hands. He's cold in the morning breeze:
a diligent angel, who worked hard for his promotions.
Suddenly he thinks he's made a mistake: all eyes,
he counts again in the open notebook
all the bodies waiting for him in the square,
camp within camp: only I
am not there, am not there, am a mistake,
turn off my eyes, quickly, erase my shadow.
I shall not want. The sum will be all right
without me: here forever (p. 32).

Pagis bears witness to the existential absurdity of the routine calling of the names in the camps, and he responds to the way that the individual's proper "name"—a designated number—effectively delegitimizes individuality. Here the anonymous victim's identity is reduced to a nameless "I." The cynically calculating logic of the German death machine ("[t]he sum will be all right without me") reconstitutes itself through the anonymous lives it consumes, leaving behind a vacuum of the "here forever," a present uninhabited by presence. In Pagis's lyric, death is a well-oiled system, life an ephemeral accident. Consistently we confront an art that makes unsparing demands on our assumptions about the meaning of survival, suggesting that existential responses have as much ethical validity as the relentless cataloging of facts. Pagis makes us uncomfortably aware of the impossibility of reaching any form of enduring affirmation of the selfhood that has been taken away.

The ironically titled "How To" tragically refutes both the possibility of a collective phoenix reborn from the atrocity of genocide and the notion of a reborn self.

The death mask is prepared
from the negative of the face.
After the soul has left, cover
the face with soft clay,
then peel it off, slowly.
In it, you get a large mold:
instead of the nose a hole,
instead of the eyesockets two blobs.
Now pour the plaster, premixed,
into the mold, wait
till it hardens,
then separate the parts:
in the positive, the nose juts out again,
the eyesockets collapse. Now
take the plaster face
and cover your face of flesh with it
and live (p. 117).

Pagis's deconstructive manual of metamorphosis (a resounding rebuke in a confident age of instant healers) creates an intricate link between personal ordeal, the unspeakable, and the presumptions made about the identity of the survivor. His darkly imagined meditation on the difficulty of ever finding refuge in the self that lingers in the wake of catastrophe conjures up the pure sense of what another survivor, Charlotte Delbo, proposes: "There comes to mind the image of a snake shedding its old skin. . . . How does one rid oneself of something buried far within: memory and the skin of memory. It clings to me yet. Memory's skin has hardened, it allows nothing to filter out of what it retains, and I have no control over it" (Delbo, p. 77). In the devastating indictment of "Draft of a Reparations Agreement," Pagis somberly concurs, acerbically interrogating the assumptions of the orderly world: "Everything will be returned to its place / paragraph after paragraph / The scream back into the throat / The gold teeth back to the gums." Speaking for many in his generation, the poet elegiacally refuses the possibility of "making good," challenging the grounds of the controversial financial reparations by the West German government in the postwar period (controversial because some Holocaust survivors felt the reparations were "blood money," a banal expiation of German guilt). Consistent with this post-Auschwitz vision of an irreparably fragmented world, "Footprints," the poet's most autobiographical work, presents memory itself as a chaos of associations, producing a confusion of collective and personal images that defy the linear container of traditional autobiography: "Frozen and burst, clotted / scarred / charred, choked" (p. 36).

Though Pagis is a poet who came to rest uneasily in Zion, his is a poetics that resists a fixed dwelling place (modern Israel is rarely glimpsed in his lyrics) but rather enacts a space of exile where existence is set loose from essence, identity, and territory. Skepticism toward the meaning of revival and arrival is memorably expressed in "Instructions for Crossing the Border," where the narrative voice muses to himself "You've got a decent coat now / A repaired body, a new name / Ready in your throat" followed by the hauntingly spare imperative: "Go. You are not allowed to forget" (p. 34). In this poet's response to the spatial and temporal dislocations wrought by the Holocaust there is no hope of assembling the fragments into anything resembling a plot. Instead, each new fragment is a branching forth of the text that must emerge, in spite of everything, as these lines, from "Autobiography," eloquently merging Genesis and Holocaust anguish, bear witness:

you can die once, twice, even seven times,
but you can't die a thousand times.
I can.
My underground cells reach everywhere.

When Cain began to multiply on the face of the earth,
I began to multiply in the belly of the earth,
and my strength has long been greater than his.
His legions desert him and go over to me,
And even this is only half a revenge (p. 5).

It is as if for Pagis, there was only one deadly plot, which compels the moral imagination to give it compelling expression, again and again. And yet, though often described as a poet of the "unspeakable," certainly his wide range encompasses much more; as Robert Alter cogently observes, "his imaginative landscape extends from the grim vistas of genocide to the luminous horizon of the medieval Iberian peninsula" (p. xvi).

Late Works

Whereas many of Pagis's later works offer science fiction themes (though the Holocaust is still a stubborn presence hovering in the background), *Last Poems*, published posthumously, offers unflinching but gently witty poems almost constantly occupied with dying and death: his father's, his own impending departure, and of course innumerable anonymous others. This morbid reality is characteristically met with humor, wry drollery, and a sardonic, unflinching gaze. In a sense, the Holocaust is as present as ever. For instance, in "Sports," his conscience reproaches him: "You have some nerve to live and swim / Among the drowned, and turn it / Into sport!" (p. 121). But in the late works, Sidra Ezrahi notes a startling shift, claiming that, after prolonged deferral, Pagis moved "from an amnesiac poetry to a remembering prose" ("Reclaiming a Plot," p. 158). Ezrahi sees a deliberate but only partially successful effort to reclaim the lost terrain of childhood. Perhaps because Pagis, like Celan, had long ago elected to reject "the privileged status of the survivor," Ezrahi's Pagis remains uninterested in the prospects of either personal or collective history "as an intelligible narrative" (pp. 159–160).

After writing poetry for four decades, Pagis dedicated his last few years to a series of experiments in prose form. The late work "Art of Contraction" reveals a struggle to express repressed memory through minimalist aesthetics: "Finally, after he hangs it on the wall, he understands: this painted blade of grass, which implies the entire meadow, also denies the entire meadow" (p. 87). In this futile struggle to recover the shattered Eden of his lost childhood, the poet negates the rhetoric of conventional memoir and representation as powerfully as his earlier verse. With few exceptions, Pagis resisted the kind of self-referentiality or autobiographic self-naming that might prevent the reader from probing the deep mysteries of his art. He preferred an active reader who would continue to make new discoveries, along new paths, though in the end this might mean that only the melancholy imperative of an urgent but still undeciphered address to an uncertain reader would remain. Hence, as if in an epilogue to his entire oeuvre, his "For a Literary Survey" remarks on its own omissions, a fitting text for a universe haunted by an absent God:

> You ask me how I write. I'll tell you, but let this be confidential. I take a ripe onion, squeeze it, dip the pen into the juice, and write. It makes excellent invisible ink: the onion juice is colorless (like the tears the onion causes), and after it dries it doesn't leave any mark. The page again appears as pure as it was. Only if it's brought close to the fire will the writing be revealed, at first hesitantly, a letter here, a letter there, and finally, as it should be, each and every sentence. There's just one problem. No one knows the secret power of the fire, and who would suspect that the pure page has anything written on it? (p. 85).

In her evocative criticism Ezrahi calls this mystery "a wry counterstrategy of intimation" that beckons the reader to further speculation on the vast absences and irrevocably lost worlds of the past ("Reclaiming a Plot," p. 170).

Pagis's verse first appeared in English translation as *Points of Departure* (1981), and Stephen Mitchell would prove to be his most gifted and devoted translator. Pagis's Hebrew verse, including the best of his Holocaust lyrics, is readily available to the English-language reader, thanks to the translations by Mitchell (*The Selected Poetry of Dan Pagis*), who was awarded the Harold Morton Landon Translation Award for his efforts. This notable selection ranges over the whole of the poet's oeuvre, including not only the well-known short poems but experimental fragments that tease the reader with their enigmatic quality. Without embracing a victim's role, Pagis's oeuvre is a rich constellation of sounds and silences, an intense appraisal of the emotional and intellectual legacy of the Holocaust. His works have been widely translated (individual and whole works) into Afrikaans, Czech, Danish, Dutch, English, Estonian, French, Greek, Hungarian, Italian, Japanese, Polish, Portuguese, Romanian, Serbo-Croatian, Spanish, Swedish, Vietnamese, and Yiddish.

Bibliography

Primary Sources

Poetry

The Shadow Dial. 1959.
Late Leisure. 1964.
Transformation. 1970.
Brain. 1975, 1977.
Twelve Faces. 1981.
Double Exposure. 1983.
Last Poems. 1987.
The Selected Poetry of Dan Pagis. 1989.

Scholarly Works

The Poetry of David Vogel. 1966; 4th ed., 1975.
The Poetry of Levi Ibn Altabban of Saragosa. 1968.
Secular Poetry and Poetic Theory—Moses Ibn Ezra and His Contemporaries. 1970.
Change and Tradition: Hebrew Poetry in Spain and Italy. 1976.
The Riddle. 1986.
Hebrew Poetry of the Middle Ages and the Renaissance. 1991.

Children

The Egg That Tried to Disguise Itself. 1973.

Secondary Sources

Alter, Robert. "Introduction." In *The Selected Poetry of Dan Pagis*. Translated by Stephen Mitchell. Los Angeles: University of California Press, 1989, pp. xi–xvi.

———. "Dan Pagis and the Poetry of Displacement." *Judaism: A Quarterly Journal of Jewish Life and Thought* 45, no. 4 (fall 1996): 399–402.

Carmis, T. "Dan Pagis: Words of Farewell." *Orim* 2, no. 2 (spring 1987): 76–78.

Delbo, Charlotte. "Voices." In Art from the Ashes: A Holocaust Anthology. Edited by Lawrence L. Langer. Oxford: Oxford University Press, 1995, pp. 77–92.

Ezrahi, Sidra Dekoven. *By Words Alone: The Holocaust in Literature*. Chicago: University of Chicago Press, 1980.

———. "Dan Pagis—Out of Line: A Poetics of Decomposition." *Prooftexts* 2, no. 1 (January 1982): 78–94.

———. "Reclaiming a Plot in Radautz: Dan Pagis and the Prosaics of Memory." In *Booking Passage: Exile and Homecoming in the Modern Jewish Imagination*. Los Angeles: University of California Press, 2000, pp. 157–178.

Pagis, Ada. *LevPitomi* (Sudden Heart). Tel Aviv: Am Oved, 1995.

Sokoloff, Naomi. "Transformations: Holocaust Poems in Dan Pagis' Gilgul." *Hebrew Annual Review* 8 (1984): 215–240.

Zierler, Wendy. "Footprints, Traces, Remnants: The Operations of Memory in Dan Pagis' *Aqebot*." *Judaism* 41, no. 4 (fall 1992): 316–333.

Archives

Pagis, Dan. *Transformations*. Pagis reads his work in both English (trans. by Stephen Mitchell) and Hebrew. Recorded at the Harvard Poetry Room. Watershed, 1979. 51 minutes.

Joseph Papiernikov
(1899–1991)

EMANUEL S. GOLDSMITH

Joseph Papiernikov achieved recognition as the first Yiddish poet to settle in Palestine-Israel with the express purpose of continuing his work as a Yiddish writer there. He arrived in 1924 and for almost seven decades lived and worked in what he called "the land of the second beginning," producing a body of work that reflects virtually every aspect of life in the old-new country. Even before the appearance of his first book of poems (*In Zunikn Land* [*In the Sunny Land*]) in 1927, thousands of workers and pioneers enjoyed his poems at public gatherings and celebrations, and welcomed the poet into their midst. His work also made its way to Jews in the Diaspora where it had great influence.

Varied Output

Papiernikov's contribution to Yiddish letters cannot be limited to his *Eretz Yisrael* poems. His second volume consisted of poems of social protest and the call to freedom, justice, equality, and revolution, which was never absent in his work. His poems about his native Poland and the Holocaust are regarded as significant achievements. He also wrote a great deal of love and nature poetry, as well as a large number of purely lyrical poems and poems about the creative process. His generous output was matched by the originality and quality of his work. He was both a major Yiddish writer and a major poet of Israel despite the fact that he wrote in Yiddish rather than Hebrew.

Papiernikov was born into a poverty-stricken family in Warsaw in 1899. His father supported his wife and their six children with his small butcher shop, while sustaining himself morally through his activities as a devoted Zionist organizer and fund-raiser. The poet's mother was a quiet woman whose only failing was an overdeveloped sense of justice. This led to frequent arguments with her husband, who was more devoted to the community than to providing a livelihood for his family. The conflicts, tensions, and bitterness of his childhood became the source of the elegiac tone of much of the poet's work.

Educated in the traditional *heder* and in a Russian *gymnasium*, Papiernikov developed his musical ability as a singer in a celebrated synagogue choir. He later composed tunes for many of his own poems which attained popularity the world over. Both his Zionism and his devotion to the Yiddish language were nurtured by the Left Poaley Zion organization of which he was a devoted member.

Pioneer Poet

Except for a stay in Poland from 1929 to 1933, Papiernikov lived in Israel from 1924 until his death in 1991. He became the leading writer of the group organized around the Yiddish journal *Onheyb* (Beginning). His experience as a pioneer paving the highways of the new country gave meaning to his life and depth to his poetry. His work reflects the struggle of the young pioneers to conquer the soil and make the desert bloom, as well as their dedication, readiness to sacrifice, and profound joy. His poems neither sentimentalize nor idealize but are rich in imagery, rhythm, feeling, and poetic diction.

Papiernikov's unique voice in Yiddish poetry thus derives from an unusual merging of his personal odyssey with the aspirations and experiences of the pioneers and laborers of Eretz Yisrael. Despite the poet's strong individuality, throughout his work the individual and the collective merge. He was indeed the troubadour or *minesinger* of Israel reborn.

Influence of Reisen

Throughout his career, Papiernikov's work had a close affinity with the work of the celebrated Yiddish poet Abraham Reisen (1876–1953). Papiernikov, like Reisen, often strikes an elegiac tone, resolved by an aphoristic insight summarizing the poem. Despite their clarity and folklike quality, the poems often reveal deep feeling, serious reflection, and a familiarity with Jewish folk wisdom. The tone of Papiernikov's most famous lyric, set to his own melody, is strongly reminiscent of Reisen.

It may well be that I build castles in the air,
It may well be that my God does not exist,
In dreams I see clearly, in dreams I feel better,
In dreams the skies are bluer indeed ("Zol Zayn").

Papiernikov's poems dealing with the rise of Nazism and the Holocaust began appearing in 1937 and were published in book form in Tel Aviv in 1944 (*Unter Shvartse Himlen* [Beneath Black Heavens]) and 1945 (*Mayn Brenendiker Shtam* [My Burning People]). They were reprinted in his *Geklibene Lider* (Selected Poems), (1947) and in *Iber Khurves* (Over Ruins), a volume devoted to his work on the Holocaust (1967).

When the Devil Has the Word

"I have lost myself in the jungle of the twentieth century" (*Iber Khurves* [Over Ruins], Tel Aviv: Hamenorah, 1967, p. 24), wrote Papiernikov in an early response to the ascending Nazi barbarism. "I have lost myself in the evil and wickedness of our time" (p. 24). Humanity has sunk lower than the wild chimpanzee and orangutan. The poet is compelled to choke the poems back—how can one write poems when the world lies dead at one's feet, each day of survival is a miracle, and the rhythm of poems recalls feet marching toward death?

A time of dark spirits,
When the devil has the word
And all tablets have been broken,
Robbery and death made holy—
Is no time for the singing
Of a poet, or a singer
Whose quivering lyre
Once spoke to every heart,
Rushed from person to person
Through darkest tunnels
In order to reach conscience,
Sympathy and empathy ("Far Shvartse Rukhes").

Hitler, Mussolini, Goering, and their ilk appropriated the poet's lyre and his poems now recall only the sounds of lead on tin and steel on stone. His muse has left him to comfort his brothers, the soldiers who have gone to battle.

Blood, blood; the horizons are
All drenched with blood
Ignited by the front lines
Of battlefields of death.
These are the fields on which my muse
Sheds blood too,
Sheds blood but also comforts ("Af di Shlakht-Felder").

In several poems Papiernikov praised and encouraged the Soviet Red Army, in which he saw hope of vanquishing the Nazi foe.

Not everything is as the enemy might wish,
Not all is lost and buried.
Even beneath the earth freedom fighters
Like silent volcanos threaten with their fire . . .

Not everything is as the enemy might wish,
Not all is lost and buried
As long as the Red Armies exist,
And behind enemy lines there are partisans ("S'iz Nokhnisht Azoy").

Poems of Poland

The largest group of Papiernikov's Holocaust poems concerns the poet's feelings toward his Polish homeland before, during, and after the war. In light of Poland's mistreatment of its Jews, even before the conflagration, he finds it difficult to refer to the land of his birth as his fatherland. He feels constrained to return his Polish passport because he has become only a stepchild of his native land. If there are still any yearnings for his birthplace in his heart, they are for a new Poland in which people might finally find life worthwhile.

Nevertheless, when the Germans invade Poland feelings of sympathy are stirred within the poet's breast. He is especially overcome with trepidation for his elderly parents, his five siblings, and the entire Jewish community.

I do so want to see my home now!
The home of my family
Which I once compared
To a sad, sparse forest
Sparse—but full of shadows
Cast by its many trees! ("Mayn Geburtsland").

Eventually he learns of the death of his father, brother, and uncle in the Warsaw ghetto. How his mother died remains a mystery. "She must have died"

(*Iber Khurves*, p. 40), he writes, "like a willow beside a brook of Jewish blood and tears" (p. 40).

The poet recalls the history of Polish antisemitism in his poem "Polonia Capta." When the Poles needed help in their struggle for independence, they joined hands with the Jews, but afterwards they conveniently forgot the contributions of Berek Yoselovitsh and other Jewish fighters for Poland's freedom. Before World War II, Poland lost its head in antisemitic debaucheries and could demonstrate its heroism and strength only by oppressing its Jewish population.

Implications of the Holocaust

The most moving of Papiernikov's poems are those in which he records his gradual realization of the immensity of the tragedy and its implications for the future of the Jewish people.

My heart bleeds, bleeds, as if it were slit
By the murder of women, children and elders,
As if the knife's blade had reached me from afar
In order to annihilate me together with them ("In Avekgeroybte Lender").

Whence, in the forest's destruction,
Shall my people, burned to its knees,
Now garner strength in order to become the source
Of rebirth, continuity and revival? ("Funvanen. . .").

The poet calls for revenge and takes heart in the partisans, the Red Army soldiers, and all the Jews who resisted the foe.

How can one forget for a minute
That he has become a mourner for millions,
A mourner who comforts himself that many
Defended life with teeth and nails,
Protected it and held it tightly,
Did not go to the slaughter like sheep but were
Martyrs for the millions
Whose blood will never cease crying for justice? ("In Troyer").

The Holocaust poem by Papiernikov that became most familiar to Yiddish readers and was set to music by the poet himself was "Beneath the Little Polish Trees." The poet Bialik had written many years before the Holocaust about little Jewish children at play beneath the little green trees of the Eastern European landscape. Papiernikov's poem, written in the style of Bialik, laments the little Moyshes and Shloymes who no longer frolic beneath the little Polish trees. It became almost a hymn of the Holocaust.

Beneath the little green Polish trees
Little Moyshes and Shloymes no longer play,
Little Sorehs and Leyehs no longer play
In the grasses or beneath the snowfalls.
The little Polish trees are in mourning.
Dead are Jewish homes large and small,
Dead are little Jewish streets, destroyed the little houses
Where children hide in holes like mice ("Unter di Poyleshe Beymelekh").

Perhaps the most moving and memorable of all of Papiernikov's post-Holocaust poems is "To God in Heaven." Words of protest directed at God may be found throughout the Jewish literary tradition. In the Hebrew Bible they are uttered by figures such as Abraham, Moses, Job, and the Psalmist. The Hasidic leader Levi Isaac of Berdichev, among others, was famous for taking the Almighty to task, especially during the High Holy Day season. Protest is also prominent in Yitzhak Katzenelson's "Song of the Murdered Jewish People" and in the work of many other Yiddish and Hebrew Holocaust writers. Papiernikov's poem is remarkably poignant because of the fact that as a conscientiously secular writer he almost entirely avoids the mention of God in his work. After the Holocaust, however, there is simply no one else to turn to.

If I believed in God in heaven,
I'd turn away from Him today:
—I've served You long enough
With prayers and thanks and praise!
—Enough of a merciful and gracious God
Who was blind and deaf,
Saw not and heard not
As toward the gates of mercy
There stretched from the hellish earth—
A sea of hands, of pleading hands,
A sea of eyes with supplications and cries—
From the forest of Jews that burned (and burns)
On the burning, alien soil of the Exile ("Tsu Got in Himl").

The overwhelming significance of Papiernikov's Holocaust poetry lies in the linkage of the tragedy of the Holocaust with the generation of transplanted pioneers who created modern Israel while shedding tears for their decimated people.

Bibliography

Primary Sources

In Zunikn Land (In the Sunny Land). 1927.
Royt af Shvarts (Red on Black). 1929.
Goldene Zamdn (Golden Sands). 1932.
Unter Fayer (Beneath Fire). 1939.
Unter Shvartse Himlen (Beneath Black Heavens). 1944.
Geklibene Lider (Selected Poems). 1947.
Iberblayb (Remnant). 1949.
Frunkht fun Vint (Fruits of the Wind). 1952.
Mayn Shir Hashirim (My Song of Songs). 1955, rev. ed. 1966.
Di Zun Hinter Mir (The Sun Behind Me). 1961.
Fun Tsveytn Breyshis (Of the Second Beginning). 1964.

Iber Khurves (Over Ruins). 1967.
In Likht fun Fargang (In the Light of Sunset). 1969.
In Vaysn Elter (In My White Old Age). 1976.
Mayn Antologye (My Anthology). 1978.
Frunkht fun Vint (Fruits of the Wind). 1980.
Di Grine Rase (The Green Race). 1983.
Banayung (Renewal). 1985.
In a Nay Likht (In a New Light). 1987.

Secondary Sources

Fertsik Yor Papiernikov in Erets Yisroel. Tel Aviv: Farlag Y. L. Peretz, 1958.
Glatstein, Jacob. *Mit Mayne Fartogbikher*. Tel Aviv: Farlag Y. L. Peretz, 1963.
Lis, Abraham. *In Mekhitse fun Shafer*. Tel Aviv: Farlag Y. L. Peretz, 1978.
Ravitsh, Melekh. *Mayn Leksikson*. Montreal, 1958.
Sfard, Dovid. *Mit Zikh un mit Eygene*. Tel Aviv, 1984.
Shargel, Yankev Tsvi. *Fun Onheyb On*. Tel Aviv, 1977.

Interview and Memoirs

Interview by Y. Pat. In *Shmuesn mit Shrayber in Yisroel*. New York: Der Kval, 1960, pp. 199–210.
The two volumes of Papiernikov's memoirs are *Heymishe un Noente* (1958) and *Fun Alts Tsu Bislekh* (1974), both published in Tel Aviv by Farlag Y. L. Peretz.

Dorit Peleg
(1954–)

DVIR ABRAMOVICH

Dorit Peleg's first opus, *Una* (1988), is an innovative work about the second generation and how it is inevitably tied to the past. Like other "bearing witness" works, it tackles the dilemma of finding the right literary vehicles for meaningfully connecting with and encoding past trauma.

Peleg's parents survived the Holocaust, her mother by pretending to be an Aryan. Her father, who was interned in one of the camps, never spoke about this. Most of their family members perished in the Holocaust.

In the face of the harmful effects of Holocaust silence, the healing work of mourning of the second generation exhibits those lacerating, yet suppressed genocidal traumas and seeks to reverse the destructive and displacing effect of silence. It ferrets out the suffocatingly intense psychological burden of the Holocaust that cripples the collective and individual identity of young Israelis and underpins the reality of the nameless horrors that exist even after fifty years. Above all, the healing work of mourning is about the relationship of the Sabra generation (native-born Israelis) to the Holocaust, its memorialization, and the resolution of the psychic trauma infusing their present lives. It explores the second generation's painful search for an avenue by which they can bear witness to and repair the wounded self that carries the indelible imprint of a terror previously ignored or suppressed.

Psychological Approach

Una does not treat the Holocaust from an external, historical perspective. Rather, it is daringly rooted in the metaphorical, propelled by the heroine's interior journey as she separates herself from the here and now, and spiritually travels to foreign sites of scorched earth in search of relief. In that regard, Peleg chose to situate her literary engagement with the Holocaust in the psychological realm to remind us of the psychic difficulties of writing about the holocaust. In place of mimetic Holocaust historiography, Peleg dramatizes the emotional conflict, a battle that is waged exclusively within the title character's soul and that pulls the reader into the midst of a personal holocaust. The employment of a psychiatrist as the medium for the heroine to air her grievances and come to grips with loss and suffering looms large over the course of the narrative, accentuating the psychological nature and structure of the tale as well as Peleg's desire to work along the lower levels of consciousness in pouring forth the young woman's torrent of agony.

In an interview with Rachel Sahar, Peleg, a native-born Israeli, admitted that all through her youth she continuously tried to ignore the inescapable truth that in one way or another, the *Shoah* had stamped itself indelibly on her psyche:

> For many years I did not deal with the Holocaust. My father never said a word about the camps. I was restless. I called this adventurism and went on trips around the world. A by-product of the travels was the recognition that there was antisemitism. At a certain stage I understood that in the main this was a journey inwards. And there inside, I was surprised to discover the Holocaust (pp. 23–24).

Moreover, Peleg discovered that her soul was preserving "inherited destinations," as she calls them. The bond was so strong that even places she did not visit were embedded in the same incomprehensible, hereditary manner. When viewing Claude Lanzmann's *Shoah* she accurately identified sites plucked out of the imagination. She also found that fear and discord were passed on to her as a legacy: "I'm talking about a struggle to escape emotion, hurt, exposure and a yearning for human contact. This bi-polarity contains also the desire to move away from the pain and the past and the desire to completely feel it" (Timan, p. 23). At one point, she says, "I was sentenced to adapt the Holocaust" (Timan, p. 23).

In not avoiding the pain of the past or participating in the process of collective repression, Peleg reminds the Israelis of the function of memory. Importantly, the book is dedicated to Peleg's father, himself a Holocaust survivor, echoing Nava Semel's dedication to her parents, who endured the camps. This is further evidence of the author's belief that although she was not seared by the Nazi fire, she must imaginatively and unequivocally affirm the event's bestiality. Much of the text's strength is due principally to its ability to illustrate strikingly how the present generation is dramatically affected by the *Shoah* though they did not personally witness its death cycle.

Main Plot

The main plot concerns the attempted Holocaust evasion of Una, a woman in her early thirties, who runs a successful travel agency in New York. Living with her boyfriend, Adam, on the thirty-fourth floor of an apartment building in Manhattan, her life is a well-made tapestry of bourgeois comforts. At first it seems as if she is the typical career woman, dynamic and content with her life. She dwells within a safe space, at a distance from the European catastrophe. Yet the threads of her tranquil existence begin to unravel when she is pursued by the phantasmagorical figure of Ana, a twelve-year-old girl whose existence is guyed in the *Shoah*. Incredulously, their lives intermingle to form a tortuous synthesis, as the chimerical creation begins to dominate Una's dreams and ultimately assumes a corporeal form. Before long, the Holocaust girl, an embodiment of Una's suppressed ego, who, in a succession of wild dreams, haunts Una's mind, begins to get under the woman's skin, shattering her complacency toward the events of the past and making her feel the possibility of another life, far removed from her own. The Holocaust girl is able to draw Una into her chaotic subworld without warning, opening a doorway to a predatory Holocaust landscape. Una attempts to resist, vigorously trying to negate the phantom girl's disruption of her placid existence and disaffirming any connection to the *Shoah* past. She refuses to admit a nexus with the darkness that coerces her to engage the memories of the European catastrophe. In one passage, she bitterly protests the growing success of her doppelgänger in drawing her into the foreign sphere:

> I can't anymore doctor. I've run out of strength. I simply can't see the things that she is forcing me to see. . . . What is she doing there? Since when has her over there become here? It scares me even more doctor. . . . And I feel that with this she is getting close to me, somehow, and this scares me, and above all it tires me. After a night of these dreams I am finished, as if I have walked with her all this way in the mountains. . . . And the cold. I have never felt this so strong (Hakibutz Hamenchad, 1988, p. 103)

Despite the agency of a psychiatrist, it should be clear that the girl "is not a suppressed biographical memory, but rather a fantastic cultural presence. The girl's simultaneous existence in the world of the Holocaust and in contemporary Manhattan embodies the persistence of the Holocaust past in the modern present" (Morahg, p. 165).

This is consistent with Gilead Morahg's assessment that the novel is about the heritage of denial steadfastly embraced by the second and third generations, resisting any encroachment of Holocaust memory into their present lives. He aptly opines that

> The struggle between Una and the girl . . . is an anatomy of the involuntary emergence of communal memory and the struggle to come to terms with it. . . . It forces the realization that the Holocaust then and there is still very much part of the contemporary now and here, and that the self will remain deformed and incomplete until it affirms its present affinity with the traumas of the communal past (Morahg, p. 156).

Una denies the relevance of the Holocaust in her life, yet despite herself, grudgingly acknowledges the presentness of the past in response to a vision the phantom provides of a great mass of victims being marched toward a death camp. Although Una claims no connection to them and to have no empathy for them, they have indeed disturbed her peace and she prays they will disappear "just so they wouldn't be here . . . so undeniably present . . . and with them their plague, their tragedy, the curse that they bear" (pp. 74–75).

Struggle for Sanity

The operating tenor of the book is the heroine's struggle to maintain her wholeness and sanity while her soul is assailed by the young girl who initially shared her reluctance to associate with the victims in her own survival strategy, fearing that joining them would be fatal. Just as Una wants distance from the Holocaust confrontation, so the Holocaust girl is shown to have sought separation from the victims of Auschwitz. She watches a selection "from the outside, from behind the double fence . . ." (p. 189) and keeps her distance. She continues to watch a woman whose courageous support of a fellow prisoner impressed her, "Just watching her day after day through the fence, walking, eating, carrying heavy rocks from the limestone quarry . . . and maybe one day I will cross the fence and go in and touch her hand" (p. 193). The tension the girl experiences between the desire for community with her own kind in the camp and the contrary desire for survival links her to Una and the second-generation Israeli dilemma between Holocaust silence and acknowledgment. Her eventual entry into the camp, sanctioned by the woman she has been watching, foreshadows Una's acceptance of the past.

Paradoxically, the name Una does not suggest unity, as its meaning indicates, but rather a split of the one woman into two and the shared repulsion-attraction toward the *Shoah* history of the girl. In essence, she becomes the locus for a battle between warring personalities. Slowly, we witness a kind of dreamscape scenario, underscored by the ever-present girl who is determined to plunge Una into her own consciousness and who wants the contemporary female to enter her fictional Holocaust space and reality. At the same time, she seeks to forcibly invade Una's seemingly wholesome life.

Ana will not allow Una to forget. The border between the sleeping and the conscious collapses into one, so much so that at times the reader is unaware of who grasps the narratorial torch. Again and again, the edges blur and the dividing line between reality and fantasy blends into an embroidery sewn with a wild mix of imaginative fervor. All these incoherencies leave the reader blinking and groping in desperate attempts to follow. Compositionally, the lack of a unified authorial voice and the dissonant time and place reflects the fragmented identity of the modern woman who is trapped between two worlds. One can imagine that the materialization of the Holocaust girl and its pervasive immanence in Una's life is, in fact, the imaginative model adopted by members of the second and third generations in their response to the collective disaster that struck their forbears.

It has been pointed out by Dan Daor that the novel is hallmarked by the motif of integration and disintegration, whereby one's roots are exposed and then uprooted, aided and abetted by the constant movement that dapples the nucleus narrative. This constant motion is very much in evidence throughout. For instance, there is the Holocaust girl who wanders through the forests and towns of Europe, the endless march of the Jews to Auschwitz, Una's journey to the United States, and the conflicting dual motion encased within her soul that terrifyingly threatens to disintegrate her psyche. Una's persistent refusal to admit the Holocaust into her universe is expressed by the odd fact that although she runs a travel company, she never avails herself of the opportunity of free travel. The rejection of a physical voyage corresponds to the psychological refusal to join the Holocaust girl on her journey through "Planet Auschwitz." Primarily, every movement in the novel is a rasping quest for a way to confront and admit the Holocaust, as Lawrence Langer puts it, into our lives.

Formally, the story is told through various, subtly interlocking viewpoints, fusing poetry and prose with often difficult but provocative images that are laced with technical innovations. Peleg juggles a complex assemblage of narrative styles in her attempt to tackle her subject matter in indirect and alternative modes. One of Peleg's prevalent themes is the recognition that presenting the unimaginable through invention and reconstruction is necessary in second-generation Holocaust texts.

At heart, the novel presents the recto and verso of characters divided between two opposing, clashing worlds, which in today's cultural milieu are destined never to meet. Therein lies the rub. In the main, *Una* is about the uneasy relationship between the postwar generation and the survivors and the intractable trope of spiritual separation that the contemporary generation insists on. As Gershon Shaked correctly asserts, texts such as Peleg's

> reveal the weakness of the "native" Israelis, who cannot cope with the Holocaust and its survivors. They attempt to correct, as it were, in their writings and fictions the distortions and the harm wrought by members of their generation orally and in reality. Their fiction must be seen as a kind of testimony by guilty *sabras*, who as the children of a historical group whose best sons were murdered or destroyed spiritually, are attempting to repent (Shaked, p. 280).

Symbolism

As the narrative progresses, it becomes more and more apparent that the young girl seeks to impose on Una a life that, as Yudkin puts it, "has been determined by events that have taken place earlier, relationships from distant years, and even by factors from generations gone by." He adds, "Trauma has been inflicted on the present generation and thus has made a permanent imprint on the psyche. Yet, somehow the generation following in its wake is also deeply influenced" (Yudkin, pp. 175–176). Notably, the fear of the second generation to imagine the suffering, to connect with the ubiquitous ghosts of the past as represented by the girl, is emplotted in the text by the symbol of the fence in its various permutations. The barbed wire of the ghetto or of the death camp also becomes a denominator of the second generation's desire to break through the repression and denial, to move beyond the trauma of unhealed wounds and to reconcile with those who stood on the other side. At one point the phantom girl, who until then had followed the procession of Jews on their inexorable march into the camp, says:

> Outside the barbed wire inside of me I stand, with open arms / Maybe they will come and cut them off / Should I draw them back? Should I hide them / This question sours my life / I stretch my hands out to my loved one, who has lost its hair and is pale as a shadow / From day to day he becomes more pale / More thin / More my lover (pp. 206–207).

Soon afterwards, in an act of total identification, Una's merged psyche crosses the line and joins the column of Jews as they walk past the iron gates: "I don't want to remain outside, I said to myself, because with an intolerable sharpness how cold, dark and alone it is beyond the gate . . . and I stretched out my hands and ran towards them and they opened their arms and welcomed me, straight inside themselves" (p. 214). Moreover, once she has chosen to enter the death milieu from which there is no escape, the girl "coordinated her steps to theirs and walked with them in one rhythm as if she had always walked with them, through all the years, the stops and roads" (p. 214).

Resolution

In the end the two personalities meld into one, as the split self is increasingly effaced and Una discovers that she can overcome her fears of integrating with the terrors of the past. Una becomes an imaginative witness to the atrocities, demolishing the comfortable patina she has constructed around herself to shield her from the Holocaust. The binary oppositions of young and old, past and present, the glamorous woman and the unclean orphan, are dissolved as the two personas learn to coexist. It can be argued that the young girl survived the carnage and breathed its horrific smoke so she could become a living monument and transmit, through her troubled eyes, her codified experiences onto the adult woman. As the tale draws to a close, Una unmistakably incorporates the enigmatic presence of the *Shoah* girl into her psyche:

> Her image quivers in the darkening light like a butterfly during twilight. Don't go, I call out to her again. Maybe she'll agree to stop and listen to me, maybe she will return. I won't try and put you in the closet anymore. We'll walk together down the street. It's autumn soon and the leaves will all turn red. . . . It's a shame you won't see them. . . . Don't go, I keep pleading with her. Suddenly, it becomes very important for me that she doesn't go. I know that if she does, something will be absent, something that I don't want to live without. I don't want her to go. Because if she does I will also sink back into my kingdom of shadows. . . . Her vision is so sharp and clear. . . . And I want from now on to see clearly. And I am willing to pay the price (pp. 218–219).

It is of particular salience that Una reaches the conclusion that she must open up psychically as well as accept and acknowledge the Holocaust on her own terms, without the aid of the psychiatrist she has been seeing, and underlines the message that ultimately, engaging with the traumatic past must be done alone. In the final analysis, the expedition into the past that Una undertakes through the figure of the Holocaust girl allows her a liberating understanding and reconciliation that will enable her to deal with her afflicted neuroses. By mentally exploring her own crippled identity she is able to resolve the inherited but unresolved neuroses that raid her private serenity, and contend with the enduring scar that seems impossible to erase. Gilead Morahg focuses on the book's coda and remarks that:

> As she concludes the process of Holocaust recuperation with a definitive move towards psychological integration, Una . . . prepares to engage life with a greater degree of openness and willingness to risk. Many of the old fears are still there, but they are countered by newly found measures of awareness and determination (Morahg, p. 180).

One of the chief tasks of books such as *Una* is to inscribe, externalize, and incorporate the Holocaust into the shared national identity by providing the uninitiated reader with the emotion and intellectual textual space to enter this horrific realm, which they had hitherto suppressed to achieve psychological distance. One may suggest that Peleg understands, as Dominick LaCapra notes, that

> The *Shoah* calls for a response that does not deny its traumatic nature or cover it over through a "fetishistic" or redemptive narrative that makes believe it did not occur or compensates too readily for it . . . what is necessary is a discourse of trauma that itself undergoes—and indicates that one undergoes—a process of at least muted trauma insofar as one has tried to understand events and empathise with victims (LaCapra, pp. 220–221)

At the epicentre of Peleg's narrative is an overwhelming confrontation with the painful past that denies closure of this century's darkest moment, declaiming explicitly that memory and its preservation have not dimmed.

Bibliography

Primary Sources

Una. 1988.
Miss Fanny's Voice. 2001.

Secondary Sources

Daor, Dan. "Review." *Ha'artez* (17 June 1988): n.p.

LaCapra, Dominick. *Representing the Holocaust*. Ithaca: Cornell University Press, 1994.

Morahg, Gilead. "Breaking Silence: Israel's Fantastic Fiction of the Holocaust." In *The Boom in Contemporary Israeli Fiction*. Edited by Alan Mintz. Hanover: University Press of New England, 1997.

Sahar, Rachel. "Yalduta Hashniya." *Yediot Akhronot* (18 March 1988): 23–24.

Shaked, Gershon "Afterword." In *Facing the Holocaust: Selected Israeli Fiction*. Edited by Gila Ramras-Rauch and Joseph Michman-Melkman. Philadelphia: The Jewish Publication Society, 1985.

Timan, Miki. "Masa mikri letokh Hashoah." *Maariv* (24 June 1988): 23–24.

Yudkin, Leon. *A Home Within: Varieties of Jewish Expressions in Modern Fiction*. Middlesex: Symposium Press, 1996.

GEORGES PEREC
(1936–1982)

ANDREW LEAK

GEORGES PEREC WAS born in 1936 in the 19th arrondissement of Paris to Polish Jewish parents who had emigrated to France in the 1920s. His father, Icek Judko Perec, died in 1940 of wounds received on the very eve of the armistice between France and Germany. In 1941 Perec's mother, Cyrla (née Sculewicz), put her son on a Red Cross convoy that carried him to the relative safety of the so-called *zone libre*—the southern part of France that was not immediately occupied by the Germans after France capitulated in 1940—where he lived out the war in Villard-de-Lans. His mother never succeeded in joining her son, however. She was rounded up in one of the police raids of 1943; interned at Drancy, a concentration camp on the outskirts of Paris used as a detention and transit center; and deported thence to Auschwitz, from where she never returned. When France was liberated in 1944, Perec returned to Paris to live with a paternal aunt and uncle.

The laconic statement of these bare biographical facts—and indeed Perec's even more laconic summary of them: "the war, the camps"—conceals the very origin and motive force of his prodigious creativity. Few critics would apply the designation "holocaust writer," in an exclusive sense, to Perec's literary output, yet equally few would deny the importance of the Holocaust—and more especially the death at Auschwitz of his mother—for an understanding of Perec's literary project. Readers of Perec's first works, however, could have had little inkling of the significance of Perec's personal history for an understanding of his work. The first three novels disoriented readers by their apparent diversity. *Les choses* (1965) was the prize-winning story of a young couple, working in the then new area of market research, who were bewitched, bothered, and bewildered by the glittering enticements of the consumer society in which they lived. *Quel petit vélo à guidon chromé au fond de la cour?* (1966) was the account of the farcical attempts of a group of friends to save one of their number—a national serviceman—from being sent to fight in Algeria during its wars of independence from France. The hilarious mixing of registers, the use of pastiche and parody, and the attempt to work into the text every rhetorical figure and device known to humankind were the first signs of the experimentalism and the linguistic fireworks that were to characterize Perec's work, and for which he is probably still most readily remembered by general readers. *Un homme qui dort* (1967) was a negative image of *Les choses*: the depressive tale of a young man who—like Melville's Bartleby—one day simply opts out of life and embarks upon a course of pathological withdrawal from external reality.

W or the Memory of Childhood

Not until 1975 was the work published that serves as the basis for the unequivocal claim for the status of Perec as a Holocaust writer. In 1969–1970 the literary journal *Quinzaine Littéraire* published a serialized *récit* titled "W" that was the reconstruction of a story Perec had made up as a child, largely in the form of cartoonlike line drawings. However, *W ou le souvenir d'enfance* (W or the Memory of Childhood), as it was published in 1975, contains *two* texts, one in italics, the other in roman type, that alternate chapter for chapter. The first of these texts is the story published in the *Quinzaine Littéraire*; the other is an attempted autobiographical account of the author's childhood up until age about ten. The italic text begins with the first-person narration of one Gaspard Winckler. Winckler is a deserter living under a false identity provided for him by a support network. One day, he is summoned to a meeting with the mysterious Otto Apfelstahl, who informs him that the child whose name and identity he had been given disappeared when the yacht on which he was cruising foundered and sank "somewhere near Tierra del Fuego." The bodies of the child's mother and the crew members had been recovered but the child's body had not, raising the possibility that he may have survived. Winckler is invited to set off in search of the lost child. At this point (the end of Part 1) the first-person narrator disappears and is replaced in Part 2 by a third-person narrator who describes, in quasi-anthropological style, life on W, an island "at the ends of the earth" (*W ou le souvenir d'enfance*, p. 89, translation by Andrew Leak) entirely governed by the Olympic ideal. There is a minute description of the complex rules that regulate every aspect of life on W: the relations among the four villages, the athletic meetings that occur regularly among them, the system of prizes and honors disputed by the athletes. But the dystopian nature of this society becomes gradually apparent: the struggle for sporting supremacy is revealed to be a struggle for life; the triumph of the victors is fragile and short-lived; the punishments for the losers are cruel and arbitrary; "victory" itself depends on the caprice of the judges and officials who interpret the rules in an unpredictable manner; and children are the products of the systematic mass rape of the females in monthly "games" expressly designed for that purpose. In the final chapter of the W story, the reader learns that the "athletes" wear striped apparel, that the high jumpers have shackled ankles, that the long-jumpers land in pits filled with excrement. The chilling final paragraph leaves us in no doubt as to what we have been witnessing:

> He who, one day, penetrates into the Fortress will at first find only a succession of long, grey, empty rooms . . . he will have to carry on walking for a long time before he discovers, buried in the depths of the earth, the remains of a world that he will think he had forgotten: piles of gold teeth, wedding rings, glasses, piles and piles of clothing, dust-covered files, stocks of poor quality soap (p. 218, translation by Andrew Leak).

The autobiographical chapters, written later and intercalated into the fictional narrative, progress in counterpoint to the latter. They also fall into two parts. The first part begins provocatively with the statement "I have no memories of childhood" (p. 13, translation by Andrew Leak); the second part begins "Henceforth the memories exist" (p. 93, translation by Andrew Leak) but insists on the dislocated, fragmentary, floating nature of these problematic memories, most of which appear to be more constructed or fantasized than real: "The memories are bits of life torn from the void. No mooring ropes. Nothing to anchor them down, nothing to fix them. Virtually nothing to validate them" (p. 94, translation by Andrew Leak). The compositional labor of *W ou le souvenir d'enfance* involved the attempt to uncover the threads that might tie these unlikely "memories" together, the discovery of a level at which a thread of reality can be perceived to run through them. For the autobiographical chapters are connected to each other and to the fiction of W by means of what Perec biographer Bernard Magné has termed textual "sutures": individual letters, words, phrases, or scenes that occur in necessarily different contexts in both the fiction and the autobiography and that create a system of echoes between these accounts, a doubling the effect of which can best be described as uncanny. The task allotted to the reader of *W ou le souvenir d'enfance* is therefore one of connecting or binding (*relier*) by a process of continual rereading (*relire*). These insistent echoes culminate in a moment of fusion between fiction and autobiography when, in the penultimate chapter of the roman-type text, we read: "Later, I went with my aunt to see an exhibition on the concentration camps. . . . I remember photos showing the walls of the ovens [*sic*] lacerated by the fingernails of those who had been gassed."

The researching and writing of *W* marked a distinct shift in Perec's attitude toward his Jewishness, toward the events of the Holocaust, and especially toward the role played by "la guerre, les camps" in his own history. The aspiring young writer of the late 1950s certainly did not think of himself primarily, if at all, as a Jewish writer (despite his romantic identification with Franz Kafka) and even less as a Holocaust writer: his self-image was that of a leftist intellectual attempting to find a style that was both literary and committed but that would avoid the pitfalls both of Sartrean *engagement* and of the disengaged *nouveau roman*. The publication of *W* also led readers to reevaluate Perec's previous output; some noted, for example, that his very earliest works included enthusiastic review articles of Robert Antelme's *L'espèce humaine* (an account of Antelme's internment in the German concentration camps of Buchenwald and Dachau) and Alain Resnais's film, *Hiroshima mon amour*, written by Marguerite Duras; the discrete references in *Un homme qui dort* to "wearers of invisible stars" (*Un Homme qui Dort*, p. 114, translation by Andrew Leak) or to the Gestapo's Paris torture center in the rue de Saussaies now seemed to be imbued with further significance. In particular, the publication of *W* prompted a rereading of Perec's 1969 novel *La disparition*. This three-hundred-page detective novel had initially been reviewed primarily as the spectacular fruit of Perec's involvement with the experimental group OuLiPo; it is a lipogrammatic composition that entirely dispenses with the most commonly used letter in French: E. But the dedication of *W* was "Pour E" (pronounced like "eux," the French word for "them"). In light of this, *La disparition*—the very title of which is a euphemism in French for death—can be read as an hommage to those who disappeared so dramatically from the author's life, a kind of controlled repetition of the original trauma. The whole of Perec's artistic project begins now to take on a different tonality: "I write because they have left their indelible mark in me and because its trace is writing; their memory is dead to writing; writing is the memory of their death and the affirmation of my life" (*W ou le souvenir d'enfance*, p. 59, translation by Andrew Leak).

Tales of Ellis Island

No evaluation of Perec as a "Holocaust writer" would be complete without mentioning *Récits d'Ellis Island* (*Tales of Ellis Island*). Perec's collaboration in 1978–1979 with French filmmaker Robert Bober on a film project about the former immigration center on Ellis Island in upper New York Bay marked a further stage in his questioning of a past that for much of his life he had avoided confronting: "What I, Georges Perec, have come to question here is wandering, dispersion, diaspora. For me, Ellis Island is the very place of exile" (*Récits d'Ellis Island*, p. 56, translation by Andrew Leak). It is doubtless no coincidence that the slow tracking shots and haunting still photography of the film are as reminiscent of the remains of a concentration camp as they are of a disused immigration center, or that the mass of bric-a-brac left behind by the lucky immigrants should evoke the "piles of gold teeth, of wedding rings" of W's empty fortress. Neither is it an accident that Perec's commentary on this place where "destiny took the form of an alphabet" (p. 49, translation by Andrew Leak) should contain numerous echoes of *Un homme qui dort, La disparition*, and *W*.

Criticism and Contribution

The annual bulletin of the Association Georges Perec attests to the ever-growing body of critical work devoted to Perec's writings. In France, he is now regarded—along with such figures as Claude Simon and Alain Robbe-Grillet—as one of the major French writers of the late twentieth century. His critical reputation in the English-speaking world is also well established; although owing to the unique kinds of wordplay that characterize his writing, aspects of Perec's work will remain a closed book for those unable to read him in French.

Perec's oblique contribution to Holocaust writing has to be set first within the context of his peculiar personal circumstances. Unlike the Nobel Prize–winning novelist Elie Wiesel, who experienced the atrocity firsthand, or the novelest Patrick Modiano, who was born after the events, Perec lived through the Holocaust without experiencing it directly; he was both present at and absent from those events. He tells how, as a child, he had almost to infer the disappearance of his mother from the whispered allusions of his entourage. The word "Auschwitz" was, in a sense, taboo. But in this respect his experience rejoins that of the wider French society of the postwar years: turned toward reconstruction, and facing the new challenges of the Cold War, France simply pretended that nothing had happened. A collective amnesia or, at most, a myth of glorious resistance occupied the place where Vichy, zealous collaboration, and the deportation of seventy thousand Jews should have been. It took twenty years and the work of an outsider—the American historian Robert O. Paxton—for the taboo to begin to be lifted. The process is far from complete today. When he died in 1982, Perec was working on a complex novel titled *"53 Jours."* The innermost layer, the core of the mystery of this Russian-doll (stories within stories) narrative, was to concern precisely the bringing to light of a concealed story of wartime betrayal and collaboration. The answer to the mystery is said to reside, at one point, in a war grave by the side of a mountain road in the Vercors, in the French Alps just a few miles from where the child Perec had survived, even as those closest to him were disappearing, somewhere "at the ends of the earth," without a trace.

Bibliography

Primary Sources

"Robert Antelme ou la Vérité de la Littérature." *Partisans* no. 8 (January–February 1963).

"La Perpétuelle Reconquête." *La Nouvelle Critique* no. 116 (May 1960).

Les Choses (*Things*). 1965.

Quel Petit Vélo à Guidon Chromé au Fond de la Cour? (Les Lettres Nouvelles). 1966.

Un Homme qui Dort (*A Man Asleep*). 1967.

La Disparition (*A Void*). 1969.

W ou le souvenir d'enfance (W or the Memory of Childhood). 1975.

Récits d'Ellis Island (Tales of Ellis Island). 1980. With Robert Bober.

"53 Jours" (*"53 Days"*). 1989.

Secondary Sources

Béhar, Stella. *Georges Perec: Ecrire Pour ne pas Dire*. New York: Peter Lang, 1995.

Bellos, David. *Georges Perec. A Life in Words*. London: Harvill, 1993.

Burgelin, Claude. *Georges Perec*. Paris: Seuil, 1988.

Cahiers Georges Perec, no. 2, *W ou le souvenir d'enfance. Une Fiction*. Paris: Université de Paris VII, 1988.

Magné, Bernard. *Georges Perec*. Paris: Nathan, 1999.

Van Montfrans, Manet. *Georges Perec. La Contrainte du Réel*. Amsterdam: Rodopi, 1999.

Archives

The "Fonds Perec," which contains, besides much else, manuscripts and typescripts of Perec's works, is housed at the Bibliothèque de l'Arsenal in Paris. The archives may be consulted on Thursday afternoons throughout the year.

GISELLA PERL
(1900–1988)

MYRNA GOLDENBERG

BORN ON 10 December 1900 (according to the United States Social Security Death Index; other less authoritative sources identify both 1905 and 1910 as the year of her birth) in Sighet, Hungary, Gisella Perl broke both gender and religious barriers to become a physician. Not only did she overcome the *numeris clausis* restrictions, quotas that limited the number of Jews who could be admitted to institutions such as medical schools, but she also had to challenge her father, who feared that she would stray from Judaism if she pursued a profession. She kept her promise to Maurice Perl that she would remain a "good, true Jew," and, with the fee from her first patient, bought him a prayer book in which she had his name inscribed. For decades, she held onto the memory of her father, Maurice Perl, who carried the book as he was being led to the gas chamber.

Deportation to Auschwitz

Perl had a lively practice as an obstetrician and gynecologist in Sighet until the Germans occupied Hungary in 1944. Her memoir opens with a portrait of Dr. Kapezius, a physician with the German chemical company I. G. Farben, who, in early winter 1943, had sought to meet Dr. Perl and her husband in order to reminisce about Berlin during the Weimar Republic. Although she did not trust him completely, she invited him to their home and enjoyed a memorable evening of music and culture. In March 1944, the Germans confined the Jews of Sighet to a ghetto. Perl was told to establish a ghetto hospital with a maternity ward. Her husband, the president of the ghetto's Jewish Council, was powerless to relieve terrible conditions. Within a couple of weeks, the ghetto was deported to Auschwitz. At Auschwitz, Dr. Kapezius sought her out again and ordered her to be the camp gynecologist—without instruments or medicine.

I Was a Doctor in Auschwitz relates Perl's experiences as a practicing doctor in the death camp and her acute sensitivity to the physical and emotional suffering of the women she treated. Published in 1948, this very early memoir records the brutality and dehumanization of the camp in vivid details and with stark frankness. Physical conditions and the lack of sanitary or medical necessities comprise most of Perl's recollection, and she describes the privations at Auschwitz unsparingly:

> No one who had to live without the small comforts of even the poorest kind of life can imagine what it is to have to do, for instance, without paper. There was, of course, no toilet paper. . . . We got into the habit of tearing tiny squares of material off our shirts, drying our eyes with them first, then using them to clean our rectum. However careful we were, the shirts got shorter and shorter until there was nothing left but the shoulder straps and a narrow strip around our chests (*I was a Doctor in Auschwitz,* Salem, N.H.: Ayer Company Publishers, 1984, p. 33).

After someone denounced the women's practices, the SS held a shirt inspection, and the prisoners were beaten for "having damaged 'camp property' " (p. 34).

Perl also focuses on the impossibility of providing more than "many, many delusive, hollow words of comfort" to the women in her care. "I speak and speak of the past, because the present is unbearable and there is no future—and the past gives strength to bear all" (pp. 98–99). She notes that talk was not only her most important palliative, but was also a form of sustenance and nurturing among the women. Although Perl minimizes the success of her efforts to take care of her patients, another survivor, Elsa Kraus, later testified that Perl's courageous and successful attempts to provide clinical care restored her eyesight. Perl had diagnosed Kraus's temporary blindness as a vitamin deficiency, and over the next several weeks used "camp connections" to get the necessary daily injections that cured Kraus.

Perl provides a sharp picture of the infamously cruel SS guard Irma Griese: "One of the most beautiful women . . . Her body was perfect in every line, her face clear and angelic and her blue eyes the gayest, the most innocent eyes one can imagine" (p. 61). She follows with a description of Griese's sexual pleasure at watching her perform surgery on women whose infected breasts had been the target of Griese's braided wire whip. Griese also ordered a terrified Perl to perform an abortion on her.

Reducing suffering and saving pregnant women became Perl's reason to survive. Perl saved hundreds, perhaps thousands, of women by performing abortions. The SS officers had encouraged pregnant women to identify themselves, deceiving them with promises of special care and double bread rations. Perl then accidentally witnessed their form of special care: the women were "beaten with clubs and whips, torn by dogs, dragged around by the hair and kicked in the stomach with heavy German boots. Then, when they collapsed, they were thrown into the crematory—alive" (p. 80). The policy of the Nazis, she came to understand was to "immediately put to death all Jewish, Polish, Russian, and French women who were pregnant, in the gas chamber, and in the crematorium" (*Time*, pp. 56–57). Her reaction was immediate and unwavering:

> Horror turned into revolt . . . and a new incentive to live. I had to remain alive. It was up to me to save all the pregnant women in Camp C from this infernal fate. It was up to me to save the life of the mothers, if there was no other way, than by destroying the life of their unborn children (p. 81).

Perl explains how she ran from barrack to barrack, delivering babies or inducing labor, always "in the dark, always hurried, in the midst of filth and dirt" (p. 81). Much later, as an obstetrician in New York and Israel, before each delivery, she addressed God: "God, you owe me a life, a living baby" (Brozan, p. C20).

War's End and After

In late January 1945, conditions improved briefly for Perl when she was escorted to a work camp in Hamburg to be the hospital physician of Dege-Werke, a rubber factory, where she characterized herself as a partisan saving lives of overworked women who reported to the infirmary. She defied orders by nursing sick prisoners back to health or concealing their illness. On 7 March 1945, she and a few other Jewish prisoners were transported to Bergen-Belsen: a "dung-heap . . . While in Auschwitz extermination was regulated by careful planning, here mass dying was a consequence of lack of planning" (p. 165). In Bergen-Belsen, she watched lice cover prisoners' bodies, rats eat prisoners alive, prisoners open the "bodies of the recently dead and [eat] their livers, their hearts, their brains" (p. 167). On 8 March she found the bodies of her brother and sister-in-law among the piles of Bergen-Belsen corpses.

After liberation, Perl searched for her family, only to learn that her husband had been beaten to death and her son gassed. Despondent, she tried to poison herself and was taken to a convent in France to recover. She came to the United States in March 1947 and began speaking as a witness, identifying herself as Ambassador of the Six Million. In September 1948, her work in the camps became the subject of a *Time* magazine piece that lauded her courage in defying the Germans by denying them the deaths of pregnant women and their unborn children. At the same time, the article generated controversy over her practice of abortion; for instance, *Time* cited a physician who condemned her in the name of Catholicism for what the Church considers "wholesale slaughter of infants . . . whether it be done by the brutal Nazis, or by a sentimental and well-meaning female medical personality." The *Time* article gave rise to a sophisticated short piece in *Partisan Review* that, in itself, responded to criticism of her actions. Hans Meyerhoff opened his *Partisan Review* essay with a reference to a private bill, introduced on 21 January 1948, to grant Dr. Perl her American citizenship:

> The woman doctor is Dr. Gisella Perl, whose parents, husband, and son were killed by the Germans. The House approved a bill granting her permanent residence after its author, Representative Sol Bloom (D., N.Y.), outlined her efforts on behalf of "simple humanity as an enforced member of the medical staff of the German Auschwitz concentration camp whose duty [it was] to report to the German authorities every morning the number of pregnant women in the camp. . . . These women were systematically put to death." As soon as Dr. Perl learned of what happened to these women, she went through the camp every night and performed abortions on all the pregnant women so that there would be none. . . . It is estimated that, in this way, she saved the lives of more than 3,000 women.

Late in 1947, Eleanor Roosevelt approached Perl at a lecture where both were honored guests and urged her to resume her medical career. Mrs. Roosevelt also invited her to lunch at the White House, but Perl demurred until Mrs. Roosevelt assured her that she would serve a kosher lunch. Perl's lunch with Eleanor Roosevelt led to a meeting with Representative Bloom, the January 1948 congressional bill, and ultimately the resumption of her practice, which she opened in 1951 in an office outfitted with "Sol Bloom furniture." Working under Dr. Alan F. Guttmacher, chair of obstetrics and gynecology and family-planning pioneer, she later joined the obstetrics staff at Mount Sinai Hospital and became an expert in infertility. In New York, and later at Shaare Tzedek Medical Center in Jerusalem, Auschwitz and Bergen-Belsen patients flocked to "Gisi Doctor," her nickname in Auschwitz. Perl moved to Israel in 1979 and lived a productive life, devoted to healing, until her death on 24 November 1988. Her memoir is a tribute to her friendships with other female physicians and nurses who, she suggests, were resistance fighters by practicing medicine and saving lives.

Bibliography

Primary Source

I Was a Doctor in Auschwitz. 1948.

Secondary Sources

Brozan, Nadine. "Out of Death, a Zest for Life." *New York Times*, 15 November 1982, p. C20.

Cosner, Shaaron, and Victoria Cosner. *Women Under the Third Reich: A Biographical Dictionary*. Westport, Conn.: Greenwood Press, 1998.

Gilbert, Martin. *The Holocaust: A History of the Jews of Europe During the Second World War*. New York: Henry Holt, 1985.

Heinemann, Marlene E. *Gender and Destiny: Women Writers and the Holocaust*. Westport, Conn.: Greenwood Press, 1986.

Kraus, Elsa. Testimony # 0.69/40, Yad Vashem Archives. Jerusalem, Israel.

Lifton, Robert Jay. *The Nazi Doctors: Medical Killing and the Psychology of Genocide*. New York: Basic Books, 1986.

Meyerhoff, Hans. "A Parable of Simple Humanity." *Partisan Review* (September 1948) 966–971.

"Not So Simple." *Time* (20 September 1948): 56–57.

Patterson, David. *Sun Turned to Darkness: Memory and Recovery in the Holocaust Memoir*. Syracuse: Syracuse University Press, 1998.

Rittner, Carol, and John K. Roth, eds. *Different Voices: Women and the Holocaust*. New York: Paragon House, 1993.

CARYL PHILLIPS
(1958–)

WENDY ZIERLER

CARYL PHILLIPS, NOVELIST, essayist, editor, and playwright, was born in St. Kitts, West Indies, on 13 March 1958 and moved to England when he was only a few months old. He grew up in Birmingham and Leeds and was educated at Queen's College, Oxford. He has held teaching positions and visiting lectureships at the Universities of Ghana, the West Indies, and Poznan, and at Amherst College, and is currently professor of English and Henry R. Luce Professor of Migration and Social Order at Barnard College. Phillips's sense of double estrangement as a West Indian migrant to England and as a descendant of African slaves has fueled his ongoing literary interest in the subjects of diaspora and memory. The author of six novels and several play scripts for stage, film, radio, and television, Phillips is best known for his depiction, in such novels as *Cambridge* (1991) and *Crossing the River* (1993), of issues relating to the history of the African Diaspora and for his postmodern use of polyphonous and disjointed forms of narration. Phillips has also evinced a persistent literary interest in the history of European persecutions of Jews, in general, and the Holocaust in particular. Phillips's major contribution to Holocaust literature has involved bringing the technique of multiple and shifting narration to bear on the twin subjects of Jewish and black suffering. Perhaps more than any other fiction writer, Phillips has helped draw together the histories of African slavery and the Holocaust in a meaningful and compelling literary conversation.

Holocaust Writings

Phillips's earliest discussions of the Holocaust came in *The European Tribe* (1987), a collection of travel essays that expose the endemic racism of Europe. Throughout this collection, Phillips makes clear the extent to which the history of European antisemitism has informed his own sense of alienation and estrangement as a European black. In an essay describing his visit to the Jewish ghetto of Venice, "the original ghetto, the model for all others in the world—places characterized by deprivation and persecution" (*European Tribe*, New York: Farrar Straus and Giroux, 1987, p. 52), Phillips presents a self-image that is bound up with the history of the Jew in Europe. "I will always remember the words of Frantz Fanon," Phillips writes, that "[w]henever you hear anyone abuse the Jews, pay attention, because he is talking about you" (*European Tribe*, p. 54). In another essay, "Anne Frank's Amsterdam," Phillips describes how his adolescent encounters with the horrors of the Holocaust precipitated his first foray into the realm of fiction writing:

> I watched the library footage of the camps and realized both the enormity of the crime that was being perpetrated, and the precariousness of my own position in Europe. . . . "If white people could do that to white people, then what the hell would they do to me?" After that programme I wrote my first piece of fiction. A short story about a fifteen-year-old Jewish boy in Amsterdam who argues with his parents because he does not want to wear the yellow Star of David. He is just like everyone else, he says, but his parents insist. Eventually there comes the knock on the door and his family is taken to the cattletrucks for "resettlement." En route the boy somehow manages to jump from the wagon, but in doing so he bangs his head. He lies bleeding by the railway embankment and it is only the sunlight shining on his yellow star that attracts a farmer's kindly attention. The boy is taken to the farmhouse and saved (*European Tribe*, p. 67).

Implied by the ending of this story is that only by donning an overt (albeit stigmatic) badge of Jewish identity and cultural memory can the boy be saved. In his adult writings about black slaves as well as Jews, Phillips has proven less optimistic about salvation, but equally concerned with how an awareness of one's people and one's past makes possible both physical and cultural survival.

With his third novel, *Higher Ground: A Novel in Three Parts* (1989), Phillips began to incorporate the Holocaust into his fictive explorations of exile and memory. Holocaust references first appear in the second part of the novel, "Cargo Rap," an epistolary novella, written from the perspective of a young African American man named Rudy, who is sent to jail for attempting to steal forty dollars. In his letters, the increasingly radicalized Rudy repeatedly misappropriates Holocaust terminology to describe his own experience of incarceration, referring to solitary confinement as "Belsen" and to the prison guards as "Gestapo," and speculating as to whether "in Nazi Germany they used to keep the lights on as a form of torture" (*Higher Ground*: *A Novel in Three Parts*, New York: Viking, 1989, p. 72). Rudy is an articulate and impassioned speaker on behalf of black power, but he is also deeply chauvinistic, self-righteous, and ultimately misguided, drawing on the experience of the Holocaust not so much to empathize with others as much as to claim the self-righteous "higher ground" of ultimate victimhood. "Higher Ground," the last of the three parts of the novel, corrects Rudy's misappropriation by focusing on the story of a Polish Jewish refugee named Irene, who was sent to England by her parents at age eighteen to escape the Nazis, and who remains plagued by the memories of her family, whom she has lost to the *Shoah*. The novella begins in the present day with a description of an emotionally shattered Irene, who "was forever crying" and "had developed a habit of letting her chin drop forward so that it touched her chest" (*Higher Ground*, p. 175). Irene inhabits a shadowy world, where memories and nightmarish visions swirl around her inexplicably, as in the following passage:

> A cat screamed like a child. The lamp posts had small heads and long necks . . . The snowflakes spun with a religious monotony that made her want to sing. Instead Irene laughed and imagined God shaking a great celestial saltcellar before he ate up his children (p. 176).

Memories bleed from her mind, "like blood from a punched nose" (p. 180), and she is neither able nor entirely willing to staunch the flow. Although the novella begins several years after the Holocaust, Irene's past continually overtakes her present, an emotional state that is underscored by Phillips's nonlinear narration, which shifts continually back and forth in time. As the novella unfolds, facts about Irene's family and the worsening condition of their lives under Nazi occupation interlock with recollections of her painful voyage to England, her unsuccessful marriage, and the loss of a baby. After a brief unconsummated relationship with a West Indian man—evidence of Phillips's desire to link his own diasporic history with that of the Jews—Irene begins to realize that she can never recover a real sense of home or happiness. The novella ends ominously with Irene reciting the words of the *shema*, evocative of the Jewish traditions of monotheistic faith as well as tragic martyrdom. This liturgical reference echoes the epigraph to the novel, taken from a gospel song—"*Lord plant my feet on higher ground*"—thereby linking black and Jewish spiritual aspirations.

The Nature of Blood

Phillips's most significant contribution to Holocaust literature is his sixth novel, *The Nature of Blood* (1997). A literary work of considerable technical virtuosity and ambition, this novel consists of several interweaving stories that loop and twist around one another, revealing a complex and wrenching depiction of the "nature of blood" in all of racial, familial, tribal, life-giving, and life-taking connotations. The central plot chronicles the experience of a young German Jewish girl named Eva Stern who survives the death camps only to take her own life in a London hospital after being betrayed by a former British soldier. Eva's story, like that of Irene in *Higher Ground*, winds back and forth in time, as do the other four narrative strands that lace in and out of her account.

In addition to Eva's story, the novel traces the exploits of her uncle, Stephen Stern, a former doctor who leaves his wife and child behind in Nazi Germany to immigrate to Palestine and become a leader in the Jewish underground army. The exact nature of Stephen's activities is never elaborated, although his surname, reminiscent of the radical "Stern Gang," establishes a connection between *Shoah* and *gevurah* (heroism), more specifically, between the tragedies of the Holocaust and the idea of Zionist redemption in its most radical form. Stephen's narrative frames the novel and culminates with a meeting in present-day Tel Aviv, between the aging former Zionist hero and a young Ethiopian immigrant named Malka—one of many connections made in the novel between the lives of blacks and Jews. Malka's sense of alienation and displacement as a black Jew in Israel and Stephen's abiding loneliness in his old age all point to a lingering personal sense of disappointment with the idea of Zionist redemption.

As in Phillips's twin essays on Venice in *The European Tribe*, *The Nature of Blood* also reaches back in time to tell two stories from Renaissance Venice, one black and one Jewish. The black story is the Venetian-based Shakespearean tragedy of Othello. Asked about what Othello has to do with the *Shoah*, Phillips told one interviewer "what makes it belong is loneliness, isolation, sense of betrayal, all things that befell Jewish people in the fifteenth century and during World War II" (Kalman Naves, p. J1) To be sure, Phillips's decision to redramatize the story of Othello also has a great deal to do with his desire to draw links between the racially motivated sufferings of blacks and Jews in Europe, between "Shylock and Othello as archetypal victims of a European modernity" (Cheyette, p. 64).

The Jewish story is a powerfully understated third-person account of a blood libel in fifteenth-century Venetian town of Portobuffole, which led to the burning at the stake of a several prominent Jews. The Portobuffole narrative, which includes references to the Italian origins of the term "ghetto" and the Venetian requirement that the Jews distinguish themselves "by yellow stitching on their clothes" (*Nature of Blood*, p. 52), clearly locates the Holocaust on a historical continuum of Christian European persecutions of the Jews. The account of the execution of the Jew Servadio and his two "co-conspirators" culminates with an image of the executioner putting in a long shovel between the burning coals, pulling out a heap of white ash and throwing it into the air, whereupon it "dispersed immediately" (p. 155)—an image that prefigures and alludes to the white ash of the Holocaust crematoria.

As each of the narrative strands progress, the shifts and disruptions become even more frequent and frantic, mirroring the various dislocations and memory fractures that beset the characters in the stories. Within individual narrative strands, Phillips also experiments with narrative point of view. In the Eva narrative, in particular, Phillips alternates between first-person and third-person narration and interposes parenthetical interior reflections and italicized dream sequences. Toward the end of the novel, Phillips interrupts narration to include "scientific commentary" on post-Holocaust survivor trauma and to insert mock-encyclopedia entries for such words and concepts as GHETTO, VENICE, SUICIDE, and OTHELLO. The result of this technique of extreme narrative fragmentation and experimentation is a novel that argues strenuously against the idea of a unified, univocal history of the Holocaust, that insists instead on employing various perspectives and stylistic registers and on juxtaposing the Holocaust against other historical instances of racially motivated bloodshed.

The Nature of Blood is a self-consciously literary work that strives to be seen in the context of a tradition of literary responses to tragedy and catastrophe. In addition to the obvious references to Shakespeare and to Renaissance Jewish history, Phillips also alludes to specific works of Holocaust literature. It is no accident that Eva Stern's sister and her boyfriend, like those of Anne Frank, are named Margot and Peter, and that while living in the ghetto, Eva befriends a woman named Rosa, who, like the protagonist of Cynthia Ozick's astonishing short story, is repeatedly pictured with a shawl, or that the encyclopedia entries recall the fourth section of David Grossman's *See: Under Love*. Scholar Alan Mintz has advocated reading Holocaust literature—Hebrew works in particular—in light of the "vertical axis of literary tradition, which extend[s] back to the Middle Ages and the Bible." *The Nature of Blood*, the chief protagonist of which bears the name Eva, evocative of the biblical mother of the first murdered child, reflects a similar albeit wider conception of the tradition, inscribing a Holocaust story within the long, sordid history of discrimination and violence based on race and blood.

Critical Reception

While Phillips's novels dealing with the history and legacy of African slavery have been almost universally acclaimed, *The Nature of Blood* has received mixed reviews. Matthew Gilbert describes Phillips's use of fragmented narrative as "junky," "theatrical," and "willfully enigmatic" (Gilbert, p. N22). Jamal Mahjoub contends that the novel adds very little to the distinguished and well-established literature of the Holocaust and fails, in its connection between the Holocaust and the establishment of the State of Israel, to confront the political consequences of Zionism (Mahjoub, p. 61). Most trenchantly, Hillary Mantel charges Phillips with trying "to lay claim to other people's suffering," an impulse she deems "indecent" and "colonial" (Mantel, p. 39). In contrast, other critics have lauded Phillips's technique and have concurred with Paul Gilroy that there is indeed "something useful to be gained from setting these histories closer to each other" (Gilroy, p. 217). Peter Rushforth praises the intricate and seamless intertwining of the various tales in this novel, which he describes as "masterly"—"an unflinching confrontation with some of the darkest passages of human history" (Rushforth, p. 35). Bryan Cheyette commends Phillips's "project of challenging separatisms and nationalisms from all sides" (Cheyette, p. 63). Similarly, James Shapiro applauds Phillips's readiness to challenge the "current literary tribalism" that "would mark off black experience as the domain of blacks, restrict the telling of women's lives to other women, and leave the Holocaust to the Jews" (Shapiro, 7:7).

Bibliography

Primary Sources

The European Tribe. 1987.
Higher Ground: A Novel in Three Parts. 1989.
Cambridge. 1991.
Crossing the River. 1993.
The Nature of Blood. 1997.

Secondary Sources

Cheyette, Bryan. "Venetian Spaces: Old-New Literatures and the Ambivalent Uses of Jewish History." In *Reading the 'New' Literatures in a Postcolonial Era*, 53–72. Edited by Susheila Nasta. Cambridge, U.K.: D. S. Brewer, 2000.

Gilbert, Matthew. "Across Time and Cultures, The Bitter Legacy of Hate." *Boston Globe* (1 June 1997), p. N22.

Gilroy, Paul. *The Black Atlantic: Modernity and Double Consciousness*. Cambridge, Mass.: Harvard University Press, 1993.

Kalman Naves, Elaine. "Fueled by Diligence and Passion." *The Montreal Gazette*, 14 June 1997, p. J1.

Ledente, Bénédicte. "Caryl Phillips." (Website including biographical and bibliographical information: http:/www/ulg.ac.be/facphl/uer/d/german/ L3/cpintro.html.

Mahjoub, Jamal. Review of *The Nature of Blood. Wasafiri* 28 (Autumn 1998): 61–62.

Mantel, Hillary. "Black Is Not Jewish." Review of *The Nature of Blood. The Literary Review* (1 February 1997): 39.

Rushforth, Peter. "Memory Is My Only Home." *Dimensions* 11, No. 2 (1997): 35–39.

Schoffman, Stuart. "What Are We Doing Here?" Review of *The Nature of Blood. Jerusalem Report* (7 August 1997): 48–49.

Shapiro, James. "Diasporas and Desperations." *New York Times*, 25 May 1997, 7: 7, column 1.

Phillips's manuscript collection is found in the Beinecke Library, Yale University, New Haven, Connecticut.

Marge Piercy

(1936–)

S. LILLIAN KREMER

KNOWN PRIMARILY AS an eco-feminist, utopian writer, Marge Piercy is a prolific novelist and poet. She acknowledges Simone de Beauvoir as "a tremendously important model" among those who wrote political fiction. Piercy also acknowledges her Jewish grandmother's distinctive storytelling and her mother as instrumental in her development as a writer ("Autobiography" in *Contemporary Authors*, p. 272). Born on 31 March 1936 in Detroit, Michigan, to Robert and Bert Bunnin Piercy, she grew up in a working-class neighborhood. Her relationship with her gentile Welsh immigrant father was emotionally distant. Raised as a Jew by her mother and grandmother, Piercy cites her parents' marriage as one reason she has married Jewish men, Michel Schiff, Robert Shapiro, and Ira Wood.

Piercy left Detroit at age seventeen with a scholarship for the University of Michigan where she earned a Bachelor of Arts degree. She later completed studies for a Master of Arts at Northwestern. As a political activist strongly committed to civil rights and antiwar movements during the sixties, Piercy was associated with the Students for a Democratic Society (SDS) and later became an important voice in the women's movement, championing the cause in essays and fiction. She has repeatedly acknowledged that "her political engagement has empowered her as a writer and that it has influenced the content of her writing" (Shands, p. 17). Attributing her realization of the importance of politics to the Holocaust, she observed, "the Holocaust made me feel that being political is a necessity and that only fools and the very naive permit themselves the luxury of remaining aloof from the political process" ("The Dark Thread of the Weave," p. 182). With fifteen collections of poetry, fifteen novels, and numerous short stories and essays to her credit, Piercy's major themes center on sexism, racism, leftist social and economic concerns, turbulence of the revolutionary life, and women's response to marginalization and the violence of a patriarchal society. She is committed "to a redressing of grievances and to a vindication of the rights of all oppressed . . . [to] decoding of cultural constructions of power and powerlessness, . . . as they intersect with issues of [gender] ethnicity and class" (Shands, p. 174).

Jewish Issues

Piercy avoided Jewish issues early in her writing career, convinced that publishers would reject such work. Nonetheless, her Jewish identity remained strong and it has found an increasingly important presence in her later poetry and fiction. Writing about the Holocaust and World War II was long in her plans, for those events "changed the lives of everybody [she] knew" (Kremer Interview). Deeply affected during her childhood by the responses of her grandmother and mother to Holocaust coverage in the Jewish press, to their realization "that Jews were being rounded up, put in camps, and that many were being killed" ("Dark Thread," p. 173), Piercy links her mother's wartime observation of the world's indifference to the slaughter of European Jewry and her own moral commitment to "Remember always" ("Dark Thread," p. 172). Like many American Jews, Piercy has pondered how she might have behaved and what her fate might have been had she been there: whether she would have resisted, or been spared for slave labor, or subjected to medical experiment, or sent to the gas chamber ("Dark Thread," p. 179). Marriage to Michel Schiff, a French Jew whose family experienced the war in France and as refugees in Switzerland, created an opportunity for her to talk intimately with people possessing direct *Shoah* knowledge. *Gone to Soldiers* (1987) is her monumental World War II novel integrating *Shoah* documentary evidence in a fictional context.

Blended Genres and Choral Voices

Through skillful juxtaposition of narrative modes, including refugee interview, diary, journalistic report, dramatic conflict, and dream fantasy, Piercy dissolves boundaries between discourses to create an epic novel encompassing the European and the Pacific theaters of war, as well as the American homefront, extending the war novel from the training camp and battle zone perspectives to encompass partisan sabotage, torture chamber, concentration camp, research center, and the homefront. Like other feminist authors who eschew single dominant authoritative points of view, Piercy composed *Gone to Soldiers* as a choral work, a cantata privileging multiple points of view and multiple stories, a method attesting to the diversity of *Shoah* experience.

The novel links the stories of two generations of a family with those of professional associates directly engaged in war-related work and the Holocaust. The prewar history of the extended family is quickly sketched through the matriarchal lines of four sisters living in Paris, Shanghai, and Detroit, a reflection of Jewish migration and settlement patterns during the late nineteenth and early twentieth centuries. The strongest, most fully realized characters in the Holocaust chapters are the Lévy-Monot family, especially the father and eldest daughter. The father fights initially with the French army and after its defeat and his escape as a POW, joins the forces of the Jewish resistance. The eldest daughter, Jacqueline, transforms herself from an arrogant adolescent Franco-assimilationist to a resistance fighter and Zionist. Of the younger sisters, Naomi is sent to safe haven in the United States, and her twin, Rivka, disappears with their mother into the clutches of the pro-Nazi French, first incarcerated in Drancy and then Dora Nordhausen. For a Holocaust perspective beyond the knowledge of the victims, the novelist incorporates the vantage point and objective voice of the social scientist as prologue and journalist as epilogue to Holocaust events. Through interviews with German refugees, the Abra chapters (the chapters focusing on the character of Abra) convey early periods of German anti-Jewish discrimination and Nazi dominion. The chapters chronicle German-Jewish misreading of the Nazis as a temporary aberration, the growth and empowerment of Hitler's paramilitary terror squads, support for the Nazis by German industrial barons, and collapse of the opposition's delusions that the major world powers would contain Hitler. Abra's interviews capture the essence of the betrayal German Jews felt and introduce the novel's French Holocaust drama. Similarly, a foreign correspondent, Louise Kahan, provides evidence denied the victims of the large-scale German plunder in a detailed inventory of currencies, art treasures, Jewish ritual artifacts, and personal possessions of victim populations.

France: Occupation and Collaboration

Although *Gone to Soldiers* is fiction, Piercy explains that nothing happens "that had not happened somewhere in the time and place of the work's setting" ("After Words," pp. 702–703). Jacqueline's diary and Naomi's impressionistic speculations and nightmares link public events and private responses, thereby affording Piercy opportunities to develop characters who engage readers and to chart the chronology of the German occupation of the north of France and the establishment and conduct of the pro-Nazi Vichy government in the south. It is through the effective fusion of narrative methods that readers learn of Parisian Jewish immigrants suffering expropriations, curfews, hostage-taking, arrests, and executions, and of the December 1941 arrest of a thousand French Jews, "including all the lawyers who practice at the Paris bar, . . . doctors, writers, and intellectuals" (*Gone to Soldiers*, p. 83). That event demonstrated that the early differentiation between French and immigrant Jews was transitory, that French-born Jews would suffer the same fate as the foreign born. Jacqueline's diary charts the early occupation from the decree compelling the Jews of France to wear the yellow star embossed with the black lettered word *JUIF*, to the roundup and imprisonment of indexed Parisian Jews. Woven among Jacqueline's extended responses to specific edicts are brief third-person accounts of the diminishment of Jewish presence in French society.

The power of Piercy's synthesis of documentary and cantata is revealed in her exposition of French complicity in the 16 July 1942 roundup, arrest, and internment in Vel d'Hiv of almost half the indexed Parisian Jews. Her presentation distinguishes varieties of Holocaust experience and interpretation based on each reflector's physical and political circumstances. Her distance from the events and her reliance on biased news accounts of the event truncate Jacqueline's entry. The victim's perspective appears in Naomi's imagined account of her twin's experience, and a Jewish political perspective from Daniela, a more knowledgeable character with connections to the organized Jewish resistance. Similarly, the Drancy children's deportations are addressed twice; once, when Jacqueline learns from her resistance network that German quotas are being met with "a mass deportation of very young children, many of whom had already lost their parents" (p. 217) and again in an emotionally wrought impressionistic account of the deportation filtered through Naomi's reverie that functions to record the operation and to imagine her fate had she remained in France.

Jewish Resistance: Not to the Slaughter like Sheep

Paralleling her frank and explicit treatment of French collaborationist initiatives is Piercy's effort to debunk the myth that the Jews went passively to slaughter. She pays homage to men and women who fought Fascism in the cafés of Paris, the countryside hideouts, the Montaigne Noire, and the torture chambers of the Milice and Gestapo. Her resistants are modeled on French Jews of exclusive Jewish Resistance units and participants in French units, where they comprised "15 to 20 percent of the active membership . . . although they constituted less than one percent of the French population" (Poliakov, p. 261). The novel's resistance sections benefited from extensive historic research and knowledge Piercy gained from stories of her husband's family and their friends. The fictional resistance centers on the Lévy-Monot patriarch's roles as masquiard leader and commander with the "Armand-Jules," the Jewish army, in Jacqueline's and Daniela Rubin's work. Both women supplied false Aryan documents to fugitive Jews, and served as couriers, saboteurs, and guides leading downed Allied pilots over the heavily patrolled borders into Spain. In addition, Jacqueline performs the dangerous task of finding safe housing for children who could pass as Gentiles, and guides the inconcealable across the Pyrenees for eventual emigration to Palestine. Reflecting historic circumstances, the novel's dominant resistance figures drawn from the ranks of the Jewish Scout Movement, Zionist organizations, and the Jewish immigrant communities, are shown disrupting German goals and assisting Allied preparation for the cross-Channel invasion. In keeping with her focus on authentic portrayal based on research revealing "how very active women were in the Resistance" (Kremer Interview), the feminist author highlights women's resistance roles. Because they were thought to be less vulnerable than men to suspicion of being resistance fighters and because it was easier for women than for men to conceal their Jewish identity, women were particularly numerous as couriers.

Concentration Camp Universe

Piercy circumscribes her fictional treatment of the concentration camps, albeit moving beyond her original intention to present only Naomi's imagined scenes of Dora-Nordhausen (Kremer interview). Two chapters set in Auschwitz and portions of several others suggest the full range of camp themes and depict the physical and psychological struggles of prisoners while addressing the moral and political implications of the Holocaust. The dramatic presentation of Jacqueline's and Daniela's imprisonment in Auschwitz and Bergen-Belsen portrays the women's ignominy as they are stripped, tattooed, shaved of head and body hair, arbitrarily and frequently beaten, starved, and subjected to hard labor.

The hunger and degrading squalor is heightened by the presence of well-fed SS men and women in immaculate uniforms, and is reinforced by the slave labor designed to destroy the workers. Inmates carry huge stones from one end of camp to another, or run double-time while staggering under the weight of heavy sacks of cement. When the prisoners are leased to German industry, the Krupp guards drive them mercilessly. SS and industrial slave masters alike abuse the women verbally and physically, dispensing random blows and exacting hard labor on starvation rations—a system invented to exhaust, to punish, to kill. The women are ordered to strip and parade before SS men and Krupp entrepreneurs who add sexual mockery to economic exploitation.

Only after the women have been interned for several weeks does Piercy employ third-person narrative and archetypal Holocaust imagery to render Auschwitz-Birkenau during 1944 when Hungarian Jews by the hundreds of thousands were being gassed:

> Every day and every night the sky was red with flames, while heavy ash filtered down on them. . . . Every night large piles of bodies were burned in enormous pyres all around the camp, because the crematoria were overloaded. Ash fell from the sky like oily black snow. The stench of burned flesh hung in the air with the stench of decay. Sometimes half an inch of ash lay on everything (*Gone to Soldiers*, p. 574).

Gendered Suffering and Coping Patterns

Because birth and motherhood made women a target population in the camps, it is not surprising to find inmate response to pregnancy, abortion, and infanticide in the work of a feminist like Piercy. These subjects enter the novel through secondary characters who collaborate in hiding pregnancy and birth from camp guards. Escaping Dr. Mengele's detection during the arrival selection meant the prisoner was spared immediate gassing or admission to the medical experimentation block where "He liked to cut open pregnant women, or experiment with the effects of starvation on the fetus or the new born child" (p. 575). The woman endures the birth of her child without benefit of anesthesia in silence, but her infant must die to save the mother's life and those of the conspirators. The scene echoes testimony on clandestine camp deliveries and pays tribute to the selfless heroism of endangered women providing medical assistance and psychological succor to an inmate violating Nazi decrees.

Piercy's fidelity to women's Holocaust experience and commentary appears also in her treatment of women's bonding in pairs or larger surrogate family groups, in recognition that "women tended to try to replicate their lost families" and that "their survival depended on it" (Kremer interview). The importance she attaches to female bonding is evident in the multiple fictive unions she creates, recalling women's testimony describing biological and constructed sisterly and maternal unions. The devotion of mothers and daughters to each other's survival is exemplified in the relationship of Chava and Rivka Lévy-Monot, the generosity of the starving mother "splitting her piece of daily bread and giving half to Rivka, . . . [each watching] the other's few things, the can in which the watery soup was ladled, the scrap of rope, the leg wrappings, the clogs that could not be replaced: any of these stolen could mean death" (p. 433); sustaining each other spiritually and physically, "sometimes Maman sang her Yiddish songs, . . . as they picked the lice from each other, the lice that gave them ulcers and brought typhus that killed" (p. 434).

Bonding that took the form of old-timers or "old numbers" advising the newcomers, a recurrent theme in women's Holocaust writing, is represented in the Auschwitz reunion of Jacqueline with her aunt, who provides her with boots and good counsel. The older woman's survival is the result of her accounting job, which also allowed her to locate her niece, although both are so physically transformed that neither recognizes the other. Characteristic of many old-timers who shared their survival strategies and "organized" food or clothing for newcomers, Jacqueline's aunt Esther parlays the privilege of an office job to trade with warehouse workers to assist others in their battle for survival. Esther also offers sage advice, warning the newcomer to avoid the hospital, where Dr. Mengele uses human subjects for medical experiments, and counseling her to look lively and masquerade as a factory worker so that she will be considered work-worthy, hence fit to live. She arms Jacqueline with the will to survive by suggesting that she think of her mother and sister as among the living. Her parting message is one of support and resistance, urging a dependable union between Jacqueline and Daniela, one in which they watch out for each other, protect each other's property, and imploring her "remember, if you die, they win" (p. 573).

Cooperative association and mutual assistance characterize the camp relationships of all Piercy's women. They help each other stand through the long roll calls, pick lice from each other, nurse one another through typhus, and support each other through hunger by sharing their memories of food. Beyond much-needed physical support, the women also nurture each other intellectually, culturally, and spiritually. Jacqueline teaches English and Daniela Hebrew to barracks mates for whom the lessons offer temporary respite from the hunger, terror, and pain and are a means of feeling human again. Spiritual sustenance is also gained from another inmate lighting makeshift Sabbath candles, "candles of rags or scraps stolen under the pain of death" (p. 575) and from the Bergen-Belsen women celebrating Passover, a seder without food, "slaves telling the story of slaves who had risen up, who had escaped" (p. 607) and finally, developing Zionist postwar plans, insisting they will be a family and go to the land of Israel.

The Long Hatred: Antisemitism

More than most authors, Piercy employs the dramatic and reflective contexts of the novel to expose the diverse social and political manifestations of antisemitism. Her fiction is corroborated in the work of historians who relate the success of Germany's war against European Jewry in some measure to the continent's enduring Christian antisemitic sympathies manifested in centuries of edicts, expulsions, pogroms, and mass murders. Piercy directs the reader's attention to the traditional economic, political, social, religious, and militant forms of antisemitism practiced in Christian nations as a critically generative and supportive agency of Nazi efforts to annihilate world Jewry. Whether in violent pogroms of nineteenth-century Russia or in the social and economic structures of the Western nations, antisemitism is a leitmotif in chapters devoted to nine of the novel's major and minor characters. Piercy's depiction encompasses European and American institutions: church, business, university, press, government, and military, and includes personal antisemitic expressions within the family and social spheres.

Underscoring the pervasiveness of Christian Holocaust culpability, Piercy juxtaposes the novel's violent European antisemitic expressions with social, political, and economic American variations she experienced while growing up in Detroit. Housing covenants kept Jews out of neighborhoods; job discrimination was prevalent. On the airwaves, Reverend J. Frank Norris ranted against "the international godless Jewish conspiracy" (p. 275), "Father Coughlin . . . spewed out his diarrhea of the mouth against Jews from all the radios in the Catholic neighborhoods" (p. 109), and the Ku Klux Klan propagated and inflamed antisemitic passions in the streets. Pervasive antisemitism flourishing during the 1930s and 1940s in Congress and the State Department comes under particular scrutiny in the novel. Chapters devoted to the intelligence services argue that London and Washington knew what the "Final Solution" meant and that through the passive neglect or active hindrance of America and Britain, along with French collaboration, Hitler's goals were significantly advanced. Piercy's ire and political invective are boldly directed at British and American failure to intervene in the genocide process by bombing the rail lines to the killing centers. Even more forceful is her criticism of obstructionist policies thwarting Jewish immigration and rescue, British refusal to allow Jews entry to Palestine, and American failure to assign priority to the rescue, suppressing information about the mass killings and thwarting Jewish organizational rescue efforts by curtailing Jewish immigration to the United States. The media come under criticism for suppressing news of German atrocities, as does the Office of War Information for its "policy of putting out no information on what was known about the [concentration] camps and the fate of the Jews in Europe" (p. 340).

Holocaust Transformation: Post-*Shoah* Jewish Identity

The Jacqueline that readers encounter at the outset of the novel is an exemplar of Alain Finkielkraut's French Israelite paradigm, that is, a Jew who is culturally French and either ignorant or dismissive of Jewish identity. She is shaped by her French education and the phenomenon Hannah Arendt characterizes as the circumstance of the self-hating Jew living "In a society on the whole hostile to Jews . . . [where] it is possible to assimilate only by assimilating antisemitism also" (Arendt quoted by Marks, p. 147). The Jewishly-estranged Jacqueline has lived in an antisemitic society and absorbed its pathology. Jacqueline's transformation is marked by authentic self-definition stemming from experience with antisemitic persecution juxtaposed with respect for Orthodox and Zionist Jews who retain their religious and political convictions under duress. She participates in religious observance; lights makeshift candles, recites Sabbath prayers, and celebrates Passover with barrack mates. She will strive to realize her father's dream of her people's regeneration through adherence to Judaism and establishment of a Jewish homeland rather than live as a marginalized citizen on a continent where one-third of world Jewry has been reduced to ash. *Shoah*-transformed, Jacqueline articulates a bill of accusation against French officials who willingly passed antisemitic legislation, indexed Jews and their properties, and arrested and deported them.

Estrangement from her compatriots is the product of Jacqueline's Holocaust-wrought understanding that Jews are hated, not for what they have done, but simply for being; that antisemites make Jews "stand for an evil they invent and then they want to kill it in us" (p. 255). She now counts herself among the Jewish "we" and the gentile French have become "they," the "others." Drancy was transmogrified as a way station to Auschwitz and Frenchmen willingly turned France into Vichy and replaced French ideals of liberty, equality, and fraternity with tyranny, bigotry, and fratricide. Now, Jacqueline, like her father, rejects postwar repatriation. No longer content to be a Diaspora Jew, the Israelite in a France that views the Jew as Other; no longer grateful for a host nation's mere tolerance, she has a new perception of Jewry's place in the world.

Survivor Syndrome/Survivor Mission: From the Killing Fields of Europe to Creation of a National Homeland

Unlike most American writers who focus on survivor syndrome, Piercy only touches briefly on the theme in wartime and postwar contexts. Beneath her superficial adjustment to a life of school and friends in her American safe harbor, Naomi endures Holocaust anxieties in silence for she correctly recognizes that language is insufficient to convey her knowledge to the innocents about her. Cognizant of how different she is from her American peers who never witnessed bombs falling, cities burning, or crematorium chimneys spewing smoke and ash, the survivor is reluctant to speak of the Holocaust to non-witnesses. The burden of her experience and the knowledge of mass murders she acquires from the Yiddish press is borne in isolation. Her silence is predicated on the wish to please her benefactors and the desire to fit in with schoolmates, an attitude common among children who were being protected either by non-Jews or in a predominantly non-Jewish society during the war. Naomi experiences Holocaust trauma in memories, dreams, and imagined sequences of the July 1942 Paris roundup, Vel d'Hiv, Drancy, and Dora-Nordhausen incarcerations. During the Detroit race riot, when she overhears her American teachers speaking of massing combatants, of people coming with guns, "She wonder[s] if this [is] an invasion" (p. 304). A classmate's suggestion that she join the Jewish group and step away from her black friend prompts Naomi to assume "they'll come to take us away. . . . They'll separate us out the way they took Maman and Rivka" (p. 306).

Classic symptoms of survivor syndrome follow Jacqueline's liberation from Bergen-Belsen. Starvation and typhus have shriveled her to seventy-one pounds. Disoriented, she believes she is back in the camp. She is haunted by nightmare-ravaged sleep, in which ill-clad women are lined up for the winter *appell* (roll-call square), the woman beside her clubbed to death. In dream, "She smelled the burning flesh, . . . saw the open glazed eyes of [the] dead . . . the smear on the wall that was the brains of a child dashed to death by a grinning guard . . . the blood pouring from the severed breast of a woman with a dog set on her, tearing now at her throat" (pp. 641–642). The nightmare landscape is the essential reality; the hospital is "an unplace, among unpeople" (pp. 641–642).

Less interested in the psychology of the survivor than the political implications of the Holocaust, Piercy shifts the focus from Holocaust paralysis to regeneration and renewal. As an accidental survivor of the Paris roundup, Jacqueline is motivated to join the resistance. In the postwar period, she first works for a Displaced Persons office and then is dedicated to building a Jewish nation. "She belonged to no one but the friends who had survived and who were going, as Jews, to make a place where Jews could never be stateless" (p. 683). Regeneration as an Israeli is the former assimilationist's political response to *Shoah* tragedy. Similarly, her return to Judaism, echoed by choral characters Oscar and Louise Kahan, approaches the theme of Jewish religious continuity for Israeli and Diaspora Jews who read the Holocaust as an orienting event in history and a transformative agent in their own lives. Jacqueline's changing discourse signifies her political transformation. As a young Francophile, her tone was that of a French citizen confident of her place in French cultural life and estranged from Judaism. As a hounded Jew of Nazi-occupied Europe, she alternates between caustic lapses into Nazi-Deutsch and resistant defiance; as an Auschwitz survivor, her voice is again double-edged, she is at once the Holocaust-burnished victim and the triumphant Zionist, a self-defined Jew who delivers political speeches rejecting the Hannah Arendt banality of evil thesis, denounces European antisemitism, and champions Jewish self-determination.

Critical Reception

Piercy's awards include two Borestone Mountain Poetry Awards, a National Endowment for the Arts Fellowship, and the Literature Award from the (Massachusetts) Governor's Commission on the Status of Women, the Sheaffer PEN/New England Award for Literary Excellence and the Arthur C. Clark Award for the Best Science Fiction Novel Published in the United Kingdom. There is broad agreement among literary critics that the distinction of the Piercy canon springs from the union of the personal and the political. Characteristic is Susan Mernit's observation that Piercy "sees human beings as interconnected in a social network, having both duties and responsibilities to one another; and it is this conviction, more than anything, that makes her fiction political" (p. 18). *Gone to Soldiers* is consistent with and extends Piercy's narrative pattern of relating the personal to the political, compellingly addressing racism and sexism in the private sphere and in the public realm. Sue Walker contends that "*Gone to Soldiers* should establish Piercy as one of the leading novelists of our time" (p. 146). Kerstin Shands considers it "the masterpiece among Piercy's novels" (Shands, p. 20) and numerous feminist critics laud Piercy for audaciously invading the male territory of war fiction and bringing a feminist point of view to the subject. She has contributed to keeping Holocaust memory alive by grounding her fiction in verifiable details of Holocaust history, producing a work that is at once politically sophisticated and deeply moral.

Bibliography

Primary Sources

Novels

Going Down Fast. 1969.
Dance the Eagle to Sleep. 1970.
Small Changes. 1973.
Woman on the Edge of Time. 1976.
The High Cost of Living. 1978.
Vida. 1979.
Braided Lives. 1982.

Fly Away Home. 1984.
Gone to Soldiers. 1987.
Summer People. 1989.
He, She and It. 1991.
The Longings of Women. 1994.
City of Darkness, City of Light. 1996.
Storm Tide (with Ira Wood). 1998.
Three Women. 1999.

Drama

The Last White Class (coauthored with Ira Wood). 1980.

Essays

Parti-Colored Blocks for a Quilt (essays on poetry). 1982.

Guide for Writers

So You Want to Write: How to Master the Craft of Fiction and the Personal Narrative. 2001.

Memoir

Sleeping with Cats. 2002.

Poetry Collections

Breaking Camp. 1968.
Hard Loving. 1969.
4-Telling Poems. 1971.
To Be of Use. 1973.
Living in the Open. 1976.
The Twelve-Spoked Wheel Flashing. 1978.
The Moon Is Always Female. 1980.
Circles on the Water. 1982.
Stone, Paper, Knife. 1983.
My Mother's Body. 1985.
Available Light. 1988.
The Earth Shines Secretly: A Book of Days (illustrated by Neil Blaine). 1990.
Mars and Her Children. 1992.
What Are Big Girls Made Of? 1997.
Early Grrrl: The Early Poems of Marge Piercy. 1999.
The Art of Blessing the Day: Poems with a Jewish Theme. 1999.

Selected Short Stories

An excerpt from "Maud Awake." *December Magazine* 4 (winter 1963): 184–190. Also in *The Bold New Women*. Edited by Barbara Alson. Greenwich, Conn.: Fawcett, 1965. Rpt. in *Modern Girl* 1 (August 1971): 22–27.
"Going over Jordan." *Transatlantic Review* 22 (fall 1966): 148–157.
"Love Me Tonight, God." *Paris Review* 43 (summer 1968): 185–200.
"A Dynastic Encounter." *Aphra* 3 (spring 1970): 3–10. Rpt. in *The Looking Glass* (1977).
"And I Went into the Garden of Love." *Off Our Backs* (summer 1971): 2–4.
"Do You Love Me?" *Second Wave* 1, no. 4 (1972): 26–27, 40.
"Somebody Who Understands You." *Moving Out* 2,no. 2 (1972): 56–59.
"Little Sister, Cat and Mouse." *Second Wave* 3, no. 1 (fall 1973): 9–12.
"God's Blood." *Anon* 8 (1974): 50–59.
"Like a Great Door Closing Suddenly." *Detroit Discovery* (March/April 1974): 45–50.
"The Retreat." *Provincetown Poets* 2, nos. 2–3 (1976): 9–11.
"The Cowbirds in the Eagle's Nest." *Maenad* 1, no. 1 (fall 1980): 17–32.
"I Will Not Describe What I Did." *Mother Jones* 7, no. 11 (February/March 1982): 45–56.
"Spring in the Arboretum." *Michigan Quarterly Review* 21, no. 1 (winter 1982): 96–99.

Selected Criticism and Essays

"The Foreign Policy Association: Fifty Years of Successful Imperialism." *CAW* 1 (February 1968): 6–10.
"The Grand Coolie Dam." *Leviathan* (November 1969): 16–18.
"Women's Liberation: Nobody's Baby Now." *Defiance* 1 (1970): 134–162.
"Tom Eliot Meets the Hulk at Little Big Horn: The Political Economy of Poetry." With Dick Lourie. *Triquarterly: Literature in Revolution* 23–24 (spring 1972): 5791.
"Through the Cracks." *Partisan Review* 41, no. 2 (1974): 202–216.
"The White Christmas Blues." With Uta West. *Provincetown Advocate*, 9 January 1975.
"Writer's Choice." *Partisan Review* 42, no. 1 (1975): 156–157.
"From Where I Work." *American Poetry Review* 5, no. 2 (March/April 1976): 11.
"From Where I Work." *American Poetry Review* 6, no. 3 (May/June 1977): 27.
"Feminist Perspectives." *Sojourner* 4, no. 4 (January 1979): 7.
"Inviting the Muse." *Negative Capability* 2, no. 1 (winter 1981): 5–15. Reprinted in *Poets' Perspectives: Reading, Writing, and Teaching Poetry*. Edited by Charles R. Dude and Sally A. Jacobsen. Portsmouth, N.H.: Boynton/Cook, 1992.
"Memory Annex." *Ariadne's Thread: A Collection of Contemporary Women's Journals*. Edited by Lyn Lifshin. New York: Harper and Row, 1982, pp. 58–61.
"Lost and Found." Foreword to *The Zanzibar Cat* by Joanna Russ. Sauk City, Wisc.: Arkham House, 1983, pp. vii-xii.
"On Jewish Identity." *Smate* 2.8 (1984): 25–27.
"Poets on Poetry." *Literary Calvacade* (October 1984): 24–25.
"Autobiography." *Contemporary Authors Autobiography Series*, vol. 1. Edited by Dedria Bryfonski. Detroit: Gale, 1984, pp. 267–281.
"E. M. Broner." *Contemporary Novelists*. 4th ed. London: St. James Press, 1986, pp. 144–146.
"Joanna Russ." *Contemporary Novelists*. 4th ed. London: St. James Press, 1986, pp. 791–792.
"Me and My Novel." *The Boston Review* 12, no. 3 (June 1987): 19.
"Of Arms and the Woman." *Harper's Magazine* 274, no. 1645 (June 1987): 30–32.
"A Symposium on Contemporary American Fiction." *Michigan Quarterly Review* 27, no. 1 (winter 1988): 105–107.
"Rooms without Walls." *Ms.* (April 1988): 36–37.
Foreword. *Back Rooms: Voices from the Illegal Abortion Era*. Edited by Ellen Messer and Kathryn E. May. New York: St. Martin's Press, 1988, pp. i–x.
"What Rides the Wind." *Tikkun: A Bimonthly Jewish Critique of Politics, Culture & Society* 4, no. 2 (March/April 1989): 58–62.
"A Writer's Garden." *Organic Gardening* 36, no. 6 (June 1989): 72.
"What I Do When I Write." *Women's Review of Books* 6, nos. 10–11 (July 1989): 25–26.
"Active in Time and History." *Paths of Resistance: The Art and Craft of the Novel*. Edited by William Zinsser. Boston: Houghton Mifflin, 1989, pp. 90–123.
"The Dark Thread in the Weave." *Testimony: Contemporary Writers Make the Holocaust Personal*. Edited by David Rosenberg. New York: Random House, 1989, pp. 171–191.

"Simone de Beauvoir." *Daughters of de Beauvoir*. Edited by Penny Forster and Imogen Sutton. London: Women's Press, 1989, pp. 112–123.

"Autobiography." *Cream City Review* 4, no. 1 (spring 1990): 3–5.

"Starting Support Groups for Writers." *Literacy in Process*. Edited by Brenda Miller Power and Ruth Hubbard. Portsmouth, N.H.: Heinemann, 1991, pp. 14–18.

"How I Came to Walt Whitman and Found Myself." *Massachusetts Review* 33, no. 1 (spring 1992): 98–100.

Foreword to *Lost in Space* by Marleen S. Barr. Chapel Hill: University of North Carolina Press, 1993.

Other Works

Edited and Introduction to *Early Ripening: American Women's Poetry Now*. New York: Pandora, 1987.

Broadsides and Chapbooks

(List Compiled by Marge Piercy)

A Work of Artifice. Detroit: Red Hanrahan Press, 1972.

"Closing."

"For Shelter and Beyond." *Woman's Day* broadside. 26 August 1976.

In the Dark All Cats Fly. Iron Mountain Press broadside. 1988.

"For the Young Who Want To." The Zoland Books Poetry Postcard Collection. 1989.

Secondary Sources

Allison, Dorothy. "Marge Piercy Makes War." Review of *Gone to Soldiers*. *Village Voice*, 19 May 1987, 45.

Arendt, Hannah. Letter to Kurt Blumenfeld. Quoted by Elaine Marks in *Marrano as Metaphor: The Jewish Presence in French Writing*. New York: Columbia University Press, 1996.

Barr, Marlene S. *Feminist Fabulation: Space/Postmodern Fiction*. Iowa City: University of Iowa Press, 1992.

Doherty, Patricia. *Marge Piercy: An Annotated Bibliography*. Westport, Conn.: Greenwood, 1997.

Finkielkraut, Alain. *The Imaginary Jew*. Translated by Kevin O'Neill. Lincoln: Unversity of Nebraska Press, 1994.

Hansen, Elaine Tuttle, and William J. Scheik. "A Bibliography and Writings by Marge Piercy." *Contemporary American Women Writers*. Edited by Catherine Rainwater and William Scheick. Lexington: University of Kentucky Press, 1985, pp. 224–228.

Henderson, Katherine Usher. "Marge Piercy." *Inter/view: Talks with America's Writing Women*. Edited by Katherine Usher Henderson and Mickey Pearlman. Lexington: University of Kentucky Press, 1990, pp. 65–71.

Kremer, S. Lillian. "Marge Piercy." *Women's Holocaust Writing: Memory and Imagination*. Lincoln: University of Nebraska Press, 1999, pp. 176–211.

Kress, Susan. "In and Out of Time: The Form of Marge Piercy's Novels." *Future Females: A Critical Anthology*. Edited by Marleen S. Barr. Bowling Green: Bowling Green State University Popular Press, 1981, pp. 109–122.

Levitsky, Holli. "Marge Piercy (1936–)." *Contemporary Jewish-American Novelists: A Bio-Critical Sourcebook*. Edited by Joel Shatzky and Michael Taub. Westport, Conn.: Greenwood Press, 1997.

Linkon, Sherry Lee. "A Way of Being Jewish That Is Mine: Gender and Ethnicity in the Jewish Novels of Marge Piercy." *Studies in American Jewish Literature* 13 (1994): 93–105.

Lodenson, Joyce R. "Political Themes and Personal Preoccupations in Marge Piercy's Novels." Edited by Sue Walker and Eugenie Hamner. *Ways of Knowing: Essays on Marge Piercy*. Mobile: Negative Capability Press, 1991.

Mernit, Susan. "Suburban Housewife Makes Good." *The Women's Review of Books* 1, no. 11 (August 1984): 18.

Montresor, Jaye Berman. "Marge Piercy." *Jewish American Women Writers: A Bio-Bibliographical and Critical Sourcebook*. Edited by Ann R. Shapiro, Sara R. Horowitz, Ellen Schiff, and Miriyam Glazer. Westport, Conn.: Greenwood Press, 1994.

Nowik, Nan. "Mixing Art and Politics: The Writings of Adrienne Rich, Marge Piercy, and Alice Walker." *Centennial Review* 30 (spring 1986): 208–218.

Poliakov, Leon. "Jewish Resistance in France." *YIVO: Annual of Jewish Social Science* 8 (1953): 252–263.

Rigney, Barbara Hill. *Lilith's Daughters: Women and Religion in Contemporary Fiction*. Madison, Wisc.: University of Wisconsin Press, 1982.

Robson, Ruth. "Women's Writing/Male Subjects." *Kalliope* 9, no. 3 (1987): 72–78.

Shands, Kerstin W. *The Repair of the World: The Novels of Marge Piercy*. Westport, Conn.: Greenwood Press, 1994.

Walker, Sue, and Eugenie Hamner, eds. *Ways of Knowing: Essays on Marge Piercy*. Mobile: Negative Capability Press, 1991.

Interviews

Kremer, S. Lillian. Interview with Marge Piercy. 26 May 1988.

Rodden, John. "A Harsh Day's Light: An Interview with Marge Piercy." *The Kenyon Review* 20, no. 2 (spring 1998): 132–143.

Sanoff, Alan. "A Woman Writer Treads on Male Turf." *U.S. News & World Report*, 8 May 1989, p. 74.

Walker, Sue, and Eugenie Hamner. *Ways of Knowing: Essays on Marge Piercy*. Edited by Sue Walker and Eugenie Hamner. Mobile: Negative Capability Press, 1981.

JÁNOS PILINSZKY

(1921–1981)

RICHARD CHESS

JÁNOS PILINSZKY WAS born 27 November 1921 in Budapest, Hungary, where his father was a postmaster with a law degree. Pilinszky finished secondary school and then studied at Péter Pázmány University, both in Budapest, though he never took his doctorate. Poor health and his status as a student resulted in his receiving several deferments from military service. He was finally called up in November 1944, and he served with Axis forces as a laborer. This service brought him face to face with extermination camps. His active service ended when he suffered serious illness and was sent to a United Nations Relief and Rehabilitation Agency in Frankfurt. His poetry of witness led some to speculate about his actual internment in a camp as a political prisoner. When asked if he was ever interned in a camp as a political prisoner, Pilinszky replied, "It's so much besides the point! Tolstoy did not participate in the Napoleonic wars, either" (quoted in *Metropolitan Icons*, edited and translated by Emery George, Lewiston, N.Y.: Mellen Press, 1995, p. xx; all page citations and quotations from Pilinszky's work hereafter refer to this volume). Pilinszky was, however, an eyewitness to the suffering and crimes of which he writes, and his identification with the victims was intense. (George pp. xx–xxi)

Pilinszky discusses the centrality of the Holocaust to his vision in an essay entitled "Instead of an *ars poetica*":

> Today, Auschwitz is a museum. Within its walls, the past—and in a certain sense, the past that belongs to every one of us—is here present with that infinite weight and that plainness that is at all times reality's innermost virtue; and for its doors having been closed, it has become more real, more valid still. . . .
>
> All that happened here is scandal insofar as it *could* happen, and sacred without exception insofar as it *did* happen (George p. xxi).

His first book of poetry, *Trapéz és korlát* (Trapeze and Parallel Bars), was published in 1946. His second poetry collection, *Harmadnapon* (On the Third Day), which includes most of his major Holocaust poems, was published in 1959. He published four more books of poetry and altogether published 214 poems in his lifetime. His writing also includes three verse tales for children, four minimalist plays, interviews and conversations, and two large volumes of collected occasional prose. Many of the essays were first published in the Catholic weekly *Új Ember* (New Man), of which Pilinszky, a Catholic existentialist himself, was a contributing editor from 1957 until his death. (George xxii–xxiii)

Pilinszky lived his entire life in Hungary, but, significantly, in 1969, 1972, 1976, and 1980, he traveled to England, where he met a number of leading English-language poets including Ted Hughes, who published the first translations of Pilinszky into English in 1976. During his career Pilinszky received three prominent awards for his writing: the Baumgarten Prize in 1947, the Attila József Prize in 1971, and the Kossuth Prize for lifetime achievement in letters in 1980 (George xxiv). He died in Budapest of a sudden heart attack on 27 May 1981.

Major Holocaust Poems

Pilinszky's second book, *Harmadnapon*, contains the greatest number of his poems about war and the Holocaust, including "Harbach 1944," "French Prisoner," "On a KZ Lager's Wall," "Ravensbrück Passion," "Frankfurt," and "Apocrypha." In these poems in particular, published in 1959, one senses the continuing presence of the Holocaust, a presence that, paradoxically, becomes more "real" over time. Though Auschwitz's doors had been closed fourteen years before the publication of this book, the facts of what happened there were then, in 1959, continuing to be brought out into the open and the meanings of those facts were only beginning to become clear. What Pilinszky witnessed when he served in the army at the end of the war—human suffering, deprivation, degradation, and death—shaped his vision of humankind. In his poems, he represents humans reduced to the status of beasts, struggling to survive in a godless world in which perpetrator and bystander alike share in the responsibility for the crimes of the Holocaust. The following statement, addressed to a victim in the poem "On a KZ Lager's Wall," can be read as a central theme of Pilinszky's Holocaust poetry: "Where you fell, there you will remain" (p. 29). The horrific events he witnessed in 1944 and 1945 remain fixed in his memory and serve as the point from which all of his poems of memory and invention depart.

The poems include many documentary details such as images of men harnessed to the shaft of an enormous cart and a prisoner gorging on a stolen turnip. But the poems go beyond documentation. Using figurative language, the poems try to suggest the quality of existence to which prisoners of labor and extermination camps have been reduced: one in which intellect, spirit, and emotion cease to function. All that remains is the physical, but even their bodies betray them. In "Harbach 1944," for instance, the "gigantic cart" the men pull "grows with the growing night." As the malnourished prisoners continue to haul their ever-increasing burden, "dust, hunger," and even their own "trembling" "take a bite" from "their bodies" (p. 21). Everything—the environment, their own basic needs and uncontrollable physical functions—turns against them.

All civilizing elements of life taken from them, the starving prisoners, now just bodies themselves, regard each other as merely bodies and ultimately as potential food. Rather than seeing himself as different from the victims, Pilinszky argues that his relations to others, too, even in the post-Holocaust period, are cannibalistic. In "Paraphrase," a poem that represents a general condition of being resulting from the war, Pilinszky willingly offers his body "for everyone's nourishment": "I give myself to the world /as living food" (p. 13). Having characterized his bed as a trough from which he feeds his heartbeat to others, in the poem Pilinszky concludes:

. . . whoever in the end is no one's,
is everyone's morsel.
Destroy me, then, terrible love.
Kill me. Don't leave me to myself (p. 15).

In the absence of relationship with a significant other or of God (one connotation of the statement "whoever in the end is no one's"), the latter a terrible loss for a Catholic, the only act of "love" left is for one human to kill (to eat) another.

The loss of hope or belief in grace or redemption is a theme also suggested by "Harbach 1944." After describing how the prisoners "totter / in one another's footsteps" (p. 21) as they drag the heavy cart, Pilinszky suggests that they are entering some body of water: not one in which they will be cleansed and healed but one in which they will drown: "to their knees they wade" (p. 21). From there, "they dip their faces aloft . . . as if they sniffed/heaven's faraway troughs" (p. 23). If heaven is a trough, then those who regard it as such have been reduced to the condition of hungry farm animals. Indeed, in the next stanza "heaven" is characterized as "some . . . pen," "wildly" opening "its gates to the hinges" (p. 23). Alas, even this debased vision of heaven as pigpen is reduced further. The poem's final characterization of heaven and its beckoning gates—"death has flung itself open" (p. 23)—implies that heaven as an idea of redemption—an image of the Kingdom of God—has itself been executed. The salvation these prisoners long for is not life after death but rather death itself, an end to physical suffering.

Any attempts to return to the old, prewar order is futile, Pilinszky argues in "Apocrypha." In this poem, the speaker sees himself as a kind of prodigal son returning home after the war. When he arrives, "the old order receives [him] back," and he "prop[s his] elbows on the windswept stars" (p. 49). What he quickly discovers, however, is that he no longer shares a common language, a "human language," with which to converse with others.

I don't understand human speech,
and of your language I speak not a word.
My word is more homeless than the Word!
I *have* no word.
  Its dreadful weight
tumbles down through air,
a tower's body gives off sounds (p. 51).

In the absence of a common language, every man having become his own tower of Babel, civilization collapses.

Human life, of course, continues after the war, but it is characterized by the alienation of one person from another, even among people who have shared common experiences. This is a central theme of Pilinszky's powerful "KZ Oratorio." The "Oratorio" features three speakers: a young girl, a young boy, and an old woman. By their costumes—striped prison uniform, black dress, gray smock—we can tell that they are inmates or former inmates of concentration and extermination camps. In the "Oratorio," we are offered fragments of each of their stories of wartime and postwar experiences. There is little continuity in the dialogue, thus very little direct interaction among the characters. The inability to focus on and sustain discussion on one topic at a time implies an inability to form community, society. Standing side by side, the three characters speak of a common experience but fail to weave a whole fabric of the threads of their experiences.

Language—oral or written—in the post-Holocaust world may fail to communicate. Visual imagery, however, may take its place as the dominant mode of communication. This idea is suggested by Pilinszky's "Ravensbrück Passion." In the beginning of this poem, one prisoner "steps out from among the rest" and appears to us "like a projected picture" (p. 31). "Fearfully alone," he stands before us, seeming at once "gigantic" and "minuscule": monstrous and insignificant. Then, forgetting "to let out a shout," he "fall[s] down in a heap" (p. 31). This poem, offering us a Christ figure for our time, is a good example of Pilinszky's vision of the Holocaust as "humanity crucified" (p. xxviii). Unlike Christ himself, however, this victim, whose haunting silence remains with us, comes not to redeem but rather to indict us. The implications of this poem are stated explicitly in the conclusion of "On a KZ Lager's Wall": "you will not yield any more now," the final quatrain begins, concluding, "Mutely, even mutely, you testify against us" (p. 29).

Underlying these dark, apparently hopeless poems is, ultimately, a modest desire to contribute something morally useful to the world. This desire is expressed in "Admonition," a kind of *ars poetica*:

Not breathing. Panting.
Not the wedding table. The falling
scraps, the cold, the shadows.
Not movement. Clutching at straws.
The hook's silence: note that.

. . . .

Then perhaps in your lifetime still
you may release as news
what alone is worth your while releasing.

Scribe:
then perhaps you will not have been here in vain (p. 129).

In his poetry, János Pilinszky offers us a vision, writes Ted Hughes, of "humanity stripped of everything but the biological persistence of cells" (Hughes, p. 9). In Pilinszky's post-Holocaust world, men are at once turned against and thrust upon one another in the most horrific ways. Neither God nor Christ appears to offer hope for redemption. Yet, it is in the very "moment closest to extinction," argues Hughes, that Pilinszky locates the source of creativity. Against the limitations of language, János Pilinszky crafts poems that in the very fabric of their being breathe and sway readers toward life.

Poetry translated by Emery George.

Bibliography

Primary Sources in Hungarian

Trapéz és korlát: Versek (Trapeze and Parallel Bars: Poems). 1946.

Aranymadár: Mesék (Golden Bird: Fairy Tales). 1957.

Harmadnapon: Versek (On the Third Day: Poems). 1959.

Rekviem (Requiem). 1964.

Nagyvárosi ikonok: Összegyüjtött versek 1940–1970 (Metropolitan Icons: Collected Poems, 1940–1970). 1970.

Szálkák (Splinters). 1972.

Végkifejlet: Versek és színmüvek (Dénouement: Poems and Plays). 1974.

A nap születése (Birth of the Sun). 1974.

Kráter: Összegyűjtött és új versek (Crater: Collected and New Poems). 1976.

Válogatott művei (Selected Works of János Pilinszky). 1978.

Szög és olaj: Próza (Nail and Oil: Prose). 1982.

Beszélgetések Pilinszky Jánossal (Conversations with János Pilinszky). 1983.

A mélypont ünnepélye: Próza (Celebration of Nadir: Prose). 1984.

Összegyűjtött versei (Collected Poems of János Pilinszky). 1987.

Kalandozás a tükörben: Mese (Adventures in the Mirror: Fairy Tale). 1988.

Primary Sources in English

Selected Poems. Translated by Ted Hughes and János Csokits. 1976.

Crater: Poems 1974–1975. Translated by Peter Jay. 1978.

The Desert of Love: Selected Poems. Translated by János Csokits and Ted Hughes, with a memoir by Ágnes Nemes-Nagy. 1989.

Sixty-Six Poems. Translated by István Tótfalusi. 1991.

Conversations with Sheryl Sutton: The Novel of a Dialogue. Translated by Peter Jay and Éva Major. 1992.

Wüstenei der Liebe/The Desert of Love. (Poems in English and German translation.) Translated by Hans-Henning Paetzke, Eva Czjzek, János Csokits, Ted Hughes, et al. 1992.

Metropolitan Icons: Selected Poems of János Pilinszky in Hungarian and in English. Edited and translated by Emery George. 1995.

Secondary Sources

Csokits, Janos. "János Pilinszky's 'Desert of Love': A Note." In *Translating Poetry: The Double Labyrinth.* Edited by Daniel Weissbort. Iowa City: University of Iowa Press, 1989, pp. 9–15.

Gifford, Henry. "Final Realities." *Times Literary Supplement,* 21 January 1977, p. 50.

Hughes, Ted. "Postscript to János Csokits' Note." In *Translating Poetry: The Double Labyrinth.* Edited by Daniel Weissbort. Iowa City: University of Iowa Press, 1989, pp. 9–15.

Nemes-Nagy, Ágnes. "János Pilinszky: A Very Different Poet." *Hungarian Quarterly* 22, no. 84 (winter 1981): 54–59.

Sanders, Ivan. "The Holocaust in Contemporary Hungarian Literature." In *The Holocaust in Hungary Forty Years Later.* Edited by Randolph L. Braham and Bélá Vago. New York: East European Monographs, 190. Columbia University Press, 1985, pp. 191–202.

Spilleth, Meg. "The Insistent Silence of Grace." *Pequod* 38 (1994): 101–106.

Interview

Interview by Janos Szilagyi. In *New Hungarian Quarterly* 21, no. 77 (spring 1980): 114–122.

HAROLD PINTER

(1930–)

CHARLES V. GRIMES

THE BRITISH DRAMATIST Harold Pinter has made the Holocaust a theme in a number of works. Born in 1930 to Jewish parents in London, Pinter was evacuated to Cornwall during World War II. He disavows religious belief but remains conscious of his identity as a Jew: "I was never a religious Jew . . . but I'm still Jewish" (*Various Voices*, New York: Grace Press, 1998, p. 69). Pinter responds personally and artistically to Jewish suffering through history (Knowles p. 4; Billington, 1996, p. 81). Much of his theater engages ethical issues connected to the Holocaust, particularly the abuse of power and the amorality of a world of oppressors and oppressed. The genocide arguably appears sub rosa in several plays, as Pinter creates a world of officialized violence and deadly persecution. After 1980, Pinter's plays began to reference politics openly, depicting abuse of power as a historical constant. Thus he sees nothing unique about Nazi evil qua evil; the powerful impose their will without mercy or morality. Pinter views the Holocaust as distinctive because of its perpetrators' careful, rational, self-approving manner: "The Holocaust was probably the worst thing that ever happened, because it was so calculated, deliberate and precise, and so fully documented by the people who actually did it" (*Various Voices*, p. 65). In *Ashes to Ashes* (1996), Pinter dramatized the Holocaust openly, allowing readers to see the significance of the genocide to his previous work.

The Holocaust in the Background: *The Birthday Party, The Dumb Waiter, The Hothouse, Mountain Language*

The Birthday Party (1958) is a complex allegory in which Jewishness, guilt, and police-state terrorism figure prominently. Stanley Weber, a failed pianist, is confronted by Goldberg and McCann, who seek to abduct him on behalf of an unspecified "organization." Goldberg invokes his Jewishness while accusing Stanley of heresy, interrogating him until he loses his mind. Is Stanley to be seen as a Jewish victim of Gestapo-like tactics? Does Goldberg's Jewishness suggest a universal, not strictly German, tendency to violence and oppression? The year 1957's *The Dumb Waiter* features two characters like Goldberg, killers employed by an "organization." Ben is the perfect conscienceless functionary while Gus is dimly ethical. The critic D. Keith Peacock writes, "The question of responsibility for causing someone's death, which had recent historical parallels in the Nuremberg War Crime Trials of only eleven years earlier, is the central concern of the play" (*Harold Pinter and the New British Theatre*, Westport, Conn.: Greenwood Press, 1997, p. 71). The play does not refer to the Holocaust, but Peacock's notion is not inappropriate—the play concerns the legitimation and banalization of violence and evil. Both plays imply that obeying an organization, however murderous, is a universal capacity. Thus Pinter assigns Nazi-like qualities to the Jew Goldberg and Englishmen Ben and Gus. Pinter believes seeing ourselves as innocent while labeling others "monsters" is morally fallacious: "we have an obligation to subject our own actions and attitudes to . . . critical and moral scrutiny" (Hern, p. 9). Self-criticism is a prime duty, to be placed ahead of judging others: "We must pay attention to what is being done in our name" (Billington, 1996, p. 323).

The Hothouse (written 1958, performed and published 1980) takes place in a Soviet-style psychiatric jail, an asylum, or perhaps a concentration camp. Rosette C. Lamont sees the play as a parable of the genocide. The inmates have numbers instead of names, and in the hothouse as in the German camps, a "medical" establishment supports a vast killing operation (p. 42). The head of the hothouse investigates the killing of a female inmate who, against the rules, has just given birth. Lamont notes allusions to Nazi sterilization programs and to the death-camp policy of killing new mothers and their infants (pp. 42, 44). The play's vocabulary, Lamont argues (p. 44), reveals its historical source: Colonel Roote remembers his predecessor giving a speech to "row upon row of electrified faces" (compare the electrified fences surrounding the camps) in a room filled to "suffocation" (p. 38); Roote even exclaims: "It's damn hot, isn't it? It's like a crematorium in here" (p. 94). Lamont connects the institution's desire for order and cleanliness to Nazi ideology about subversive, "dirty" Jews (p. 46). Similarly, in Pinter's political plays after 1980, his villains use metaphors of infection to describe their enemies while praising themselves as "clean" (*Party Time*, p. 38). And like National Socialism, which extensively propagandized German youth, the hothouse seeks to substitute the state for the family as the source of identity and love. Any powerful government is capable of stripping its citizens of human dignity, as in the hothouse one of its workers, "Lamb," is first tortured, then scapegoated for the hothouse's misdeeds. *Mountain Language* (1988) exemplifies Pinter's political theater. The play's setting is a prison where the regime isolates, tortures, and finally subjugates "mountain people" for no reason other than their ethnic differences.

Pinter as Director of Holocaust Plays

Pinter's career as a director underscores his political turn. Jane Stanton Hitchcock's *Vanilla*, Donald Freed's *Circe and Bravo*, and Jean Giraudoux's *The Trojan War Will Not Take Place*, all of which Pinter has directed, concern abuse of power. This theme links Pinter's political productions to his works that specifically allude to the Holocaust. Also, Pinter seems to use directing to prepare for his writing: *Party Time*, about ultrarich fascists, was written a year after he directed Hitchcock's *Vanilla*, on the same theme, while *Ashes to Ashes* premiered the year after Pinter staged Ronald Harwood's *Taking Sides*, which also addresses Nazi Germany.

Pinter directed *The Man in the Glass Booth* by Robert Shaw in London (1967) and New York (1968); he also helped rewrite the script during rehearsals. In a grotesque inversion, Arthur Goldman, a Jewish businessman, assumes the identity of Colonel Dorff, a sadistic Nazi. Unlike Adolf Eichmann, who pleaded that he had never victimized Jews in a direct, sadistic manner, Dorff at his trial revels in his viciousness. He calls the Jews sheep, mocks them as the chosen people, and refers to the cooperation of the *Judenrate* with the Final Solution—one thinks of Hannah Arendt's controversial discussion of Jewish complicity in *Eichmann in Jerusalem*. Goldman as Dorff claims that if Hitler had chosen the Jews to lead, they would have followed. This assertion of moral equivalence leads an Old Woman to unmask Goldman as not Dorff but a Jewish survivor. Even when unmasked as innocent, Goldman continues his charade—reviewer Walter Kerr noted that Pinter's directing emphasized a wish for martyrdom, perhaps inspired by survivor's guilt, as motivation for Goldman's impersonation. This compelling play is often revived. However, the literary critic Robert Skloot claims that the play evades honest engagement with the moral issues of the Holocaust (*The Darkness We Carry*, pp. 83–87). Edward Isser observes that Goldman's antisemitic accusations of Jewish complicity and moral equivalence between Jews and Nazis are never rebutted in the play, and he argues that these themes typify British Holocaust drama (*Stages of Annihilation*, pp. 49–51). Seeing oppression as universal leads Pinter to present Nazism as an example of radical evil rather than in its singularity. If the Holocaust is not unique, it is not necessarily unforgivable. Thus, Michael Billington notes that Pinter, through *The Man in the Glass Booth* (Robert Shaw, New York: Samuel French, 1967), sought to ask whether "the Germans should be absolved for the killing of the Jews" (p. 194).

In 1995 Pinter directed Ronald Harwood's *Taking Sides*, about the "denazification" of German conductor Wilhelm Furtwängler. Was Furtwängler a tool of the regime or an apolitical artist? Major Arnold, a former insurance investigator and proud philistine, treats Furtwängler as a hypocrite who benefited from Hitler's patronage, while Captain Wills, a German-born Jew, wonders whether he, in the conductor's place, would have chosen exile over comfort. Though Harwood intends a balanced debate, he ignores counterexamples such as Bertolt Brecht and Thomas Mann, who chose exile and spoke out against the Nazis. Also, Furtwängler's notion that music transports us above politics meets no objection. Compare George Steiner: "We know now that a man can read Goethe or Rilke in the evening, that he can play Bach and Schubert, and go to his day's work in Auschwitz in the morning" (*Language and Silence: Essays on Language, Literature, and the Inhuman*, New York: Atheneum, 1967). Ultimately, Furtwängler is exonerated, but Major Arnold spreads media disinformation about him: is this justice or vengeance? Through this final ambiguity, the play criticizes postwar attempts by the conquering nations to assess Germany's guilt for its Nazi past.

Fred Uhlman's *Reunion*: The Rise and Legacy of Nazism in Germany

German guilt is a theme in Pinter's screenplay of Fred Uhlman's novella *Reunion*, filmed in 1988. The 1977 novella, by German-born Uhlman, who opposed the Nazis and emigrated to England in 1933, narrates a prewar friendship between a young Jew, Hans Schwarz, and an aristocratic German, Konradin von Hohenfels. Konradin's antisemitic parents pressure him until he renounces his friendship with Hans. Hans's parents send him to America, and Konradin decides Hitler is Germany's best hope. Ultimately, Hans, middle-aged and calling himself Henry, discovers that his friend was executed for involvement in the 20 July 1944 plot to assassinate Hitler, an ill-fated coup attempt in which a cadre of German officers led by Claus von Stauffenberg bombed Hitler's headquarters but failed to kill him.

Pinter's treatment of German resistance qualifies Konradin's betrayal of Hans, and German guilt in general, by pointing to a "good Nazi" who gave his life to oppose Hitler. However, Pinter's portrayal of the resistance as unequivocally heroic conflicts with historical assessments. Hannah Arendt, for example, views the conspirators as opportunistic and nationalistic; Theodore S. Hamerow and Daniel Goldhagen note that many resisters subscribed to antisemitism and early Nazi ideology. But Pinter complicates the issue of German guilt by inventing scenes in which Henry, visiting Stuttgart in 1988, encounters sinister-seeming Germans who appear to hide their complicity in the Nazi past. A childhood friend mysteriously denies knowledge of Konradin, apparently still believing him a traitor to Germany. Henry rages at an antisemitic taxi driver, asserting that he must acknowledge his country's deeds.

Ashes to Ashes: The Holocaust and the Present

Ashes to Ashes (1996), greeted as Pinter's best work in years, represents his most direct investigation of Nazi genocide. This play approaches the Holocaust allusively, as Rebecca, an Englishwoman in her forties, confronts her husband, Devlin, with stories evoking genocidal horror. Since the play is set in the present, her stories cannot be "true" in the sense that they happened to her; but they are real because they, or something very like them, occurred to others. Pinter presents Holocaust history as memory; and genocidal imagery affects Rebecca even though she, like Pinter, did not experience Nazism firsthand. Rebecca describes an abusive affair with a certain "courier," "guide," or "guard," who took part in an "atrocity" (London and Boston: Faber and Faber, 1996, p. 41). Her stories blend the historical with the contemporary, alluding to Nazi Germany and evoking "ethnic cleansing" in 1990s Europe, while her accounts of sexual abuse link political fascism to private life. Devlin denies that Rebecca truly knows the horrors she narrates: "What authority do you think you yourself possess which would give you the right to discuss such an atrocity?" Rebecca replies, "I have no such authority. Nothing has ever happened to me" (p. 41). Through Rebecca, Pinter illustrates imagination as moral engagement. Rebecca tells stories to acknowledge human victimization, just as Pinter tries to awaken audiences to historical suffering. Through Devlin, Pinter dramatizes the conflict between personal experience as inviolate and private, and human experience as shared, thereby suggesting how we rationalize moral indifference to others.

Rebecca's final silence is ambiguous. Lawrence L. Langer proposes that Holocaust literature may invoke both the "redemptive" and the "grievous power of memory" but should not emphasize the former, positive quality over the ultimate reality of catastrophic loss (*Admitting the Holocaust:* p. 6). Critics Francis Gillen and Katherine H. Burkman stress redemption, arguing that Rebecca transcends victimhood through empathizing with others. An alternative reading privileges grief and loss, portraying Rebecca's silence as isolation and the stilling of her empathetic voice much as dissent is silenced in Pinter's political plays. Is Rebecca's silence the renunciation of speech, of memory, of human connection? In this reading the present no longer allows the presence of the past, and we may witness the end of witness, the disappearance of testimony to the death-camp universe. Langer asserts that something in psychology or society works against remembering extreme victimization: "[H]umiliated memory negates the impulse to historical inquiry. Posterity not only can do without it; it prefers to ignore it" (*Holocaust Testimonies*, p. 79).

Pinter began writing *Ashes to Ashes* after reading Gitta Sereny's *Albert Speer: His Battle with Truth*. Rebecca's visit with her lover to a "factory" is based on Speer's 1943 visit to Dora, an underground work camp built to produce V-2 rockets (Sereny, p. 404; see also Jean Michel's *Dora*, pp. 61–63). As Rebecca is opposed, perhaps silenced, by an unwillingness to attend to historical memory, *Ashes to Ashes* points to "compassion fatigue" (p. 344), Sereny's term for the feeling that there is so much suffering, it is useless or impossible to pay heed. In 1985 Pinter remarked: "[N]ow it's only too easy to ignore the horror of what's going on around us" (Hern, p. 9). Sereny sees Speer's Nazi-like qualities as empathetically limited rather than knowingly evil (p. 719), while historian Joachim Fest analyzes Speer's substitution of professional expertise for moral responsibility—traits that also describe Devlin. Perhaps influenced by Sereny's notation that two-thirds of the Holocaust's victims were women and children (p. 344), in her final story, Pinter's Rebecca tries to rescue a baby but surrenders it to her guard-lover. This narrative illustrates the destruction of the innocent, while reversing the familiar, sentimental paradigm of rescue, a staple of movies such as *Schindler's List*.

Pinter describes himself as having "been haunted by [Nazi] images for many years" (*Various Voices*, p. 64). He has compared the Holocaust to current arms-dealing and oppression sponsored by Western democracies, equating Nazi genocide to other atrocities: "[I]n *Ashes to Ashes* I'm not simply talking about the Nazis, I'm talking about us and our conception of our past and our history" (*Various Voices*, p. 66). This emphasis parallels his assumption that political violence is historically omnipresent.

Bibliography

Primary Sources (including Holocaust plays Pinter has directed)

The Room. 1957.
The Birthday Party. 1958.
The Caretaker and *The Dumb Waiter*. 1960.
A Slight Ache, The Collection, The Dwarfs. 1962.
The Homecoming. 1965.
A Night Out, Night School, Revue Sketches: Early Plays. 1967.
The Lover, Tea Party, The Basement: Two Plays and a Film Script. 1967.
The Man in the Glass Booth, by Robert Shaw. (New York: Samuel French, 1968.) Stage production directed by Harold Pinter. (With uncredited revisions to Shaw's script by Pinter.) With Donald Pleasence, Jack Hollander, and F. Murray Abraham. Royale Theatre, New York. Opened 26 Sept. 1968.
Landscape and *Silence*. 1969.
Old Times. 1971.
Five Screenplays: The Servant, The Pumpkin Eater, The Quiller Memorandum, Accident, The Go-Between. 1971.
No Man's Land. 1975.
The Proust Screenplay: A la recherche du temps perdu. With Joseph Losey and Barbara Bray.
Betrayal. 1978.
The Hothouse. 1980.
The French Lieutenant's Woman: A Screenplay. 1981.
Other Places: A Kind of Alaska, Victoria Station, Family Voices. 1983.
"Precisely." 1985.
One for the Road. 1985.
Mountain Language. 1989.
Reunion. Screenplay by Harold Pinter. Director: Jerry Schatzberg. Performers: Jason Robards, Christian Anholt, Samuel West. Les Films Ariane, 1989. (Can be rented from Facets Video.)
The Comfort of Strangers and Other Screenplays (*Reunion, Turtle Diary, Victory*). 1990.
The Dwarfs Novel. 1990.
The Heat of the Day. (Screenplay of Elizabeth Bowen's novel.) 1990.
Party Time and *The New World Order*. 1993.
Moonlight. 1993.
The Trial: Adapted from the Novel by Franz Kafka. 1993.
Taking Sides, by Ronald Harwood. (London: Faber, 1995). Stage production directed by Harold Pinter. With Michael Pennington and Daniel Massey. Minerva Theatre, Chichester, England. Opened 18 May 1995.
Plays One through *Plays Four*. 1996.
Ashes to Ashes. 1996.
Various Voices: Prose, Poetry, Politics. 1998.
Celebration. 1999.

Secondary Sources

Arendt, Hannah. *Eichmann in Jerusalem: A Report on the Banality of Evil*. Revised ed. New York: Penguin, 1977.
Baum, Rainer C. "Holocaust: Moral Indifference as *the* Form of Modern Evil." *Echoes from the Holocaust: Philosophical Reflections on a Dark Time*. Edited by Alan Rosenberg and Gerald E. Myers. Philadelphia: Temple University Press, 1988, pp. 53–90.
Bauman, Zygmunt. *Modernity and the Holocaust*. Ithaca, N.Y.: Cornell University Press, 1989.
Billington, Michael. *The Life and Work of Harold Pinter*. London: Faber, 1996.
Burkman, Katherine H. "Harold Pinter's *Ashes to Ashes*: Rebecca and Devlin as Albert Speer." *Pinter Review* (1997/98): 86–96.
Engelmann, Bernt. *In Hitler's Germany: Daily Life in the Third Reich*. Translated by Krishna Winston. New York: Pantheon, 1986.
Gillen, Francis. "History as a Single Act: Pinter's *Ashes to Ashes*." *Cycnos* 14 (1997): 91–97.
Hamerow, Theodore S. *On the Road to the Wolf's Lair: German Resistance to Hitler*. Cambridge, Mass.: Harvard University Press, 1997.
Isser, Edward R. *Stages of Annihilation: Theatrical Representation of the Holocaust*. Cranbury, N.J.: Associated University Presses, 1997.
Knowles, Ronald. *Understanding Harold Pinter*. Columbia: University of South Carolina Press, 1995.
Lamont, Rosette C. "Harold Pinter's *The Hothouse*: A Parable of the Holocaust." *Pinter at Sixty*. Edited by Katherine H. Burkman and John L. Kundert-Gibbs. Bloomington: Indiana University Press, 1993, pp. 37–48.
Langer, Lawrence. *Admitting the Holocaust: Collected Essays*. New Haven: Yale University Press, 1991.
———. *Holocaust Testimonies: The Ruins of Memory*. New York: Oxford University Press 1994.
Merrit, Susan Hollis. "Harold Pinter's *Ashes to Ashes*: Political/Personal Echoes of the Holocaust." *Pinter Review* (1999/2000): 73–84.

Michel, Jean. *Dora*. Written in association with Louis Nucera and translated by Jennifer Kidd. New York: Holt, Rinehart and Winston, 1980.

Muller, Ingo. *Hitler's Justice: The Courts of the Third Reich*. Translated by Deborah Lucas Schneider. Cambridge, Mass.: Harvard University Press, 1991.

Sereny, Gitta. *Albert Speer: His Battle with Truth*. New York: Knopf, 1995.

Silverstein, Marc. " 'Talking about Some Kind of Atrocity': 1971. *Ashes to Ashes* in Barcelona." *Pinter Review* (1997/1998): 74–85.

Skloot, Robert. *The Darkness We Carry: The Drama of the Holocaust*. Madison: University of Wisconsin Press, 1988.

Uhlman, Fred. *Reunion*. New York: Farrar, Straus and Giroux, 1977.

Archives

Relevant documents such as working manuscripts, notes, and letters related to Pinter's works can be found in the Pinter Archives, housed at the British Library, London.

Interviews

Hern, Nicholas. "A Play and Its Politics: A Conversation between Harold Pinter and Nicholas Hern." *One for the Road*. By Pinter. New York: Grove Press, 1986, pp. 5–24.

Ciment, Michel. "Visually Speaking: An Interview with Harold Pinter on *Reunion*." *Film Comment* 25, no. 3 (May/June 1989): 20–22.

CHAIM POTOK

(1929–2002)

S. LILLIAN KREMER

CHAIM POTOK WAS born in New York on 17 February 1929 to Polish Jewish parents, Benjamin Max and Mollie (Friedman) Potok. He was educated at Yeshiva University, where he earned the B.A. summa cum laude in 1950; at the Jewish Theological Seminary, where he received the M.H.L. and rabbinic ordination in 1954; and at the University of Pennsylvania, where he earned a Ph.D. in philosophy in 1965. Following service as a U.S. Army chaplain in Korea (1956–1957), Potok married Adena Sarah Mosevitzky and began a distinguished teaching and publication career in Jewish studies. He taught at the University of Judaism in Los Angeles (1957–1959), served as scholar in residence at Har Zion Temple in Philadelphia (1959–1963), and taught at the Jewish Theological Seminary Teachers' Institute (1963–1964). His career in publishing has included positions as managing editor of *Conservative Judaism* (1964–1965). As special projects editor for the Jewish Publication Society (since 1974), he has collaborated with other scholars and rabbis to prepare the new authorized translation of the Hebrew Bible. *Wanderings: Chaim Potok's History of the Jews* (1978) is a compendium of scholarship about Jewish civilization and its relation to the myriad cultures with which Judaism has come into contact. Among Potok's honors are the Edward Lewis Wallant Award (*The Chosen*, 1967), the Anthenaeum (*The Promise*, 1969), the national Jewish Book Award for Fiction (*My Name Is Asher Lev*, 1972), the Jewish Cultural Achievement Award, and the O. Henry Award.

The Holocaust

Jewish history, including repeated outbreaks of antisemitism and its 1939–1945 genocidal manifestation, resonate throughout Potok's fiction. Because the author believes "The Jew sees all his contemporary history refracted through the ocean of blood that is the Holocaust" (*Wanderings*, New York: Alfred A. Knopf, 1978, p. 398), the *Shoah* is always in the background of his fictional universe and its impact on survivors and American Jews is explored. Rather than treating the Holocaust directly, Potok generally introduces the topic indirectly. He focuses instead on postwar restoration through renewal of Judaism and Jewry in America and Israel. His characters are most often devout Jews, conversant in Jewish theology, liturgy, Talmudic studies, and rabbinic commentary, and are frequently presented in the context of synagogue, yeshiva, and observant Jewish homes.

Survivor Trauma

An early short story, "The Dark Place Inside" (in *Dimensions in American Judaism*, fall 1967), portrays an Israeli Holocaust survivor suffering the trauma of his losses sixteen years after their origin. Having escaped death in a mass shooting when he fell into heavy brush a moment before the bullets met their marks and survived as a fugitive in the barn of a Polish peasant, Levi Abramovich mourns the loss of four sons who "had walked the narrow corridor and tasted the smoky waters of poison gas in the shower house, together with their mother" (p. 35). The survivor generally suppresses his Holocaust memories, but they occasionally erupt and overpower his capacity for postwar Israeli regeneration. The text charts his transformation from matter-of-fact dismisser of the ineffectual God to despairing protestor. He expresses the utter desolation of the alienated believer, "I believe in perfect faith that You are unworthy of my perfect faith" (p. 39).

The Chosen

Much more typical of Potok's treatment of the Holocaust in the early phase of his writing is *The Chosen*, with its look at the impact of the Holocaust on religious American Jews. Set in the Jewish Williamsburg neighborhood of Brooklyn, the novel follows two sets of fathers and sons and their variant practice and study of Judaism against the backdrop of the Holocaust and the establishment of the State of Israel. These historic forces remain in the novel's background while the religious issues dividing Jewish orthodoxy claim the novelist's central interest. Nevertheless, the *Shoah* is a leitmotif and an important influence on characters' lives. The young men, Danny Saunders and Reuven Malter, discuss Hitler's war against Jewry in the context of general war news. The Hasid, Reb Saunders, speaks "of the Jewish world in Europe, of the people he had known who were now probably dead, of the brutality of the world" (*The Chosen*, Greenwich, Conn.: Fawcett Publications, 1967, p. 180) interpreting this catastrophe in the context of historic anti-Jewish persecutions. Although Saunders reluctantly accepts the Holocaust as "the will of God" (p. 181), a divine mystery of inaction, he is deeply troubled by it. David Malter, the progressive Orthodox scholar, rejects Reb Saunders's meek submission, arguing instead "We cannot wait for God. If there is an answer, we must make it ourselves" (p. 182). His response is to put all his effort into "the education of American Jewry and a Jewish state in Palestine" (p. 213). For Malter, the way to derive meaning from the slaughter of six million Jews is to embrace a program of repair, for American Jews to replace the lost treasures of Judaism, and by training teachers and rabbis, thereby generating a religious renaissance. In the immediate aftermath of the Holocaust and before the establishment of the State of Israel, Malter is convinced that unless Judaism is rebuilt in America, it will perish. When the modern State of Israel is born, he also works assiduously to realize the Zionist goal of a Jewish homeland, modeling a course that his son takes to heart.

The Promise

Potok's second novel elaborates post-Holocaust consciousness and sensibilities of survivors and observant American Jews. *The Promise* follows the careers of Reuven Malter and Danny Saunders and returns to indirect representation of the Holocaust. The drama takes the form of a theological confrontation between orthodox and progressive scholars who teach Reuven and Danny. The lives and pedagogical philosophies of the teachers, a survivor and an American Jew, have been shaped by the Holocaust. As a postdoctoral scholar studying the Vienna Circle positivists before the outbreak of war, Abraham Gordon realized that few Jews would survive Hitler's Europe. He remapped his career, rejecting a philosophy position at Harvard to take a seminary position and play a role in rebuilding American Judaism. Years later, academic conflict erupts between Gordon and Rav Kalman, a Holocaust survivor, although each is dedicated to Holocaust repair by strengthening Judaism. Rav Kalman fiercely protects ultra-orthodox interpretation of the sacred texts in order to honor God's word and the memory of *Shoah* victims whose lives were devoted to the Torah and God. Kalman's colleagues, survivors of the "sulfurous chaos of the concentration camps" (*The Promise*, New York: Fawcett Publications, 1969, p.13), remain steadfast traditionalists, staunchly opposed to changes of orthodox worship, practice, and scholarship. Undefeated by the physical enemy in Europe, they are prepared to do battle with those they perceive as Judaism's spiritual enemies. They bear Holocaust witness through their determination to live according to the commandments, to defend the Torah, and revitalize the *Yiddishkayt* (Jewishness) the Nazis sought to destroy.

Adhering to his indirect approach to Holocaust representation, Potok employs conversation by third parties to chart Kalman's Holocaust biography of a two-year incarceration in a German concentration camp in northern Poland, the murder of his wife and children in a mass killing of Jews in Russia, and his subjection to Nazi medical experimentation and sterilization. David Malter draws an analogy between Kalman's resistance to Nazism and his resistance to weakened religious observance: "He was not of those who believed in going willingly to the crematoria. He was with the partisans and killed German soldiers for Torah. Now he defends it with words" (p. 280). Even as he is the victim of Rav Kalman's fierce orthodoxy, Abraham Gordon addresses the philosophic implications of Kalman's Holocaust suffering:

> The concentration camps destroyed a lot more than European Jewry. They destroyed man's faith in himself. I cannot blame Rav Kalman for being suspicious of man and believing only in God. Why should anyone believe in man? There are going to be decades of chaos until we learn to believe again in man (p. 315).

Despite their antipathy for one another's pedagogy, orthodox and progressive Torah scholars of Potok's fiction are committed to Holocaust repair through the survival and flourishing of Judaism and the Jewish people.

In the Beginning

Potok's fourth novel, *In the Beginning* (1975), brings historic antisemitism and its *Shoah* manifestation to the thematic core and dramatic center of the novel. The bustling streets of a Bronx multiethnic neighborhood, where Potok spent his childhood, and where American-born children inherit their immigrant parents' fears and prejudices, provide the urban backdrop for antagonistic encounters between Jew and Gentile. Eddie Kulanski, son of Polish immigrants, is presented as hating Jews with "a kind of mindless demonic rage" (*In the Beginning*, Greenwich, Conn.: Faucett Publications, 1975, p. 11), expressing animosity that "bore the breeding of a thousand years" (p. 11). Albeit in childish overtones, Eddie parrots the oft-repeated Christian charge of Jewish influence and affluence. He spews the old world venom in his mother tongue, using the Polish epithet, *Anonymowe Panstwo* ("Anonymous Empire"), reiterating the slander propagated in *The Protocols of the Elders of Zion* that Jews secretly conspire first to destroy Christian countries and then to dominate the world.

Exemplifying Potok's method of using the novel to inform readers of Jewish history are several expository speeches such as that by an older cousin, who debunks the *Protocols* conspiracy theory, and a Christian neighbor who identifies the deicide libel as the source and fuel of nearly two thousands years of European antisemitism. He informs the Jewish child of church doctrine and books that perpetuate the infamy. David finds corroboration for his neighbor's account in the Christian Bible, where he finds "rage and scorn directed at the scribes and Pharisees" in Matthew, Mark, Luke, and John and in antisemitic commentary published in contemporary Catholic textbooks.

Whereas most Jewish American writers of Holocaust literature cite ample evidence of historic antisemitism, very few treat the Jewish response. Potok does, dramatizing both passive and assertive responses. A descendant of a victim of an east European massacre, Max Lurie (David's father) argues against the passive Jewish mentality that tries to negotiate peace when armed resistance is required to counter enemies bent on Jewish annihilation. The bitterness of Lurie's tone is unprecedented in the fiction created by American-born novelists, but it has an authentic ring in light of the Polish–Jewish interwar history that motivates the character's speech.

Potok's pattern of indirect Holocaust presentation appears in his integration of pre-Holocaust anti-Jewish persecutions, Hebrew liturgy, and Jewish legend. A *Yom Kippur* memorial lament for Torah sages martyred during Roman dominion stimulates grief for an anonymous Jew murdered in Berlin. Biblical and mythological constructs flood David's consciousness as he imagines a deluge cleansing Polish cities, a purgation in whose aftermath "the Angel of Death would have less of a job to do because goyim would not kill Jews" (p. 96). The novel's most sustained use of Jewish legend is its adaptation of the sixteenth-century Golem of Prague myth. The golem was fashioned from lifeless, shapeless matter by a person who knew God's Ineffable Name and who could thereby breathe life into the homunculus, who would then use his enormous strength to protect powerless Jews from potent enemies. David's golem fantasies coincide with the Third Reich's heightening anti-Jewish violence. He imagines a Nazi demonstration, flags and banners waving; torches smoking; and twenty thousand brown-shirted men shouting and saluting. In the child's fantasy he performs heroically, shouting down the Nazis, quelling demonstrations, and spying on Nazi strategy sessions. Another time he imagines a holocaustic conflagration, a synagogue aflame, and envisions himself plunging swiftly through smoke and fire toward the ark to save the endangered Torah scrolls. As Nazi harassment of German Jews escalates, the golem recedes and David retreats into silence. Potok concludes this section of the novel by juxtaposing the end of the golem reveries with Germany's invasion of Poland and cessation of mail from the family in Poland.

The final segment of the novel is set in the Holocaust era and its immediate aftermath. It deals with heightened American antisemitism, thereby sustaining the focus on the connection between Christian and Nazi anti-Jewish violence. As in the Third Reich, aggressive rhetoric foments physical attacks in America. Inspired by Father Charles E. Coughlin and his Social Justice movement, roaming gangs of hooligans ambush American yeshiva boys and old Jews in the presence of police officers who stand by idly. Genteel antisemitism takes the form of curtailed immigration quotas and other obstruction of efforts to rescue European Jews.

Although massive Jewish losses were known by 1942, the concentration camp atrocities and mass murders become apparent to the public only at war's end. Potok registers the impact of Holocaust loss on Jewish immigrants whose families were being destroyed in Europe through David's mother, who becomes mute in reaction to news that the many branches of her large family were transferred from Auschwitz to Bergen-Belsen and that no one survived. More than 150 family members perished, a fate similar to that suffered by the Potoks. The novelist, who was David's age at war's end, draws on his own memories in writing of the character's reaction to "newspaper photographs, the memorial assemblies, the disbelief in the faces of friends, the shock as news came of death and more death" (*Wanderings*, p. 388).

Only when he writes of the Bergen-Belsen photographs does Potok register Holocaust atrocities graphically: "Grotesque forms with skeletal arms and legs and rib cages and heads lay stacked like macabre cordwood on a stone ramp" (*In the Beginning*, p. 408). He notes the enormity of the crimes, "hills of corpses, pits of bones, the naked rubble of the dead and the staring eyes and hollow faces of the survivors" (p. 400). David is overwhelmed by a photograph of dead children, "eyes and mouths open, bodies twisted and frozen with death" (p. 400). In addition to realistic rendering, Potok composes an imagistic reverie in which David sees the Bergen-Belsen news photos while walking along a parapet overlooking the Hudson River. The river begins to flow red; the entire world is red. A freight train passes, a central holocaustic vision for David and the postwar reader of the transports that crisscrossed German-occupied Europe; trains behind whose sealed doors "a multitude of writhing human beings packed together riding in filth and terror" (p. 412) move relentlessly toward death.

The novel's final Holocaust reference appears years later when David, now a biblical scholar, travels to Germany to inspect a manuscript. There, he sets out on his quest "into the final beginnings" of his family. Standing at the entrance to Bergen-Belsen he reads the numbers of the dead and laments his family losses. Because he follows the scholarly path of his martyred uncle, David's family perceives him to be "the resurrection of the dead" (p. 219). The novel concludes with David's recitation of the Kaddish, a prayer filled with hope for Jewish survival, on the site that witnessed the murder of hundreds of thousands of Jews.

Biblical allusion pervades the novel's regenerative theme. The title, *In the Beginning*, is derived from the first word of the Hebrew Bible, *Bershith.* Toward the end of the Book of Genesis, Joseph recapitulates the lesson of his career, that God brings good out of evil; that He will bring the Jewish people out of Egypt and to the land promised to the patriarchs. During the worst period of Holocaust suffering, the nineteen-year-old David recalls his *bar mitzvah* Torah reading, the entry of the Jews into Egypt, and its accompanying prophetic reading from Amos, a prophecy of restoration of the fortunes of the Jewish homeland and those who would rebuild the ruined cities and inhabit them. This work is the culmination of Potok's interpretation of the Holocaust through a religious/dialogical framework in which he uses the discourse of repair (*tikkun olam*) and restoration rather than the more common American approach of psychiatric rhetoric of post-traumatic stress, survivor guilt, nightmare, and depression.

The Later Fiction: Resurrected Holocaust Memories

In contrast to the earlier fictions that conclude with visions of Jewish regeneration through spiritual rebuilding in America and nation building in Israel, recent narratives supplant the thesis of collective renewal, positing only rhetorical consolation that Holocaust confrontation frees the individual psychologically. *The Gift of Asher Lev* (1990), sequel to one of Potok's most successful and memorable works, *My Name Is Asher Lev* (1972), returns to the controversial Jewish painter, now living in French exile in expiation for the agony his early crucifixion paintings inflicted on his Hasidic community. Lev, who endeavors to record the anguish of the world, has enjoyed a successful career, but is now blocked. Although he is married to a Holocaust survivor, a hidden child, whose entire family was killed in the concentration and death camps, he has not broached the Holocaust in his art. His work depicts other suffering produced by twentieth-century political and social outrages. Not until Lev returns to the community he offended, makes them the gift of his son to stand in his stead as a dynastic Hasidic rebbe, and begins to treat the Holocaust in his painting is he able to work meaningfully again. The novel's religious drama is rendered successfully; but its Holocaust treatment, in light of Potok's original intention of showing the artist wrestling with the aesthetic problem of Holocaust representation, is peripheral and insufficiently developed.

Holocaust memory, its function, retrieval, and pertinence to contemporary life are central to Potok's later fiction. The American and European-born, middle-aged secular men in "The Trope Teacher" (found in Old Men at Midnight, 2001) and "The Canal" (1993) suffer the burden of repressed Holocaust memory. Walter Benjamin, a World War II military historian, is unable to write his memoir until he recalls memories of his beloved childhood trope teacher, an immigrant who prepared him for his *bar mitzvah* by teaching him proper cantillation and later disappeared into the concentration camp universe. Encouraged by another writer to excavate these repressed memories, Benjamin confides that as a soldier in World War II, he imagined seeing his teacher's corpse in a mass grave near one of the concentration camps his company helped liberate. The story of the trope teacher emerges piecemeal in a fractured narrative by the memoirist, recalling the self-interrupted narratives of survivors coping with traumatic memory. The central character of "The Canal" confronts fragmented memories of his childhood in Krakow, specifically "gruesome details of his escape, . . . from Nazi violence by jumping into a canal" (Buning, p. 11). Years after the war, Amos Brickman, a successful architect, is compelled to return to his birthplace, to visit Auschwitz and the crematorium at Birkenau before he can continue productive work. Named allegorically to suggest his profession and the prophet Amos, who announced restoration and rebuilding following disaster, Brickman accepts a commission to build an ecumenical church near a Philadelphia canal. It is the site visit for this commission that is the catalyst for the architect's return to Europe. There, he faces the deeply traumatic memory of his escape from the Nazis by diving into a local canal.

Because the Holocaust is a secondary element in Potok's canon, criticism has understandably focused on his major themes of the Jewish encounter with modernity through psychology, art, communism, and modern antisemitism, rather than the *Shoah*.

Bibliography

Primary Sources

Fiction

The Chosen. 1967.
The Promise. 1969.
My Name Is Asher Lev. 1972.
In the Beginning. 1975.
The Book of Lights. 1981.
Davita's Harp. 1985.
The Gift of Asher Lev. 1990.
I Am the Clay. 1992.
Old Men at Midnight. 2001. Contains novellas "The Ark Builder," "The War Doctor," and "The Trope Teacher."

Children's Books

The Tree of Here. 1993.
The Sky of Now. 1994.
Zebra and Other Stories. 1998.

Nonfiction

Jewish Ethics (14 volumes). 1964–1969.
The Jew Confronts Himself in American Literature. 1975.
Wanderings: Chaim Potok's History of the Jews. 1978.
Ethical Living for a Modern World: Jewish Insights. 1985.
Theo Tobiasse: Artist in Exile. 1986.
The Gates of November: Chronicles of the Slepak Family. 1996.
My First Seventy-Nine Years. Isaac Stern's autobiography, with Isaac Stern. 1999.

Selected Short Stories

"Reflections on a Bronx Street." In *May My Words Feed Others*. Edited by Chayym Zeldis. New York: A. S. Barnes and Co., 1974, pp. 50–57.
"The Dark Place Inside." *Dimensions in American Judaism* (fall 1967): 35–39.
"A Tale of Two Soldiers." *Ladies' Home Journal* 98 (December 1981): 16–19.
"The Gifts of Andrea." *Seventeen* 41 (October 1982): 152.
"Long Distance." *American Voice* 4 (fall 1986): 3–16.
"The Seven of the Address." In *Winter's Tales: New Series 8*. Edited by Robin Baird-Smith. New York: St. Martin's, 1993, pp. 77–99.
"Moon." In *Prize Stories, 1999: The O. Henry Awards*. Edited by Larry Dark. New York: Doubleday, 1999, pp. 202–223.
"Finding Ruth." *TriQuarterly* (winter 2000): 186–203.

Novellas

"The Trope Teacher." *TriQuarterly* 101 (winter 1997/1998): 15–83.
"Het cijfer zeven" (The Seven of the Address). 1990. Published in the Netherlands.
"De troop-leraar" (The Trope Teacher: A Ghost Story for Our Times). 1992. Published in the Netherlands.
"Het Kanaal" (The Canal). 1993. Published in the Netherlands.
"The Golem's Hand." 1995. Published in Italy.

Plays

The Chosen. Musical adaptation of the book. 1988.
Out of the Depths. 1990.
Sins of the Father: The Carnival and The Gallery. Two one-act plays, premiered 24 May 1990.
The Play of Lights. One-act play. 1992.

Selected Periodical Publications

"The Naturalism of Sidney." *Conservative Judaism* (winter 1964): 40–52.
"Chaim Potok's Answers to Five Questions." *The Condition of Jewish Belief: A Symposium*. New York: Macmillan, 1966, pp. 171–179.
"Provisional Absolutes." *Commentary* 39 (May 1965): 76–78; 40 (September 1965): 22.
"Martin Buber and the Jews." *Commentary* 41 (March 1966): 43–49.
"The State of Jewish Belief." *Commentary* (August 1966): 125–127.
"Interaction in the Adopted Land." *Saturday Review* 51 (7 December 1968): 37–40.
"Jews of the 1970's." *Ladies Home Journal* (December 1969): 134.
"Rebellion and Authority: The Adolescent Discovering the Individual in Modern Literature." *Adolescent Psychiatry* 4 (1975): 15–20.
"Judaism under the Secular Umbrella." *Christianity Today* 22 (8 September 1978): 14–21.
"Reply to a Semi-Sympathetic Critic." *Studies in American Jewish Literature* 2 (spring 1976): 30–35.
"Culture Confrontations in Urban America: A Writer's Beginnings." In *Literature and the Urban Experience: Essays on the City and Literature*. Edited by Michael C. Jaye and Ann Chalmers Watts. New Brunswick: Rutgers University Press, 1981, pp. 161–167.
"What Will You Do When April Comes? Treaty of Peace Between the Republic of Egypt and the State of Israel." *Moment* 7 (March 1982): 13–24.

"The Barbra Streisand Nobody Knows." *Esquire Magazine* (cover story). October 1982.
"The Bible's Inspired Art." *New York Times Magazine* (3 October 1982): 58–69.
"Torah, Torah, Torah. Streisand Seems Fascinated by Tribulations She Had to Endure Making 'Yentl.' " *Philadelphia Daily News*, 8 December 1983.
"The Culture Highways We Travel." *Religion and Literature* 19, no. 2 (summer 1987): 1–10.
"Russia and the Jews: Photos of a Turbulent Past." *New York Times*, Arts & Leisure Section, 21 February 1988.
"Text and Texture: Early Adventures in the Fourth Dimension." In *Sign and Witness*. New York: New York Public Library, Oxford University Press, 1988.
"A Planet in Exile (Experiences and Problems of Secular Jewish Life)." *Du die Zeitschrift der Kultur* 10 (1990): 20–25.
"The Invisible Maps of Meaning: A Writer's Confrontations." *TriQuarterly* 85 (spring 1992): 17.
"A Subtle Effort to Deconstruct the Shtetl." *New York Times* 144 (23 October 1994): 44.
"The Mourning Road." *Philadelphia Magazine* 89, no. 11 (November 1998): 96–97.

Introductions and Forewords

From the Corners of the Earth: Contemporary Photographs. Bill Aron. Jewish Publication Society. 1985.
Last traces: The Lost Art of Auschwitz. Joseph P. Czarnecki. Atheneum. 1989.
The Jews in America. Collins. 1989.
Tales of the Hasidim. Martin Buber. Pantheon Books. 1991.
The Book of Jonah. Ismar David. Chiswick Book Shop, Southbury, Conn. 1991.
Graven Images: Graphic Symbols of the Jewish Gravestone. Arnold Schwartzman. Abrams. 1993.
I Never Saw Another Butterfly: Children's Drawings & Poems. Edited by Hana Volavkova. Pantheon/Schocken Books. 1993.
Reclaiming the Dead Sea Scrolls: The History of Judaism. Lawrence H. Schiffman. Jewish Publication Society. 1994.
The Holocaust Museum in Washington. Jeshajahu Weinberg and Rina Elieli. Rizzoli. 1995.
As a Driven Leaf. Milton Steinberg. Behrman House. 1996.

Book Reviews

Review of *The Dean's December* by Saul Bellow. *Philadelphia Magazine* 73 (April 1982): 130–144.
Review of *Him with His Foot in His Mouth* by Saul Bellow. *Philadelphia Inquirer*, 20 May 1984.
Review of *The Chronicle of the Lodz Ghetto*, edited by Lucjan Dobroscycki. *Philadelphia Inquirer*, 30 September 1984.
Review of *Love and Exile: A Memoir* by Isaac Bashevis Singer. *Philadelphia Inquirer*, 11 November 1984.
Review of *Stories for Children* by Isaac Bashevis Singer. *Philadelphia Inquirer*, 11 November 1984.
Review of *The Burn* by Vassily Aksyonov. *Philadelphia Inquirer*, 9 December 1984.
Review of *Exodus and Revolution* by Michael Walzer. *Philadelphia Inquirer*, 21 April 1985.
Review of *Zuckerman Bound* by Philip Roth. *Newsday*, 23 June 1985.
Review of *From the Fair* by Sholom Aleichem. *New York Times*, 14 July 1985.
Review of *The Siege* by Conor Cruise O'Brien. *Newsday* 2 March 1986.
Review of *Semites and Anti-Semites* by Bernard Lewis. *Philadelphia Inquirer*, 31 August 1986.
Review of *Jewish Self-Hatred: Anti-Semitism and the Hidden Language of the Jews* by Sander L. Gilman. *Philadelphia Inquirer*, 11 January 1987.
Review of *Twilight* by Elie Wiesel. *Philadelphia Inquirer*, 22 May 1988.
Review of *The Death of Methuselah and Other Stories* by Isaac Bashevis Singer. *Moment* (January/February 1989).
Review of *From Beirut to Jerusalem* by Thomas L. Friedman. *Washington Post*, 16 July 1989.
Review of *The Lost Childhood* by Yehuda Nir. *Newsday* 29 October 1989.
Review of *Lodz Ghetto* by Alan Adelson and Robert Lapides. *Philadelphia Inquirer*, 26 November 1989.
Review of *Writing into the World* by Terrence Des Pres. *Philadelphia Inquirer*, 24 March 1991.
Review of *Jewish-American History and Culture*, edited by Jack Fischel and Sanford Pinsker. *Philadelphia Inquirer*, 15 March 1992.
Review of *The New Israelis* by Yosi Melman. *Washington Post*, 22 November 1992.
Review of *Strange Pilgrims* by Gabriel Garcia Marquez. *Philadelphia Inquirer*, 17 September 1993.
Review of *The Waterworks* by E. L. Doctorow. *Philadelphia Inquirer*, 12 June 1994.
Review of *God* by Jack Miles. *Philadelphia Inquirer*, 16 April 1995.
Review of *The Origin of Satan* by Elaine Pagels. *The Forward*, 2 June 1995.
Review of *The Moor's Last Sigh* by Salman Rushdie. *The Forward*, 29 December 1995.

Interviews of Chaim Potok

"Judaism under the Secular Umbrella." Interview by Cheryl Forbes. *Christianity Today* 22 (8 September 1978): 14–21.
"Chaim Potok." Interview by Harold Ribalow. In *The Tie That Binds: Conversations with Jewish Writers*. New York: Barnes, 1980.
"A Conversation with Chaim Potok." Interview by Martin Bookspan. *The Eternal Light* 1453. Transcript of NBC Radio Network Broadcast (22 November 1981). New York: Jewish Theological Seminary of America, 1981.
"Interview with Chaim Potok, July 21, 1981." By S. Lillian Kremer. *Studies in American Jewish Literature* 4 (1984): 84–99.
"When Cultures Collide." Interview by Alan Abrams. *Jewish News* (22 June 1984): 13ff.
"Interview with Chaim Potok, July 1983." By S. Lillian Kremer. In *Dictionary of Literary Biography Yearbook: 1984*. Edited by Jean W. Ross. Detroit: Gale, 1985, pp. 83–87.
"An Interview with Chaim Potok." By Elaine Kauvar. *contemporary Literature* 27 (fall 1986): 291–317.
"An Interview with Chaim Potok." By Wendy Herstein. *The World & I* (August 1992): 309–313.
"The Odyssey of Asher Lev." Interview by Aviva Kipen. *Jewish Quarterly* (spring 1993): 1–5.
"A *MELUS* Interview: Chaim Potok." By Laura Chavkin. *MELUS* 24, no. 2 (summer 1999): 147–157.
Walden, Daniel, ed. *Conversations with Chaim Potok*. Jackson: University Press of Mississippi, 2001.

Secondary Sources

Abramson, Edward A. *Chaim Potok*. Boston: Twayne, 1986.
Andouard-Labarthe, Elyette. "Ethnicité et religion dans les romans de Chaim Potok: Actes du colloque des 25 & 26 No-

vember 1983." In *Le Facteur religieux en Amerique du Nord, V: Religion et groupes ethniques au Canada et aux Etats unis*. Edited by Jean Beranger and Pierre Guillaume. Talence: Maison de Sciences de l'Homme d' Aquitaine, 1984, pp. 193–214.

Buning, M. "Chaim Potok." In *Post-War Literatures in English: A Lexicon of Contemporary Authors*. Edited by Hans Bak et al. Alphen aan den Rijn: Samson Uitgeverij; Groningen: Wolters-Noordhoff, 1988, 1–15.

———. "*The Chosen* van Chaim Potok." *Joods Amerikaanse Literatuur* [Free University, Amsterdam] 3 (1989): 45–69.

Fagerheim, Cynthia. "A Bibliographic Essay." *Studies in American Jewish Literature* 4 (1985): 107–120.

Fry, A. J., Derek Rubin, Peter Jan de Voogd, and J. B. Weenink. *Joods-Amerikaanse Literatuur*. Amsterdam: VU Uitgeverij, 1987.

Guttman, Allen. "The Postwar Revival of Peoplehood." In *The Jewish Writer in America: Assimilation and the Crisis of Identity*. New York: Oxford University Press, 1971, pp. 120–128.

Kremer, S. Lillian. "Chaim Potok." In *Dictionary of Literary Biography. Volume 28: Twentieth-Century American-Jewish Fiction Writers*. Edited by Daniel Walden. Detroit: Gale, 1984, pp. 232–243.

———. "Eternal Light: The Holocaust and the Revival of Judaism and Jewish Civilization in the Fiction of Chaim Potok." In *Witness through the Imagination: Jewish American Holocaust Literature*. Detroit: Wayne State University Press, 1989, pp. 300–323.

———. "Chaim Potok." In *Dictionary of Literary Biography. Volume 152: American Novelists since World War II, Fourth Series*. Edited by James Giles and Wanda Giles. Detroit: Gale, 1995, pp. 202–215.

———. "Chaim Potok (1929–)." In *Contemporary Jewish American Novelists: A Bio-Critical Sourcebook*. Edited by Joel Shatzky and Michael Taub. Westport: Greenwood, 1997, pp. 284–294.

Loreto, Paulo. "Chaim Potok's Plea for Jewish 'Gentleness' as an Answer to Hatred." In *Reclaiming Memory: American Representations of the Holocaust*. Edited by Pirjo Ahokas and Martine Chard-Hutchinson. Turku, Finland: University of Turku, 1997, pp. 149–160.

Marovitz, Sanford E. "A Jew Is a Jew Is a Jew: The Dilemma of Identity in American Jewish Fiction." In *Chu Shikoku: Studies in American Literature* [Japan] 14 (1978): 1–18.

———. "Freedom, Faith, and Fanaticism: Cultural Conflict in the Novels of Chaim Potok." *Studies in American Jewish Literature* 5 (1986): 129–140.

Morton, Brian. "Banished and Banished Again." *Times Literary Supplement* (2 November 1990): 1182.

Parker, Peter, ed., and Frank Kermode, consulting ed. *A Reader's Guide to Twentieth-Century Writers*. New York: Oxford University Press, 1996.

Walden, Daniel. "Chaim Potok, Zwischenmensch ('Between-Person') Adrift in the Cultures." *Studies in American Jewish Literature* 4 (1985): 19–25.

———, ed. *The World of Chaim Potok. Studies in American Jewish Literature* 4 (1985). (Special Potok issue).

Yudkin, Leon I. "From the Periphery to the Centre." In *Jewish Writing and Identity in the Twentieth Century*. London: Helm, 1982, pp. 112–128.

Francine Prose

(1947–)

GARY WEISSMAN

FRANCINE PROSE IS the author of ten novels, two short-story collections, a book of novellas, several children's books and numerous uncollected stories, essays, articles, and reviews. She was born on 1 April 1947 in Brooklyn, New York, to two physicians, Philip and Jessie (née Rubin) Prose. After receiving her B.A. in English from Radcliffe College in 1968 and her M.A. in English from Harvard University in 1969, Prose taught creative writing at Harvard from 1971 to 1972. In 1973 she published her first novel, *Judah the Pious*, which won the Jewish Book Council Award. Written in the tradition of Hasidic folklore, this tale, like much of Prose's early work, involves storytelling that interlaces history, legend, and the fantastic.

In 1976 Prose married artist Howard Michels. Their home was in upstate New York for several years, though they often resided elsewhere when Prose accepted visiting teaching positions at institutions including the University of Arizona, Warren Wilson College, Sarah Lawrence College, and the Iowa Writers Workshop. In 1996 Prose moved with her husband and two sons, Bruno and Leon, back to New York City, where she has taught creative writing at the New School for Social Research. Prose's more recent fiction presents darkly comic portraits of contemporary life, often focusing on hapless family and sexual relations. In addition, Prose writes art and book reviews, travel pieces, and essays for such newspapers and periodicals as *New York Times*, *Wall Street Journal*, *Harper's*, *ARTnews*, and *Elle*. Among her often controversial essays is "I Know Why the Caged Bird Cannot Read" (*Harper's*, 1999), an indictment of how high school students study literature. Her list of widely taught books of "dubious literary merit" includes "Elie Wiesel's overwrought *Night*" (pp. 78–79).

Prose has also cotranslated into English three books by Ida Fink, a Holocaust survivor living in Israel who writes autobiographical Holocaust-related fiction in Polish. These include the collections *A Scrap of Time and Other Stories* (1987) and *Traces: Stories* (1997), and the novel *The Journey* (1992). In her fiction, Prose addresses the Holocaust in her novella "Guided Tours of Hell" (from *Guided Tours of Hell: Novellas*, 1997). Her own relation to the Holocaust is the subject of an essay titled "Protecting the Dead," (found in *Testimony*, 1989).

"Protecting the Dead"

Prose's essay, commissioned for the collection *Testimony: Contemporary Writers Make the Holocaust Personal* (1989), also appeared in *Tikkun* (May/June 1989). "Protecting the Dead" is Prose's candid reflection on her own perception of the Holocaust from childhood to the present. She is curious to know "how a protected American child comes to apprehend it: how the knowledge of the Holocaust—and of suffering in general—is romanticized, sentimentalized, glamorized, personalized, abstracted, denied, internalized, and finally—if not understood—then seen, insofar as possible, without the blinders of sentiment and confusion" ("Protecting the Dead," *Testimony*, New York: Random House, 1989, p. 105).

Prose recalls how as a child she regarded the Holocaust as "something dark, mysterious, forbidden, tragic—at once terrible and exciting" (p. 101). She obsessively reread *The Diary of Anne Frank*, finding in its "story of a girl who had a love affair and a girl who died" a kind of suffering that seemed romantically appealing (p. 102). She knew that the Holocaust involved real suffering on an almost unimaginable scale, but writes that "the knowledge was abstract for me, distanced; only much later did it become what I would call 'real' " (p. 105).

Prose found "that suffering no longer seemed . . . abstract, romantic, desirable, or voluptuous, but rather ugly, terrifying, deeply moving, and entirely real" after her children were born (p. 112). "Of course the birth of true compassion need not come through the bearing of children," she writes, but from "any experience that ties one to life, that makes one see it as precious and fragile" (p. 112). In realizing that the suffering and evil of the Holocaust were real—"not Hollywood, not glamorous"—she came to understand that "the issues the Holocaust raises are the most important there are" (p. 108); but this realization, accompanied by "true compassion" (p. 112), also makes thought of the Holocaust much harder for her to bear.

While translating Ida Fink's stories, Prose felt overcome with sorrow and, closing her eyes, escaped into sleep. Prose chose not to see *Shoah*, and when a documentary about "a group of now-elderly Hungarian concentration-camp survivors who return to the camps as tourists" appears on television, she wants to change the channel (p. 99). Still, Prose writes, the Holocaust is very much on her mind, its images "always present" in her head (p. 108). She is mindful of the "moral and spiritual obligation" to remember the Holocaust (p. 113), to imagine it without transforming it into something "terrible and glamorous, dark-toned and nostalgic, a black-and-white or sepia film" (p. 101). Thus, she writes, "It is important not to let the words vanish, to remember, to keep repeating: The Holocaust happened. It was not glamorous or romantic" (p. 114).

"Guided Tours of Hell"

The heartfelt understanding of the Holocaust that Prose portrays in "Protecting the Dead" is dramatically absent from her 1997 novella, "Guided Tours of Hell." Instead, the characters who populate her story—attendees of the First International Kafka Congress in Prague—display a tendency to romanticize and glamorize the Holocaust, as well as an inability to overcome the self-involvement that impedes them from empathizing with its victims.

Inspired by Prose's trips to Paris, Prague, and the Theresienstadt camp ("Francine"), *Guided Tours of Hell: Novellas* (1997) contains the sixty-six page title story and "Three Pigs in Five Days," the story of a troubled couple, Nina and Leo, whose relationship is tested by a tour they take of the catacombs and other death-related sites in Paris. In "Guided Tours," where the participants in the Kafka conference take a tour bus to a nearby Nazi concentration camp (dramatically, albeit erroneously, referred to as a death camp throughout the novella), the nature of such tourism is questioned: "Isn't there something by definition obscene about guided tours of hell—except, of course, if you're Dante?" (*Guided Tours*, New York: Henry Holt and Company, 1997, pp. 10–11). Prose's protagonist, a third-rate playwright and occasional adjunct professor named Landau, reflects that the camp, where guards now take tickets and sell postcards, is no longer hell: "The smoldering pit where hell used to be has closed up like a wound, and crowds of people pay money to inspect the jagged scar" (p. 66).

Landau's objections to the tour appear to compensate for his own failure to realize the camp's horror. Looking into rooms crammed with wooden bunks, he tries in vain to imagine them populated by "jammed-together skeletal Jews," but sees only "walls, scratched paint, bare bunks. No one's staring at him with raccoon eyes, and frankly, Landau's just as glad. The whole trip is filthy, filthy. What people will do for sensation!" (p. 21).

In fact, Landau spends little time trying to imagine what Jews suffered in the camp; he is preoccupied, instead, by a drama involving himself and three other conferees. These are Eva Kaprova, the conference's director who, "fortyish and sexy in that sour Eastern European way," is its "only viable female" (p. 9); Natalie Zigbaum, a homely and bitter Slavic languages professor from Vassar; and Jiri Krakauer, the renowned Holocaust survivor, celebrated author, and Princeton professor who is the conference's star participant. The drama involves the sexual power plays among them: "all through the conference [Landau] has noticed Natalie finding reasons to be near him, noticed Natalie eyeing him even as he eyes Eva Kaprova, who has been eyeing Jiri Krakauer. In other words, the usual daisy chain, even here in the death camp" (p. 13).

Underlying the "daisy chain" is Landau's intense rivalry with Jiri, whose charisma, literary celebrity, academic success, and stature as a Holocaust survivor make Landau painfully aware of his own mediocrity. As the conferees tour the very camp where Jiri was a prisoner, Landau's thoughts alternate between self-loathing and harsh criticism of his rival, "that terrible poet and memoirist whose only claim to fame is that he survived two years in the camp, where he somehow conducted a love affair with Kafka's sister, Ottla" (p. 4). Listening to Jiri, "Landau can't help thinking he sounds . . . rehearsed. Isn't there something monstrous about telling this over and over, the Holocaust as a party piece to amuse one's dinner companions! But isn't that the point, in a way: to tell it again and again and never stop repeating . . . It's Landau who's the monster, judging Jiri for sounding practiced" (pp. 48–49).

The drama culminates in the former SS canteen, now a restaurant. There Jiri tells the highly dubious story of how he used to have sex in the canteen's kitchen with the Kommandant's girlfriend, a Jewish prisoner who worked as a pastry chef, while the Kommandant was nibbling cream puffs in the canteen. When questioned by Landau, Jiri attacks him and like-minded American writers and academics for leading meaningless lives. "The dirty truth is, you envy us, you wish it had happened to you," he says. "You wish you'd gotten the chance to survive Auschwitz or the Gulag" (p. 60). Even here in the camp, Jiri says with remarkable acumen, Landau is "fighting some little fight in [his] head," engaging in "some ridiculous ego drama about writing or women" (p. 63).

In response, Landau accuses Jiri of lying. In this effort to take the survivor's place as the guardian of memory and protector of the dead, Landau "feels like a hero" ready to defend the Holocaust against Jiri's distortions (p. 64); but when the enraged Jiri suddenly faints, Landau flees outside, where, recalling the dismal life he will return to following the conference, he thinks that Jiri was right. Landau does wish he had been thrown into "the abyss"—if not to have survived it, then to have disappeared in its depths.

Critical Reception

Guided Tours of Hell has been widely praised by reviewers. Prose's novellas have been described as "small, wonderfully well-observed tales" (Borchardt, pp. 56–57), full of wry humor (St. Andrews, p. 78) and characters who are not idealized but "selfish, envious, cowardly, guilt-ridden, limited, real" (Kessler, p. 232). Commentator Katie Bolick states that while Prose's fiction has been described as "withering" and "mocking," her writing is not cynical: "Trapped within their own heads, victims to the nervous dins of their own inner voices, her characters are nevertheless endearingly rendered." But there is arguably little to find endearing about the characters in "Guided Tours." In the novella—which Prose says is about "unrestrained and inappropriate egoism" ("Francine Prose")—not only Landau but "dull ugly" Natalie ("Guided Tours," p. 34) and "Mr. Professional-Survivor" Jiri (p. 28) are largely repellent characters.

Though written in the third person, Prose's fiction provides the intimate access to characters' inner lives that might be associated with first-person narration. In the *New Leader* Rosellen Brown states that when reading "Guided Tours" we are "listening to the endless complaint" inside Landau's head; David Lodge writes in the *New York Times* that "Landau seems to be reporting on himself from an ironic, third-person distance, despairingly observing his own contradictions, impotence and bad faith." The blurred line between the narrator and Landau seems to extend to other characters as well. Prose writes that Natalie "seems to have read Landau's mind, to know what he's been thinking" (p. 17), and the same can be said of Jiri. These characters all seem remarkably privy to each other's thoughts and speak them with the same mocking, knowing voice, which is that of the third-person narrator. This voice is like a weapon for performing character assassination that keeps changing hands among Landau, Natalie, and Jiri. The only ones above the fray appear to be Prose and her readers.

How do readers respond to the caustic voice that speaks in "Guided Tours"? In the *Library Journal* Patricia Ross writes that Prose's "uncanny ability to express the nasty, sordid, and petty secret thoughts of her characters" makes for insightful, thought-provoking writing that is nevertheless "not pleasant reading" (p. 91). However, most reviewers appear to enjoy this "irresistibly readable" novella (Lodge). Rosellen Brown suggests that Prose's novella—in which "all the props are poised for the dagger of her ironic wit"—is both enjoyable and discomforting to read, stating: "It is an unsettling pleasure to dislike Landau only slightly less than he dislikes himself." Yet, in an unusually negative review that appeared in the *Washington Post*, Michael Mewshaw contends that Prose's dagger ultimately provides little in the way of complex understanding. "Prose doesn't allow the characters much room for development after their early annihilating introductions," he writes, "nor does she offer the reader many insights that exceed the characters' limitations."

Brown, by contrast, claims that Prose confronts readers with "the paradoxes of late 20th-century consumer-friendly horror-grazing," challenging us "to understand the complexities of memory and mourning without degrading them, to grant them a human face but not replace them with all-too-human self-aggrandizement" (p. 24). Mewshaw may fail to recognize this challenge because readers of this novella encounter only negative examples: that is, much self-aggrandizement but no understanding that (as Prose puts it in "Protecting the Dead") the Holocaust happened, it was not glamorous or romantic. Furthermore, Prose's characters are so unattractive as to discourage the identification that might lead readers to reflect on how they too participate in "consumer-friendly horror-grazing."

Conclusion

No alternative to Holocaust commemoration-through-consumerism factors in the novella. The camp is adjoined by "parking lots crammed with dusty cars, campers, and fully loaded German-made RVs" (*Guided Tours*, p. 11); the tour guide, Jiri, presents the camp as the dramatic nightmare setting for his sexual escapades; "a certain wax museum aesthetic prevails" in the camp's sick bay, now dubbed "Dr. Adolf's Chamber of Horrors" (p. 22); and the SS canteen has been transformed into a restaurant, complete with waiters in tuxedos, to feed hungry tourists. While these descriptions may be read as a critique of Holocaust consumerism, they may also be taken as the details Landau fixates upon in lieu of a more earnest engagement with the camp and the Holocaust.

Perhaps the most curious aspect of "Guided Tours of Hell" is that the excesses of Holocaust consumerism, which distort the event to make it "consumer-friendly," are represented by the figure of the survivor. Is Jiri meant to caricature actual survivors who are too "professional" and egocentric in their relation to the Holocaust, or is he the embodiment of the kind of survivor that consumers of Holocaust horrors fully deserve? In either case, it is the survivor who symbolizes how the Holocaust has been eroticized, personalized, and otherwise distorted. Whereas Jiri reflects the glamorous, sex-laden versions of the Holocaust that appealed to Prose during her childhood, the novella includes no one and nothing like the elderly Hungarian survivors she cannot bear to watch on television as they "return to the camps as tourists." Thus, ultimately in this novella it may be Prose who divests the Holocaust of its horror by fabricating a tourist-friendly death camp in which there is truly no trace of the real suffering that occurred there. In place of the hell of the Nazi camps, Prose substitutes another kind of hell more suited to her ironic wit—one best described by Sartre's terse formulation: hell is other people.

Bibliography

Primary Sources

Judah the Pious. 1973.
The Glorious Ones. 1974.
Stories from Our Living Past. 1974.
Marie Laveau. 1977.
Animal Magnetism. 1978.
Household Saints. 1981.
Hungry Hearts. 1983.
A Scrap of Time and Other Stories (by Ida Fink; translator, with Madeleine Levine). 1988.
Bigfoot Dreams. 1989.
"Protecting the Dead." In *Testimony: Contemporary Writers Make the Holocaust Personal*. Edited by David Rosenberg. 1989, pp. 98–114.
The Journey (by Ida Fink; translator, with Johanna Weschler). 1992.
Primitive People. 1992.
The Peaceable Kingdom: Stories. 1993.
Hunters and Gatherers. 1995.
Dybbuk: A Story Made in Heaven. 1996.
Guided Tours of Hell: Novellas. 1997.
The Angel's Mistake: Stories of Chelm. 1997.
Traces: Stories (by Ida Fink; translator, with Philip Boehm). 1997.
You Never Know: A Legend of the Lamed-Vavniks. 1998.
"I Know Why the Caged Bird Cannot Read." In *Harper's* 299 (September 1999): 76–84.
Blue Angel. 2000.
The Demon's Mistake: A Story from Chelm. 2000.

Secondary Sources

Borchardt, Georges. "Guided Tours of Hell." *Publisher's Weekly* 243, no. 44 (October 1996): 56–57.
Brown, Rosellen. "Where Love Touches Death." *New Leader* (16 December 1997): 24+.
Kessler, Rod. "Guided Tours of Hell." *The Review of Contemporary Fiction* 17, no. 3 (fall 1997): 232.
Lodge, David. "Excess Baggage." *New York Times*, 12 January 1997, sec. 7: 7.
Mewshaw, Michael. "Lovers and Other Strangers." *Washington Post*, 12 January 1997: X3.
Ross, Patricia. "Guided Tours of Hell." *Library Journal* 121, no. 19 (15 November 1996): 91.
St. Andrews, B. A. "Guided Tours of Hell." *World Literature Today* 71, no. 4 (autumn 1997): 788.
Thibodeaux, Troy L. "Francine Prose." In *Dictionary of Literary Biography*, vol. 234. Edited by Patrick Meanor and Richard E. Lee. Detroit: The Gale Group, 2001.

Interviews

"Francine Prose." *Bookreporter.com*, 28 July 2000, http://www.bookreporter.com/authors/au-prose-francine.asp.
Bolick, Katie. "As the World Thrums: A Conversation with Francine Prose." *The Atlantic Online* (11 March 1998), http://www.theatlantic.com/unbound/factfict/ff9803.htm.

ANNE RABINOVITCH

(1945–)

JULIETTE DICKSTEIN

BORN IN THE French Alps in 1945, Anne Rabinovitch, the daughter of Wladimir Rabinovitch ("Rabi"), the famous lawyer, judge, and scholar of French Jewry (see *Anatomie du judaïsme français* (Anatomy of French Jewry); *Un peuple de trop sur la terre* (One People Too Many on the Earth); and *Varsovie* (Warsaw), is best known as one of France's leading English-language literary translators. She has translated Margaret Atwood, Saul Bellow, Jerzy Kosinski, Doris Lessing, Norman Mailer, Daphné du Maurier, Joyce Carol Oates, Israel Joshua Singer, and Jane Urquhart, among many other celebrated authors. Rabinovitch studied literature and theater in Grenoble and San Diego, and has a master's degree in literature, as well as a doctorate in contemporary American Jewish theater. She has also published four novels, *L'hiver au coeur* (Winter of the Heart, 1983), *Les étangs de Ville-d'Avray* (The Marshes of Ville-d'Avray, 1987), *Pour Budapest il est encore temps* (For Budapest There Is Still Time, 1990), and *Comme si les hommes étaient partis en voyage* (As If the Men Had Left on a Journey, 1995). She has earned her rightful place not only among other French Jewish writers of her generation, but also within the established French literary canon.

Writing and Family History

Rabinovitch began writing fiction after her father's tragic death in a car accident in 1981. At that time she also began to explore, literally and figuratively, his Ashkenazic Jewish heritage, the contemporary landscape of Eastern and Central Europe, and the violent impact of the Holocaust on her psyche.

During World War II, Wladimir Rabinovitch went into hiding in the south of France, while his wife, Germaine, an art teacher who was not Jewish, stayed in their house in the Alps with their first-born daughter, Sol. The impact of these years on the Rabinovitch family cannot be overstated. Not only did the family endure incredible hardship, but the circumstances of the French state's institutionalized persecution of its Jews motivated Wladimir Rabinovitch, when he resumed his legal career after the war, to examine the history of French Jewry, especially the relationship between French jurisprudence and the Jews of France. Although Rabinovitch was born after the war, these dark years have left indelible scars. This is made manifest in her novels, which present tired and psychologically weakened women who are disconnected and isolated from other people, and who also seek this condition: "Fabrizio expects her to be pretty, charming, dazzling, as if life were an easy load to carry," states the narrator of *Comme si les hommes étaient partis en voyage*. "She sends him a book on the Prague Ghetto with synagogues and Jewish cemeteries. To tell him what he doesn't want to hear, to construct walls between them" (L'Harmattan, 1995, p. 37). (All translations from the French are my own.)

Eastern and Central European Influences

Rabinovitch's texts cover an enormous amount of territory, psychological and geographic. Each novel recounts the inner world of a Parisian artist whose life is punctuated by travels to Israel, Eastern and Central Europe, and the United States, as well as by her obsessive relationships with different men and a fixation on the lost world of Ashkenazic Jewry. Rabinovitch describes the Eastern and Central European backdrop that figures in her writings as a kind of "interior course inscribed in geography" (personal interview, 1995). The path of travel begins with *L'hiver au coeur* in

Poland at the time of Jaruzelski's military coup in 1981, and ends in the early 1990s with *Comme si les hommes étaient partis en voyage*, after the fall of Communism, when the protagonist, Lilith, is able to return to Vilnius, her father's birthplace—Wladimir Rabinovitch's actual birthplace: "The plane flies over the Tatras, behind her Bratislava, Prague and Budapest. The journey begun years ago. History has allowed her" (p. 38).

As a result of traveling to Eastern and Central Europe, Rabinovitch's protagonists not only bear witness to major historical events of the post-World War II era, but also experience the awakening of their Jewish collective memory of the war. In *L'hiver au coeur*, Milena, a French writer, embarks for Poland soon after the death of her father, hoping to reunite with her estranged Polish lover, Wojtek, a leader in the Solidarity movement. While the novel chronicles the whirlwind of events leading up to Jaruzelski's military coup, it also brings our attention to the suffering endured by the post-Holocaust generation.

> Nothing makes sense anymore, neither my love for Wojtek nor the occurrences of my thoughts. Yesterday and tomorrow no longer exist. Perhaps I will never leave this country, caught in the wheels of a gigantic mechanism I am not able to discern. . . . And if they decided to reopen the camps. Not one has been destroyed. In Auschwitz, everything has remained in place. Nathan, Treblinka survivor, the first man I knew—émigré in Israel, uprooted in France. Killed himself with gas. Intense blue of the dawn. I was haunted by narratives of the Holocaust during my entire adolescence (Barrault, 1981, p. 79).

Awakening Jewish Memory

The awakening of Jewish memory is represented by temporal instability in the text. Moments in time are transposed onto each other: Poland in the 1980s merges with Poland of the 1940s; Wojtek, the distant Polish lover, evokes memories of Milena's first love affair with a Treblinka survivor who ultimately took his own life.

Rabinovitch has not directly experienced the trauma of World War II, yet in her writings and her travels she retraces the steps of deportation taken by the previous generation: "I did not live through the Holocaust, but I was infinitely and profoundly aware of what happened . . ., in part because of the literature I read as an adolescent, and in part because of the dramatic lighting that is projected onto these childhood years . . ., I have dreams of being arrested, chased . . ." (interview, 1995). While Rabinovitch may suffer unconsciously from this dark chapter in history, her protagonists consciously seek experiences of dislocation and rupture: "I like encounters and ruptures. The rest is only suffering and deception" (*Les étangs*, Actes Sud, 1987, p. 84). They travel to foreign lands and lie in different beds in order recreate an inherent feeling of absence and longing, and also to compensate for the tainted history and the absent memory they have inherited: "Above them, in the sky, the Castle of Prague. She has come too late for Kafka and for Central Europe, too late for memory" (*Comme si*, p. 86). Indeed, they attempt to defy the fact that they were born after the almost total destruction of European Jewry by bearing witness, albeit retrospectively, to what happened: " 'Look at this staircase. It is constructed with Jewish tombstones.' Lilith leans over, she recognizes a few letters rubbed out by peoples' steps" (*Comme si*, p. 54).

Jewish tombstones destroyed and wrested into staircases: the brutality of this image attests to the violence of a Jewish world marked by persecution, exile, and destruction. Through writing, Rabinovitch not only repeats experiences of violent rupture, but also attempts to reverse this antisemitic act of effacement by inscribing Jewish memory onto the white page. Like the work of her contemporaries, Rabinovitch's writing serves a commemorative function whereby the literary text becomes a memorial representing a destroyed Jewish world. Her writing also becomes a space where post-memory crystallizes: the past refuses to go away; it haunts her writing with unrelenting force. In the following passage, the phenomenon of post-memory is artfully demonstrated by Rabinovitch through Lilith, the protagonist of *Comme si*, who experiences, in one fleeting instant, different moments in time and place.

> In Manhattan, there is not a bit of land for her. She sees again the tombs of the Lithuanian children in Bagneux, the Hebrew inscriptions, the bouquets of rhododendron, the small rocks. She is next to her grandmother in the summer light; she has the same blue stare. She reads her name, Lilith (p. 8).

That the Jewish cemetery is the center of this description brings to the fore the significance of the Jewish cenotaph, which brings together different moments and people in time and place: Manhattan; the French Jewish cemetery, Bagneux, where the Lithuanian children are buried; and the two Liliths. As this passage suggests, the past lives in the present, takes over the present; it is not something static and immovable.

Although Rabinovitch remembers and pieces together a lot of history in her writing, she does not try to reconstruct the past. Rather, she chooses to remain in the present among the ruins, graves, and ghosts, both personal and collective. Her writing imitates, like a palimpsest, layers of history and memory, real and imagined as well as personal and collective. It is therefore difficult, if not impossible, to categorize Rabinovitch's novels as any particular genre of fiction: historical, realist, experimental, or autobiographical. Inherently hybrid, her work resists classification. Nonetheless, historical moments—recent wars, revolutions, and political events—provide contextual frames. Experiences of great loss (personal and collective), impossible love affairs, and the death of Rabinovitch's father (which is represented in all of her novels), are indeed punctuated by violent historical crises: The Six-Day War in 1967, the Yom Kippur War in 1973, Jaruzelski's military coup in 1981, the Israeli-Lebanese War in 1982, and the fall of Communism in 1989. Touched by explosive episodes, her narratives cannot accommodate such a saturation of history and thus do not conform to any traditional structure. Different stories and different moments in time interrupt each other, journeys abroad become confused, the protagonists' numerous fleeting love affairs converge and form an indeterminate portrait of the lover. Indeed, Rabinovitch's texts represent consequences of the traumatic history of the Holocaust for the self and also for writing. Violent experiences of exile and rupture are represented thematically as well as textually. Rabinovitch's staccato fragmented style, her sentences absent of verbs, and her intensely purified language reflect a fractured world marked by the passage of time and by loss. The opening passage of *Comme si les hommes étaient partis en voyage* inaugurates the movement of reflection:

> The first night. The impression of never having left. Sirens scream along Third Avenue, agonize in the distance. In the midst of her insomnia, Lilith strangely thinks of the final scene in one of Bellow's novels which describes the burial of an old poet.
>
> Needles scattered on the floorboards of the room. The particular odor of wax in New York apartments. Streets winter, the clouds of vapor that escape from the bowels of the city. The central heat resonates like the engine of a ship, it punctuates time (p. 7).

From the onset, the text introduces us to the fictional world of the writer: "the final scene in one of Bellow's novels which describes the burial of an old poet." Through its denotative discourse, the above passage informs us that we are about to begin a journey, one that is first and foremost concerned with writing. While Rabinovitch and her generation may have been born too late for memory and for Central Europe, they were born with the gift of language and words. This gift, which manifests itself most profoundly in the ability to articulate the wrenching pain of the post-Holocaust condition, has enabled Rabinovitch to make connections to the past. Exiled from the destroyed world of her ancestors, Rabinovitch appeals to words in order to express this loss and to investigate its traces.

Bibliography

Primary Sources

"Un monde que j'ignorais m'appartenir" (A World I Forgot Belongs to Me). *Esprit* (July–August 1969): 117–123.

"Comme si les hommes étaient brusquement partis en voyage" (As If the Men Had Left on a Journey). *Le Monde* 23 (December 1981): 33.

L'hiver au coeur (Winter of the Heart). 1981.

Les étangs de Ville d'Avray (The Marshes of Ville-d'Avray). 1987.

Pour Budapest il est encore temps (For Budapest There Is Still Time). 1990.

Comme si les hommes étaient partis en voyage (As If the Men Had Left on a Journey). 1995.

Secondary Sources

Dickstein, Juliette. "*Born After Memory: Repercussions of the Second World War on Postwar French Jewish Writing.*" Ph.D. diss. Harvard University, 1997.

Interview

Interview with Juliette Dickstein. October 1995. Unpublished.

HENRI RACZYMOW

(1948–)

JULIETTE DICKSTEIN

HENRI RACZYMOW WAS born in Paris, France in 1948 and educated at the Sorbonne; he holds a master's degree in modern literature. Having taught in public schools since 1972, he presently teaches in an Orthodox Jewish girl's school in Paris. Raczymow's first book, *La saisie* (The Repossession, 1973), which was published in 1973, won the prestigious Fénéon prize. Since then, Raczymow has written numerous novels, stories, essays, cultural criticism, and literary portraits devoted to Jewish themes as well as to pertinent arguments in the world of letters and ideas, from Proust to Yiddish culture. His novel *Un cri sans voix* (A Voiceless Cry, 1985) was translated into English as *Writing the Book of Esther* in 1997. In the late 1970s, Raczymow participated with journalist Luc Rosenzweig and historian Annette Wieviorka in the founding of *Traces*, a journal of contemporary Jewish culture in France. Throughout the years he has been a steady contributor to other intellectual Jewish journals such as *L'Arche* and *Pardès*, as well as to the avant-garde journals *Tel Quel, L'infini*, and the review, *Les Temps Modernes*, which was founded by Jean-Paul Sartre and Simone de Beauvoir.

Family History

Raczymow came of age during the 1960s in Paris, in the midst of ideological, political, and artistic upheaval, and like most of his contemporaries, joined the ranks of disgruntled students during the riots of May 1968. The watershed of his teenage years, however, the Six-Day War, occurred one year earlier: "I experienced a tremendous rupture in my life and a sudden awakening" (Liberman, p. 3). By the time Raczymow decided to enlist in the Israeli army, the war was over. Nevertheless, at the age of nineteen he began to question and to explore a culture and a religion from which he had felt estranged, and "which had been hidden by his parents, children of immigrants who wanted to leave the ghetto and the Yiddish of their own parents . . ., and who were atheists without any connection to the synagogue" (Liberman, p. 3). (Unless otherwise noted, all translations from the French are my own.)

Raczymow's mother, Anna Davidowicz, was born in 1928 in Paris after her family's recent emigration from Dusseldorf. Raczymow's father, Isaac (Etienne), also born in Paris in 1925 of immigrant parents from Poland, fought with the Jewish communist partisans, the FTP-MOI (Francs Tireurs Partisans/Main-d'Oeuvre immigrée) during World War II, and identified himself, first and foremost, as a member of the French Resistance. The Davidowicz family, however, were "assignés à résidence," that is, forced to stay in a specific place of residence by the Vichy government under the law of 4 October 1940, enacted to control the activities and property of foreign-born Jews. The Davidowiczs were assigned to the region of the Charentes. The Raczymow and Davidowicz families both lost parents and siblings in the death camps of Poland. Raczymow's mother's brother, Heinz, was arrested by the French gendarmes in the Charentes and deported to Majdanek, the camp near Lublin, Poland, where he died. Raczymow's paternal grandmother was arrested and deported during the "rafle du Vel' d'hiv,' " the largest mass arrest of Jews in France during the war; she was never seen again. The Velodrôme d'hiver, the sports stadium in the fifteenth arrondissement (neighborhood) of Paris, became a squalid, disease-ridden holding tank for arrested Jewish families waiting to be sent to camps in the East. The French police rounded up 12,884 men, women, and children. Of the 4,051 children deported, not one survived.

Much of this horrific history surfaces in Raczymow's writings, fiction and nonfiction. His most recent work, *L'homme qui tua René Bousquet* (The Man Who Killed René Bousquet, 2001), is a psychological investigation of Christian Didier who, on 8 June 1993, shot and killed the ex-Vichy chief of police, René Bousquet, who was responsible for organizing and carrying out the "rafle du Vel' d'hiv,' " among other heinous acts. His murder took place only a couple of weeks before he was to be tried for crimes against humanity. The 343 pages that comprise *L'homme* document the misadventures of Christian Didier, and probe how a man with no personal connection to what happened to the Jews of France during World War II, sought revenge on Bousquet and assassinated him outside his apartment door, and then held a press conference in front of the Parisian Town Hall. The book is written in a journalistic style that is interspersed with literary allusions and quotes from the visionary poet Arthur Rimbaud to the Surrealist André Breton in an attempt to make associations between literary representations of murder and actual homicidal acts. It also poignantly communicates Raczymow's "raison d'écrire" (reason for writing): Without having asked him to do so, Didier, indeed, sought revenge in his place; what happened to the Jews of France is Raczymow's inheritance, not Didier's. Raczymow must live with this history and endure the ensuing guilt "d'être né trop tard" (for being born too late).

The Post-Holocaust Generation

Born in the wake of the almost complete destruction of European Jewry, Raczymow belongs to a generation of French Jews that has inherited the trauma of the German occupation and Vichy France's collaborationist regime, and to an age group of authors who repeatedly return to the war years in their writing to look for answers to questions that plague their existence. "I have always felt like a plant that has sprung from the manure heap of the Occupation," states writer Patrick Modiano (Assouline, 34–46). Faced with a past that is not his own, yet still a part of him, Raczymow endures guilt and shame for not having experienced what his elders suffered: "What right do I have to speak if I am neither a victim, survivor, nor witness of the event?" ("Memory Shot Through with Holes," p. 180). Raczymow does speak about the Holocaust and communicates what it feels like to be born on the heels of an annihilated universe:

> In everyone there is an unfillable void, but for the Ashkenazic Jew born in the Diaspora after the war, the symbolic void is coupled with a real one. There is a void in our memory formed by a Poland unknown to us and entirely vanished, and a void in our remembrance of the Holocaust through which we did not live. We cannot even say that we were almost deported ("Memory Shot Through with Holes," 1994, p. 180).

Much scholarship has focused on the work of the Holocaust generation, the generation that was deported, survived, and struggled, and continues to struggle to write about this dark chapter in their personal and collective history and memory. Psychoanalyst Dori Laub, who has worked extensively with trauma victims, especially Holocaust survivors, explains how necessary it is for them to articulate the traumatic experience to someone who listens and who can testify to the reality of the experience endured. In *Se Questo É un Uomo* (1947 If This Is a Man, translated by Stuart Woolf, New York: Penguin, 1979, pp. 34–36), Primo Levi, who was deported from Italy to Auschwitz in 1944, expresses the need to transmit the experience, "the need to tell 'others,' to have 'others' participate" (p. 8). Charlotte Delbo, who was deported to Auschwitz from France in one of the last convoys, writes about her experiences in an unadorned, neutral language. (See her trilogy, *Auschwitz et après* [Auschwitz and After].)

While the Holocaust generation of writers has been most concerned with aesthetic and epistemological questions that treat linguistic and thematic problems of representation, the post-Holocaust generation has demonstrated an obsession with the war years and with the notion of memory itself, precisely because they were born on the cusp of one of the darkest periods of history. Academics and journalists have been turning their attention to this postwar generation of artists, writers, and historians, from the critical essays of Alain Finkielkraut, whose term "imaginary Jew" has codified the particular condition of postwar Jews who live in an imaginary world marked by an intense experience of suffering they have not endured, to the photographs and installations of Christian Boltanski, which recall the fragility of life and the specters of the past. The historiography of Henry Rousso examines how contemporary French society has remembered and dealt with the aftermath of the Vichy years; Marianne Hirsch, whose writings focus on the aftermath of the Holocaust in the works of second-generation writers and artists, has formulated a new term, "post-memory," to describe the condition of the child of the post-Holocaust generation whose life is overwhelmed by family memories that predate his or her birth. This has been perceived by clinical psychologist Nathalie Zajde, who has published a remarkable study of the children of Holocaust survivors in France, *Enfants de survivants* (Children of Survivors), which analyzes, through case studies, interviews, and research, how post-Holocaust Jews in France profoundly suffer from troubles they associate with events experienced by their parents and grandparents during the war. French psychoanalyst Nadine Fresco, the daughter of Holocaust survivors, qualifies this particular suffering as an illusory pain where amnesia has taken the place of memory. Indeed, the novels of Patrick Modiano, Anne Rabinovitch, Miriam Annisimov, and of course Henri Raczymow treat the aftermath of traumatic history and the ensuing problematics that concern writing or creation in general: How does one narrate and what does one narrate, when the events you are trying to remember happened before you were born?

Writing

Although much of Raczymow's written work communicates the consequences of being born immediately after the catastrophe of the Holocaust, what he qualifies as the "problematic of deficiency inherent in postwar Jewish identity," his earlier writing was strongly influenced by the aesthetic and ideological theories of the postwar avant-garde—the nouveau roman, or New Novel. The "New Novelists" (Alain Robbe-Grillet, Nathalie Sarraute, Claude Simon) avoided certain conventions proper to literary realism in their own texts: traditional character and plot development, a chronological ordering of events; in short, a readable literary work à la Balzac. Raczymow's *La saisie*, *Scènes* (Scenes, 1975) and *Bluette* (Small Spark [Light and Witty Literary Work], 1977) are highly experimental, self-reflexive investigations of the nature, act, and purpose of writing. Characters and plot development break down, chronological time is subjected to forces of distortion and aberration—rendering, at times, past and present indistinguishable from each other—and proper names and personal pronouns are confused and impossible to distinguish from one another. At times, language and its referential activity appear to be in such a state of crisis that one understands more is at stake in the narrative than a simple literary "*exercise de style*." Robbe-Grillet's famous dictum: "To tell a story has become practically impossible" (*Pour un nouveau roman* [For a New Novel], Paris: Gallimard, 1964, p. 33), may sound to some like a cliché, yet it is still meaningful not only to a discussion of Raczymow's work, but also in general to any consideration of the consequences of the Holocaust for writing.

Over time, as Raczymow started to explore his Jewish identity in greater depth, critics began to trace his transformation from "new novelist" to "new Jewish novelist." In the early 1980s, "Raczymow entered a new stage in his literary itinerary," writes scholar Ellen S. Fine. "Called by critics *le nouveau roman juif* ("new Jewish novel"), his fiction began to integrate the self-reflective mode of the nouveau roman with the telling of Jewish tales and legends" (p. 47). Gilles Pudlowski situates Raczymow "half-way between the French avant-garde and the Yiddish novelists of the past" (p. 54). In "*La mémoire trouée*" ("Memory Shot Through with Holes"), an essay devoted to memory, writing, and Jewish identity, Raczymow discusses the influence of the New Novel on his writing and the subsequent emergence of his Jewish identity:

> The theories of the "new novelists" appealed to me. They took delight in repeating that they had nothing to say, that they needed to devise new forms of fiction. I thought I was attracted to such theories for purely ideological or esthetic reasons, but that was not at all true. Some years later I came to understand that I did not have nothing to say. Like many others I could have said, or written, just about anything. Rather, I had to say nothing, which is not the same thing. As the years went by, as I wrote more, I discovered that the nothing I had to say, to write, to explore—the nothing I turned into sentences, narrative, books—the nothing I could not escape saying as a positive nothing, was my Jewish identity (translated by Alan Astro pp. 98, 99).

Raczymow's texts may share a good deal with the "new novelists." The difference, however, between "having nothing to say," and "having to say nothing" is a minimal yet decisive discrepancy that distinguishes his work from theirs. Inscribed in the space of absence are the vanished world of Eastern European Jewry and the historical reality of the Holocaust. The reader has only to note the number of blank spaces that are represented either thematically or textually in Raczymow's works to realize how dominant a role absence plays. In fact, absence is so paramount that it takes on signifying powers and can be read as a trace, a mark that bespeaks the "nothingness" of his Jewish identity. "What does it mean to be a Jew?" Raczymow asks. "It does not mean something that is plentiful, paradoxically, it means something that is lacking . . . a kind of insufficient way of being" (interview, 1996).

La saisie, Raczymow's first book, relates the story of a man named Irtych who has lost all of his belongings and furniture in a repossession ("*saisie*"), including the magazine pictures he had pasted on the wall of his apartment. Dispossessed of all of his belongings—with the exception of a wooden chair on which he sits—faced with a completely bare and empty apartment, Irtych begins to fill the blank page not only with an inventory of his lost possessions, but also with his fragmentary memories of a previous life in a foreign country and an entire inheritance that has been taken from him by some unnamed group of people. Absence marks *La saisie* textually: included in the text are actual spaces or holes that appear whenever Irtych speaks about the blankness of the walls, "the   of the walls." Absence even determines the narrative structure of the text in the sense that it lacks a certain traditional, logical development of events. The ordered universe of the realist novel is more than missing; it is completely turned upside down.

Although Raczymow claims that this work is completely devoid of Jewish subject matter, he also acknowledges the Jewish dimension that permeates all of his work, which he describes as a "disappointment that pushes him towards something else"—could it be his lost Jewish heritage? (Liberman, p. 3). Estranged from the past and his own language, Irtych is emblematic of the post-Holocaust Jew living in the Diaspora, who takes recourse in writing in order to compensate for imperfect memory, and to fill the gaps of the absent past of prewar (Jewish) Poland.

Several years later, these questions become more obviously the focus of Raczymow's work. *Contes d'exil et d'oubli* (*Tales of Exile and Forgetfulness*, 1979), Raczymow's first overtly "Jewish" book, portrays the lost world of pre-World War II Poland through the eyes of Matthieu Schriftlich, the narrator/protagonist, who is haunted by the ghosts of his ancestors murdered in the crematoria. He struggles to reconstruct the landscape of this tragically destroyed world, and pushes his grandparents, aunts, and uncles to tell him about the past. What ensues are fragmented stories about the Polish villages Konsk and Kaloush, the imaginary lake Kamenetz "swallowed up by the mist of postwar Poland" (p. 63), tales about Simon Davidovicz, the peddler, Rabbi Schlomo Gruenflamm, Matthieu's great great grandfather, and Mati Oksenberg, his ancestor "whose repose is protected by no cemetery" (p. 87). Matthieu's relatives relate their memories of Poland with reluctance and consider his desire to uncover the past a rather dubious project: "You must forget Kaloush, what's dead will not come back to life." Consequently, Matthieu questions his right to stir up these memories and his right to disturb the dead: "Yes, does he have the right to disturb the dead?" (p. 103). The refusal or inability of the older generation to communicate their memories of the past alienates him from the history of prewar Jewish Poland, and pushes him to appeal to his imagination to complete the story; it also forces him to struggle with the ensuing emotions of what can be called "second-generation survivor guilt." Nowhere is this more apparent than in his novel, *Un cri sans voix* (A Voiceless Cry, 1985), where the narrator, Mathieu Litvak, wrestles with his identity as a writer whose inspiration feeds on the memories of his relatives who perished in the crematoria.

The story begins one summer evening in 1982 during the Israeli-Lebanese war when Mathieu reads in the newspaper, after the Israeli invasion of southern Lebanon, that a "Genocide without precedent in the entire history of humanity" has just taken place (p. 3). The paper's appropriation of the specific language of the Holocaust is a watershed for Mathieu that unleashes his obsession with the fate of the European Jews, and in particular, his memory of his sister Esther, who committed suicide seven years earlier by gassing herself in her oven. Her suicide, the result of an overidentification with the death camps, begins to haunt Mathieu unrelentingly. Born on 2 August 1943, the day of the Treblinka uprising, Esther's experience of survivor guilt is so strong that it ultimately destroys her. Her family responded to her death by not speaking about it and by making it a taboo subject. Mathieu responds to this fixation on his sister's life and death by usurping her avocation, her story and her "stories." By writing her story in her place he is able to explore his own relationship to this traumatic history, his own obsession and guilt for being born too late.

The first section of the novel is Esther's ghetto diary as imagined by Mathieu. The diary is Mathieu's fictional chronicle of daily life in the Warsaw ghetto as experienced by those he transposed from his family and friends, interspersed with other fictional and historic characters. It is an account of the events, dates, organizations, and figures that shaped ghetto life: the erection of the ghetto walls; the Nazi establishment of the Judenrat (Jewish Council); the pedagogue Janusz Korczak's orphanage; and other well-known writers and ghetto personalities such as Shlomo Huberband, Yitzhak Katzenelson, and Adam Czerniakow; the Zionist group Hashomer Hatzair; the filming of the ghetto by the Germans; the deportations; and the preparations for the ghetto uprising. Mathieu writes the book he assumes his sister would have wanted to write if she had been born in Poland and lived in the ghetto during the 1940s. The second section of Raczymow's novel treats Mathieu's relationship to his sister, her fate, and the shadow her life and death have cast over him: "The great superiority of Esther, her incontestable superiority was that she was endangered. Mathieu, born after the war, will never be able to catch up to her" (pp. 115–116). Mathieu probes the life and death of his sister and the activities of other members of his family who survived the war. Similar to Contes, Mathieu pushes his relatives to tell him stories. Although they recount their experiences in Poland, they do so in a familiar fragmentary style, which mixes together contemporary politics, daily life in the Warsaw ghetto, Hassidic tales, and biblical stories.

Whereas the first section of *Un cri* chronicles the breakdown of Jewish life in the Warsaw ghetto and demonstrates how all attempts to represent or understand this horror ultimately fail, the second section further explores the epistemological and existential questions with which all post-Holocaust literature must contend: how to represent what happened and how to understand it. One of the most disturbing examples is a conversation Mathieu has with his relative Simon about the question of Jewish passivity. Mathieu is completely obsessed with how a group of four hundred Jews could be led into a camp by only two SS officers:

> For Mathieu that was the real question: the passivity of the victims, indeed their complicity with the executioners in the extermination. . . . The silence of the Jews before the gas chamber.
> The silence of the Jews one meter from the gas chamber. The only cry of the Jews reverberates once the doors are closed. A mute cry. An S.S. officer could see them scream through the peephole, but not hear them. A mute cry. How can a cry be mute?
> We agree equally on three things, a Hassidic rabbi mentioned to someone who asked him what makes a Jew a Jew: An upright kneeling, a mute cry, an immobile dance . . ."What are you saying," asked Simon. Do you mean that it was in the gas chambers that the Jews satisfied this Rabbi's avowal?
> —No, I don't mean anything," replied Mathieu. It's only literature . . ." (pp. 156–157).

No answer or deep meaning can be extracted from the words of the rabbi; the fate that met the Jews in the gas chambers cannot be explained or interpreted as any kind of fulfillment. Moreover, the literary text cannot draw conclusions. It is without any totalizing function. This does not mean that the writing of this novel is something meaningless or gratuitous. Mathieu writes with definite purposes: to become closer to his sister and to explore his own relationship to the Holocaust. He writes, however, not to understand in philosophical terms how such an event could happen in our "civilized," modern world, but rather to document and to record history. *Un cri sans voix*, therefore, ends on a curious note. Mathieu decides not to tell his child the story of his sister's suicide and her obsession with the destruction of Polish Jewry.

> My child will be saved from the past. He will not be tainted. He will really be a postwar child. . . . I will never speak to him about Esther. Her name will be silenced. My book will have effaced her. Curiously, words were necessary for that. Words and not silence (pp. 213–214).

Mathieu writes in order to erase the silence, the trauma of his sister's suicide—the trauma of the war. He writes for the historical record, so that his child will have historical knowledge without the trauma of history. "My child must live," he states, "and not only survive" (p. 214). In writing his "Book of Esther," Mathieu attempts to narrate differently from his parents, aunts, and uncles whose fragmented and aborted tales succeeded only in transmitting a traumatic experience of the past. Mathieu's project is, on the contrary, one of articulation and inscription. By writing the imagined life of his sister, and by transcribing the stories told to him by his family members—fragmented stories shot through with holes—Mathieu Litvak moves beyond the silence and the taboo that have been placed on talking and writing about the horror that met the Jews of Europe. ("Esther's book," of course, recalls the biblical "Book of Esther," one of the most important stories of Jewish resistance, which recounts the story of the beautiful Esther's power to deliver the Jewish people from domination under the Persian King Ahasuerus and his despotic minister, Haman. It is a story the Jewish people retold during times of extreme hardship.)

Conclusion

Raczymow's narrators and protagonists strive to make connections and create narratives. "Writing was and still is the only way I can tell myself about the past, the whole past, even if it is by definition a recreated past," Raczymow states in reference to the function writing serves with respect to re-membering, that is, piecing together the fragments of a ravaged history ("Memory Shot Through with Holes," p. 180). Raczymow may have trouble recalling the horrific events of World War II, but he has, nonetheless, accomplished a significant mnemonic feat, for his work, like that of his contemporaries, has helped all of France to remember the French state's collaboration with the occupying Germans and its participation in the deportation of over 75,000 Jews of France. Raczymow's work, however, also bears witness to another reality, no less real and no less significant than that of the older generation who lived through World War II: rebuilding a new life in the wake of historical catastrophe, and moving beyond the overpowering memory of this past.

Bibliography

Primary Sources

La saisie. (The Repossession). 1973.
Scènes (Scenes). 1975.
Bluette (Small Spark [Light and Witty Literary Work]). 1977.
Contes d'exil et d'oubli. (Tales of Exile and Forgetfulness). 1979.

Tales of Exile and Forgetfulness (excerpt). Translated by Alan Astro. *Yale French Studies: Discourses of Jewish Identity in Twentieth-Century France* 85 (1994).

Rivières d'exil (Rivers of Exile). 1982.

"*On ne part pas* (One Does Not Leave)." 1983.

Un cri sans voix (A Voiceless Cry, *Writing the Book of Esther*). 1985, 1997.

Maurice Sachs ou les travaux forcés de frivolité. 1988.

Le cygne de Proust (Proust's Swan). 1989.

Ninive. 1991.

Territoires du Yiddish: de la création vivante à la désolation (Pardès 15) (Yiddish Landscapes: From Living Creation to Desolation). 1992.

Bloom & Bloch. 1993.

La mort du grand écrivain (The Death of the Great Writer). 1994.

Quartier Libre (Free Neighborhood). 1995.

Le Paris intime et littéraire de Marcel Proust (Marcel Proust's Intimate and Literary Paris). 1997.

Pauvre Bouilhet (Poor Bouilhet). 1998.

L'homme qui tua René Bousquet. 2001.

Major Essays

"Pourquoi écrire," (Why Write). *Traces* 3 (1981): 98–99.

"Aujourd'hui, le roman juif?" (Today, the Jewish Novel?). *Traces* 3 (1981): 71–108.

"Les gestes sont morts." *Tel Quel* 87 (1981): 102–104.

"La mémoire trouée." *Pardès* (1986): 177–182.

"Memory Shot Through with Holes." Edited and translated by Alan Astro. *Yale French Studies: Discourses of Jewish Identity in Twentieth-Century France* 85 (1994): 225–227.

"La langue perdue." *L'infini* 33 (spring 1991): 43–46.

"Fin du peuple ashkénaze." ("End of the Ashkenazy People." A Thousand Years of Ashkenazy Culture). *Mille ans de cultures ashkénazes*. Edited by Jean Baumgarten. Paris: Liana Levi, 1994, 609–616.

Edited Volumes

Littérature et judéité dans les langues européennes. Paris: Les Editions du Cerf, 1995.

Translations from the Yiddish by Raczymow

Asch, Schalom. *Varsovie*. Translated by Aby Wieviorka and Henri Raczymow. Paris: Mémoire du Livre, 2001.

Secondary Sources

Assouline, Pierre. "Modiano: lieux de Memoire," *LIRE* 176 [May 1990]: 34–46.

Berger, Alan. *Children of Job: Second-Generation Witnesses to the Holocaust*. New York: State University of New York Press, 1997.

Epstein, Helen. *Children of the Holocaust: Conversations with Sons and Daughters of Survivors*. New York: G.P. Putnam's Sons, 1979.

Fine, Ellen S. "The Absent Memory: The Act of Writing in Post-Holocaust French Literature." In *Writing and the Holocaust*. Edited by Berel Lang. New York: Holmes & Meir, 1988.

Finkielkraut, Alain. *Le juif imaginaire*. Paris: Editions du Seuil, 1980.

———. *The Imaginary Jew*. Translated by Kevin O'Neill and David Suchoff. Lincoln: University of Nebraska Press, 1994.

Fresco, Nadine. "La diaspora des cendres." *Nouvelle revue de psychanalyse* 24 (1981): 205–220.

Friedlander, Judith. *Vilna on the Seine: Jewish Intellectuals in France since 1968*. New Haven: Yale University Press, 1990.

Hartman, Geoffrey H., ed. *Holocaust Remembrance: The Shapes of Memory*. Cambridge: Blackwell, 1994.

Hirsch, Marianne. "Family Pictures: *Maus*, Mourning, and Post-Memory." *Discourse* 15, no. 2 (winter 1992–1993): 3–29.

Koster, Serge. *Trou de mémoire*. Paris: Criterion, 1991.

Liberman, Jean, comp. "Dialogue entre Regine Robin et Henri Raczymow." *La Presse Nouvelle Hebdomadaire* (7 September 1979): 3–5.

Marks, Elaine. *The Marrano as Metaphor: The Jewish Presence in French Writing*. New York: Columbia University Press, 1996.

Pudlowski, Gilles. "Le bon vieux temps du ghetto: Henri Raczymow et le 'nouveau roman juif.' " *Les Nouvelles Littéraires* (13 May 1982): 53–55.

Rosenzweig, Luc. *La jeune france juive: conversations avec des juifs d'aujourd'hui*. Paris: Editions Libres-Hallier, 1980.

Rousso, Henry. *Le syndrôme de Vichy: de 1944 à nos jours*. Paris: Editions de Seuil, 1990.

———. *The Vichy Syndrome: History and Memory in France since 1944*. Translated by Arthur Goldhammer. Cambridge: Harvard University Press, 1991.

Sicher, Efraim, ed. *Breaking Crystal: Writing and Memory After Auschwitz*. Urbana & Chicago: Illinois University Press, 1998.

Zajde, Nathalie. *Enfants de survivants*. Paris: Edition Odile Jacob, 1995.

Zeitlin, Froma. "The Vicarious Witness: Belated Memory and Authorial Presence in Recent Holocaust Literature." *History and Memory* 10 (1998): 5–42.

Interview

Interview with Juliette Dickstein. 5 October 1996. Unpublished.

MIKLÓS RADNÓTI

(1909–1944)

RITA HORVÁTH

MIKLÓS RADNÓTI WAS born to Jakab Glatter and Ilona Grosz in Budapest on 5 May 1909: Radnóti's mother and twin brother died during his birth. His father, a salesman, soon married Ilona Molnár, whom the child adored, not knowing that she was not his birth mother. In 1914 his sister, Ágnes, was born. Radnóti's father died of a stroke in 1921, when Radnóti was only twelve years old. Because of insurmountable financial difficulties, his stepmother and sister were forced to move away, a devastating blow for the boy. Amidst these traumatic events, Radnóti learned about the circumstances of his birth, and an uncle, a successful textile merchant, became his guardian. He wanted Radnóti to follow in his footsteps in the textile business and directed his education accordingly: Radnóti graduated from a high school of commerce in 1927, and studied for a year in the School of Textile Production and Technology in Reichenberg (Liberec), Czechoslovakia. After returning to Hungary, he worked as a clerk in his uncle's business. However, Radnóti began to write poetry in adolescence and soon began to publish in journals. He also met the love of his life, his muse, Fanni Gyarmati, in the autumn of 1926. Together they joined the Hungarian Youth's Bálint Balassa Literary Club and worked on the publication of the club's journal: *Haladás* (Progress). Radnóti very consciously developed his poetic skills and took an active part in literary life. His first volume of poetry, *Pogány köszöntő* (*Pagan Salute* [unless indicted otherwise, I use Emery George's translations]), was published in the spring of 1930. He soon realized that working in the textile business was incompatible with his vocation as a poet. Consequently, he took a supplementary examination and enrolled in the Ferenc József University in Szeged, majoring in Hungarian and French. He joined the Szeged Youth Arts College and took a special interest in folklore and the life of the peasants. Both Communist and Christian ideals attracted him. After graduation, he moved back to the capital and vigorously participated in its literary life, but he was never given a teaching position because of his Jewish background. He supported himself by publishing poems, translating foreign literature into Hungarian, and giving private lessons. Radnóti and Fanni Gyarmati married in 1935. Radnóti was taken to forced labor three times: from September until December 1940; from July 1942 until the spring of 1943; and for the last time on 18 May 1944. He arrived at the Bor *lager*-complex (Serbia) on 2 June. By the end of August the Germans had liquidated the *lagers* in the vicinity of Bor and many forced laborers were sent in a forced march toward the west. On 8 or 9 November 1944, Hungarian soldiers, with the help of two Austrian SS soldiers, shot the exhausted poet in the neck along with twenty-one other men, into a mass grave near the village of Abda in northwest Hungary. The mass grave was exhumed on 23 June 1946 and the poet was identified. On his body, the so called "Bor notebook" was found containing his last poems. His stepmother and his sister, who became a journalist and poet, were both murdered in Auschwitz.

Oeuvre

Radnóti's life and oeuvre is wrought with a major paradox from the point of view of Holocaust literature. He suffered a typical Jewish fate during the Holocaust but he did not construct a Jewish identity. In a letter to a literary critic, Aladár Komlós, written on 17 May 1942, in which the poet refused to give manuscripts to the Hungarian Jewish Almanac, "Ararát-almanach," because it was a denominational publication, he pointedly formulated his convictions about his identity. Radnóti emphasized that he did not feel himself to be a Jew; he had not had a religious upbringing, and historical forces—alien to his personality—transformed his Jewishness into his major "life problem."

He stated that he identified himself as a Hungarian poet despite having experienced the extreme humiliation of forced labor, expulsion from the Hungarian literary scene, and denial of teaching privileges, and had no illusions about what the future had in store for him. He espoused this view, widespread among highly assimilated Jews in Hungary, with exceptional consistency. For example, he wrote "Nem tudhatom . . ." ("I Cannot Know . . ."), a patriotic poem, concerning the devastation of his homeland by bombardments. When he read this poem on New Year's eve of 1943 to a circle of predominantly Jewish intellectuals, the fact that a person banished from Hungarian society could write such a tender confession of love to Hungary, startled his audience.

Radnóti took significant steps to make his chosen identity evident. As a poet he used the name Radnóti instead of Glatter. Radnót is the Hungarian name of a small settlement in Transylvania from which his parents came. In 1934 he wanted to change his name officially, but the Ministry of Interior approved only a variant: Radnóczi. Thus, he continued to use the name Radnóti as his artistic name. On 2 May 1943, he converted to Christianity together with his wife. He was baptized by his mentor, a poet and Piarist monk also of Jewish origin, Sándor Sík. In the previously mentioned letter to Aladár Komlós, Radnóti wrote that he wanted to convert much sooner, but thought he might have been treated differently from Jews. By the spring of 1943 it became obvious that conversion would not provide any escape from the Jewish fate, so Radnóti felt free to express his feeling that the poetry of the New Testament was as much his as that of the Old Testament. This expression of his motivation to convert indicates that it was an act of more fully embracing European culture as a whole.

Radnóti forged an identity as the heir and repository of the values of the entire European culture—humanism, human dignity, the power of reason, art, compassion, and sensitivity to social injustice—which was attacked and eradicated by Fascism. A crucial step in constructing this identity was Radnóti's use of various traditional closed forms, especially the elegaic distich, verse epistle, hymn, and the eclogue written in hexameters. His first volumes of poetry were written under the influence of the avant-garde, predominantly expressionism and surrealism. Neoclassicism was a determinative factor in European literature; it was also a clearly discernible tendency among Hungarian poets belonging to the "third generation" of poets affiliated with the periodical *Nyugat* (*West*). Radnóti's abandonment of free verse in favor of classical versification was the most radical among his peers: Zoltán Nadányi, Jenõ Dsida, Sándor Weöres, and Zoltán Jékely. Classical subjects, such as bucolic idylls, had already attracted him in his avant-garde experimental phase. Radnóti's poem "Ó, régi börtönök" ("O Peace of Ancient Prisons"), dated 27 March 1944, provides a clear indication that his purpose in turning to strict traditional versification was to find a weapon against the entrapping historical situation and a way to assert traditional values. In this poem, Radnóti likens reality to a cracked pot that does not hold its form and spreads its corrupt shards. He then juxtaposes this pot with the poet, who "speaks in form" until he is allowed to live.

Although he did not identify himself as a Jew, he gave a truly exceptional and very personal poetic voice to the Jewish experience of the Holocaust in Hungarian because of his identity as a Hungarian poet. His last poems are generally seen as voicing the collective fate of the Jews. For example, when a group of Jewish architects prepared a plan for the Holocaust Museum in Budapest in 2000, they proposed carving Radnóti's poem, "Erõltetett menet" ("Forced March"), in huge letters on one of the major walls of the building complex. This poem, which was written in Bor following a forced march from one of its satellite *lagers*, *Lager* Heidenau, to the main camp and in anticipation of a much longer march toward Hungary, captures in its rhythm and form the painfully achieved monotony of the march. In these marches the person, who is reduced to "an errant mass of pain," must decide anew at every moment whether to trudge on and whether to get up when fallen to avoid being killed instantly. The first half of the poem amply indicates that there is no chance for a forced laborer to return to a world of normalcy, beauty, and love, because it depends upon his own as well as his loved ones' and home's survival. Thus, the speaker calls anyone who does not choose death a fool. After stating all this, however, irrational hope emerges, leading to a decision to continue the fight for survival. The speaker is fully aware of the irrational nature of any hope because his main argument for continuing to struggle is tied to the moon, which is traditionally associated with lunacy: "just look at tonight's full moon" (*The Complete Poetry*, edited and translated by Emery George, Ann Arbor, Mich.: Heatherway, 1980, p. 275). Nevertheless, the speaker in the poem makes the "foolish" decision to get up and fight for survival. "Forced March" is written in strict form, following that of Walter von der Vogelwide's elegy: "Oweh, war sint verschwunden." Even the space after the caesura in the middle of the Niebelungen line is observed. Facts such as the forced march, actual deaths of companions, anticipation of one's own death by a shot in the neck, and the terrible opposition between getting up and staying down are also the topics of Radnóti's last poem, "Razglednica (4)" ("Picture Postcards [4]"), written just days before his own death.

In constructing his identity Radnóti also gave a major poetic voice to the times preceding the Holocaust, which were filled with fear and growing anticipation of complete catastrophe. He prepared himself for almost ten years for the inevitable and violent death forced upon him by historical circumstances of which he was keenly aware. His thorough preparation, both on the conscious and unconscious levels, for his own murder starkly contrasts and conflicts with the extraordinary love of life that radiates from his writings. He frequently captures natural idylls and idyllic situations connected to love through very precise observations of minute details. For example, he closes "Tétova óda" ("Hesitant Ode") with a description of the exact moment at which his beloved falls asleep by showing her palms closing and opening involuntarily. From 1933, fear of violent death resonates in his landscapes, as the first poem of *Újhold* (*New Moon*, 1935), "Mint a bika" ("Like a Bull"), dated 22 August 1933, indicates. The title of his next volume makes the poet's evaluation of his situation painfully clear: *Járkálj csak, halálraítélt* (*Keep Walking, You, the Death-Condemned!* 1936, translated by Clive Wilmer and George Gömöri). These volumes are full of tortured premonitions of his own death. Death is omnipresent; it saturates the landscape and penetrates the idylls that are deeply intertwined with the poet's love for his wife.

In "Sem emlék, sem varázslat" ("Not Memory, Nor Magic") the poet reckons with the fact that the idylls he captures in his poetry will not save him from the murderously mad world surrounding him. In a confessional poem, "A félelmetes angyal" ("The Terrible Angel"), the "I" of the poem realizes that his love cannot save him from the self-destructive madness threatening from inside as the consequence of the childhood traumas, which haunted Radnóti's entire existence. Both his poetry and his lyrical autobiographical prose piece, *Ikrek hava* (*Under Gemini*, 1959, translated by Kenneth and Zita McRobbie), are permeated with an overwhelming sense of guilt and existential despair. Probably because of this confessional voice, a major Hungarian poet, János Pilinszky, asserted that only Sylvia Plath could have translated Radnóti's poetry into English. Because Radnóti realized that engulfing madness threatened him from every corner, writing, especially about idylls, became a life function and an expression of selfhood. However, in many of his last poems, written in the labor camp and during forced marches—"À La Recherche . . .," "Levél a hitveshez" ("Letter to My Wife"), "Hetedik ecloga" ("Seventh Eclogue"), "Razglednica" ("Picture Postcards [1]") and "Forced March"—the memory of idylls also became a source of strength. Although he prepared himself for a violent death by recording enveloping fear, Radnóti realized that fear itself interfered with his sole aim: the production of great poetry. He therefore aimed to eliminate fear. In "Örizz és védj" ("Guard and Defend Me," translated by Jascha Kessler), the poet invokes pain and consciousness to save his words from the falsifying effects of fear as an ars poetica.

His identity as a poet miraculously provided Radnóti with strength to keep writing until the very end of his life. In the "Seventh Eclogue" he describes the inhuman conditions in the labor camp as he writes the poem at night while the others are sleeping. He dwells on the details of the wretched insect-ridden life of the shaven-headed prisoners behind the barbed wire. Insects so dominate the prisoners' existence that Radnóti documents how in the evenings the fleas continue their attacks, but the flies, at least, are asleep. So complete is the dehumanization that the poet calls himself a "captive beast" and compares his writing, without diacritics, in the dark barracks to the blind groping movement of an earthworm.

The extreme care with which Radnóti ensured the survival of his poems, stemming from the monomaniacal strength of his identity, is also truly exceptional. On the night before leaving home for the last time to report for forced labor, he sent his newest poems to a friend, Iván Boldizsár. At the time of the liquidation of the *lagers* around Bor, he made copies of some of his poems written in the camp and gave them to friends. Into the notebook in which he wrote his last poems, he inscribed in five languages—Hungarian, Serb, German, French, and English—that it contained the poetry of the Hungarian poet, Miklós Radnóti. He requested that the notebook be forwarded to a friend whose name and address he carefully included.

The great number of various English translations of Radnóti's poems illustrate both the need to relate these magnificent poems and the emerging frustration with the results. While Wilmer and Gömöri emphasize the formal difficulties in translation, literary scholar Mihály Szegedy-Maszák identifies as the main difficulty, the fact that the entire Hungarian literary tradition resonates, especially in Radnóti's late work, as the poet consciously equated his motherland with the Hungarian cultural and linguistic heritage. Thus, for non-Hungarian-speaking audiences, the grandeur of Radnóti's poetry has been tempered by its resistance to translation.

Obviously, Radnóti's last poems, written amidst the events of the Holocaust, are very different from works about the Holocaust by survivors who lived with their experiences for a long time before writing. Radnóti's poems, which are very well known in Hungary, continue to greatly affect readers. They structure the experiences of survivors and assist the imagination of those who try to conceive of forced labor.

Bibliography

Primary Sources

Poetry

Pogány köszöntő (*Pagan Salute*). 1930.
Újmódi pásztorok éneke (*Song of Modern Shepherds*). 1931.
Lábadozó szél (*Convalescent Wind*). 1933.
Ének a négeről, aki a városba ment (*Song of the Black Man Who Went to Town*). 1934.
Újhold (*New Moon*). 1935.
Járkálj csak, halálraítélt! (*Keep Walking You, the Death-Condemned!*). 1936.
Meredek út (*Steep Road*). 1938, 1990.
Válogatott versek, 1930–1940 (Selected Poems). 1940.
Naptár (*Calendar*). 1942.
Tajtékos ég (*Sky with Clouds*). 1946.
Radnóti Miklós versei (Miklós Radnóti's Poems). 1948.
Radnóti Miklós válogatott versei (Miklós Radnóti's Selected Poems). 1952.
Radnóti Miklós versei és műfordításai (Miklós Radnóti's Poems and Translations). 1954.
Versek és műfordítások (Poems and Translations). 1954.
Radnóti Miklós összes versei és műfordításai (Miklós Radnóti's Complete Poetry and Translations). 1956, 1959, 1963, 1965, 1969, 1970, 1972, 1974, 1987.
Radnóti Miklós válogatott versei (Miklós Radnóti's Selected Poems). 1956, 1962.
Válogatott versek (Selected Poems). 1960.
Eclogák (Eclogues). 1961, 1979.
Sem emlék, sem varázslat: Radnóti Miklós összes versei (Not Memory, Nor Magic: Miklós Radnóti's Complete Poetry). 1961.
Versek (Poems). 1961.
Radnóti Miklós válogatott művei (Miklós Radnóti's Selected Works). 1962.
Radnóti Miklós összes versei (Miklós Radnóti's Complete Poetry). 1963.
Radnóti Miklós összes versei és műfordításai (Miklós Radnóti's Complete Poetry and Translations). 1966.
1944—(Bori Notesz) (1944—Bor Notebook). 1970, 1971, 1974, 1985.
Radnóti Miklós legszebb versei (Miklós Radnóti's Most Beautiful Poems). 1972.
Válogatott versek és müfordítások (Selected Poems and Translations). 1973.
Esti mosolygás (Evening Smile). 1974, 1978.
Naptár (*Calendar*). 1975, 1997.
Radnóti Miklós művei (Miklós Radnóti's Works). 1976, 1978.
Válogatott versek és műfordítások (Selected Poems and Translations). 1976.
Bori notesz: Hasonmás kiadás (Bor Notebook: Facsimile). 1978.
Hommage A Radnóti (Homage to Radnóti). 1979.
Radnóti Miklós válogatott versei (Miklós Radnóti's Selected Poems). 1979.
Radnóti Miklós versek és műfordítások (Miklós Radnóti's Poems and Translations). 1985.
Napló (Diary). 1989.
Nem bírta hát . . .: Radnóti Miklós utolsó versei (They Just Couldn't Bear It . . .: Miklós Radnóti's Last Poems). 1989.
Virágének (Flower Song). 1989.
Sötét órák (Dark Hours). 1992.
Radnóti Miklós összes versei és versfordításai (Miklós Radnóti's Complete Poetry and Translations). 1993, 1994.
Válogatott versek (Selected Poems). 1994, 1996.
Erőltetett menet: Válogatott versek (Forced March: Selected Poems). 1995, 1996.
Radnóti Miklós versei és versfordításai (Miklós Radnóti's Poems and Translations). 1996.
Radnóti Miklós: Radnóti Miklós általános és középiskolások számára (Miklós Radnóti: Miklós Radnóti for Pupils of Primary and Secondary Schools). 1997.
Radnóti Miklós válogatott versei (Miklós Radnóti's Selected Poems). 1998.
Útravaló Radnóti Miklós tollából (Provisions for the Journey from Miklós Radnóti's Pen). 1998.
Egy vers egy rajz (One Poem One Drawing). 1999.
Radnóti Miklós összegyűjtött versei és műfordításai (Miklós Radnóti's Collected Poems and Translations). 1999.

Prose, Diary, Essays, Studies, and Articles

Kaffka Margit művészi fejldése (Margit Kaffka's Artistic Development). 1934, 1934.
Ikrek hava: Napló a gyerekkorról (*Under Gemini: A Prose Memoir*). 1940.
Tanulmányok, cikkek (Studies, Articles). 1956.
Ikrek hava: Napló a gyerekkorról (*Under Gemini: A Prose Memoir*). 1959, 1960.
Ikrek hava: Napló a gyerekkorról (*Under Gemini: A Prose Memoir*). 1969, 1973.
Próza: Novellák és tanulmányok (Prose: Short Stories and Studies). 1971.
Négy Radnóti-levél (Four Letters by Radnóti). 1973.

English Language Collections of Miklós Radnóti's Works

Miklós Radnóti: 33 Poems. 1992.
Foamy Sky: The Major Poems of Miklós Radnóti. Princeton, N.J.: Princeton University Press, 1992.

Secondary Sources

Bibliographies

Radnóti Miklós: Bibliográfia. Compiled by Mariann Nogy. Budapest: Petöfi Irodalmi Múzeum, 1989.
Vasvári, István. *Radnóti Miklós: Bibliográfia*. Budapest: FSZEK, 1966.

Books after 1986 and Articles after 1988 (the years in which Mariann Nagy completed her bibliography)

Aczel, R. L. "The Poetry of Miklós Radnóti." *The Slavonic and East European Review* (July 1989): 459–460.
Andai, Ferenc. "Radnóti Heidenauban: A költö halálának ötvenedik évfordulóján." *Kortárs* 4 (1994):114–128.
Benedek, István. "A halál költöje." *Új Magyarország* 259 and 277 (1995):17.
Beney, Zsuzsa. "Bevezetés a költészet olvasásába. Radnóti Miklós: 'Töredék' címü versének értelmezése." *Irodalomismeret* 4 (1994):8–16.
Beney, Zsuzsa. "Radnóti Miklós: Erőltetett menet." *Irodalomtörténet* 2–3 (1995): 469–482.
———. "Radnóti angyalai." *Irodalomtörténet* 1–2 (1996): 184–204.

———. "Radnóti Miklós: Mint a bika." *Új Holnap*, no. 5 (1996):46–56.

———. "Naptár: Radnóti Miklós verse." *Irodalomtörténet* 1–2 (1998):97–108.

Birnbaum, Marianna D. "The Poetry of Miklós Radnóti." *Slavic and East European Journal* (fall 1989):470–471.

Bognár, Béla. *Gyötrelmek útja: Dokumentum-regény*. Györ: Györ-Sopron Megyei Tanács, Radnóti Miklós Emlékbizottság és Irodalmi Társaság, 1987.

Forche, Carolyn. "The Poetry of Witness." In *The Writer in Politics*, William H. Gass and Lorin Cuoco, eds. Carbondale, Ill.: Southern Illinois University Press, 1996.

Géfin, László K. "Help Me, Pastoral Muse: The Virgilian Intertext in Miklós Radnóti's Eclogues." *Hungarian Studies* 1 (1996): 45–57.

George, Emery. "Miklós Radnóti: Diarist." *Cross Currents* 11 (1992): 153–161.

Gömöri, György. "Miklós Radnóti and the Bible." *Hungarian Studies* 1 (1996): 3–12.

Gömöri, György, and Clive Wilmer, eds. *The Life and Poetry of Miklós Radnóti: Essays*. Boulder, Colo.: East European Monographs, 1999.

Hernádi, Miklós. "Radnóti in English." *The Hungarian Quarterly*, no. 141 (1996): 118–121.

Horgas, Béla. "Tünöistenkeresés." *Tiszatáj* 1(1993): Melléklet (supplement) 1–15.

Hulesch, Ernö. *Stációk: Dokumentumriport Radnóti Miklósról*. Györ: A Györ Megyei Lapkiadó Vállalat, 1989.

———. *Tarkólövés: Dokumentumriportok Radnóti Miklósról*. Györ: Hazánk, 1997.

———. *Tarkólövés: Dokumentumriportok Radnóti Miklósról*. Györ: SZIF—Universitas Kft, 1999.

Köbányai, János. "Az apokalipszis krónikásai: Azonosságok Ámos Imre és Radnóti Miklós életében, halálában." *Népszava* 112 (1999): II.

Köbányai, János. "Radnóti és Ámos: Az apokalipszis aggadája." *Magyar Nemzet* 129 (1999):16.

Lengyel, András. " 'Hösi és tevékeny szerepvállalás': Radnóti identitás alakítási igényéröl." *Valóság* 11(1992):54–70.

Melczer, Tibor. "Elöhangok a bori Radnótihoz." *Új Magyarország* 260 (1994):13–14.

Moncorgé, Patricia. "Miklós Radnóti (1909–1944)." *Cahiers d'études hongroises*, no. 7 (1995):234–247.

Nemes, István. " 'Megjártam érted én a lélek hosszát.' Radnóti Miklós: Levél a hitveshez." *Dunatáj* 1(1995):23–28.

Német, G. Béla. "Tragikum az életrajzban—Tragikum a versekben (Radnóti Miklósról)." *Irodalomismeret* 4 (1994): 3–7.

Orosz, Magdolna. " 'Wenn schwarz der Tau tropft von den kehlen Weiden': Gerg Trakl in der ungarischen Übersetzung von Miklós Radnóti." *Berliner Beiträge zur Hungarologie*, no. 8 (1995):123–161.

Ozsváth, Zsuzsanna. "From Cain to Nahum: Shifts and Changes in Radnóti's Poetic Vision." *Hungarian Studies* 1 (1996): 29–44.

———. *In the Footsteps of Orpheus: The Life and Times of Miklós Radnóti*. Bloomington and Indianapolis: Indiana University Press, 2000.

Pomogáts, Béla. "Az otthont keresö költö: Háborús idökben Radnótiról." *CET* 6–7 (1999):11–19.

Réz, Pál (Selected, edited, and compiled). *Eröltetett menet: In memoriam Radnóti Miklós*. Budapest: Nap Kiadó, 1999.

Rónay, László. "Hösi önfeláldozás: Radnóti Miklós halálának ötvenedik évfordulójára." *Magyar Nemzet* 260 (1994):19.

———. "A költö és a próféta vándorútja." *Parnasszus* 1 (1995): 18–22.

Serey, Éva Á. " 'S mit érek én?' Ötven éve halt meg Radnóti Miklós." *Magyar Hírlap* 260 (1994): Melléklet (supplement) 2.

Szabó, Ferenc. "Lágerfények közt varázslat: 50 éve ölték meg Radnóti Miklóst." *Távlatok*, no. 20 (1994):760–762.

Szabolcsi, Miklós. "Idöszerü-e a Radnóti magatartás?" *Irodalomtörténet* 1 (1995): 84–91.

Szegedy-Maszák, Mihály. "National and International Implications in Radnóti's Poetry." *Hungarian Studies* 1 (1996): 13–28.

———. "Radnóti Miklós és a holocaust irodalma." *Literatura* 2 (1996):216–231.

Vilcsek, Béla. *Radnóti Miklós: Élet-kép sorozat*. Budapest: Elektra Kiadóház, 2000.

Lev Raphael

(1954–)

VICTORIA AARONS

LEV RAPHAEL, THE AUTHOR of the popular Nick Hoffman academic mystery series, is primarily known as a writer of mysteries and gay literature. He has also written fiction about second-generation Jews in America and refugees of the Holocaust, though he is less known uniquely as a writer of Holocaust fiction. Originally a New Yorker, born in 1948 to Holocaust survivors, Raphael received a Master of Fine Arts in creative writing from the University of Massachusetts at Amherst, where he was awarded the prestigious Harvey Swados Fiction Prize, and a Ph.D. in American Studies at Michigan State University, where he later taught creative writing. A university professor for thirteen years, Raphael, a self-defined "escaped academic," currently devotes his professional life to writing in an impressive array of genres. His writing includes short stories, a novel, nonfiction essays, book-length works, book reviews, reportorial pieces, and articles on a wide variety of topics for an equally wide range of journals and newspapers. In all of these genres and in most of his works, Raphael deeply engages the issues of being gay and Jewish in America.

Early in his literary career, Raphael wrote both a collection of short stories, *Dancing on Tisha B'Av* (1990) and a novel, *Winter Eyes* (1992), in which the Holocaust and its aftermath figure prominently, particularly in the tension between survivors of the *Shoah* and their American-born children, children who are made insecure by their parents' past and who suspect, as does the narrator in the short story "Fresh Air," that they were born "for reasons of history . . . of necessity, of duty to the past" (*Dancing on Tisha B'Av*, New York: St. Martin's Press, 1990, p. 109). The child of Holocaust survivors, Raphael was raised by parents who consciously disavowed Judaism. Despite their willful renunciation, Raphael self-consciously defines himself as a Jewish writer and, perhaps in opposition to his parents' silence regarding Judaism and the Holocaust, became a bar mitzvah at the age of thirty. In explaining the Jewishness of one of his recurring characters, Stefan Borowski, who was raised by his parents as a Christian, Raphael describes his own motivation for creating such a character as a kind of testimony, a bearing witness to those denied their Jewish heritage, who feel an immense loss, as had he. As Raphael puts it, "I'd met a lot of people who'd had their Jewishness hidden from them by their parents. . . . It's a devastating experience, and I felt I had to pay tribute to their suffering" (White, p. 5).

Being Gay and Jewish in America

Dancing on Tisha B'Av, which received the 1990 Lambda Literary Award and for which St. Martin's Press is currently planning a tenth anniversary edition is, undeniably, Raphael's most explicitly Jewish collection of stories, including the much acclaimed title story, "Dancing on Tisha B'Av." The singularly distinguishing feature of these stories is the intersection of Judaism and homoeroticism, a concern that differentiates Raphael from other second-generation witnesses to the Holocaust. The gay son of Holocaust survivors, Raphael grapples in his fiction with the social marginalization and personal anxieties of being gay and a Jew in America, especially a Jew whose connection to the Holocaust is only one generation removed.

To be a gay in straight America, as the characters in Raphael's fiction reveal, means living as objects of derision. Raphael's gay characters are denied claims to place, ownership, and identity. From Raphael's point of view, their experience is not unlike the experience of ghettoized Jews prior to their transport and incarceration in concentration camps, a denial as imagined by the gay sons of survivors who people Raphael's fiction. Raphael likens the public contempt and ostracism directed against gays in twentieth-century America to the persecution of Jews in Nazi Germany. The graffiti painted on the Michigan State campus—"white scrawling letters chalked inside jagged circles: KILL ALL FAGS, DEATH TO HOMO QUEERS . . . FAGGOTS MUST DIE"—becomes, in the short story "Abominations," a reminder for his character of "Germany in the Thirties, with JUDEN RAUS . . . whitewashed across Jewish-owned storefronts, synagogues collapsing in flame, religious Jews beaten, bloody, dead" (*Dancing on Tisha B'Av*, pp. 215, 229). Though implicitly acknowledging the historical complexity of such an analogy, for Raphael, contemporary debasement and hatred directed against gays become a reenactment of the war against the Jews a half century past, not an approach similar to that of Lesléa Newman, another late twentieth-century Jewish writer, in her story "A Letter to Harvey Milk."

Although Raphael continues this insidious connection between the persecution of the Jews preceding and during the Holocaust throughout the stories collected in *Dancing on Tisha B'Av*, such a sense of shared persecution does not, for him, necessarily result in the easy construction of a universal community of sufferers, of those who might come together in some kind of solidarity or mutual recognition of victimization. In this, Raphael indicts the Jewish community, as in the title story, "Dancing on Tisha B'Av," where in the synagogue, the gay protagonist and his lover, part of the *minyan*, are denied a community of worshipers. They are, in fact, driven from the synagogue: "Get out," one member of the congregation demands, "I won't let you touch that Torah" (p. 12).

Such hostility and rejection from the Jewish community, particularly the Orthodox, is, for Raphael's gay Jewish characters, compounded by the willed and willful silence of their parents, parents who deny both the reality of their gay sons as well as the place of the Holocaust in their past and in current family dynamics. In story after story in *Dancing on Tisha B'Av*, the children of Holocaust survivors keenly feel the shadowy presence of an inheritance they believe enshrouded by a silence so palpable that it is given voice; it has taken up residency, crowding out these characters' passage into adulthood and the accompanying autonomy that would freely accommodate their choices; "the cruelty of silence," as one of Raphael's characters puts it ("The Tanteh," p. 21). For, although the characters who have survived the *Shoah* maintain an uncomfortable and precarious silence around their children, they cannot become other than they are, the products of the legislated attempts to drive them from their homes, tear them away from their families, and exterminate them. For these survivors, everything and everyone they encounter, outside the cloistered confines of the family, are perceived as a threat, a dangerous reminder of the past. Initially afraid of her children's friend, the mother, a survivor, in the short story "Inheritance," readily sees in him "a vicious reminder of the madness in her world: '*Shaydim*' . . . Yiddish for evil spirits" (p. 183). That this fear is the involuntary inheritance that Raphael's survivors bequeath to their offspring fills them with dread, with a sense of their own failures and disqualifications, the inadequacy of their own limited imaginations: "I wanted to know," reveals the American-born narrator in the short story "Witness," "but I never would. I was only an American, and did not understand the terrible things" (p. 205).

Collective Guilt

While some of the stories in *Dancing on Tisha B'Av* portray Holocaust survivors who want to pass on stories of their experiences and thus educate their American-born children in the atrocities of the past, most of the survivors in the stories in this collection express a desire to mute the past. In a story central to this collection, "War Stories," however, these two seemingly disparate responses to the aftermath of the Holocaust merge. Here, the two parents, both survivors, represent the two approaches or responses to their past and to their child's place in their history. In "War Stories," the protagonist, Marc, endures his father's silence, a survivor of the Holocaust who "rarely spoke to him . . . never mentioned the War. If anyone did he would announce, 'I'm walking out of this room' " (pp. 23–24). Marc's response to his father's silence is one of resentment complicated by his utter helplessness at the "gap of comprehension that was between them" (p. 24). The real conflict, however, resides in Marc's feelings toward his mother, a Holocaust survivor who constantly speaks of "dates and camps and trains and punishments and bombings," stories that grew "intolerable as she forced word after word on him" (p. 24). Caught between a deafening silence on one hand, and an equally deafening monologue on the other, the American-born protagonist is deeply conflicted, feeling both guilt and betrayal.

Like many second-generation children of Holocaust survivors, Marc believes that he wants to hear the detailed and unabridged stories of his parents' experiences during the Holocaust, wanting to know what they endured and how they survived. Like other characters in literature by children of Holocaust survivors, he feels a sense of betrayal when his queries are met with silence. Deeply conflicted, he both does and does not want to hear the stories of his parents' past and feels a kind of betrayal when it is thrust upon him and he is forced to hear what can only make him feel trapped in a past that does not belong to him. Marc, "feeling the ruin," but "listening to her War stories [as] the price he had to pay for his mother's love," is drawn into her world at the expense of his own (pp. 23, 25). For this particular character, the father's silence is preferable, but at an equally unbearable cost, especially because it makes him complicitous in a web of betrayals, a form of conspiring with the enemy and, at the same time, victimized by an ubiquitous yet impenetrable antagonist, as put by the narrator of "Inheritance," as "nowhere to hide" (*Dancing on Tisha B'Av*, p. 187).

More often than not, however, for Raphael's older children of Holocaust survivors, the unrelenting silence that characterizes their relationships with their parents fills them alternately with guilt and with rage and with a kind of shame that is compounded for many of them by being gay. The silence of these children, born of their fear of their parents' reaction to their sexual disclosure, mirrors the silence on the part of the Holocaust survivors themselves. Such secrecy, then, is for both a matter of hidden identities. Like Stefan Borowski, the central character in Raphael's novel, *Winter Eyes*, Raphael's characters fear that their parents' silence about the Holocaust, their rejection of Jewish identity, and their bitterness toward the idea of God all stem from their disappointment in their offspring.

The problem of what it means to identify oneself as a Jew becomes the central issue for both second-generation children and their parents. For the survivors, what it means to be a Jew, even under the seeming protection of America, is enshrouded by memories of persecution, death camps, and loss. It is, for them, the measure of how they have suffered and continue to, if only in memory. For the children of survivors, what it means to be a Jew can only be tinged with their parents' frozen silence, fear, and continuing sense of marginalization. Their parents' revocation of Jewish history and a personal Jewish past is compounded for the gay sons of survivors, because their sexual identities are framed as antithetical to Judaism, as a disgrace: "It's sick, like the Nazis. . . . Men with men. It's like the Nazis, disgusting" ("Caravans," in *Dancing on Tisha B'Av*, p. 81). And so they feel themselves to be doubly ostracized: by a society that continues to see gays as deviant, and thus a threat, and by the only community, an insular and protective community of Jews, from which they might attain some measure of comfort. Finally, the lives of the second-generation American-born are eclipsed by their parents' unrelenting pasts, whose stories, once told, are like offerings, unwitting invitations to step back and thus step into the identities of the European Jews whose visions of horror become their own.

God and the Holocaust

Such unease in Raphael's fiction introduces the central issue of theology, or rather how one, after the Holocaust, can identify with God. Ironically, because the children of Holocaust survivors in these stories were raised to be ignorant of Jewish belief and ritual, or desperately, because they were denied such identification, many of Raphael's children of survivors try to reconstruct Jewish observance and practice. This return to formal Judaism is a characteristic pattern in the fiction of American Jewish writers, even those without direct Holocaust connections, for example the fiction of Tillie Olsen (the often anthologized novella "Tell Me a Riddle") and that of Allegra Goodman (particularly in *The Family Markowitz*). But Jewish ritual itself becomes, for the survivor, an affront. Raphael's short story "The Tanteh" (*Dancing on Tisha B'Av*), for example, centers on a woman who survived the horrors of the Holocaust only to be constantly reminded of them by the rituals of ordinary Jewish middle-class life, her attempts at silence prodded into outburst, a defensive attack on one who would bring her "stories" to life: "a Nazi . . . perverse . . . a snake of disapproval and contempt, spying on her soul" (p. 21). In response to the blessing recited over the lighting of the Sabbath candles, she bitterly acknowledges the representation of such incantations in the history of the all too immediate past. "They prayed. . . . And still they died" (p. 17). Her cynical interpretation of Jewish history sees everything through a post-Holocaust lens, including the narrator's attempts to write about her as "survivor." The *tanteh* (aunt) responds to such seeming intrusions as a preemptory denial of Judaism and a rejection of any notion of God, considered superstitious at best, compliant at worst. Similarly, as part of a recurring theme throughout *Dancing on Tisha B'Av*, the child of survivors tells his father that he would like a bar mitzvah—"though I had no real idea what was involved or what it meant." His father responds with the accumulated and undisguised outrage of the apostate: "You don't need all that *chazerai* . . . nonsense. . . . There's no God, no Torah; it's only lies" ("Caravans," p. 73). This persistent denial of the covenant in Lev Raphael's fiction leaves the children of Holocaust survivors empty, at a loss, all the more difficult to come to terms with the Holocaust and with their identity as Jews and as gays, bereft of all but "a Jew in name alone" ("Caravans," p. 76).

Critical Reception

Lev Raphael's Holocaust fiction has received less critical attention than have his mysteries, his gay fiction, and his essays about gay culture. Nonetheless, *Dancing on Tisha B'Av*, in particular, has received some critical acclaim, its stories noted primarily for their deft interweaving of the "dual identity" of being gay and Jewish, Raphael's "grand theme" (Olsen, p. 13). Several of Raphael's short stories have been anthologized, including "History (with Dreams)," published in *American Jewish Fiction*, the widely read collection of American Jewish fiction, placing him in the tradition of writers such as Abraham Cahan, Bernard Malamud, and Cynthia Ozick. Gerald Shapiro, in *American Jewish Fiction*, suggests that Raphael writes "directly about [his] Jewishness" and in response to the perceived "disappearance" of Jewish culture and religious belief in contemporary American literature. In doing so, Lev Raphael contributes to and has become part of the rich and continuing presence of Jewish writing in America.

Bibliography

Primary Sources

Dynamics of Power: Building a Competent Self (with Gershen Kaufman). 1983; revised edition published as *Dynamics of Power: Fighting Shame and Building Self-Esteem*, 1991.
Dancing on Tisha B'Av. 1990.
Stick Up for Yourself: Every Kid's Guide to Personal Power and Positive Self-Esteem (with Gershen Kaufman). 1990.
The Last Novels of Isaac Mayer Wise. 1991.
Edith Wharton's Prisoners of Shame: A New Perspective on Her Neglected Fiction. 1991.
"On a Narrow Bridge: A Jewish Writer's Journey." *Reconstructionist* (1992): 23.
Winter Eyes: A Novel About Secrets. 1992.
Coming Out of Shame: Transforming Gay and Lesbian Lives (with Gershen Kaufman). 1996.
Journeys and Arrivals: On Being Gay and Jewish. 1996.
Let's Get Criminal: An Academic Mystery. 1996.
The Edith Wharton Murders. 1997.
The Death of a Constant Lover. 1999.
Little Miss Evil: A Nick Hoffman Mystery. 2000.

Anthologies That Include Works by Lev Raphael

Men on Men 2. Edited by George Stambolian. New York: Penguin, 1988.
American Jewish Fiction. Edited by Gerald Shapiro. Lincoln: University of Nebraska Press, 1998.
Certain Voices. Edited by Darryl Pilcher. Boston: Alyson, 1991.
The Faber Anthology of Short Gay Fiction. Boston: Faber and Faber, 1991.

Reviews by the Author

Review of "Forgotten Victims of the Holocaust." *Lambda Book Report* 4 (September/October 1995): 32.
Review of "*God's Phallus and Other Problems for Men and Monotheism*." *Lambda Book Report* 4 (March/April 1995): 43.
"Why Are They Bashing *Dancer from the Dance*?" Review of *Dancer from the Dance*. *Lambda Book Report* 4 (January/February 1995): 10.
Review of "*BAD Chili*." *Lambda Book Report* 6 (March 1998): 30.

Secondary Sources

Berger, Alan L. *Children of Job: American Second-Generation Witnesses to the Holocaust*. Albany, N.Y.: State University of New York Press, 1997.
Brinker, Ludger. "Lev Raphael (1954–)." In *Contemporary Jewish-American Novelists: A Bio-Critical Sourcebook*. Edited by Michael Taub and Daniel Walden. Westport, Conn: Greenwood Press, 1997.
Buchbinder, David. "Gaiety of Tisha B'Av: Sexuality, Subjectivity, and Narrative Closure in the Work of Lev Raphael." *Canadian Review of American Studies* 28 (1998): 163–176.
Olson, Ray. "Lev Raphael." *Booklist* (July 1, 1996): 13.

Interviews

"An Interview with Lev Raphael." *Frontiers* 1 (March 1991): 42.
Gans, Ronald. "An Interview with Lev Raphael." *Christopher Street* 13 (1990): 31–32.
Glatzer, Jenna. "Interview with Lev Raphael." *Absolute Write* (2001): 1–15.
Han, Paul. Interview. "Author Speaks on Holocaust Day." *Yale Daily News* 12 (April 1991): 6.
White, Claire E. "A Conversation with Lev Raphael." *Writers Write: The Internet Writing Journal* (1999). www.writerswrite.com/journal/archives.htm

PIOTR RAWICZ

(1919–1982)

LEA WERNICK FRIDMAN

PIOTR RAWICZ–SURVIVOR, writer, scholar, poet, journalist and bon vivant–produced one of the earliest, most important experimental novels written about the Holocaust. *Blood from the Sky* is loosely autobiographical. First published in 1961 in France, it won the prestigious Prix Rivarol. Strangely, for all of its inventiveness, literary flair, and seriousness, the book has been seriously neglected in the critical literature.

Life

Piotr Rawicz was born in the Polish city of Lvov (now Ukraine) on 12 July 1919 to Helena Sabina and Salomon Rawicz . Rawicz's father was a well-known lawyer and his mother, a poet. Arrested and tortured by the Gestapo in Zakopane, Poland, Rawicz did not give away the names of friends during the harsh interrogations. He was deported to Auschwitz in 1942 where he used a medical note to explain his circumcision and passed as a Ukrainian. In 1944 Rawicz was sent to another camp, Leitmeritz, in Czechoslovakia, until 1945. At the end of the war Rawicz remained in Poland working as a journalist, traveling and writing poetry.

Moving to Paris in 1947, Rawicz earned degrees in Sanskrit from the Sorbonne and in Hindi from the Ecole Nationale for Living Oriental Languages. He was fluent in many languages and their literatures, including Ukrainian, Chocklis, Russian, Polish, German, French, Sanskrit, Hindi, English, Yiddish, and Hebrew. A familiar figure in intellectual and scholarly circles, Rawicz became press attaché to the Polish legation, wrote regularly for *Le Monde*, served as diplomatic correspondent to a number of foreign newspapers, and as contributing editor to *European Judaism*. He committed suicide in 1982 in the apartment of his wife, Anna, a filmmaker, several weeks after her death from cancer.

Writings and Critical Discussion

Among survivor writers, Rawicz is unusual for his artistic daring as well as for the way he combines European learning and sophistication with a broad-ranging knowledge of Jewish theology, history, and literature. Two of his novels—one about his Holocaust experiences and the other, a commentary on contemporary France—were published along with numerous essays, journalistic articles, and some poetry. A long personal journal in the possession of a nephew remains unpublished along with a third novel written in several languages including Sanskrit. Aside from Anthony Rudolf's slim volume, *Engraved in Flesh*, only scattered articles, parts of chapters, and brief references to Rawicz and his work exist.

There are no detailed treatments that view *Blood from the Sky* in the literary context of the French "new novel" or of European modernist experimentation, movements whose innovations he embraces even as he scathingly undermines their assumptions. Rawicz is an important example of the highly complicated, albeit little-understood, relationship between Holocaust literary works and the literary milieus out of which they emerge. That relationship, however, can be understood once we understand the ways in which the subject matter of the Holocaust shapes its literary representation. Formal and thematic concern with questions of representation, and more specifically with questions of representational limit, is the single most important identifying feature of Holocaust literary narrative and of what we might more generally identify as traumatic narrative. The discussion that follows will focus in large measure on this fundamental issue.

Blood from the Sky

The novel is a brilliant example of what I shall call "traumatic narrative," narrative that must figure out how to tell the story that cannot be told ("One by one—words—all the words of the human language—wilt and grow too weak to bear a meaning," translated by Peter Wiles, New York: Harcourt Brace, 1964, p. 132). Should it be told in the first or in the third person? In prose, poetic, or dramatic form? Or, all of the above? Rawicz's novel is not only a closely observed record of ordinary Jews, indeed ordinary Germans and Ukrainians acting out the lethal events of 1939 through 1945, it is at the same time a speculative novel that wrestles with the all too immediate technical question of how to tell the story at hand: the story for which, finally, there are no words.

Blood from the Sky is divided into three sections. Part I deals with the liquidation of the Jewish ghetto in an unnamed Ukrainian town. Part II is about the journey of the protagonist, Boris, and his companion from one hideout to the next posing as Ukrainian lovers. Part III recounts the capture and prison experience of the protagonist, who outwits his captors and bluffs his way into a gentile identity.

The novel begins as a first-person narrative with the meeting of the narrator and Boris in a café in the Montparnasse section of Paris. For the first fourteen chapters of the novel, Boris gives testimony: he tells the story of the liquidation of the Jewish ghetto in the town of his birth and ancestry, including snippets of the rich lore of its past and traditions, and of the fortunes and misfortunes of the Jewish hospital ("an important political and commercial meeting point," Boris calls it, p. 91) and provides vignettes of townspeople, all of whom are targeted for imminent extermination: David the boiler stoker in the hospital, Leo L., president of the Jewish Council, Senator Gordon, Dr. Hillel, Old Yaakov the busy gravedigger, and various former girlfriends. We learn about the businessman Garin and his failed scheme to provide the Reich with workers and Jews with papers that would spare their lives. There are episodes of near brushes with discovery and death in which Boris's quick wits, light hair, and expensive clothing save him and his companion, Naomi, from recognition as Jews.

The Witness Disappears

Boris and the narrator leave the café in chapter fifteen. When the story of the town and its liquidation resumes in the next chapter, Boris has indeed left the world of the novel for good—at least as witness. Our final glimpse of the ghetto's demise—the horrific narrative of the massacre of a group of children found accidentally by three off-duty German SS—is pieced together from Boris's journal, which the narrator receives months after the meeting with Boris. The witness thus disappears from the witness stand just before the narrative of the horrific massacre begins: an important formal shift in narration that marks a boundary (or limit) between what can and cannot be said. The formal retreat from a testimonial first-person to a more distant and constructed third-person narration brings this boundary into view, pulling the wordless spaces that exist on the far side of representational limit into the novel. It is—formally speaking—in the space of this wordlessness that the story of the massacre unfolds in all of its horrifying detail.

Like the dead Jews of the town of his birth, Boris and the rest of his story must, from this point forward in the novel, be culled and constructed from a document. There is a novelistic point being made within the "fiction" of the novel that has to do with Boris and the parts of him that die along with the Jews from his town. If for the first half of the novel the distinction is intentionally blurred between the "I" of the narrator and the "I" of Boris telling his story to the narrator in the café, there is a literal splitting that occurs at this point between them: between the "I" of the narrator and the "he" that is now Boris; between the present of a story being told and the past of a story that can never be fully told. The substitution of a document for testimony, of Boris's journal for his living voice and presence, just as the liquidation of the town is about to be completed, inscribes a hole into all that remains of the narrative, so that Boris's absence and the deaths of the Jews of the ghetto to which it is linked underpin the remainder of the novel like a bass whose deep tones undergird the music of the orchestra.

Works of Holocaust literature must inevitably deal with the limits of words, description, and narration. They must invent ways to remain faithful to, and at the same time, circumvent those limits. Rawicz's novel is full of "holes," of stories left out or left incomplete: how did Boris escape the mass shooting he so evasively recounts in chapter two of the novel? How do Boris and Naomi escape the ghetto? What happens to Naomi after Boris is arrested at the outset of Part II? What happens to Boris after the evening he spends in Montparnasse with the narrator? And what are we to make of a narrative in which the narrator discusses a chapter of Boris's journal that he then tells us he has decided to skip?

In this way the larger black hole of a historical destruction outside the novel overwhelms and displaces the fates of individual characters, leaving holes in their individual narratives just as the narrator/editor has left holes and gaps in his rendering of Boris's story and thus, in the idea of narrative itself. Where the conventional telling of a story—the narration and representation of a sequence of events—is no longer possible, narrative shifts to a very different modality: that of witness. Indeed, *Blood from the Sky* makes use of a chain of witnesses. Boris bears witness to the narrator during their time spent together in the café; the narrator, in turn, brings Boris's testimony to the reader who, in this way, takes his or her place in a human chain of transmission.

But transmission, even within a modality of witness, is not finally possible in *Blood from the Sky*. As Boris slips out of the narrative, leaving the narrator to bring editorial coherence to the narrative and dramatic fragments, poetic stammerings, philosophic rantings and probings of states of consciousness that make up Boris's journal, witnessing itself appears to have broken down. The turning from conventional (or representational) storytelling to a modality of witness is a familiar feature of Holocaust literary narrative, although Rawicz's treatment and subversion of this modality—its reinvention as a constructed document—is an ingenious twist, not merely on the modality of witness involved, but on the deeper issue of language and the limits of representation.

The "Tool" of Identity

Blood from the Sky is a novel that mixes up the identities of the writer, of the narrator, of the Jewish protagonist, Boris, and of his gentile alias, Yurigoletz, whose birth certificate Boris has accidentally found on the streets of the ghetto. Parts II and III of the novel are the story of an aftermath: of the life of hiding that follows the liquidation of the ghetto and of the imprisonment that follows Boris's arrest. It is the fraught tale of murderous hatred of Jews around which central themes of otherness, identity, human connection, love, hate, and God are gathered, picked apart, examined. Staying at an inn while in hiding, Boris regularly plays the piano in the evenings for a German general and for the chief of police. Boris wonders about the "solidarity . . . springing up between me and the companions of my musical evenings" (p. 233). He notes how "the hatred in my heart had burned out . . ." and questions himself: "Was Boris any closer to me than Yuri? Was he any more real? My two halves seemed to be melting away" (p. 233). Later, imprisoned for months in a cell with gentile petty criminals who, taking him for a Jew, ostracize and humiliate him, he finds himself unable "to stave off the feeling of warm friendship that was invading his entire being" (p. 274) despite dogged attempts to withdraw from the hostile group.

Indeed, Boris's life hangs on the question of identity, and the question of his identity hangs upon the question of the "tool"—the penis—and its circumcision. Who is Boris really? What God is his God? What people is his people? By the end of the novel Boris has convinced his German and Ukrainian interrogators that he is the Gentile, Yuri Goletz, son of a Ukrainian farmhand, a nationalist and patriot who has only contempt for his Ukrainian countrymen who have welcomed Germans into their midst. And he has convinced them that his circumcision was medical in origin, a treatment for an attack of "phimosis." Boris, waiting for his medical examination, contemplates the organ of identity in question, his penis—the organ that will determine his fate, that is used during interrogations as a vehicle of torture, that is the ancient ritual mark of his connection to his God and to his people, and that is the seat of his sexuality and generativity into the future. In a mystical turn of mind, Boris wonders. "Did this door still open onto God? Did it at least open onto the Divine . . . are the Covenant with God and physical passion sharing the same site and founded in the same crucible, the same thing?" The question is real for Boris and for Rawicz for whom the mystical and ontological are no less urgent than are the mysteries of human connection, identity, and love.

Few works of Holocaust literature have ranged so freely, so imaginatively, so inventively over the charred landscape of murder, genocide, torture, and loss. For all of its linguistic, digressive, and transgressive exuberance, its formal irreverence, and thematic richness, *Blood from the Sky* is a novel that speaks with raw honesty to the terror of the human condition in the aftermath of the Holocaust as well as to the different, but equally terrifying, Jewish condition after the Holocaust. It remains for future scholars to explore its agonized and bracing vision.

Bibliography

Primary Sources

Le Sang du Ciel (Blood from the Sky). 1961.
Bloc-Notes d'un Contre-Revolutionaire (ou la Geule de Bois). 1969.
"The Companion of the Dream." *European Judaism* 9 (1970).
Review of Solzhenitsyn's *August 1914*. *Le Monde*, 2 July 1971.
"Singing Meat." *European Judaism* 11 (1971).
"Fragments." *European Judaism* 13 (1972).
Solzhenitsyn: Colloque de Cerisy. Edited by Tarr. "Ethique et Esthetique: le Rapport a L'Occident." 1974.
Solitude de Juize dans la Creation Littéraire. Edited by J. Halperin and G. Levitte. World Jewish Congress, Paris: Presses Universitaires Paris de France, 1975.
Introduction to *Le Lion du Saint Sabbath* by Adolf Rudnicki. Gallimard, 1979.
Introduction to *Sablier* by Danilo Kiš. 1982.
"Salt and Pepper." *European Judaism* 23 (1978).

Secondary Sources

Alexander, Edward. *The Resonance of Dust: Essays on Holocaust Literature and Jewish Fate*. Columbus: Ohio State University Press, 1979.

Alvarez, A. "The Literature of the Holocaust." *Beyond All This Fiddle*. New York: Random House, 1968.

Bourniquel, Camille. "Piotr Rawicz: *Le Sang du Ciel*." *Esprit* 29, no. 7 (1961): 658.

Dayan Rosenman, Anny. "Piotr Rawicz, La Douleur d'Ecrire." *Les Temps modernes* (March–April 1995).

Fridman, Lea Wernick. "The Literary Act of Witness: Narrative, Voice, and the Problematic of the Real." In *Words and Witness: Narrative and Aesthetic Strategies in the Representation of the Holocaust*. Albany: State University of New York Press, 2000, pp. 99–126.

Hamaoui, Lea (Fridman, Lea W.). "Art and Testimony: The Representation of Historical Horror in Literary Works by Piotr Rawicz and Charlotte Delbo." *Cardozo Studies in Law and Literature* 3, no. 2 (fall 1991).

Rudolf, Anthony. *Engraved in Flesh*. London: Menard Press, 1996.

Solotaroff, Theodore. "Anna Langfus and Piotr Rawicz." In *The Red Hot Vacuum*. Boston: Godine, 1979.

Sungolowsky, Joseph. "Piotr Rawicz: *Le Sang du Ciel*." *French Review* 36, no. 6 (May 1963): 655.

Interviews

Interview by Nicole Dethoor. *Combat*, 5 October 1961.

Interview by Anna Langfus. *L'Arche*, February 1962.

Interview. *From Bergen-Belsen to Jerusalem: Contemporary Implications of the Holocaust*. Edited by Emil Fackenheim. Jerusalem Institute of Contemporary Jewry, 1975.

Interview by G. Dubowski. *Theatre en Pologne* 24, nos. 6–7 (1982).

CHARLES REZNIKOFF

(1894–1976)

RANEN OMER-SHERMAN

THE CHILD OF Russian immigrants who fled the 1881 pogroms, Charles Reznikoff (1894–1976) was born in Brooklyn, New York. In his early years he witnessed the arrival of his paternal grandparents from Russia and the immigrant struggles of numerous relatives. Their experiences, together with the childhood beatings by antisemitic street bullies Reznikoff himself endured, emerged as important themes in his entire oeuvre, even before he turned to the subject of the Holocaust. In his early adolescence, Reznikoff's family moved to Brownsville, a section of Brooklyn that was isolated from Jewish neighborhoods, and the adult poet would darkly invoke it as a site where "the hatred for Israel smoldered" (*Complete Poems II*. Santa Rosa, Calif.: Black Sparrow Press, 1977, p. 151). His autobiographical poems are filled with accounts of how he had to rush home from high school to avoid the taunts of children leaving their grade school. A particularly traumatic experience was the sight of his uncle and grandfather returning from breaking their fast on Yom Kippur, with gruesome injuries after being attacked by an antisemitic gang. Reznikoff studied journalism at the University of Missouri in 1910 and law at New York University Law School, where he graduated second in the class of 1915. He also served briefly in the U.S. army.

With Louis Zukofsky and George Oppen, Reznikoff founded the Objectivist Press in the early 1930s. His poetic influences came from a diverse range of modernist movements, including imagism, objectivism, and German expressionism. Beginning in 1918 and during the next sixty years, Reznikoff published nineteen individual collections of poetry, as well as three novels, numerous translations, and historical and edited works. In most of this prodigious body of work, the poet emphasizes a subjectivity linked to exile and loss after catastrophe. During the last years of his life Reznikoff occupied himself with writing *Holocaust* (1975), a major work modeled on his long sequential rendering of American courtroom trials, and *Testimony* (1978), which consisted of his unique "translation" of the transcripts of the Eichmann and Nuremberg trials into condensed, spare language.

Holocaust

Reznikoff's late work, *Holocaust* (1975), is organized under twelve loosely chronological sections that coalesce into an unprecedentedly comprehensive representation of the wreckage of the Nazi years: "Deportation," "Invasion," "Research," "Ghettos," "Massacres," "Gas Chambers and Gas Trucks," "Work Camps," "Children," "Mass Graves," "Marches," "Escapes," and perhaps the most nightmarish section of all, "Entertainment," which documents the sadistic excess of Nazi violence. The poem culminates in a representation of the Warsaw Ghetto Uprising (1943) and the escape of six thousand Danish Jews to Sweden with the help of non-Jewish fellow citizens, a movement that takes the reader from atrocity to the fulfillment of human struggle, compassion, and communal responsibility. It is a relentlessly "documentary" work, and Reznikoff's wife, Marie Syrkin, would later recall how her husband "refused to use any material from numerous first-hand witness reports. Only the records of the Nuremberg Trial and of the Eichmann Trial were to be his sources; nor would he allow himself any subjective outcry. The bare facts, as selected by him, would speak for themselves: there would be no tampering with the experience through imagery or heightened language" (p. 64).

As Janet Sutherland observes in her study of Reznikoff's poetic rendering of courtroom testimony, the poet's alterations contain few distortions of the original. Condensing and paraphrasing, occasionally omitting repetitive material, Reznikoff transforms his reader into a participating witness to the witnesses, one whose focus on the human scale of history is gradually intensified. To understand the ambition and significance of Reznikoff's project, it is worth considering, as Janet Sutherland has in her meticulous study, the relation between the last poem from the "Ghetto" sequence and the transcript source. Reznikoff writes:

> One of the S.S. men caught a woman with a baby in her arms.
> She began asking for mercy: if she were shot
> The baby should live.
> She was near a fence between the ghetto and where Poles lived
> And behind the fence were Poles ready to catch the baby
> And she was about to hand it over when caught.
> The S.S. man took the baby from her arms
> And shot her twice,
> And then held the baby in his hands.
> The mother, bleeding but still alive, crawled up to his feet.
> The S.S. man laughed
> And tore the baby apart as one would tear a rag.
> Just then a stray dog passed
> And the S.S. man stooped to pat it
> And took a lump of sugar out of his pocket
> And gave it to the dog (*Holocaust,* Santa Rosa, Calif.: Black Sparrow Press, 1975, pp. 28–29).

The corresponding transcript from the Eichmann trial read as follows:

> *Q* Do you remember another scene with Kidash with a woman and an infant of about one and a half years?
> *A* The place we were in hiding bordered with the Aryan part and there was a fence there. This Kidash caught a woman with a baby in her arms of about 18 months. She held the baby in her arms and began asking for mercy that she be shot first and leave the baby alive. From behind the fence there were Poles who raised their hands ready to catch the baby. She was about to hand the baby over to the Poles. He took the baby from her arms and shot her twice and then took the baby into his hands and tore him as one would tear a rag (*The Eichmann Trial in Jerusalem,* 2.5.61.Pp 1, Qq1, Session 24). quoted in (Sutherland, p. 303).

The Eichmann transcript goes on to describe the stray dog, the laughter, the solicitous lump of sugar. Clearly Reznikoff, writing during the years of shameful silence, when the public was not yet inundated with the wealth of Holocaust memoirs and witness accounts now available, felt compelled to ask readers to subject themselves to its carnage to an unprecedented degree.

Contribution to Holocaust Literature

Reznikoff's contribution to the literature of the Holocaust has been sorely neglected and underestimated, particularly his monumental, unsparing record of atrocity, *Holocaust*, which appeared many years before the subject was given serious literary attention by Jewish Americans. Perhaps this is due, in part, to the book's unsparing exposure of the reader to relentless details of inhumanity. As Anne Stevenson grimly observes, "when we come to the end of *Holocaust* (granted, it is a poem, not a play) we want to find a place to be sick. No poet has ever written a book so nakedly shocking, so blatantly calculated to make us feel that the Nazi persecution of the Jews can *never* be fictionalized or abstracted into 'literature' " (p. 184). Because Reznikoff refuses readers the conventions of artistic *catharsis*, few readers seem to have felt comfortable with the book's message of the seemingly infinite capacity of human beings to inflict unprecedented cruelty on one another.

Even Reznikoff's neglected 1944 novel, *The Lionhearted*, ostensibly exploring the persecutions against the Jews during the 1189–1199 rule of Richard I (its ironic title refers to the Jews of England, not to Richard) was written in such a way that its martyrdoms inevitably commented on contemporary persecutions. As Sylvia Rothchild points out, years before the genocidal extermination "had a name and a literature to describe it," Reznikoff sought to commemorate the event (Rothchild, p. 289). In a three-page poem that appeared in *Inscriptions* (1944–1956), Reznikoff addressed a subject that would remain for decades to come an unmentionable topic.

> One man
> escapes from the ghetto of Warsaw
> where thousands have been killed or led away in tens of thousands, hundreds of
> thousands, hundreds of thousands,
> to die in concentration camps,
> to be put to death in trucks, in railway cars, in gullies of the woods
> in gas chambers,
> and he who escapes—
> of all that multitude—
> in his heart the word *Jew* burning
> as it burned once in Jeremiah
> when he saw the remnant of Judah
> led captive to Babylon
> or fugitives,
> from that man
> shall spring again a people
> as the sands of the sea for number,
> as the stars of the sky.
> *Blessed are You, God of the Universe,*
> *delighting in life* (ll. 60–61).

Originally titled "A Compassionate People," this lyric appeared as American Jewry was receiving the darkest reports about the fate of European Jews during World War II, and it led off the thirtieth-anniversary issue of the *Menorah Journal.* It is useful to compare Reznikoff's haunting juxtaposition of extermination and continuity, a nightmare of the secular world and divinity, with his conclusion to *Holocaust* (1975):

> Fishing boats, excursion boats, and any kind of boat
> Were mustered at the ports;
> And the Jews were escorted to the coast by the
> Danes—
> Many of them students—
> And ferried to safety in Sweden:
> About six thousand Danish Jews were rescued
> And only a few hundred captured by the Germans.
> (*Holocaust,* pp. 77–78)

What both poems have in common, the lyrical poem of the 1940s and the spare, sober lines from the poet's last year, is a shared ethos that underwrites Reznikoff's entire oeuvre. What is sometimes called the "Doctrine of the Saving Remnant," a theological notion that derives from Genesis 45:7, constitutes an undeniable but muted presence in *Holocaust.*

Having published most of his early poetry and prose in the *Menorah Journal*, Reznikoff shared the world view of its editors, who, having rejected what they saw as Zionism's cynical perspective on Jewish continuity outside Palestine, exhibited an upstart confidence in Judaism's viability in exile. Although Reznikoff's radically unsentimental, violent, and unvarnished record of atrocity dares not speak of hope, its mitigating clause embraces the totality of the Holocaust, which meant its rescuers and survivors, as much as its sadists and corpses. Reznikoff's almost theological faith in the remnant is just as ardent an ideology as classical Zionism. After the Holocaust it became even more vital for Reznikoff to keep faith with the tradition of the "faith in the remnant" in its philosophic and cultural entirety. The prophetic imperative of the Jews' ultimate survival and creativity in their dispersal remained every bit as binding on his poetry as the actuality of persecution. In recent years many who endured the Holocaust have embraced the same trope that Reznikoff found so morally compelling, using "saving remnant" as a substitute for the popular (if problematic) term "survivor." As Samuel Norich observes, "that term ["survivor and children of survivors"] may be fine for external consumption, but for understanding ourselves and the sources of our parents' motivation, *sheris ha'pleyte* tells us more. Perhaps we can even get America to use the term 'saving remnant' " (Norich, p. 3).

Any reader looking to Reznikoff's work for spiritual consolation will be disappointed. *Holocaust* is relentless in its immediacy, horror, and bleakness. It is one of the most graphic accounts of atrocity ever produced. Outside of the epic narrative's final seven lines and a few other instances of human compassion scattered throughout the text (as rare as they were in the historical record to which Reznikoff bears witness), the reader is subject to the bleak truth of what he gleaned from poring over witness, perpetrator, and survivor accounts in the Eichmann and Nuremberg transcripts. Without embellishing or didactic commentary, Reznikoff transforms the unthinkable acts of his sources into a powerful narrative. As Sylvia Rothchild cogently observes, Reznikoff's "Auschwitz was not Elie Wiesel's holy mystery or William Styron's 'fatal embolism in the bloodstream of mankind' but a real place where men and women lived and died without witnesses and mourners" (Rothchild, p. 295).

The abruptness of the documentary account, with its condensed speeches juxtaposed with Reznikoff's refusal to pass judgment, places a special burden on the reader to form his or her own moral response to the text:

> A number of Jews had to drink sea water only
> To find out how long they could stand it.
> In their torment
> They threw themselves on the mops and rags
> Used by the hospital attendants
> And sucked the dirty water out of them
> To quench the thirst
> Driving them mad (*Holocaust,* p. 22).

The Post-Holocaust Jewish American Poet

Even during the years that he pored over the legal records of atrocity that composed *Holocaust*, Reznikoff refused to see himself primarily as a mourner. By rejecting this label he was able to pursue a difficult tradition that was far more important to him: the *creative* marginality of Jewishness in its historic relation to the host culture. In its ambivalent and competing identifications, Reznikoff's poetry comments on the enlarged and ultimately permeable borders of all the worlds he inhabits, while aspiring to avoid the exclusionary practices of any particular majority culture. Preservation of this enigmatic space has important consequences for his approach to the Holocaust. Despite the singularity of the Holocaust, Reznikoff seems to have been fully prepared to envision American Jewry as sharing the contingency of history with other minority groups in a cosmopolitan milieu.

Reznikoff's historical poems and verse plays, and even the historical novel *The Lionhearted*, illustrate ways of existing between the polarities of absolute absorption by and absolute expulsion from non-Jewish populations. Whatever they may have wished, the Jews Reznikoff writes about rarely succeeded in insulation, as is evident in a heritage of dynamic exchanges, in other words, Judaism's contributions to, and borrowings from, host cultures. Hence, though the Holocaust is often encoded in his most Jewish verse, so too is the richness of cultural pluralism and exchange. In Reznikoff's simultaneous nod to both this spirit of the past—the enduring vitality of Judaism as a textual, rather than territorial, ethos — and his incomparable struggle to look ahead to a Judaism that might survive even the Holocaust, we find what is perhaps the most explicitly prophetic moment in his entire oeuvre:

As when a great tree, bright with blossoms and heavy with fruit,
is cut down and its seeds are carried far
by the winds of the sky and the waves of the streams and seas
and it grows again on distant slopes and shores
in many places at once,
still blossoming and bearing fruit a hundred and a thousandfold,
so, at the destruction of the Temple
and the murder of its priests, ten thousand synagogues
took root and flourished
in Palestine and in Babylonia and along the Mediterranean;
so the tides carried from Spain and Portugal
a Spinoza to Holland
and a Disraeli to England (*Complete Poems*, vol. II, p. 60).

Despite his immersion in Holocaust materials Reznikoff was more forgiving than most Jewish American poets when it came to the problematic relation of T. S. Eliot and, especially, the fascist Ezra Pound, whose antisemitic lyrics created poetry that many now feel helped engender a fatal culture of indifference. When asked in his final interview, which took place only ten days before his death, how a poet "so deeply Jewish" could be inspired by the blatantly antisemitic Ezra Pound, Reznikoff did not evade the question but stressed his lifelong interest in an ethos of influx, experimentation, exchange, and adaptation: "I don't see why I can't benefit from the work Pound did, whatever his prejudices. I was very interested in the music of everyday speech and in free verse, and along came Pound, experimenting with these very things. I found all that very useful and illuminating; and frankly, I'm still very grateful for those ideas. Whatever motivated his antisemitism—and remember, this was no Hitler—it isn't related to what he taught me as a poet" (Rovner, p. 1976).

This stubborn desire to learn from and communicate with the non-Jewish world eventually brought Reznikoff some degree of international recognition and modest material reward. Years after his *Family Chronicle* (1963), an examination of immigrant life, had been rejected by Jewish publishers, the new British publishing firm Norton Bailey (which had no Jewish editors) was impressed enough to make it their inaugural venture. The work was then enthusiastically reviewed by the London critics. It was an Irishman, Seamus Cooney, who edited Reznikoff's *Collected Works*, and C. P. Snow, a British literary critic, who wrote a moving introduction to the New Directions paperback edition. Reznikoff's response to this unexpected attention juxtaposes his understatedly wry modernism with his modest desire to situate himself in some way within Jewish textual tradition: "You never can tell who will be moved by what you write. That's as true today as it was in the time of Amos the Prophet. The king wanted to have him thrown in jail for what he was saying—but he kept on" (Rovner, p. 18). Reznikoff's reply underscores his enduring cosmopolitan credo—his sense that Judaism, and individual Jews, were invigorated by their openness to surrounding cultures.

In spite of his marriage to the Zionist activist and polemicist Marie Syrkin, Reznikoff's post-Holocaust resistance to the Zionist insistence on ending exile may be at least partially accounted for by his unequivocal representations of Judaism as an extraterritorial culture, a textual landscape enriched by a living stream of ideas (even from antisemites), enlivened by its propinquity to other discourses, one in which Jews were not so tribally bound that they could not interact on a par with members of other groups. An example of Reznikoff's beliefs about the open-endedness of contingency appears in the poem "Samuel": "Chance planted me beside a stream of water; content, I serve the land, whoever lives here and whoever passes" (*Complete Poems*, vol. I, p. 73).

Today we know how well this "chance"—the Jews' intellectual gamble on America—has paid off. By the late twentieth century unprecedented numbers of widely read Christian journals published articles that urged Christians to study rabbinics as a wellspring of religious insight. Post-Holocaust Protestant and Catholic theologians and professors of religious studies read and teach Martin Buber, Gershom Scholem, and Abraham Joshua Heschel (pre-eminent twentieth-century

Jewish theologians whose religious thought has had a profound impact on Christianity and Judaism alike). But for the wary poet such blessings do not mean that the stream where the poet "think[s] in psalms" is "homeland," or that America is his Zion, but rather, as he patiently explains in the title chosen for both a prose work and a poetry collection, "Babylon." The diasporic setting that most interests Reznikoff (apart from New York City) is Babylonia, because this is the archetypal site where Jews learned to assert themselves vis-à-vis others. His poetry shares a recognition of the singularity of Judaic experience that George Steiner, a cultural critic and ardent diasporist, so aptly describes: "when the text is the homeland, even when it is rooted only in the exact remembrance and seeking of a handful of wanderers, nomads of the word, it cannot be extinguished" ("Our Homeland, the Text," *Salmagundi* (winter/spring 1985) 66:24). The medieval persecutions that set the stage for *The Lionhearted*, the various narrative versions of his family's immigrant struggle against American antisemitism, and the capsule histories of his poetry are filled with centuries of risks and losses, but for Reznikoff the sacrifice on which Steiner speculates—the stasis of a material homeland—is the one that causes him misgivings: "Locked materially in a material homeland, the text may, in fact, lose its life-force, and its truth values may be betrayed." This is especially apparent in "The Black Death," where the poet commits himself to the power of the surviving remnant (rather than the historical-messianic emphasis of the Zionist), to a construction of transcendence and a way of honoring a tradition that is not engulfed by the waves of history. Reznikoff never pretended to move beyond the Holocaust and refrained from systematizing the unspeakable.

At the age of sixty-nine Reznikoff received an award for his poetry from the National Institute of Arts and Letters that read simply: "To Charles Reznikoff, born by the waters of Manhattan. Mr. Reznikoff was educated for the law but has instead dedicated his life to giving sworn testimony in the court of poetry against the swaggering injustices of our culture and on behalf of its meek wonders." Thanks to Black Sparrow Press, a rush of publications followed, and Reznikoff lived to see several volumes of his poetry appear in print: *By the Well of Living and Seeing: New and Selected Poems 1918–1973* (1974); *Holocaust* (1975); and *The Complete Poems* (1976). On the evening of 22 January 1976, Reznikoff remarked to Syrkin: "You know, I never made money but I have done everything that I most wanted to do," then died of a heart attack. He was buried in the Old Mount Carmel Cemetery in Brooklyn, where his epitaph from *Separate Way* (1936), reads: "And the day's brightness dwindles into stars" (*Complete Poems*, vol. I, p. 167).

Though much neglected in canonical studies of American poetry, Reznikoff was always a poet's poet, respected by figures as disparate as Ezra Pound (despite the latter's antisemitism), William Carlos Williams, and Allen Ginsberg. Critical interest in Reznikoff is increasingly reflected in the pages of journals such as *Sagetrieb*, and in 1984 the National Poetry Foundation included a volume of essays by Paul Auster, David Ignatow, and Harvey Shapiro among others dedicated to examining Reznikoff's legacy in its "Man and Poet" series. Among the most important recent critical works on Reznikoff are *A Menorah for Athena: Charles Reznikoff and the Jewish Dilemmas of Objectivist Poetry* (2001), a work that delineates how, for Reznikoff, the linked concepts of race, homeland, and state fundamentally undermine the ethical possibility of dialogical openness and the realm of poetry itself. In *Diaspora and Zionism in Jewish American Literature*, Ranen Omer examines the relation between diasporic continuity and the Holocaust in Reznikoff's lyrics.

Bibliography

Primary Sources

Nine Plays. 1927.
The Lionhearted: A Story About the Jews in Medieval England. 1944.
Inscriptions: 1944–1956. 1959, self-published.
By the Waters of Manhattan: Selected Verse. 1962.
Holocaust. 1975.
Testimony: The United States 1885–1915: Recitative. 1978.
The Complete Poems of Charles Reznikoff: 1918–1975. 1976.

Secondary Sources

Bernstein, Charles. "Reznikoff's Nearness." *Sulfur* 32 (spring 1993): 6–38.
Finkelstein, Norman. "Tradition and Modernity, Judaism and Objectivism: The Poetry of Charles Reznikoff." In Rachel Blau DuPlessis. *In The Objectivist Nexus: Essays in Cultural Poetics*, Edited by Rachel Blau DuPlessis. Tuscaloosa, Ala.: University of Alabama Press, 1999, pp. 191–209.
Fredman, Stephen. *A Menorah for Athena: Charles Reznikoff and the Jewish Dilemmas of Objectivist Poetry*. Chicago: Chicago University Press, 2001.
Hatlen, Burton, ed. Charles Reznikoff Special Issue, *Sagetrieb* 13, nos. 1 and 2 (spring/fall 1994).
Hindus, Milton, "Charles Reznikoff." In Carole S. Kessner. *The "Other" New York Jewish Intellectuals*. New York: University Press, 1994, pp. 247–267.
Norich, Samuel. "Choosing Life." *Forward* (21 January 2000): 1, 3.
Omer, Ranen. *Diaspora and Zionism in Jewish American Literature*. Hanover and London: University Press of New England, 2002.

———. " 'Palestine Was a Halting Place, One of Many': Diasporism in the Poetry of Charles Reznikoff." *Melus* 25, no. 1 (spring 2000): 147–180.

Rothchild, Sylvia. "From a Distance and Up Close: Charles Reznikoff and the Holocaust." In *Charles Reznikoff: Man and Poet*. Edited by Milton Hindus. Orono: National Poetry Foundation/University of Maine, 1984, pp. 289–296.

Rovner, Ruth. "Charles Reznikoff—A Profile." *Jewish Frontier* (April 1976): 14–18.

Stevenson, Anne (with Michael Farley). "Charles Reznikoff in His Tradition." In *Charles Reznikoff: Man and Poet*. Edited by Milton Hindus. Orono: National Poetry Foundation/University of Maine, 1984, pp. 177–185.

Steiner, George. "Our Homeland, the Text." *Salmagundi* 66 (winter/spring 1985): pp. 4–25.

Sutherland, Janet. "Reznikoff and His Sources." In Milton Hindus (ed.). *Charles Reznikoff: Man and Poet*, 1984, pp. 297–307.

Syrkin, Marie. "Charles: A Memoir." In Milton Hindus (ed.). *Charles Reznikoff: Man and Poet*, 1984, pp. 37–67.

Adrienne Rich

(1929–)

DONNA KROLIK HOLLENBERG

Ever since her first book of poems won the Yale Younger Poets Award in 1951, the poetry and essays of Adrienne Rich have been mainstays of contemporary American literature. Widely recognized as one of the most eloquent voices of the women's movement, she has written about the politics of sexuality, race, language, and power from her experience as a white, Jewish, lesbian feminist, in nineteen books of poetry and three volumes of essays. Rich is committed to claiming and exploring the complexities of North American cultural and historical identity. Her life and work are marked by change and growth both in lived commitments and in subject matter, reflecting aspects of her evolution from wife and mother to lesbian lover and from social Christian to self-determined Jew. Raised in a family of mixed religious background, she did not come to terms with her Jewishness until well into adulthood, but upon doing so she discovered a connection that is fundamental to her spiritual continuity. Rich is a social poet dedicated to documenting the history of the dispossessed and to extending the range of individual and social accountability. Her response to the Holocaust is part of that endeavor.

Adrienne Rich was born 16 May 1929 in Baltimore, Maryland, the elder of two daughters of Arnold Rich, a Jewish doctor and professor of pathology at Johns Hopkins University, and Helen Jones Rich, a Protestant pianist and composer who gave up a possible musical career to raise a family. She earned an A.B. from Radcliffe College in 1951, published her first book of poems the same year, and married Alfred H. Conrad, a Jewish economist teaching at Harvard, in 1953. Within the next six years she bore three sons.

In her early books, as well as in the autobiographical essay "When We Dead Awaken," Rich considers the effects of female socialization upon her life and work as a poet. Rich's keen social conscience led her to become increasingly active in New Left politics in the 1960s and after. She became radicalized as a feminist and a lesbian, an aspect of her identity that was enhanced by the beginning of her life with the Jamaican-born writer, Michelle Cliff, with whom she coedited the lesbian-feminist journal *Sinister Wisdom*. Her work is marked by intense self-scrutiny and also by empathy for others, particularly for women from less privileged backgrounds. It is thus characteristic that she accepted the National Book Award in 1974 with Audre Lorde and Alice Walker in the name of all women who are silenced.

The Importance of Identity

For Rich, the psychology and politics of gender identity are inextricably linked to the psychology and politics of race and class, and she is also attuned to the impact upon identity of geographical and historical location. The works of her middle period indicate the development of a deepening and expanding historical and moral imagination. As she put it in her 1983 essay, "Resisting Amnesia: History and Personal Life," she is "pursued by questions of historical process, of historical responsibility, questions of historical consciousness and ignorance and what these have to do with power." The beginning of this phase of her poetic development can be traced to the new clarification she achieved in *Sources* (1983), the sequence of twenty-three poems in which she reevaluates her own ethnic identity by considering the psychological legacy of her father and her husband, both deracinated Jews, whose sense of identity as men was compromised by the anti-semitism of American culture and, in her husband's case, whose alienation led to his death. More specifically, she associates their deracination, as well as her own, with downplaying their Jewishness and with denying the psychological impact of the Holocaust.

As Rich tells us in this poetic sequence, she had been brooding over this aspect of her identity since adolescence. Her family had had little to do with her father's Jewish kin in the American South, whose lives, she realized later, must have been circumscribed by antisemitism. Similarly, through "the immense silence" around the subject of the Holocaust, she was spared knowledge of the devastation of the Jews of Europe. Early in *Sources*, in an attempt to account for this silence, she remembers her dead father's "rootless ideology / his private castle in the air," and with this memory comes a voice of self-rebuke and challenge: "From where does your strength come, you southern Jew? / Split at the root, raised in a castle of air?"; "With whom do you believe your lot is cast?" (*Sources*, Woodside, Calif.: Heyeck Press, pp. 11, 12). Later in the poem Rich achieves a new understanding of and compassion for her father's historical situation. She writes, "I saw the power and arrogance of the male as your true watermark; I did not see beneath it the suffering of the Jew, the alien stamp you bore, because you had deliberately arranged that it should be invisible to me" (*Sources*, p. 15). She rejects his deracination and also the related ambivalence of her dead husband, "who had tried to move into the floating world of the assimilated who know and deny they will always be aliens" (*Sources*, p. 25). In the course of the poem she works through remembered conflicts with both men to reach a fundamental sense of herself as a Jewish woman. As part of this process she acknowledges her connection with the dead Jews of Europe: "The Jews I've felt rooted among / are those who were turned to smoke" (*Sources*, p. 24).

Simultaneously with the writing of *Sources*, Rich was exploring her Jewishness in an essay entitled, "Split at the Root," written for the lesbian-feminist collection, *Nice Jewish Girls*. Rich points out that, in the South in the 1940s, the word "Jew" was not used by polite Gentiles. Perhaps this is why, as a high school student, she learned some things about World War II—about the Battle of Britain, the noble French Resistance fighters, and the starving Dutch, for example—but nothing about the resistance of the Warsaw Ghetto. In a particularly moving section of the essay, she describes going alone, sometime in 1946, to a local theater to see films of the Allied liberation of the Nazi concentration camps. She felt overwhelmed at those photos of heaps of corpses, with whom she knew she was connected, but there was no one in her world with whom to discuss her feelings. In her words: "Writing this now, I feel belated rage that I was so impoverished by the family and social worlds I lived in, that I had to try to figure out by myself what this did indeed mean for me. That I had never been taught about resistance, only about passing. That I had no language for antisemitism itself" (*Blood, Bread, and Poetry*, New York: Norton, p. 107). In an unconscious repetition of the silence within her own childhood, although she and her husband raised their three sons as Jews, they did not tell them about the Jewish children, like themselves, who were murdered in Europe in their parents' lifetimes.

Perhaps because Rich continues to feel this history of denial within herself like "an injury," she has been increasingly determined to speak out as a Jew. In all of her books of poetry since *Sources*, there are poems that view the world from a Jewish perspective or reflect on some aspect of the Holocaust or World War II. For example, *Sources* is reprinted as the first part of *Your Native Land, Your Life* (1996), a book that also contains the poem "Yom Kippur 1984," written after her move that year to Santa Cruz, California. It is a long meditation on the meanings of solitude and community in the context of violence against minority groups in America. *Time's Power* (1989) contains the poem "The Desert as Garden of Paradise," about the meanings of the physical site of monotheism, and a group of imaginary "Letters in the Family," one of which is to Chana Senesh, a heroine of the Jewish Resistance. *An Atlas of the Difficult World* (1991) contains three relevant poems: "Tattered Kaddish," which draws on the Jewish praise of life even in the event of suicide, "1948: Jews," which considers her mother's antisemitism within the context of her role as wife; and the long sequence, "Eastern War Time," in which Rich attempts to atone for her schoolgirl ignorance of the Holocaust through poems of memorial. *Dark Fields of the Republic* (1995) contains the sequence "Then or Now," inspired by the letters between Hannah Arendt and Karl Jaspers, and *Midnight Salvage* (1999) contains the poems "Char," a tribute to the French poet's courage and moral balance while fighting in the French Resistance, and "1941," a poem about the imaginative limits of those, like herself, who are indirectly affected by the tragic fate of the European Jews. Visibility and consciousness of Jewish identity was also the mission behind the Jewish feminist journal *Bridges*, which Rich confounded and published from 1989 to 1992.

Poetic Strategies

Among the poems mentioned above, the two sequences—"Eastern War Time" and "Then or Now"—are particularly significant for those interested in the effects of the Holocaust upon the inner lives of contemporary Americans. In both Rich uses the common language of direct communicative statement that has characterized her most recent books, inviting the ordinary reader into cultural participation. Her main formal strategy is a complex layering of tones and allusions within the structure of the sequences themselves. She builds on "the technique of weaving, a way of interlacing voices, echoes or motifs" that Willard Spiegelman has described as her characteristic way of "creating a whole from disparate parts" (p. 383). This is a process-oriented poetics in which the poet dramatizes her quest for a deeper understanding of her own subject position.

For example, in the ten-part sequence "Eastern War Time," Rich dramatizes contemporary post-Holocaust consciousness as a process in which memory and empathy are both liberating and limiting, especially when she considers the continuing impact of the European tragedy upon people today. In the first four sections she remembers the circumstances of her own earlier ignorance during the war within the context of American antisemitism and the accompanying silence of denial; these memories are clearly liberating. Then the associations become more complicated. In the next four sections, she pictures first the past lives of imagined contemporaries in Europe who would then have been youthful survivors of suffering and loss, and then she considers the present lives of all people, including herself, who search for but do not find "the end of degradation" (*Atlas*, New York: Norton, p. 41). This group ends with a poem set in the contemporary Middle East, where a woman "wired in memories" of recent violence to members of her family is "forbidden to forget" (p. 42). The last two sections are a response to the mixed messages of memory: ". . . Memory speaks: / You cannot live on me alone / you cannot live without me" (p. 43).

Rich has a healthy skepticism about the intrinsic moral and social value of memory. She implies that memory and empathy are valuable only insofar as they awaken in readers a desire to effect real social change.

This sense of the poet's social responsibility is also evident in the five-part sequence "Then or Now," in which Rich uses historical interlocutors to achieve an overtly didactic purpose. A meditation on guilt and innocence in the context of the Holocaust, this poem draws on the relationship between Hannah Arendt and Karl Jaspers to explore our contemporary psychological, social, and moral condition. The poem explores overlapping psychological, moral, and social aspects of guilt, its implications for connections between people, and the role of artists and intellectuals in establishing or destroying these connections. The sequence is organized around the time frames suggested by the words in the title: the first two poems are set in the 1940s ("then") and the last three in the 1990s ("now"). By considering the ways in which concepts of guilt and innocence were still tainted by widespread pathological indifference to the Holocaust beginning in the aftermath of Nazi rule, Rich shows the ways in which attention to the inadequacy of that response can prevent a similar brutal indifference to other, present tragedies. Arendt and Jaspers are apt interlocutors, as both wrote about the problem of German guilt from this common point of orientation. As I have written elsewhere, "In the course of the poem Rich dramatizes a creative relationship to guilt that she invites readers to share. She transforms anxiety about guilt into a mission of social responsibility" (Hollenberg, p. 378). In both of these sequences Rich demonstrates the ancient role of poetry in keeping memory and spiritual community alive. Written out of the deep tangle of her own longings and anguish about the Holocaust, these works are exemplary efforts. They show that, despite the silences that dominated the immediate aftermath, the impact of the Holocaust need not be spiritual stasis.

In fact the possibility that empathy with survivors may prevent moral complacency is the theme of "1941," a poem from her 1993 book, *What Is Found There*. Here post-Holocaust consciousness is a form of haunting, in which Rich necessarily falls short in an attempt to share the continuing pain of a fictive European Jewish survivor. Having called this counterpart to mind, Rich is careful to respect her difference, describing herself as "(like you, not with you)." As the poem progresses, instead of empathy, she gains further insight into the ethical dilemma her project entails. As she tries to envision her counterpart's present feelings toward a homeland wherein she once hid among farm animals for protection, Rich confronts the limits of her imaginative task. The poem ends abruptly with the poet questioning herself about the right to speak:

How did you get here anyway?
Are you the amateur of drought? the collector
of rains? are you poetry's inadmissable
untimely messenger?
By what right?
In whose name?
Do you (*What Is Found There*, New York: Norton, p. 24)

Yet the imaginative effort itself *is* salutary, not least for the participation it inspires in readers. That final, incomplete question, "Do you," speaks volumes. The words it fails to express take readers by the throat. For Adrienne Rich, today more than ever, the poet's role is to locate and document the ruptures of imagination implicit in our communal history. She continues to write poems, about Jewish subjects as well as others, that keep pain vocal so that it cannot become "normalized and acceptable" (*What Is Found There*, p. 242). In this more-recent example of post-Holocaust consciousness, as in the earlier poems mentioned, Rich employs such fierce attention and skill that the poems themselves are artful figures of moral transformation and of yet untold possibility. Hers is a revolutionary art driven by the desire for a better world.

Rich's work has been widely reviewed and has provided the occasion for extended critical analysis. Discussions of it are included in surveys of contemporary poetry by David Kalstone (1977), Suzanne Juhasz (1978), Cary Nelson (1981), Deborah Pope (1984), Wendy Martin (1984), Charles Altieri (1984), Alicia Ostriker (1986), Paula Bennett (1986), Helen Vendler (1988), and Walter Kaladjian (1989). Book-length studies of Rich's poetry include those by Myriam Diaz-Diacaretz (1984), Claire Keyes (1986), and Alice Templeton (1994). Collections of essays solely on Rich include those edited by Barbara Charlesworth Gelpi and Albert Gelpi (1975 and 1993), Jane R. Cooper (1984), and Craig Werner (1988). As Alice Templeton has pointed out, in the 1970s and 1980s critical discussion centered on the following themes: "the connection between poetry and political change, Rich's reading and writing of women's history in her poetry, language as both a liberating and constraining cultural legacy, the poet's engagement in a radical feminist discourse, Rich's feminist ethics, her place in American poetic tradition, and the poetry's intertextual resonances with the work of other poets" (1993, p. 335). Since then, critics have addressed Rich's extension of feminist analysis to ideological systems other than sexual difference, including the deforming power of racism and antisemitism. They have also begun to assess more positive aspects of her claims as a Jewish writer, analyzing ways in which these claims affect her handling of poetic traditions as well as her formal experiments. For example, new critical perspectives include a discussion of Rich's reworking of the poetic tradition of lamentation to feature mourning as a potentially redemptive communal enterprise (Shreiber), and an exploration of the influences of nonliterary forms such as maps and photographs on her poems about the psychosocial effects of the Holocaust (Jacobs).

Bibliography

Poetry

A Change of World. 1951.
The Diamond Cutters and Other Poems. 1955.
Snapshots of a Daughter-in-Law: Poems 1954–1962. 1963.
Necessities of Life: Poems 1962–1965. 1966.
Selected Poems. 1967.
Leaflets: Poems 1965–1968. 1969.
The Will to Change: Poems 1968–1970. 1971.
Diving into the Wreck: Poems 1971–1972. 1973.
Poems: Selected and New, 1950–1974. 1975.
Twenty-One Love Poems. 1976.
The Dream of a Common Language: Poems 1974–1977. 1978.
A Wild Patience Has Taken Me This Far: Poems 1978–1981. 1981.
Sources. 1983.
The Fact of a Doorframe: Poems Selected and New 1950–1984. 1984.
Your Native Land, Your Life: Poems. 1986.
Time's Power: Poems 1985–1988. 1989.
An Atlas of the Difficult World: Poems 1988–1991. 1991.
Collected Early Poems 1950–1970. 1993.
Dark Fields of the Republic: Poems 1991–1995. 1995.
Midnight Salvage: Poems 1995–1998. 1999.

Prose

Of Woman Born: Motherhood as Experience and Institution. 1976.
On Lies, Secrets, and Silence: Selected Prose 1966–1978. 1979.
Blood, Bread, and Poetry: Selected Prose 1979–1985. 1986.
What Is Found There: Notebooks on Poetry and Politics. 1993.
"Poetry, Personality, and Wholeness: A Response to Galway Kinnell." 1997.

Selected Secondary Sources

Birkle, Carmen. *Women's Stories of the Looking Glass: Autobiographical Reflections and Self-Representations in the Poetry of Sylvia Plath, Adrienne Rich, and Audre Lorde*. Munich, Germany: Fink, 1996.

Davidson, Harriet. " 'In the Wake of Home': Adrienne Rich's Politics and Poetics of Location." In *Contemporary Poetry Meets Modern Theory*. Edited by Anthony Easthope and John D. Thompson. Toronto: University of Toronto Press, 1991.

Dickie, Margaret. *Stein, Bishop, and Rich: Lyrics of Love, War, and Place*. Chapel Hill: University of North Carolina Press, 1997.

Gelpi, Albert. "The Poetics of Recovery: A Reading of Adrienne Rich's *Sources*." In *Adrienne Rich's Poetry and Prose*. Edited by Albert Gelpi and Barbara Charlesworth Gelpi. New York: W. W. Norton, 1993.

Helle, Anita. "Elegy as History: Three Women Poets 'By the Century's Deathbed.' " *South Atlantic Review* 61, no. 2 (spring 1996): 51–68.

Hirsh, Elizabeth. "Another Look at Genre: Diving into the Wreck of Ethics with Rich and Iragaray." In *Feminist Measures: Soundings in Poetry and Theory*. Edited by Lynn Keller and Christine Miller. Ann Arbor: University of Michigan Press, 1994.

Hollenberg, Donna K. "Holocaust Consciousness in the 1990s: Adrienne Rich's 'Then or Now.' " *Women's Studies* 27 (1998): 377–387.

Jacobs, Joshua S. "Mapping after the Holocaust: The 'Atlases' of Adrienne Rich and Gerhard Richter." *Mosaic* 32, no. 4 (December 1999): 111–127.

Kirby, Kathleen. "Thinking Through the Boundary: The Politics of Location, Subjects, and Space." *Boundary 2* 20, no. 2 (summer 1993): 173–189.

Klein, Karen. "Adrienne Rich: 'Stuck to Earth.' " In *Daughters of Valor: Contemporary Jewish American Women Writers*. Edited by Jay L. Halio and Ben Siegel. Newark: University of Delaware Press, 1997.

Rugoff, Kathy. "Sappho on Mount Sinai: Adrienne Rich's Dialogue with Her Father." In *Multicultural Literatures Through*

Feminist/Poststructuralist Lenses. Edited by Barbara Frey Waxman. Knoxville: University of Tennessee Press, 1993.

Shreiber, Maeera. " 'Where Are We Moored?': Adrienne Rich, Women's Mourning, and the Limits of Lament." In *Dwelling in Possibility: Women Poets and Critics on Poetry*. Edited by Yopie Prins and Maeera Shreiber. Ithaca, N.Y.: Cornell University Press, 1997.

Spiegelman, Willard. " 'Driving to the Limits of the City of Words': The Poetry of Adrienne Rich." In *Adrienne Rich's Poetry and Prose*. Edited by Albert Gelpi and Barbara Charlesworth Gelpi. New York: W. W. Norton, 1993.

Templeton, Alice. "Contradictions: Tracking Adrienne Rich's Poetry." *Tulsa Studies in Women's Literature* 12, no. 2 (fall 1993): 333–340.

———. *The Dream and the Dialogue: Adrienne Rich's Feminist Poetics*. Knoxville: University of Tennessee Press, 1994.

MORDECAI RICHLER

(1931–2001)

MICHAEL GREENSTEIN

MORDECAI RICHLER WAS born 27 July 1931 in Montreal, Quebec, Canada, to Leah (née Rosenberg) and Moses Isaac Richler. From 1944 through 1949 he attended Baron Byng High School, and from 1949 through 1951 Sir George Williams University in Montreal. Much of his writing life was spent in England, and for years he divided his time between London and Canada, the two poles playing a major role in settings for his fiction. Among his awards are the following: Canada Council junior arts fellowship (1959), Guggenheim Foundation creative-writing fellowship (1961), Canada Council senior arts fellowship (1967), Governor-General's award (1969, 1972).

Growing up in Montreal, Richler experienced two forms of antisemitism: racial and religious prejudice from French-Canadian Catholics, and socioeconomic discrimination from English-Canadian Protestants. The hypocrisies of a conservative Canadian establishment are targets for Richler's satire, which attacks antisemitism at home and abroad. In his early fiction he sends a naïve gentile Canadian to Europe to mediate between Jewish characters and Germans; in his more mature novels, Jewish protagonists confront ex-Nazis both realistically and mythologically so that stereotypes become archetypes. He portrays a decadent post-Holocaust world in an expressionistic mode, exposing both the distorted viewpoints of survivor and ex-Nazi.

To understand Richler's fictional approach to the Holocaust it is helpful to examine his essay, "The Holocaust and After" (in *Shovelling Trouble*, 1972), first published in 1966. He begins by stating bluntly that he still considers Germans an abomination more than twenty years after the end of World War II, for he has been reading memoirs about life in the Warsaw ghetto, Terezin, Treblinka, and Janowska. After describing Chaim Kaplan's *Scroll of Agony* and Leon Wells's *The Janowska Road*, he takes a strong moral stance: "Let no one ask why there wasn't more resistance" (Toronto: McClelland and Stewart, 1972, p. 87). He then offers accounts of his own visits to Munich in 1955 and 1963 where he encounters a disturbing poster about Dachau that he uses in two of his novels. By the mid-1960s he discovers in Germany and elsewhere that films and fiction about the Nazis have become sexually appealing to the masses. That kind of "kitsch" is immoral, as is the habit of universalizing the Holocaust and appropriating it for a number of political causes from the far Left to the Jewish fixation with it as a means of solidarity and group identity. He also criticizes the use of numbers such as six million as a catchall or cliché that reduces individual and collective horrors, and concludes by praising Elie Wiesel's *Night*, but is critical of much of Wiesel's other writing that "spins tales" about the death camps. In Richler's own fiction, he tries to avoid spinning tales or sensationalizing the Holocaust.

The Acrobats

Early in his first novel, *The Acrobats* (1954), Richler introduces a kind-hearted bar keeper, Chaim, who has settled in Valencia after the war in the spring of 1946 with a forged passport, having given his American passport to a thin, frightened boy with a number and symbol on his arm, so that the survivor from Warsaw could be reunited with his sister in America: "He thought about the Warsaw ghetto where those who were not burnt now walked in the cold desert land, tugging at their beards, mourning murdered sons and murdered daughters, wondering if it was truly hot in the Promised Land" (London: André Deutsch, 1954, p. 17). Chaim's wandering thoughts form part of Richler's mental peregrinations in postwar Europe. Even though the novel is set in Spain, Richler covers the entire continent throughout his fiction and goes back in time to the Inquisition. From the Inquisition to the

Spanish Civil War to the Holocaust, he confronts injustice and inhumanity in all of his novels. The desert and the Promised Land are both Jewish and universal concerns in his treatment of the Diaspora and Zion.

Chaim's teacher, Rab Moishe, maintains that Jews perished because they spoke of the Holy Ark as a box and the synagogue as a resort for vulgar ignoramuses. Richler satirizes not only those vulgar worshipers but also the Rab Moishes of this world who cling to an outmoded faith in the face of catastrophe. Because Richler refuses to believe in a God who would permit the deaths of millions of innocent women and children in the Holocaust, he denounces any rabbinic justification about Jewish suffering for sins committed.

Typical of Richler's fictional universe is its mixture of Germans, Jews, and Canadians and a subsequent confusion of their identities in a grotesque world. Less than a decade after the war, Richler pits Chaim against Nazi Colonel Kraus who works for him in his Spanish club. Kraus's memories take him back to Munich, 1921, when he was part of a crowd of 5,600 listening to "the angry man in the brown trenchcoat gesticulating wildly, his voice hysterical" (p. 57) telling them the truth about the International Jewish Stock Exchange. Throughout the 1930s Kraus served the Nazis in Spain and returned there after the war. He dislikes Spain because Spaniards are effeminate, Semitic, godless, and poor soldiers. Orderly Kraus had been at Maidanek where his sister worked at the *Vernichtungslager* (extermination camp) checking cremated victims for gold teeth and overlooked rings. In a dialogue between brother and sister she tells him to beware of their enemies and not show any signs of weakness.

Kraus's sister pays Chaim a visit: she has hard, blue eyes, as opposed to Chaim's liquid, grey eyes, and a sharp-lined face that is bony and dry. Their antagonistic dialogue correlates with their contrasting appearances. When he asks her if she enjoys the Spanish festival, she replies in the negative, whereupon Chaim asks if she would prefer the festival at Bayreuth or Munich. She responds coldly, "You do not like Germans" (p. 18). A melancholy clown, Chaim shrugs his shoulders and asks why he should dislike Germans, listing Bach, Beethoven, Mozart, and Goethe. When he mentions Karl Marx, Fräulein Kraus reminds him that Marx was a Jew. A self-proclaimed fascist, she denies any prejudice against Jews, only against communists. Wondering if he should judge the past and the present, Chaim drinks to cope with the trauma of history, and thinks about the war against Hitler when heaps of Jews were murdered and made into soap or lampshades.

Later the Canadian protagonist, André Bennett, who learns about history from Chaim, asks Kraus if he collects lampshades and what kind of soap he uses. The confrontation between André and Kraus takes place against a backdrop of *fallas* (a Spanish festival in which effigies are burned) going up in flames, particularly one of a wooden gypsy. This symbol connotes European decadence in the present and the past—tradition as destruction. The deaths in the novel come as aftershocks of the war: Kraus kills his rival André, and Kraus's sister commits suicide, hanging herself with the skipping rope her brother used when he was in training for the Olympics. Kraus escapes to West Germany and is successful in carrying his Nazi past with him. Chaim philosophically sums up fate: "Nothing is ever resolved, but it's always worth it" (p. 202). Oxymoronic Chaim, the melancholy clown whose name means "life," offers hope and stands in as Richler's spokesperson after the Holocaust, which forces Jews and Gentiles alike to be acrobats of history.

In the triangular relationship between Jew, Canadian, and German, Chaim serves as André's teacher, introducing him to Jewish sources such as Hillel, Shamai, and Maimonides. André, in turn, in an effort to exorcise the Nazi within himself, provokes Kraus. That is, the "innocent" Canadian Gentile recognizes his own potential for antisemitic behavior and wrestles with that feeling by learning from Chaim and by opposing Kraus.

A Choice of Enemies

Richler's third novel, *A Choice of Enemies* (1957), is also set in Europe, and the first intrusion of the Holocaust occurs in a Munich poster:

DACHAU
Bus Leaves Every Saturday at 1400
VISIT THE CASTLE
AND THE CREMATORY
(Toronto: McClelland and Stewart, 1977, p. 14)

Throughout his fiction, Richler uses signs for a variety of effects, but this abruptly introduced poster without any commentary startles the reader. This juxtaposition of castle and crematory underscores the banality of evil in post-Holocaust Europe; similarly, the weekly routine departure of the bus tour collapses history in the cold horror of Dachau's ovens.

As the novel's title implies, each character has a choice of enemies, and the reader as well may choose a series of enemies from a wide range of characters. At Munich's military camp we meet Ernst Haupt, who belonged to the Hitler Youth Movement but claims that his father spent the war years as a prisoner in

Belsen. From his escape from East Germany at the beginning of the novel to his resurfacing as Joseph Rader in Montreal at the end of the novel, Ernst's identity remains somewhat vague. At the opposite end of Richler's character spectrum (or perhaps the opposite side of the same coin), Karp is a survivor of the concentration camps and as evasive about his identity as Haupt. Richler probes hidden traumas in the post-Holocaust clashes of these two characters. Castrated in the camps and without any first name, he is dehumanized—a fish out of water and a link in the food chain who contemplates characters "like a meal" (p. 28). With his peculiar physique, Karp is a startling figure as he massages his cane: "His face was round, but his limbs were so thin that his belly, sudden as it was huge, sprung forth as a surprise. Karp had a hurt flatulent face and protuberant eyes" (p. 29). Richler portrays the survivor as a grotesque figure, far from sympathetic, yet his face is "hurt," while the contrast between thin limbs and protruding stomach hints at the horror he had been through a decade earlier. When one of the American-Jewish characters drops a Yiddish phrase, Karp states emphatically that he does not speak the language even though one might assume that he does from his past.

Like many other characters in this existential novel about "choice," Karp acts in bad faith, going out of his way to abandon his Jewish past, which has involved so much suffering. Having starved in the concentration camp, he overcompensates by becoming a fastidious gourmand, aping the ways of his British neighbors. Richler simultaneously uses and challenges stereotypes. At times, landlord Karp appears like a caricature out of T. S. Eliot or even a Victorian one in his resemblance to Charles Dickens's Fagin. More than a century after Fagin roasts his sausage, Richler's survivor prepares his meal in London while waiting to confront Ernst. "With manifest skill Karp injected a ham with a hypodermic of brandy, massaged the ham's surface with honey, stuck cloves in here and there, and eased the pan into the oven" (p. 123). His injection recalls Nazi experiments, and his repeated fiddling with the oven gas evokes images of the gas chambers from which he has escaped. This domestic scene with Karp sipping his sherry is not nearly so innocent when set against the backdrop of world events. It would be far too glib to label Karp (or his creator) as a self-hating Jew, for he has been traumatized by his camp experience and adopts assimilation into the gentile world as a survival strategy.

Richler's gentile protagonist, Norman Price, provides a vehicle for examining Jewish characters and their relationships with Gentiles. Surrounded by a host of Jewish friends, Norman belongs to a minority; Richler often explores such religious reversals in his fiction. Karp worships Norman and constantly seeks his approval, but Norman rebuffs him: "The best ones were killed, Karp. Only the conniving evil ones like you survived" (p. 146). A protagonist who suffers from more than amnesia, Norman may not be taken as a spokesperson for Richler, whose opinions are far different. If Norman has his nightmares from the war when his plane crashed and burned, his insult to Karp throws the survivor and former *Sonderkommando* (crematoria worker) into turmoil. His plans for survival topple, for his cultivation of gentile culture is for naught. Richler enters the survivor's mind where past and present comingle, the gaunt face of *Obersturmführer* (the Nazi camp commander) Hartmann changing to Norman's face and back again to Hartmann. Although Hartmann had shot thousands of Jews, what remains most vivid in Karp's memory is an incident with one young girl who survived the crematorium because she fell with her face against the wet concrete. She was not asphyxiated because zyclon gas does not work under humid conditions. When Hartmann discovers that she has survived, he shoots her. By delineating the specifics of this example instead of relying on statistics, Richler makes the Holocaust more graphic to the reader.

In the absurd post-Holocaust world of *A Choice of Enemies*, Karp goes to Israel where his credibility is called into question because he survived. Tragic fate does not stop after 1945. Ernst escapes to Canada, "heroically" saves a Montreal Jew, and marries a German widow who is proud of the fact that her late father served in the SS. The novel's politics veer from Franco's Spain to McCarthyism in the United States. Richler unveils blindnesses and difficulties in the middle of the twentieth century where political extremes have resulted in millions of deaths.

Cocksure

In *Cocksure* (1968) Richler continues in his Gothic vein, particularly where Germans are concerned. Among the team of "efficiency experts" (New York: Simon and Schuster, 1968, p. 30) from Frankfurt are Herr Dr. Manheim and his three secretaries. Two of them are male and wear black leather coats, while the third, Fräulein Ringler, has a dueling scar on her cheek. Miss Fishman, the British secretary who had come to England from a displaced person's camp after the war, attacks Fräulein Ringler with a letter opener because her necklace had belonged to Miss Fishman's mother, who had been killed in the ovens of Treblinka. Richler's black humor is very troubling at this point, but in delineating a specific case within the overall framework of the Holocaust, his biting satire shocks the reader out of complacency. Miss Fishman's mother was the one-millionth Jew to be burned, "not counting half or quarter Jews or babies who weighed under nine pounds before being flung into the ovens" (p. 31). Richler marks the event graphically, describing how flowers and Chinese lanterns decorated Treblinka in honor of Miss Fishman's mother. The leaders of other concentration camps are invited for this occasion, but Richler's narration of this "ring-a-ding" night and "sentimental barbecue" goes beyond aesthetics of atrocity.

Lord Woodcock intervenes between Miss Fishman and Fräulein Ringler. After the war he compiled a book about all the charitable acts of German behavior on behalf of Jews during the Nazi era: a sergeant offering marmalade to children before they were led off to the gas chambers, a general refusing to drink with Eichmann, a professor quoting Heine in front of a Nazi. When Miss Fishman calls Fräulein Ringler a "German bitch," Lord Woodcock reprimands her, arguing that she herself sounds like a Nazi. He then tries to placate her by stroking her number-tattooed arm and by quoting from scriptures concerning the extermination of nations. Self-righteous Woodcock clearly represents British bogus with regard to antisemitism, and gentile insensitivity to Jewish Holocaust suffering.

Mortimer Griffin, the innocent Canadian antihero in the novel, explains to Woodcock how he expected Jewish soldiers, with the Allied forces, to take revenge after the war and hunt down former SS men, but acts of vengeance had been scarce. Woodcock tells Griffin that after the war he had traveled to Germany with some saintly Jews to plant botanical gardens. German onlookers maintained that nothing would grow because the Jews were ignorant in agricultural matters and refused to use chemical fertilizers. The gardens bloom in abundance, however, because of rare fertilizers underground—rivers of human blood, mashed bone, and burned flesh. Richler oversteps the bounds of propriety once again by explaining that to this day the fertilizer accounts for the succulent asparagus of the Schwarzwald and fine Rhine vintages, "thereby bringing dividends to gourmets the world over, regardless of race, color, or creed" (p. 33). Richler's brutal satire levels all of humanity, victor and victim alike; it serves as a constant reminder that the Holocaust will not simply disappear through collective amnesia or indifference in a post-Holocaust world. Variations of Nazism abound as new tyrants emulate and adapt Nazi methods in Richler's ever-darkening, increasingly pessimistic vision of the post-Holocaust world.

The British response to *Cocksure*'s satire ranges from Anthony Burgess's approval to Philip Toynbee's qualified criticism that it is not possible to detect Richler's moral stance in the fiction and that not all Germans should be portrayed negatively. Most Canadian critics have agreed with Toynbee that *Cocksure* lacks a moral center.

St. Urbain's Horseman

Three years separate *Cocksure* from Richler's more sophisticated distancing from the Holocaust in *St. Urbain's Horseman* (1971). Where Richler's earlier novels are more compressed, *St. Urbain's Horseman* ranges widely and expansively, drawing on history, fantasy, and myths to complement contemporary realistic events. The novel opens with Jake Hersh obsessing about Mengele: "Sometimes Jake wondered if the *Doktor* . . . slept with his mouth open" (Toronto: McClelland and Stewart, 1976, p. 3). At first it is not clear to whom Richler is referring, for his technique of indirection distances and involves the post-Holocaust reader. Mengele is not mentioned at the beginning, so the *Doktor* allusion is unspecified. Even when the narrator or Jake continues to imagine his antagonist's mouth, Josef Mengele's identity is not fully revealed.

Jake invents the figure of the Horseman, a postmodern golem based on the folkloric figure created in the sixteenth century by Rabbi Lowe of Prague to defend the Jews from a pogrom, and who will avenge Jewish suffering in the post-Holocaust era by tracking down and torturing Mengele, extracting the gold fillings from his teeth. Where André Bennett and Norman Price are Christian mediating forces between Jew and Nazi in Richler's early fiction, in *St. Urbain's Horseman*, Jake Hersh confronts Nazis head-on with the help of Cousin Joey, a combination of Hersh's real cousin and the eponymous equestrian or Pegasus. This literary globetrotter enables Richler to discard the unities of time and place; from the comfort of his domestic setting in London, Jake is able to project himself into vast distances and various time zones in his tracking of Nazis. No matter where Josef Mengele hides in South America's jungles, Joseph Hersh will track him down.

Jake Hersh is on trial in London, though he is innocent. He, in turn, puts the Nazi past on trial; the trials overlap in a surrealistic blur. Jake's walls are lined with photographs of wartime Nazi leaders. Jake has written a film script in which he imagines history reversed, with the Nazis victorious over England. Jake's film script, *The Good Britons*, is accompanied by a letter addressed to the *Sturmbannführer* (the Nazi camp leader) and signed by Jakob Von Hersh. Richler's satire attacks not only Nazis but also British anti-semitism.

Jake's imagination pursues Nazis, but he also empathizes with their victims, for example, as he studies photographs of a bewildered Jewish boy on a Warsaw street. The boy's eyes are filled with fear as he raises his arms above his head along with other Jews huddled together. Four German soldiers pose for the photographer who remains unseen and one of the soldiers points his rifle at the little boy. The photograph may be familiar enough, but Richler defamiliarizes it somewhat by following his objective description with a testimony quoted in italics: "*Children scratched their arms and with their own blood would write on the barracks walls, as did my nephew, this child here, who wrote: 'Andreas Rappaport—lived sixteen years*' " (p. 73). The contrast between Jake's domestic comforts and his examined, middle-aged life, and the doomed children of the Holocaust jolts Jake and the reader out of any complacency, for complacency itself is a form of complicity. Rappaport's signature in blood on wood contrasts sharply with the lengthy narrative of *St. Urbain's Horseman*. We are left to imagine the rest of Andreas Rappaport's life cut so short. Richler's presentation of photographs captures, in brief, some of the horror of the Holocaust.

From the child's photograph Jake turns to a photograph of a beautiful Jewish woman sitting naked before a pit, while German soldiers smirk in the background in contrast to her sorrowful look. She will die within seconds; the photograph lives on in memory for generations. Again quotation marks and italics follow the photograph as if to frame the historic moment. This time Richler re-creates a dialogue of German testimony, presumably from the Nuremberg trials where Friedrich Wilhelm Boger is asked how many were murdered at Auschwitz. He responds that it is approximately the number given by Rudolf Höss, that is, two million. The vagueness of millions, more or less, stands in relief to the photograph of individual suffering. By highlighting an individual case and surrounding it with statistics of millions, Richler effectively bears witness to the *Shoah*. He goes one step further: Jake has a nightmare in which extermination officers enter his house and violently kill his own children. What begins as a comfortable domestic scene in London in the 1970s ends up as a recapitulation of the Holocaust a generation earlier. The chapter ends with more Nuremberg testimony in italics: "*A terrible stench came out of the car, like the plague. These prisoners were loaded onto the trucks directly and dumped into the pit next to Crematory II*" (p. 73). Some of them were still alive, and Mengele was always present.

In Frankfurt, the Horseman sits in the court presided over by Judge Hofmeyer, while a witness remembers that Mengele remained sober, with his thumbs in his pistol belt, while Dr. Rohde and Dr. König always got drunk. There follows a description of the terrible conditions of the women's block where washing and drinking took place right beside the latrine. Female guards beat the inmates with clubs as the SS passed by and watched. Lice and rats destroyed bodies, but when Mengele arrived he gassed the entire block. All confiscated valuables go "to storehouses with the collective name Canada, so called because of the country's reputation as a land of immense riches" (p. 176). Richler contrasts the hell of the Holocaust with the fantasy of Canadian abundance.

In Israel, Richler's Horseman follows the history of Dr. Rudolph Kastner, a leader of Hungary's Jewish community, who in 1944 contacted one of Eichmann's Hungarian assistants to negotiate the freedom of 1,700 Jews from among 750,000 to be deported. Kastner's relatives and many wealthy Jews were saved with the $1.6 million ransom. Kastner settled in Israel but was accused of collaborating and put on trial in 1953 and again in 1957; he was acquitted, but shortly thereafter shot dead in the street by a Hungarian Jew.

Visiting his cousin Chava's kibbutz in search of the Horseman, Jake learns that Cousin Joey would show up inebriated at the Kibbutz of the Survivors of the Warsaw Ghetto, near Haifa, with its museum and archives of the Holocaust. Chava displays her collection of old photographs of Göring's wife shopping on the Theatinerstrasse, and the Von Papens posing on a leather chesterfield. These domestic photographs point to the banality of evil and contrast with the Jewish families and homes described in *St. Urbain's Horseman*.

Also in Chava's possession are more documents pertaining to Mengele, who lived in Munich until 1951, then fled to Buenos Aires and Paraguay in 1955. There is a declaration signed by Dr. Nyiskizli Miklos, chief physician at the Auschwitz crematoria, admitting that he reported directly to Mengele in Berlin. As Chava complains about the price of apartments in Tel-Aviv, Jake reads on about Mengele's selection of aged, crippled, feeble women and children under 14, sending them to the left, while able-bodied men and women were sent to the right. This historic description is interrupted by Chava serving tea. Then the historic document in italics continues with the details of how the gas canisters were applied to the pipes leading into the gas chambers. Once again, this alternation between past and present brings the past into sharper focus for the reader, making the unreality of Auschwitz more real.

Still in pursuit of Cousin Joey, the Horseman, Jake flies to Munich where the narrative is again interrupted by an account of the past set in italics, rendering the gruesome events even more graphic. These italics highlight the distortion of bodies being gassed and intertwined in their futile struggle for air. Their faces are blue and bloated, their noses and mouths bleeding (p. 262). Jake tours the *jazzkellers* of Schwabing, which seem like the lowest regions of hell—"Gehenna" (p. 262). He would like to set fire to the place, shout "murderers" at passersby, and when he bumps into one woman, excusing himself in Yiddish, he wishes instead that he could have stamped on her. "Hatred was a discipline" (p. 262), and Richler's fiction is very disciplined even in its most outrageous moments. Jake comes across exactly the same poster that Richler had introduced almost twenty years earlier in *A Choice of Enemies*:

DACHAU
Bus Leaves Every Saturday at 1400
VISIT THE CASTLE
AND THE CREMATORIUM

The *Bürgurbraukeller*, now an American Army Services Club, was a Nazi shrine where Hitler led his followers to the Bavarian parliament in 1923. At this army base, less than ten miles from Dachau, Jake meets Rabbi Irwin Meltzer to inquire after Joey, who had told the rabbi that any God who allowed six million Jews to perish could not exist. Joey blasphemes and tells the rabbi that the Lord was finally denied when some Orthodox Jews at Auschwitz refused to fast on Yom Kippur for the first time in their lives. Jake studies the Munich phone book to find four listings for "Goering," no Eichmanns, but lots of Himmlers. Jake's obsession with the Holocaust goes beyond Richler's earlier obsession with absurdity and is replaced now with post-Holocaust affirmation.

Drunk in Germany, Jake interchanges roles with Joey, insulting Germans who killed six million Jews. He tells Canadian soldiers that Joey Hersh, alias Jesse Hope, is the golem or Jewish Batman who has moved on to Frankfurt to attend the proceedings against Robert Karl Ludwig Mulka, Friedrich Wilhelm Boger, Dr. Victor Capesius, and others of Auschwitz-Birkenau. Their testimony serves as a refrain throughout the novel, a reminder of Mengele's presence not only during the war but in its aftermath as well:

> "Mengele cannot have been there all the time."
> "In my opinion always. Night and day" (p. 271).

Also repeated from an earlier section in the novel is the description of the women's block. After all the testimony giving gory details of children being shot or carried to Crematory IV, the narrator concludes, "If God weren't dead, it would be necessary to hang Him" (p. 272).

Joey also travels to Galway, Ireland, to investigate SS Colonel Otto Skorzeny, who settled on a large estate. Although Skorzeny was acquitted by a U.S. tribunal at Dachau in 1947, his wartime activities were sinister. On 20 July 1944, after Stauffenberg's bomb failed to kill Hitler, Skorzeny went to the Bendlerstrasse and put handcuffs on the plotters. After the trial he went to Spain, South America, and then to Galway where many former Nazis became gentlemen farmers.

When Jake learns of Joey's death in an airplane crash in South America, he relates an incident about Mengele from Simon Weisenthal, head of the Documentation Center on Nazis in Vienna. An Israeli woman, who had been in Auschwitz, visits her mother in Bariloche in the Andes. At the local hotel she recognizes Mengele, who notices the number on her lower left arm. A few days later her body is found in the mountains—a climbing accident, according to the local police.

The novel ends with Jake awakening from his Horseman nightmare. He goes to his study, crosses out "died" in his journal, and writes instead "presumed dead," referring to Cousin Joey. He then returns to bed and falls into a deep sleep beside his wife. History is a nightmare from which Jake Hersh awakens and returns to domestic comfort, but in chronicling the Holocaust obsessively he shows his moral commitment and vicarious heroism. Jake's aggressive behavior toward former Nazis is in part a reaction to the passivity of his parents' generation, which remained silent and tried to placate Canadian antisemites in much the same way that Jews of Eastern Europe behaved historically in hostile environments.

Joshua Then and Now

Joshua Then and Now (1980) continues Richler's involvement with the Spanish Civil War and the Holocaust with Joshua Shapiro taking over from Jake Hersh. All of the altercations between Jew and German in this novel turn on misunderstandings of identity—distortions of history whereby the boundaries between Jew and Nazi become blurred. On a flight to Ibiza, Joshua remembers Dr. Mueller's taunting words, "*Are you a man or a mouse?*" (p. 112). In their dialogue Joshua and Mueller spar. On Ibiza an aging Jewish couple, the Freibergs, open a new hotel, and Joshua and Mueller are both invited to the opening. The Freibergs left Hamburg after *Kristallnacht*, then moved to

Paris, Vichy, Arles, Barcelona, and finally settle on Ibiza. Joshua is upset that the Freibergs are willing to serve Mueller, and Joshua deliberately addresses Mueller in Yiddish. At the table, Mueller jokingly tells Joshua that if he had a gun he would shoot him. Later exploring a campfire in the hills, Joshua comes across Mueller and points a rifle at him, for Mueller is constantly playing out his "American" Western fantasies. Joshua constantly pesters him about his wartime activities. Mueller's repeated response is: "Are you a man or a mouse?" Uncertain of which Germans are guilty of perpetrating the Holocaust, Richler continues to hunt real and imaginary Nazis in almost all of his fiction where Jewish and German ghosts abound. The scars of World War II linger in his novels, and his satire defies any kind of cosmetic solution.

At the same time that Joshua battles Nazism in Europe, he also conducts a war against Nazi sympathizers in Canada, in keeping with Richler's revenge on more than one front. Joshua travels from Montreal to Ottawa for the Annual Day of the Mackenzie King Memorial Society. Richler satirizes the former Canadian prime minister, William Lyon Mackenzie King, who was born in Berlin, Ontario, and in 1938 met with Hitler whom he admired and with whom he identified. "Wee Willie," as Richler refers to him, predicted that Hitler would "rank some day with Joan of Arc among the deliverers of his people, and if he is careful may yet be the deliverer of Europe" (p. 162). Richler mocks such false martyrdom as Joshua and his fellow Jews descend upon King's estate, reducing its ruins to further ruin. The "then" and "now" of the novel's title point to historical perspectives—the present taking revenge on past persecution.

Jewish involvement in Spanish history also forms part of Richler's fictional project as Joshua fantasizes about Jewish forces in the International Brigades fighting fascism during the Spanish Civil War. Complicating Jewish efforts on behalf of the Republicans and European Jewish powerlessness in the Holocaust is Joshua's exposure to the long history of Spanish persecution of its Jews from the Inquisition. On Ibiza, Joshua encounters Carlos, a descendant of conversos who reclaims his Jewish heritage, studying Hebrew and planning to settle in Israel. After saving money for ten years, Carlos ultimately settles in South America because the law of return to Israel does not apply to him or hundreds of other conversos whose mothers were officially Catholics. As soon as Joshua learns of Carlos's fate he makes one final stop at the site of Dr. Mueller's former villa, which has now been converted into a six-story condominium, the Don Quixote Estate. With this discovery Joshua laughs until he almost cries, for Richler's vision is tragicomic: against the tragic history of the Holocaust, Josh the joker tilts at a comedy that seeks to restore and integrate justice and Jewish humanitarian values.

Bibliography

Primary Sources

The Acrobats. 1954.
Son of a Smaller Hero. 1955.
A Choice of Enemies. 1957.
The Apprenticeship of Duddy Kravitz. 1959.
The Incomparable Atuk. 1963.
Cocksure. 1968.
Hunting Tigers Under Glass. 1968.
The Street. 1969.
St. Urbain's Horseman. 1971.
Shovelling Trouble. 1972.
Joshua Then and Now. 1980.
Solomon Gursky Was Here. 1989.
Barney's Version. 1997.

Secondary Sources

Brenner, Rachel. *Assimilation and Assertion: The Response to the Holocaust in Mordecai Richler's Writing*. New York: Peter Lang, 1989.

Craniford, Ada. *Fiction and Fact in Mordecai Richler's Novels*. Lewiston: Edwin Mellen, 1992.

Darling, Michael, ed. *Perspectives on Mordecai Richler*. Toronto: ECW Press, 1986.

Davidson, Arnold. *Mordecai Richler*. New York: Frederick Ungar, 1983.

Ramraj, Victor. *Mordecai Richler*. Boston: Twayne, 1983.

Ravvin, Norman. *A House of Words: Jewish Writing, Identity, and Memory*. Montreal: McGill-Queen's University Press, 1997.

EMANUEL RINGELBLUM

(1900–1944)

NECHAMA TEC

EMANUEL RINGELBLUM WAS born in 1900, in Buczacz, a small town in eastern Poland. In the spring of 1944, on the ruins of the Warsaw ghetto, a German bullet interrupted his life. Murdered with him were his wife Judith and teenage son Uri. Ringelblum's existence was filled with extraordinary achievements in the intertwined roles of scholar, historian, educator, political activist, and communal welfare worker.

Ringelblum's contributions are open to scrutiny, but information about his personal life is sparse, limited to a few scattered facts, leaving a multitude of unanswered questions. Of his wife, Ringelblum's own chronicles note that she held a managerial position in a ghetto welfare organization, and that during a deportation she protected one of her employees by bribing a policeman with a loaf of bread (*Kronika Getta*). Equally little is known about Ringelblum's early family life. Dislocated by the disasters of World War I, the Ringelblums had to flee Buczacz. Financial losses followed. The family's middle-class standing changed to the poverty level. After dangerous travels, the Ringelblums settled in another small town, Nowy Sacz. Here, as a high school student, Ringelblum contributed to the family's income by tutoring. He further distinguished himself from other teenagers by his eagerness to learn and his desire to impart knowledge to the less fortunate. On his own, he became immersed in the serious study of sociology, economics, Jewish history, and literature, which became lifetime interests (Eisenbach, p. 23). About that time, too, Ringelblum joined the Poalei Zion Left movement. Political interests prompted him to set up study groups that benefited young Jewish laborers. Eager to improve the lot of the socially and economically disadvantaged, Ringelblum recognized the close connection between improved education and political awareness.

In 1919, he graduated from high school and enrolled at Warsaw University in the Humanities. As a history student, he aimed at acquiring the skills for critical evaluation of original historical sources. Focusing on Warsaw Jews, he began with an exploration of their early history. Soon he was fortunate to have as one of his mentors the renowned historian Ytzchak Schiper. Ringelblum also joined a group of young historians who studied Jewish history within its broader societal contexts. They felt that the exploration of the history of a specific group ought to include simultaneous attention to broader societal processes and developments. One of these young historians was Raphael Mahler, who became an outstanding authority on pre-World War II Polish Jewry. Ringelblum and Mahler's close scholarly cooperation was sealed by their equally close friendship, ending only with Ringelblum's death (Gutman, "Emanuel Ringelblum," p. 7).

A book based on Ringelblum's doctoral dissertation, titled "The Jews of Warsaw from the Earliest Times to Their Last Expulsion in 1527" was published in 1932. Ringelblum's next project covered the history of Warsaw Jews up to the eighteenth century. Skillful at extracting broader economic, political, and sociological implications from historical evidence, the young scholar concluded that Jewish economic circumstances depended on the political and social climates that prevailed at different times in Poland. Throughout his life, he retained a special sensitivity to the complex integrative processes he was convinced operated among the various societal realms.

By 1939 Ringelblum's research, a body of 126 publications, had been praised for its systematic, innovative reliance on archival sources, and for his profound grasp of Polish history. He was also commended for his intellectual honesty. Still, Ringelblum's wide range of scholarly activities and publications left room for communal work. Dedicated to the welfare of Jewish students, he played a leading role in establishing an academic section of young Jewish historians. Although he had to supplement his income with private tutoring, he also taught without pay the economically disadvantaged youths of his political party, the Poalei Zion Left. He soon became the coeditor of the party's publication *Free Youth* (*Freie Jugend*). In appreciation, Ringelblum was elected to the party's central committee. This participation further sensitized him to the economic hardships most Jews had to endure in prewar Poland.

Neither Ringelblum's commitment to scholarly excellence nor his extensive publications led to an academic appointment. In all of Poland, in fact, there was only one chair in Jewish History, at Warsaw University. It was occupied by the renowned historian Meir Balabat. After spending a year in Vilna to support his family, Ringelblum returned to Warsaw and accepted a teaching position at a progressive middle school for girls in Warsaw. He also worked in the historical section of YIVO, at the Jewish Historical Institute based in Vilna, which led to an appointment as chairman of YIVO's circle of young historians. This is when he met Itzchak Giterman, the head of the American Joint Distribution Committee in Poland. Subsequently they became good friends and together established a YIVO branch in Warsaw.

Ringelblum's teaching career came to an abrupt stop in 1938 when the Germans expelled seventeen thousand Polish Jews who lived in Germany. In accordance with a newly established Polish law, about five thousand of these new arrivals were stateless. When Poland refused to admit any of these refugees, the Germans deposited them in a no-man's-land along Poland's border. In response to this crisis, Itzchak Giterman asked Ringelblum to help him improve the condition of these destitute Jews. Ringelblum's organizational talents immediately translated into innovative self-help measures. He organized a cadre of 10 percent of the five thousand stateless Jews for extensive training in communal operations, which eventually resulted in the establishment of impressive economic, educational, and cultural facilities.

Ringelblum's work with these refugees lasted only several weeks, but contained important lessons for the future. By putting him into direct daily contact with the displaced, it gave him additional exposure to the sufferings of the Jewish people. At the same time the job created opportunities for collecting information about the history of the Third Reich. Through refugee stories Ringelblum gained new insights into the social, economic, and political forms of discrimination. These indirect exposures to Nazi cruelty offered Ringleblum significant evidence of contemporary German-Jewish history. What he heard, he recorded and kept in his Warsaw apartment; the notes remained there through 1939. Some think that Ringelblum wanted to use these materials for a book about the Jews in the Third Reich (Eisenbach, p. 10).

In August 1939, Ringelblum interrupted his work with the Joint Distribution Committee to attend the twenty-first World Zionist Congress in Geneva, Switzerland, as an observer for the Poalei Zion Left. Upon his return, he resumed work in Warsaw with the Joint Committee. Again he became immersed in relief activities with refugees who kept pouring into the capital. Colleagues and friends who wanted to escape the Nazi invasion urged him to join them, but he refused, electing to help the Warsaw Jewish community in a variety of efforts including civil defense and care of the wounded. Despite growing hardships, Ringelblum felt morally bound, both as a Jew and as a historian, to stay in Poland to promote Jewish welfare (Eisenbach, p. 10; Szulkin, p. 118).

The German occupation of Warsaw started with directives that underscored Gentile-Jewish differences. Oppressive measures against the Jews followed; widespread food shortages affected them much more than the Gentiles. This was followed by frequent direct and violent attacks on Jews, with the help of young Polish collaborators. As noted by Ringelblum,

> Mass pillaging of Jewish shops and homes began. Bands of German soldiers went from one flat to another and emptied them of everything. A local element acquainted with the terrain was needed here, which could play the part of an intermediary. This commendable role was played by the antisemitic mob, which served as informer giving information as to which homes and shops belonged to wealthy Jews. . . . From the moment the Polish antisemites helped the Germans drive the hungry Jews away from the soup vats, the "street" became a link between the Polish antisemites and the Nazis. The "street" supplied them with steady prey (*Polish-Jewish Relations*, Jerusalem: Yad Vashem, 1974, pp. 41–42).

Ringelblum plunged into activities that aimed at relieving the suffering of Jewish refugees from different areas as well as local Jews who had lost their homes. He was instrumental in establishing the House Committee, a cooperative tenants' self-help organization that organized soup kitchens, collected and distributed clothes and medications among the most impoverished Jews, and offered educational and cultural activities. Eventually, too, these self-help organizations functioned as cover-ups for underground operations. It is estimated that in the Warsaw ghetto alone the number of active Home Committees grew to over a thousand (Ringelblum, "The History of Social Aid During the War," Jerusalem: Yad Vashem, 1986, pp. 338–344).

Eventually, Ringelblum's dedication culminated in the role of founder, organizer, and coordinator of the most extensive archival depository of World War II Jewish history (Gutman, "The Chronicler," p. 16). These underground archives were variously identified as "Ringelblum's Archives," or by the cryptonym ARG, or as *Oneg Shabbath*, a Hebrew term signifying pleasure of the Sabbath, to camouflage the illegal purposes of Ringelblum's meetings with his archival coworkers (Sakowska, "Wstep," p. 14). The OS Archives, the most important materials on Jewish World War II history, grew out of Ringelblum's continuously expanding involvements with scholarly, political, and communal welfare pursuits. He himself traced the origin of this archival undertaking to his 1938 relief work with Jews expelled from Germany. Ringelblum's daily exposures to refugee stories alerted him to Nazi terror; his contacts with a wide circle of communal leaders supported the evidence. Indeed, there was a significant fit between Ringelblum's contacts with the refugees, his contacts with different communal leaders, and his passion for gathering information about unfolding history.

Acknowledging that his 1938 relief work opened the door to the collection of historical materials, Ringelblum traced the actual start of the underground archives to October 1939. At first, the recording of evidence was a one-man operation. During the day, while Ringelblum attended to his duties as a relief organizer and listened to other communal leaders, he made informal notes. In the evening, in the privacy of his home, he edited the written material, adding comments about the facts before him. His early writing was filled with allusions, referring to some people by code names. Sometimes, he wrote the evidence in the form of letters so as to distract the likely enemy reader from learning about the true purpose of the writing material. Often, what he wanted to convey was unorganized. It would have been hard for the uninitiated to decipher the evidence. Probably at the beginning of this historical journey Ringelblum expected to be the future writer who would transform this material into a comprehensively written history of the Jews in the Third Reich (Gutman, p. 13). With the upsurge of German anti-Jewish atrocities, Ringelblum perhaps realized that his survival was not certain and began to scrutinize his records for their accessibility to future historians. He must have felt that a more orderly presentation of data would be needed. He was also eager to amass as much historical evidence as possible with as much objectivity and validity as possible, aiming at establishing a historical chronicle rather than a personal diary. On rare occasions when family members or friends appeared in his accounts, their presence was intertwined with the story and was of some historical relevance.

When the recorded information grew into hundreds of pages, Ringelblum realized that his solitary method of gathering data would have to change because he could not handle the growing evidence by himself. By May 1940 he had decided that his archival collection had to become a communal undertaking, and had begun to recruit a group of dedicated coworkers. Some of them were writers, teachers, scientists, and social activists. All shared his enthusiasm for the preservation of contemporary Jewish history and were not deterred by dangers inherent in the gathering of these illegal materials. This initial nucleus of participants labored under strict conspiratorial circumstances.

As the founder and chief organizer of this vast undertaking, Ringelblum wanted to document life in all its complexity. He instructed those who joined him to collect information that would yield multifaceted data about Jewish communal life under the German occupation. The underground archivists collected evidence and wrote reports about ghetto councils (*Judenrate*); the ghetto police known as the *Ordungspolizei*; the Polish policemen, many of whom collaborated with the German authorities; Polish blackmailers; and Poles who risked their lives to save Jews. Additional reports dealt with newly emergent groups: refugees, beggars, smugglers, Nazi collaborators, orphans, and others. In 1940, for example, Ringelblum wrote that

> The Jewish woman sustains the family by standing for hours in dangerous food lines, by intervening with the authorities—German soldiers and the Gestapo—by accepting jobs, jobs that promise only meager benefits. Gone is the elegant lady with the fancy hats. We see instead simply dressed women with kerchiefs on their heads constantly searching for ways to support their families (*Kronika Getta*, p. 67).

He also commissioned Cecylia Ślepak to research the fate of Jewish women during the war. This project was based on in-depth interviews with fifteen women from a variety of social backgrounds. Results offer unusual insights into these women's coping strategies and fates. The study ended in 1942 when Slepak was sent to her death in Treblinka.

Ringelblum was especially sensitive to and burdened by the sufferings of Jewish children. To their pain and his own anguish he returns continuously: "Mortifying and incredible are the street children who beg for alms simultaneously reminding us of their homelessness. Each evening at the corner of Leszna and Karmelicka Streets the children are there, their faces flooded with bitter tears. After these encounters sleep eludes me for most of the night. The few pennies I offer them fail to ease my conscience" (*Kronika Getta*, p. 347).

When instructing his coworkers and contributors, Ringelblum invited them to include their personal stories and observations. At the same time he urged them to report facts with utmost objectivity. To increase objectivity, Ringelblum charged several individuals to report independently on similar topics, and encouraged the use of partly standardized questionnaires rather than informal interrogation. He wrote that it would be easier for future historians to arrive at the core truth of history if they could rely on several descriptions of the same phenomena (Sakowska, "Wstep," p. 14).

Despite the supervision and concerted efforts, errors appeared here and there. There was often no possibility to properly verify information received. All that was written down, however, had been heard by someone. Occasionally what was heard might have been an unsubstantiated rumor; but rumors if talked about or heard are evidence. Ringelblum was sensitive to the possible interdependence of facts. He was convinced that if presented in an orderly fashion, all facts, ugly or uplifting, would be useful to those who would be reconstructing history. With time, he probably lost some confidence that he himself would be the author of such a history, but despite dark forebodings he was convinced that the risks and difficulties entailed in the clandestine collection and preparation of these materials were worthwhile.

As 1942 Warsaw ghetto deportations raged, these archivists continued their research, engaged in a race with time. Unable to protect the people, they concentrated on saving their history. This is when Ringelblum and his partners took steps to safeguard their treasures. The OS archives were sealed in ten large units that consisted of metal boxes and milk bottles. Two parts of these units were buried in the ghetto in August 1942 at 68 Nowolipki Street. By February 1943 the rest of the archival materials were buried at 36 Swietokrzycka Street. Two parts of the archives were later retrieved, one in 1946, the second in 1950. The third section was lost (Eisenbach, p. 18).

By 1942, most of the ghetto underground knew about concentration camps and death camps. In 1942 Dawid Nowodworski, who had escaped from Treblinka, supplied the underground and the archivists with detailed evidence about this death camp, its operations, and the deportees' ignorance of the fate that awaited them. The ghetto chroniclers were eager to share this information with the world. Even earlier, at the beginning of February 1942, three young Jewish men had escaped from the death camp Chelmno. One of them, identified as Szlamek, with a probable last name of Bajler, presented Hersch Wasser, the secretary of the Ringelblum archives, with testimony containing vivid descriptions about the gassings of Jewish and some Gypsy inmates in special trucks. Later in 1942 the chroniclers succeeded in transferring documents about death camps to the Polish government in London (Sakowska, "Archiwum Ringelbluma," No. 3–4, pp. 153–160). This information also became the basis for Jewish underground reports about death camps in general (Sakowska, "Szlamek," pp. 131–152).

When the 1942 deportations stopped, the population of the Warsaw ghetto was reduced to an estimated fifty to fifty-five thousand inmates. Reflecting on this devastation, Ringelblum began to question whether the Jews should not have met the enemy's assaults with armed resistance. Acknowledging that initially his attitude toward the use of armed opposition had been ambivalent, he seemed to regret his past lukewarmness, and now considered armed resistance the only option for the Jews. In the latter part of 1942, after the Warsaw ghetto population had been reduced to about 16 percent of its pre-deportation size, Ringelblum and his archival staff joined the National Committee of the Underground. From then on he took an active part in organizing resistance with the main underground group, ZOB. By 1943, he was also in touch with the smaller Jewish national underground (ZKN). He was particularly touched by the role of women couriers:

> The heroic girls, Chaijke and Frumke—they are a theme that calls for the pen of a great writer. Boldly they travel back and forth through the cities and towns of Poland. They carry "Aryan" papers identifying them as Poles or Ukrainians. One of them even wears a cross which she never parts with except when in the Ghetto. They are in mortal danger every day. They rely entirely on their "Aryan" faces and on the peasant kerchiefs that cover their heads. Without a murmur, without a second's hesitation, they accept and carry out the most dangerous missions (*Notes from the Warsaw Ghetto*, p. 273).

By February 1943, the ghetto underground had persuaded Ringelblum to relocate, with his family, to the forbidden Christian world. There they moved into a large bunker on Grojecka Street. The Polish owner of the place, Władysław Morczak, agreed to hide thirty-four Jews. Here Ringelblum continued to write. On 18 April 1943, he smuggled himself into the ghetto; the next day, the Warsaw ghetto Uprising began. For a while there was no news of him. Three months later, in July 1943, a letter reached the Polish underground with the information that Ringelblum was an inmate in the Trawniki camp. The Jewish and Polish underground cooperated in smuggling him out of Trawniki. A Polish courier, Tadeusz Pajewski, who was employed as a train conductor, along with a female courier associated with the Jewish underground, Róża Kossower (Emilka), succeeded in bringing Ringelblum to Warsaw, disguised as a conductor.

Ringelblum returned to the bunker he had left three months earlier, and continued writing. He once more became immersed in contemporary history, but he ceased reporting about current events. He finished a two hundred-page sociological and historical monograph about the Trawniki camp, which was subsequently lost, as well as biographical sketches of Warsaw ghetto figures who were dedicated to the social, cultural, and educational welfare of the ghetto. He also wrote a systematic study of wartime Polish-Jewish relations. Among his other writings was a monograph on the fate of Jewish intellectuals, writers, artists, and scientists, and on the Jewish underground movement. Additional essays dealt with a few broad subjects: the role of the Jewish police during deportations; Nazi policies toward the Jews who went into hiding, and others (Gutman, "Emanuel Ringelblum, the Chronicler of Warsaw," pp. 11–13). Ringelblum handed over some of his finished writings to Adolf Berman, a member of the Jewish underground who occasionally visited him. Among his writings illegally sent abroad was a report about the final liquidation of the Warsaw ghetto, which was widely publicized in the Polish underground press (Sakowska, "Archiwum Ringelbluma," vol. 3–4, p. 160).

On 7 March 1944, the bunker on Grojecka Street was discovered by the Gestapo. All the Jews, among them the Ringelblum family, were arrested. Also arrested were the Poles: their main protector, Morczak, his family, and his assistant Mieczyslaw Wolski. All were transferred to the Pawiak prison and subsequently executed on the ruins of the Warsaw ghetto. According to one report, a small group of Jewish craftsmen who worked at the Pawiak prison offered to rescue Ringelblum by dressing him as one of them and by smuggling him out. He rejected this plan when he learned that his wife and son would not be included (Gutman, "The Chronicler," pp. 15–16).

All concur that Emanuel Ringelblum was a multifaceted giant. The scope of his interests and involvements defies a summary description. Among the many scholars who recognize Ringelblum's contributions are Israel Gutman and Joseph Kermisz. Gutman's assessment is that "Ringelblum's work forms, without a doubt, the most important and detailed source of information about the Holocaust period and its universal significance" (Gutman, "The Chronicler," p. 16). Kermisz concurs that "this work, unparalleled in its range and its sense of responsibility for the truth in history as it really was, constitutes a testimony to human courage and a memorial for the Jewish historiography of that terrible period" (Kermisz, "Introduction" in *Polish-Jewish Relations*, Jerusalem: Yad Vashem, p. xxxix).

While the Germans succeeded in murdering millions of Jews, including Ringelblum and most of his dedicated partners, they could not kill the fruits of their self-sacrificing, compassionate labors. Just as Ringelblum had wanted, his work touched on all aspects of wartime Jewish existence. Impeccable scholarly research, exceptional organizational skills, and ability to coordinate the expansion of activities were all compressed into Ringelblum's short life. Guiding all these pursuits was his selfless dedication to the welfare of the Jewish people and to the improvement of their economic, social, and political lives. Ringelblum's effectiveness reached beyond his grave and the graves of those he loved, including the dedicated coworkers whose contributions he fully recognized.

Just as Ringelblum and all the OS archivists had wanted, humanity is the inheritor and guardian of the contemporary history record they left behind.

Bibliography

Primary Sources

Archiwum Ringelbluma Getta Warszawskie, lipiec 1942–styczen 1943 (*Ringelblum's Warsaw Ghetto Archives, July 1942–January 1943*). Edited by Ruta Sakowska. Warszawa: Panstwowe Wydawnictwo Naukowe, 1980.

Kronika Getta Warszawskiego (*Warsaw Ghetto Chronicle*). Edited by Tatiana Berenstein, Artur Eisenbach, Bernard Mark, and Adam Rutkowski. Warszawa: Czytelnik, 1983.

Notes from the Warsaw Ghetto: The Journal of Emanuel Ringelblum. Edited by Jacob Sloan. New York: Schocken Books, 1975.

Polish-Jewish Relations During the Second World War. Edited by Joseph Kermisz and Shmuel Krakowski. Jerusalem: Yad Vashem, 1974.

"The History of Social Aid in Warsaw During the War." In *To Live with Honor and Die with Honor, Selected Documents from the Warsaw Ghetto Underground Archives.* Edited by Joseph Kermisz. Jerusalem: Yad Vashem, 1986.

Secondary Sources

Eisenbach, Artur. "Wstep." *Kronika Getta.* 5–27.

Gilbert, Martin. *The Holocaust.* New York: Holt, Rinehart and Winston, 1985.

Gutman, Israel. "Emanuel Ringelblum, the Chronicler of the Warsaw Ghetto." *Polin, a Journal of Polish-Jewish Studies* 3 (1988): 5–16.

———. *The Jews of Warsaw, 1939–1945.* Bloomington: Indiana University Press, 1982.

Kermisz, Joseph. "Introduction." In Emanuel Ringelblum, *Polish-Jewish Relations During the Second World War.* Edited by Joseph Kermisz and Shmuel Krakowski. Jerusalem: Yad Vashem, 1974. vii-xxxix.

———. "Introduction." *To Live with Honor and Die with Honor, Selected Documents from the Warsaw Ghetto Underground Archives.* Edited by Joseph Kermisz. Jerusalem: Yad Vashem, 1986. xliv.

Sakowska, Ruta. *Dwa Etapy*. Warszawa: Wydawnictwo Polskiej Akademii Nauk, 1986.

———. *Ludzie Z Dzielnicy Zamknietej*. Warszawa: Panstwowe Wydawnictwo Naukowe, 1975.

———. "Szlamek." Ucieknier z Osrodka Zaglady W Chelmie N/Nerem. *BZIH* 3–4 (1984): 131–152.

———. "Archiwum Ringelbluma—Ognem Konspiracji Warszawskiego Getta." Czesc II *BZIH*, No. 1 (1990): 79–95.

———. "Archiwum Ringelbluma—Ogniwen Konspiracji Warszawskie Getta." Czesc III *BZIH*, No. 3–4 (1990): 153–160.

———. "Wstep." *Archiwum Ringelbluma Getta Warszawskie*. 14.

Szulkin, Moshe. "Dr. Emanuel Ringelblum, Historyk I Orgnizator Podziemnego Archivum Ghetta Warszawskiego." *BZIH* 86–87 (1973): 111–125.

JONATHAN ROSEN

(1963–)

EVA FOGELMAN

JONATHAN ROSEN WAS born in New York on February 25, 1963. His parents, Robert and Norma, represent one version of the two worlds he straddles—the American and European Jewish worlds. There is a juxtaposition between Rosen's maternal American Jewish family life and the horrendous fate of his father's family perpetrated by the Nazis. His grandmother was shot when she was deported to the eastern front, and his grandfather was killed in Buchenwald. At age thirteen, Rosen's own father left Vienna in 1938 on a *Kindertransport* and found refuge in Scotland. Rosen realizes that he is living between tragic awareness of his past and modern American prosperity, feeling as if he is straddling two varied realities.

Education and Career

Rosen, who grew up in a "house full of books" (*The Talmud and the Internet: A Journey between Worlds*, New York: Farrar, Straus and Giroux, 2000, p. 26) chose a professional path that was inspired by his writer mother and a father who was a retired professor of comparative literature.

Rosen received a B.A. from Yale University in 1985 with honors and won a prize in English literature. He continued his education with an M.A. degree in English Literature in 1987 with a Mellon Fellowship in the Humanities.

Rosen then embarked on a major career as a freelance writer and journalist. In 1990 he created and began editing the Arts and Letters section of the English *Forward*. There he wrote a weekly column on Jewish culture and serialized fiction and nonfiction; his topics included Art Spiegelman's *Maus* and Philip Roth's *Operation Shylock*. Rosen reviews books and writes essays and articles about American literature and contemporary Jewish concerns and has been a regular reviewer for the *New York Times Book Review*, *Slate*, and the *Wall Street Journal*. In addition, Rosen has published essays in the *New York Times Magazine*, the *New York Times Book Review*, the *New Yorker*, and the *American Scholar*. His work has been anthologized. He also has a special interest in bird watching and has written about this in the *New Yorker*.

Rosen's first novel, *Eve's Apple* (1997), focused on a man's attempt to help a woman with an eating disorder. The man was madly in love with the woman and morbidly fascinated with her illness. *Eve's Apple* was optioned as a movie by Oprah Winfrey for ABC, for which he wrote the screenplay. In 2000, Rosen's personal memoir in the form of a meditation, *The Talmud and the Internet: A Journey between Worlds*, was published.

Rosen has lectured to both academic and general audiences. In 1991 he was a writer in residence at Yeshiva University, where he taught fiction writing and organized readings.

Major Titles, Themes, and Concerns

The focus of Jonathan Rosen's lyrical meditation, *The Talmud and the Internet*, echoes the theological themes in the creative texts of the second generation surveyed by Alan Berger in his *Children of Job* (1997). Berger's book attempts "to respond to the ancient question of how to live Jewishly after a catastrophe" (Berger, p. 19).

The theme of Jewish identity in *The Talmud and the Internet* is covered in Nessa Rapoport's (2000) review, where she explains that the purpose of Rosen's journey is to "find a home within exile." For Rosen, living after the Holocaust is not centered in the redemptive spirit of Israel, but rather in the Diaspora. The result is an inspired integration of a fragmented Jewish and American life. Rosen explains: "The Talmud offered a virtual home for an uprooted culture, and grew out of the Jewish need to pack civilization into words and wander out into the world" (*The Talmud and the Internet*, p. 14). He continues, "The Internet, which we are continually told binds us all together, nevertheless engenders in me a similar sense of Diaspora, a feeling of being everywhere and nowhere. Where else but in the middle of Diaspora do you need a home page?" (p. 14).

Another major theme in *The Talmud and the Internet* is a universal second-generation focus of mourning dead relatives one never knew. A mourning person begins in shock and denial, then moves to confrontation, which evokes a flood of feelings of anger, rage, helplessness, guilt, and a need to undo the suffering, sadness, grief, and depression. Ultimately these feelings need to be constructively channeled. The final stage in the mourning process is a search for meaning. Rosen's ingenious juxtaposing of the Talmud and the Internet is the backdrop for his own mourning process and ultimate search for meaning. As he mourns, the personal and the conceptual are intertwined. This is the book's basic theme.

Similar to other children of Holocaust survivors, Rosen was probably unaware of his own need to mourn his father's mother, who was killed before he was born. Dealing with this second-generation experience in the present inevitably leads to an unconscious need to mourn unknown relatives. As a Jew, Rosen is cognizant that the mourning process in Judaism is imbedded in a historical context. He searches Jewish history to examine what enabled the people and their culture to survive after major destructions.

Through modernity Rosen opens the door of knowledge to traditional Judaism and its rich texts. As a scholar of American literature, Rosen fills the *The Talmud and the Internet* with literary references to answer philosophical questions of life and death, and analogies that are truly stimulating and unexpected. Rosen makes reference to *The Education of Henry Adams* (1907), who saw the Jews and himself coming from a dead culture. Classics such as T. S. Eliot's *The Waste Land*, *The Odyssey*, *Mr. Sammler's Planet*, and *Remembrance of Things Past* are interspersed in the narrative as well.

In his earlier work, *Eve's Apple* (1997), Rosen was reluctant to make the protagonist in the novel a member of the second generation, but he had come "to discover that [he] had written a post-Holocaust novel anyway. A young man fantasizing about saving an emaciated young woman is inevitably emblematic of certain Holocaust-induced feverish dreams" ("Writing under the Shadow of the Holocaust," paper presented at the writing the Jewish Future Conference, National Foundation for Jewish Culture, San Francisco, February 1998, p. 5).

For Rosen "writing under the shadow of the Holocaust is not the same thing as writing about the Holocaust" (*The Talmud and the Internet: A Journey Between Worlds*, p. 5). He continues, "I know in advance that writing about the horrors of the Holocaust is beyond my abilities, my ambition, and perhaps beyond what I feel art can accomplish. Ultimately, my challenge is how to do justice to the lives and experiences of both my grandmothers—the woman who died at 95 surrounded by family members who loved her, and the woman who was murdered in the forest of Eastern Europe" (pp. 5–6).

Critical Reception

The Talmud and the Internet: A Journey between Two Worlds has been widely and favorably reviewed. Cynthia Ozick captures this "gemlike" (Anne Fadiman, *The Talmud*, book jacket) book when she writes: "Once in a very great while you will come upon a book which signals instant recognition: that it has the quality of permanence, that just as you cherished it in the reading, so will newer generations." Ozick continues: "It honors father and mother and grandparents; it thinks into both past and future; it shines with beauty and originality" (book jacket).

The reviews of *The Talmud and the Internet* have been laudatory. Ron Rosenbaum was excited to read a book that "links ancient and modern sensibilities in a way that's both impressively cerebral and highly personal" (book jacket).

Sandee Brawarsky considers the book to be "original, compelling and soulful . . . packed with ideas, literary references and fine writing. The brief book is both family history and cultural history" (p. 39). For example, Rosen features his father who "left Vienna in 1938 on a Kindertransport, which sent some ten thousand Jewish children from Germany, Austria, and Czechoslovakia to safety in Britain" (*The Talmud and the Internet*, p. 50). Rosen then likens his father's escape to that of Yochanan ben Zakkai, both of whom turned their back on a dying world and were reborn into a new one. Rosen tells us the Talmudic story of ben Zakkai, "a great sage of the first century, who found himself living in besieged Jerusalem on the eve of its destruction by Rome" (*The Talmud and the Internet*, p. 15). When he realized the temple and Jerusalem were doomed, he got his students to hide him in a coffin and carry him outside the city walls.

> But unlike ben Zakkai, he [his father] was fleeing one Diaspora for another, and there was no clear culture telling him how to live. The culture he longed for had itself longed for a vanished world. The Talmud supplanted the Temple. But what supplants the Talmud? (*The Talmud and the Internet,* p. 50).

In her review, Nessa Rapoport discusses the paradox Rosen negotiates in *The Talmud and the internet.* "With the destruction of the Second Temple and the ensuing exile from their land, Jews lost their geography but survived by making a virtual place of their texts." Rosen, like many in the post-Holocaust generation, is searching for continuity after the cataclysmic destruction of European Jewry, "to make each fragment [of the past] feel whole" (Rapoport). Rapoport points out that Rosen recognizes exile as a human condition while retrieving a "venerable tradition in order to embrace uncertainty more knowledgeably."

The theme of continuity is symbolized in the Talmud itself because the beginning of the Talmud is a link to a destroyed past. The Talmud becomes central after the Second Temple was destroyed by the Romans in A.D. 70. Sandee Brawarsky (2000) points out that the internet is also born out of "loss of books and objects" (p. 39). In Rosen's own life continuity is represented by the birth of his daughter.

Reviewers of *The Talmud and the Internet* did not emphasize that Rosen's personal journey is part of the collective second-generation voice and a literary genre that is becoming distinct. Sandee Brawarsky, in her interview with Rosen, differentiates an important theological element in the book. Rosen asks religious questions but does not dwell on God. "The lack of overt God-references in second-generation texts" is explained by Alan Berger, who refers to Irving Greenberg's theory that in "an age of extreme hiddenness God must be discovered everywhere" (*Children of Job,* p. 26). A dialectic involving mending the self and mending the world impacts the second generation's understanding of God. Rosen's work shows "a commitment to creating life and to learning more about and bearing witness to the Holocaust" (*Children of Job: American Second-Generation Witnesses to the Holocaust*, p. 27).

Bibliography

Primary Sources

"Breaking Glass." *New York Times Book Review*, 10 November 1996, end page.

Eve's Apple. 1997.

Review of *The Iron Tracks* by Aharon Appelfeld. *New York Times Book Review*, 15 February 1998, 8.

Review of *Damascus Gate* by Robert Stone. *New York Times Book Review*, 26 April 1998.

"Writing under the Shadow of the Holocaust." Paper presented at the Writing the Jewish Future Conference, National Foundation for Jewish Culture, San Francisco, February 1998.

"Endless Visibility." In *Oxford Book of Jewish Stories*. Edited by Ilan Stavans. New York: Oxford University Press, 1999, 455–458.

The Talmud and the Internet: A Journey between Worlds. 2000.

"Writers on Writing: A Retreat from the World Can Be a Perilous Journey." *New York Times*, 7 May 2001, pp. Arts 1–2.

"The Uncomfortable Question of Anti-Semitism: Waking up to My Father's World." *New York Times Magazine*, 4 November 2001, 48–51.

Review of *The Collected Stories of Isaac Babel*. *New York Times Book Review*, 18 November 2001, 10.

"Trivialization of Tragedy." In *Best Contemporary Jewish Writing*. Edited by Michael Lerner. New York: Jossey Bass, 2001, 230–240.

"Grace, Punishment, and the Torah." *The American Scholar* 71, no. 1. (winter 2002): 61–70.

Secondary Sources

Berger, Alan L. *Children of Job: American Second-Generation Witnesses to the Holocaust*. Albany: State University of New York Press, 1997.

Brawarsky, Sandee. "A Dialogue across Time." Review of *The Talmud and the Internet*. *The Jewish Week*, 1 September 2000, 39.

Eder, Richard. "Before High Tech, There Was a Higher Authority." Review of *The Talmud and the Internet*. *New York Times*, 15 September 2000.

Linton, Eric. Review of *The Talmud and the Internet*. *Star Ledger*, N.J., 15 October 2000.

Mnookin, Seth. Review of *The Talmud and the Internet*. *Brill's Content*, September 2000.

Rapoport, Nessa. "Review of *The Talmud and the Internet*: A Journey of Great Questions and Great Souls." *Los Angeles Times*, 23 September 2000.

Rolston, Holmes III. Review of *The Talmud and the Internet*. *The Chronicle of Higher Education*, 27 October 2000, B6.

Schacter, Erica. Review of *The Talmud and the Internet*. *Wall Street Journal*, 22 September 2000, W13.

Schoffman, Stuart. "Making Sense of the Jumble." Review of *The Talmud and the Internet*. *The Jerusalem Report*, 10 October 2000, 53.

Shapiro, Susan. "Fiddler on the Web: A Writer Links His Past, Present and Future in a Great New Memoir." Review of *The Talmud and the Internet*. *New York Post*, 24 September 2000.

Ulin, David L. "World Wide Wonder." *Newsday*, Review of *The Talmud and the Internet*. 17 September 2000.

———. "Discovering the Symmetry of the Talmud and Internet." Review of *The Talmud and the Internet*. *Los Angeles Times*, 29 September 2000, E1, E4.

NORMA ROSEN

(1925–)

S. LILLIAN KREMER

BORN IN NEW York on 11 August 1925 to Rose Miller and Louis Gangel, Norma Rosen reports that she was "born of an immaculate Jewish conception . . . [of] parents, who were Jews by birth, refrained from intercourse with the Jewish religion and proudly passed me, in an untainted state, into the world" (*Accidents of Influence*: *Writing as a Woman and a Jew in America*, Albany: State University Press of New York, 1992, p. 128). Following a first marriage, during which she published under the name Norma Stahl, in 1960 she married Robert Rosen, a professor of comparative literature, one of the fortunate few to escape Nazi Europe on a children's transport to England. The Rosens have two children, a daughter, Anne Beth, and a son, the writer Jonathan Aaron Rosen. Marriage to Rosen, who had been Judaically educated, brought the writer into closer proximity with Judaism because her husband wished to maintain a Jewish lifestyle. The novelist's formal studies in Jewish religious thought and philosophy with a noted Judaic scholar have been a lasting influence on her thinking (Klingenstein, "Norma Rosen," p. 351). The marriage also brought her into more intimate contact with *Shoah* history, which, in turn, strongly influenced her intellectual and artistic life.

Career

Educated at Mount Holyoke College in Massachusetts, Rosen studied modern dance with Jose Limon and choreography with Martha Graham, was elected to Phi Beta Kappa, and graduated cum laude in 1946. After teaching English and dance at a private girls' academy for three years, she earned a master's degree from Columbia University with a thesis on Graham Greene. Studies in book design at New York University led to a job with Harper and Row in New York, working on all stages of book production. She left the firm in 1959 when her first two stories were published. Following summer writing at the MacDowell Colony in New Hampshire, Rosen won a Eugene F. Saxton Grant in 1960 to complete her first novel, *Joy to Levine!* (1962).

Rosen continued to publish short fiction and novels and enjoyed an active teaching career in creative writing at many institutions including the New School for Social Research, the University of Pennsylvania, Harvard, Yale, Barnard College, and New York University. *Joy to Levine!* was acclaimed for its wit and compassion by the *Times Literary Supplement* reviewer and described as "beautifully poised between pathos and comedy" in *Harper's*. It was followed by a collection of short fiction, *Green: A Novella and Eight Stories* (1947); the novels *Touching Evil* (1969), *At the Center* (1982), and *John and Anzia* (1989); a collection of critical and personal essays, *Accidents of Influence: Writing as a Woman and a Jew in America*; and *Biblical Women Unbound* (1996), an innovative *midrash* giving voice to more than a dozen silent biblical women whose counterlives she invents, and five contemporary women reevaluating their lives in light of the Ruth and Naomi paradigm.

Jewish and Holocaust Interests

Accidents of Influence gives voice to Rosen's thoughts on Judaism, antisemitism, Holocaust writing, and women's experience. In addition to the essays discussing her own Holocaust writing and her theories about Holocaust literature, she struggles to understand how otherwise brilliant intellectuals like T. S. Eliot, Paul de Man, and Simone Weil could succumb to or perpetuate antisemitism. Other essays admonish Jewish-American writers for producing "a literature of contempt" against their own people and praise gentile writers George Eliot and Charles Dickens for balanced portraits of Jews. Still others examine the place of women in Judaism. Rosen's insights in this volume led one reviewer to describe her as "blessed with a probing eye and critical perspective" (Avery, p. 142).

Rosen addresses the feasibility and propriety of writing about the Holocaust in her 1974 essay, "The Holocaust and the American Jewish Novelist." She asks "How could the virtues of fiction—indirection, irony, ambivalence—be used to make art out of this unspeakable occurrence?" Convinced that the Holocaust is "the central occurrence of the twentieth century . . . the central human occurrence," Rosen describes herself as a "witness-through-the-imagination," a "documenter of the responses of those who had heard the terrible news" (*Accidents of Influence*, p. 9). Treating the *Shoah* as a recurrent theme in fiction and essays, Rosen propels readers to contemplation of the Holocaust through the mediating lens of Americans who wrestle with the philosophical and social implications of the event. Her characters truly grapple with "the knowledge that human beings—in great numbers—could do what had been done" (p. 12). Thirteen years and several Holocaust works later, in "The Second Life of Holocaust Imagery" (1987), she argues that the paradox for novelists working in this sphere lies

> in the tension between writing and not writing about it. If the writer treats the subject, the risk is that it may be falsified, trivialized. Even a "successful" treatment of the subject risks an aestheticizing or a false ordering of it, since whatever is expressed in art conveys the impression that it, too, is subject to the laws of composition. Yet not to write means omitting the central event of the twentieth century (p. 49).

Touching Evil

Removed in time and space from the Holocaust landscape, but powerfully impacted by its enduring resonance, Rosen's American women in *Touching Evil* absorb the testimony of eyewitnesses and take that history to heart. Set in America in 1961, during the Jerusalem Eichmann trial, the novel portrays Jews only as imagined Holocaust victims and televised court witnesses. Past and present collide and merge as the novel alternates between recollections of 1944, the year the protagonist, Jean Lamb, learned of the *Shoah* through newspaper photographs of concentration camps, and the 1961 Eichmann trial, the vehicle through which a younger woman, Hattie Mews, first encounters the Holocaust and Jean confirms the centrality of the catastrophe in her life. Hattie's response reveals intense dismay at first discovering this radical evil, while Jean is a "reflector . . . distanced from her own revelation" (Kremer interview). Setting the fiction during the trial and creating its aura by portraying the American women's response rather than reciting the testimony, Rosen relies on readers' knowledge of the legal proceedings and the Holocaust to suggest the content of the trial and reminds us that our perspective limits and influences our understanding. The burden of the novel is its thesis that the *Shoah* must not be conveniently put to rest; that it ought to continue to influence our thinking.

That pre-Holocaust normality is forever lost is manifest in Rosen's representation of the Gentile Americans' obsession with the Holocaust. For Jean, "there were two kinds of people, . . . those who knew and those who didn't know. And it had nothing to do with reading newspapers" (*Touching Evil*, New York: Harcourt Brace World, 1969, p. 77). She embraces a lover primarily because he had been a camp liberator, and her friendship with Hattie is *Shoah* predicated. Because Jean's Holocaust epiphany occurred while making love, her response is personal denial, rejection of marriage and childbearing, and a feminist rebuttal of the Hitlerian universe. In choosing deprivation, she allies herself with her European sisters and testifies to humanity's loss of Jewish progeny. Hattie's response to the television coverage of the trial echoes Jean's earlier reaction to newspaper photographs of the camps. The pregnant Hattie, like Rosen who watched the trial during her own pregnancy, absorbs the Holocaust experience, takes it thoroughly into her consciousness, senses it in her body. The two Gentile American women become witnesses for those Jewish women who did not live to testify to the devastation. They empathize powerfully and repeatedly with the women of the camps: Jean with the woman who "was shot but did not die and dug her way from under a mountain of corpses that spouted blood" (p. 221); Hattie with a far-gone pregnant woman on a forced march and with another giving birth in lice-infested straw. *Touching Evil* is distinctive in its feminist perspective and its deliberation of American reaction to the Holocaust. The Holocaust becomes the categorical imperative for Rosen's characters. *Shoah* imagery and associations inform their thinking, their speech, and a chorus of voices that surround them, voices that appropriate and misappropriate Holocaust terms. Contemporary events, people, and conditions evoke Holocaust classifications and definitions. A neighbor describes a personal betrayal as "telling the police where Anne Frank is hiding," a person of ignoble behavior is described as "a gold tooth salvager" or "an informer" (p. 60).

Rosen's fiction is uncommon among American Holocaust titles in its religious speculation. Like Elie Wiesel's adolescent survivor, Eliezer, whose faith was temporarily extinguished in the flames that consumed his family and who condemned the God who tolerated the extermination centers, Jean Lamb judges and denounces divine failure. Jean's assertion of God's Holocaust complicity is reminiscent of Eliezer's anguished misgiving about blessing the name of God. Her prayer-parody is a vitriolic denunciation of the merciless God of Auschwitz: "God of the medical-experiment cell block . . . God of the common lime pit grave . . . God of chopped fingers . . . of blind eyes, God of electrodes attached at one end of a jeep battery and at the other to the genitals of political prisoners" (p. 233). By introducing this mode, Rosen evokes the voices and contributes to the convention of Yiddish and Hebrew prayer-parody and countercommentary through which textual subversion imitates *Shoah* rupture.

Holocaust transmission is thematically and structurally significant in the novel. Rosen's narrative design employs a manuscript within a manuscript within a manuscript for the characters' subjective responses. This device complements the newspaper accounts and trial testimony through which Rosen conveys historic evidence. Jean's letters and Hattie's diary entries reveal the connection between receiving the news and making it one's own. The distance between listening and telling is traversed as Jean's revelatory memory is sparked by trial testimony. Acting both as Jean's foil and as her double, Hattie embraces the responsibility for transmitting Holocaust history to the next generation through her diary, a form that evokes victim and survivor diaries and testimonies and simultaneously suggests how personal the Holocaust has become for this "witness through the imagination" ("The Holocaust and the American-Jewish Novelist," *Midstream* 20, rpt. in *Accidents of Influence*, pp. 3–17). The need to continue to bear witness is manifested in testimonial voices at the Eichmann trial two decades after the atrocities, and in Hattie's writing. The pattern of transmission is established for another generation: as history has been passed from Jean to Hattie, so it will be from Hattie to her daughter. Each woman bears witness directly, Jean in her diary-letters and Hattie in manuscripts for a play, a memoir, a novel.

The Quarrel with God

The 1990s brought an explosion of second-generation Holocaust writing to American literature. Norma Rosen introduced a second-generation character as early as 1982 in the protagonist of *At the Center*. Hannah Selig is the daughter of Hasidic Holocaust survivors who were brutally murdered in their New York apartment. Hannah's consequent lapse of faith is expressed in her quarrel with God, which takes the form of journal arguments with her rabbi and God, and rebellion against Judaic law and values. Like many later second-generation characters who feel responsibility for pleasing or protecting their parents, Hannah believes she is being punished for her transgressions: refusing to marry, desire to attend university, desire to leave the community. As Ruth Rosenberg observes,

> It is after she has tested all the strictures that she arrives at cabalistic insight. . . . the vision of her parents' congregation that the work of creation is unfinished. Human beings must assume the obligation of completing that work, of uplifting the divine sparks, of redeeming the earth from evil. By participating in the suffering of others at The Center, the abortion clinic founded by an idealistic doctor . . . Hannah is enabled to return with renewed commitment to the Hasidism she had sought to escape (Rosenberg, p. 251).

Hannah ultimately inspires one of the clinic doctors to return to Judaism.

Concurrent themes of protest against God's Holocaust silence and the validity of religious practice in the post-Holocaust era take a more prominent place in Rosen's short fiction and later essays. Authorial protest against God's silence in the face of the *Shoah* finds expression in an essay on the biblical Jonah. In this text, Rosen invents a fantastic narrative illuminating the biblical text, a *midrash* of Jonah inside the great fish receiving images of future "scenes of inquisitions and expulsions and ghettos and pogroms and, at last, death camps and crematoria" (*At the Center*, Boston: Houghton Mifflin, 1982, p. 93). Divine forgiveness and rescue of the pagan sinners of Nineveh, is contrasted with God's failure to intervene on behalf of millions of innocents who perished in the Holocaust, remaining an enigma for the faithful Jonah.

Short Fiction

Unlike the characters of *Touching Evil*, those of Rosen's short fiction are Jews and Gentiles, wives of survivors or empathetic citizens, who respond to the horrific ordeal European Jews experienced. These narratives generally turn from the "witness through the imagination" of non-Jews to the Holocaust concerns and impressions of Jewish Americans and Holocaust survivors. Rosen continues to maintain distance, never setting the fiction directly in the Holocaust arena, yet her Holocaust-haunted characters grow ever more complex as they live with knowledge of the *Shoah*. An important aspect of her achievement in short fiction is the delineation of the consequences of the Holocaust in the lives of people who were not there, the wives and children of survivors and those related only by humanitarian concern. Recurrent figures are a male survivor and an American wife who exhibits various degrees of sensitivity to and understanding of her husband's Holocaust background and its influence on his postwar decisions. Another construct is the postwar encounter of survivors and Jewish Americans meeting and occasionally confronting Germans with Holocaust history. Themes often emerge in this writing exploring the impact of the Holocaust on the second generation, the children of victims and perpetrators and problems inherent in Holocaust transmission.

"The Cheek of the Trout," an autobiographical story, engages the theme of Holocaust confrontation. The narrative is set in postwar Vienna, the city of the survivor's birth and brief residence, where he and his American wife meet Austrians and Germans. Clearly, his enjoyment of the city is clouded by memories of lost family and his own flight in a children's transport. The city's history is revealed in its cemetery, modest stones testifying to the Holocaust slaughter of Vienna's betrayed Jews: ["Vergast Belsec, Gestorben in Theresienstadt, . . . Verschleppt nach Auschwitz. Umgekommmen in Dachau. Ermordet in Belsen"] ("Gassed in Belsec, Died in Theresienstadt . . . Departed to Auschwitz, Succumbed in Dachau, Assassinated in Belsen") ("Cheek of the Trout," p. 402). As the Americans prepare to dine with a German couple young enough to be free of Holocaust taint, the American wife imagines the German husband's father counseling his son not to be apologetic to Jews for his grandfather's membership in the Nazi party or his own role as an SS officer. There is logic in the elder's advice that the younger generation is free of the sins of the fathers, but his discourse reveals his sustained Nazi sympathies. The "confrontation" amounts to little. The Americans acknowledge their difficulty with Germans and Austrians old enough to have been involved in Hitler's war. The Germans agree that it is a "natural" and "understandable" reaction. The American contains her fury and Rosen opts instead for a symbolic condemnation of the perpetrator generation. The evening and the story end with reference to the dinner menu. The couples have been dining on trout, Rosen's allusion to Schubert's composition, "Die Forelle" ("The Trout"). Thereby, she subtly signifies the ease with which the Nazis moved between art and atrocity, the practice of concluding the day's labor as concentration camp commandants with an evening of beautiful German music.

The novelist moves from confrontations imagined by her characters to an actual clash of Jew and German in "The Inner Light and the Fire." Here, Rosen dramatizes the encounter through the agency of an innocent American woman determined to reconcile victim and perpetrator's heir. The American decides that her Jewish tailor, Mr. Shneider, a survivor, must meet her new German friends, Walter, a visiting academic, and Gretel, his wife, in order that he "forever after take them into account when he thinks of Germans" (p. 5). What the Germans are to take from the meeting is left unarticulated.

Unlike other survivors of Rosen's fiction, who are reticent to speak of their wartime experience, Shneider is forthcoming and the American woman thinks she wants him to share his wisdom, his legacy of "Man in extremis" (p. 5). Yet when he reveals his story, she reacts as though she were being assaulted. As the survivor enumerates degrees of persecution, the American auditor is impatient because the details might wound the cultured Germans. To each charge Shneider recites, she inaudibly adds "thump" suggesting that his hammering the truth home is offensive. Thereby, the American assigns blame to the victim of Nazi brutality and consigns vulnerability to the descendants of criminals. In contrast to Gretel, who claims to be unaware of her country's Holocaust crimes, Walter confesses that his family knew what was happening and recalls walking with his father in the fields where he saw a hundred ghost-like women herded to work. Lest we conclude that Walter is apologizing for Germany's criminal past, Rosen conveys the limitations to full witness common to many of his countrymen. Walter's ardent disclaimer of continued German antisemitism is marked "with just a trace of residual national pride that pokes, hard as a rock, through the soft snowblanket of general atonement" (p. 7).

Although the American woman and the German couple are eager to put the past behind them and bask in self-delusive optimism, Shneider cuts through such deceptions, offering his testimony to help convict Nazi criminals who have thus far eluded justice. His witness is expanded from unofficial purveyor of the news in an American living room setting in the manner of the ancient mariner, and concludes in the mode of official witness in a German war crimes trial against a camp commandant. Through Shneider's pained speculation that the aged criminal will evade punishment, Rosen expresses her moral outrage at the failure of society to demand justice for the victims. The final section of the narrative returns the reader to the American's consciousness through a Holocaust nightmare that clarifies Holocaust reality for her. The crying voice she hears affirms that Holocaust memory cannot, and ought not, be put to rest. Thus, in an ironic reversal, the American who thought the Holocaust victim needed to be unburdened of Holocaust memory is herself transformed by the encounter.

In the symbolic and multileveled short story, "Fences," whose title alludes to concentration camp fences as well as the psychological barriers survivors erect and dismantle between themselves and nonwitnesses, Rosen returns to the theme of religious response to the *Shoah*. Here, she develops the delicate psychological balance of survivors in dialogue and dramatic presentation more thoroughly than before, and introduces the theme of Holocaust impact on the second generation. A family member's discovery of a package containing her dead father's prayer shawl is the catalyst for debate regarding transmittal of Holocaust memory and assumption of Judaic religious identity for post-Holocaust generations.

The narrative's survivor chorus consists of two men, one who escaped the conflagration and the other who experienced it directly. Edward left his mother and elder sister behind when he escaped from Vienna in a children's transport bound for England, following his father's murder in an early concentration camp. The family lodger, Frederick, was an adult during the war and suffered the loss of his wife and child. A muted voice is that of Edward's older sister, Bryna, who remained in Austria with their mother. Representative of survivors "Coddling the flesh because the heart won't heal" ("Fences," p. 81), Bryna is more psychologically fragile than Edward and Frederick and fearful at the prospect of looking at her father's deteriorated prayer shawl.

The lodger exhibits the characteristics described in clinical psychiatric writings on survivor syndrome. Unmarried, he lives in a rented room in another survivor's apartment and is silent about his lost family. Contemptuous of inauthentic interest in survivors, he charges that postwar attention comes cheaply, "How fascinated they are by us now. Not while it was happening, no. But now, later they want to know everything" (p. 80).

Perhaps because Frederick no longer has a child to protect, as does Edward, he permits his rage to emerge unbridled while commenting on the world's indifference to the slaughter of European Jewry. Frederick articulates a dilemma at the center of Rosen's Holocaust writing: "Between the reality-witnesses and the imaginers there can be no accord. The imaginers . . . wish in subtle ways to extract meanings that the survivors themselves avoid" (p. 80). Frederick attests to the difficulties of Holocaust transmission explicitly and evokes a quintessential Holocaust image to articulate the story's theme: "All around there are electrified fences. As the grandparents could not get out, so no one else can get in" (p. 77).

Although Rosen does not explain the family's Holocaust silence, it may be attributed to the parents' effort to shield their ten-year-old son, and to Edward's effort to cope with contemporary life. Initially, Edward fears that the sight of the prayer shawl will lead to painful questions from Daniel, yet it is at his son's urging that Edward's memories take voice. In response to the child's question about when his grandfather stopped wearing the prayer shawl—a query phrased in euphemistic diction that evades Holocaust reality—the father responds forthrightly, abandoning a protective veneer: "When did my father die, do you mean, Daniel? He was taken to a concentration camp when I was your age. After six months he died" (p. 79). In contrast to this direct approach, Edward later hesitates to answer Daniel's question about his grandmother's history. He seeks not to spare his son, but to award his mother an extra moment of life, if only metaphorically, as he revels in memory of her nurturing role, before disclosing that she was transported "to the East, and shot . . . in a field of snow" (p. 81).

Edward transmits more than Holocaust history to his son. He transmits the Judaic heritage in the act of sharing the prayer shawl, the *tallith*, with him. Enacting the ritual associated with donning the *tallith*, emblematic of embracing the commandments, he covers his head and upper body in the column of black and white striped fabric and recalls for his son how he shared a similar religious experience with his father. In Edward's gesture of draping the prayer shawl over his amenable son, Rosen symbolically intimates and then explicitly declares the survival of Jewry and continuity of Judaism in the post-Holocaust era. This gesture is confirmed in Rosen's explanation of the prayer shawl's durability through its many migrations in wartime and in peace, thereby signifying that Judaism and the Jewish people will persist given the devotion of adherents who cherish and transmit the legacy to future generations prepared to embrace it.

Paralleling Frederick's role is Daniel's American mother, who wavers between engagement and withdrawal. Sensitive to her husband's psychic trauma, yet protective of her young son's innocence, she observes the conferral scene with trepidation, mentally urging her son to resist vicarious association with his father's Viennese tribulations. Aware of the perils of "imaginary shifting into other people's lives," Rebecca fears that the impressionable boy will be permanently scarred by Holocaust knowledge. Paradoxically, anxiety for her son leads to the mother's epiphany, "with the clarity of sudden electrification" (p. 82). The visual stimulus of the prayer shawl's broad black stripes against the white of the bedspread lead the parents to polar perspectives. For Edward, the black stripes spread out against the white background suggest Torahic calligraphy. For Rebecca, Judaically unschooled, the black stripes evoke only concentration camp uniforms. She sees the tallith on her ten-year-old son's shoulders as metaphor for his assumption of the mantel of oppression. Edward perceives that his son is accepting a sacred inheritance. Before Rebecca can remove the prayer shawl, Frederick thwarts her renunciation. Formerly secretive about his family, Frederick now shares a photograph that Rebecca presumes to be either his son or the young Frederick himself. This gesture heralds the beginning of Frederick's healing, a sign that he welcomes communication and causes Rebecca to refrain from intruding on the father-son transmittal scene as a sign that she accepts their commitment to a Jewish future. Here, as in much of Rosen's increasingly Jewish writing, she is asserting that collective Jewish memory must include the Holocaust, and that the *Shoah* no longer obviates faith in God and Judaic observance. The American wife realizes at last what her survivor husband has long known, that Holocaust restoration lies in the individual's voluntary acceptance of Jewish identity and building Jewish community.

Critical Response

Rosen's careful meditation about the Holocaust and her exploration of the radical change visited upon humanity by the *Shoah* have earned her well-deserved critical acclaim. Representative is Sidra DeKoven Ezrahi's conclusion that in *Touching Evil*, Rosen achieves "a partial balance between the narrative of commonplace events in the lives of a few people in New York in 1961 and the subterranean forces of Holocaust evil and suffering which constantly threatens those events" (pp. 209–210). Alan Berger concludes that Rosen, far from universalizing the Holocaust, "wishes the Jewish experience to be read as a cipher of the human condition, . . . [making clear that] survival has moral implications and thus is much more than . . . Darwinian survival" (pp. 172–173). Norma Rosen has contributed significantly to the endeavor of creative writers to understand a hitherto unimaginable evil, not by re-creating the Holocaust universe but by rendering Holocaust metamorphosed lives, lives transformed by malevolence so absolute that it overwhelms earlier concepts of good and evil. In this manner Rosen effectively demonstrates that the *Shoah* is and should be of concern to thinking people, convincingly illustrating that "the central question was—and is still—how to write as a Jew after the Holocaust" (*Accidents of Influence*, p. 42). In the process, the daughter of parents estranged from Judaism became a Jewish writer, honoring the moral injunction to remember collective Jewish history.

Bibliography

Primary Sources

Books

Joy to Levine! 1962.
Green: A Novella and Eight Stories. 1967.
Touching Evil. 1969.
A Family Passover (coauthored with Anne Rosen and Jonathan Rosen). 1980.
At the Center. 1982.
John and Anzia: An American Romance. 1989.
Accidents of Influence: Writing as a Woman and a Jew in America. 1992.
Biblical Women Unbound: Counter-Tales. 1996.

Selected Articles and Short Fiction

"Apples." *Commentary* 27 (January 1959): 43–53.
"The Open Window." *Mademoiselle* 48 (April 1959): 169–178.
"What Must I Say to You?" *New Yorker* 39 (26 October 1963): 48–53.
"Sister Gertrude." *Redbook* 122 (November 1963): 60–61.
"A Thousand Tears." *Redbook* 123 (June 1964): 42–43.
"Sheltering a Life." *Redbook* 125 (October 1965): 88–89.
"Walking Distance." *Commentary* 52 (November 1971): 63–68.
"Mount Holyoke Forever Will Be." *New York Times Magazine*, 9 April 1972, 37ff.
"A Forum: Women on Women." *American Scholar* 41 (autumn 1972): 599–627.
"Traveling Toward the Inner Life." *Ms.* (November 1972): 77, 111–112, 115.
"Living in Two Cultures." *Response: A Contemporary Jewish Review* 6 (winter 1972–1973): 105–111. Reprinted in *Accidents of Influence*. Albany: State University of New York Press, 1992, pp. 127–132.
"Making Connections." *Hadassah Magazine* 54 (June 1973): 12–13.
"Who's Afraid of Erica Jong?" *New York Times Magazine* 28 July 1974, 8–9; 8 September 1974, 21.
"The Holocaust and the American-Jewish Novelist." *Midstream* 20 (October 1974): 54–62. Reprinted in *Accidents of Influence*. Albany: State University of New York Press, 1992, pp. 3–17.
"What is Hanukkah but the Symbol of Few against Many?" *New York Times*, 9 December 1982, C2.
"The Inner Light and the Fire." *Forthcoming: Jewish Imaginative Writing* 1, nos. 3/4 (fall 1983): 4–9.
"Hunting Metaphors and Nazis." Review of *Invisible Mending* by Frederick Busch. *New York Times*, 1 April 1984, S7, P12.
"The Miracle of Dora Wakin's Art." *Lilith* 12/13 (winter/spring 1985): 22–25.

"Fences." *Orim* 1 (spring 1986): 75–83.

"The Second Life of Holocaust Imagery." *Midstream* (1987). Reprinted in *Accidents of Influence*. Albany: State University of New York Press, 1992, pp. 47–54.

"Justice for Jonah, or, a Bible Bartleby." In *Congregation: Contemporary Writers Read the Jewish Bible*. Edited by David Rosenberg. New York: Harcourt Brace Jovanovich, 1987. Reprinted in *Accidents of Influence*. Albany: State University of New York Press, 1992, pp. 87–96.

Contributor to "The Holocaust." *Witness*, 1987.

"The Cheek of the Trout." *Testimony: Contemporary Writers Make the Holocaust Personal*. Edited by David Rosenberg. New York: Times Books, 1989, pp. 398–411.

"Notes toward a Holocaust Fiction." *Testimony: Contemporary Writers Make the Holocaust Personal*. Edited by David Rosenberg. New York: Times Books, 1989, pp. 392–398. Reprinted in *Accidents of Influence*. Albany: State University of New York Press, 1992, pp. 105–110.

"Fraud by Friendship." *New York Times Magazine*, 26 August 1990, 24.

"The Literature of Contempt." *Accidents of Influence*. Albany: State University of New York Press, 1992, pp. 41–46.

"Dialogue on Devotion." In *Reading Ruth: Contemporary Women Reclaim a Sacred Story*. Edited by Judith A. Kates and Gail Twersky Reimer. New York: Ballantine Books, 1994.

"The Lovemaking of I. B. Singer." *Commentary* 101 (March 1996): 40–45.

"My Son, the Novelist." *New York Times Magazine*, 3 August 1997, 60.

"The Holocaust and Popular Literature: History, Morality and Mass Art." *A Journal of Holocaust Studies* 11, no. 2 (1997): 17–21.

"Elixir." *Academic Questions* 12, no. 1 (winter 1998–99): 54.

"Poetry after Auschwitz." Review of *Fugitive Pieces* by Anne Michaels. *Partisan Review* 65, no. 2 (spring 1998): 330–333.

"Going over the Ground." Review of *The Iron Tracks* by Aharon Appelfeld. *Partisan Review* 66, no. 2 (spring 1999): 313–317.

"*Which Lilith?: Feminist Writers Re-create the World's First Woman*." Review. *Bridges* 8, nos. 1–2 (2000).

"The Orphan Lover." *The Antioch Review* 59, no. 4 (fall 2001): 690–699.

Interview

Interview with S. Lillian Kremer. 19 May 1988. Unpublished.

Secondary Sources

Alexander, Edward. *The Resonance of Dust*. Athens: Ohio University Press, 1979.

Avery, Evelyn. Review of *Accidents of Influence*. *MELUS* 19, no. 4 (winter 1994): 141–143.

Berger, Alan. *Crisis and Covenant: The Holocaust in American Jewish Fiction*. Albany: State University of New York Press, 1985.

Ezrahi, Sidra DeKoven. *By Words Alone: The Holocaust in Literature*. Chicago: University of Chicago Press, 1980.

Goldberg, Marilyn. "The Soul-Searching of Norma Rosen." *Studies in American Jewish Literature* 3 (1983): 202–211.

Klingenstein, Susanne. "Destructive Intimacy: The *Shoah* between Mother and Daughter in Fictions by Cynthia Ozick, Norma Rosen, and Rebecca Goldstein." *Studies in American Jewish Literature* 11, no. 2 (1992): 162–173.

———. "Norma Rosen." *Jewish American Women Writers: A Bio-Bibliographical and Critical Sourcebook*. Edited by Ann R. Shapiro, Sara R. Horowitz, Ellen Schiff, and Miriyam Glazer. Westport, Conn.: Greenwood Press, 1994, pp. 350–357.

Kremer, S. Lillian. "The Holocaust in Our Time: Norma Rosen's *Touching Evil*." *Studies in American Jewish Fiction* 3 (1983): 212–222.

———. "The Holocaust and the Witnessing Imagination." *Violence, Silence, and Anger: Women's Writing as Transgression*. Edited by Deirdre Lashgari. Charlottesville: University Press of Virginia, 1995, pp. 231–241.

———. "Norma Rosen: An American Literary Response to the Holocaust." *Daughters of Valor: Contemporary Jewish American Women Writers*. Edited by Jay L. Halio and Ben Siegel. Newark: University of Delaware Press, 1997, pp. 160–174.

———. "Norma Rosen." *Women's Holocaust Writing: Memory and Imagination*. Lincoln: University of Nebraska Press, 1999, pp. 214–235.

Rosenberg, Ruth. "Norma Rosen's *At the Center*: A Literary Onomastic Interpretation." *Literary Onomastics Studies* 11 (1984): 165–177.

———. "Norma Rosen." *Dictionary of Literary Biography*. Vol. 28: *Twentieth-Century American Jewish Writers*. Detroit: Gale Research Company, 1984, pp. 248–252.

THANE ROSENBAUM
(1960–)

ANDREW FURMAN

THANE ROSENBAUM WAS born in New York on 8 January 1960. His parents, Norman and Betty Rosenbaum, were both Holocaust survivors. His mother was interned at Maidanek and his father survived several death camps, including Bergen-Belsen. The Rosenbaums met in 1950 in Stuttgart, Germany, and emigrated to the United States. They raised their son, an only child, in Washington Heights in Manhattan until 1969, when they moved to Miami Beach. Thane Rosenbaum received a B.A. from the University of Florida in 1981; in that same year, both of his parents died within two months of one another, his father from a series of heart attacks and his mother from pancreatic cancer.

Rosenbaum went on to earn an M.A. in public administration from Columbia University in 1983 and a law degree from the University of Miami in 1986. He worked for several years as a corporate lawyer at the Wall Street law firm Debevoise and Plimpton. But, as Rosenbaum wrote in the Yiddish newspaper *Forward*, "the seduction of money . . . never could quite compensate for the damage done to the soul from all those days spent without purpose" ("Stepping Out of the 'Corporate Yuppie' Lane," p. 16). In 1992, Rosenbaum resigned from Debevoise and Plimpton to pursue a writing career. He began by writing a novel-in-stories, *Elijah Visible* (1996), that focused on the legacy of the Holocaust that haunts his protagonist, Adam Posner, a child of survivors. *Elijah Visible* won the annual Edward Lewis Wallant Award for the best work of Jewish-American fiction.

In November of 1996, Rosenbaum became the literary editor for *Tikkun*, a Jewish magazine of politics, culture, and society. His debut novel, *Second Hand Smoke*, a National Jewish Book Award Finalist, was published in 1999. In addition to his fiction writing, Rosenbaum has established himself as a prolific essayist and book reviewer for such prestigious publications as *The New York Times* and *The New York Times Book Review*, *The Wall Street Journal*, *The Miami Herald*, *Tikkun*, *The Washington Post*, *The Los Angeles Times*, and *Newsday*. He also teaches human rights and law and literature at Fordham Law School. Rosenbaum's second novel, *The Golems of Gotham*, is forthcoming from HarperCollins. The novel, which completes Rosenbaum's post-Holocaust trilogy, is a mystical ghost story set in New York City.

Major Titles, Themes, and Concerns

As S. Lillian Kremer has suggested, "Contemporary Jews increasingly feel that, geography aside, they were present at Auschwitz. American Jews carry the psychological burden of Auschwitz and Chelmno and Dachau and Bergen-Belsen and Treblinka and all the other Nazi death factories where their relatives died brutal deaths" (Kremer, p. 15). While the European atrocity left a deep impact on all Jews in America, the psychological burden to which Kremer refers weighs most heavily on the children of survivors and has manifested itself in the current surge of novels and short stories that the second generation has contributed to the burgeoning canon of Jewish-American Holocaust fiction. In his powerful collection of interconnected stories, *Elijah Visible*, and in his debut novel, *Second Hand Smoke*, Rosenbaum explores with great intensity the special burdens of the second generation in America as he grapples artistically with the seemingly ineffable horrors committed against his parents and, more specifically, with the legacy of those horrors visited upon him.

To engage these burdens in *Elijah Visible*, Rosenbaum creates in this collection a single protagonist, Adam Posner, but varies the details surrounding Posner's identity from one story to another. In one story, for example, Posner is a lawyer in an elite New York firm; in another story, he is an abstract expressionist painter; in another he is a teacher. He grows up in Atlantic City in one story, in Miami in another, and in still another, in New York. In Adam Posner, then, Rosenbaum creates a mosaic figure to capture the complex, nuanced, and, above all, fractured existence of the Holocaust survivor's child in America. The name Adam suggests rebirth or regeneration, and throughout the collection Rosenbaum scrutinizes the possibility of such continuity. Through the many Adams, Rosenbaum dramatizes the second generation's vicarious psychological immersion in the Holocaust, its responsibility to reconstruct and remember the experiences of survivor parents, and its struggle to maintain religious faith in a post-Holocaust America seemingly devoid of redemptive possibilities.

In the first story of the collection, "Cattle Car Complex," Rosenbaum tersely dramatizes the vicarious suffering of Adam Posner. The overarching point of this opening story is that the past, specifically the Holocaust experiences of Posner's parents, bears down heavily on this American Adam. The Holocaust has scarred Posner, precluding any meaningful relationships in his life. Not even a pet greets him at his barren apartment. More subtly, the Holocaust guides Posner's career choice. He reluctantly decides to become a lawyer to ensure his own financial safety. The comfortable trappings of Posner's life and his relative physical safety in America contrast mightily with his parents' predicament during the Holocaust; they survived cattle cars and concentration camps.

When Posner's elevator breaks down, trapping him indefinitely in the "hollow lung of the skyscraper," he suffers a psychological trauma that exemplifies the presence of the Holocaust in his life (p. 3). His claustrophobia in the elevator transports Posner, psychologically at least, to a Nazi cattle car in Holocaust Europe. Rosenbaum takes pains to emphasize (in this story and in others) that Posner inherits the legacy of suffering from his parents, "inherited their perceptions of space, and the knowledge of how much one needs to live, to hide, how to breathe where there is no air. . . . He carried on their ancient sufferings without protest—feeding on the milk of terror; forever acknowledging—with himself as proof—the umbilical connection between the unmurdered and the long buried" (pp. 5–6).

Still, if the Posner of Rosenbaum's collection inherits the Holocaust legacy of his parents "through his veins," as he mentions in the story "Elijah Visible" (*Elijah Visible: Stories*, St. Martin's Press, 1996, p. 5), it is just as true that experience, itself, cannot be inherited. A double bind, Rosenbaum suggests, plagues the second generation. Posner cannot get the Holocaust out of his mind; but, at the same time, he remains painfully aware that his treacherous imagination, rather than memory, burdens him. In another story, "An Act of Defiance," from the same collection, Posner reflects, "My imagination had done all the work—invented suffering, without the physical scars, the incontestable proof" (p. 59). Thus, in several stories, Posner must satisfy his inexorable desire to learn all he can about the Holocaust generally, and about his parents' experiences specifically. He must uncover the details that will sharpen the frustratingly nebulous images of terror that haunt him. Unfortunately, Posner's parents and other survivor relatives prove especially reluctant to share their stories with Posner. The memories are too painful, the truth too horrific for words. Besides, why burden the next generation with such stories?

One sees this relational dynamic emerge poignantly in "The Pants in the Family," which might well be described as a meditation on the incommunicable nature of the Holocaust. A short narrative of a dramatic moment in Posner's childhood frames a central narrative of the circumstances surrounding his mother's death during his adolescence. Through the acuity of a third-person narrator, Rosenbaum describes an episode on the Atlantic City pier when Posner's father abandons his son for a brief but scary moment. Baited by a barker at the shoot-out gallery—"Your kid will remember this day, when his pop chickened out of a fight" (p. 39)—he releases Adam's hand and, replacing it with a rifle, shoots down every one of the animal targets with ease. The tale evokes the estrangement between the Holocaust survivor parent and the second-generation child. At the carnival, the father's past rushes upon him in a flash of memory and separates him from his confused son, psychologically and physically.

In the story's central narrative, Rosenbaum dramatizes the extent of the elder Posner's psychological disorientation as Adam, now the narrator, must make the final medical decisions for his dying mother. When the doctor tells Adam that he really should speak to his father, Adam cries, " Leave him alone, he won't be able to handle it . . . the man's been through enough. He's old and weak, and has been disappointed before by bad news. Just look at him . . . what else do you need to know?" (p. 41). At sixteen, Adam must wear the pants in the family. His father, emotionally embattled and suffering from heart troubles, simply does not have the strength.

As Adam's father nears his own death, he becomes more communicative with his son and regrets having imposed a silent childhood upon him. Still, he does not understand why his son wishes to know about the past: " You think you need to know. . . . Do you want to know whether I ever killed someone? How will that change anything? What mystery will that answer?" (pp. 50–51). While one senses that certain experiences will remain forever inscrutable, Adam's father realizes an emotional connection with his son through piercing the silence that had defined their relationship.

If the unbridgeable chasm dividing memory from imagination in *Elijah Visible* represents Adam Posner's greatest burden as a second-generation survivor in America, the waning of religious faith and adherence following the Holocaust also bears down heavily on Rosenbaum's protagonist. Alienated from Jewish ritual and belief, Adam Posner cannot turn to religion for solace. Rosenbaum dramatizes in several stories the especially keen spiritual crisis of the second-generation American through Adam Posner, who must reckon not only with his own post-Holocaust religious doubts but with an American zeitgeist of secularism and crass materialism that exacerbates his spiritual crisis.

In "Romancing the *Yohrzeit* Light," Rosenbaum evokes the crisis poignantly as Posner's religious alienation wars against a curious exigence to commemorate his mother in a religiously meaningful way on the first anniversary of her death. The Posner of this story, an abstract expressionist painter, arguably represents the most disaffected Posner of the collection. Though Posner's mother, Esther, observed the Sabbath rituals and kept a kosher home, Adam "ate all manner of spineless fish, and the commingled flesh of unhoofed animals. His hot dogs didn't answer to a higher authority other than his own whim of which sidewalk peddler to patronize" (p. 17). Adam lives close to several synagogues in New York but avoids them at all costs "as though they were virtual leper colonies" (p. 17). Not only does he ignore the high holidays, but he does not even know what time of year to expect them.

Posner's mother laments her son's renunciation of Judaism. She realizes that her son's refusal to observe Jewish rituals proffers upon Adolf Hitler a posthumous victory and castigates Adam, who dons the obligatory black leather of the artist: "I didn't survive the camps so that you could walk around looking and acting like a camp guard. Look at you. Nothing Jewish that I can see" (p. 20). She also does not hesitate to denounce the paganism of her son's art. She pleads with him to paint something Jewish, to abandon the gloomy nihilism that pervades his work. Pointing to one canvas in particular, she opines, "Thank God your father has been dead all these years—because *this* . . . would have killed him" (p. 20). Importantly, Posner's mother does not encourage her son's identification with the Holocaust. A Jewish identity, Rosenbaum suggests, should not be rooted solely in one's remembrance of the European atrocity but in the rich legacy of Judaism that was almost completely snuffed out in the catastrophe.

Rosenbaum emphasizes the importance of Jewish ritual rather than Holocaust remembrance alone. Posner's memory of his mother's implacable religious faith following her Holocaust experiences impels him to honor her on the first anniversary of her death by seeking out a *Yohrzeit* candle (the plain but long-burning candle that, in accordance with Jewish ritual, mourners light on each anniversary of a loved one's death). Rosenbaum's narrative leads one to anticipate a hopeful conclusion. After purchasing the *Yohrzeit*, Posner's art suddenly loses its characteristic dreariness. He paints discernable figures, including several portraits of his mother, in bright, warm colors. Rosenbaum, however, suddenly deflates one's anticipation of Posner's Jewish renewal (or *t'shuvah*) as carnal impulses compete with his theological stirrings. In short, his passion for a non-Jewish woman, Tasha (a Swedish fashion model), interferes with his religious commemoration of his mother. This particular second-generation witness, Rosenbaum suggests, cannot embrace Judaism, given the competing influences in post-Holocaust America and, tragically, remains hopelessly lost without Judaism.

Rosenbaum tempers the cynicism of "Romancing the *Yohrzeit* Light" somewhat in the titular story of the collection, "Elijah Visible." The story opens as Adam Posner, celebrating Passover with his cousins, bemoans the thinning of religion in their lives. Exasperated by the Elvis Costello music blaring in the background and the prosaic American fashion magazines littering the Passover table, he cries, "You call *this* a Seder?" (p. 89). The desultory Seder illustrates, above all, the result of the silence between the generation of Holocaust survivors and their children. The survivor parents do not discuss their Holocaust experiences, nor do they educate their children in Torah Judaism. Raised to "ignore the lineage that was unalterably theirs," Adam and his cousins cling to near vacuous Jewish identities (p. 95).

However, a letter that Adam and his cousins receive from their cousin Artur, the last surviving relative of their parents' generation, jolts Adam from his spiritual complacency. Illustrative of the presence of the European past on the second generation, cousin Artur (who fled to Palestine after surviving Auschwitz) wishes to meet his cousins in America. He wishes to tell them about their family's history in Europe. Their cousin Artur represents the final link to a past that they must claim. Even though Elijah does not make an appearance at the Posner cousins' seder, Artur, by story's end, is on the way. The second generation, Rosenbaum suggests, might yet achieve *t'shuvah*.

In *Elijah Visible*, Rosenbaum dramatizes the near rupture of Jewish existence, but he also envisions the restoration of Jewish continuity through the piercing of the silence between Holocaust survivors and second-generation children; through the defiant humor of Posner's uncle Haskell, who uses the numbers of his Holocaust tattoo to triumph at an Atlantic City roulette wheel; through the similar defiance embodied in the Holocaust survivors' mantra at Cohen's summer cottages—"Leisure *Macht Frei*" (Leisure Will Make You Free); and through the sizzle of a match that poignantly triggers Posner's memories of his mother over the Shabbat candles.

In his debut novel, *Second Hand Smoke*, Rosenbaum revisits—with a renewed and redirected intensity—several of the themes he engaged in *Elijah Visible*. Most broadly, and as his fiercely accurate title suggests, Rosenbaum once again explores the toxic legacy that Holocaust survivors unwittingly but ineluctably pass on to their children. The novel revolves around Duncan Katz, a Nazi hunter for the Operation of Special Investigations and the son of two Holocaust survivors. His father is the silent and inscrutable Yankee (nee Herschel) Katz, who feverishly and mysteriously pecks away at his typewriter but refuses to answer Duncan's query, "Father, what happened to you during the war?" (*Second Hand Smoke*, St. Martin's Press, 1999, p. 31). His mother, Mila, is an indomitable woman who (guilt-ridden over her abuse and abandonment of an infant son she conceived just after the war) cannot bring herself to raise her second son, Duncan, with loving kindness and instead ruthlessly trains him to avenge their shattered lives: "Capeless and without a cowl, or even a phone booth, Duncan knew that what his mother really wanted was not a son, but a comic-book superhero" (p. 32).

Mila sees to it that Duncan forswears traditional Jewish bookishness for a black belt in karate by age nine. To the horror of even her tough cronies in Miami Beach's Jewish Mafia, she constantly tests her son's strength by subjecting him to everything from street brawls in the urban ghettoes of New Jersey to wilderness survival training in the Rockies. Traditional modes of Jewish existence, Mila believes, were discredited and made obsolete upon God's silence at Auschwitz.

Here, Rosenbaum engages what has now become a central theme in his work, the rupture and discontinuity that lamentably define Jewish existence after the Holocaust. The center of Judaism, Torah, evidently cannot hold after the atrocity in Europe. Additional scenes that exemplify this rupture pervade the novel. *Second Hand Smoke* evocatively opens, for example, with Duncan's decidedly "unkosher" *bris*. Echoes of *Elijah Visible* resound in such scenes of discontinuity and rupture.

Importantly, however, there are several crucial distinctions between *Elijah Visible* and *Second Hand Smoke*. Perhaps most significantly, Rosenbaum redirects his artistic energies toward a new emotional vista in his novel. Whereas the overarching tone of *Elijah Visible* might best be described as elegiac and mournful, Rosenbaum's novel is decidedly more red in tooth and claw. Put another way, whereas Rosenbaum's first book is a book primarily about loss, his debut novel is primarily about the rage that accompanies such loss and, even more specifically, the destructive power of this rage. The novel reaches its denouement as his protagonist travels to Warsaw to find Isaac, a sort of Zen master, who helps Duncan to eschew the self-destructive rage that has defined his existence. Only through Duncan's releasing his anger does Rosenbaum glimpse the possibility of a restored, albeit revised, Jewish continuity.

With *The Golems of Gotham*, Rosenbaum completes—in stunning fashion—his post-Holocaust trilogy of fiction. While rage and sadness loom large across the fictional landscape of the novel, a Jewish imp of mischief seems to have willed *The Golems of Gotham* into being. The novel opens audaciously as Lothar and Rose Levin, Holocaust survivors living in Miami Beach, commit a dramatic double-suicide in their synagogue during the Shabbat service. The narrative then jumps several years into the future to focus upon the Levins' only child, Oliver, a bestselling mystery writer suffering from writer's block, and his daughter, Ariel, who seeks to unblock her father's mind and heart by summoning her dead grandparents to return to them as golems. Through Hudson River mud and the magic of her violin, Ariel manages not only to summon the golems of Lothar and Rose, but also the golems of six famous writers (Jerzy Kosinski, Paul Celan, and Primo Levi, among them), all of whom survived the Holocaust, wrote trenchantly and poignantly about the atrocity, and ultimately took their own lives.

Having returned to the world of the living, albeit in ghostly form, the golems take it upon themselves to "fix" not only Oliver, but modern-day New York. In their headlong rush to greet the new millennium, the residents of this rather bleak, soulless Gotham (emblematic of cosmopolite citizenry worldwide) have failed to learn the lessons from the fire. "The century and millennium were ending," Oliver reflects, "but we had focused so little on the time that had just passed, the one we had lived through, squandered, and violated" (*The Golems of Gotham*, HarperCollins, 2002, p. 108). To restore memory to Gotham's residents, the golems begin by eradicating all the vestiges of the Nazis that endure. Fashion tattoos disappear from New Yorkers' arms, barbers suddenly cannot give crew cuts, showerheads (which can never be trusted again) stop working and force New Yorkers to take baths, and the city trains and subways come to a screeching halt. Rather than provoke anarchy on the streets, New Yorkers begin to embrace a new, more contemplative, ethos. A "renewed spiritual community" begins to take hold on the Upper West Side (p. 103). "Nobody was anonymous, or godless, anymore," Rosenbaum writes. "The city that once felt crowded but lonely was suddenly overrun with yentas, but was also suffused with warmth and connection" (p. 103).

Still, the golems eventually lose faith in the redemptive possibilities in Gotham, owing largely to the ways in which the Holocaust has been trivialized in art and film to appeal to the mass market. "The Holocaust was now a legitimate, moneymaking commodity," Rosenbaum writes (p. 294). He takes particular aim at the "good-guy-triumphs-over-bad-guy sanctimony" of *Schindler's List*, and the execrable humor of *Life Is Beautiful*, "popcorn for emotionally desensititized audiences" (pp. 292–293). In keeping with the mythical tradition, Rosenbaum's golems eventually turn against the very community they had sought to redeem. They wreak havoc, darkening the skies, leveling Yankee Stadium, and eerily—given the events of 11 September 2001—"fusing the World Trade Center together like Siamese twin towers" (p. 339).

How, exactly, should the thoughtful citizens of New York and the world remember the Holocaust and honor its victims as the catastrophe retreats further and further into the past? This is the conundrum at the center of *The Golems of Gotham*, and the trilogy as a whole. Rosenbaum's anxiety is not so much that we will forget the Holocaust entirely, but that we will domesticate it beyond all recognition to accommodate our contemporary sensibilities, just as we have done to other, once venerable, holidays like Labor Day, Veteran's Day, and even Passover. "Every year, in almost every seder I've ever been to," Oliver observes, "when Jews sit down to read from the Hagaddah, more and more of the story gets left out" (p. 268). Just as it is incumbent upon Jews, first and foremost, to commemorate the Jewish Exodus from Egypt during Passover, they must never forget that the Holocaust was about mass murder. Yet, Rosenbaum also suggests, to wholly immerse oneself in the catastrophe is to court an unearned and grotesque affinity with the actual victims. "The golems inside you now need to die, Oliver," Primo Levi's golem advises toward the end of the novel (p. 366).

Rosenbaum will undoubtedly face intense scrutiny for the way in which he fictively imagines this addendum to the lives of these famous Holocaust survivors, just as Philip Roth encountered criticism for imagining Anne Frank's miraculous survival in his novel, *The Ghost Writer* (1979). Rosenbaum, however, manages successfully to honor, rather than desecrate, the memories of his real-life subjects through the postmodern framework of his narrative and the moral rigor of his post-Holocaust vision. The reader is ever aware that the golems and the novel are products of Oliver Levin's imagination, finally freed by his willingness to confront rather than ignore his painful legacy. Indeed, while we cannot allow ourselves to be held hostage by the brutal past, we are all haunted, or *should* be, Rosenbaum suggests, by the ghosts of the Holocaust. We should all see the streaks of blood, if only in our imaginations, that the golems of Gotham leave in their wake.

Critical Reception

Rosenbaum has enjoyed a largely favorable critical reception. As one would expect of a relatively new writer, most of the critical discussion regarding Rosenbaum's work has been carried out in book reviews; and both of Rosenbaum's works were widely reviewed in leading national publications. Marcie Hershman called *Elijah Visible* "as vibrant and provocative a collection of short fiction as I've read in years. . . . The collection's ingenious structure mimics the pull between inheritance and impermanence, as story after story slightly rearranges the reader's assumption of who Adam is" (p. 242). Alan Berger, writing in *Tikkun*, argued that "Thane Rosenbaum's taut prose conveys with sensitivity and insight the experience of receiving his Holocaust legacy" (p. 85). Reviewing *Second Hand Smoke* for the *New York Times Book Review*, Richard Lourie observed, "The overheated atmosphere of the novel reminds one of Isaac Babel's *Tales of Odessa* and, more recently, *An Impossible Life*, by David Black, with a touch of *Maus* . . . and the film *Life Is Beautiful*. But in a style very much his own Rosenbaum depicts the painful comedy of being a regular American kid raised to be an angel of retribution" (p. 7). In her review of the novel, Janet Burstein focused upon Rosenbaum's painful depiction of Mila Katz, "who reconfigures our image of the destructive Jewish mother. . . . A feminist reader will quickly identify Mila as one of the harsh, castrating mothers who disfigure Western literature from Grimm to Disney and Philip Roth. But the identification is mistaken. Mila has been shaped by forces undreamt of in earlier literature" (p. 73). Sanford Pinsker, the reviewer for the *Wall Street Journal*, lauded *Second Hand Smoke* as "superb, if deeply disturbing, writing. . . . What remains, long after the final page has been turned, is a portrait of a man at war with ghosts of the Holocaust and himself" (p. W10).

More lengthy considerations of Rosenbaum's work are just beginning to emerge. In his important study, *Children of Job: American Second-Generation Witnesses to the Holocaust*, Alan Berger usefully limns several of the stories in *Elijah Visible*, paying particular attention to the theological implications embedded in the work. Berger insightfully argues that the collection's titular story "specifically links survivor testimony and the role played by Elijah the prophet. Like Elijah of antiquity, survivor testimony is holiness in disguise" (p. 81). In "Traumatic Memory and American Jewish Writers: One Generation after the Holocaust," Janet Burstein places Rosenbaum's work in the context of other recent works written by second-generation writers such as Melvin Bukiet and Helen Epstein. She explores the ways in which Rosenbaum, and other second-generation writers, evoke traumatic memory in their work, and thus clarify the "labor of mourning" (p. 188). Rosenbaum's stories, according to Burstein, impressively "make one feel the premature loss of childhood as a salient feature of a past that cannot wait much longer to be mourned" (p. 190).

In my book, *Contemporary Jewish-American Writers and the Multicultural Dilemma: The Return of the Exiled* (2000), I devote a chapter to Rosenbaum's *Elijah Visible* and *Second Hand Smoke*. I discuss Rosenbaum's work in the context of the Jewish-American literary tradition and the contemporary multicultural literary curriculum as well.

Conclusion

Owing largely to the simultaneous breadth and depth of Rosenbaum's vision, his work represents an invaluable contribution to the canon of Jewish-American Holocaust fiction. As a second-generation writer, Rosenbaum realizes painfully the unimaginable nature of the Holocaust. That he can never truly comprehend the horrors experienced by his parents is both his burden and his muse. His protagonists' psychological immersion in the Holocaust raises essential questions that face both the children of survivors and the broader Jewish-American community today: What are the theological implications of the Holocaust? How and to what extent should Holocaust remembrance inform the contemporary Jewish-American ethos? Can Holocaust education and Torah Judaism peacefully coexist? Might they even bolster one another to forge a stronger Jewish-American identity? These and other Holocaust-related issues will undoubtedly keep Rosenbaum writing novels for quite some time.

Bibliography

Primary Sources

Elijah Visible: Stories. 1996.
"Stepping Out of the 'Corporate Yuppie' Lane." 1997.
"Imagining a Life after the Unimaginable." 1998.
"Artist v. Critic: Wanting to Be True to History and Also to the Imagination." 1999.
Second Hand Smoke. 1999.
"The Writer's Story, and the Lawyer's." 2000.
The Golems of Gotham. 2002.

Secondary Sources

Berger, Alan L. *Children of Job: American Second-Generation Witnesses to the Holocaust*. Albany: State University of New York Press, 1997.
———. "Witnesses Once-Removed." *Tikkun* (September/October 1996): 85–86.
Burstein, Janet. "Legacy of Pain." Review of *Second Hand Smoke*. *Tikkun* (May/June 1999): 73–74.
———. "Traumatic Memory and American Jewish Writers: One Generation after the Holocaust." *Yiddish* 11 no. 3–4 (1999): 188–197.
Dickstein, Morris. "Ghost Stories: The New Wave of Jewish Writing." *Tikkun* (November/December 1997): 33–36.
Furman, Andrew. *Contemporary Jewish-American Writers and the Multicultural Dilemma: The Return of the Exiled*. Syracuse: Syracuse University Press, 2000.
Hershman, Marcie. Review of *Elijah Visible*. *Ploughshares* 22 (fall 1996): 242.
Kremer, S. Lillian. *Witness Through the Imagination: Jewish-American Holocaust Literature*. Detroit: Wayne State University Press, 1989.
Lourie, Richard. "Payback." Review of *Second Hand Smoke*. *New York Times Book Review* 11 (April 1999): 7, 31.
Pinsker, Sanford. "Dares, Double-Dares, and the Jewish-American Writer." *Prairie Schooner* 71.1 (spring 1997): 278–285.
———. "Review of *Second Hand Smoke*. *Wall Street Journal* (9 April 1999): W10.
Sicher, Efraim. "In the Shadow of History: Second Generation Writers and Artists and the Shaping of Holocaust Memory in Israel and America." *Judaism* 47.2 (spring 1998): 169–185.

BLANCA ROSENBERG
(1913–1998)

TOBE LEVIN

ONCE LYDIA HAD pulled the Star of David off Blanca's sleeve, things moved quickly. Equipped with the authentic birth certificate of deceased Ukrainian Catholic Bronislava Panasiak, the distressed woman would soon be boarding the night train to Lvov, barely escaping the last gasp of the Kolomyja Ghetto. Soon to know the persecutions visited on desperate Jews by a Polish cottage industry of extortionists and antisemites, Blanca would resist on the Aryan side.

At war's end, Joseph Korzenik, Rosenberg's closest living relative, offered Blanca his admiration. Although he had gone through six different camps, he called her a "heroine": "You were out here, fighting for survival, surrounded by enemies, alone, always looking over your shoulder, never knowing where the next threat would come from" (*To Tell at Last, Survival under False Identity 1941–45*, University of Illinois Press, p. 163). "I didn't argue, (p. 163)" she replied.

Biography

Blanca Rosenberg was born in Gorlice, Poland, in 1913, to Eli, a businessman, and Elenore Nebenzahl, a homemaker who insisted on her daughter's education. Six years after Rosenberg's birth her brother Romek was born, and six years later twin boys. Romek and Rosenberg, while in Kołomyja, learned of their parents' and brothers' as well as Rosenberg's two-year-old son, Zygmund Rosenkranz's deportation. They were all murdered in Belzec. Romek, who looked Jewish, was convinced that Rosenberg's Aryan appearance and unaccented Polish would permit her to endure. In a selection process, during which he was sent to the right to death, he challenged the decision, seeming indifferent to his own murder but adamant that his sister survive in order to relate their experiences. Blanca Rosenberg's manuscript, written in Polish in 1951, reveals atrocities in occupied Poland, both in the ghettos and outside.

Selected as the best book of Holocaust and Jewish Resistance Literature by the Israeli committee of the Egit Grants, Rosenberg's *To Tell at Last. Survival under False Identity 1941–45* (1993) places the vexed issue of resistance in a gendered context. It also expresses survivor guilt; reveals the rabid avarice of a Polish citizenry keen to stalk and shake down anyone remotely resembling a Jew; and honors the rare but blessed among the Gentiles to whom, with luck, survivors owed their lives. Read with an eye to postmodern elevation of the nomadic and rootless, it raises harrowing questions of choice and coercion in which hiding-in-the-open erases the self. It also celebrates a friendship begun in 1941 over a discussion of classic Polish literature while two people sat on a parachute factory bench. The incidents are commemorated in *The Jewish Week* in 1993. "Fifty years later," the photo caption reads, "Rosenberg, left, and [Maria] Rosenbloom share a special bond" (Kalish, p. 12). Maria, like Rosenberg, escaped from the Kolomyja Ghetto to Lwow where she had been a university student. Rosenberg joined her there once denunciation in Warsaw was imminent. The two went through many ordeals on the Aryan side; both labored, as *Hausdame* (Rosenberg) and loud-mouthed servant (Rosenbloom), for the German accountant Schmidt in Warsaw; Rosenberg helped Rosenbloom join her as a maid in Heidelberg; both worked after liberation for the U. N. High Commission for Refugees (UNHCR) and the Jewish Joint (the American Jewish Joint Distribution Committee that aided Jewish refugees after World War II); and both emigrated to the United States where they completed their college degrees. Maria Rosenbloom, professor (Emerita) of Social Work at the City University of New York, was among the first to integrate Holocaust studies into her field. Blanca Rosenberg, having read law in Kracow, enjoyed a distinguished career at the

Columbia University Graduate School of Social Work. In addition, Rosenberg became a psychotherapist. To honor the late associate professor, following her death at age eighty-five, the Blanca Rosenberg Scholarship was established. This award is given to students "with a professional interest in aiding the victims of relocation and immigration traumas" (*Columbia University School of Social Work* [CUSSW] Newsletter).

The Kołomyja Ghetto

The term "relocation trauma" is an understatement in light of Rosenberg's experience. In 1936, she married physician Wolf Rosenkranz (they were divorced after the war) and moved to his hometown. In 1939, Kołomyja became part of the Ukraine (Soviet Union) and was thereby spared hostilities until 1941. Once Hitler invaded Russia, however, Ukrainian gangs began attacking Jews. Under banners reading, "Death to the Yids and Bolshies," males were conscripted and forced, by truncheon and lash, to topple the statues of Lenin and Stalin—benign treatment when compared to the bloodbaths soon to pollute the Szeparowce woods, where victims of several *Aktions* (the brutal rounding up and shooting of Jewish civilians) dug their own graves. Of fifteen thousand Jewish inhabitants, a mere several hundred would survive. First came the Wild Action, followed by the Intelligentsia Action, which exterminated "two hundred physicians, lawyers, engineers, teachers, accountants and other educated professionals on the roster of Jews in Kolomyja" (Rosenberg, p. 22). Deportations soon followed.

After conquest, Nazi measures were rapidly imposed in Kołomyja, as vicious as anywhere else in occupied Poland. Jews were now forced to wear a star, obey a curfew, avoid walking on sidewalks, and shun fraternizing with Gentiles. Before ghettoization, the Germans relied on the native gentile population to identify Jews. Then ghettos ensued, and food grew scarce. "We became experts in malnutrition, our own and that of others. First the flesh began to hang off the bones, revealing their shapes and sizes. Then the feet and legs began to swell. After that the stomach started to protrude until people began to look like balloons with appendages" (p. 46). Soon, people began to die of starvation.

The Distinction of Gender

Though it seems to Mary Lowenthal Felstiner that "Rosenberg . . . recall[s] not so much a female as a human and Jewish hell" (Felstiner, p. 9), women (and children) suffered differently from men. On the outside, the circumcised males could be given away by their "Mark of Cain" (male circumcision) (p. 132), but, as admitted at Rosenberg's and Maria's arrest in Warsaw, "it's hard to tell with women" (p. 116). Yet, within the ghetto "only young men qualified for work cards" (p. 34) while at selections, witnessed by both Rosenberg and her cousin Korzenik, "mothers and children [were sent] to the left, males to the right" (p. 162). Rosenberg, like many mothers, struggled with maternity. Should she place her son, Zygmund, with a gentile family? Despite an offer, she found it impossible:

> Even the knowledge of what other mothers had been through . . . did not move me. Some had been forced to abandon babies in their cribs; others saw their children suffocate in airless hiding places. We had all seen the Germans catch a child on the street and use the toddler for target practice. A friend had even throttled her own son to protect the hiding place of a hundred others. The luckiest children I knew had died by the cyanide their mothers had saved the instant they had been discovered (p. 49).

Given prewar gender expectations, the genocidal targeting of Jewish women was bewildering. "We soon learned that most of those . . . carried off [in the first *Aktion*] were women and children. It was hard for us to understand what this meant. For us, war was still fought between men" (p. 21).

The fact that this war was not fought between men resonated in the bitter question of resistance. When asked later "in all innocence" why the victims had not died fighting, "we described women holding babies in their arms, clutching the frail hands of children" (p. 28). Women, socialized not to individualism but to family responsibility and collective care, found insurgency prohibitive, for "Who among us would have . . . attack[ed] a guard when the result would be not just our own death but that of a hundred more, all still clinging to life? We could not choose for others, and so we could not choose for ourselves" (p. 29).

The *Szmalcownicy*: Extortionists

If on the Aryan side females had an advantage—being checked for their religion, they wouldn't be told to "pull down [their] drawers" (p. 131)—they were equally prey to the *Szmalcownicy*, "parasites . . . doing a flourishing trade in extortion and blackmail" (p. 106). Rosenberg and Maria would have to buy deliverance again and again, so often, in fact, that the memoir's examples confirm the generalization: "For every one person who helped, thousands made a business of taking Jewish money and then collecting a bounty for Jewish lives. The worst of them were the apartment building caretakers" (p. 133). Life on the outside was experienced as flight. Denounced by one concierge after another, the women changed apartments, changed jobs, and fled from Warsaw to L'vov and back, always nervous about police registrations and the *Kennkarte* (official IDs). So essential were these documents that, once jostled on a tram, Maria lost her handbag; it flew out the back. As the vehicle sped on, she jumped after it, incurring a concussion and a broken nose.

emergency housing or payoffs to save other Jews. Once slaving as maids in Heidelberg, they continued their mutual support. Excellent actresses, they performed (almost) to perfection. One near slip occurred, however, when Rosenberg's employer caught her enjoying Rilke at the university on her day off. Having earlier mentioned prewar education, Rosenberg managed to divert suspicion. But far from experiencing exhilaration in the liberty to self-create, she felt oppressed, and once reverted. During one incident, while hysterical with fever, she "began swearing that [she] was a Jew . . . condemned for abandoning [her] child" (p. 153). Fortunately, in the Heidelberg hospital, she shouted it in Polish.

The Resistance and the Righteous

The accident led to one of several encounters with the righteous. Maria's physician appeared to know who his desolate clients really were, but far from denouncing them, he refused payment. Exposed in L'vov by one of Maria's former classmates—only one step ahead of the Gestapo, Rosenberg and Maria, disguised as peasants, were greeted at the train station by wanted posters of themselves—the young women found an ally in Stach, a possible police headquarters spy. They were arrested on arrival. The two women had disembarked from the train in the midst of the Warsaw Ghetto Uprising, which made authorities more than usually vigilant. Stach effected their release. Additional assistance came from a shoemaker who allowed Maria to take refuge in his shop. Throughout the ordeal, Gentiles had sent letters, received parcels, and offered food to Jews. Romek's employer Lydia, who procured the birth certificate and insisted that Rosenberg use it, as well as the unnamed Gentile who carried the circumcised baby boy, Rosenberg's son, to Gorlice, reveal that not everyone was corrupted. Once, in fact, Rosenberg, who regularly attended mass, wanted to know how the Catholic Church, maintaining "a silent complicity" in Jewish suffering, would advise if she confessed, " 'father, I'm breaking the law. I'm hiding a Jew.' " The young priest answered: " 'It is no sin, my child. In the sight of God it is a good deed' "(p. 133). The rarity of this response brought tears to the penitent's eyes.

Mainly, Jews were left to take care of their own. Once in a position to do so, Rosenberg and Maria, employees in a German firm in Warsaw, helped with

Survivor Guilt and Romek's Legacy

The euphoria of freedom jackknifed into despair, for lives had been secured but "what were they worth?" (p. 156). Pursued by "unmarked graves . . . air rancid with . . . decomposing bodies . . . suffocated, mutilated, martyred children. How would we . . . live with the memories and . . . guilt?" (p. 156), survivors asked. Rosenberg never forgot that "right before his death, her brother sent her a message to escape and 'tell the world' " (Shapiro). The writing, "critical for . . . healing," fulfills "Romek's legacy at last" (p. 173). And Rosenberg hopes, too, that it "may . . . serve the cause of peace" (p. 173).

Bibliography

Primary Sources

To Tell at Last: Survival under False Identity 1941–45. 1993.

Secondary Sources

"Blanca Rosenberg Scholarship Established." *CUSSW Alumni Newsletter*. Winter 1999. http://www.columbia.edu/cu/ssw/alumni/newsletter/wi n99/rosenberg.html (Accessed 11 August 2001).

Felstiner, Mary Lowenthal. "Overcoming Silence." *The Women's Review of Books*. Vol. XI, no. 1 (October 1993): 9–10.

Kalish, Jon. "Two against the World. Soulmates since the Holocaust, Blanca Rosenberg and Maria Rosenbloom Survived against All Odds. Theirs Is the Story of a Friendship That Wouldn't Die." *The Jewish Week* (December 3–9, 1993): 12–13.

Shapiro, Susan. Review of *To Tell at Last: Survival under False Identity 1941–45*. *New York Times* (October 10, 1993). N.p. From the publisher's files.

CHAVA ROSENFARB

(1923–)

GOLDIE MORGENTALER

CHAVA ROSENFARB IS not only one of the most important Yiddish novelists of the second half of the twentieth century, she is also, sadly, one of the last. Rosenfarb's primary topic is the Holocaust and she is one of the few Yiddish writers who is herself a Holocaust survivor and whose work on the Holocaust is cast primarily as fiction rather than as memoir or autobiography.

Life

Chava Rosenfarb was born on 9 February 1923 in Lodz, Poland, the elder of two daughters of Abraham Rosenfarb, a restaurant waiter, and his wife Simma. Her parents were Bundists, members of the Jewish Socialist Party of Poland and Russia, and sent her to a Yiddish secular school for her primary schooling. She then attended a private Jewish high school, from which she graduated in 1941. By that time, Rosenfarb and her family had been incarcerated in the Lodz ghetto, and it was in the ghetto that she received her high school diploma.

It was also in the ghetto that she began seriously to write poetry, waking up at dawn from her bed of chairs and composing her poems in the hours before going to work at her various ghetto jobs. Through her poetry Rosenfarb made the acquaintance of Simcha-Bunim Shayevitch, the great ghetto poet and author of the epic poem "Lekh-Llekho." She became Shayevitch's protegée and it was he who introduced her to the writers' group of the Lodz ghetto, who quickly recognized her talent and accepted her, at age seventeen, as their youngest member.

When it became clear that the Lodz ghetto was to be liquidated by the Nazis in August of 1944, Rosenfarb and her family, as well as Shayevitch and the family of Henekh Morgentaler, the man who would become her husband, all hid in an alcove behind a false door in the Rosenfarbs' apartment. They were discovered by the Nazis a few days later, on August 23, and deported to Auschwitz. At Auschwitz, the knapsack containing Rosenfarb's poems was taken away. Rosenfarb, her mother, and sister survived the selection and were sent from Auschwitz to a labor camp at Sasel near Hamburg, where they were put to work building houses for the bombed-out Germans of that city. There she begged one of her German overseers for something to write with. He gave her a pencil stub and with this she recorded on the ceiling above the uppermost bunk on which she slept, the texts of the poems that had been taken away from her. She then memorized the poems and later included them in the first volume of poetry she published.

From Sasel, Rosenfarb, her mother, and sister were sent to Bergen Belsen, where, suffering from typhus, she was liberated by the British army in 1945. Once recovered, she traveled throughout the devastated postwar German countryside seeking news of her father, only to learn that he had died in the last transport out of Dachau, when the train on which he and the other inmates had been riding was bombed by the Americans. In 1945 Rosenfarb, her mother, and sister crossed the border illegally into Belgium, where she lived as a displaced person until her marriage and emigration to Canada in 1950. She lived in Montreal from 1950 to 1998, bore two children, took an active part in the Yiddish cultural life of this "Jerusalem of the North," and did most of her writing there. She currently resides in Toronto.

Holocaust Influences and Major Works

Rosenfarb was profoundly affected by her experiences during the Holocaust, and her prodigious output of poetry, novels, short stories, plays, and essays all deal with this topic in one way or another. She began as a poet, publishing her first collection of poetry, *Di balade fun nekhtikn vald* (The Ballad of Yesterday's Forest) in London in 1947. This was followed by a book-length poem about her father, *Dos lid fun yidishn kelner Abram* (The Song of the Jewish Waiter Abram, 1948); and the poetry collections *Geto un andere lider* (Ghetto and other Poems, 1950) and *Aroys fun ganeydn* (Out of Paradise, 1965). Rosenfarb's play *Der foigl fun geto* (The Bird of the Ghetto, 1958) about the martyrdom of the Vilna partisan leader, Isaac Wittenberg, was translated into Hebrew and performed by the Habimah, Israel's National Theatre, in 1966.

Finding that neither poetry nor drama could begin to express the depths of her feelings about the Holocaust, Rosenfarb turned to fiction. In 1972 she published, in Yiddish, *Der boym fun lebn* (The Tree of Life). This monumental three-volume epic chronicles the destruction of the Jewish community of Lodz during World War II. From the first, the book was hailed as a masterpiece by the critics. In breadth and scope there is, in fact, nothing quite like this novel in Yiddish literature and possibly not in the literature of any other language, a fact noted repeatedly by reviewers.

The Tree of Life follows the fates of ten Jewish inhabitants of Lodz who live through the terrible events of the years 1939 through 1944, that is, from before the beginning of the war, when life was still "normal," until the liquidation of the ghetto in August and September 1944. The ten characters include Samuel Zuckerman, a factory owner before the war, and Itche Mayer, a carpenter with four sons, each of whom is a member of a different political party.

There is also Mordechai Chaim Rumkowski, the head of the Lodz ghetto, and Simkha-Bunim Berkovitch, the poet. There is the doctor, Michael Levine, who corresponds compulsively with a woman he loved in Paris before the war but never sends the letters; Rachel Eibushitz, a politically committed high school student; her boyfriend David, a diarist; Adam Rosenberg, a prewar industrialist and Kripo (German criminal police) spy; Miss Diamond, a high school teacher and Polish patriot; and Esther, a great beauty and ardent Communist, who is active in the ghetto underground and whose wish to have a baby in the ghetto seals her doom.

Because these ten characters come from all walks of life, the novel recreates, in all its complexity and particularity, an entire Jewish ghetto community and then unflinchingly chronicles its destruction. The novel describes, in detail, everyday life in the ghetto workshops and food distribution centers. It describes the gatherings of the ghetto intelligentsia and of the various political parties—the Zionists, Communists, and Bundists—and it does not shy away from describing the activities of the ghetto spies and informers.

While most of Rosenfarb's characters are fictitious, some are based on actual people, like the poet Shayevitch, who appears here under the name of Berkovitch. The most important historical portrait is that of Mordechai Chaim Rumkowski, the "eldest" of the Jews in the Lodz ghetto. Rosenfarb describes the ironic road that Rumkowski traveled from being the founder and director of an orphanage before the war, to being the puppet leader of the ghetto, put in place by the Nazis, who, in one of the novel's most chilling accounts of a historical event, demands that the mothers of the ghetto willingly give up their children to the Nazis for the good of the collective.

> From an elevated platform the white prophetic head of Rumkowski surfaced at last. The sky had acquired a pair of hands which rose above the black mass of the throng. The sky had acquired a mouth which through thunder and lightning pronounced the judgement: "Mothers, you must give up your children!" . . . Words like mountains rolled down upon the sea of heads.
> "Mothers!" the Presess called. "Save the ghetto! If we don't give up the children . . . We shall be erased from the face of the earth. If life continues, you will have other children. Mothers! Make this sacrifice for the people . . ." (Carlton, Australia: Scribe Publications, 1985, p. 828).

The Yiddish press immediately hailed the publication of The Tree of Life, repeatedly emphasizing its unique place in the literature of the Holocaust. In unanimously awarding Rosenfarb Israel's highest literary honor, the Manger Prize for 1979, the jury concurred: "[*The Tree of Life*] is a work that rises to the heights of the great creations in world literature and towers powerfully over the Jewish literature of the Holocaust, the literature which deals with the annihilation of European Jewry, in particular Polish Jewry" (taken from Jury's decision for the Manger Prize, 1979).

Rosenfarb followed The Tree of Life with the novel *Bociany* in 1983, named after an imaginary Polish village. *Bociany* was translated into English by the author herself and published in 2000 in two volumes as *Bociany* and *Of Lodz and Love*. The translations won Rosenfarb the John Glassco Prize of the Literary Translation Association of Canada in September 2000. Although these novels do not deal directly with the Holocaust, they actually constitute a prequel to The Tree of Life, giving the early history of some of the characters who appear in that novel. The Holocaust hangs like an unspoken presence over the lives of the Jews described in *Bociany*.

Rosenfarb had always been reluctant to write about the horrors of the concentration camp in her fiction. She purposely ended The Tree of Life at the point where her characters were deported from the ghetto as a way of saying that she could describe their fates no further. The last few pages of the novel are thus purposely left blank, to imply that the horror was too great to be put into words. It was not until 1992 that Rosenfarb finally felt herself capable of attempting a description of the camps in her as-yet untranslated novel *Briv tsu Abrashen* (Letters to Abrasha). The story is told through a series of letters penned after the war by Miriam, a Holocaust survivor, to a man recovering from tuberculosis in a sanatorium in Germany, whom Miriam believes to be her former teacher and friend Abrasha. Miriam recounts the events of her incarceration in Auschwitz, Sasel, and Bergen Belsen where she was liberated. Some of these descriptions make for harrowing reading, especially the scene in which Miriam loses her mother during the selection at Auschwitz. *Briv tsu Abrashen* is, in many ways, Rosenfarb's most powerful novel, although its unflinching descriptions of the death camps and their horrors make it an emotionally wrenching book to read.

Essays, Short Stories, and Honors

Rosenfarb was a frequent contributor of essays to the Yiddish literary journal *Di goldene keyt* (The golden chain), where in the early 1980s she also began to publish a series of short stories about the lives of Holocaust survivors in Canada. Whereas all of Rosenfarb's novels are set in Poland in the early decades of the twentieth-century, her short stories travel the Atlantic to Canada and take as their subjects the tragedy's aftermath. One of these stories, "The Greenhorn," about a newly arrived Holocaust survivor working his first day at a Montreal sweatshop, was translated by Miriam Waddington for her anthology *Canadian Jewish Short Stories* and has since been reprinted in other anthologies. Another story, "Edgia's Revenge" (published in English in *Found Treasures: Stories by Yiddish Women Writers*) describes the unhealthy symbiotic relationship of two women survivors who meet again in Montreal after the war. Rella, the story's narrator, had been a concentration camp kapo during the war, with the power of life and death over the other inmates. Her one good deed had been to save Edgia's life. In the postwar years the two women act out the repercussions of that one good deed in an endless to-and-fro of guilt and dependence that is only resolved when one of them commits suicide.

Rosenfarb's important essay on the problems of being a Yiddish woman writer ("Feminism and Yiddish Literature: A Personal Approach") appeared in English in *Gender and Text in Modern Hebrew and Yiddish Literature*. She has contributed essays and reviews to the Montreal *Gazette*, as well as to numerous Yiddish-language publications. She is also the winner of numerous literary awards. In addition to the Manger Prize and the John Glassco Award for Literary Translation mentioned previously, she has twice won the Canadian Y. Y. Segal Prize, as well as the Award of the American Association of Professors of Yiddish in 1998. She has also twice won the New York Prize of the Congress for Jewish Culture, Israel's Sholem Aleichem Prize, and the Argentinean Niger Prize in 1972.

Despite all these honors and awards, her work is not as well or widely known as it deserves to be, largely, one suspects, because she writes in Yiddish. She expressed the pain of being a Yiddish writer and a survivor quite poignantly in her lecture "Confessions of a Yiddish Writer," delivered at the Jewish Theological Seminary, New York, in 1991:

> What affects me the most is the continual sense of isolation that I feel as a survivor—an isolation enhanced by my being a Yiddish writer. I feel myself to be an anachronism wandering across a page of history on which I don't belong. If writing is a lonely profession, the Yiddish writer's loneliness has an additional dimension. Her readership has perished. Her language has gone up with the smoke of the crematoria. She creates in a vacuum, out of fidelity to a vanished language—as if to prove that Nazism did not succeed in extinguishing that language's last breath. If creativity is a life-affirming activity, the lack of response to creativity and being condemned to write for the desk-drawer are stifling, destructive experiences. Sandwiched between these two states of mind, struggles the spirit of the contemporary Yiddish writer.

Bibliography

Primary Sources

Novels

Briv tsu Abrashen (Letters to Abrasha). 1992. Excerpted in English translation in *The Gazette* (Montreal), 7 May 1995.
Bociany. 1992, 2000.
Of Lodz and Love. 2000.
Botshani. 2 vols. 1983.
Ets Hakhayim (The Tree of Life). 3 vols. 1978, 1985.
Der boym fun lebn (The Tree of Life). 3 vols. 1972.

Short Fiction

"A Friday in the Life of Sarah Zonabend." In *Contemporary Jewish Writing in Canada*. Translated by Goldie Morgentaler. Edited by Michael Greenstein. University of Nebraska Press, 2002.
"The Greenhorn." In *Not Quite Mainstream: Canadian Jewish Short Stories*. Translated by Goldie Morgentaler. Edited by Norman Ravvin. Calgary and Montreal: Red Deer Press/Insti-

tute for Canadian Jewish Studies, 2001. Also in *Canadian Jewish Short Stories*. Translated by Miriam Waddington. Edited by Miriam Waddington. Toronto: Oxford University Press, 1990, pp. 111–122.

"Letters to God." *Di goldene keyt* 140 (1995): 51–72.

"Edgia's Revenge." In *Found Treasures: Stories by Yiddish Women Writers*. Translated by Goldie Morgentaler. Edited by Frieda Forman, et al. Toronto: Second Story Press, 1994.

"Royt feigele" (Red birdie). *Di goldene keyt* 139 (1994): 86–98.

"François." *Di goldene keyt* 135 (1993): 16–47.

"In serengeti." *Di goldene keyt* 128 (1990): 115–156.

"Letste leibe" (Last love). *Di goldene keyt* 110–111 (1983): 117–140.

Poetry

Aroys fun gan-eydn (Out of Paradise). 1965.

Geto un andere lider (Ghetto and other poems). 1950.

Dos lid fun dem yidishn kelner Abram (The song of the Jewish waiter Abram). 1948.

Di balade fun nekhtikn vald (The ballad of yesterday's forest). 1947; republished *Di balade fun nekhtiken vald un andere lider* (The ballad of yesterday's forest and other songs) in conjunction with *Fragmentn fun a tog-bukh* (Fragments of a diary). 1948.

Individual Poems in Journals and Anthologies

The Last Lullaby: Poetry from the Holocaust. Edited and translated by Aaron Kramer. Syracuse: Syracuse University Press, 1998.

"Aquarium." Translated by the author. *Judaism* 45, no. 1 (winter 1996): 58.

"Tokhter." *The Yiddish Pen* 7 (February 1995): 4.

"Two Poems by Hava Rosenfarb." Translated by the author. *The Bridge: Australian Jewish Quarterly* 7, no. 3 (January 1973), 35–36.

"I Would Go into a Prayer Room." Translated by Abraham J. Karp. *Conservative Judaism* 20, no. 4 (summer 1966): 23.

"Praise." Translated by the author. *Prism International* 5, no. 2 (autumn 1965): 30–33.

"Ikh un mein kholem." In *Yiddish*. New York: Congress for Jewish Culture, 1961, 69.

"Dos lid fun Atalia." *Zamlbikher*. Edited by H. Leivik and Y. Opatoshu. New York: Grenich, 1948, 335.

Memoirs and Essays

"Writing in a Language Foreign to Nearly All." *The Gazette* (Montreal), 14 August 1999, Book Section, I, 1–2.

Yiddish Poets in Canada. Mississauga: Publications for the Jewish Studies Program at University of Toronto, 1994.

"Paul Celan and His Colleagues." *Di goldene keyt* 138 (1994): 53–70.

"Laterna Magica: Prague Travelogue." *Di goldene keyt* 137 (1993): 119–137.

"Feminism and Yiddish Literature: A Personal Approach." In *Gender and Text in Modern Hebrew and Yiddish Literature*. Edited by Naomi B. Sokolof, et al. New York: The Jewish Theological Seminary of America, 1992.

"Isaac Bashevis and Sholem Asch." *Di goldene keyt* 133 (1992): 75–104.

"My Debut." *Midstream* 35, no. 3 (April 1989): 26–29.

"Bergen-Belsen Diary." In *Kiddush Hashem*. Edited by S. Niger. New York: Cyco Publishing House, 1948, 775–779.

Plays

Der foigl fun geto (The bird of the ghetto). Montreal: H. Morgentaler, 1958.

Journals That Include Works by Chava Rosenfarb: *Di zukunft* (literary monthly, New York, N.Y.); *Mir zainen do* (New York, N.Y.); *Loshn un lebn* (London, England); *Foroys* (Mexico City, Mexico); *Undzer tseyt* (New York, N.Y); *Undzer gedank* (Melbourne, Australia); *Melbourner bleter* (monthly for literary and social affairs, Melbourne, Australia.); *Montrealer heftn* (Montreal, Canada).

Secondary Sources

Cooper, Judy, "Chava Rosenfarb's *The Tree of Life*." Broadcast on Radio Australia, May 26, 1989.

Duhl, Lisa. *Rocking an Empty Cradle: A Psychological Study of Yiddish Holocaust Lullabies: Isaiah Spiegel, Chava Rosenfarb*. Ph.D. diss., California School of Professional Psychology, University of California, Berkeley, 1999.

Elberg, Yehuda. "Chava Rosenfarb." In *Undzer vort*. Paris, 1974.

Emiot, Israel. "A Great Book About Lodz." *Jewish Daily Forward*. New York, 29 July 1972.

Jonasovitch, Isaac. "*Der boym fun lebn*." *Folk un Medine*. Tel Aviv (summer 1975): 33.

Kahan, Isaac. "Chava Rosenfarb's trilogie, der boym fun lebn." *Di Tsukunft* (October 1973): 372–377.

Lev, Yacov. "Chava Rosenfarb's Trilogie, *Der boym fun lebn*." *Undzer Shtimme*. Paris (June 1973): 118–135.

Mlotek, Yossl. "Editorial: *Der boym fun lebn*." *Kultur un lebn*. New York (May–June 1973): 3–4.

Morgentaler, Goldie. "Land of the Postscript: Canada and the Post-Holocaust Fiction of Chava Rosenfarb." *Judaism* 49, no. 2 (spring 2000): 168–183.

Naves, Elaine Kalman. "Chava Rosenfarb's *The Tree of Life*," a two-part documentary on *Ideas*, Canadian Broadcasting Corporation, Radio 1. 6 and 13 February 2001.

———."Chava Rosenfarb." In *Putting Down Roots: Montreal's Immigrant Writers*. Montreal: Véhicule, 1998.

Rak, Meyer. "Chava Rosenfarb and Her Great Trilogy about the Holocaust." *Kultur un lebn*. New York (August–September 1973): 10, 11, 14.

Ravvin, Norman. "Ghost Writing: Chava Rosenfarb's *The Tree of Life*." In *A House of Words*, Montreal: McGill-Queens, 1997.

Sharlett, Jeffrey. "More Objective than Tears: A Profile of Chava Rosenfarb." *Pakn Treger* 25 (summer 1997): 50–65.

Yanovsky, Joel. "Standard-Bearer for Yiddish: For Chava Rosenfarb, Writing in Her Native Tongue Is a 'Sacred Duty.' " *The Gazette*, Montreal, 1 April 2000, Book Section, 33.

PHILIP ROTH

(1933–)

S. LILLIAN KREMER

LIKE THE GREAT satirists of the past, Philip Roth's concerns are significant public and private subjects—genocide, war, the foibles of modern democracies, family life, the individual's inner turmoil, and the writer's imagination and craft. His prolific career has been marked by extremes of low comedy and high seriousness, prompting his critics and readers to receive him as both *enfant terrible* and literary elder statesman. Born to Herman and Besse Finkel Roth in 1933, the writer grew up in a working-class Jewish neighborhood of Newark, New Jersey. He was graduated from Bucknell University *magna cum laude* and Phi Beta Kappa with a B.A. in English in 1954. He received an M.A. in English at the University of Chicago in 1955 and stayed on as a doctoral student in English until he left the program in 1957. By then, four of his stories had won awards and two had been reprinted.

Critical recognition of Roth's artistic imagination is evidenced in myriad awards, honors, and grants, including the National Book Award in 1960 and 1995, the Jewish Book Council of America Daroff Award, the National Book Critics Circle Award in 1987 and 1992, the PEN\Faulkner Award in 1993, a Pulitzer Prize in 1998, election to the National Institute of Arts and Letters, the Houghton Mifflin Literary Fellowship, the National Institute of Arts and Letters Grant, a Guggenheim Fellowship, a Ford Foundation Grant, and a Rockefeller Fellowship. He has contributed to literary studies as the general editor of the Penguin "Writers from the Other Europe" series and as a teacher at several universities and the Iowa Writers' Workshop.

Throughout his career, Roth has experimented with narrative strategies ranging from the realistic novel and the comedy of manners to postmodernist fantasy and metafiction. Self-reflexivity and the exploration of the nature and status of fiction are dominant components of Roth's oeuvre. His protagonists are generally products of middle-class, religiously nonobservant, ethnic Jewish families in Newark, New Jersey, confronting personal and public aspects of modernity. Most have studied and taught literature at the university level and have become writers. His artistic and intellectual second generation American Jews are joined by Israelis, often encountering a panorama of socio-political issues, questioning the accepted order, and challenging conventional behavior and attitudes. Motivated by an abiding interest in exploring their Jewish identities, they struggle with critical questions of our time—among them overt and genteel manifestations of antisemitism, Holocaust representation and legacy, communist totalitarian repression in eastern Europe, American and Mideast policy and politics, and the ethics of social, aesthetic, and political choices. Targets of Roth's satire include bourgeois Jewish parents, academics, novelists and literary critics, politicians, and journalists. With a deft talent for speech mimicry, Roth moves adroitly from the socio-linguistic matrix of urban and suburban American Jewish life of the fifties to ardent Arab and Israeli political discourse.

Early Work

Roth treated the Holocaust directly only once, in an unpublished play that explored the dynamics of Jewish responses to ghettoization. At the same time he was writing the stories of *Goodbye Columbus*, he wrote "A Coffin in Egypt," set in the Vilna ghetto from 1941 to 1943. A major interest in the play, according to Steven Milowitz, is the interaction of four characters that each respond to the Nazi system in a manner "depending on his/her former life, perceptions and ardent beliefs" (Milowitz, p. 17). Some cooperate with the Nazi bureaucracy and others join the religious and political opposition. Center stage is given to the Holocaust transformation of an insignificant member of the prewar Jewish community who rises to prominence as the Nazi appointed mayor of the Jews, his supporter and opponents including a rabbi who refuses to recognize his leadership and another who sees the need for compromise, and a communist who also rejects the Nazi installed leader. Duped by the Nazis to believe that by cooperating with deportation demands the ghetto will prosper and countless Jewish lives will be saved, the leader is resigned to follow orders and proud of his negotiation to send 5,000 young, strong workers to a new work camp in Kovno, thereby saving them and an additional 5,000 needed to replace them in Vilna. But the train halts and the young, healthy Jews are massacred. The mayor now knows the truth, and in the final act, after a speech reminiscent of that delivered by Jacob Gens, the historic chief of the Vilna ghetto, he takes responsibility for providing Jews for deportation in an effort to save a remnant. But, unlike Gens who was shot by the Nazis, he joins the last convoy to the extermination camp. Each of the play's acts concludes with the mourner's prayer for those killed, for those who lose their innocent belief in rescue through work, for the world, "a psalm of memory . . . an impetus for Roth's efforts" (Milowitz, p. 20).

More characteristic of the place of the Holocaust in Roth's work is his exploration of the American response, or lack thereof, to the *Shoah* and Holocaust survivors as seen in "Eli, The Fanatic," the best short fiction in the *Goodbye Columbus* collection. This tale is a satiric attack on assimilated, Jewishly uneducated American Jews who are so paralyzed by their fear of antisemitism that they not only conceal outward manifestations of their own ethnic identity, but seek to impose that model on observant Jews who have recently arrived in their suburban neighborhood. Believing their acceptance in the pristine, largely Protestant suburb is threatened by the visibility of eighteen Hasidic child Holocaust survivors and their two adult black-garbed and skull-capped teachers living in an old mansion housing their yeshiva, the assimilated Jews threaten legal action for violation of residential zoning laws.

The focus of the story is on the transformation of the lawyer retained to negotiate with the survivors. Dealing with the Holocaust survivors is at once traumatic and redemptive for Eli Peck. Guilty for persecuting the persecuted children who flee in fear at his approach, Eli eventually succumbs to the Talmudic wisdom of the survivor-mentor whose veiled reference to German law and single overt reference to family losses and subjection to Nazi medical experimentation reveal that there are times when the law is not the law. In an effort to placate his clients and benefit the survivors, Eli sends his own suits for the survivors to wear in public. In turn, the Hasid delivers a box with his attire to Eli's home. The guilt-ridden American dons the Hasidic suit in metaphoric acceptance of his true identity and claims a Judaic legacy for his newborn son. Eli's behavior is unintelligible to the wooden sensibilities of his neighbors, who assume he has had a nervous breakdown. The community's effort to tranquilize the "new" Eli is ineffectual. The drug "did not touch [his soul] down where the blackness had reached"("Eli, the Fanatic," *Goodbye Columbus* Boston: Houghton Mifflin, 1959, p. 216). Eli—whose Hebrew name means "ascend," "uplift," and "exalted"; whose biblical namesake acted as judge and High Priest of the sanctuary—has, by donning the black suit as a token of Jewish identity, become the overt critic of Woodenton's lapsed Jews and the covert critic of Jewish-American silencing of the Holocaust in exclusive embrace of American prosperity and the good life. Post-*Shoah* Jewish American self-erasure coupled with indifference to Holocaust history and harassment of *Shoah* survivors prompts the yeshiva head to inquire whether news of the Holocaust reached America. This compelling question and the casting of the religiously observant *Shoah* survivor as moral guide to lapsed American Jews are illustrative of Roth's enduring indirect approach to the *Shoah*.

The World according to Nathan Zuckerman

The acerbic reception from some critics regarding Roth's satiric presentation of Jewish characters in *Goodbye Columbus* provided Roth a dominant theme of his oeuvre: the life and work of the post-Holocaust Jewish American writer and the relationship of artistic integrity to communal responsibility. In addition to responding in polemical essays, Roth refuted his critics in the *Zuckerman Bound* collection (comprising *The Ghost Writer* [1979], *The Anatomy Lesson* [1981], *Zuckerman Unbound* [1981], and "The Prague Orgy") through the persona of Nathan Zuckerman, whose career encounters many of the same vicissitudes Roth's has.

The Ghost Writer, Roth's portrait of an artist as a young Jew, is the retrospective narrative of a successful novelist. The work draws upon the *Bildungsroman*/ quest conventions to explore critical questions about art and the writer's moral relationship to community and, incidentally, raises questions about Jewish-American *Shoah* response. The first part of the novella, "Maestro," focuses on Nathan's effort to select a literary master on whom to model his career. He ponders whether to pursue restraint and an orderly approach to life and art, or to become a public celebrity. Striving to clarify his identity as a writer and a Jew, Nathan makes a pilgrimage to the Berkshire home of a famous reclusive Jewish American writer, E. I. Lonoff, whom he covets as his spiritual father. Beyond the master's dedication to art, the novice is attracted to Lonoff's work for the feelings of kinship he expresses toward his fictional Jewish immigrants, "for our pious, unknown ancestors, . . . [and] the sense given by such little stories of saying so much" (*Zuckerman Bound*, New York: Farrar, Straus, & Giroux, 1985, p. 13). Zuckerman is in awe of the Lonoff hero who, a decade after Hitler, "seemed to say something new and wrenching to Gentiles about Jews, and to Jews about themselves" (p. 13).

Adopting the Joycean pattern in the "Nathan Dedalus" chapter, Roth maps the young writer's relationship to his past, to his family and community. He introduces passages that echo the criticism he received for *Goodbye, Columbus*, in the paternal Zuckerman's accusation that one of Nathan's stories disparages Jews and will promote antisemitism. Failing to convince his son to retract his story, Zuckerman enlists the help of a highly regarded local judge, a representative of the parochial world from which the young writer seeks escape. In a hilariously censorious letter posing a series of hostile questions, the sanctimonious Judge Wapter echoes Roth's early critics, like Marie Syrkin, condemning Nathan's story as one that would satisfy Julius Streicher or Joseph Goebbels. Wapter closes by advising Nathan to see the Broadway production of *The Diary of Anne Frank*, implying that for a generation, like Nathan's, without Jewish memory or knowledge, Anne Frank and the Holocaust are touchstones of Jewish identity and authenticity. Wapter's Nazi analogy infuriates Nathan, leading to his quip that American Jews are "not the wretched of Belsen." Zuckerman sees these worlds as essentially different precisely because of the Holocaust and objects to Wapter's suggestion that American Jews base their identity on Holocaust history, which is not theirs to appropriate.

As in *The Ghost Writer*, the most interesting questions in *The Anatomy Lesson* and *Zuckerman Unbound* explore the nature of the artist; the relation of the artist to his work, his family, and his community; the connections between the writer and his roots. The trilogy's first volume concludes with a validation of Zuckerman's literary voice. The second and third books close with metaphors of loss and silence. In the second volume, loss of family and neighborhood signify diminished literary subject; in the third, physical pain and loss of literary voice parallel a blocked writing career. Bereft of subject, the author cannot write. Unlike the writers Roth's literary men admire—Kafka, James, Chekhov—Zuckerman's imagination has become detached from the world and constrained by the circumscribed universe of the text. In a final epiphany, he realizes that he has become too self-absorbed to write good fiction.

Holocaust Presence and Absence in Roth's Fictional Universe

Addressing the place of the Holocaust in the Jewish American consciousness and as subject for the writer in *Reading Myself and Others*, Roth observes: "For most reflective American Jews . . . it is simply there, hidden, submerged, emerging, disappearing, unforgotten. You don't make use of it—it makes use of you" (New York: Farrar, Straus, & Giroux, 1975, p. 130). Although he neither re-creates the concentrationary universe nor introduces survivors as protagonists in his fictional world, the Holocaust theme is a recurrent presence in the work. The occasional survivor, as in "Eli, the Fanatic," appears as a voice of judgment, a moral mentor, and Holocaust consciousness becomes a more visible component of the fiction as he attacks both *Shoah* indifference and misappropriation as touchstone of Jewish American identity construction. The young Roth, who recurrently turned to the high mindedness of literature to explore social issues, initially entered the Holocaust terrain through the door of a literary text, *The Diary of Anne Frank*, or to be precise through his critique of the Broadway play's misappropriation of the diary. As Roth had earlier metamorphosed Franz Kafka into a Newark Hebrew schoolteacher in "Looking at Kafka," Zuckerman transmogrifies Lonoff's refugee-protégé in *The Ghost Writer*, Amy Bellette, as Anne Frank, secret Holocaust survivor, whom he imagines sacrificing reunion with her father in order that, through her assumed death, her art and Holocaust witness may live. The Anne of Zuckerman's imagination is the novice writer devoted to free thought and nonconformity, but also the means for his imagined redemption in his father's eyes. Through his reconfigured Anne, Nathan acts out his anxiety about the double burden of the Jewish writer: aesthetic distance from those he writes about and responsibility to their history.

Roth may have committed a lapse of aesthetic judgment in appropriating the Holocaust victim for Nathan's redemptive marriage fantasy, but he tempers his approach with a thoughtful meditation on antisemitism and critiques of the American revision and trivialization of the diary by persuasively dislodging Anne from the mythic attic sentimentalist of the Francis Goodrich and Albert Hackett production. Roth introduces a far more intellectually and morally astute Anne of the Westerbork transport, Anne of Auschwitz and Belsen, who "had not come to hate the human race for what it was . . . but she did not feel seemly any more singing its praises" (p. 146). Through Zuckerman, Roth reminds readers that although the Holocaust fate of European Jewry is generally met with indifference, Anne's story became popular precisely because

> the young girl of her diary was . . . only dimly Jewish . . . the daughter of the father who calmed her fears by reading aloud to her at night not the Bible but Goethe in German and Dickens in English. . . . To expect the great callous and indifferent world to care about the child of a pious, bearded father living under the sway of the rabbis and the rituals—that was pure folly. . . . To ordinary people it would probably seem that they had invited disaster by stubbornly repudiating everything modern and European—not to say Christian (p. 144).

In taking this approach, Roth is among the first to question the stereotypes and clichés of American Holocaust representation and response. He confronts the existing "*Shoah* etiquette" of sentimentalization, dejudaization, sanitation, and trivialization of Holocaust reality as instruments that metamorphose tragedy into kitsch.

"The Prague Orgy," the epilogue written for the *Zuckerman Bound* collection, restores Nathan Zuckerman to literature as a regenerated novelist, reformed man, and returned Jew, and again invokes the Holocaust via Anne Frank's image. Zuckerman is reunited with his heritage, to Jewish history and culture, through his association in Prague with a persecuted Czech-Jewish writer and an oppressed gentile actress who made a bad career choice by playing the martyred Anne Frank and by abandoning her husband for a Jew. In Soviet-dominated Czechoslovakia there is no aesthetic distance between the self and the roles one plays. Consequently, the actress who plays Anne Frank convincingly is branded a Jew-lover in a nation whose official Cold War policy is anti-Zionist and where Anne Frank herself is viewed not as a writer who told the truth about totalitarianism, but as a "curse and a stigma" (p. 759). The persecuted couple seeks Zuckerman's aid in recovering the Yiddish stories of the writer's father, a Holocaust victim, shot by the Nazis in 1941. Zuckerman undertakes the mission that parallels Roth's rescue of east European fiction as general editor of "Writers from the Other Europe." He secures the manuscripts, only to have the police seize them and expel him on trumped up charges that he is a "Zionist agent." In Kafka's city, Zuckerman, like Joseph K, is arrested although he has committed no crime and the murdered Jew's manuscript is confiscated by a successor totalitarian regime.

Unlike Zuckerman of the earlier novels, who championed self and a psychoanalytic interest in self-definition, the redeemed Zuckerman of the epilogue is rooted in history. Retrieving the fiction of a Nazi-persecuted Jewish writer in a post-Holocaust Communist nation, where storytelling is a form of political resistance, is a fitting objective for the redeemed author cognizant of his link to Jewish history and literary precursors. With the epilogue, *Zuckerman Bound* is framed by literary-cultural pilgrimages to spiritual fathers: to the contemporary fictional master who wrote about Jewish characters and life and to Kafka, whose fiction many regard as a prophetic announcement of the Holocaust universe. In privileging these spiritual fathers, Zuckerman attains artistic maturity and history, and Roth adds his voice to the debate on *Shoah* representation, Holocaust misappropriation, and Holocaust silence. The significance of Roth's trajectory is mapped by the Israeli critic Hana Wirth-Nesher, who contends that "Philip Roth's long odyssey from Newark to Prague is also a turning point in the American Jewish literary tradition, for it marks the passage from a literature of immigration and assimilation into a literature of retrieval, of the desire to be part of a Jewish literary legacy alongside the European and American literary traditions" (p. 228).

Self-Reflexive Metanarratives

Having made a pilgrimage to his literary Jerusalem in Prague, Zuckerman is primed to encounter geographic Jerusalem in *The Counterlife*, where he further refines and comes to terms with his post-*Shoah* diasporic Jewish identity. Following examination of the sources of fiction and the relationship between fiction and autobiography in *Zuckerman Bound*, Roth produced two self-reflexive metanarrations. *The Counterlife* and *Operation Shylock* continue to pose questions about the writer's art, the conflict between the writer's personal and artistic commitments, and the conflict between the writer's responsibilities to himself and others. But unlike the earlier novels in which Roth scrupulously adhered to the conventions of realism, he now violates them to challenge the realistic view of fiction in an exploration of the purposes of storytelling. He departs from his earlier references to other writers that were designed only to illuminate his themes. They are now part of his explorations of Jewish identity and history.

Creation of new identities through the imagination is the subject of *The Counterlife*. Five sections of the novel juxtapose alternative lives and interpretations of the characters. Each first person narrative presents interlocking personal and public histories from disparate points of view and is countered by a story in which Nathan and his younger brother, Henry, live lives counter to the other's and counter to his own, comment on each other's lives, and offer corrections and counter-interpretations, ultimately transferring the hermeneutic responsibility to readers.

Complementing the novel's postmodernist self-reflexivity is a return to Jewish history and identity, sharp polemical exchanges by advocates of disparate post-Holocaust Jewish ideologies and identity perspectives, a brief evocation of the Holocaust, and a long ideological debate about Arab-Israeli relations. Bakhtinian dialogic prevails in the "Judea" and "Aloft" debates, yielding a full spectrum of contradictory discourses and possibilities for post-Holocaust diasporic and Israeli self-definition and political positions. Among the identity constructs Roth examines are the religious-secular and Israeli-diasporic polarities. Whereas Henry rejects his profligate life in America to embrace Zionism and Orthodox Judaism, Nathan remains a devout diaspora assimilated Jew. "Christendom," the final chapter, addresses Nathan's amended thinking, a revision and obligation developed in direct reaction to his encounter with post-Holocaust antisemitism and anticipation of fatherhood. Married to his fourth Christian wife, Nathan is now living in England where he had come to seek refuge in a counterlife as "Maria's husband." However, his enjoyment of English pastoral life is shattered by repeated encounters with genteel British antisemitism. The concluding image of the novel, Zuckerman's erect circumcised penis, signifies not the sexual virility of the trilogy, but reestablishment of Nathan's bond to the Jewish past through insistence on circumcision for his son. Choosing the most elemental sign of the covenant, he affirms his connection to Jewish history and community.

Overt discussion of the Holocaust enters *The Counterlife* briefly but forcefully in the "Aloft" chapter, set on a flight from Jerusalem to London. Jimmy Ben-Joseph, a demented Jewish American, threatens to blow up the El Al plane, but is subdued by an Israeli security guard. During the aborted highjacking of the airliner, and in earlier conversation with Zuckerman, Ben-Joseph argues that Jews must "Forget Remembering," that only by abandoning Holocaust memory and its inherent reminder to the Gentiles of their sins, can Israel enjoy international support. Jews, he asserts, must lose their suffering or the world "will annihilate the State of Israel in order to annihilate its Jewish conscience." Although the view is preposterous, especially as propounded by a character who has been used for comic relief earlier in the novel and is now a "wanna-be" terrorist, Roth situates this theme in so shocking a context that it is not easily dismissed as mere lunacy. Embedded in Jimmy's yoked construction are two political observations: recognition of "Holocaust fatigue" as articulated either by those who object to the attention given the subject or those who wish to conceal *Shoah* crime. Roth challenges the legitimacy of Holocaust silence not only by attributing the speech to a deranged person, but by encouraging readers to consider the view through the lens of political reality.

With *Operation Shylock*, Roth revisits many of his major themes—coalescence of the real and the fantastic, the writer's relationship to his work, and Jewish history and identity. But he redirects his self-reflexive mode to the *Shoah* and Israel as the polar elements of late twentieth-century Jewish identity formation. Unlike the American Jews of his early fiction, whose ignorance of Jewish culture and history marks their personalities, the personae of *The Counterlife* and *Operation Shylock* are passionate about the Holocaust, Israeli security, and politics. Against the backdrop of the Intifada and the Demjanjuk trial, historic events that lend an aura of authenticity to his fantasy, Roth introduces a confrontation between a character named Philip Roth, to whom he attributes his own books under their real titles, and an impostor calling himself Philip Roth, whom the fictional Roth derisively renames Moishe Pipik. Recovering from a Halcion-induced emotional breakdown, the beleaguered novelist departs for Israel to interview the acclaimed Holocaust novelist Aharon Appelfeld and to confront the man usurping his persona and making public pronouncements in his name. Pipik, who dresses like Roth, copies his mannerisms, and can recite Roth's childhood history, is the founder and moving force of Anti-Semites Anonymous and an avid promoter of repatriation of Israelis of European and American origin and descent to the lands of their birth. Obsessed by the fear that Zionism is the latest threat to the Jewish people and that it will induce an Arab-wrought holocaust, Pipik wants to save Israeli Jews from annihilation by expelling them from the Mideast. The impostor fantasizes repatriation of Israelis culminating in "a historic day for Europe, for Jewry, for all mankind when the cattle cars that transported Jews to death camps are transformed . . . into decent, comfortable railway carriages carrying Jews by the tens of thousands back to their native cities and towns" (*Operation Shylock: A Confession*, New York: Simon & Schuster, 1993, p. 45).

By situating the American writer in Jerusalem at the time of the Demjanjuk trial and the raging Intifada,

Roth focuses our attention on two temporal turning points in twentieth-century Jewish history, the genocide of European Jewry and the regeneration of an independent Jewish nation. Although Roth treats Palestinian suffering sympathetically, he advocates the necessity for the Jewish homeland. *Operation Shylock* is not a representation of the *Shoah*, yet the text interrogates Holocaust memory by charting Jewish-American identity in relation to such remembrance in the Demjanjuk trial. That, in turn, evokes the impact of the Eichmann trial on Jewish-American and Israeli consciousness and the connection for the post-Holocaust Jew between the actual European Holocaust and the intended Arab annihilation of Israel. Roth's sensitivity to Jewish survival readily emerges in depiction of the trial testimony of Holocaust survivors coupled with reflection on the murder of Leon Klinghoffer by Palestinian terrorists aboard the cruise ship *Achille Lauro*. The portrayal of British antisemitism was confined to the occasional statement of a passerby or of a Christian family member in *The Counterlife*. Roth's satire of the public manifestation of antisemitism is more biting in his *Operation Shylock* ridicule of the London press caricature of Menachem Begin standing over a pyramid of dead Arabs while it sentimentally and fallaciously ennobled the Intifada and downplayed Arab murders of Israelis.

Roth's more nuanced approach to the *Shoah* is also signaled in his differentiation of an American writer's sympathetic *Shoah* interest and an Israeli survivor's knowledge based on experience. He describes Aharon Appelfeld, "Hiding as a child from his murderers in the Ukrainian woods while I was still on a Newark playground playing fly-catcher's-up had clearly made him less of a stranger than I to life in its more immoderate manifestations" (p. 111). But it is also Roth's feeling of connectedness to, and *Shoah*-separation from, Appelfeld as fellow Jew that accounts for his response to the impostor who demands to know why Philip rejects him but speaks with Appelfeld. Philip explains, "Because . . . of Aharon's and my distinctly radical twoness . . . because each recognizes in the other the Jewish man he is not; because of the all but incompatible orientations that shape our very different lives and very different books and that result from antithetical twentieth-century biographies" (pp. 200–201). Roth's position can only be that of historic "postmemory," the term Marianne Hirsch introduces in *Family Frames* to identify a position between the personal experience of memory and the lessons of history. Michael Rothberg judges that "the manner in which [Roth's] writing intersects with the Holocaust demonstrates the extent to which the postmemory predicament has come to be shared (albeit with crucial psychic and historical differences) by Jewish Americans more broadly" (p. 189).

Critical Reception

A remarkably prolific writer producing a book almost every other year, Roth has been a controversial and celebrated author since he published his first novel in 1959. Critical reaction to Roth's fiction has been mixed, for he is a writer about whom neutrality is difficult. While detractors found his early characters and his views of American society disturbing, supporters heralded an original new voice, applauded his satirical talents, marveled at his facility for reproducing the language around him, and appreciated the moral concerns underlying the comic surface of his fiction. Condemned by some as a self-hater and antisemite, Roth has also been hailed as an original, provocative voice, as the true chronicler of secular American Jews. Discussions of Roth's work generally center on his place in the American tradition, the Jewish-American canon, literary influences—especially that of Kafka and James, analysis of his comic-satiric voice, the influence of psychoanalytic theory on the fiction, and Roth's contribution to postmodernism's fixation on metafiction and self-reflexivity. Throughout Roth's prolific career, critics of the stature of Alfred Kazin, Harold Bloom, and Robert Alter have praised the novelist's comic invention and moral intelligence, his superb rendering of a Jewish-American voice into fiction, and his provocative delineation of the Jewish writer determined to express himself freely, unencumbered by the restraining voices of his critics. Alfred Kazin reads Roth as a second generation Jewish writer whose concern is the self-conscious middle-class Jew whose identity is problematic; Sanford Pinsker finds an ambivalent, even troubled response to the Jewishness in Roth's protagonists; and Hermione Lee judges his incorporation of a Yiddish-American voice into fiction to be the most spectacular of contemporary Jewish American writers. By mid-career, detractors of Roth's ethnic Jewish characters were replaced by critics of his political and sexual satire and by others who found his focus on Zuckerman obsessive. Critical ire has been supplanted by near universal praise for the later novels' postmodernist subjects and style, technical brilliance, and mature engagement of substantive subjects. Illustrative of the widespread positive reading is Harold Bloom's assessment of *Zuckerman Bound* meriting "something reasonably close to the highest level of aesthetic praise for tragicomedy" (p. 1), and his praise of Roth's morality, distinguishing his "negative exuberance" not in the service of "negative theology, but [intimating] instead a nostalgia for the morality once engendered by the Jewish normative tradition" (p. 2). Roth's mature, more substantive and complex treatment of Jewish history prompted Hillel Halkin's observation that "a sheer, almost abstract passion for being Jewish seems to grow stronger in Roth's work all the time" (p. 48). Mark Shechner maps the trajectory of Jewishness in Roth's fiction, observing that it has shifted from "a Jewishness of sensibility and self-consciousness . . . a psychological condition and a form of disablement, for which Kafka supplied the metaphor, . . . and psychoanalysis the treatment" to the Jewishness of the later period, "a historical Jewishness and source of meaning" (p. 224). Representative of the most recent criticism that is focused on Roth's Jewish subjects are Alan Cooper's *Philip Roth and the Jews*, Andrew Furman's *Israel through the Jewish-American Imagination*, and Steven Milowitz's *Philip Roth Considered: The Concentrationary Universe of the American Writer*. Milowitz reads Roth's work as having extended the Holocaust universe from the ghettos and camps to include "the altered universe that is born as a result of unprecedented evil" (p. 2). Whereas most Jewish-American writers have been reticent to deal with Israel, Roth has, in the opinion of Andrew Furman, who reads his Israeli novels from a postcolonialist perspective, "engaged Israel with far greater intellectual rigor than any other contemporary Jewish-American writer" (p. 128). Writing in a countercurrent to the postmodernist vogue that denies the idea of meaning in life and art, that separates life and art in equally meaningless realms, Roth opposes the view of history as an unintelligible flux of phenomena. He rejects the postmodernists' view that efforts of the designing or ordering imagination to discover or impose meaning are absurd or fraudulent, and affirms that truth exists beyond as well as in the text; that texts may be read for enlightenment as well as pleasure taken in their artifice. Roth's best work combines Judaic moral conscience with postmodern artifice by which he fashions a literary universe.

Bibliography

Primary Sources

Novels

Goodbye, Columbus and Five Short Stories. 1959.
Letting Go. 1962.
When She Was Good. 1967.
Portnoy's Complaint. 1969.
Our Gang (Starring Tricky and His Friends). 1971.
The Breast. 1972.
The Great American Novel. 1973.
My Life as a Man. 1974.
The Professor of Desire. 1977.
The Ghost Writer. 1979.
A Philip Roth Reader. 1980.
The Anatomy Lesson. 1981.
Zuckerman Unbound. 1981.
Zuckerman Bound: A Trilogy and Epilogue. 1985.
Deception: A Novel. 1990.
Operation Shylock. 1993.
Sabbath's Theater. 1995.
American Pastoral. 1997.
I Married a Communist. 1998.
The Stain. 2000.

Nonfiction Books

Reading Myself and Others. 1975.
The Facts: A Novelist's Autobiography. 1988.
Patrimony. 1991.
Shop Talk: A Writer and His Colleagues and Their Work. 2001.

Selected Essays, Interviews, and Short Stories

"The Box of Truths." *Et Cetera* (October 1952): 10–11.
"Armando and the Fraud." *Et Cetera* (October 1953): 21–28.
"The Day It Snowed." *Chicago Review* 8 (1954): 34–45.
"The Final Delivery of Mr. Thorn." *Et Cetera* (spring 1954): 20–28.
"The Contest for Aaron Gold." *Epoch* 7–8 (fall 1955).
"The Kind of Person I Am." *New Yorker* 34 (29 November 1958): 173–178.
"Recollections from Beyond the Last Rope." *Harper's* 219 (July 1959): 42–48.
"On the Air." *New American Review* 10 (1970): 7–49.
"Very Happy Poems." *Esquire* 57 (January 1962): 79–86.
"The Psychoanalytic Special." *Esquire* (November 1963): 106–110, 172–176.
"Most Original Book of the Season." Excerpts of Roth's interviews of Milan Kundera. *New York Times Book Review* 85 (November 30, 1980): 7.
"Smart Money." *New Yorker* 56 (2 February 1981): 38–44.
"The Collar." *Esquire* 100 (October 1983): 136–138.
"His Mistress's Voice." *Partisan Review* 53, no. 2 (1986): 155–176.
"Pictures of Malamud." *New York Times Book Review* 91 (20 April 1986): 1.
"Joe College: Memories of a Fifties Education." *Atlantic* 260 (December 1987): 41–48.
"A Talk with Aharon Appelfeld." *New York Times Book Review* (28 February 1988): 29.
"Kafka Would Have Savored the Irony of Being a German Treasure." Letter. *The New York Times* (24 November 1988).
"A Conversation in Prague." *New York Review of Books* (12 April 1990): 14–22.
"A Bit of Jewish Mischief." *New York Times Book Review* 98 (7 March 1993): 1.
"The Ultimatum." *New Yorker* 71 (26 June, 3 July 1995): 114–127.
"Drenka's Men." *New Yorker* 71 (10 July 1995): 56–66.

Manuscripts

"A Coffin in Egypt." Third draft ms. The Philip Roth Collection, 28 October 1959.
"Introduction: *Goodbye, Columbus*, German Edition." The Philip Roth Collection.
"The Last Jew." Draft ms. The Philip Roth Collection.
"The Mistaken." Ms. The Philip Roth Collection.

The Philip Roth Collection. Manuscript Division of the Library of Congress, Washington D.C.

"The Sex Fiend." Ms. The Philip Roth Collection.

"Writing About Jews – Draft." The Philip Roth Collection.

Secondary Sources

Bibliographies

Baumgarten, Murray, and Barbara Gottfried. "Philip Roth." *Bibliography of American Fiction, 1919–1988*. Two volumes. Edited by Matthew J. Bruccoli and Judith S. Baughman. New York: Facts on File, 1991, vol. 2, pp. 429–431.

Leavey, Ann. "Philip Roth: A Bibliographic Essay (1984–1988)." *Studies in American Jewish Literature* 8 (fall 1989): 212–218.

Rodgers, Bernard F. *Philip Roth: A Bibliography*. New Jersey: Scarecrow Press, 1984.

Books

Baumgarten, Murray, and Barbara Gottfried. *Understanding Philip Roth*. Columbia: University of South Carolina Press, 1990.

Bloom, Harold, ed. *Philip Roth*. Modern Critical Views. New York: Chelsea House, 1986.

Cooper, Alan. *Philip Roth and the Jews*. Albany: State University of New York Press, 1996.

Halio, Jay L. *Philip Roth Revisited*. New York: Twayne, 1992.

Jones, Judith Paterson, and Guinevera A. Nance. *Philip Roth*. New York: Frederick Ungar, 1981.

Lee, Hermione. *Philip Roth*. London: Methuen, 1982.

McDaniel, John N. *The Fiction of Philip Roth*. Haddonfield, N.J.: Haddonfield House, 1974.

Meeter, Glenn. *Philip Roth and Bernard Malamud: A Critical Essay*. Columbia: University of Missouri Press, 1973.

Milbauer, Asher Z., and Donald G. Watson, eds. *Reading Philip Roth*. New York: St. Martin's Press, 1988.

Milowitz, Steven. *Philip Roth Considered: The Concentrationary Universe of the American Writer*. New York: Garland, 2000.

Pinsker, Sanford. *The Comedy That 'Hoits': An Essay on the Fiction of Philip Roth*. Columbia: University of Missouri Press, 1975.

———, ed. *Critical Essays on Philip Roth*. Boston: G. K. Hall, 1982.

Rodgers, Bernard E. *Philip Roth*. Boston: Twayne, 1978.

Searles, George J. *The Fiction of Philip Roth and John Updike*. Carbondale: Southern Illinois University Press, 1985.

Walden, Daniel, ed. *The Odyssey of a Writer: Rethinking Philip Roth*. Special issue of *Studies in American Jewish Literature* 8 (fall 1989).

Articles and Essays

Alter, Robert. "Defenders of the Faith." *Commentary* 84 (July 1987): 52–55.

Appelfeld, Aharon. "The Artist as a Jewish Writer." *Reading Philip Roth*. Edited by Asher Z. Milbauer and Donald G. Watson. New York: St. Martin's Press, 1988, pp. 13–16.

Beatty, Jack. "*The Ghost Writer*." *New Republic* (6 October 1979): 36–40.

Bell, Pearl K. "Roth and Baldwin: Coming Home." *Commentary* (December 1979): 72–74.

Bellow, Saul. "The Swamp of Prosperity." *Commentary* (July 1959): 77–79.

Berger, Alan L. *Crisis and Covenant: The Holocaust in American Jewish Fiction*. Albany: State University of New York Press, 1985, pp. 153–160.

Bilik, Dorothy Seidman. *Immigrant-Survivors*. Middletown, Conn.: Wesleyan University Press, 1981, pp. 11–13, 45, 191n.

Brent, Jonathan. "The Unspeakable Self: Philip Roth and the Imagination." *Reading Philip Roth*. Edited by Asher Z. Milbauer and Donald G. Watson. New York: St. Martin's Press, 1988, pp. 180–200.

Budick, Emily Miller. "The Haunted House of Fiction: Ghost Writing the Holocaust." *Common Knowledge* 5, no. 2 (fall 1996): 121–135.

Ezrahi, Sidra DeKoven. *By Words Alone: The Holocaust in Literature*. Chicago: University of Chicago Press, 1980.

———, Daniel Lazare, Daphne Merkin, et al. "Philip Roth's Diasporism: A Symposium." *Tikkun* 8, no. 3 (1993): 41–42.

Furman, Andrew. "The Ineluctable Holocaust in the Fiction of Philip Roth." *Studies in American Jewish Literature* 12 (1993): 109–122.

Gilman, Sander L. "The Dead Child Speaks: Reading *The Diary of Anne Frank*." *Studies in American Jewish Literature* 7 (spring 1988): 9–25.

Gittleman, Sol. "The Pecks of Woodenton, Long Island, Thirty Years Later: Another Look at 'Eli, the Fanatic.' " *Studies in American Jewish Literature* 8 (fall 1989): 138–142.

———. "Witnessing the Holocaust in American Literature: A Note to Bonnie Lyons." *Yiddish* 7, no. 4 (1990): 36–38.

Greenstein, Michael. "Ozick, Roth and Postmodernism." *Studies in American Jewish Literature* 10 (spring 1991): 54–64.

Halkin, Hillel. "How to Read Philip Roth." *Commentary* 97 (February 1994): 43–48.

Hendley, W. Clark. "An Old Form Revitalized: Philip Roth's *Ghost Writer* and the *Bildungsroman*." *Studies in the Novel* 16 (1984): 87–100.

Hirsch, David H. *The Deconstruction of Literature: Criticism after Auschwitz*. London: University Press of New England, 1991.

Howe, Irving. "Philip Roth Reconsidered." *Critical Essays on Philip Roth*. Edited by Sanford Pinsker. Boston: G. K. Hall, 1982, pp. 229–244.

Kellman, Steven G. "Philip Roth's *Ghost Writer*." *Comparative Literature Studies* 21 (1984): 175–185.

Kremer, S. Lillian. "Philip Roth (19 March 1933 –)." *Dictionary of Literary Biography*. Volume 173. *American Novelists since World War II, Fifth Series*. Edited by James R. Giles and Wanda H. Giles. Detroit: Gale Research, 1996, pp. 202–234.

———. "Philip Roth's Self-Reflexive Fiction." *Modern Language Studies* 28, no. 3 (1998): 57–72.

Lehmann, Sophia. " 'And Here [Their] Troubles Began': The Legacy of the Holocaust in the Writing of Cynthia Ozick, Art Spiegelman, and Philip Roth." *CLIO: A Journal of Literature, History, and the Philosophy of History* 28, no. 1 (fall 1998): 29–52.

Lowin, Joseph. "Philip Roth and the Novel of Redemption." *Jewish Book Annual* 47 (1989–1990): 83–98.

O'Donnell, Patrick. "The Disappearing Text: Philip Roth's *The Ghost Writer*." *Contemporary Literature* 24.3 (1983): 365–378.

Pinsker, Sanford. "Jewish-American Literature's Lost-and-Found Department: How Philip Roth and Cynthia Ozick Reimagine Their Significant Dead." *Modern Fiction Studies* 35, no. 2 (summer 1989): 223–235.

———. "Marrying Anne Frank: Modernist Art, the Holocaust, and Mr. Philip Roth." *Holocaust Studies Annual* 3 (1985): 43–58.

Quart, Barbara Koenig. "The Rapacity of One Nearly Buried Alive." *Massachusetts Review* 24 (autumn 1984): 590–608.

Ravvin, Norman. "Strange Presences on the Family Tree: The Unacknowledged Literary Father in Philip Roth's *The Prague Orgy*." *English Studies in Canada* 17, no. 2 (1991): 197–207.

Rubin, Derek. "Philip Roth and Nathan Zuckerman: Offenses of the Imagination." *Dutch Quarterly Review* 13, no.1 (1983): 42–54.

Rubin-Dorsky, Jeffrey. "Philip Roth's *The Ghost Writer*: Literary Heritage and Jewish Irreverence." *Studies in American Jewish Literature* 8, no. 2 (fall 1989): 168–185.

———. "Philip Roth and American Jewish Identity: The Question of Authenticity." *American Literary History* 13, no. 1 (2001): 79–107.

Shechner, Mark. "Philip Roth." *Critical Essays on Philip Roth*. Edited by Sanford Pinsker. Boston: G. K. Hall, 1982, pp. 117–132.

———. "The Road of Excess: Philip Roth." *After the Revolution: Studies in the Contemporary Jewish American Imagination*. Bloomington: Indiana University Press, 1987, pp. 196–242.

———. "Zuckerman's Travels." *American Literary History* (spring 1989): 219–231.

———. "Philip Roth." *Contemporary Jewish-American Novelists*. Edited by Joel Shatzky and Michael Taub. Westport, Conn.: Greenwood, 1997, pp. 335–354.

Shostak, Debra. " 'This Obsessive Reinvention of the Real': Speculative Narrative in Philip Roth's *The Counterlife*." *Modern Fiction Studies* 37 (summer 1991): 197–216.

Sokoloff, Naomi. "Imagining Israel in American Jewish Fiction: Anne Roiphe's *Lovingkindness* and Philip Roth's *The Counterlife*." *Studies in American Jewish Literature* 10 (spring 1991): 65–80.

Solotaroff, Theodore. "The Diasporist." *The Nation* (7 June 1993): 778–84.

Spargo, R. Clifton. "To Invent as Presumptuously as Real Life: Parody and the Cultural Memory of Anne Frank in Roth's *The Ghost Writer*." *Representations* 76 (fall 2001): 88–119.

Tintner, Adeline. "*The Prague Orgy*: Roth Still Bound to Henry James." *Midstream* 31 (December 1985): 49–51.

Trachtenberg, Stanley. "In the Egosphere: Philip Roth's Anti-Bildungsroman." *Papers on Language and Literature* 25, no. 3 (1989): 326–341.

Van Oostrum, Duco. "A Post Holocaust Jewish House of Fiction: Anne Frank's *Het Achterhuis* (The Diary of a Young Girl) in Philip Roth's *The Ghost Writer*." *Modern Jewish Studies* 9, nos. 3–4 (1994): 61–75.

Wilson, Matthew. "*The Ghost Writer*: Kafka, *Het Achterhuis*, and History." *Studies in American Jewish Literature* 10.1 (spring 1991): 44–53.

———. "Fathers & Sons in History: Philip Roth's *The Counterlife*." *Prooftexts* 11, no. 1 (January 1991): 41–56.

Wirth-Nesher, Hana. "The Artist Tales of Philip Roth." *Prooftexts* 3 (September 1983): 263–272.

———. "From Newark to Prague: Roth's Place in the American-Jewish Literary Tradition." *Reading Philip Roth*. Edited by Asher Z. Milbauer and Donald G. Watson. New York: St. Martin's Press, 1988, pp. 17–32.

Selected Interviews

Appelfeld, Aharon. *Beyond Despair: Three Lectures and a Conversation with Philip Roth*. Translated by Jeffrey M. Green. New York: Fromm International Publishing Corporation, 1994.

"Jewishness and the Younger Intellectuals." Symposium. *Commentary* (April 1961): 11–12.

"Symposium: Second Dialogue in Israel." *Congress Bi-Weekly* 30 (16 September 1963): 4–85.

Mangione, Jerry. *Philip Roth*. National Educational Television, 1966.

Finkielkraut, Alain. "The Ghosts of Roth." *Esquire* (September 1981): 92–97.

"Philip Roth Talks about His Work." *London Review of Books* 9 (5 March 1987): 7–9.

Machan, Linda. "Philip Roth Faces 'The Facts.' " *Boston Globe* (4 October 1988): 65.

Milbauer, Asher Z., and Donald G. Watson. "An Interview with Philip Roth." *Reading Philip Roth*. New York: St. Martin's Press, 1988.

Searles, George J., ed. *Conversations with Philip Roth*. Jackson: University of Mississippi Press, 1992.

Jerome Rothenberg

(1931–)

HILENE FLANZBAUM

JEROME ROTHENBERG has had an impressive career, one that has spanned over forty years, and one that grows increasingly important and influential with each generation. Always an innovator with respect to language, he has also been a leader in setting the political agenda for contemporary poets. His experimentation with style and language has brought him respect, and even reverence, from the avant garde of contemporary poets. In all areas, Rothenberg has appeared to be ahead of his time, rejecting the formal aesthetics of modernism before it was popular to do so, and discovering a vitality and political imperative in poetry at a time when the most critically acclaimed poets were insisting "that poetry makes nothing happen." As influential as his poetry has been, his additional roles as an anthologist, a canon-maker, a critic, and a cultural historian have made him appear prophetic and brought him almost a legendary status in American and international letters.

Biography

Born in New York City to Morris and Esther (Lichtenstein) Rothenberg, and educated at the City College of New York, Rothenberg published his first book of poetry in 1960, and at this writing has published over fifty books of poetry, most of which demonstrate his proclivity to work in experimental and innovative forms. Early in his career, Rothenberg began exploring alternative poetic structures, using found poetry and collage, and working on the development of experimental dialogues and narrative. He then combined these postmodern explorations with his interest in oral culture and the primitive languages of man. In his anthology *Technicians of the Sacred* (1968), he recovered long abandoned sites of poetry: picture poems, dreams and visions, and the scenarios of ritual events. From there, he rapidly moved on to studying American Indian poetry, collaborating with the Seneca to translate a series of Navajo horse blessings and editing *Shaking the Pumpkin: Traditional Poetry of the Indian North Americas* (1972). Around this time, Rothenberg's interest in Native Americans and other cultures that stressed the orality of poetry led to the founding of a magazine, *Alcheringa*, which he coedited from 1970 through 1976.

Shaking the Pumpkin and *Alcheringa* began Rothenberg's career as an editor and anthologist. In 1978 Rothenberg published *A Big Jewish Book: Poems and Other Visions of the Jews from Tribal Time to the Present*. Reconstructing oral traditions through sacred and secular poetry, this anthology provided a history of Jewish consciousness that emphasized the mystical side of the tradition; many of its works were newly translated or uncovered. In another groundbreaking anthology edited almost twenty years later, *Poems for the Millenium, The University of California Book of Modern and Postmodern Poetry: From Fin-de-Siecle to Negritude* (Vol. 1) (1995) and in the second volume, *From Postwar to Millenium* (1998), Rothenberg constructs a new poetic canon—one that values internationalism, political commitment, and radical experimentation with language.

In the 1960s, while Rothenberg devoted his poetry to studying the sounds and rhythms of Native American discourse, he was paying close attention to cultural particularities, origins, and natural idioms of speech. He labeled this poetry "ethnopoetics," a type of poetry that brought together poetic and anthropological consciousness. The first goal of this linkage was to translate archaic poetries; the second was to show that many of the concerns of contemporary culture appear in much earlier civilizations. Another major anthology appeared on this topic, *Symposium of the Whole: A Range of Discourse toward an Ethnopoetics* (1983), which he coedited with Diane Rothenberg. Clearly, ethnopoetics has been a major contribution to postwar American poetry, and is perhaps Rothenberg's single most noted accomplishment.

Using ethnopoetics, Rothenberg explored both the cultural myth and archetype of the Native American experience, but he also easily connected contemporary Jewish American culture to that of Native Americans. In fact, Rothenberg moves easily between these models, often interchanging the two identities. This could have been a politically dangerous technique, yet critics have extensively praised Rothenberg's ethnopoetics. Paula Gunn Allen writes: "Because Jerome Rothenberg understands his own origins, because he knows his fathers and how his being arises of/from theirs, he can accept and articulate his Seneca experience justly." It is possible to reverse this claim; that is, that Rothenberg's initial interest and success in describing Native American history and devastation led him to articulate the history and devastation of his own ancestors. Whatever the case, there can be no doubt that Rothenberg's descriptions of Jewish American culture are interwoven with his work on Native Americans.

According to Gary Pacernick, Rothenberg "has written the spiritual autobiography of his Jewish past in *Poland/1931*" (Pacernick, p. 31). The critic quotes Rothenberg's intention for the book as published in a 1974 interview: "to create through those poems an analogue, a presentation of the Eastern European Jewish world from which I had been cut off by birth, place, and circumstance, and to which I no longer have any way of returning, because it doesn't exist in that place any longer" (Pacernick, p. 32).

Rothenberg's most vivid descriptions of the experiences of Eastern European Jewish immigrants arise in tandem with the experience of the Native American. In one of his most successful and widely anthologized poems, "Cokboy I and II," Rothenberg writes "saddlesore I came / a jew among / the indians" (*Poland/1931*, New York: New Directions, 1974, p. 143). The term "Cokboy" evokes several things: first it is used to suggest an Eastern European mispronunciation of cowboy, thus satirizing the traditionally hostile relationship between cowboys and Indians; second, the term obviously suggests male genitalia. This suggestion is metaphorically accurate because "Cokboy II" especially takes up issues of transcultural intercourse and reproduction, or more precisely, miscegenation. The poem tells us that in this respect, Jews and Native Americans are alike because they have miscegenated their tribes into evisceration. An entire culture "marries" America. Interestingly enough, Rothenberg uses the Native American experience to highlight the Eastern European Jew's differences from an indigenous American culture, and to discuss how assimilation through intermarriage has worked on both ethnicities. It is, as Rothenberg claims in four recurring and consecutive lines in "Cokboy II," an "America[n] disaster" (p. 151). Both ethnic identities have been obliterated by the "Marriage of America" to their cultures and now the Cokboy "got nothing left to say" (p. 151). As Rothenberg said in "Ethnopoetics at the Millenium," a lecture he gave to the Modern Language Association in 1994, "Ethnopoetics focus[es] on ancient and autochthonous cultures (often under threat or long since blown away)." In these poems, the civilization of the Eastern European Jew is just as extinct as the Native American's.

In this discussion of "Cokboy," the reader can see how Rothenberg's ethnopoetics could be useful beyond Native-American discourse; it proved uniquely suited to the American 1970s, a decade in which many ethnic minorities became interested in uncovering their own cultural identities. Yet in a crucial way Rothenberg's devotion to ethnopoetics should not be confused with the more leisurely pursuit of one's roots that became popular at this time. For Rothenberg, ethnopoetics is a way of seeing and saving the world. He has explained that "A poetics for me is as personal (as distinguished from an imposed) theology might be for a person with a serious belief in God or a metaphysics for another kind of searcher after what is real or true or both." (*Ethnopoetics at the Millenium*, lecture to the Modern Language Association, 1994). Rothenberg believes that his identity is formed by the history of his ethnic culture.

More important to this discussion, however, is that in *Poland/1931*, Rothenberg focuses on describing the disappearance of Jewish cultural identity, which in that text occurs by assimilation. Once the poet begins to explore the disappearance of his culture, and to examine the fate of his own ancestral lineage, he discovers, as did so many Jewish Americans of Eastern European descent, that he did not have to delve too far before coming face to face with the Holocaust. As he explains in the introduction to *Khurbn and Other Poems* (1989), (Khurbn in Yiddish is "the destruction"), "those in my own family had died without a trace." One uncle, the poet continues, survived only long enough to shoot himself in the head when he heard about the murders of his wife and children. In this way, Rothenberg shows that Jewish ethnopoetics will always be saturated with the memory of the Holocaust. Rothenberg's eclectic interests, and his dedication to cultural idiosyncrasies and exploration of lineage all brought him quite naturally to an important discussion of the Holocaust.

In three collections *Poland/1931* (1969), *A Book of Testimony* (1971), and *Esther K. Comes to America* (1973), which have been aggregated in one volume titled *Poland/1931* (1974), Rothenberg adapts the methods he used to discuss Native American culture to describe his own. He discovers a unique Jewish sensibility by reemphasizing the Eastern European past of the large majority of Jewish Americans. This trilogy, which many critics believe contains Rothenberg's most important work, examines the impact of ethnicity, religion, and time on the formation of ethnic identity—and introduces the subject of the Holocaust.

While *Poland/1931* (1969) skillfully traces the idioms and customs of his ancestral lineage, it is much more than a personal narrative. What Rothenberg attempts is the reconstruction of an entire ancestral world for the Eastern European Jewish immigrant. Calling upon the Kabbala, Hasidism, and modern Jewish philosophers, and integrating them with the distinctive voices he has imagined from his past, *Poland/1931* might be considered the collective memory of an entire generation of Jewish Americans that descended from Eastern Europe. Although this story has been told before, Rothenberg's stylistics in this volume (and others) is hardly conventional. Through surreal, dark, and occasionally barbaric images, half-finished sentences, and random allusions split evenly between popular movies and Jewish mysticism, Rothenberg succeeds in presenting the consciousness of an entire generation of Jewish immigrants that was rapidly Americanizing. As that Americanization process took place, their memories of Poland were consolidated into lore.

For Rothenberg, then, the issue becomes the way that Jewish immigrants remember their native land. Despite the beautiful images that Rothenberg can summon ("& so we live without associations / in the past we live / nourishing incredible polands / lazy and alive remembering" "The Fish," *Poland/1931*, New Directions, p. 15), what he cannot avoid is the destruction soon to follow. That knowledge cannot be forgotten; no nostalgia for a "tender" Polish past will be possible. In many of the poems here, the beautiful images of Poland are undercut by images of death. Even a paean to "Beards" ends with the ominous line, "how many would die rather than have their beards cut?" (p. 19). This inevitable connection between Poland and death is the central motif in two of Rothenberg's volumes. After the Holocaust, it will simply not be possible to think of Poland without thinking about the virulent antisemitism and the obliteration of almost the entire Jewish population. In the poetry of *Poland/1931*, Rothenberg acknowledges this, but still seems determined to present that world as it once was—in plenitude.

In order to more fully examine Rothenberg's contribution to Holocaust literature, however, *Poland/1931* should be considered alongside *Khurbn* (1989). What binds these two books is memory: in both volumes, Rothenberg is doing more than narrating a story of someone else's experiences. He seems to remember a past that he never had, but seems to have inherited by the virtue of being Jewish. This method becomes much more prominent in *Khurbn*, where the reader can actually hear the voices of those about to be murdered. The pairing of these two volumes not only highlights the great loss engendered by the Holocaust, but also casts a large shadow on the earlier one. In the first, Rothenberg examines Poland at the height of its Jewish civilization; *Khurbn* focuses on that same civilization after World War II. Of all Rothenberg's work, *Khurbn* is his most complete document on the Holocaust.

In addition to ethnopoetics, Rothenberg has other theoretical proclivities that take him directly to the subject of the Holocaust: his interest in experimental forms and linguistic innovation. Rothenberg's dedication to stretching poetic forms beyond their conventional limits finds a formidable challenge when he tries to represent the Holocaust, a topic that has always been in the treacherous waters between language and representation.

In the introduction to *Khurbn*, Rothenberg responds to this challenge head on, claiming that the poetry in this volume is "an answer to the proposition—by Adorno and others—that poetry cannot or should not be written after Auschwitz" (*Khurbn*, New Directions, p. 4). Rothenberg knows that this frequently cited statement by the twentieth-century German critic, Theodor Adorno, has exercised a lasting hold on Jewish writers and critics. Rothenberg also certainly knew that Adorno had made this statement, not as an imperative to silence writers, but rather to question the philosophically complex relationship between morality and formal aesthetics in a work of art. Is what is beautiful automatically good? Is what is good beautiful? If certain formal properties of art are met, then should the piece be considered beautiful, and therefore "good," even if the content (or morality) of the piece is questionable?

What Adorno's statement tells us, and what is undoubtedly true, is that these considerations take on additional complexities when dealing with the subject of the Holocaust. For instance, if poetry by its very observance of formal properties is considered "beautiful," wouldn't that mean that a poem about the Holocaust could be beautiful? Experiencing beauty brings human beings satisfaction and stasis. No beauty, no satisfaction, no stasis, Adorno believed, should be drawn from the experience of the Holocaust. With this statement, Rothenberg would strongly concur, yet his agreement does not signal that one should be silent about the Holocaust. Rather, Rothenberg believes that poetry need not be beautiful; he begins "Nokh Aushvits (After Auschwitz)" with the line "the poem is ugly." A few lines later, he writes "no / not a moment's grace nor beauty to obstruct / whatever the age demanded / . . . or the poem / shit poured on wall & floor" (p. 18). "Whatever the age demanded" recalls Ezra Pound's defense of the unconventionality of modern poetry in "Hugh Selwyn Mauberley" (1919) where Pound wrote these famous lines: "The age demanded an image / for its accelerated grimace." Rothenberg, in fact, has been compared to Pound more than once. The poets share an interest in the primitive origins of poetry, and as critic Jonathan Cott said in the *New York Times Book Review*, both Pound and Rothenberg fought, or have been fighting, the "revolution of the word."

But if 1919, the year Pound wrote "Mauberly," demanded an image to match the age's pain, what does the post-Holocaust world require? And what does the post-Holocaust artist need to do to meet that requirement? It would seem to be much more. According to Rothenberg, the poet must fight "his rage for beauty must make a poem / so ugly it can drive out the other voices / like artaud's squawl the poem addressed / to ugliness must resist / even the artistry of death" ("Nokh Aushvits" [After Auschwitz], in *Khurbn & Other Poems*, New York: New Directions, 1983, p. 18). So the poet must resist beauty and render destruction. It should be noted that not only does Rothenberg continue to answer Adorno here, he enlarges upon an anti-modern doctrine of aesthetics; modernism assured readers that the artwork would organize the chaos of the world, and that "order" was beauty. In fact, the "rage for beauty" that Rothenberg summons invokes Wallace Stevens's "The Idea of Order at Key West," a central poem of the modernist tradition that similarly "rages for order" with the belief that establishing order establishes beauty.

Rothenberg defies order and beauty throughout *Khurbn*, even in the title of the volume itself. In the introduction to the text, Rothenberg explains his discomfort with the word Holocaust: "too Christian and too beautiful, too much smacking of a sacrifice. . . . The word with which we spoke of it was the Yiddish-Hebrew word Khurbn" (p. 3). Rothenberg also explains his method of writing *Khurbn* in this introduction; he writes it because he returns to the hometown of his parents, Ostrow-Mazowiecka.

> I hadn't realized . . . that the town was only fifteen miles from Treblinka, but when we went there (as we had to), there was only an empty field & the thousands of large stones that make up the memorial. . . . The absence of the living seemed to create a vacuum in which the dead—the dibbiks who had died before their time—were free to speak. It wasn't the first time I had thought of poetry as the language of the dead, but never so powerfully as now (p. 3).

Although these statements seem to be straightforward, in this formulation Rothenberg confronts yet another landmine in Holocaust studies by maintaining that the voices of the dead "speak through him" (pp. 3–4): "The poems that I first began to hear at Treblinka are the clearest message I have ever gotten about why I write poetry" (Preface in *Khurbn & Other Poems*, p. 4).

Such statements may at first strike us as just personal, and maybe a bit melodramatic, yet in casting his remarks this way, Rothenberg actually engages in yet another argument about the politics of Holocaust representation. The notion that only actual survivors can adequately recount the events of the Holocaust—or that only they have the right to tell the story—had long been a precept in Holocaust studies. Jewish American writers had, of course, not fully obeyed this commandment, much to the consternation of some, and from there the debate ensued. Interestingly enough, and quite possibly in response to these concerns, in *Khurbn* Rothenberg does not speak for the survivors, he speaks for the victims and therefore neatly sidesteps this argument. That distinction, of course, is largely theoretical, for Rothenberg, a nonsurvivor, is still writing about a taboo topic. However, he offers an original solution to the windy debate, as well as an eerily effective technique to render the event itself.

The poems in *Khurbn* recount many of the horrors of the Holocaust by using a method that might be compared to the dramatic monologue. Because Rothenberg is being "spoken through," each of these poems adopts the voice of someone who perished. In "Dos Oysleydkin" ("The Emptying"), for instance, the speaker narrates the liquidation of the ghetto: "at honey street in ostrova / where did the honey people go?" (p. 6). In the poems, the speaker continues to experience the worst the Nazis had to offer. In "Der Gilgul" ("The Possessed"), Rothenberg writes in the voice of an inmate of a concentration camp: "Each night another would hang himself. Airless boxcars. Kaddish. 'What will they do with us?' " (p. 16). Rothenberg fills *Khurbn* with the voices of the dead, writing in "Di Toytes Kloles" ("The Maledictions"): "Let his words be the poem & the poem be what you wouldn't say yourself" (p. 33).

While of great interest to scholars of Holocaust literature, *Khurbn* did not attract the kind of critical attention that *Poland/1931*, commonly perceived to be his major work in the Jewish American canon, did. Nor has *Poland/1931*, important as it remains to the Jewish American literary canon, achieved the status of ethnopoetics in the discussion of Rothenberg's great influence on his and future generations. Rothenberg is often, in fact, left out of discussions of Holocaust literature, as well as anthologies of Jewish American literature. The reasons for this stem partially from his great versatility: he cannot be easily assigned a label. Second, his writing is very difficult and theoretical, characteristics that often alienate readers. Third, when he challenged the tenets of modernism, he lost some powerful friends. Yet Rothenberg's stature has grown with the importance of postmodernism. As poets and literary critics have rejected many of the values of modernism, rejecting ideas of universality in favor of cultural specificity, ethnopoetics has been even more fervently embraced. Moreover, many of today's most critically esteemed poets cite Rothenberg's experimentation with language as a major influence on their own work. With these changes in evaluation, Rothenberg's reputation has continued to advance. While *Poland/1931* and *Khurbn* significantly contribute to the canon of Holocaust literature, Rothenberg's influence in the national and international poetry canons will continue to be felt for many generations.

Bibliography

Primary Sources

Esther K Comes to America. 1973.
Poland/1931. 1974.
The Pirke and the Pearl. 1975.
Gematria Twenty-Seven. 1977.
Abulafia's Circles. 1979.
Vienna Blood and Other Poems. 1980.
Pre-Faces and Other Writings. 1981.
Altar Pieces. 1982.
That Dada Strain. 1983.
Fifteen Flower World Variations: A Sequence of Songs from the Yaqui Deer Dance. 1985.
New Selected Poems 1970–1985. 1986.
Further Sightings and Conversations. 1989.
Khurbn and Other Poems. 1989.
The Lorca Variations, I–VIII. 1990.
Seven Flag Poems. 1990.
In a Time of War. 1993.
Gematria. 1993.
The Lorca Variations, 1 to 33. 1993.
An Oracle for Delfi. 1995.
Pictures of the Crucifixion. 1996.
Seeding and Other Poems. 1996.
A Paradise of Poets. 1999.
Poems for the Game of Silence, 1960–1970. 2000.
Quasha, George, and Jerome Rothenberg, editors. *America a Prophecy, A New Reading of American Poetry for Pre-Columbian Times to the Present*. New York: Random House, 1973.

Books edited by Jerome Rothenberg

Symposium of the Whole: A Range of Discourse Toward an Ethnopoetics, with Diane Rothenberg. Berkeley: University of California Press, 1983.
Technicians of the Sacred: A Range of Poetries from Africa, America, Asia, Europe & Oceania. New York: Doubleday-Anchor, 1968; Rev. ed. Berkeley: University of California Press, 1985.
A Big Jewish Book: Poems & Other Visions of the Jews from Tribal Times to the Present, with Harris Lenowitz. New York: Doubleday-Anchor, 1978; abridged and reprinted as *Exiled in the World*. Port Townsend, Washington: Copper Canyon Press, 1989.
Shaking the Pumpkin; Traditional Poetry of the Indian North Americas. New York: Doubleday-Anchor, 1972; Rev. ed. New York: Alfred van der Marck Editions, 1986; Albuquerque: University of New Mexico Press, 1991.
The Book, Spiritual Instrument. New York: Granary Books, Incorporated, 1996.
Revolution of the World: A New Gathering of American Avant Garde Poetry, 1914–1945. Cambridge: Exact Change, 1997.
From Fin-de-Siecle to Negritude. Vol. 1 of *Poems for the Millennium: The University of California Book of Modern & Postmodern Poetry*, with Pierre Joris. Berkeley: University of California Press, 1995.
From Postwar to Millennium. Vol. 2 of Poems for the millennium: The University of California Book of Modern & Postmodern Poetry. Berkeley: University of California Press, 1998.

Secondary Sources

Bartlett, Lee. *Talking Poetry: Conversations in the Workshop with Contemporary Poets*. Albuquerque: University of New Mexico Press, 1987.
Chametzky, Jules et al., ed. *Jewish American Literature: A Norton Anthology*. New York: Norton, 2001.
Cott, Jonathan. "Conversations with American Writers." *New York Times Book Review*, 13 January 1985.
Gitenstein, Barbara. *Apocalyptic Messianism in Contemporary Jewish American Poetry*. Binghamton: State University of New York Press, 1986.
Pacernick, Gary. "Jerome Rothenberg: Mythic Memory." In *Memory and Fire: Ten American Jewish Poets*. New York: Peter Land, 1989.
Zalenski, John. "Rothenberg's Continuing Revolution of the Word." *North Dakota Quarterly* 55, no. 4 (fall 1987): 202–216.

DAVID ROUSSET

(1912–1997)

COLIN DAVIS

IN THE YEARS immediately after World War II, French accounts of the German concentration camps tended to focus on their political significance rather than on the barbarities of genocide and the Final Solution. David Rousset was instrumental in establishing this tendency with two books written and published shortly after the end of the war, *L'Univers concentrationnaire* (The Concentrationary Universe) (1946) and *Les Jours de notre mort* (The Days of Our Death) (1947). The first, in barely more than one hundred pages, combines anecdotal memory and Marxist analysis to propose an interpretation of the camps as "the gangrene of a whole economic and social system" (*L'Univers concentrationnaire*, Paris: Minuit, 1965, p. 118; translations throughout by Colin Davis). The second extends this to over nine hundred pages, giving a detailed panorama of the concentrationary universe that expands upon and fills in the gaps of the earlier work. It is presented as a novel, roving freely between different locations and characters; but the author insists that there is no fabrication in the work: "The facts, the events, the characters are all authentic. It would have been puerile to invent when reality far exceeded the imaginary" (*Les Jours de notre mort*, Paris: Hachette, 1993; volume 1, p. 9).

Rousset was born on 18 January 1912. He studied philosophy and literature at the Sorbonne and became a teacher and socialist militant in the 1930s. Arrested as a member of the Resistance in October 1943, he was deported to Germany in 1944 and spent the rest of the war in Buchenwald, Porta Westphalia, Neuengamme, and the salt mines of Helmstedt. After the war he was involved in politics, founding the short-lived Rassemblement Démocratique Révolutionnaire with Jean-Paul Sartre and others in 1948, incurring the wrath of the French Communist Party for being one of the first to denounce the Stalinist gulags (forced labor camps), and later becoming a left-wing supporter of Charles de Gaulle. He died on 15 December 1997. He wrote and collaborated on a number of books on political issues, including the gulags, but he remains best known for his two books on the German camps, the first impressive for its concision and intellectual sweep, the second imposing for its determination to recount the camps in as much detail as possible.

Auschwitz or Buchenwald?

Les Jours de notre mort reads like a novel of initiation for both its characters and its readers. It begins with a mass hanging, then describes the deportation of a fresh convoy of prisoners; it goes on to chronicle in immense detail the experiences of a huge cast of characters and the structure of the concentration camp world; it recounts the final, anguished months of the camps, when the prisoners lived in fear of being executed en masse, and it culminates in their eventual liberation. The focus throughout is on the political organization in the camps, as the Communists struggle with common criminals for control of key positions in the camp administration so that they can ensure the survival of their own comrades. The solidarity of the Communists becomes a vital defense against the dangers of separation, demoralization, starvation, or brutalization at the hands of the SS and the common criminals. For this reason it is Buchenwald, with its highly developed political organization, rather than Auschwitz, which appears as the keystone for understanding the concentrationary system (Caron, p. 71). *L'Univers concentrationnaire* describes Buchenwald, Neuengamme, Sachsenhausen, and Dachau as examples of "the models of the 'normal' camps that underpin the concentrationary universe" (p. 34), whereas Auschwitz and Neue-Bremm are brutal exceptions. But even here, Rousset insists that the difference is of degree, not nature. Because the principal significance of the camps and the world they constitute is political, Buchenwald is more representative than Auschwitz; and by the same token the focus is on Communists rather than Jews as the prisoners whose experience provides the key for understanding the camps.

In recent years the Holocaust has tended to overshadow other aspects of the history of the camps. In this context, the relative lack of importance accorded the Jews in Rousset's work, as in the accounts of such politically like-minded survivors as Robert Antelme, is a salutary reminder that the camps were not originally or primarily set up for the purpose of genocide. Readers expecting accounts of selection and systematic extermination will be surprised by the relative scarcity of references to Jews. The political prisoners see them as a group apart, failing to achieve the solidarity of the Communists because of their lack of organization and common purpose. Prisoners of all nationalities are relieved when a new group of Jews arrive because they know the Jews will attract the worst treatment, which might otherwise fall on them. Even as liberation approaches and the Communists decide to protect the Jews and treat them as comrades, they remain suspicious and acknowledge the need to discipline them if they do not fall into line. Although Rousset certainly does not endorse any form of antisemitism, the Jews appear as if from a different universe:

> They come from the East. They left Auschwitz weeks earlier. They don't say much. They have strange eyes. Martin and I stayed a long time, watching them. In their silence, they evoke a world even more terrible than ours. They bear the mark of the Beast: terror in their features, in their gestures, in their eyes. Bodies saturated with terror (vol. 2, pp. 529–530).

In moments such as this, it becomes apparent that the Buchenwald-centered interpretation of the camps is not exhaustive, despite the enormous length and detail of *Les Jours de notre mort*. Passages of the book are set in Auschwitz, which cannot be entirely assimilated to the politically inspired perspectives of the novel. But except in rare moments, Rousset's account of the camps focuses on political struggle rather than racial persecution. It is only through the political optic that the camps can be understood and survival becomes possible.

Making Sense

What is perhaps most surprising about *L'Univers concentrationnaire* and *Les Jours de notre mort*, given that they describe the terrible conditions in which prisoners lived and died, and given how close the books are to the events they describe, is that they appear surprisingly unaffected by the traumatic nature of the experiences they recount. Curiously placid, they oscillate between anecdotal narrative and broad interpretation of the world of the camps. The camps form a structured universe with its own laws, which Rousset explicates at length. Crucial here is that the experience of Buchenwald does not entail, as it did for other survivors, a catastrophe for Rousset's beliefs and sense of self. Preexisting aesthetic and ideological frameworks continue to provide the means to contain and to explain experience. In *L'Univers concentrationnaire* Rousset refers persistently to literary models that make the concentrationary world intelligible. The epigraph is taken from Alfred Jarry's *Ubu enchaîné* (1900), introducing from the beginning reference to Jarry's grotesque, cruel, and violent character, Ubu. Subsequently, it is suggested that Ubu is more than a simple point of comparison; he provides a model for the world into which the prisoners are plunged. The camps are "of ubuesque inspiration" (p. 10), a chapter of the book is entitled "Les Ubuesques" (The Ubuesques), and the SS are described as worshipers of an "Ubu-God" (p. 71). Other literary references offer the reader a means of understanding the camps and their inhabitants. One prisoner is described as "a Shakespearean character"; another roams through "Dantesque corridors" (p. 27). This is "a world like Céline's with Kafkaesque echoes" (p. 43), in which Ubu and Kafka have become "material components of the world" (p. 120).

These are references to a world that is hellish, violent, senseless, and cruel. They also serve, however, to give the camps a point of comparison outside themselves, thus anchoring them in a culture shared by readers who did not experience them directly. Here there is none of, for example, Elie Wiesel's impassioned insistence that the camps are beyond comparison and comprehension, that they bring to light the inadequacy of preexisting cultural, ideological, philosophical, or theological norms. On the contrary, Rousset offers a world different from ours, but nevertheless comparable to it. He describes how life has begun to mirror art; and although the result may be a Kafkaesque nightmare, it is somehow less nightmarish for being described as Kafkaesque. Cultural paradigms still work; they are capable of offering a means of holding together the fragments of experience in something like a meaningful whole. Although the victims of the camps are described as "separated from others by an experience impossible to transmit" (*L'Univers concentrationnaire*, p. 117), the thrust of Rousset's writing is to show that the truth of the camps can be known and communicated. There are no pieties about the unspeakable here. This affirmation of the value of art explains the presentation of *Les Jours de notre mort* as a novel. The validity of literary form has not been destroyed. The ambitions of the text are panoramic, so that each of its parts contributes to the fuller picture that gradually emerges. Rousset does not claim to give a stenographic transcription of words and thoughts; rather he aims through fiction to attain the truth behind the detail: "The words convey the anxieties that existed and that have been kept in memory, without worrying about the manner in which mortal lips formulated them at that time" (vol. 1, p. 9).

Rousset reaffirms a faith in the continuing pertinence of fiction and of established cultural models. Literature helps to make the camps intelligible by giving structure to individual experience and subsuming it under the banner of more general truths. Literary representation is tantamount to a promise of meaning; it thus becomes, for both the prisoner and the author, part of a strategy of survival. The prisoners who are most at risk are the ones whose suffering seems to them to be groundless and meaningless: "All of them were in a bad state. They had nothing to hold on to. Things got dislocated in their heads, and in the camps that was the end" (*L'Univers concentrationnaire*, p. 41). To survive means to understand. The camps are thus consistently presented not as scenes of senseless suffering, but as material to be interpreted. In this context, the maintenance of intellectual structures from before the war is as vital as food and water. Seeing the camps as bearing a meaning that will be useful and usable after the war becomes the very condition that makes survival possible:

> Since Buchenwald, continually, I had attempted to understand, to observe scrupulously (and the constant thought that I was living an exceptional experience, full to bursting with creative lessons, made a huge contribution to my physical and moral resistance), to form close links with the German communists, so to prepare, thanks to this cordial cohabitation and to this daily, necessarily sincere appreciation . . . a climate favorable for a shared political analysis after the war: our experience of the camps must be of help to us. For one and for all, in order to construct the socialist United States of Europe (vol. 2, pp. 78–79).

Literature helps ensure the transmissibility of experience, but the key to interpretation here is political. The solidarity of the Communists in Buchenwald and other camps strengthens their chances of survival both physically and intellectually. They help each other avoid the worst transports and obtain less hazardous jobs or extra rations; they also encourage each other to cling to prewar political beliefs, which sustain them. The lengthy political discussions of *Les Jours de notre mort* record the continuing endeavor to refine a materialist interpretation of the concentrationary world. We learn about the history of the camps, the political and legal conditions that produced them and within which they evolved, and the economic and social organization within them. The camps are both a world apart—a universe or a planet, as Rousset repeatedly suggests—and a phenomenon with clear lessons for the world outside. Fascism is "the expression of degenerate capitalism" (vol. 1, p. 368); the oppression and survival of the Communists are part of their ongoing struggle against capitalism. Understanding the camps entails placing them within their proper political context and grasping their universal significance. The strength of the Communists, and their advantage over other prisoners, resides in their solidarity and their confidence that the collective struggle against the SS has a meaning that surpasses and makes sense of individual suffering.

The Avoidance of Trauma

For Rousset and his comrades, then, the Marxist paradigm that served before the war has lost none of its validity. Indeed, the camps confirm the truth of the beliefs for which they were deported. Although individual selves die or lose faith, there is here no generalized crisis of the self or of belief. This confidence in intelligibility helps the Communists survive and remain so untraumatized. Critics of concentration camp literature have sometimes avoided the trauma of the material by finding in it lessons and reasons for hope that the texts themselves barely support. Lawrence Langer has written powerfully about the "culture of consolation" that leads one to find prospects of value and redemption where none survive (Langer, pp. 9–11). Rousset's writing shows how this avoidance of trauma is also at work within concentration camp literature itself. There is suffering, but no fundamental questioning of the structures of identity and belief that sustain the individual. At the end of *L'Univers concentrationnaire* Rousset records the dignity and courage of his comrades and insists that, despite everything, "The balance is not negative" (p. 119). Others would emerge from the camps with the sense that they had left behind an essential part of themselves, that they had in some sense died despite their physical survival. One thinks for example of Elie Wiesel's *La Nuit*, which ends with the narrator looking in a mirror and seeing a corpse; or of Jorge Semprun, whose novels often enact the death he escaped. In this context, Rousset's works are shocking for the positive spin they put on the concentrationary experience. Values are maintained, lessons are learned, dignity is reaffirmed, solidarity triumphs, and at the end the writer discovers the most surprising thing of all—health, and a joy in living:

> It is still too soon to draw up the positive balance of the concentrationary experience, but from now on it's proving to be rich. A dynamic realization of the power and the beauty of the fact of living itself, brutal, entirely stripped of all superstructures, of living even through the worst crises or the most serious setbacks. A sensual freshness of joy constructed on the most complete knowledge of ruin and, in consequence, a hardening in action, a stubbornness in resolve, in short a greater and more intensely creative health (p. 119).

This astonishing cheerfulness is made possible by Rousset's belief in his ability to grasp, to encapsulate, and to communicate the truth of individual and collective experience from a secure Marxist perspective. Writing itself becomes bound up with the avoidance of trauma, as the future author of *Les Jours de notre mort* begins, in discussion with a fellow prisoner, to plan the book he will one day write:

> Better still, by becoming an attentive listener, Martin helped me to come to a clearer understanding of our concentrationary adventure. I thought in front of him. Together we planned a book, a book I was to write, once I was free again, if death didn't come first. We discussed the order of chapters, we examined the subject that was reworked every day. . . . I brought back from these brief moments an exultation in life, a taste for creation, a feeling of power, which was in defiance of all the humiliations we suffered (vol. 2, pp. 229–30).

Here, the links between comradeship, understanding, writing, and the avoidance of trauma emerge clearly. Each feeds into the other, and the future book (the book one is reading) serves as a source of joy, a reason to live, and a shield against the degradations of the camp. Here at least, literature is a defense against the most horrific aspects of experience; and this function is reinforced because of its pretensions to authenticity and truth. Although *Les Jours de notre mort* is "constructed with the technique of a novel," it contains no "fabulation"; although it does not purport to record literally what people said and thought, it claims to be faithful to its subject (vol. 1, p. 9). The fictional element here is not a distortion, an error, or a lie, rather the distillation of the truth within and beyond the anecdotal.

This is, however, not the only view of the processes of fictionalization suggested in *Les Jours de notre mort*. Rousset describes Russian prisoners who tell stories in which it is impossible to discern the degree of truth (vol. 2, p. 101). Even in his own case, he admits the impossibility of distinguishing between reality and deliberate mystification (vol. 2, p. 79). More revealing still is the case of Pierre, a prisoner who protects himself by living his life as if it were a story: "He combated his terror by recounting to himself the drama in its future version for adolescents . . . Pierre still only thought (it was his way of strengthening his resistance) from the inside of his own story" (vol. 2, pp. 332–333). Here, the defensive function of storytelling is primary. Pierre recounts his own story to himself as he lives it, in order to confer on it the coherence and grandeur of literature. Fiction is thus a strategy of resistance against terror. It is not a vehicle of truth, and its effectiveness as a defense is not assured because it portrays things as they really are; on the contrary, it is effective because it distracts from the present terror by placing it within a broader imaginary frame.

One way of understanding this alternative view of fiction is by distinguishing between the reality Rousset aims to portray and the Real in the sense of the French psychoanalyst Jacques Lacan. The Real is a traumatic kernel beyond representation and symbolization, which, if encountered, may annihilate the structures of meaning and identity. Literature, in *Les Jours de notre mort*, appears as a means of encapsulating reality, but fiction emerges also as the avoidance of the Real. This then raises the question: Might Rousset's account of the reality of the camps be the fictional ruse that enables him to sidestep the trauma of the Real? Might Pierre be the author's self-portrait, as he contains the terror of the camps within a frame that gives it sense and coherence? The effectiveness of the narrative as a defense would thus be attributable to its status as fiction, rather than its truth. What guards the author of *L'Univers concentrationnaire* and *Les Jours de notre mort* against trauma is that the camps make sense. It may be that the sense they made was in part a fiction or an error. Certainly, Rousset's belief that the concentration camps were only intelligible in the context of capitalism turned out to be disastrously wrong, and after the war he made enemies of former Communist friends by denouncing concentration camps wherever they occurred, including in the Soviet Union. But, however erroneous, the intelligibility found in the camps by the political deportees was nonetheless effective in ensuring their solidarity and survival. Rousset's distinctive contribution to the literature of the camps lies in his refusal to be panicked by their enormity and horror. For him, the camps offer lessons to be learned. Political and aesthetic paradigms still work, and the present—however traumatic—can still be understood using the tools of the past, which point in turn toward action for the future.

Bibliography

Primary Sources

L'Univers concentrationnaire (The Concentrationary Universe). 1946.

Les Jours de notre mort (The Days of our Death). 1947.

Le Pitre ne rit pas (The Clown Doesn't Laugh). 1948.

Pour la vérité sur les camps concentrationnaires (For the Truth on the Concentration Camps). With Théo Bernard and Gérard Rosenthal. 1990.

La Société éclatée (The Shattered Society). 1973.

Sur la guerre (On War). 1987.

Secondary sources

Bataille, Georges. "Reflections on the Executioner and the Victim." *Yale French Studies* 79 (1991): 15–19.

Brossa, Alain, et al. *Lignes*. Paris: Léo Scheer, 2000.

Caron, David. "Deux récits, deux exigences: *Les Jours de notre mort* de David Rousset et *La Nuit* d'Elie Wiesel." *Nottingham French Studies* 36, no. 2 (1997): 71–82.

Gartland, Patricia. "Three Holocaust Writers: Speaking the Unspeakable." *Critique: Studies in Contemporary Fiction* 25, no. 1 (1983): 45–56.

Langer, Lawrence. *Admitting the Holocaust*. New York: Oxford University Press, 1995.

TADEUSZ RÓŻEWICZ

(1921–)

DOROTA GLOWACKA

TADEUSZ RÓŻEWICZ IS one of Poland's best-known and most innovative poets and playwrights of the postwar period. He belongs to the first generation that grew up in free Poland, after the country gained independence in 1918, and whose optimism was shattered by World War II. The experience of war and the disintegration of fundamental values in its wake have been central in shaping Różewicz's worldview and his literary itinerary.

Partisan, Poet, Individualist

Tadeusz Różewicz was born on 9 October 1921, in Radomsko, the son of Stefania (from the Gelbard family) and Władysław Różewicz, who worked as a minor clerk. During the war, he completed a clandestine military school and joined the Polish Home Army, the armed forces of the anti-Communist Polish government in exile, where, from 1943 to 1945, he was a member of an underground detachment. The volume *Echa leśne* (Echoes from the Forest), written for his fellow partisans under the pseudonym "Satyr" and distributed through a makeshift secret press, was a poetic record of his experiences in the forest as a soldier.

Różewicz never associated with a particular literary school or movement, choosing the life of artistic solitude. For many years he lived in Gliwice, a mining town in Silesia, away from major cultural centers. In 1968 he moved to Wrocław, one of Poland's largest cities, where at the age of eighty-one he still resided, although he stood aloof from mainstream cultural and political establishments.

Różewicz's works have been translated into more than forty languages. He received numerous honorary doctorates and awards, including state awards and literary prizes in Poland and abroad, and he was nominated for the Nobel Prize for literature several times. His honors include the Polish Minister of Culture and Art Award (1962), the Polish State Prize for Literature (1966), the Poet's Award (1971), the Austrian State Prize (1981), the Polish Cross of Merit (1996), and the Nike 2000, the most prestigious Polish literary award, presented annually for the best book of the preceding year.

The Voice of the Lost Generation of World War II

Różewicz debuted in 1947 with a collection of poems titled *Niepokój* (Anxiety), soon followed by *Czerwona rękawiczka* (A Red Glove) in 1948. The poems in both volumes speak to the situation of the entire generation of survivors (*ocalonych*) and convey their profound sense of moral crisis after the catastrophe that swept away all the metaphysical foundations of Western civilization. In the poem "The Survivor" (in *The Survivor and Other Poems*, translated by Magnus J. Krynski and Robert A, Maguire, Princeton, N.J.: Princeton University Press. 1976), Różewicz writes:

> I am twenty four
> led to slaughter
> I survived
> These labels are empty and synonymous
> man and beast
> love and hate
> friend and foe
> light and dark (p. 7).

His writings have always been iconoclastic with respect to the Polish cult of heroic martyrdom. Instead, they reveal the prosaic truth about the war: the struggle for survival, the primitive fear, and the crude physiology of the body brutalized by violence, which often affect man's moral choices and integrity. In the poem

"Syn marnotrawny" (Prodigal Son), naturalistic images of death and physical decay correspond to the horror and moral anxiety experienced by a witness:

I saw the earth
that through the rain
of tears and blood
shone
with the cadaverous light
of a cooling corpse (quoted in Burkot, p. 57, translation by Dorota Glowacka).

Many of the early poems are written in the form of a dark lament or elegy, conveying the unspeakable pain of mourning for the dead, as in "Mother of Hanged Men":

with leaden feet she paces
the concrete streets
the mother of the hanged
the moon around her neck. (*They Came to See a Poet,* p. 28).

These sentiments, as well as Różewicz's vision of postwar devastation devoid of tragic pathos, are akin to Tadeusz Borowski's arid "landscape after the battle," in which the belief in the sanctity of human life has been taken away and the entire heritage of Western values has been revealed as a deception. Rather than victimization or righteous indignation about the crimes perpetrated upon his nation, Różewicz's survivor feels a sense of responsibility for the horror, disturbingly blurring the line between the victim and the executioner:

I am twenty years old
I am a murderer
I am an instrument
blind as an axe
in the hands of an executioner ("Lament," from *"The Survivor" and Other Poems,* p. 5).

Despite total moral devastation, however, the poet insists on the need for a new order and sees poetry as a possible ground where primary meanings can be rediscovered.

Holocaust Remembrance

With other Polish writers of the postwar period (such as Jan Józef Szczepański, Adolf Rudnicki, or Zofia Nałkowska), Różewicz shares a stunned horror at the persecution and extermination of Polish Jews. Several poems (for example, "Stone Imagination," "She Looked at the Sun," "Warning") as well as short stories from the volumes *Opadły liście z drzew* (Leaves Fell from Trees, 1955), *Przerwany egzamin* (An Interrupted Exam, 1960), and *Wycieczka do muzeum* (An Excursion to the Museum, 1966), contain vignettes describing Jewish suffering and death, the horror of which cancels the meaning of "victory" and the joy of liberation:

in the eye of a passing stranger
who has survived the war
darkness pierces
light and joy
through the sun I see
a black sewer
a pit dank fetid
at the bottom
a little Jewish girl
who on liberation day
came out of hiding
after many years
she looked at the sun
stretched out her arms went blind ("She Looked at the Sun," from *"The Survivor" and Other Poems,* p. 43; translation modified).

The poems "Massacre of the Boys" and "Pigtail," from the volume *Pięć poematów* (Five Poems, 1950), often anthologized in collections of Holocaust literature, are a moving tribute to the children who perished in death camps:

In huge chests
clouds of dry hair
of those suffocated
and a faded plait
a pigtail with a ribbon
pulled at school
by naughty boys ("Pigtail" from *They Came to See a Poet,* p. 43).

The sparse, concrete images, uncluttered by metaphor, already pose questions about the nature of Holocaust memory, insisting on the human, individual dimension of the Holocaust death and warning against the anonymity, depersonalization, and moral vacuity of rites of remembrance. This theme is especially pronounced in a chilling short story, "Wycieczka do muzeum" (An Excursion to the Museum, 1959), a reflection on the Auschwitz death camp, which in 1948 was turned into a state museum. Stanisław Burkot (p. 143) points out that the processions of the condemned to the gas chambers, as described with macabre precision by Borowski (in *This Way for the Gas, Ladies and Gentlemen*), are paralleled in Różewicz's story by a steady stream of tourists, turning the horror into a grotesque spectacle and the memory of the dead into classifications of inanimate objects. Narrated as a cacophony of voices—conversations between the tourists and fragments of texts recited by the guides—the memory of horror becomes the object of an empty and monotonous ritual. The tourists at Auschwitz are either indifferent (even bored) or driven by the curiosity for snuff shows: " 'Where is the hair? They said there was hair, and I don't see any hair. Ignac, do you know where the hair is, and the prostheses?' 'What do you need the prostheses and the hair for?' " (in *Proza*, Kraków: Wydawnictwo Literackie, 1990, p. 182). The concentration camp deaths are a spectacle to be consumed by the ravenous masses (and one of the visitors complains, "Man, I'm hungry. Maybe they'll buy us some dinner here," p. 189). The story is an unsparing, even farcical, reflection on the culture of ritualistic memorialization stripped of meaning.

Later Works on the Holocaust

In the late twentieth-century, Różewicz returned to Holocaust motifs, lending his voice to the discussion in contemporary Poland about the place and significance of the extermination of the Polish Jews in Polish history and culture and about the meaning of this atrocity for the world at large. In his last play, *Pułapka* (The Trap, 1979), Różewicz reinvents the life of Franz Kafka and imagines him and his family among Holocaust victims. In a long poem, *"recycling"* (1998), he ponders questions of global amnesia, an amnesia that has been reinforced rather than prevented by mass production and commercialization of the Holocaust ("on her head / recently shaved for the movie / she sports a smart crew cut"; from *recycling*, (translated by Barbara Plebanek and Tony Howard, Todmorden, U.K.: Arc, 2001, p. 31); the scandalous revelations about the Nazi gold in Swiss and Swedish banks ("gold laundered in Europe and America / erupts in stains / bleeds"; *recycling*, p. 35), Holocaust denial ("but the Holocaust never happened / it was dreamed up by jewish / usurers bankers and communists / in league with the gypsies"; (p. 41), and the eruption of antisemitic sentiments: "you can read more and more on the walls / of our towns slogans in polish 'gas the jews' and in german '*jude raus*' / just thoughtless youths / just naughty boys children"; (p. 38–39). The theme of his 2001 volume, *Nożyk profesora* (Professor's Knife), is announced by the illustration, on the back cover, of the monument to the victims of the Holocaust at Yad Vashem. The collection is a poetic reminiscence on the *Shoah* dedicated to Różewicz's life-long friend Mieczysław Porębski, a prominent art historian and a survivor of Auschwitz. Różewicz continues to insist on the indelible place of the past in the present, and says of his work: "I throw a bridge that connects the past with the future" (*Nożyk profesora* (Professor's Knife), Wrocław: Wydawnictwo Dolnośląskie, 2001, p. 7).

"To Create Poetry After Auschwitz"

In "I Did Espy a Marvelous Monster" (from *Conversation with a Prince and Other Poems*, translated by Adam Czerniawski, London: Anvil Press, 1982), Różewicz announces, matter-of-factly: "at home a task / awaits me: / To create poetry after Auschwitz" (p. 185). Aware of the poet's paradoxical position between speech and silence, he ponders Theodor Adorno's famous dictum that to create poetry after Auschwitz would be barbarous. Aesthetics, the discourse of beautiful lies, has proven incapable of conveying the moral and philosophical dilemmas of the new times. The motif of death—brutal and direct—is intertwined with questions about the death of poetry, and the impasse of artistic practice arises from the poet's traumatic encounter with the atrocities of war. The heritage of war in Poland, contaminated by death, cannot be converted into aesthetic notions.

Różewicz, often dubbed an antipoet, stubbornly rejects both classical poetic forms and the legacy of modernist avant-gardes, aware of their insufficiency to describe the existential condition of man "after Auschwitz." At the same time, Różewicz, perhaps the most prolific contemporary Polish writer, believes in the poet's unceasing task to continue reinventing language—in the face of "nothing." In the search for a new idiom, he blurs the line between poetic and nonpoetic experience, creating a reticent, blunt, and prosaic "poetics of the rubbish heap," while his typical protagonist speaks in the voice of an anonymous, simple man, the very antithesis of the Polish romantic hero. The raw texture of his poetry, which critics have called "naked" or "somatic" poetry, conveys the desire to approach the unspeakable by exhausting language, stripping it from the layers of words and concepts.

Różewicz presents the tension between language's inadequacy to describe reality and the poet's task to reinvent the world in language as a fissure between the poet and the world. His kaleidoscopic collages, strewn with counterpoint and contrast, disclose poetry as a site of ontological struggle where meanings are created and dismantled at the same time. Różewicz's deceptively simple poetry is deeply self-reflective, revealing the author's extensive study of contemporary philosophers, especially Karl Jaspers, Bertrand Russell, Ludwig Wittgenstein, and Martin Heidegger.

For Różewicz, poetry is acting and the words are facts: the poet is morally responsible for what he creates. Despite a notorious absence of didacticism in his poetry, he is often described by critics as an uncompromising moralist. In "Beyond Words," he writes:

Blood-smeared
what are you piecing together
what is your burden
I am piecing together words
I carry my time (*They Came to See a Poet,* p. 59).

A poet is a witness, and his craft an unceasing vigil. In Różewicz's poems from the 1950s, the lyrical protagonist often speaks in the voice of the camp victim as in the poem "Równina" (Flat Country): "I am a man / marked with a number for slaughter" (quoted in Drewnowski, p. 112). At the same time, the task of "poetry after Auschwitz" is to remind us that we must not relieve ourselves from the responsibility for the horror:

little children who offered bouquets of flowers
are guilty
lovers are guilty
guilty are poets
guilty are those who ran away
and those who stayed
those who were saying yes
those who were saying no
and those who said nothing
the dead are taking stock of the living
the dead will not rehabilitate us ("Posthumous Rehabilitation," in *Conversation with a Prince,* p. 65).

In its nature, therefore, poetry is ethical; by producing an existential shock, by "doing" rather than producing aesthetic experiences, poetry constantly thwarts the desire for comfort and forgetfulness.

Różewicz's courage and tenacity in revealing national stereotypes, debunking social myths, and shattering familiar metaphors (the traits that also bring to mind S. I. Witkiewicz [Witkacy] and Witold Gombrowicz) are perhaps unparalleled in Polish literature. He has been unrelenting in his assaults on the taboos of Polish literature, and from the beginning of his career he has been a target of attacks and the focus of a quarrel in literary criticism. He has been accused of nihilism, cynicism, antipatriotism, insult, and even high treason. In a way, public and critical reactions to Różewicz's work have always been a litmus test of changing moods, tensions, and ideological struggles in postwar Poland. Similarly, his popularity and even rise to stardom in his native country at the end of the twentieth century reflected changing sensibilities in a nation which was dramatically confronting the ghosts of its wartime past. The Nike 2000 award for his 1999 volume *Matka odchodzi* (Mother Departs) was thus a belated—and well deserved—recognition of Różewicz's preeminent place in Polish postwar culture.

Bibliography

Primary Sources in Polish

Niepokój (Anxiety). 1947. Poems.
Czerwona rękawiczka (A Red Glove). 1948. Poems.
Pięć poematów (Five Poems). 1950. Poems.
Równina (Flat Country). 1954. Poems.
Opadły liście z drzew (Leaves Fell from Trees). 1955. Short stories.
Srebrny kłos (A Silver Ear of Corn). 1955. Poems.
Formy (Forms). 1958. Poems.
Przerwany egzamin (An Interrupted Exam). 1960. Short stories.
Rozmowa z księciem (Conversation with a Prince). 1960. Poems.
Et in Arcadia ego. 1961. Poems.
Głos anonima (The Anonymous Voice). 1961. Poems.
Grupa Laokoona (Laokoon). 1961. Play.
Nic w płaszczu Prospera (Nothing Dressed in Prospero's Cloak). 1962. Poems.
Świadkowie czyli nasza mała stabilizacja (Witnesses; or, Our Little Stabilization). 1962. Play.
Akt przerywany (The Interrupted Act). 1964. Play.
Śmieszny staruszek (A Funny Old Man). 1964. Play.
Twarz (The Face). 1964. Poems.
Wyszedłz domu (Gone Out). 1965.
Wycieczka do muzeum (An Excursion to the Museum). 1966. Short Stories.
Przyrost naturalny (Birth-Rate). 1967. Play.
Spaghetti i miecz (Spaghetti and the Sword). 1967. Play.
Twarz trzecia (The Third Face). 1968. Poems.
Regio. 1969. Poems.
Śmierćw starych dekoracjach (Death in the Old Sets). 1970. Novella.
Przygotowanie do wieczoru autorskiego (Preparations for a Poetry Reading). 1971. Prose.
Do piachu (Six Feet Under). 1972. Play.
Białe małżeństwo (White Marriage). 1973. Play.
Odejście głodomora (Hunger Artist Departs). 1976. Play.
Duszyczka (Animula). 1977. Prose.
Próba rekonstrukcji (An Attempt at Reconstruction). 1978. Prose.
Pułapka (A Trap). 1979. Play.
Tarcza z pajęczyny (The Cobweb Shield). 1980. Prose.
Na powierzchni poematu i w środku (On the Surface of the Poem and Inside). 1983. Poems.
Echa leśne (Echoes from the Forest). 1985. Poems.
Proza (Prose Works). 1990.
Płaskorzeźba (Forms in Relief). 1991. Poems.
Nasz starszy brat (Our Elder Brother). 1992. Poems.
Zawsze fragment. Recycling. (Always the Fragment. Recycling). 1998. Poems.
Matka odchodzi (Mother Departs). 1999. Poems and prose.
Nożyk profesora (Professor's Knife). 2001. Poems.

Primary Sources in English

Faces of Anxiety. Translated by Adam Czerniawski. 1969.
The Card Index and Other Plays. Translated by Adam Czerniawski. 1970.
Selected Poems. Translated by Adam Czerniawski. 1976.
The Survivor and Other Poems. Bilingual edition. Translated by Magnus J. Krynski and Robert A. Maguire. 1976.
Conversation with a Prince and Other Poems. Translated by Adam Czerniawski. 1982.

They Came to See a Poet. Translated by Adam Czerniawski. 1991.

Forms in Relief and Other Works. Bilingual edition. Translated by Richard Sokoloski. 1994.

Reading the Apocalypse in Bed. Translated by Adam Czerniawski, Barbara Plebanek, and Tony Howard. 1998.

recycling. Translated by Barbara Plebanek and Tony Howard. 2001.

Secondary Sources

Błoński, Jan. "Szkice do portretu współczesnego." In *Poeci i inni* (Poets and Others). Kraków: Wydawnictwo Literackie, 1956.

Burkot, Stanisław. *Tadeusz Różewicz*. Warsaw: Wydawnictwa Szkolne i Pedagogiczne, 1987.

Drewnowski, Tadeusz. *Walka o oddech: O pisarstwie Tadeusza Różewicza* (A Struggle for Breath: On the Writings of Tadeusz Różewicz). Warsaw: Wydawnictwa Artystyczne i Filmowe, 1990.

Filipowicz, Halina. *The Laboratory of Impure Forms: The Plays of Tadeusz Różewicz*. New York: Greenwood, 1991.

Guderian-Czaplińska, Ewa, and Elżbieta Kalemba-Kasprzak. *Zobaczyć poetę: Materiały konferencji "Twórczość Tadeusza Różewicza." UAM Poznań, 4–6.11.1991* (To See a Poet: Proceedings of the Conference "The Work of Tadeusz Różewicz"). Poznań: Zakład Teatru i Filmu IFP UAM. Wydawnictwo WIS, 1993.

Kisiel, Marian, and Włodzimierz Wójcik. *Słowo za słowo: Szkice o twórczości Tadeusza Różewicza* (Word for Word: Sketches on the Works of Tadeusz Różewicz). Katowice: FA-art, 1998.

Wyka, Kazimierz. *Różewicz parokrotnie* (Several Times Różewicz). Warsaw: Państwowy Instytut Wydawniczy, 1977.

Żukowski, Tomasz. "Zagłada a język poetycki Tadeusza Różewicza" (The Holocaust and Tadeusz Różewicz's Poetic Language). In *Literatura polska wobec Zagłady* (Polish Literature and the Holocaust), 141–165. Warsaw: Żydowski Instytut Historyczny, 2000.

ADOLF RUDNICKI

(1912–1990)

MONIKA ADAMCZYK-GARBOWSKA

ADOLF RUDNICKI WAS born on 19 February 1912 in Żabno. He received a traditional Jewish education together with a secular one. After graduating from a trade high school in 1931, he worked as a banking clerk. Although he knew Hebrew and Yiddish from home, like a number of Jewish writers in the interwar period he chose Polish as his language of artistic expression. As he stated about himself much later in "Stara Ściana" (The Old Wall) published in volume three of *Sto jeden* (One Hundred One): "I belonged to those creatures that started worshipping two gods rather early. Polish legends interposed themselves on Jewish ones, got entangled, mixed together" (Rudnicki, 1988 p. 27).

With his debut novel *Szczury* (Rats) in 1932, Rudnicki attracted the attention of reviewers, among others Karol Irzykowski, an influential critic in the period between the wars. The novel was marked by the writer's interest in Freudian psychoanalysis and can be interpreted as a voice of the lost generation in the eastern European context. His second novel *Żołnierze* (Soldiers), published the following year, constituted an insightful rendering of Polish society and its conflicting minorities in the 1920s and 1930s. In 1936 he published *Niekochana* (The Unloved One), one of his best known works, a study of unreciprocated love. The figure of a sensitive, devoted woman, appearing in this novella under the name of Noemi, will appear frequently throughout Rudnicki's oeuvre. *Niekochana* was followed by *Lato* (Summer) and *Doświadczenia* (Experiences).

Rudnicki fought in the September campaign of 1939 after Poland had been attacked by Nazi Germany. After the collapse of the Polish army, he managed to escape to Lvov (in Soviet occupied Poland), and he stayed there between 1940 and 1941, working for *Nowe Widnokręgi* magazine. After the Nazi invasion of the Soviet Union, he moved to Warsaw in 1942, where he lived in hiding during the occupation; he was active in underground publishing and fought in the Warsaw Uprising of 1944. During the years 1945–1949, he lived in Lodz where he worked as an editor of *Nowa Kuźnica* weekly. After his return to Warsaw, he regularly contributed (1953–1968) to *Świat* weekly where he published his cycle *Niebieskie kartki* (Blue Pages). In 1955 and 1966 he received the State Award for his work. In 1968 at the time of the antisemitic campaign in Poland, instigated by some antagonistic groups in the Communist Party, he moved to France, but he returned to Warsaw in the mid-1970s. His last works combine literary criticism with personal observations, a number of which are devoted to his European literary masters (for instance Fyodor Dostoyevsky and Isaac Babel) and the Polish literati he personally knew (for instance Antoni Słonimski).

Rudnicki's Work

Rudnicki is sometimes called a "lyrical naturalist"; he combines elements of fiction with reportage, memoirs, and autobiography. After the war, he did not change his technique of elaborate psychological realism but adapted it to his new subject matter, mainly focused on the Holocaust experience, as recorded in the cycle *Epoka pieców* (The Epoch of Crematoria). This cycle constitutes one of the most compelling voices on the topic of the Holocaust in Polish literature among writers who were adults during the war and is comprised of collections of stories and novellas of different lengths and characters. While Tadeusz Borowski or Zofia Nałkowska, the Polish gentile writers of his generation, present their characters mainly by how they act, Rudnicki depicts both the victims and the survivors by how they think and feel, giving readers complex psychological portraits of his characters. He becomes a chronicler of the destroyed Jewish world, giving grim historical truth a lyrical note. By the mid-1950s, he stopped writing about the Holocaust, and, as one of his biographers, Józef Wróbel, observes, Rudnicki felt that he was not working up to his potential. The situation in Polish literature of that time, when the war theme was suddenly being treated as a historical topic and when the prevailing tendency, politically imposed, was to write about the "bright socialist future," most probably affected Rudnicki's work.

After the war, Rudnicki looked critically at his own works written before the war's outbreak, claiming that the events of the war and occupation made his works look as if they were from a completely different era. He argued that he looked at them with disgust, as if they were some worthless and lifeless manuscripts left somewhere in an attic. He felt guilty about the crisis in the world and considerd the focus on aesthetic values, characteristic of his earlier work, as immoral. He writes in "Kartka znaleziona pod murem straceń" (A Sheet of Paper Found at the Execution Wall) in *Sto jeden*, volume 1:

> The war had aged what I have written by a thousand years. I read myself full of astonishment. I read with anger and disapproval. I read and do not recognize . . . The war has already destroyed them, though it has not touched their physical form. The impact of the great conflagration has deprived their pages of readability, deformed them like a bridge into whose trusses a missile has been fired. Life has left them, as it has left the steppes under the crushing weight of tanks. My art seems to be wretched. Wretched! (p. 207).

Rudnicki also blames himself for not recording earlier the Jewish world that was destroyed during the war. This does not mean that he did not treat Jewish topics at all in the 1930s. For example, in *Lato* (Summer, published in 1938), he presented scenes of Jewish life in Kazimierz on the Vistula (known in Yiddish as Kuzmir), a picturesque shtetl frequented by artists and literati, and he included a description of a pilgrimage to Ger (Polish Góra Kalwaria), the seat of the famous Hasidic rebbe. In the preface to the reissue of *Lato* in 1959, he states that he finds comfort in the fact that he recorded at least this much, and he treats his prose devoted to those topics as a small memorial candle. One must add, however, that in *Lato* the writer looks at the Jewish world from the point of view of the outsider, an assimilated artist who by no means identifies himself with the presented milieu. Nevertheless, when read today, fragments of *Lato* still resonate with ominous tones and can be intepreted as containing new meaning.

Rudnicki mourns the destroyed Jewish world in a number of works, for instance, in the essay "Spalony świat Egona Kaganowskiego" (The Burned World of Egon Kaganowski) devoted to the Yiddish writer whose work Rudnicki did not appreciate enough earlier, he pays tribute in retrospect as a representative of unassimilated Polish Jews who wrote in Yiddish rather than Polish. Rudnicki admits that under the influence of the destruction, he became more sensitive to the world of Polish Jews and less critical of its flaws.

Some of Rudnicki's stories are based on real events and are set partly in Lvov, reflecting the experience of that period in the writer's life. For example, the character Stefan Konecki from the story "Wielki Stefan Konecki" ("Great Stefan Konecki") is based on the life of Ostap Ortwin (Oskar Katzenellenbogen, 1876–1942), a socialist critic from Lvov who was murdered by the Nazis under unknown circumstances. *Wniebowstapienie* (*Ascent to Heaven*) is based on a story recorded in the book by Władysław Bartoszewski and Zofia Lewinówna about the righteous Poles (published in English as *Righteous among Nations: How Poles Helped the Jews, 1939–1945*). In both of Rudnicki's stories, one finds devastating passages of the persecution of Jews soon after the Nazis replaced the Soviets in the summer 1941. There is the merciless "elimination" of the old and handicapped and the desperate attempts at survival of those who feared their deaths, as well as other scenes of humiliation and perverse cruelty.

Rudnicki also sees the Holocaust in the context of earlier sufferings of Jews in the Diaspora. As he states in *Ascent to Heaven*:

> There are words that have an identical meaning when translated into another language; yet somehow they mean less; there is no equality in the total of national experiences. No other nation has so many synonyms for suffering as have the Jews. The Book of Job was not written by a Frenchman, or even a Russian. Everybody knows that what the Germans did during the Second World War has no equivalent in history, yet it was all contained within the Jews' ancient vocabulary (Polonsky, p. 95).

Rudnicki's writing deals with Polish Jewish relations; for instance, he presents how Nazi propaganda deepened the gaps between the two communities, as symbolically rendered in a meat shop advertisement in "The Great Stefan Konecki" in volume 2 of *Sto jeden*:

> Olejniczuk's butcher's stall was closed, but someone kept changing the sign on the door. The first one read: For Aryans, 10 dkg meat without bones; for Jews, 5 dkg meat without bones. The second sign: Aryans, 10 dkg meat without bones; Jews, 5 dkg (no mention of bones). There still was no meat, but a third sign appeared anyway: Aryans, 10 dkg meat without bones; Jews receive no meat. The stall was always closed, but the great deceit changed color in nuances. The enemy fed the imagination (Rudnicki, p. 218).

A number of his stories are devoted to the ghetto life, especially in Warsaw. Rudnicki records the reactions of crowds around a burning ghetto, the loneliness of the ghetto inhabitants doomed to distraction (destined for death by the war troops liquidating the ghetto), the helplessness of Jews hiding on the Aryan side, and the necessity to talk about what happened. In "Wielkanoc" (Easter) he writes:

> Some arrived, others went away. While day lasted they stuck under the wall. They looked, discussed, regretted. They regretted the goods, the wealth, the gold—the legendary gold, but above all they regretted the apartments and houses, "the finest you could find". They said: "Couldn't King Hitler solve this question some other way?" (pp. 194–195).

In the very short sketch "Benio, zwycięzca Hitlera" ("Benio, Hitler's Conqueror), Rudnicki commemorates the ghetto's idiot jester, mentioned in a number of reports from that time as the author of numerous jokes and sayings flavored with black humour. Rudnicki calls him in volume 2 of *Sto jeden* "a spark of light brightening the gloomy pages" (p. 270).

Ascent to Heaven, one of Rudnicki's best novellas, is a good example of his favorite approach in which a love story is shown against merciless destiny. Love is manifested as an entanglement in a hopeless relationship in a world ruled by coincidence. For unclear reasons, the musically talented character Raisa from an Orthodox Jewish merchant family marries the artistically inclined psychiatrist Sebastian Goldman who, as it turns out, is mentally unbalanced. Thanks to her "good" Aryan looks, Raisa is able to move around freely, becoming a breadwinner in occupied Warsaw, while, on account of his "bad" Jewish looks, Sebastian has to stay inside. However, Sebastian rebels against his confinement, preaching some unrealistic theories on how to combat the Nazis and pretending that there are no Germans in Warsaw. Eventually Sebastian is murdered by the Gestapo, and Raisa dies in a bombing during the Warsaw Uprising of August 1944.

The title of the novella is ironic since the stimulus behind Raisa's "ascension" is the man she loves, who does not deserve the sacrifice Raisa is making by risking her life for him.

> Never speak evil of women! Much more than men, they know how high love can lead, and they pray and watch daily, for their ascent to heaven to be achieved through love. Close your eyes, strain your ears, and you will hear their great cry, their daily prayer for an ascent to heaven. Raisa's ascent to heaven was now seated beside her: a man stepping along a narrow plank between two worlds, contemplating views that no one else but he had ever contemplated; a being with whom it was more difficult to reach an understanding than with the river flowing below, or the pine growing beside them; someone with whom nature was playing, showing its fans again and again; a lunatic, a being without one chink through which another man could penetrate (Polonsky, p. 120).

The story, like many others by Rudnicki, is constructed on paradoxes and coincidences. The narrative is intermingled with authorial comments referring to the plight of the Jews, universal human evil, and the repetitive character of history. In the first edition, there were also some comments written under the influence of Stalinist socialist realism, but, as in other works, they were removed by the writer in later editions. The titular "ascension" is a semi-ironic, semiserious reference to the Madonna. Raisa resembles the images of the Madonna not only because of her angelic looks (according to the prevailing Polish Christian representation of the Virgin Mary as a fair skinned, blue-eyed blond) but also because of her total devotion to her childlike husband. She is a victim not only of history but also of the men in her life, especially her father, who by wanting to protect her against marrying a non-Jew indirectly contributes to her death, and her mentally unbalanced husband to whom she acts as a surrogate mother. In the depiction of both the main protagonist and marginal characters, Rudnicki shows his mastery of intricate psychological portrayal.

Just as a number of Rudnicki's heroines resemble Raisa in their devotion and sensitivity, so do a number of male characters resemble Sebastian—artistically and intellectually inclined writers and professionals, who, by any means available, attempt to separate themselves from the dehumanized reality and to avoid being touched by barbarity.

In *Kupiec łódzki* (The Merchant of Lodz), Rudnicki draws a portrait of Chaim Rumkowski, called the king of the Lodz ghetto. Rudnicki does not fictionalize the story but remains within the bounds of an essay and intellectual argument. He describes Rumkowski as a petty bourgeois. Rumkowski believed that by offering the Nazis unlimited services he would save lives. He accepted the Nazi elimination of the sick, the handicapped, and the elderly, believing that he understood the Germans and wanting to trade with them as he did with merchants. He was an obsessive bureaucrat, everything was registered, and he indulged in his power. Rudnicki quotes from historical sources and enters into a polemic with Rumkowski's defenders who have claimed that by Rumkowski's strategy he managed to save some people from death. Rudnicki leaves no doubt that Rumkowski's behavior was wrong. Rudnicki openly states that Rumkowski might have been guided by illusions up to a certain point, but that afterward, especially after the great deportations of

1942 and the suicide of Adam Czerniakow, the head of the Judenrat in the Warsaw ghetto, to protest deportations of children, Rumkowski's main aim was to secure his own safety. Rudnicki's work resembles the story "Śmierć liberała" ("The Death of a Liberal") by Artur Sandauer, in which Doctor Kirsche, the head of the Judenrat in an unnamed town, makes deals with the Nazi commissar and deludes himself with the "cultured" behavior of the "civilized" Germans. While Doctor Kirsche ends up on a mound of corpses, shot by his Nazi "friend," *Kupiec łodzki* concludes with a macabre and grotesque scene of Rumkowski being taken to the crematorium in a parlor car.

In Rudnicki's "The Clear Stream" the devastation of Warsaw is portrayed through the eyes of Abel who arrives there from Lodz. The whole city is in ruins, burned-out houses and empty windows mark the moonlike landscape. Nevertheless, when Abel reaches the former Jewish quarter, he cannot believe his eyes:

> Expecting devastation he had expected it on the scale of other districts, he had expected traces, which would make it possible to re-create what had once been here. There were no traces. There were no houses more or less burned, more or less destroyed—there were simply no houses at all. . . . There, downtown, were corpses, here, there was not even a corpse. In this spot the city had been pulverized, not one stone was left on another. . . . And though more dead lay under these fields of rubble than in a hundred cemeteries, nothing here resembled a cemetery. There was the nothingness of an obliterated city whose ephemeral, indistinct and delusive form loomed in the mind of the spectator (pp. 258–259).

That is where Abel met his wife, Amelia. Their relationship was affected by the war. He spent the war years in an internment camp, while she was first in the ghetto and later on the Aryan side. Amelia was involved with a different man and gave birth to a child. As Amelia states:

> Death came to live in our midst and changed much in our conception of life. A man, who went away, went away into darkness and usually did not return. Feelings should not be stored up. They had to be paid at once. Women gave themselves to men as if they were giving them their due, as if they were repairing a wrong. And then it appeared that there are a hundred kinds of love and that each one of them is good. And each one of them is acceptable (pp. 273–274).

There is no doubt that in the radically transformed world, any re-creation of their former life is impossible.

Rudnicki often uses biblical imagery. As Ruth Schenfeld observed, some of his stories resemble exegesis or midrash. This is visible in the titles of his pieces like "Ofiarowanie Izaaka" (The Sacrifice of Isaac) and "Ginacy Daniel" (The Dying Daniel). His characters sometimes also have biblical names like the above-mentioned Abel and Daniel. Likewise, on a stylistic level, Rudnicki often alludes to the Bible. For instance in "Easter," he opens the piece with a matter-of-fact statement as to when the massacre started and then quickly moves to a passage from Psalm 69: "My heart awaits derision and pain; I waited for one to take pity on me and there was none, I searched for one who would give me joy, and did not find one. And they gave me wormwood for food and when I thirsted, they gave me vinegar to drink." This seems to be suitable means of expression, as "the language of the fathers became once again a living language" (p. 191).

Rudnicki's later work focuses on contemporary problems and the position of the artist in society. His impressionistic essays constitute a loosely structured chronicle of artistic and intellectual life in postwar Poland. Some critics, for instance Artur Sandauer, a very influential albeit equally controversial Polish-Jewish critic, accused Rudnicki of narcissistic tendencies (going so far as calling him a kind of martyrological primadonna) and excessive pathos and moralizing. Sandauer sees his narcissistic tendencies in the fact that Rudnicki often focuses on the plight of writers, as if their deaths were objectively a greater loss than the murder of millions of other victims. He accuses Rudnicki of egocentrism, of too great a focus on creating his own image, and of trying to serve as the exemplary Jewish writer.

Rudnicki wrote a preface to the Polish edition of Dawid Sierakowiak's diary from the Lodz ghetto first published in Poland in 1960 and edited a collection of texts about Auschwitz *Lest We Forget* (the English language edition published in Poland in 1955). In the preface to the latter, he stresses the necessity to remember and to make people read and popularize

> the books that reveal the bare truth about death camps, not avoiding these books as some would like to, but rather making them generally known and even reading them aloud in the big stadiums of large cities, before big audiences listening in solemn silence" (Rudnicki, p. 12).

Rudnicki is a difficult writer for critics and bibliographers because he constantly changed his works and put them in different cycles; he eliminated and replaced words and passages, changed details of place and time, and rearranged the order. An attempt was made to put his main works in three volumes edited by Józef Wróbel. Rudnicki's works have been translated into French, English, German, Hebrew, Russian, Czech, Slovak, Serbo-Croatian, and Hungarian. Rudnicki died in Warsaw on 15 November 1990.

Bibliography

Primary Sources

Szczury (Rats). 1932.
Żołnierze (Soldiers). 1933.
Niekochana (The Unloved One). 1936.
Lato (Summer). 1938.
Doświadczenia (Experiences). 1939.
Czysty nurt (The Clear Stream). 1946.
Józefów (Juzefov). 1946.
Koń (Horse). 1946.
Major Hubert z armii Andersa (Major Hubert from Anders Army). 1946.
Profile i drobiazgi żołlnierskie (Soldier Profiles and Miscellaneous Pieces). 1946.
Uśmiech żandarma (The Gendarme's Smile). 1946.
Wrzesień (September). 1946.
Wielkanoc (Easter). 1947.
Szekspir (Shakespeare). 1948.
Ucieczka z Jasnej Polany (A Flight from Yasna Polana). 1949.
Pałeczka, czyli każdemu to, na czym mu mniej zależy (A Baton, or Everybody Gets What He Cares Less For). 1950.
Wybór opowiadań (Collected Stories). 1950 (revised edition 1976).
Kartki sportowe (Sport Pages). 1952.
Żywe i martwe morze (The Dead Sea and the Living Sea). 1952 (extended edition 1955).
Młode cierpienia (Youthful Sufferings). 1954.
Manfred (a play). 1954.
Niebieskie kartki. Ślepe lustro tych lat (Blue Pages. A Blind Mirror of These Years). 1956.
Niebieskie kartki. Prześwity (Blue Pages. Vistas). 1957.
Krowa (Cow). 1959.
Narzeczony Beaty. Niebieskie kartki (Beata's Fiance. Blue Pages). 1960.
Obraz z kotem i psem (A Picture with a Cat and a Dog). 1962.
Kupiec łódzki. Niebieskie kartki (The Merchant of Lodz). 1963.
Pył miłosny. Niebieskie kartki (Love Dust. Blue Pages). 1964.
Weiss wpada do morza. Niebieskie kartki (Weiss Is Falling into the Sea. Blue Pages). 1965.
50 opowiadań (50 Stories). 1966.
Wspólne zdjęcie. Niebieskie kartki (A Group Photo. Blue Pages). 1967.
Teksty małe i mniejsze (Small and Smaller Texts). 1971.
Noc będzie chłodna, niebo w purpurze (The Night Will Be Cool, the Sky Purple). 1977.
Daniela naga (Naked Daniela). 1978.
Zabawa ludowa. Niebieskie kartki (A Folk Dance. Blue Pages). 1979.
Rogaty warszawiak (The Stubborn Varsovian). 1981.
Sto jeden (One Hundred One). vol. 1, 1984; vol. 2, 1985, vol. 3, 1988.
Krakowskie Przedmieście pełne deserów (The Cracow Suburb Full of Desserts). 1986.
Teatr zawsze grany (Theatre That Is Always On). 1987.
Sto lat temu umarł Dostojewski (Dostoyevsky Died One Hundred Years Ago). 1989.
Opowiadania (Stories). 1996.

Secondary Sources

Baumgarten, Murray. *Expectations and Endings: Observations on Holocaust Literature*. Working Papers in Holocaust Studies III, Holocaust Studies Program. New York: Yeshiva University, 1989.
Błoński, Jan. "Is There a Jewish School of Polish Literature?" In *Studies from Polin: From Shtetl to Socialism*. London and Washington, D.C.: Littman Library of Jewish Civilization, 1993.
Ezrahi, Sidra DeKoven. *By Words Alone. The Holocaust in Literature*. Chicago and London: The University of Chicago Press, 1980.
Polonsky, Antony, and Monika Adamczyk-Garbowska. *Contemporary Jewish Writing in Poland: An Anthology*. Lincoln and London: University of Nebraska Press, 2001.
Rudnicki, Adolf. Preface to *Lest We Forget*. Warsaw: "Polonia" Foreign Language Publishing House, 1955, pp. 7–12.
Schenfeld, Ruth. "Korzenie kulturowe Adolfa Rudnickiego." In *Literackie portrety Żydów*. Edited by Eugenia Łoch. Lublin: Wydawnictwo UMCS, 1996, pp. 31–44.

MAREK RYMKIEWICZ

(1935–)

KATARZYNA ZECHENTER

JAROSŁAW MAREK RYMKIEWICZ, the son of Hanna Baranowska (a physician) and Wladysław Rymkiewicz (a writer and a literary critic), was born in Warsaw on 13 July 1935, where he spent most of World War II. After 1945 he lived in Łódź where he studied Polish philology at the Łódź University (UŁ). After receiving his doctorate in 1966 he began working at the Institute of Literary Studies at the Polish Academy of Sciences (IBL PAN) in Warsaw. He was dismissed from his post in 1985 for political reasons and reinstated in 1989 after Poland regained independence. He has received multiple prizes for his novels, essays, and translations, including the prestigious Kościelski Prize (1967), S. Vincenz Prize (1985), Z. Hertz Prize, and Polish PEN Club Prize. Together with his wife, Ewa Suliborska, and a son, he lives in Milanówek near Warsaw.

Rymkiewicz as a Poet

Rymkiewicz, although primarily a poet, is also known as a brilliant literary critic, essayist, translator from English and Spanish, and a novelist. He is one of the founders of the neoclassical movement in Polish postwar poetry. Rymkiewicz's poetry is a dialogue between two prominent themes—culture and existence—often expressed through questioning the sense of history. Rymkiewicz's literary output includes thirteen volumes of poetry. He is also the author of one volume of scholarly prose, *Myśli różne o ogrodach. Dzieje jednego toposu.* (Various Thoughts on Gardens, 1968), devoted to the changes in the imagery and role of a garden, and eight volumes of essays. In his essays he combines intimate biographical knowledge of his subjects with unusual and original interpretations uniting fiction and facts—the most typical feature of his prose. His best-known collections of essays are devoted to Polish romantic poets: Adam Mickiewicz, Juliusz Słowacki, and Aleksander Fredro.

Rymkiewicz as a Prose Writer

Although Rymkiewicz is primarily a poet, he is better known as the author of two influential novels that not only achieved popular success but also contributed to the two most important debates of the 1980s: that involving martial law (1981) and Polish-Jewish relations. The first novel, *Rozmowy polskie latem 1983* (Polish Conversations in Summer, 1983), is set in the realistically described Poland of the 1980s after the imposition of martial law, with shortages of goods and suppression of the press. The novel discusses the meaning of being Polish and the Polish preoccupation with achieving lasting independence. The protagonist, Mr. Mareczek (the first name of the narrator alludes to Rymkiewicz himself), attempts to understand how future Poles will perceive the communist past and the meaning of martial law. Rymkiewicz's second novel, entitled *Umschlagplatz* (1988), had a much greater impact and was translated into French (1989), German (1993), and English (1994). Instytut Literacki, the largest Polish émigré publishing house, originally published *Umschlagplatz* in Paris in 1988 as the novel could not appear in communist Poland. It was reprinted a few times by underground publishing houses in Poland but officially appeared in 1992 after the communists lost power. The same year Rymkiewicz received a prestigious award from the journal *Odra* for both of his novels.

Umschlagplatz in the 1980s Discussion on the Polish-Jewish Relationship

Umschlagplatz was written during a time of increased interest in the Polish-Jewish past. The collapse of communism allowed the Poles to search for answers about their history and culture, including topics that until now were officially considered taboo or that could not be analyzed due to existing censorship. As censorship diminished, the lively interest in Polish Jewry blossomed with festivals of Jewish culture in Kraków, literature, monuments, exhibitions, and performances throughout the country. Rymkiewicz belongs to a large group of Polish writers, usually from the prewar generation, such as Zbigniew Herbert, Tadeusz Konwicki, Czesław Miłosz, or Andrzej Szczypiorski, who support the idea of Poland as a multiethnic state and who believe that Polish culture is not complete without its Jewish component. The renewed interest in the Polish-Jewish past had another angle as well—the possibility of exploring difficult aspects of Polish-Jewish relations, which until the 1980s were denied, such as the existence of antisemitism, indifference to the fate of Polish Jews after the war, and the feeling of shame after the events of 1968 with its official campaign of antisemitism. This debate, which continues to the present day, began with Jan Błoński's article "The Poor Poles Look at the Ghetto," published in the progressive Catholic weekly *Tygodnik Powszechny* (11 January 1987). Rymkiewicz's novel is, by all accounts, one of the most important voices in this debate, as it is devoted to the feeling of guilt stemming from the postwar indifference to the fate of Polish Jews. It has received a lot of critical attention and was reviewed by major Polish journals as it coincides with and supports "the spontaneous outburst of interest, curiosity, desire to know" the world of Polish Jewry, a desire which many critics consider long overdue.

The Symbolic Meaning of *Umschlagplatz*

Rymkiewicz's novel focuses on the symbolic meaning of *Umschlagplatz*, which denotes a small square in German-occupied Warsaw from which the Germans sent more than 300,000 Jews to their death, and thus a place which "may well be the only place of its kind" in the world (p. 7). Rymkiewicz's work is both a novel (he employs fictional Jewish characters although their names are borrowed from prewar guides or other actual prewar sources), and a record of his research to establish the actual plan of the square during World War II. More importantly, however, the novel is a document not of what happened to Jews in occupied Warsaw, but rather a study of how and why these events were forgotten in postwar Poland. In his conversations with his fictional Jewish wife, Hania, Rymkiewicz/the narrator torments himself with questions about the postwar years, the government's antisemitic campaign of 1968 in which those who opposed the government were labeled as Jews and ostracized or forced to emigrate, and most of all, how to understand those who, after the war, preferred not to remember the tragic fate of Polish Jewry. Consequently, the novel should be read on two major levels. The basic and the most obvious one is the documentation of Rymkiewicz's effort to create a reliable and most probably the only precise and detailed plan of the *Umschlagplatz* in 1942 and 1943 (that is, from 22 July to 12 September 1942 and in January, April, and May of 1943) when the mass deportations to the Treblinka death camp took place. Much more consequential, however, is the level of ethical questions and Rymkiewicz's attempt to understand the implications of the existence of such a place for the contemporary inhabitants of Warsaw and, more broadly, for all Poles: "we, who live in its immediate vicinity, in the very heart of Warsaw, ought to reflect on what it means for us, not in terms of the past, but in terms of our own reaction to what once happened there" (p. 7) and answer "what does *Umschlagplatz* signify in Polish life and Polish spirituality" (p. 8).

The Historical Aspect of *Umschlagplatz*

Creating the detailed plan of the *Umschlagplatz* took Rymkiewicz two years of study and meticulous research through various documents, plans, and memoirs of the survivors. He begins with a basic yet still unanswered question: when was the name *Umschlagplatz* used for the first time? To establish this and find answers for many other equally fundamental questions, Rymkiewicz compared documents and written accounts, read between the lines of various testimonials trying to establish the number and the look of buildings in which Jews waited for deportation or were held overnight on the *Umschlagplatz*, the color of the walls in these buildings, the number of windows, the number of gates in this part of the ghetto, the existence of barbed wire or a fence surrounding the square, and other, even the most minute, details. He concluded that the Germans introduced the name *Umschlagplatz* sometime before July 1942; in prewar Poland the place was called Transfer Square and was an important center for the Jewish wholesale trade. July 1942 marks the beginning of mass deportation from the Warsaw ghetto, although even earlier the *Umschlagplatz* was used by the Germans to disembark Jews from western Europe before they were resettled in the ghetto. Until 1946 the Polish name of the square was still used by some of the survivors, but then it was completely replaced by the German word *Umschlagplatz*, which implied a symbolic "limbo, gate to the underworld, antechamber of death" (p. 47) although the process of symbolization had begun during the war. Rymkiewicz was, however, unable to discover many details, for instance the exact number of buildings on the *Umschlagplatz*, although some details such as the existence of a hospital or a building where the Jews were held overnight, are certain. Eventually, he tried to catalog the few remaining houses that survived the ghetto uprising, the destruction afterwards, and finally the Warsaw Uprising in 1944. He counted around forty or fifty houses but realized that sooner or later "the ghetto will be just one house. After which there will not be a single house left" (p. 310) as the houses gradually succumb to old age and are demolished. The disappearance of the houses, however, suggests a more dramatic process of forgetting the past and the indifference resulting from it, indifference that Rymkiewicz finds deeply disturbing.

The Issues of Forgetting in *Umschlagplatz*

Establishing the accurate plan of the *Umschlagplatz* is only a starting point in Rymkiewicz's quest for understanding the symbolic meaning and the ethical ramification of the actual place, a meaning which, according to Rymkiewicz, cannot be compared with anything else in the world. He is preoccupied with the concept of moral responsibility in broader terms and looks at the events in occupied Warsaw not from the point of view of German moral responsibilities for genocide (Rymkiewicz avoids the term "Nazis" and uses only the word "Germans" as it is used in the memorials of the survivors), but in the narrower context of an issue between Poles and Jews: "I don't care about the Germans. . . . The Germans will atone for their deeds until the end of time, but that's an issue for their conscience, not mine. For me the issue is between Poles and Jews" (p. 26).

One of the reasons for Rymkiewicz's moral torment is an actual photograph of him and his sister as small children in the summer of 1942 in Otwock, at the time when the extermination of the Jews from Otwock and Warsaw began: "it is obscene that we survived at all, when those other children, the Jewish children went to the gas chambers and crematoria. It was a most obscene idea on the part of the Polish or the Jewish God" (p. 26). Rymkiewicz/the narrator argues with his sister that their survival is simply indecent, while she argues that one snapshot of two Polish children does not encompass the horrors of the war reality and that death could be simply a matter of minutes after taking that photo of her and her brother. Rymkiewicz/the narrator, however, juxtaposes their photo from July 1942 with perhaps the best-known photo from the Warsaw ghetto—that of a Jewish boy in a peaked cap and knee-length socks with his raised hands—a photo taken probably in July or August 1942 or during the ghetto uprising. After describing the photo, which shows a group of nineteen Jews and four Germans with automatic pistols aimed at the Jews, Rymkiewicz/the narrator enters into an imaginary dialogue with the boy, Artur Siemiątek who, like Rymkiewicz, was born in 1935. He suggests that the symbolic exchange of their positions carries some of the terrible burden of a Polish Jew during the war: "I'll lift my arms up now, and you put yours down. They may not notice. But wait. I have got a better idea. We'll both stand with our arms up" (p. 326). The symbolic sharing of the fate of a Jew by a Pole does not, however, bring catharsis. *Umschlagplatz* is, after all, presented as the ultimate end of Polish Jewry, a feeling supported by the last sentence of the novel—the dramatic words of Marek Edelman, the only surviving leader of the Warsaw Ghetto Uprising, who believes that "there are no more Jews in the world. This nation does not exist. It will never exist again. . . . There are no Jews left. And there'll never be any Jews again" (p. 327). In such a context, Rymkiewicz's novel becomes a desperate attempt to remember and to atone for the postwar indifference toward Polish Jews, although "no other book could properly testify to the past, or provide the restitution we Poles owe to our Polish Jews. . . . Who knows, my novel, in which authentic facts are mixed with fiction, may also be an act of restitution. That is how I conceived it, and that is the best that I can do" (p. 319).

Bibliography

Primary Sources

Poetry

Konwencje (The Conventions). 1957.
Człowiek z głową jastrzębia (A Man with a Head of a Hawk). 1960.
Metafizyka (Metaphysics). 1963.
Animula (The Animula). 1964.
Anatomia (The Anatomy). 1970.
Co to jest drozd? (What is a Thrush?). 1973.
Wybór wierszy (Selected Poems). 1976.
Thema regium (Thema Regium). 1978.

Poezje wybrane (Selected Poems). 1981.

Ulica Mandelsztama i inne wiersze z lat 1979–1983 (Mandelshtam's Street and Other Poems 1979–1983). 1983.

Mogiła Ordona i inne wiersze z lat 1979–1984 (The Ordon's Tomb and Other Poems 1979–1984). Warsaw 1984.

Moje dzieło pośmiertne (My Posthumous Work). 1993.

Prose and Drama

Czym jest klasycyzm? Manifesty poetyckie (What is classicism? Poetic manifestos). 1967.

Myśli różne o ogrodach. Dzieje jednego toposu (Various thoughts on gardens: The Story of One Topos). 1968.

Kochankowie piekła. Tragifarsa w dwóch aktach według Calderona. (The lovers of Hell: Comedy in two acts). 1975.

Aleksander Fredro jest w złym humorze (Alexander Fredro is in a bad mood). 1977.

Król Mięsopust. Porwanie Europy (The king of carnival: The rape of Europe). 1977.

Dwie komedie (Ułani; Dwór nad Narwia.) (Two comedies: [The Ulhans. Manor house at Narwia River]). 1980.

Juliusz Słowacki pyta o godzinę (Juliusz Słowacki asks the time). 1982.

Wielki książę z dodaniem rozważań o istocie i przymiotach ducha polskiego (The great prince and his thoughts about the essence of Polish soul). 1983.

Rozmowy polskie latem 1983 (Polish conversations in summer 1983). 1984.

Żmut (Zmut). 1987.

Umschlagplatz (Umschlagplatz). 1988.

Baket (Baket). 1989.

Kilka szczegółów (A few details). 1994.

Mickiewicz, czyli wszystko. Z J. M. Rymkiewiczem rozmawia A. Poprawa (Mickiewicz—That is everything. A. Poprawa Talks with J. M. Rymkiewicz). 1994.

Do Snowia i dalej . . . (To Snowie and further. . .). 1996.

Secondary Sources

Adamczyk-Garbowska, Monika. "A New Generation of Voices in Polish Holocaust Literature." *Prooftexts: A Journal of Jewish Literary History* 9, no. 3 (1989): 273–287.

Barańczak, Stanisław. *Etyka i poetyka. Szkice 1970–1978.* Kraków: 1981, pp. 161–166.

Bernstein, Michael André. "Victims-in-Waiting: Backshadowing and the Representation of European Jewry." *New Literary History* 4 (1988): 625–651.

Błoński, Jan. *Odmarsz.* Kraków: 1978.

Levine, Madeline. "Wrestling with Ghosts: Poles and Jews Today." *East European Studies. Occasional Paper* 36 (March 1998).

Michlic, Joanna. "*Umschlagplatz.*" *Polin: A Journal of Polish-Jewish Studies* 6 (1991): 333–338.

Polonsky, Antony, ed. *My Brother's Keeper? Recent Polish Debates on the Holocaust.* New York: Routledge, 1990.

Poprawa, Adam. "Najwieksza synagoga." *Res Publica* 9 (1988).

———. *Kultura i egzystencja w poezji Jarosława Marka Rymkiewicza.* Wrocław: 1999.

Przybylski, Ryszard. *To jest klasycyzm.* Warsaw: 1978.

Roztropowicz, Clark Joanna. "*Umschlagplatz.*" *The Polish Review* 33, no. 3 (1988): 359–363.

Segal, Harold B. *Stranger in Our Midst. Images of the Jew in Polish Literature.* Ithaca: Cornell University Press, 1996.

NELLY SACHS
(1891–1970)

KATHRIN M. BOWER

LEONIE (NELLY) SACHS was born 10 December 1891 in Berlin. The only daughter of Georg William Sachs (1858–1930), a wealthy rubber manufacturer and inventor, and Margarete Sachs, née Karger (1871–1950), Nelly experienced a sheltered and often lonely childhood. Her parents belonged to the Berlin Jewish community in name only, and she remained largely ignorant of Jewish tradition and religion until well into her adult years. As a result of her education in an assimilated household, Nelly developed strong affinities with German Romanticism (particularly with the poet Friedrich Novalis) and Christian mysticism (most prominently with Jakob Böhme). A painfully shy, sensitive, and introspective child, Nelly did not fare well in public school, and her parents had her tutored privately at home.

After completing her formal education in 1908, Sachs devoted herself to writing poetry and painting watercolors. This was also the year in which she met the love of her life, a divorced older man whom she was forbidden to marry. The unhappy outcome of this doomed affair threw Sachs into deep despair and she languished in bed for over a year, suffering from depression and anorexia, until she was gradually able to regain her strength and stability, in large part through writing poetry. She later maintained that the love affair that inspired such excess of feeling and despair was the real stimulus for all of her subsequent writing, and that it was then that she had first recognized that writing enabled her to survive. Long after this incident, Sachs referred to the therapeutic power writing held for her in a statement that is quoted repeatedly in Sachs scholarship: "Had I not been able to write, I would not have survived. Death was my teacher . . . my metaphors are my wounds" (Dischner, 1966, p. 108).

After the death of William Sachs in 1930, Nelly and her mother moved to a smaller apartment in Berlin. The peaceful, reclusive existence they shared met an abrupt end when Hitler came to power and increasingly repressive measures against the Jews forced Sachs to confront her identity. While she had never felt much affinity with Judaism before 1933 and regarded herself as a product of the German cultural tradition, she responded to the identity imposed upon her by the Nazis by delving into the roots of a tradition that had hitherto been foreign to her. She was particularly drawn to the Hasidic tales in Martin Buber's translation as well as the tenets of Jewish mysticism. In the mid-1930s she became an active member of the Jewish cultural association in Berlin, and her poems were read at association events between 1936 and 1938. It was here that Sachs became familiar with the work of another famous Berlin poet, Gertrud Kolmar, who unlike Sachs, would not survive the Holocaust. In January 1939 the Third Reich implemented a mandatory second-name policy for all Jewish residents: men would take the second name Israel, women would be called Sara. Nelly Sachs's last published poem in Germany before she fled the country appeared in April 1939 in the monthly bulletin of the Jewish cultural association under the name "Nelly Sara Sachs."

Flight and Exile

After *Kristallnacht* in November 1938, Sachs realized it was unsafe to remain in Germany any longer, and set about finding a place of refuge for herself and her mother. Sweden was a logical choice. Since the age of fifteen, Sachs had been corresponding with Selma Lagerlöf, a Swedish novelist whose legends and sagas had captivated her and inspired her to write a collection of her own, *Legenden und Erzählungen* (Legends and Stories, 1921), which she had sent to Lagerlöf as a token of her admiration. Obtaining visas for herself and her mother, however, proved an arduous task, and even with the benevolent intercession of the aging Lagerlöf, the situation seemed hopeless. The Swedish government would only accept refugees who could prove that their stay in the country was solely for purposes of transit to another safe haven, preferably the United States. Sachs was fortunate in having friends willing to sponsor her in America so that her visa papers would be acceptable. Just as the tension and danger were reaching nearly unbearable proportions—she had already received her deportation papers—the visas arrived, and Sachs and her mother were able to escape in May 1940, on the last flight from Berlin to Stockholm. Without the courageous support of friends and the assistance of both Lagerlöf and Prince Eugen of Sweden, Nelly and her mother would have been transported to the camps, with little or no hope of survival.

Sachs greeted her new home with a mixture of gratitude and apprehension. She did not speak the language, and she and her mother had been forced to leave all their valuables behind. Destitute and dependent upon the goodwill of the Stockholm Jewish community, Sachs set about learning Swedish and within a few years became adept enough to earn a modest living as a translator. By the late 1940s, Sachs was recognized as an accomplished translator of modern Swedish poetry, and by the end of her life her translation work spanned seven volumes. Several scholars have argued that it was this exposure to modern Swedish poetry and the task of translation that brought about a dramatic shift in Sachs's own writing. She left behind the traditional rhyme and strophes that characterized her early poetry and began writing free verse flush with genitive metaphors and anguished language. While changes in form may have been influenced in part by her contact with contemporary Swedish poetry, her content and imagery were undeniably the result of her growing knowledge of the events of the Holocaust and the ever-widening circle of victims it claimed. In 1943 Sachs learned of her lover's death as well as of the deportations of Jews to Auschwitz. She was filled with sorrow and despair about the fate of friends and relatives, feelings mingled with a sense of guilt at having escaped their fate, and turned to her poetry as a vehicle for bearing witness to the memories of the dead and an instrument of mourning.

The poem cycles "Dein Leib in Rauch durch die Luft" (Your Body in Smoke through the Air), "Gebete für den toten Bräutigam" (Prayers for the Dead Bridegroom), and "Grabschriften in die Luft geschrieben" (Epitaphs Written in the Air), and the lyric drama *Eli. Ein Mysterienspiel vom Leiden Israels* (*Eli: A Mystery Play on the Suffering of Israel*), were all written between 1943 and 1945 and include some of her most powerful and best-known work. In these poems, Sachs begins to develop the repertoire of images that come to characterize her poetry of mourning and remembrance. Most resonant are the repeated references to sand, shoes, and dust. In laments to the dead she asks who has emptied the victims' shoes of sand and reflects on the force of death that inevitably turns all mortals to dust. Sand and dust combine to represent mortality and the cycle of death and regeneration that spares neither the innocent nor the guilty, but is also representative of the countless victims turned to dust and ashes in the Holocaust. The reference to shoes filled with sand evokes not only the victims' nearness to death, but also the figure of the Wandering Jew, the tribes of Israel cast into the desert, and the exile bereft of home.

Sachs's own sense of exile and her desire to find a home at least for her writings galvanized her search for a publisher. In the immediate aftermath of the war, this proved difficult despite the moving force of her poems. Eventually, with the assistance of a German friend, she was able to find a sympathetic ear among the editors of the Aufbau Verlag in Soviet-occupied eastern Germany, and the press published the collection *In den Wohnungen des Todes* (In the Habitations of Death) in 1947. It was the publication of this volume that established Sachs's reputation as the "Dichterin jüdischen Schicksals" (poetess of Jewish fate). The dedication that opens the collection—"to my murdered brothers and sisters"—demonstrates the degree of Sachs's identification with the victims as well as the newfound strength of her sense of kinship with the Jewish people. Two years later, she was again forced to search for a home for her poems, and found one this time with an Amsterdam publisher known for its support of exile writers. *Sternverdunkelung* (Darkening Star) was published by Bermann Fischer Verlag in 1949. Although celebrated in critical reviews, the book found little appeal with the public, and unsold copies were pulped. Germany in 1949 was more concerned with reconstruction and the conflicts of a divided nation than with pangs of conscience and reminders of a past most wanted to forget.

In February 1950 Margarete Sachs died. Nelly felt her loss acutely; her mother's death after a long illness was the catalyst for a psychological crisis she sought to overcome by writing and intensive study of Jewish mysticism, particularly the *Zohar* (Book of Splendor). Although she was now alone in Sweden, Sachs had no intention of returning to Germany and felt that she was too old to start a new life in Israel. Sweden had become and would remain her adopted homeland—she became a citizen in 1952. But Sachs never relinquished her love for the German language, and used German exclusively as her idiom, producing in bursts of creative intensity an ever-growing body of poetry and lyric drama. One exception in this string of lyric is a short prose piece she published in a small journal in 1956. Entitled "Leben unter Bedrohung" (Life under Siege), this essay is the only prose piece Sachs ever made public that directly addresses the conditions of terror and persecution she had experienced in Germany. It is based on an event in 1938, when she was arrested by the Gestapo and interrogated. Sachs was so shaken by this experience that she suffered a temporary paralysis of the larynx and was unable to speak for a week. This terror-inspired muteness is transformed into metaphors of silent suffering in her poetry and can be found even in her late work (as in "Als der große Schrecken kam" [When the Great Terror Came]). Drawing on her own experience of terror, Sachs speaks there for the multitude of victims whose voices had been silenced in a realm where words themselves had become refugees.

Fame and Psychosis

After over a decade of near obscurity, Nelly Sachs's poetry was "discovered" in Germany in 1959, following the publication of two volumes by German presses and an influential essay on her work by Hans Magnus Enzensberger in the journal *Merkur*. Sachs's 1957 volume *Und niemand weiß weiter* (And No One Knows Further) and 1959 collection *Flucht und Verwandlung* (Flight and Transformation) extended the themes of persecution, suffering, and death found in her first two books of poetry, but also broke new ground in the form of poetic reflections on exile, the regenerative power of the word, the longing for dialogue, and the possibility of transcendence. It was particularly her treatment of language in these poems that caught Enzensberger's eye, and in his essay "Die Steine der Freiheit" (Stones of Freedom) he portrays Sachs as a healer of the German language and her work as a refutation of Theodor Adorno's dictum that there could be no poetry after Auschwitz. At the end of 1959 Sachs was named the recipient of the prestigious Droste prize, and in May 1960 made her first trip back to the country of her birth to receive the award.

The year 1959 also marked the debut broadcast on Swedish radio of an opera version of Sachs's play *Eli* (a radio play version adapted by Alfred Andersch had been broadcast in Germany in 1958), but Sachs's feeling that she had been betrayed by the composer, Moses Pergament, and misunderstood by the public planted the seeds of a persecution complex. The prospect of setting foot on German soil filled her with both hope and anxiety, and the tensions of the trip combined with concerns about the reception of her work took a toll. When she returned to Sweden in the summer of 1960, she suffered a nervous breakdown and was admitted to a psychiatric ward in a Stockholm hospital after being diagnosed with paranoid psychosis. This would be the first in a series of psychiatric treatments and extended stays in clinics and also the first warning sign of Sachs's growing paranoia and persecution mania, which deprived her of sleep and put a tremendous strain on her friendships.

One friend who could relate to Sachs's anxiety and paranoia was the poet Paul Celan, with whom Sachs had begun corresponding in 1957. Their letters attest to the depth of their growing friendship as well as to the strong affinity they felt for each other as poets and survivors. Both were concerned about the resurgence of antisemitism in Germany and about the fragile condition of the fledgling state of Israel. Yet Sachs's concern for Israel was mixed with a powerful fear that the persecuted could become persecutors, a fear that began to take alarming proportions in her mind when she learned of the Eichmann trial in Jerusalem. During the period of the trial, from 1961 to 1962, Sachs's delusions of persecution increased and she was convinced that she was being terrorized by Nazi spies in her Stockholm apartment building as punishment for Eichmann's arrest.

Under the influence of these paranoid fears and the psychiatric treatment, including electroshock therapy, designed to eliminate them, Sachs produced the cycle "*Noch feiert Tod das Leben*" (Death Still Celebrates Life), containing poems on Hasidic themes, syntheses of Jewish and Christian iconography, death and regeneration; and part of the cycle *Glühende Rätsel* (Glowing Enigmas). Despite the radical nature of the therapy she received, Sachs later remarked that the treatment designed to make her forget was unsuccessful in erasing the parts of her memory that continued to plague her ("I cannot work after the shock treatments—because I forget everything—only what I am supposed to forget, I don't forget" (*Briefe der Nelly Sachs*, Edited by Ruth Dinesen and Helmut Onüssener, Frankfurt am Main: Suhrkamp, 1984.)

Celebrated Poet or Mascot of Reconciliation?

Ruth Dinesen, the author of the most detailed biography of Nelly Sachs, has argued that after the publication of *Flucht und Verwandlung* in 1959, Sachs was no longer concerned with attempting to reconcile her dual identity as German and Jew and came to resent being pigeonholed as a distinctively Jewish poet. According to Dinesen, Sachs perceived this reductive label as one of the bases for the persecution she felt pursued her. Other scholars (including Bahr and Vaerst) have noted the shift in Sachs's later work away from resonant images that evoke the genocide and the broader history of Jewish suffering to a sparer, more condensed, and hermetic language. What is clear from Sachs's correspondence is that she had a strong aversion to organized religion and orthodoxy of any kind. In an environment where denominational faith had been deeply destabilized, Sachs turned to a synthetic and unbounded spirituality combining those elements of Jewish, Christian, and Eastern beliefs that appealed to her: "The not-bound, the fluid, the always possible is perhaps the only solace after the terrible experiences" (*Briefe*, p. 87).

The categorization of Sachs as a "poet of Jewish fate" was one that confined her, but it also served to cement her reputation and recognition as a Holocaust poet. While this perception has exercised an enormous influence on the criticism and reception of her work, it is her association with the Holocaust and her poetic tributes to the dead that garnered her the Peace Prize awarded by the German Book Trade Association in 1965 and, a year later, the Nobel Prize. In the presentation of the Peace Prize, Sachs was once again lauded as a healer of the German language and as a voice of reconciliation. Several critics have argued that Sachs served as a mascot for Germany's demonstration of remorse for its past, while others have maintained that her poetry offered German readers the kind of aesthetic distance from the horrors of the Holocaust that made the past easier to bear. The splitting of the 1966 Nobel Prize for Literature, awarded to Sachs and to the Israeli novelist Shmuel Yosef Agnon, was a more obvious cause for controversy because of the Nobel committee's rationale that the two writers were both Jewish and that their works together represented the fate of Israel.

The ironies of identity and public recognition culminated in Sachs's award of honorary citizenship in 1967 by Berlin, the city where she was born and had spent over half of her life, but to which she had returned only once—in 1965—since her flight from Nazi Germany. In 1967 Sachs's health worsened; she suffered a heart attack and a recurrence of crippling paranoia, which again required psychiatric treatment. In 1969 she underwent extensive surgery for colon cancer and spent months convalescing in the hospital, but never fully recovered and died on 12 May 1970, one month after her friend and kindred poetic spirit Paul Celan had committed suicide in Paris. Sachs was buried in the Jewish cemetery in Stockholm. The safe haven she had found thirty years earlier thus became her final resting place.

Neglect and Revival

After Sachs's death, the second volume of her collected poems, *Suche nach Lebenden* (Search for the Living), was published, as a companion to *Fahrt ins Staublose* (Journey into the Vacuum), which contained poetry from 1943 to 1960. These two volumes, together with *Zeichen im Sand* (Signs in the Sand), her collected lyric drama, comprise the body of writing for which Sachs is known today. But the reception of this work has been uneven, subject to the vicissitudes of public and critical attention that inevitably turns on her designation as a poet of the Holocaust. Despite her status as a Nobel prizewinner and despite ever-growing interest in Holocaust literature, the volumes containing her dramatic works and correspondence are out of print, and the poetry collections are difficult to come by. In contrast, the more recent publication of Sachs's correspondence with Paul Celan has been given wide distribution, and appeared in English translation soon after the German edition came out. This phenomenon only adds fuel to a hypothesis expressed by Michael Krämer that Sachs's reception has been eclipsed by Celan's dominance as the representative German-Jewish poet of the Holocaust.

In fact, existing scholarship has often compared Sachs to Celan, but others to whom she is compared also include Else Lasker-Schüler, Gertrud Kolmar, and Rose Ausländer, as well as Franz Kafka and Heinrich Heine. These comparisons place Sachs's work in the contexts of broader debates about German Jewish identity, exile, the Diaspora, and estrangement. Numerous secondary studies have done much to illuminate central aspects of Sachs's work beyond the association with the Holocaust, such as the influence of Romanticism (Berendsohn; Michel; Beil); her appropriations of mysticism and religious imagery (Michel; Bower); the ethics of her poetic project to awaken a sense of responsibility and moral awareness in her readers toward the memory of the victims of the Holocaust (Bower; Langer); and the modernity of her use of language (Dischner; Dinesen). But recognition has come in waves, the first in the 1960s following her "discovery" in Germany and the Nobel award, a second in the 1970s after her death. The marked drop in critical recognition in the 1980s has been attributed by one scholar to the suffering tone of Sachs's poems and her image as a persecuted Jew (Falkenstein, p. 89), but this hypothesis sheds little light on the revival of interest in her work during the 1990s. Despite this recent upward trend in Sachs's standing among scholars, there are no indications that a critical edition of her collected works or an expanded volume of her correspondence can be expected in the near future, nor has her work become more accessible to English-speaking audiences. The two existing translations of her work in English, *O the Chimneys* (1967) and *The Seeker* (1970), were hastily produced and do not do justice to the force of her language.

In the Habitations of Death

Although Sachs herself never experienced the horrors of the concentration camp universe, the strength and degree of her identification with the victims and their suffering inspired her to turn her poetic voice to the task of bearing witness. In her letters from the 1940s, she repeatedly stated that her name and her person were not important, that it was the voice of the Jewish people that spoke from her poems and had to be heard (*Briefe*, pp. 54, 177). The first volume of poetry Sachs published after the Holocaust, *In den Wohnungen des Todes*, contains poems written after her flight to Sweden and the end of the war that can be read most directly as testaments to the victims and the memory of their suffering. The poem that opens the collection is entitled "O die Schornsteine" (O the Chimneys). In spite of what appears to be a literal reference to the crematoria in the camps, the imagery and use of metaphor in this poem are indicative of Sachs's attempts to represent the unrepresentable. The poem speaks not of extermination camps but of habitations of death, not of burned individual bodies, but of the collective body of Israel going up in smoke, not of selections and mass murder, but of chimneys as fingers marking the boundary between living and dying. The language of poetry must be distinct from the language of the witness even as the poem testifies to the suffering of the victims. For this reason, Sachs's poems aim toward transfiguration rather than realism, not only because the event itself has rendered poetic traditions and conventional imagery obsolete, but also in order to express the implications of the horror rather than the horror itself.

In den Wohnungen des Todes consists of individual and collective testimonials to the dead, laments on the continuity of Jewish suffering, and attacks on the apathy and complicity of the bystanders. The bluntly accusatory tone of "Ihr Zuschauenden" (You Onlookers), addressing those who did nothing to intervene as their neighbors were murdered, refuses to accord these bystanders a position of moral ambiguity, unequivocally denouncing their indifference as a criminal act. Their punishment is to be haunted by the gaze of the eyes of the dead. Yet it is not only the complicit who are destined to be tormented by the past. In "Chor der Tröster" (Chorus of Consolers), Sachs addresses the problem of mourning a catastrophe of such proportions that it has left no one untouched. In the aftermath of the Holocaust, life cannot continue as before; the gap between yesterday and tomorrow is too wide to be bridged by either language or gestures. Sachs likens this rupture in time to a wound that should not be allowed to heal, a wound in the collective memory of a people that refuses consolation but must be expressed.

The cycles "Gebete für den toten Bräutigam" (Prayers for the Dead Bridegroom), dedicated to the memory of Sachs's murdered lover; "Grabschriften in die Luft geschrieben" (Epitaphs Written in the Air), poems bearing the initials of Sachs's friends and acquaintances who had perished in the Holocaust; and "Chöre nach der Mitternacht" (Choruses after Midnight) combine the pain of personal loss and individual suffering into a dirge to the collective memory of all the victims. Many of the images in these first poems smithed in the fires of a growing realization of the extent and dimensions of the Holocaust would become recurring metaphors in Sachs's work: flames to evoke both divine inspiration and destruction; smoke as the incineration of a people and a cipher of loss; dust and ashes as memory traces as well as symbols of the cycle of death and regeneration; night as the realm in which dreams, memories, and myth combine to reveal the convergence of cosmic and human time; butterflies as liberated souls; fish as representatives of mute suffering; abandoned objects as silent witnesses to persecution and death; the refugee as a seeker filled with restless longing for community and God.

In *Eli*, a lyric drama on the suffering of Israel written during the same period as *In den Wohnungen des Todes*, Sachs attempted to link the genocide with the Hasidic belief in the *lamed vov*, the thirty-six righteous born into each generation who carry the weight of the world on their shoulders without knowing it. The shoemaker, Michael, is one of the thirty-six, and witnesses the deaths of Jewish villagers at the hands of Nazi soldiers. One death in particular, that of the shepherd boy Eli, killed because he threw back his head and played a desperate plea on his flute to God, consumes him, and the bulk of the play is devoted to Michael's search for Eli's murderer. Michael's special status is visible to others in the form of a mark on his forehead, and the power associated with this sign becomes manifest at the end of the play after he has a vision that leads him to the killer. The final scene transports the action from the level of history to that of myth as the remorseful murderer turns to dust before Michael's eyes and Michael himself ascends into the heavens. God's intervention is a signal that there is a divine justice, but the balance of good and evil in the universe remains beyond human comprehension. *Eli* is the only one of Sachs's lyrical dramas performed during her lifetime, and she was adamant that Michael be portrayed as a miracle worker and a conciliatory figure rather than one filled with hatred and vengeance. While the radio play adaptation by Alfred Andersch remained true to Sachs's original text, Moses Pergament's opera version achieved the effect that she had feared, and the connection to the healing figure of Hasidic lore as well as the emphasis on responsibility over revenge were lost.

An Era of Victims and Perpetrators

In her second volume of poetry, *Sternverdunkelung*, Sachs moved away from the direct references to the event of the Holocaust common to her earlier poems, toward more universal images of persecution and suffering. It is here that she began to explore what would become a central theme in her later work: the cyclical and reversible positions of victim and perpetrator. The clear opposition of the two in representations of the Holocaust was disturbed in Sachs's mind by subsequent events—most significantly the establishment of the state of Israel with its dual role as a Jewish safe haven and aggressive independent state, and the 1948 assassination of Swedish diplomat Folke Bernadotte by Jewish extremists in Jerusalem. In a poem entitled "Auf daß die Verfolgten nicht Verfolger werden" (In Hope That the Persecuted Do Not Become the Persecutors), Sachs portrays the conflict between the persecuted and the persecutors as an eternal cycle in which now one, now the other plays the role of the victimizer. In the process, history itself becomes but a manifestation of the dictates of a cosmic time in which the hunter and the hunted are constantly in pursuit of each other.

Sachs produced many variations on the theme of pursuit and persecution in her work, alternately referring to the opposition as victim and perpetrator, victim and executioner, hunter and hunted, victor and vanquished, but the underlying message is the same: our time is an age of victims and perpetrators, our existential condition is one of perpetual fear, our landscape is a landscape of screams ("Landschaft aus Schreien"), and to be human is to be guilty (see "Beryll sieht in der Nacht" and "Nachtwache"). The guilt of humanity is manifest in Sachs's poetry and drama in the images of those who watched and did nothing—the bystanders who out of apathy, complacency, or self-interest did not intervene. Without being actively involved in murder and destruction, these bystanders are nevertheless accomplices to evil, and belong on the side of the perpetrators. In a letter of 1948, Sachs argued that it was this phenomenon more than anything else that enabled the Holocaust: ". . . how easy it would have been to save the small Jewish population back then, if, yes if, the half-heartedness were gone from the world" (*Briefe*, p. 89). Sachs remained far from sanguine that revelation of the Holocaust's horrors would inspire greater empathy in the future. In an untitled poem from *Sternverdunkelung*, she wonders whether a horde of prophets would have the power to penetrate humanity's deaf ear and awaken the people from their complacent sleep. She implicitly compares the prophets' search for a listening ear ("an ear like a homeland") to the exile's longing for a home (*Fahrt ins Staublose*, Frankfurt am Main: Suhrkamp, 1988, p. 93), but leaves the reader with the sense that humankind remains mired in petty concerns, blind, deaf, and unfeeling even in the face of divine communication.

In the lyric drama "Abram im Salz" (Abram in Salt) allusions to acts of persecution by the Nazis against their victims are masked behind a mythical constellation of figures. This figurative strategy universalizes the victim and victimizer while bringing together legend and lived history. The lack of historical specificity is designed to illustrate the cyclical, eternal nature of the struggle between the hunter and the hunted, or as Sachs puts it in her notes to the play in *Zeichen im Sand* (p. 346): "the eternal contest on earth between the hunters and the hunted." The central conflict in the play is between Nimrod, king of the hunters, representing the Nazi perpetrators, and the young Abram, representing the collective suffering of Israel, and is set in a landscape of salt where all inhabitants are driven by thirst. Abram emerges from his torment and touches the wound of God, a signal that suffering is both a prerequisite for communication with the divine and a path to redemption.

Suffering and Salvation

In her poetry of the 1950s and 1960s (*Und niemand weiß weiter*, *Flucht und Verwandlung*, *Die Suchende*), Sachs began to focus more on the condition of the exile and refugee, drawing on religious and literary sources ranging from biblical figures whose faith and loyalty were tested by God (Abraham, Jacob, Job) to female icons of exile, wandering, and banishment that have their roots in Romanticism and mysticism (Mélusine, Genoveva, and Shekhinah). In the figure of the bereaved wanderer, the seeker compelled by longing for what has been lost, be it loved ones, community, homeland, or God, Sachs makes the link between remembrance and redemption. The seeker's desire to return to a remembered or imagined state of wholeness is a spiritual search that leads her to the border between life and death, a privileged position from which she can commune with the victims and serve as their voice to the living.

Sachs's portrayal of persecution and suffering as ineluctable conditions of human existence is at once mirrored and mitigated by the religious conception of Jewish history as a repeating sequence in which destruction precedes regeneration and death necessarily begets life. It is only through loss or absence that longing is born, and with it the hope for new life. The searching that characterizes her later poetry represents the hope that new life will rise from the ashes, that through suffering and seeking, one will find redemption. The conception of suffering as a path to God and to creative inspiration runs through Sachs's work. Critical praise for Sachs as a healer of the German language fit well, during her lifetime, into her mysticism-infused perception of the regenerative potential of the word and the indestructible integrity of the alphabet ("Beryll sieht in der Nacht," "Flucht und Verwandlung," "Glühende Rätsel," "Teile dich Nacht"). Language itself had been abused and corrupted; the old words were not adequate to bear witness to the catastrophe or to herald a new beginning. Sachs referred to the inadequacy of existing language on many occasions in her letters, while emphasizing that the wounds inflicted on it and on the victims must be preserved in the form of suffering that becomes inseparable from language itself (*Briefe*, pp. 85, 110). In her poetry, her frequent use of the dash at the end of a line is at once a visualization of a cut or rupture in meaning and an admission that the new language to express the inexpressible remained beyond her grasp.

Sachs in the Context of Holocaust Studies

It is one of the paradoxes of Nelly Sachs's reception as a writer that the association with the Holocaust that brought her critical recognition also served as an obstacle to the wider dissemination and analysis of her work. Bahr and others have argued that Sachs's status as the poet of Jewish fate placed a kind of halo around her writing that prompted uncritical affirmation rather than critique. Other scholars have insisted that in reading Sachs as a Holocaust writer, important aspects of her work have been neglected. It is undeniable, however, that her writing would not have developed as it did without the impact of the genocide, and even in studies that focus on Sachs's mysticism, modernism, or representative qualities as a German Jewish poet, there is agreement on the central significance of the Holocaust.

The most contested issues in Sachs scholarship include her use of language, which has been variously called cathartic, psalmic, transcendent, modernist, and, in reference to the late poems, hermetic; the appropriate or inappropriate nature of her metaphors; and more sweeping concerns about the representation of the Holocaust. As the distance between scholars and the actual event of the Holocaust lengthens, more and more studies are devoted to questions of how the Holocaust can and should be represented. In the process, scholars without any experience of the event, lacking an essential sensitivity and awareness, pass judgments on the appropriateness or authenticity of imagery and language, and impose aesthetic standards on Holocaust literature that at times belie its ethical foundations as a literature of witness, testimony, mourning, and remembrance. While Sachs's metaphors (which at times cross the line between pathos and sentimentalization) and images (presenting a diverse array of naïve, clairvoyant, and violent visions) can and should be subject to critical analysis, the key significance of her work for future generations lies elsewhere. In its unfolding as a complex yet very human testimonial to the struggle for spiritual balance, meaning, and hope, Nelly Sachs's writing enjoins the reader to continue what is at once an individual and collective task: to mend a world that seems to have learned all the wrong lessons from the Holocaust and appears bent on perpetuating the very cycle of victims and perpetrators Sachs believed could one day be brought to an end.

Translations from the German by Kathrin Bower throughout.

Bibliography

Primary Sources

Legenden und Erzählungen (Legends and Stories). 1921.
In den Wohnungen des Todes (In the Habitations of Death). 1947.
Sternverdunkelung (Darkening Star). 1949.
Eli. Ein Mysterienspiel vom Leiden Israels (*Eli: A Mystery Play on the Suffering of Israel*). 1951.
"Leben unter Bedrohung" (Life under Siege). 1956.
Und niemand weiß weiter (And No one Knows Further). 1957.
Flucht und Verwandlung (Flight and Transformation). 1959.

Fahrt ins Staublose (Journey into the Vacuum, Collected Poems I). 1961.
Zeichen im Sand (Signs in the Sand, Collected Lyric Drama). 1962.
Ausgewählte Gedichte (Selected Poems). 1963.
Das Leiden Israels (The Suffering of Israel). 1964.
Glühende Rätsel I und II (Glowing Enigmas I & II). 1964.
Späte Gedichte (Late Poems). 1965.
Die Suchende (The Seeker). 1966.
Landschaft aus Schreien (Landscape of Screams). 1966.
Simson fällt durch Jahrtausende (Samson Falls through Millennia). 1967.
O the Chimneys: Selected Poems, translated by Michael Hamburger and others. 1967.
Verzauberung (Enchantment). 1970. [Late lyric drama]
The Seeker and Other Poems, translated by Ruth Mead, Matthew Mead, and Michael Hamburger. 1970.
Suche nach Lebenden (Search for the Living, Collected Poems II). 1971.
Teile dich Nacht (Separate Night). 1971.
Gedichte (Poems). 1977.
Briefe (Letters). 1984.
Paul Celan/Nelly Sachs: Briefwechsel (*Paul Celan/Nelly Sachs: Correspondence*). 1993.

Archives

Documents, letters, and unpublished manuscripts are housed in the following archives:
Nelly Sachs Archive, State Library, Dortmund, Germany.
Nelly Sachs Archive, Royal Library, Stockholm, Sweden.

Secondary Sources

Bahr, Ehrhard. *Nelly Sachs*. Munich: C. H. Beck, 1980.

———. " 'My Metaphors Are My Wounds': Nelly Sachs and the Limits of Poetic Metaphor." In *Jewish Writers, German Literature: The Uneasy Examples of Nelly Sachs and Walter Benjamin*, edited by Timothy Bahti and Marilyn Sibley Fries. Ann Arbor: University of Michigan Press, 1995. 43–58.

Bahti, Timothy, and Marilyn Sibley Fries, eds. *Jewish Writers, German Literature: The Uneasy Examples of Nelly Sachs and Walter Benjamin*. Ann Arbor: University of Michigan Press, 1995.

Beil, Claudia. *Sprache als Heimat: Jüdische Tradition und Exilerfahrung in der Lyrik von Nelly Sachs und Rose Ausländer*. Munich: tuduv, 1991.

Berendsohn, Walter. *Nelly Sachs: Einführung in das Werk der Dichterin jüdischen Schicksals*. Darmstadt: Agora Verlag, 1974.

Bower, Kathrin. *Ethics and Remembrance in the Poetry of Nelly Sachs and Rose Ausländer*. Rochester, N.Y.: Camden House, 2000.

Dinesen, Ruth. *Nelly Sachs: Eine Biographie*. Translated by Gabriele Gerecke. Frankfurt am Main: Suhrkamp, 1992.

Dischner, Gisela.

———. *Poetik des modernen Gedichts: Zur Lyrik von Nelly Sachs*.Bad Homburg/Berlin/Zürich: Verlag Gehlen, 1970.

———. *apropos Nelly Sachs*. Frankfurt am Main: Verlag Neue Kritik, 1997.

Domin, Hilde. "Offener Brief an Nelly Sachs." In *Nelly Sachs zu Ehren. Zum 75. Geburtstag am 10. Dezember 1966*. Frankfurt am Main: Suhrkamp, 1966: 191–197.

Enzensberger, Hans Magnus. "Die Steine der Freiheit" (Stones of Freedom). In *Nelly Sachs zu Ehren*. Frankfurt am Main: Suhrkamp, 1961: 45–51.

Falkenstein, Henning. *Nelly Sachs*. Berlin: Colloquium Verlag, 1984.

Fritsch-Vivié, Gabriele. *Nelly Sachs*. Reinbek bei Hamburg: Rowohlt, 1993.

Holmqvist, Bengt, ed. *Das Buch der Nelly Sachs* (The book of Nelly Sachs). 1968. Frankfurt am Main: Suhrkamp, 1977.

Kessler, Michael, and Jürgen Wertheimer, ed. *Nelly Sachs: Neue Interpretationen* (Nelly Sachs: New Interpretations). Tübingen: Stauffenburg, 1994.

Lagercrantz, Olof. *Versuch über die Lyrik der Nelly Sachs*. Translated by Helene Ritzerfeld. Frankfurt am Main: Suhrkamp, 1967.

Langer, Lawrence. *Versions of Survival: The Holocaust and the Human Spirit*. Albany: State University of New York Press, 1982.

Lermen, Birgit, and Michael Braun. *Nelly Sachs 'an letzter Atemspitze des Lebens.'* Bonn: Bouvier Verlag, 1998.

Nelly Sachs. Munich: Edition Text + Kritik, 1979.

Nelly Sachs zu Ehren. Frankfurt am Main: Suhrkamp, 1961.

Nelly Sachs zu Ehren: Zum 75. Geburtstag am 10. Dezember 1966. Frankfurt am Main: Suhrkamp, 1966.

Ostmeier, Dorothee. *Sprache des Dramas—Drama der Sprache. Zur Poetik der Nelly Sachs*. Tübingen: Niemeyer, 1997.

Rudnick, Ursula. *Post-Shoa Religious Metaphors: The Image of God in the Poetry of Nelly Sachs*. Frankfurt am Main: Peter Lang, 1995.

Vaerst, Christa. *Dichtung- und Sprachreflexion im Werk von Nelly Sachs*. Frankfurt am Main: Peter Lang, 1977.

LEENY SACK
(1951–)

ELLEN SCHIFF

THE THEATER ARTIST Leeny Sack's address is the intersection of Holocaust and feminist issues. Her work differs from that of dramatists like Liliane Atlan and Charlotte Delbo, who wrote numerous plays about women and the *Shoah*, in that Sack creates performance pieces rather than scripts for actors. Sack's métier is closer to that of solo performance artists like Margo Lee Sherman, with her guided tour of the Auschwitz victim Charlotte Saloman's paintings, and the actor George Bartenieff, who, with playwright Karen Malpede, has made a one-man show of Victor Klemperer's *I Will Bear Witness*. Like Deb Filler, whose autobiographical one-woman shows *Punch Me in the Stomach* and *Filler Up* are ironically humorous, Sack is a second-generation narrator. The Holocaust is in her blood.

Leeny Sack's best-known performance piece is titled *The Survivor and the Translator* (1980). Its subtitle firmly states her identity and her artistic intent: "A solo theatre work about not having experienced the Holocaust, by a daughter of concentration camp survivors."

Sack's mother, Gina Rachman, was liberated from Auschwitz in 1945. She traveled through Europe in search for her brother. A lead sent her to Dachau where Joel Sack, who had been imprisoned there, now headed the Jewish Information Office, which reunited survivors. Although unsuccessful in locating her brother, Gina Rachman and Joel Sack found each other. In 1947, one of Sack's relatives, living in America, heard his name on a radio broadcast listing survivors and promptly sponsored the immigration of both the young couple and Gina Sack's mother, Rachela Rachman, also a survivor of Auschwitz. Leeny Sack was born in Brooklyn in 1951. She grew up speaking English and Polish in a household where lost family members were frequently recalled in everyday conversations. Sack recalls her parents or her grandmother sitting with her at bedtime, telling stories about their wartime experiences. She too told stories. An unusually creative child, she also drew and wrote poetry. "I dreamed poetry when I was a little kid," she recalls (interview).

But Sack's dreams were stained by the Holocaust, a formidable presence in her life from earliest childhood. She remembers "a feeling of terror of mass graves and anonymous death" and the urgent need to find a way to escape them. Her fears soon led her to recognize acting as a route to immortality. As a little girl she perceived that famous actors in the movies "died" but were still alive. At nine, she decided to be an actress. Over parental objections, she enrolled in Saturday acting classes at the American Academy of Dramatic Arts. As a high-school junior, she took an intensive summer course in theater and experimental film at the Lawrenceville School that opened her eyes to unconventional possibilities in presenting content. Between 1969 and 1971, she attended the Juilliard School, Drama Division.

Then Sack began to work with influential mentors. Elaine Summers trained her in kinetic awareness, an exploration, through movement, of the biokinetic and psychophysical languages of the body. This contemplative process freed Sack from inculcated restraints, enabling her to investigate ranges of motion, voice, behavior, and expression. Ultimately, Sack herself earned certification as a master teacher of kinetic awareness. As a member of the Performance Group, Sack worked under Richard Schechner, the founder and director of the important off-off Broadway vanguard theater. Here she learned the difference between acting and performing. Her 1975 performance as Kattrin in Brecht's *Mother Courage and Her Children* was hailed by the *SoHo News* as one of the year's ten best. Sack's development as a theater artist was also influenced deeply by Jerzy Grotowski. Workshops with members of his Polish Laboratory Theatre strengthened her ability to connect sound and spirit and to use this connection to bridge the material and the immaterial.

When Sack decided in 1978 to create a solo piece, all the experiences of her life coalesced. She realized that she viewed her initial theme—women/ madness/ God—through what she knew about the Holocaust. Listening to a recording she had made of her grandmother's wartime accounts, she was again struck by the nonlinear and incomprehensible nature of the material. The task was to shape this "narrative" into verbal and physical languages that would be comprehensible in performance. For two years she worked, first alone, then in collaboration with colleagues Steven Borst, Sabrina Hamilton, and Chloe Wing to develop a vehicle for her unrelenting material. Gina Sack came to rehearsals, providing her daughter a layer of protection and healing.

The Survivor and the Translator premiered in May 1980. Following her New York performances, Sack took the work on tour for six months to Florence, Amsterdam, Paris, Brussels, Antwerp, Milan, Cardiff, and London. She performed the work's harrowing testimony section at the World Gathering of Holocaust Survivors in Jerusalem in 1982.

Alone on stage for the stunning sixty-five minutes of *The Survivor and the Translator*, Sack brings to life her Survivor grandmother, the flat-voiced Translator of her grandmother's wartime memories, and the Second Generation performer who did not experience the Holocaust but strives to integrate the testimony into her identity—and to exorcise it. "The story I tell," she explains, "was slipped under my skin before I could say yes or no or Mama. I sit inside the memory of where I was not" (Skloot, p. 120).

Sack wears huge headphones taped to a battered suitcase, its interior stuffed with memories, its shabby exterior typifying the countless bags left in the death camps. She struggles with the imperative to find ways to relate the material that she "hears." She begins with the Sabbath blessing, perhaps seeking solace in the continuity of ritual. But she is not consoled; instead her prayer dissolves into frenzy. Sack runs in place on a metal cot whose assaulted springs make a noise that sounds uncannily like the wheels of a train, an effect she heightens by making a high-pitched noise, "like a train whistle," she writes, "or a scream" (Skloot, p. 121).

In a fevered mélange of Polish and halting English, she begins to "translate" from her grandmother's account. The rush of emotionally charged memories overflows the grandmother's experiences and invades the granddaughter's. Sack speaks alternately in the first person and in the third, not always distinguishing which pronoun refers to herself, so that the two women seem ultimately to fuse. In the early sections of the performance, she speaks in the halting, groping-for-words idiom that characterizes simultaneous translation. In the riveting half-hour monologue that ends the piece, her words circle, their uncertain syntax bespeaking the near impossibility of finding language equal to the memories, as here:

> What do you want more? Auschwitz? There was in Auschwitz when. We worked in the fields. We pulled out these from the ground and or we planted in the ground. We planted. Graves we dug. But they had to give these people work. Sometimes came still some uh people from other countries. From. So then was. Were. They were there and saw. They couldn't so much see but for sure they saw. How. When they came. When this smoke. And a big chimney. Big such. And from this smoke came this smell and this gray sky so they know that people are burning there. Of course. I didn't think about would I. You lived with the hour (Skloot, pp. 143–144).

The intimate relationship between women that gives *The Survivor and the Translator* its substance and tone and the connotation of some of its props—a Sabbath candle, a rocking chair, a wedding dress—mark it as a profoundly feminist work. Still, the refrain that punctuates the text—"Where is my mother? I don't see my mother. Where, where is my mother?"—is in the words both of the survivor's son and of her daughter. These questions, in Polish and in English, serve as the work's epigraph. They take *The Survivor and the Translator* beyond feminism and underscore its universality.

The Survivor and the Translator opened in May 1980 at the Performing Garage to excellent reviews. The *New York Times* found Sack "wonderfully persuasive" (Shepard). "Acted with conviction and great tenderness," said *The Village Voice* (Laschener); "one of the great performances of the year," declared *The Soho News* (Shewey). The twenty-nine-year-old actress won the weekly *Villager*'s Outstanding Solo Performance Award. Later, in London, *Time-Out* gave it its Most Memorable Show Award.

Sack's subsequent work has taken her in new directions. Although the succeeding theater pieces do not treat the *Shoah* explicitly, the shadow of the Holocaust informs their concern with loss and recovery, memory and retrieval, splitting and reintegration, and the imperative to connect inner experience with kinetic testimony.

Paper Floor (1984) was an investigation of the connection between preconscious imagery and the physical act of writing. Sack led eight participants through meditation into a presleep stage, then encouraged them to capture their mental formations, images, and words by writing or drawing them on the paper-lined floor, which, at day's end, was richly covered with words, signs, and lines.

Our Lady of the Hidden Agenda (1986–1988) was a solo performance piece about the physical manifestations of spiritual phenomena. Sack receives letters and cards from a writer who describes stigmata she developed in her journey from doubt to faith. Sack is skeptical, but as she expresses her disbelief, she discovers stigmata in the palms of her own hands.

(Neo-Ventriqual) THOUGHT-CLOUDS (1993–1996) was a solo performance piece developed through lengthy experimentation with slide photography and ventriloquism ("neo-ventriqual" refers both to ventriloquism and to the chambers of the heart). The two media are used to portray Sack's relationship with her mother and her responses to her mother's death. In its final scene, Sack retrieves bones from a dirt-filled table and reassembles them as a clear vision of her mother comes into focus.

In *Patient/Artist*, an autobiographical work in progress, Sack explores illness, surgery, and power relationships through an interplay of ventriloquism, projections, and dolls.

NEA Interarts Series Grants supported both *Paper Floor* and *Our Lady of the Hidden Agenda*. With a New York Foundation of the Arts Special Opportunity Stipend, Sack attended the nineteenth annual International Ventriloquists' Convention in Kentucky to research her "neo-ventriqual" piece, *THOUGHT-CLOUDS*. Sack has been a visiting artist at the Foundation Corps de Garde in Groningen, Holland (1981), Nova Scotia College of Art and Design (1987), Minneapolis College of Art and Design (1988), and Trinity College in Hartford, Connecticut (1992 and 1994). She taught at New York University's Tisch School of the Arts, Experimental Theater Wing from 1983 to 1989. She regularly conducts performer-process workshops at colleges and universities in the United States, abroad, and at Pangea Farm, a center for the study and practice of contemplative and performing arts cofounded by Sack, the therapist Norman Rosenberg, and naturalist Laura Rosenberg. From 1983 to 2000, Sack and Norman Rosenberg led seminars, workshops, and retreats at the Buddhistisches Zentrum, a Buddhist center near Vienna. Those with whom they have done this healing work include the sons and daughters of Nazis. In 2002 she began research on her next project, *Thinly Veiled*, an exploration of assumed identity and exposure.

Bibliography

Primary Sources

The Survivor and the Translator. In *Out from Under: Texts by Women Performance Artists*. Edited by Lenora Champagne. New York: Theatre Communications Group, 1990.

The Survivor and the Translator. In *The Theatre of the Holocaust*, vol. 2. Edited by Robert Skloot. Madison: University of Wisconsin Press, 1999.

Secondary Sources

"Currents and Comments." In *Parabola: Myth and the Quest for Meaning*, V; 4:100.

Guttman, Melinda Jo. "I Translate, Therefore I Am," *The SoHo News*, 21 May 1980, 59.

Helbing, Terry. "Sack Proves Strength Versatility As Actress," *The Villager*, 8 May 1980, 15.

Laschener, Sara. "In Dreams Begins Responsibility." *The Village Voice*, 2 June 1980, 87.

Shepard, Richard F. "Theater: 'The Survivor' Starring Leeny Sack." The *New York Times*, 10 August 1980, 50.

Shewey, Don. "Playing Around." *The SoHo News*, 27 August 1980, 48.

Steinman, Louise. "The Storyteller." In *The Knowing Body: Elements of Contemporary Performance and Dance*. Boston: Shambhala Publications, 1986, pp. 140–144.

"The Survivor and the Translator." *The Drama Review* 24, no. 3 (T87, September 1980): 113–116.

Interview with Leeny Sack by Ellen Schiff, 10 July 2001.

JULIE SALAMON
(1953–)

EVA FOGELMAN

JULIE SALAMON WAS born in rural Seaman, Ohio, on 10 July 1953. Both her parents, originally from Czechoslovakia, had survived concentration camps. Her mother, Lilly, born in Huszt, was deported with her parents to Auschwitz in May 1944. The transport was greeted by Dr. Joseph Mengele, and Lilly's mother was sent to a line that was destined for the gas chamber. Due to the tumult of their arrival at night, Lilly had no visual recall of what happened to her father. At the end of the war Lilly was deported to Zittau, a labor camp in eastern Germany near the Czech border. After liberation she fled to Prague, where she met Dr. Sanyi Salamon, whose wife and daughter had been gassed upon arrival to Auschwitz. Sanyi had been sent to Dachau for treating an injured partisan. Three weeks before liberation, he had escaped from a death march into the woods and had joined a partisan troop. Lilly and Sanyi Salamon married in 1946 and arrived in the United States on 27 January 1947.

After a frustrating period in New York, in 1953 the Salamons moved to Seaman, Ohio, and their second daughter, Julie, was born soon after. Because Salamons were one of the only Jewish families in Seaman, they had limited opportunities for Jewish culture and learning. Julie's father, who was a secular Jew before the Holocaust, wanted his family to maintain their Jewish identity. He took the initiative to read the weekly Torah portion every Saturday morning and drove two hours every Sunday in order for the children to have Hebrew lessons. Adherence to their Jewish heritage was also marked by support of Israel as a Jewish homeland and visiting local synagogues on international travel.

Julie Salamon attended Tufts University near Boston, where she majored in Chinese history and wrote for the school newspaper. Salamon received a law degree from New York University but opted to work at the *Wall Street Journal* covering commodities. In 1983, after five years of business writing, Julie was offered the opportunity to be the film critic for the *Wall Street Journal* and remained in that position for eleven years. In 2000 she began working as the television critic for *The New York Times.*

While riding the New York subway to view movies, at the age of 30, Salamon wrote her first novel, *White Lies* (1987), which "in outline is autobiographical . . ." (Caplan, p. 8). Salamon's reporting became a hit when her book *The Devil's Candy* (1991) was the "one good thing to come out of the . . . making of the *Bonfire of the Vanities*" (Ansen, 1991, p. 78). Salamon's *The Christmas Tree* (1996) was on *The New York Times* bestseller list. She received the Front Page Award from the Newswomen's Club of New York, as well as several Pulitzer nominations and the Ohio Ana Library Association Award for *The Net of Dreams* (1996).

Major Themes and Concerns

The diverse literary accomplishments of Julie Salamon all evidence her strong interest in social justice and second generation Holocaust themes of intergenerational *Shoah* response and post-Auschwitz Jewish identity. Salamon joins other journalists who are children of Holocaust survivors, such as Helen Epstein, Joseph Berger, and David Lee Preston, in grappling with uncovering hidden family histories through others and directly, via their own ancestry. The intergenerational psychological dynamic of choosing an occupation related to the survivor-parent ordeal is not uncommon. The occupations, however, are as diverse as helping professions in law, medicine, mental health, teaching, performing, or visual arts. Salamon acknowledges, "I think I wouldn't have become a writer" had it not been for the fact that "there were so many things left unanswered when my father died" (Eshman, 1996). She "loved [her father,] worshipped him, feared him, sometimes, but didn't know him" (*The Net of Dreams: A Family's Search for a Rightful Place*, New York: Random House, 1996, p. 158). How could she know him? He never told her that he had a wife and a child who were killed in the war, not even when he was dying. Instead of being angry at her father's silence, Julie Salamon challenged herself to transform her feelings into creative ventures. She spoke with many people to piece together the family history of her father, who was the youngest of seven children, "a miracle child of 'elderly' parents" (*A Net of Dreams*, p. 157).

For some second generation, the pervasive discontinuity between the past and present is bridged by a physical connection to the places that were destroyed. Such a journey was undertaken by Julie Salamon, her mother, and her stepfather, although initially under the guise of going to write about the making of Steven Spielberg's *Schindler's List*. When Lilly Salamon, an inmate of Auschwitz, accompanied Julie Salamon to the set design of *Schindler's List*, the film became a less compelling subject for a book than her own family's connection to the extermination camp. In *The Net of Dreams* the professional and personal intertwine, and the reader witnesses the process Julie Salamon follows to search her roots.

Communication between the generations is a major theme in the novel *White Lies* as well as in *The Net of Dreams*. Salamon makes "the reader a part of the process of self-discovery" (Eshman, 1996). On one hand, Salamon heard almost no details of her father's ordeals, although she explains that she felt it viscerally at age fifteen or sixteen when she saw him lighting a memorial candle at a Holocaust commemoration ceremony. On the other hand, her mother spoke incessantly about the past. Salamon explains in an interview with *The New York Times* that her mother "never finishes the story. She would always be getting up to do something" (Haberman, *New York Times*, pp. C1, C4). Salamon clearly breaks the barrier in communication with her mother by striving to construct a sequential narrative for *The Net of Dreams*. At various times the process is painful for both mother and daughter. When Julie realizes that her mother skips over the last time she saw her father, Julie probes deeper until her mother recalls that painful moment. Breaking the silence not only enhances intimacy between the generations, but facilitates a sense of rootedness and a less fragmented self.

A point of curiosity for the member of the second generation is the desire to know to what the survivor parent attributes his or her survival. Salamon's mother describes meeting a "Gypsy woman," not a real Gypsy, "but a nice Jewish woman who had learned from a Gypsy" (*Net of Dreams*, p. 111). In the barracks in Lager C of Auschwitz, this very small pretty woman, who came from Hungary, had learned how to read palms from a Gypsy woman. She said, "You'll come out. You'll survive. As a matter of fact, you will be very happy. You will be very lucky in marriage and in life" (*Net of Dreams* p. 112). This prediction kept Lilly optimistic. She says, "I just believed it, that nothing could happen to me, that I'll come out. I just didn't know how and when and what" (*Net of Dreams*, p. 112). After hearing this spiritual encounter, the journalist part of Salamon wanted facts and feelings. Her mother reveals a shameful part of herself, "I never worry about the past or the future, I worry about today. I think that's why I survived it better than other people" (*Net of Dreams*, p. 112).

The significance of Salamon's portrayal of her parents in *The Net of Dreams* is that they are flesh-and-blood human beings who had a life prior to being sent to the concentration camps. Salamon dispels the myth and stereotype of the Holocaust survivor-victim, portrayed in film and journalistic accounts as emotionally disturbed, with women shown as depressed and suicidal and men shown with out-of-control aggression. The reader is privy to how survivors mobilized whatever emotional and physical strength they could muster in order to begin new families, careers, and communities. The idiosyncratic after-effects, the silence of the father, the mother who stuffs cookies into her purse, lurk in the background, rather than in the foreground of their being.

Julie Salamon's fictionalized second-generation character, called Jamaica, departs from the clichéd identity of the emotionally-disturbed person. Rather, Jamaica—based on Julie herself—functions as a vehicle to promote social justice. Jamaica works as a journalist who exposes the plight of second generation welfare mothers. In his discussion of the tendency of second generation writers to universalize the Holocaust through their presentation of social justice themes, Alan L. Berger situates Julie Salamon among Carol Ascher and Lev Raphael, who write to "protest against injustice" (p. 126). Alan L. Berger has suggested that other second-generation writers such as Carol Ascher and Lev Raphael write in order to "protest against injustice" (p. 126). Berger interprets these authors' efforts to turn history into story, thereby hoping to come to grips with what remains an "unmasterable trauma" (pp. 126–127). He concludes that "by writing the story of their parents' survival and its impact on their own lives, these second-generation witnesses hope to share the message of common human vulnerability, thereby helping to prevent Holocaust modes of thought from operating in the world" (p. 127).

Finding out the story is a phase in the mourning process that second-generation individuals, knowingly or unknowingly, undergo. Moving beyond shock, denial, and confrontation, a second-generation writer such as Julie Salamon is able to transcend overidentification with victimhood. Other children of survivors tend to relive the pain and suffering of the Holocaust victims by being victims in their personal life. Such a dynamic may be exacerbated by feeling survivor guilt, and hence not allowing oneself to enjoy the present. While children of survivors such as Salamon are driven by a moral imperative to make a difference and search for meaning beyond their parents' persecution, others continue to fear the external world and find it difficult to trust.

Critical Reception

Although Salamon is best known for her "mesmerizing best-seller" *The Devil's Candy* about Brian DePalma's film *The Bonfire of the Vanities* based on Tom Wolfe's novel, her creative writing career was launched with a second-generation novel entitled *White Lies*.

The *Kirkus* review recognizes *White Lies* as a promising but flawed first novel. The anonymous reviewer praises Salamon for her effort to be original about contemporary issues and morals. To Lore Dickstein (1988) *White Lies* had no nucleus to integrate its unrelated digressive parts. The coherence of the "second-generation self" in *White Lies* is imbedded in the core of Jamaica's moral compass, which manifests itself in a desire to fight for just causes.

White Lies is also a novel that has merited critique in an academic literary review of American second-generation witnesses to the Holocaust, Alan Berger's *Children of Job*. Berger alludes to the strength of the novel in its portrayal of a complex second generation character, rather than a unidimensional stereotype caricature. A few of the psychological dynamics illustrated in the life of Jamaica are "guilt, alienation, identity, communication between the generations, the struggle between forgetting and remembering the Holocaust" (p. 97) and "contrast of attitudes toward survivors" (p. 109).

Historian Deborah Lipstadt praises Salamon for her writing on the postwar period:

> This is a compelling story of discovery. On one level it is the author's discovery of her parents' past, but on a deeper level it is the story of a child of survivors learning that she cannot get on with her life until she has come to terms with what is not only her parents' story but also her own.

Salamon's ability to penetrate the abyss of the destruction of European Jewry, and her inner yearning to confront moral issues makes her a writer to keep watching.

Bibliography

Primary Sources

Review of *Children of the Holocaust* by Helen Epstein. 1979.
White Lies. 1987.
The Devil's Candy. 1991.
The Net of Dreams: A Family's Search for a Rightful Place. 1996.
The Christmas Tree. 1996.
"Walls That Echo of the Unspeakable." *The New York Times*, 7 September 1997.
Facing the Wind. 2001.
"The Lifetime Reporting Trip." In *Second Generation Voices: Reflections of Children of Holocaust Survivors and Perpetrators*. Edited by Alan and Naomi Berger. 2001.

Secondary Sources

Berger, Alan L. *Children of Job: American Second-Generation Witnesses to the Holocaust*. Albany: State University of New York Press, 1997.
Bolton, Judith. Review of *White Lies*. *Hartford Courant*, 25 December 1988.
Bolton-Fasman, Judith. Review of *The Net of Dreams: A Family's Search for a Rightful Place*. *Baltimore Jewish Times*, 17 May 1996.
Caplan, Lois. Review of *White Lies*. *St. Louis Jewish Light*, 20 January 1988, p. 8.
Crittenden, Yvonne. Review of *The Net of Dreams*. *Toronto Sun*, 12 May 1996. http:www.canoe.ca/JamBooksReviewsN/netofdreams-salamon.html.
Dickstein, Lore. Review of *White Lies*. *The New York Times*, 7 February 1988.
Dunford, Judith. Review of *The Net of Dreams: A Family's Search for a Rightful Place*. *Newsday*, 17 March 1996, pp. 35–36.
Elliott, Roberta. Review of *White Lies*. *Jewish Week*.
Eshman, Robert. Review of *The Net of Dreams*. *Jewish Journal*, 3 November 1996.
Haberman, Clyde. Review of *The Net of Dreams*. *The New York Times*, 22 May 1996, pp. C1, C4.
Heymann, Susan. Review of *The Net of Dreams*. *Los Angeles Times Book Review*, 23 June 1996.
Levin, Donna. Review of *The Net of Dreams*. *San Francisco Chronicle*, 7 April 1996.
Lipstadt, Deborah. Review of *The Net of Dreams*. *Washington Post Book Review*, 1996.
Lorber, Helene. Review of *The Net of Dreams*. *Free Press*, 3 April 1996, p. 7D.

Richmond, Theo. Review of *The Net of Dreams. The New York Times Book Review*, 31 March 1996.

Roberts, Larry. Review of *The Net of Dreams. Blade*, 5 May 1996.

Salony, Mary. Review of *The Net of Dreams. Library Journal*, 15 April 1996.

Skolow, Raymond. Review of *White Lies. The Wall Street Journal*, 3 February 1988.

Stewart, James B. Review of *The Net of Dreams. Facing the Wind: A True Story of Tragedy and Reconciliation. The New York Times Sunday Book Review*, 1 April 2001, p. 10.

Vromen, Galina. Review of *The Net of Dreams: A Family's Search for a Rightful Place. The Jerusalem Report*, 25 July 1996, p. 44.

Wertheimer, Linda K. Review of *The Net of Dreams. Orlando Sentinel*, 25 April 1996.

DIANE SAMUELS
(1960–)

CLAIRE M. TYLEE

DIANE SAMUELS WAS born in Liverpool in 1960. Her father, Rubin Samuels, was born in Liverpool in 1937; her mother, Elaine Samuels (née Davies) was born in Southport in 1935. After reading history at Cambridge University, Samuels trained as a drama teacher at Goldsmiths', University of London, then taught in inner London schools for five years before becoming a full-time dramatist. She lives in London with her husband and two sons and lectures part-time at Middlesex University. A number of her plays and adaptations have been produced on stage, but *Kindertransport* is the first to be published. It remains her best-known work. Since its London premiere in 1993, this prize-winning play (1992 Verity Bargate Award, 1993 Meyer Whitworth Award) has been broadcast on BBC Radio 4 and performed worldwide; a screenplay is in preparation. This is the only work by Samuels connected with the Holocaust.

The *Kindertransports*

The German word "*Kindertransport*" (literally, the transportation of children) carries a special, emotional meaning in English. It refers to the campaign to rescue Jewish children from Nazi-controlled Europe in the last nine months before Britain declared war on Germany in September 1939. These rescued children (*Kinder*) hold a special place in both the history of World War II and in contemporary British culture: a million and a half Jewish children perished as a result of the war. In her foreword to the 1995 publication of *Kindertransport* Samuels identifies several incidents that led her to write the play and comments on her research for it. She dedicates the play to all the Jewish *Kinder* who were saved by the *Kindertransports*, including Bertha Leverton and others who talked to her about their experiences. It was Leverton who organized the fiftieth anniversary celebration and reunion of the *Kinder* in June 1989. Despite earlier publications by Karen Gershon, it was only then that the full extent and continuing impact of the *Kindertransports* started to be recognized. Since 1989 there have been an exhibition, books, and several film and television documentaries retelling the events.

Refugees had been leaving Germany from the early 1930s, some with help from concerned individuals and organizations, but a sudden sense of urgency was impelled in Britain by the pogrom of *Kristallnacht* in November 1938. The Refugee Children's Movement was set up by the British Inter-Aid Committee (BIC) in association with existing Jewish, Christian, and nondenominational councils to rescue children, both Jewish and "non-Aryan Christian," from Germany, Austria, and Czechoslovakia. In fact, children were also rescued from France, and some arrived by air. The BIC had already brought out 470 children since 1936 but had been hampered by red tape. The new plan involved financial bonds and guarantees to the British Home Office concerning the children's welfare; in return, the Home Office simplified the travel documents required. The first trainloads arrived in England on 10 December 1938 and continued for nine months. By August 1939, 9,354 children had been rescued under the scheme. They were aged from a few months to seventeen years. Although some went to relatives or hostels, most were fostered, many by non-Jewish families. Their individual stories are hugely varied, as can be seen from the books edited by Leverton and Gershon and the personal memoirs by *Kinder* such as Karen Gershon and Vera Gissing. While some were eventually reunited with their parents and some reemigrated to America or Israel, about 6,000 *Kinder* were absorbed into British society. Samuels's *Kindertransport* tells the fictional story of one such girl and reveals what the costs of assimilation and survival might have been.

Play: *Kindertransport*

By its very title *Kindertransport* refers to European history, and actual historical events are alluded to in the course of its action. Yet it is not a conventional history play. It does not attempt to present a story set in the past, nor is it written in realist mode. This makes it unlike many British Holocaust plays that are set in the war years (for instance, Pip Simmons's *An die Musik* or Julian Garner's *The Flight into Egypt*). It is also different from two other women-centered Holocaust plays by female dramatists, written to tell the experiences of real refugee women: Sue Frumin's *Housetrample* and Julia Pascal's *Teresa*. By contrast, *Kindertransport* is a fictional memory play, set in present-day London but interwoven with scenes from wartime Hamburg and Manchester. It makes use of double casting and expressionist devices such as "the Ratcatcher" to indicate the haunting, nightmarish, threatening quality of a past that has persisted into the present.

Critical Responses

London theater critics, while applauding the play's seriousness, were wary that *Kindertransport* was subject to the charge of "hitching a ride on the back of other people's sufferings." Some worried that its dedication hinted at moral blackmail and emotional arm-twisting. However, only one critic believed that the play was set within the context of the Holocaust merely to heighten the impact of its central mother-daughter conflicts. In general they found that the play had moral integrity, that it was conscientiously researched, and that it genuinely honored the refugee children whom it commemorated. There was agreement that the play was moving, unpredictable, and skillfully constructed; but there was strong disagreement as to whether its documentary edge preserved it from lapsing into melodrama. Whereas one (male) critic, Simon Round in the *Jewish Chronicle*, found "the intensity of anguish almost unbearable," another (male) critic, David Murray in *The Financial Times*, condemned the "ritualised screaming matches" and "obscure motivations" as typical of a "woman's play" weakened by the absence of men. On the whole *Kindertransport* was praised for its uncompromising intelligence; it investigated the effects of traumatic dislocation, counted the costs of emotional survival, and boldly refused a redemptive ending: "some wounds are too deep to heal."

Feminist Drama

Like the plays by Frumin and Pascal, *Kindertransport* came out of the postwar women's movement in Britain. It investigates the emotional bonds between mothers and daughters across three generations. The cast of six calls for one male actor who doubles in several minor roles, including the Ratcatcher, but the interest centers on one woman, Eva/Evelyn, now age sixty. Both as child and adult, daughter and mother, Eva/Evelyn links the other three women in the play. This focus on female relationships, particularly on "mothering," was the common theme of a new tradition of feminist plays that formed the backbone of the women's movement in Britain from 1970, including Nell Dunn's *Steaming* and Caryl Churchill's *Top Girls*. These and other writings by women revealed a muted area of culture, women's intimate experiences, and made possible the gradual breaking of other silences. Taboo subjects such as illegitimacy, rape, and breast cancer were broached. What had been repressed as personal trauma now appeared as the hidden underside of the social fabric, catastrophic consequences of the larger political system and its values. Samuels draws on this feminist heritage, using the supportive structure of studio drama to show how the war ruptured female bonds.

British National Identity and Jewish Identity

Kindertransport also reveals two other muted areas of British culture: war trauma and the state of unbelonging. It accomplishes this through the translated voice of the "other," a German Jewish refugee girl who survives psychologically by naturalizing as English. Against the dominant, victorious history of Britain in World War II, so familiar as "Our Finest Hour," Samuels sets a tiny fragment of that nation: Evelyn. Samuels has said that when, during the fiftieth anniversary of the *Kindertransports*, many people who had been silent started to identify themselves as refugees, it was "as if a dark national secret had come to light." Her play reveals one such silence—a personal war trauma from the dark underside of Britain's national history. A British audience is encouraged to empathize with Evelyn, a stereotypically middle-class Englishwoman, before discovering that she is/was also stereotypically "other," both Jewish and German at the outbreak of World War II. She is not only alien with regard to religion and language but from *the* enemy nation.

Gradually we see what her survival has cost her and the impact this has had on her daughter, Faith, whom she has kept in ignorance. Evelyn and Faith are an integral part of contemporary British society; Evelyn's past is therefore part of the British past, and that includes the loss of her father in Auschwitz. It also includes Evelyn's cold rejection of her birth mother, Helga, in favor of her adopted Christian mother, Lil. Querying Britain's xenophobia, Samuels's *Kindertransport* challenges its audience to accept the Holocaust as part of a composite British national identity. The children's story, *Der Rattenfänger*, the legend of the Pied Piper, is used as a thread to link Evelyn with Eva and also represents the common culture linking England with Germany. In the legend, one crippled child survives. Evelyn, psychologically scarred, finally acknowledges her German Jewish past but nevertheless confirms her commitment to her adopted Anglo-Christian identity.

However, when she destroys her personal documents at the end of the play, Evelyn retains for Faith two books that Helga had given her fifty years before: not only *Der Rattenfänger* but also a copy of the Haggadah. Thus, she leaves options open for Faith to recover her links to the German past and also to her Jewish heritage. The Haggadah has a particular symbolic significance for Jewish members of the play's audience. It is the Hebrew text of the traditional Jewish Passover ceremony that celebrates the escape from slavery and the survival of the Jewish people. The Jewish escape from Nazi Europe is often regarded as another such Exodus. So the sacred book may be seen to counterbalance the Nazi evil represented by the Ratcatcher's physical presence on the stage. That evil has continued to affect Evelyn, for she is paranoically secretive, still feels resentment against Helga for having "abandoned" her, and can scarcely recall her Jewish upbringing. Yet Faith has already unwittingly enacted the role of the youngest child at the Passover ceremony—to ask questions about the past. So the saving and transmission of both books, even though neither Faith nor Evelyn can read either of them, resonates ironically. Together the texts have a symbolic force, powerfully suggesting that the women's lives have a mythical, historical, and sacred meaning that transcends their own understanding.

Survival

The play affects not only British and Jewish audiences. Acclaimed productions from Japan to South Africa demonstrate the international appeal of its depiction of war's traumatic effects on children. Many societies have collective ceremonies of World War II remembrance and mourning that focus on national war memorials. Particularly where a survivor feels excluded from the nation (for instance, Japanese Americans), the public performance of personal acts of recollection and resolution in plays like *Kindertransport* may also aid healing. When Evelyn as an adult decides to tear up her past, saying that she absolutely refuses to give up, Lil calls her a survivor. Evelyn replies: "Is that what I am? Yes. No matter what happens, no matter what anyone anywhere does. No matter how the skies may blaze and the earth tremble, it must continue. Mundane, ordinary life. Most people don't begin to know the value of it." Samuels says the past "is a part of the inner life of the present." *Kindertransport* enables audiences everywhere to recognize that inner life and to contemplate what may prevent reconciliation with the wounding past that still lurks within the everyday life of survivors.

Bibliography

Primary Sources

Kindertransport. 1995.

"About Now." In David Edgar, ed. State of Play. 1999.

Secondary Sources

Berghahn, Marion. *German-Jewish Refugees in England: The Ambiguities of Assimilation.* Basingstoke: Macmillan, 1984. Republished as *Continental Britain: German-Jewish Refugees from Nazi Germany.* Oxford: Berg, 1988.

Drucker, Olga Levy. *Kindertransport.* New York: Holt, 1992.

Frumin, Sue. *The Housetrample.* In *Lesbian Plays: Two*, edited by Jill Davis. London: Methuen, 1989.

Gershon, Karen, ed. *We Came as Children: A Collective Biography.* London: Gollancz, 1966; New York: Harcourt, 1996.

———. *Bread of Exile.* London: Gollancz, 1985.

Gissing, Vera. *Pearls of Childhood.* London: Robson, 1988.

Gottlieb, Amy Zahl. *Men of Vision: Anglo-Jewry's Aid to Victims of the Nazi Regime 1933–45.* London: Weidenfeld & Nicolson, 1998.

Harris, Mark Jonathan, and Deborah Oppenheimer. *Into the Arms of Strangers: Stories of the Kindertransport.* London: Bloomsbury, 2001.

Hirschfield, Gerhard, ed. *Exile in Great Britain: Refugees from Hitler's Germany.* Leamington Spa: Berg, 1984; Atlantic Highlands, N.J.: Humanities, 1984.

Leverton, Bertha, and Schmuel Lowensohn, ed. *I Came Alone: The Stories of the Kindertransports.* Sussex: Book Guild, 1990.

Leverton, Bertha, and Bea Green, ed. *Kindertransport 60th Anniversary 1939–1999.* London: ROK, 1999.

Newman, Rabbi Jacob. *Kinder Transport: A Study of Stresses and Traumas of Refugee Children.* Privately published by the author.

Pascal, Julia. "Teresa." In *The Holocaust Trilogy*. London: Oberon, 2000.

Sicher, Efraim. "The Burden of Memory: The Writing of the Post-Holocaust Generation." In *Breaking Crystal: Writing and Memory after Auschwitz*, edited by Efraim Sichler, 19–88. Champaign: University of Illinois Press, 1998.

Theatre Record (20 May–2 June 1996): 691–694; (9–22 September 1996): 1147–1151.

Turner, Barry. *. . . And the Policeman Smiled*. London: Bloomsbury, 1990.

Documentary Films

The Children Who Cheated the Nazis: Great Britain: 2000. Sue Read. Gold Reed Productions.

Into the Arms of Strangers. Great Britain: 2000. Mark Jonathan Harris. Warner Bros.

Als Sie nicht mehr deutsche sein dürfen: Über die Kindertransport nach England. Great Britain: 1989. Sabine Bruning and Peter Merse Burger.

My Knees Were Jumping: Remembering the Kindertransports. USA: 2000. Melissa Hacker.

ARTUR SANDAUER
(1913–1989)

MADELINE G. LEVINE

SANDAUER WAS ONE of the most influential literary critics in postwar Poland. A born polemicist and brilliant interpreter of both prose and poetry, he was a man of strong opinions, provocatively expressed. A Jew from the Polish provinces who barely escaped death during the Holocaust, he became one of the most important arbiters of Polish high literary culture. Sandauer spoke and wrote about himself as a split personality—a fate he ascribed to all assimilated Jews in Poland—and the vehemence with which he established himself after the war as a voice to be reckoned with in Polish literary circles appears to have been, in some measure at least, his defiant response to both the Holocaust itself and to pre- and postwar antisemitism in Poland. He would neither accept being marginalized nor would he curry acceptance by adopting a conciliatory tone even during the years of high Stalinism. His insistence that Polish literature must open itself to experimental writing and "outsider" sensibilities implicitly rejects, as well, the notion that what is "Polish" is the preserve of ethnic Poles.

Surviving the War

Sandauer was born in Sambor, a provincial town in the then-Austrian province of Galicia, now a city in Ukraine, not far from his friend Bruno Schulz's Drohobycz. Sandauer's parents raised their children to think of themselves as Poles; the family "religion" was socialism. Sandauer graduated in 1936 from Jan Kazimierz University in Lwów, having concentrated in classical philology; in 1937 he moved to Kraków and began working as a freelance literary critic for various leftist journals. He returned to Sambor as soon as the war broke out in order to be with his family. Sambor was under Soviet rule from mid-September 1939 until shortly after the June 1941 German invasion of the Soviet Union; during that time Sandauer worked as a high school Russian teacher—a position that led indirectly to his survival. When the Sambor ghetto was being liquidated in the summer of 1943, one of his former students happened upon the scene and, horrified at finding his teacher there, managed to arrange a hiding place for Sandauer, his mother, and sister (the father had already been killed). The Sandauers survived the war thanks to this young man and the Ukrainian peasants who kept them concealed in their attic for fourteen months until the Red Army liberated Sambor.

Sandauer seems to have emerged from the Holocaust with a strong sense of self-loathing expressed as contempt for Jews who could not bring themselves to oppose Nazi rule. During the first postwar years, while reestablishing himself as a literary critic, he hesitated over how he wished to define his identity and where his allegiances belonged. He moved back and forth between Paris and Kraków, even attempting in 1948 to join a newly formed Israeli army in France (he was rejected as physically unfit), yet when his mother and sister emigrated to Israel in 1950, Sandauer, now married, opted to remain in Poland. In 1955 he traveled to Israel as an official representative of the Polish-Israeli friendship society; this trip resulted in a slim illustrated travelogue, *W 2000 lat później: Pamiętnik izraelski* (1956; Two Thousand Years Later: An Israeli Memoir), depicting Israel as an exotic land whose citizens are pursuing an entirely different destiny from that of the East European Jews like him who have chosen the path of assimilation.

Short Stories

Sandauer's other self-consciously Jewish writings form, as it were, a pair of parentheses around his life's work as a literary critic. *Śmierć liberała* (1947; The death of a liberal) is a disturbing collection of six linked short stories about life and death in an unnamed ghetto. The protagonists of these stories all collaborate one way or another in the death of other Jews. Sandauer's narrative tone is cynicism with contempt for those who deluded themselves into thinking they cared about others, while their sole goal was to save their own skins; his greatest disdain is reserved for the *Judenrat* elite. The title story introduces the fictional Dr. Herbert Kirsche, the ghetto's *Judenrat* president, who fancies himself a brilliant strategist and thinks his conversations about Goethe with "his" Gestapo agent have earned him respect and a special dispensation for the ghetto. The narrator of this story, one of a tiny group preparing for armed rebellion, is rebuked by Kirsche for placing his own need to rebel above the community's survival. In the end, no rebellion takes place and the narrator is vindicated only by outliving Dr. Kirsche: "He fell onto the heap of corpses, the last man from our town" (*Proza*, Warsaw: Czytelnik, 1983, p. 16). In the sardonically titled story "Limited Liability Partnership," the main character is Dr. Jassym, who is in charge of the *Judenrat* records office. Dr. Jassym delights in the precision with which he maintains his card files, working around the clock to keep up with the necessary transfer of records from the file cabinets containing the names of the living to the files holding the records of the dead. In a grotesquely comic scene, Dr. Jassym is confronted by a man who has tried to work the system and declared himself dead twice over, but now wants to be resurrected so he can go on drawing rations. Dr. Kirsche reappears in this story, demanding that Jassym select, overnight, half the ghetto population for deportation—or rather, as Kirsche prefers to put it, that he save 3,500 people by listing them as exempt from the order. Because time is so short, Kirsche and Jassym select the survivors according to the length of their surnames—long names take too much time to list. Just as grotesque is the story "A Night of Law and Order" which depicts the roundup of the condemned, conducted by the Jewish police under the supervision of the Ukrainian police, with everyone, the hunters and the hunted, focused solely on saving their own skin.

In "A Memoir of Nonsense" the reader learns only in the story's final pages that he has been reading the journal of a now-dead survivor of the mass deportation. The writer of the journal had been given shelter, but fled with another survivor in hopes of joining up with partisans. He did not join the partisans and took his own life instead, having arrived at the unbearable conclusion that only someone who is fighting for something higher than life itself can risk his life. "And I? . . . What was I dying for? For a faith that I did not profess? For a people with whom I felt no bonds? I was dying for nonsense, that's what!" (p. 58). The last story in the volume bears the hopeful title, "A Matter of Dignity," but "dignity" turns out to be the protagonist's request to be executed first. This story, and thus the book *The Death of a Liberal*, ends with the narrator's bitter gloss: "And that is his revenge. Let us not deprive those who are dying of their final consolation" (p. 111).

Memoirs

Sandauer returned to the subject of the Holocaust in his memoir, *Zapiski z martwego miasta* (*Autobiografie i parabiografie*) (1963; Notes from a dead city [Autobiographies and parabiographies]), which he began writing in 1948. Dedicated to the Małankiewicz family in whose attic he survived the Holocaust, this book begins as a straightforward autobiographical narrative about Sandauer's prewar life, including mention of antisemitism among some Polish intellectuals, but records the wartime and Holocaust experience through a fictional alter ego—Mieczysław Rosenzweig—a self-hating Jewish intellectual whose assimilation, unlike Sandauer's, took the form of internalizing the views of Polish right-wing nationalism. In 1982 Sandauer returned to Jewish themes with the publication of his extended, penetrating essay on the representation of Jews in Polish literature and the paradox of being a Jew who claims Polish culture as his own: *O sytuacji pisarza polskiego pochodzenia żydowskiego w XX wieku (Rzecz, którą nie ja powinienem był napisać . . .)* (1982; On the situation of the Polish writer of Jewish descent in the 20th century: Something that I ought not to have written . . .). Here he argues that assimilation is impossible; that the "too heavy" heritage of Jewishness leads Polish Jewish writers to one of two outcomes: the inauthenticity of denying their Jewish identity or the self-demonization and self-hatred of embracing it. As for himself, Sandauer has this to say in closing, "Assimilation proved impossible; what turned out to be possible, however, was an analysis of this impossibility" (Warsaw: Czytelnik, 1982, p. 97).

Sandauer returned once more to autobiography in the posthumously published volume *Byłem . . .* (1991; I was). Here, too, as in his "Notes from a Dead City," he does not speak directly of his own experience of the Holocaust; instead, his family's fourteen months in hiding are described by his sister (these pages, at least, are attributed to his sister), who writes only briefly about the physical difficulties of their life. Sandauer supplements his sister's narrative by reminding the reader that they had lots of reading material while in hiding and that during those fourteen months he translated into Polish (from memory) a lengthy poem by Mayakovsky; he even provides samples of his excellent translation, as if to prove the Holocaust did not scar him in the least. An embittered and difficult personality, Sandauer died believing, apparently, that he was the victim of an informal conspiracy of Polish scholars who were borrowing his ideas but erasing his name from the history of Polish letters. None of Sandauer's books has been translated into English.

Bibliography

Primary Sources

Śmierć liberała (The Death of a Liberal). 1947.
Theokritos—twórca sielanki (Theocrites—Creator of the Pastoral). 1955.
Poeci trzech pokoleń (Poets of Three Generations). 1955.
W 2000 lat później. Pamiętnik izraelski (Two Thousand Years Later: An Israeli Memoir). 1956.
Moje odchylenia (My Deviations). 1956.
O jedności treści i formy (On the Unity of Content and Form). 1957.
Zapiski z martwego miasta (Notes from a Dead City). 1963.
Stanowiska wobec . . . (Positions About . . .). 1963.
Dla każdego coś przykrego (Something Bad for Everyone). 1966.
Samobójstwo Mitrydatesa (The Suicide of Mithridates). 1968.
Liryka i logika (Lyric and Logic). 1969.
Przyboś. 1970.
Matecznik literacki (Literary Nursery). 1972.
Teoria i historia (Theory and History). 1973.
Poeci czterech pokoleń (Poets of Four Generations). 1977.
Bóg, Szatan, Mesjasz i . . .? (God, Satan, Messiah and . . .?). 1977.
Białoszewski. 1979.
O sytuacji pisarza polskiego żydowskiego pochodzenia w XX wieku. (Rzecz, którą nie ja powinienem był napisać . . .) (On the Situation of the Polish Writer of Jewish Descent in the 20th Century: Something that I Ought Not to Have Written . . .). 1982.
Proza (Prose). 1983.
Pisma zebrane (Collected Works). 4 vols. 1985.
Byłem . . . . (I Was). 1991.

Secondary Sources

Baran, Józef, ed. "*Śnił mi się Artur Sandauer*": *Rozmowy i wspomnienia*. Hereditas Polono-Judaica 2. Kraków: Centrum Kultury Żydowskiej na Kazimierzu w Krakowie, 1992.
Lam, Andrzej. "Sandauer, Artur." In *Literatura polska. Przewodnik encyklopedyczny*. Vol. 2. Warsaw: PIW, 1985, pp. 334–335.
Wróbel, Józef. *Tematy żydowskie w prozie polskiej 1939–1987*. Kraków: Towarzystwo Autorów i Wydawców Prac Naukowych "Universitat," 1991.
Wołowiec, Grzegorz. *Nowocześni w PRL. Przyboś i Sandauer*. Wrocław: Fundacja na Rzecz Nauki Polskiej, 1999.

JEAN-PAUL SARTRE

(1905–1980)

JONATHAN JUDAKEN

As a result of his contributions to philosophy, literature, literary criticism, theater, and his political interventions, Jean-Paul Sartre emerged as the most recognized French intellectual in the wake of World War II. His vast body of work contains some significant contributions to the literature on the Holocaust, especially his analysis of the victims in *Réflexions sur la question juive* (*Anti-Semite and Jew*, 1946) and his exploration of the culpability of the perpetrators dramatized in *Les séquestrés d'Altona* (*The Condemned of Altona*, 1959).

Biography

Born in Paris on 21 June 1905, Jean-Paul was the only son of Anne-Marie (née Schweitzer) and Jean-Baptiste Sartre. The cousin of Albert Schweitzer, he was reared to exceed his relative's cultural renown. His father died when he was fifteen months old, and he was raised by his doting mother and his maternal grandfather, Charles Schweitzer, a published educator of German. An early leucoma in the right eye gave him his distinctive bespectacled, cross-eyed look.

Sartre was educated in the elite Lycée (high school) Henri IV and studied at Lycée Louis-le-Grand for his entrance in 1924 into the École Normale Supérieure, the final training ground for France's intellectual elite, where he was a schoolmate with other famous French thinkers including Paul Nizan, Raymond Aron, Jean Hyppolite, and his lifelong companion, Simone de Beauvoir. After passing the *agrégation* exam with the top mark in 1929, he took a position in Le Havre before a one-year stint at the French Institute in Berlin just after Adolf Hitler was appointed chancellor in 1933. Having already published some of his early philosophical investigations, Sartre would spend the year revising his literary masterpiece, *La Nausée*, (*Nausea*, 1938), immersing himself in Martin Heidegger's existential critique of Edmund Husserl, and completing his phenomenological analysis of consciousness, *La transcendance de l'ego* (*The Transcendence of the Ego*, 1937.

Sartre returned to a France embroiled in the Franco-French conflicts of the 1930s and his literature began to address the social divisions engendered by the rise of fascism and antisemitism, especially his short story "L'enfance d'un chef" ("The Childhood of a Leader"), published in a collection titled *Le Mur* (*The Wall*), which appeared in 1939, a year after the critical success of *La Nausée*. It narrates the evolution of a young, provincial French boy, Lucien Fleurier, anguished in his search for meaning, who finds purpose among the cadres of the *camelots du roi*, "the hawkers of the king," who sell the royalist and antisemitic newspapers of the extreme-right Action Française and served as the shock troops in their battles. With his star rising in French intellectual circles, Sartre was called to the front as the German *Blitzkrieg* rolled across Poland in September 1939.

Sartre wrote at a furious pace during the nine months of the "phony war" before the German attack on France in May 1940. His posthumously published *Les carnets de la drôle de guerre* (The War Diaries, 1983) both testifies to the life of ordinary soldiers on the Maginot front and contains the outlines of subsequent work including his philosophical magnum opus, *L'étre et le néant* (*Being and Nothingness*, 1943). Sartre also completed *L'âge de raison* (*The Age of Reason*, 1945) the first volume of his trilogy, *Les chemins de la liberté*, (*The Roads to Freedom*). When the German *Blitzkrieg* roared through the Ardennes, he was among the 1,700,000 soldiers captured. While a prisoner of war in Stalag 12D, he began his foray into theater, writing *Bariona; ou, Le fils du tonnerre* (*Bariona, or The Son of Thunder*), a play about a small Jewish village confronting Roman domination on the night preceding the birth of Christ, which intended to inspire the other prisoners on Christmas eve. After his release in April 1941, he returned to Paris and started Socialisme et Liberté, a short-lived resistance group.

For the remainder of the war, Sartre endured the conditions of forced accommodation—in his own words, as "a writer who resisted, not a resistor who wrote." His choices under the occupation were ambivalent: he advanced his own career by pursuing publishing opportunities that required the Nazi censor's imprimatur, while writing occasional pieces for the clandestine press, leading eventually to membership in the writers' committees that served as the intellectual wing of the resistance movement. In the immediate postwar climate and until the 1960s, his ideas about the anguish of the human condition, freedom conjoined with responsibility, the political role of the intellectual, and his effort to fuse existentialism and Marxism dominated the intellectual scene. His funeral following his death in 1980 was a mass public commemoration of one of France's great intellectual luminaries.

Writing on the Holocaust

In the immediate postwar period, Sartre did not directly assess the singularity of the *Shoah.* While the German existentialists Hannah Arendt and Karl Jaspers reflected on the radical novelty of the Nazi extermination and the general question of German guilt, and members of the Frankfurt School, Theodor Adorno and Max Horkheimer, explored the links between Western instrumental rationality, culture, and the Holocaust, the *Shoah* was not directly discussed by Sartre. He did write about the conditions under German occupation, especially in a series of newspaper articles that appeared just after the liberation of Paris (August 1944), and he theoretically explored the existential conditions of human freedom in *Being and Nothingness* and in the plays *Les mouches* (*The Flies*, 1943) and *Huis clos* (*No Exit*, 1944). There is, however, no sustained exploration in Sartre's work on the role of the Vichy authorities in the collaboration of the more than 75,000 French Jews killed during the war or on the Holocaust more generally.

Despite this silence, the collaboration of the French state and the complicity of average citizens in the mass murder reverberate throughout his postwar work. His association with the Rassemblement Démocratique Révolutionaire (1947–1949), where he was a leading member of a group of dissident leftist intellectuals that attempted to forge a third way between the inequities of capitalism and the oppression of Stalinism, and his response to the Arab-Israeli conflict, where unlike most leftist intellectuals he refused to accede to the Arab position, notably reveal that his ethical and political theory, as well as his practical interventions, were significantly impacted by National Socialism and the Holocaust. His most poignant considerations of the issues raised by the Holocaust are his *Réflexions sur la question juive* (*Anti-Semite and Jew*), his play *Les séquestrés d'Altona* (*The Condemned of Altona*), and the published dialogue with Benny Lévy, *L'espoir maintenant* (*Hope Now*).

Anti-Semite and Jew

Sartre's *Réflexions sur la question juive*, written between the liberation of Paris and the opening of Auschwitz, is a highly influential examination of the victims of antisemitic subjugation. While he only refers to the Vichy authorities and to the Final Solution to "the Jewish Question" in a couple of moments in the text, this short book became a major contribution to postwar debates about antisemitism, Jewish identity, and the possibility of "Jewish emancipation" after the Holocaust. Sartre's failure to discuss directly the novelty of the racial state, however, makes the text somewhat anachronistic; it explains more about antisemitism in the Third Republic (1870–1940) and under democratic regimes than the forms of persecution experienced by Jews during World War II.

Anti-Semite and Jew is a phenomenological analysis of "the Jewish Question" in France. The text has four parts: part 1 was called "Portrait de l'antisémite" (Portrait of an Anti-Semite) when it was first published in December 1945 in one of the first issues of *Temps modernes* (Modern Times), the journal created by Sartre after the war. Part 2 discusses the liberal-democratic or Enlightenment solution to "the Jewish Question," which Sartre rebukes, calling it "the politics of assimilation" (*Reflexions sur la question juive*, Paris: Gallimard, 1954, p. 57). Part 3 considers the interrelation of what he calls the "authentic" and "inauthentic" Jew, and part 4 proposes a new French revolution as the solution to "the Jewish Question."

Part 1 and part 3, the two longest sections of the text, contain the two major theses that structure Sartre's analysis. In part 1, Sartre develops his first axiom that the antisemite is a man of "*mauvaise foi*" or self-deception: "Antisemitism, in short, is fear of the human condition" (p. 64). Here, Sartre's analysis amplifies his portrait of Lucien in "L'Enfance d'un chef" in terms of the basic categories developed in *L'être et le néant*.

Sartre's contribution to theorizing antisemitism is his insistence that to understand it you cannot reduce it only to economic, historical, religious, or political analyses, which do not reveal it as an existential choice. Rather, antisemitism must be understood as an inauthentic response to man's situation in the world and being-with-others. The antisemite fears the limits of the human condition (death, change, a world shared with others who call into question your essence and values). Sartre targets the antisemitism of writers like Éduoard Drumont, Charles Maurras, and Maurice Barrès, who provided the intellectual foundation for Vichy state antisemitism, condemning their assertion that "the Jew" has contaminated the essential values of French culture and tradition. He thus disparages French cultural racism, which uses "tradition" as a homologue for race in German antisemitism. He does not, however, discuss the specifically Nazi eliminationist antisemitism or its French lineage. The focus of Sartre's analysis is existential, castigating all antisemites who legitimate their choices through the typology of the degenerate Jewish Other. Anti-semites avoid responsibility by projecting it onto their image of "the Jew" who serves as a free-floating symbol of what must be eliminated to redeem the modern world.

Like the antisemite, "the Jew" is condemned to confront the human condition: to assume in freedom the responsibility of his situation. Sartre's second axiom, explored in part 3, is that a defining factor in the Jewish situation is that "the Jew is a man that other men consider a Jew: that is the simple truth from which we must start" (pp. 83–84). Sartre here renders in existential terms the inescapability of Jewishness characteristic of Nazi racial definitions. Every Jew must confront the possibility that the racial state, the individual antisemite, or an everyday non-Jewish citizen may apprehend him as "the Jew," this possibility thus becoming a constitutive factor for the Jewish situation.

Sartre further argues that Jews can respond to this situation either authentically or inauthentically. Inauthentic Jews deny the abjection of the antisemitic gaze, wanting their Jewish difference to pass entirely unnoticed. This results in embracing rationalism, universalism, an abstract relation to money, and denying Jewish uniqueness. The only authentic response for "the Jew" is to understand the shared nature of his condition with other Jews, necessitating the recognition of Jewish abjectness and taking pride in his situation. Following logically from his second axiom, the authentic Jew necessarily takes on the description of "the Jew" by the antisemite: "He knows that he is separate, untouchable, execrable, proscribed, outlawed, and it is as such that he claims responsibility [for his situation]" (p. 166). Therefore, Jews are condemned to choose between the Scylla of inauthenticity or the Charybdis of martyrdom.

Sartre's vision of Jewish authenticity, consequently, remains mired in contradiction, occasionally slipping into reiterating antisemitic stereotypes. Because of his lack of understanding of Jewish culture and history, he never adequately challenged the antisemite's description of "the Jew," a point he later came to recognize. Thus, Sartre sometimes equivocates on whether Jews are a race, identifies "the Jew" with mammon and a love of money, reiterates the image of "the wandering Jew," and repeats the Enlightenment and Hegelian notion that Jews are "quasi-historical" and that Judaism is atavistic or anachronistic in the modern period. Perhaps most perniciously, Sartre's opacity concerning the collaboration of Vichy in the *Shoah* was part of a wider French collective amnesia that would persist until the student revolts of May 1968.

Despite the problems of *Anti-Semite and Jew*, Sartre's account would become an ur-text for intellectual reflections on "the Jewish Question" in the postwar period. It was the starting point for postwar Jewish thinkers like Albert Memmi and Robert Misrahi and Jewish radicals of the May 1968 generation like Benny Lévy, Pierre Goldmann, and Alain Finkielkraut. Sartre's anti-essentialist thesis that "the Jew" is a construct of the specular gaze of the French antisemite and his emphasis on Jewish alterity as the paradigm of the Other in French and Western culture also influenced postmodern interrogations of "the Jewish Question."

The Condemned of Altona: Perpetrators and Collective Responsibility

First performed in September 1959, Sartre's most sustained meditation on the culpability of the perpetrators of the Holocaust is his play *The Condemned of Altona*, a work that has received insufficient attention by scholars of Holocaust literature. The play was written in the context of Sartre's denunciation of torture and terror tactics in the Franco-Algerian war and his simultaneous effort to integrate the existential conception of freedom into a Marxist framework that achieved fruition with the publication of the *Critique de la raison dialectique* (*Critique of Dialectical Reason*, 1960). The drama represents the dilemmas of the von Gerlachs, a family of wealthy industrialists who do not support Nazism but who benefit from their collusion with the regime. The play operates on three intertwined levels: it interrogates the interpersonal relations of the family members; it deals with personal guilt and responsibility for the events of World War II and the Holocaust as a part of a wider German collective accountability; and it considers the interconnection between the modes of reproduction operating in the family and the mode of industrial production. Sartre's success at linking these three levels in the drama reveals the fecundity of literary representations of the Holocaust, since historiographical approaches have not adequately connected them.

The central character of the drama is Franz, the heir of the family fiefdom who transgresses the interests of the family when he tries to help a Polish rabbi attempting to escape from a concentration camp built on property sold to the Nazis by the von Gerlach patriarch. To save his son, the father reports this "crime" to the authorities rather than having him get caught by them. Shattered, Franz seeks to overcome his impotence by enlisting to fight on the eastern front. After the war, cognizant that he is a perpetrator of Nazi atrocities who is nevertheless only a banal cog in the machinery of destruction, Franz voluntarily sequesters himself in the attic in the family home after listening to the proceedings of the Nuremberg trials. There, in a quasi-delirious state, he serves as a perpetual witness to Nazi horrors and the brutality of the twentieth century, constantly serving to remind the family of their responsibility even as they have become an industrial power in the rebuilding of the German Democratic Republic. The drama unfolds when it is revealed that the father is dying and seeks reconciliation with his son, whom he has not spoken to since the Nuremberg trials; it concludes with achieving this reconciliation, when the two of them commit suicide together. The play thus powerfully dramatizes the contradictions of perpetrators who are at the same time victims of historical processes they are powerless to control and condemned to responsibility for their actions and for the significance of the traumatic past. In a parallel fashion to the way Sartre's *Réflexions* applied the terms of *Being and Nothingness* to the concrete situation of Jews, *The Condemned* applies Sartre's existential Marxism to an analysis of the Holocaust.

Hope Now: Sartre's Final Reflections on "the Jewish Question"

The last controversy of Sartre's life resulted from his revisiting his lifelong reflections on "the Jewish Question" in dialogue with the young radical philosopher Benny Lévy, a former leader of the French Maoists and subsequently an adherent of Orthodox Judaism. Originally published in *Nouvel Observateur* in March 1980 and later repackaged by Lévy into a book called *L'éspoir maintenant*, the interviews caused a scandal because Sartre radically reassessed some of the fundamental tenets of his philosophical system, including his early conception of consciousness and Marxism as the basis for his political thought. Perhaps most shockingly, this infamous atheist stressed the importance to non-Jews like himself of the Jewish concept of the coming Messiah as a point of departure for rethinking the question of justice. In the midst of the controversy, Sartre entered Broussais hospital and died on 15 April 1980.

Through his reflections on these questions, Sartre left a mark on the literature of the Holocaust by contributing some key concepts that have influenced how the *Shoah* is assessed as well as two major works that have contributed to our understanding of the events from the perspective of both the victims and the perpetrators.

Bibliography

Primary Sources

L'imagination (*Imagination: A Psychological Critique*). 1936.
La transcendance de l'ego: Esquisse d'une description phénoménologique (*The Transcendence of the Ego: An Existentialist Theory of Consciousness*). 1937.
La nausée (*Nausea*). 1938.
Esquisse d'une théorie des émotions (*The Emotions: Outline of a Theory*). 1939.
Le Mur (*The Wall*). 1939.
L'imaginaire (*Psychology of the Imagination*). 1940.
L'être et le néant (*Being and Nothingness*). 1943.
Les Mouches (*The Flies*). 1943.
Huis clos (*No Exit*). 1944.
Les chemins de la liberté, vol. 1: *L'âge de raison* (*Age of Reason*). 1945.
Les chemins de la liberté, vol. 2: *Le sursis* (*The Reprieve*). 1945.
Baudelaire (*Baudelaire*). 1946.
L'existentialisme est un humanisme (*Existentialism*). 1946.
Morts sans sépulture (*The Victors*). 1946.
La putain respectueuse (*The Respectful Prostitute*). 1946.
Réflexions sur la question juive (*Anti-Semite and Jew*). 1946.
Les jeux sont faits (*The Chips Are Down*). 1947.
Situations I (Situations I). 1947.
L'engrenage (*In the Mesh*). 1948.
Les mains sales (*Dirty Hands*). 1948.
Situations II (Situations II). 1948.
Les chemins de la liberté, vol. 3: *La mort dans l'âme* (*Troubled Sleep*). 1949.
Entretiens sur la politique (Interviews on Politics). 1949.
Situations III (Situations III). 1949.
Le diable et le bon dieu (*The Devil and the Good Lord*). 1951.
Saint Genet, comédien et martyr (*Saint Genet*). 1952.
L'affaire Henri Martin (The Henri Martin Affair). 1953.
Kean (*Kean*). 1954.
Nékrassov (*Nekrassov*). 1955.
Les séquestés d'Altona (*The Condemned of Altona*). 1959.

Critique de la raison dialectique, preceded by *Questions de méthod* (*Critique of Dialectical Reason*). 1960.
Les Mots (*Words*). 1963.
Situations IV (Situations IV). 1964.
Situations V (Situations V). 1964.
Situations VI (Situations VI). 1964.
Les troyennes (The Trojan Women). 1965.
Situations VII (Situations VII). 1965.
L'idiot de la famille, vols. 1 and 2 (*The Family Idiot*). 1971.
Situations VIII (Situations VIII). 1972.
Situations IX (Situations IX). 1972.
Un théâtre de situations (A Theater of Situations). 1973.
On a raison de se révolter (We Have Reason to Revolt). 1974.
Situations X (Situations X). 1976.
Les carnets de la drôle de guerre (*The War Diaries*). 1983.
Cahiers pour une morale (*Notebooks for an Ethics*). 1983.
Lettres au Castor et à quelques autres, vols. 1 and 2 (*Quiet Moments in a War*). 1983.
Le scénario Freud (*The Freud Scenario*). 1984.
Critique de la raison dialectique vol. 6 (Critique of Dialectical Reason, vol. 7). 1985.
Mallarmé (*Mallarmé*). 1986.
L'espoir maintenant: Les entretiens de 1980 (*Hope Now*). With Benny Lévy. 1991.

Secondary Sources

Charmé, Stuart. *Vulgarity and Authenticity: Dimensions of Otherness in the World of Jean-Paul Sartre*. Amherst: University of Massachusetts Press, 1991.

Cohen-Solal, Annie. *Sartre: A Life*. Translated by Anna Cancogni. New York: Pantheon, 1987.

Contat, Michel, and Michel Rybalka. *The Writings of Jean-Paul Sartre*, vol. 1, *A Biographical Life*. Translated by Richard C. McCleary. Evanston, Ill: Northwestern University Press, 1974.

Hayman, Ronald. *Sartre: A Biography*. New York: Carroll & Graf, 1987.

Hewitt, Nicholas. "Portrait de l'antisémite dans son context: Antisémitisme et judéocide." *Etudes sartriennes I, Cahiers de Sémiotique textuelle 2* (1984): 111–122.

Hollier, Denis, ed. *October 87* (winter 1999). Special issue: *Jean-Paul Sartre's "Anti-Semite and Jew."* Cambridge, Mass.: MIT Press, 1999.

Judaken, Jonathan. "The Mirror Image and the Politics of Writing: Reflections on 'the Jew' in Sartre's Early Thought." *Historical Reflections/Réflexions Historiques* 25, no. 1 (spring 1999): 33–59.

———. "The Queer Jew: Gender, Sexuality, and Jean-Paul Sartre's Anti-Antisemitism." *Patterns of Prejudice* 33, no. 3 (July 1999): 45–63.

Kritzman, Lawrence. "Critical Reflections: Self-Portraiture and the Representation of Jewish Identity in French." In *Auschwitz and After: Race, Culture, and "the Jewish Question" in France*. Edited by Lawrence D. Kritzman. New York: Routledge, 1995: 98–118.

Lévy, Benny. *Le nom de l'homme: Dialogue avec Sartre*. Paris: Verdier, 1984.

———. "Sartre et la judéité." *Études sartriennes II-III, Cahiers de Sémiotique textuelle* 5–6 (1986): 139–149.

Marks, Elaine. "The Limits of Ideology and Sensibility: J. P. Sartre's *Réflexions sur la question juive* and E. M. Cioran's *Un peuple de solitaires*." *French Review* 45, no. 4 (1972): 779–788.

Meschonnic, Henri. "Sartre et la question juive." *Études sartreinnes I, Cahiers de Sémiotique textuelle* 2 (1984): 123–153.

Misrahi, Robert. "Sartre et les juifs: Une histoire très étonnante." *Les nouveaux cahiers* 16, no. 61 (summer 1980): 2–12.

Suleiman, Susan. "The Jew in Sartre's *Réflexions sur la question juive*." In *The Jew in the Text: Modernity and the Construction of Identity*. Edited by Linda Nochlin and Tamar Garb. London: Thames and Hudson, 1995.

SUSAN FROMBERG SCHAEFFER
(1941–)

S. LILLIAN KREMER

INFLUENCED BY THE narrative experiments of Henry James, William Faulkner, Virginia Woolf, and Vladimir Nabokov, Susan Fromberg Schaeffer is interested in realism and fantasy, and occasionally bases novels on historical or biographical fact, using settings ranging from nineteenth-century New England to World War II and the Vietnam era. European Jewish life, intergenerational family conflict, urban conditions, the Holocaust, the Vietnam War, photography, and mental illness are among her subjects, with memory and the presence of the personal and historic past persistent interests. Schaeffer is the author of many novels, several short story collections, collections of poetry, and scholarly articles as well as book reviews.

The American writer was born on 25 March 1941 in New York to Irving Fromberg, a law school graduate who worked in the wholesale clothing industry, and Edith Levine Fromberg, a Spanish teacher. Schaeffer earned her B.A., M.A. with honors, and Ph.D. with honors from the University of Chicago. She has enjoyed a long teaching career as a professor of English at the Illinois Institute of Technology (1965–1967) and then at Brooklyn College of the City University of New York (since 1967), where she has been appointed the Broeklundian Professor of English. Among the honors she has received are the John Simon Guggenheim Fellowship, the Lawrence Award for Fiction, the Edward Lewis Wallant Award for Fiction, the Friends of Literature Award, and the O. Henry Award. She is married to fellow English professor Neil Jerome Schaeffer, with whom she has two children.

Anya

Schaeffer attributes the genesis of her second novel, *Anya*, to discovery that an antique dealer she knew was a Holocaust survivor and to her subsequent desire to understand what the Holocaust "really meant instead of what it was supposed to mean" (1988 Kremer Interview). Before her interviews with this survivor, Schaeffer's interest in the subject had been minimal. She had seen *The Diary of Anne Frank* and heard of the Holocaust in her youth "as a cautionary tale." Despite her previous disinterest in the subject, Schaeffer spent ten months of protracted discussion and research with the antique dealer for a novel that would make the experience of survivors accessible. In her Wallant Prize acceptance speech, she credited her with providing her "the bones of the dinosaur," but ascribed her impressions of European Jewish family life to conversations with her own grandparents and to study of photographs of Vilna's streets as they appeared before and after a bombing raid and as they look following rehabilitation. Schaeffer said in 1988 that she had conducted interviews with fifteen to twenty people when she was writing the book, and that although she shared their goal of preserving *Shoah* history, her interests diverged from theirs because she "wanted to write a book which began with a normal life" (Kremer Interview), whereas survivors needed to talk about their experiences when they really became dreadful, and needed to tell her about their treatment when they were rounded up, suffered in the ghetto, and were put on trains and shipped to concentration camps.

Acrimonious public encounters with the unnamed survivor and her husband, followed by an accommodation, make it clear that *Anya* is based mainly on the biography of Anya Savikin Brodman, who recorded the history of three generations of her family for Schaeffer, who then incorporated the family names and Holocaust experience in her book, save for changing the name of Anya's second husband. While Schaeffer's book reflects the experience common to many survivors, *Anya* is primarily a composite of a single survivor's testimony, Schaeffer's invention, and superb writing.

As Marlene Heinemann observes, Schaeffer's fiction attains immediacy and authority by its "imitation of a memoir through the first-person narrator, who relates her memories of the collision of her life with the Holocaust" (Heinemann, p. 120). By her rhetorical adoption of the survivor's voice and meticulous integration of historical detail with novelistic artifice, Schaeffer establishes an authentic aura. The novel's elegiac "Prologue" and "Epilogue," set in the America of 1973, frame the Holocaust chronicle and attest to the permanent physical and psychological impact of the event on the lives of survivors. "In History" introduces the reader to the vibrant social and cultural tapestry of Vilna, home to a population of Poles, Lithuanians, Russians, and Jews, on the verge of World War II. The reader learns of the Savikin family's privileged economic and social lives, the protagonist's promising medical career, her courtship and marriage, the couple's move to exhilarating and cosmopolitan Warsaw, and the birth of their child—indices by which to measure the coming metamorphosis and obliteration of European Jewish life.

Anti-Jewish violence emerges in the novel's third section, "Biblical Times," whose title alludes to an ancestor's characterization of an onerous period as "living through biblical times, [when] the living will come to envy the dead" (p. 149). The family experiences what Jews, collectively, experienced during the Nazi occupation: exclusion from hitherto public places, curfews, confiscation of personal property, dismissal from employment, mandatory wearing of yellow stars, subjection to state-choreographed street violence, and forced separation from the non-Jewish population in sealed ghettos, followed by death or deportation to the camps.

The political sophistication of Schaeffer's treatment is evident in her juxtaposition of the fall of two Polish cities: Warsaw's rapid collapse in the face of Hitler's *Blitzkreig* and the relatively slow capitulation of Vilna. In Warsaw, Anya's experience begins abruptly with her young family's flight across the beleaguered city, dodging falling bombs and tumbling buildings. By virtue of her Aryan appearance, Anya safely ventures outdoors, during a lull in the bombing. There she witnesses the campaign isolating Warsaw Jews for degradation and humiliation: dark-haired Jewish women hauled off to the forest to be raped and murdered; young Jewish males abducted from homes and public thoroughfares, conscripted for hard labor from which they will never return; and old Orthodox men beaten and humiliated by soldiers hacking off their beards and earlocks, defiling their religious garments, and burning their holy books. When Anya returns to Vilna, she finds the city within the Russian sphere of influence, under the 1939 Hitler-Stalin Non-Aggression Pact. Vilna remains a relatively safe domain for Jews, who are subject to Russian exploitation and thievery but retain their freedom. When the Germans occupy Vilna in 1941, anti-Jewish violence accelerates, culminating in mass killings and ghettoization. The brutal beating and deposit of the family patriarch's unrecognizable body, with hundreds of others, in public gardens ringed with barbed wire is an evocation of the brutal July 1941 assault on the Jews of Vilna and a visual foreshadowing of the approaching genocide.

Among Schaeffer's most memorable contributions to American Holocaust literature are her renditions of ghetto and labor camp. Notwithstanding her disinclination to read the voluminous histories of the period, Schaeffer's extensive interviews with Anya Savikin Brodman enabled her to depict ghetto conditions and administrative conduct in ways that parallel the accounts of historians, particularly the studies by Leonard Tushnet in *Pavement of Hell* and of Yitzhak Arad's *Ghetto in Flames*. Like these detailed histories, this survivor-inspired novel portrays the ghetto as a scene of starvation, rampant disease, and arbitrary and deliberate brutality. *Anya*'s setting is the larger of two Vilna ghettos, located near the medieval town ghetto, the worst section of the city, its buildings rotting and its plumbing primitive, thus an effective physical and psychological antechamber to the labor and concentration camp universe. As in all the ghettos, sustaining life in Vilna depended on one's capacity to supplement starvation rations through smuggling, purchasing food clandestinely, or obtaining a privileged job rewarded with extra rations or offering opportunity for theft. During early days the family secures additional food because one son-in-law works with the ghetto police, another with the Jewish Council, and Anya smuggles in small quantities upon her nightly returns from work as a masseuse for Gestapo wives. Although there are housing and food advantages accrued by working for the Jewish Council and in the Gestapo office, such work is also hazardous. The Gestapo retaliates against all the privileged workers and their families for an alleged infraction by a German of the racial laws prohibiting sexual liaison with Jews. The Savikins lose six family members in this assault. Following the torture and execution of Anya's husband on a false charge, the family of eleven is reduced to three, and Anya becomes the sole protector and provider. The threats presented by hunger, disease, overcrowding, and primitive sanitation are joined by ever more frequent death selections of children, the aged, and the infirm.

While male and female authors share similar presentation of ghetto physical conditions, women's Holocaust writing more often addresses family matters, chiefly the separation of mothers and children, the heightened danger to mothers of young children, and the physical and psychological suffering of children. Anya's struggle to preserve the life of her child is underscored by frantic attempts to secure food, medication, and hospitalization when Ninka contracts diphtheria, an illness that will condemn the child to lethal injection if the Germans discover her condition. The absurdity of struggling to heal Ninka so that the Germans can later kill her is the catalyst for Anya's decision to smuggle her daughter out of the ghetto. Unlike most parents, she is able to save her child by placing her in the home of a surrogate family through the intervention of organized resistance forces and the cooperation of the ghetto's Jewish leader, Jacob Ganz (Gens). Authenticity is again achieved by casting the Jewish ghetto leader as facilitator of the child's escape in concert with the United Partisan Organization, for Gens did allow the partisans to operate. Had Anya failed to smuggle Ninka to safety, her fate would have been that of other children who were snatched from ghetto rooms and hiding places and given death injections, or like that of the babies pulled from mothers' arms and smashed against walls, their brains splattering. Guard dogs attack mothers who resist. During the ghetto liquidation, Anya watches as some mothers surrender their children on command because childless women are employable and therefore worthy of life.

"The Lion's Jaws" chronicles Anya's ordeal in Riga's infamous work camp, Kaiserwald, where half the inmates were women working for the *Wehrmacht* and *Luftwaffe*. Here, Schaeffer renders the sexual assault women suffered as part of the degrading camp initiation ritual. She writes self-damning dialogue for the soldiers and juxtaposes the women's pain with the soldiers' pornographic sadism. Schaeffer's discourse, selection and arrangement of detail genders the humiliation with emphasis on women's sexual vulnerability: mauled breasts, probed rectums, and chemically burned vaginas—transparently mischaracterized by the women's tormentors as medical procedures "for their own good." Comparison with camp induction scenes written by survivors Primo Levi, Elie Wiesel, and the American novelist Richard Elman suggests that while men experienced humiliation during admissions procedures, their discomfort was based on denial of autonomy and assaults on social or professional status, rather than on sexual self-image and gendered social role.

In contrast to the survivor-modeled Anya, Schaeffer's Erdmann shares traits with the privileged male prisoners, known as "cousins," who assisted female prisoners. These benefactors, working as camp doctors, Kapos, block leaders, and labor supervisors would, for political or personal motives, provide their favorites extra food, better jobs, and advance warning of "actions." Crucial to Anya's camp survival, eventual escape, and reunion with her daughter is the assistance of a Jew masquerading as a German soldier. For Aryan-featured Anya, he secures a position as a cleaning woman in the camp commander's quarters, where she is able to pilfer extra food and to work in relatively comfortable physical circumstances, compared to poorly clad fellow inmates working outdoors. Anya makes herself indispensable to the commandant as a Russian translator assisting with his interrogations of prisoners of war. Guarded less closely, she begins to consider escape and reunion with Ninka, especially after Erdmann implores her to flee before a scheduled tattooing. Although historical documentation exists of Jews working secretly within the Nazi war machine, Erdmann is a fictional construct, the most far-fetched of the novel; he exemplifies the American tendency to favor individual heroism, even in the Holocaust universe.

Schaeffer is one of the few novelists who have explored the toll of separation on mother and child through both maternal trauma and the child's psychic wounds. Unlike the relationship her mother and Anya enjoyed before the war, Anya's relationship with her own daughter is shaped primarily by suffering and separation. Their bond undergoes radical emotional shifts, from hate to love, suspicion to trust, resentment to attachment. Grateful for Ninka's safety, Anya nonetheless resents not only her benefactor's usurpation of the maternal role, but also her daughter's transference of filial affection to the Lithuanian woman whom she now calls "Mommiti." When Anya finally locates her daughter, at war's end, in a Catholic orphanage where she has been placed after her surrogate parents' arrest, mother and child are strangers once more. Ninka remains emotionally divided, continuing to claim her fabricated Lithuanian identity, prating Catholic prayers while vehemently spurning her true identity. At this stage, Ninka views adults as temporary protectors, and asks Anya how long she will keep her. Only when Anya is able to prove her identity by referring to an old favored toy is Ninka convinced of their relationship. She is then ready to relinquish her assumed identity and claim the mother who has repeatedly risked her life to find her daughter.

Like many Jewish writers, Schaeffer effectively balances treatment of the Holocaust as an unprecedented atrocity and as yet another chapter in the long history of European antisemitism. She overtly links Nazi racism and traditional Christian attitudes, placing the Holocaust within a two-thousand-year cycle of anti-Jewish violence. Aside from the courageous efforts of a few righteous Gentiles—a former servant who brings food to the ghetto and a couple who shelter Anya's child—Christians menace Jews at each stage of the narrative: in Mrs. Savikin's recollection of Czarist law, which prescribed a Pale of Settlement segregating Jews to prescribed areas where they could live and work; in her account of Russian White guards raping Jewish women; in citation of prewar Polish economic and cultural prejudice rendered in exclusionary university quotas and in physical assaults on Jewish university women by their Polish classmates, whose goal was to "go after the faces of the beautiful girls, [with iron nails] and demolish them" (p. 59). Polish collaboration in the Nazi genocide spans the novel's social strata: peasants descend on the Jewish home like vultures, "robbing our house as if they were plundering our graves" (p. 170); lawyers neglect professional ethics and refuse their services to Jews. More sinister is the identification and denunciation of Jews to the Nazis, leading to certain death. Even in the postwar period Polish antisemitism continues unabated, as Holocaust survivors encounter hostility from neighbors who refuse to return homes and other possessions to their Jewish owners.

Anya's changing response to antisemitism signifies the evolution of her Jewish identity. Gone is girlish guilt, manifested in self-mutilation for having escaped unscathed while her classmates were disfigured. Gone are the timidity and terror that gripped her while Poles looted her home. Gone is prewar passivity in the face of overt bigotry. Schooled in ghetto and labor camp, Anya now responds assertively. During her fugitive period, she risks denunciation during a clandestine visit with Ninka when she rebukes a servant in the rescuer's employ for giving Ninka antisemitic drawings and for instructing the child to avoid Jews or risk being devoured. After liberation she confronts the usurpers of her family home and demands the return of her mother's jewelry to provide food for herself and her child.

In contrast to the "Prologue's" brief, dramatic, and metaphoric introduction to survivor hardships, the epilogue, "And Then There Were None," continues Anya's story reflectively and expansively, encompassing twenty-five years of the postwar period and establishing the searing, long-term influence of the *Shoah* on the survivor. Holocaust disruption remains a factor in Anya's life and in that of her second husband. Early expectations for postwar regeneration are erased with the brutal realization of Holocaust-wrought limitations. Anya suffers chronic depressive states, a guilt complex, nightmares, psychosomatic complaints, and a self-image as "one of the walking dead" (p. 474). Career interests and professionalism have lost their significance. Attempts to recoup her medical career, even in the amended role of nurse, fail. Anya retreats to an antique shop, a confined space she characterizes as "so tiny sometimes I feel as if we are living in a coffin" (p. 471). The claustrophobic environment can stand for camp incarceration, the cause of Anya's depression. Guilt vexes her conscious hours and invades her dreams, for she irrationally blames herself for failing to save her family. Her decision to remarry is founded on pride in her second husband's successful delivery of his father's murderer to trial. The couple live and work in a run-down neighborhood in order to be among fellow survivors, the only people they trust and the only ones who "can understand what it was like" (p. 475). The couple aborts a pregnancy to avoid afflicting a child with the psychological freight of their trauma. Anya's postwar parenting is dominated by her Holocaust history, revealing many of the patterns observed in survivors—overprotectiveness, overidentification with one's children, and obsession with health. She remains forever wounded, forever disillusioned; nothing will reconstitute the wholeness of her being. It is in her fiercely protective relationship with Ninka, who is both a link to the past and hope for the future, and in her concern for the welfare of Ninka's children, that Anya's postwar commitment to the continuity of Judaism and the Jewish people is manifest. Schaeffer paints a vivid portrait of survivor duality in Anya's daily struggles with death and life that is similar to the "permanent irresolution" Henry Greenspan encountered in interviewing survivors (Greenspan, p. 48).

Tormented by memory, Anya seeks psychiatric help to suppress her Holocaust recollection. The psychiatrist rejects her plea, and helps her understand that to record the events as she experienced them is more than mere reiteration of remembered detail; that, as Shoshana Felman has written, "To testify is thus not merely to narrate but to commit one's self, and to commit the narrative, to others: to take responsibility . . . for history—or for the truth of an occurrence, for something which, by definition, goes beyond the personal, in having general (nonpersonal) validity and consequences" (Felman, p. 204). The novel's themes of memory and silence, memory and voice, are brought to fruition in Anya's comprehension of the futility of oblivion and of the concomitant moral imperative to sustain Holocaust memory and commemorate the martyred millions. That the commemoration will not be restricted to the private realm but chronicled for future generations is signified in the protagonist's closing affirmation that she is transcribing her testimony. With this American novel's early linkage of Holocaust memory and testimony, Schaeffer invites consideration of a theme that has, two decades later, become central to critical inquiry by scholars examining the relationship between literature and testimony, between the writer and the witness, between the act of witnessing and writing.

Critical Reception

Schaeffer's meticulous recreation of prewar European middle-class Jewish life and the enormous breadth of her Holocaust canvas has earned accolades from readers and critics. Recipient of the Friends of Literature Award and the Edward Lewis Wallant Award, *Anya* has been cited for its comprehensive and authentic Holocaust representation. Typical of the critical acclaim is Edward Alexander's assessment of *Anya* as an "extraordinary achievement . . . probably the best American literary work on the Holocaust" (Alexander, p. 133). Although he faults Schaeffer's focus on the domestic, "at the expense of thorough probing into the complexities of human responses to radical evil," Alan Mintz is impressed with her ability to "get inside Anya's world," especially since he reads the novel's evocation of the years before and during the war as "entirely an act of the imagination" (Mintz, p. 90). Writing of the proliferating realistic American Holocaust literature during the 1960s and 1970s, Sidra DeKoven Ezrahi cites *Anya* as "a consummate example of the appropriation of the Holocaust and of the pre-Holocaust heritage through the vicarious acquisition of the details that constituted the events" and concludes that such a novel could not have been written "before scholarship and testimony had provided compensation for the existential distance" (Ezrahi, p. 215). Alan Berger attributes the novel's "wealth of detail concerning prewar family life in Poland" to its basis in a survivor's story (Berger, p. 12). While critics have acknowledged Schaeffer's use of survivor testimony, they have neither identified Anya nor raised the Brodman family assertions that Schaeffer's book is not a work of the imagination. Documents in the Brodman family's possession authenticate that Anya Savikin Brodman provided substantial history to Schaeffer and that the authentic quality of the European voice is the result of the novelist's access to the survivor's testimony in a series of tapes made over many months of collaborative work. Although no systematic enumeration is available of the proportion of invention and reconstruction, the book evinces access to territory American novelists had not insufficiently explored or incorporated. At the time of its publication, no other American-born writer had so realistically, systematically, and comprehensively delineated the ghetto and labor camp of the Nazi universe.

Bibliography

Primary Sources

Fiction

Falling. 1973.
Anya. 1974.
Time in Its Flight. 1978.
The Queen of Egypt and Other Stories. 1980.
Love. 1981.
The Madness of a Seduced Woman. 1983.
Mainland. 1985.
The Dragons of North Chittendon. 1986.
The Injured Party. 1986.
The Four Hoods and Great Dog. 1988.
Buffalo Afternoon. 1989.
First Nights. 1993.
The Golden Rope. 1996.
The Autobiography of Foudini M. Cat. 1997.

Poetry

The Witch and the Weather Report. 1972.
Granite Lady. 1975.
Rhymes and Runes of the Toad. 1975.
Alphabet for the Lost Years. 1977.
The Bible of the Beasts of the Little Field. 1980.

Scholarly Articles

"The Unwritten Chapters in the Real Life of Sebastian Knight." *Modern Fiction Studies* 13 (winter 1967–1968): 427–442.
"The Editing Blinks of Vladimir Nabokov's *The Eye*." *University of Windsor Review* 8.1 (1972): 5–30.
"Bend Sinister and the Novelist as Anthropomorphic Deity." *Centennial Review* 17 (spring 1973): 115–151.
" 'It Is Time That Separates Us': Form and Theme in Margaret Atwood's *Surfacing*." *Centennial Review* 1974.
"Under the Chronoscope: A Study of Peter Redgrove's *Wedding at Nether Powers*." *Poetry Review*. London: Redgrove Special Issue (September 1981): 45–48.
"The Unreality of Realism." *Critical Inquiry* 6 (summer 1982): 727–737.
"Making New or Making Known: The State of Fiction Today." *Great Ideas Today*, an annual publication of *The Encyclopedia Britannica*, 1984.
Introduction. *Villette*. By Charlotte Bronte. New York: Bantam, 1986, pp. 7–23.
Introduction. *Wuthering Heights*. By Emily Bronte. NAL/Signet, 1993.
Memories Like Splintered Glass: Growing Up in New York. Unpublished memoir. 1993.

Speeches

Edward Lewis Wallant Prize Acceptance Speech. 27 April 1975.

Secondary Sources

Alexander, Edward. *The Resonance of Dust: Essays on Holocaust Literature and Jewish Fate*. Columbus: Ohio State University Press, 1979.

Berger, Alan. *Crisis and Covenant: The Holocaust in American Jewish Fiction*. Albany: State University of New York Press, 1985.

———."Holocaust Survivors and Children in *Anya* and *Mr. Sammler's Planet*." *Modern Language Studies* 16.1 (winter 1986): 81–87.

Bilik, Dorothy S. *Immigrant Survivors: Post-Holocaust Consciousness in Recent American Literature*. Middletown, Ct.: Wesleyan University Press, 1981, pp. 101–111.

———."Susan Fromberg Schaeffer." In *Jewish American Women Writers: A Bio-Bibliographical and Critical Sourcebook*. Edited by Ann R. Shapiro, Sara R. Horowitz, Ellen Schiff, and Miriyam Glazer. Westport, Ct.: Greenwood Press, 1994, pp. 368–375.

Castro, Ginette. "*Anya* de Susan Fromberg Schaeffer ou le rachat du temps." *Multilinguisme et Multiculturalisme en Amerique du Nord: Temps, mythe et histoire*. Bordeaux: PU de Bordeaux, 1989. 109–120.

Ezrahi, Sidra DeKoven. *By Words Alone: The Holocaust in Literature*. Chicago: University of Chicago Press, 1980.

Felman, Shoshana, and Dori Laub. *Testimony: Crises of Witnessing in Literature, Psychoanalysis, and History*. New York: Routledge, 1992.

Gottschalk, Katherine K. "Paralyzed in the Present: Susan Fromberg Schaeffer's Mothers or Daughters." In *Mother Puzzles: Daughters and Mothers in Contemporary American Literature*. Edited by Mickey Pearlman. Westport, Ct. Greenwood Press, 1989, pp. 141–157.

Greenspan, Henry. "Imagining Survivors: Testimony and the Rise of Holocaust Consciousness." In *The Americanization of the Holocaust*. Ed. Hilene Flanzbaum. Baltimore: Johns Hopkins University Press, 1999.

Heinemann, Marlene E. *Gender and Destiny: Women Writers and the Holocaust*. Westport, Ct.: Greenwood Press, 1986.

Kremer, S. Lillian. "Holocaust Survivors: Psychiatric and Literary Parallels." *Proteus: A Journal of Ideas* 12.2 (fall 1992): 27–31.

———."Susan Fromberg Schaeffer." In *Women's Holocaust Writing: Memory and Imagination*. Lincoln: University of Nebraska Press, 1999, pp. 119–148.

Kress, Susan. "Susan Fromberg Schaeffer." In *Twentieth Century American-Jewish Fiction Writers*. Edited by Daniel Walden. Detroit: Gale, 1984. Vol. 28 of *Dictionary of Literary Biography*.

Mazurkiewicz, Margaret. "Susan Fromberg Schaeffer." In *Contemporary Authors: New Revision Series*. Vol.18. Eds. Linda Metzger and Deborah A. Straub. Detroit: Gale, 1986.

Mintz, Alan. "Mothers and Daughters." *Commentary* 59 (March 1975): 88–90.

Mintz, Jacqueline A. "The Myth of the Jewish Mother in Three Jewish American Female Writers." *Centennial Review* 22.3 (1978): 346–355.

Pearlman, Mickey. "The Power of Memory, Family, and Space." In *American Women Writing Fiction: Memory, Identity, Family, Space*. Lexington: University Press of Kentucky, 1989, pp. 137–146.

Interviews

"A Conversation with Susan Fromberg Schaeffer." With Harold U. Ribalow. *The Tie That Binds: Conversations with Jewish Writers*. Edited by Harold U. Ribalow. San Diego and New York: A. S. Barnes, 1980, pp. 77–92.

Interview with S. Lillian Kremer. Unpublished. Brooklyn, New York: 18 May 1988.

"Susan Fromberg Schaeffer." With Mickey Pearlman. *Inter/view: Talks with America's Writing Women*. Edited by Mickey Pearlman and Katherine Usher Henderson. Lexington: University Press of Kentucky, 1990, pp. 58–63.

ROBERT SCHINDEL

(1944–)

MICHAEL OSSAR

ROBERT SCHINDEL WAS born toward the end of World War II on 4 April 1944 in Bad Hall near Linz in Upper Austria. Official records list his surname as Soël, the pseudonym adopted by his parents, René Hajek and Gerti Schindel, who as Jewish communists fled their native Austria for France. In 1943, as part of an effort by Austrian communists to form resistance groups, they returned to Austria, disguised as Alsatian *Fremdarbeiter*, the Nazi term for foreign workers, where they were arrested (his mother four months after Robert's birth) and taken to Auschwitz. Schindel's father was murdered in Dachau on 30 March 1945. Robert was cared for by the *Nationalsozialistische Volkswohlfahrt*, a Nazi social welfare agency, as a supposedly Catholic "orphan of asocial parents of unknown origin" and later, by foster parents. His mother survived Auschwitz and Ravensbrück and returned to Vienna from Sweden, where she was reunited with her son. Schindel attended elementary school from 1950–1954 and then the federal Realgymnasium in Vienna from which he was expelled for bad conduct in 1959. He spent the next few years at a variety of odd jobs, first as an apprentice for the Viennese publishing house Globus, then as a dishwasher in Paris and Sweden. Following his parents' political views, he was an active member of the Communist Party from 1961–1967. In 1967 he earned his high school equivalency certificate and enrolled as a student of law and philosophy at the University of Vienna. During this period, the height of the European student revolts, he was a leader of the *Kommune Wien*, inspired by a similar commune in Berlin and the most radical among the Viennese student groups. He remained active in Maoist circles until 1978. At this time in his life, he deemphasized his Judaism and even took part in an anti-Zionist demonstration to disrupt the Viennese Jewish community's celebration of the thirtieth anniversary of the founding of Israel. In 1979, however, he forswore his radical politics and became increasingly interested in the situation of his fellow Austrian Jews, joining the IKG, the Jewish Community of Vienna, in the early 1980s.

Schindel began writing poetry in the late 1950s. In 1968 he wrote a radio play for Radio Austria and more poetry and prose which was published by the Gruppe Hundsblume, which he founded together with Christof Šubik. During this period he worked at numerous odd jobs: as a postal and railway worker, as editor of the literary magazine *Hundsblume* (1970–1971), as a librarian in the main library of Vienna (1975–1980), as a member of the editorial staff of Agence France Presse (1981–1983), and as a social worker for the unemployed (1983–1986). His first large prose work, *Kassandra* (Cassandra), was written between 1967 and 1968 and was published in 1970. He calls it a novel but puts its generic designation in parentheses. In fact, the difficult hundred-page work consists of ten different *Figuren* (figures), evoking a variety of dreams, autobiographical memories, fairy-tale motifs, and allusions to people living and dead. The work is loosely connected by two female personae: Miriam (reminiscent of a figure in a very beautiful poem by the Jewish poet Paul Celan) and Kassandra, prophetess and daughter of Priam and Hecuba. Although Schindel wrote the "novel" at a time in his life when he tended to repress his Jewishness, the Holocaust figures among the threatening aspects of the world, together with the Vietnam War and a society dominated by capitalist greed and oppression. His other important work of 1970, the collection of poems *Zwischen den Mauschellen des Erklärens* (Between the Blows of Explanation), is very much a product of the period of the student revolution, with its vulgar language and political themes recapitulated from the prose work, even as it anticipates later works such as *Ohneland* (Withoutland).

In the wake of the anti-Waldheim campaign of 1986 (of which he was one of the leaders), Schindel decided to devote all his energies to his writing and to the emerging Jewish literary scene in Vienna. His poems on the nascent Jewish intellectual culture in Vienna, *Ohneland* (1986), were published by perhaps the leading German publishing house, Suhrkamp. This was followed by three other volumes of poetry, *Geier sind pünktliche Tiere* (Vultures are Punctual Beasts) in 1987, *Im Herzen die Krätze* (Rash in the heart) in 1988, and *Ein Feuerchen im Hintennach* (A Flame in Retrospect) in 1992, all published by Suhrkamp. Most of the poems in *Ein Feuerchen im Hintennach*, written between 1986 and 1992, are reminiscences of Hamburg, Vienna, and the postwar Paris of the Romanian poet Paul Celan. They are love poems, or explorations of how a child of Holocaust victims is to look at the Holocaust in retrospect and to treat it in poetry. In a sense, the poems are an attempted reply to Theodor Adorno's dictum in his 1951 essay "*Kulturkritik und Gesellschaft*" (Cultural Criticism and Society) that to write poetry after Auschwitz is barbarism.

The difficult title poem in *Ein Feuerchen in Hintennach* (interpreted by Gerlinde Ulm Sanford) describes, in six parts and ninty-six lines, the feelings of a child of Holocaust victims caught between memories of the fate of his family and the present of his now pleasant life in Vienna with his German lover and his politically radical friends. The speaker visits Bergen-Belsen and is obsessed with memories of Anne Frank, who died there in the same month as Schindel's father, and at the same time reflects on the meaningless rituals of politicians and on the NATO troop maneuvers that disturb the rest of the dead. Finally, he returns to his home, Vienna, with its Lethe/Danube and its so-called "Emperor of Forgetfulness," President Kurt Waldheim, whose memory of his wartime role was clouded by his "Waldheimer's disease."

Schindel's most famous novel, *Gebürtig* (*Born-Where*, 1995) also appeared in 1992. In 1994 he published a book of short stories, *Nacht der Harlekine* (Night of the Harlequins) and a volume of essays, *Gott schütz uns vor den guten Menschen* (May God Protect Us from Good People) in 1995. The latter consists of seven essays. "Der Friede wird fünfzig" (Peace Is Fifty Years Old) reflects on Europe in 1995, its peace and its wars, and Germany and the moral conflict posed by its policy on asylum seekers. The essay begins with a very moving personal description of Schindel's mother's flight to Sweden and his youth in Austrian communist circles. "Judentum als Erinnerung und Widerstand" (Judaism as Memory and Resistance) deals with the survivors of the Holocaust and their children and questions of Jewish identity and assimilation. It regards the secular traditions and the memory of the Enlightenment as essential to a self-definition of contemporary Judaism. "Literatur—Auskunftsbüro der Angst" (Literature—Information Bureau of Anxiety) is the text of a series of lectures on literature that Schindel gave at the University of Vienna between 1992 and 1995. "Über Hiob" (On Job), which deals with the implications of the Holocaust for the concept of divine justice, is a homage to the Austrian novelist Joseph Roth (alluded to in *Gebürtig*) and his novel *Hiob* (Job). "Wer der Folter erlag, kann nicht mehr heimisch werden in der Welt" (He Who Succumbed to Torture Can No Longer Find a Home in This World) is an extended reflection on the Viennese exile, resistance fighter, and Holocaust-survivor Jean Améry and his view of man's need for a homeland, no matter how problematic the notion of "homeland" might be. Finally, "Erich Friedpreisrede" (Speech on the Acceptance of the Erich Fried Prize) describes Schindel's complicated feelings on accepting the Erich Fried Prize in Tel Aviv (Fried was an Austrian émigré who lived in England and was a severe critic of Israel), on his family history, on his relationship with the German writers Walter Jens and Wolf Biermann, and on the neo-Nazi movement in Germany and Austria.

Immernie (Alwaysnever), published in 2000, is a series of poems divided into six sections called chapters. The poems deal with themes such as the Turkish slaughter of the Armenians, the war in Bosnia and Kosovo, the death of friends, the cities of Rome and Venice (which also plays a part in *Gebürtig*), the poet's body, the Swiss landscape, Algeria, Paris, the Gulf War, and the Holocaust. Particularly beautiful are the love poems. Schindel is currently working on a continuation of *Gebürtig*, tentatively titled *Der Kalte* (The Cold Man).

Robert Schindel has been honored with numerous literary prizes, among them the Förderpreis Literatur der deutschen Industrie (1989), the Förderpreis zum österreichischen Literaturpreis (1992), the Förderpreis zum Marburger Literaturpreis (1992), the Dr. Emil-Domberger-Literaturpreis der B'nai B'rith Européen (1992), and the Erich-Fried-Preis für Literatur und Sprache (1993). He was selected as Stadtschreiber von Klagenfurt (1995–1996). He is considered one of the most important voices in the emerging group of Jewish (or partly Jewish) writers and intellectuals in Vienna and elsewhere in Austria, a group that includes Ruth Beckermann, Doron Rabinovici, Robert Menasse, Elfriede Jelinek, and Anna Mitgutsch. The reception of Schindel's major work, *Gebürtig*, was overwhelmingly positive, though some reviewers (Sibylle Cramer, Werner Fuld, Klaus Kastenberger, and Wendelin Schmidt-Dengler) criticized Schindel's linguistic excesses, his somewhat overwrought prose, and his often frankly vulgar language. Others (Wolfgang Zwierzynski) found the language appropriate and refreshing in its irreverence and even bitterness.

Memory: Individual and Collective

In his important study of psychic disorders, *The Man Who Mistook His Wife for a Hat*, Oliver Sacks demonstrates how a full personality cannot exist independently of memory. He tells the story of Jimmie the "lost mariner," a man who in all respects functions normally except that he has no memory of a large part of his past life, his actions since 1945, or even his very recent actions. When he is introduced to someone, he forgets that person just a few moments later. His friends and relatives, all those in whom he had invested a lifetime of emotion and whose fates were intertwined with his own in ways too complicated to trace over decades of his life, are now strangers to him. Sacks shows how the person we are at a particular moment depends not just on ourselves, but also on our stars, external events, and the entire fabric of our lives. But if we cannot survey, remember, examine, and reflect on this fabric, then we have no access to large parts of ourselves. Memory proves to be bound up with the notion of identity and self-definition: If what we are is in some sense related to the sum total of our actions, then we are unable to define ourselves when our memory of these actions is blocked or distorted. Like the Spanish filmmaker Luis Buñuel, whom he quotes, Sacks avers that our memory is our coherence, our reason, our feeling, our action, and that without memory we are nothing. Other writers, J. M. Barrie and Max Frisch (in *Biografie*), for example, have been captivated by the question of how personalities are forged by experiences: Is there, for instance, an immutable core at the bottom of personalities that would cause people to make the same choices, fall in love with the same spouses, become fascinated by the same ideas, experience the same emotions when confronted with the same stimuli should they be given the chance to alter their fates?

The concept of memory, however, is anything but simple or axiomatic. On the contrary, it proves on closer examination to be highly ramified and highly problematic. We can repress unpleasant memories, memories of painful times in our lives or of shameful things we have done. But as Freud has taught us, this act of repression can avenge itself in a variety of ways, and these memories can come back to haunt the person who repressed them. We can, on the other hand, "recover" memories of things that never happened to us, sometimes so vividly that we are willing to testify about them to help convict the people who allegedly perpetrated them and to punish them for what they did not do. Our relationship to memory is a complicated and dynamic one, like wrestling with an unruly pet—sometimes we imagine memory is under our control, and we discover to our surprise that it has a will of its own.

Gebürtig

Robert Schindel, in his seminal novel *Gebürtig*, about the lives of Jews and Austrians in Vienna of the 1980s, proceeding from Sacks's observation but from the opposite starting point, shows how, for a certain group of people, Jews and non-Jews, living in a certain place forty years or more after World War II, memory defines and molds not only their past but also their present, taking possession of them and holding them prisoner. These people no longer have the ability or the luxury of seeing the world except through the glasses of the past, so that not only their modes of thought but also the very sense data on which these modes act are not of their choosing. To the casual observer these people appear to be free, but in reality they are captives—not of the Nazis, like their parents, but of their memories.

In fact, Schindel's book can be read as a sermon on *Die Unfähigkeit zu trauern*, 1967 (*The Inability to Mourn*, 1975), the text of Alexander and Margarete Mitscherlich's influential Freudian analysis of postwar Germany and its collective memory, its problematic relationship to its past. The Mitscherlichs distinguish between the mourning that occurs when one loses a loved object perceived as outside and distinct from oneself and the melancholy that occurs with the loss of an object seen as an extension or a mirror of one's sense of self. In the latter case, the bereaved party suffers not only the loss of the loved object but also the destruction of the illusion of omnipotence. In the case of postwar German society attempting to come to terms with the loss of Adolf Hitler and the shattering of the corporate, integrated Nazi society, the *Volksgemeinschaft* (national community), it was the latter, narcissistic orientation that prevailed. The Germans were unable to reach the stage of mourning because they were able to remain mired in narcissism by transferring their emotional identification from Hitler to the Western allies, by contriving to obscure the reality of the twelve years of the Thousand Year Reich, and by claiming for themselves the status of victim (for example, they suffered in the bombing of the civilian populations of Berlin and Hamburg and Dresden, and they suffered deportations from the eastern territories). Ruth Beckermann coins the term "to de-realize" to denote this phenomenon: "To de-realize means to justify immoral modes of action with the exceptional circumstances of the war, and thus, as with all sins of omission, to deny the necessity of consistency" (Beckermann, p. 28). The result was a collective denial of the past. These three mechanisms identified by the Mitscherlichs played a role not only in Germany but also in postwar Austria. Indeed, the third mechanism, the appropriation of the status of victim, was for the Austrians even more pronounced than it was for the Germans because of the Austrian mythology that regarded Austria as the first victim of Nazi aggression, a myth generally based on the so-called Moscow declaration of the allies of 1943 (which was intended to separate Germany from Austria), but belied by newsreels of jubilant Austrians welcoming Hitler into Vienna after the *Anschluss* of 1938—the rape of a not too unwilling virgin, as one observer characterized it.

Corresponding to the imponderable irruptions of memory, of the past into the present, the narrative structure of *Gebürtig* is quite complicated: The story is supposedly told by Alexander (Sascha) Grafitto, the twin brother of Danny Demant, editor for a publishing house, but the book also includes diary notes, flashbacks, a novel within a novel, interior monologues, fairy tales, a film within a film within the novel, exchanges of letters, dreams, and a bewildering variety of filmic fades from past to present. Both time and space seem capable of coming loose at a moment's notice and spinning out of control, so that, for example, a corner of Vienna in 1984 may suddenly be occupied by the ghosts of people who populated it years before. Without warning, characters are liable to dissolve into their fathers or brothers. Indeed, the reader will often have to read far into a passage before it is clear from just whose perspective it is being seen. This game Schindel plays with narrative perspective evokes in the reader an extreme disorientation, a sense of being in constant danger of sliding down the slope of the past. In fact, the very existence of Sascha Grafitto is a mystery: When Danny tells his lover the story of his family, he fails to mention having a brother at all, much less a twin.

But not only does the narrative structure of the novel conspire to conflate past and present, the characters themselves are beset by memories of their own pasts and those of their families that occupy and take possession of them, so that the main work of the novel proves to be a coming to terms with the past as a necessary precondition of finding a way to exist in the present: *Vergangenheitsbewältigung* (confronting the past) as a path toward *Gegenwartsbewältigung* (confronting the present). In *Civilization and Its Discontents*, Sigmund Freud imagines a visitor to Rome who is able to perceive in each part of the Eternal City not only its present state but also, simultaneously, the countless layers of the past of that place. He asks the reader to consider such a gifted observer as a metaphor for the human psyche, able to encompass at one and the same time the totality of its experiences. This is the situation of the characters in Schindel's novel, both Jewish and non-Jewish Austrians. Like scorpions in a bottle, they are paradoxically bound together by their pride and self-hatred, by their necessity to define themselves, and by a sense of being tied to and defined by their respective pasts that makes both Jewish and non-Jewish Austrians pariahs: the one group because it will always be thought of as the Other, as outsiders, as eternal victims; the other because it will forever be thought of as perpetrators of the Holocaust. Schindel suggests that the Germans and Austrians will never forgive the Jews for Auschwitz, for having caused them to become murderers, and, to heighten the indignity, for remaining around to serve as a constant admonition. It is the variety of the characters' attempts to discover their individual relationship to these two groups, either to acknowledge membership in them or to disavow them and break loose, that constitutes the topography of the novel.

Gebürtig has three main plots and a variety of sub plots of which a striking feature is that the Jewish characters almost without exception seek out Christian partners: Danny Demant, who abandons his first lover, Wilma Horvath, for his second, the doctor Christiane Kalteisen; the banker and novelist, Emanuel Katz and his blond, blue-eyed Käthe; the sociologist Mascha Singer, Erich Stiglitz and her "Styrian drunks"; Sonja Okun and the theatrical director Erich Stellein; the playwright Herrmann Gebirtig and the journalist Susanne Ressel; the poet Paul Hirschfeld and his Christian lover. It is as if, in constructing this series of difficult and problematic relationships, Schindel were setting up and conducting an experiment devised to test the truth of the so-called German-Jewish symbiosis, a hypothesis rejected by Gershom Scholem, a philosopher of Jewish mysticism and the Kabbalah, after the *Shoah* and in 1986 reinterpreted by Dan Diner, a professor of Jewish history and culture at the University of Leipzig, as a "negative symbiosis."

The first of the three large plot lines is actually a novel within the novel, written by Danny Demant's friend, the banker Emanuel Katz. It is the story of Herrmann Gebirtig, a nearly sixty-year-old survivor of the Holocaust who has emigrated to New York, where he now lives on the East Side as a world-famous playwright. One writer has suggested that Gebirtig, named after the Yiddish poet Mordechai Gebirtig, is an allusion (or perhaps a homage) to the Hungarian émigré George Tabori, author of a number of provocative plays including *Die Kannibalen* (*The Cannibals*, 1974) in 1969, *Jubiläum* (Jubilee) in 1983, and *Mein Kampf* (My Struggle) in 1987. Schindel's Gebirtig however is a writer of comedies. One day, the journalist Susanne Ressel is hiking on a mountain near Vienna with her father, Karl, a lifelong member of the Austrian Communist Party, volunteer against Franco in the Spanish Civil War, and resistance fighter under Hitler. While they are having lunch, Karl recognizes Anton Egger, who had been a brutal guard in the concentration camp in which Karl had been imprisoned. Egger, who earned the sobriquet "the skull-cracker of Ebensee" in recognition of his favorite method of execution, is arrested. Soon afterward, Karl dies of a heart attack. Egger denies being the guard in question, and because of the infirmity and unreliability of all the other living witnesses Susanne's only hope of identifying Egger rests on Herrmann Gebirtig. Gebirtig, however, has vowed neither to set foot in his homeland ("Naziland") nor to allow his works to be published or his plays to be performed there. Susanne flies to New York and eventually persuades him to return to Vienna to testify. The scenes describing Gebirtig's feelings as he visits his beloved Altaussee, his old neighborhood in Vienna, the scene of his father's law office, as well as when he meets his former landlord and gradually falls in love with Susanne are among the most poignant in the novel. He ends up shaking the hand of the son of his old concierge and a former SA member, Heini Hofstätter (although he notes "only the dead can forgive"), and decides to settle in Vienna, where so much has changed since the war—"a good place to die in" (*Unzugehörig: Österreicher und Juden nach 1945*, Vienna: Löcker Verlag, 1989).

Ruth Beckermann recalls a similar story told by Günther Anders in his diary about Vienna in 1950:

> He walks along the street with a casual acquaintance. A man comes towards them, whom his companion greets with exquisite politeness. Anders is completely astonished, since this is the very same neighbor who had denounced his friend during the Nazi period for failure to fly the swastika flag. To the question why he did not simply politely ignore the man instead, the answer Anders hears is: "You see, Herr doctor, Herr Dr. R and I, we go way back, after all. Decades, in fact. And before Hitler he was really a fine person, really a gentleman. And now he is again" (Beckermann, p. 27).

Officials of the city of Vienna succeed in persuading a reluctant and intractable Gebirtig to accept a medal in a public ceremony, described in a series of brilliantly satirical scenes that deconstruct Viennese cultural politics and reveal the supposed honor to be part of an ongoing public-relations campaign to polish the image of the "world capital of antisemitism," as Schindel once called this city with which he is bound by a love-hate relationship. But just after Gebirtig has instructed his agent to conclude an agreement with a German publisher, the jury's verdict is announced: Despite Gebirtig's positive identification, Egger is released for lack of evidence that "Herr Eigler" is identical with the skull-cracker of Ebensee Egger. Schindel relates the news of the acquittal in a short paragraph. Why devote more attention to it, he told an interviewer. It would be like saying that it rained today in Vienna, something unremarkable that happens all the time. Without taking leave of Susanne, Gebirtig flies back to New York on the next plane. One is reminded of Kurt Tucholsky's (the German satirist and journalist who committed suicide in 1935) remark, quoted by Ruth Beckermann: "My life is too valuable for me to sit down under an apple tree and to ask it to bear pears" (Beckermann, p. 97). In a recent interview with Clemens Berger, Schindel remarks that acquittals of Nazi war criminals by "SA-men disguised as jurors" (*Interview with Clemens Berger*, "Ich war Kein Schlechter Ping-Pong Spieler." In *Göttinger Zeitschrift für neue Literatur*, 1998) were a frequent occurrence in the Austria of the 1960s, mentioning in particular Franz Murer, the "butcher of Vilna," who is now living a pleasant life in Murau and whose son is a representative of the Freedom Party (the party of the right-wing politician Jörg Haider), and also the cases of the Maurer brothers and Novak. Novak was an Austrian implicated in the assassination of Chancellor Dollfuss and later as an assistant to Eichmann, in charge of arranging the transport of Jews (especially Hungarian Jews) to death camps. After the war, he was not arrested by Austrian police, even though he lived under his real name until the publicity surrounding the Eichmann trial necessitated the assumption of a pseudonym in 1961. In 1964, he was sentenced to eight years. However, after a complicated series of appeals and retrials, he was acquitted and set free in 1966. Similarly, the Maurer brothers were released from their sentence in April 1964. Schindel tells Berger that these people would probably be condemned today, but that in the private consciousness of a majority of his compatriots they would still be mentally exculpated according to the principle "let the old men die in peace."

Especially interesting from a structural point of view is Schindel's decision to make the story of Herrmann Gebirtig, Susanne and Karl Ressel, and Alfons Egger fictional, a novel within a novel instead of giving it an independent status equal to that of the other main plots of *Gebürtig*. This is particularly so in view of the threads that connect the story of Egger's crimes and his acquittal to a number of actual quite similar cases, as Schindel himself indicated in the interview quoted above. Why should Schindel have resorted to this narrative technique that generally has a distancing effect, considering the obvious emotion he has invested in the story of Gebirtig and his relationship to Vienna, a relationship that largely mirrors his own? Furthermore, the closeness of the name of Gebirtig and the name of the novel, *Gebürtig*, also indicates an essential nexus. Is the reader to ascribe a lesser degree of reality to the story of Egger's trial and acquittal because it is "fictional"? Is he or she to interpret the story as a reflection of the psychological complexities of its putative author, Emanuel Katz, and therefore as a kind of special pleading rather than an objective analysis of the mood of postwar Vienna in the 1980s? If one examines Katz's background, one discovers numerous points of tangency with Schindel's own. Katz, now thirty-five, lived with his family until the death two years before of his father, a Hungarian Jew who had been rescued by Raoul Wallenberg. Katz moves out of his parents' apartment, plunges into a kind of religious orthodoxy, and immerses himself in literature about the Holocaust, eventually irritating his coffeehouse friends with his monomania and provoking Danny to splash a glass of wine in his face. Liberated by this deed, Katz shaves off his beard and begins his novel. Katz's mother, Amalie, survived three years in Auschwitz/Birkenau under unspeakable conditions and now regards her survival as a curse. When she dies later in the novel in a wonderfully and movingly described scene, it is clear that she is willingly renouncing an existence that has been a burden and a source of guilt for her. In her delirium she thinks of the last time she stood on the threshold of death, in the camp, and how she had asked a Yugoslav doctor for an orange, for her the symbol of a finer land, as it had been for Goethe. At his mother's deathbed, Katz asks himself why he is writing about this fictional Jew Gebirtig, who lives on the East River in New York, instead of telling the story of his parents.

Like the poet Paul Hirschfeld, Katz feels drawn to tall, blond non-Jewish women for whom he is an exotic object of fascination, but unlike Hirschfeld he wears his Judaism like a badge. When he visits his lover Käthe and her two brothers, Hans and Holger ("breakfast-roll-blond monsters"), in Hamburg-Altona his refusal to ignore their antisemitic provocations leads to an explosion, and he abruptly leaves for Vienna. His words to Hans and Holger define his philosophy:

> "I'm sorry," he said maliciously, "that I barge into the middle of this conversation with my [announcement] of my heritage. It has to do with the compulsion I've been suffering from for a while now. You see, I have a testing-obsession . . ."
>
> "You know," he said, with his back to the others, "I myself find it tasteless to say all the time 'how are you, the weather's lousy, and by the way, I'm a Jew. A Jew.' On the other hand, that way I put the ground under my feet. Because," and Katz turned around and gazed at the Germans, "if someone then says, 'Jews are people too' or 'but that doesn't matter,' or 'one of my best friends is a Jew' or even 'we're sorry, but what happened, happened,' then somehow everything is clear and I can hit the road" (pp. 114–115).

The second plot line tells the story of Konrad Sachs, a prominent journalist who writes on cultural topics for the respected Hamburg *Echo* and lives in a wealthy suburb of Hamburg with his wife, Else. On the day after his forty-fourth birthday, Sachs is jogging and he runs into his college friend Herrmann Eggenberger, son of Alois Eggenberger, a Nazi and friend of his father's. The chance encounter with Eggenberger tears open the wound of Konrad's past—his discovery in a library in Munich of the dossier on his father, Ernst Sachs, who was a prominent Nazi judge, who later became the governor-general of Poland (the King of Poland, as he was called), and was eventually condemned at the war crimes trials in Nuremberg to be hanged. Konrad, who played as a little boy in Auschwitz, had been dubbed the Prince of Poland by Alois Eggenberger. He becomes increasingly obsessed with the question of the guilt he has incurred by loving this mass murderer and choosing to be his son. His dreams and his waking life are invaded more and more frequently by this other person, the Prince of Poland, who fights to gain control of his personality. After meeting Emanuel Katz, author of the novel about Gebirtig, and plagued by his demons, Sachs leaves his wife and his friend, the director Peter Adel (modeled on the Peter Zadek, who famously urged that Rainer Maria Fassbinder's play *Der Müll, die Stadt, und der Tod* [Garbage, the City and Death] should be performed in 1985 even though it was antisemitic). Sachs moves to Munich and then to Frankfurt, horrifies a prostitute by telling her his story, and eventually contacts Katz and Danny, hoping to find in them confidants to whom he can confess his torments. Finally, after a car accident puts them both in the hospital, Danny advises Sachs to publicly reveal his secret. Sachs writes a series of articles and a book about his father and eventually finds a kind of peace that eludes all the other characters in the book. Sachs's story is evidently modeled on that of Niklas Frank, a writer for the Hamburg magazine *Der Stern* and son of Hans Frank, governor-general of Poland.

The third main plot tells the story of Danny Demant, born in 1941, in Moussac on the Vienne in the unoccupied zone of France. His parents were communists who had fled there and were active in the French resistance. His father, Heinrich, who worked under a false name for the German quartermaster corps in Marseille, passing information about the Allies and distributing anti-Nazi propaganda, is captured and brought first to Auschwitz, then Dachau, and eventually Mauthausen, where he is executed. His mother, Ida, is protected by the mayor and the citizens of the little French town and survives the war, returning to Vienna, the city she loves, where Danny's grandfather, Simon, and great-grandfather had run an inn. Danny's story is essentially the story of his love affair with the Catholic doctor Christiane Kalteisen, who is introduced in the third section of the prologue (a scene which is recapitulated from another narrative point of view in the last section of the last chapter titled, "Hitze" [Heat], which actually takes place after the action of most of the novel). We see Christiane abandon her husband and arrive at Danny's doorstep just before his Christmas open house party, we see him fall in love with her and leave his lover, Wilma. We see him visit her in her home village, Lilienfeld an der Traisen and play with her two daughters. We see Christiane leave him, travel to Paris, where she lives for a time with a Dutch drug dealer, and then return to Danny. In all of this, Danny and Christiane play a role somewhat similar to that played by the Jewish novelist Heinrich Bermann and his sometime friend, the non-Jewish composer and aristocrat Georg von Wergenthin in Arthur Schnitzler's novel, *Der Weg ins Freie*, 1908 (*The Road to the Open*, 1923) about another group of Viennese intellectuals, Jews and non-Jews, at the turn of another century. Each pair serves as a sounding board for the ramified, sometimes poignant and sometimes terrifying, difficulties in the way of personal relationships between Jews and non-Jews in a country in which there had been formal legal equality since 1867–what Schindel calls a "glass wall" (*Gebürtig* [*Born-where*], Frankfurt am Main: Suhrkamp, 1992, pp. 12, 179). In a scene in the Zeppelin coffeehouse, Danny says of his friend Mascha:

> Finally, she reproaches me for wanting to be like all the others, for wanting to hide my Jewishness, and so forth. This makes me quite furious. How does she get off, constantly using the bones of the Jews as organ-pipes to blare out her jarring song again and again? I say so and she cries.
>
> On the way home, Christiane tells me that she is completely on Mascha's side and proposes the theory that as a woman and a Jew, [Mascha] has it twice as hard with such screwed-up men. I stare at her, astonished, pull her gently to myself, and ask her just how she so suddenly acquired a Jewish soul, even if it was only a female one (p. 337).

Each man—Georg, Heinrich, and Danny—is captivated and ensnared by a love affair and at the same time drawn back by a fear of giving himself entirely to the woman he loves, an inability to accept commitment that finds expression both in the title of Schnitzler's novel, *Der Weg ins Freie*, which has the sense of the path to freedom, and in the working title of Schindel's forthcoming sequel to *Gebürtig*, *Der Kalte* (The Cold Man).

In Schnitzler's novel the hero, aristocrat and composer Georg von Wergenthin, describes the same phenomenon from a Christian point of view: " 'Another one of these guys,' " he thought to himself, 'whom one has insulted. It was really completely impossible to deal with these people in a normal way' " (*Der Weg ins Freie*, in *Die erzählenden Schriften*, Erster Band, Frankfurt am Main: S. Fischer Verlag, 1961, p. 670). And elsewhere he remarks when his interlocutor superfluously, he believes, announces to him his Judaism: "He knew it already and didn't hold it against him; but why did they always start to talk about it themselves? No matter where he went, he was always running into Jews who were ashamed that they were Jews or who were proud of it and were afraid people would think they were ashamed" (p. 661).

Both Schnitzler's and Schindel's novels describe the difficult relationship between a group of Viennese Jewish and Christian intellectuals and artists at the two turns of the twentieth century: in the case of Schnitzler, the beginning; in the case of Schindel, the century's end. And as the above quotation indicates, the same ructions and anguish that agitated the Jews of 1908, that had afflicted Bermann and Ehrenberg and Nürnberger, questions of assimilation, of self-hatred, of the role of Zionism, of self-assertion, of constant self-consciousness and a sense of otherness and alienation, afflicted Danny Demant and his circle. Schnitzler has one of his characters tell Georg the story of Oskar, the son of the industrialist Salomon Ehrenberg and a fop who will do anything to be accepted into Christian aristocratic circles and only refrains from converting because he knows he will be disinherited if he does. One day, Oskar's father observes him crossing himself as he hurries by a church, whereupon his father crosses the street and publicly boxes his son on the ear, a scene that has its counterpart in the open house party in *Gebürtig*, where Hanna Löwenstein excoriates Katz for his attraction to blond Christian women or the scene later in the story where Hanna teases Katz for the failure of his relationship with the non-Jew Käthe in the presence of Paul Hirschfeld, Danny's friend of thirty years and an assimilationist:

"I know," he mollified her malicious glee, "you were right for the wrong reasons."

"For all reasons," she said. "Because of the big picture. These things always end this way."

"I don't believe that," said Paul Hirschfeld and thought of a blond actress he planned to meet in half an hour in order to begin an affair. "It happens to you, of course, with your constant sniffing for antisemitism."

"A Jew's a Jew," said Hanna.

"What crap," said Hirschfeld, annoyed. "That's our own self-inflicted idiocy. First of all I'm a human being, only then a Jew or Eskimo or pan-German."

"You'd like that to be true," snorted Katz and poured Paul's vodka down his throat. Hirschfeld pursed his lips: "Judeocentrists," he said to Katz and Löwenstein. And he grimaced and said in Yiddish: "Ä chund hat geschissen. Is das git far die Jidden?" [A dog shat. Is that good for the Jews?] (p. 142).

The attitudes, the problems, the roles that are played seem the same in Schnitzler and in Schindel even if they are played by different actors. And yet, there is a difference, and it is crucial. In between the Christian Socialist Vienna of Karl Lueger, the openly antisemitic mayor of Vienna (from 1897 until his death in 1910) at the turn of the twentieth century and the antisemitism of Vienna at the turn of the twenty-first century lies the Holocaust. The political conflicts that in Schnitzler's novel had been ominously simmering in the background have in the meantime boiled over in Schindel's. All the Jewish characters in *Gebürtig* are marked by the Holocaust or obsessed by it in one way or another: Danny, Alexander Grafitto, Heinrich Demant, Ida Demant, Josef Demant, Siggi Demant, Elisabeth Katz, Amalie Katz, Emanuel Katz, Mascha Singer, Herrmann Gebirtig, Daniel Lebensart (based on Simon Wiesenthal), Sonja Okun, Ilse Jakobsohn-Singer, Peter Adel, and Hanna Löwenstein. These characters gradually come to realize the fact that the past has taken possession of their entire world to the point of their not being able to pronounce geographical place names like Mauthausen (a lovely town where one of them had played as a child) or Galicia without hearing resonances of the Holocaust. Every street corner of Vienna is occupied by the ghosts of people who once inhabited it and now no longer exist. When Christiane innocently speaks of a murderer who once raged in her idyllic village, Danny cannot help thinking of another kind of murder and the absurdity of calling this man a mass murderer.

Problems of self-identity and self-definition have always loomed large in the Jewish consciousness, as they have for Germans (as the controversy of the comments Lorenz Meyer, General Secretary of the Christian Democratic Party, made regarding the so-called "Leitkultur" [leading culture] and the question of whether it is appropriate to say that one is proud to be a German demonstrated in November 2000). But while in Schnitzler's novel, memories play a negligible role in these struggles at self-definition, in Schindel's novel, they are decisive: Characters morph and transmute themselves bewilderingly into their ancestors before our eyes, sometimes in the space between the beginning and the end of a sentence. If we accept Buñuel's and Sacks's insight that memory is essential to the process of self-definition, and if we accept the Mitscherlichs' notion of the collective consciousness of a nation, then *Gebürtig* demonstrates the truth of Diner's assertion that with the passage of time the hold of memory, of the past, and of the Holocaust on Jews, Austrians, and Jewish Austrians has become greater, not less.

Bibliography

Primary Sources

Franz Dörr: Ein Mensch ohne Reue und Gewissen (Franz Dörr: A Man with Neither Regret Nor Conscience). 1968.

Drei Miniaturen: Erzählungen (Three Miniatures: Stories). Coauthored with Wolfgang Murawatz. 1970.

Kassandra (Cassandra). 1970.

Zwischen den Maulschellen des Erklärens (Between the Blows of Explanation). 1970.

Brockt sie frisch von den Weibern: Prosa (Pluck Them Fresh from the Women: Prose). 1971.

Haikus im Ruderleiberl (Haikus). 1971.

Im Büro kannst auch vom Sessel fallen (You Can Fall Out of Your Chair in Your Office, Too) Coauthored with E. A. Richter. 1978.

Auf der Strecke (Stuck on the Road). 1980.

Bitter Sweet: Brechts Liebe in Augsburg (Bitter Sweet: Brecht's Love in Augsburg). 1981.

Der Mai ist vorbei (May Is Gone) Coauthored with Peter Henisch. 1982.

Ohneland: Gedichte vom Holz der Paradeiserbäume 1979–1984 (Withoutland: Poems from the Wood of the Paradise Trees 1979–1984). 1986.

Geier sind pünktliche Tiere: Gedichte (Vultures Are Punctual Beasts: Poems). 1987.

Im Herzen die Krätze: Gedichte (Rash in the Heart: Poems). 1988.

"Judentum als Erinnerung und Widerstand" (Judaism as Memory and Resistance). 1989.

"Antisemitismus: 'Der Vater aller Vorurteile' " (Antisemitism: The Father of All Prejudices). 1991.

Ein Feuerchen im Hintennach: Gedichte 1986–1991 (A Flame in Retrospect: Poems 1986–1991). 1992.

Gebürtig (*Born-Where*). 1992.

"Literatur—Auskunftsbüro der Angst" (Literature–Information Bureau of Anxiety). 1992.

Die Nacht der Harlekine: Erzählungen (Night of the Harlequins: Stories). 1994.

Gott schütz uns vor den guten Menschen: Jüdisches Gedächtnis, Auskunftsbüro der Angst (May God Protect Us from Good People: Jewish Memory, Information Bureau of Anxiety). 1995.

Immernie (Alwaysnever). 2000.

Secondary Sources

Adorno, Theodor W. "Kulturkritik und Gesellschaft." In *Kulturkritik und Gesellschaft I: Prismen. Ohne Leitbild*. Frankfurt am Main: Suhrkamp, 1977, pp. 11–30.

Adunka, Evelyn. "Die Wiener jüdische Gemeinde und der Anti-Semitismus nach 1945." In *Studien zur Geschichte der Juden in Österreich*. Edited by Martha Keil and Eleanor Lappin. Bodenheim: Philo, 1997, pp. 205–222.

Améry, Jean. *Jenseits von Schuld und Sühne. Bewältigungsversuche eines Überwältigten*. Stuttgart: Klett, 1966.

Anonymous. "Gläserne Wand." *Der Spiegel*, no. 18 (27 October 1992): 245.

Beckermann, Ruth. *Unzugehörig: Österreicher und Juden nach 1945*. Vienna: Löcker Verlag, 1989.

Briegleb, Klaus. "Negative Symbiose." In *Gegenwartsliteratur seit 1968*. Edited by Klaus Briegleb and Sigrid Weigel. München: Hanser, 1992, 117–152.

Broder, Henryk. "Heimat, Nein Danke!" In *Ich liebe Karstadt und andere Lobreden*. Augsburg: Ölbaum, 1987.

Broder, Henryk, and Michael Lang. *Fremd im eigenen Land*. Frankfurt am Main: Fischer, 1979.

Broder, Henryk M. *Der ewige Antisemit: Über Sinn und Funktion eines beständigen Gefühls*. Frankfurt am Main: Fischer 1986.

Bunzl, Matti. "Political Inscription, Artistic Reflection: A Recontextualization of Contemporary Viennese-Jewish Literature." *German Quarterly* 73, no. 2 (spring 2000): 163–170.

Cramer, Sibylle. "Büchermarkt. Aus dem literarischen Leben. Robert Schindel, Gebürtig." *Deutschlandfunk*, 19 April 1992.

Derman, Sabine. "Ein Kaffeehausliterat: Robert Schindel, Lyriker und Romancier." *Lesezirkel*, May 1991.

Diner, Dan. "Negative Symbiose: Deutsche und Juden nach Auschwitz." *Babylon* 1 (1986): 9–20.

Embacher, Helga. *Neubeginn ohne Illusionen: Juden in Österreich nach 1945*. Vienna: Picus, 1995.

Epstein, Helen. *Die Kinder des Holocaust: Gespräche mit Söhnen und Töchtern von Überlebenden*. München: Beck, 1979.

Fried, Erich. *Gegen das Vergessen*. Köln: Bund-Verlag, 1987.

———. *Nicht verdrängen, nicht gewöhnen: Texte zum Thema Österreich*. Edited by Michael Lewin. Vienna: Europa, 1987.

Fuld, Werner. "Nächte unterm Schuldgestirn. Erpreßte Solidarität: Robert Schindels Roman 'Gebürtig,'" *Frankfurter Allgemeine Zeitung* no. 89 (14 April 1992): L4 (Beilage).

Fürst, Werner. "Denn sie wissen (nicht), was sie tun: Die Kinder der Täter und die Kinder der Opfer in Schindels Roman 'Gebürtig.' " *Tiroler Tageszeitung*, 18–20 April 1992, p. 13.

Geiger, Thomas. "Niemand marschiert mit vollem Bauch: Der österreichische Autor Robert Schindel über sein Land und politische Zustände." *Berliner Zeitung*, 28 January 1993.

Gilman, Sander L. *Jewish Self-Hatred: Anti-Semitism and the Hidden Language of the Jews*. Baltimore and London: Johns Hopkins University Press, 1986.

Grotz, Elisabeth. "Ich hätt noch gern ein Maul voll Schweigen." *Der Standard*, 6 March 1992, p. A8 (Beilage).

Haider, Hans. "Gespräch mit Schindel. Sieben Worte im voraus." *Die Presse (Wien)*, 22 February 1992, p. 7.

Hardtmann, Gertrud. *Spuren der Verfolgung: seelische Auswirkungen des Holocaust auf die Opfer und ihre Kinder*. Gerlingen: Bleicher Verlag, 1992.

Herzog, Andreas. "Von Juden, Deutschen und Österreichern." *Israel Nachrichten*, 5 June 1992.

———. " 'Zwischen Assimilation und Judentum': Jüdische Autoren in der Geschichte deutschsprachiger/österreichischer Literatur—Perspektiven neuerer Forschungen." In *Geschichte der Österreichischen Literatur Teil I*. Vol. 3, Edited by Donald G. Daviau and Herbert Arlt. Österreichische und Internationale Literaturprozesse. St. Ingbert: Röhrig, 1996, pp. 76–95.

Hirt, Elisabeth. "Von Dogmen und Küssen: Interview mit Robert Schindel." *Die Linke (Magazin)*, 19 September 1986.

Holloway, Evelyn. "Schattenschrift: Jüdische Identität in der modernen Literatur. Zu den österreichischen Schriftstellern Franz Kafka, Ruth Klüger, Robert Schindel." *Literarität*, pp. 39–43.

Huber-Lang, Wolfgang. " 'Bin nur der Saujud': Gespräch." *Wirtschaftswoche*, 21 April 1994.

Höbel, Wolfgang. "Wien ist kein guter Platz zum Sterben: Nach drei Gedichtbänden legt Robert Schindel seinen ersten Roman vor: 'Gebürtig.' " *Süddeutsche Zeitung*, 26 March 1992, II (Beilage).

Kaindlstorfer, Günter. "Die Odysseen eines Poeten: Ein Porträt des Dichters Robert Schindel." *Neue Arbeiter Zeitung*, 25 November 1988.

———. " 'Auf Wiederschaun, Herr Schindel' Gespräch." *Der Falter*, 7–13 August 1992.

Kaiser, Konstantin. "Ausharren in der Angstschicht: Der Wiener Dichter Robert Schindel." *Die Presse*, 5–6 September 1987.

———. "Kühler Kopf und warme Füsse." *Literatur und Kritik*, no. 263/264 (1992): 99–102.

Kastenberger, Klaus. "Fürze zum Frühstück, nach ihrem Geschmack." *Der Falter*, 15–21 May 1992, p. 30.

Kaukoreit, Volker. "Robert Schindel: Von Juden und Nichtjuden." *Marabo Magazin*, February 1993.

———. *Robert Schindel*. Kritisches Lexikon zur deutschsprachigen Gegenwartsliteratur (KLG). München: Edition text + kritik. 1995.

Kernmeyer, Hildegard. "Gebürtig Ohneland. Robert Schindel: Auf der Suche nach der verlorenen Identität." *Modern Austrian Literature* 27, no. 3–4 (1994): 173–192.

Kippenberger, Susanne. "Die ganze Welt ist ein Fussboden: Robert Schindel, Schriftsteller aus Wien." *Der Tagesspiegel*, 26 March 1992.

Knott, Marie Luise. "Der Glücksfall eines strittigen Romans: Eine lebhafte Debatte mit dem Autor Robert Schindel im Literarischen Colloquium am Wannsee." *Der Tagesspiegel*, 13 May 1993.

Konzett, Matthias. "The Politics of Recognition in Contemporary Austrian Literature." *Monatshefte* 90, no. 1 (1998): 71–88.

———. "Austrian Literatures in a Culture of Amnesia." Conference presentation. Historical Memories/Historische Gedächtnisse Conference. Vienna, 1998.

Kos, Wolfgang. *Eigenheim Österreich: Zu Politik, Kultur und Alltag nach 1945*. Vienna: Sonderzahl, 1994.

Kraft, Helga. "Post-*Shoah* Jewish Culture in Germany and Austria: An Introduction." *German Quarterly* 73, no. 2 (spring 2000): 145–150.

Kramer, Theodor. *Verbannt aus Österreich*. London: Austrian PEN, 1943.

Kugler, Gisela. "Platz zum Widerspruch: Robert Schindels Debütroman 'Gebürtig.' " *Südkurier*, 9 January 1992.

Kunisch, Hans-Peter. "Personengeflecht von stiller Dramatik: Robert Schindels Roman 'Gebürtig.' " *Aargauer Tagblatt*, 2 May 1992.

Köppen. "Auschwitz im Blick der zweiten Generation: Tendenzen der Gegenwartsprosa (Biller, Grossmann, Schindel)." In

Kunst und Literatur Nach Auschwitz. Edited by Manuel Köppen. Berlin: Erich Schmidt Verlag, 1993, pp. 67–82.

Kübler, Gunhild. "Unterm Schuldgestirn leben: Robert Schindels Roman 'Gebürtig.' " *Neue Zürcher Zeitung*, no. 66 (20 March 1992): 43.

Linsmayer, Charles. "Lokaltermin in Mauthausen: Zu Robert Schindels Buch über Söhne und Töchter der Auschwitz-Opfer und -Täter." *Der Bund*, 25 April 1992, 9 (Beilage).

Lorenz, Dagmar C. G. "The Legacy of Jewish Vienna." In *Insiders and Outsiders: Jewish and Gentile Culture in Germany and Austria*. Edited by Dagmar C. G. Lorenz and Gabriele Weinberger. Detroit: Wayne State University Press, 1994, pp. 293–300.

———. "Pasts in the Present: Vienna Jewish Literatures of the 1980s." Conference presentation. Historical Memories/ Historische Gedächnisse Conference. Vienna, 1998.

Martin, Marko. "*Gebürtig*, Der versperrte Weg in die Normalität. Ein Gespräch mit dem österreichischen Autor Robert Schindel zu seinem ersten Roman Gebürtig." *Freitag*, 31 July 1992.

Menasse, Robert. *Überbau und Underground. Die sozialpartnerschaftliche Ästhethik: Essays zum österreichischen Geist*. Frankfurt am Main: Suhrkamp, 1997.

Mitscherlich, Alexander and Margarete. *The Inability to Mourn: Principles of Collective Behavior*. Translated by Beverley R. Placzek. New York: Grove, 1975.

Nabbe, Hildegard. "Die Enkelkinder des Doppeladlers: Einblendung von politischer Vergangenheit in den Alltag der Gegenwart in Robert Schindels Roman *Gebürtig*." *Modern Austian Literature* 32, no. 2 (1999): 113–124.

Obermüller, Klara. "Scham, Sühne, Schuld. Robert Schindels *Gebürtig*." *Die Weltwoche* no. 18 (30 April 1992): 71 (Beilage).

Oxaal, Ivar, Michael Pollak, and Gerhard Botz, eds. *Jews, Antisemitism and Culture in Vienna*. London and New York: Routledge & Kegan Paul, 1987.

Paetzke, Iris. "Aus der Hauptstadt des Antisemitismus." *Basler Zeitung* no. 91 (16 April 1992): 2 (Beilage).

Part, Matthias. " 'Es gibt Leute, die den Juden wegen Auschwitz böse sind': Gespräch." *Salzburger Nachrichten*, 14 July 1994.

Pfoser, Alfred. "Vergangenheitsbewältigung auf wienerisch. Aufsehenerregendes Debüt: Der Roman 'Gebürtig' von Robert Schindel im Suhrkamp Verlag." *Salzburger Nachrichten*, 21 March 1992, VIII (Beilage).

Plath, Jörg. "Gebürtig." *Freitag*, no. 32 (31 July 1992).

Pollak, Anita. "Die gläserne Wand." *Kurier*, 14 March 1992.

Posthofen, Renate. "Erinnerte Geschichte(n): Robert Schindels Roman *Gebürtig*." *Modern Austrian Literature* 27, no. 3–4 (1994): 193–211.

Pulver, Elsbeth. " 'Meine Horchlappen wachsen und wachsen': 'Gebürtig–Der erste Roman von Robert Schindel." *Schweizer Monatshefte* no. 6 (1992): 509–511.

Rabinovici, Doron. " 'Gebürtig': Ein Roman von Robert Schindel." *Illustrierte Neue Welt*, March 1992, p. 15.

Rieger, Bernd. "Lächeln ist ein Erbe unseres Stammes: Gespräch." *Kleine Zeitung*, 9 October 1994.

Rosenstrauch, Hazel. " 'Wurzel aus Jude mal Kommunist, gebrochen durch achtundsechzig.' " *Listen* no. 27 (1992): 14–15.

Rothschild, Thomas. "Die gläserne Wand der Vergangenheit." *Frankfurter Rundschau*, 28 March 1992.

———. "Kosmetik als Politik: Welche Rolle spielt der Schriftsteller Robert Schindel im österreichischen Staatstheater?" *Wespennest* no. 93 (1993): 63–67.

Rybarski, Ruth. "Die unterste Falte der Seele." *Profil* no. 18 (28 April 1992): 88–89.

Sacks, Oliver. *The Man Who Mistook His Wife for a Hat and Other Clinical Tales*. New York: Simon and Schuster, 1998.

Sanford, Gerlinde Ulm. "Zaubernähen, Immernie, Frostesonnen, nullerlei: Zu Robert Schindels 'Liebliedern' und ähnlichen Gebilden." *Modern Austrian Literature* 27, no. 3–4 (1994): 155–171.

———. "Wortschöpfungen und Wortverfremdungen in Robert Schindels Lyrik." *Jura Soyfer: Zeitschrift der Jura Soyfer Gesellschaft* 4, no. 2 (1995): 19–24.

———. "Robert Schindel und der Holocaust." *Jura Soyfer: Internationale Zeitschrift für Kulturwissenschaften* 5, no. 2 (1996): 12–19.

Schobel, Eva. "Der Schindel: ein österreichischer Dichter, und der Mai ist vorbei." *Frankfurter Rundschau*, 10 June 1989.

Schwarz, Robert. " 'Die Nacht der Harlekine' by Robert Schindel." *World Literature Today* 68, no. 4 (autumn 1994): 807–808.

Sichrovksy, Peter. *Born Guilty: Children of Nazi Families*. Translated by Jean Steinberg. London: I. B. Tauris & Co., 1988.

———. *Strangers in Their Own Land: Young Jews in Germany and Austria Today*. Translated by Jean Steinberg. New York: Basic Books, 1986.

Šlibar, Neva. "Anschreiben gegen das Schweigen. Robert Schindel, Ruth Klüger, die Postmoderne und Vergangenheitsbewältigung." In *Jenseits des Diskurses. Literatur und Sprache in der Postmoderne*. Edited by Albert Berger and Gerda Elisabeth Moser. Vienna: Passagen, 1994.

Spörk, Ingrid. "Robert Schindel's Novel *Gebürtig* Continues the Development of Jewish Writing in Austria after the *Shoah*." In *Yale Companion to Jewish Writing and Thought in German Culture 1096–1996*. Edited by Sander Gilman and Jack Zipes. New Haven, Conn., and London: Yale University Press, 1997.

Söllner, Werner. "Die Helden sitzen im Angstgehäuse." *Die Welt*, 7 March 1992.

Vogl, Walter. " 'Mauthausen ist eine schöne Stadt': Messerscharfer Witz aus dem Geiste des Galgens. Robert Schindel und sein Roman 'Gebürtig.' " *Die Presse*, 16 April 1992, VII (Beilage).

Wantoch, Erika. "Von '68 zu '38: Gespräch." *Profil* no. 51–52 (21 December 1987).

Wichmann, Dominik. " 'Es geht hier eigentlich nicht um Juden': Schriftsteller Robert Schindel über den Dauerstreit zwischen Hrdlicka, Biermann und Broder." *Süddeutsche Zeitung*, 7 February 1995.

Winkels, Hubert. "Doppellämmer und Tätersöhne: 'Gebürtig': Das Romandebüt des Lyrikers Robert Schindel." *Die Zeit* no. 16 (10 April 1992): 4 (Beilage).

Wüterich, Werner. "Auskunftsbüro der Angst: Porträt des Wiener Dichters und Kaffeehausliteraten Robert Schindel." *WochenZeitung*, 22 October 1993.

Zwierzynski, Wolfgang. "Von Schuld, Scham und Lüge: Zu Robert Schindels Roman 'Gebürtig.' " *Schaffhauser Nachrichten*, 10 November 1992.

BERNHARD SCHLINK

(1944–)

MARIANNE M. FRIEDRICH

THE RENDITION OF the Holocaust has repeatedly been characterized by the split between two fundamentally heterogeneous and mutually exclusive worlds of experience: the banality of evil on the part of the perpetrators and the monstrosity faced by the victims. Bernhard Schlink suggests that these two perspectives are not mutually exclusive. He tries to demonstrate "how human beings are capable of committing the most horrible crimes without being monsters" (quoted in Möckel, p. 69). In *Der Vorleser* (*The Reader*, 1995) the rendition of a close encounter with a perpetrator may be seen as resulting to a high degree from Schlink's own experiences.

Biographical Data

Bernhard Schlink was born on 6 July 1944 in Grossdornberg, near Bielefeld in northern Germany. His father, Edmund, had been a professor of Lutheran Theology in Giessen, but had been dismissed by the Nazi regime because he was a member of the Confessing Church, a Protestant resistance movement. He subsequently became a minister in Bielefeld, where, during the war, the police repeatedly harassed him because of his subversive sermons. Bernhard Schlink remembers that as a young man he was deeply impressed by a later book of his father's sermons, in which his father had stressed reconciliation and working together, rather than against one another, to rebuild the destroyed Germany.

Schlink's mother is Swiss and comes from a background of Calvinism-informed Reformed Protestantism. In an interview, the author comments: "My preoccupation with moral questions, particularly questions of guilt, I got from my mother. Compared to my father's Lutheran orientation, the Reformed Protestants have a more difficult time with moral questions and questions of guilt" (Kammann interview).

After the end of World War II, Schlink's father resumed his academic career, teaching Systematic Theology, and the family moved to Heidelberg. The author grew up there, the youngest sibling among two sisters and a brother. He studied law in Heidelberg and Berlin, and in 1975 he completed his studies in Heidelberg with a dissertation on Constitutional Law, followed by an academic teaching qualification in Administrative Law in 1981.

Looking back at his student years, Schlink recalls that, despite the 1945–1946 Nuremberg trials, the truth of the Holocaust did not seem to seep into German public consciousness until the early 1960s, especially during the 1963–1968 Frankfurt trials of Auschwitz guards (Smith interview). The author himself observed one of those. Schlink belongs to the second postwar student generation, the "68 generation," who rebelled and often protested violently against what their parents had done. Personal encounters with the Nazi past, Schlink recalls, were almost a daily experience. During semester breaks, for example, he worked on an assembly line in a metal factory, where he had long conversations with the workers about the war. One Romanian migrant worker in particular, a former member of the SS, who was well aware of having participated in unforgivable crimes, left a lasting impression (Smith interview), and may have been seminal in the creation of *The Reader*'s character Hanna, who comes from Siebenbürgen (Transylvania), a German enclave in Romania. Schlink also recalls his disappointments discovering that two of his favorite teachers, one in high school and one at the university, were former Nazis (Kammann interview).

The core issue of the second generation, the question of *Vergangenheitsbewältigung*, coping with the past, has been one of Schlink's major interests throughout his professional life. Since 1992, he has been teaching at the Humboldt University in Berlin, with an emphasis on Constitutional Law and Philosophy of Law. In 1994 he was elected dean of the School of Law. In addition, he has been serving since 1988 as a judge on the Constitutional Court of North Rhine-Westphalia. His special interest in comparative studies and international perspectives on constitutional law has prompted Schlink's intermittent teaching abroad. He was a visiting professor at the University of Aix-en-Provence in 1985. In the United States he taught at Stanford University in 1974–1975 and at Yeshiva University in New York in 1993–1994 and 1997–1998.

Schlink has published widely on law. He authored a well-known basic textbook on Constitutional Law (17th reprinting in 2001). In addition, his *Vergangenheits Schuld und gegenwärtiges Recht* (Past Guilt and Present Law) is a collection of his publications over the years that specifically address retroactivity and other conflicting legal aspects of *Vergangenheitsbewältigung* that arise from the momentous change of political systems that occurred after the war and again after Germany's 1990 reunification. These articles and lectures are of particular interest with regard to the central part 2 of *The Reader*.

Schlink's Development as a Writer of Novels: Prizes and Awards

Before the publication of *Der Vorleser*, which catapulted him into international recognition, Schlink distinguished himself in Germany as the writer of prize-winning crime novels: *Selbs Justiz* (Selb's Justice, 1987), *Die gordische Schleife* (The Gordian Loop, 1988), and *Selbs Betrug* (Selb's Betrayal, 1992). A third novel about the detective Selb, titled *Selbs Mord* (Selb's Murder), was under way in 2002 as the last part of a trilogy dealing with the major phases of Germany's postwar history in chronological succession.

In these German detective novels, the Third Reich past reaches into the present. Beside an obvious connection in their narrative approach, the thematic connection of all of these crime novels with *The Reader* is apparent in various respects. *Die Gordische Schleife* and *Selbs Betrug* were awarded German literature prizes in the crime novel category. A German screen adaptation of *Selbs Justiz*, titled *Der Tod kam als Freund* (Death Came as a Friend), was released in 1991.

The worldwide success of *The Reader* remains—at least partially—a puzzle to many critics. The book has been translated into thirty languages and has won a great number of prestigious prizes internationally; it reached the best-seller lists in many countries. In Germany, *Der Vorleser* already belongs to the canon for high school students. In America, the book is being taught in college courses. Following Oprah Winfrey's book club selection (February 1999), *The Reader* rocketed to number one on the best-seller list. A screen adaptation by Anthony Minghella, the director of *The English Patient*, is under way.

Schlink's collection of short stories, *Liebesfluchten* (Flights of Love), appeared in 2000, its first American edition in 2001, and in 2002 the author was working on a new novel, *Verrat und Heimkehr* (Betrayal and Returning Home).

Der Vorleser (*The Reader*) in the Context of German Holocaust Literature

West German postwar literature in general has continually been aware of the Holocaust in ever new endeavors of representation, including the many narrative strategies of silence. A first wave of German Holocaust literature in the 1950s and early 1960s was mainly documentary in approach. The second wave, starting in the mid-1960s, reflected a new political emphasis in writing, followed, in the third phase of the 1970s and 1980s, by an interest in introspective autobiographies. Simultaneously, a distinctive group of novels about mothers and fathers indicates the second generation's continued desire to explore the parental role in the Third Reich.

The year 1995, in which *Der Vorleser* was published, appears to mark a new interest in history among German writers. In the latest Holocaust novels, the motifs of silence, of forgetting, and of blindness persist.

Synopsis of The Reader

The Reader incorporates two major themes of the writers of the second generation: the generational discord characteristic of the novels about fathers and mothers, and autobiography. Schlink, however, takes a new approach in dealing with the Holocaust. Not only does he, in contrast to the earlier documentary literature, switch his focus from the victims to his protagonist's personal encounter with a perpetrator, he also replaces the bond between fathers and their children with a bond of passionate love. This provocative strategy, linking romance to the Holocaust and presenting it in the course of an introspective autobiography, generates a closeness, which requires the narrator's most personal response to his examination of a perpetrator. It enables the author, by way of a pointed allegory, to demonstrate and explore in detail the core issues of postwar Germany's dealing with its Nazi past, and particularly the conflicts of the "68 generation" in their relation to their fathers.

The protagonist in *The Reader*, Michael Berg, tells the story of his life in a linear chronology. The chapters are short and the plot is streamlined, reminiscent of detective novels. In view of the novel's distinct realism, the contemporary problematics of representation, questions of how to deal adequately with the precarious subject matter of the Holocaust in particular, do not appear to be much of a concern to this author. Rather, Schlink feels strongly that the horrors of the Holocaust must not lead to silence. He asks: "Should we only fall silent in revulsion, shame, and guilt? To what purpose?" (*The Reader*, p. 104). Writers must continue, he asserts, to convey the Holocaust imaginatively in order to preserve its memory for future generations; it must be integrated into the collective memory on three levels simultaneously—the scholarly, the documentary, and the artistic (Kübler interview).

Schlink's clear and unadorned language enhances the authenticity of the text, in which at times the dividing line between fiction and reality appears to be blurred. With only minor deviations, Michael's and the author's biographies are strikingly parallel; Michael's family situation and background, his father's career as a professor at Heidelberg (specializing in Kant and Hegel), his own interest in literature and the *Odyssey* in particular, his student years, and his professional life as a professor of law all mirror Schlink's biography. In addition, the realistic and precise description of the fictional space (Heidelberg, Frankfurt, and the Rhine-Main-Neckar area), as well as the almost identical chronology of Michael's life with that of Schlink's contribute to the authenticity of the novel.

The timing and location of the novel's trial call to mind the Auschwitz trials in Frankfurt. More significant, however, particularly in terms of the character of Hanna and the particulars of her trial, are the striking parallels with the Majdanek trial in Düsseldorf (1975–1981), in which out of five female camp guards the exceptionally cruel camp guard Hermine Ryan was sentenced to life in prison. In fact, Schlink's text contains a direct allusion to Hanna as being similar but different from "the Mare" (p. 119). By comparison, in the novel, partially due to its consistent first-person perspective, Hanna's conduct at the camp remains underdeveloped. A few critics see this as a considerable disadvantage.

In the retrospective chronological rendition of his life, the narrator in *The Reader* drastically expands or reduces its scale of representation to suit exactly his purpose to explore and read the mind and mysterious past of a perpetrator.

The book is divided into three almost equally long parts. The first part covers only nine months and centers around the illicit love between the fifteen-year-old Michael Berg and the thirty-six-year-old Hanna Schmitz, a streetcar conductor. They meet in the fall of 1958, when Hanna helps the boy, who is suffering from an attack of explosive vomiting on his way home from school. After his recovery, a few months later, Michael, following his mother's advice, visits Hanna with flowers to thank her. He suddenly feels forcefully drawn to her, but his moral upbringing keeps him at first from going back to her. Finally, realizing full well that he is making his desire an "entry into a strange moral accounting" (p. 19), he is drawn into a passionate sexual relationship. He meets Hanna almost daily, following a ritual: "reading to her, showering with her, making love to her, and lying next to her for a while afterwards" (p. 43).

This secret romance appears to be endangered by discord, each time the lovers meet outside of Hanna's simple dwelling, in the streetcar, and during a bicycle outing to Amorbach at Easter. Moreover, Michael does not understand Hanna's sometimes rude, or even sadomasochistic behavior, and he is puzzled by her reticence about her past. He begins to distance himself from her and starts dating Sophie, a classmate. Suddenly, in the summer of 1959, Hanna leaves her job for no apparent reason, and disappears without any notice. Michael is devastated by the loss; he feels guilty of having neglected and betrayed Hanna.

Part 2 begins seven years later. Michael has begun to study law; as he and his classmates are observing the trial of five female concentration camp guards, he recognizes Hanna as one of the defendants. It develops that between 1942 and 1945 she served as a guard in Auschwitz and at a satellite camp near Kraków. Hanna and the other guards are accused of two charges: selecting inmates to be sent to Auschwitz on a regular basis, and failing, after an air raid, to unlock the doors of a burning village church, into which several hundred Jewish women, who had been on their death march, were locked to spend the night. The dramatic scene in which the judge confronts Hanna directly with her crime culminates in Hanna's incisive question: "What would you have done?" (p. 111). Apparently, Hanna honestly does not know how she could have acted differently.

Hanna is charged with an additional cruelty, as a witness testifies that she selected particularly frail Jewish women and ordered them to read to her before they were sent to Auschwitz. Significantly, Hanna is also, falsely, accused by her codefendants of having been in charge of the guards and having written the report about the church incident, which she denies. Later, however, for no apparent reason, Hanna admits to this charge, accepting a much harsher sentence than that given her impudent codefendants.

In a separate scene in the woods, Michael broods over Hanna's inexplicable and inconsistent conduct in court. By intuition, he suddenly discovers the underlying motive for it; it is the second grave secret of her life. Hanna is illiterate. She could not have written the report. It is inconceivable to Michael that Hanna's moral blindness should be so extreme that this appears more shameful to her than being a murderer. It becomes increasingly clear to him, though, that the obsession to conceal her illiteracy has determined all her actions in life. This is why, when young, she preferred joining the SS to being promoted at the Siemens factory, and why, years later, she left her job in Heidelberg, when promotion was imminent: She could not bear to be exposed as an illiterate.

Undecided whether to help Hanna by disclosing this crucial information about her illiteracy to the court, Michael first consults his father as an authority in matters of morality and ethics. His father advises him in abstract terms that he has the moral obligation to discuss the matter with the person involved, but should leave the final decision to that person. Next, Michael visits with the presiding judge, but in their encounter the essential topic is not even touched on. In the end, Michael does not try to talk to Hanna, nor does he disclose her secret. Hanna is sentenced to life in prison.

The lengthy recounting of the central trial covers a relatively short period of only four months. By contrast, the novel's fast-moving part 3 sums up the twenty years in Michael's life after Hanna's sentence. Michael finishes law school and marries Gertrud, a young lawyer; he becomes a professor of the History of Law, and after the birth of a daughter is divorced. He does not visit Hanna, but following his divorce, he resumes the former ritual of reading to Hanna; he sends her tapes, but never adds a personal note. Highlights of the concluding chapters are (1) the significant news that in prison Hanna has learned to read and to write, (2) Michael's first visit at Hanna's prison, where he sees Hanna for the first time in eighteen years, and (3) the second visit, after Hanna has committed suicide the night before she was to be released. The bookshelf Hanna has left behind—containing major Holocaust literature—proves that before her death she had been preoccupied for years with rereading and deciphering the past. To fulfill Hanna's last wish, Michael visits the Jewish "daughter" in New York, a witness at the trial and only survivor of the church burning, who refuses Hanna's modest donation intended as a gesture of atonement.

Condemnation versus Love

As Michael rereads the past, he finds that condemnation versus love of parents is the central moral dilemma, the tragic fate of his generation, "a German fate" (p. 171). It is the core issue in his personal biography as well. During the trial, Michael becomes increasingly and painfully aware of its tragic impact on him personally. Throughout his life, he wrestles desperately with reconciling his compassion for Hanna with the undeniable atrocities of her acts. But as his conflict between condemning Hanna and feeling compassion for her unfolds, it transcends the German generational issue and becomes an allegory for a universal moral problem.

Jeremiah P. Conway argues that in *The Reader* Schlink challenges the widely held position that compassion for the guilty is neither possible nor desirable: Michael comes to understand that "[c]ompassion . . . is due even to those who suffer by their own fault" (Conway, p. 296). That, of course, is basically a Christian position, and many critics do not approve. They claim that Schlink is confused, lacks a moral compass, or does not offer satisfying resolutions to the issues he presents.

The Context of Collective Guilt

The experience of the trial changes Michael as he is trying to come to terms with his parents' generation. At the beginning, he enthusiastically joins in the self-righteous attitudes of his fellow students, who are convinced of their own innocence: "Exploration! Exploring the past! We students in the seminar considered ourselves radical explorers. . . . Our parents had played a variety of roles in the Third Reich. . . . We all condemned our parents to shame, even if the only charge we could bring was that after 1945 they had tolerated the perpetrators in their midst" (pp. 91–92).

Michael gradually recognizes his own entanglement in guilt and his responsibility for it: "I had to point at Hanna, but the finger I pointed at her turned back to me. . . . I tried to talk myself into a state of innocence in which children love their parents. But love for our parents is the only love for which we are not responsible" (p. 170). He feels "guilty of having loved a criminal" of his own free choice (p. 134).

As the trial proceeds during the summer of the 1968 student upheavals, Michael distances himself from the other students. Convinced of their own innocence, they dissociate themselves from their parents and "thus from the entire generation of perpetrators, voyeurs, and the willfully blind, accommodators and accepters" (p. 171). By contrast, he has come to see this dissociation as an attempt to "drown out the fact that their love for their parents [makes] them irrevocably complicit in their crimes" (p. 171). As Michael's love for Hanna has led to his personal entanglement in guilt, the second generation's love for their parents involves them in collective guilt. Michael realizes that, in addition to his personal guilt, he cannot deny participating in his generation's collective guilt: "the concept of collective guilt . . . was a lived reality" (p. 169).

The concept of collective guilt is not elaborated on in the novel. Schlink has addressed collective guilt elsewhere, in "Recht—Schuld–Zukunft" ("Law—Guilt—Future", in *Geschichte—Schuld—Zukunfte* [History—Guilt—Future], ed. Jörg Calliess, Loccumer Protokolle 66/87: Loccum, 1987, pp. 57–78). He explains that according to law collective guilt does not exist. In a strictly legal sense, only a single person can be guilty for his or her own deeds; a transfer of guilt from one person to another, or from one generation to the next, is not possible. If members of the second generation cannot be guilty in any legal sense, how do we explain the feelings of shock, embarrassment, and shame among so many of them when confronted with victims or evidence of Nazi crimes? To explain this conflict, which becomes so evident in the story, Schlink offers an illuminating inquiry into the history of criminal law.

Schlink points out that, in contrast to the principle of individual guilt in current criminal law, the old Germanic law was based on a concept of collective guilt. If an individual committed a crime, the whole tribe was responsible for it. The tribe could expel the perpetrator and would no longer be responsible. But if they kept him within their community, they would be exposed to feud or revenge ("Recht-Schuld-Zukunft," p. 63). In addition, children were legally responsible for the crimes of their parents in certain cases. Enmeshment in the web of guilt was far-reaching; not only the perpetrator but everyone who remained in solidarity with the perpetrator after the deed was caught in it. "The concept of guilt," Schlink emphasizes, "is not only connected with the norms of the current law but is linked to other equally valid norms as well, the norms of religion, morality, ethics, and tact. I believe that these norms exist" ("Recht-Schuld-Zukunft," p. 66).

In summary, he concludes, the loss of the custom of expelling or punishing the perpetrators generates new guilt, for the contemporaries of the perpetrators as well as for their children. The Germans became guilty in this way. Their entanglement in guilt is tragic. After 1945, attempts at renunciation, at expelling or punishing, could not succeed because of the great numbers involved. What was left was the possibility of dissociation either by way of a massacre, "a night of long knives," which would have included the innocent, or through legal proceedings, which were bound to fail in the face of organized crimes. A third alternative did not exist ("Recht—Schuld—Zukunft," p. 69).

Other Legal and Moral Issues

Michael Berg's critical account of the trial in *The Reader* raises issues that help to explain why the postwar legal system was bound to fail in dealing with the Holocaust. The law students watching the trial, for example, discuss the inadequacies caused by the prohibition of retroactive justice (p. 90), which disregards, as their professor points out, the moral aspects of culpability (p. 91). The prohibition of retroactive justice made consistent punishment and elimination of perpetrators extremely difficult. It had been suspended during the Nuremberg trials, as Schlink points out in a legal paper dealing with retroactivity, but was guaranteed within the German criminal law ("Bewältigung von Vergangenheit durch Recht," p. 443).

Throughout Michael's detailed account of the proceedings he offers professional criticism. He comments, for example, that a more competent defense could have pointed out that the defendants had acted under compulsion within a hierarchy of responsibilities (pp. 113–114). He also observes that the older defense lawyers are former Nazis. The judge, too, it is suggested, is a former Nazi. Above all, Hanna's sentence is "the most grotesque oversimplification of all" (p. 179), a grave "miscarriage of justice" (p. 158).

Why does Michael not act to prevent this miscarriage of justice? Why does he remain silent about Hanna's illiteracy, entangling himself in additional moral guilt by thus betraying her? At this point of the plot development, the clear and comfortable division between good and evil, between those who are unequivocally guilty and those who only seem to be innocent and not involved, appears to be provocatively undermined. Michael does not act because he cannot resolve a basic conflict, that he wants "simultaneously to understand Hanna's crime and to condemn it" (p. 157). Another answer lies in his self-analysis: "This juxtaposition of callousness and extreme sensitivity seemed suspicious even to me" (p. 89). Schlink has commented on his protagonist, "Michael is frozen inside, because he never confronts Hanna or his guilt, his entanglement in the past. He kept himself from fully maturing" (Smith interview). Schlink sees this lack of maturity, a mental paralysis and "numbness" as typical of the second generation. The deforming psychological effects of the Holocaust are still painfully noticeable in the present. If parents as perpetrators or as victims remain silent about their traumas, they cannot communicate with their children openly. Children in turn cannot learn the openness and trust necessary for them to find their identity and develop into mentally healthy and strong adults ("Bewältigung," p. 439). This lack of communication and trust, a major theme throughout *The Reader*, is emphasized in conversation between Michael and his undemonstrative father (pp. 139–144).

The Paradox of Evil

As Michael tries to understand Hanna, she mysteriously appears to combine in her character both the monstrosity and the banality of evil. Throughout his life he continues to ask himself, "Was she vain enough, and evil enough, to become a criminal simply to avoid exposure" of her illiteracy (p. 133)? Or should he believe, to the contrary, that "Hanna had not decided in favor of crime, she had decided against a promotion at Siemens, and fell into a job as a guard" (p. 133)? Did Hanna become guilty through a conscious act of evil, or did she "fall" into evil through her vanity, a trifling weakness? The narrator here touches on ultimate questions about the origin and the paradox of evil (see Ricoeur, p. 146). The banality of evil is presented as resulting from the possibility Hanna always has of making her own choices. The theme of the banality of evil is further epitomized and carried to an extreme in Michael's shocking encounter with the taxi driver, a former Nazi.

Critical Response to *The Reader* and the Significance of Illiteracy

The monstrosity of Hanna's crime is provocatively undermined through the introduction of her illiteracy. Understandably, Hanna's illiteracy has been subject to much critical attention. Cynthia Ozick argues that it is "her exculpation" (Ozick, p. 115). This "anomaly," she holds, is not representative of Germany's high level of *Kultur*; it "sweeps away memory" (pp. 118–119). Ian Sansom believes that Michael accepts Hanna's illiteracy as "a total and simple explanation for her crimes" (Sansom, p. 10). Stuart Parkes does not see any clear moral or message in the theme of illiteracy (Parkes, p. 119). Eva Hoffman contends that in linking illiteracy and brutality Schlink is introducing false explanatory ideas about the Holocaust; the notion that Hanna did not know what she was doing because she could not read is a dubious premise for a novel (Hoffman, p. 35).

In Germany, several critics argue along similar lines. Others seem to agree with the literary scholar Volker Hage, who contends that Hanna's inability to read must be interpreted beyond its literal sense: "Hanna did not and does not even approximately understand what happened back then, she is incapable of deciphering what she has caused and experienced" (Hage, p. 29). Schlink himself seems to agree with this reading in stating that many criminals are illiterate.

Hanna's illiteracy as implicating a severe lack of insight, a mental blindness and imprisonment, is a theme developed at the metaphorical level as well. It is epitomized in Hanna's helpless question to the judge and by her seeming to fear the shame of a personal failing, being unable to read, more than the shame of being a murderer. It is also implied in the narrator's commentary at the pivotal point when Hanna has learned to read: "Illiteracy is dependence [*Unmündigkeit*]. By finding the courage to learn to read and to write, Hanna had advanced from dependence to independence [*Mündigkeit*], a step towards liberation [*ein aufklärerischer Schritt*]" (p. 188). The German text here clearly refers to Theodor Adorno's influential lectures on Germany's coming to terms with the past, *Erziehung zur Mündigkeit* (Education Toward Adult Responsibility). The reference is lost in translation, as is the literal sense, "a step toward *enlightenment*," as opposed to the free translation "a step toward *liberation*." Adorno's concept of *Mündigkeit* resists a satisfactory translation; it may be said to be the self-reliant, Kantian decision-making of the individual, based on his ability to make full use of his potential for reasoning ("Erziehung zur Mündigkeit," p. 133). According to Adorno, the most basic prerequisite for *Mündigkeit* is *Aufklärung* (enlightenment) about the self, to strengthen an individual sense of identity and self-reliance (through psychoanalysis), and about the past, to develop historical consciousness and understanding.

Michael has helped Hanna to achieve the first liberating step toward "enlightenment" by resuming the habit of reading to her on tape while she is in prison. As *Vor-leser*, one who reads to someone, he takes on the role of guardian of her education, including her education toward *Mündigkeit*. He has been selecting books for her all along: world literature, as well as texts most representative of the rich German cultural heritage, as, for example, works of the Enlightenment, with its emphasis on moral and ethical absolutes. Playwrights of that period, like Lessing (*Emilia Galotti)* and Schiller (*Intrigues and Love*), considered their plays and the theater itself a "school of the world of morals" (J¢rgensen, p. 274). They saw their mission as sharpening the moral awareness of their audiences by focusing on a hero's tragic entanglement in guilt, which often resulted in self-imposed death. Early in their relationship Michael reads *Emilia Galotti* and *Intrigues and Love* to Hanna and they attend a performance of Schiller's play together. The intertextual relevancy of other books mentioned in *The Reader* deserves to be investigated further. In reading from the rich heritage of the German past, Michael is trying to reclaim it, to reinscribe it step by step in the historic memory, to bridge the gap created by the Holocaust.

Hanna's imprisonment turns out to be her liberation toward "enlightenment." She takes on the past by immersing herself in Holocaust literature from the perspectives of both perpetrators and victims. Her studies lead her to the self-analysis Adorno thought necessary. Hanna's first step toward an "enlightened maturity" includes signs of her spiritual awakening as well; she is living a life of "meditation," as in a "convent" (p. 207). Her last words to Michael before her death are an expression of her utmost loneliness: "[W]hen no one understands you, then no one can call you to account. Not even the court could call me to account. But the dead can. Here in prison they were with me a lot" (p. 198).

In the face of enormous guilt, Michael has reached the limits of what one can be or do for another human. His communication with Hanna has remained "frozen," blocked to the very end. Ultimately, Michael has never resolved his traumatic conflict: the aftereffects of the Holocaust reach into the present.

Bibliography

Primary Sources

Selbs Justiz (Selb's Justice). 1987.

"Recht—Schuld—Zukunft" (Law—Guilt—Future). In *Geschichte—Schuld—Zukunft* (History—Guilt—Future). Edited by Jörg Calliess. Loccumer Protokolle 66/87: Loccum, 1987, pp. 57–78.

Die Gordische Schleife (The Gordian Loop). 1988.

Selbs Betrug (Selb's Betrayal). 1992.

Der Vorleser (*The Reader*). 1995

Selbs Mord (Selb's Murder). 2001.

"Die Bewältigung von Vergangenheit durch Recht" (Coming to Terms with the Past through Law). In *Vergangenheitsbewältigung am Ende des 20. Jahrhunderts* (Coming to Terms with the Past at the End of the 20th Century). Edited by H. Koenig. Opladen-Wiesbaden: Westdeutscher Verlag, 1998, pp. 433–451.

Liebesfluchten (*Flights of Love*). 2000.

Vergangenheits schuld und gegenwärtiges Recht (Past Guilt and Present Law). 2002.

Secondary Sources

Adorno, Theodor. "Erziehung zur Mündigkeit." *Erziehung zur Mündigkeit: Vorträge und Gespräche mit Hellmut Becker 1959–1969*. Edited by Gert Kadelbach. Frankfurt: Suhrkamp, 1970.

———. "Was bedeutet Aufarbeitung der Vergangenheit?", *Erziehung zur Mündigkeit: Vorträge und Gespräche mit Hellmut Becker 1959–1969*. Edited by Gert Kadelbach. Frankfurt: Suhrkamp, 1970.

Barner, Wilfried et al. (eds.) *Geschichte der deutschen Literatur von 1945 bis zur Gegenwart*. München: C. H. Beck, 1994.

Braese, Stephan. *In der Sprache der Täter*. Opladen/Wiesbaden: Westdeutscher Verlag, 1998.

Conway, Jeremiah P. "Compassion and Moral Condemnation: An Analysis of *The Reader*." *Philosophy and Literature* 23.2 (1999): 284–301.

Diner, Dan. "Der Holocaust im Geschichtsnarrativ." In *In der Sprache der Täter*. Edited by Stephan Braese. Opladen/Wiesbaden: Westdeutscher Verlag, 1998, pp. 13–30.

Friedlander, Saul. *Probing the Limits of Representation*. Cambridge: Harvard University Press, 1992.

Görtz, Franz Josef, Volker Hage, and Hubert Winkels (eds.) *Deutsche Literatur 1995*. Stuttgart: Reclam, 1996.

Hage, Volker. "Im Schatten der Tat." *Der Spiegel* [Hamburg], 20 Nov. 1995.

Hinderer, Walter. *Arbeit an der Gegenwart: Zur deutschen Literatur nach 1945*. Würzburg: Königshausen & Neumann, 1994.

Hoffman, Eva. "The Uses of Illiteracy." *New Republic*, 23 Mar 1998, pp. 33–36.

J¢rgensen, Sven Aage. *Geschichte der deutschen Literatur: Aufklärung, Sturm und Drang, frühe Klassik*. Vol. 6. München: C. H. Beck, 1990.

Köster, Juliane. *Bernhard Schlink: Der Vorleser*. München: Oldenbourg Schulbuchverlag, 2000

Möckel, Magret. *Bernhard Schlink: Der Vorleser*. Hollfeld: C. Bange Verlag, 2000.

Ozick, Cynthia. *Quarrel and Quandary*. New York: Alfred A. Knopf, 2000.

Parkes, Stuart. "The Language of the Past: Recent Prose Works by Bernhard Schlink, Marcel Beyer, and Friedrich Christian Delius," in Williams/Parkes/Preece, 1998, pp. 115–132.

Parry, Ann. "The Caesura of the Holocaust in Martin Amis's *Time's Error* and Bernhard Schlink's *The Reader." European Studies*, xxix (1999): 249–267.

Ricoeur, Paul. *Fallible Man*. Trans. Charles Kelbey. New York: Fordham University Press, 1986.

Sansom, Ian. "Doubts about *The Reader*." *Samalgundi* (Fall/Winter 1999/2000): 3–16.

Schlant, Ernestine. *The Language of Silence: West German Literature and the Holocaust*. New York: Routledge, 1999.

Schmitz, Thorsten. "Die Stute von Majdanek" ("The Mare of Majdanek"). *Süddeutsche Zeitung* Magazin, no. 50, 13 Dec. 1996: 17–26.

Williams, Arthur, Stuart Parkes, and Julian Preece (eds.) *'Whose Story?' – Continuities in Contemporary German-Language Literature*. Bern: Peter Lang, 1998.

Winkels, Hubert. "Zur deutschen Literatur 1995," in Görtz/Hage/Winkels, 1996, pp. 5–27.

Interviews and Archives

Interview by Dinitia Smith. "Seeking Guilt, Finding Fame." *New York Times*, 30 Mar. 1999.

Interview by Petra Kammann. "Der Erzähler." *Buchjournal* [Frankfurt], Frühjahr 2000.

Interview by Gunhild Kübler. "Als Deutscher im Ausland wird man gestellt." *Weltwoche* [Zürich], 27 Jan. 2000.

Interview by Sieglinde Geisel. "Der Botschafter des deutschen Buches." *Neue Zürcher Zeitung*, 27 Mar. 2000.

Translations from the German throughout by Marianne M. Friedrich.

HELEN SCHULMAN
(1961–)

GARY WEISSMAN

HELEN SCHULMAN WAS born on 30 April 1961 in New York City, the daughter of David Schulman, a child psychiatrist, and Gloria (née Yevish) Schulman, a social worker. After attending the Bronx High School of Science, she earned a B.A. from Cornell University in 1983 and an M.F.A. from Columbia University in 1986. She has taught fiction workshops and literature courses at Emory University, New York University, and Bard College, and currently teaches in the Graduate Writing Division at Columbia University.

Overview of Work

Schulman's first book, the short story collection *Not a Free Show* (1988), was praised by reviewers. In the *New York Times Book Review*, Martin Kirby described the collection as "evidence of a genuine literary talent" (p. 7). The story he identified as the collection's best—"James Dean's Widow," about a young woman whose parents take her on a trip to Hawaii in an effort to lift her spirits after her husband's death—introduces a theme that has since pervaded Schulman's fiction. This theme, developed through prose infusing despair with humor, concerns how the living deal with the haunting, premature death of a loved one.

Schulman's first novel, *Out of Time* (1991), revolves around twenty-year-old Ken Gold's death in a car crash; loosely connected chapters, set years before and after the crash, explore his death's impact on the living. Schulman's next novel, *The Revisionist* (1998), concerns thirty-nine-year-old David Hershleder, whose failure to come to terms with his mother's death finds expression in his obsession with the Holocaust, denier-turned-author of an exhaustive study of the Nazi gas chambers. In Schulman's third novel, *P.S.* (2001), Louise Harrington, a thirty-eight-year-old divorcée and college admissions coordinator, is startled to come across an application from someone whose identity appears nearly identical to that of her old high school crush, who died in a car accident twenty years before.

Schulman also has written several screenplays and co-edited *Wanting a Child* (1998), an anthology of personal essays and short stories recounting the experiences of writers whose difficult efforts to have children have involved miscarriage, stillbirth, in vitro fertilization, adoption, or surrogacy. Part of the first chapter of *The Revisionist*, published as a short story under the same title in *The Paris Review* in 1995, won the Pushcart Prize. *The Revisionist* is Schulman's only work to date relating to the Holocaust.

The Revisionist

Toward the end of *The Revisionist*, Dr. David Hershleder, a Jewish neurologist in New York who is used to diagnosing patients, receives his own diagnosis: "Survivor shock. It's like a disease. Grief. Trauma. Mourning. And let me tell you, it can be inherited" (New York: Crown Publishers, Inc., 1998, p. 221). If Hershleder inherited his mother's grief and trauma, he never learned to mourn. His mother and her sister, smuggled out of Germany in a trunk after *Kristallnacht*, were the only ones in the family to survive the Holocaust. Whenever the young Hershleder asked his mother about this, she would cut him short and retreat to the bedroom with a headache. Only in her later years, when Adela Hershleder left her husband to pursue a degree in Holocaust studies at City College, did she want to talk about it. For Hershleder it was too late: "He'd been trained too well, and he'd avoided the subject at all costs" (p. 91). He also avoided his own Jewishness by marrying a non-Jew, and any emotional connection to others by living safely inside his own head.

Given that the predicament of the "second generation," or the children of Holocaust survivors, is the main subject of fiction by second-generation writers, Schulman's portrayal of Hershleder is notable for being authored by someone who is not the child of a survivor. Still, Schulman writes that as a child she inherited "fear, separation anxiety and heavy sadness" from her grandmother, who had left Austria for America after World War I while her four siblings died in Nazi death camps. Schulman, who shared her childhood bedroom with her grandmother, writes that "the Holocaust for me was both a history lesson and an almost silent, ever-present companion" ("Author Notebook"). *The Revisionist*, she states, was written in part to fulfill "the debt I owed my grandmother and my family, now dead, to bear witness for them" ("Author Notebook"). Yet perhaps because she lacks the stories that second-generation writers "inherit" from their parents, her novel bears witness to the Holocaust only indirectly, through the theme of Holocaust denial.

The impetus for Schulman's novel was an article about French pharmacist Jean-Claude Pressac, author of *Auschwitz: Technique and Operation of the Gas Chambers* (New York: Beate Klarsfeld, 1989), a monumental study documenting the development of the killing facilities at Auschwitz-Birkenau. Schulman was fascinated by how Pressac, influenced by Holocaust deniers, undertook his research intending to substantiate their claim that homicidal gas chambers had never existed at Auschwitz. "The idea that someone could embrace such lies outraged me, and this guy's retreat from these lies intrigued me somehow even more," writes Schulman ("Author Notebook"). Reading as much as she could about Holocaust denial, Schulman—already troubled by some of her students' ignorance of the Holocaust—was amazed at the abundance and accessibility of material portraying the Holocaust as a hoax.

Fascinated that Pressac "found the strength and the courage to refute his own position and turn himself around," Schulman originally planned to write about a Pressac-like figure (Steiker). Instead, her novel focuses on someone who shares her fascination with such a figure. *The Revisionist* concerns Hershleder's obsession with Jacques LeClerc, a French chemist who had been a "revisionist" (the term Holocaust deniers use to describe themselves) before writing his 1,032-page study of the Nazi gas chambers. Hershleder imagines the Frenchman to be a man of science very much like himself—except that LeClerc has managed to turn his life around.

Hershleder's own life is a mess: his inability to communicate with others causes him to avoid and mistreat his patients, and has led his wife, Itty, to throw him out of the house and take another lover. "I'd hoped you'd take this time to take a good, hard look at yourself, not spend it hunting Nazis," Itty tells him (*The Revisionist*, p. 120); but Hershleder believes that LeClerc's example can help him to do just that: "LeClerc had taken a good hard look at himself and in due course he'd learned to accept the truth. In some strange way, wasn't that exactly what his own wife had been begging him to do? LeClerc's study sounded like an exemplary example of self-examination" (p. 72).

After finding little in the study to account for LeClerc's courageous act of self-examination, Hershleder decides to approach him through David Josephson, an old acquaintance who happens to have translated LeClerc's study into English. A series of misadventures takes Hershleder to Los Angeles and then to Paris, where, with Josephson translating, he and LeClerc look over charts and graphs and discuss the operation of the gas chambers late into the night. Pushed to reveal what gave him "the guts to rethink his life" (p. 213), LeClerc can only respond, "The facts. I studied the facts" (p. 220). Asked to explain his initial attraction to revisionism, he says, "I don't like Jews" (p. 224)—giving voice to Schulman's belief that Holocaust denial is essentially "plain old antisemitism" (Steiker).

The metaphor of "the revisionist" is spelled out when Josephson reproaches Hershleder for joining LeClerc in discussing the extermination in purely technical terms that dehumanize the dead. "What are you denying?" he asks Hershleder (*The Revisionist*, p. 221), and "Who's the real revisionist here, you or him?" (p. 222). Hershleder admits what he has been denying only later, after returning to New York and opening himself up to an old college girlfriend. Then, as if for the first time, he remembers that his mother did not die of an accident or an aneurysm, as he told his wife and others, but killed herself by laying her head in the oven and turning on the gas.

The Revisionist begins with Hershleder, curiously repressing the fact that his wife threw him out of the house months ago, traveling home to discover that he no longer lives there; it ends with a wiser Hershleder returning home once more to tell Itty what he has learned about "his own attempt to deny all the lousy things that had happened to him" by "revising history" (pp. 243–244). The novel concludes with Hershleder still uncertain whether his wife will take him back, but grateful that he can finally open himself up to her.

Critical Reception

While praising Schulman's tragicomic novel for its humor and intelligence, reviewers have disagreed over its treatment of the Holocaust. *The Revisionist* suggests an analogy between Holocaust revisionism and what Schulman has described as "the ways in which many of us both willingly and unwittingly revise our own personal histories" ("Author Notebook"). More specifically, the revisionist's denial of the Holocaust becomes a metaphor for Hershleder's repression of painful events in his own life. Some reviewers have found fault with the connection this metaphor suggests between Hershleder's personal troubles and the incomparable horror of the Holocaust. "Although handled with seeming decency and taste, the Holocaust theme, juxtaposed with Hershleder's more mundane problems, seems forced and almost exploitative," comments *Kirkus Reviews*. On the other hand, Earl L. Dachslager, writing in the *Houston Chronicle*, states that the novel's focus on Hershleder's personal failings reminds us that the Holocaust was not only a "history-altering event" but also a "person-altering event."

Many reviewers appear to forget that Hershleder's problems are, in fact, closely related to the Holocaust. The novel's protagonist is often described as a thirty-nine-year-old man experiencing a midlife crisis; that his mother narrowly escaped the Holocaust appears almost incidental—possibly because the novel does not sufficiently render Hershleder's identity as the son of a Holocaust survivor. This identity might have been conveyed through Hershleder's dealings with his family, but, as Brian Morton writes in his *New York Times* review, too few scenes explore "Hershleder's relationships with his mother, his wife and his children, all of whom are rather lightly sketched."

Morton sees this as the one shortcoming in an otherwise boldly original novel. He contends that though the parallels drawn between Hershleder's marital woes and the Holocaust may appear "dubious" and even "grotesque," "Schulman deals gracefully with the problem by keeping an ironic distance from her protagonist's quest. She isn't endorsing Hershleder's feverish speculations about the similarities between himself and LeClerc; she's observing them, with a skeptical eye." Schulman even has Hershleder come to question his preoccupation with LeClerc: "He wondered how he ever, ever thought any of this could possibly relate to him, to David Hershleder and his tiny, personal problems" (p. 223).

Some reviewers have criticized Hershleder's identification with LeClerc for being implausible or unconvincing (Pinsker, *Kirkus Reviews, Publishers Weekly*); Morton interprets it as a sign of his derangement. Still, one can infer why Adele Hershleder's son would identify with the former Holocaust denier. Schulman writes that Hershleder, in his work as a neurologist, felt at home with anything two-dimensional: papers, charts, brain maps; it is the third dimension, populated by actual patients, that "scared him half to death" (*The Revisionist*, p. 2). Thus, it is not surprising that Hershleder should be drawn to LeClerc's version of the Holocaust, composed as it is of architectural drawings and technical analyses characterized by "neurotic attention to minutiae, to detail" (p. 83). Hershleder finds through LeClerc a two-dimensional version of the Holocaust, one unpopulated by the actual victims, including his mother.

Although Pressac's study has been criticized for its unemotional, technical language, Schulman's LeClerc seems quite unlike Pressac. For whereas LeClerc appears an unrepentant antisemite, swayed only by "the facts" from his revisionist views, Pressac, in his study's postscript, tells how in the end it was not the archival documents that "turned [his] initial ideas inside out," but the testimony of a Jewish Auschwitz survivor who told him his story in detail one afternoon. "For him, it was very painful," writes Pressac. "As for me, I could never be the same again . . . I had the impression of lifting the lid of the cauldron of Hell, a thing I am in no hurry to do again" (p. 561). LeClerc, by contrast, has never peered into the cauldron. He represents, in short, a way to accept the fact of the Holocaust without facing up to its true horror—and without mourning the dead. Curiously, Hershleder and perhaps the novel itself never seem to realize this; for even at its conclusion Hershleder can tell Itty, "In fact, I was a lot like that antisemite LeClerc, except he could face up to the truth" (p. 244).

Bibliography

Primary Sources

Not a Free Show. 1988.
Out of Time. 1991.
Wanting a Child [co-edited anthology]. 1998.
The Revisionist. 1998.
"Author Notebook." Random House, 1998. http://www.randomhouse.com/boldtype/1098/schulman/notebook.html
P.S. 2001.

Secondary Sources

Dachslager, Earl L. "Revising History—The World's and One's Own." *Houston Chronicle*, 30 December 1998. http://www.chron.com/cgibin/auth/story/content/chronicle/ae/books/9899/01/03/revisionist.html

Kirby, Martin. "Crypto-intellectual Neurotics and Others." *New York Times Book Reviews*, 17 July 1988, p. 7.

Morton, Brian. "Deconstructing Life." *New York Times*, 1 November 1998.

Pinsker, Sanford. "Second Thoughts on the Holocaust and Other Matters." *Hadassah Magazine*, August/September 1998. (http://www.hadassah.org/News/archive/1998/AugSep98/BOOKS.HTM)

Pressac, Jean-Claude. *Auschwitz: Technique and Operation of the Gas Chamber*. Translated by Peter Moss. New York: Beate Klarsfeld Foundation, 1989.

Review of *The Revisionist, Kirkus Reviews*, 15 July 1998.

Review of *The Revisionist. Publishers Weekly* 245, no. 25 (22 June 1998): 82.

Steiker, Valerie. "A Holocaust Denier Inspires a Novel: Helen Schulman Talks About 'The Revisionist.' " *Forward* 4 (September 1998): 11.

ANDRÉ SCHWARZ-BART

(1928–)

D. MESHER

THE LAST OF the Just (1960) by André Schwarz-Bart was one of the first great novels of the Holocaust and, in its portrayal of Christian responsibility for Jewish suffering, one of the most controversial as well. The novel was first published in France in 1959, a year after Elie Wiesel's memoir *Night*, at a time when the term "Holocaust" had not come into common usage to describe the destruction of European Jewry during World War II. Indeed, though writing fiction, Schwarz-Bart felt it necessary to include a short list of texts at the beginning of the novel to support the historical underpinnings of the work. The Catholic Church's sins of commission and omission during the Holocaust were not yet widely documented, let alone the subject of an official apology. The French were still in denial about their wartime record: the stunningly quick military defeat, followed by widespread collaboration with the Germans and the Vichy government, and in particular the dubious distinction of being the only nation in occupied Europe to voluntarily transport Jewish countrymen to death camps, even before requested to do so by the Nazis. Wiesel grew up in Transylvania, and only came to France after the war; his memoir was written in French, but had nothing to do with France. Schwarz-Bart was, however, born in France (in 1928, albeit of parents who had immigrated there from Poland). He joined the French resistance as a boy of fifteen after his parents had been deported to the camps. His eloquent condemnation, in particular of the church's historical antisemitism as the root cause of the Holocaust, brought both high praise (*The Last of the Just* was awarded the 1959 Prix Goncourt) as well as outspoken denunciation by those defending the church. This was only one of a variety of attacks in the French press in the months after the novel's publication, during what Francine Kaufmann has termed "L'affaire Schwarz-Bart," in which the author was variously condemned by Jews, Christians, Marxists, Zionists, and even former resistance fighters (pp. 10–11, 24–25). Now, more than forty years later, Holocaust historians have largely rejected the central premise of *The Last of the Just*—a direct causal link between the church's historical demonizing of the Jews and the Holocaust—but the novel remains a brilliant and haunting re-creation of nearly a millennium of Jewish history in Europe.

Life

Only fourteen years old when the Germans arrested much of his family for deportation in 1942, Schwarz-Bart soon joined the French resistance and was once captured in Limoges by military authorities, from whom he escaped with the aid of partisan irregulars operating in Haute-Vienne. After the war he held a series of jobs, often as a laborer, including stints of factory work and mining, but also working as a librarian and salesman. While a student at the Sorbonne, Schwarz-Bart worked at a Jewish orphanage and, in 1952, was secretary of the Union of Jewish Students of France; later, he also studied at the University of Paris. *The Last of the Just* brought him immediate recognition, but also seems to have exhausted his literary resources. In 1961 he married a woman originally from the Caribbean island of Guadeloupe with her own literary ambitions. Subsequently, Schwarz-Bart published, under his own name, two novels with strongly Caribbean components that now appear to have been written, or at the very least in collaboration with, his wife, Simone Schwarz-Bart. The first of these, entitled *Un Plat de porc aux bananes vertes* (1960, A Plate of Pork with Green Bananas), is the story of an old black woman, now confined in an institution for the aged in France, but with vivid memories of her home on Martinique. The second, which has been translated into English as *A Woman of Solitude* (1973), is an eighteenth-century story of a woman named Solitude who is born into slavery on Guadeloupe, after her mother is abducted from Africa. In 1972 Simone Schwarz-Bart published her first solo novel, translated as *The Bridge of Beyond*; no further works, whether individual efforts or collaborations, have appeared under the name of André Schwarz-Bart.

The Last of the Just

Initial criticism of *The Last of the Just* in France was severe, with charges leveled against Schwarz-Bart of historical inaccuracy, plagiarism, and distortion, in part because of the structure of the novel and the interpretation of Christian-Jewish relations in Europe on which it is based. Though many of these criticisms were unfounded, the second edition of the novel corrected a few minor errors and included a note on the author's sources.

The novel starts with the assertion that, if it is to be "a true history of Ernie Levy," the main protagonist living in "the second quarter of the twentieth century," it must begin "much earlier, toward the year 1000 of our era, in the old Anglican city of York" (New York: Atheneum, 1960, p. 3). Schwarz-Bart's plan was to recount representative catastrophes in the Jewish experience in Europe through the involvement of generations of a single family, the Levys, beginning with the massacre of the Jews of York on 11 March 1185. Quoting passages from a contemporary source, Schwarz-Bart recounts the York bishop's incitement of the violence, and the fate of a small remnant of the Jewish community that sought refuge in a tower and, under siege for six days, chose to take their own lives rather than fall into the hands of their Christian attackers. As Schwarz-Bart reminds his reader, "this anecdote in itself offers nothing remarkable."

> In the eyes of Jews, the holocaust of the watchtower is only a minor episode in a history overstocked with martyrs. In those ages of faith, as we know, whole communities flung themselves into the flames to escape the seductions of the Vulgate. It was so at Speyer, at Mainz, at Worms, at Cologne, at Prague during the fateful summer of 1096. And later, during the Black Plague, in all Christendom. (p. 4)

Thus Schwarz-Bart introduces his thesis: that the Jewish experience in Europe has been a linear progression of ever-escalating attacks by Christians (identified above by the Latin version of their bible, the *Vulgate*), culminating in the Holocaust—though it is important to remember that the term "Holocaust" was not generally applied to the destruction of European Jewry during World War II when Schwarz-Bart used it in the passage above. As Lawrence Langer explains, the structure of the novel suggests that Schwarz-Bart "would pit the full weight of generations of Jewish suffering against that single culminating instant of Jewish extinction in the gas chambers of Auschwitz" (p. 252). One can easily imagine how Christians who opposed the Nazis on the basis of their faith (as well as those who did not) might have reacted negatively to such a blanket condemnation of their religion, especially considering the heinousness of the crimes with which it was being associated. Even today, European history texts often ignore the atrocities committed against Jews by marauding crusaders, and present the Spanish Inquisition as primarily involved in countering the Reformation. In 1959, *The Last of the Just* may have been the first systematic exposure of tainted church history that many Europeans had ever read.

The Last of the Just, however, goes well beyond the factual background of Jewish persecution. The novel is a blend of one part history (the fate of the Jews in Europe from the Middle Ages onward), one part folklore (the Jewish legend of thirty-six secret saints), and one part fiction (the involvement of a single family in many of the major events of Jewish history in Europe for almost a millennium). Schwarz-Bart, for example, alters the infamous episode at York by having a single survivor—Rabbi Yom Tov Levy's infant son, who somehow survives the mass suicide. According to the novel's fictional thirteenth-century source, the result of Yom Tov Levy's martyrdom is a promise by God to that son, Solomon Levy, that "to all his line, and for all the centuries, is given the grace of one *Lamed-Vovnik* to each generation" (p. 6).

In its way, this use of Jewish folklore is every bit as controversial as the novel's use of Jewish history. To begin with, the legend of the *Lamed-Vav* (the Hebrew letters signifying "36") originates in a Talmudic saying of Abbaye, that in each generation there are at least thirty-six saints (Sanhedrin 97b; Sukkot 45b). Perhaps taking a cue from the biblical story in which God agrees to save Sodom if only ten righteous men can be found there (Genesis 18:23–33), Jewish traditions teach that the world itself is saved by the existence of these thirty-six just individuals, that a new saint is born before one of the thirty-six dies to ensure the continued salvation of the world, and that the identities of the thirty-six are secret. Beyond the anachronism of a thirteenth-century Italian Jew using the Yiddish phrase "*Lamed-Vovnik*," which combines Ashkenazi-accented Hebrew with a Slavic suffix, the whole notion that the identity of one of the "secret" just men in each generation would be revealed is seemingly contrary to the intent of the tradition. Yet Schwarz-Bart makes his point, about the iniquity of the persecution as well as the martyrdom of the persecuted, precisely by assigning the fictional Levy family one just man in each generation.

This association of the Levys with the *Lamed-Vav* has a special consequence because, in *The Last of the Just*, there can be no question as to whether God exists. After all, in each generation for almost a thousand years, one Levy has served as incontrovertible proof that God not only exists, but intercedes, however belatedly or ineffectively where suffering is concerned, in human affairs. The result is a novel in which God can be condemned, but not dismissed outright. Schwarz-Bart's formulation is part of a repeated theme throughout much of Holocaust literature, and modern Jewish thought in general: the question whether, if God does not exist, can the Jews? If there is no God, after all, then there can be no chosen people, and the Jews' centuries of suffering cannot be part of some divine plan. As one character in the novel puts it, "if God is in little pieces, what can it mean to be a Jew?" (p. 92). Edward Alexander notes that a "tension between the impulse to see the Holocaust as another tragic event within the history of an ever dying and therefore eternally Chosen People and the contrary impulse to see it as the end of Jewish history and a denial of the Jewish God continues to the end of the novel, and beyond it" (p. 221). That tension, however, is controlled by the novel's central premise: the existence of the Levys' just men not only reaffirms the place of the Jews in some divinely ordained historical process but, at least within Schwarz-Bart's fiction, validates God's existence even in the aftermath of the Holocaust.

It is the third element in Schwarz-Bart's symbolic recreation of Jewish history that requires the greatest suspension of the reader's disbelief: the personal involvement of members of a single family, the descendants of Rabbi Yom Tov Levy of York, in almost every major catastrophe to befall the Jews of Europe in the last eight hundred years. In the first chapter of the novel alone, Solomon dies at an auto-da-fé ordered by the "sainted King Louis" of France; his son, Manasseh, returns to England, where he too successfully defends Jews under indictment for religious offenses, and ends up a victim of the Inquisition himself; his son, Israel, was among those Jews banished by the edict of expulsion from England and eventually dies of shame in Toulouse after having accepted his role in an annual Easter humiliation of Jews. The next Levy, Mattathias, flees the French edict of expulsion into Spain, only to die there on the Inquisition's "immense white slab of the *quemadero* in Seville" (p. 11). In the following generation, the mystical Joachim endures the explusion from Spain; his escape to Portugal ends in slavery and death, and his own son, Chaim, is raised in a convent and ordained a priest. But Chaim remains faithful to his roots. "Leaving for Rome in soutane and biretta, he ended at Mainz in black caftan and sugar-loaf hat. . . . A few months later, betrayed by a co-religionist, he is escorted back to Portugal," torture, and death (pp. 12–13). This litany of suffering for the Jews in general, and the Levys in particular, continues many more generations until, at the end of the chapter, another Chaim Levy arrives in the late eighteenth century Pale of Jewish Settlement, land Russia annexed after its wars with Poland. There he settles in "the small town of Zemyock, in the canton of Moydin, in the province of Bialystok" (pp. 20–21).

Having covered six hundred years of Levy family history in the first chapter, the novel then begins to telescope down. Chapter two deals with only four generations of Levys and ends with the departure of Benjamin, the father of the main protagonist Ernie, from Zemyock; Ernie himself is born in chapter three, which ends in 1933. The next ten or eleven years are described at a much slower, more horrifying pace through the rest of the novel. This change in tempo and scope is part of Schwarz-Bart's careful structure, which also intentionally avoids descriptions of relative happiness, such as Chaim's life in Zemyock. "Lest the reader see a romance in it," according to the text, "none of that can be the object of a historical narrative" (p. 25). The comment is only partly facetious because the point of the Jewish experience in Europe—certainly Schwarz-Bart's point—is better made without reference to happy times. Its ringing condemnation of the victimizers is accomplished not by falsifying any of the historical details that are presented, but by omitting others that might detract from that goal.

Benjamin eventually settles in the German town of Stillenstadt, where he hides his identity as a Levy. To his father, who comes with his wife to join their son in Germany, Benjamin discounts the virtues of being one of the thirty-six. "You know very well that to be a *Lamed-Vovnik* is worth hardly anything in this world," Benjamin says, "and maybe not even in the next" (p. 119). Benjamin is dismissive of the Levy family history, and terms suffering as an ideal, "the virus of Zemyockism" (p. 131), an error left behind in the move from Poland, but German enlightenment is soon shown to be little different from Polish pogroms. Lured by a beautiful young girl named Ilse, with "corn-silk blond hair" (p. 135), Benjamin's son Ernie is victimized by a gang of German children who reenact "the trial of Jesus," and assign Ernie the part of "the Jews" (p. 136). After the children use rocks to beat Ernie bloody and senseless, Schwarz-Bart's narrator intrudes into the story to emphasize the author's point: "Although its origin would always remain mysterious, in time the act of aggression against Ernie took its place in the series of antisemitic acts that announced Adolf Hitler's rise to power . . . it was the year 1933" (pp. 139–140). At least within the novel, this establishes a direct link between the Holocaust and traditional Christian teachings that Jews are Christ-Killers.

Ironically, this central point in Schwarz-Bart's deconstruction of the Holocaust, so reviled by its early Christian critics, has also been undercut by historians of antisemitism and the Holocaust, who have come to believe that an important change in German attitudes toward the Jews occurred in the decades leading up to World War I. Explaining a theory first advanced by historian Uriel Tal in 1969—ten years after the publication of *The Last of the Just*—Michael R. Marrus identifies "two strands of anti-Jewish thought in Germany, traditional and radical."

> The former was largely Christian in inspiration and rested its opposition to Jews essentially on their rejection of the religious faith of the majority; the latter was violently anti-Christian in inspiration, pagan in its models for the ideal society, and racist in its definitions of Jews. This second blend of antisemitism proved much more dynamic, virulent, and uncompromising. Relatively the weaker of the two before 1914, radical antisemitism grew much stronger in Germany and Austria in the postwar period, eventually with disastrous consequences. This version, of course, became the mainspring of the Nazis' anti-Jewish ideology (p. 11).

Similarly, Lucy Dawidowicz might have been describing parts of *The Last of the Just* in saying that "a line of antisemitic descent from Martin Luther to Adolf Hitler is easy to draw," but she goes on to emphasize that "modern German antisemitism had more recent roots than Luther and grew out of different soil" (p. 23). Important as this distinction may be historically, however, it certainly does not excuse failure of Christian churches and clergy to actively oppose and condemn publicly the destruction of European Jewry, whatever the historical reasons behind Nazi attitudes toward Jews, nor does it significantly weaken Schwarz-Bart's impassioned condemnation. As Dawidowicz herself concludes, "modern German antisemitism was the bastard child of Christian antisemitism with German nationalism" (p. 23).

The rest of the novel is a martyrology of Ernie Levy, who dies not one death but three. When Ernie saves an old woman from an attack of the Nazis' S.A. (*Sturmabteilung* or Storm Troopers), his grandfather recognizes him as a just man and, "in a hoarse voice, as if strangled by all the years of silence he had imposed upon it, told the prodigious history of the Levys from beginning to end" (p. 165). Ernie, however, romanticizes that family legacy, and almost immediately undertakes "the dream of his own martyrdom" (p. 167). In increasingly bizarre scenes, young Ernie becomes a "Just Man of the flies," both celebrating and massacring insects in great numbers; next, after another encounter with Ilse and her friends, Ernie commits suicide, like "hundreds and hundreds of little German-Jewish school boys" (p. 255). This "first death of Ernie Levy" is not, however, entirely successful—Ernie's grandfather believes that "the Eternal, in his infinite pity, had restored life to the little angel," but not "his soul" (p. 256). And, as *Kristallnacht* comes and goes and the Levys escape Germany and move to France, "the late Ernie Levy" decides to become a dog, crawling on all fours, barking without talking, eating raw meat. The point of Ernie's doghood is not entirely clear in the novel. Certainly, it is a measure of his rejection of and isolation from the rest of humanity because, "despite his age, a certain vigor, and his extraordinary appetite, the late Ernie Levy seemed to be doggedly alienating himself from human affections" (p. 290). Ironically, then, Ernie's eventual death as a dog, his second death, allows him to be reborn as a human, because "while Ernie Levy felt himself die, and come to life, and die again, his heart, sweetly, opened to the light, as it had done long ago" (p. 302).

Cleansed of both romanticizing death and excoriating life, Ernie is now ready for his final demise, in the gas chambers of Auschwitz. To take us there, Schwarz-Bart resets elements from the biography of Janusz Korczak, the writer and educator who ran an orphanage in the Warsaw ghetto and sacrificed his own life in order to accompany his young charges to their deaths. Ernie first voluntarily enters Drancy, the most infamous of the French concentration camps, in order to be with Golda, with whom he has fallen in love. Once in the camp, he again volunteers, this time for transportation to Auschwitz, along with Golda and fifteen hundred orphans. In explaining his decision to the camp's secretary, Ernie sounds perhaps a little too messianic: "M. Blum, wherever there are Jews, there is my kingdom!" (p. 359). Finally, in Auschwitz, he volunteers for the gas chambers to Mengele himself (p. 371).

For Schwarz-Bart, the death of Ernie Levy is the death of Jewish history as we know it. As the last of the Levys, and therefore the last of their line of the *Lamed-Vav*, Ernie's martyrdom completes the cycle of European persecution begun in 1185 in York. Stanley Brodwin has noted, however, that the neatness of this ending has any number of difficulties underlying it. "The absolute certainty in God's mercy and justice which had always validated the martyr's sacrifice," according to Brodwin, "is nevertheless made problematical here by the nature of the Holocaust as a unique apocalyptic 'end' of Jewish history and by the lurking doubt that Ernie himself did not believe in his 'illusion' of redemption except as it brought solace to others" (p. 85). By this point in the novel, Ernie has become a symbolic figure whose lurking doubts only help to humanize his sacrifices. On his way to the gas chamber, Ernie prays for the termination of Jewish history, and the deliverance of the Jews:

> "O God," the Just Man Ernie Levy said to himself as bloody tears of pity streamed from his eyes again, "O Lord, we went forth like this thousands of years ago. We walked across arid deserts and the blood-red Red Sea in a flood of salt, bitter tears. We are very old. We are still walking. Oh, let us arrive, finally!" (p. 372).

That fervent wish is echoed in the famous ending of the novel—a prayer interspersed with the names of the camps and ghettos where millions of Jews lost their lives.

> And praised. *Auschwitz.* Be. *Maidanek.* The Lord. *Treblinka.* And praised. *Buchenwald.* Be. *Mauthausen.* The Lord. *Belzec.* And praised. *Sobibor.* Be. *Chelmno.* The Lord. *Ponary.* And praised. *Theresienstadt.* Be. *Warsaw.* The Lord. *Vilna.* And praised. *Skarzysko.* Be. *Bergen-Belsen.* The Lord. *Janow.* And praised. *Dora.* Be. *Neuengamme.* The Lord. *Pustkow.* And praised . . . (p. 374)

Bibliography

Primary Sources

Le Dernier des justes 1959. *The Last of the Just* 1960.
Un Plat de porc aux bananes vertes (A Plate of Pork with Green Bananas). 1967.
La Mulatresse Solitude 1972. *A Woman Named Solitude* 1973. 1972.

Secondary Sources

Alexander, Edward. *The Resonance of Dust: Essays on Holocaust Literature and Jewish Fate.* Columbus: Ohio State University Press, 1979.
Brodwin, Stanley. "History and Martyrological Tragedy: The Jewish Experience in Sholem Asch and André Schwarz-Bart." *Twentieth Century Literature* 40, no. 1 (1994): 72–91.
Dawidowicz, Lucy. *The War against the Jews, 1933–1945.* New York: Holt, Rinehart and Winston, 1975.
Kaufmann, Francine. *Pour relire* Le Dernier des justes: *Réflexions sur la Shoah.* Paris: Meridiens Klincksieck, 1986.
Langer, Lawrence L. *The Holocaust and the Literary Imagination.* New Haven: Yale University Press, 1975.
Marrus, Michael R. *The Holocaust in History.* New York: Meridian, 1989.

MOACYR SCLIAR

(1937–)

JOSEPH ABRAHAM LEVI

SON OF JOSÉ Scliar and Sara Slavutsky, Moacyr Jaime Scliar was born in Pôrto Alegre, Brazil, on 23 March 1937, and raised in a predominantly Jewish neighborhood, later the scene of his stories of Jewish life in this part of Brazil. After Jewish primary school, Scliar attended the Colégio de Nossa Senhora do Rosário (Our Lady of the Rosary), where he was the victim of antisemitism. Later, Scliar frequented the Colégio Júlio de Castilhos, a more liberal and politically active school. Scliar's early Marxist ideals and his dreams of living on a kibbutz, which were guided by his messianic visions, were ultimately replaced by his interest in human suffering and social injustice. In 1962, Scliar received a degree in medicine, with a specialization in public health, and saw publication of *Histórias de médico em formação* (Stories of a Doctor-in-the-Making). Since then, he has dedicated himself to writing and to practicing medicine.

Scliar remains one of Brazil's most prolific writers, with award-winning novels, short stories, and chronicles published on an almost yearly basis and translated into more than ten languages. In 1970, he spent three months teaching public health in Beersheba, Israel. Two years later, Scliar began writing for regional and national newspapers. Then in 1978, Scliar was nominated director of the Ministry of Health for the state of Rio Grande do Sul. He has been married since 1965 to Judith Oliven, an ESL (English as a Second Language) teacher who is of German descent, The couple has one son, Roberto. Among Scliar's many awards are the Minais Gerais Academy of Letters Prize (1968), the Érico Veríssimo Novel Prize (1977), the Art Critics Association of São Paulo Prize (1980), the House of the Americas' Prize (1988), and the Jabuti Prize (1988).

Jewish Brazilian vs. Brazilian Jewish: A Case of Dual Identities

Despite the fact that Brazil is a nation of immigrants, literature that explores immigrant, ethnic, or religious minorities is still scarce. Scliar is perhaps the first Brazilian to openly declare himself as an ethnic author, "a writer who writes on Jewish themes" (Igel, p. 111). Though Jewish, he views himself as a "cultural hybrid," with roots in both Brazilian and Russian Jewish culture, as his name demonstrates. The name Moacyr, given to him by his mother, who was also instrumental in awakening his interest in fantastic tales and East European Jewish folklore, is a native Guarani word meaning "son of suffering"; while the name Scliar is of Russian Jewish origin and refers to "the eye." This blend of cultures, as well as the dilemma that it carries, is evident in all his characters who "remain a [cultural] enigma. They are neither typical Jews nor typical Brazilians. They are hybrids" (Glickman, "Scliar, Moacyr," p. 469).

Instead of hybrid, Scliar's essence is basically dual, where both Judaism and Brazilianess live side by side, causing a feeling of displacement. The author's crisis is transposed to his characters. Thus, most of Scliar's literary production is centered around Jewish issues within a Brazilian context—such as Jewish immigration, first-generation Jewish experience, and the double predicament of assimilation/integration into mainstream Brazil—including the Holocaust and its repercussions on Brazil and on Brazilians. His characters are secular Jews who have a Jewish ethnic background. The religious aspects of Judaism are therefore always explained in terms of cultural behavior; they become the source of clashes or comparisons against mainstream Catholic Brazil, by nature a syncretic nation. Scliar is, in a sense, the pioneer of "the novel of Jewish-Brazilian expression" (Vieira, "Scliar, Moacyr," p. 314).

Nazism, the Holocaust, and Post-Holocaust Experience

I identify with the millions of human beings with whom I share the Judaic condition. I suffered with those who were persecuted, I died with those who were exterminated . . . I don't accept the fact that a Jew can possibly be indifferent to Judaism. Such alienation is not possible, even in a country like Brazil where identities are often hidden in what I have called "the mix" (Sadow, p. 60).

Scliar uses a plethora of Jewish themes—from biblical stories and parables to Ashkenazi customs and folklore, Sephardism (as it pertains to the history of Brazil), as well as the Holocaust and its aftermath—as a springboard for most of his works related to Pôrto Alegre and its Jewish population. As a secularist, Scliar recognizes the "contradictions and idiosyncrasies" of all religions and consequently focuses on "the rich cultural past" of Judaism, a religion that he otherwise sees "without a future" (Van Steen, p. 175). Scliar contextualizes the Holocaust as an issue of social and cultural engagement in post-Holocaust Brazil. He sees the Holocaust and the post-Holocaust experience as living lessons from which humanity, particularly Brazilians, can learn how to cope with evil and to overcome it.

The tale "*Na minha suja cabeça, o Holocausto*" (Inside My Dirty Head, the Holocaust), from his 1986 collection *O olho enigmático* (*The Enigmatic Eye*), the 1981 novel *Max e os felinos* (*Max and the Cats*), and the 1978 short story "*Pega pra kapput!*" (It All Went Kaput!) are perhaps the only instances in which Scliar directly approaches the theme of the Holocaust and the post-Holocaust experience in the Diaspora. In "*Na minha suja cabeça, o Holocausto*," the narrator—here an amoral and filthy, eleven-year-old Jewish boy, whose father lost his siblings to the Holocaust—has to undergo a double awakening in order to finally accept and come to terms with his own background. Living in 1949 "safe" Brazil, the "filthy boy," representative of the world's immediate postwar insensibility to the Holocaust, has rejected his father's past and his own identity implicit in it. The narrator's dream that Mischa, a Holocaust survivor, is accused of being a Ukrainian Gentile by a Holocaust victim whose camp number he (Mischa) has usurped, may be the narrator's expression of his own self-hatred and guilt for not wanting to understand the reality of the Holocaust. Oneiric episodes, triggered by the presence of Mischa, lead the narrator to finally comprehend "his ethnic identity." The narrator dreams that Mischa, with his concentration-camp numbers tattooed on his arm, washes the boy's mouth with soap bars made of human flesh: "I wake up sobbing. . . . And it is this suffering that I, for lack of a better word, call the Holocaust" ("Na minha suja cabeça, o Holocausto," in *O olho enigmático* [*The Enigmatic Eye*], Rio de Janeiro: Editora Guanabara, 1986, p. 116). This is the turning point. The boy is now aware of the meaning of suffering and accepts his father's Holocaust legacy. Second generation guilt and self-hatred give way to a final reconciliation: accepting two identities and realizing that the two can indeed cohabit.

Directly linked with the Holocaust and immigration to Brazil is the adventure novel *Max e os felinos*, set in Germany and Brazil, during and following World War II. Scliar constructed the narrative under a layer of Ashkenazi folklore and myths, over which he weaves the topoi of the problems of adaptation to the new land. Max Schmidt comes from a family of German furriers, in the business by disgrace: his father would say that their profession was "corrupt," "a thing for Jews to do" (*Max e os felinos* [*Max and the Cats*], Pôrto Alegre: L&PM Editores, 1981, p. 78). Max's views of the Jewish people as a "filthy and penurious race" eventually change when he befriends Harald, a socialist Jew who is later killed by Nazis in Berlin. Having avenged the murder of his friend and achieved an epiphany, Max, as a fugitive, sets sail for South America, on board a vessel whose cargo is destined for a zoo. The escape from Nazism is symbolized here by the near death of these wild animals during a shipwreck. Troubled by the ambivalence of his obligations toward homeland and his simultaneous aversions for antisemitism and abuse of power, Max experiences nightmares and hallucinations and fights his demons, which take the form of felines. Max perceives Brazil, unlike Germany with its pervasive racism and xenophobia, as the promised land for all. However, he is disappointed when he sees young members of the Ação Integralista Brasileira (Brazilian Integralist Action)—a fascist party founded in 1933 that condemned liberalism, international capitalism, socialism, and Judaism—parading and flaunting their intolerance. Max is haunted by the jaguar, symbol of Germany and antisemitism, and all Holocaust victims. Finally, Max discovers that the jaguar is within himself and that only through discipline can this animal be tamed. The evils within and without, Max realizes, must be subdued in order not to unleash episodes of personal, national, or worldwide intolerance.

Dualism is also found in the short story "*Pega pra kapput!*" (It All Went Kaput!) in which, aside from the pervading fantasy and mordacity (pungency) of the story, the evil of the Holocaust resurfaces in Brazil. After the fall of the Third Reich (1933–1945), Hitler seeks to escape, disguised as a Jew. An almost-blind rabbi, fresh from the concentration camp, performs circumcision on the Führer; however, the old man cuts off Hitler's only testicle. On its way to Argentina, the relic, religiously kept in a jar, falls into Brazilian waters and is later found by a woman whose husband "lost many relatives" to the Holocaust (Scliar, "Pega pra Kapput!" in *Pega pra Kapput* [It All Went Kaput!].

Pôrto Alegre: L&PM Editores, 1978, p. 72). Opening this Pandora's flask unleashes a series of misadventures that lead to her husband's death and an apparent curse on herself: whenever she opens something, a disaster occurs. Nineteen years later, an international neo-Nazi conspiracy is set up to recover the relic, "the essence of Nazism . . . embryo of the Führer" (Scliar, pp. 33–34). Though the threat is eventually defeated, the novel's conclusion is left open: Evil still exists. The souvenir, Hitler's testicle, is in a jar somewhere in Brasília for someone to claim; the negative power of this talisman could be restored since "Arianism has [now] been resuscitated," and "the Fourth Reich [may be] coming" (Scliar, p. 56).

Though not autobiographical, almost all of Scliar's books contain personal experiences in which Judaism and fantasy predominate, the former helped by the latter. Also contained in his work are local "history and folklore in order to evoke Brazil's paradoxical realities: *gaúchos* drinking *mate* while conversing in Yiddish; biblical stories intertwined with Indian legends" (Glickman, "Scliar, Moacyr," p. 464). Scliar's synthetic and concise style thus combines a fantastic imagination and a sharp sense of humor. On the other hand, his characters realistically find themselves ill at ease with the society in which they live. Though feeling that they belong to Brazil, culturally and politically, they are always battling between their inner identity as Jews and their sociopolitical space.

Scliar's importance in Holocaust and post-Holocaust literature rests upon the emphasis on the inner conflicts of his Jewish characters who are faced with yet another dilemma: how to reconcile their ethnic diversity with their Brazilianness. His Jewish novels/characters, even if not directly connected with the Holocaust, still call for a reflection on the human suffering that the Jews experienced from the crypto-Jews of colonial Brazil (1500–1822), to their treatment during dictatorship (1964–1988).

Robert DiAntonio, Nora Glickman, Laura Estelle Pirott-Quintero, and Nelson Harry Vieira, among others, interpret Scliar's Jewish perspective as the key element in approaching multicultural Brazil, vis-à-vis identity and ethnicity issues. There is also the view that the Jewish reality of Scliar's fictional universe is also created to fulfill his quest for an inner belonging and, on a wider level, to reconstruct an outer connection to his readers and his country. In both cases, there is a dilemma: how to reconcile both being Jewish and Brazilian without giving up the essence of the former or the reality of the latter. Scliar's success rests in having revisited Jewish traditions—mainly Ashkenazi with a few Sephardic—and strategically placing them within the context of Brazilian reality. Scliar's Judaism is principally the microcosm of Pôrto Alegre, which, as a centrifugal force, develops into the macrocosm of Rio Grande do Sul and its adjacent states. His Judaism is thus of southern, middle-class, and urban culture, and of Eastern European tradition. What makes Scliar special is the fact that he skillfully managed to bring to the surface an otherwise marginalized and second-class literature in Brazil.

Bibliography

Primary Sources

Histórias de medico em formação (Stories of a Doctor in-the-Making). 1962.

O Carnaval dos animais (The Carnival of the Animals). 1968.

A Guerra no Bom Fim (The War in Bom Fim). 1972.

O exército de um homem só (The One-Man Army). 1973.

Os deuses de Raquel (*The Gods of Raquel*). 1975.

A balada do falso Messias (*The Ballad of the False Messiahs*). 1976.

Os mistérios de Pôrto Alegre: coletânea de crônicas publicadas em Zero Horas (The Mysteries of Pôrto Alegre: Collection of Chronicles Published by [the Newspaper] Zero Horas). 1976.

Histórias da terra trêmula (Stories of the Tremulous Earth). 1977.

Mês de cães danados (Month of Damned Dogs). 1977.

O ciclo das águas (The Cycle of Waters). 1977.

Doutor Miragem (Doctor Mirage). 1978.

Pega pra kapput! (It All Went Kaput!). 1978. Coauthored with Josué Guimarães, Luís Fernando Veríssimo, and comic-book illustrator Edgar Vasques. In *The Collected Stories of Moacyr Scliar*. Translated by Eloah F. Giacomelli. Albuquerque, N.M.: VNMP, 1999 Scliar.

O anão no televisor (The Dwarf in the Television Set). 1979.

Os voluntários (The Volunteers). 1979.

O centauro no jardim (The Centaur in the Garden). 1980.

Cavalos e obeliscos (Horses and Obelisks). 1981.

Max e os felinos (*Max and the Cats*). 1981.

A festa no castelo (The Party in the Castle). 1982.

A estranha nação de Rafael Mendes (*The Strange Nation of Rafael Mendes*). 1983.

A massagista japonesa (The Japanese Masseuse). 1984.

Dez contos escolhidos (Ten Chosen Short Stories). 1984.

Moacyr Scliar: seleção de Regina Zilberman (Moacyr Scliar: Short Stories Selected by Regina Zilberman). 1984.

Os melhores contos de Moacyr Scliar (The Best Short Stories by Moacyr Scliar). 1984.

O olho enigmático (*The Enigmatic Eye*). 1986.

Introdução à prática amorosa (Introduction to the Practice of Love). 1988.

No caminho dos sonhos (On the Pathway of Dreams). 1988.

Um seder para os nossos dias (A Seder for Our Days). 1988.

A orelha de Van Gogh (Van Gogh's Ear). 1989.

Os cavalos da República (The Horses of the Republic). 1989.

Um país chamado infância (A Country Called Childhood). 1989.

O tio que flutuava (The Uncle Who Fluctuated). 1990.

Cenas da vida minúscula (Scenes from a Minuscule Life). 1991.

Sonhos tropicais (Tropical Dreams). 1992.

Uma história só pra mim (A Story Only for Me). 1994.

Contos reunidos (Collected Short Stories). 1995.

Dicionário do viajante insólito (Dictionary of the Unusual Traveler). 1995.
Minha mãe não dorme enquanto eu não chegar e outras crônicas (My Mother Does Not Go to Bed until I Arrive Home and Other Chronicles). 1995.
Um sonho no caroço do abacate (A Dream in the Avocado Seed). 1995.
Oswaldo Cruz: entre micróbios e barricadas (Oswaldo Cruz: Between Microbes and Barricades). 1996.
A majestade do Xingu (The Majesty of the Xingu). 1997.
O amante da Madonna e outras histórias (The Madonna's Lover and Other Stories). 1997.
Os contistas e outras histórias (Short-Story Writers and Other Stories). 1997.
Histórias para (quase) todos os gostos (Stories for (Almost) All Tastes). 1998.
A colina dos suspiros (Hill of Sighs). 1999.
A mulher que escreveu a Bíblia (The Woman Who Wrote the Bible). 1999.
Os leopardos de Kafka (Kafka's Leopards). 2000.
Pique-nique (Picnic). 2000.
Entre o Shtetl e o Gulag: Vozes do judaísmo russo (Between the Shtetl and the Gulag: Voices from Russian Jewry). n.d.
Vasques. n.d.

Articles and Other Creative Works
"O relógio" ("The Clock"). 1952.
Em busca da juventude (*Looking for Youth*). 1956.
Tempo de espera (*Time of Waiting*). 1960.
"*Três histórias de busca. 1. Temporal. 2. Relógio. 3. O ato consumado. Peixes. Almôço de domingo*" ("*Three Stories of Pursuit. 1. Storm. 2. Clock. 3. Consummated Act. Fish. Sunday Lunch*"). 1962.
"Amai-vos" ("Love One Another"). 1966.
"O cão" ("The Dog"). 1969.
"Começo e fim" ("Beginning and End"). 1970.
"Irmãos" ("Brothers"), and "Lavínia" ("Lavínia"). 1970.
"A guerra no Bom Fim" ("The War in Bom Fim"). 1971.
"Nós, o pistoleiro, não devemos ter piedade" ("We, the Gunman, Should Not Have Mercy"). 1973.
"Os leões" ("The Lions"). 1973.
"Nos subterrâneos da Rua da Praia" ("In the Underground Passages of the Rua da Praia"). 1974.
"O dia em matamos James Cagney." ("The Day in Which We Killed James Cagney"). 1974.
"Pausa" ("Pause"). 1975.
"A balada do falso Messias" ("The Ballad of the False Messiah"), "Magrinho que virou pandorga" ("The Skinny Boy Who Became an Obese Woman"), and "Nos subterrâneos da Rua da Praia" ("In the Underground Passages of the Rua da Praia"). 1976.
"Da mesa da cozinha. Moacyr Scliar para Maurício Rosemblat" ("From the Kitchen Table. Moacyr Scliar for Maurício Rosemblat"). 1976.
"Manual do pequeno terrorista" ("Manual of the Small Terrorist"). 1976.
"Relações de Produção" ("Relationships of Production"). 1976.
"Festa das luzes. Festa da liberdade" ("Festival of Lights. Festival of Freedom"). 1977.
"Pausa" ("Pause"), and "Cego" ("The Blind"). 1977.
"A ilha" ("The Island"), "O velho Marx" ("Old Marx"), "Nos subterrâneos da Rua da Praia" ("In the Underground Passages of the Rua da Praia"), and "Os passarinhos imobiliários" ("Immovable Birds"). 1978.
"História pôrto-alegrense" ("Story from Pôrto Alegre"). 1978.
"The Prescript" and "Fishing Tournament." 1978.
"Os amores de um ventríloquo" ("The Loves of a Ventriloquist"). 1979.
"O dia em que matamos James Cagney" ("The Day in Which We Killed James Cagney"). 1979.
"A pausa" ("The Pause"). 1980.
Authored scripts for the television shows "Série Obrigado Doutor" and "Série Especial—O Pacto," TV Globo, 1980. [Privately owned, *Rede Globo* is Brazil's number one television station]
"Cinco e uma paixão" ("Five and One Passion"). 1980.
"Confissões de um abstêmio" ("Confessions of a Teetotaler"). 1980.
"Der Angeklagte" ("The Accused") and "Die Kuh" ("The Cow"). 1980.
"O cão" ("The Dog"). 1980.
"O mistério dos hippies desaparecidos" ("The Mystery of the Missing Hippies"). 1982.
"Der alte Marx" ("Old Marx"). 1982.
"Jantando com a contestação" ("Dining with Protest"). 1982.
"Os leões" ("The Lions"). 1983.
"Cego e amigo Gedeão à beira da estrada" ("The Blind and Friend Gideon at the Edge of the Road") and "Nós, o pistoleiro, não devemos ter piedade" ("We, the Gunman, Should Not Have Mercy"). 1984.
"Como era bela a escravatura" ("How Beautiful Slavery Was"). 1984.
"Literatura e exílio" ("Literature and Exile"). 1985.
"O homem da ampulheta" ("The Man of the Sand-Glass"). 1985.
"Judíos en Brasil, de la Inquisición a la pregunta por el futuro" ("Jews in Brazil, from the Inquisition to the Question of the Future"). 1986.
"Judaísmo e literatura" ("Judaism and Literature"). 1986.
"Mário Quintana, por amigos." 1986.
"The Prophets of Benjamin Bok/Os profetas de Benjamin Bok." 1981.
A condição judaica: das tábuas da lei à mesa da cozinha (*The Jewish Condition: From the Tablets of the Law to the Kitchen Table*). 1985.
Moacyr Scliar Reads from His Works. 1985.
Cenas médicas: pequena introdução à história da medicina (*Medical Scenes: A Short Introduction to the History of Medicine*). 1987.
Do mágico ao social: a trajetória da saúde pública (*From the Magical to the Social: The Trajectory of Public Health*). 1987.
"El Bom Fim de Pôrto Alegre" ("The Bom Fim of Pôrto Alegre"). 1990.
"Este país, la memoria" ("This Country, the Memory"). 1990.
Caminhos da esperança. A presença judaica no Rio Grande do Sul. Pathways of Hope. The Jewish Presence in Rio Grande do Sul. 1988.
"O homem da ampulheta" ("The Man of the Sand-Glass"). 1989.
Do Éden ao divã: humor judaico (*From Eden to the Sofa: Jewish Humor*). 1991.
Maurício: a trajetória, o cenário histórico, a dimensão humana de um pioneiro da comunicação do Brasil (*Maurice: The Trajectory, the Historic Scenery, the Human Dimension of a Pioneer of Brazilian Communication*). 1991.
"The Plagues." 1991.
"Pai e filho" ("Father and Son"). 1992.

Se eu fosse Rothschild. Citações que marcaram a trajetória do povo judeu (*If I Were Rothschild: Quotations that Marked the Trajectory of the Jewish People*). 1993.

Sobre Pôrto Alegre (*On Pôrto Alegre*). Coedited with Carlos Augusto Bisson. 1993.

"Inside My Dirty Head—The Holocaust." 1994.

Judaísmo: dispersão e unidade (*Judaism: Dispersion and Unity*). 1994.

"Living on Literature or for Literature?" 1995.

A paixão transformada: história da medicina na literatura (*Passion Transformed: History of Medicine in Literature*). 1996.

Exposição. O casamento judaico. 13 de outubro a 14 de novembro de 1996 (*Exhibition. Jewish Wedding. October 13 to November 14, 1996*). Exhibition catalog coauthored with Henry I. Sobel (Pôrto Alegre: Museu Judaico de Porto Alegre, 1996).

"O exame pré-nupcial: um rito de passagem da Saúde Pública/ Premarital Examination: A Rite of Passage in Public Health." 1997.

Moacyr Scliar (*Moacyr Scliar, Prose Works. Selections*). [sound recording]. 1998.

"A Centaur in the Garden." 1999.

Secondary Sources

DiAntonio, Robert Edward. "Redemption and Rebirth on a Safe Shore: The Holocaust in Contemporary Brazilian Fiction." *Hispania* 74, no. 4 (December 1991): 876–882.

DiAntonio, Robert Edward, and Aaron DiAntonio. "Jewish Brazilian Writing." *Jewish Spectator* (spring 1988): 53–55.

Glickman, Nora. "Los felinos indomables de Moacyr Scliar." *Revista Hispánica Moderna* 44, no. 1 (June 1991): 150–151.

———. "Scliar, Moacyr." In *Jewish Writers of Latin America: A Dictionary*. Edited by Darrell B. Lockhart. New York: Garland, 1997.

Igel, Regina. "Jewish Component in Brazilian Literature: Moacyr Scliar." *Folio* 17 (1987): 111–118.

Morganti, Vera Regina, ed. *Moacyr Scliar Autores gaúchos*. Vol. 9. Pôrto Alegre: Instituto Estadual do Livro, 1985.

Pirott-Quintero, Laura Estelle. "A Centaur in the Text: Negotiating Cultural Multiplicity in Moacyr Scliar's Novel." *Hispania* 83, no. 4 (December 2000): 768–778.

———. *Hybrid Identities: The Embodiment of Difference in Contemporary Latin American Narratives*. Ann Arbor: University Microfilms International [UMI], 1998.

Sadow, Stephen A. "Moacyr Scliar. Brazil." In *King David's Harp: Autobiographical Essays by Jewish Latin American Writers*. Edited by Stephen A. Sadow. Albuquerque: University of New Mexico Press, 1999.

Steen, Edla van. "Moacyr Scliar." In *Viver e escrever*, 3 vols. Edited by Edla van Steen. Pôrto Alegre: L&PM Editores, 1981.

———. "Moacyr Scliar faz no Brasil a literatura da Diáspora." *Estado de São Paulo* (19 January 1975): 23.

Vieira, Nelson Harry. *Jewish Voices in Brazilian Literature: The Discourse of Alterity*. Gainesville: University Press of Florida, 1995.

———. "Moacyr Scliar: Social Difference and the Tyranny of Culture." In *Jewish Voices in Brazilian Literature: The Discourse of Alterity*. Gainesville: University Press of Florida, 1995.

———. "Scliar, Moacyr." In *Dictionary of Brazilian Literature*. Edited by Irwin Stern. New York: Greenwood Press, 1988.

———. "Jewish Resistance and Resurgence as Literary Symbols and Metaphors for Brazilian Society and Politics." In *Proceedings of the Ninth World Congress of Jewish Studies, Jerusalem, August 4–12 1985*, Division B, vol. 3, *The History of the Jewish People* (*The Modern Times*). Jerusalem: World Union of Jewish Studies, 1986.

———. *Judaic Fiction in Brazil: To Be and Not To Be Jewish*. Pittsburgh: Department of Modern Languages, Carnegie Mellon University, 1986.

———. "Post-Holocaust Literature in Brazil: Jewish Resistance and Resurgence as Literary Metaphors for Brazilian Society and Politics." *Modern Language Studies* 16, no. 1 (1986): 62–70.

W. G. SEBALD

(1944–2001)

ERNESTINE SCHLANT

W.G. SEBALD WAS BORN in 1944 in Wertach, Allgäu. He studied in Freiburg, Germany; in the French-speaking part of Switzerland; and in the United Kingdom, taking up a teaching position in Manchester in 1966. Beginning in 1970, he taught German and European Literature at the University of East Anglia in Norwich, where he became professor of European Literature in 1988 and where, from 1989 to 1994, he was the first director of the British Centre for Literary Translation. While he used the initials of his first two names "Winfried Georg" in his professional writings, "Maximilian," that is, "Max," his second middle name, was reserved for his private life. This distinction casts an interesting light on his concept of the writer vis-à-vis the private person. Sebald died in a car accident in December 2001.

Career and Themes

Sebald began his literary career as a scholar and academic who was predominantly interested in Austrian literature of the nineteenth– and–twentieth centuries. In these studies he pursued themes that would provide a major focus for his creative writings; he showed his continued preoccupation with these themes in his critical studies of 1998, *Logis in einem Landhaus* (Lodgings in a Country House) and the novel *Austerlitz* of 2001.

One of the most dominant of these themes is alienation, uprootedness, and the simultaneous emotions of homesickness. He posits the theory that "possibly the provincialism of the home country (*das Winkelwesen der Heimat*) provokes emigration into the most distant countries" (*Beschreibung des Unglücks*, Frankfurt: Fischer Taschenbuchs, 1994, p. 10) and sees this theory exemplified in Austria's imaginative literature as well as in the lives of its authors, if one admits that "emigration"—the crossing of borders into the "irrevocable loss of familiarity" (*Beschreibung des Unglücks*, p. 10)—includes not only geographical, but spiritual and intellectual dislocation as well. Sebald was most likely drawn to this insight because he himself was an "emigrant."

It should not surprise that in his scholarly work Sebald shows a particular interest in Jewish writers as "emigrants" par excellence and what it meant to be Jewish in Austria during the time between emancipation to the ultimate destruction in the Holocaust. For example, Sebald's essay (in *Unheimliche Heimat*, Frankfurt: Fischer Taschenbuchs, 1995, p. 141) on the Holocaust survivor and essayist Jean Améry, who like Primo Levi and Paul Celan ultimately committed suicide, is a sensitive and imaginative projection into someone physically, emotionally, and psychologically tortured and uprooted, and full of resentment, yet plagued by homesickness "as by the fierce phantom pain of a part of the body long amputated" (p. 141). The complex interplay of being an "emigrant" and of having to cope with the contradictory emotions of longing for and repulsion of one's home country find their most permanent expression in melancholy. Without exception, Sebald's work is steeped in melancholy.

Sebald's literary prominence as it emerged in the 1990s is also confirmed in numerous and prestigious prizes and awards. In 1991 he received the Lyrikerpreis Fedor-Malchow; in 1994, the Johannes-Bobrowski Medaille, the prize of Literatour Nord, and the Berlin Literatur-Preis; in 1996, the Mörike-Preis of the city of Fellbach; in 1997 the Heinrich-Böll Preis; and in 2000, the Joseph-Breitbach Preis, and the Heinrich-Heine Preis of the city of Düsseldorf.

The Novels

It is difficult to assign genre-sanctioned terminology to Sebald's literary work. The ruptures, fissures, overlaps, and gaps that mark so much of post-Holocaust discourse, the heaving repetitiveness of unfinished sentences (so characteristic of Gert Hofmann, for example, or of Imre Kertész) give way, in Sebald's writings, to a destruction of form: hybrid texts that eliminate the borders between invented scenes, memoirs that more than anything else chart the retrieval of painfully "forgotten" memories, diaries that do not signal whether they are "authentic" or fictitious, protagonists' interpretations and projections that dive in the uncertain waters of subjective remembrances and truths for the solid rock bottom of facts. The universe of his fiction is structured on involuted, multilayered time dimensions, on correspondences with elusive meaning, on the scattered pieces of a four-dimensional puzzle. And always, Sebald integrates the process of finding the "stories" he writes, and his reflections as he researches and assembles them, into a work-in-progress, thereby undermining any perspectival authority.

Sebald first attracted critical attention with his prose narrative *The Emigrants* (1992). This hybrid work consists of the portraits of four emigrants, three of them Jewish, and spans German-Jewish relations over the last century. Although practically all the events narrated occur in different pasts, the narrative times intersect with "recovered" times and on occasion lead up to a narrated present.

Dr. Henry Selwyn, the Jewish protagonist of the first portrait, emigrated with his parents from Lithuania as a small boy; accidentally stranded in England, he chooses the path of assimilation and makes good as a doctor, yet feels that in the process he has lost his soul, and with approaching age confesses to the narrator his increasing homesickness. Eventually he commits suicide by directing a favorite object, his hunting rifle, on himself. Paul Bereyter of the second portrait was once the narrator's teacher. Only as an adult, and in ever-renewed starts, does the narrator come to realize the tragedy in Bereyter's life. He was one quarter Jewish and therefore exposed to all the misery meted out by the Nazi regime: the woman he loves disappears in the Holocaust; his Jewish father dies in the early years of the Nazi regime, consumed by the injustices done to Jews; his non-Jewish mother follows her husband as ostracism, denigration, and expropriation of their department store become too much to bear. Yet, ironically, he is not exempt from the duties of the Nazi regime and must serve in the military during World War II. In the post-Nazi era, Bereyter, a deeply wounded person without faith or energy to begin anew, again settles in his hometown, revulsed by its shabby behavior toward his family and humiliated by a homesickness that overcomes his longing to be elsewhere. He commits suicide by allowing a train, symbol of his desire not to be where he finds himself, to run over him. Ambros Adelwarth, the narrator's uncle and elusive third protagonist, emigrated at the turn of the century as a young hotel trainee to the United States. He becomes the butler for a New York Jewish family, and then companion to their ingenious, but increasingly disturbed son, Cosmo. Cosmo dies in a mental institution in upstate New York. Ever more despondent after Cosmo's death, Ambros follows his beloved to the same institution where he dies as a result of excessive electroshock therapy. The British painter Max Ferber, living in Manchester, escaped as a young boy from Nazi Germany to be with his uncle in England, but his parents perished in the Holocaust. In this final portrait, with its intricate maze of recaptured and narrative times, the narrator presents his thoughts on the possibilities of post-Holocaust art and, through access to the memoirs of Ferber's murdered mother, pays moving homage to the traditions, and to the loyalties, of German Jewry before the Holocaust. To the emigrant eyes of the author, Manchester, an English city, is ironically the symbol of a once successful coexistence of emigrant Germans and Jews. Ferber, in the post-Nazi era, chooses to live in this now decaying city that belches smoke and ashes from industrial chimneys that evoke the crematoria of the concentration camps, and he understands his life as serving "under the chimney," wrestling in his art with giving shape to absence and loss.

Austerlitz, published in 2001, pieces together, mostly through conversations between the narrator and the protagonist, the life of a young boy born in Prague who, at four years of age, is sent on a children's transport to England to escape Nazi persecution. In infrequent conversations that extend over many years, he tells the narrator of an unloved upbringing in England; of the accidental discovery in his teens of his Jewish identity; of his unsuccessful attempts to repress his past, form human bonds, and build a career as a scholar of fortress architecture (fortresses that were useless as military strongholds in modern warfare, but widely used as prisons and places of torture in the Nazi regime); of increasing anxiety attacks and loss of memory; and ultimately of his search for his parents. He traces his mother to her disappearance in a transport that left Terezin for the east, and, at the end of the narrative, begins a search for his father, who escaped to France. Throughout his adult life he is overwhelmed by a sense of having been "expelled and extinguished." Rare moments of recaptured time and the Proustian moments of involuntary memory assert the authenticity of his experiences, yet they are too tenuous to overcome the devastations of a lifetime.

Conclusion

As supported by his numerous literary awards, Sebald's work enjoys considerable critical recognition in Germany. In the United States, *The Emigrants* has been very favorably received (*Austerlitz*, published in 2001, has not yet been translated), while *Vertigo* (1990, the peregrinations of four historic personalities) and *The Rings of Saturn* (1995, the author/narrator's meanderings along the east coast of England), reflective and melancholy works that do not focus on the Holocaust, have attained near-cult status.

For a non-Jewish German writer, it takes courage not to suppress suffering experienced or perpetrated, and to open up to a sense of overwhelming loss and bereavement. Allowing melancholy as "a kind of labor of mourning" to surface is a precarious and dangerous undertaking ("Konstruktionen der Trauer. Zu Günter Grass 'Tagebuch einer Schnecke' und Wolfgang Hildesheimer 'Tynset,' " *Der Deutschunterricht* 35, no. 5 [1983]: 32–33). More than half a century after the defeat of the Nazi regime and the perpetration of hitherto unimaginable crimes, the time should have come for writers who are, according to Sebald, "predestined to be the conscience of the new society" ("Konstruktionen," p. 33) to approach the labor of mourning and to let pain and sorrow emerge. Among the several generations of postwar non-Jewish German writers, Sebald is one of the very few who has allowed this sorrow to surface and to restitute—through the work of art—the individuality of lives lost. Perhaps he is helped in accomplishing this unique feat by being an emigrant.

Bibliography

Primary Sources

Carl Sternheim. Kritiker und Opfer der Wilhelminischen Ära (Carl Sternheim. Critic and Victim of the Wilhelmian Era). 1969.

Der Mythos der Zerstörung im Werk Döblins (The Myth of Destruction in the Oeuvre of Alfred Döblin). 1980.

"Konstruktionen der Trauer. Zu Günter Grass 'Tagebuch einer Schnecke' und Wolfgang Hildesheimer 'Tynset.' " *Der Deutschunterricht* 35, no. 5 (1983): 32–46.

Die Beschreibung des Unglücks. Zur österreichischen Literatur von Stifter bis Handke (The Description of Fatalities). 1985.

A Radical Stage. Theatre in Germany in the 1970s and 1980s (Editor). 1988.

Nach der Natur. Ein Elementargedicht (Following Nature; An Elemental Poem). 1988. Photographs by Thomas Becker.

Unheimliche Heimat. Essays zur österreichischen Literatur (Uncanny Home Country. Essays on Austrian Literature). 1991.

Die Ausgewanderten. 1992. (*The Emigrants*). 1996.

Die Ringe des Saturn. Eine englische Wallfahrt. 1995. *The Rings of Saturn*. 1998.

Logis in einem Landhaus. Essays (Lodging in a Country House: Essays). 1998.

Luftkrieg und Literatur (Air War and Literature). 1999.

Schwindel. Gefühle. 1990. *Vertigo*. 2000.

Austerlitz. 2001.

Radio Plays

Max Aurach. Bavarian Broadcasting, 20 May 1994.

Aurachs Mutter. Bavarian Broadcasting, 10 February 1995.

Secondary Sources

Aciman, André. "Out of Novemberland: 'The Rings of Saturn.' " *The New York Review of Books*, 3 December 1998, 44–47.

Angier, Carole. "Who Is W. G. Sebald?" *The Jewish Quarterly* 43, no. 4 (winter 1996/1997): 10–14.

Doerry, Martin, and Volker Hage. "Ich fürchte das Melodramatische. Spiegel-Gespräch mit W. G. Sebald." *Der Spiegel* 11 (2001): 228–234.

Isenschmid, Andreas, et al. "Überblick und Debatte: W. G. Sebalds 'Luftkrieg und Literatur.' " In *Deutsche Literatur 1998. Jahresüberblick*. Stuttgart: Reclam, 1999, pp. 249–290.

Juhl, Eva. "Die Wahrheit über das Unglück. Zu W. G. Sebalds 'Die Ausgewanderten.' " In *Reisen im Diskurs. Modelle der literarischen Fremderfahrung von den Pilgerberichten bis zur Postmoderne*. Heidelberg: Universitätsverlag C. Winter, 1995, pp. 640–659.

Kastura, Thomas. "Geheimnisvolle Fähigkeit zur Transmigration. W. G. Sebalds interkulturelle Wallfahrten ins Leere." *Arcadia* 31, nos. 1–2 (1996): 197–216.

Lane, Anthony. "Higher Ground. Adventures in Fact and Fiction from W. G. Sebald." *The New Yorker* (29 May 2000): 128–136.

Löffler, Sigrid. "Dienst unter dem Schlot. Ein Schriftsteller wird entdeckt." *profil* 19, no. 4 (1993): 104–106.

Loquai, Franz, ed. *Far from Home: W. G. Sebald. Sammlung von Rezensionen*. Bamberg: Universität Bamberg, 1995.

Parry, Ann. "Idioms for the Unrepresentable: Post-War Fiction and the *Shoah*." *European Studies* 27 (December 1997): 417–432.

Schlant, Ernestine. *The Language of Silence: West German Literature and the Holocaust*. New York: Routledge, 1999, 224–234.

Silman, Roberta. "In the Company of Ghosts: 'The Rings of Saturn.' " *The New York Times Book Review*, 26 July 1998, 6.

Weber, Markus R. "Phantomschmerz Heimweh. Denkfiguren der Erinnerung im literarischen Werk W. G. Sebalds." In *Neue Generation—Neues Erzählen. Deutsche Prosa-Literatur der achtziger Jahre*. Edited by Walter Delabar, et al., eds. Opladen: Westdeutscher Verlag, 1993, pp. 57–67.

———."W. G. Sebald." *Kritisches Lexikon zur deutschsprachigen Gegenwartsliteratur*. Edited by Heinz Ludwig Arnold. Munich: edition text and Kritik, Stand vol 1. April 2000.

Williams, Arthur. "The Elusive First Person Plural: Real Absences in Reiner Kunze, Bernd-Dieter Hüge, and W. G. Sebald." In *"Whose Story?"—Continuities in Contemporary German-Language Literature*. Edited by Arthur Williams, Stuart Parkes, and Julian Preece. Frankfurt/Main: Peter Lang, 1998, pp. 85–113.

LORE SEGAL
(1928–)

CLAIRE M. TYLEE

LORE SEGAL (NÉE GROSZMANN) was born in Vienna in 1928, the only child of a bank accountant. After the Anschluss, she escaped to London on the first train of the Kindertransport in 1938. Her parents, impoverished by the Nuremburg Laws, followed in time for her eleventh birthday. However, they only gained entry on a domestic service visa, so Lore continued to live with foster families throughout the war. She graduated in English from the University of London in 1948. Then, her father having died in 1944, she reluctantly followed her mother, uncle, and grandparents to the Dominican Republic before immigrating to New York in 1951. There she married in 1960, had a son and a daughter, and was widowed. As is movingly recounted in the documentary *Into the Arms of Strangers: Stories of the Kindertansport* (2001), Segal's elderly mother, Franzi, lives in the same apartment block in New York and they still have breakfast together.

Segal taught English and creative writing at a number of American universities before holding chairs in English at the University of Illinois and The Ohio State University.

She is perhaps best known for her work in the field of children's literature, particularly for her translation of tales from the Brothers Grimm in *The Juniper Tree* (1973). Among her three adult novels, two are connected with the Holocaust. The middle novel, *Lucinella* (1976), continues the trajectory of a Jewish heroine loosely identical with the characters Lore, in *Other People's Houses* (1964), and Ilke Weissnix in *Her First American* (1985). Ilke's brief trip to Europe raises issues of memory about the Holocaust and the postwar attitude of Germans, which critics have linked to novels by other American novelists such as Cynthia Ozick. However, *Other People's Houses* is the book that deals most closely with events between 1937 and 1951, and consequently raises problems about Jewish self-identity in the wake of the Holocaust.

Other People's Houses

Granted scant critical attention in Britain, *Other People's Houses* has been translated into German and was strongly praised in the United States. Eli Wiesel stated that few personal documents dealing with that period moved him to such depths; Evelyn Torton Beck appreciated its tone as "nowhere self-pitying, always understated, slightly distanced and ironic." It is Segal's wit that most distinguishes this autobiographical novel from others by second-generation Holocaust survivors. Responding to the Nazification of Austria, World War II, and the immediate postwar world through the eyes of an intelligent but naive child, the book is often surprisingly funny. The humor is painfully deepened for adult readers by ironic awareness of what the child does not, despite her curiosity, fully understand. A striking instance of her detached, laconic mode is her account of the sacking of her grandparents' home by the Hitler Youth Brigade:

> Ladders had been put against the ledge, and boys and girls from the village, still in their uniforms, had climbed up and were sitting in our windows. They stayed all night. Now and then, one of the boys would swing his legs over the sill and step into the room with us. There were some books they didn't approve of, and possessions they did, and they carried everything portable away (*Other People's Houses,* New York: New Press, 1994, pp. 18–19).

The novel breaks into two. Each chapter is self-contained, devoted to a phase in the life of Lore or her family. The first eight chapters, which constitute Part I, begin in 1937 Vienna and cover the period from the Nazi annexation of Austria, when Lore is ten, to her graduation from London University at the age of 21. Those years turned her into "an Anglophile forever," as her writing itself evidences. Critics find this part of the novel superior to the second. It was published separately in England in 1974 as a book for children, with a preface by Naomi Lewis. Fortuitously the enforced peripatetic life of a refugee gives the novel a picaresque form. Although not a rogue, yet certainly with the outsider's sharp eye, Lore travels through the various strata of English society. To this pitiless little alien, the representatives of Little England are as comical as any character in Austen. Segal shares that satiric vision: the snug, narrow-minded English families her heroine encounters are, although kindly, almost willfully uncomprehending of the child's difficulties and the evil she has escaped.

Part II of *Other People's Houses* consists of four chapters that detail the years spent in the Dominican Republic by Lore, her mother, grandmother, and uncle, and their time reunited in New York until she makes a home of her own with a Jewish-American husband. What binds the two parts together is the relationship between Lore, her mother, and her uncle. The wry sense of humor that seasons the novel is inherited from Franzi, as is Lore's resilience. They help defend her from the egoistic self-pity she inherits from her father, an exasperating man broken by his humiliating experiences. Yet the novel displays a compassion toward his suffering that the child could not share with her mother. Despite its sadness, the novel, like Lore herself, gravitates toward hope and new life.

Its title notwithstanding, *Other People's Houses* is more valuable as a self-portrait of a self-conscious teenager who eavesdropped than as a picture of English or Dominican society. Not only was this one of the first books by a child-refugee (since the fiftieth anniversary of the *Kindertransport* rescue scheme, there have been dozens of *kinder* memoirs); it is also a most self-revealing coming-of-age novel. Its distinctiveness can be highlighted by setting it alongside the memoir of another such refugee-child from an assimilated Jewish family who also graduated in English from the University of London to become a professional writer: Eva Figes's *Little Eden: A Child at War* (1978). The similarities and differences are striking. Figes was four years younger than Segal with a smaller brother. Her father was a prosperous businessman in Berlin who was interned after Kristallnacht. After his release very ill, the family gained visas in 1939 to escape together to London. There he enlisted in the Pioneer Corps and remained a hero for Eva. She was deliberately sheltered by her mother from understanding what was happening in Germany until after the war. Following an unpleasant year at a council school in London, she was evacuated to a genteel boarding school in Cirencester, Gloucestershire. Figes's picture of that school, Akenside, run by two maiden ladies in a Victorian villa parallels Segal's picture of Adorato, the Georgian house in Allchester owned by Mrs. Dillon and Miss Douglas where Lore stayed while she was attending the nearby private high school.

Both books dissect the class distinctions and conservatism of English country-town society, but for Eva, Cirencester was "a sanctuary," a childhood paradise of security before she learned about the Holocaust. Lore was never shielded from knowledge of the adult world and had personally endured antisemitic malice from other children. Once in England she shouldered the responsibility for getting her parents out of Austria and became her mother's confidante as her father suffered a series of strokes. He had lost his job and home, been arrested and beaten by SS guards, and suffered from increasingly poor health. He became not only financially dependent on his far younger, more resourceful wife, but also emotionally dependent. The reader can hardly help sharing Lore's relief when he dies, having "witnessed" his cutting tongue and continual complaining, and the familiar sense of unease and panic he engenders in Lore's chest.

While the book's comedy gives it its distinctive charm, its dispassion masks fear and pain. This mask gauges the author's success at assimilation to Englishness (although Lore rejected both Anglicanism and Judaism). There is a striking lack of emotional response following the roar of grief at the jettison of the symbolic rotting sausage, Lore's secret emotional link with her mother. Thereafter, as another refugee notices, Lore rapidly adopted an English chilliness. She became false and alienated, ill at ease with herself. The narration telescopes events from 1946 to 1951, distancing the reader as Lore herself is distanced. What is particularly marked is the absence of any reference to the newsreels of Belsen that ended Figes's childhood. Nor does Segal mention the rise in antisemitism in Britain in those years. She was studying in London while there were frequent public meetings in all parts of the capital concerning the presence of Jews in British society; Jewish families in the East End were being terrorized by Fascist thugs and Jewish commando groups were leading the fight back. This was the period of Jewish militancy in Palestine. Killings and bombings there triggered anti-Jewish riots in many cities around Britain in 1947. Segal appears to have lived in a kind of limbo from 1944. After Chapter 7, the book becomes evasive and diverts attention away from Lore herself.

Segal claims in the foreword to the 1994 republication of *Other People's Houses*, that it was her early experiences as a refugee that turned her into a writer. She says that her discovery (at the age of ten) of a love of words was refined by her efforts to see and report objectively, both about others and about herself. Too objectively perhaps, in her effort to acquire a stance acceptable to her English hosts? Through a letter to the refugee committee and by stories for her first foster parents, she tried to enable people in England to understand what was happening to her parents: "It was the novelist's impulse not to explain or persuade but to force the reader's vision: see what I saw, feel what it felt like" (p. x). She develops an explanation of this aesthetic in "Memory: The Problems of Imagining the Past" (Lang, *Writing the Holocaust*, 1988). Segal may have been successful in forcing the reader to see what she could see, but the reader also sees what Lore did not see or feel as she became increasingly alienated. Segal displays her own adolescent susceptibility to genteel English behavior. At the age of ten she learned to cut herself off from emotions that she could not otherwise control, what she called "a survival trick with a price-tag" (*Other People's Houses*, p. xi). Apparently, grief for her father was frozen more than twenty years. She claims that a 1968 trip back to the places of her childhood in Austria, to write *Her First American,* enabled her to recover the feelings from which she had dissociated. Yet they are not manifested in the novel itself which critics praised for its drollery. The price of safety was high indeed.

Bibliography

Primary Sources

Other People's Houses. 1964. Republished: New York: New Press, 1991.

"Euphoria in the Rootcellar." *New American Review* 10 (1970): 160–173.

The Juniper Tree and Other Tales (with Maurice Sendak). 1973.

Lucinella. 1976.

Her First American. 1985.

"An Absence of Cousins." *New Yorker* (17 August 1987): 22–29.

"Memory: Problems of Imagining the Past." In *Writing the Holocaust*. Edited by Berel Lang. New York: Holmes and Meier, 1988, pp. 58–65.

"The Bough Breaks." In *Testimony: Contemporary Writers Make the Holocaust Personal*. Edited by David Rosenberg. New York: Random House, 1989, pp. 231–248.

"Money, Fame, and Beautiful Women." *New Yorker* (August 28, 1989): 28–36.

"At Whom the Dog Barks." *New Yorker* (3 December 1990): 44–49.

"Fatal Wish." *New Yorker* (1 July 1991): 26–37.

"William's Shoes." *New Yorker* (25 November 1991): 48–54.

"The Talk in Eliza's Kitchen." *New Yorker* (6 April 1992): 28–37.

"The Reverse Bug." In *The Schocken Book of Contemporary Jewish Fiction*. Edited by Ted Solotaroff and Nessa Rapoport. New York and London: 1992.

Secondary Sources

Beckman, Morris. *The 43 Group*. London: Centreprise, 1992.

Berger, Alan L. "Jewish Identity and Jewish Destiny, the Holocaust in Refugee Writing: Lore Segal and Karen Gershon." *Studies in American Jewish Literature* 11, no. 1 (1992): 83–95.

———. "Theological Implications of Second Generation Literature." In *Breaking Crystal: Writing and Memory after Auschwitz*. Edited by Efraim Sicher. Chicago: University of Illinois Press, 1998, pp. 252–275.

Berghahn, Marion. *German-Jewish Refugees in England: The Ambiguities of Assimilation*. Basingstoke: Macmillan, 1984.

Cavanaugh, Philip G. "The Present Is a Foreign Country: Lore Segal's Fiction. " *Contemporary Literature* 34, no. 3 (1993): 475–511.

Cooper, Howard, and John Morrison. *A Sense of Belonging: Dilemmas of British Jewish Identity*. London: Weidenfeld, 1991.

Figes, Eva. *Little Eden: A Child at War*. London: Faber; New York: Persea, 1978.

Harris, Mark Jonathan, and Deborah Oppenheimer. *Into the Arms of Strangers: Stories of the Kindertransport*. London: Bloomsbury, 2001.

Hirshfield, Gerhard, ed. *Exile in Great Britain: Refugees from Hitler's Germany*. Leamington: Berg; New Jersey: Humanities, 1984.

Kushner, Tony. "Anti-Semitism and Austerity: The August 1947 Riots in Britain." In *Racial Violence in Britain 1940–1950*. Edited by Penikos Panayi. Leicester: Leicester University Press, 1993, pp. 149–168.

———. *The Persistence of Prejudice: Antisemitism in British Society during the Second World War*. Manchester: Manchester University Press, 1989.

Sicher, Efraim. "The Burden of Memory: The Writing of the Post-Holocaust Generation." In *Breaking Crystal: Writing and Memory after Auschwitz*. Chicago: University of Illinois Press, 1998, pp. 19–88.

Documentary Films

Read, Sue. *The Children Who Cheated the Nazis*. Great Britain: 2000. Gold Reed Productions.

Harris, Mark Jonathan. *Into the Arms of Strangers*. Great Britain: 2000. Warner Bros.

Rafael Seligmann

(1947–)

KATHRIN M. BOWER

RAFAEL SELIGMANN WAS born in 1947 in Tel Aviv to German Jewish parents who had fled to Palestine in 1934. His father, Ludwig Seligmann, was a commercial clerk and his mother, Hannah (née Schechter) had been a textile worker before marriage. Despite the reasons behind the move to Palestine, the Seligmanns remained strongly bound to their German heritage and raised their son with German as his first language. When Rafael was ten, his parents returned to Germany and settled in Munich. Since the end of the 1970s, Seligmann has worked as a journalist while pursuing other career interests. He studied political science and history in Munich and Tel Aviv and wrote his doctoral dissertation on Israeli security politics. From 1980 to 1984 he lived in Bonn, West Germany, where he worked as a political adviser for the Christian Democratic Union and as a reporter for *Die Welt.* In 1985, he founded the *Jüdische Zertung* (Jewish newspaper). From 1985 to 1988 he taught at the University of Munich. He became known as a fiction writer with the publication of his controversial first novel, *Rubinsteins Versteigerung* (Rubinstein's Auction), in 1989. As of 2001, Seligmann had published five novels, a book on German-Jewish and German-Israeli relations, and numerous essays and was living in Berlin with his wife and son.

Major Themes

Over the years Seligmann has produced numerous essays on a wide variety of topics, including post-Holocaust commemorative practice and the debates surrounding Holocaust representation, the history of anti-semitism, contemporary politics between Germany and Israel, and the implications of German unification for German-Jewish relations. But a recurring theme in his writing is the critique of the persistent stereotypes that hinder dialogue and debate between Jews and non-Jews. Seligmann's focus on stereotypes and his condemnation of attitudes that elevate dead Jews over living members of the community is bound up with the concerns about Jewish identity and post-Holocaust consciousness that permeate his entire oeuvre. Seligmann has repeatedly decried the reduction of Jewishness to an identification with the Holocaust and a community of victims, or *Opfergemeinschaft*, rather than an affinity with Jewish culture, tradition, and religious belief. He is acerbic in his criticism of so-called *Vergangenheitsbewältigung* (coming to terms with the past), arguing that it is of no use if unaccompanied by a *Bewältigung der Gegenwart* (coming to terms with the present). Commemorative politics for superficial political or personal ends represent "Zerredung" (talking to death) of the past, he says in *Mit beschränkter Hoffnung* (With Limited Hope, Hamburg: Hoffmann and Campe, 1991, p. 172) rather than any kind of substantive confrontation with the impact of the Holocaust on contemporary German-Jewish relations.

Seligmann's critical stance toward what he terms the *Holocaust-Kult*—and the appropriation of the Holocaust by both Jews and non-Jews who use the past to manipulate the present—in combination with the perceived irreverence of his fictional portrayals of Jews as morally ambiguous characters has earned him the epithet *Nestbeschmutzer* (nest-dirtier) from within Jewish ranks in Germany. Seligmann's response to his accusers has been to highlight his goal of normalization through provocation. By offering exaggerated images both of Jewish and non-Jewish Germans, Seligmann aims to spark controversy and debate that will eventually lead to an examination of the realities of German-Jewish relations.

He also maintains that the aggression and hatred expressed by his characters are emotions that have been repressed in the majority of Jewish writing about contemporary Germany. In Seligmann's view, Jews in

Germany feel compelled either to justify their decision to live in the country that launched the Holocaust or to distance themselves from their Jewish identity. Commenting on the two most often-cited rationales for Jewish life in Germany, namely, to prevent Hitler from achieving a posthumous victory in the form of a Jew-free Germany and for Jews to serve as emissaries of German-Jewish reconciliation, Seligmann argues that the latter leads to the avoidance of conflict he observes in contemporary German-Jewish writing ("What Keeps the Jews in Germany Quiet?" in *Reemerging Jewish Culture in Germany*, edited by Sander Gilman and Karen Remmler, New York: New York University Press, 1994, pp. 175–176).

In his own assessment of his status and career as a novelist, Seligmann regards himself as a pioneer chronicler of a largely unrepresented frontier of contemporary German-Jewish relations (see especially "German Jewry Squawking at the Approach of Danger," in *Speaking Out: Jewish Voices from United Germany*, edited by Susan Stern, Berlin: Edition Q, 1995, p. 175). It is for this representation that Seligmann has been most widely recognized—and criticized. Reception of his work has been mixed and reflects divergent responses ranging from critical dismissal to high praise. On the one side are those who see his writing as ammunition for antisemites and thus condemn it outright as detrimental to the Jewish cause. On the other side are those who laud his efforts to undermine the preconceptions that make any form of self-affirming Jewish identity impossible in the first place. Negative critiques of his fiction tend to foreground his uneven abilities as a novelist and the kitsch that imbues the portrayals of his male protagonists' sexual exploits, particularly their irrepressible lust for the German *Schickse*.

The Novels

The fascination with sex and the *Schickse* in Seligmann's fiction has led to repeated comparisons with Philip Roth—the character Rubinstein in Seligmann's first novel has been described as "a Munich Portnoy full of chutzpah" (quoted in Blumenthal, p. 20)—but Seligmann himself finds such comparisons misplaced (*Mit beschränkter Hoffnung*, p. 185). Seligmann's best received novel thus far, *Rubinsteins Versteigerung*, has been the primary focus of critical reception in English and is also the only work that has been translated in part into English to date. This largely autobiographical work addresses the conflicted situation of the children of Holocaust survivors living in Germany, where they must deal not only with their own struggles to define themselves but also with the legacy of their parents' suffering. Over the course of the novel, Jonathan Rubinstein develops from an awkward but obstreperous teenager—impatient with his parents' Holocaust trauma and their decision to return to Germany from Israel—into a young man aware of the complexities and contradictions of contemporary Jewish life. After testing and abandoning his youthful plan of "going up" to Israel, Jonathan comes to a realization and acceptance of his identity as a German Jew. This in itself represents a considerable achievement, particularly since Jonathan's fear that he will lose his strength because of "the neurotic situation of a Jew in Germany after Auschwitz" (Frankfurt: Eichborn, 1989, p. 104) is never completely laid to rest. In this context, the novel's closing sentence, "I am a German Jew" (p. 189), retains a note of ambiguity, at once affirmative and resigned.

The three novels following *Rubinsteins Versteigerung*—*Die jiddische Mamme* (The Yiddish Mama, 1990) which satirizes the stereotype of the domineering Jewish mother; *Der Musterjude* (The Model Jew, 1997), an exposé of philo-Semitism in contemporary German society; and *Schalom meine Liebe* (Shalom My Love, 1998), a journey of self-discovery that takes the protagonist from Germany to Israel and back—focused on the lives of the younger generation whose attitudes toward Jewishness were complicated by the Holocaust trauma their parents both suffered from and exploited. Seligmann's 1999 novel, *Der Milchmann* (The Milkman), however, is told from the perspective of the survivor generation. Inspired by a supposedly true story and dedicated to the murdered relatives of his mother's family, *Der Milchmann* is the first novel in which Seligmann portrays the experience of the Holocaust itself.

The opening chapter describes the protagonist's chance discovery of a crate of milk powder that has fallen from a freight train near the concentration camp. Jakob Weinberg, whose later nickname serves as the novel's title, originally plans to keep all the milk for himself, but finds that he is too weak to carry the crate back to the camp alone. The implausibility of the incident, which judging from Jakob's words takes place in Auschwitz, and the prisoners' success at getting the crate back to the barracks undetected is offset by harsh depictions of inmate interaction and camp life. Neither the protagonist nor his fellow prisoners are idealized in Seligmann's portrayal, and the battle over the milk powder that ensues when the prisoners return to the barracks reveals the contradictory emotions that arise under conditions of extremity, ranging from compassionate friendship to unvarnished greed and self-interest. Although Jakob has demonstrated that he himself belongs to the latter category, his observations of his fellow prisoners only serve to confirm his loss of faith in God and he even goes so far as to claim in his Yiddish-tinged German that "God is a German. Hitler is God" (Munich: DTV, 1999, p. 21). After the orgy of milk drinking has been broken up by SS guards who beat the prisoners brutally, Jakob has the revelation that his barracks will be exterminated the next day. To save his own skin, he steals a wedding ring hidden in the clothes of an injured prisoner and uses it to bribe his way into another barracks. To ensure that the head count of prisoners in his adopted barracks will be the same in the morning he drags the body of a sickly prisoner into the latrine and assumes the vacant place on the bunk. The rule of self-preservation he has learned in the camp causes him to disregard the value of any life but his own. His strategy proves successful: while his old barracks is eliminated, he survives.

The rest of the novel is set in Munich, Germany, where Jakob is now an old man with a legendary past, the product of his own self-transformation from villain to hero. Based on a story he invented about his camp experience in which he figures as the selfless savior of his barracks by providing his fellow prisoners with a case of milk powder, Jakob has earned the nickname "Milkman," a term of respect used by both friends and admirers. While Jakob's far from milk-white lie separates him from the benevolence of Jurek Becker's *Jakob the Liar*, the allusion to Becker's novel is as deliberate as the associations to the biblical figure of Jakob and his deceitful machinations. The dissonance between the protagonist's real behavior and that of the persona he invents after the fact points to a theme of recurring relevance in Seligmann's writings: the critique and simultaneous deconstruction of the myth of the "good" Jew.

Weinberg on the eve of his seventieth birthday is increasingly haunted by the past and the remainder of the story is largely devoted to the psychological turmoil characterizing his life as a survivor in Germany. As a Polish Jew, Jakob has no national affiliation to justify his choice of residence, and he attempts to deal with this difficulty obliquely by forcing his daughter to marry an Israeli soldier and emigrate to Israel. Through this vicarious act of "patriotism," Jakob seeks to assuage his own doubts about what keeps him in Germany and simultaneously keep his destabilized Jewish identity in balance. Seligmann portrays the Jewish community in postwar Munich as crippled by the loss of faith experienced by the survivor generation and hamstrung by an identity crisis in which Israel and antisemitism have taken the place of belief in God.

In Jakob's case, he views the fact of his survival itself as the sign of his moral superiority and as the validation of his sense of entitlement. His continual reference to his suffering as a justification for his behavior sparks vehement arguments with his children. In one such exchange, Udo, Jakob's son, accuses his father of exploiting his KZ experience to excuse his actions and his hatred of the Germans: "Your concentration camp number is a seal of quality without an expiration date" (p. 100). Jakob's behavior and attitudes are portrayed as alternately schizophrenic and pathetic. His abhorrence of the Germans is contradicted by his passionate relationship with his non-Jewish German lover and his insistence on driving a Mercedes, while his ostensible patriotism for Israel is weakened by his lack of desire to live there.

These are precisely the contradictions that Seligmann has raised in his earlier works, but the difference here is his detailed depiction of the trauma that dominates the survivor's situation and psyche and the dilemma of locating Jewish identity in culture and community without an allegiance to God. While Weinberg appeared to be an exception in Seligmann's novels because of the difference in generation, the question he faces is one common to all of Seligmann's protagonists: what does it mean to be Jewish in Germany? The solution Seligmann proposes is to move away from a victim mentality that identifies Jewishness with the Holocaust, and instead to embrace Jewish culture and Jewish tradition as part of Germany's history going back more than a thousand years. The intent of such a shift in attitudes would be to free both Jews and non-Jews from a relationship in which the Holocaust obstructs interpersonal interaction as well as personal growth.

For scholars of the Holocaust and its repercussions for German-Jewish relations, Seligmann's significance lies in his critique of Holocaust memory politics as well as in his satirical exposés of the anti- and philosemitic stereotypes that continue to color German-Jewish interaction. His use of satire and exaggerated imagery to deconstruct the very stereotypes that hinder the encounter between Jews and non-Jews are intended to shake his readers into an examination of their own preconceptions and stimulate dialogue. Not until Jews cease to be held to a higher moral standard will both Jews and non-Jews be able to confront the complexities of their shared existence in Germany and begin to come to terms with the present.

Translations from the German by Kathrin Bower throughout.

Bibliography

Primary Sources

Rubinsteins Versteigerung (Rubinstein's Auction). 1989.
Die jiddische Mamme (The Yiddish Mama). 1990.
Mit beschränkter Hoffnung (With Limited Hope). 1991, 1993.
"From *Rubinstein's Auction*." 1994.
"What Keeps the Jews in Germany Quiet?" 1994.
"German Jewry Squawking at the Approach of Danger." 1995.
Der Musterjude (The Model Jew). 1997.
Schalom meine Liebe (Shalom My Love). 1998.
"Playing Ass." 1998.
"The Underling." 1998.
"Zionism." 1998.
Der Milchmann (The Milkman). 1999.

Secondary Sources

Blumenthal, Michael. "A German Jew's Frontal Assault on Complacency." *International Herald Tribune*, 18 May 2000.

Gilman, Sander. *Jews in Today's German Culture*. Bloomington: Indiana University Press, 1995.

Gilman, Sander, and Jack Zipes. "Introduction: Jewish Writing in German through the Ages." In *The Yale Companion to Jewish Writing and Thought in German Culture, 1096–1996*. Edited by Sander L. Gilman and Jack Zipes. New Haven, Conn.: Yale University Press, 1997. pp. xxvii–xxx.

Gilman, Sander, and Hartmut Steinecke, eds. *Deutsch-jüdische Literatur der neunziger Jahre. Die Generation nach der Shoah*. Berlin: Erich Schmidt Verlag, 2002.

Koch, Gertrud. "Corporate Identities: Zur Prosa von Dische, Biller und Seligmann." *Babylon* 7 (1990): 139–142.

Nolden, Thomas. *Junge jüdische Literatur*. Wurzburg, Germany: Köngishausen und Neumann, 1995.

Remmler, Karen. "1980: The 'Third Generation' of Jewish-German Writers after the *Shoah* Emerges in Germany and Austria." In *The Yale Companion to Jewish Writing and Thought in German Culture, 1096–1996*. Edited by Sander L. Gilman and Jack Zipes. New Haven, Conn.: Yale University Press, 1997. pp. 796–804.

Robertson, Ritchie. "Rafael Seligmann's *Rubinsteins Versteigerung*: The German-Jewish Family Novel before and after the Holocaust." *Germanic Review* 75, no. 3 (2000): 179–193.

Zipes, Jack. "Jewish Consciousness in Germany Today." *Telos* 93 (1992): 159–172.

NAVA SEMEL
(1954–)

DVIR ABRAMOVICH

NAVA SEMEL, BORN in 1954 in Tel Aviv, Israel, earned her M.A. in art history, and served as an art critic in the Israeli press. Semel has worked as a TV, radio, and recording producer and as a journalist. She has written poetry, prose for children and adults, and television scripts, and has translated plays. Semel has received several literary prizes, including the American National Jewish Book Award for children's literature, the 1994 Women Writers of the Mediterranean Award, the 1996 Israeli Prime Minister's award for Literature, the 1996 Austrian Best Radio Drama Award, and the 1999 Ze'ev Award. Many of her works have been adapted for radio, film, and television, and the stage. She is also a member of the Massua Institute of Holocaust Studies and a member of the Yad Vashem board of governors.

Kova Zehuhit (A Glass Hat)

"Through my story-telling I embraced my mother's personal account of pain and loss, and the scar she would carry for the rest of her life," writes Nava Semel. "In the process I was conscious of the virtues of healing, yet I was also well aware of the fact that a complete repair, *tikkun*—wasn't possible" (*Kova Zehuhit*, Tel Aviv: Sifriyat Hapoalim, 1998, p. 416).

Within the cannon of second-generation Holocaust fiction, Nava Semel's oeuvre, in particular the collection of short stories titled *Kova Zehuhit* (A Glass Hat), is worthy of special study. Semel's collection of stories was the first Israeli work to give literary voice to the sons and daughters of the survivors, a poignant pipeline to the world of those unique relationships. Semel's symbiotic nexus to her parents is evidenced by the dedication, "To my mother who survived and to my father who accompanied." In a breathtaking introduction to *Kava Zehuhit*, Nurit Govrin proffers an explanation for the book's title as a metaphor for the enduring burden projected upon the children of survivors (all translations of *Kova Zehuhit* are by Dvir Abramovich):

> This glass hat, its touch is cold. It is transparent and insulated, burdensome and not isolated, vulnerable and may break into pieces at any moment. More than it protects it exposes and bears great danger. It concentrates the sunrays and amplifies the heat underneath so much so it can cause fire. The glass hat recalls the glass bell in which divers go down to the depths of the ocean to watch what is happening there without being injured. Yet, as opposed to the glass bell the hat cannot provide similar protection. As well, it hints at the glass cage where the war criminal Eichmannn was placed during his trial in Jerusalem (pp. 9–10).

In common with other texts bearing witness, the theme of a survivor's daughter struggling with the intense pain of her mother's memory is explored at many levels. Semel replays the difficulty of children living with survivor parents, presenting their anxieties as childhood fragments from a broken home movie. Sooner or later, each tale focuses on the dark underside of the individual to whom a particular pathology has been bequeathed. One of Semel's fundamental concerns is that the second generation must, in order to attain insight into their parents' Holocaust trauma, understand the essence of the extreme horror the victims experienced. Only then can the contemporary hero reclaim the empathic identification abnegated by the conventional boundaries of the dominant Israeli culture. Semel believes that this process permits survivor children to enter the world of their parents, assume their trauma within their current lives, and feel the pain of their own personal holocaust. She suggests that this is a necessary development, enabling the second generation to deal with the trauma. Semel elucidates the process:

> I see writing as my quest along the axis of time, like those young Israelis who try to mark dates. I do not do it out of nostalgia, but from a deep need to seek the primeval components under our Israeli shield that are still in operation today. First, we had to trace them down, then admit that they exist, and not run away from their consequences. Writing about the scar of the Holocaust is my rebellion against the rigid model of the neo Israeli, supposedly untainted by the past. We are coming to terms with that inner drum that echoed in the Israeli psyche all those years, but we pushed it aside and refused really to listen (p. 416).

This theme is very much in evidence in the story "A Private Holocaust." The central figure is Dafna, a young Kibbutz woman in London trying to break into show business. She is the daughter of Holocaust survivors, and her parents' past has become a central psychic event in her life. Like other contemporary protagonists, she is forced to confront the dilemma of understanding her bereaved parents on the one hand, and achieving autonomy on the other. The nightmare of Europe is resurrected in the context of her childhood, partly through her father, but especially through her mother. Her father would tell bedtime stories, never reading from the book, but inventing his own Holocaust-derived tales. After the scene in which Bambi's mother is burned in the forest, Dafna asks him if it hurts when one is burned. He responds, "It hurts very much, but at first you choke from the smoke and don't feel a thing" (p. 41).

Dafna's mother was previously married and had two children who, along with their father, were murdered in the chaos of Europe. Dafna symbolizes, for the mother, the family that perished. Her mother imposes the identity of the children on the living daughter, and Dafna is unable to liberate herself from her mother's "Holocaust cape" (Wardi, pp. 27–35). Aware of her role in the family, Dafna feels antagonistic emotions, "How she deceived her. She would tell her every birthday: You are the eldest, you are my only one. She was after all a *substitute* [italics added] for the others. Why didn't she tell her: You are my only one that remained. *I gave birth to you so God forbid I will not forget the ones before* [italics added]" (p. 60). Still, this resentment is accompanied by an idealization of her mother. In an incident bearing a striking resemblance to one in the Gila Almagor novel *Summer of Aviya*, when her mother arrives at a rehearsal for a *Shavuot* play, a flood of nervous feelings well up in Dafna and she is unable to recite her lines. She manages only to mumble a few incomprehensible words.

The prevailing pattern of the survivor parents' reluctance to talk about the destruction of their identities is repeated here. Haunted by history and deprived of knowing what marked her from an early age as a memorial candle, Dafna discovers some old photographs of her mother and her murdered brother and sister. Dafna's interior thoughts reverberate, "These are your dead siblings. They were born before you were" (p. 47).

The common features of posttraumatic syndrome such as anxiety, reactive depression, and brooding absorption in the past characterize the mother's behavior. Semel paints a portrait of a mother possessed by a death-in-life burden, having endured the destruction of her personality in the unspeakable horror of the camps. She denied Dafna a normal expression of parental love. In addition to never holding or hugging her child, she lived as if savoring the opportunity to carry the weight of the dead on her shoulders, always walking as if behind her daughter stood the shadows of her murdered children, generating the sense that to be loved one needed to be dead. Dafna recollects her mother's reaction to moments of happiness, such as her father dancing with the young girls of the Kibbutz, "mother twists her face and a line of contempt broadens across her face. How dare people be happy? A family is a kind of hump connected to the shoulders" (p. 48).

The mother's overprotectiveness encourages Dafna's excessive dependence on her; the mother wills her to stay in the kibbutz. It is evident that Dafna's sojourn in London is an act of rebellion—the first time she fulfills her own desires rather than those of the mother—trying to "break the chain," as she puts it. Nevertheless, the mother makes it difficult. Dafna receives a letter from her father saying that the mother is ill and pleading with her to return at once. She believes her mother's illness is self-induced to exploit her feelings of guilt. She phones the airline several times and repeatedly hangs up at the last moment. Her decision to remain in England affirms Dafna's earlier rage against the overwhelming depression that dominates her environment, denying the relevance of Holocaust history to her, and to her generation's, life:

> Leave me out of all this. Why do you keep dealing with the Holocaust? We lock the ceremonies away for one day in the year. It has been, it is finished, we are another generation, and we are the new children. Don't lumber us with your fur of fears. We are new. Shem, Cham and Yefet. Throwing covers over their father's nakedness. All these things happened in a place far away. That period stuck only to the pages of the books. It does not touch me. I seek to find myself, I am after a new girl (pp. 47–48).

Traveling to an audition, she stumbles upon a robbery in progress and is taken hostage by the bandit. The kidnapping triggers a doppelgänger effect; while enduring the violence and rape, she becomes the mother who survived the Nazi camps. The narration shuttles between description of the daughter's capture and her mother's savage persecution. At times the reader is unsure who is being tormented. Significantly, the entire episode is encoded with terms referencing the systematic dehumanization and extermination her mother witnessed. When the felon pushes her, it is as if she is an obstinate cargo animal (pp. 51–52). Mumbling in English, she remembers how her mother used to rebuke her in broken Polish (p. 54). In the car, she notices her captor's sports shoes, an image she associates with the boots of Joseph Mengele, clanking along the camp's stones, whose selection her mother escaped and whose face she will remember for eternity (p. 55). Later, as Dafna is allowed outside her hijacker's car to urinate, she takes off her pants and envisages her mother naked, dissolving the margins of time and space, "They take off their clothes. Mother stands and the secret of her organs is revealed. No coverings for the soul, no covering for her box. She places her hand over her nakedness. The master of dogs checks her body" (p. 58). Themes of exposure and nakedness abound in religious and secular Hebrew Holocaust fiction as a symbolic analogue to the victim's experience in the *Shoah* (Ramras-Rauch and Michman-Melkman, p. 5).

The sound of a train in the English countryside evokes the image of a train transporting Jews to Auschwitz, where they are forced to send postcards to their relatives assuring them they are well. She believes that when she and her captor stop, they will be at the gates of Auschwitz. She is unsure of when his dirty hand grabbed her, now or thirty-nine years ago. Once released, Dafna crawls to the nearest house in the English village, and bangs on the door. At that moment, the mother's actions following her release fold into the daughter's narrative. The emphasis here, again, is in the simultaneous participation and sharing of the daughter in imagery from the mother's past. The daughter's identification with the mother reaches its crescendo in the scenes leading to and after Dafna's rape, where the two women become one. At first, she remembers her mother's disgust when she cut her hair severely short, her turning away and screaming, "It's repulsive. You look just like me. Then" (p. 62). Lying battered on the floor of a deserted cottage, bleeding from his blows, a significant breach occurs; the daughter makes her mother's Holocaust experience an integral component of her being and identity, now comprehending the realities of the "unlived life" through her present suffering. Being taken prisoner provides Dafna compelling access to the mother's life, allowing the daughter to enter and actualize her world. The entire episode employs quintessential Nazi terminology to delineate Dafna's imprisonment, framing a narrative that articulates and evokes the reality of traumatic shock within a post-Holocaust society. Ultimately, the experience leads the daughter to empathize with her mother's degradation and despair. Dafna has adopted her mother's experiences as her own, in the ultimate form of inherited pain and identification. By having this modern-day drama unfold against the background of the Holocaust, Semel shows how the deep residue of the Holocaust is powerfully present in the lives of young Israelis.

Essentially, "A Private Holocaust" embodies, through rhetorical strategies, the psychological research of the postgenocide generation. It has been noted that in their dreams and fantasies, the second generation share a group memory of the actual cruelties suffered by their parents, tracing a psychic imprint, filling a blank space from secondary knowledge about the experience and remembering events not personally experienced (H. Barocas and C. Barocas, p. 331).

By becoming a participant and co-owner of the traumatic event, a movement toward real understanding emerges, as the daughter feels the injury of the survivor that had previously been impossible. While she still does not wholly accept her mother's utter lack of optimism and affection, a space has been created for a process of healing between the two, for the daughter has now opened the way for reassessment of her mother's neuroses and psychological scarring. The two opposing worlds have united within a single psyche. Like her mother, she has been starved, debased, and beaten. It is only in this way that she can forgive her mother:

> This is how she sits, her closed mother, burrowing inside her secrets, inside the end of her shame. *You are free of any guilt,* and I did not know. The Children will never return. But I am a new girl, the reincarnation of the dead girl, from the pictures, my half sister. I will never replace them, because there is no relief for the skin that has been cut. The mother's body kept walking, but the foetuses landed and returned, planted inside her bitter tidings. . . . Her mother did not perform the *Kriah* over her children. Even the release of the mourning was not allowed. . . . The sorrow sank inside of her as pregnancy past its term. She did not repeat their names, even in a dream. She was not allowed to long for them. They urged her to forget, to quickly produce copies of her kids. And in the same way that she failed in her second marriage, she perhaps failed with her copied daughter (pp. 65, 67, italics added).

As she flies back to Israel, wearing one of the sweaters her mother knitted for her, which she has never worn before, Dafna recognizes the inescapable connection to her mother's history:

> That invisible cord has been woven inside of her. Now she knows, the first children of her mother have been gathered inside her. A cloud that formed many years be-

fore her birth will not disintegrate easily. *Maybe every man experiences the epiphany of a personal Holocaust* (p. 69) [Italics added].

The key motif of visiting the death camps by the postgenocide generation can be found in the story "Epilogue." The main plot concerns a thirty-year-old woman visiting with her father, who is returning to Birkenau—the site of his nightmare. As she enters the gates of the camp, she reflects, "I imagined in my soul, that I stayed here before. Perhaps it is the rotten fruit of the genetic memory. Like a light bulb the address kept blinking in my head" (p. 212). Although a mother herself, she reflects that within the immediacy and the emotional engagement of Birkenau, she feels again like a child, like the children whose shoes are now falling to pieces inside the glass windows (p. 213). In the mountain of shaven hair she sees her mother's curls, but despite feeling the immediate and present imprint of the place, despite the unmediated experiential and temporal biographical relationship that has opened up, she is unable to touch or lay flowers at the crematorium as the Poles do. Instead, she searches for shards of prayer in her head that will attenuate the scream of pain she cannot utter, "Life had been hurled to the ground and lost consciousness and every man who left came out with a broken, bleeding wound. My father . . . held on to me and cried bitterly, and the snow landed on his face and mingled with the tears but could not freeze them" (p. 212).

Soon afterwards she returns alone to the crematorium. Walking along the blackened walls she whispers a prayer she remembers, yet she does not dare touch, afraid to desecrate or to permit the place to make a mark on her. Although she wishes to mourn her parent's traumatic past, as well as her own, she refuses to cry, "My lips were dry but I did not drink. I did not empty my body's refuse and a thin pain plucked my guts. I shall not leave my footprints here, I swore, except my footsteps. And the vindictive snow will erase them" (p. 213). Through the excursion into the heart of darkness the daughter is capable of voicing her pain. Broadly speaking, this artifice refers to the recurring comingling of memory, imagination, and fact, for the second-generation writers who displace (from the limited knowledge possessed by survivor children) onto themselves an imagined involvement in the atrocities. At heart, it describes the importance and difficulty of communicating the destructive calamity of the Holocaust to the third generation so as to sustain the fading memory and legacy of the eyewitnesses.

Bibliography

Primary Sources

Kova Zehuhit (A Glass Hat). 1985.
Isha Al Niyar (Bride on Paper). 1996.
Morris Havivael Melamed La'uf (Flying Lessons). 1990.
Rally Masah Matarah (Night Games). 1994.

Secondary Sources

Barocas, H., and C. Barocas. "Wounds of the Fathers: The Next Generation of Holocaust Victims." *International Review of Psychoanalysis* 6 (1979): 331–340.
Govrin, Nurit. Introduction to *Kova Zehuhit*, by Nava Semel. Tel Aviv: Sifriyat Hapoalim, 1985.
Lev, Eleonora. *Sug Mesuyam Shel Yatmut: Edut Al Masa*. Tel Aviv: Am Over, 1989.
Ramras-Rauch, Gila, and Joseph Michman-Melkman, eds. *Facing the Holocaust: Selected Israeli Fiction*. Philadelphia: The Jewish Publication Society, 1985.
Wardi, Dina. *Memorial Candles*. London & New York: Routledge, 1992.

Jorge Semprun

(1923–)

COLIN DAVIS

EARLY IN THE morning of 25 April 1985 Juan Larrea, the protagonist of Jorge Semprun's novel *La Montagne blanche* (1986), recounts his experiences as a prisoner in Buchenwald to his closest friends and then takes his own life by swimming out to sea. He has not yet fully confronted the trauma of Buchenwald, and suppressing his memories of it for forty years has only served to augment its power. Semprun's endeavor in his novels and autobiographical writing is to find ways of coping with the memory of Buchenwald that will enable him to avoid Larrea's fate. Yet Larrea's suicide is in a sense also his author's death, or one of his author's deaths. "Juan Larrea" was in fact one of the names used by Semprun during his years of involvement in the clandestine struggle against Francisco Franco's fascist regime in Spain. The fictional Larrea dies so that Semprun can survive. Rafaël Artigas, in the novel *L'Algarabie* (1981), bears another of the names used by Semprun; like Larrea he is destined to die at the end of the novel. It is as if Semprun is killing off his alter egos in order to make his own survival possible, but at each stage something of himself is also lost. Whether fiction or autobiography, his work can be read as the ceaseless endeavor to reassemble the fragments of memory while also preserving himself against its deadly potential.

Life and Work

Semprun was born on 10 December 1923 in Madrid to an affluent and well-connected family with Republican sympathies. During the Spanish Civil War the family went into exile, and Semprun pursued his education in Paris, first at the Lycée Henri IV and then as a student of philosophy at the Sorbonne. He joined the Communist Party, was arrested in 1943 for Resistance activities, and was deported to Buchenwald, where he remained until its liberation in April 1945. Returning to Paris, he began to write an account of his time in Buchenwald, which he subsequently abandoned. After a period working as a translator for UNESCO, he became a leading member of the Spanish Communist Party and, under the name Federico Sánchez, organized its clandestine work in Madrid. While in hiding in Madrid in 1961, he began to write what would be his first novel, *Le Grand Voyage* (1963), which recounts the train journey that would lead a Communist Resistance member named Gérard to Buchenwald. "Gérard" had been the name by which Semprun was known in the Resistance, and in his first novel as in all his subsequent books—whether novels or autobiographical texts—Semprun uses a sophisticated literary form to explore his own memories. *Le Grand Voyage* was heralded by György Lukács, among others, as the work of a major writer. By this time, however, Semprun's relations with his Communist colleagues were strained, and he was first relieved of his responsibilities and then expelled from the party in 1964 for political differences. Semprun then pursued a career as a writer of novels, memoirs, and film scripts, working on films most notably with the directors Alain Resnais (*La Guerre est finie*, *Stavisky*) and Constantin Costa-Gavras (*Z*, *L'Aveu*, *Section spéciale*). Between 1988 and 1991 he served as minister of culture in the socialist government in Spain. Throughout his career he has written mainly in French. His characters are typically haunted by memories of the concentration camps, but frequently the theme is kept in the background. He has written more directly about Buchenwald and the problems of living with its memory in four books: *Le Grand Voyage*, *Quel beau dimanche!* (1980), *L'Écriture ou la vie* (1994) and *Le Mort qu'il faut* (2001).

Much postwar debate about literature in France has been driven by the conflict between proponents of committed literature, spearheaded by Jean-Paul Sartre, and experimentation, as found in the work of the New

Novelists (such as Nathalie Sarraute, Alain Robbe-Grillet, and Michel Butor) or the writers involved with the journal *Tel Quel*. For proponents of committed literature it was vital to accept the political responsibility of literature, whereas for the experimental writers the role of art was to explore language, experience, and representation without the constraints of established political doctrine. The differences between these groups have sometimes been exaggerated, but even so Semprun is unusual in that his writing draws from both sides, combining political and ethical subject matter with an abiding concern for questions of form. For him, the experience of the concentration camps cannot be adequately narrated or understood in traditional forms. Straightforward testimony and chronological sequence may faithfully reproduce facts, anecdotes, and clichés, but they will never enter into the heart of the matter. Typically, Semprun begins from a particular moment and then moves backward and forward in time, building up a complex narrative in which each instant is overlaid with reminiscences and anticipations of numerous others. *Le Grand Voyage*, for example, describes the train journey to Buchenwald, but it constantly flashes back to Gérard's earlier life and forward to his experiences after his liberation. *Quel beau dimanche!* focuses on one Sunday in Buchenwald but also draws on its narrator's postwar life and shows how his eventual break with Communism led to a radical reassessment of his experience in the camp.

In *L'Écriture ou la vie* Semprun describes how testimony requires literary form if the substance and density of experience are to be recreated: "Only the artifice of a controlled narrative will succeed in transmitting partially the truth of testimony" (*L'Écriture ou la vie*, Paris: Gallimard, 1994, p. 23). This recognition of the importance of form is allied with two further views that put Semprun at odds with many others who survived the camps. He insists that there is nothing unique about the difficulty of bearing witness to the camps ("But there is nothing exceptional about this: it is the case with all great historical experiences," p. 23), and he also repudiates the common assertion that the extreme suffering of the prisoners cannot be communicated to others. For Semprun, the camps like everything else are entirely susceptible to literary representation, even if the labor of narration will never be complete:

> You can always say everything, all things considered. The ineffable which we will be told about endlessly is nothing more than an alibi. Or a sign of laziness. You can always say everything, language contains everything. . . . [y]ou can say everything about this experience. You just have to think about it. And work at it. To have time, no doubt, and the courage, to undertake a narrative which is unlimited, probably interminable, illuminated—and also circumscribed, of course—by the possibility of carrying on into infinity (pp. 23–24).

The work of memory and of understanding is thus also a struggle with form and language. Semprun's work can be read as an interminable narrative that constantly repeats and revises the past, adding to earlier accounts, changing details, or offering new perspectives. The boundaries between fact and fiction are never clearly drawn; some of Semprun's books are described as novels on their title pages, but the distinctions between these and more overtly autobiographical texts are never watertight. In Semprun's view, moreover, that something is fictional does not mean it is not also true. For example, the novel *L'Évanouissement* (1967) describes an episode from the protagonist's Resistance past involving a Jewish companion called Hans, who had also appeared in *Le Grand Voyage*. In *L'Ecriture ou la vie* Semprun says that the incident did indeed take place, but that the person involved was neither Jewish nor called Hans. This, however, does not mean that the fictional account of the incident was false, as Hans was invented to represent real Jewish companions-in-arms who took part in the struggle against the German occupation: "So there the truth is reestablished: the total truth of a narrative which was already truthful" (p. 46). There is no contradiction between the different versions of the story, and no need to choose between the literal truth of one and the fictional truth of the other. Fiction and testimony together reveal aspects of meaning and experience that may be explored from many angles.

Semprun's books constitute a vast echo chamber in which the same memories and incidents are revisited: a massive, ongoing interrogation of identity and history. His work is also a commentary on itself, observing the entanglements of past and future, the difficulties this entails for the reader, and the shifts in the narrator's understanding of what has happened to him. Neither the past nor the identity of the narrator is fixed. The same incidents return, but sometimes appear quite different. One story recounted on several occasions illustrates how memory is never settled once and for all: In *Quel beau dimanche!* the narrator tells how, on arrival in Buchenwald, he was asked his profession for the camp records. He answered that he was a student of philosophy. Told, "Das ist doch kein Beruf" (But that isn't a profession), he considered replying with the pun, "Kein Beruf, nur eine Berufung" (Not a profession, only a vocation), but thought better of it (Paris: Grasset, 1980, p. 95). When the same anecdote is repeated in *L'Écriture ou la vie*, the narrator says that he did make the pun; later, however, he is shown his camp registration card and learns that the fellow prisoner taking down his details perhaps saved his life by recording a more practical profession. When the incident recurs yet again, in *Le Mort qu'il faut*, the narrator again claims to have made the pun and concludes with the assumption that the prisoner duly put him down as a student of philosophy. In a sense, the discrepancies in these accounts barely matter. Even so, they illustrate that the meaning of the past can be revisited and transformed in any future narration. One account may be complemented or contradicted by another. If the boundaries between fact and fiction are not clearly established, neither is the past: In Semprun's four different accounts of Buchenwald, there are distinct shifts in the significance he attributes to his experience there, shifts that tie his narrative to his own political development after the war, and more generally to the evolution of European Communism.

The Communist Phase

It took Semprun sixteen years of literary silence and political activity before he could return to his abandoned ambition to write about Buchenwald. He needed time to forget before he could undertake the labor of remembering. The similarity between his position in hiding in Franco's Spain and his imprisonment in Hitler's Germany seems to have provided him with both the occasion and the form he needed. *Le Grand Voyage* was greeted in 1963 as one of the first French novels of real literary merit to deal with the deportation, and its author was awarded both the Prix Formentor and the Prix littéraire de la Résistance.

The novel describes the thoughts, memories, and subsequent experiences of its narrator, a Spanish Communist named Gérard, as he travels in the train that will take him and his fellow deportees to Buchenwald. One of the most striking features about Gérard, as he discusses the deportation with his fellow prisoner *le gars de Semur* (the lad from Semur), is his self-confidence. Although references in the novel to life after the liberation from Buchenwald show a young man haunted by the past, sometimes overwhelmed by painful memories and struggling to forget what he has experienced, private trauma does not on the whole shake his political and intellectual security. As with other Communist deportees, Gérard's worldview is confirmed rather than threatened by his imprisonment. For him, capture, torture, and deportation are entirely intelligible as the consequences of his political commitment and the resistance against Nazism. The barbaric behavior of the German occupiers serves only to justify any actions taken against them. After the war, David Rousset in *L'Univers concentrationnaire* (1946) and Robert Antelme in *L'Espèce humaine* (1947) had established the terms of the Communist interpretation of the camps, which underpins the relative emotional calm of *Le Grand Voyage*. As Semprun would later write in *Quel beau dimanche!* the situation of the political deportees made perfect sense:

> In the Nazi camps, the situation of the political deportee . . . was clear: the SS were our enemies, their ideology was what we abhorred, so we knew very well why we were in Buchenwald. We were there because we had taken risks and decisions, freely, which had led us to where we were. We knew why we were in Buchenwald. In some way it was only natural that we were there. It was natural that, having taken arms against Nazism, the sanction for our arrest would be deportation (pp. 215–216).

Le Grand Voyage is informed throughout by this sense that deportation can be fully understood as the consequence of the armed political struggle against Nazism. This in turn is an episode in the fight against capitalism. Thus, for Gérard, the war is not a matter of good French against bad Germans, but of oppressed against oppressor. As he insists to the initial consternation of the "lad from Semur," there are concentration camps in France, run by the French, just as there are camps in Germany. This rocks his companion's understanding of the war as a conflict between nations, but it entirely corresponds to the Communists' understanding of it in class terms. Imprisonment confirms his commitment, rather than bringing it into question: "I have never understood so well why I was fighting. . . . Because it is quite simply a question of installing the classless society" (Paris: Gallimard, 1963; Folio edition, p. 56). Deportation is merely a consequence of political action, and the barbarity of the camps is merely an extreme instance of the barbarity of capitalism. So, while Buchenwald threatens the prisoners' physical survival, it does not undermine the political faith that brought them there. As a result, there is really nothing to be learned from the camps that a Communist did not already know. Buchenwald brings out the best and worst in men: some steal the bread of others for their own benefit, whereas some put their own well-being and lives at risk to help their comrades. But there is nothing surprising in this: "The camps are limited situations, in which the rift between men and others is made more brutally. In fact, we didn't need the camps to tell us that man is capable of the best and the worst. It's sorrowfully banal, this observation" (p. 72).

Still, reticence is palpable in the book. Much more is said about the journey to Buchenwald and the period after liberation than about life as a prisoner; and the novel ends with the deportees' arrival in the camp, when what awaits them is still unknown. Moreover, there are moments suggesting how limited the narrator's account may be. His belief that the end of Nazism would necessarily entail the end of Franco's regime in Spain ("but it's clear, there isn't the shadow of a doubt," p. 92) is discredited by history. He records in distressing detail how the SS set their dogs on a group of Jewish children, then calmly murder them, on their arrival from Poland (pp. 192–197); no attempt is made to explain this horror politically. Such passages perhaps anticipate the revision of his understanding and political views that later works would document. Indeed, as Semprun was writing *Le Grand Voyage* the process that would lead to his expulsion from the Spanish Communist Party and his disillusionment with Communism were already under way. But on the whole, and despite the rapidity with which the narrative moves between the narrator's past, present, and future, *Le Grand Voyage* is characterized by intellectual and political self-confidence. This is the work of a man who refuses self-pity and retains the beliefs that helped him survive the camps.

The Return of Trauma

Semprun began to write *Le Grand Voyage* sixteen years after the liberation of Buchenwald, and it was finally published eighteen years after the end of the war. A further seventeen years would separate *Le Grand Voyage* from *Quel beau dimanche!* his next sustained treatment of the camp experience. In the meantime, Semprun had been expelled from the Communist Party and had become well-known as a novelist and screenwriter. His period of renewed silence about the camps coincides with a loss of the political faith that had guided the composition of *Le Grand Voyage*. The trauma the earlier book had largely succeeded in avoiding now erupts belatedly, because the structures that had held it at bay have broken down. Crucially also, *Quel beau dimanche!* is set inside the camp, describing one day in Buchenwald, whereas *Le Grand Voyage* had said relatively little about life as a prisoner. This suggests that, in some sense, Semprun in 1980 is more imprisoned within Buchenwald than he had been earlier. The defining change is the collapse of his belief in Communism, given poignancy by growing and incontrovertible evidence of the Soviet gulags (forced labor camps).

Quel beau dimanche! is both the narrative of a day in Buchenwald and an account of how events after the war retrospectively changed the overall significance of earlier experience. A precedent for Semprun's decision to focus on a single day is Aleksandr Solzhenitsyn's *One Day in the Life of Ivan Denisovich*. This book was published in France in 1963, the same year as *Le Grand Voyage*, and Semprun perceived it as undermining the significance of his own novel. In Buchenwald, the Communists had been sustained by the belief that the camp was an excrescence of capitalism: in the Soviet Union such camps could not exist. Through the 1940s and 1950s, despite mounting evidence of the gulags, many French Communists simply refused to believe what was to them politically inconceivable. Once the reality and brutality of the Soviet camps was acknowledged, it would no longer be possible to view concentration camps as solely a product of capitalism. Reading *One Day in the Life of Ivan Denisovich*, and also Varlam Shalamov's *Kolyma Tales*, Semprun's narrator finds his experiences in Buchenwald anticipated and repeated in the gulags; this transforms the meaning of his own memories. The trauma, here, does not come from the experience of Buchenwald itself; *Le Grand Voyage* indicated that Buchenwald could be survived and recounted. Rather, trauma arises at the point where the experience of Buchenwald is reencountered years later in accounts written from inside a very different political system—precisely the system for which the Buchenwald Communists had been struggling.

Reading *One Day in the Life of Ivan Denisovich*, Semprun rediscovers the traumatic core his political commitment had enabled him to resist. Nearly twenty years after liberation, a new intellectual and emotional disarray emerges. Semprun loses what he calls "that innocence of memory" (*Quel beau dimanche!* p. 384). It is not that *Le Grand Voyage* was untruthful, but its truth has, in retrospect, been invalidated:

> My whole narrative in *Le Grand Voyage* was linked silently, without being made explicit, without making a meal of it or being high-handed about it, to a Communist vision of the world. The whole truth of my testimony had as an implicit but constraining reference point the horizon of an unalienated society: a classless society in which the camps would have been inconceivable. The whole truth of my testimony bathed in the holy oils of this latent good conscience. But the horizon of Communism was not that of the classless society, I mean: its real, historical horizon. The horizon of Communism, inevitable, was that of the gulag. At a stroke, the whole truth of my book became mendacious (pp. 384–385).

The narrative of the camps takes a new turn. It is not just that memories can always be augmented; more disturbingly, their significance can in retrospect be shattered. Just as Communism could no longer appear as a triumphal march toward the classless society, memory could no longer be conceived as the slow reconstruction of the stable reality of the past. An experience which for the narrator of *Le Grand Voyage* had been difficult but tolerable becomes, in Semprun's later writing, almost unbearable because there is no longer any framework to guarantee its intelligibility. Trauma lies not in the event itself, but in its unanticipated recollection, perhaps years later. When, in *La Montagne blanche*, Juan Larrea is assailed, forty years after his liberation, by memories of Buchenwald he has no reason to believe the experience served a higher purpose, and no resources to resist the call to death. The self-inflicted violence or murder of Semprun's alter egos in his novels of this period from 1967–1987 (*L'Évanouissement*, *La Deuxième Mort de Ramón Mercader*, *La Montagne blanche*, *netchaïev est de retour*) can be interpreted as an attempt to ward off the newly provoked trauma by directing its catastrophic effects at his fictional surrogates. The political faith that had sustained *Le Grand Voyage* has given away to a political and emotional disarray that threatens to be fatal.

The Reinvention of Sense

After *Quel beau dimanche!* another fourteen years passed before Semprun wrote again at length about his experience of deportation in *L'Écriture ou la vie* (1994), and then another seven years before *Le Mort qu'il faut* (2001), which is described on its final page as a kind of sequel to *Le Grand Voyage*. These most recent books mark a new phase in Semprun's approach to Buchenwald. Many familiar elements are still present. Characters and episodes from previous books reappear; and the texts follow the narrator's memory as it wanders backward and forward through time, each moment complexly related with many others. But in this latest phase there is also a renewed sense of calm, which can be linked to the reemergence of sense in the experience of Buchenwald, discovered after the collapse of the Communist paradigm. It is also significant that since 1987 Semprun has not published any more books that are explicitly novels. His novels often enacted the killing off of fictional alter egos; now the need to preserve himself by killing his doubles seems to have passed.

It is not that the entrapment of memory in Buchenwald has been overcome. *L'Écriture ou la vie* begins immediately after the liberation of the camp; the narrator is no longer a prisoner, yet it is clear that being outside is, for the survivor, only another form of being inside. Liberation does not signal the end of the camp experience. The book describes the long period of forgetting the narrator had to undertake after his return from Buchenwald. He abandons his initial attempt to write about his experience because, by dwelling on his memories, he was also sapping his ability to live. As the title suggests, for a long period he believed himself obliged to choose between writing and life.

Semprun's most recent works, however, show a renewed self-confidence as he returns to the process of revising the past. The narrator of *Quel beau dimanche!* finds that the meaning of his experience has been shattered by the revelation of the gulags. By contrast, the narrators of *L'Écriture ou la vie* and *Le Mort qu'il faut* rediscover the shards of meaning by looking elsewhere in their memories. The past is recalled differently, and a different past is constructed. In *L'Écriture ou la vie* the narrator describes an encounter, shortly after the April 1945 liberation of Buchenwald, with an American soldier of German Jewish origin. The two men discuss how the experience of the camp might be recounted, and the narrator insists that mere anecdotal, factual narratives inevitably miss the essential. Asked if he knows what the essential is, he indicates that he does; what he then goes on to suggest, though, is very different from the Communist interpretation implied over thirty years earlier in *Le Grand Voyage*: "The essential? I think I know, yes. I think I am beginning to know. The essential is to manage to go beyond the evidence of horror in order to attempt to reach the root of radical Evil, *das radikal Böse*" (p. 98).

The reference to Kant's "radical Evil" is deliberate, and it is developed further in *Le Mort qu'il faut*, where the narrator reveals that Kant's *Religion within the Limits of Reason Alone*, in which the theory of radical Evil is developed, was one of the last books he read before his capture and deportation. According to Kant, Evil is an ineradicable natural propensity, chosen by the will as one of the possible expressions of its freedom. Kant's view of Evil now replaces those of Hegel and Marx in providing the intellectual framework in which the past makes sense. This coincides with, and elucidates, the introduction of a figure previously absent from Semprun's memories: the Muselmann (Muslim), one of the prisoners who have given up on life and who survive in a form of spectral existence. *Le Mort qu'il faut* recounts how the narrator befriends, to some extent identifies with, and attempts to save one such Muslim. The absence of the Muslims earlier is explained by the fact that they do not fit with the Communists' interpretation of the camps as a site of resistance:

> The Muselmänner [Muslims] disturb him, that's the truth of the matter. By their mere existence they confuse the picture he has made of the concentrationary universe

> [*l'univers concentrationnaire*]. They contradict, even deny, the behavior which seems to him to be indispensable for survival. The Muselmänner introduce into his ideological horizon an element of elusive uncertainty because, by their very nature, their unproductive marginality, their apathy, they escape the Manichaean logic of resistance, the struggle for life, survival.
>
> The Muselmänner are beyond these notions, beyond life and survival. All our efforts to stick together, to act well, must seem incongruous to them. Even derisory. What's the point? (*Le Mort qu'il faut,* Paris: Gallimard, 2001, pp. 35–36).

The allusion to David Rousset's book *L'Univers concentrationnaire*, marks the distance Semprun has traveled from the interpretation of the camps as an expression of capitalist exploitation, as influentially proposed by Rousset. The Muselmann is presented as a blind spot in such a reading, and he calls for a new account, which Semprun finds in Kant. In this version, the camps are explained in terms of Evil and freedom rather than as the product of historical conditions; Semprun's narrator now insists that he had learned long ago the significance that has only belatedly emerged in his writing: "a year in Buchenwald had taught me concretely what Kant says, that Evil isn't inhuman but, quite to the contrary, a radical expression of human freedom" (p. 61).

Semprun has undertaken a long journey to get to this point, longer than he can have imagined when he entitled his first book *Le Grand Voyage*. Then, the sense to be ascribed to the camp experience seemed settled; but it was already dissolving, and Semprun's later works trace the shattering of the intellectual, political, and emotional supports that had initially made survival possible. His commitment to and subsequent disillusionment with Communism mirrors the rise and fall of one of the most idealistic and bloodiest political adventures of the twentieth century. His discovery of the truth about the gulags destroys the sense of the Communist struggle in Buchenwald. More recently, although the pain of memory has not disappeared, there are signs that, for Semprun at least, the sense of disarray may be overcome. Individual suffering replaces collective struggle, and human freedom appears as more important than economic and social conditions. But some factors remain constant throughout Semprun's writing: the conviction that only sophisticated literary forms are adequate to the complexity of experience and memory; and the emphasis on comradeship, on the human decency and solidarity which ensure that radical Evil is not the final word. Of course, it is inherent in Semprun's view of narrative as interminable that the final word will never be spoken. Memory is unstable and the meaning of the past is never finally fixed; even if Semprun's narrators seem to have regained confidence in the meaning of their experience, the thrust of his writing nevertheless suggests that further revision is always possible. That past may always need to be reinvented once again in the light of an ever-changing present.

Bibliography

Primary Sources

Le Grand Voyage (The Long Journey). 1963.
L'Evanouissment (The Fainting). 1967.
La Deuxième Mort de Ramón Mercader (The Second Death of Ramon Mercader). 1969.
Autobiografia de Federico Sánchez (The Autobiography of Federico Sánchez). 1977.
Quel beau dimanche! (What a Fine Sunday!). 1980.
L'Algarabie (Algarabia). 1981.
Montand, la vie continue (Montand, Life Goes On). 1983.
La Montagne blanche (The White Mountain). 1986.
Netchaïev est de retour (Netchaïev Is Back). 1987.
Federico Sánchez vous salue bien (Federico Sánchez Says Hello). 1993.
L'Écriture ou la vie (Writing or Life). 1994.
Mal et modernité (Evil and Modernity). 1995.
Se taire est impossible (To Remain Silent Is Impossible). With Elie Wiesel. 1995.
Le Retour de Carola Neher (The Return of Carola Neher). 1998.
Adieu, vive clarté . . . (Farewell, Bright Light . . .). 1998.
Le Mort qu'il faut (The Necessary Dead Man). 2001.

Secondary Sources

Caroll, David. "The Limits of Representation and the Right to Fiction: Shame, Literature, and the Memory of the *Shoah*." *Esprit créateur* 39, no. 4 (Winter 1999): 68–79.
Davis, Colin. "Understanding the Concentration Camps: Elie Wiesel's *La Nuit* and Jorge Semprun's *Quel beau dimanche!*" *Australian Journal of French Studies* 28, no. 3 (1991): 291–303.
——— and Elizabeth, Fallaize. "Recalling the Past: Jorge Semprun's *La Montagne blanche* (1986)." In *French Fiction in the Mitterrand Years: Memory, Narrative, Desire*. Oxford: Oxford University Press, 2000, pp. 61–82.
Gartland, Patricia. "Three Holocaust Writers: Speaking the Unspeakable." *Critique: Studies in Contemporary Fiction* 25, no. 1 (fall 1983): 45–56.
Johnson, Kathleen. "Narrative Revolutions / Narrative Resolutions: Jorge Semprun's *Le Grand Voyage*." *Romanic Review* 80, no. 2 (March 1989): 277–287.
King, J. H. "Jorge Semprun's Long Journey." *Australian Journal of French Studies* 10 (1973): 223–235.
Nicoladzé, Françoise. *La Deuxième Vie de Jorge Semprun: Une écriture tressée aux spirales de l'histoire*. Castelnau-le-Lez: Climats, 1997.
Silk, Sally. "The Dialogical Traveler: A Reading of Semprun's *Le Grand Voyage*." *Studies in Twentieth-Century Literature* 14, no. 2 (summer 1990): 223–240.

ALAN SHAPIRO

(1952–)

RICHARD CHESS

ALAN SHAPIRO WAS born in 1952 in Boston. He received his B.A. from Brandeis University in 1974 and was a Stegner Fellow in Poetry at Stanford University in 1975. Shapiro is the author of six books of poetry, including *After the Digging* (1981), *The Courtesy* (1983), *Happy Hour* (1987), *Covenant* (1991), *Mixed Company* (1996), and *The Dead Alive and Busy* (2000). He has also published a critical study, *In Praise of the Impure: Poetry and the Ethical Imagination* (1993), and *The Last Happy Occasion* (1996), as well as a memoir, *Vigil* (1997). He has received many prestigious awards, including two grants from the National Endowment for the Arts, a Lila Wallace-Reader's Digest Award (1991), the O. B. Hardison Jr. Poetry Prize (1999), and the Kingsley Tufts Poetry Award (2001). He teaches poetry and creative writing at the University of North Carolina at Chapel Hill.

Through study, ritual, chance meetings with survivors or children of survivors, and acts of the imagination, American Jews engage in the process of transforming the Holocaust from a catastrophic historical event that happened "over there" to personal and collective memory of an event, the impact of which continues to be felt now, here in America. We can see this process enacted in Alan Shapiro's poetry, beginning with "On the Eve of the Warsaw Uprising," published in his second book, *The Courtesy*, and continuing to "The Sanctuary," a poem published in his sixth book, *The Dead Alive and Busy.*

The Courtesy

"On the Eve of the Warsaw Uprising" (from *The Courtesy*) centers on a child's fascination with Elijah's cup, the ceremonial cup dedicated, during a Passover seder, to the prophet who, according to legend, visits Jewish homes on Passover and who, one day, will herald the coming of the Messiah. Impatient with his family's lengthy seder, the boy suddenly became attentive when the seder arrived at the dedication of Elijah's cup:

> But when that wine was poured, the door left open,
> waiting seemed almost holy: a worshipper,
> the candle flame bowed in the sudden draft.
> And for a moment I thought I'd behold
> Elijah's glad lips bend out of the dark
> to brighten and drink up into His Light
> the Red Sea in the glass
> that never parted (*The Courtesy*, Chicago: The University of Chicago Press, 1983, p. 5).

His anticipation transforms his vision: a candle that moments ago was just a candle now appears as "a worshipper." Alas, the "Red Sea" of wine never parts, the messenger never appears. To the boy's disappointment is added his confusion that no one ever asks, "Where was Elijah?"

As an adult, the point of view from which the poem is told, he comes to a new understanding of what role, if any, Elijah might play in a post-Holocaust world.

> And now I think, knowing what I know,
> if anyone had ever come to us,
> he could have come only to keep watch
> and not to drink; to look upon the glass,
> seeing within the wine, as from across
> the whole of night, the small flame still as God;
> someone who would have known the numberless
> doors that have been opened, to be closed;
> the numberless who watched till they became
> the shimmer in the wine he looked upon (p. 6).

This poem represents the coupling of the story of the Exodus with one part of the story of the Holocaust—a reference to the Warsaw Ghetto Uprising, which began on 19 April 1943, the eve of Passover. As such, the poem reflects a general movement in post-Holocaust

Jewish experience of joining the Holocaust to other catastrophic Jewish events throughout history and of including allusions to them in Jewish rituals. In this case, the Passover theme of liberation from slavery is overshadowed by the theme of Elijah's (and by implication, God's) failure to rescue the Jews from the Holocaust. In ancient Egypt, God engaged with history; in Poland, during World War II, God was disengaged from history as "the numberless . . . watched [the door awaiting sign of their redemption] till they became the shimmer in the wine he looked upon" (p. 6).

Through the practice of ritual and by means of the religious imagination, the postwar American Jew learns one facet of the Holocaust experience: God's apparent failure to save the Jews. Personal encounters with refugees or survivors are another means by which Jews of Shapiro's generation either acquire knowledge of the events of the Holocaust or encounter worldviews shaped by antisemitism. "Simon, the Barber" (from *The Courtesy*), another poem told from the point of view of an adult recalling a childhood experience, represents the encounters of a Jewish-American child coming of age in the 1960s and an older Jewish refugee from Europe. Characterized by his Yiddish-inflected English—"So? Vhat kind of haircut? I haven't got all day," the barber says to the boy—Simon looks disdainfully upon the secular world of the speaker who, as the poem informs us, is the same age as the barber's son (p. 21). Simon sees the world divided between Jews and "goyim" (Gentiles), all of whom were "Jew haters, / remember. God forbid you should forget" (p. 21). This hardened attitude toward non-Jews reflects the experiences of one who has experienced the worst expressions of antisemitism, if not in concentration camps (the poem does not indicate specifically whether Simon is a survivor) then in pogroms before the war. Ironically, in America, Simon encounters a new kind of enemy: his own son and other kids his son's age as they rebel against their parents' values:

> you were surrounded
> by enemies more dangerous than any
> you had fled—your children, your own seed;
> all that you had suffered and survived
> and learned, mere ashes in our prayer for the dead (p. 23).

As a boy, the speaker of the poem rejected the attitudes and approaches to Judaism ("mere ashes in our prayer for the dead") of men like Simon, but as an adult recalling his boyhood encounters with Simon, the speaker has come to understand and respect the "legacy" Simon passed on to him: a legacy of persecution and suffering, caution and survival.

Covenant

In his Holocaust poems, Shapiro represents well the experiences of American Jews of the postwar generation as they became aware, often as adults, of the immensity of the Holocaust. With knowledge acquired as adults, they came to perceive the subtle and sometimes profound influence the Holocaust has had and continues to have on their lives, shaping their identities as Jewish men and women. Through personal experience, religious ritual, and acts of the imagination—the religious, historical, and literary imagination—they bring the Holocaust to America. The latter is seen vividly in "Mud Dancing" (from *Covenant*), Shapiro's most sophisticated and original poem on the Holocaust.

Set at the Woodstock Music Festival in 1969, and in particular in a mud hole where naked young men and women are dancing "knee deep in mud," the poem invokes the ghosts of victims of the Holocaust who are drawn to the scene because of its familiarity, its odd and ironic similarity to a concentration camp.

> Anonymous as steam, in the steam teased
> from the mud-hole at the field's edge
> where we gathered, the unhallowed dead,
>
> the herded up, the poured out like water,
> grew curious about us (*Covenant*, Chicago: The University of Chicago Press, 1991, p. 15).

Gone is the anticipation and longing for vision expressed in "On the Eve of the Warsaw Uprising." Collapsed is the distance between the old and the young, and the old world and the new. Erased, too, is the distance among Poland, Germany, and New York State. While the poem itself is an act of imagining, the act of imagining is not represented in the poem: what was imagined now simply is; the dead of the Holocaust are present at Woodstock and they suffer what they see:

> . . . us—naked as they were
> once, our numbers so like theirs,
>
> and the air, too, a familiar newsreel
> dusk of rain all afternoon.
> It could almost have been themselves
>
> they saw (p. 15).

But unlike the victims of the Holocaust, these festival goers, "unpoliced and under no one's orders / but the wiry twang and thump / we danced to," choose to cover their bodies with mud as they attempt to overcome the limits of individuality and to achieve a "single fluency" of communal being.

Reminded of "the muddy / gestures of their" own "degradation," the ghosts of the Holocaust are confused by what they are witnessing, wondering if this is "some new phase of their affliction," "the effect of yet some new device" (p. 16).

Having absorbed its history, Shapiro is no longer free to enjoy the luxuries of his generation of American Jews—of rebellion, of idealizing free of "the shalts and shalt / nots of you and me, mine and not yours"—without considering them in the context of the Holocaust. Addressing their master, History, personified as a German matron, the victims of the Holocaust are given the final words in this poem:

Frau History, they asked, *is this the final*
reaving of what we loved well, that we should
swarm now in the steam over the indistinguishable

garments scattered everywhere in piles, that
we should need, even now, to sort through them,
to try to lift in vaporous hands

the immovable rough granite
of this sleeve or collar, that vest,
those sandals, the flimsiest top? (p. 16).

Mixed Company

The passage from childhood and adolescent innocence, Shapiro suggests in his poems, is conducted by means of the study of history. His knowledge of the history of the Holocaust enables him to understand now, as he looks back on Woodstock, Passover seders from his childhood, and childhood haircuts, what he could not understand when he first had those experiences. Similarly, when he now thinks back on his childhood friend Gary, as he does in "The Basement" (from *Mixed Company*), he finds himself more interested in Gary's nanny Helen, "the only German Jew I knew," than he is in his old friend. Helen, the speaker of the poem realizes, serves as his "personal link to what [he] can't imagine" (*Mixed Company*, Chicago: The University of Chicago Press, 1996, p. 67).

The speaker of "The Basement" recalls Helen's accented English—"can I get you zumzing, Gary, you vant zumzing now"—and how his friend Gary mocked her by calling her Zumzing (p. 65). But, either "unmindful of the teasing, or inured to it," Helen stood ready to serve and please Gary no matter how he treated her (p. 65). Even as a boy, the speaker sensed that Helen seemed "strangely dour, / joyless, like someone on indefinite probation for some crime / nothing she could ever do could quite make up for" (*Mixed Company*, p. 65).

Among the games they played—the three of them—in Gary's basement, was one of prisoners and guards, the goal of which was for the prisoner to storm the gate and break free, and another in which one child was "buried under cushions" for a period until he roared back to life. Later in his life, the speaker would read about the children's games in the ghettoes and camps—role-playing Germans and Jews. Realizing only many years later that Helen, during the war, would have been about the age of Gary and the speaker when they played these games, the speaker senses that Helen's perceptions of the games must have been radically different from their own: "I wonder now what she was seeing, or / wanted to see as she looked on, waiting until the play / got too rough" (pp. 66–67). Rather than imagining what Helen's life was like in a ghetto or a camp, Shapiro tries to imagine how she perceived and experienced life after the Holocaust in America.

This leads to further speculation on the motives for Helen's apparent acts of kindness to Gary—was she spoiling him or using him as "her puppet of a secret brooding on what couldn't be forgotten" (p. 67). The fact that these speculations are presented in the form of questions implies that there are limits to what one can, finally, know about the Holocaust and the experiences of its victims and survivors. But the conclusion of the poem, in which the speaker recalls the pleasure Helen took in watching Gary and the speaker, bored after a period of playing with model trains, "rampage" over and pull apart the replicas of German stations (Stuttgart, Munchen, Wurzburg, Berlin) through which Gary's toy trains passed, leaves no doubt as to the speaker's understanding of Helen's pleasure: through their play, the boys were enacting Helen's own revenge fantasy.

The Dead Alive and Busy

In "The Basement" Shapiro attempts to understand the psychology of the survivor. In "The Sanctuary," a poem in *The Dead Alive and Busy*, Shapiro represents a rescue fantasy, a fantasy represented in other Holocaust poems written by American Jewish poets. In "The Sanctuary" we see Shapiro again bringing the Holocaust home by comparing the speaker's aging father to a prisoner in a concentration camp. Alluding to a story he read "somewhere in a book about the camps," Shapiro describes a prisoner who "every morning, till his final morning," went through the routine of bathing himself but using only "imagined water / flowing from an imaginary tap" (*The Dead*

Alive and Busy, Chicago: The University of Chicago Press, 2000, p. 18). Similarly, the speaker's aging father goes through the nightly routine of eating dinner but, because his "palsied hand" shakes so much, by the time the fork reaches his mouth there is nothing on it. Thus, he eats mostly "air for dinner" (p. 18). Both men persist in their seemingly futile activities.

As he informs us in the poem, the speaker is composing the poem itself, the creation of a "kind of sanctuary," a place where the prisoner's and the father's "bodies in the motion of a dream / of normalcy are held, preserved, protected" (p. 19). Unlike the worlds in which they actually dwell, in this "sanctuary" the prisoner bathing with "imagined water" and the aging father consuming "phantom food" are "subservient" only "to the rules of grammar." Thus Shapiro replaces the rules of the Nazis and the rules of nature with the more civilized, less harmful rules of grammar. In doing so, Shapiro implicitly offers one response to Adorno's often-cited statement that after Auschwitz, there can be no poetry. What are the purposes of poetry after Auschwitz? One purpose, as witnessed in this and the other poems we have considered, is to link personal experience—the subject of many contemporary American poems—to historical events. Another is to create a place of refuge, a sanctuary, where "bad as it surely is" in the world, for the moment of the poem "it can't get worse" (p. 19).

Bibliography

Primary Sources

After the Digging. 1981.
The Courtesy. 1983.
Happy Hour. 1987.
Covenant. 1991.
In Praise of the Impure: Poetry and the Ethical Imagination: Essays, 1980–1991. 1993.
Mixed Company. 1996.
The Last Happy Occasion. 1996.
Vigil. 1997.
The Dead Alive and Busy. 2000.
Song and Dance: Poems. 2001.

Secondary Sources

Hadas, Rachel. "Three Lives." *Yale Review* 85, no. 3 (July 1997): 119–128.

Ingalls, Zoe. "Up against Pain and Loss, a Poet Goes One-on-One with a God." *The Chronicle of Higher Education* 47, no. 42 (29 June 2001): A48.

Pinsky, Robert. "Tidings of Comfort and Dread: Poetry and the Dark Beauty of Christmas." *New York Times Book Review* (4 December 1994): 37.

SIMKHA-BUNIM SHAYEVITCH

(1907–1944)

GOLDIE MORGENTALER

THE NAME AND literary accomplishments of Simkha-Bunim Shayevitch, the great poet of the Lodz ghetto, would have been totally lost to history were it not for the fact that after the war, two of his poems and two of his letters were found in the rubble of what was left of the ghetto. These two poems, "Lekh-lekho" and "Spring 1942" constitute the only remaining legacy of this supremely gifted poet.

Early Life

Shayevitch was born in 1907 in Lenczyce, a small town near Lodz in central Poland. The only son in an impoverished family of nine children, he was ordained a rabbi, but never practiced. When Shayevitch's family moved from Lenczyce to Lodz, he joined them and found work in a textile factory. Although deeply attached to his pious family, Shayevitch felt the pull of secular culture, which caused a painful rift with his orthodox parents. To help patch over this rift, Shayevitch continued to wear Hasidic clothing until the outbreak of World War II. His outmoded dress and extreme shyness are often noted in the accounts of those who knew him before the war.

Shayevitch began his writing career with a novel called *The American*, published in the mid-1930s. Another novel, *On the Road to Blenkitna*, was due to be published by the Yiddish PEN club on the very eve of the war. It never appeared. After the German invasion of Poland, Shayevitch moved with his wife and daughter into a one-room dwelling in the Lodz ghetto. His parents and sisters found lodging nearby. With no means of support he lived under the constant threat of starvation, his worries divided between caring for his own family and for his parents and sisters. Until the beginning of 1941, he and his dependents lived on handouts from the Jewish ghetto administration, which he badgered with letters begging for help. At length, he was given the job of janitor at the place where vegetable rations were distributed to the ghetto population. This job permitted him to write in the intervals between work.

Patronage was a way of life in the ghetto and nothing better expresses the torment of Shayevitch's position than the letters he wrote to a Mr. Sh. (full name unknown) Rosenstein, a functionary of the Jewish ghetto government. Two of these letters from late 1941 survived the war. There Shayevitch writes: "In the month of Sivan my father died, and after thirty days so did my mother. Now I am forced to watch my five-year old daughter and my wife waste away" (*Lekh-lekho*, edited by Nachman Blumenthal, Lodz: Central Jewish Historical Commission, 1946, p. 23). In another letter he pleads: "Please trust the possibilities that lie dormant within me. Play for me the role of the High Priest who enters the Holy of Holies to kindle the flame of the menorah."

"Lekh-lekho"

By the end of 1941, the situation in the ghetto had worsened. One by one Shayevitch lost the members of his family to hunger and disease. That winter, too, mass deportations started from the ghetto. It was then that Shayevitch put aside the long verse epic he was working on and wrote "Lekh-lekho" (Go Forth), taking the title from the biblical injunction of God to Abraham. "Lekh-lekho" is addressed to the poet's five-year-old daughter, Blimele.

Treating its title with tragic irony, "Lekh-lekho" evokes biblical episodes as a way of comparing the traditional Jewish past with the tragic historical present, for instance, in this description of the deportations (all verse translations by Goldie Morgentaler):

But for this present catastrophe
There is no Jeremiah to cry his lamentation.
He does not accompany his people into exile
To console them, as once he did by the rivers of Babylon (p. 35).

"Lekh-lekho" is full of homey details, of the father telling his daughter what to pack for the journey, including soap for washing her shirt and a special comb for delousing. He lists all the things they will have to leave behind, including the poems he has not yet finished writing. Occasionally, bitterness overwhelms the father, as when he speaks of his beloved Yiddish authors, then suggests the fate that awaits them when the pages of their books will be used as toilet paper by those who remain behind.

By the end of the poem, Shayevitch makes explicit the comparison to the biblical "lekh-lekho" where God enjoined Abraham to go forth and enter the land that He would show him and there He would make of him a great nation. "And now," says the poet, "must this great nation indeed go forth on its unknown, far off way / Sick and tired—broken vessels / That cannot find a shore" (p. 42). Despite this the poem ends on a note of hope:

Although under our steps is death,
Above our heads hovers the emanation of God.
So, child, let us go out with a new readiness for sacrifice
And with the old name of the one God (p. 45).

"Spring 1942"

"Lekh-lekho" was written in February 1942. Shayevitch returned to the theme of expulsion a few months later in "Spring 1942," which is in many ways a darker continuation of "Lekh-lekho." Both poems were written at a time when it was not yet clear where the mass deportations were leading, but Shayevitch sensed that they were death sentences. In "Spring 1942" he contrasts the hopeful onset of spring with the horrors of ghetto life, and especially with the deportations of April 1942. Written on Passover eve, the poem is divided into ten sections, each of which begins like an incantation with the phrase, "And in an hour of good fortune / Spring is here again—"(*Lekh-lekho*, pp. 51–62).

The poem is written in blank verse and takes the form of a psalmodic chant. Shayevitch is constantly plagued by the question of why God sentenced the Jews to death, but where "Lekh-lekho" ended with hope, "Spring 1942" ends with a call for revenge against those who slaughtered an innocent people. Both "Spring 1942" and "Lekh-lekho" describe the poet's ambivalent and complex reaction to God, a reaction that swings from humility to open revolt, from faith and hope to utter resignation.

Not long after Shayevitch finished his poems, Rosenstein managed to find him a position in the gas kitchen, where the ghetto inhabitants went to cook their rations. By way of thanks, Shayevitch gave Rosenstein the two poems, "Lekh-lekho" and "Spring 1942," thereby unwittingly ensuring their survival after the war.

Later Life

Shayevitch lost his wife and children during the Sperre (house arrest) that took place in the ghetto in September 1942. The Sperre was supposed to result in the deportation of children under ten and of the elderly, although in fact the Germans took whomever they pleased. Shayevitch's wife had just given birth to a son. Desperate for food, Shayevitch left his family one morning to get rations. He returned to find the door open, his wife and children gone.

The Yiddish novelist, Chava Rosenfarb, met Shayevitch in the ghetto shortly after he lost his wife and children. It was to her that he read aloud sections of his unpublished long verse poem about the Lodz ghetto, which he never finished. Chapters 23 and 24 of this poem described the deportation of Shayevitch's wife and children and were written in 1943, a year after the event. Shayevitch wrote other poems during his incarceration in the ghetto, all of which have been lost. One of these, "Israel Noble," told of a young man who is caught trying to escape from the ghetto. The poem was intended as a composite portrait of the brave souls who had attempted to escape. Those who failed were hanged in the public square, while the rest of the ghetto inhabitants were forced to look on.

When rumors circulated that the Lodz ghetto was to be liquidated, Shayevitch organized a hiding place in the apartment of Chava Rosenfarb's parents. There, a group of nine people hid for three days. On 28 August 1944 they were discovered and transported to Auschwitz. At Auschwitz the bag containing Shayevitch's manuscripts was torn from his hands. From Auschwitz, Shayevitch was transported to the concentration camp at Kaufering, near Dachau. He continued to compose poems even in the camps. He was among the last group of inmates sent to the gas chamber.

The two poems and two letters that Shayevitch sent to Rosenstein were published after the war by the Jewish Historical Commission in *Lekh-lekho*. This small paperback also reproduces Shayevitch's handwritten manuscript. The two poems were written in columns on both sides of a book-keeping ledger.

Shayevitch's influence on Yiddish writers after the war was considerable, despite the meagerness of his output, and there are several Yiddish commentators on his work. Unfortunately, he is less well known to an English-speaking readership, although sections of his poems have appeared in English translation. In *Against the Apocalypse*, David Roskies classifies "Lekh-lekho" as "an unmistakably modern response to catastrophe, in which the oldest and newest strata of Jewish culture come together in a ragged formation of humanism and transcendental faith, artistic self-awareness and the intimacy of prayer" (p. 217).

Bibliography

Primary Sources

Lekh-lekho (Go Forth). Edited by Nachman Blumenthal. Lodz: Central Jewish Historical Commission, 1946.

Shayevitch's poems can be found in *Truth and Lamentation: Stories and Poems on the Holocaust*, Urbana: University of Illinois Press, 1994; and *The Golden Peacock: A Worldwide Treasury of Yiddish Poetry*. Edited by Joseph Leftwich. New York: T. Yoseloff, 1961.

Secondary Sources

Blumenthal, Nachman. Introduction and Notes to *Lekh-lekho*, by Simka-Bunim Shayevitch. Lodz: Central Jewish Historical Commission, 1946.

Fuchs, Chaim Leib. *Lodsh shel maleh: dos yidishe geistige un derhoybene lodsh*. Tel Aviv: Y. L. Peretz, 1972.

Goldkorn, Itzhak. "Simkha-Bumin Shayevitsh." In *Lodsher portretn: umgekumene yidishe shreyber un tipn*. Tel Aviv: Hamenorah, 1963.

Mark, Ber. *Di umgekumene shreyber fun di getos un lagern un zayere verk*. Warsaw: Yidish Bukh Farlag, 1954.

Rosenfarb, Chava. "A videh fun a mekhaber." *Di goldene keit* 81 (1973): 127–141.

Roskies, David G. *Against the Apocalypse*. Cambridge: Harvard University Press, 1984.

Singer, S. D. "Simkha-Bunim Shayevitch." *Undzer veg* 39, no. 4 (April 1966): 12–14.

ARANKA SIEGAL

(1930–)

TOBE LEVIN

ON 9 MAY 1944, the cattle car delivered Rise Rosner Davidowitz, Aranka Siegal's mother, to the platform in Auschwitz-Birkenau. When the baton signaled to the right to life, with daughters Piri, Siegal's nickname (thirteen) and Iboya (sixteen), she chose the left. Scooping up Joli (three) and taking Sandor (six) by the hand, she told an astonished SS, "They need me more." To the girls, "she said, Be brave and look after each other" (Siegal; Farrar, Straus & Giroux, p. 70). Of this gesture, Siegal writes in her book, *Grace in the Wilderness: After Liberation 1945–1948*, "It was her last act as our mother, setting an example to last us a lifetime" (Siegal, p. 70).

A half century later, Siegal (born on 10 June 1930 in Beregszász, Hungary), the fifth of her mother's seven children, and her sister Iboya remain together in Aventura, Florida. Only three of the children survived. Etu, Siegal's sister, made it on false papers and now lives in Israel. On 19 April 1945, after the two youngest suffered Auschwitz-Birkenau, Christianstadt (a labor sub-camp of Gross-Rosen), and a death march to Bergen-Belsen, Marshal Montgomery's first army rescued them.

The Swedish Red Cross had brought the children to Hälsingborg where Swedish kindness permitted some wounds to heal. First placed in a school to compensate for their interrupted education, the refugees later went out on their own, supporting themselves as factory workers. "Adopted" by a Swedish couple, Siegal dated a gentile Swede but tore herself away to remain with Iboya and to join relatives in the United States.

Eventually, Siegal entered college at the State University of New York at Purchase. Here Siegal earned a B.A. in social anthropology. Later, with her husband, Gilbert, she raised a son and daughter in Hartsdale, New York. A Holocaust educator for thirty years, she gives seminars for teachers, as well as television and radio interviews.

Her two books answer a pressing emotional need, to inform future generations. *Upon the Head of the Goat: A Childhood in Hungary 1939–1944* (1981) speaks with a young girl's voice, but it details Hungary's increasingly severe anti-Jewish measures, including expropriation, ghettoization, and deportation. *Grace in the Wilderness* (1985) flashes back to camp experience, while foregrounding re-entry into a teen's "normal" life with its concerns for acceptance and romance.

Upon the Head of the Goat

A Newbery Honor Book, *Upon the Head of the Goat* earned the Boston Globe-Horn nonfiction award, the B'nai Brith Janusz Korczak Award, as well as enthusiastic endorsement from Nobel Laureate Isaac Bashevis Singer. Organized in three sections according to geographic venue, Komjaty, Beregszász, and The Ghetto, its major themes include: the application of increasingly repressive legislation in Hungary; that nation's subjection to lightning implementation of the Final Solution in springtime 1944; generations' differing perceptions of nationality and assimilation; Jewish identity related to passing as Christian; resistance including an "underground railroad" and Zionist forgery; emotional ties to family; and, above all, gendered Holocaust experience.

Mrs. Davidowitz's—Siegal's mother—hometown, Komjaty, in disputed Ukrainian territory, is where Siegal spent her summers as a child. It is here that she keeps her pious but realistic grandmother, Babi, company. A speaker of Hungarian, Ukrainian, and Yiddish, Siegal as the child-narrator, Piri, nine years old in 1939, begins her memoir during a battle between Hungary and Ukrainian resistance fighters. Receiving her first taste of war while playing, she stumbles upon soldiers' bodies in the Rika, which reminds her of the fate of men. Would this be her little brother's, her stepfather's end? The irony here lies in this gesture toward the conceivable violence among males. Unthinkable is Nazi brutality toward females, though the majority of rural and small town Hungarians murdered in 1944 were women and children, able-bodied Jewish men having been conscripted into labor battalions long before.

The domestic side of wartime deprivation, most insidious for Jewish households, comprises a theme throughout *Upon the Head of a Goat.* In Komjaty, Babi is presented as hard-working and self-supporting. In a poignant scene, she is depicted as the antithesis of Nazi anti-Jewish propaganda that she and a friend find in Babi's newspaper. As they try to sound out "rounding up" and "slave labor," "Kamenets-Podolski" and "Novi Sad," they know they are reading about Poland, where Hitler is. "Who is Hitler?" Molcha asks. "Babi says . . . a madman . . . turning everybody against the Jews." "Why?" "It says here that we are bad risks and eat up too much of the bread. We cause bread shortages." "But we only eat our own bread, so how can we cause a shortage?" "I don't know" (Siegal, New American Library, p. 14). Evidence of housewives' industrious self-sufficiency renders the charge of Jewish parasitism incomprehensible to the girls. The scapegoat theory of the memoir's title can offer the only explanation but has its own ironic twist. The biblical animal expiated Hebrew sins; the Nazis and their accomplices used Jews to service theirs.

Babi, who refuses to leave, despite the urgings of her children in America, encourages Rise, Siegal's mother, to send the girls there. After Piri has returned to Beregszász, Babi sells her land, but it is too late: passage cannot be booked. "Only your own can feel your pain" (Siegal, p. 26), Babi warns Rise, who, like Piri, argues first that assimilation into Hungary's multicultural society has been successful. "In Beregszász I . . . did not choose my friends or separate them by religion. On our street lived Hungarian, Czechoslovak, Russian, and Jewish families. My mother was friendly with all of them." But segregation follows, proving Babi right. The answer to Piri's question—"pogroms, scapegoats—was this what being a Jew meant?" (Siegal, p. 12)—seems to be "yes."

Typical of her age, Piri worries, on returning after a year in Komjaty, that social conditions will have changed, her playmates will now be distant because she's Jewish. Soon, in fact, friends invite the sisters to go caroling, as they have done every year, but Rise's head-shake sends the neighbors scurrying, and no other singers come. Mrs. Davidowitz, Siegal's mother, defines a ghetto as "a place for people who have been separated from the rest of the community" (Siegal, p. 118). This disengagement proceeds, occasionally with subtlety, as neighbors no longer chat over the back fence, and, at other times, with violence. Called "Dumb Jew bitches" (Siegal, p. 45), Piri and Iboya are pursued by rowdies. It is the spring of 1941.

In 1942, refugees begin spilling into Beregszász. The Davidowitzs sneak the lost souls over to Mrs. Silverman's, often with the warning, "Take off your headscarf and try not to look Jewish" (Siegal, p. 55). As Piri notes: "I learned to recognize them from a distance. Most . . . were women, some older, some young. . . . Their bodies drawn in almost to a curl, they moved fast, yet hesitated . . . scanning the space around them. Sometimes they asked me for help and sometimes I . . . whispered swiftly in Yiddish, 'Follow me at ten paces behind, and I will take you to shelter' " (Siegal, p. 56).

Iboya, too, does rescue work, smuggling escapees under a tarpaulin when transporting one-armed Mr. Schwartz's fish, while another relative, Aunt Luiza, forges documents for the Zionist underground. Discovered by the Gestapo, which punishes entire families, Luiza throws herself under an oncoming train. Violence also visits Dr. Feher, who is driven to suicide by the rape of his wife and daughter, the rapes resulting from the pro-Nazi Hungarians flexing their muscles in early 1944.

The passage delineating a woman's response to imminent ghettoization deserves lengthy quotation:

> Mother turned her flour sack upside down to bake the last . . . bread. "I am not going . . . to save the growing yeast for the next baking," she said. "There is no next. . . . [For] who will be here to bake bread?" I had once asked Mother about the neat little ball of dough she always saved . . . tucked inside a flowered tin box for the following Friday ['s baking]. She had answered, " . . . when I first moved to Beregszász [my] mother gave me . . . her growing yeast to take with me. She got her original ball of dough from her mother. This way the bread we bake stays the same for generations." "Are you going to give me a ball of the dough when I get married?" I asked.
> "Of course," she had answered. (Siegal, pp. 120–121)

" 'Bread mildews, but toast keeps' " (Siegal, p. 121). Rise turns her last slices into zwieback, her ingenuity having been previously shown when she purchased a sheep to provide milk and cheese. But a neighbor alerts the police, and those who come to confiscate the ewe walk off with the radio, too.

Among the recurrent themes in Holocaust memoirs are those Siegal treats exposing a policy of expropriation of Jewish property and the danger of denunciation faced by Jews passing as Christians. In the first instance, she links Nazi theft with the economic advantage of Jewish victimization to non-Jewish countrymen. Not only do the occupying Germans demand twenty thousand pengö for release of elders held captive in the synagogue, but Rise discovers the garnet earrings, which she had given her daughter Lilli, in a strange Polish woman's ears. The theme of passing appears when Rise, disguised as Christian, finds that Lilli's Jewish behavior has betrayed her. When she is summoned to Poland to rescue her granddaughter, Rise braves the hostile public only to learn that her daughter Lilli had endangered her Christian persona when she innocently "cracked the egg on the edge of the bowl and carefully pulled the shell apart to examine the yolk for bloodspots. She poured it from one half shell to the other before scrambling it, never realizing that only a Jewish woman does that" (Siegal, p. 81). The Polish hosts, now aware of harboring a Jewish family, ask them to leave immediately. A payoff brings only a single night's reprieve. That such an apparently minor gesture could lead to discovery and deportation suggests the cultural difficulty Jews in open hiding encountered every moment of their fugitive existence.

Housed within the roofless walls of a brick factory, made to sleep on damp ground, and fed stale bread, the Jews of Beregszász endure for less than two weeks before their transport to Auschwitz on 9 May 1944. Despite the compression of time, however, mortification, resourcefulness, and resistance characterize ghetto experience, as well as Rise's resilience in defeat. Happy that her family is still intact, she resumes the tasks of daily life whose increasing scarcity challenges her ingenuity. An artist at "making do," Piri's mother dramatically illustrates her skill, demanding and achieving some improvements even in the ghetto.

Emblematic of the humiliation visited upon the Jews and suggestive of the excremental environment of the concentration camp universe is the presence of open latrines in full view of the roads and guards, the restricted access to water, and the enforced idleness, which occasioned Rise to protest to the Judenrat, "These are people, not cattle. If they can't do anything for themselves . . . they will soon turn into just what the Germans want to believe we are—dirty vermin" (Siegal, p. 135). Demanding outhouse walls and the means to keep clean, Rise suggests, "Scare them, if necessary; tell them that if an epidemic of typhus breaks out, it will spread to the city" (Siegal, p. 141).

As Rise challenges with arguments, the few men of appropriate age discuss armed resistance. Aware of the overwhelming odds, however, they can accomplish little. The young people, meanwhile, do what young people do, they meet and date. Though only thirteen, Piri goes with Henri in the ghetto, snatching her first taste of love. The fact that he appears on the loading ramp only four meters away makes the final humiliation even more intolerable: the "leering German," with "sausagy breath," tobacco-stained teeth, and an "iron grip" on Piri's neck reaches "into [her] bloomers and [feels] inside [her] private parts" (Siegal, p. 183). Then they board.

Grace in the Wilderness

The closing scene from Siegal's first book recurs, as a flashback, in her second book *Grace in the Wilderness*. In Sweden, a flirtatious young man has just tried out his beer-infested German: " 'Ich liebe dich, Fräulein' " (Siegal, p. 206), evoking "a frightened little girl about to be loaded onto a train to Auschwitz. A crude man not much older than Hasse, speaking German and reeking of sausage and beer, . . . searched her private parts and laughed at her shame" (Siegal, p. 207).

Despite considerable treatment of survivor trauma, *Grace in the Wilderness* opens within hours of rescue and thereafter relegates horror to the crevices of the mind. The Auschwitz experience is not directly dramatized but rather intrudes on a seemingly smooth return to "normalcy" which, however, must be continually wrested from recurring nightmares, reservoirs of distrust, isolation, and difference, even among the "generous Swedish people" to whom the text is dedicated. For the most part, Piri takes pleasure in her adopted family, her relationship to a boyfriend, and her rapport with young people, despite the chasm separating her recent experience from theirs.

Under the sign of hope, three themes stand out: the miracle of survival, the purpose of survival, and the exercise of choice, even in the jaws of hell. The "miracle" (Siegal's word) was effected by Mrs. Berger, Rise's friend from Beregszász, who, in a flashback, happened to be returning from "Canada," the camp warehouse of confiscated prisoner property, just as Iboya, without Piri, was chosen for transport to Christianstadt. "Mrs. Berger looked around and . . . with one hand . . . pulled a crying mother out of the transport and deposited her back with her daughter, while with [the] other . . . she swung [Piri] over into the moving line" (Siegal, p. 68). Survival often depended on sisters (real or camp) remaining together; in Sweden, Iboya insists, "Mrs. Berger's presence was more than chance. She was sent to spare you . . . [by someone] like Mother . . . [who] watches over us. I . . . believe that" (Siegal, p. 68).

Life's blessings overwhelm Iboya during a summer in the countryside, where inhabitants are "not too different from the farmers in Komjaty" (Siegal, p. 66), inspiring her to feel "grateful that at least two of us survived and that we have each other. Now it is up to us to do something worthwhile with our lives, something to count for having been spared" (Siegal, p. 67).

Reception

Like the best memoirists, Siegal feeds detail to memory, including minutiae "of daily life that the more massive, historical accounts of the Holocaust omit" (Lisagor, *Philadelphia Inquirer*). As a reviewer at the *Minneapolis Tribune* notes, "Piri's days [hit readers] with an impact that six millions' summarized [martyrdom] always lacks," and Jean Strouse in *Newsweek* adds, "you [sense] the power . . . of particular experience." A writer for the *New York Times* agrees. Reflecting a favorable broad reception for both books, Betsy Hearne praises the second volume's focus on the teen survivor who expresses "the feelings Anne Frank never lived to enter in her diary" (Hearne).

Critics highlight the gendered dimension. Impressive to a writer for *Newsweek*, for instance, is Mrs. Davidowitz, who, on arrival of the Germans, teaches "her girls to make themselves look old and ugly. ('What does violation mean?' [Piri asks.])." Yet "resiliency of the human spirit" (*Kirkus*) is what most reviewers see as the author's prime achievement. Of the debut work, a critic for the *Baltimore Sun* writes, "It is not without hope—and therein lies its strength," true, in fact, for both of Siegal's books.

Bibliography

Primary Sources

Upon the Head of the Goat: A Childhood in Hungary 1939–1944. 1981.

Grace in the Wilderness: After the Liberation 1945–1948. 1985.

Secondary Sources

Review of *Upon the Head of the Goat*. *The Baltimore Sun*.

Hearne, Betsy. Review of *Grace in the Wilderness: After the Liberation 1945-1948*. *New York Times Book Review*, December 8, 1985.

Review of *Grace in the Wilderness: After the Liberation 1945-1948*, *Kirkus Review*.

Lisagor, Nancy. Review of *Upon the Head of the Goat*. *Philadelphia Inquirer*, January 24, 1982: 11–M.

Review of *Upon the Head of the Goat*. *Minneapolis Tribune*.

Strouse, Jean. "In the Wilderness." *Newsweek*, January 18, 1982.

Isaac Bashevis Singer

(1904–1991)

S. LILLIAN KREMER

Brought to the attention of the English reading public through Saul Bellow's translation of "Gimpel, the Fool," Nobel Laureate Isaac Bashevis Singer, was born in Poland in 1904 to Pinhos Mendel, a Hasidic rabbi and his wife, Bathsheba Zylberman Singer, a descendent of a non-Hasidic Orthodox rabbinic line. Singer had a traditional Judaic education, but influenced by his older brother, the writer Israel Joshua Singer, he left the rabbinical life for the world of modern Yiddish literature. In Warsaw he worked as a translator and proofreader for *Literarische Bletter*, a Yiddish literary magazine that published his first stories. He was enthralled by the literary ambiance of Warsaw, then the center of Yiddish literary life, and following a brief venture in Hebrew, dedicated himself to write exclusively in Yiddish. In 1932 he became editor of *Globus*, a Yiddish literary journal that serialized his first novel, *Satan in Goray* (1935).

By the mid-1930s, family and public events including the rise of Nazism caused Singer to immigrate to the United States where he joined his brother. There, he started to write for the Yiddish daily, *The Forward*, in which he presented serious fiction under his own name and journalism under the pen names Varshofsky (Warshafsky)—("The Man from Warsaw") and D. Segal (Hadda, p. 349). *The Forward* published most of Singer's stories and serialized his novels before their publication in book form and translation into English and other languages. In a prolific career, Singer produced a series of novels delineating the history and lives of Polish Jewry from the sixteenth- through the twentieth-centuries.

Although he did not experience the Holocaust directly, as did most of his family, the *Shoah* is an ever-present motif in much of his fiction as is the eastern European Jewish life destroyed in the Holocaust. He memorializes and honors those who perished in the ghettos and camps; keeps their Yiddish language vibrant, their traditions and customs accessible, and reminds the world of their suffering.

Gathering Storm

Singer's work offers sustained presentation of the causal relationship of traditional Christian antisemitism and Nazism, evocation of earlier diasporan catastrophes as "so many announcements of the Holocaust, of which they are prototypes" (Alexander, *Resonance of Dust*, pp. 149–50), and thorough exploration of survivor trauma and theological implications of the Holocaust for religious and secular Jews. An early novel, *The Family Moskat* (1950), correlates family history with historic events, traces Polish Jewry's encounter with modernity, and concludes with the last peacetime Passover and a graphic rendition of the German bombardment of Warsaw. Singer's prose creates powerful visual images of homes, shops, and factories ablaze, their contents strewn wildly about the streets. The imagery charts the abrupt shift from ordinary domestic life to the horrors of war, from the losses sustained by individuals to the collective loss of the city.

Survivors

Like many authors writing in the aftermath of the *Shoah*, Singer avoids representation of the Holocaust universe. Although significant portions of the past reach his readers via the mediating and interpretive filter of his narrators' response to their subjects, Singer's primary subject is the difficulty of survival after the Holocaust. Singer's focus is how to live with the knowledge of the *Shoah* and the consequences of survival, how to be a Jew in the post-Auschwitz age. *Enemies, A Love Story* (1966), Singer's first published novel set in America, focuses on a community of Holocaust survivors, sharply schematizing characters according to their survival traumas. Herman Broder was a fugitive suffering deprivations and anxieties as a hidden Jew, but avoiding the extremities of ghettos, camps, and crematoria that marked the fate of his fellow Polish Jews. Broder, his wives, and a supporting émigré cast of semi-ghosts enact diverse philosophic, social, and psychological versions of survival "as if they were now the central bearers of Jewish fate and as if the definition and resolution of the ultimate questions of philosophy, politics, and religion can never again be made without reference to their experience" (Alexander, *Isaac Bashevis Singer*, p. 99).

Broder's postwar private life is Holocaust-determined; his public life is Holocaust-haunted. Concluding that the Nazis killed his wife and children, Broder expresses his gratitude to his wartime benefactor by marrying her, but insists on a childless marriage, believing it is irrational to have children in a world where innocents are subject to Nazi brutality. He alternately envisages their American home as a prewar paradise and as a wartime shelter. Yadwiga shares her husband's postwar obsession, reenacting her role as protector. Because Broder has nothing in common with the woman who had been his family's servant, he becomes embroiled in an extramarital affair with Masha, a woman with whom he formed a romantic liaison in a Displaced Persons Camp. Masha's feigned pregnancy resulting in a bigamous marriage, followed by the sudden appearance of Tamara, Broder's first wife, who had escaped from a mass grave where she and her children were left for dead, heighten the Holocaust-wrought tensions Broder is already experiencing.

Broder remains psychologically trapped in his Polish hayloft, his survival marred by Holocaust memories, disorientation, and recurrent bouts of terror approximating wartime anxiety. The survivor is haunted by recollections of hunger and thirst, numbness in his hands and feet, high fevers induced by insect and rodent bites, and lengthy deprivations of daylight—the elements that characterized three years of confinement in a hayloft. Guilty for having escaped the degradation and brutality of incarceration suffered by fellow Jews, Broder fashions an American life that is an equivalent for the war; "he creates situations so absurdly painful, so anxiety-ridden, so oppressive, that vicariously he experiences in New York what he has missed in Europe" (Gittleman, p. 312).

Characteristic of Broder's post-Holocaust trauma is his continuing fear of capture by Nazis and rage against a world that has failed to bring war criminals to justice, a world impervious to victims but rebuilding Germany. Perpetually searching for sanctuary, he studies urban streets to memorize the land "as if America were destined for the same destruction as Poland" (*Enemies, A Love Story*, Farrar, Straus & Giroux, 1972, p. 133) and plans how to make his Coney Island apartment a more comfortable and secure hiding place than was his Polish hayloft. Broder's revenge fantasies are fueled as the surviving remnant suffer, ignored by the nations that acquiesced to their earlier persecution, while the builders of gas chambers and industrialists who worked millions of slave laborers to death thrive and neo-Nazism is on the rise in Germany and America.

Masha, Broder's Holocaust soul mate, expands the novel's Holocaust exposition and the spectrum of Holocaust response. Weighing only seventy-two pounds at liberation, her face permanently bayonet-scarred, Masha's physical condition is emblematic of her battered psyche. Emotionally incapacitated and existentially directed by Holocaust experience, Masha attributes her postwar physical lethargy and psychological paralysis to concentration camp conditioning. She plays *Shoah* Scheherazade for Broder with stories from ghetto, camp, and postwar Polish ruins to satiate his psychic need for vicarious Holocaust suffering.

At the Edge of the Abyss and Beyond

Shosha (1978) is Singer's transition Holocaust novel that reiterates the Holocaust eve themes of *The Family Moskat* and introduces a new mediating voice, Aaron Griedinger, the autobiographical narrator-protagonist. It is through his recollection of prewar orthodox and secular intellectuals and literati—most doomed to the crematoria and lime pits—and post-*Shoah* accommodation that readers understand the dynamics of survival. The epilogue, set in Israel thirteen years following the *Shoah*, is an elegy for Polish Jewry and dialogue on post-Holocaust Jewish sensibility. Survivors confide their Holocaust histories and postwar observations of survivor life and tribulations to the now successful Yiddish writer, either as comment on the authenticity of his writing or expecting that he will write their stories. Consistent with Singer's pattern of approaching and transcending the abyss, silence prevails between the announcement of the anticipated German invasion of Poland and the epilogue. Singer relies on his readers to know the Holocaust history that shapes the postwar persona.

Although Singer does not suggest a direct connection between the Holocaust and political establishment of the State of Israel, the epilogue considers post-

Auschwitz Jewish identity and prevailing contrasts between the European and Israeli attitudes toward Jewish self-defense. In conversation with the narrator, Haiml, one of the old Warsaw friends attributes the change in Jewish sensibility to the Holocaust and Zionism's determination that Jews face their aggressors with armed resistance: "here no one went like a sheep to the slaughter. Our lads from Warsaw, Lodz, Rawa Ruska, and Minsk suddenly turned into heroes like the fighters in the time of Masada" (*Shosha*, translated by Joseph Singer and Isaac Bashevis Singer, Farrar, Straus & Giroux, 1978, p. 265). Israelis and Holocaust survivors recognize that although antisemitism endures, the historic Jewish pattern of passive resistance does not.

Singer's Israel is a land of survivors. Like the American survivors of his earlier fiction, the survivors residing in Israel continue to suffer physical and psychological Holocaust wounds. Haiml, too, lives with memories of Holocaust loss, even while taking pride in the new assertive Jew. Anticipating a theme that has since materialized in second- and third-generation Holocaust literature, Singer's new Israeli articulates doubts that the victim generation and its children will recover without scars, and puts his hope in future generations: "Perhaps their grandchildren will be normal if the Almighty doesn't send a new catastrophe down upon us" (*Shosha*, p. 274).

Shoah Incomprehensibility: Failed Dialogue

In two short stories, "The Mentor" (from *A Friend of Kafka and Other Stories*, 1970), set in Israel, and "Hanka" (from *Passions and Other Stories*, 1975), set in Argentina, Singer again uses a scribal narrator to interrogate and record Holocaust survivor trauma. The autobiographical narrator records Holocaust experience revealed to him by a survivor. As the author exchanges news with compatriots he hasn't seen either since leaving his village in 1922, or since emigrating from Poland in 1935, they lament lost neighbors and families who perished in Nazi ghettos and concentration camps or in Russia. In an inversion of roles, a former student, Friedl, becomes mentor to the narrator, who in turn will become the transmitter of her tale. Reversing the mentor-student relationship, she poses rhetorical questions to the teacher, philosophical questions that have been implied throughout Singer's Holocaust oeuvre: "where shall we go from here? Where does the Holocaust road lead? What path shall mankind take from the Holocaust abyss?" ("The Mentor," *A Friend of Kafka and Other Stories*, Farrar, Straus & Giroux, 1970, p. 12). The story offers no resolution; it simply articulates the central questions.

In "Hanka," which shares both theme and narrative method with "The Mentor," the narrator encounters the *Shoah* through the eyes of his cousin, the lone survivor of her immediate family. Cast in the role of Holocaust guide, Hanka maps the troubled course of her parents who reared their children "to be one-hundred-percent Poles" ("Hanka," *Passions and Other Stories*, Farrar, Straus & Giroux, 1975, p. 13), believing assimilation is the remedy for traditional Polish antisemitism. Just as Friedl remains psychologically and spiritually unhealed in the aftermath of the Holocaust, so too, Hanka remains a perpetual Holocaust victim. An ambulatory corpse, she argues against facile expectations of postwar rehabilitation. Completing the frustrating reunion is the narrator's recognition of the incomprehensibility of the Holocaust for those who were not direct witnesses. His innocence precludes thorough understanding of his cousin's encounter with absolute evil. He cannot break through the wall, just as the author has consistently evaded setting his novels in the concentrationary landscape.

Post-*Shoah* Theodicy and Judaism

In addition to his depiction of psychological survivor trauma, Singer's main contribution to Holocaust literature rests on his explorations of the varieties of Jewish religious responses to the *Shoah*. Like most Jewish theologians, Singer's characters reject attempts to explain the Holocaust as punishment for sin. Some concur with Richard Rubenstein's judgment that the only response to the death camps is the rejection of God; others favor Emil Fackenheim's insistence on reaffirming God and Judaism; and others adopt Eliezer Berkovits's acceptance of the hidden face of God and his view that the Holocaust is unique in the magnitude of its destruction, but not in the theological dilemma it presents to religious faith.

Central themes of Singer's Holocaust writing, the nature of evil and the nature of God in an evil universe, emerge in *The Family Moskat* in Asa Heshel Bannet's attribution of evil to God, in his argument that Hitler is a functional part of the cosmos. The English version of the novel concludes with a nihilistic pronouncement, "Death is the Messiah. That's the real truth" (*The Family Moskat*, Fawcett Publications, 1950, p. 608). The Yiddish edition, however, reflecting the diversity of Jewish Holocaust responses, petitions for messianic deliverance. Emphasizing the incongruity of the Nazi invasion coinciding with the *Rosh HaShanah/Yom Kippur* holy season, worshipers chant the traditional prayers, praise God, and weep for their dead. In a sermon focused on the holiday themes of mercy and judgment, the rabbi explains God's withdrawal from human affairs, "For the sake of free choice the Infinite made Himself Finite. For the sake of free choice, the evil powers were created" (Yiddish edition, chapter 65, translated by Isaac Bashevis Singer and Joseph Landis, *Yiddish* 6 [summer–fall 1985], p. 106). As the bombs fall, Asa's impulse is to hurl the Bible to the ground. Instead he kisses it in recognition of the majesty of Jewish morality. Congruent with the theme of Jewish continuity is the Yiddish edition's concluding scene—Zionists gathering in the forest to escape to Israel. In sharp contrast to the English version's pessimistic conclusion, the Yiddish edition ends in hope, the promise of Moses, "Rise up and fear not. Yours is the final victory. Unto you will come the Messiah" (Yiddish edition, Landis translation, chapter 65, p. 116). One can only speculate that Singer wrote the endings that he believed would be convincing to his audiences, that even a post-Holocaust Yiddish audience had not abandoned messianic belief, whereas an English language audience was receptive to a darker conclusion.

Shadows on the Hudson, posthumously published in English (1998), but originally serialized in *The Forward* between January 1957 and January 1958, introduces the breadth of Jewish theological, cultural, and political opinion of a cast of Holocaust survivors trying to reconstruct their lives in America. Much of their conversation focuses on Jewish suffering under the tyrannies of Stalin and Hitler, and "exploration of the paradox that the same twentieth-century horrors that have made it impossible to believe in God have demonstrated the necessity for believing in Him more than ever" (Halkin, p. 75). Like Singer's late work, most of the religious debate of this early post-Holocaust novel clearly favors the traditionally orthodox. The work is presented as a long letter written from a Jerusalem retreat by one of the guests who attributes his return to Judaism to his witness of religious life of the ultra-Orthodox community, and his recognition that the restrictions and prohibitions of Jewish law are essential to moral behavior. Singer's later theme of American materialism and assimilation as destructive of Jewish continuity is evident in a minor key in this mid-1950s novel.

Holocaust survivors in *Enemies* occasionally echo Richard Rubenstein's recognition of the meaninglessness of existence in a universe shaped neither by divine plan nor divine concern, a universe without transcendental purpose. Broder laments God's passivity and ironically correlates divine impotence with human impotence: "if a God of mercy did exist in the heavenly hierarchy, then He was only a helpless godlet, a kind of heavenly Jew among the heavenly Nazis" (p. 123). His post-Holocaust ambivalence toward religious observance is characteristic; he fasts on *Yom Kippur* but refrains from communal synagogue prayer. He prays when he is not contending with God. Masha, who shares none of the compunctions of the orthodox, bluntly indicts God as a Nazi collaborator, a butcher God. Rejecting theories of the retributive and regenerative powers of suffering, she argues that even if it had been God's purpose to strengthen Jewish devotion through suffering, the Nazi scourge was immoral. Like Broder, Masha believes that history is a cycle of persecution; but unlike Broder, she denounces God for normalizing such history. Orthodox foil characters, who reject both Masha's contemptuous censure and Broder's traditional protest, round out Singer's multifaceted treatment of survivor religious response in this novel. Masha's mother, Shifrah Puah, and Tamara's uncle, Reb Nissen, remain religiously observant and community directed, escaping the isolation and anger that drive Broder to protest and Masha to suicide. These pious Jews cling even more tenaciously to Orthodox Judaism after Holocaust devastation.

Whereas the older generation's Jobian faith remains unshaken, Tamara represents the younger generation of assimilated Polish Jews whose Holocaust metamorphosis begins in apostasy and secular assimilation and ends in affirmation. In her pre-Holocaust youth, Tamara sought to supplant Orthodox Judaism with secular social reform, to replace religious messianism with Marxist messianism. After a brief return to Judaism in response to recognition of Communism's flaws and antisemitism, the Holocaust was reason to reject God once again. Her post-Holocaust spiritual return and commitment to Orthodox Judaism derives from a Fackenheimian conviction that only through the practice of Judaism will Jews deny Hitler a posthumous victory.

Much of Singer's fiction protests God's Holocaust-era silence, employing language rooted in the biblical patriarchs and prophets. He acknowledges God's sovereignty, while denouncing divine failure to uphold the covenantal obligations. Through Broder's voice, Singer explores the thesis that God is in league with the devil and Hitler. He rejects that idea in the authorial voice and contends that people will embrace it only in moments of great despair (Lee, p. 156). He argues that God is unjust and that man has the right and moral obligation to protest God's injustice. Because he believes God tolerates human evil to insure the principle of free will, he argues that man must protest human and divine injustice. In spite of God's Holocaust silence, Singer maintains that the Jew must continue to honor Israel's covenant with God. God has faltered, but it remains the duty of the observant Jew to faithfully honor Torahic law.

Anticipating the redeemed protagonist in *The Penitent* (1983), Broder struggles to free himself from the "licentiousness into which he had sunk when he had strayed from God, the Torah, and Judaism" (p. 169). Because the civilized and cultured West spawned and tolerated Nazism, Broder condemns the moral failure of the religious and secular West. He rejects philosophers Berkeley, David Hume, Benedict de Spinoza, Gottfried Liebnitz, Georg Friedrich Hegel, Arthur Schopenhauer, and Friedrich Nietzsche, for one could be a devotee of their thought and a Nazi; one could be a paragon of European culture and perpetrate or facilitate atrocities. Repudiating Western secular philosophy, he seeks a redemptive model in Western religion, but disavows Christianity, refusing to embrace "a faith which had, in the name of God, organized inquisitions, crusades, bloody wars. There was only one escape for him: to go back to the Torah, the Grmara, and the Jewish books. . . . Since he was suffocating without God and the Torah, he must serve God and study the Torah" (pp. 170–171). Emblematic of his spiritual return is his decision to live by the commandments, to father a child, to abandon ghost writing, and to teach. Broder's good intentions wait on action. In post-Holocaust America, barren of the vibrant Judaism that flourished in Eastern Europe before the faithful were murdered by Hitler and Stalin, Broder's resolution weakens. In contrast to the repentance and redemption quests of Singer's old-world Orthodox Jews who "lived in a world where Jews still had a culture and a language and an inner world of their own, one which could sustain waverers"(Alexander, *Isaac Bashevis Singer*, p. 109), the efforts of the transplanted European will be more difficult because, in his view and Singer's, American Jewry lacks an encompassing Jewish civilization. Singer leaves Broder's spiritual quest open-ended, but Tamara's speculation that he has found his hayloft suggests a possibility of spiritual return.

Singer entrusts the next Jewish generation to two women of strong faith: to Yadwiga, a righteous Gentile who risked her own life to save a Jewish life and later converted to Judaism; and to Tamara, redeemed apostate, a Jewish mother bereft of her children in the *Shoah*, who establishes a Jewish home for Yadwiga and her baby above the Jewish bookstore she operates. Restoration and regeneration from Nazism, Singer implies, is within Judaism's ethics, sacred literature, and community, concluding with symbols of hope, rebirth, and regeneration.

Theodicy Revisited

The pivotal question of *Shosha* centers on divine purpose in the Holocaust. Where was the benevolent God during the twelve-year Nazi annihilation of one-third of the world's Jewish population? Obsession with the mystery of faith in an age of atrocity emerges as a leitmotif in the characterization of Morris Feitelzohn, a Spinozan, who adamantly decries faith in a benevolent deity. In 1939, Feitelzohn argued that Jews deluded themselves and others by creating the illusion of a just and merciful God, but the epilogue reveals that this debunker of Jewish illusions recanted while in hiding. During the darkest period of the Holocaust, he was moved by the heritage of generations and replaced his ridicule of the faithful with rage against God—rage expressed in the context of religious faith.

Foil to the pre-penitent Feitelzohn is Moishe, the protagonist's brother, a young rabbi modeled on, and named for, I. B. Singer's younger brother who perished in the Holocaust. In contrast to the pre-Holocaust Spinozan's contempt for Jewish perpetuation of the just and beneficent God, the young rabbi remains faithful to the law and rituals of Orthodox Judaism, trusting God's intended continuity of the Jewish people. Thus, while lighting the Hanukkah candles in commemoration of a Jewish victory over ancient oppressors, he draws an analogy to the Hitlerean persecution and its anticipated defeat. He is spiritually sustained by belief that the Messiah will come either when the world merits him because of its goodness or because of its terrible evil. He accepts Hitler's war against the Jews as the possible "birth pains of the Messiah."

Singer's early Holocaust victims are often distinguished from his survivors by their affirmative voices and conviction in the probability of divine intercession and a providential reading of history. They regarded Hitler as another in the catalog of historic anti-Jewish tyrants, a Czar, a Chmielnicki, a Petluria. Although the young rabbi hopes for divine deliverance, he also knows the doctrine of *Hester Panim* (the hidden face of God), which explains that God occasionally chooses to allow evil to run its course in affirmation of the principle of free choice. Because he accepts these two explanations for God's silence, he is prepared to die a martyr's death in sanctification of the Holy Name.

To those who have followed Singer's prolific career, *The Penitent*, which many critics regard as Singer's least successful novel—one critic derisively proclaiming it "more monologue than novel" (Halio, p. 41) and another "an unrelieved philippic against modernity" (Epstein, p. 37)—criticism of Enlightenment secularism comes as no surprise. Yet for many, the stridency of its orthodox polemics is unwelcome. The late novel resurrects and develops the sacred passion previously reserved for minor characters who held fast to the values of traditional rabbinic and Hasidic Judaism despite Holocaust history. The protagonist, Joseph Shapiro, is a reformed reprobate who prospered in America but discovers that worldly success led to his spiritual demise. Because the Holocaust was the pivotal event in Shapiro's life, his categorical imperative, he measures morality and spiritual lapses by Holocaust standards. Thus, he views his ethical failure as betrayal of "the Jews who had donned prayer shawls and phylacteries and gone off to the cemeteries to die martyrs' deaths" (*The Penitent*, Farrar, Straus & Giroux, 1983, p. 27). His guilt is manifested in troubled sleep, in nightmares of hiding from the Nazis and discovering that he is a Nazi among Jews "dressed . . . in a brown uniform and a swastika" (p. 27). He repudiates post-Enlightenment Europe and its German paradigm of high culture on the grounds that one "could be versed in all their philosophies and still be a Nazi" (p. 44). Because he sees an intimate connection between Christian and Nazi antisemitism, like Herman Broder, he believes that Western religion and philosophy are morally bankrupt and so justifies his rejection of those systems in favor of a spiritual return to Orthodox Judaism.

Return to Judaism is the novel's central theme and provides both the drama and resolution to the Jew's problem in the modern age. The penitent's return to orthodoxy is neither easy and direct nor free of nagging reservations. An inner voice mocks the spiritual quester, ridiculing his worship of a callous deity: "Where was He when the Jews of Poland dug their own graves? Where was He when the Nazis played with the skulls of Jewish children? If He does exist and He kept silent, He is as much a murderer as Hitler" (p. 47). A Hasidic rabbi, who remained pious despite hard labor and beatings at Majdanek concentration camp, enacts the role of Shapiro's spiritual mentor and leads the quester back to orthodoxy. The first stage of Shapiro's repentance takes him from American business to Jewish synagogue and study hall. The second stage involves a journey from New York to Jerusalem. Although Singer has set several works in Israel, implicitly suggesting a connection between his treatment of the Holocaust and its antithetical historic expression, it is not until *The Penitent* that he moves from the tentative suggestion of *Shosha*'s epilogue about the survival of Israel as negation of Hitler's plan to destroy Jewry to forthright and developed assertion that commitment to the Jewish state is as central to Holocaust repair and restoration as is renewed commitment to Judaism. Congruent with dedication to Judaism in *The Penitent*, is commitment to Israel, where one can live in an ultraorthodox community without the temptations of American materialism.

Shapiro's *Shoah* regeneration is cast in the mode of Jewish mysticism's Lurianic Kabbalists, whose response to God's withdrawal from history is even greater effort to usher in the messianic age. Jewish mysticism stresses both God's manifestation and hiddenness and man's obligation to honor the Sinai compact, to exert human effort in the restorative process regardless of God's self-restrictions. The peace that Shapiro finds, eludes Singer, who wrote in the epilogue "I'm still as bewildered and shocked by the misery and brutality of life as I was as a six-year-old child . . . there isn't and cannot be a justification for the pain . . ." and noted in his conversation with Richard Burgin, "I believe that God is a silent God" (*Conversations*, p. 93).

Critical Reception

Critical attention has focused most heavily on the author's style of storytelling, Singer the traditionalist and Singer the modernist, the Yiddish world he memorialized, and his use of the supernatural, the oscillation between faith and doubt so many of his characters struggle with, and the supernatural dybbuks and imps of his short fictions. As Janet Hadda observes, "The Yiddish press . . . acknowledged Bashevis's sophistication, but it viewed his accomplishments with suspicion and dislike" (Hadda, p. 353). Irving Howe summarizes Singer's reputation among Yiddishists, acknowledging their praise for his prose style and unease with his "modernist" subjects including his emphasis on sexuality, "concern for the irrational, expressionist distortions of character, and a seeming indifference to the humane ethic of Yiddishism" (Howe, p. 65). Howe's own judgment is more appreciative of Singer's "total command of his imagined world; . . . his use both of traditional Jewish materials and his modernist attitude towards them; . . . [his] serious if enigmatic moral perspective; and his [mastery] . . . of Yiddish prose" (Howe, p. 67). Writing about *Shosha*, Robert Alter's commentary may stand for much of Singer's oeuvre: "the novel succeeds in plangently rendering the process of questioning the place of man in the frightful flux of being, and that is what gives conviction to his literary pursuit of a vanished past" (Alter, p. 22). Most critics, like Lawrence Friedman, recognize that "The tragic knowledge that the Jewish community of Poland was snuffed out by Hitler is never far from the surface of Singer's fiction" (Friedman, p. 288).

The public affection and critical acclaim Singer garnered is evidenced by his many literary awards and honors, including the Louis Lamed Prize for *The Family Moskat* in 1950 and for *Satan in Goray* in 1956; National Institute of Arts and Letters and American Academy award in literature, 1959; the Daroff Memorial Fiction Award, Jewish Book Council of America award in 1963 for *The Slave*; Newbery Honor Book Award, 1967, 1968, and 1969; National Endowment for the Arts grant, 1967; National Book Award for Children's Literature, 1970; National Book Award for Fiction, 1974; Agnon Gold Medal, 1975; and the Nobel Prize for Literature, 1978.

Bibliography

Primary Sources

Novels Originally in Yiddish

Der Satan in Gorey (Satan in Goray). 1935, 1955.
Di Familie Mushkat (*The Family Moskat*). Two volumes, published under name Isaac Bashevis. 1950.
The Magician of Lublin. 1960.
The Slave. 1962.
Sonim, di Geshichte fun a Liebe (*Enemies, A Love Story*). 1966, 1972.
Der Certificat (*The Certificate*). 1967, 1992.
The Manor. 1967.
The Estate. 1969.
Shosha. 1978.
Reaches of Heaven: A Story of the Baal Shem Tov. 1980.
Isaac Bashevis Singer: Three Complete Novels. Includes *The Slave*, *Enemies: A Love Story*, and *Shosha*. 1982.
The Penitent. 1983.
The King of the Fields. Limited edition. 1988.
Shoym (*Scum*). 1991.
Meshugah. 1994.
Shootns baym Hodson (*Shadows on the Hudson*). Originally serialized in *The Forward* in 1957–1958. 1998.

Collected Short Stories Originally in Yiddish

Gimpel the Fool and Other Stories. 1957.
The Spinoza of Market Street and Other Stories. 1961.
Short Friday and Other Stories. 1964.
Selected Short Stories of Isaac Bashevis Singer. 1966.
The Séance and Other Stories. 1968.
A Friend of Kafka and Other Stories. 1970.
An Isaac Bashevis Singer Reader. 1971.
A Crown of Feathers and Other Stories. 1973.
Passions and Other Stories. 1975.
Old Love and Other Stories. 1979.
The Collected Stories of Isaac Bashevis Singer. 1982.
The Image and Other Stories. 1985.
Gifts. 1985.
The Death of Methuselah and Other Stories. 1988.

Children's Books Originally in Yiddish

Zlateh the Goat and Other Stories. 1966.
The Fearsome Inn. 1967.
Mazel and Shlimazel; or, The Milk of a Lioness. 1967.
When Schlemiel Went to Warsaw and Other Stories. 1968.
Elijah the Slave: A Hebrew Legend Retold. 1970.
Joseph and Koza; or, The Sacrifice to the Vistula. 1970.
Alone in the Wild Forest. 1971.
The Topsy-Turvy Emperor of China. 1971.
The Wicked City. 1972.
The Fools of Chelm and Their History. 1973.
Why Noah Chose the Dove. 1974.
A Tale of Three Wishes. 1975.
Naftali the Storyteller and His Horse, Sus, and Other Stories. 1976.
The Power of Light: Eight Stories for Hanukkah. 1980.
The Golem. 1982.
Stories for Children. Includes stories from *Naftali the Storyteller and His Horse, Sus, and Other Stories*, *When Schlemiel Went to Warsaw and Other Stories*, and *The Power of Light*. 1984.

Autobiography Originally in Yiddish (under pseudonym Isaac Warshofsky)

Mayn Tatn's Bes-din Shtub (*In My Father's Court*). 1956; published under name Isaac Bashevis Singer 1966.
A Day of Pleasure: Stories of a Boy Growing Up in Warsaw. 1969.
A Little Boy in Search of God: Mysticism in a Personal Light. 1976.
A Young Man in Search of Love. 1978.
Lost in America. 1981.
Love and Exile: The Early Years: A Memoir. Includes *A Little Boy in Search of God: Mysticism in a Personal Light*, *A Young Man in Search of Love*, and *Lost in America*. 1984.
More Stories from My Father's Court. 2000.

Plays Originally in Yiddish

The Mirror. 1973.
Yentl, the Yeshiva Boy. With Leah Napolin. 1978. Adaptation of Singer's story produced on Broadway in 1974.
Schlemiel the First. 1974.
Teibele and Her Demon. With Eve Friedman. 1984.
A Play for the Devil. Based on Singer's story "The Unseen."

Translator into Yiddish

Pan. Knut Hamsun. 1928.
Di Vogler (The Vagabonds). Knut Hamsun. 1928.
In Opgrunt Fun Tayve (In Passion's Abyss). Gabriele D'Annunzio. 1929.
Mete Trap. Karin Michaelis. 1929.
Roman Rolan (Romain Rolland). Stefan Zweig. 1929.
Viktorya (Victoria). Knut Hamsun. 1929.
Oyfn Mayrev-Front Keyn Nayes (All Quiet on the Western Front). Erich Maria Remarque. 1930.
Der Tsoyberbarg (The Magic Mountain). Thomas Mann. 1930.
Der Veg oyf Tsurik (The Road Back). Erich Maria Remarque. 1930.
Araber: Folkstimlekhe Geshikhtn (Arabs: Stories of the People). Moshe Smilansky. 1932.
Fun Moskve biz Yerusholayim (From Moscow to Jerusalem). Leon S. Glaser. 1938.

Other

Editor with Elaine Gottlieb. *Prism* 2. 1965.
Visit to the Rabbinical Seminary in Cincinnati. 1965.

The Hasidim: Paintings, Drawings, and Etchings. With Ira Moscowitz. 1973.
Nobel Lecture. 1979.
The Gentleman from Cracow; The Mirror. Illustrated by Raphael Soyer. Introduction by Harry I. Moore. 1979.
Isaac Bashevis Singer on Literature and Life. 1979.
The Meaning of Freedom. 1981.
My Personal Conception of Religion. 1982.
One Day of Happiness. 1982.
Remembrances of a Rabbi's Son. Translated by Rena Borrow. 1984.
Conversations with Isaac Bashevis Singer. With Richard Burgin. 1986.
The Safe Deposit and Other Stories about Grandparents, Old Lovers and Crazy Old Men. Masterworks of Modern Jewish Writing Series. Edited by Kerry M. Orlitzky. 1989.

Selected Introductions and Prefaces

Yoshe Kalb. I. J. Singer. 1965.
The Adventures of One Yitzchok. Yizchok Perlov. 1967.
Hunger. Knut Hamsun. 1967.
"The Fable as Literary Form." Introduction to *Aesop's Fables*. Translated by George Tyler Townsend. 1968.
An Anthology of Modem Yiddish Poetry. Edited by Ruth Whitman. 1979.
My Love Affair with Miami Beach. Richard Nagler. 1991.

Sound Recordings

"Isaac Bashevis Singer Reading His Stories" (contains "Gimpel the Fool" and "The Man Who Came Back").
"Isaac Bashevis Singer Reading His Stories in Yiddish."

Selected Periodical Publications

"The Everlasting Joke." *Commentary* 31 (May 1961): 458–460.
"The Poetry of Faith." *Commentary* 32 (September 1961): 258–260.
"A New Use for Yiddish." *Commentary* 33 (March 1962): 267–269.
"Realism and Truth." Translated by Adah Auerbach Lapin. *The Reconstructionist* 15 (June 1962): 5–9.
"Why I Write in Yiddish." *Pioneer Woman* 38 (January 1963): 13.
"What It Takes to Be a Jewish Writer." Translated by Mirra Ginsburg. *National Jewish Monthly* 78 (November 1963): 54–56.
"Scholem Aleichem: Spokesman for a People." *New York Times* (20 September 1964), Section 2: 1, 4.
"Rootless Mysticism." *Commentary* 39 (January 1965): 78–79.
"Indecent Language and Sex in Literature." Translated by Mirra Ginsburg. *Jewish Heritage* 8 (summer 1965): 51–54.
"Hagigah." *American Judaism* (winter 1966–1967): 18–19, 48–49.
"The Future of Yiddish and Yiddish Literature." *The Jewish Book Annual* XXV. New York: Jewish Book Council of America, 1967, 70–74.
"The Extreme Jews." *Harper's* (April 1967): 55–62.
"Civilizing the Shtetl." *Jewish Chronicle* (8 December 1967): i–ii.
"On Translating My Books." Papers Delivered at Conference on Translation of Literature. New York City. PEN American Center. May 1970.
"Yiddish Tradition vs. Jewish Tradition: A Dialogue." With Irving Howe. *Midstream* (June–July 1975): 33–38.
"Roth and Singer on Bruno Schulz." *New York Times Book Review* (13 February 1977): 5, 14, 16, 20.
"The Golem Is a Myth for Our Time." *New York Times* (12 August 1984): H1.
"The Mistake." With Rina Borrow and Lester Goran. *New Yorker* (4 February 1985): 36–40.
"Dazzled." With Dvorah Menashe. *New Yorker* (18 March 1985): 40–43.
"New Yiddish Frontiers." *Yiddish* 6, nos. 2–3 (summer–fall 1985): 141–148.
Nobel Lecture. Reprinted in *Yiddish* 6, nos. 2–3 (summer–fall 1985): 169–172.
"We Must Preserve the Heritage of Yiddish." Translated by Sol Liptz. *Yiddish* 6, nos. 2–3 (summer–fall 1985): 135–139.
"When the Old World Came to Sea Gate." Translated by Elizabeth Shub. *Yiddish* 6, nos. 2–3 (summer–fall 1985): 121–125.
"Yes . . ." *Yiddish* 6, nos. 2–3 (summer–fall 1985): 159–167.
"Yiddish, the Language of Exile." *Yiddish* 6, nos. 2–3 (summer–fall 1985): 127–133.
"The Impressario." *Harper's* (April 1986): 57–61.
"The Recluse." With Deborah Menasche. *New Yorker* (21 July 1986): 30–33.
"Disguised." With Deborah Menasche. *New Yorker* (22 September, 1986): 34–38.
"The Bitter Truth." *Playboy* (April 1988): 64–66.
"The Last Gaze." *Partisan Review* 55, no. 2 (spring 1988): 210–218.
"The Missing Line." *Partisan Review* 55, no. 2 (spring 1988): 205–210.
"Problems of Yiddish Prose in America (1943)." Translated by Robert H. Wolf. *Prooftexts* 9, no. 1 (January 1989): 5–12.
"Writing: A Love Story." *Seventeen* (January 1991): 95–97.
"Concerning Yiddish Literature in Poland (1943)." *Prooftexts* 15, no. 2 (May 1995): 113–127.
"Shadows on the Hudson." *Tikkun* 13, no. 1 (January 1998): 60–62.
"The Last Demon." *Parabola* 24, no. 4 (winter 1999): 47–54.
"He Wants Forgiveness from Her." *New Yorker* (21 August–28 August 2000): 154–156.
"A Guest in the Shtibl." *New Yorker* (21 August–28 August, 2000): 156–169.
"Reb Yekl Safir." *Book* (November 2000): 61.

Works Translated into Other Languages

"Un ami de Kafka." Translated by Marc Pierre Castelnau. *Nouvelles Litteraires* (20 August 1970): 1, 6.
"Litteratur og fridom." *Samtiden: Tidsskrift for Politikk, Litteratur og Samfunnssporsmal* [Oslo, Norway] 91, no. 5 (1982): 61–64.

Contributor

Tully Filmus: Selected Drawings. Edited by Anatol Filmus. Philadelphia: Jewish Publication Society of America, 1971.
Miami Beach. Gary Monroe. Bowling Green, Ohio: Forest & Trees, 1989.

Secondary Sources

Bibliographies

Bryer, Jackson R., and Paul E. Rockwell. "Isaac Bashevis Singer in English: A Bibliography." In *Critical Views of Isaac Bashevis Singer*. Edited by Irving Malin. New York: New York University Press, 1968, pp. 220–265.
Miller, David. *A Bibliography of Isaac Bashevis Singer, January 1950–June 1952*. Working Papers in Yiddish and East

European Jewish Culture. Vol. 34. New York: YIVO Institute for Jewish Research, 1979.

———. *Bibliography of Isaac Bashevis Singer: 1924–1949.* New York, Berne, Frankfurt on the Main: Peter Lang, 1983.

Books

Alexander, Edward. *Isaac Bashevis Singer.* Boston: Twayne, 1980.

———. *Isaac Bashevis Singer: A Study of the Short Fiction.* Boston: Twayne, 1990.

Allentuck, Marcia, ed. *The Achievement of Isaac Bashevis Singer.* Carbondale: Southern Illinois University Press, 1969.

Buchen, Irving H. *Isaac Bashevis Singer and the Eternal Past.* New York: New York University Press / London: University of London Press, 1968.

Friedman, Lawrence S. *Understanding Isaac Bashevis Singer.* Columbia: University of South Carolina Press, 1988.

Hadda, Janet. *Isaac Bashevis Singer: A Life.* Oxford: Oxford University Press, 1997.

Kresh, Paul. *Isaac Bashevis Singer: The Magician of West 86th Street.* New York: Dial, 1979.

Lee, Grace Farrell. *From Exile to Redemption: The Fiction of Isaac Bashevis Singer.* Carbondale and Edwardsville: Southern Illinois University Press, 1987.

Malin, Irving, ed. *Critical Views of Isaac Bashevis Singer.* New York: New York University Press, 1969.

———. *Isaac Bashevis Singer.* New York: Ungar, 1972.

Milbauer, Asher Zelig. *Transcending Exile: Conrad, Nabokov, I. B. Singer.* Miami: Florida International University Press, 1985.

Miller, David Neal. *Fear of Fiction: Narrative Strategies in the Works of Isaac Bashevis Singer.* Albany: State University of New York Press, 1985.

———, ed. *Recovering the Canon: Essays on Isaac Bashevis Singer.* Leiden: E. J. Brill, 1986.

Siegel, Ben. *Isaac Bashevis Singer.* Minneapolis: University of Minnesota Press, 1969.

Sinclair, Clive. *The Brothers Singer.* London: Allison & Busby, 1983.

Tuszyńska, Agata. *Lost Landscapes: In Search of Isaac Bashevis Singer and the Jews of Poland.* Translated by Madeline G. Levine. New York: William Morrow, 1998.

Articles and Essays

Abitebuol, Maurice. "*The Penitent* de Isaac Bashevis Singer ou l'exil et le Royaume." *Caliban* 25 (1988): 13–23.

Alexander, Edward. "The Destruction and Resurrection of the Jews in the Fiction of Isaac Bashevis Singer." In *The Resonance of Dust: Essays on Holocaust Literature and Jewish Fate.* Columbus: Ohio State University Press, 1979.

———. "Isaac Bashevis Singer and Jewish Utopianism." *The Jewish Idea and Its Enemies.* New Brunswick and Oxford: Transaction Books, 1988.

Alter, Robert. "Review of *Shosha.*" *The New Republic* (16 September 1978): 20–22.

Baumgarten, Murray. "Intersections and Modern Urban Identities: Isaac Bashevis Singer, American Jewish Writers, and the Jewish Street." *Judaism* 49, no. 3 (summer 2000): 322–341.

Berger, Alan L. "Isaac Bashevis Singer." In *Crisis and Covenant: The Holocaust in American Jewish Fiction.* Albany: State University of New York Press, 1985, pp. 79–88.

Bilik, Dorothy S. "Singer's Diasporan Novel: *Enemies, A Love Story.*" *Studies in American Jewish Literature* 1 (1981): 90–100.

Chandler, Marilyn R. "Death by the Word: Victims of Language in *Enemies, A Love Story.*" *Studies in American Jewish Literature* 1 (1981): 101–106.

Cheyette, Bryan. "Angels and Dybbuks." Review of *Meshugah. Times Literary Supplement* (3 February 1995): 21.

Cohen, Josh. " 'Disgrace of Revelation': I. B. Singer's Holocaust Impiety." *Textual Practice* 12, no. 3 (winter 1998): 443–457.

Elikan, Marc. "La Litterature yiddish et un de ses representants, Isaac Bashevis Singer." *Etudes de Lettres* 2 (April–June 1989): 7–23.

———. "Perdu et retrouvé: La fiction 'américaine' d'Isaac Bashevis Singer." Actes du XIIe congrès de l'Association Internationale de Littérature Comparé: Munchen 1988. *Espace et frontières dans la littérature.* Edited by Roger Bauer, Douwe Fokkema, Michael de Graat, John Boening, Gerald Gillespie, Maria Moog Grunewald, Virgil Nemoianu, Joseph Ricapito, and Manfred Schmeling. Munich: Iudicium, 1990, pp. 159–164.

Elman, Richard. "Antic Arts: Spinoza of Canal Street." *Holiday* 38 (August 1965): 83–87.

———. "Bashevis." *Tikkun* 9, no. 1 (January 1994): 63–68.

Epstein, Joseph. "Our Debt to I. B. Singer." *Commentary* 92, no. 5 (November 1991): 31–37.

Field, Leslie. "The Early Prophetic Singer: *The Family Moskat.*" *Studies in American Jewish Literature* 1 (1982): 32–36.

Forrey, Robert. "The Sorrows of Herman Broder: Singer's *Enemies, A Love Story.*" *Studies in American Jewish Literature* 1 (1981): 100–106.

Friedman, Lawrence S. "Isaac Bashevis Singer." *Dictionary of Literary Biography Yearbook: 1991.* Detroit: Bruccoli Clark Layman, 1992, pp. 283–293.

Gladsky, Thomas. "The Polish Side of Singer's Fiction." *Studies in American Jewish Literature* 5 (1986): 4–14.

Glatshteyn, Yankev. "Singer's Literary Reputation." In *Recovering the Canon: Essays on Isaac Bashevis Singer.* Edited by David Neal Miller. Leiden: E. J. Brill, 1986, pp. 145–148.

Guzlowski, John. "Isaac Singer and the Threat of America." *Shofar: An Interdisciplinary Journal of Jewish Studies* 20, no. 1 (2001): 21–35.

Hadda, Janet. "The Double Life of Isaac Bashevis Singer." *Prooftexts* 5, no. 2 (May 1985): 165–181.

———. "Isaac Bashevis Singer in New York City." *Judaism* 46, no. 3 (summer 1997): 346–364.

Halio, Jay L. "The Individual Struggle for Faith in the Novels of I. B. Singer." *Studies in American Jewish Literature* 10, no. 2 (spring 1991): 35–43.

Halkin, Hillel. "The Posthumous Penitent." Review of *Shadows on the Hudson. Commentary* 105, no. 6 (June 1998): 73–75.

Howe, Irving. "I. B. Singer." *Encounter* 26 (March 1966): 60–70.

"Isaac Bashevis Singer." *Contemporary Authors.* Galenet. 2002. Hale Library. Kansas State University. Manhattan, KS. 3 May 2002, http://www.infotrac.galegroup.com.

Kremer, S. Lillian. "Kaddish and Resurrection: Isaac Bashevis Singer's Holocaust Memorial." In *Witness through the Imagination: Jewish American Holocaust Literature.* Detroit: Wayne State University Press, 1989, pp. 181–217.

Lainoff, Seymor. "Prison as Metaphor in the Fiction of Malamud, Singer, and Roth." *Yiddish* 11, no. 3–4 (1999): 64–69.

Landis, Joseph. "I. B. Singer: Alone in the Forest." *Yiddish* 6, no. 2–3 (summer–fall 1985): 5–23.

Lee, Grace Farrell. "Isaac Bashevis Singer: Mediating between the Biblical and the Modern." *Modern Language Studies* 15, no. 4 (fall 1985): 117–123.

Magentsa-Shaked, Malka. "Singer and the Family Saga Novel in Jewish Literature." *Prooftexts* 9, no. 1 (January 1989): 27–42.

Miron, Dan. "Passivity and Narration: The Spell of Isaac Bashevis Singer." *Judaism* 41, no. 1 (winter 1992): 6–17.

Roskies, David. "Reclaiming Isaac Bashevis Singer." Special issue of *Prooftexts* 9, no. 1 (1989).

Schulz, Max F. "The Family Chronicle as Paradigm of History: *The Brothers Ashkenazi* and *The Family Moskat*." In *The Achievement of Isaac Bashevis Singer*. Edited by Marcia Allentuck. Carbondale: Southern Illinois Press, 1969, pp. 77–92.

Sherman, Joseph. " 'Can These Bones Live?': Destruction and Survival in Isaac Bashevis Singer's *Enemies, A Love Story*." *English Studies in Africa: A Journal of the Humanities* (Johannesburg, South Africa) 26, no. 2 (1983): 141–152.

———. "The Gates of Zion and the Dwellings of Jacob: Zion and Zionism in the Works of Isaac Bashevis Singer." *Theoria* (Pietermaritzburg, Natal, South Africa) 69 (May 1987): 29–39.

———. "Guilt as Subtext: I. B. Singer's Memoiristic Fictions." *Studies in American Jewish Literature* 13 (1994): 106–123.

Shmeruk, Chone. "The Polish–Jewish Relations in the Historical Fiction of Isaac Bashevis Singer." *The Polish Review* 32, no. 4 (1987): 401–413.

Siegel, Ben. "The Jew as Underground/Confidence Man: I. B. Singer's *Enemies, A Love Story*." *Studies in the Novel* 10 (1978): 397–410.

Waxman, Barbara Frey. "Isaac Bashevis Singer." In *Dictionary of Literary Biography: Twentieth-Century American Jewish Fiction Writers*. Edited by Daniel Walden. Detroit: Bruccoli and Clark, 1984, pp. 297–305.

Wirth-Nesher, Hana. "Orphaned Fictions: Hindsight in Isaac Bashevis Singer's *The Family Moskat* and *Shosha*." In *Recovering the Canon: Essays on Isaac Bashevis Singer*. Edited by David Neal Miller. Leiden: E. J. Brill, 1986, pp. 39–49.

Wisse, Ruth. *The Schlemiel as Modern Hero*. Chicago: University of Chicago Press, 1971, pp. 60–67.

Yungman, Moshe. "Singer's Polish Period: 1924–1935." *Yiddish* 6, nos. 2–3 (summer–fall 1985): 25–38.

Interviews

Andersen, David M. "Isaac Bashevis Singer: Conversations in California." *Modern Fiction Studies* 16 (winter 1970–1971): 424–439.

Axelrod, D. B., S. Barkan, and J. C. Hand. "An Interview with Isaac Bashevis Singer." *Tel Aviv Review* 1 (January 1988): 304–311.

Blocker, Joel, and Richard Elman. "An Interview with Isaac Bashevis Singer." *Commentary* 36 (November 1963): 364–372.

Burgin, Richard, and Isaac Bashevis Singer. *Conversations with Isaac Bashevis Singer*. New York: Doubleday, 1985.

Gilman, Sander L. "Interview/Isaac Bashevis Singer." *Diacritics* 4 (spring 1974): 30–33.

Lee, Grace Farrell. "Stewed Prunes and Rice Pudding: College Students Eat and Talk with Isaac Bashevis Singer." *Contemporary Literature* 19 (autumn 1978): 446–458.

Pinsker, Sanford. "Isaac Bashevis Singer: An Interview." *Critique* 11 (1969): 26–39.

Ribalow, Reena Sara. "A Visit to Isaac Bashevis Singer." *The Reconstructionist* 30 (29 May 1964): 19–26.

Rosenblatt, Paul, and Gene Koppel. *Isaac Bashevis Singer on Literature and Life*. Tucson: University of Arizona Press, 1971.

Israel Joshua Singer
(1893–1944)

ANITA NORICH

Singer was the second child in a family of Yiddish writers that included his elder sister, Esther Singer Kreitman, and his younger and now more famous brother, Isaac Bashevis Singer. Born in the small town of Bilgoray, in the Lublin province, Singer spent much of his childhood in Leoncin, another small town in the Warsaw province. He received a traditional Jewish education and was influenced by the opposing strains of Jewish thought represented by his mother's rationalism and his father's Hasidic enthusiasm. When he was fourteen, the family moved to the Hasidic court at Radzimin. Later Singer moved to Warsaw and worked as an unskilled laborer and proofreader; he also studied painting and hid in an artists' atelier to avoid the military. By 1918, when he traveled to the Soviet Union, he had already begun publishing his earliest stories. Singer's literary success began with the publication of "Perl" ("Pearls," 1922), a short story that won the attention of Abraham Cahan, the powerful editor of the New York Yiddish daily, the *Forverts* (The Forward). Singer served as a correspondent for the newspaper, reporting on his travels throughout Poland, the Soviet Union, and, in 1932, the United States, where he finally settled in 1934, continuing to write fiction and journalistic essays (under the name G. Kuper, his wife's maiden name) until his sudden death at the age of fifty.

Singer's Place in Yiddish Literature

Singer was a remarkably successful and admired literary figure, most of whose works were translated into English during his lifetime to much acclaim. His novels and short stories examine the political and cultural upheavals in Jewish life between the two world wars and on two continents. They compel his readers to identify and confront the multiple strands that formed the fabric of interbellum Jewish life and of modern Yiddish literature, portraying a seemingly endless series of wars, class conflicts, pogroms, shifts in borders, and messianic ideologies, critiquing every one of the many choices available to Jews of the period: traditional religious life, secularism, Yiddish culturalism, Zionism, socialism, even individualism. Singer's primary theme is the ultimately destructive nature of any messianic belief in religious, social, or historical resolutions for the problems that beset the individual and the Jews. His stories are marked by relentlessly critical attacks on contemporary Jewish life and by a radical pessimism about its future. For a post-Holocaust audience turning to Yiddish texts as a kind of memorial to the dead, Singer's harsh depictions of Jewish culture in Poland were jarring. Thus, Singer suffered the fate of many modernist, socially critical Yiddish writers whose texts found a limited responsive audience after the Holocaust, when Yiddish literature was often read through the distorting prism of its demise.

A Place for Yiddish Culture

By the time Singer arrived in New York, he had been writing for almost two decades. Like others before him, he fled Europe, but not primarily because of poverty or antisemitism. He sought in America what he had not found in Poland or Russia: a cultural haven free of the internal political and literary squabbles of Yiddish cultural life. The U.S. Yiddish world, he would find, had similar internecine fights, but he seemed to suffer less from them in his new home. His first novel, *Shtol un Ayzn* (1927, *Blood Harvest*) generated considerable controversy about the place of politics in fiction. Accused of not understanding politics and convinced that his critics were merely Communist or socialist party hacks, Singer renounced Yiddish literature for a while, turning to journalism instead. Four years later, however, he published his second and most successful novel, *Yoshe Kalb* (1932, *The Sinner*), a psychologically astute novel about a man who adopts two personalities and remains, until the end, an enigmatic figure. In addition to volumes of short stories, he published three more novels after his arrival in the United States: *Di brider Ashkenazi* (1936, *The Brothers Ashkenazi*), *Khaver Nakhmen* (1938, *East of Eden*), and *Di mishpokhe Karnovski* (1943, *The Family Carnovsky*). Adapted for the stage, *Yoshe Kalb* was performed in New York in 1932 and became one of the most critically acclaimed and financially successful plays ever produced in the Yiddish theater; less successful adaptations of his other novels followed: *Di brider Ashkenazi* in 1938, *Khaver Nakhmen* in 1939, and *Di mishpokhe Karnovski* in 1943.

In *Yoshe Kalb*, the last novel he produced in Warsaw, Singer was already pointing toward a new location for his imagination. The novel depicts Polish Hasidic life and religious institutions in unremittingly negative terms and seeks a sense of community and identity elsewhere. Yoshe becomes a combination of the myth of the Wandering Jew and a Christ-like figure who cannot be rooted in any particular time or place. Singer never believed that Yiddish culture had a particular geographical boundary or home and, like Yoshe, sought a place in which to locate his imagination. The United States proved to be at least a more open environment than Poland, as increasingly frightening antisemitic attacks occurred in Poland throughout the 1930s.

In the midst of World War II Singer adopted an explicit, if short-lived, ideological stance in sympathy with Zionist goals. In a 1942 essay, "A tsvey toyznt yoriker toes" (A two-thousand-year-old mistake) he called for a place where Jews could live normal lives, a place where they were not intruders within foreign borders. His reluctant acceptance of a nationalist ideology was an expression of the horror with which he heard increasingly tragic news from Poland, and the problem he had long perceived in finding a home for the Jewish imagination. Striking in his short stories is the lack of a material sense of place, even when his characters are men who cultivate the land. The Polish countryside and the Catskills are largely indistinguishable from one another in these stories. In part, this is a reflection of the problem of national identity that Jewish writers from Eastern Europe could not escape, even in the safety of New York.

Family Sagas

After the rise of Nazism, Singer wrote two family sagas that wrestled with the relationship between historical events and their literary representation. *The Brothers Ashkenazi* (1934–1935) and *The Family Carnovsky* (1940–1941) were, like each of his texts, serialized in the daily Yiddish press. They present Jewish history as inexorably cyclical, repeating itself in every generation, even when the rest of the world moves on. The contemporary loss of national identity, the attenuation of cultural identity implied by assimilation, and the more overt threats to Jewish lives are thus seen as differing in degree but not in kind from past events. This does not, however, suggest any particular way of responding to the growing Nazi threat. *The Brothers Ashkenazi* is a history of twin brothers and of the city of Lodz. Written in the first years of Nazi rule, it ends with World War I, the Russian Revolution, and the establishment of an independent Poland, but for Jews these events have less resonance than the saga's depiction of the famous 1918 pogrom in Lemberg, in which the fates of the religious and the Marxist, the assimilated and the traditional Jew, are all identical.

By the time Singer wrote *The Family Carnovsky*, he was explicitly coming to terms with the early years of what was already being called in Yiddish *khurbn*: destruction or Holocaust. His inability to conclude this tale may well be to his credit because it points to his unwillingness to either romanticize or condemn Jewish life in response to this incomprehensible fate. The novel traces three generations through half a century, ending almost at the moment of publication. It is schematic in its presentation of place and character, following the family from a Polish *shtetl* to Berlin to New York. The eldest Carnovsky, Dovid, flees the *shtetl*, seeking to live by the principles of Moses Mendelssohn and the Haskalah (Jewish Enlightenment). His son, Georg, is intended to embody the ideal of living as "a Jew at home and a man in the street," but the German street quickly dominates and tells him that he will be considered an outsider—a Jew—everywhere. Germany's escalating antisemitism and Georg's marriage to a Gentile destroy Dovid's faith in Mendelssohn. The marriage is condemned by the Jewish family and by the family of German Nazis; only the Jewish grandparents are reconciled to the child born of this union. Georg, who is prohibited from practicing medicine in Nazi Germany because he is a Jew, is thrust back into the Jewish world. Georg's own son, Yegor, is the most extreme expression of the failure of the golden rule. He is completely removed from the Enlightenment attempt to be both a Jew and a citizen of the world, identifying instead with his uncle's vicious antisemitism and hating all indications of his father's Jewish legacy. In New York, Yegor casts his lot with Nazi sympathizers, returning to his father only when he has killed his former Nazi employer and is himself shot.

In a melodramatic conclusion, he returns, bleeding and unconscious, to his father's doorstep.

At the end of the novel, Singer leaves Yegor's fate uncertain, a sign of the difficulty of conceiving of a coherent conclusion to the conflicts of the novel and current history. Singer's energies were no doubt elsewhere. His correspondence during the period is full of increasing concern about his family's fate under the Nazis. He could not maintain contact with his mother and youngest brother, who were caught in the war's upheaval. Neither survived the war, though Singer died still uncertain of their fates.

Telling Interesting Stories

In his prose fiction and in numerous essays, Singer displayed a view of social reality as the primary constraint on artistic creativity, and also its primary subject. Also consistent in his work was his disavowal of any political solution to the problems besetting contemporary Jews. The corrupting influence of politics always seemed more acute to Singer within Yiddish culture than in other cultures because the Jews were, he explained, always living *in extremis*, forced to respond to uniquely cataclysmic upheavals. The unfolding *khurbn* could only confirm this sense of the political and personal situation of the Jew. In his attempt to come to terms with the impending disaster in Europe, Singer suggested, somewhat disingenuously, that he sought only to tell interesting stories. His fictions offer no resolutions to the tensions in which his characters find themselves, telling instead of the modern Jewish writer's responsibility to articulate these dilemmas and analyze them. In the end, the most positive sign of Singer's fiction is the ongoing audience it invites.

Bibliography

Primary Sources

Perl (Pearls). 1922.

Af fremder erd (On Foreign Ground). 1925.

Shtol un Ayzn (*Steel and Iron*, *Blood Harvest*). 1927, 1935, 1969.

Nay Rusland (New Russia). 1928.

Yoshe Kalb The Sinner, *Yoshe Kalb* 1932, 1933, 1965.

Di brider Ashkenazi (*The Brothers Ashkenazi*). 1936, 1985.

Friling (Spring). 1937.

Khaver Nakhmen (Comrade Nakhmen, East of Eden). 1938, 1939.

Di mishpokhe Karnovski (*The Family Carnovsky*). 1943, 1969.

Fun a velt vos iz nishto mer (*Of a World That Is No More*). 1946, 1970.

Dertseylungen (Stories). 1949.

Secondary Sources

Einhorn, David. "Y. Y. Zinger un di yidishe literature fun zayn dor." *Forverts* (19 February 1943).

Gris, Noakh. "Y. Y. Zinger." *Di tsukunft* 90 (January 1984): 19–26.

Howe, Irving. "The Other Singer." *Commentary* 31, no. 3 (1966): 76–82.

Magentsa-Shaked, Malka. "Singer and the Family Saga Novel in Jewish Literature." *Prooftexts* 9 (January 1989): 27–42.

Mayzl, Nakhmen. "Y. Y. Zinger—der mentsh un kinstler." *Yidishe kultur*, no. 6 (March 1944): 18–26.

Norich, Anita. *The Homeless Imagination in the Fiction of Israel Joshua Singer*. Bloomington: Indiana University Press, 1991.

Ravitch, Melekh. "I. J. Singer: On the Twenty-Fifth Anniversary of His Death." Translated by Sol Liptzin. *Jewish Book Annual* 26 (1968–1969): 121–123.

Schwartz, Maurice. "Y. Y. Zinger—der dramaturg." *Forverts* (8–11 March 1944).

Sinclair, Clive. *The Brothers Singer*. London and New York: Allison & Busby, 1983.

JOSEPH SKIBELL

(1959–)

SANFORD PINSKER

JOSEPH SKIBELL WAS born in Lubbock, Texas on 18 October 1959, the son of Irvin and Shirlene (Lezan) Skibell. This has always struck Skibell as something of an anomaly because, he claims, his "DNA was prepared for eastern Europe." He grew up around eastern European Jews: his grandfather Archie Skibell and great-uncles Albert and Sidney Skibell, all sons of great-grandfather Chaim Skibelski, the eventual protagonist of Joseph Skibell's novel, *A Blessing on the Moon* (1997). Small wonder that living on what Skibell calls "the very edges of the diaspora" often struck him as both unreal and, in an odd way, unnatural. His soul belonged somewhere else. At the age of eighteen Skibell left home ("Enough was enough," he later insisted)—to study at the University of Texas at Austin (1978–1981), supplemented by summer courses at Yale University (1980) and the University of Chicago (1981). From 1993 to 1996 he studied at the Texas Center for Writers at the University of Texas, receiving an M.F.A. in 1996.

Skibell and the Holocaust

Whatever may be said of those who experienced the Holocaust firsthand, at least they had a standard of what was "normal" from which to judge that which became abnormal, and often horrific. They could, if they chose, remember what their lives in Eastern Europe were like before the Nazi shadow swept over them. They carried memories inside them—everything from the rhythm of religious observance and internecine Jewish quarrels about Zionism or socialism to the Yiddish folktales and songs that made their world so distinctive, and particular. By contrast Skibell, born in a very different time and place, had no such benchmarks, and so had to struggle to recapture, if only through the imagination, some sense of those members of the Skibelski family (as they called themselves in Eastern Europe) that Joseph Skibell never had the chance to know.

His family's silence about the eighteen members who perished in the Holocaust only compounded the problem. They simply "disappeared," as Skibell puts it, never to be heard of or talked about again. In an interview published in the June 1997 issue of *The Algonkian*, a periodical about books, authors, and publishing, Skibell says "no one ever talked about it. This silence, I think, haunted me as a child and formed my character in a number of ways which eventually were not that pleasing to me." Many children of survivors tell similar stories about the wall of silence that shut them off from their parents or grandparents, and how this rupture caused pain on both sides of the wall. What makes Skibell's situation different, however, is that although his parents were not Holocaust survivors, he felt a need to write his way to something akin to transcendence nonetheless. As he puts it in the same *Algonkian* interview, "the book [*A Blessing on the Moon*] is an attempt on my part to recover from the silence of a family history that, except for a clutch of photos and whatever is encoded genetically, has all but disappeared. It is an imaginative reconstruction, of course, not a historical one, and because of that, I feel it is somehow truer."

A Blessing on the Moon

A Blessing on the Moon was long in the making, especially if one considers the years during which the material gestated in the author's head. Filling in the silences of his childhood was for Skibell a preoccupation, if not an obsession. The material, in a word, chose him, rather than the other way around; this is an important consideration whenever the question about appropriate material is raised. Skibell had to write about his great-grandfather, a man he never knew, because it was Chaim Skibelski who haunted him.

Skibell's novel began as a failed play, and then found itself taking shape, finding its "voice," as it were, in a short story. As Skibell tells us, his aborted play got as far as a monologue by the ghost of the main character's great-grandfather (he enters with "gunshot wounds in his face . . . and starts to speak"). He kept rewriting the scene—some fifteen times, in fact—and each time found himself stuck. Chaim Skibelski was a haunting voice, but one that wanted to speak in prose rather than in stage dialogue. Skibell finally realized that he had no choice; this ghost not only wanted to be a fictional character, but also wanted to be the center of the story. The result was a tale that won first prize in a competition sponsored by *Story* magazine, but, more important, that became a chapter in what would eventually become *A Blessing on the Moon*. At long last, the disparate stories of his childhood, the haunting Grimm Brothers tales that seemed to foreshadow the Holocaust as well as Yiddish folktales and songs, came together, allowing Skibell both to reimagine his great-grandfather and to tell his story.

For the post-Holocaust writer, realism, narrative unity, and other standard benchmarks of conventional fiction are now rendered problematic. Small wonder, then, that many Jewish-American writers have been attracted to magical realism's strangely evocative blending of the fantastic and the "real," along with its penchant for fragmented plotting, kaleidoscopic dissolves, and the sheer dazzle of language that suggests fairy tale at one level and family chronicle at another. *A Blessing on the Moon* is a case in point. It is, above all else, an effort of rescue, a way of coming to terms with his great-grandparents who, along with all of their daughters and one son, perished in the Holocaust. Of the best representatives of post-Holocaust literature we can say this: They bear witness through the imagination, and as such, become increasingly important as the number of those who can offer firsthand testimony becomes smaller every year. Skibell adds an important dimension to this formula because he means to give voice to those in his family who for so long had been silenced. What he means to do is create a world much closer to the horrific one Jerzy Kosinski projected in *A Painted Bird*—that is, a fictional construct in which matter-of-factness is forced to share floor space with the magical. As his narrator points out at a crucial point in the novel: "But that's impossible," I say [referring here to the moon being pulled from the heavens by a boat laden with silver]. "Impossible? Of course," says Kalman, giggling behind me. "Nevertheless, it's true"—true, that is, as the best fiction always discovers a truth deeper than the surface truths of fact and methodical measure.

The novel's odd yoking of the incredible and the all too true begins from the first page. When the elderly Chaim Skibelski climbs out of the mass grave into which the Nazis have consigned him (along with nearly three thousand of his Jewish neighbors), he does not quite realize that he is dead. Such is the bitter premise established on the novel's opening page, and it is this aesthetic decision that simultaneously makes *A Blessing on the Moon* so startlingly original and that dooms it to a mug's game of constantly raising the ante. For Skibell, magical realism occurs when his protagonist describes himself running out of a mass grave "with the dirt still in my mouth. I had to spit it out as I ran." Realism appears when he first sees a watery reflection of his face as it really is:

> One side is entirely missing, except for an eye, which has turned completely white. Barely hanging in its socket, it stares at itself in an astonished wonder. My grey beard is matted thick with blood, and broken bits of bone protrude here and there through the raw patches of my flesh.

From there bad news moves inexorably to worse as Skibelski (now invisible to everyone except a morally sensitive Polish teenager) learns that death serves up more questions than answers, and more magical realism than anything else.

For a dead man, Chaim Skibelski is a lively narrative presence, given to flights of language so delicate (however incongruous) that they make the heart crack. For the first generation of Holocaust writers, breaking the silence about what had happened to them required a rigorous attention to facts that seemed to defy description, much less meaning. Skibell, by contrast, has found a new way to probe the very essence of the horror; his radical inventions (a rabbi transmogrified into a crow a luxury hotel in which the Jewish dead are given soups that taste just like mother's, and steam baths that are really gas chambers in disguise) promise to change the very definition of writing about catastrophe. Terms such as "dry wit" or "radical understatement" hardly describe the power that Skibelski's offhand observations unleash. As Ann Patchett, writing in the pages of the *Boston Globe* put it, Skibell has "turned the full light of his extraordinary talent and vision to one of history's darkest moments and taught us to see it again." Most reviewers agreed, many commenting on Skibell's dazzling style and his way of turning the Holocaust into a surrealistic fantasy, but not all: Alvin Rosenfeld, writing in the pages of *The Forward*, found Skibell's comically bickering characters both "jarring" and "grotesque." Even more disturbing than the imposition of lighthearted humor, Rosenfeld feels, is Skibell's sheer audacity as a fiction writer. He seems blind to the "sheer inadequacy of the literary imagination to position itself at the slaughter pits and render that horror in plausible ways."

By contrast, Michelle Ephraim, writing in the *Chronicle of Higher Education*, argues that Skibell takes "a leap of faith," one that risks a trust of and openness to the public. His novel "does not insist that the reader react with shock or guilt; it defies the pressure to be an overly prescriptive, educational tool. Instead, the novel assumes the reader's ethical autonomy." If his excessive magical realism causes us to see the Holocaust in new ways, so be it. That is precisely what the best fiction always docs.

Seeing is, of course, related to the moon, and the odd light that it casts over Chaim Skibelski's imaginary world. Conspicuous by its absence during most of Skibelski's adventures, Skibell's tone implies, is a case of the natural world responding to the systematic destruction of its local Jews. Not surprisingly, the Poles, now comfortably ensconced in the Skibelskis' former house, have quite another explanation: "The yids disappear and the moon disappears and you're telling me they didn't take it." Moreover, one peasant observes, "you think they'll stop with the moon . . . Soon they'll want the stars and then the entire planetary system!"

The novel ends on the twin notes of epiphany and healing as the traditional Hebrew blessings for a new moon are recited, and the moon itself is restored. Skibell reminds us in his *Algonkian* interview that

> In Jewish thought, we are taught to look at everything that happens to us as a blessing, Good or bad. There is only one God, after all, who is the source of everything, so everything is a blessing. Or should be seen as such. It's not always easy to do.

Certainly it is not easy to do if the subject at hand is the Holocaust, but a kind of redemption—a blessing, if you will—is what Skibell's novel is about. He seems to be saying that imagination has the power to bring his dead great-grandfather back from the silence that formerly surrounded him, that the world's hatred is finally no match against the world's love, and that prayer can help even the natural order of the heavens reestablish itself.

Bibliography

Primary Source

A Blessing on the Moon. 1997.

Interview

"Interview." *Algonkion* (June 1997).

SIMJA SNEH
(1914–1999)

DARRELL B. LOCKHART

SIMJA SNEH IS WITHOUT a doubt a seminal figure in Holocaust literature written in Spanish. This is of particular significance because his native languages were Yiddish and Polish. Born on 15 October 1914 in Pulawy, Poland, he was educated in Hasidic studies by *melamdim* (private tutors) in Hebrew and in literature by his uncle Itzjak Weintraub. He finished his secondary education at the gymnasium Prince Czartorysky, which had a *numerous clausus* policy effectively limiting the number of Jewish students permitted to attend. Having studied history and philosophy at the Free University of Warsaw, he worked as a teacher and journalist. With the emergence of Nazism and Hitler's military aggression, Sneh was compelled to become a soldier, fighting with the Polish army under General Anders and with the Jewish Brigade of the British Army in Italy.

He arrived in Argentina under precarious circumstances. Wounded while fighting and then hospitalized, he later met a Dutch soldier who was going to Argentina and who promised to carry a letter to Sneh's friend Joseph Lenger. Incredibly, Lenger was located; he arranged for Sneh to travel to Buenos Aires from London, but the Argentine consul informed him that Jews were currently not allowed into the country and refused to grant him a visa. Sneh was not discouraged; he made the trip and entered the country illegally. He quickly adapted to life in Buenos Aires, teaching Yiddish and Hebrew in the Jewish school system of Buenos Aires. In addition, he worked as a journalist for a variety of Jewish and mainstream newspapers and periodicals. Although Sneh wrote several books in Yiddish and Hebrew and thus might have adhered to traditional Hebrew or Yiddish lamentation conventions or midrashic and biblical themes, his Spanish works follow a documentary or testimonial style, as found in Latin American realism. His works have earned the Tzví (Zwi) Kessel award (1952), the Sash of Honor from the Argentine Writers Association (1977), and the Fernando Jeno prize from Mexico. Sneh worked for many years in the Department of Culture of the AMIA (Asociación Mutual Israelita Argentina), one of the major Jewish institutions in Buenos Aires. In fact, he was there on 18 July 1994 when the building was destroyed by a terrorist car bomb, killing over 80 people. Miraculously, Sneh survived the attack. His life and works are defined by survival, endurance, and strength. Simja Sneh passed away in April 1999.

El pan y la sangre

Sneh's first volume of stories to appear in Spanish was *El pan y la sangre* (Bread and Blood, 1977). Sneh's experience as a *Shoah* survivor serves as the source from which the characters, places, and circumstances in these stories emerge. Dedicating the book to his perished parents, two brothers, and two sisters, Sneh states "este libro es mi autobiografía, sin ser, en absoluto, la historia de mi vida" [This book is my autobiography, without being, by any means, the story of my life (Sudamericana, p. 7)]. Although there is no direct treatment of specific ghettos or concentration camps in *El pan y la sangre*, the deceptive cruelty by which the Nazis lured Jews to their deaths is evoked by the story titles, which, while apparently simple, hide the violence they often contain. Titles like "Una mosca" (A Fly), "Sangre" (Blood), "Pan" (Bread), "El roble" (The Oak Tree), or "El muñeco de nieve" (The Snowman) give little indication of the horror and anguish they contain. For example, in "El muñeco de nieve" Sneh turns what is usually a whimsical creation of joyful children into a nightmarish act of violent cruelty and human depravity as he meticulously describes the sadistic SS torture and murderous freezing of a Jewish man. Sneh holds nothing back. His descriptions are at times disturbing in their portrayal of cruelty, pain, and suffering, and yet there are more tender moments, even if they evoke nostalgia for what has been lost.

Critic Leonardo Senkman focuses on two stories from *El pan y la sangre* to provide an analysis of what he finds to be one of the main leitmotifs in Sneh's writing: the depiction of survivor guilt manifested in feelings of guilt for being alive, shame for receiving reparation monies, and constant mental anguish from memories that cannot be shaken. "Sombras" (Shadows) foregrounds the problematic relationship of Argentina with Europe (and especially Germany) during World War II, shown principally through the illicit dealings of one of the characters with German business interests, from which he becomes very wealthy. Sneh pits two Jewish friends against each other to contrast the different Argentinian reactions—specifically among Jews—to the war. Iósel sends his fiancée to Argentina when war erupts while he stays behind in Poland to fight in the resistance. After the war he too immigrates to Argentina, where he discovers that his fiancée has married his friend Miguel Weinblat. Even when presented with the opportunity to make a lot of money, Iósel prefers to work as a humble *cuentenik* (peddler) in northern Argentina. On his deathbed he rebukes his old friend Miguel for becoming rich from his business dealings with Nazis while he was in a concentration camp. This final reprimand is the impetus for the story. Chastised into pondering the immorality of his actions, Miguel is haunted by guilt and shame. "El cheque" (The Check) also deals with the issue of guilt, but from a different angle. In this case the protagonist is a Holocaust survivor who undergoes psychoanalysis to help him deal with the extreme guilt he feels for being the only survivor in his family. The eponymous "check" refers to reparation monies he receives, which only add to his feelings of guilt. He realizes that therapy is futile, and that he will not be able to overcome his mental anguish. Senkman summarizes the meaning of the Holocaust in Sneh's writing: "For Sneh there is no consolation in surviving the Holocaust. There is no dignity among the living, even for those who fought the Nazis. There can be none" (p. 388 translation mine).

Sin rumbo

While *El pan y la sangre* alone is a significant contribution to Holocaust writing, Sneh's true masterpiece is to be found in his subsequent work, *Sin rumbo* (Aimless, 1993) completed just two years prior to his death. Published between 1993 and 1997 (in Spanish), the six-volume text is over sixteen hundred pages in length. It was originally written in Yiddish as a trilogy and serialized between 1947 and 1952 in the Yiddish periodical *Di Presse* in Buenos Aires. The first volume was published as a book entitled *Na'Venad* (Aimless) (1952) and earned him the Zwi Kessel award from Mexico. The six volumes of *Sin rumbo* were published by Editorial Milá, the press operated by the AMIA. The volumes are prefaced by enthusiastic commentaries from Argentine writers and critics Ernesto Sabato, Ricardo Feierstein, Marco Denevi, Samuel Tarnopolsky, Santiago Kovadloff, and Leonardo Senkman. Each also contains a variety of photographs, copies of handwritten letters, and other visual documents that add to this work, which is part testimonial narrative, part memoir, part novel, and part historical document. *Sin rumbo* is divided into three parts: The first part (volumes 1 and 2) begins with the German invasion of Poland and Sneh's escape to the east, where he joins the Red Army and fights against the Nazi advance. It chronicles his regiment's travels across the Soviet Union toward Asia, the creation of the Polish army by General Anders, his enrollment in the army, and his departure for the Middle East. The second part (volumes 3 and 4), covering 1942 to 1944, describes in some detail the climate of antisemitism among Anders's own troops. He also writes of the British Army's creation of the Jewish Brigade, how he comes to join it, and its campaign in Italy. In the two volumes dedicated to his experience in the Jewish Brigade, Sneh details the gamut of emotions felt by the soldiers, from elation at having the chance to fight back to frustration at having to follow British command. He also speaks extensively about the often troubled relationship between foreign Jews and *sabras*. Some of this frustration is illustrated in the following passage.

> News has arrived from the Jewish Brigade: they are on the front lines. The newspapers publish stories about Nazi prisoners led by Jewish soldiers with Stars of David on their shoulders. Why take prisoners? Why do we need prisoners? They have to be fed and taken care of so nothing happens to them. After the conflict is over they will be set free and sent back to their German homes. Of course, international laws and norms exist that prohibit the killing of prisoners; it's clear that such matters are governed by treaties, agreements, and codes. But let the English, the North Americans and the French adhere to them. Everyone, everyone but us. Where are our prisoners to be found? Who will return our dead to us from the gas chambers? Take heed, cold world made of stone! (Vol. 4, pp. 129–130, translation mine).

The third part (volumes 5 and 6) takes place toward the end of the war up to mid-1947. He continues the narration of his experience with the Jewish Brigade in northern Italy, and later his transfer to Holland and

Belgium. He describes his search for survivors in Poland, always confronted with antisemitism, as seen in the following passage.

> The one-time Polish neighbors who lived near Jewish quarters of the city related details of the annihilation to the soldiers (of the Jewish Brigade). The tone of their voice and the look in their eyes revealed a sort of poorly disguised satisfaction. They seemed to enjoy what they had seen (Vol. 5, p. 151, translation mine).

The defining characteristic in the narrative is the experience of a soldier fighting in several different campaigns against Nazism, a perspective unique in the body of Holocaust writing from Latin America. Likewise, it stands as a substantial social and historical record of the Holocaust, and certainly the single most important Holocaust work written in Spanish. Together *El pan y la sangre* and *Sin rumbo* constitute a remarkable legacy of an even more remarkable human being who overcame incredible odds and left the world a gift of momentous significance.

Critical Reception

Criticism of Sneh's works is not abundant despite the fact that his literary corpus is quite extensive. This may be due to the fact that the Spanish-language version of *Sin rumbo* is still relatively recent. Nevertheless, the volumes do contain some significant commentary by leading authors and critics. One of Simja Sneh's most ardent supporters, Argentina's greatest living author and intellectual, Ernesto Sabato, praises Sneh for his courage and for his ability to reach all mankind through the universality of his work:

> These voices, these memories, this knot in the throat that appears time and again, much like the icons of that other Jew who painted fiddlers on rooftops, transcend the limits of any ghetto to reach the soul of all feeling men, because all great artists achieve this miracle of universality. Thus, through the words of he who speaks to us from Yiddish in Spanish, we as humanity comprehend what we hope for, feel, love, and suffer on all parts of the earth (pp. 492–493).

Bibliography

Primary Sources

Na'Venad (Aimless). Buenos Aires: Editorial Undzervort, 1952.
El pan y la sangre (Bread and blood). 1977, 1986.
Sin rumbo (Aimless). 6 vols. 1993.

Secondary Sources

Sabato, Ernesto. "Sneh, Simja." In *Jewish Writers of Latin America: A Dictionary*. Edited by Darrell B. Lockhart. New York: Garland, 1997, pp. 489–494.

Senkman, Leonardo. "Sobrevivir el holocausto: bochorno y culpa." In *La identidad judía en la literatura argentina*. Buenos Aires: Pardés, 1983, pp. 384–389.

JOSHUA SOBOL

(1939–)

STEVEN DEDALUS BURCH

JOSHUA (YEHOSHUA) SOBOL was born in Tel Mond, an agricultural village close to Tel Aviv in, then, Palestine in 1939. His father was a Russian agronomist, his mother was from Poland, and his grandmother, in whose home he grew up, was a Zionist and a former Bundist. His early career included writing and publishing short stories written during his experience as a member of Kibbutz Shamir. In 1965 he went to Paris and studied philosophy at the Sorbonne, returning to Israel as a teacher after his graduation in 1970.

In 1971 his first produced play, *The Days to Come*, premiered at the Haifa Theater, home to most of his plays for the next sixteen years. Politically leftist and sharply critical of his government, Sobol caused several controversies with his outspoken views, expressed not only in interviews and in essays but in his plays, in which he frequently dramatizes historical events and characters in order to address moral and political questions of current Israeli life.

The Vilna Trilogy

In 1984, *Ghetto*, the first of Sobol's Vilna Trilogy, premiered in Haifa and then received a hugely successful production at the Volkstheater in Berlin under the direction of Peter Zadek. Since then, the play has been seen around the world in more than sixty productions and has brought Sobol numerous best play awards from Germany, Japan, England (the coveted Olivier Award), and most recently, the United States (the Jefferson Award for best production). It has also brought vociferous complaints from many audiences that have been disturbed by the play's painful portrait of Jews attempting to survive the Nazis seemingly at any cost.

In the Vilna Trilogy (*Ghetto*, 1984, *Adam*, 1989, *Underground*, 1991) Sobol attempts to put an entire society on stage by interrogating the memories of Holocaust survivors and to examine that society's response to the moral cataclysm caused by the Holocaust. Using historical facts, diaries, and first-hand recollections of survivors from the Vilna Ghetto, Sobol explores what he perceives as the central moral question of that time: How can any individual choose good, when choosing good over evil is not an option? In the plays' central linking character, Jakob Gens (ca. 1899–1943), the historical leader of the Vilna Ghetto, Sobol creates one of the most emotionally and morally complex roles in modern theater. Sobol's trilogy, with its extraordinary stagecraft demands, incisive characterizations, and troubling morality, may yet come to be recognized as one of the true landmarks in the theater of our time.

Vilna had a Jewish population, before World War II, of over 70,000, which constituted the largest single ethnic bloc of the city. This community had existed and flourished since the end of the fifteenth century, and it was renowned as the Jerusalem of Lithuania for its wide cultural life, many rabbinical scholars, and centers of Talmudic learning. But by the time of the Nazi invasion, in the summer of 1941, there were no recognized Jewish organizations to deal with the incursion. Beginning in July 1941, the Germans kidnapped Jewish men from the streets and from their homes. Officially reported as having been sent to work camps, these men were taken to Ponar, a popular picnic area just outside the city limits, where they (and later women and children) were shot in a continuous series of mass slayings. These executions were not known among the majority of the Jewish population. By the time the slayings became public knowledge, it was too late.

During the first week of September 1941, six wounded women escaped to Vilna from the pits at Ponar and were secretly taken to the Jewish hospital on Zawalna Street. There they told their stories of being led blindfolded to the pits and shot. Fearing reprisals if the Germans heard about the survivors, the hospital personnel, along with police chief Jakob Gens, kept the stories secret. But very shortly after this, widespread, ongoing *Aktionen* (organized progroms) by the Nazi *Einsatzkommando* (SS special action groups) succeeded in liquidating over 50,000 men, women, and children (mostly at Ponar) and herding the remaining 20,000 Jews into two small ghettoes.

A Jewish council (*Judenrat*) was established in the ghetto but was formally dissolved by the Germans on 10 July 1942, and full power was transferred to the head of the Jewish police, Gens. During the two years of its existence, until the ghetto was liquidated on 20 September 1943, an extraordinary attempt was made by several individuals and hastily set up organizations to save the remaining Jews from extermination by bullet, starvation, and disease. It is in this two-year period, from the women survivors' escape from Ponar to the liquidation of the ghetto, that Sobol sets the action of his three plays.

Ghetto addresses the formation of a ghetto theater; *Adam* recounts the horror of the day when the ghetto's inhabitants were persuaded to surrender the leader of the underground resistance to the Nazis; and *Underground* dramatizes the work of the hospital wards, which, under the auspices of false documents, secretly treated cases of typhus and illegal pregnancy. All three plays are presented through the troubled memories of three of the Vilna Ghetto's former inhabitants: the lone survivor of the theater company, the mistress of a resistance leader, and a homeless psychotic.

In *Ghetto*, as Jewish bodies are perishing under Nazi torture, an almost quixotic attempt is made by several people to salvage the Jewish soul by preserving Jewish culture through the formation of a theater company that would perform skits, musical numbers, and full-scale dramas for the ghetto's inhabitants and, occasionally, the Nazis. Sobol intersperses his community's story with various songs and skits from the historical theater's actual repertoire, creating a highly theatrical play within a play as the ghetto theater's performers are able to mix satirical commentary on their situation within their musical numbers. Noting the play's affinities with Bertolt Brecht's epic theater and the German satirical cabaret of the 1920s, Yael Feldman acknowledges that the "impact of the original ghetto songs and the sketches of musical review, staged as they are within the horror of liquidation, is nothing less than chilling" (" 'Identification-with-the-Aggressor" or the 'Victim Complex,' " p. 166).

The play introduces five figures from the historical files of the Vilna Ghetto. Preeminent among them is Jewish Chief of Police Jakob Gens, who became the head of the ghetto when the Germans disbanded the *Judenrat* and transferred its power to him. *Ghetto* also dramatizes the collaboration by Gens and the Jewish police in the liquidation of Oshmyany, a smaller ghetto in a suburb outside of Vilna, and in the hanging of six Jewish criminals for a murder committed during a robbery in the ghetto. The remaining four characters are Hermann Kruk, the Bundist librarian who at first opposed the formation of a theater company (and whose actual diary provided much first-hand information for Sobol); Hans Kittel, the music-loving Nazi officer who directly carried out the orders of liquidation; Weiskopf (no first name is given), a tailor who convinced Kittel and other Nazis to let him open a factory to restore uniforms for German soldiers; and Srulik (Israel Segal), a ventriloquist whose response to an unseen interviewer's question about the very last performance of the theater company provides the play with its narrative frame.

According to Sobol, in his "A Theatre in the Wilna Ghetto," published by Theatre Communications Group, Gens's attachment to the principle of preserving Jewish culture at a time when the ghetto was being slowly destroyed came from his "conviction that normalization and productivization . . . were the key to saving as many people as possible [and he] regarded the theatre not only as a source of livelihood and employment for the actors but also as an invaluable emotional outlet which would boost morale and help to normalize ghetto life" (p. 228). On the question of morale, Gens was quickly proven right. No fewer than 111 performances were given in the first year, and from January 1942, when the ghetto's theater opened, to the liquidation in September 1943, the ghetto's population of twenty thousand people bought seventy thousand tickets.

Over the objections of the Bundists, especially Kruk, who attempted to stop the cultural activity by displaying banners and handbills declaring, "In a cemetery there can be no theatre" (p. 227), Gens pushed through his plans for a vigorous renewal of cultural life in the ghetto and in the course of the play finally succeeds in winning over many to his viewpoint, including Kruk. But along with this robust cultural activity, Gens also ruled the ghetto as an autocrat, attempting to stave off the coming extermination by convincing the Nazis that it was in their interest to keep the ghetto alive and productive during the war. The way that Gens bought time from the Germans (for he was convinced that Germany was losing the war) was to "collaborate" in the liquidation of the population through negotiation, consortment, and bribery. When groups of Jews were demanded for execution or removal to the camps, Gens frequently reduced their numbers by weeding out the elderly, the infirm, the criminal.

When he could not bargain, Gens resorted to trickery. In *Ghetto* Sobol dramatizes one such occasion when in 1941 the Germans ordered all inhabitants of the ghetto to register. Yellow certificates allowed Jews to work, and their families were issued blue tickets. But the tickets only recognized four members per family: husband, wife, and two children. In November another round-up occurred, requiring all Jews without certificates and tickets to be deported. As families passed through the ghetto gate, Gens stood and supervised the removal of Jews without certificates. As related by Kruk with grudging astonishment, a family of five came through, and Gens hit one of the boys with a cane and separated him from the family. Savage indignation swept through the crowd. Then a family of three passed through. Gens stopped them and berated the father of this family for failing to keep track of all his sons, and pushed the other family's boy into this group, causing Kruk to sardonically observe, "And Jakob Gens, the Jewish Jew-killer, saves another child" (p. 182).

Gens's policy was ruthless but simple: save as many Jews as he could by whatever means at his disposal; delay the implementation of the final liquidation; and hope that the Russians would arrive before that fateful day. Driven as he was by a profound sense of compassion for his people, Gens was ruthless against those who threatened to undermine the entire scheme. In June 1942, his police hanged six men in the ghetto. Five had been convicted of murder during the course of a robbery, an incident Sobol recreates in the second act of *Ghetto*. The sixth had stabbed a policeman who recovered from his wound. But this sixth man was a Gestapo informer, and Gens took the opportunity of ridding the ghetto of a lethal troublemaker (Tushnet, p. 172).

On still another occasion, a partisan was discovered at the ghetto gate to have a revolver and, in a panic, shot and killed one of the Jewish policemen; Gens personally pursued him and shot him to death. Yet Gens was also respectful toward the partisan underground movement, tacitly approving their activities while keeping the peace. After his police caught partisan member Moshe Shutan, Gens taunted him by asking how many dozens of Jews of the ghetto's 20,000 inhabitants the partisans would save. Interviewed on a film directed by Josh Waletsky four decades later, Shutan reflected, "His [Gens's] arguments—given his point of view—left me helpless. I couldn't argue with him" (*Partisans of Vilna*). Gens then issued Shutan a work permit and allowed him to rejoin his resistance group in the forest.

On 14 September 1943, Gens was arrested, accused of aiding the partisans (he had covered their escape into the forest through an elaborate ploy of organizing mass deportations of the ghetto inhabitants to work camps in Estonia) and was executed the same day. The day before, he was warned of what the Germans were planning to do to him and was advised to flee the ghetto. Fearful of German reprisal against the remaining inhabitants of the ghetto in retaliation for his escape, he refused (Tushnet, p. 196; Arad, p. 425). Nine days later on 23 September 1943 the ghetto was liquidated. Between mass executions at Ponar and transfers to the death camp at Majdanek and to labor camps in Estonia, only 2,000 to 3,000 of the ghetto's original inhabitants survived.

From the ghetto's beginning, Gens's policies made him enemies, yet many believed in him and felt that, hard though his way was, he was doing his best to save as many Jews as he could. Gens instilled a Work to Live ideology which, even though opposed by the FPO (*Fareinikte Partizaner Organizatzia*, or United Partisans' Organization), is presented sympathetically by Sobol and historians Yitzhak Arad and Leonard Tushnet, among others, as a sound strategy, despite its ultimate failure. Still, hatred for Gens and his seeming complicity with the Nazis was intense if not widespread within the ghetto. In 1942, a remarkable "trial" was held at one of the school clubs Gens had helped organize. The historical figure of King Herod the Great was placed on trial, with students acting as prosecutor and defender before a court made up of scholars. Fifteen-year-old diarist Yitskhok Rudashevski was chosen to prosecute, and in his diary, as well as in his brief, he clearly analogized Herod, the corrupt Jewish ruler of imperial Rome, with Gens. Of what Gens felt or said about the trial, there appears to be no record. But Gens knew full well how he appeared to many in the ghetto. At a literary gathering to award a prize to a novelist and a poet, Gens gave a remarkable speech, acknowledging that in his efforts to save as many Jews as possible he stood before them willingly with blood on his hands: "And in order to save even a small part of the Jewish people, I alone had to lead others to their deaths. And in order to ensure that you go out with clear consciences I have to forget mine and wallow in filth" (Tushnet, p. 169–170).

Sobol uses a large portion of this speech to end the second act of *Ghetto*. By this point in the play the audience has seen Gens bribe the enemy, procure prostitutes, host an orgy for the Germans, begin the theater company, hang Jewish criminals, bully his Jewish opposition and threaten them with reprisal, and set up factories for Jewish and German mercenaries. At this point in the play he is drunk and alone on stage. It is to the audience that he addresses these extraordinary words, taunting them with their easy and speedy judgment. And of course the audience will judge him. History and Sobol's play demand it. But Sobol and the historical Gens also demand that the audience examine their "clear consciences." In the play, Gens's final words to the speech are a taunt to his audience: "A clean conscience for Jakob Gens? I couldn't afford one!" (p. 203). As if, Sobol is saying, the audience can.

A respectful but uneasy relationship between Gens and the resistance reached a crisis on 15–16 July 1943, in a betrayal remembered afterward as Witenberg Day. Slightly fictionalized by Sobol as the core event of the second play of the trilogy, *Adam*, this historical crisis occurred when a minor Communist Party activist, after arrest and torture by the Gestapo, named Isaac Witenberg as the head of the FPO, the partisan resistance group. Fearful that this would bring on the liquidation that he had anticipated for so long, Gens called a secret meeting of the leaders of the FPO. As the meeting progressed, Gens's Jewish police entered and arrested Witenberg, but within minutes, as Witenberg was being led to jail, the resistance mobilized and rescued him, whereupon he went into hiding.

At first, the remaining resistance leaders were convinced that Gens had betrayed them to the Germans and would not listen to Gens's explanation. Knowing that this rescue would surely bring the Gestapo into the ghetto and that the Nazis would seek reprisals as well, Gens hastily called a public meeting. At the top of his voice Gens asked the crowd if the safety of the ghetto should be imperiled because of one man. The crowd yelled back to give Witenberg up and save the ghetto. Chaos ensued as the crowd began to rush around the ghetto searching for the hidden Witenberg. Finally, Gens convinced the leaders that the Gestapo had no information about the resistance, that this was not a conspiracy against them, and that if they gave up Witenberg, Gens would do everything in his power to free him. After a long night of painful reflection and recrimination, the leaders asked Witenberg to give himself up. He did and was taken into custody and presumably tortured. The next day, he was found dead from poisoning, most likely cyanide potassium. According to Yitzhak Arad's history of the Vilna Ghetto, Gens had supplied Witenberg with the poison just prior to Witenberg's surrender (p. 393), a scene dramatized by Sobol in *Adam* in which the two men grimly share their hope that the ghetto can be kept alive for just another four or five months (p. 329).

In his introductory essay to *Adam*, Michael Taub remarks that Gens's seeming collaboration with the Nazis and his moral ambiguity are seen by an idealist in the first play as reprehensible, but that Sobol is attempting to contest a range of conventional notions regarding heroism and collaboration with one's enemies (*Israeli Holocaust Drama*, p. 15). In *Adam*, Sobol focuses on the two days of the Witenberg affair and deliberately and dramatically contrasts Gens with the principled leaders of the underground resistance.

Adam's structure as a memory play is more complex than *Ghetto*'s, with the events of the past occurring simultaneously on stage with their remembrance by Old Nadja, a retired actress who was also Adam's (Witenberg) lover in the ghetto. Old Nadja's reconstruction of the events of Witenberg Day occur during Israel's 1982 war against the PLO camps in Lebanon. Drawing an implied parallel between the Vilna resistance fighters and the Palestinian guerrillas, Sobol investigates the destructive arguments advanced by idealists with guns. At this period in the ghetto's existence, Gens was almost literally sitting on a powder keg. The revolt in the Warsaw Ghetto in the spring of 1943 resulted in Holocaust architect Heinrich Himmler's orders for the liquidation of all the large ghettoes. Gens knew about the resistance and tacitly supported it as long as the leaders did not threaten the safety of the ghetto. But when a communist agent was arrested and gave the Gestapo the name of Isaac Witenberg, Gens feared the Germans' discovery of the resistance movement's existence.

As dramatized by Sobol and confirmed by the participants of this event, Gens's only hope was to turn Witenberg over to the Gestapo, to hope the Nazis knew nothing about the resistance, and to try to buy some time before the liquidation order became a reality. The crux of the play is the heroes' realization and agreement that to betray their leader might mean survival for themselves and the ghetto. In the world of Gens and Sobol, idealism means death and destruction. Earlier in the play, Sobol dramatizes this in an exchange between Gens and the Nazi officer Kittel, who does not want the ghetto liquidated because it will mean his being sent to the Russian front, and who acknowledges to Gens that Germany is run by idealistic fanatics who will destroy the entire country.

What dominates this exchange is the tone of moral fatigue between the two pragmatic antagonists. On the one hand, Kittel's Germany is portrayed as plunging into a nonstop orgy of self-destruction through the idealism of its leaders, and on the other hand, Gens's ghetto is threatened with destruction because of the idealism of its freedom fighters. Essentially, both men are powerless to stop these events, yet each attempts to finesse, to negotiate, and to bargain away the coming reality.

At the end of the third play in the trilogy, *Underground* (which deals with the successful efforts to hide a typhus epidemic in the ghetto from the Germans), Gens and Kittel continue their negotiating ploys until there is nothing left to negotiate: the order for liquidation has come, and the Nazis know that Gens has used the transfers of the ghetto inhabitants to Estonia as a smoke screen to cover the evacuation of the partisans to the forest. Gens is under arrest, and the leader of the Germans, Neugebauer, is ready to execute him, as he did historically, according to an eyewitness (Arad, p. 425). Kittel makes one last attempt to negotiate for the life of Gens: urging Gens to tell them where the remnants of the partisans are hidden in the ghetto so his life will be spared. As imagined by Sobol, it is a powerful conclusion to his themes as Gens refuses Kittel and goads the Nazis into killing him on the spot:

> You can kill me. It's easy to kill a man. A bubble of air in the veins, a drop of filth in the blood.
> (*Kittel aims at Gens' chest.*)
> I am a man and you are that filth that kills me. FIRE!
> (*Kittel fires a shot. Blackout.*) (pp. 42–43).

The mirror image Sobol has constructed of these two morally tired pragmatists is destroyed in this final confrontation. By killing Gens, Kittel acquiesces in the Nazis' decision to liquidate the ghetto, thereby ensuring his own probable destruction at the collapsing Russian front. In the history of the Vilna Ghetto and in Sobol's trilogy, Jakob Gens emerges as a deeply complex character who was obviously aware of the corruption done to his soul. But Sobol does not see such corruption as evil in itself. In fact, this corruption presages a greater good because it declines judgment and accepts the existence of an Other. In his lecture "Theatricality of Political Theatre," published in *Maske und Kothurn* in 1987, Sobol detailed his thoughts:

> I think the human being is impure. Purity is not a human attribute. I know myself and I'm not pure, my thoughts are not pure, my feelings are not pure, nor my dreams are pure and God knows what else. The moment you cannot accept any more your impurity . . . is the moment you start dealing with this point of reversal. You start to project the fear of your impurity on everyone. This fear is projected on everyone who looks different, smells different, everyone who behaves differently, talks differently, or prays differently to his God, and immediately he is a candidate for annihilation. . . . The drama of our time is the desperate struggle of human beings, individuals, and some groups against this leading tendency. . . . I feel attracted to subjects and events which have to do with this clash between those who have the passion to destroy and those who have the passion to resist it and say no. There is no purity, let us be as we are. Do not ask us to be pure, to be saints. We are impure, and let us live like this (pp. 111–112).

Commentary

Not everyone agrees with Sobol, however. When *Ghetto* first opened in New York in 1989, *New York Times* critic Frank Rich refused to look at the play's morally conflicted characters as anything but stereotypes, especially the money-grubbing Weiskopf, and dismissed Sobol's Brechtian play within a play as a musically inferior *Cabaret*. More critically damning was an article by Holocaust survivor and Nobel Prize winner Elie Wiesel, who was distressed at Sobol's unflattering portrait of the Jews in the ghetto, calling it not just false and nasty but " 'Hilul hashem'—blasphemy or profanation" (p. 38).

Also troubling to many, especially in Sobol's native Israel, is his use of the story of the Vilna ghetto to advance his leftist, seemingly anti-Zionist political views. To Sobol's many detractors in his country, he appears to equate the racism of the Nazis with the "need" by Jews to preserve a specifically Jewish state. Indeed, as Yael Feldman correctly points out, Sobol's choice of his materials is deeply influenced by Israel's political crises in the 1980s, and Sobol quite deliberately and provocatively sets up parallels between the arguments advanced by his characters in the Vilna ghetto with those resembling the critics and defenders of Israel during the Lebanon War ("Whose Story Is It Anyway?" pp. 225–226). Clearly these plays are not intended to be seen solely as a documentary recreation of one small corner of the Holocaust. In *Ghetto*, the Bundist scholar and librarian Kruk's argument against Zionist philosophy is energetically rebutted by none other than the Nazi scholar Dr. Paul who, as indicated by Sobol in his stage directions, is meant to be played by the same actor who enacts the role of Kittel.

Making two appearances, first in act two and the second time in act three, Dr. Paul is based on another real-life model working out of the Rosenberg Foundation, for "the investigation of Judaism without Jews" (p. 189), to record and preserve Jewish culture before it is obliterated forever. In the mouth of the Nazi, the faux Jew, Sobol relates a Hasidic legend of a king who has had a fight with his son and has banished him from the castle. Later, thinking better of his deed, the king sends a messenger to find his son and ask him what three wishes he would have. The messenger returns with the reply of "bread, clothing, and a place to sleep" (p. 191). From this, the king determines that his son has truly forgotten to be a prince because a prince would have only asked for one wish: to return to the castle where the other three wishes would automatically be granted. Sobol, through Dr. Paul, intends that Israel be seen as the castle, yet in Kruk he provides an alternative reading:

> you've got it all wrong. The son understood the situation perfectly. He wished for what he needed: Men aren't at

> home because of any particular soil—they're at home with their heritage, with their traditions. *That's* the loss they must guard against. Without culture, they lose their identity (p. 192).

Against this, Dr. Paul argues that Kruk's belief that "socialism in the Diaspora would allow for the survival of Jewish culture" (p. 191) and that Kruk's brand of Zionism will leave it "to the Genses of this world" (p. 192) who, as Jews, are "horrifying caricatures—something you might see in a funhouse mirror" (p. 191). In the third act, when Gens asserts that he will order Hebrew and "Palistinography" to be taught in the schools (p. 206) and further asserts that anyone "not in agreement with the new policy of nationalism is hereby barred from all key positions" (p. 206), Kruk (Sobol) retorts that the Germans have succeeded.

Some of Sobol's defenders have denied that he equates Zionists with Nazis, arguing, like Rachel Shteir, that Sobol's image of the funhouse mirror is only a critical trope for examining Israel's current crisis (p. 41). Certainly Sobol himself has elaborated on this metaphor, considering the funhouse mirror as a distortion of the same image, an image that Sobol finds in the traditional carnival, as he writes in his "Theatricality of Political Theatre":

> [the world] is a carnival . . . life is turned inside out, it is "le monde a l'envers," the world we know is capsized, turned upside down. All the laws, taboos, and restrictions are abolished for the duration of the carnival. There is no more hierarchy, no respect, no manners prevail. There is no longer any difference between people . . . You go out in the streets and take part in the carnival . . . This special kind of mixture is probably one of the characteristics of the Nazi era, when the king of a carnival became the leader of a nation. As a result, history became a bloody carnival (pp. 108–110).

Sobol further cites that what happened to the populace of the ghetto was a "desacralization of human reality. . . . Desacralization of human values, profanation of anything that is saintly, anything valuable in human life" (p. 109). During the carnival "rationality and irrationality no longer exclude each other, they now complement each other and become two facets of the same phenomenon that is the human being" (p. 109).

Sobol is deeply interested in how a society, any society (especially one that prides itself on its moral and cultural values) can lose its bearings and bring down a reign of terror on a minority group. In his trilogy, there is a troubling and troubled response to what many in his homeland accept in the current Israeli-Palestinian situation. Racial and cultural purity was once used by the Kittels and the Rosenbergs to kill an entire people and eradicate their culture. Jakob Gens becomes the dramatist's stratagem to cut through all questions of purity and morality by forcing himself and those around him to accept a moral equivalence between themselves and their annihilators. Only by doing that could a town (and by extension, a culture) survive. Only by accepting the blood on his hands and by "plunging . . . into the sewer, and [leaving his] conscience behind" (*Ghetto*, p. 203) could a moral man save himself and that culture. By showing Gens weeding out the nonproductive "undesirables" from the ghetto, Sobol holds up the funhouse mirror to the Nazis and forcefully rebuts the criticism of Wiesel and others, arguing against any portrayal of Jews as martyrs.

Other scholars, among them Lawrence Langer, Freddie Rokem, and Robert Skloot, while acknowledging the validity of some of the criticism of Sobol's detractors, nevertheless praise these plays for their theatrical energy and approvingly note the provocative arguments that anyone, even a Jew, can become a Nazi (Rokem, "On the Fantastic," p. 48). Throughout Sobol's Vilna Trilogy, the character of Jakob Gens looms, making audiences mindful of the many sacred and profane contradictions that can reside in the human character and obviously did reside in him. Bully, killer, liar, tyrant, betrayer, Jakob Gens never lost sight of his self-proclaimed mission: to save his people and to save their culture. Sobol has rescued a man from history's footnotes, put him on the stage, and made him ask the audience all the troubling, unanswerable questions. In his speech to the writers, Gens said that he was willing to be judged for his actions. Sobol provokes his audience throughout his trilogy to ask themselves: can they, dare they, be the judges?

Bibliography

Primary Sources

"A Theatre in the Wilna Ghetto." 1987.
Ghetto. 1987.
"Theatricality of Political Theatre." 1987.
Underground. 1991.
Adam. 1996.
"Erotic/Neurotic?" 1999.

Interviews

Baraitser, Marion. "On Throwing Stones: A Meeting with Joshua Sobol." *Jewish Quarterly* (spring 1999): 68–70.

Langworthy, Douglas. "When Choosing Good Is Not an Option: An Interview with Joshua Sobol." *Theatre* 22, no. 3 (summer-fall 1991): 10–17.

Rees, Roland. *Fringe First: Pioneers of Fringe Theatre on Record.* London. Oberon Books. 1992.

Plays

The Father. (date unknown).
The Days to Come. (1971).

Status Quo Vadis. (1973).
Sylvester '72. (1974).
The Joker. (1975).
Night of the Twentieth. (1976).
The Gog and Magog Show. (1976).
The Tenants. (1977).
Crisis. (1977).
Homeward Angel. (1978).
Wedding Night. (1978).
The Next Day. (1978).
Let There Be a Hole. (1979).
The Last of the Workers. (1980).
The Wars of the Jews. (1981).
The Soul of a Jew. (1982).
The Sailor's Revolt. (1983).
Ghetto. (1983).
The Last Striptease. (1984).
People in the Night. (1984).
Passodoble. (1984).
Shooting Magda. (1985).
King of Israel. (1986).
The Jerusalem Syndrome. (1988).
Adam. (1988).
Underground. (1989).
Solo. (1991).
A & B. (1991).
Eye to Eye. (1991).
Aleph-Beit. (1992).
Love for a Penny. (1994).
Beautiful Tony. (1995).
Honey: A Land Flowing with Real Estate and Honey. (1997).
Village. (1997).
Alma. (1998).
Strangers. (1999).
A Heart Which Yearns for Songs. (2000).
Magna Carta. (2000).
Falco—A Cyber Show. (2000).
Schneider Und Shuster. (in progress, 2000).

Secondary Sources

Arad, Yitzhak. *Ghetto in Flames*. Jerusalem: "Ahva" Cooperative Printing Press, 1980.

Bernstein, Michael André. "Victims-in-Waiting: Backshadowing and the Representation of European Jewry." *New Literary History* 29, no. 4 (1998): 625–651.

Diner, Dan. "Historical Understanding and Counterrationality: The *Judenrat* as Epistemological Vantage." *Probing the Limits of Representation*. Edited by Saul Friedlander. Cambridge, Mass.: Harvard University Press, 1992.

Feldman, Yael. "Whose Story Is It, Anyway? Ideology and Psychology in the Representation of the *Shoah* in Israeli Literature." *Probing the Limits of Representation*. Edited by Saul Friedlander. Cambridge, Mass.: Harvard University Press, 1992.

———. " 'Identification-with-the-Aggressor' or the 'Victim Complex'? Holocaust and Ideology in Israeli Theatre: Ghetto by Joshua Sobol." *Modern Judaism* 9, no. 2 (May 1989): 165–178.

Isser, Edward R. *Stages of Annihilation: Theatrical Representations of the Holocaust*. Madison, N.J.: Fairleigh Dickinson University Press, 1997.

Lichtenstein, Leonie. "Rushdie, Steiner, Sobol and others." *Encounter*. (Sept/Oct 1989): 34–42.

Rich, Frank. "Ghetto: A Review." *New York Times* May 1, 1989.

Rokem, Freddie. "On the Fantastic in Holocaust Performances." *Staging the Holocaust: The Shoah in Drama and Performance*. Edited by Claude Schumacher. Cambridge, Mass.: Cambridge University Press, 1998.

———. "Hebrew Theater from 1889 to 1948." "Yehoshua Sobol—Between History and the Arts." *Theater in Israel*. Edited by Linda Ben-Zvi. Ann Arbor, Mich.: The University of Michigan Press, 1996.

Rothstein, Mervyn. "When Art Becomes a Matter of Life or Death." *New York Times* (April 30, 1989): 1–8.

Rudashevski, Yitskhok. *The Diary of the Vilna Ghetto*. Translated by Percy Matenko. Israel: Ghetto Fighters' House, 1973.

Segev, Tom. *The Seventh Million*. Translated by Haim Watzman. New York: Hill & Wang, 1993.

Shteir, Rachel. "In Search of Sobol." *Theatre* 21, no. 3 (summer-fall 1990): 39–43.

Skloot, Robert. *The Darkness We Carry*. Madison, Wis.: The University of Wisconsin Press, 1988.

Strine, Mary S. "Art, Activism, and the Performance (Con)Text: A Response." *Text and Performance Quarterly* 12 (October 1992): 391–394.

Taub, Michael. "The Challenge to Popular Myth and Conventions in Recent Israeli Drama." *Modern Judaism* 17, no. 2 (1997): 133–162.

———. "Israeli Theatre and the Holocaust." *Israeli Holocaust Drama*. Syracuse, N.Y.: Syracuse University Press, 1996.

Trunk, Isaiah. *Judenrat: The Jewish Councils in Eastern Europe under Nazi Occupation*. New York: Stein and Day, 1972.

Tushnet, Leonard. *The Pavement of Hell*. New York: St. Martin's Press, 1972.

Waletszky, Josh, dir. *The Partisans of Vilna*. Cielsa Productions Foundation, Inc, 1986.

Wiesel, Elie. "Art and the Holocaust: Trivializing Memory." *New York Times* (11 June 1989): 1–38.

ISAIAH SPIEGEL

(1906–1991)

BEN FURNISH

YIDDISH WRITER ISAIAH Spiegel was born in the Balut area near Lodz, Poland, on 14 January 1906. His parents were weavers of modest means. He received a traditional *heder* and Talmud Torah education, although he recalled his family as being more culturally than religiously Jewish. He went on to a normal school and teachers college. Influenced by the writers Itzhak Katzenelson and M. Broderzon, Spiegel began to publish his work in 1922. He became a teacher of Yiddish language and literature at the Medem School in Lodz.

After the 1939 Nazi takeover of Poland, Spiegel was interned in the Lodz ghetto, where he remained until shortly before its liquidation in 1944. His wife, his parents, and three of his sisters died in the Nazi camps, and his daughter died of starvation in the ghetto. Spiegel continued to write stories throughout the war years. He managed to bury many of these manuscripts in a cellar before his deportation to Auschwitz, where the rest of his manuscripts were taken from him and destroyed. Before the Soviet liberation of Auschwitz, Spiegel was evacuated to a slave camp in Saxony. After the war's end, he returned to teaching in Lodz and was able to recover some of the manuscripts he had buried. He revised these and rewrote other stories from memory, publishing them in the volumes *Malkhus Geto* (Ghetto Kingdom), *Shtern Ibern Geto* (Stars over the Ghetto), and *Mentshn in Tehom* (People in the Abyss).

In 1948, Spiegel moved to Warsaw to head the Polish Yiddish Writers Association. In 1951, he moved to Israel, where he worked as a government clerk until retiring in 1964 because of poor health. He continued to write literature in Yiddish about the Holocaust, publishing several books as well as stories and poems in *Di Goldene Kayt*, *Tsukunft*, and other Yiddish periodicals. Among several other awards, he received the Itsik Manger Prize, the most prestigious Yiddish literary award, in 1972. He lived in Israel until his death in 1991.

Major Works

For English-language readers, Spiegel is known chiefly for the stories and poems originally written while he was living in the Lodz ghetto. The Holocaust forms an unavoidable backdrop to every character's and story's situation, but Spiegel maintains sufficient control to accentuate the humanity of his characters rather than allowing the Holocaust's enormity to overwhelm his depiction of their particular concerns and motivations, even though each story typically describes how the Holocaust ultimately overwhelms each character's life.

The first and perhaps best-known of his stories to be translated into English, "A Ghetto Dog," was included in Irving Howe and Eliezer Greenberg's *A Treasury of Yiddish Stories* and performed by Lauren Bacall in the National Yiddish Book Center's Jewish literature series on National Public Radio. "A Ghetto Dog" is typical of Spiegel's stories in centering on memorably crafted individual characters and their conflicts. Anna Nikolaievna Temkin, a thoroughly assimilated widow who lives alone with her dog Nicky, rejoins the Jewish people when a German soldier forces her from her home and into the newly created ghetto: "When the German had opened [her door] that morning, he had aroused the little woman from her torpor and reminded her that she was a Jew and that heavy days had come for her and all the other Jews" (From A Treasury of Yiddish Stories, edited by Irving Howe and Eliezer Greenberg, New York: Penguin, 1990, p. 617 [reprinted of 1954 Viking edition]).

There she is assigned a room with Big Rose, a prostitute who initially scorns her dog Nicky—and scorns Anna as an apostate. Eventually, the two women and the dog come to care for each other, until the day when the Germans confiscate all Jewish-owned animals in the ghetto. Anna refuses to relinquish Nicky's leash to a German soldier and is herself herded with the doomed dogs as the story ends. That her fate foreshadows that of the ghetto's other Jews is clear.

The published story "A Ghetto Dog" departs considerably from its original, "The Death of Anna Yakovleva Temkin," which Spiegel wrote while in the ghetto. The original, written in first person rather than third, is a character sketch that describes how Spiegel observed Temkin while on his daily walking surveys of the ghetto. Temkin suffers a breakdown and eventually dies when a soldier stabs her "and withdraws the bayonet quickly like a knife from bread." Spiegel added the dog and Rose in the revision, and in so doing rendered the story a composite of several characters and events he recalled from his own observations. In interviews with Yechiel Szeintuch, Spiegel stressed that he drew all of the material for this story and for all of his ghetto fiction from actual people and events. Spiegel's job with the *Judenrat* (Jewish council) required him to traverse the ghetto on foot regularly at all times of the year, and gave him a particularly detailed, long-term, firsthand perspective on human existence in the ghetto.

Spiegel's fiction moves beyond simple documentary by revealing, as Jacob Glatstein noted, the larger symbolic truths that his material typifies. Spiegel remarked that the Jews who had the greatest difficulty of all in surviving ghetto conditions were the assimilated, of whom Temkin and the German Jews in the story "Jews" are key examples. Almost the only irony Spiegel permits himself in his fiction is his exploration of these characters' involuntary return to the community of Jews with whom—despite their cultural alienation—they share a common fate.

"Ghetto Kingdom," the title story to Spiegel's first fiction collection, exemplifies his use of what he calls "the laconic vision," an approach to fiction that is deceptive in its apparent simplicity as it exploits the symbolic and artistic dimensions of its narrative with keen economy. Perhaps the only developed character in this brief story is the ghetto itself, as Spiegel's description captures a range of essential qualities about ghetto existence from morning to night in a swift, almost aerial view, as in this glimpse of the marketplace:

> A Jew is shuffling around. In his hand he holds three potatoes, two of which are completely wholesome; the third is rotten. A small crowd of Jews is gathering around him, gazing at the treasure. The Jew does not let the potatoes out of his hand. Anybody who wants to buy them will have to do so without touching them. Nobody takes them. But it is good just to look at a potato, a real potato . . .

"Trapped" is set inside the ghetto's abandoned St. Mary Church, which now houses not worshipers but homeless Jews who take uneasy refuge there. The story ends at the church as curfew hour begins: "Boots are pounding on the other side of the wire. Germans are entering the ghetto. The Crucified One in the heart of the ghetto is now drenched in flame. His thin tortured Jewish body lies curled in a red pool of warm blood" (p. 99).

In another rare but devastating instance of irony, Spiegel thus places the image of the crucified Jewish Jesus inside the ghetto, awash in fresh blood.

In the short story "Bread," parents Shimmele and Glikke live in a deteriorating ghetto hovel. The Gentile who had lived there before the ghetto's creation had kept pigeons in a small chamber. Now brother and sister Umele and Perele like to sneak inside the chamber, because through cracks in its wall they can see outside the ghetto fence to a bakery on the Gentile side. They can see loaves of bread when these are on display in the bakery window. Before these loaves sell and disappear, the children imaginatively gorge themselves. The family's meager bread ration never satisfies; rather, each bite further stimulates their hunger. In fact, one day, father Shimmele loses control and devours his children's shares of the bread along with his own. "A father, eh? A father, is it? *Murderer!*" mother Glikke accuses him (in *Ghetto Kingdom*, 1998, p. 77). Shimmele is shocked by his own behavior. Then one day, neighbors tell Glikke that Shimmele has been taken from the street with many other area men and deported from the ghetto. The family is grief-stricken for hours. Then Glikke recalls Shimmele's bread ration and divides it between them: "And for the first time in many, many months, the children eat joyfully to their hearts' content, as does Mama Glikke" (p. 81).

In the ghetto Spiegel also wrote poetry that he buried before being deported, and recovered after the war. Some of these poems were putative lullabies, in which Spiegel—as Frieda Aaron notes—inverts the formal convention of consoling and comforting a child into sleep. One of these, "*Makh tsu di Eygelekh*" (Close Your Precious Eyes), Spiegel wrote after the death of his daughter Eva in the ghetto:

> Naked, of everything bereft
> Chased, our homes we left,
> In the pitch of night
> Pursued into the field,
> And storm, hail, and wind,
> My child, escorted us
> To the fathomless void.
> Close your precious eyes . . . (translation appears in Bearing the Unbearable: Yiddish Polish Poetry in the Ghettos and Concentration Camps, Frieda W. Aaron. Albany: SUNY Press, 1990, p. 122).

Another Spiegel lullaby, "*Nit Keyn Rozhinkes un Nit Keyn Mandlen*" (Neither Raisins Nor Almonds) adapts the famous Abraham Goldfadn theater song "*Rozhinkes Mit Mandlen*" (Raisins and Almonds). Spiegel's is one of several adaptations of this and other popular Yiddish songs to ghetto conditions across Nazi-held Europe. Whereas in Goldfadn's song, a widowed mother sings to her son about the fortune he will find when he grows up, the widowed mother in Spiegel's lullaby reassures the son that the father who has been deported will someday return bearing raisins and almonds—an impossible hope. Frieda Aaron indicates that these two poems were performed at the opening of the ghetto's cultural center and were subsequently banned by the ghetto's Jewish leader, Chaim Rumkowski, who sought accommodation with the Nazis.

Criticism

Spiegel's importance in Holocaust literature derives from historical as well as literary factors. He was one of the few already established Yiddish writers to survive the Holocaust from within, experiencing as he did nearly five years—virtually the entire span of its existence—in the Lodz ghetto as well as subsequent imprisonment in Auschwitz and in Germany. In 1986, the collected criticism on Spiegel's work was published in Yiddish in two volumes. These included articles by such figures as Avraham Sutzkever, Jacob Glatstein, Shmuel Niger, Shlomo Bickel, and Melekh Ravitch, reprinted from the leading Yiddish periodicals of the day, including *Di Goldene Keyt, Der Yidisher Kemfer, Forverts*, and *Di Tsukunft*.

These critics agree on the importance of Spiegel's work, most of all his ghetto narratives, as representing one of the earliest and most articulate eyewitness voices to emerge from the *Khurbn* (Holocaust). Spiegel not only documented the emotional landscape of the Lodz ghetto; as Shmuel Niger noted as early as 1948, he did so in a style that was at once innovative and yet quite realistic. Niger counted Spiegel among such figures as Avraham Sutzkever (Vilna), Emmanuel Ringelblum (Warsaw), and Mordecai Shtrigler (Maidenek).

After the war's end, Spiegel had revised (and in some cases rewritten from memory) the Lodz ghetto stories before their publication. In 1995, Yechiel Szeintuch and Vera Solomon published Spiegel's extant stories from the war years in their original versions in order to give readers access to them word for word as Spiegel had written them inside the ghetto. Yet publication of this edition in no way invalidates the literary quality of Spiegel's postwar revisions, which largely polish and flesh out the original manuscripts. Szeintuch and Solomon identify a shift in Spiegel's vision from a "testimonial literature" rooted in description and fact to a "commemorative literature" that more fully exploits the metaphorical possibilities of this description.

Spiegel had a long, productive postwar literary career. Important works included not only Holocaust-related novels like *Flamen fun der Erd* (Flames from the Earth) but also *Di Brik* (The Bridge), a novel about Israeli life. *Flamen fun der Erd* is by Spiegel's own account an autobiographical work; its protagonist Vigdor must watch helplessly while his young daughter dies of malnutrition, just as Spiegel's had. The Yiddish language that closely tied Spiegel to most other Jews who experienced the Holocaust became, after the war, a barrier that inhibited wider knowledge of his work even in Israel, his new home country. Jacob Glatstein sums up Spiegel's importance by calling him "a belle-lettristic prince, and his short fictions will remain a cultural treasure of the House of Israel."

Bibliography

Primary Sources

Mitn Ponim tsu der Zun (Facing the Sun). 1930.
Malkhus Geto (Ghetto Kingdom). 1947.
Shtern Ibern Geto (Stars over the Ghetto). 1948.
Mentshn in Tehom (People in the Abyss). 1949.
Un Gevorn Iz Likht (And Light Appears). 1949.
Likht funem Opgrunt (Light from the Abyss). 1952.
Vint un Vortslen (Wind and Roots). 1955.
Di Brik (The Bridge). 1963.
Flamen fun der Erd (Flames from the Earth). 1966.
Shtaygn tsum Himl (Ascent to Heaven). 1966.
Geshtaltn un Profiln (Figures and Profiles). 1971.
Di Kroyn (The Crown). 1973.
Shtern Laykhtn in Tehom (Stars Shining in the Abyss). 1976.
Tsvishn Tov un Alef (Between Z and A). 1978.
Himlen Nakhn Shturem (The Skies after the Storm). 1984.
Ghetto Kingdom (1998).

Secondary Sources

Aaron, Frieda W. *Bearing the Unbearable: Yiddish and Polish Poetry in the Ghettos and Concentration Camps*. Albany: State University of New York Press, 1990, pp. 120–124.

"Isaiah Spiegel." In *Encyclopaedia Judaica*. New York: Macmillan, 1971–1972, p. 271.

Hirsch, David H. "Introduction to the Ghetto Stories of Isaiah Spiegel." In *Ghetto Kingdom: Tales of the Łodź Ghetto*. David H. Hirsch and Roslyn Hirsch, Trans. Evanston, Ill.: Northwestern University Press, 1998, pp. vii–xxiv.

Niger, Shmuel. "Yeshayahu Shpigl." In *Yidishn Shrayber fun Tsvantikstn Yorhundert* (Vol. II). New York: Congress for Jewish Culture, 1973, pp. 314–320.

Szeintuch, Yechiel. "Ghetto Literature and I. Spiegel's Ghetto Manuscripts." In Yechiel, Szeintuch and Vera Solomon, eds.

Isaiah Spiegel: Yiddish Narrative Prose from the Lodz Ghetto. Jerusalem: Magnes Press, the Hebrew University, 1995, pp. iii-xiv.

Szeintuch, Yechiel, and Vera Solomon. "Fun Yeshayahu Shpigls Umbakante Kasav-Yadn fun Lodzher Geto." *Di Goldene Kaeyt*, vol. 130 (1990), pp. 37–39.

Yeshayahu Shpigl: In Likht fun der Kvaliker Pen: Oysdervaylte Ophandlungen vegn Zayn Shafn (Vol. 1). Tel Aviv: Israel-Book, 1986.

Yeshayahu Shpigl: In Likht fun der Farloshener Pen: Kritishe Ophandlungen vegn Zayn Shafn in Proze, Esay, Lid (Vol. 2). Tel Aviv: Israel Book, 1986.

Manès Sperber

(1905–1984)

PETER STENBERG

Manès sperber was born on 12 December 1905 in Zablotow, an East Galician *shtetl* on the Pruth River in the heart of what has become the legendary world of East European Jewry, a world that was still very much alive and real in the years before the outbreak of World War I. He died on 5 February 1984 in one of the great cities of Western Europe, Paris, where he had lived since the end of World War II. Sperber spent the first half of his life as an active participant in the revolutionary developments that resulted in the end of old Europe, in the violence of two world wars, and the second half as a prominent bilingual (French and German) essayist and novelist whose works attempt to deal with the consequences of these wars.

Childhood in East Galicia and Vienna

Sperber was brought up in the illusory security of Orthodox Jewry in Eastern Europe at the beginning of the century which was annihilated in the Holocaust. For the first ten years of his life, he moved easily into the apparently pre-ordained path of a child whose great-grandfather, Boruch, was a rabbi and whose father was a successful businessman. Like most of the three thousand residents of Zablotow, the Sperbers came from a long line of Yiddish-speaking Hassidic Jews who religiously followed the rigorous tenets that determined the way they spent their lives. But unlike most of the Jews in Zablotow, the Sperbers were rather well-off financially and undoubtedly foresaw a future for their very promising son as a prominent figure in the Jewish community. Perhaps he would go on to further schooling in the German high school in nearby Brody on the Russian border, and after that to the German university in Czernowitz or even in Vienna. For those Yiddish-speakers who could afford it, the opportunity to be educated in German was understood to offer the obvious route to one of the great cultures of Western Europe. The Sperbers belonged to this group, taking their annual summer vacations in Western European spas and being well-versed in German language and culture.

The advance of the Cossacks into the eastern parts of the Austrian empire during World War I convinced Sperber's father to make the dramatic decision to abandon his previously secure position and home. Three unsuccessful attempts to escape from increasingly threatened Galicia became full-scale flight as the actual Russian front arrived in Zablotow in the summer of 1916, and on 27 July 1916 the Sperbers completed the long train ride to Vienna. Like many East European Jews before and after, the Sperbers ended up in a very modest apartment in Leopoldstadt, the traditionally Jewish second district of Vienna. As was usually the case with such immigrants who came from a reasonably prosperous background, the Sperbers had to face a dramatic decline in social and financial status in a city where antisemitism was acceptable and even expected. Life in Leopoldstadt usually failed to fulfill the dreams that most immigrants nurtured when they left Eastern Europe, a situation that intensified dramatically with the death in November 1916 of Emperor Franz Josef, who had been seen by the Jews as the bulwark against antisemitism since his ascendance to the throne in 1848. Sperber's father viewed the post–Franz Josef era with trepidation, and it is probably no surprise that his son began to seek other solutions in the attempt to improve his own position in the dangerous world that was quickly appearing on the horizon.

Already as a thirteen-year-old at the end of the war, Sperber was drawn to the political activism of Zionism and later Communism and began to turn his back on the traditional Jewish beliefs and way of life of his parents, who would eventually emigrate to London. Young Sperber joined a leftist Zionist group, *hashomait hatzair*, and quickly abandoned traditional academic schooling to become a group leader. He later visited Israel three times without showing any interest in settling there.

The Communist Years

Sperber's interest in the Communist party and its theoretical foundations becomes evident very early in the intellectual life of this very gifted young man. He first read Karl Marx's *Das kommunistische Manifesto* (*The Communist Manifesto*) when he was fourteen, and when he was nineteen he wrote his first lengthy piece of fiction, the still unpublished Der Charlatan und seine Zeit (The Charlatan and his Times), in which a young psychologist goes to Russia, has his first doubts about the future of the state governed by the Communist party that he serves, and returns discouraged to Vienna. In many ways this early work foreshadows the future of its author. As a teenager he had become a disciple of the psychologist Alfred Adler, and in 1926 earned a degree from the International Society for Individual Psychology as a therapeutic pedagogue for disturbed children, a field in which he practiced professionally for many years. Some twenty years later, in the middle of World War II, he would return to fiction with an epic novel in which he documented his painful decade-long experiences in the service of the Communist party.

In the wake of the violence surrounding the burning of the Palace of Justice in 1927 during political demonstrations that wracked the city, Sperber left Vienna for Berlin, where he immediately became a member of the German branch of the Communist party, the largest and most important one outside of Russia. From 1928 to 1933 Sperber was an active member of the Marxist opposition to the rising Nazi party. In 1931 he undertook a three-month journey to major cities of the Soviet Union, lectured on psychology at the Seventh International Psychotechnic Congress in Moscow, and encountered the first mild rebukes from the Moscow authorities over what they considered to be critical remarks about the party. During this period, Sperber came into contact with such Communist luminaries as the prominent theoretician and former head of the Comintern, Nikolai I. Bukharin, and the leader of the short-lived Communist Republic in Hungary, Béla Kun, both of whom later became victims of the Stalinist purges of the late 1930s.

On 15 March 1933, Sperber was arrested by the Nazis, released a month later on Hitler's birthday, and forced into an exile that took him on a long journey to the locales that became central features of the trilogy *Wie eine Träne in Ozean*. They included Prague, Vienna, Zagreb, the Dalmation coast, and, finally, on orders of the party, Paris, where he spent most of the rest of his life. In the Paris of the second half of the 1930s, Sperber automatically became part of the German exile milieu, which was largely leftist-oriented if not necessarily Communist, but he also gradually moved into the circle of French intellectuals. His most important and lasting contact in this group was André Malraux, who had just published his successful novel about Communists in Asia, *La condition humaine* (*The Human Condition*), and who would become Sperber's life-long friend and supporter, later arguing that Sperber's fiction played a similar role in the presentation of the European political crisis as did his own in the context of Asia.

In the late 1930s, in the wake of the Stalinist show trials against members of the Comintern, Sperber became totally disillusioned with the workings of the party to which he had been so loyal, and turned his back on it. Sperber left the party formally in 1937. Like his friend Arthur Koestler, who entrusted him with the manuscript of *Darkness at Noon*, he became one of those prominent defectors from the Communist party who could count on the enmity of the Soviet Union for the rest of his life. In an attempt to engage himself personally against the German invasion of France, Sperber joined the French Foreign Legion in December 1939 and was assigned to an infantry battalion, but he experienced only logistical chaos rather than front-line action. Upon demobilization in August 1940 following the French defeat, he resided illegally in Cagnes-sur-Mer in unoccupied France for two years, but he fled to Switzerland in September 1942 after Malraux warned him that the Gestapo was on his trail and planned to arrest him.

Thus, Manes Sperber was a prominent witness to and participant in the major political and social crises in Europe during the first half of the twentieth century. He dealt with these experiences in two massive literary works: the 1,050-page novel trilogy *Wie eine Träne im Ozean* (*Like a Tear in the Ocean*), written between 1940 and 1951, and the three-volume autobiography *All das Vergangene* (*All the Past*), written in the 1970s. In his epic novel, Sperber describes in devastating detail the situations leading to the Moscow-ordered executions of party loyalists in central and southeastern Europe and their catastrophic effect on the morale of the members of the Comintern. Antifascists who were continuing to risk their lives in the fight against Nazi Germany and its allies gradually realize that their own party was using the same methods as the enemy. Near the end of the novel, one of his main protagonists, Denis (Dojno) Faber, who is Jewish and certainly at least a partial self-portrait of Sperber, reaches his darkest despair as he reports on the murder of one of his loyal and courageous party comrades. He concludes that it was carried out on orders from Moscow and was organized by a sadistic Croatian police officer, who had entrapped and executed a Communist agent on the first pages of the novel while working for the Fascists and now was doing the same thing but in the payment of the Communist Party (*Wie eine Träne im Ozean*, p. 982).

The Fate of the Jews in Sperber's Fiction

When Sperber began to write his novel in French exile in 1940, he certainly could not have been planning on completing the work ten years later with a lengthy episode dealing with the Holocaust, which André Malraux, in the introduction to the separately published French translation of just this episode, would call "one of the very great books about the Jewish people." In fact, Sperber had been an agnostic since he was a teenager, had shown little or no interest in his Jewish roots before the end of the war, and included almost nothing about the fate of the European Jews in the first two novels of his trilogy, although they were not completed until 1950. But he would later write that in his political activism he had, in fact, acted on the basis of the Jewish ethical teachings that were the foundations of the same religious beliefs that he openly questioned, and that his actions as a political revolutionary must be seen in this light. "And this too is my Jewishness: solidarity with those who are victims of injustice. That has been my socialism from the very beginning; it has remained my socialism despite the numerous unsuccessful and impatient efforts to bring about a world in which theory and practice would be united and remain so forever" (*Churban oder die unfaβbare Gewissheit*, Vienna: Europaverlag, 1979, p. 58).

Sperber also admitted that he had not always been able to follow these ethical tenets. "I don't dare to claim that I always carried out these commandments" (*Churban*, p. 57), and this clash between ethical and political demands forms in many ways the core of the novel. A central theme is the moral problem that confronted dedicated party members, many of whom are Jewish, in the face of increasingly immoral orders from the party, including the demand that loyal comrades and friends be betrayed and even executed. Much of the power of the novel involves the convincing presentation of the construction of a web with a center in Moscow but with increasingly self-woven threads in which courageous and dedicated revolutionaries and antifascists are eventually caught and exterminated. The eventual total disillusionment of Dojno, who has himself reluctantly carried out orders he considers immoral, and, like Sperber, decides he must defect from the party and go into a kind of resigned opposition, suggests that Sperber may have felt personally responsible for spinning part of the web.

The first two books of the novel trilogy, *The Burned Bramble* and *Deeper Than the Abyss*, exemplify in many ways the dilemma faced by the middle-aged Sperber as he looked back at the turbulent first half of his life. Here he used his experiences during his Communist period as the fictional framework in which to present the fates of a large network of figures, who act out increasingly marionette-like roles for the party in locales ranging from Norway to the Mediterranean and almost all of whom fail to survive the war. In describing the increasingly murderous relationship between the party headquarters in Moscow and party loyalists in Europe, Sperber transformed his experiences into one of the most panoramic pieces of fiction describing the catastrophe of World War II. The disaster seals the fates of most of the confronted figures, many of whom are executed in the most humiliating way by the self-destructive Soviet Russian wing of the party. Almost in passing, however, the reader realizes that many of the characters in this vast novel about the terrifying extermination of idealists are, like Sperber, assimilated Jews. This includes the two main figures who survive into the period of the Holocaust, Denis (Dojno) Faber and Dr. Edi Rubin, the latter the only character in the novel who finally attempts to act on the evidence of the Holocaust. Sperber's complete novel thus is one of the major documents about that prominent group of Jewish intellectuals and idealists who had often transformed the moral commandments of their youth into a belief in the ultimate justice of Communism, and who had then experienced the annihilation of their loyal friends and comrades on orders of a failed god in Moscow.

In this context the story of Denis Faber as a Jew in the course of World War II is an extremely sad, disillusioning, and ultimately tragic one. It is also the story of Manès Sperber and his idealistic friends of the 1920s who would turn into traitors or victims in the 1930s and first half of the 1940s. As such it is also the story of the failure of the many Jews who chose violent resistance within the framework of Communism as an answer to the Fascist threat to European order and European Jewry. Most of them die uselessly or worse, without contributing anything to any potential attempt to stop the Holocaust, although Dojno survives in almost nihilistic resignation among Tito's partisans. All this takes place outside the context of the Holocaust among Jewish party members, who are leading players in the Communist reign of self-destruction and who pay virtually no attention to apocalyptic events that point increasingly toward the full-blown attempt by the Nazis to murder all European Jews.

The catastrophe of the Holocaust could not be encompassed by the story of Denis Faber and the dozens of politicized and revolutionary men and women he meets along his path from idealism to despair. The reader wonders, for instance, if part of Dojno's final despair is not rooted in his realization that he has indeed, under extreme political pressure, sometimes failed to carry out the ethical tenets of his Jewish upbringing. And at the same time he had done nothing to try to stop the Holocaust, which was being carried out mercilessly on his own people in the very area where he had experienced his Jewish upbringing. It is an event he must have known about by the end of the war. (Sperber has written that he first heard about the Holocaust in 1943, after talking with an escapee from a concentration camp in Poland.) Sperber's complex and sometimes confusing relationship to his Judaism, at least until the second half of the century, should probably be considered within this context.

In Sperber's fictional works, neither the Zionists nor the Orthodox Jews are treated with the disdain that he reserved for the atheistic Communist Party. However, he also seems to make it clear in his writings that he did not believe that either the Orthodox Jews or the Zionists offered any kind of practical solution to the imminent threat of genocidal antisemitism that accompanied the rise of Adolf Hitler and the Nazi party to power in Germany.

The Holocaust in Sperber's Fiction

In his fictional work of more than a thousand pages, Sperber did not touch the Holocaust until the novel was virtually completed, and then it was in a chapter completely isolated from the events described elsewhere. As Jack Zipes has convincingly argued, this is the moment when Sperber recognizes that he as a Jew must face the consequences of the Holocaust he had survived in safe exile in Switzerland. "By 1945 he began raising his own Jewish questions and focusing his attention on issues pertaining to Jewish identity, the Holocaust (or "Churban" as he preferred to call it), antisemitism, Zionism and Messianism. . . . What is most significant at this point in Sperber's life and writings is that for the first time he begins to reconsider and analyze his Jewishness" (Zipes, pp. 697, 699).

In order to deal with that story, Sperber needed a different character who had not been a dedicated Communist; he sends the skeptical Dr. Edi Rubin out to report on the horrifying news. The story of his journey to the fictional *shtetl* of Wolyna begins only on page 877 of the novel. Rubin's experiences in Poland in the summer of 1942 are described in the third chapter of the final novel of the trilogy, whose title, *The Lost Bay*, refers to a gripping military action during the partisan war in Croatia, which constitutes the main part of the volume. This chapter of the novel is so isolated from the rest of the work that André Malraux convinced Sperber to publish it as a separate work of fiction that appeared in Sperber's own French translation under the title *Qu'une larme dans l'océan* (*A Tear in the Ocean*) in 1952. (Eventually the entire novel appeared under the original German name of this chapter.)

While Dojno has become a very reluctant participant in the orgy of violence in Yugoslavia, Edi Rubin's wife and child have disappeared into the furnaces of Auschwitz. Dr. Rubin, whom the reader has met early in the novel in Vienna, has been a sympathetic but somewhat unconvinced observer of the political actions of his leftist friends. In reaction to the direct evidence of the ungraspable certainty of the Holocaust, Rubin for the first time decides to take on an active role on the stage of European violence. He manages to take possession of a German military uniform and travels to Poland in order to try to save what may still be left of the East Galician Jews. He ends up in the only *shtetl* that has not been emptied of its inhabitants, Wolyna, in order to warn the remaining Jews of their imminent deportation and murder and to organize their resistance. While Wolyna is certainly reminiscent of Zablotow and the locales of Sperber's childhood, Sperber's account of Rubin's experiences there is entirely fictional, unlike many of the other episodes that take place in real locales in Yugoslavia.

Rubin goes to Wolyna, famed for its carpet weavers and musicians, because he had heard from his old friend Dojno that another former acquaintance, the Polish aristocrat Roman Skarbek, has organized a partisan resistance there, and because the Jews have already been sent to the killing camps from everywhere else in East Galicia. In Wolyna, Rubin confronts a group of Jewish inhabitants who offer a cross section of the choices faced by the *shtetl* Jews who were the main victims of the Holocaust. Distrusting the leader of the partisans, he goes to the head rabbi, the *Zaddik*, who refuses all entreaties that he must convince his people to defend themselves or to flee, insisting that the Chosen People must follow religious guidelines that exclude such actions. Most of the inhabitants follow the rabbi's decisions without question and are annihilated as soon as the Nazis arrive. Rubin, however, has a more hopeful response from the sixteen-year old son of the rabbi, Bynie, who reads Hegel and can imagine something other than simply waiting for the slaughter. He convinces twenty-eight men to join him with Rubin and the partisans.

Sperber's story is complex and focuses partly on the relationship between Poles (and in particular Polish partisans) and a Jewish population that was being exterminated on Polish soil. Rubin's suspicions about the trustworthiness of the partisan leader and fear of the possible violent antisemitic leanings of his men turn out to be misplaced with regard to the leader but completely justified with regard to his men. The (loyal) count gets distracted in an amorous encounter and his (disloyal) men proceed to kill almost all of the Jews whom Rubin has managed to convince to join the armed opposition. Bynie refuses to take up arms against the imminent Polish attack because it is the Sabbath and any defense would violate its sanctity. Once again his men accept his conclusions unquestioningly and are massacred. In these episodes Sperber seems to be attacking both the Poles for their antisemitism and Orthodox Jews for their ancient beliefs that render them incapable of dealing with the modern threat of genocide and thus incapable of defending themselves. After the ensuing slaughter, the despairing Rubin moves on with Skarbek to Warsaw, just in time to witness the Warsaw Ghetto Uprising, but here too he cannot offer any practical help and is forced to look on hopelessly from the outside.

As a consequence, Rubin too never really finds a successful alternate mode of action. Even his admiration for the courage and determination shown by the participants in the Warsaw Ghetto Uprising is of course tempered by the knowledge that in the end they are all doomed. He never finds an answer and finally simply decides to go off with one of the couriers sent by the ghetto insurgents to Palestine "not because they were asking for help—because there was no longer any hope—but because they should report to the survivors what had happened. They assumed that not all the couriers would get through, but they hoped that one of them might slip through the net" (*Träne*, p. 963). It is a bleak scenario and one that leads back to the possibility that in a nihilistic universe the only real meaning can be found in the actual spiritual foundations of each individual identity. After the war, Sperber made it clear that he felt increasingly that in his own case the spiritual foundation was rooted in his Jewish background.

At the end of the Wolyna episode, Rubin, who has long since lost his belief in God and Judaism, seems to find some solace in the example and lessons of the martyred Bynie and leaves for Palestine with somewhat less hatred and somewhat more understanding of his own identity as a Jew. For the rest of his life Sperber also underlined this part of his identity and almost came full circle in his return to Judaism. But for many Jews, it remains a somewhat problematic version of Judaism because it combines agnosticism and socialism with religious ethics, and it specifically excludes belief in Jewish rites or for that matter in God, which might well be considered a sine qua non of Judaism by believers. "So, I am an unbelieving Jew. Not a single one of the endless rituals which determine the everyday life of the believers has any validity for me any more. . . . I am a Jew because I was formed in my childhood by a total, permeating Jewish upbringing. They taught me how to recognize, understand and interpret everything according to God's commandments" (*Churban*, p. 57).

Conclusion

The distance between East Galician Zablotow, near the eastern boundary of the Austro Hungarian empire, and Paris is not so great geographically but almost infinite psychologically. It serves as an excellent measure of the expanse of a life, which, like few others, encompassed the breathtaking scope of the events that would overwhelm the world of the European Jews in the first half of the twentieth century. In the eighty years that passed between his birth and his death, the traditional world of the East European Jews disappeared forever in apocalyptic annihilation, and the boy who was an eyewitness to the violence of World War I became the young man who chose Communism in order to fight the great fight against the forces of evil that came from the west. But before that war had even started militarily, he came to the realization that this political God, too, had failed miserably and that he must thus join the battle against it. During the first forty years of his life, Manès Sperber metamorphosed from an orthodox Jewish child to a Zionist to a German-speaking psychologist, a Communist, and finally a French-speaking anti-Communist renegade.

Later on he would emphasize his Jewishness: "I am a European Jew who is always aware of being a survivor, and will never forget the years when being a Jew was a deadly crime" (*Churban*, p. 42). In the midst of the turmoil and catastrophe of the war and the Holocaust, when events piled on each other in breathtaking speed, he served various masters and described such difficult times in powerful prose works in which his own actions are often hard to accurately decipher. He portrayed himself as a Job who refused to be as patient as his namesake but whose impatience had also failed to solve the problems of a world engulfed in total chaos. As such he will remain one of the main Jewish literary figures demanding resistance, even if he never seems really convinced that his resistance had borne much fruit, nor that as a Jew he had taken on the most appropriate role in the face of such overwhelming peril.

Bibliography

Primary Sources

Alfred Adler, der Mensch und seine Lehre (Alfred Adler, the Man and his Teachings).1926.

Wie eine Träne im Ozean. Romantrilogie (*Like a Tear in the Ocean*). 1961. The three books of the trilogy appeared separately: *Der verbrannte Dornbusch* (*The Burned Bramble*, 1949); *Tiefer als der Abgrund* (*Deeper than the Abyss*, 1950); *Die verlorene Bucht* (*The Lost Bay*, 1953). Selections have appeared in English translation. The subsequent German paperback edition of the trilogy (1980) is now in its tenth edition.

Leben in dieser Zeit: *Sieben Fragen zur Gewalt*. (Life in These Times: Seven Questions about Violence).1972.

All das Vergangene (All the Past). The trilogy of autobiographical works listed below is now available in one volume under the above title.

Der Wasserträger Gottes (God's Water-Carriers). 1974.

Die vergebliche Warnung (The Futile Warning). 1975.

Bis man mir Scherben auf die Augen legt Until the fragments on are placed on my eyes). 1977.

Churban oder die unfaßbare Gewissheit (Churban or the Ungraspable Certainty). 1978.

Secondary Sources

Hemecker, Wilhelm, and Mirjana Stancic. *Ein Treuer Ketzer–Manes Sperber. Der Schriftsteller als Ideologe*. Profil, Band 6 Vienna: Paul Zsolnay Verlag, 2000.

Magris, Claudio. "Ein Versuch aus dem Nirgends: Zu Manes Sperber und seinem Werk." *Modern Austrian Literature* 12 (1979): 41–66.

Stenberg, Peter. "Remembering Times Past: Canetti, Sperber and 'A World that is No More.' " *Seminar* 17 (Nov. 1981): 296–311.

Zipes, Jack. "Manes Sperber's Legacy for Peace in *Wie eine Träne im Ozean*." *German Quarterly* 61 (Spring 1988): 249–263.

———. "Manes Sperber Pursues the Jewish Question in *Wolyna*." In *The Yale Companion to Jewish Writing and Thought in Germany 1096–1996*, 697–703. Edited by Sander Gilman and Jack Zipes. New Haven, Conn.: Yale University Press, 1997.

ART SPIEGELMAN

(1948–)

ROBERT FRANCIOSI

AMONG THE MOST unusual contributions to Holocaust literature is Art Spiegelman's *Maus: A Survivor's Tale* (1986), the acclaimed comic book memoir using cats and mice to tell the story of Vladek Spiegelman's life during and after the Holocaust. Following extensive taped interviews with his father, Art Spiegelman constructed, throughout the 1970s and 1980s, a cartoon account of the narrative and its narration, one that intricately interweaves Vladek's story with his artist son's reflections—its impact on his life and the difficulties he faced in bringing this survivor's tale to the page.

From the start the critically successful *Maus* caused readers what Spiegelman termed a problem of taxonomy. How might they categorize this strange, even disturbing, text: as Holocaust memoir? graphic novel? cartoon autobiography? In 1991 the *New York Times* faced the dilemma: It first placed *Maus II* on the fiction best-seller list; then, after a letter from Spiegelman, moved it to the nonfiction list. The use of the comics medium to record Holocaust narrative also courted confusion, even outrage, from readers whose expectations about survivors' tales had been conditioned by the writings of Elie Wiesel and Primo Levi. Nevertheless, and perhaps surprisingly, response to the *Maus* phenomenon by such Holocaust scholars as Lawrence Langer, Terrence Des Pres, and many others has been overwhelmingly positive. A question/encomium from Daniel Schwarz seems typical: "I ask myself why I—who rarely even read *Doonesbury*, wouldn't think of reading any other comics, and never had much interest in comics or cartoons—am so fascinated and enthralled by *Maus*? What is so compelling and why do I continually reread it?" (p. 301). A major source of *Maus*'s appeal is Spiegelman's ability to utilize the visual nature of comics to intermingle three compelling life narratives in his multilayered Holocaust text: Vladek Spiegelman's experiences during and after the Holocaust; the artist's narrative account of *Maus*'s multiyear composition—the literal unfolding of memory before his readers; and the son's engagement with the *Shoah* via his survivor parents.

Life

Art was born in Stockholm in 1948, the second son of Vladek and Anja Zylberberg Spiegelman, Polish Jews who, though surviving Auschwitz, lost nearly all their families, including their son, Richieu. After reuniting in Poland at the war's end, the Spiegelmans first emigrated to Sweden, then in 1950 to the United States where they settled in Rego Park, New York. During his childhood in Queens, Art cultivated an early love for comic books and *Mad* magazine, knowing from those first encounters that he wanted to become a comic book artist. At age fifteen he was a staff cartoonist for the weekly Long Island *Post*, and after graduating from New York High School of Art and Design in 1966, he attended the experimental Hamilton College in upstate New York at the State University of New York, Binghamton. Only there did the full impact of his parents' Holocaust experiences register for him: "I mean, for instance, the fact that my parents used to wake up in the middle of the night screaming didn't seem especially strange to me. I suppose I thought everybody's parents did" (*The Complete Maus*, CD-ROM). The combination of freedom from his survivor parents' everyday lives and his plunge into the 1960s drug culture eventually led to what Spiegelman has termed a "psychotic breakdown." He was hospitalized for a month in 1968 and released on the condition that he move home with his parents. A few months later his mother killed herself, leaving no note.

After Anja Spiegelman's suicide, Art moved to California where he immersed himself in San Francisco's underground comics scene. While there, he confronted both his mother's suicide, in the 1973 expressionistic *Prisoner on the Hell Planet* (ultimately reproduced in *Maus*), and his parents' Holocaust legacy, in a three-page Ur-version of *Maus*. By 1978 Spiegelman had married. He and his wife, Françoise Mouly, returned to New York, where they founded Raw Books and Graphics, a publication venture devoted to experimental comics from the United States and abroad. From this enterprise emerged *RAW* magazine, the venue where in 1980 Spiegelman would begin publishing the early chapters of *Maus: A Survivor's Tale*.

In New York, Spiegelman finally decided to use comics (or as he often terms it, "comix," a mixture of text and images) to examine the wounds the Holocaust had inflicted upon his family—his brother's death, his mother's suicide, his father's distance. To that end, Art resumed the taped interviews with Vladek Spiegelman he had first begun in 1969 before leaving for California. After Anja Spiegelman's suicide, Vladek experienced a number of setbacks: his marriage to another survivor resulted in an unhappy relationship; he endured two heart attacks; most significantly, he became estranged from his only surviving child. Some of the first words in *Maus* record this distance: "I went out to see my Father in Rego Park. I hadn't seen him in a long time—we weren't that close" (New York: Pantheon, 1986, p. 5). For Vladek, resuming the interviews became a means of reconnecting with Art.

Unlike some survivors, he was not reluctant to recount his experiences. Art reports that Vladek was in fact a very good storyteller, even though he did not feel a particular need to bear witness to the Holocaust: "What he had a need for was for his son to hang out and be around, and about the only way that I could arrange for that to happen would be with a microphone holding him at bay" (*The Complete Maus*, CD-ROM). Taping over the course of several years yielded a six-hundred page transcript telling the story of Vladek and Anja's experiences under the Nazis; the very process of interviewing his father provided Art with an equally compelling narrative in the present. As the earliest chapters of *Maus* began appearing in *RAW*, Vladek Spiegelman's health was in serious decline, and he died in 1982, four years before the first full volume's appearance.

Maus: A Survivor's Tale: My Father Bleeds History achieved immediate critical and commercial success upon the book's publication in 1986. On the strength of his initial accomplishment, Spiegelman was awarded a Guggenheim Fellowship in 1990 to complete the project, which had already consumed him for much of two decades. Part II (*And Here My Troubles Began*) appeared in 1991, garnering even more attention than the first volume. It landed on the *New York Times* best-seller list, and in 1992 the Pulitzer Prize board granted a special award to the book, which did not fit into any of its categories.

Since his work on *Maus*, Spiegelman has continued to use comics as a serious means for addressing American culture. A 15 February 1993 cover for *The New Yorker*, for example, spurred a hail of criticism because it depicted a Hasidic man embracing and kissing an African American woman. Printed six months after the riots between blacks and Jews in Crown Heights, the drawing was viewed by Spiegelman as something of a peace offering, even a valentine. When in 1999 Roberto Benigni received two Academy Awards for his Holocaust comedy *Life Is Beautiful*, Spiegelman penned another controversial cartoon for *The New Yorker*—a camp prisoner holding an Oscar statuette.

Art Spiegelman and his wife, who is now the art editor for *The New Yorker*, continue to live in New York with their two children, Nadja and Dashiell, and have edited a number of books including *Little Lit* (2000), a collection of folklore and children's tales reimagined by contemporary comix artists. Spiegelman also continues to edit *RAW* and to produce occasional comics and drawings for *The New Yorker*.

Partially published first in *RAW, Maus* has caused readers more than the problem of generic taxonomy noted by Spiegelman. The work has appeared in many forms, producing an array of overlapping and discrete texts: the three-page "Ur" version of 1972; the serial strips published between 1980 and 1991 in *RAW*; the separately issued 1986 and 1991 volumes; the single-volume cloth edition of 1996; and the Voyager CD-ROM of 1994, inspired by response to a *Maus* exhibit at the Museum of Modern Art and including, for example, transcripts of 60 percent of the interview tapes.

Origins and *Maus I: My Father Bleeds History* (1986)

Spiegelman's *Maus* project began in 1971 when he was asked to contribute a strip to *Funny Aminals* [*sic*](1972), an underground comics anthology whose only requirement of contributors was that they use anthropomorphic characters. After viewing early twentieth-century animated films featuring cats and mice and noting their similarities to racist imagery from the same time period, Spiegelman first thought to create a strip in which the Ku Klux Katz lynch several mice, but quickly dropped the idea because he did not have the necessary depth of personal knowledge to make it succeed. "And then suddenly the idea of Jews as mice just hit me full force, full blown," he told Lawrence Weschler. "I began to recognize the obvious historical antecedents—how Nazis had spoken of Jews as 'vermin,' for example, and plotted their 'extermination' " (*The Complete Maus*, CD-ROM).

In the three-page Ur-*Maus* Spiegelman anticipated many of the images and themes he would engage in the subsequent project. The opening panel from "MAUS" (as this 1972 version is titled) illustrates how he would later tap into our cultural visual memory of the Holocaust by using images familiar from newsreels, camp drawings, and photographs. (In "MAUS" he reworks a famous liberation photograph by Margaret Bourke-White, to depict mice prisoners standing inside the barbed wire fence.) Besides Jewish mice in camp uniforms, other visual devices infusing subsequent manifestations of *Maus* are present in this early three-page version—the Nazi cats, even the figure of a cat-Hitler that appeared on the covers of both later volumes. This latter image is, in this version, stamped on bags of kitty litter the Jewish mice are forced to manufacture. But the three-page "MAUS" approaches Vladek's story from a different direction than the later full version. The Holocaust tale Vladek narrates in 1972 ends at "Mauschwitz" and is told to his young son, "Mickey," as a bedtime story in the 1950s. The mouse metaphor, which Spiegelman addresses extensively in *Maus II*, is highlighted in the 1950s panels where the father speaks to his almost-sleeping son, at whose bedside sits a Mickey Mouse lamp. Despite many familiar aspects, the mood of the Ur-*Maus* is also dramatically different, particularly in the way Spiegelman depicts his father. In the 1972 effort, Vladek not only appears gentle, but his relationship with Art/Mickey seems a loving and protective one. It is with the dismantling of this earlier image of family security that *Maus I: A Survivor's Tale* begins.

Maus I's initial setting is once again Rego Park during the 1950s, the voiceover narration provided by the adult artist son: "It was summer I remember. I was ten or eleven. I was roller-skating with Howie and Steve 'til my skate came loose." Left behind by still-skating friends and in search of comfort after his fall, young Artie walks over to his father, who is busy sawing a piece of wood. Depicted across three panels, his father's response announces immediately that we have moved beyond the world of the 1972 "Mickey" and his bedtime-story-telling father. "Friends? Your friends?" he sputters in a panel cut to a close-up. Two progressively longer shots follow: "If you lock them together in a room with no food for a week . . . *then* you could see what it is, friends!" (pp. 4–5). In two pages Art Spiegelman has established the thematic and stylistic dynamics that will infuse the rest of his project. The seeming unimportance of the roller-skating scene is shaded by the gravity of the adult son's understanding that his childhood was indelibly marked by his father's Holocaust experiences. That "father" is no longer the sympathetic "Poppa" of the earlier strip, but a complex and psychically wounded individual whose life in this 1958 scene is about to pivot from a decade of recovered happiness, beginning with the birth of Artie in 1948, toward a decade that collapses in renewed tragedy with Anja Spiegelman's suicide in 1968.

Finally, this two-page "Prologue," like so much of *Maus*, invests rich layers of meaning in the details and visual movement of the panels. The last emphasizes the intensity of the unique bond between the survivor father and his son by depicting them as small figures in a large, rectangular frame, Vladek standing over Art (figure from *Maus I*, p. 5). Visually, this frame anticipates later scenes in *Maus* where the adult son lies on the floor interviewing his father, establishing that however ridiculous or annoying the aged Vladek may seem, his Holocaust narrative remains primary. Another visual foreshadowing can be found in Artie's clothing—his overalls and striped shirt usually signify his dead brother, Richieu. Finally, the stark lines of the Spiegelmans' brick home and the dark garage opening before which the two small figures stand, chillingly anticipate the drawings of Auschwitz in the second volume, *And Here My Troubles Began*.

The "Prologue" to *Maus* establishes from the start the very narrative tension that permeates both volumes and remains a main source of the texts' energy. Vladek's story of survival engages us, yet our attention is equally drawn to the son's tale and his attempts to confront a past that both is and is not his own. The story progresses as follows: In 1937 Vladek Spiegelman, a handsome Polish Jew, marries Anja Zylberberg, whose wealthy family owns a hosiery factory in Sosnowiec. Staked by his father-in-law, Vladek starts a textile factory. Soon after the birth of their son, Richieu, life becomes more difficult for the Spiegelmans; Anja suffers from depression and World War II looms. Called up as a reserve in 1939, Vladek is captured when Germany invades Poland and experiences treatment under the Nazis that foreshadows what Jews in the camps will endure: Jewish soldiers are separated from their Polish comrades, receive less food, live in worse shelter, and endure more backbreaking labor. Released, he returns to Sosnowiec, where restrictions on Jews are followed by confinement in a ghetto and ultimately "evacuation." Though his abilities to find safe hiding places are impressive, Vladek is unable to prevent the betrayal that sends him and Anja not to the safety of Hungary, but to Auschwitz. "And we knew," he tells

his son at the end of the first volume, "that from here we will not come out anymore" (p. 146).

Summarizing the first volume in terms of its "story" is far more complicated than simply telling the tale of Vladek's Holocaust past. Indeed, a mere charting of time past in *Maus I* perhaps even undercuts its biographical power as a survivor narrative. *Maus* moves beyond this sort of straightforward Holocaust narrative by intermixing stories. Maus is about not only Vladek Spiegelman, but also his son. Coming to terms with his immigrant father makes Art's story very much an American one. Recording Vladek's story forces Art to confront his mother's suicide, not merely by charting Vladek's despair over the loss of Anja, but by incorporating the entire 1973 *Prisoner on the Hell Planet* comic strip within *Maus*'s larger narrative. Facing Holocaust history for Art Spiegelman is, finally, an attempt to recover family history and to touch the enormity of mass death through its single life stories. He understands the enormous gap separating him from his father's past; regardless of how well Vladek tells the story, the boy who holds the wood in the "Prologue" and whose vacation photograph with his mother appears in the opening panel of *Prisoner on the Hell Planet* (also set during 1958) is intimately connected to that past.

Complicating Art's relationship to Vladek's experiences is his awareness that he has only half the story; his mother's version has been lost to him. So when Vladek mentions, in *Maus I*, the diaries Anja kept after the war (an account of her Holocaust past), Art is ecstatic: "Ohmigod! Where are they? I *need* those for this book!" (p. 84). By the end of the volume, though, just after Vladek has finished recounting their first moment in Auschwitz, Art learns that his grieving father burned all his dead wife's papers, including the survivor memoir she had written and hoped her son might someday find of interest. Art's furious words are enclosed in the jagged balloon that denotes anger in the world of comics: "God *damn* you! You—you murderer! How the hell could you do such a thing!" (p. 159). Vladek is so stunned by the attack that he reverses his position from the book's "Prologue," where friends do not matter, and declares that "Even to your friends you should never yell this way!" (p. 159). Although Art is somewhat chastened by the exchange, for which he apologizes, he ends the first volume with his mouse-self leaving his father and muttering, "murderer."

Closure and *Maus II: And Here My Troubles Began* (1991)

Volume one ends with unresolved tension between father and son; the second volume not only continues the emotional standoff but introduces a new dimension to Art's struggle: reaching his father and trying to convey his Holocaust experiences through the comics medium. He speculates as the book opens that his effort may have been a fool's errand. "I feel so inadequate trying to reconstruct a reality that was worse than my darkest dreams," he tells mouse-wife Françoise as they drive to the Catskills to be with Vladek, whose second wife, Mala, has just left him. "There's so much I'll never be able to understand or visualize. I mean, reality is too complex for comics . . . so much has to be left out or distorted" (New York: Pantheon, 1991, p. 16). These anxieties become a preoccupation throughout the second volume, not only because of the graphic Auschwitz material introduced, but because of Spiegelman's amazing success with the first volume. Thus, while he seemingly pushes his form to the limit as he struggles to depict Auschwitz from the inside, he must also adjust to his celebrity status garnered by the earlier volume, the book that ended at Auschwitz's gates: The drama of retelling Vladek's camp experiences is tempered by his own self-consciousness. Add in the story of Vladek's later years, his separation from Mala, their "reconciliation," his declining health, and the second volume becomes an extremely complex intermixing of narrative time.

Nowhere is this more apparent than in the opening of the second section, "Auschwitz (Time Flies)," where across four panels Spiegelman, sitting self-consciously at his drawing table and wearing an obvious mouse mask, cites a swirling array of dates and events underlining how his personal past and Vladek's Holocaust past are conflated in his present: Art began this page in February 1987; in May 1987, Spiegelman and Mouly expected their first child; forty-three years before, in May 1944, "over 100,000 Hungarian Jews were gassed in Auschwitz;" Vladek died in August 1982; Art and Françoise visited him in the Catskills during August 1979; Vladek began work as a tinsmith in Auschwitz in the spring of 1944 (p. 41). Facing the reader in the fourth frame, the cartoonist notes the successful publication of *Maus I* in 1986. Then in a large panel dominating the page, Spiegelman graphically illustrates the cost of his success, built literally upon the bodies of dead Jews (figure from *Maus II*, p. 41). Over the next few pages Art depicts his struggle to resist the commercialization of *Maus*, his anxiety concerning the prospect of drawing Auschwitz, and his need to visit a survivor therapist in order to complete the project. After his visit to the psychiatrist, he again sits at the

drafting table. This time Vladek's recorded voice pulls him (and the reader) back into the world of the camps. From that point on in "Time Flies" and, indeed, throughout the remainder of the volume, Spiegelman returns to the narrative structure that served him before: Art interacts and struggles with Vladek in the present; Vladek recounts his own struggles in the past both to survive and to reunite with his wife.

Even more so than in the first volume, though, Art Spiegelman must find a means for addressing the chasm that separates him from his father's Holocaust experiences. While *Maus I* depicted the complex, though seemingly inevitable, process by which Vladek and Anja (and Europe's Jews) arrived at the gates of Auschwitz, the second volume takes its readers within the concentrationary universe itself, surely the point at which the comics medium is most severely tested.

Visually, the deeply shaded and contrast-filled Auschwitz panels of *Maus II* at times create a woodblock effect that seems to extend the graphic scope of the comic book form. The bold vertical stripes of the camp uniforms, for example, though doubtless more vibrant than the prisoners' tattered garments, serve as distinctive visual signs of the Auschwitz world, and help to pull our eyes down the page and through the panels. Their regular use throughout the book yields even subtler effects. Nearly all present-tense panels depicting Art's wife, Françoise, for example, show her wearing a shirt with bold horizontal stripes, as if to represent both his links to and distance from the Holocaust past.

If the visual challenges of the second volume are formidable, the task of depicting Auschwitz from the inside adds aesthetic and historical urgency to the entire *Maus* project. Spiegelman must not only convey what the poet William Heyen terms the "willed chaos" of the Nazis' genocidal program, he must strive to present camp life in all its complexity. To engage the mood of Auschwitz he drew upon such noted witnesses as Primo Levi and Elie Wiesel, as well as the sketches from prisoner artists, though it was Tadeusz Borowski's *This Way for the Gas, Ladies and Gentlemen* that most affected him. To depict Auschwitz's society, Art of course relied mostly on Vladek's recollections of life in the camp, whether detailing the barter system (a ration of bread was worth three cigarettes), the kinds of labor inflicted on the prisoners, the life-or-death importance of having shoes and clothes that fit, the power and caprice of the kapos, or the absolute authority of the German guards. Yet he supplements this information with extensive research, at one point within the narrative even challenging his father on the presence of a camp orchestra: Vladek does not recall such music as he marched to work, only the guards' shouts, while Art says the orchestra is "very well documented" (p. 54).

Although committed to rendering Vladek's memory of the camp, Art also had to meet the visual demands of his form, a need best met through the photographic record as well as travel to Poland itself. Nowhere is this more evident than in his attempt to trace the extermination process. For three pages Vladek recalls how, working as a tinsmith, he helped to dismantle one of the large crematoria. His description of the facility, and his narration of the various stages of the process, are accompanied by panels depicting the gassing site—stairs leading to an undressing room, the room itself, a gas chamber with a label indicating hollow columns where Zyclon B was dropped, and ovens where the dead were burned. All are meticulously drawn, as if for a textbook, though Spiegelman remains faithful to Vladek's perspective (he had never witnessed the killing process itself) by presenting the gassing-cremation facility absent of mouse figures. Only after breaking this visual narrative with a present-tense view of Vladek does he venture to show the killing process's final fiery results—the corpse-filled trenches used during the summer of 1944, based this time not on his father's words or his subsequent visit to Auschwitz, but on a famous photograph taken by the camp underground (figure from *Maus II*, p. 72). If in creating *Maus* the son remains largely faithful to the father's narrative, his own significant Holocaust research and devotion to accuracy extends the tale beyond a particular family's drama. Their story, of course, fuels the son's passion for his project, but what often distinguishes *Maus* from other survivor memoirs is Spiegelman's self-conscious attention to Holocaust detail, to presenting an overview of the event, which he achieves by placing himself within *Maus* as both listener and interrogator.

Although calling any survivor's tale "typical" seems an insult to the trauma, the lives of Vladek and Anja Spiegelman as depicted in *Maus II* have much in common with numerous Holocaust testimonies. Just as Vladek's ability to create bunkers allow them to avoid Nazi capture until 1944, his many talents are also invaluable in Auschwitz and even allow him to smuggle extra food to his wife. He teaches English to a kapo, repairs shoes for a German officer, and quickly learns enough tinsmithing to avoid more backbreaking labor. Vladek's particular blend of strength and intelligence also help him to survive the death march from Auschwitz to Germany and the brutal conditions of the overcrowded camps there. After liberation these same qualities finally effect reunion with Anja. Her story, as in the first book, is provided only in fragments, its untold components haunting the entire *Maus* project.

PRISONERS WHAT WORKED THERE POURED GASOLINE OVER THE LIVE ONES AND THE DEAD ONES.
AND THE FAT FROM THE BURNING BODIES THEY SCOOPED AND POURED AGAIN SO EVERYONE COULD BURN BETTER.

Throughout *Maus II* Spiegelman continues to detail the complex relationship with his father, its story at times creating an ironic counterpoint to the main Holocaust narrative, as when the seemingly helpless Vladek, in the present abandoned by his second wife, describes the arduous means by which he endured Auschwitz and his persistent attempts to help Anja survive. While his physical health consistently declines throughout the present-tense telling of the second volume, his story portrays a man who moves from confinement to liberation and from weakness to strength; we see the "souvenir" photograph from which, in a clean camp uniform, he stares resolutely from the book's pages to the future.

But that future, like so much in *Maus*, is not as simple as his story's progress toward a climactic reunion with Anja first implies. Concluding his happily-ever-after scene, the gravely ill Vladek asks his son, Art, to stop the tape recorder. "I'm tired from talking, Richieu, and it's enough stories for now" (p. 136). Mistaking his living son for the child he lost during the war, Vladek reopens the dirty wound that even his extended act of telling has not fully healed. In a disturbing inversion of the original Ur-*Maus* of 1972, it is the father who falls asleep at story's end, the son now standing over him. Art's narrative strand concludes with an image of Vladek and Anja's tombstone, where they are in fact reunited in death. Beneath the stone Art signs his name and "1978–1991," these years he spent composing the *Maus* project. Evoking the haunting image of the cartoonist troubled by success built on the bodies of Holocaust dead, this frame depicts the counterweight of ghosts now pressing on him. Art's actual life extends beyond the 1991 narrative closure of *Maus*, despite the black page succeeding his final frame, but resolution for this modern child of Job is not easily achieved, as a drawing from a 1992 grouping for *Tikkun* titled "Saying Goodbye to *Maus*" conveys. In this cartoon's foreground an adult mouse artist, wearing Spiegelman's ever-present vest, plays with his young daughter who now holds a Mickey Mouse doll; in the background are shadows both disturbing and revealing. Five mice hang from ropes around their necks.

The Complete Maus

While many have engaged issues raised by Spiegelman's printed texts—the use of cartoons to approach the Holocaust, their status as text by the child of survivors, their generic position as collaborative autobiography and oral history—little attention has been given to the electronic version of *Maus*. The scholars who do comment on *The Complete Maus* (1994) tend to focus on what they consider its most valuable feature: several hours of Vladek Spiegelman's oral testimony. Marianne Hirsch notes that this data allows us to "assess the transformations and revisions the son performs on his father's words as he tried to fit them into preset cartoon bubbles" (p. 275). The father's audio testimony does, in Dominick LaCapra's words, "disrupt the narrative with the voice of the survivor and provide the possibility of readings that may diverge from those prompted by the printed version of the text" (p. 147). Spiegelman himself declares that one of the CD-ROM's "core appeals" is its ability to include Vladek's version of an anecdote, in a sense "to let him have the last word." As others have noted, though, the son seldom surrenders authorship to the father. Indeed, the steady presence of the son's voiced commentary throughout the CD-ROM tends to undercut the effect of Vladek's voice.

In a section entitled "Why a CD-ROM?" the cartoonist explains that his initial desire to adapt *Maus* to an electronic format was based upon his mistaken notion that a single disk could hold not only the printed text, but all preliminary versions of the sketches, literally thousands of pages. The CD-ROM as electronic preserve has its attractions, but overall Spiegelman's archival impulse undermines the narrative tension that is so much a part of *Maus*'s success, the taut interweaving of stories by father, son, and artist. Unfortunately the unbalanced weight of so many sketches and comments, so many supplementary materials (video of Art's visit to Poland, interviews with him, even a section entitled "Art on Art"), pushes Vladek Spiegelman's story deep into the background.

Interestingly, it is when the son refrains from assuming the historian's corrective role that *The Complete Maus* reveals its potential. In the most sustained vocal selection on the CD, Vladek describes his job of disassembling the gassing and cremation facility at Birkenau. The last two panels read: "You heard about the gas, but I'm telling not rumors, but only what really I saw. For this I was an eyewitness." Absent from this "page" of the CD-ROM is any commentary by Art, either about his father's memories or the historical details gleaned from research. In this case he apparently deemed confirmation of Vladek's account supplied by supplementary materials superfluous.

Critical commentary that is focused on how *The Complete Maus* disrupts the narrative continuity of the printed texts (often viewed as a hypertextual virtue) usually fails to note absences or the CD-ROM format's most significant impact upon the *Maus* project overall: the overemphasis of a single narrative thread —namely, the focus on artist Spiegelman's attempt through composition to come to terms with his father's Holocaust experiences. The self-referentiality of *The Complete Maus*, its screens cluttered by icons luring us toward supplementary materials, subordinates Vladek's lived experience to the life of Art's book. Appended to a long audio explanation of how he chose to end the book, for example, Art includes a note in which he imagines concluding *Maus* with Vladek's funeral, followed by a panel of the son reflecting: "I didn't feel much or think much except, 'I guess this is how my book ends.' " The artist honestly acknowledges that the construction of his book is primary for him, his only route through his father's narrative, but the ghostly presences of the printed texts dissipate in the CD-ROM, inviting criticism: Roy Rosenzweig opines, "By so lovingly and carefully bringing together all of the artifacts surrounding the making of *Maus*, the CD-ROM may enshrine Art Spiegelman as an artist and *Maus* as a work of high art. The CD-ROM becomes an object that *Maus* aficionados can take as testifying to and embodying Spiegelman's 'genius' " (p. 1639). More harshly, Michael Rothberg proclaims all the electronic appendages as "another step on the road to the Spielbergization of the Holocaust" (p. 674).

The electronic *Maus* is more a tool for scholarly study than the dynamic text some readers seek, but whatever textual energy and balance is lost in the transition from page to computer screen, the scholarly rewards of *The Complete Maus* are in fact many and valuable. Despite overemphasis on the text's visual evolution, the CD-ROM still demonstrates the potential of multimedia in general and of the aural in particular. Amid the many images, both moving and static, those of Vladek are few, his photograph appearing only a few times in the entire electronic text. The sway of the unseen is, in some respects, enhanced by the absence of a Vladek video, and most memorable are those brief moments in *The Complete Maus* when the visual surrenders to the aural force of Vladek speaking. If, as Lawrence Langer says, "oral Holocaust testimonies are doomed on one level to remain disrupted narratives, not only by the vicissitudes of technology but by the quintessence of the experiences they record" (p. xi), Vladek Spiegelman's accented voice nevertheless bodies forth the primary substance to be ruptured. Listening, we witness the elusive material compelling the cartoonist son to attempt expression of experience beyond naming. We can view an individual panel, listen to the voice actuating it, and recover afresh the dynamic power that is *Maus* at its best. We recognize what the son has realized, however much we must also register the impracticability of his task.

Bibliography

Primary Sources

"MAUS" in *Funny Aminals* [sic]. 1972.
"Prisoner on the Hell Planet." In *Short Order Comics #1*, 1973.
Whole Grains: A Book of Quotations. With Bob Schneider. 1973.
Breakdowns: From Maus to Now: An Anthology of Strips. 1977.
RAW. 1980.
Jack Survives. With Jerry Moriarty and Françoise Mouly. 1984.

Invasion of the Elvis Zombies, with Gary Panter and Françoise Mouly. 1985.

Maus: A Survivor's Tale: My Father Bleeds History. 1986.

Raw: The Graphic Aspirin for War Fever, with Françoise Mouly. 1986.

Agony by Mark Beyer, with Françoise Mouly. 1987.

Read Yourself Raw, with Françoise Mouly. 1987.

Harvey Kurtzman's Jungle Book, with Denis Kitchen. 1988.

Jimbo: Adventures in Paradise by Gary Panter, with Françoise Mouly. 1988.

Warts and All by Drew Friedman and Josh Alan Friedman, with R. Sikoryak and Françoise Mouly. 1990.

Raw: No. 2, with Françoise Mouly. 1990.

Maus: A Survivor's Tale, II: And Here My Troubles Began. 1991.

Raw: Number Three: High Culture for Low Brows, with Françoise Mouly. 1991.

Roach Killer, with Jacques Tardi and Jean-Marc Lofficier. 1992.

"Saying Goodbye to Maus," *Tikkun*. (September–October 1992): 45.

The Selected Letters of Philip K. Dick, 1977–1979, Vol. 5. 1992.

Skin Deep: Tales of Doomed Romance by Charles Burns, with R. Sikoryak and Dale Crain. 1992.

City of Glass by Paul Auster, with Bob Callahan and others. 1994.

The Complete Maus (CD-ROM). 1994.

The Wild Party: The Lost Classic, with Joseph M. March. 1994.

The Narrative Corpse, with R. Sikoryak. 1995.

Neon Lit: Barry Gifford's Perdita Durango, with Scott Gillis and Bob Callahan. 1995.

History of Comix. 1996.

Maus: A Survivor's Tale. 1996.

I'm a Dog! 1997.

Comix, Essays, Graphics & Scraps: From Maus to Now to Maus to Now. 1998.

Dr. Seuss Goes to War: The World War II Editorial Cartoons of Theodor Seuss Geisel, with Richard H. Minear. 2000.

Little Lit. Folklore and Fairy Tale Funnies, with Françoise Mouly. 2000.

Jack Cole and Plastic Man: Forms Stretched to Their Limits, with Chip Kidd. 2001.

Legal Action Comics, with Danny Hellman and R. Crumb. 2001.

Strange Stories for Strange Kids, with Françoise Mouly. 2001.

Secondary Sources

Berger, Alan. *Children of Job: American Second-Generation Witnesses to the Holocaust*. Albany: State University of New York Press, 1997.

Hirsch, Marianne. *Family Frames: Photography, Narrative, and Postmemory*. Cambridge, Mass.: Harvard University Press, 1997.

Horowitz, Sara R. "Auto/Biography and Fiction after Auschwitz: Probing the Boundaries of Second Generation Aesthetics." In *Breaking Crystal: Writing and Memory after Auschwitz*. Edited by Efraim Sicher. Urbana: University of Illinois Press, 1998.

Hungerford, Amy. "Surviving Rego Park: Holocaust Theory from Art Spiegelman to Berel Lang." In *The Americanization of the Holocaust*. Edited by Hilene Flanzbaum. Baltimore: Johns Hopkins University Press, 1999.

LaCapra, Dominick. *History and Memory after Auschwitz*. Ithaca, N.Y. Cornell University Press, 1998.

Langer, Lawrence. *Holocaust Testimonies: The Ruins of Memory*. New Haven, Conn.: Yale University Press, 1991.

Rosensweig, Roy. " 'So, What's Next for Clio?': CD-ROM and Historians." *Journal of American History* 81 (March 1995): 1621–1640.

Rothberg, Michael. " 'We Were Talking Jewish': Art Spiegelman's *Maus* as 'Holocaust' Production." *Contemporary Literature* 35 (winter 1994). 661–687.

Schwarz, Daniel R. *Imagining the Holocaust*. New York: St. Martin's Press, 1999.

Staub, Michael E. "The *Shoah* Goes On and On: Remembrance and Representation in Art Spiegelman's *Maus*." *MELUS* 20, (fall 1995). 32–46.

Weschler, Lawrence. "Art's Father, Vladek's Son." In *Shapinsky's Karma, Boggs's Bills and Other True-Life Tales*. New York: Penguin, 1990

GEORGE STEINER

(1929–)

S. LILLIAN KREMER

GEORGE STEINER'S PARENTS, Bohemian Frederick George and Viennese Elsie (Franzos) Steiner left Vienna in 1924 for Paris, where the writer was born in 1929. The family then emigrated to the United States in 1940. Steiner was educated at the University of Chicago (B. A. 1948), Harvard University (M. A. 1950), and Oxford University (D. Phil. 1955). He has and continues to enjoy an illustrious academic and literary career including work as a member of the editorial staff of the London *Economist*, as Fellow of the Institute for Advanced Study at Princeton University, and as founding fellow and Extraordinary Fellow of Churchill College at Cambridge University. In addition to lecturing at several prestigious American universities, he has taught as professor of English and comparative literature at the University of Geneva, as a Fulbright scholar in Austria, Maurice lecturer at the University of London, Leslie Stephen lecturer at Cambridge University, W. P. Ker lecturer at the University of Glasgow, visiting professor to the College of France, and First Lord Weidenfeld professor of comparative literature at Oxford University. He was named the 2001–2002 Charles Eliot Norton Professor of Poetry at Harvard.

Steiner's achievements in literature were recognized early with his reception of the Bell Prize at Harvard, a Rhodes scholarship and the Chancellor's Essay prize at Oxford, and the 1958 O. Henry Short Story Prize for "Botteghe Oscure." In addition to a Guggenheim Fellowship and the Morton Dauwen Zabel Prize from the American Academy of Arts and Letters, he has garnered honorary degrees from universities across Europe and America as well as the 1974 Remembrance Award for his essay collection addressing the *Shoah*, *Language and Silence*; the 1992 Macmillan Silver Pen Award for *Proofs and Three Parables* (1992); and the 1993 PEN Macmillan Fiction Prize. For his literary criticism Steiner received the 1998 Truman Capote Lifetime Achievement Award.

Holocaust Consciousness

Although George Steiner escaped the assemblies of Jewish children awaiting deportation, escaped being forcibly separated from his parents when the trains reached their destinations, and escaped the concentration camp slave labor, starvation, and death selections, he did not escape survivor guilt. Steiner considers himself "maimed for not having been at the roll call" (quoted in *Time*, 29 March 1982, n.p.). His essay "A Kind of Survivor" addresses how the tragedy that befell the Jews of Europe affects his attitudes toward his children, and his views of language, literature, politics, and the human condition. Steiner has recanted his earlier prescription for fictional silence on the *Shoah* in favor of bearing witness to the appalling crimes of Nazism in narrative. Because he is convinced that the Holocaust rose from the core of European civilization, Steiner has written extensively on the nature of antisemitism and its cultural context. He has examined the abuse of language as a precipitator of the *Shoah* and the *Shoah*'s representation through language. In "The Hollow Miracle" he argues:

> Use a language to conceive, organize, and justify Belsen; use it to make out specifications for gas ovens; use it to dehumanize man during twelve years of calculated bestiality. Something will happen to it. Make of words what Hitler and Goebbels and the hundred thousand *Unterstrumführer* made; conveyers of terror and falsehood. Something will happen to the words. Something of the lies and sadism will settle in the marrow of the language. (*Language and Silence: Essays on Language, Literature and the Inhuman*, Atheneum, 1977, p. 101).

Fictional Transmission

Many of the theoretical issues Steiner explores in his essays appear dramatically in the *Anno Domini* (1964) collection of three novellas and *The Portage to San Cristóbal of A.H.* (1982). Avoiding dramatic presentation of the ghettos and camps, Steiner focuses on character representations of the Nazis and their collaborators, occasionally through the perspective of survivor flashback and judgment, through self-incrimination by the villains, and more often through judgmental choral voices. Whether the scene is a French seaside village, a country mental asylum, or a South American jungle, Steiner's stage is the Nuremburg courtroom.

The stories of *Anno Domini* explore activities of the war years, the moral imperative to foster memory, and the psychological and political implications of wartime trauma and postwar response to the atrocities of the Nazi regime. In "Return No More" a prosperous industrialist and former Wehrmacht officer travels to the Normandy farmhouse where he was billeted during the war to marry the daughter of the family whose son his unit ordered hanged from the family ash tree. Claiming to have learned the value of life in their rural French village, he speaks of mutual suffering and reconciliation. He acknowledges Nazi atrocities and denounces German Holocaust amnesia and silence, echoing Steiner's views published in "The Hollow Miracle" regarding German post-1948 Holocaust silence—a desire to forget the past while privileging economic recovery, productivity, and industrial restoration. French reactions to the German's reconciliation overtures range from acceptance by villagers eager for reparations to outright rejection. At the country wedding celebration, the bride's surviving brother and his cohorts demand that the lame bridegroom dance. They join him and deliver him to the punishment he may have unconsciously sought, by trampling him to death. Despite its sympathetic rendering of the German, "Return No More" argues that there is no forgetting and no forgiving Nazi atrocity. The story may be read as a realistic prologue to the fantasy treatment of *The Portage to San Cristóbal of A. H.*

Attention shifts from the perceptions of the perpetrator to those of the bystander in the volume's second story. "Cake" presents a retrospective view of an American's transformation from innocent Harvard graduate student to politically engaged resistance agent and fugitive in Nazi-occupied France. Disgusted by what he perceived as his cowardice after witnessing SS men manhandling an old Jewish man and a young woman on a city tram, the American envies them for "the torments being wrought on them" (*Anno Domini: Three Stories*, Faber and Faber, 1980, p. 73). Like the tourist who wants to experience the real Europe, this man feels deprived to be missing the pain in his flesh that others are undergoing. No longer content to spend his efforts on violence in literature when real blood flows all around him in the prisons and Gestapo cellars, he becomes a courier for the underground only to be sequestered in an insane asylum when the Gestapo get too close to discovering him. A Jewish girl, hidden in the same sanatorium, who relates her family's *Shoah* history to him, initiates his Holocaust education. It is his love for Rahel and his postwar commemoration of her that is at the heart of his internalizing Jewish history.

Through Rahel Jakobsen's narrative, Steiner renders the "special actions" the Germans reserved for the Jews in France, delineating the change from prewar normality to disruption of emigrating and disappearing family, donning of mandatory yellow stars, followed by deportation to the concentration camps and killing centers. Functioning doubly as trope for freedom and incarceration, the insane asylum is Rahel's temporary safe haven, but also a symbol of the restricted world of the concentration camp where Rahel believes her brother was sent. The American seeks to comfort her with reminders of a civilized Germany, "the land of Schiller and Beethoven; . . . the language of Rilke" (p. 92) and by recalling the excesses of World War I anti-German propaganda, but the European Jew knows better. She prepares a memorial for her dead and introduces the theme of bearing witness. Defying those who swore "that no one would even recall the names of the dead, that their sum would be ash, . . . [that they] would have neither graves nor the fitful resurrection men are allowed in the remembrance of their children" (p. 99), Rahel made the telling and listening a holy service. In the anticipated American retelling of the history, she and her family would be remembered. During his postwar visit to Rahel's room in the asylum, the American expresses his grief for having lost her to Gestapo arrest in a Holocaust image: "I would cry out to her that since she had left me, my life was ash" (p. 111). Yet even in his anguish for a lost love, he misses the point; she did not leave him, and other Jews did not voluntarily part with their loved ones. Perhaps the point of Steiner's comment has wider implications and is meant to suggest the ashen void in European culture created by Jewish absence.

Holocaust Fantasy: Hitler Lives

Realistic presentation of historic data was long the approach to Holocaust literature of most nonwitness writers, especially because many doubted their right to imagine the concentrationary universe. Recently, this decorum has been shattered. Israeli novelist David Grossman, graphic artist Art Spiegelman, and poststructuralist theorist Hayden White paved the way for a shift away from insistence on the authentic representation of events to exploration of fantasy as a means of registering and perceiving the historically true. Arguing that realism is inadequate for Holocaust representation, White advocates writing "which lays no claim to the kind of realism aspired to by nineteenth-century historians and writers" (p. 52). The incorporation of the fantastic element of Hitler's survival in a South American jungle in *Portage to San Cristóbal of A. H.* facilitates authentic response to post-Holocaust sensibilities by allowing witness characters to document their experience realistically. By denying the code of reality, Steiner is able to use the fantastic to give Hitler voice and make the horror of his thinking concrete.

The Portage is a novel blending fantasy and the detective plot of locating and bringing the criminal to justice. The novel's action is centered on the efforts of an Israeli Nazi-hunting team to extricate Hitler from the South American jungles and swamps for trial and the obstruction they face from multinational agents. Its thematic development centers on representative post-Holocaust consciousness and response of British, French, German, Russian, Israeli, and American allegorical characters to the *Shoah* and its chief perpetrator. To map post-Holocaust thinking, the prose alternates between the tense verbal altercation of the Jews and the Holocaust architect and the sedate, supercilious, passionless voices of the international intelligence agencies analyzing the advantages and damages that would accrue to their respective nations should Hitler be put on trial. These passages are extensions of Steiner's long-term examination of language as a mirror of human psychology. Through the international characters' use and abuse of language the Holocaust-era and post-Holocaust national purposes are revealed, and in Hitler's speech Steiner once again interrogates Nazism's pervasive corruption of the German language, which he treated in "The Hollow Miracle."

Although the only overt trial in *Portage* is Hitler's, the international community is also on trial and judged corrupt. Its member nations have sought to conceal past crimes and collaboration and present errors in judgment. The indifference of the great powers to Jewish annihilation is effectively transmitted through postwar vignettes of the intelligence services in which the British concern is primarily forensic, the German is legal, the Russian is political, the French is to conceal Vichy collaboration and preserve French honor, and the American is opportunistic.

Allies and Axis representatives alike receive Steiner's censure. The Briton's remarks on the Holocaust are passionless and amoral, reflecting his government's Holocaust-era indifference to the fate of the Jews. Britain's failure to bomb the railroad lines to the concentration camps—a topic Steiner pursued in "A Kind of Survivor"—and suppression of its 1942 knowledge of mass murder of European Jewry exemplify its passivity. Ryder's acknowledgment of English passivity during the Holocaust and its vigorous obstruction of immigration by Holocaust survivors to Palestine further indict his nation. The French perspective is presented as a diary of a self-serving career intelligence officer from a Fascist family that served the Vichy government. In addition to blocking Israeli objectives of an open trial, the diarist's great interest is in suppressing evidence of French dishonor. Mass killings of Jews are a minor indiscretion but maintenance of an inviolate French political image, deceitful though it is, is sacrosanct. The counterpoint to French deception is German sentimentality and criminality introduced through the voice of an unrepentant Nazi. Dr. Röthling was exhilarated by the triumphs of the Reich, but now disdains Germans who "pretend that they are carrying our national burden, that the past lies on their shoulders and the blood on their forehead" (p. 114). Röthling strives to erase Nazi crimes from history, to enjoy sweet amnesia, to protect Germans by accusing Nazi victims who expose the hidden perpetrators of engaging in "Mere hysteria. Melodrama" (p. 114). An educated, cultured man, Röthling is the embodiment of the German who read Goethe and listened to Bach and yet had no difficulty following Hitler devotedly, working the gas chambers of Auschwitz or conducting medical experiments on humans. He is nostalgic for the war years. For him it was an opportunity to live history fully, to live heroically, to "Have crossed and recrossed Europe like Napoleon's hordes, . . . A thousand year Reich inside each of us, a millennium of remembered life" (p. 115). He regrets the diminished lives of postwar Germans who inherited Nazi ash, but neither the philosophy nor the crimes of the Reich.

Only the Israelis are obsessed with Holocaust loss and with bringing A. H. to justice. Certain both of the immensity of Hitler's crimes and of international indifference or inability to exact commensurate punishment, each member of the team imagines his own retribution. One member, who is just beginning to use future tense verbs, and who remains burdened by memories of his child burnt alive and another led by its mother into the gas, would allow Hitler freedom of movement throughout Israel on the condition that he had to identify himself "Every time he wanted food or water or shelter" (p. 62). Another, who suffered the brutal murder of his father and three children before he traversed the sewers under the ghetto wall, all the while fearful that when he emerged there would be a Nazi boot in his face, declares all punishment inadequate. He fantasizes a painful death for Hitler, a prolonged agony like that experienced by European Jews. He argues against execution because nations will claim the accounts have been settled when they can never be settled. A third, Elie Baruch, whose name evokes images of the priesthood and blessings, would leave the matter to God's judgment.

The novel's two monologues, that of the Israeli team leader and A. H., embody much of Steiner's thinking about the Holocaust and language. We never see Leiber, for he directs the operation by radio from London, Turin, and Tel Aviv, yet it is his voice that instructs the team and shapes reader perceptions. Leiber is a survivor whose Holocaust history includes having crawled out from under burnt flesh in a death pit, having witnessed "the fires of Bialka, the children hung alive" (p. 17). His is the most sustained voice of historical memory and ethical imperative. A moral tour de force, his monologue shifts from biblical diction and cadence to graphic realism and symbolic fragmentation charting the disruptive impact of Nazism on civilization and the human psyche through its manipulation of language. Referring to a theory of dichotomies, Leiber insists:

> All that is God's . . . must have its counterpart, its backside of evil and negation. So it is with the Word, with the gift of speech that is the glory of man. . . . He created on the night side of language a speech for hell. Whose words mean hatred . . . Few men can learn that speech or speak it for long. . . . But there shall come a man whose mouth shall be as a furnace and whose tongue as a sword laying waste. He will know the grammar of hell and teach it to others. He will know the sounds of madness and loathing and make them seem music. Where God said, let there be, he will unsay (p. 45).

Because he has elevated language to these cosmic proportions, Leiber urges his men to resist listening to Hitler's speech; to anticipate his every need and provide it, to gag him, and to stop their own ears as Ulysses did, rather than chance succumbing to the demonic voice and its lies.

Structurally, this monologue functions as the legal prosecution that Hitler evades in a fictional court of law, as he evaded it in history. Leiber's powerful litany of tortured and murdered Jews serves both as an indictment of the criminal and a memorial to the martyrs. It maps the excremental concentrationary world, detailing atrocities perpetrated to degrade and humiliate the victims as prelude to their murder. Steiner makes the destruction of the six million comprehensible by referencing individual cases; yet he never looses sight of the genocidal proportions of the Holocaust, citing specific camps and the magnitude of their death tolls. Leiber's description of the Nazi universe is comparable to Steiner's discussion in *Bluebeard's Castle* (1971) comparing the camps to Western civilization's artistic visions of Hell. In a catalog juxtaposing the victims' accomplishments with their psychological and physical abuse—public humiliation, rape, torture, mutilation, starvation, death by fire and gas—he pays homage to the culture that bred the victims, and implies judgment of the culture that produced the victimizers. A lengthy series of unpunctuated fragmented phrases elicits readers' imagined completion and judgment. Alvin Rosenfeld compares this portion of the monologue favorably to Paul Celan's "stuttering and hallucinatory lyricism, [in "Todesfuge"] [as] it also drives language into and beyond ellipsis, finding in fragments of speech a literary form to encompass and express brokenness" (p. 88).

Understanding that one "can imagine the cry of one, the hunger of two, the burning of ten, but past a hundred there is no clear imagining . . ." (49), Steiner recites the awesome list, Treblinka, Majdanek, Belzec, Chelmno, Sobibor, Belsen, and suggests their tragic proportions by offering a sacred litany of individual and collective losses. At the center of the catalog is the name of one not subjected to the Nazi universe, "Nathaniel Steiner who was taken to America in time" (49), an autobiographical reference to the Steiner family's escape from the physical hell, and its psychological bondage to its history.

The Connective Tissue Linking Historic Antisemitism and the *Shoah*

In essay and fiction, Steiner repeatedly marks a direct connection between pre-Nazi religiously based antisemitism and the Nazi racist variety culminating in the *Shoah*. In "Cake" (*Anno Domini*) a jealous woman betrays a hidden Jewish woman to the Nazis and warns the American that "a dirty little Jewess" is deceiving him. The admonition is catalyst for the American's spontaneous recollection of antisemitism he witnessed in his own social circle, the enrollment quotas restricting Jews in prestigous private schools, their exclusion from social clubs, and finally the ironic recognition that if he lives to preserve Rahel's history it would be in his mother's Belmont home and in "cousin Peyton's library on Mt. Auburn Street, in the Somerset Club . . . . [places where] living Jews have small welcome" (p. 99). Indeed the narrator vents his own antisemitism: "Like most people, I found that Jews left me uncomfortable; I parted from them as from a stiff chair" (p. 94), thereby characterizing the prejudice as universal and attributing it to the same motives that Steiner identifies in his analytic writing. Introducing the method to be used later in *Portage* of recasting his expository ideas in fictional form, the protagonist of "Cake" argues that a root cause of antisemitism is in gentile resentment of Jewish conscience: "By their unending misery, the Jews have put mankind in the wrong. Their presence is reproach" (p. 95). This view echoes Steiner's theory as outlined in the essays of *Bluebeard's Castle* that the Jewish insistence on moral perfectibility is a threat to the non-Jewish world that defies it through the periodic destruction of Jewry.

Given his Holocaust experience, Leiber abjures comment on the relatively harmless social expressions of antisemitism that characterize American experience. His focus is on the more deadly forms and on the assistance of willing Nazi collaborators and the passive bystanders to the Nazi genocide:

> Oh they helped. Nearly all of them. Who would not give visas and put barbed wire on their borders. Who threw stones through the windows and spat. Who when six hundred escaped from Treblinka hunted down and killed all but thirty-nine—Polish farmers, irregulars, partisans, charcoal burners in the forest—saying Jews belong in Treblinka. He could not have done it alone. I know that. Not without the helpers and the indifferent, not without the hooligans who laughed and the soft men who took over the shops and moved into the houses. Not without those who said in Belgravia and Marly, in Stresa and in Shaker Heights that the news was exaggerated, that the Jews were whining again and peddling horrors. Not without D. initialing a memo to B-W. at Printing House Square: *no more atrocity stories. Probably overplayed.* Or Foggy Bottom offering seventy-five visas above the quota when one hundred thousand children could have been saved (p. 51).

The uniquely Steinerian aspect of the speech, "Because we foisted Christ on them" (p. 51) links the *Shoah* directly to Christian anti-Judaism. Leiber, like Steiner in *Bluebeard's Castle*, views antisemitism as the rebellion of natural man against the abstractness of monotheism and the Jewish moral imperatives Jesus repeated in his teaching. He conjectures that the Jewish invention of monotheism and its subsequent moral system provoked an intolerable affront to Western civilization.

A. H. reiterates the author's accounting for antisemitism as a direct expression of gentile hatred of the Jewish inventions of God and conscience as affronts to Western paganism. Parodic distortion is at the center of his ironic analogy of the doctrine of Aryan racial superiority and the Judaic principle of covenantal election; his fallacious comparison of his *Ubermenschen* with the chosen people and his biblical justification for genocide. A. H. claims to have learned from the Bible "a device to alter the human soul," that is, "To slaughter a city because of an idea, because of vexation over words" (p. 163). Here, the language shifts from biblical diction to racial propaganda, evoking Nazi vocabulary of disease and corruption. In accord with Steiner's expository writing positing the relationship of antisemitism to the psychology of religion, A. H. blames the Jews for their idealism, whether it be in the form of monotheism, the quest for ethical perfection, or social and economic equality. Compare A. H.'s rhetorical query: "Was there ever a crueler invention, a contrivance more calculated to harrow human existence, than that of an omnipotent, all-seeing, yet invisible, impalpable, inconceivable God?" (p. 164), and Steiner's observation that although parallels exist with other hatreds that produced other massacres, there is no comparison "ontologically, not on the level of philosophic intent" ("A Season in Hell," *Bluebeard's Castle*, Yale University Press, 1971, p. 37). A logical progression of this attack is the A. H. parody of Steiner's observations that the Jewish code setting forth a system for attaining moral perfectibility affronts man's natural inclination to evil: "The Jew invented conscience and left man a guilty serf" (p. 165). This rant recalls Steiner's observation in "A Season in Hell" that

> Monotheism at Sinai, primitive Christianity, messianic socialism generated a subconscious hatred for the Jews for having "produced a summons to perfection" for "*We hate most those who hold out to us a goal, an ideal, a visionary promise which . . . we cannot reach, yet, . . . which remains profoundly desirable, which we cannot reject because we fully acknowledge its supreme value* (pp. 44–45).

Steiner's theories of the relation between Holocaust barbarism and the corruption of language find dramatic expression in the speech of A. H. who uses language as Hitler did—to lie, to distort, to misrepresent, to defile Jews and Judaism.

A. H.'s self-identification as a man of his times, one who accomplished what France, England, Russia, and even America secretly desired, has an element of truth in it as manifested in occupied Europe's collaboration with the Nazis, just as there is a kernel of truth in his assertion that the Nazi genocide led to acceptance of a Jewish homeland. Yet these clever manipulations pervert truth. In the fashion of Milton's Satan, A. H. argues that his evil is benign because it served to generate good and that he was therefore God's instrument. Although Hitler has the last speech and identifies himself as a messiah, his self-description as the Sabbatai links him to an historic false messiah. The allusion serves also as link to Leiber's reference to Nathaniel of Mainz describing the voice and language of a counter-Messiah negating the Bible and "banishing God from creation," a hate-filled voice remarkably similar to the fictional Hitler.

Critical Reception

Many who respect Steiner's essays on the Holocaust and his literary criticism, recoil in horror at his incorporation of self-parody for the speech of A. H. Beyond the offensive claim that he learned his racist philosophy from Judaism's sense of being a chosen people, the capacity for distortion in his analogy of the doctrine of Aryan racial superiority to the Judaic concept of covenantal election, are his equally outrageous claims of "biblical justification" for genocide, and his role as father of the Zionist state. Representative of the detractors' opinion is Hyam Maccoby's concern that the impact of the dramatic adaptation

> is not in the world of apocalypse, as Steiner intended, but in the world in which we live, where arguments of the kind A.H. uses are believed quite seriously by educated people; where propaganda is continually going on to diminish the significance of the Holocaust by blaming the Jews themselves for it in various ways; where, in fact, the chief effect of Hitler's peroration, presented with an air of awe and unanswerability, may well be to send away some from the theatre with anti-Jewish prejudices reinforced (p. 31).

Maccoby observes that in playing the Devil's advocate, Steiner risks attributing convincing arguments to Hitler which, apart from being uncharacteristic of the historic prototype's racist demagoguery, might be misinterpreted as valid. In *Imagining Hitler*, Alvin Rosenfeld strenuously objects to Steiner's attribution of "the authority of his own essayistic voice, but pitched now to express an exuberant mockery of his Jewish adversaries—indeed, a mockery of every major aspect of Jewish antecedence" (p. 101). While some despair that Hitler has the final word, Joseph Lowin points out that the final sound is that of hovering helicopters—a suggestion that A. H. may be brought to trial. Robert Boyers, who is dismissive of Maccoby's extraliterary objections, is not only untroubled by A. H. having the final speech, but considers it mandatory given the novel's structure and purpose:

> because it is the object of the novel to show what the power of transvaluation is all about. The final speech demonstrates that a Hitler can appropriate a Steiner for his purposes by willfully ignoring, and thus violating, the spirit and intent of Steiner's original utterances and turning them to totally alien purposes (p. 46).

Bryan Cheyette concludes that "Steiner is not simply contrasting Leiber and A. H. but is portraying them as part of the same dialectic . . . two different aspects of George Steiner" (p. 77). Despite A. H's near verbatim repetition of Steiner's assessment of the underlying causes of antisemitism, Cheyette maintains this does not give A. H. "the authority of Steiner's criticism—as those who have condemned the text have argued—but is more subtly, Steiner's most profound means of thinking against himself" (p. 77) and that "it is precisely Steiner's faith in his readers and audience, that they will offer a counter-interpretation to the language of A. H., which distinguishes his deliberately unfinished dialogue in this work" (p. 78). This assessment follows Norman Finkelstein's luminous analysis and interpretation of Steiner's appropriation of the *midrashic* mode: "the text casts its problem back upon the reader; calling for the very dialogue (or dispute) which it has in fact provoked" (p. 116).

Bibliography

Primary Sources

Books—Nonfiction

Tolstoy or Dostoevsky: An Essay in the Old Criticism. 1959.
The Death of Tragedy. 1961.
Language and Silence: Essays on Language, Literature, and the Inhuman. 1967.
Extraterritorial: Papers on Literature and the Language Revolution. 1971.
In Bluebeard's Castle: Some Notes toward the Redefinition of Culture. 1971.
Nostalgia for the Absolute. 1974.
After Babel: Aspects of Language and Translation. 1975.
On Difficulty and Other Essays. 1978.
Martin Heidegger. 1978. Revised and expanded, in America, as *Martin Heidegger: With a New Introduction*. 1991. Published in England as *Heidegger*, 1978; revised and expanded in 1992.
George Steiner: A Reader. 1984.
Antigones: How the Antigone Legend Has Endured in Western Literature, Art, and Thought. 1984.
Real Presences: Is There Anything in What We Say? 1989.
No Passion Spent. 1996.
Errata: An Examined Life. 1997.
Barbarie de l'ignorance: Juste l'ombre d'un certain ennui (With Antoine Spire and others). 1998.
Ce qui me hante (With Antoine Spire and others). 1999.
Grammars of Creation. 2001.

Books—Fiction

Anno Domini: Three Stories. 1964.
The Portage to San Cristóbal of A. H. 1981.
Proofs and Three Parables. 1992.
The Deeps of the Sea (Includes *The Portage to San Cristóbal of A. H.*). 1996.

Plays

The Portage to San Cristóbal of A. H. Adapted for stage by Christopher Hampton. In *The Theatre of the Holocaust, Volume Two: Six Plays*. Edited by Robert Skloot. Madison: University of Wisconsin Press, 1999.

Editor

Homer: A Collection of Critical Essays (With Robert Fagles). 1962.

The Penguin Book of Modern Verse Translation. Editor and author of introduction. Penguin, 1966. Reprinted as *Poem into Poem: World Poetry in Modern Verse Translation*. 1970.

Editor and author of introduction. *Homer in English*. With assistance of Aminadav Dykman. London: Penguin, 1996.

Selected Published Lectures

Has Truth a Future? Bronowski memorial lecture, 1978. London: British Broadcasting Corporation, 1978.

The Uncommon Reader. The Ben Belitt Lectures at Bennington College. Bennington College Press, 1978.

Real Presences: The Leslie Stephen Memorial Lecture Delivered before the University of Cambridge on 1 November 1985. Cambridge: Press Syndicate of the University of Cambridge, 1986.

A Reading against Shakespeare: The W. P. Ker Lecture. Glasgow: University of Glasgow, 1986.

What Is Comparative Literature? An Inaugural Lecture Delivered before the University of Oxford on 11 October 1994. New York: Oxford University Press, 1995.

Selected Periodical Publications and Parts of Books

"Lyric of Desire." *Poetry* 75 (February 1950): 267. Published under Francis George Steiner.

"Two Poems." *Paris Review* (summer 1953).

"Our Castles in Spain." *Harper's* (September 1954): 79–86. Published under F. George Steiner.

"A Preface to 'Middlemarch.' " *Nineteenth-Century Fiction* 9 (March 1955): 262–279. Published under F. George Steiner.

"Eden in Trouble." *Harper's* (April 1956): 49–53. Published under F. George Steiner.

"The Americanness of American Literature." *Listener* 62: 95–97.

"Notes from Eastern Europe." *Harper's* (June 1959): 49–54.

"George Lukács and His Devil's Pact." *Kenyon Review* 22 (winter 1960): 1–18.

"Postscript to Power." *Nation* 189 (12 March 1960): 230–232.

"Baedekers of the Heart." *Reporter* 22 (17 March 1960): 47–49.

"Old Language of the Young." *Reporter* 22 (29 April 1960): 46–47.

"America's Only Class War." *Reporter* 22 (12 May 1960): 46–48.

"Baroque Novel." *Yale Review* 49 (June 1960): 488–495.

"Genius of Robert Graves." *Kenyon Review* 22 (summer–fall 1960): 340–365, 677–679.

"Just before the Deluge." *Reporter* 24 (19 January 1961): 62–64.

"Beyond Logic." *Nation* 192 (4 February 1961): 102–103.

"Retreat from the Word." *Kenyon Review* 23 (spring 1961): 187–216.

"Literature under a Deadline." *Reporter* 28 (17 January 1963): 50ff.; (28 February 1963): 10 ff.

"A Writer's Conscience." *Times Literary Supplement* (29 March 1963): 209–210.

"Humane Literacy." *Times Literary Supplement* (26 July 1963): 539–540.

"On Paul Goodman." *Commentary* 36 (August 1963): 158–163.

"Building a Monument." *Reporter* 30 (7 May 1964): 37–39.

"The Nerve of Günter Grass." *Commentary* 37 (May 1964): 77–80.

"A Note on Literature and Post-History." In *Festschrift zum achtzigsten Geburtstag von Georg Lukacs*. Edited by Frank Benseler. Neuwid: Luchterhand, 1965, pp. 502–511.

"A Kind of Survivor." *Commentary* 39 (February 1965): 32–38.

"Dying Is an Art." *Reporter* 33 (7 October 1965): 51–54.

"To Traduce or Transfigure: Modern Verse Translation." *Encounter* 27, no. 2 (1966): 48–54.

"Old in Heart." Review of P. N. Furbank's *Italo Svevo, the Man and the Writer*. *New Yorker* (3 June 1967): 137–143.

"Of Nuance and Scruple." Discussion of Samuel Beckett. *New Yorker* (27 April 1968): 164–174.

"White Light in August." Review of Robert Jay Lifton's *Death in Life*, about Hiroshima. *New Yorker* (3 August 1968): 76–80.

"Displaced Person." Review of Alexander Herzen's memoirs. *New Yorker* (8 February 1969): 114–126.

"True to Life." Review of George Orwell's works. *New Yorker* (29 March 1969): 139–151.

"The Future of the Book: Classic Culture and Post-Culture." With Jack Lindsay and Ken Baynes. *Times Literary Supplement* (2 October 1970): 1121–1123.

"Linguistics and Poetics." *TriQuarterly* 20 (1971): 73–97.

"Future Illiteracy." *Atlantic* (August 1971): 40–44.

"The Poetics of Cultural Criticism." *Times Literary Supplement* (17 December 1971): 1565–1566.

"Whorf, Chomsky, and the Student of Literature." *New Literary History: A Journal of Theory and Interpretation*, 4 (1972): 15–34.

"Cruellest Months." *New Yorker* (22 April 1972): 134–142.

"The Writer as Remembrancer: A Note on Poetics." *Yearbook of Comparative and General Literature* 22 (1973): 51–57.

"Text and Context." *Salmagundi* 31–32 (1975): 173–184.

"Under Eastern Eyes." *New Yorker* (11 October 1976): 159–170.

"On Difficulty." *Journal of Aesthetics and Art Criticism* 36 (1978): 263–276.

"A Note on the Distribution of Discourse." *Semiotica: Journal of the International Association for Semiotic Studies* 22 (1978): 185–209.

" 'Critic'/'Reader.' " *New Literary History: A Journal of Theory and Interpretation* 10 (1979): 423–452.

"On an Exact Art (Again)." *Kenyon Review* 4, no. 2 (spring 1982): 8–21.

"The Historicity of Dreams." *Salmagundi* 61 (fall 1983): 6–21.

"Literary Theory in the University." Symposium with thirty-nine contributors. *New Literary History* 14, no. 2 (winter 1983): 411–451.

"Our Homeland, the Text." *Salmagundi* 66 (winter–spring 1985): 4–25.

"Books in an Age of Post-Literacy." Excerpt from address, April 1985. *Publishers' Weekly* (24 May 1985): 44–48.

"Language under Surveillance: The Writer and the State." *New York Times Book Review* (12 January 1986).

"Power Play." *New Yorker* (17 March 1986): 105–109.

"The Responsibility of Intellectuals: A Discussion." With Conor Cruise O'Brien, Leszek Kolakowski, and Robert Boyers. *Salmagundi* 70–71 (winter–spring 1986): 164–195.

"The Long Life of Metaphor: An Approach to 'the *Shoah*.' " *Encounter* 68 (February 1987): 55–61.

"An Examined Life." *New Yorker* (23 October 1989): 142–146.

"Levinas." *PN Review* 16, no. 6 (1990): 24–26.
"Literary Forms: A Note on Absolute Tragedy." *Literature and Theology: An Interdisciplinary Journal of Theory and Criticism* 4, no. 2 (July 1990): 147–156.
"B. B." *New Yorker* (10 September 1990): 113–120.
"Grandmaster." *New Yorker* (10 December 1990): 153–158.
"Battles of the Book: Revaluations of Scripture from Dante to de Man." *Times Literary Supplement* (20 December 1991).
"A Responsion." In *Reading George Steiner*. Edited by Nathan A. Scott and Ronald A. Sharp. Baltimore: Johns Hopkins University Press, 1994, pp. 275–285.
"Through That Glass Darkly." In *Perspectives on the Holocaust: Essays in Honor of Raul Hilberg*. Edited by James S. Pacy and Alan P. Wertheimer. Boulder: Westview Press, 1995.
"The Ephemeral Genre and the End of Literature." *New Perspectives Quarterly* 13 (fall 1996): 46–49.
"What Is Comparative Literature?" *Comparative Criticism: An Annual Journal* 19 (1996): 157–171.
"He Was Only a Boy But He Was Good in Bed." Review of Bernard Schlink's *The Reader*, translated by Carol Brown Janeway. *Observer* (2 November 1997): 15.
"The Dog Did Not Bark: A Note on Keats in Translation." In *The Persistence of Poetry: Bicentennial Essays on Keats*. Edited by Robert M. Ryan and Ronald A. Sharp. Amherst: University of Massachusetts Press, 1998, pp. 189–200.
" 'The Consciousness Industry': A Symposium." *Salmagundi* 118/119 (spring 1998): 106–190. Edited transcript of symposium, held in April 1997, about the mass media and popular culture.
"The Humanities: At Twilight?" *PN Review* 25, no. 4 (March–April 1999): 18–24.
"After the Panzers, the Plunderers." Review of Jonathan Petropoulis's *The Faustian Bargain: The Art World in Nazi Germany*. *Observer* (16 April 2000).
"At Five in the Afternoon." *Kenyon Review* 24, no. 1 (winter 2002): 81–118.

Recordings

A Necessary Treason: The Poet and the Translator. (cassette) 1970.
The Poet as Translator: To Traduce or Transfigure. 1970.

Media Adaptations

After Babel (Adapted for television as *The Tongues of Men*). 1977.

Secondary Sources

Alter, Robert. "Against Messiness." *Times Literary Supplement* (12 January 1996): 23–24.
Boyers, Robert. "Steiner's Holocaust: Politics and Theology." *Salmagundi* 66 (winter 1985): 26–49.
Cheyette, Bryan. "Between Repulsion and Attraction: George Steiner's Post-Holocaust Fiction." *Jewish Social Studies: History, Culture, and Society* 5, no. 3 (spring–summer 1999): 67–81.
Feuer, Lewis S. "Confronting Evil and Its Unreason: Rationalist Reflections on the Holocaust." *Encounter* 70, no. 5 (May 1988): 67–70.
Finkelstein, Norman. "Judaism and the Rhetoric of Authority: George Steiner's Textual Homeland." *The Ritual of New Creation: Jewish Tradition and Contemporary Literature*. Albany: State University of New York Press, 1992, pp. 97–116.
Friedländer, Saul. *Reflections of Nazism: An Essay on Kitsch and Death*. New York: Harper and Row, 1982.
Horowitz. Sara R. *Voicing the Void: Muteness and Memory in Holocaust Fiction*. Albany: State University of New York Press, 1997.
"George Steiner." In *Contemporary Authors*. Galenet. 2002. Hale Library. Kansas State University. Manhattan, KS. 24 April 2002. ⟨http://www.infotrac.galegroup.com⟩
Kremer, S. Lillian. "Nazism on Trial: The Holocaust Fiction of George Steiner." *Witness through the Imagination: Jewish American Holocaust Literature*. Detroit: Wayne State University Press, 1989, pp. 324–355.
Lowin, Joseph. "Steiner's Helicopters." *Jewish Book Annual* 41 (1983–1984): 48–56.
Maccoby, Hyam. "George Steiner's 'Hitler': Of Theology and Politics." *Encounter* 58, no. 5 (May 1982): 27–34.
McDowell, John C. "Silenus' Wisdom and the 'Crime of Being': The Problem of Hope in George Steiner's Tragic Vision." *Literature and Theology: An International Journal of Theory, Criticism and Culture* 14, no. 4 (December 2000): 385–398.
Peterson, Joan. "The Holocaust, George Steiner, and Tragic Discourse." *Rendezvous: Journal of Arts and Letters* 34, no. 1 (fall 1999): 93–105.
Popkin, Michael. "George Steiner's *Portage*: Holocaust Novel or Thriller?" *Apocalyptic Visions Past and Present: Selected Papers from the Eighth and Ninth Annual Florida State University Conference on Literature and Film*. Edited by JoAnn James and William J. Cloonan. Tallahassee: Florida State University Press, 1988.
Rosenfeld, Alvin H. *Imagining Hitler*. Bloomington: Indiana University Press, 1985.
Sharp, Ronald A. "Interrogation at the Borders: George Steiner and the Trope of Translation." *New Literary History: A Journal of Theory and Interpretation* 21, no. 1 (autumn 1989): 133–162.
———. "Steiner's Fiction and the Hermeneutics of Transcendence." In *Reading George Steiner*. Edited by Nathan A. Scott Jr. and Ronald A. Sharp. Baltimore: Johns Hopkins University Press, 1994, pp. 205–229.
Skloot, Robert. "Holocaust Theatre and the Problem of Justice." In *Staging the Holocaust: The Shoah in Drama and Performance*. Edited by Claude Schumacher. Cambridge, Mass.: Cambridge University Press, 1998, pp. 10–26.
White, Hayden. "Historical Emplotment and the Problem of Truth." In *Probing the Limits of Representation: Nazism and the "Final Solution."* Edited by Saul Friedländer. Cambridge: Harvard University Press, 1992, pp. 50, 52.
White, Nick. "The Ventriloquial Paradox: George Steiner's *The Portage to San Cristóbal of A. H.*" *New Theatre Quarterly* 18, no. 69 (February 2002): 66–90.
Wyschogrod, Edith. "The Mind of a Critical Moralist: Steiner as Jew." In *Reading George Steiner*. Edited by Nathan A. Scott and Ronald A. Sharp. Baltimore: Johns Hopkins University Press, 1994, pp. 151–179.
Young, Michael. "Real Presence and the Conscience of Words: Language and Repetition in George Steiner's *Portage to San Cristobal of A. H.*" *Style* 26, no. 1 (spring 1992): 114–128.

Selected Interviews

"La Cambridge du George Steiner." With Matei Calinescu. *Gazeta Literara* 40 (1968): 8.
"Interview with George Steiner." *Yale Theatre* 3, no. 2 (1971): 4–13.

"Two Conversations about Culture." *Time* (12 March 1973): 52.

Interview. Edited by J. F. Baker. *Publishers' Weekly* (21 April 1975): 10–12.

"George Steiner Thinks!" Interview edited by M. Posner and A. Lesley. *Macleans* 91 (20 November 1978): 12+.

"Talk with George Steiner." With D. J. R. Bruckner. *New York Times Book Review* (2 May 1982): 13+.

"George Steiner in Conversation." With Nicolas Tredell. *PN Review* 17, no. 4.78 (March–April 1991): 24–31.

"George Steiner Interviewed by Eleanor Wachtel." *Queen's Quarterly* [Kinston, ON, Canada] 99, no. 4 (winter 1992): 837–848.

"Gesprach mit George Steiner." With Michael Jakob. *Sinn und Form: Beiträge zur Literatur* [Berlin, Germany] 45, no. 4 (1993): 545–555.

"Leer el mundo." With Ramin Jahanbegloo. *Quimera: Revista de Literatur* [Barcelona, Spain] 129 (1995): 22–28.

"George Steiner: The Art of Criticism II." With Ronald A. Sharp. *Paris Review* 37, no. 137 (winter 1995): 42–102.

JEAN-FRANÇOIS STEINER

(1938–)

SAMUEL KHALIFA

JEAN-FRANÇOIS STEINER was born in 1938 to a French-Catholic mother and a Polish-Jewish father, Kadmi Cohen, who died during deportation to Auschwitz. In 1967 he married Grit von Brauchitsch, the granddaughter of the field marshal commander in charge of the Wehrmacht. In the 1994 European elections, Steiner ran alongside Flemish Nazis (*Le Monde*, 2 June 1994; *Charlie Hebdo*, special, no. 6, April 1998). In 1997 Steiner testified on behalf of Maurice Papon, a former member of the Vichy government involved in deportation of the Jews, and assisted him in his attempt to flee abroad in 1999 (*Le Monde*, 22 October 1997; *Paris Match*, 4 November 1999; *Marianne*, 1–7 November 1999).

Career Overview

Steiner has written as a journalist for *Nouveau Candide*, a far-right weekly, and as a novelist. In 1966 the twenty-eight-year-old author published a novel dealing with the history of the Treblinka extermination camp and the August 1945 prisoner revolt. *Treblinka* immediately sold over 600,000 copies and has had five reprintings, the latest edition being prefaced in 1994 by Gilles Perrault, a fellow traveler and friend of the author, who applauded it for its realistic depiction of life in an extermination camp. For Françoise Giroud writing in *L'express* (11 April 1966), "The Question is not whether it is good. It is unforgettable" (p. 27). It was also praised by François Mauriac in *Le Figaro Littéraire* (5 April 1966), who noted that he would "have the strength and courage to read through to the end before the day is over, since the ending is the deliverance from Hell for God's people" (p. 6). For the Jewish community, *Treblinka* was more controversial, bordering on outrage. Among the dozen books written by Jean-François Steiner, there are notably *Les Métèques* (1970) and *Varsovie 44* (1975). For the most part, the author's work centers around what Steiner considers to be the same issue: the remembrance of the camps and the attitude of Jews toward the Nazi oppressor.

Treblinka

Ambivalence about his own Jewish identity, stemming from his father's death and postwar feelings about Holocaust losses, greatly influences Steiner's depiction of Jews imprisoned in the Vilna ghetto and Treblinka. Steiner wrote in 1966, "The reason I wrote this book is because rather than the indignation and the emotion I was supposed to feel, I felt the shame of being one of the sons of a people who—for 6 million of them—in the end run let themselves be packed off to the slaughter house like a flock of sheep" ("L'usine à tuer les juifs," *Le Nouveau Candide*). Without considering this as evidence of Jewish self-hatred, one can recognize a denial of identity on Steiner's part, having questioned as he did, whether deliberately or not, the perception of the Jewish memory of having been "victimized."

The account of Treblinka opens with scenes in the Vilna ghetto intended to demonstrate the Nazi strategy of exterminating the Jews via deception and conditioning, and the victim population's historic submission to powerful enemies as a survival tactic. The author considers the Nazi methods of conditioning prisoners and shows the complete and utter subjection of the Jews. Steiner suggests that the ghetto population, accepting a submissive role they have borne for centuries, became docile victims anticipating that this strategy, which had proven successful in previous antisemitic persecutions, would again assure survival. Eager to minimize their own work and more easily and efficiently annihilate the population, the Nazis authorized the creation of the *Judenrat*, an administrative and executive body designed to manage ghetto existence in accord with Nazi orders while creating a false sense of security among the Jews. Jakob Gens, head of the *Judenrat* and chief of police, deceived by his Nazi manipulators into thinking he could simultaneously follow orders and help the ghetto population, is appointed to win over the trust of his own people by spreading Nazi lies. Failing utterly to address the complexity of Gens's motivation for cooperating with the Nazis (because he thought it was for the "good" of the Jews), or to address the nature of his position, which required obedience to the Nazis while trying to subvert their intentions, Steiner simplifies and demonizes Gens. Evidence of Steiner's revisionist approach to Holocaust history is found in his interpretation of Gens's agreement to turn over the ghetto's resistance leader, Itzak Wittenberg. Gens is presented as self-aggrandizing and double-dealing, interested primarily in pleasing his Nazi overlords rather than making the decision based primarily, if not solely, on the Nazi threat that the ghetto would be liquidated if the resistance leader were not turned over. Steiner does convey an accurate account of the episode in his rendition of the population's fear of liquidation and the urging by some to sacrifice Wittenberg, a view that Gens also held. In short, the author uses this incident to argue that the Jews, with their inclination to surrender, seem unsuited for rebellion. Steiner then deals with the theme of Jewish resistance in the Treblinka extermination camp. In this respect, the story of the Vilna ghetto foreshadows the Treblinka narrative.

The Vilna section is a masterful introduction to the role of language in the Nazi strategy of deception to lull the victims into compliance in their own destruction. Instead of annihilation, the victims are induced to anticipate survival through the intricate system of changing regulations about work permits entitling the bearers to life, a system that induces belief that the victim has choices and options that will lead to survival. In the Treblinka section, language takes on a more ominous role as signifiers are unrelated or opposite to the signified to deceive already preconditioned victims regarding the extermination program. The arrival platform is designed as a conventional train station to suggest normality. Prisoners are "workers"; death camp functionaries are "technicians." The unreality of the camp is designed to confuse and deceive the victims. The gas chambers are "factories"; the latrines "the house of rest"; the room where women's hair is forcibly shorn "the hairdresser's salon."

Steiner's decision to blend the historic testimony of the survivors and fictional constructs into a single narrative is responsible for both the novel's strength and its weakness. The authentic documents, as David Bond points out, are constantly offset by the fiction: "Despite the fact that it presents itself as 'history' it is saturated with techniques that one normally associates with fiction" (p. 375). In the dozen individual stories converging in Treblinka, the different types of human psyche are drawn, often in an exaggerated manner: there is the young candid girl, the upstart, the utopian, the politician, the cynic, the meticulous organizer, the coward, the traitor, and the miser. Yet the imagined speech of these victims suggests historical authenticity. The literary device is implicitly reinforced by the author's genealogy because as the son of a Jewish deportee who died, he is considered the bearer of historic memory. The superficially objective tone of the narrator does not mask Steiner's hostility toward the victims who were forced to be complicit in their own destruction. In an interview for *Nouveau Candide* when the book was launched, Steiner explained the significance of the German method:

> In Treblinka as elsewhere in all the extermination camps, the Germans had organized the "machine" as they called it, meaning the exterminating machine, in such a manner that they themselves hardly had any part in it anymore. It was the Jews who did everything. . . . It is one of the most "outrageous" aspects of the death camps that the victims themselves became accessories to their own execution, a fact which was best kept secret (Interview with Jean-François Steiner in "L'usine à tuer les juifs." *Le Nouveau Candide* 251 [13 February 1966], p. 1).

This theme of collaboration runs throughout the book:

> Physically weakened, morally broken, the Jews let themselves be led to their death like a flock of animals to the slaughter house, aiding and abetting their enemy in the extermination of their own people. And these accessories were not merely bad boys but often enough good Jews, even sometimes great Jews (*Treblinka*, New York: Simon and Schuster, 1967, p. 187).

In the later chapters—those that precede and depict the uprising in the camp—Steiner uses a technique of parallel connection. On one hand the deportees cover up the evidence and dismantle the "machine," and on the other, these same accessories to their own extermination adopt the Nazi delusionary strategy to institute a revolt. Recognizing the need to survive to bear witness coupled with realizing that Treblinka will soon have completed its mission and be destroyed, the prisoners pretend to accept the system imposed on them to lull the Nazis into confirmation of their belief that the Jews will not resist.

> The curtain was falling over the penultimate act of the drama. As in ancient tales, the adversaries/protagonists were fraternizing before getting to grips with one another. . . . In camp n° 2 too life was being lived to the full.

> Spurred on by Adolphe, whilst Djielo was devoting himself to the strategic organizing of the uprising, the camp had become a kind of fairground. All day long the men would remove, carry off and burn the bodies, but as soon as the work was over, they would sing, dance and play under the approving gaze of the Germans. . . . Orchestrated by Adolphe, camp n° 2's afternoons became nothing less than a succession of neverending parties. Singing, dancing and playing would go on till evening. Women for their part becoming intoxicated by the prevailing madness would throw themselves into this life and soon all that was missing from their quarters was a red lantern to hang up over the door. Eroticism had suddenly reached a climax despite the presence of dead bodies or maybe because of them, despite the closeness of death or because of it, despite the fear which grasped them each day a little harder or because of it (pp. 374–375).

Steiner's representations of the Jews in the Vilna leadership and in the Treblinka revolt significantly revised earlier presentations of them as faithful members of the Jewish community who were caught in no-win situations. On one hand he portrays the Jews as colluding with the Germans in a manner that led Simone de Beauvoir to observe in the Preface of the 1966 edition: "The collusion of Jewish notables with the Germans constituting the *Judenräte* is a known fact which is easily fathomable; at all times and in all countries—with a few rare exceptions—the notables collaborate with the victors—all a question of class" (p. 8). On the other hand, the noted critic of Holocaust literature, Sidra DeKoven Ezrahi, who cites Steiner in the context of a critique of documentary fiction, notes that he is guilty of many "historical inaccuracies and omissions" (p. 32) and "a simplistic reductionism in the portrayal of character and situation," and charges that "he tailors the evidence of a revolt in the death camp to a rigid procrustean concept of Jewish history" (p. 30). Ezrahi contends that *Treblinka* is a revisionistic hagiography:

> What emerges in this novel is a glorified sense of Jewish superiority and revisionist nationalism. It is an extreme example of a quality inherent in literature, something which R. J. Lifton calls the "documentary fallacy"—an overriding loyalty to the dead which generate(s) a kind of hagiographical excess, denying them the "dignity of their limitations" (p. 32).

One of her most serious charges against the book, that "Steiner's ideological commitment directs the organization of his material" (p. 31), leads to the conclusion that "The 'facts' which the author himself adduces are not always amenable to such a reading, however, and occasionally lead to editorial excesses which seriously undermine the claims of historical reconstruction" (p. 31).

The distress in some Jewish circles caused by Hannah Arendt's attribution of blame to the Jewish leadership for the success of the deportations in *Eichmann in Jerusalem* was echoed in the negative response in some quarters to Steiner's *Treblinka*. Representative was the criticism of Leon Poliakov, resistance historian, who accused Steiner of giving new life to old antisemitic themes. He sees *Treblinka* as a "need for diversion or even projection in the face of the terrifying reality of the Holocaust" (p. 37).

In contrast to this negative assessment of Steiner's presentation, the French gentile critical community unanimously welcomed Steiner's work. He was awarded the Grand Prix de la Résistance (1967), he was praised by the far-right paper *Rivarol*, which delighted in the thesis of the "collaborationist Jews." Simultaneously, intellectuals and historians supported the book despite its lack of rigor. Simone de Beauvoir, in her preface to the first edition, points out the ambiguity of Steiner's reworking of reality, but her conclusion simply reinforces this process of reconstruction:

> Each detail is guaranteed by the testimonies both oral and written which he compiled and set against one another. But he did not shy away from a certain amount of staging. In particular he reworked conversations which he could obviously not know word for word but only their content. One might reproach him with this lack of rigour; and yet he would not have been as authentic had he not delivered the story in its unfolding (Preface, *Treblinka*, p. 9).

Historian Pierre Vidal-Naquet praises the book in *Le Monde*, but revised his opinion. In an article entitled "Un Eichmann de papier" (*Esprit*, September 1980, reprinted in *Les assassins de la mémoire*, 1995), he took a stand against the merchandising of history and specifies the nature of his targets in the following manner:

> The names of Christian Bernadac, of Silvain Reiner and of Jean-François Steiner immediately come to mind. . . . I myself at the time denounced one of the most despicable of these distortions, *Et la Terre sera pure* by Silvain Reiner (published by Fayard, 1969; see *Le Nouvel Observateur*, 8 December 1969) and contributed with Roger Errera to having the book seized as a counterfeit of *Médecin à Auschwitz* written by M. Nyiszli. I did though fall into the trap laid out in *Treblinka* by Jean-François Steiner (Fayard 1966) see my article in *Le Monde*, 2 May 1966, which I do not renege on for the most part (*Les assassins* . . ., p. 193).

Pierre Vidal-Naquet's twofold reaction seems to reflect the waverings of public opinion in the face of a memory that remains beyond their grasp and misunderstood. Although *Treblinka*—published only one year before these events—encapsulates the underlying malaise in saying the unsayable, Steiner does indeed distort historical facts. Consider his comment, among many controversial passages, on the invention of gas chambers as a technical innovation, solving the question of profitability (pp. 67–68), and the manner in which he relates the murder of the guard "Ivan the Terrible" (John Demjanjuk) by a Jewish prisoner (pp. 383–384). In the 1980s, after Demjanjuk had been judged, Steiner recognized that "the story of his death, during the insurrection, was completely imaginary" (Letter from Jean-François Steiner to OSI lawyer Betty Shave, dated 2 February 1984, in *The Demjanjuk Affair*, 1994). A close reading of *Treblinka* shows that, with all the knowledge and thought about the *Shoah* acquired over the last thirty years, it is fairly easy to detect the elements of the "trap" denounced by Vidal-Naquet. Indirectly, *Treblinka* enhances a process in the French community to escape culpability.

A critical examination of *Treblinka* underscores the problem of transmission of memory and its reconstitution in the face of complex historical reality. Steiner's text and the range of critical reception reveal that what was problematic in France in the late 1960s was not only the manner in which the national community spoke of or represented the genocide or the occupation, but the manner in which Jews view their own history. The debates that arose within the Jewish community demonstrate the limitations of the idea of the "unspeakable horror." In Steiner's hands, the mythicizing of memory became a tool for the deprecation of the deportees rather than a duty of memory. Indeed, in its guise of being a historical document, *Treblinka* conveys what can be considered as a first step toward a questionable discourse, possibly even a revisionist one.

Bibliography

Primary Sources

Treblinka. Preface by Simone de Beauvoir. 1966.
Les Métèques. 1970.
Varsovie 44. 1975.
Treblinka. Preface by Gilles Perrault. 1994.

Secondary Sources

Arendt, Hannah. *Eichmann à Jérusalem. Rapport sur la banalité du mal*. Paris: Gallimard, 1966.
Bond, David. "Jean-François Steiner's *Treblinka*: Reading Fiction and Fact." *PLL*: Papers on Language and Literature 26, no. 3 (summer 1990): 370–378.
Ezrahi, Sidra. *By Words Alone. The Holocaust in Literature*. Chicago and London: The University of Chicago Press, 1980.
Forges, Jean-François. *Eduquer contre Auschwitz*. Paris: ESF Editeur, 1997.
Poliakov, Léon. "Tréblinka: vérité et roman." *Preuves*, May 1966: 23–31.
Sheftel, Yoram. The *Demjanjuk Affair: The Rise and Fall of the Show Trial*. Translated by Haim Watzman. London: Gollancz, 1994.
Todorov, Tzvetan. *Face à l'extrême*. Paris: Editions du Seuil, 1991, 1994.
Vidal-Naquet, Pierre. *Les assassins de la mémoire*. Paris: Editions du Seuil, 1995.
———. *Réflexions sur le génocide. Les juifs, la mémoire et le présent*. Paris: La Découverte, 1995.
Weil, Nicolas. "La *Shoah*, la mémoire et les historiens." *Le Monde*, 5–6 May 1996.

Interviews and Archives

"Les juifs, ce qu'on a jamais osé dire," *Le Nouveau Candide* 255, 14–20 March 1966.
"L'usine à tuer des juifs." *Le Nouveau Candide* 251, 13 February 1966.

J.J. STEINFELD

(1946–)

MICHAEL GREENSTEIN

J.J. STEINFELD WAS BORN in Munich, Germany, on 11 December 1946 to Holocaust survivors, Leon and Esther, from Poland. He holds a B.A. from Case Western Reserve University, an M.A. in history from Trent University (Peterborough, Ontario), and spent two years in the Ph.D. program in history at the University of Ottawa before abandoning graduate school in 1980 and moving to Charlottetown, Prince Edward Island. A playwright and fiction writer, he has won the following awards: Norma Epstein Award (1979), Great Canadian Novella Competition (1986), Okanagan Short Fiction Award (1984, 1990), Toronto Jewish Congress Book Committee (1990), Theater Prince Edward Island Playwriting Competition (1997, 2000). Many of his short stories deal with dramatic conflicts between the protagonist, who is a son of survivors, and some form of German antagonist—whether a person or situation.

Club Holocaust

The title alone of J. J. Steinfeld's short story "Dancing at the Club Holocaust" (*Dancing at the Club Holocaust: Stories New and Selected*, 1993) suggests not only oxymoronic qualities but also an emotional disjunction between hedonistic activities and genocide. These disjunctions operate on a number of different levels throughout the story. The opening sentence introduces a "clean, symmetrical" office in an edifice "driven into the heart of downtown Montreal" (Charlottetown, P.E.I.: Ragweed Press, 1993, p. 31). As the story unfolds, this symmetry breaks down and is replaced by another structure driven into the reader's heart. The psychiatrist's office near the top floor contrasts with the basement club, its polar opposite setting. Its window opens "an unconscious eye" over the city and seems "to tilt the office away from symmetrical perfection" (p. 31). What also tilts the story away from symmetrical perfection is the protagonist, Reuben Sklar, with his oblique story.

In the psychiatrist's office, the character sees himself through displaced anatomical parts, the unconscious eye tries to become conscious, while anatomical parts proceed from heart to eye to mouth in a slightly displaced fashion. Reuben Sklar, son of Holocaust survivors and obsessed with his parents' memories, demands to see the doctor's diplomas so he may feel safe letting a stranger into his "mouth." These anatomical parts not only suggest fragmentation, torture, and disease in post-Holocaust society, but also address the difficulties of dialogue and the virtual impossibility of comprehending the totality of the Holocaust. The talking cure between Reuben and his psychiatrist remains problematic, for the doctor refuses to believe in the existence of the Club Holocaust, which Reuben claims to frequent.

Reuben suddenly disrupts the comfort of his doctor's office when he announces that his mother used to dance before the war but killed herself afterward because she could no longer dance. Reuben withholds some of the details that are left to the reader's imagination, but mentions that the West German government paid her *Wiedergutmachung* (reparations) for her crippled legs. Having grown up knowing how his mother's legs were crippled, Reuben becomes somewhat mentally disabled and is determined to take revenge on the Nazi legacy. Reuben Sklar dances around his doctor's office like a very sad madman.

The scene shifts abruptly to a basement in New York City—the Club Holocaust—a neo-Nazi meeting place where antisemitic propaganda films are screened, and where Reuben imagines continuity between events in the 1940s and the contemporary scene a generation later. This section begins with the 1985 baseball season; the Montreal Expos are playing against the New York Mets at Shea Stadium. From this innocent American pastime linking the two cities of Steinfeld's short story, the narrator shifts immediately to Reuben watching, not the ball game, but the movie *Jud Süss* (Jew Süss), which hundreds of thousands of Germans had watched during the war. The club's host announces that this is the same film that Himmler had ordered all German soldiers and SS men to view.

As Reuben wonders about the score of the baseball game, the past flashes across the screen: long-bearded Rabbi Loew, the alleged creator of the legendary golem or Jewish monster of retribution, huddles conspiratorially close to Josef Süss Oppenheimer. Patrons at the Club Holocaust jeer in English and German, "Jew, Jew" and "*Jud, Jud*" ("like booing at a ballpark," p. 33), when the rape scene begins with Süss attacking the defenseless heroine Dorothea Strum. As Süss is placed into an iron cage in preparation for his execution, the audience becomes even more frenzied in their bilingual shouting.

The club has a cabaret atmosphere reminiscent of Berlin in the 1930s. Reuben sits in a corner as far from the stage as possible where smoke drifts and "hangs like automobile exhaust" (p. 33). This smoke-filled, time-defying, ominous world fills Reuben's imagination, and the beer-drinking crowd responds to the host's cries of "*Deutschland erwache*!" (Germany awake!). Germany is indeed awake in Reuben's mind even though he attempts a response of "*Deutschland schlafe*" (Germany sleep) before succumbing to the "*erwache*" of the crowd. The next film, *Der ewige Jude*, identifies Jews with rats and graphically portrays Jewish ritual slaughtering of animals. When *der Führer* appears on the screen, "the past completely vanquished the present for the audience" (p. 34). Steinfeld's overlapping of past and present, high-rise Montreal office and New York basement, baseball and Nazi film, creates a surrealistic, voyeuristic effect.

The psychiatrist believes that Reuben's club is a delusion or morbid fantasy, and no sooner do we observe Reuben watching the club's pornographic entertainment with grieving eyes than we transfer to Montreal where the psychiatrist comments on his patient's tired eyes. When he gives Reuben a mirror to observe his own eyes, Reuben shatters the glass and deliberately cuts himself with the shards. Implicit in the story's glass imagery, from the sheet of polished glass protecting the doctor's desk, to his long window, to the broken mirror, is *Kristallnacht*. Similarly, when Reuben looks out the doctor's office window he sees "Buchenwald, Dachau, Treblinka, Belsen, Auschwitz, and Ravensbrück" (p. 36). The broken mirror also represents the necessity of both mimetic and nonmimetic representation of the Holocaust—the need for distortion and fragmentation in a post-Holocaust rearview mirror. Reuben reenacts the grotesqueries of Club Holocaust when he asks the psychiatrist if he would have kissed Hitler to save his own life. This question not only reveals Reuben's disturbed state of mind, it also implicates the doctor and challenges his objective distance. Reuben's madness mirrors the insanity of the Nazis.

Once again the narrative shifts to the dance floor of the Club Holocaust where couples dance while the film plays in the background. Reuben thinks of the *Totentanz* in *Paracelsus* (1943), a German opera about a medieval alchemist by Richard Wagner, the antisemitic German composer, and wants to perform his own Dance of Death but feels paralyzed: "His mother's legs were his; he was almost all the way back" (p. 38). Dancing in the story becomes a metaphor for uniting with the past, for Steinfeld's story dances between past and present settings. Once again the story shifts abruptly to the doctor's office where Reuben accuses his doctor of being a comfortable Jew and his own ex-wife, likewise, a comfortable Jewish wife. Reuben describes how he had lost his tenured academic position: During a costume party someone came disguised as Hitler; Reuben was sufficiently offended that he urinated on "Hitler," who turned out to be the dean. In the story's final section we return to New York with Reuben, who gets drunk before visiting the club. Avenging his parents, he sets fire to the club, screams "*Ich bin ein Jude*," (I am a Jew) and performs his *danse macabre*. Amid retributive flames he feels happy for the first time in his adult life because "damaged decades coalesce" (p. 41). Reuben Sklar achieves catharsis through his post-Holocaust burnt offering. Reuben and Steinfeld force discomfort and memory upon the reader, and that very discomfort is a means of keeping the past alive.

Other Short Stories

"The Chess Master" is the first story in *Dancing at the Club Holocaust*, dedicated to Holocaust survivors and their families. A story within a story and a story about a story, "The Chess Master" progresses like a chess game with chess as a metaphor for life. The story opens with Lionel Siedelman, a son of survivors, standing outside of Kruger's Grocery, a German store in Toronto where old men gather to play chess. Lionel taunts the owner, Heinrich Kruger, with "*sholom, sholom*," and wants to break the store's window, an act of revenge for *Kristallnacht*.

The first section ends with Lionel shattering the glass; the blood that flows flashes back years earlier to the chess matches between Lionel and Heinrich's brother, Ernst. Lionel also has a brother, Zvi, who accuses the Krugers of being Nazis and then commits suicide. Ernst, the chess master, teaches Lionel that "concentration" is essential to winning, and part of the story revolves around that word, for the concentration camps lurk in the background, and the short story itself is a concentrated form of the novel Lionel writes at the end of the story. The interplay between brothers dead and alive, past and present, short story and novel, resembles a chess game with its complex moves; at times the brothers are merely pawns, at other times they are players responsible for history's moves. Chess and writing, nightmares and obsessive revenge form Steinfeld's subject matter. Visiting blind Ernst at the hospital, Lionel traces his mother's camp number on the old man's left forearm, thereby linking victimizer and victim. The story ends with a description of Lionel's novel, which opens with a grocery in flames.

Steinfeld's Holocaust obsession continues in "The Apostate's Tattoo" (*The Apostate's Tattoo*, 1983). History professor Sam Morgan changes his name to Shlomo Markovitz and begins to study Hebrew and Yiddish after visiting his parents' birthplace in Poland and his own birthplace in a Displaced Persons Camp in Germany. Mysteriously he goes around quoting the slogan above the entrance to Auschwitz—"*Arbeit macht frei*" (Work makes one free)—and decides to get his arm tattooed with a number in order to complete his identification with the inmates of concentration camps. By mistake, he tells the tattooist to put the number on his right forearm, and when he realizes his error he becomes disturbed, at which point the story ends. The misplaced number, like the displaced camp of his birth, points to the absurdity of the post-Holocaust world trying to come to terms with the tragedy of the earlier generation. Steinfeld makes history repeat itself in distorted focus.

In "Ida Solomon's Play" (*Dancing at the Club Holocaust: Stories New and Selected*, 1993) the narrator assumes the role of her mother who was born in Poland in 1921 and died in Toronto in 1977, and performs the eight stages of her life nightly. She "dissolves" her own forty-one years into any of the stages of her mother's life from a dancing teenager to her lonely suicide. The play consumes the narrator and the line between reality and theater blurs: she goes to a bar and announces that she was in a concentration camp. The play becomes a way to confront the past. "The past is a tangible character in the play" (p. 70). Steinfeld resorts to and relies upon the uncanny to collapse Holocaust and post-Holocaust worlds with second-generation survivors literally and figuratively reenacting the lives of their parents in the camps. At a bar the narrator encounters a suicidal man who turns out to be a survivor just like Ida Solomon. The narrator embraces the old man with the tattooed arm and searches for Ida. The story ends with the narrator's dilemma: "I no longer want to be my mother in the play. . . . I want the play to end, but I cannot under any circumstances allow my mother to die and remain lost to me, not again, never again" (p. 74). Against an individual's will, Holocaust history repeats itself, for Ida Solomon lives in memory and in a life re-created.

"The Heart" (*Dancing at the Club Holocaust: Stories New and Selected*, 1993) is situated in Charlottetown, Prince Edward Island, Steinfeld's current "home" where very few Jews live. This eastern Canadian province on the Atlantic Ocean keeps him in touch with his past on the other side of the ocean. Artist Isaac Katzman frequents a local bar where an older German, Herr Wilhelm, is one of the regulars. The bartender mediates their antagonistic dialogue, which focuses on the German's mysterious jewelry box that Isaac wants to open because he has heard that the petrified heart of a Jew from the war is inside. Eventually Isaac manages to open the box, which turns out to be empty, and Isaac concludes the story with, "If not a petrified heart, you could have had a dangerous device for forgetfulness" (p. 94). Isaac fights against forgetfulness; he paints to expel his ghosts and demons, but he would need six million tattoos to be successful. Filled with the smoke of history, he moves from city to city across Canada, "engaging in bruising memory dances" (p. 91). He dumps an armload of Elie Wiesel's books on Herr Wilhelm's table and gives him his portrait in an SS uniform with a sky full of coruscating hearts of Jews. The darkened bar revives memories of German bars, tattoos in Prince Edward Island overlap with the numbers on his dead parents' forearms, and the animosity between sons of survivors and Germans pervades "The Heart." Tattoos signify concentration camps and Steinfeld's post-Holocaust fiction tries to burn the memory into the flesh of his innocent readers.

"Starring at Auschwitz" (*Dancing at the Club Holocaust: Stories New and Selected*, 1993) is a variation on the themes Steinfeld employs in his other Holocaust stories. Daniel Nathanson, the son of survivors, is writing a play, *Arbeit Macht Frei*, about his parents' experiences at Auschwitz. He becomes so involved with this work that he transforms everyday life in Toronto a generation after the Holocaust into Europe during World War II. "He thought about Auschwitz as a high-rise with intercoms and garbage chutes, savage little guards pressing the buttons, the inmates squeezed together a thousand to a room" (p. 128). When his friend Abe Gordon, another son of survivors, visits him, they decide to go to the circus where Abe performs as a clown. Daniel takes his girlfriend Sally, a prostitute, to the circus where his imagination transforms all the performers into inmates of the camps, the trailers into a railroad car, and the clown's costume into a yellow star at Auschwitz. By the end of the story he walks arm in arm with Sally and Abe, shouting "to the gas chambers," the "play about Auschwitz finishing by itself" (p. 139). Imagination and reality, European past and Canadian present collapse in Steinfeld's mixed genres of fiction and drama. He sees the *Shoah* as an overwhelming tragedy—all too real, surreal, and impossible.

Bibliography

Primary Sources

The Apostate's Tattoo. 1983.
Our Hero in the Cradle of Confederation. 1987.
Forms of Captivity and Escape. 1988.
Unmapped Dreams. 1989.
The Miraculous Hand and Other Stories. 1991.
Dancing at the Club Holocaust: Stories New and Selected. 1993.
Disturbing Identities. 1997.
Should the Word Hell Be Capitalized? 1999.
Anton Chekhov Was Never in Charlottetown. 2000.

Secondary Sources

Berger, Alan L. *Children of Job: American Second-Generation Witnesses to the Holocaust*. Albany: State University of New York, 1997, pp. 75–79.

GERALD STERN

(1925–)

SANDFORD PINSKER

GERALD STERN WAS born in Pittsburgh, Pennsylvania, on 22 February 1925. The son of Harry and Ida (Barach) Stern, he grew up in the middle-class section of Bellvue. His father was a clothing salesman and later a buyer of goods destined for closeout sales.

Stern attended the University of Pittsburgh, receiving his B.A. in 1947. In 1949 he received an M.A. from Columbia University and did postgraduate study there from 1950 to 1952. Stern has worked at a number of colleges and universities but he is most associated with the Creative Writing Program at the University of Iowa, where he taught for many years. He has won a number of awards for his collections of poetry, including a Lamont Prize for *Lucky Life* (1977) and a National Book Award for *This Time: New and Selected Poems* (1998).

Stern's Generation of Poets

Stern belongs to a generation of Jewish-American poets, born in the 1920s, that includes Harvey Shapiro (b. 1924), Anthony Hecht (b. 1923), Ruth Whitman (b. 1922), Louis Simpson (b. 1923), John Hollander (b. 1929), Allen Ginsberg (b. 1926), Maxine Kumin (b. 1925), and dozens of others. They are a disparate group and no easy generalization about Jewish-American poetry can pin them down. Some were interested in language or politics, or both—without much overt concern about their Jewishness.

Stern likes to talk about his own poetry as staking out a place that no one else wanted: weeds and waste places, urban cafeterias and largely abandoned rural locales. To all of these he brings a vision that is at once elegiac and celebratory. For those who define Jewish poetry narrowly—either as verse written in Jewish languages (Hebrew, Yiddish, or Ladino) or as a poetical commentary on sacred texts—Gerald Stern's poetry, like that of Karl Shapiro and Delmore Schwartz, Stanley Kunitz and Allen Ginsberg, is neither described nor well served by such rigid categorization. Rather, one detects a Jewish sensibility at work in each of these very different writers, but especially so when Stern writes about occasions (such as seeing a dead animal on the highway) that leave him no choice but to, in his words, "behave like a Jew."

Consider, for example, the cultural juxtapositions in a signature Stern poem, "Weeping and Wailing" (found in *Paradise Poems*, 1984):

> I like the way my little harp makes trees
> leap, how putting the metal between my teeth
> makes half the animals in my back yard quiver,
> how plucking the sweet tongue makes the stars
> live together in love and ecstasy.
>
> I bend my face and cock my head. My eyes
> are open and listening to the sound.
> My hand goes up and down like a hummingbird.
> My mouth is opening and closing. I am singing
> in harmony. I am weeping and wailing (Random
> House, 1984).

On the literal level, Stern's speaker is playing a Jew's harp, or in the folk idiom, a "juice harp": a musical instrument made in the shape of David the Psalmist's lyre and played by placing it into one's mouth and then plucking its flexible metal tongue. As the speaker's hand "goes up and down like a hummingbird," the sound produced reminds him, unconsciously, of Orpheus, whose songs made the trees dance and the wild animals tame, as well as of the psalms that celebrate God's creation. The result is a poem of harmony, of a oneness with the world. But it is also a song filled to the brim with minor chords, with a recognition—however unconscious it may be—that "love and ecstasy" are inextricably bound to "weeping and wailing."

Indeed, all that Stern, the poet, can do is keep faith with the imperative sounded again and again throughout Jewish history—to *schrebt un farschrebt* (to write and record). However, it is also true that when Stern's efforts at imaginative reconstruction touch on the Holocaust (as happens most strikingly in poems such as "Adler," "The Dancing," "Soap," "The Jew and the Rooster Are One," and "The War Against the Jews"), the result is a peculiar identification with those Jews singled out by fate and geography for extermination.

Holocaust Influence

Because Stern has an abiding sense of Jewish history, it is hardly surprising that he would be marked by the catastrophe of the Holocaust. But the roots of his empathy for victims and nascent feelings of survival guilt may be linked to an event that occurred much earlier—the death of his only sibling, Sylvia, who died at the age of nine from spinal meningitis. Stern was a year younger at the time. The effect traumatized his mother and, for Stern, found its way into poems such as "Joseph's Pockets," Sylvia," and "Expulsion." In *The Terror of Our Days: Four American Poets Respond to the Holocaust*, Harriet L. Parmet persuasively argues that the death of his sister was "the one loss he forcibly takes beyond familial boundaries in his poetry—to the afflicted family at large—the annihilation of his brethren, the six million European Jews."

Stern's identification, his sense of guilt because the vagaries of geography and timing saved him while so many others were systematically murdered, is poignantly expressed in these lines from "Soap":

> I write this poem, for my little brother, if I
> should call him that—maybe he is the ghost
> that lives in the place I have forgotten, that dear one
> that died instead of me—oh ghost, forgive me!
> (pp. 77–80).

Many would have preferred that Stern *not* write this poem, partly because of the grotesque images he presents in its opening lines: "Here is a green Jew / with thin black lips . . . And here is a blue Jew. It is his color, you know." There were other objections as well: those with a deep skepticism about the very enterprise of "Holocaust poetry," especially when written by a nonparticipant, felt that "Soap" was exploitive if not downright trivializing. It was, in short, Stern's riskiest attempt to write about the Holocaust. To speak of green Jews and blue Jews, of human beings turned into boutique soap bars, is to pile grotesquerie atop grotesquerie. The poem has images so stark, so shrill, that, as Richard Chess argues in *Poetry East*, it becomes "a selfish act of invention." Other critics, however, view the poem's string of negatives ("I don't like to see . . . I don't want to see . . .") quite differently. They provide the poem's necessary counterweight and tension.

As Stern commented to Gary Pacernick in an unpublished 1996 interview:

> I actually remember starting "Soap" in a little store in Iowa City that was selling soap, and horrified by the kind of graceless accumulation of soap for its own sake. . . . But as the poem came into being, as I got into that animal, that poem, it took over, my memory took over and my horror and my anger and my pity and, most of all, my guilt as an American Jew of a certain age who, if I'd been born in Europe, would probably have been dead but was not because I was American. A very common subject for American Jews in my generation.

No doubt there are some who would argue that Stern has no business appropriating the guilt that Holocaust survivors often feel, that Jewish-American "survivor guilt" is, by definition, a misnomer. Stern's efforts to imagine himself as a surviving American cousin not only struck most readers as authentic, but also as part of his general vision as a weeper and wailer, a man who takes a sympathetic measure of God's creatures and the mystery of God's world.

There are times when the collective unconscious, rather than personal experience, provides the "memories" of east European Jewry, and there are times when Stern quite consciously crafts literary allusions into the fabric of his verse. "The War Against the Jews," for example, not only makes a conscious use of the title Lucy Dawidowicz gave to her pioneering study of the Holocaust, but adopts the central devise in Delmore Schwartz's famous story, "In Dreams Begin Responsibilities."

In Schwartz's story, the protagonist watches uneasily as a film documentary of his parents' lives winds slowly through the movie theater of his mind. He sees them as a young, courting couple and watches in eerie fascination as the seeds of their psychic destruction are planted and move inevitably toward the moment of his conception. But try as he will, he cannot stop the film or cancel its terrible consequences. By contrast, Stern's poem is set in a crowded German railway station as its inhabitants are blissfully unaware of the tragic fate about to unroll. As Stern puts it, he "would give anything to bring them back," to stop the dream from which he cannot awaken, the nightmare of history that begins when the German soldier blows his whistle and the Jews are forced to board the trains that will take them to their deaths. The wry understatement of Stern's poem accounts for its enormous power.

Irving Feldman expresses something of the same wish in "The Pripet Marshes" as he imagines an east European shtetl "the moment before the Germans arrive." Feldman also wants to stop time in its tracks, because "there isn't a second to lose":

I want to snatch them all back,
For, when I want to, I can be God.
No, the Germans won't have one of them!
This is my people, they are mine.

For Stern and many other Jewish-American writers of his generation, "survival guilt" takes on new meanings that distinguish it from those Holocaust survivors wracked by the question of why they lived when other members of their families did not. "Why did God spare *me*?" cannot be answered, even by those who tick off such factors as a stubborn will to live, faith, courage, and, of course, luck. As for those like Stern, an ocean away from the disaster, guilt is a function of being spared an immediacy that the imagination does its best to correct. Much the same fusion of Eastern Europe and America can be found in poems as different as "Behaving Like a Jew," "The Rose Warehouse," and "Bread Without Sugar." As Parmet points out,

> history matters [in "The Rose Warehouse"] in ways that strike one as Eastern European, "Jewish," rather than American, even though the locale is pure Northeastern U.S.A. . . . He does not so much recapture the past as much as relive it, and his memory is burdensome as well as comforting. The opening of "The Rose Warehouse" is chatty and ironic, but its ending is sinister, as he binds the Jewish custom of mourning to the Holocaust (p. 142).

Parmet is referring to lines such as "some German Jews talking about Berlin / the town that had everything; / some man of love / who dug his own grave and entered there."

Only a handful of Stern's poems are ostensibly about the Holocaust, although it could be argued that all his poems, whatever the subject at hand, are suffused with Jewishness and strains of Jewish mysticism, along with an unflinching sense that the long shadow of the Holocaust falls over virtually everything.

Bibliography

Primary Sources

Pineys. 1971.
The Naming of Beasts. 1972.
Rejoicings: Selected Poems 1966–1972. 1973.
Lucky Life. 1977.
The Red Coal. 1981.
Paradise Poems. 1984.
"What is the Sabbath?" *American Poetry Review* 13 (January/February 1984): 17–19.
Lovesick. 1987.
Selected Essays. 1988.
New and Selected Poems. 1989.
Leaving Another Kingdom: Selected Poems. 1990.
Bread Without Sugar. 1992.
Odd Mercy. 1995.
This Time: New and Selected Poems. 1998.
Last Blues. 2000.

Interviews

Hamilton, David. "An Interview with Gerald Stern," *The Iowa Review* 19, no. 2 (1968): 32–65.
Hillinghouse, Mark. "An Interview." *American Poetry Review* 13 (March/April, 1984): 19–31.
Knight, Elizabeth. "A Poet of the Mind: An Interview with Gerald Stern." *Poetry East*, no. 26 (fall 1988): 32–48.
Moyers, Bill. "The Power of the Word, Part 4: 'Voices of Memory' " (containing a conversation with Gerald Stern). Alexandria, Va.: Public Broadcasting System, 1989, Video recording.
Pinsker, Sanford. "The Poetry of Constant Celebration: An Afternoon's Chat with Gerald Stern." *Missouri Review* 13, no. 2 (1984): 55–67.

Secondary Sources

Chess, Richard. "Stern's Holocaust." *Poetry East* (fall 1988): 150–159.
Parmet, Harriet L. *The Terror of Our Days: Four American Holocaust Poets Respond to the Holocaust*. Lehigh University Press, 2001.
Pinsker, Sanford. "Weeping and Wailing: The Jewish Songs of Gerald Stern." *Studies in American Jewish Literature*, no. 2 (1990): 186–196.
Somerville, Jane. "Gerald Stern: The Poetry of Nostalgia." *The Literary Review* 28, no. 1 (fall 1984): 99–124.
———. "Gerald Stern Among the Poets: The Speaker as Meaning." *American Poetry Review* 17, no. 6 (1988): 55–67.
———. *Making the Light Come*. Wayne State University Press, 1990.

ARYEH LEV STOLLMAN

(1954–)

EFRAIM SICHER

ARYEH LEV STOLLMAN is a rabbi's son and a graduate of Yeshiva University. He works at Mount Sinai Medical Center in New York City. *The Far Euphrates* (1997), which won a 1997 Lambda award for gay writing and a place on the American Library Association's 1998 Notable Book list, is his first novel. Not only is its powerful prose disturbing, the novel is also troubling because it destabilizes safe assumptions about history and memory. The memory of the Holocaust passed down to the generations who did not experience it personally has inflicted a searing burn on Jewish identity, and in recent years the literary imagination has recast Judaism's ancient traditions in the darkness of Auschwitz. The revelation of the horror of absolute evil, it seemed to some, challenged the viability of Israel's covenant with G-d and overshadowed the revelation at Sinai. So it is not surprising that Jewish suffering should be seen as marking them like the sign of circumcision, as if they were biologically destined for destruction.

In *The Far Euphrates*, a fictional memoir of growing up Jewish in a quiet suburb of Windsor, Ontario, the Holocaust is only a generation away: the grandparents have moved back to their native Germany in rejection of their son's career as a rabbi and his marriage. A rabbi's son, Alexander is a sole survivor of his mother's miscarriages, a "real survivor" (*The Far Euphrates*, p. 70), and he feels guilty for being the cause of her obsessive concern for his strange dreaminess. He is taken to an eccentric, dwarf, gypsy fortune-teller named Mademoiselle Dee-Dee, who receives him in bed in a wealthy mansion amid fantastic splendor. The gypsies, the reader is told, survived Auschwitz because they knew the future and the past meant nothing to them. Mademoiselle Dee-Dee is one of two seers in the novel who have a fateful effect on Alexander's destiny and who make warnings about his hearing. The other seer is the Lubavitcher Rebbe, the late Rabbi Menachem Mendel Schneersohn.

Alexander is marked for life by his relationship with a pair of twins, Hannalore and Bernhard, who were subjected to the notorious Nazi medical experiments performed by the infamous Dr. Mengele. As a result, Hannalore suffers a gender mutilation which points to a confusion in Alexander's own identity and to his discovery, at age sixteen, of his homosexuality and his heritage. Hannalore wears women's clothing and a crucifix as sexual and religious disguises when she works for the wealthy Ford family at Grosse Pointe. She asks to be buried with the crucifix, carrying a Holocaust survivor's denial of the secret past beyond the grave. The secret makes Alexander a carrier of memory for the childless Cantor as well as the bearer of a terrible secret.

At the same age as the twins when they suffered in the Holocaust, Alexander internalizes their experience by shutting himself in his bedroom and retreating from the world for a year, during which, as in similar stories of lonely adolescence, he discovers his self, his body, and his relationship with history. The retreat emulates the Divine *tsimtsum*, a withdrawal into self at the time of the Creation, which is part of the novel's mystical aura rather than a serious engagement with Cabbala (as in Michal Govrin's novel *The Name*). On another level, the self-cocooning risks a denial of the disasters that accompany the *hester panim*, the "hiding" of G-d's presence that the Bible warns will come with divine punishment. The Holocaust, it seems, is too unbearable a punishment to be easily reconciled with acceptance of divine justice. The ancient question of suffering in the biblical story of Job remains unanswered: why do the evil prosper and the good suffer?

Stollman offers a meditation on the aftereffects of death and destruction, yet readers are left with a strange impression of Judaism and Jewishness. The Cantor, for example, has in common with Cynthia Ozick's "Pagan Rabbi" a penchant for palm trees, and the boy's father, who cultivates an *asherah* (sacred cult-tree) in the garden, has dreamed up a wild theory that the Jews' origins in Mesopotamia and their wanderings contain the secret of the fall from Eden and their subsequent troubles. Alexander's father tells him,

> Our forefathers, strangely enough,—and this I believe is the real root of mankind's problem—originally came not from Kana'an, not from an earthly Jerusalem, but from the far Euphrates with its source in Eden, from an impossibly remote and primordial home. We cannot forget it, or ever find it again. I believe this fact has afflicted us to the present day (p. 163).

Such an itinerary traces the root cause of the cosmic disaster to the expulsion from Eden. Jewish history is made to bypass the biblical account of Abraham's covenant with G-d, the redemption from Egypt, and the gift of the Torah on Mount Sinai. Instead, Jewish history entails an apocalyptic journey that leads to Germany and to catastrophe. The story continues to riots in Detroit, and then to a mysterious, precious stone that finds its way to Alexander and that is mixed up in some inexplicable manner with the rescue of Holocaust victims. It is a journey from the far Euphrates through Alsace, where the river is shaped like a kiss, to closure in Montreal, on an island between two rivers "frozen in time" (p. 199). The story ends with the sudden death of Alexander's father in Iraq, just as he is following in the footsteps of his grandfather and embarking on a journey into Mesopotamia. Life is a long search for meaning in the Divine pattern, and the Jews are accompanied in exile by the *Shekhinah* that, as the Lubavitcher Rebbe explains in the novel, is the female emanation of G-d who takes part in human suffering and joy.

The eloquent prose seduces readers into a cabalistic belief in the creative power of words. The healing lies in a discovery of G-d's mercy and loving kindness that is expressed in the words of the kaddish that sanctify the Divine Name in the kaddish, the mourner's prayer for the dead, something that puts Stollman in M. J. Bukiet's category of "mourners" in contemporary Jewish-American fiction (p. 45). But healing may come at the price of rupture, as in the perforation of Alexander's ear-drum, and the wound can be both blessing and curse. Moreover, as Alexander discovers in his relationship with the invalid girl Marla, healing is a *tikkun* (mystical repair) that might be achieved by ordinary mortals rather than by gifted angels. It is surely no accident that the author is an interventionist neuroradiologist, for the question of why children suffer is at the heart of the narrative of Alexander's spiritual search. Drawn, like him, to the scene of a gruesome road accident in which two children died, Marla calls him "Mrs. Lot" because—like the wife of Lot in the Bible who looked back at the destruction and was paralyzed—he is fixated by death. She is also dying, and Alexander's hospital visit to her is a *khesed* (loving kindness) that puts him in league with the angels.

The *Illuminated Soul* uses *midrash* in an original way that brings Jewish concepts from cabala to bear on daily living. As in *The Far Euphrates*, a gifted Jewish boy growing up in Windsor meets an enigmatic figure from Jewish Eastern Europe of the past, Eva Higashi. Mrs. Higashi is carrying with her a rare illuminated manuscript that has been saved from the Holocaust. The scroll, thought lost, is also sought by a Nazi professor and contains a mysterious legacy that illuminates Joseph's life with beauty and meaning. The strength of this novel is not related exclusively to the Holocaust, partly because it takes a broader view of time and history and partly because Eva Higashi is left as a mysterious emblem, one of those figures who enter our lives momentarily and change us indelibly.

Although Stollman's work may be read as Holocaust fiction, its understanding of the universal meaning of the Holocaust may risk the further devaluation of survival and witnessing. Yet it does claim a place in the canon of post-Holocaust literature that deals with the theological and psychological effects of that cosmological rupture and seeks in its own understated way to attempt a small *tikkun*.

Bibliography

Primary Sources

"The Creation of Anat." 1992.
"The Dialogues of Time and Entropy." 1993.
"The Seat of Higher Consciousness." 1993.
"Die Grosse Liebe." 1996.
"The Adornment of Days." 1996.
The Far Euphrates. 1997.
"How the Torah Illuminates the Anatomy and Fluidity of Time." 1999.
"Mr. Mitochondria." 2000.
The Illuminated Soul. 2002.

Secondary Sources

Bukiet, Melvin Jules. "Machers and Mourners." *Tikkun* 12, 6 (November–December 1997): 44–46, 76.
Sicher, Efraim. "The Future of the Past: Countermemory and Postmemory in Contemporary American Post-Holocaust Narratives." *History and Memory* 12, no. 2 (2000): 56–91.

WILLIAM STYRON

(1925–)

DANIEL R. SCHWARZ

STYRON WAS BORN on 11 June 1925, the only child of William Clark Styron, an engineer who worked in the shipbuilding yards at Newport News, Virginia, and Pauline Margaret Abraham, an American musician trained in Vienna. Styron attended Davidson College for one year before enlisting in the Marine Corps. He received officer training at Camp Lejeune in North Carolina and later at Quantico, but never saw the battlefield. Following discharge from the military in 1945, he attended Duke University, where he received his Bachelor of Arts degree. He then worked in New York City as associate editor for McGraw-Hill Publishing Company. At the end of six months he was fired—an event that, Styron wrote to his father, freed him to devote all his time to writing (Casciato and West, p. 3; Ruderman, pp. 4, 6).

With the encouragement of Hiram Hadyn of the New School of Social Research, Styron published his first novel, *Lie Down in Darkness*, in 1951. Receiving the Prix de Rome Fellowship in 1952, he visited Paris en route to Rome and met the American writers Peter Matthiessen and George Plimpton, and others, with whom he cofounded the *Paris Review*. While in Rome in 1953 Styron married Rose Burgunder, a young Jewish poet. From the outset, Styron used his fiction to confront social and historical issues. *The Long March* (1956) is based on a thirty-five-mile training march forced on Styron and other marines who were recalled to duty during the Korean War. Throughout the 1960s, Styron continued to write book reviews and essays for journals; he also became active in civil rights and politics, serving as a delegate to the 1968 Democratic Convention (Ruderman, pp. xiii, xiv). The *Confessions of Nat Turner*, based on the only known insurrection led by a slave, was published in 1967 and received not only the Pulitzer Prize for literature and the Howells Medal for Fiction (1970), but also negative reviews from African American critics who considered Styron's portrayal of Turner inadequate.

In the following decades, Styron continued to publish and to receive recognition for his work. Styron's works include his play *In the Clap Shack* (1973), his screenplay '*Dead*!' coauthored with John Phillips (1973), *Set This House on Fire* (1960), *Sophie's Choice* (1979), *This Quiet Dust: and Other Writings* (1982), *Darkness Visible: A Memoir of Madness* (1990), *A Tidewater Morning: Three Tales from Youth* (1993), and *The Way of the Warrior* (2001). *Sophie's Choice* garnered for Styron the first American Book Award for fiction (1980); in 1988 Styron was granted the MacDowell Medal, awarded by the MacDowell Colony for outstanding contribution to American culture.

Sophie's Choice

William Styron's *Sophie's Choice* is a medley of genres: Kunstlerroman, romance, and Holocaust story. The semiautobiographical narrator, Stingo, is a veteran of World War II, an aspiring young southern writer living in Brooklyn who becomes close friends with Nathan, a brilliant but emotionally disturbed and drug-addicted Jew, and his gentile lover, Sophie. Sophie is a Polish refugee and Auschwitz survivor, who, in a series of monologues, gradually reveals her complicated past to Stingo. Thus the novel has two narrators, Stingo and Sophie; the latter's narrative is framed by Stingo, who is in love with Sophie.

Conscious of writing in the American tradition, and indeed as heir to Herman Melville and F. Scott Fitzgerald, Stingo echoes *Moby Dick*'s opening, "Call me Ishmael": "Call me Stingo, which was the nickname I was known by in those days, if I was called anything at all" (New York: Random House, 1979, p. 5). Like Nick Carraway in *The Great Gatsby*, Stingo writes with the burden of his experience as an engaged character. Stingo is an Ishmael figure who is obsessed not with Captain Ahab's quest for the whale, but with the quest of his demonic and psychotic double, Nathan, for Sophie's love. Nathan is Sophie's other self: the Jew who has been trying to rescue her from her own history and whom she has unsuccessfully tried to insulate from the knowledge of her father; her husband (Josef), who garroted those who betrayed Jews; and Höss, the Auschwitz commandant.

Styron uneasily combines the verisimilitude of documentary—including numerous references to those who wrote about the Holocaust—with the fictional lives of his characters. Stingo's retrospective tale is about events that took place in 1947, but he tells his audience that it was not until 1967 that he began to think of his book, and even "the preparation I went through at that time required that I torture myself by absorbing as much as I could find of the literature of l'univers concentrationnaire" (p. 216).

The older Stingo is trying to write the Great American novel, a historical novel that addresses the horrors of the twentieth century, even while dramatizing the growth of consciousness of the representative southern voice recalling the American tragedy of the Civil War. Most readers can see that having the American Civil War and Holocaust metaphorically represent one another is a far-fetched and insensitive comparison. At times the speaker's polemics objectionably universalize the Holocaust, particularly in view of his own romanticizing of the Poles as victims of the same magnitude as the Jews and his use of the word "torture" to describe his own act of reading about the Holocaust (p. 216).

Sophie is a riddle, and we cannot always know how her psyche and memory distort events. Sophie's disingenuousness struggles with her desire to tell, to reveal her story. Like Stingo, we are blocked by Sophie's evasions. Sophie's choice—her selection of her male child as the one who will live and her daughter as the one who will die—is the novel's crystallizing moment. The title refers most obviously to a grotesque choice she had to make at Auschwitz between saving her son and saving her daughter. Sophie has a need—a compulsion—to tell, to explain, to extenuate, and finally to understand; thus she reveals her darkest secrets to Stingo. Another choice that receives continuing focus is her decision to leave the younger Stingo for the destructive and psychotic Nathan, who has already abused her. After initiating Stingo into adult sexuality, she returns to Nathan, and she and Nathan commit double suicide. As Kurtz is for Marlow in Joseph Conrad's *Heart of Darkness*, another text that influenced the writing of *Sophie's Choice*, the manic-depressive Nathan is the nightmare of her choice. Discourse dominates the story as she wanders back and forth over the same terrain; the same is true for Stingo, who strays far and wide in his narration.

Sophie's Choice is about the relationship between memory and narrative. Sophie's narrative of the war years is a model of refracted memory; her narrative is shaped by whether Nathan or Stingo is her audience. For Sophie the past is a harrowing present. To avoid Nathan's torturing her with accusations of collaboration, she withholds information from Nathan. That her narrative to the psychotic Nathan is shaped by her fear of his abusive personality is a radical version of how expectations shape narratives. Indeed, his coercive power is part of his appeal to her, in much the same way as she had been magnetized and intimidated by her father during her youth in Poland.

How, we might ask, could her father, a law professor and antisemite who wanted to deport Jews to Madasgacar, make Sophie his factotum? In what becomes her characteristic way of making major decisions, she lets the choice be made for her. At age sixteen, Sophie made the choice to follow her father, perhaps in a foreshadowing of later magnetic attraction to powerful figures like Höss, Nathan, and Professor Durfield, a Nazi functionary she met while working as her father's secretary, and to whom she was sexually attracted, and even her female lover, Wanda.

The reader comes to understand that Sophie's choice includes not only whether to narrate the truth as she knows it, but also how much of the truth to narrate. Yet she is often not in control of her telling, and her own trauma shapes not only her efforts to recapture the truth and the concomitant repression and sublimation, but also her conscious lies and evasions. How do we know whether Sophie was simply seducing commandant Höss at Auschwitz at the behest of the partisan resistance or if she was doing it for herself? She tells Stingo both versions. She uses her father's antisemitic pamphlet to insinuate herself into Höss's good grace with the idea that she will seduce him and he will let her son, her lone surviving child, be part of the *Lebensborn* program. We do know that a combination of guilt, pain, and anger drives her telling. After speaking of how she begged Höss to save her son, the narrator observes: "Sophie halted, gazing again for long moments into that past which seemed now so totally, so irresistibly to have captured her" (p. 285); she continues: "People acted very different in the camp, some in a cowardly and selfish way, some bravely and beautifully—there was no rule. No" (p. 286).

A recurring theme in Holocaust narratives is that with power comes the power to name and the power of language; Höss, like Sophie's father before him, can articulate his wishes without any sense of propriety: "Sophie kept her eyes shut as the flow of his weird Nazi grammar, with its outlandishly overheated images and clumps of succulent Teutonic word-bloat, moved its way up through the tributaries of her mind, nearly drowning her reason" (p. 281). Sexually attracted to Nathan, she allows him to appropriate the same linguistic power.

We need to ask whether a Jewish reader responds differently to Styron from the way a non-Jewish reader does, even a non-Jewish southern reader. Styron's retrospective narrator is conscious of building on a prior tradition of Holocaust writing and evokes his predecessors by name: "Tadeusz Borowski, Jean-François Steiner, Olga Lengyel, Eugen Kogon, André Schwarz-Bart, Elie Wiesel and Bruno Bettelheim . . . George Steiner" (p. 218). At times, the narrator is doing what he says he will not do, that is draining the Holocaust of its substance by using it contextually rather than as the essential event. While Styron often eloquently *imagines* the Holocaust, his claim that Sophie's tortures were the equal with Jews' is a dubious claim that cannot be measured. At times, discriminating readers feel Styron's moral blindness. The lives of by far the largest group of Holocaust victims should not be consigned to background anonymity, while the suffering of Poles is foregrounded. Certainly a far greater percentage of Poles survived than Jews.

Styron is often insensitive to repeating shibboleths about how Jews behave or invoking Jewish stereotypes. Take Sophie's outburst of antisemitism: "Oh, it was so very Jewish of Nathan to do that—he wasn't giving me his love, he was buying me with it, like all Jews. No wonder the Jews were so hated in Europe. . . . All my childhood, all my life I really hated Jews. They deserved it, this hate. I hate them, dirty Jewish cochons" (p. 353). The narrator is not above joining in the chorus of antisemitism and is fussily conscious in Brooklyn of living with Jews as when he goes to meet the stereotypical Leslie Lapidus and speaks of "the intense Jewishness of the little scene" (p. 162). To the resistant reader, Stingo's antisemitic tirade—even if Styron is trying to reveal his narrator's parochialism and insularity—is especially tasteless in a novel in which the Holocaust plays a large role.

To be sure, the wordiness of Stingo's monologue itself is ironized by the devastating silence of the Holocaust, of Auschwitz, if not Nathan's and Sophie's death. Yet, as Barbara Foley comments, "Those narrative forms—both factual and fictive—that rely upon an informing teleology, generally prove inadequate to the task of encompassing the full significance of Holocaust experience" (p. 353).

Bibliography

Primary Sources

Books

Lie Down in Darkness. 1951.
The Long March. 1956.
Set This House on Fire. 1960.
The Confessions of Nat Turner. 1967.
In the Clap Shack. 1973.
Sophie's Choice. 1979.
This Quiet Dust: And Other Writings. 1982.
Darkness Visible: A Memoir of Madness. 1990.
A Tidewater Morning: Three Tales from Youth. 1993.
The Way of the Warrior. 2001.

Introductions

A Death in Canaan, by Joan Barthel. 1976.
The Big Love, by Florence Aadland. 1986.
To Reach Eternity: The Letters of James Jones, edited by George Hendrick. 1989.
Fathers and Daughters, by Mariana Cook. 1994.

Selected Periodical Publications—Fiction

"The McCabes." *Paris Review* 7 (autumn–winter 1959–1960): 12–28.
"Marriott, the Marine." *Esquire* 76 (September 1971): 100–104, 196, 198, 200, 202, 204, 207, 208, 210.
"Dead!" Coauthored with John Phillips. *Esquire* 80 (December 1973): 161–168, 264, 266, 270, 274, 277–278, 280, 282, 286, 288, 290.
"The Seduction of Leslie." *Esquire* 86 (September 1976): 92–97, 126, 128, 131–134, 136–138. Excerpt from *Sophie's Choice.*
"My Life as a Publisher." *Esquire* 89 (March 1978): 71–79.

Selected Periodical Publications—Nonfiction

"Letter to an Editor." *Paris Review* 1 (Spring 1953): 9–13.
"The Prevalence of Wonders." *Nation* 176 (2 May 1953): 370–371.
"The Paris Review." *Harper's Bazaar* 87 (August 1953): 122, 173.
"If You Write for Television . . ." *New Republic* 140 (6 April 1959): 16.
"Mrs. Aadland's Little Girl, Beverly." *Esquire* 56 (November 1961): 142, 189–191.
"The Death-in-Life of Benjamin Reid." *Esquire* 57 (February 1962): 114, 141–145.
"As He Lay Dead, a Bitter Grief." *Life* 53 (20 July 1962): 39–42.
"Aftermath of Benjamin Reid." *Esquire* 58 (November 1962): 79, 81, 158, 160, 164.
"Two Writers Talk It Over." *Esquire* 60 (July 1963): 57–59. Taped conversation between William Styron and James Jones.
"An Elegy for F. Scott Fitzgerald." *The New York Review of Books* 1 (28 November 1963): 1–3.
"A MacArthur." *The New York Review of Books* 3 (8 October 1964): 3–5.
"Truth and Nat Turner: *Jeanne.*" *Nation* 206 (22 April 1968): 544–547.
"The Shade of Thomas Wolfe." *Harper's* 236 (April 1968): 96–104.
"My Generation." *Esquire* 70 (October 1968): 123–124.
"On Creativity." *Playboy* 15 (December 1968): 138.
"The Uses of History in Fiction." *Southern Literary Journal* 1 (spring 1969): 57–90.

"Kuznetsov's Confession." *New York Times*, 14 September 1969, IV, 13.

"A Friend's Farewell to James Jones." *New York* 10 (6 June 1977): 40–41.

" 'Race Is the Plague of Civilization': An Author's View." *U.S. News & World Report* 88 (28 January 1980): 65–66.

"Almost a Rhodes Scholar: A Personal Reminiscence." *South Atlantic Bulletin* 45 (May 1980): 1–7.

"A Conversation." *Esquire* (January 1982): 86–93. William Styron talks with Candace Bergen.

"Why Primo Levi Need Not Have Died." *New York Times* (19 December 1988): A17.

"A Literary Friendship." *Esquire* 111 (April 1989): 154–155, 158, 160, 162, 164, 165.

"Nat Turner Revisited." *American Heritage* 43 (October 1992): 64–73.

"Profits and Pills: Prozac Days, Halcion Nights." *Nation* 256 (4 January 1993): 1, 18, 20, 21.

"The Enduring Metaphors of Auschwitz and Hiroshima." *Newsweek* 121 (11 January 1993): 28–29.

Secondary Sources

Aldridge, John W. "Styron's Heavy Freight." *Harper's* 259 (September 1979): 95–98.

Bell, Pearl. "Evil and William Styron." *Commentary* (August 1979): 57–59.

Caputo, Philip. "Styron's Choices." *Esquire* (December 1986): 136–159.

Casciato, Arthur D., and James L. W. West III, eds. *Critical Essays on William Styron*. Boston: G. K. Hall, 1982.

Chametzky, Jules. "Styron's *Sophie's Choice*: Jews and Other Marginals." In *Our Decentralized Literature: Cultural Mediations in Selected Jewish and Southern Writers*. Amherst: University of Massachusetts Press, 1986.

Cologne-Brookes, Gavin. *The Novels of William Styron: From Harmony to History*. Baton Rouge: Louisiana State University Press, 1995.

Crane, John Kenny. *The Root of All Evil: The Thematic Unity of William Styron's Fiction*. Columbia: University of South Carolina Press, 1984.

Dickstein, Morris. "The World in a Mirror: Problems of Distance in Recent American Fiction." *Sewanee Review* 89 (1981): 386–400.

Evanier, David. "Looking into the Void." *National Review* XXX, 35 (31 August 1979).

Foley, Barbara. "Fact, Fiction, Fascism: Testimony and Mimesis in Holocaust Narratives." *Comparative Literature* 34, no. 4 (fall 1982): 330–360.

Friedman, Melvin J. "The 'French Face' of William Styron." *The International Fiction Review* 10, no. 1 (1983): 33–37.

Kort, Wesley. "Styron's Corpus and Sophie's Choice." *Christianity and Literature* 30, no. 2 (winter 1981): 64–70.

Kreyling, Michael. "Speakable and Unspeakable in Styron's *Sophie's Choice*." *Southern Review* 20 (1984): 546–561.

Langer, Lawrence L. "Fictional Facts and Factual Fictions: History in Holocaust Literature." In *Reflections of the Holocaust in Art and Literature*. Edited by Randolph L. Braham. New York: Columbia University Press, 1990, 117–129.

Ozick, Cynthia. "A Liberal's Auschwitz." In *The Pushcart Prize: Best of the Small Presses*. Edited by Bill Henderson. New York: Pushcart Book Press, 1976, 149–153.

Pearce, Richard. "Sophie's Choices." In *The Achievement of William Styron*. Edited by Robert K. Morris with Irving Malin. Athens: University of Georgia Press, 1981, 284–298.

Rosenfeld, Alvin. "The Holocaust According to William Styron." *Midstream* 25 (December 1979): 43–49.

Rubenstein, Richard L. "The South Encounters the Holocaust: William Styron's *Sophie's Choice*." *The Michigan Quarterly Review* 20, no. 4 (fall 1981): 425–442.

Ruderman, Judith. *William Styron*. New York: Ungar, 1987.

Saposnik, Irving S. "Bellow, Malamud, Roth . . . and Styron? or One Jewish Writer's Response." *Judaism* 31, no. 1 (1982): 322–332.

Schwarz, Daniel R. "The Ontological Problems of Docufiction: William Styron's *Sophie's Choice*." In *Imagining the Holocaust*. New York: St. Martin's Press, 1999.

Seeskin, Kenneth. "Coming to Terms with Failure: A Philosophical Dilemma." In *Writing and the Holocaust*. Edited by Berel Lang. New York: Holmes and Meier, 1988.

Sirlin, Rhoda. *William Styron's Sophie's Choice: Crime and Self-Punishment*. Ann Arbor: University of Michigan Press, 1989.

Stern, Frederick C. "Styron's Choice." *The South Atlantic Quarterly* 82, no. 1 (1983): 19–27.

Trouard, Dawn. "Styron's Historical Pre-Text: Nat Turner, Sophie, and the Beginnings of a Postmodern Career." *Papers on Language and Literature* 23, no. 4 (1987): 489–497.

Vice, Sue. *Holocaust Fiction*. New York: Routledge, 2000.

Wesker, Arnold. "Art between Truth and Fiction." *Encounter* LIV, no. 1 (January 1980): 55–56.

West, James L. W., III, ed. *Conversations with William Styron*. Jackson: University Press of Mississippi, 1985.

———. *William Styron: A Descriptive Bibliography*. Boston: G. K. Hall, 1977.

Wiesel, Elie. "Art and the Holocaust: Trivializing Memory." *New York Times*, 11 June 1989, sec. 2, 1.

ABRAHAM SUTZKEVER

(1913–)

RUTH WISSE

ONE OF THE great poets of the twentieth century, Abraham Sutzkever was a survivor of the ghetto of Vilna and the unofficial Jewish poet laureate in its aftermath. His life and work attest to the creative vitality of Yiddish during the period when it was crushed and all but abandoned. As against the philosopher Theodor Adorno's egregious formulation, "To write poetry after Auschwitz is barbaric," Sutzkever considered poetry the most effective rival of barbarism and felt that he owed his survival to its autonomous standards of judgment. From his earliest emergence as a poet to the work of his ripest last years, he experienced writing as a metaphysical feat, transcending the realities from which it emerges.

Youth and Early Career

Sutzkever was born 15 July 1913 in Smorgon, a small industrial city southwest of Vilna, Lithuania. His mother, Reina, was the daughter of the Mikhalishok rabbi, and his father, Hertz, a good Talmud scholar, came from a local family of leather merchants. In 1915, during World War I, the Russians plundered the city in advance of the German armies and expelled its 25,000 Jews. The couple with its three children, of whom "Abrasha" was the youngest, fled to Omsk, Siberia, for the duration of the war. Conditions there were difficult, and the father's death at age thirty plunged the family into even greater want. But Sutzkever transfigured his childhood into an adventure of artistic self-discovery. His first long poem, *Siberia* (1936, published in its final form by UNESCO in 1953 with illustrations by Marc Chagall), evokes a frozen Eden of sharply engraved sound and sensation:

Sunset over icy roads
Colors suffuse my mood. A little hut
Shines across the way in the valley.
Covered with a flurry of sunset.
Amazing forests sway against the panes;
Magic sleighs go ringing by.
Doves coo in the attic, coo my face
Out of its shell. Beneath the ice,
Striped with flashes of lightning crystals,
The Irtish ripples as if it were not real.
And there, under hushed cupolas,
A seven year old child—a world—grows tall

(translated by Chana Bloch).

The rest of the poem, of which this is the opening stanza, shows the poet hatched in his world of wonders, as fully formed in his seventh year as God's own world on the seventh day of creation.

Siberia sets out the poet's myth of origin and his artistic ideal. It transforms the Russian symbol of cruel exile into a pristine wonderland. The boy's father is portrayed not as the Jewish teacher that he was, but playing the fiddle so vibrantly that a wolf is drawn to the window "to sniff the flesh of the music." When, after the father's death, the boy considers joining his parent in his new hut in the snow, he is lured back to life by the dove he carries in his bosom, a fluttering symbol of the inspiration that turns memory into art. In this way the transition from generation to generation, instead of being fraught with conflict as it is in most modern Jewish narrative, appears seamless and so natural that one does not even notice how the father's religion has given way to the son's poetry. The modern Abraham comes not from the desert, with God's legacy in the form of Torah and Commandments, but from the opposite direction as witness of God's splendors. Writing not at the beginning of civilization, but facing the threat of its decline, the poet uses ice, with its properties of keeping things fresh, as metaphor for the poetic act, in defiance of death, forgetfulness, and decay.

The society within which Sutzkever composed this poem bore little resemblance to its landscape. At the end of World War I, Reina Sutzkever settled with her three children in Vilna, the Lithuanian capital that was then part of the newly independent Poland. Jewish Vilna between the wars was a community of some 65,000, about a third of the city's total population. Famed for its Jewish learning, Jewish Vilna still boasted the study house of the Vilna Gaon (genius), Rabbi Elijah Ben Solomon Zalman (1720–1797), but it also contained a network of modern Jewish schools and institutions and a politically active Jewish youth. The Yiddish poet Moyshe Kulbak was an instructor in the local Jewish Teachers' Seminary. Jews were restricted by Polish nationalist policies from advancing as they might have in business and the professions, but they tried to compensate for these economic and political disabilities through autonomous social and cultural institutions. Sutzkever attended a Hebrew-Polish high school, read assiduously at the Jewish Strashun Library, and later studied old Yiddish poetry at the YIVO Institute for Jewish Research that was established in Vilna in 1926 as a center of research and scholarship. Along with other youngsters from his poor Snipeshok suburb, he joined the Jewish scouting organization led by Dr. Max Weinreich (co-founder of the YIVO), which promoted physical well-being and Yiddish culture.

The divergent paths of Vilna youth were represented by his family and friends: his older sister, who wrote poetry in Russian, died of meningitis at age thirteen; his older brother, a passionate Zionist who spoke Hebrew with their mother, went to settle in "Eretz-Israel" (Land of Israel). Sutzkever's childhood love, Freydke Levitan, whom he married in 1939, worked in the bibliographic section of the YIVO and shared his passion for exploring the countryside. A close friend, Miki Chernikhov (later Michal Astur), introduced Sutzkever to Russian literature. He read Polish poetry on his own and attended lectures on Polish literature by Professor Manfred Krydl at the Vilna University.

A local literary and artistic coterie calling itself Yung Vilna formed in 1929, about the time Sutzkever began writing poetry. It organized exhibitions and public readings and between 1934 and 1936 published three issues of a little magazine. The group, made up of painters, writers, and poets of various Jewish backgrounds, levels of education, and artistic temperaments, projected a collective image of social responsiveness to the times. Though some members, such as Leyzer Volf and Shmerke Kaczerginski, were his friends and neighbors, they initially discouraged the membership of this "Ariel" in their group, objecting to his exotic themes and his indifference to political issues. Indeed, most of Sutzkever's early lyrics explored the poet's affinity with nature and looked to poetry as an *alternative* to pressing social and political concerns. Of an evening, he writes: "So what remains for me to do at such an hour, / Oh, world mine in thousand colors? / Just / To gather in the knapsack of the wind / The red beauty / And bring it home for supper" (*A. Sutzkever: Selected Poetry and Prose*). Sutzkever found his first important critical support abroad, when Aaron Leyeles published his verse in the New York "Introspectivist" Yiddish literary journal, *Inzikh*, in 1935. Local recognition followed. In 1937 the Yiddish PEN Club of Warsaw put out Sutzkever's maiden book, *Lider*, containing the first version of *Sibir*. His second book, *Valdiks* (Of the Forest), appeared under the imprint of Yung Vilna in 1940, after the outbreak of World War II and the Soviet conquest of the city, when Vilna was briefly part of an independent Lithuania. Abraham Novershtern notes the divergence between the contents of the book and its timing: "monumentalism in a time of destruction, poems of nature with wars raging all around, overture of youth when the *khurbn* (Holocaust) is already at the door."

World War II

The Germans invaded the Soviet Union on 22 June 1941 and captured Vilna two days later. Mass roundups and murders began immediately, mostly at Ponary, a wooded area ten kilometers from the city. Dodging the manhunt through the summer, Sutzkever adopted the habit of dating his poems precisely and of circulating them in several copies to enhance their chances of surviving. In his memoir *Of the Vilna Ghetto* (1944–1946), he describes some of the circumstances in which the poems were written. At the beginning of July, along with two other Jews, he was forced to "perform" for some German officers' amusement. "The Circus" (early July 1941) frames his own humiliation as part of the "dance" that the Jewish people have too long performed for its executioners: "If only to be offerings of a bloody Lord / let frogs be born instead of us." A second poem, "I Lie in This Coffin," of 30 August, is based on a night Sutzkever spent hiding in a casket. The narrow lyric explores the paradox that creative energy issues from inside the poet's "wooden clothing," and that his proximity to his dead sister activates the dormant connection with her: "From here, where all / flesh is taken to eternity, / I call / to you, sister, and you / in your distance / still hear me." The Houdini-like poet carries out death-defying acts of poetry within tightening artistic constraints.

At the beginning of September, the Germans drove all remaining Vilna Jews into two adjacent ghettos and began liquidating first one, then the other. The poem, "Glust zikh mir tsu ton a tfile" (I feel like saying a prayer, Vilna ghetto, 17 January 1942), registers the nadir of the poet's confidence in the efficacy of speech or in the presence of any listener:

I think I just thought of a prayer,
But I can't imagine who might be there.
Sealed in a steel womb,
How can I pray? To whom?

Star, you were once my dear friend,
Come, stand for the words that have come to an end.
But dear, dear star,
I understand, you're too far.

Still, someone in me insists: pray!
Tormenting me in my soul: pray!
Prayer, oh wildest surmise,
I still babble you till sunrise

(translated by C. K. Williams).

But most of Sutzkever's ghetto writings reaffirm his faith in the communicative powers of poetry. His threnody on the murder of his mother applies the principle of metonymy to survival. The poet hears the mother's posthumous counsel to accept the verdict of their parting because "if you remain / I will still be alive / as the pit of the plum / contains in itself the tree, / the nest and the bird / and all else besides" ("Mayn mame," *Burnt Pearls: Ghetto Poems*). A popular Yiddish lullaby, in chain formation, tells of a king who had a queen who had a vineyard, with a tree, a nest, and inside a bird that flew away. Inverting the song's pattern, the poet finds in the laws of nature assurance that the fragment will some day regenerate the whole. The principle of *tsimtsum*, creative self-contraction, defines the mission of poetry within a time of slaughter.

Nature becomes more precious than ever as the part of existence that is impervious to the Nazis. In "A Pack of Music" (December 1941), the poet feels regret as he warms his hands over a pile of steaming horse manure: "Too little have I known, have I listened / To the greatness of smallness. / Sometimes, / The warm breath of a pile of dung / may become a poem, a thing of beauty" (*A. Sutzkever Selected Poetry and Prose*). Having once cast himself as the impresario of nature's majestic perfection, the poet is humbled to discover bounty in its most menial aspects. In another poem, "A Flower" (29 May 1943), a man pays the price of seven lashes for trying to smuggle a flower into the ghetto. "My neighbor bears the mementos with no regrets: / spring breathes through and colors his tortured flesh— /that's how much he wanted it to flourish" (*Burnt Pearls: Ghetto Poems*). The advent of nature in the ghetto is not always redemptive. A butterfly that first enlivens a roomful of schoolchildren finally becomes the theater of their execution ("Es flit arayn a flaterl," 5 May 1943).

Sutzkever was a moving spirit of the cultural resistance to the Germans in the intervals between mass deportations. The ghetto diarists Herman Kruk and Yitshak Rudashevski describe the inspiration of his personality and his work. His poem "The Grave-Child" won the Ghetto Writers' Union literary prize for 1942. Set to music, his poem, "Beneath the Whiteness of Your Stars" (22 May 1943) became a popular song. He commemorated other cultural leaders of the ghetto, including the musicologist and choir leader Yankev Gershteyn ("On the Death of Yankev Gershteyn," 28 September 1942) and the teacher Mira Bernstein ("Di lererin Mire," 10 May 1943). The ghetto poems were later collected in *Di festung* (The Fortress, 1945).

Sutzkever and his wife were put to work for the so-called Alfred Rosenberg staff, sorting out cultural treasures of Jewish Vilna for shipment to Germany to form part of the projected "Science of Jewry without Jews" (*Wissenschaft des Judentums ohne Juden*). The YIVO building, where their work was situated, stood outside the ghetto. The poet and his wife hid some of the most precious books and documents for eventual recovery after the war, and they helped to smuggle arms into the ghetto for the resistance movement.

Sutzkever joined the United Partisan Organization (FPO) that was consolidated in January 1942 among the various political youth factions. Such poems as "Lid tsu di letste" ("Song for the Last," 16 March 1943) and "A nem ton dos ayzn" ("Take Up Arms," 13 April 1943) reflect its militant mood. "Di blayene platn fun Rom's drukeray" ("The Lead Plates of Rom's Printing Press," 12 September 1943) describes the ghetto resistance melting down the lead of Vilna's most prestigious Jewish publishing house for bullets. The smelting of the metal under fire marks the actual and symbolic metamorphosis of the pacific Jews into fighters:

Letter by melting letter the lead
Liquefied bullets, gleamed with thoughts:
A verse from Babylon, a verse from Poland,
Seething, flowing into the one mold.
Now must Jewish grit, long concealed in words,
Detonate the world in a shot!

(translated by Neal Kozodoy).

Fused images of the poem correspond to the compressed Jewish historical experience: When the ghetto fighters hear in their doomed struggle the echo of the collapsing walls of ancient Jerusalem, they are obstinately reinvigorated by the memory of those who fought for their people and their faith.

The capture and execution of commander Itsik Wittenberg by the Gestapo in July 1943 fractured the unity of the FPO that had planned to defend the ghetto until its final hour. Groups began leaving the ghetto through the sewers to join partisan units in the forests. Sutzkever, Freydke, and Shmerke Katcherginsky left with one such group on 12 September. They trekked 120 kilometers through German-patrolled territory to join the Jewish unit Nekome (Vengeance), around Lake Narocz. Shortly after their arrival, under Soviet orders, the five hundred Jewish partisans were forcibly disbanded and left to fend for themselves against the Germans and units of Polish rightists. Sutzkever evokes this desperate period in the prose poem "The Ring" in the cycle *Green Aquarium* (1953–1954).

One striking feature of Sutzkever's wartime poetry is its formal regularity. The poems clench themselves tightly, insistent on closure, pitted by their elegance against all that would grind them into formless oblivion. Sutzkever is a master of rhyme, linking apparent disparate features of language for witty effect, and he creates new words as his subject requires. In later appreciation of Sutzkever's creativity during wartime, his colleague of Yung Vilna, the poet and novelist Chaim Grade, said that providence had placed Sutzkever in hell just to see whether the chief celebrant of nature's harmony could be crushed. In Sutzkever's version of his testing, the Angel of Poetry had struck a bargain with him: "If your song inspires me, I will protect you with a flaming sword. If not—don't complain . . . My conscience will remain clean."

Inside the ghetto Sutzkever had given his poem "Kol Nidre" to a partisan courier to transmit to the Yiddish poet Peretz Markish in Moscow. Although Stalin had previously forbidden Jewish national expression, after the German invasion of 1941 he permitted the formation of the Jewish Anti-Fascist Committee (JAFC) to stoke anti-Nazism at home and win Jewish influence abroad. Members of the committee were deeply stirred by Sutzkever's dramatic monologue of a ghetto Job, who kills the last of his remaining five sons as the alternative to having the Germans burn him alive. Through the intervention of Justas Paleckis, president of the Lithuanian government-in-exile, a small plane was sent to a landing strip in an area held by the partisans to transport Sutzkever and his wife to Moscow. An article about his arrival by Ilya Ehrenburg in *Pravda*, 29 April 1944, was the first official Soviet mention of the Holocaust, and it brought the poet mail from all over the country. Sutzkever became even more prominent after his testimony at the Nuremburg trials on 27 February 1946. One of four Soviet witnesses, and the first to testify on behalf of the Jewish people, he gave details of the mass killings and deportations and of the murder of his mother and of his new-born son in the ghetto hospital. After one bloody German *aktion*, he reported, "It looked as if a red rain had fallen."

Postwar

Sutzkever returned to Vilna immediately after its liberation by the Soviet army on 13 July 1944 and stayed through September, retrieving hidden materials and trying to reestablish for the trickle of survivors such core institutions as a school, museum, and library. Back in Moscow, he realized that he was on the brink of another Jewish tragedy. The writers he befriended, Peretz Markish, Dovid Bergelson, Dovid Hofshteyn, Shmuel Halkin, and the director of the Moscow Jewish Theater, Solomon Mikhoels, sensed that the period of relative artistic openness they had enjoyed as Jews after the Nazi invasion was coming to an end. Convinced that "the poison of the ghetto had cauterized all his fears," Sutzkever made bold interventions to protect writers from political denunciations and to obtain government help for Jewish refugees. He and Freydke along with their infant daughter, who had been born in Moscow, were allowed to leave the Soviet Union as Polish refugees in 1946, shortly prior to Stalin's liquidation of the JAFC and its leadership. He later wrote about his interaction with the Russian Jewish intelligentsia in poems and a series of memoirs.

During the years in Russia, Sutzkever deviated from the short lyrical forms he favored to try to convey the scale of the national tragedy. "Epitaphs" (Vilna Ghetto-Moscow-Łodz, 1943–1946) projects with virtuoso variance the voices of twenty-seven Nazi victims. *Geheymshtot* (Secret City; Moscow-Łodz-Paris, 1945–1947), is an epic narrative in 241 stanzas of amphibrach tetrameter, conceived during Sutzkever's return to the ruins of Vilna. It records the efforts of ten Jews, a symbolic *minyan* of men and women and a newborn infant, to escape the destruction of Vilna by constituting a community in the sewers beneath it. The ode "To Poland" (July–September 1946) is a leavetaking from Polish soil and the Polish culture he had loved. Khone Shmeruk notes that despite its autobiographical form, the poem was already perceived by those who heard Sutzkever read it in Łodz in manuscript form as "the most adequate expression of the painful moods and feelings" of those who had remained alive in Poland.

As though fated to be at the center of Jewish history-in-the-making, Sutzkever moved with the refugee tide through Łodz to Paris, and from there he came to Palestine in 1947 on the eve of the establishment of Israel. His second epic narrative, *Gaystike erd* (Spiritual Soil, 1961), dramatized the journey of refugees from Europe to Palestine aboard the same ship, the *Patria*, that had brought the Sutzkevers, and the efforts of this saving remnant to resettle the country under Arab attack. Although the struggle to revive Hebrew as the language of the emerging Jewish state was fought largely at the expense of Yiddish, Sutzkever ignored the language war and established a literary quarterly under the auspices of the Histadrut, Israel's Labor Federation. The journal's title, *Di goldene keyt* (The Golden Chain) taken from a drama by I. L.Peretz, refers to the unbroken Jewish tradition and culture. As Peretz once created a "home" for Yiddish literature in Warsaw (1891–1915), Sutzkever turned Tel Aviv into the locus of Yiddish creativity in the postwar years, inspiring the return to Yiddish of the American poet Y. L.(Judd) Teller, the upsurge in Israel of a literary group, "Young Israel," and the productivity of untold writers and scholars whom he plied for contributions.

Sutzkever was himself inspired by his physical encounter with the land of Israel. In *Poems of the Negev*, he found in the desert something akin to the spacious stretches of Siberia, space where the solitary inhabitant can once again take his bearings in the greater scheme of things. He brought into Yiddish verse the unfamiliar sounds of Arabic, the names of wadis, the representation of bedouins and Sephardic Jews, forging new links between his earlier history and the old-new homeland. But neither the relative tranquility of his domestic life nor the excitement of national homecoming relieved the pressure from the dead he had left behind. At the place where Moses is presumed to have interred the bones of Joseph, the poet mourns that the bones of Joseph under sand remain estranged from the bones of Joseph under Poland. Instead of being organically absorbed into the new soil, "They cut like knives and glow like coals."

A recurring theme is the yearning of the living for the dead, and of the dead to have their yearning redeemed. An untitled lyric, dated 1947 to mark the poet's arrival in the land of Israel (the opening poem of *In the Chariot of Fire*, 1952), evokes the blessing *shehekhiyonu* that the Jew recites when he reaches a festive landmark, but from the conditional perspective of someone who knows he might *not* have reached this shore. The improbability of survival permeates the joy of homecoming. Had he not come to Israel, the poet knows he would have expired, *fargoyt*—a neologism meaning, turned into Gentile—yet his longing would have reached the land on its own. Here, the poetic act speaks for that part of the people that will never reach its destination.

Responding to invitations from Jewish communities, Sutzkever traveled all over the world. On an extended trip to Africa in the 1950s, he explored its desert and jungle and visited with the King of the Zulus. In poems that followed, collected in the series *Elephants at Night*, his own past was refracted in new images of caged tigers, a plague of termites, a pygmy dance, and a monkey merchant. "Elephant Graveyard" conveys the sorrow of the wise beasts when their time comes to die, and lesser animals—jackal and human—poise to profit from their remains. The quasi-primitive "Song of the Lepers" invites the Warrior to dip his arrows in the blood of the pariahs in order to acquire its fatal properties. "We alone, we have no fingers, / We cannot charge the enemy— / Warrior, dip your arrows in our blood." The poem draws its emotional force from the superimposition of two conditions—the actual lepers in their frustrated isolation and the implied Jews (or any other victim group) in their historic role as impotent target. The alien context involves readers in this call for vengeance before they can sort out its points of reference.

Through the twist of historical fate, the ordinary life of Vilna's Jews posthumously had become the most exotic of all landscapes, and Sutzkever, the involuntary explorer of a legendary universe. In a lullaby to his second daughter ("Toys," 1956) the poet asks the child to show special tenderness to her playthings because he recalls seven streets filled with dolls in the city that is without a child. Sutzkever conveyed this sense of deranged reality in the series of prose-poems *Green Aquarium* and poetic stories *Messiah's Diary* (1975), *Where the Stars Spend the Night* (1979), and *Prophecy of the Inner Eye* (1989). In these works, everyday expressions and events and casual acquaintances of the past acquire legendary significance through the unaccountable manner in which they were overtaken by destruction. David Roskies calls this "mythopoetic narrative," autobiography experienced as legend, documenting life's private victories over death and the hard-won struggle of language against mortality.

In Israel, Sutzkever published most of his poems in his own journal, *Di goldene keyt*, then collected them in a series of books. He was awarded every major Yiddish literary prize, and won the Israel Prize in 1985. He was made an honorary citizen of Tel Aviv. Internationally acclaimed, his work has been translated into many languages, including Hebrew, English, French, Swedish, Polish, Russian, Spanish, and Indonesian.

Poems from a Diary

Most critics consider the high point of Sutzkever's writing the series of lyrics he wrote between 1974 and

1981 and collected as *Poems from a Diary*. Yoking the formal properties of the poem to the prosy function of the diary entry, they embrace incongruity as the basis of life. Most of the lyrics, in four rhymed quatrains, rest on plain observations or memories that reveal, through associated images, their metaphysical implications. They explore in particular the commingled properties of poetry, which is faithful to the real yet impervious to its restrictions. "Trees are made into marvelous paper. And I—the reverse / I transform paper into trees / into the tree of life." The words "transform, transforming, transformation," appear eight times in sixteen lines, conveying the many varieties of inspired magic that connect the poet to "the cosmic poet" who is his heir. However suspect, its transcendent potential makes poetry and art indispensable to the true witness.

Paradox figures in these poems not as a vehicle of bafflement, but rather to reinforce the conviction that the dead do not die. Ontology is not subject to material proofs. A poem's opening questions—"Who will last? What will last?"—might apply to the poet's language, his civilization, or life itself. In reply, it offers proofs of endurance in such images as a thread of foam along the sea, and "a bit of cloud snarled on a tree" (translated by Cynthia Ozick). We are invited to seek assurance of survival in apparent signs of impermanence; a single syllable can regenerate its creation in the manner of Genesis. The poem tosses back the opening question rhetorically, "God will last, isn't that enough?" It has no patience for those who seek more tangible evidence of eternity.

Another poem begins, "The funeral's early, the concert is late. / I go to both (such is my fate)" (1975; translated by Cynthia Ozick). Through this homespun linkage and a further series of contrarieties, the poet affirms that the coupling of death and music, of mortality and art, is as primal as the coupling of woman and man. He resists all attempts to isolate the full from the empty, light from shadow, scythe from stalk, there from here, is from was. The plausibility—and the moral necessity—of pairing opposites is conveyed through rhyming couplets and a fusion of high and low imagery.

Conclusion

Both the growing distance and the immediacy of the *khurbn* come through in a poem of 1981 in which the poet receives from a former beloved in his native city a letter with an enclosed blade of grass from Ponary. This plucked memento releases memories of the poet's passion and the murder of his world which were consummated in that same place. It becomes, through the poem that preserves it, legendary conductor of the music of the burning children and the gift that the poet will bring to his Lord from his native city when he is returned to dust.

Sutzkever formed his idea of poetry in the interwar period and subjected his subsequent experience to its criteria. Although his biography situates him prominently among "poets of the Holocaust," he resists any such confining definition, since it was not Hitler who determined his approach to art and reality, but his approach to art and reality that determined his response to Hitler. His work registers the tension between history and poetry—history as destruction and chaos, poetry, the creative reach of the moral imagination. The poet's control is the sign of his determination to undo historical "reality" by linking the worlds of the dead and living so as to transcend their separation.

Bibliography

Primary Sources

Nowersztern, Abraham. *Abraham Sutzkever Bibliography*. Tel Aviv, 1976. (Comprehensive)

Major Books of Poetry

Lider (Poems) 1937.
Valdiks (Of the Forest) 1940.
Di Festung (The Fortress) 1945.
Yidishe Gas (Jewish Street) 1948.
Geheymshtot (Secret City) 1948.
In fayer-vogn (In the Chariot of Fire) 1952.
Sibir (Siberia; illustrations by Marc Chagall) 1953.
Fun dray veltn (Of Three Worlds) 1953.
Ode tsu der toyb (Ode to the Dove) 1955.
In midber sinay (In the Sinai Desert) 1957.
Oasis (Oasis) 1960.
Gaystike erd (Spiritual Soil) 1961.
Poetishe verk (Collected Works, 2 vols.) 1963.
Firkantike oysyes un moyfsim (Square Letters and Signs) 1968.
Tsaytike penimer (Ripe Faces) 1970.
Di fidlroyz (The Fiddlerose) 1974.
Lider fun togbukh (Poems from a Diary) 1977.
Fun alte un naye ksavyadn (From Old and New Manuscripts) 1982.
Tsviling-bruder (Twin Brother) 1986.
Der yoyresh fun regn (The Heir of the Rain) 1992.
Tsevaklte velt (Shaken World) 1996.

Prose Poems and Poetic Stories

Griner akvarium: dertseylungen (Green Aquarium; introduction by Ruth R. Wisse) 1975.
Dortn vu es nekhtikn di shtern (Where the Stars Spend the Night) 1979.
Di nevue fun shvartsaplen: dertseylungen (Prophecy of the Inner Eye; introduction by Ruth R. Wisse) 1989.

Memoir

Vilner geto (The Vilna Ghetto) 1944.
International Military Tribunal. *Trial of the Major War Criminals*. Nuremberg, 1947: 306.

Secondary Sources

Nowersztern, Abraham. *Abraham Sutzkever on His Seventieth Birthday* (Yiddish and Hebrew). Much more than a catalogue of the exhibition held at the Jewish National and University Library of Jerusalem in November 1983, this is the most complete biographical work on the poet to date.

Books translated into English

A. Sutzkever: Selected Poetry and Prose. Translated from the Yiddish by Benjamin Harshav and Barbara Harshav, with an introduction by Benjamin Harshav. Berkeley, 1991.

Burnt Pearls: Ghetto Poems. Translated by Seymour Mayne, with an introduction by Ruth R. Wisse. Oakville, Ont., 1981.

The Fiddle Rose. Translated by Ruth Whitman, Detroit, 1990.

Selected Works about Sutzkever

Kaczerginski, Shmerke. "A. Sutzkever." In *Shmerke Kaczerginski Memorial Book*, Buenos Aires, 1955, pp. 295–315.

Leftwich, Joseph. *Abraham Sutzkever, Partisan Poet.* London-New York, 1971.

Miron, Dan. *Snow on the Dove's Wings: Encounters with the Poetry of Avrom Sutzkever* (Hebrew). Tel Aviv, 1999.

Roskies, David G. *Against the Apocalypse: Responses to Catastrophe in Modern Jewish Culture.* Cambridge, Mass., 1984: chapters 8–10.

Sadan, Dov et al., eds. *Pedigree of the Poem: For Abraham Sutzkever on His Seventieth Birthday* (Hebrew and Yiddish). Tel Aviv, 1983.

Shazar, Zalman, Dov Sadan, and M. Gros-Tsimerman, eds. *Festschrift in Honor of Abraham Sutzkever's Fiftieth Birthday* (Yiddish). Tel Aviv, 1963.

Spiegel, Isaiah. *Abraham Sutzkever's Poems from a Diary* (Yiddish). Tel Aviv, 1979.

Szeintuch, Yekhiel. "Yiddish and Hebrew Literature under the Nazi Rule in Eastern Europe: Yitzhak Katzenelson's Last Bilingual Writings and the Ghetto Writings of A. Sutzkever and I. Spiegel" (Hebrew). 2 vols. Ph.D. diss., Hebrew University, 1978.

Wisse, Ruth R. "The Last Great Yiddish Poet?" *Commentary* (November 1983): 41–48.

Yanasowicz, Yitzhak. *Abraham Sutzkever: His Poetry and Prose.* Tel Aviv, 1981.

Erwin Sylvanus

(1917–1985)

ANAT FEINBERG

ERWIN SYLVANUS'S PLAY *Korczak und die Kinder* (*Korczak and the Children*) is one of the earliest attempts in German drama to come to terms with the Nazi past and in particular with the Holocaust. Addressing the experience of the Holocaust in untraditional theatrical language, the play is the most original German contribution to the so-called theater of the Holocaust in the 1950s. Notably, it has been Sylvanus's most successful play, having enjoyed, since its premiere (at Krefeld, 1 November 1957), nearly a hundred productions on German stages alone, and having been translated and performed in fifteen languages.

Life and Career

Born in Soest, Westphalia, 3 October 1917, Sylvanus was a young man when he embarked on his literary career, writing poetry and prose in the spirit of National Socialist ideology (*Jahresring* 1936, *Sülzhayner Elegie* 1938, *Der ewige Krieg* 1942). After his *Abitur* (school-leaving examination), he joined the fascist Labor Service (*Arbeitsdienst*), served in the *Wehrmacht*, and was severely wounded in World War II. He subsequently spent many years in hospitals and convalescent clinics. From 1954 he lived as a freelance writer in Völlinghausen, Westphalia, and later on the Greek island of Aegina. Sylvanus died in 1985, leaving behind an enormous yet still unresearched archive (at the State Library of Dortmund) including manuscripts, letters, and private documents. His postwar oeuvre, mostly plays, radio plays, and television scripts, seeks to alert and protest against animosity, violence, tyranny, and inhumanity. Among these works are not only the Holocaust plays *Korczak und die Kinder* (1957) and *Exil—eine Reise in die Heimat* (*Exile—A Journey to the Homeland*, 1981) but also *Jan Palach* (1972), which deals with the suppression of the Prague Spring revolution in 1968, and *Victor Jara* (1974), depicting the life of the freedom fighter and folksinger who was murdered by the Chilean military junta.

Korczak und die Kinder

It was a Holocaust play that marked the breakthrough in the literary career of Sylvanus, advancing him to the forefront of the postwar German stage. *Korczak und die Kinder*, "a dramatic requiem" (M. Kesting), was not the first German play to deal directly with the murder of Europe's Jews, but it is true that the reluctance of the Germans to confront and reflect upon their collective and individual experiences during the Third Reich, and in particular on their active or passive involvement in the extermination of the Jews, was mirrored in the theater after 1945. The rebuilt stages in postwar Germany revived the classics, imported foreign plays banned by the Nazi authorities, or sought to entertain a demoralized public with undemanding drama. The handful of German plays written in the early 1950s that sought to confront the past did not attempt to engage the memory and consciousness of the audience so much as to refute the thesis of collective guilt. These plays (for example, Ingeborg Drewitz's *Alle Tore waren bewacht [All gates were guarded*, 1956] or Wolfgang Altendorf's *Thomas Adamsohn*, 1956), mostly realistic in style, with a poignant moralizing element, and tinged by melodramatization, featured protagonists who represent the Bad as well as the Good. Among the latter were not only Jewish victims, but also individual Germans: persons who put up resistance to the regime, expiating and atoning Nazis, or officers in uniform who try to help individual Jews.

Not surprisingly, none of those few early plays seeking to awaken that which had been repressed collectively as well as individually was a hit. The only play to capture the hearts of German spectators and become a commercial success, ironically, was the American dramatization (by Frances Goodrich and Albert Hackett) of the *Diary of Anne Frank*. Opening in Germany in 1956, this received seventy-five different productions within the following two years, thirty-three of them in the German Democratic Republic. Spectators must have quickly realized that here was no piece of accusation, no matter of vendetta. Instead they were being offered the heart-wrenching story of the young Anne, a concrete, individualized case of suffering with which they could empathize, as did the spectator who—according to Theodor W. Adorno—maintained that "Yes, this girl at least should have been spared" (*Erziehug zur Mundigkeit*, Frankfurt, 1963, p. 26, trans. by Anat Feinberg). Adorno pointed to the danger latent in such plays: A single case, meant to represent the mass, turns precisely through this individualization into an alibi.

It was in reaction to the avid yet insouciant reception of *Anne Frank* that Erwin Sylvanus felt the need to frame the experience of the Holocaust in a form other than cumbersome dramatic realism with its didactic overtones and tendency toward shallow emotionalism. "Tears for the Jews—this is still fashionable," the first actor in his play remarks cynically, alluding to the enormous popularity of *Anne Frank*. Sylvanus seeks not to stage the past, as do some of the earlier plays, so much as to activate both actors and spectators. He sets out to contest repression and forgetfulness, to challenge the conspiracy of lies and self-deception with which postwar society tried to protect and dissociate itself from its own history.

It was by chance that Sylvanus came upon the story of the well-known Polish Jewish educator Dr. Janusz Korczak, who had chosen to accompany the children of his orphanage to the gas chamber in August 1942. Writing for a small provincial ensemble with limited financial means, and hoping at best for three performances, Sylvanus created a play for four adult actors and a child, dispensing with scenery and costumes. He readily admitted that he relied on only one historical source (an article published in the German monthly *Kulturprobleme des neuen Polen* in September 1956), and made it quite clear that he never intended to write a biographical study in scenes. While invoking a referential authority—a need common to writers on the Holocaust—he nonetheless allowed himself poetic license.

The play is structured as a rehearsal. Five actors are preparing a theatrical presentation based on the story of Korczak, who dedicated his life to the well-being of two hundred orphans and did not forsake them in the terrible final moments, although he could have saved himself. Central to the narrative is the concept of the lie, the illusion. Korczak's one "lie" was keeping the truth about their final destination from the children. Yet the dramatist's real aim is to document not only the crime against the Jews but what amounted to a collective conspiracy of silence after 1945, and the reluctance to shoulder guilt. The historical case is then only one aspect of the rehearsal, which becomes, in fact, the play itself. No less important is the way the actors relate to this rehearsal, both cognitively and emotionally. Making use of techniques from the epic theater and from Luigi Pirandello's theatrics, constantly blurring the lines demarcating reality from illusion, exploring the overlap of past and present and the interchangeability of roles, the playwright presents the last journey of Dr. Korczak and his orphans as a provocation. The audience is forced to transcend the limits of its own stifled imagination in order to accommodate this inconceivable event and reflect on it.

Sylvanus uses a variety of techniques to keep the audience "estranged" from the happenings on stage. The plot is revealed at the very beginning of the performance. Moreover, the narrator, in the role of a show master, warns the spectators that they should leave the theater if they have come expecting entertainment or mere relief. "Nobody forces you to stay. Why should you care about what happened between 1940 and 1942?" he remarks. The interaction with spectators—at times a game at the expense of spectators—is designed to shock and taunt. Another device to secure attention is that of multiplying the assumed identities of the participants: their role and function are protean, determined by the changing requirements of the action. This regulates the degree of identification of the actor with his assumed identity, and forestalls an emotive presentation of the dramatic argument. The actress, for example, alternates among three roles: the wife of an SS officer, a German mother, and a Jewish nurse working in Korczak's orphanage. The child actor undertakes the role of two youths: Jürgen, the German, and David, the Jew. Sylvanus aims at a two-pronged effect: the actors feel their way into the experience of both victim and victimizer; spectators are denied any possible identification. The reality of the performance encroaches time and again upon the historical narrative, and the dynamics of the rehearsal dictates the nature of the presentation. The actors address each other by their real names, while spectators watch them bickering over the casting and voicing their resentment or dissatisfaction with a given line. Seeking relentlessly to break down theatrical illusion, the playwright forces the spectator to participate in the performance, to take a stance. Sylvanus maintained that the production of the play in different countries would vary depending on the political context, as well as on the collective and individual history of both performers and spectators; the experience of a specific nation with Nazi occupation and with antisemitism would determine the character of the performance.

Nearly twenty-five years after the premiere of *Korczak und die Kinder*, for which he was awarded the Leo Baeck Prize (1958), Sylvanus attempted another treatment of the Holocaust experience. Interestingly, in the interim he had dealt repeatedly with Jewish themes, both historical and religious. *Exil—eine Reise in die Heimat* (premiered in Bruchsal, April 1981) is based on a historical-literary text, Paul J. Schrag's *Heimatkunde* [*Local History*], 1979), which itself is an adaptation of documentary evidence, relying on oral and written testimonies of people who either experienced or witnessed the events. As in Schrag's book, Fritz Kusel, a Jewish survivor, is the protagonist, but by no means the only victim. Sylvanus expands the figures of Imhoff, a homosexual, and Maus, a conscientious Catholic, two non-Jewish victims in Nazi and post-Nazi Germany. The biting irony of the play is that Kusel, a victim of discrimination and persecution and the only one of the three friends to survive, is himself guilty of intolerance as he hesitates to light a candle in memory of his friend the homosexual. As in *Korczak*, Sylvanus eschews sentimentalization of the dramatic material. He seeks to alienate the audience and provoke them into awareness and critical judgment, making use of devices common in the political theater, such as photographs and slogans, a dummy of Hitler, and the broadcasting of infamous Nazi songs. Furthermore, the plot fabula is interspersed with elements of the traditional Jewish *Purimspiel*. The colorful theatrical presentation of the biblical story, an improvised entertainment which disrupts the main plot, operates as a deliberate fallacy. The Purim story illustrates by way of negation: Hitler *cannot* be analogized to the biblical villain Haman, and there is no miraculous intervention in the modern event. The Holocaust is not the climax in a long history of persecution; it is unprecedented, unique.

Bibliography

Primary Sources

Jahresring (Annual Ring). 1936.
Sülzhayner Elegie (Sülzhayner Elegy). 1938.
Der ewige Krieg (The Eternal War). 1942.
Der Dichterkreis (Poets' Circle). 1943.
Die Muschel (The Shell). 1947.
Der Paradiesfalter (The Paradise Butterfly). 1949.
Soester Friedensspiel (The Peace Play of Soest). 1953.
Hirten auf unserem Felde (Shepherds in our Fields). 1956.
Korczak und die Kinder (Korczak and the Children). 1957. Two English translations are available. See *Postwar German Theatre*, edited by Michael Benedikt and George E. Wellwarth. London: Macmillan, 1968; and Eva Boehm-Jospe, *Korczak and the Children*. New York: Samuel French, 1970.
Die Lex Waldmann (Waldmann's Law). 1958.
Sieger ohne Sieg (Winners without Victory). 1958.
Die nächtliche Tat (The Nightly Deed). 1959.
Zwei Worte töten (Two Words Kill). 1959.
Emil Schumacher. 1959.
Geburtstag (Birthday). 1960.
Unter dem Sternbild der Waage (Under the Scales in the Zodiac). 1960.
Der rote Buddha (The Red Buddha). 1961.
Kafka und Prag. 1963.
Loew. 1963.
Scharrett. 1964.
Der Rabbi. (The Rabbi). 1964.
Kinder von Theresienstadt heute (Children from Theresienstadt Today). 1965.
Durchlöcherte Rinde (Perforated Bark). 1965.
CV 180. 1965.
Zick-Zack. (Zigzag). 1967.
Der werfe den ersten Stein (He who Throws the First Stone). 1968.
Ulrich Bräker. 1969.
Familie in der Krise (Family in Crisis). 1974.
Jan Palach. 1972.
Victor Jara. 1974.
Sanssouci. 1974.
Im Sprunge verharrend (To Hold Still while Jumping). 1975.
Brennen mußich—Licht werden (Burn Must I—Become Light). 1977.
Lessings Juden (Lessing's Jews). 1978.
Papiertheater (Paper Theater). 1978.
Dieter Hirschberg. 1978.
Exil—eine Reise in die Heimat (Exile—A Journey to the Homeland). 1981.

Secondary Sources

Feinberg, Anat. "Erwin Sylvanus and the Theatre of the Holocaust." *Amsterdamer Beiträge zur neueren Germanistik* 16 (1983): 163–176.
Kesting, Marianne. "Erwin Sylvanus." *Panorama des zeitgenössischen Theaters*. Munich: Piper, 1962: 234–238.
Müller, Hans-Christian. "Der Nachla ß Erwin Sylvanus' in der Stadt- und Landesbibliothek Dortmund. Ein Arbeitsbericht." *Literatur in Westfalen*. Edited by Walter Gödden and Winfried Woesler. Paderborn, Munich, Vienna, Zurich: Ferdinand Schöningh, 1992: 245–251.
Wiemer, Elisabeth. " 'Korczak und die Kinder'—Der Welterfolg eines westfälischen Dichters." In *Aus Nichts schafft Gott, wir schaffen aus Ruinen! Grabbe-Jahrbuch 1986*. Edited by Winfried Freund and Karl-Alexander Hellfaier. Emsdetten: Lechte Verlag, 1986: 109–117.

ANDRZEJ SZCZYPIORSKI

(1924–2000)

MONIKA ADAMCZYK-GARBOWSKA

ANDRZEJ SZCZYPIORSKI CAME FROM a family with Socialist views. His father, active in the Polish Socialist Party, was a member of the parliament before the war. During the war Szczypiorski fought in the Warsaw uprising of August 1944 as a soldier of the People's Army, and after the failure of the uprising was sent to Sachsenhausen concentration camp. In 1946 and 1947 he studied political science in Warsaw, interrupting his studies because of the growing political restrictions that affected, among other things, university curricula. Until 1956 he had problems publishing his works because his father was in exile and the family was treated with suspicion by the Stalinist authorities. After the October thaw in 1956 and political changes introduced by the Gomulka government, his father returned to Poland and Szczypiorski began developing his career in the new political climate. In 1956 through 1958, he was a cultural attaché at the Polish Embassy in Copenhagen. Upon his return to the country, he worked with Polish Radio and with various prestigious periodicals of that time, including *Polityka* and *Odra*. From 1968 on, when he refused to support intervention in Czechoslovakia and opposed the antisemitic campaign instigated by the Communist Party in his journalism, he inclined more and more to the opposition movement. In 1981, under martial law, he was interned, and after the fall of Communism in 1989 became a senator of the Republic of Poland.

In his work he constantly returns to World War II and his experiences from that period. He tries to test simplifications and stereotypes of national and ethnic groups, and exhibits a very self-critical attitude toward Poles. This is especially true of novels like *Czas przeszly* (1961, *Past Tense*) or *Za murami Sodomy* (1963, *Behind the Walls of Sodom*). In his other books he addresses contemporary issues under the guise of a historical facade (for example, *Msza za miasto Arras* (1971, *Mass for the Town of Arras*), which refers to the events of March 1968 although its action takes place in the fifteenth century. He wrote reportage, radio broadcasts, and film scripts, and under the pseudonym of Maurice S. Andrews, he wrote detective stories.

Początek

Szczypiorski's most popular novel directly addressing the problem of World War II and the Holocaust is *Początek* (1986, *The Beginning*, rendered into English as *The Beautiful Mrs. Seidenman*). Written in 1986, it was first published in Paris and then in the underground publishing house Przedświt. It could only be published officially in Poland in 1989. It was translated into many languages and particularly appreciated in Germany, Austria, and Switzerland.

Początek shows the Holocaust through the vicissitudes of more than a dozen characters who have survived, showing the irony of their fates: a Jewish woman rescued during the war must leave Poland in 1968; a Jewish boy who, during the war, did not want to deny his Jewish heritage although threatened by death, tries to erase it completely after the war. Szczypiorski presents the entire gamut of attitudes Poles revealed toward Jews during the Warsaw ghetto uprising: a collaborator who made a fortune on blackmailing Jews; an old professor who suffers a heart attack while seeing the ghetto in flames; and young Polish people on the infamous merry-go-round, set up by the Nazis just beyond the ghetto walls during the liquidation of the ghetto in April 1943.

Szczypiorski perceives the Holocaust in the context of all totalitarianisms of the twentieth century, reflecting upon a certain repetitiveness of human suffering. The language is, on the whole, matter of fact, but in some parts becomes loftier, as in depictions of the scene of the events, a particular Polish landscape:

> Here was the center of the earth, the axis of the universe, where stupidity was interlaced with the sublime, odious betrayal with the purest self-sacrifice. . . . Here was the center of the earth, the axis of the universe, the accumulation of brotherhood and hatred, closeness and strangeness, for here were fulfilled the joint destinies of peoples most distant one from the other. In these mills by the Vistula God made Polish flour for the Polish hungry, Polish flour, heavenly manna, Mosaic and Christian, of the old and the new covenant, for all the martyrs and scoundrels, the saints and the villains of this world (London: Weidenfeld & Nicholson 1989, p. 38).

The action of the novel takes place mainly in the Warsaw of 1942 and 1943 and the 1980s, but there are a number of reminiscences from other periods of the past (as far back as the Russian revolution of 1905) and from other places, for instance Russia, France, and Israel. The twenty-one chapters, loosely constructed and juxtaposed with each other, are connected by the figure of the omniscient narrator and Pawel Krynski, a Pole who constitutes the writer's alter ego. Pawel was in love with beautiful Irma Seidenman and friends with Henryk Fichtelbaum (both assimilated Jews), whose sister he helped to save during the Holocaust. Szczypiorski indirectly presents the situation in the Warsaw ghetto that serves as a background for various attitudes of Jews, Poles, and Germans. He shows the tragedy of the Jews by creating characters who, no matter what they do or where they come from, have practically no chance of survival. Among Polish characters, apart from noble or indifferent individuals, he creates villains like Beautiful Lolo, a *szmalcownik*, a person specializing in "hunting" Jews in hiding or turning them over to the German authorities. He finds joy in blackmailing both them and their Aryan hosts:

> Lolo found joy in hunting. When he came upon a Jew more worthy of attention slinking through the streets, frightened but full of determination, he would tail him, letting the Jew understand that the game was up. . . . Then they would clinch the deal. Lolo took money, jewelry, even clothing. . . . While he was at it Lolo would also fleece the Jew's Aryan hosts, who in their panic would give him whatever he wanted. . . . He was never sure of being able to strike a deal with his Aryan countrymen. This kind of Polish "Sabbath goy" who hid a few Jews, could be doing it for profit but also for lofty and humane reasons, and that always made Beautiful Lolo anxious, for the devil alone knew if a Pole like that, molded from such noble clay, wouldn't inform the underground of Lolo's visit, if he wasn't himself up to his ears in the underground, if he wouldn't bring trouble down on Beautiful Lolo's head (pp. 77–78).

The novel undoubtedly makes for good reading and is intellectually accessible for young people; it has been used for educational purposes in Polish schools. However, a more demanding reader can accuse the writer of simplifications and perceive the novel as a roman à these novel. Iwona Irwin-Zarecka states, for instance, that the book is "a work of reassurance, a quasi-didactic presentation of Germans-Poles-Jews in the trying times" and that the economy of expression leads to "a flattening of situations into tableau-like 'messages' which should be immediately comprehensible to the reader" (Irwin-Zarecka, p. 275). She also explains the novel's enormous popularity in Germany (*Początek* became a bestseller in Germany under the title *Schöne Frau Seidenman*) by the fact that it not only contains "good Germans" but also makes Nazi crimes milder by emphasizing the cruelties of Soviet totalitarianism:

> A West German reader, confronted with this view in the midst of a highly publicized historians' debate, could easily fit the novel into a larger framework of efforts to de-emphasize the uniqueness of Nazism. Coming from a Polish writer, the soothing of German conscience is undoubtedly even more effective (p. 278).

Some motifs from *Początek* are continued in *Noc, dzień i noc* (1990, *Night, Day, Night*). The book is constructed as a monologue of the main character Antoni Rudowski, severely tested by Stalinism, with a foreign journalist, periodically interwined with chapters in third-person narration showing a number of the same events from a different point of view. Again the writer focuses on paradoxical human fates under the Nazi occupation and after the war. For instance, a devoted non-Jewish wife who managed, thanks to her stamina, to save the life of her Jewish husband but dies at the conclusion of the war of some unexpected ailment at the time when there was finally a chance for them to start a normal life. Among more memorable characters is survivor Szyja Gutmajer, a black marketeer who indulges in sex during the day and spends sleepless nights recalling his murdered relatives; he ends up murdered in his own bed.

The 1990s

In the 1990s Szczypiorski became very involved in political life and was treated as a moral authority by some and attacked by others. In his journalism he often addressed the Holocaust and antisemitism. A very significant analysis of the Polish attitude toward the Holocaust was given in his essay "Marzec i Polacy" (1998, "March 1968 and Poles") in which, among other things, he claims that "Jews have the right to come to terms with their past, but Christians do not have such a right. Jews can even allow themselves to forget about the Holocaust. Christians are not allowed to do this," and states explicitly that Christians who do not realize the scope of Jewish suffering "do not have God in their hearts" (p. 12). Those largely rhetorical but thoroughly genuine statements, dictated by passion and involvement, have reverberated in numerous discussions of historical and political importance conducted in Poland and Germany.

Bibliography

Primary Sources

Z daleka i z bliska (From Far and Near). 1957.
Czas przeszly (Past Tense). 1961.
Godzina zero (The Zero Hour). 1961.
Lustra (Mirrors). 1962.
Portret znajomego (An Acquaintance's Portrait). 1962.
Ucieczka Abla (Abel's Escape). 1962.
Za murami Sodomy (Behind the Walls of Sodom). 1963.
Polowanie na lwy (Lion Hunting). 1964.
Podróż do krańca doliny (A Journey to the End of the Valley). 1966.
Msza za miasto Arras (*Mass for the Town of Arras*). 1971. English edition, 1993.
I minęli Emaus (And They Passed by Emaus). 1974.
Zlowić cień (*The Shadow Catcher*). 1979. English edition, 1997.
Początek (*The Beginning*). 1986. English edition, *The Beautiful Mrs. Seidenman*. 1989.
Noc, dzień, noc (Night, Day, Night). 1990.
Autoportret z kobieta (Self-Portrait with Woman). 1994. English edition, 1995.
Grzechy, cnoty, pragnienia (Sins, Virtues, Desires). 1997.
"Marzec i Polacy" ("March 1968 and Poles"). *Gazeta Wyborcza*, 17 August 1998.

Secondary Sources

Bugajski, Leszek. *Szczypiorski*. Warszawa: Agencja Autorska, 1991.
Irwin-Zarecka, Irena. "Challenged to Respond: New Polish Novels about the Holocaust." In *Bearing Witness to the Holocaust*. Edited by Alan L. Berger, Lewiston: The Edwin Mellen Press, 1991, 273–283.
Jażdżewska-Goldsteinowa, Ewa. *"Początek" Andrzeja Szczypiorskiego*. Warszawa: WS: 1995.

WŁADYSŁAW SZLENGEL

(1914–1943)

MADELINE G. LEVINE

WŁADYSŁAW SZLENGEL WAS THE most significant Polish-language chronicler in verse of the Warsaw ghetto. Until he died in a bunker during the Warsaw Ghetto Uprising in April 1943 (the exact date of his death has not been established), Szlengel wrote and recited poems that reflected, recorded, and probably helped to shape the changing moods of the ghetto population. Not all of his poems and occasional prose pieces survived their author's death and the destruction of the ghetto. Some of his manuscripts were found in the Ringelblum Archives; poems attributed to him have been discovered in copies by various hands and recorded, from memory, in survivors' memoirs. The first publication of a significant number of Szlengel's poems (a collection of nineteen, including several of his most important works) was in *Pieśń ujdzie cało. Antologia wierszy o Żydach pod okupacją niemiecką* (The Song Will Survive: An Anthology of Poems about the Jews under German Occupation), compiled by the Polish-Jewish scholar Michał Borwicz and published in 1947. In 1977, Polish scholar Irena Maciejewska assembled, based on painstaking archival research, a slim volume of Szlengel's verse which, following the poet's recorded intentions for an eventual collection of his poetry, she published under the title *Co czytałem umarłym* (What I Read to the Dead, 1977). Szlengel used that title for an essay he wrote in February 1943, as an introduction to and explanation of his work as "a poet of anno domini 1943, seeking inspiration in the gloomy chronicle of his days." In 1979 Maciejewska published a revised, enlarged edition of *Co czytałem umarłym*, containing some thirty poems and a half-dozen variant readings, the essay "What I Read to the Dead," and three very short prose pieces.

Perhaps it is unfair to form judgments on the basis of so slight a corpus, but the extant poems suggest that Władysław Szlengel, though an important voice, was not a major poetic talent. Life confronted him, however, with a monumental subject to write about and, in a handful of stunning poems, he rose to the challenge. In his last months he had come to see it as his duty to write "document-poems on the wall of my ship." He writes in the prefatory essay "What I Read to the Dead": "I want to enrich (a bad word choice) future history with anecdotes, documents and illustrations" (*Co czytałem umarłym*, PIW, p. 38). He knew only too well that if he had any readers, they would belong to the future, for the ghetto was doomed and his own days numbered.

Influences

Born in Warsaw into a middle-class family, Szlengel was among the first generation of young Polish citizens to be educated in the newly re-created state of Poland. Extravagant hopes were placed in this generation, almost giddy expectations that its members would enjoy the fruits of a new freedom that would bring with it great progress and even prosperity. Little more than a decade after independence was regained it became clear, however, that those high hopes would be dashed for all of Poland's citizens, not least among them the Jews who made up some 10 percent of Poland's population at the time. Reflecting the growing tensions in the political realm, by the mid–1930s alarming images could be found in the work of virtually all the major Polish writers of the time, including the poems of the most important Jewish poet writing in Polish—Julian Tuwim. Immensely popular in his time, Tuwim was famous for his lexically innovative, often insouciant and witty, but increasingly vitriolic verse, and for his cabaret performances designed for the entertainment of Warsaw middle-brow, middle-class audiences, large numbers of whom were Jews. Szlengel had to have known and followed Tuwim's development; no Jew in interwar Poland who elected to write poetry in Polish, rather than Yiddish, could have been unaware of or indifferent toward Julian Tuwim.

Szlengel's practice of the profession of poet suggests that in fact he was profoundly influenced by Tuwim's approach to poetry. Szlengel began pursuing a literary career in his teens, writing for local newspapers, for the Polish-language Jewish press, and eventually for a humor magazine aimed at a non-Jewish Polish readership. He was drawn to the theater, and by the late 1930s had left Warsaw for Bialystok, where he worked as a narrator of performances by the Polish Theater of Miniatures and as the theater's literary director. The outbreak of war in September 1939 caught him in that eastern Polish city; it is assumed that he took up arms in the brief, futile defense of Poland. He returned to Warsaw in 1940 and from then until his death shared the fate of the doomed Warsaw Jews. Once the ghetto was established in 1941, Szlengel became a frequent performer at the "Sztuka" (Art) nightclub—the largest and most prosperous club inside the ghetto walls. Władysław Szpilman, a well-known pianist and composer, remembers Szlengel performing nightly in a comic routine called "The Living Journal," in which the performers, using "camouflaged allusions," poked fun at the Germans (Szpilman, p. 65). The verses or skits that Szlengel recited in his comedy routines are either not extant or not collected in Maciejewska's edition of *Co czytałem umarłym*. Reflections of the scenes Szlengel observed in "Sztuka" and other gathering places where ghetto inhabitants sought distraction from their fraught reality can be found, however, in such sardonic poems as "Cyrk" (Circus), "Dajcie mi spokój" (Don't Bother Me), or "Wiersz o dziecięciu kieliszkach" (Poem About Ten Shot Glasses), in which the speaker seems to relish the false sense of bravado that comes with progressive drunkenness, but ends with a sardonic warning not to drain the bottle because tomorrow will only be worse.

Bitterness in Szlengel's Poetry

Bitterness is the predominant tone in Szlengel's poetry—bitterness born of and mixed with a terrible yearning for the city and the life from which he was severed. As he explains in his short prose piece, "Do polskiego czytelnika" (To the Polish Reader), his ghetto poems are dominated by "my profound and hopeless yearning for Warsaw" (p. 55). One of Szlengel's most haunting poems, "Okno na tamtą stronę" (Window onto the Other Side), is a prisoner's tortured cry for connection with the beloved city outside the ghetto walls, a city he gazes at yearningly, "stealing" its forbidden sights from his window, and waiting for a response that he knows will never come.

> My eyes stare greedily,
> stuck like knives into the breast of the night,
> into the silent Warsaw evening, into my blacked-out city . . .
> (. . .)
> I shut my eyes and whisper:
> "Warsaw . . . speak to me . . . I am waiting . . ." (pp. 59–60).

That no response will come from the other side, that Polish Warsaw has turned away from its Jews, is the painful theme of Szlengel's deceptively simple, ironic poem "Telefon" (Telephone). The speaker in this poem craves contact with someone from his former life; he wants, literally and symbolically, to be connected. He lifts the telephone receiver only to be struck by the hurtful realization that there is no one among the Polish population to whom he can turn:

> And suddenly I think: By God,
> I really have no one to call,
> in nineteen thirty-nine
> I went down a different road (p. 61).

And so, at once pathetically and bitterly, the speaker dials the recorded time operator, attributing to this neutral, disembodied voice all the compassion and solidarity that he can no longer imagine coming from a living human being. She, at least,

> . . . remembers so clearly,
> we were bound by a common fate,
> she does not fear speaking with me,
> and she has such a soothing voice (p. 63).

Here, as elsewhere when he speaks of Polish attitudes toward the Jews, Szlengel seems to be expressing more the muted pain of a spurned admirer than outright anger.

Strange though it may seem, Szlengel, so acutely and bitterly aware of the impenetrable wall between Poles and Jews, allowed himself to fantasize briefly in verse about the common humanity of Germans and Jews. In "Dwaj panowie na śniegu" (Two Men in the Snow), the speaker addresses a German soldier, suggesting that both of them—the Jew and the German—are being manipulated by a third power who has neither of their interests at heart. This is a variation on the common-humanity trope familiar to us from *All Quiet on the Western Front* and similar pacifist literature. In Szlengel's version, the Jew reminds the soldier that the falling snow does not discriminate between them and appeals to him to walk away from enmity: "Let's go our separate ways . . . let's go on home." No response, of course, is forthcoming. In this and other poems, Szlengel's message is clear: the ghetto's agony is as invisible and muffled as if it were completely buried under an annihilating blanket of snow.

A number of Szlengel's poems are framed as "neutral" reports on life in the ghetto, but even these do not conceal the author's bitterness, his disgust at what Jewish lives have been reduced to, his envy of Poles and their romantic heritage of armed rebellion. "Rzeczy" (Things) records with suppressed emotion, in the dry tone of a bill of lading, the procession of household articles moving through the streets of Warsaw as the Jews are relocated into the ghetto; the second part of the poem takes the form of an inventory of all the goods left behind, now the property of the Aryan inheritors of Jewish households. In "Romans współczesny" (Contemporary Romance) love is reduced to a partnership in smuggling the bare necessities of life across the wall (the last line of each quatrain refers to "butter, eggs, cheese"). In "Za pięć dwunasta" (Five Minutes to Midnight) and "Kontratak" (Counter attack), both written during the ghetto's final months, Szlengel, aligning himself with the ghetto resistance movement, issues a frenzied appeal for armed resistance and prays for a chance to die in battle.

Szlengel's surviving oeuvre provides no clues as to the poetic path he might have followed had he survived the Holocaust, nor is it likely that we will ever know how he would have attempted to situate himself within the body of Polish poetry, had he not been compelled to become his people's poetic voice.

Bibliography

Primary Sources

Co czytałem umarłym (What I Read to the Dead). 1979.

Secondary Sources

Borwicz, Michał, ed. *Pieśń ujdzie cało: Antologia wierszy o Żydach pod okupacją niemiecką*. Warsaw: Centralna Żydowska Komisja Historyczna w Polsce, 1947.

Ringelblum, Emanuel. *Kronika getta warszawskiego: wrzesień 1939—styczeń 1943*. Warsaw: Czytelnik, 1983.

Szpilman, Władysław. *Pianista: warszawskie wspomnienia 1939–1945*. Edited by Andrzej Szpilman. Cracow: Wyd. Znak, 2001.

George Tabori

(1914–)

ANAT FEINBERG

"THERE ARE TABOOS that must be broken or they will continue to choke us," George Tabori wrote upon the 1969 German premiere of *Cannibals*, a shockingly grotesque play about the inmates of a concentration camp who, in desperation, prepare to eat one of their fellow inmates in order to survive. This provocative debut marked the direction Tabori's work would take in Germany and Austria in the years to come. In his so-called Holocaust plays and in his productions foregrounding Jewish fate, Tabori confronted the history of Jewish suffering and the systematic murder of European Jewry during World War II in a way that is both daring and highly original. A controversial writer and subversive theater director, Tabori is undoubtedly one of the foremost figures in contemporary German theater.

Life and Career

A Hungarian-born Jewish holder of a British passport, Tabori wrote his plays in English and produced them on German-speaking stages. Born in Budapest in 1914, Tabori witnessed Hitler's rise in Berlin before he emigrated to London in 1935 to join his brother, Paul, a versatile author and a leading figure in the expanding community of European artists in exile during the Nazi era in Germany (1933–1945). Tabori's work as a journalist and BBC broadcaster took him from 1940 to 1942 to Bulgaria, Turkey, and Jerusalem. The year he spent in Jerusalem left him indifferent to the idea of a Jewish homeland and to Zionist activities. Years later he would explain: "One is reminded by the others that one is a Jew." "I have suppressed the Jewish in me," he admits. "After Auschwitz, at the latest, I had to face the fact that I am Jewish" (Koelbl, p. 234).

Tabori's year in Jerusalem was followed by another in Cairo (1943), where he worked for British intelligence and wrote his first novels. An offer to work as scriptwriter for Metro-Goldwyn-Mayer took him in 1947 to Hollywood, where he worked with directors Alfred Hitchcock and Joseph Losey and ran into the community of German writers and artists living in American exile. The most significant of those casual encounters was no doubt the meeting with the German playwright Bertolt Brecht, whose plays he helped translate into English and stage. Tabori's most valuable contribution to the dissemination of Brecht's works in the United States was the production entitled *Brecht on Brecht* (1961).

Tabori's career in the theater began with director Elia Kazan's production of *Flight into Egypt* on Broadway, in 1952. Addressing the plight of refugees and exiles, the play received lukewarm reviews. Nearly twenty years in the United States did not bring about his breakthrough as dramatist that Tabori so keenly longed for. Ironically, Germany offered him a second chance and proved the ideal matrix for his unconventional theatrical vision and his prodigious gift as dramatist.

Cannibals

Tabori settled in Germany in 1970, following the controversial reception of *Cannibals*, which raised interest in the work of the unorthodox theater man. His compelling stage vision of the concentration camp universe broke new ground, avoiding the sentimental impression of German Holocaust plays of the 1950s as well as the impartial scrutiny of the causes, manifestations, and moral implications of fascism that marked German documentary theater in the 1960s. For the first time, German theatergoers were challenged by a play that focused on the meticulously implemented genocide, and notably these victims were depicted neither as saints nor as martyrs. As if this were not complicated enough, the taboo breaker was a Jew, a newcomer to the local scene, who dedicated the play, "a black mass," to the memory of his father, Cornelius Tabori, who perished in Auschwitz.

Born out of pain and gnawing guilt, this unconventional elegy to his father depicts people trapped in a humanmade hell, where some of the victims manage to retain a human image while others submit to the Nazi commandant by consuming morsels of the flesh of Puffi, a prisoner in a concentration camp. *Cannibals* inaugurates Tabori's experimentations with the theater as a locus of remembrance (German, *Gedächtnisort*). The performance is meant to be a visceral experience for both actors and spectators, in which the past is evoked, retrieved, relived, and reflected upon. The emphasis is on the actual, immediate experience, on the presentness of the past. Tabori generates an effect of synchronicity or temporal overlap by casting the same actors as the victims and as the victims' sons; the sons, even as they enact their stories, confront their fathers, and question their decisions and choices. The personages who participate in the mnemonic ceremony are examples of the camp's victims: a Gypsy, a Greek, a homosexual, Jews. Tabori's black mass, partly inspired by Sigmund Freud's *Totem and Taboo*, reverberates with allusions to Christian sacrament and to Jewish liturgy. "Only few of us have succeeded in remembering what we wish to forget, and we can only forget what we have truly remembered," writes Tabori in his typically tortuous manner. Jews and Germans alike, albeit for different reasons, try to disremember, to suppress, only to be overtaken by memory at one point or another. This is what Tabori's father, Cornelius, did, believing he could shake off his Jewish heritage and slip into a new identity as a cosmopolite. "No, you don't become a Jew. You are merely reminded that you are one," realizes Uncle in *Cannibals*, who is modeled on Cornelius Tabori.

Improvisations on Shylock

No less original and daring was Tabori's rendition of Shakespeare's *Merchant of Venice* in 1978: dispensing with the love scenes playing in Belmont, he offered his German audience *Improvisations on Shylock*. Tabori was one of the first to imbed Shylock's story in the context of the Holocaust. His first staging of the play was in the United States (Stockbridge, Massachusetts, 1966), tellingly entitled *The Merchant of Venice as Performed in Theresienstadt*, in which Jewish prisoners perform Shakespeare's play for a Nazi audience. Conceived for a German audience, *Improvisations on Shylock* evolved into a theatrical meditation on antisemitism or "6,000 years of injuries," a genuine effort by "the wound to understand the knife." The performance focused on the Jewish trope of the maltreated, downtrodden, and persecuted victim with no trace of the bittersweet or black humor permeating so many of Tabori's so-called Holocaust plays. Tabori had hoped to stage the performance in the former concentration camp of Dachau; actors and spectators were supposed to be bussed from the theater to the railway station in nearby Munich, escorted by a Bavarian band, and later on to the site of the camp. Official refusal forced Tabori to change his staging concept. In a boiler room of an abandoned plant, with a big incandescent bulb glaring unrelentingly over a grand piano in the center, spectators watched the stereotypical Jew—multiplied. The performance was a perplexing investigation of Shylock, or "Shylockism," with each actor offering his own interpretation of Shylock. "We managed in our best moments to consternate and to hurt. The audience. Ourselves," recalls one of the actors. His observation points to the gist of Tabori's "theatre of embarrassment" (*Theater der Peinlichkeit*). The performance sought to taunt and disconcert, to shock, to offend and injure, to get under the skin. According to Tabori: "One way to avoid embarrassment is to wipe out the cause for it."

My Mother's Courage

The year 1979 saw the premiere of *My Mother's Courage*, Tabori's subversive reply to Brecht's much acclaimed *Mutter Courage* (*Mother Courage*). Basing his text on his mother's own story, Tabori relates how fifty-five-year-old Elsa, arrested in Budapest in the summer of 1944 and deported with four thousand other Jews, saved herself by maintaining that her arrest was unlawful. Instead of proceeding to Auschwitz, Elsa found herself on a train heading back to Budapest. The play, originally a short story, is Tabori's love song to his mother, who died in 1963; it is suffused with tenderness and lyricism, a homage to a woman who plucked courage almost unawares and pulled herself out of hell. What Tabori loosely calls his dialectical approach, a theatrics promoting subversion, interpolation, fragmentation, and the inversion of expectations, is evident in *My Mother's Courage*, both the text and the production. Tabori presents the audience with what may be called a mock fairy tale of modern times—a tale of petrifying danger, miraculous deliverance, and a happy ending—which is overturned by ironic twists. "A fairy tale, but no one would be saved from getting baked in the oven, except for one," in the words of the narrator son in the play. "My answer to Holocaust"—this was the title of the original production in its early phase, and Tabori meant it in two ways. Rehearsed in the spring of 1979, this was his reply to the American television melodrama *Holocaust*, which was screened on German television in January, raising an unprecedented interest in the *Shoah*. Beyond that, this was his private confrontation with a theme that had haunted him for years, as well as a studied reaction to the mystification and mythologization of the Holocaust.

Jubilee

Written and staged by Tabori to mark the fiftieth anniversary of the National Socialists' rise to power in Germany, *Jubilee* (1983) is yet another example of Tabori's theater of remembrance. Set in a cemetery on the banks of the Rhine, Tabori's eerie *danse macabre* features Arnold, the musician; his wife, Lotte; her spastic niece, Mitzi; Helmut, the homosexual; and his lover, Otto the barber. Each of these victims of the Nazi regime—Jews and non-Jews alike—recalls a private jubilee or cutoff date. Exposing the wounds and reawakening pain, *Jubilee*—a collage—calls for a total immersion in memory, in traumatic pain, while deliberately blurring the demarcations between theater and life, reality and nightmare, past and present. Here, as in other plays and productions, Tabori seeks to free our confrontation with the past from the conventions and taboos that burden and strain, distort and falsify it, from sentimental pity, sanctimonious judgment, and the hypocritical philosemitism that is in many cases the reverse of antisemitism. There is no place for a mystical reverence for the victims, for tears or solemn self-incrimination, such as pervade officially staged commemorations and many plays or other productions.

Mein Kampf

Best-known among Tabori's plays is undoubtedly *Mein Kampf* (1987). This farce, presenting a fictitious encounter between Adolf Hitler and the Jew Shlomo Herzl in a Viennese flophouse around 1907, was a sensational hit upon its premiere in Vienna in 1987. Not only did the play place Tabori at the forefront of contemporary German drama, it also became his *billet d'entrée* to the big institutional theaters. Shlomo, a spirited storyteller and master of caustic wit, lovingly mothers the newly arrived Hitler and teaches him how to behave, much to the amazement and remonstrance of inmate Lobkowitz "the Loon," a former kosher cook who plays at being God. Shlomo painstakingly grooms the aspiring candidate for his fateful interview at the Academy of Art and consoles him when he fails, all the while advising his frustrated, highfalutin roommate to go into politics. When Frau Death looking for a certain Adolf Hitler visits the home of the destitute, Shlomo chats with her while his chum hides in the toilet; later he finds out that the lady in black was not interested in Hitler "as a corpse," but rather she meant to recuit him "as a criminal, as a mass murderer, as an exterminating angel" (*Theaterstücke* 2, p. 194, trans. in Carl Weber, *DramaContemporary: Germany*). The "Great Love Story [of] Hitler and His Jew" ends with the gruesome mock-religious sacrifice of Mitzi, Shlomo's beloved chicken, as a menacing foreboding. It exemplified Tabori's belief that "the content of every joke is a catastrophe."

The play displays a sophisticated intelligence reveling in verbal acrobatics, slapstick, comic squirmings, and makeshifts. In the vein of diasporic Jewish humor, Shlomo's joke often expands into an anecdote. And most striking is his Talmudic disquisitional style, Shlomo's hairsplitting mode of logical argumentation reminiscent of the *pilpul* (Talmudic method of study and exposition). Flying in the face of spectators' expectations, Tabori does not recoil from injecting humor into moments of horror and pain, shaking up the audience through shocking jokes and offputting quips. "I am regularly berated for making people laugh about such holy subjects as Hitler or Auschwitz or sex," concedes Tabori, who considers laughter a legitimate, healing, cathartic reaction. Tabori provokes a pained laughter here as in his other plays, biting, terrifying, macabre. "Humor is no laughing matter," he maintains. For many spectators, critics, opponents, and admirers alike, this tastelessness, this crudeness, is the hallmark of Tabori's theater, which Jörg Gronius termed "theatre of embarrassment" (Gronius and Kässens, eds., pp. 9–24).

Other Works

Although Tabori's plays, novels, and essays cover a wealth of topics, he has become widely known for the above-mentioned Holocaust plays. And yet, his nonconformist, deliberately provocative approach to delicate subjects is already apparent in his earlier "American" phase. *The Niggerlovers* (1967) depicts the dialectics of victims and victimizers against the background of multiethnic, multicultural New York. *Pinkville* (1971) is an antiwar play written in the wake of the Vietnam War, showing the process of dehumanization and brutalization that war entails. Other memorable plays include *Masada* (1988), in which two survivors of the mass suicide reflect on questions such as the right to live, the guilt of the survivor, and the duty to bear witness; *Weisman and Copperface* (1990), a "Jewish Western," an enormously funny yet moving play in which Tabori pits two subalterns—The Jew and the American Indian, two cantankerous pariahs squabbling somewhere in the wilderness of the Rocky Mountains about hegemony and justice, voicing rival claims to victimhood and vying for the monopoly of suffering; and *Goldberg Variations* (1991), a pastiche made up of various Old and New Testament episodes in which a congenial duo—director Mr. Jay and his assistant, Holocaust survivor Goldberg—embodies the dyadic tension between theater makers, master and assistant, father and son, while echoing other couples, from slapstick masters Laurel and Hardy to Samuel Beckett's tramps or Tabori's own pairs, such as Shlomo and Hitler in *Mein Kampf* and Weisman and Copperface. As a director of his own plays and plays by other dramatists, Tabori offered a fresh approach to theater making marked by originality and vigor. The defiant outsider, Tabori resolved to tear off the figleaf, as he called it, hampering the vitality of theater making in Germany.

Conclusion

Although Tabori was revered and celebrated, his career, first in the United States, later in Germany, was fraught with disappointments, crises, and even scandals. And yet, the gray-haired iconoclast became both a cult figure and the doyen of the German theater, seen by many as the honorific Jew, a witness of our century, a vestige of the renowned tradition of European Jewish culture that was brutally severed by the Holocaust.

Bibliography

Primary Sources

Beneath the Stone the Scorpion. 1945.
Companions of the Left Hand. 1946.
Original Sin. 1947.
The Caravan Passes. 1951.
The Emperor's Clothes. 1953.
Flight Into Egypt. 1953.
The Journey. 1958.
The Good One. 1960.
Brecht on Brecht. 1967.
The Niggerlovers. 1967.
The Cannibals. 1974.
Son of a Bitch. Erzählungen (Stories). 1981.
Unterammergau oder die guten Deutschen (Unterammergau or the Good Germans). 1981.
The Cannibals. 1982.
Jubilee. 1983.
Spiele: Peepshow, Pinkville, Jubiläum. (Plays: Peepshow, Pinkville, Jubilee). 1984.
Meine Kämpfe (My Wars). 1986.
Masada. 1988.
Weisman and Copperface. 1990.
Betrachtungen über das Feigenblatt: Handbuch für Verliebte und Verrückte. (Reflections on the Figleaf: Handbook for Lovers and Lunatics). 1991.
Goldberg Variations. 1991.
Theaterstücke (Plays). 2 vols. 1994.
Die Ballade vom Wiener Schnitzel. (The Ballad of the Wiener Schnitzel). 1996.
Mein Kampf: Farce. 1996.
My Mother's Courage. 1999.
Autodafé. Erinnerungen. 2002.

Secondary Sources

Bayerdörfer, Hans-Peter, and Jörg Schönert, eds. *Theater gegen das Vergessen: Bühnenarbeit und Drama bei George Tabori*. Tübingen: Niemeyer, 1997.

Feinberg, Anat. *George Tabori*. Munich: Deutsce Taschenbuch Verlag, forthcoming 2003.

———. *Embodied Memory: The Theatre of George Tabori*. Iowa City: University of Iowa Press, 1999.

———. "The Taboos Must Be Broken: George Tabori's Mourning Work in *Jubiläum*." In *Staging the Holocaust*. Edited by Claude Schumacher. Cambridge: Cambridge University Press, 1998.

Fischer, Barbara. *Nathans Ende? Von Lessing bis Tabori*. Göttingen: Wallstein, 2000.

Garforth, Julian A. "George Tabori's Bair Essentials—A Perspective on Beckett Staging in Germany." *Forum Modernes Theater* 1 (1994): 59–75.

Gronius, Jörg W., and Wend Kässens, eds. *Tabori*. Frankfurt: Athenäum, 1989.

Guerrero, Chautal. *George Tabori im Spiegel der deutschsprachigen Kritik*. Cologne: Teiresias Verlag, 1999.

Hadomi, Leah. "The Historical and the Mythical in Tabori's Plays." *Forum Modernes Theater* 1 (1993): 3–6.

Höyng, Peter, ed. *Verkörperte Geschichtsentwürfe: George Taboris Theaterarbeit*. Tübingen: Francke Verlag, 1998.

———. "George Tabori's 'Brecht on Brecht' Production: A Success Story." *Brecht Yearbook* 24 (1999): 97–107.

Isser, Edward R. "Contaminated by Death: The Theatre of Tabori and Szajna." In *Stages of Annihilation: Theatrical Representations of the Holocaust*. Madison, N.J.: Fairleigh Dickinson University Press, 1997.

Koelbl, Herlinde. *Jüdische Portraits: Photographien und Interviews*. Frankfurt: S. Fischer, 1989.

Marschall, Brigitte. "Verstrickt in Geschichte(n): Im Würgegriff des Überlebenskampfes George Taboris." *Maske und Kothurn* 1–4 (1991): 311–325.

Ohngemach, Gundula. *George Tabori*. Frankfurt: Fischer, 1989.

Radtke, Peter. *M.—Wie Tabori: Erfahrungen eines behinderten Schauspielers*. Zurich: Pendo, 1987.

Strümpel, Jan. *Vorstellungen vom Holocaust: George Taboris Erinnerungs-Spiele*. Göttingen: Wallstein, 2000.

Text + Kritik 133: *George Tabori*. Munich: Edition Text, 1997.

Welker, Andrea, ed. *George Tabori: Dem Gedächtnis, der Trauer und dem Lachen gewidmet*. Weitra: Bibliothek der Provinz, 1994.

Welker, Andrea, and Tina Berger, eds. *George Tabori: Ich unite meine Tochter läge tot zu meinen fußen und hätle die Juwelen in der Ohren. Improvisati oven über Shakespeare's Shylock*. Munich: Hauser Verlag, 1979.

Zipes, Jack. "George Tabori and the Jewish Question." *Theater* 29, no. 2 (1999): 98–107.

NECHAMA TEC

(1931–)

ROCHELLE G. SAIDEL

NECHAMA TEC WAS born in Lublin, Poland, in 1931, the daughter of Estera and Roman Bawnik. Her father's chemical factory was taken over by the Nazis in 1939, but the German commissioner in charge of the factory allowed her father to continue working. When the family was forced to leave their home, they moved into a room in the factory. By the time Lublin was proclaimed *Judenrein* in November 1942, the family had obtained false papers and traveled to Warsaw by train. After a few weeks there, Nechama and her sister moved in with a Christian family in rural Otwock, about a half hour train ride away. Her family then moved to Kielce and lived with another branch of the same Christian family until the end of the war. Nechama was at first left in Otwock so that her family's departure would not arouse their hosts' suspicion, and she was extremely frightened that she would never be reunited with her parents and sister. However, her sister, Gisa, who was four years older, later returned and took her by train to join her parents in Kielce.

The two girls posed as visiting nieces of the Christian family and appeared in Otwock and Kielce openly, while their parents did not officially exist. Nechama, known as Krysia, eventually sold bread on the black market to augment the family's finances. After the German surrender to the Russians, Nechama and her family left Kielce for Lublin. They complied with the wishes of the family that had hidden them and left Kielce without revealing that they were Jews. Their protectors did not want their friends and neighbors to know they had helped a Jewish family survive.

Dry Tears—Tec's Memoir

Most of this information on Tec's life during World War II was in the first edition of her memoir, *Dry Tears* (1982), which ended with the family's return to Lublin in the spring of 1945, and her feeling that she was a stranger in her hometown. For the 1984 paperback edition by Oxford University Press, she added an epilogue that provided insights into the difficulties of postwar life in Poland. The antisemitism and threats to her family became so grave that she and her sister were sent to Lodz, where they again assumed non-Jewish names and identities. Finally, later in 1945, the family left Poland for the American zone of Germany and then lived for a while in a displaced persons' camp. The epilogue skips the intervening time and ends with Tec's current residence in Connecticut. Between her time in the displaced persons' camp and her immigration to the United States with her husband, Leon Tec, in 1952, she was briefly in Israel in 1948 and then studied in Switzerland. She has a Ph.D. in sociology from Columbia University and is a full professor of sociology at the University of Connecticut. She has also been a Senior Research Fellow at the U. S. Holocaust Memorial Museum and Scholar-in-Residence at the International Institute for Holocaust Research at Yad Vashem, Jerusalem. Nechama and her husband are the parents of two children, Leora and Roland.

Tec's memoir is a mixture of childhood memories and adult reflections on the psychological and physical ordeals suffered as a child during the Holocaust. Her descriptions of her relationships with her parents, her Christian rescuers, and her own inner struggles provide insights into the life-threatening situation she survived.

Although Tec's memoir is a literary representation of the *Shoah*, her intention was simply to tell her own story. She had avoided the Holocaust in general, and her own story in particular, since the end of World War II. However, in the mid-1970s her memories compelled her to begin her memoir. She wrote by hand for six to seven hours a day, remembering how she passed as a Christian and how her family and Christian rescuers interacted with her and each other during those years. Tec's training as a sociologist, along with her talent for writing in an engaging and skillful manner, results in a memoir that is both analytical of the situations that she faced and a fascinating narrative.

An example of her ability to combine childhood memories with adult reflection is her description of the time that her mother came to take her home from the Majdan Tatarski ghetto, on the outskirts of Lublin, where she had been staying with friends:

> My mother, her shoulders stooped, walked in front of me. As we neared the ghetto gate, she lovingly reached for my hand. I was overcome by a wave of sad tenderness. "Oh, Mama, how good it is to have you!" I thought. Majdan Tatarski was behind me. I had spent only a few months there, but the time seemed much longer. I had learned so much about life, made so many friends, received so much attention and love (p. 30).

This is but one example of Tec's approach to memory from the dual perspective of a child and adult.

Throughout the memoir, Tec describes the anxiety of being in "open hiding." She felt especially vulnerable when her parents and sister went on to a safer haven in Kielce, leaving her in Otwock. She had no guarantee that she would ever be reunited with them, and the time she spent without them seemed like an eternity.

> An extra layer of secretiveness, combined with a fear of discovery, became part of my being. . . . All my life revolved around hiding; hiding thoughts, hiding feelings, hiding my activities, hiding information. Sometimes I felt like a sort of fearful automaton, always on the alert, always dreading that something fatal might be revealed (p. 109).

Dry Tears was first published in 1982 by Wildcat Publishing Company in Westport, Connecticut. Two years later Oxford University Press reissued the book as a paperback, and it remains in print. In advance praise of *Dry Tears*, Geoffrey Hartman, professor of comparative literature at Yale University, wrote that Tec's memoir rendered "with such honest yet compassionate detail the struggle of Jews to 'pass' as Christians among antisemitic people who sheltered them, loved them, lived off them, and finally, after the war, were ashamed rather than proud of having taken [them] in." According to the late historian Lucjan Dobroszycki, editor of *The Chronicle of the Lodz Ghetto, 1941–1944*, Tec's work "will take its place among the best memoirs of the Holocaust years." *Dry Tears* received the Merit of Distinction Award from the Anti-Defamation League of B'nai B'rith, and has been translated into Dutch, German, and Hebrew.

Tec's Book on Christian Rescuers

Seeking answers beyond her own story, Tec turned her scholarly attention to Holocaust literature about Jews who survived with the help of Christian rescuers. In an effort to better understand the question of Jews surviving by passing and what made some Christians risk their lives in order to help Jews survive, she began to research archival materials. Her research and subsequent interviews culminated in the publication of her second book, *When Light Pierced the Darkness: Christian Rescue of Jews in Nazi-Occupied Poland* (1986). The book is based on sixty-five interviews with Jews and rescuers, as well as primary sources in archival collections, sometimes translated from Polish by the author. Her book is based on the cases of 308 survivors and 189 rescuers, and includes research of primary sources in archival collections of the Jewish Historical Institute in Warsaw, the YIVO Institute for Jewish Research in New York, and Yad Vashem in Jerusalem, as well as interviews with rescuers in Poland. Tec's ability to conduct interviews in Polish, French, Hebrew, and Yiddish, as well as English, gave her the opportunity to talk to people in the language in which they were most comfortable. This resulted in the interviewee providing information that might not otherwise have been revealed.

Tec summarized her conclusions as follows:

> I have tried to demonstrate the presence and describe the meaning and interrelationships among six basic characteristics and conditions associated with the rescuers. . . . (1) individuality, (2) independence or self-reliance in pursuing their personal values, (3) matter-of-fact views about rescue, which come together with the insistence that there was nothing heroic or extraordinary in their protection of Jews, (4) long-lasting commitment to aid the needy, a commitment that began before the war and that in the past infrequently involved Jews, (5) the unplanned and gradual beginning of rescue, at times involving a sudden even impulsive move, and (6) universalistic perceptions of the needy that overshadow all other attributes except their dependence on aid (*When Light Pierced the Darkness,* Oxford University Press, p. 205).

She accomplished her goal of "mixing numbers with descriptions of detailed life experiences," so that she "reconciled and achieved a certain balance between an observer and a participant, between objectivity and involvement" (p. 205).

While the research provides new insights and testimony from both rescuers and the rescued, neither this nor any other such project can ever really be completely systematic or comprehensive. However, Tec had two distinct advantages over most American scientific researchers armed with a doctorate in sociology, which helped her to gather significant data. First of all, she is not only a sociologist but also a survivor herself. As Tec states, "Invariably I was told that were I not a Holocaust survivor they would not have talked to me" (p. 200). Secondly, her fluency in Polish, German, Hebrew, and Yiddish provided her with the opportunity to speak with people in the language in which they were most comfortable. Only five of the sixty-five people she interviewed in Poland, Israel, and the United States chose to speak in English (p. 202).

A Jewish Rescuer Who Became Catholic

While working on *When Light Pierced the Darkness*, Tec came across the case of Oswald Rufeisen, a Polish Jew who converted to Catholicism. He did not fit solely into either of Tec's categories—rescued Jews and Christian rescuers. In fact, he was both. *In the Lion's Den: The Life of Oswald Rufeisen* (1990) is Tec's biography of a Jew who passed as a Gentile during the war, became the trusted aide of the head of the gendarmerie in western Belorussia for nine months, and thus was able to save the lives of hundreds of Jews. Although Rufeisen was somewhat older than Tec (nineteen), male, and directly involved with the Nazi bureaucracy, like the author he was a Jew posing as a Christian in "open hiding." He warned the Jews remaining in the Mir ghetto about their impending liquidation, and hundreds were able to escape to the forest. Rufeisen also acquired weapons for them, so they could defend themselves against hostile gentile partisans. He ultimately admitted he was Jewish, escaped, and found refuge in a convent with the Order of the Sisters of Resurrection. There he underwent a spiritual transformation and converted. When the convent became too dangerous, he sought a haven in the Nalibocki forest and joined the partisans. By March 1945 he was able to return to Poland and entered a monastery in Czerna, where he became Brother Daniel. At the age of 30 in 1952 he became a Catholic priest. Still wanting to fulfill the Zionist aspirations of his youth, he applied for a transfer to the Carmelite monastery in Haifa. In Israel, Rufeisen, or Father Daniel, provoked one of the state's first "Who-is-a-Jew" crises when he tried to immigrate to Israel as a Jew under the Law of Return.

In the Lion's Den was the result of an eight-year association between Tec and Rufeisen, whom she interviewed numerous times in Haifa. She also interviewed other people important to his unusual and significant story.

Jews Rescuing Jews

While working on *In the Lion's Den*, Tec became more aware of the fact that other Jews she had interviewed had also helped Jews. As she described in *In the Lion's Den*, Rufeisen operated in the Nalibocki forest, and had even met with Tuvia Bielski, head of a Jewish family partisan group. This led to her next book, *Defiance: The Bielski Partisans* (1993), a study of the rescue of Jews by Jews. This book is based on interviews with partisan leader Tuvia Bielski (two weeks before his death in 1987) and other members of the partisan movement who had settled in Israel or the United States. Tec presents an extensive history of this partisan group, which created a forest community of men, women, and children that numbered more than twelve hundred Jews by 1944. The many instances of Jews rescuing Jews have often been overlooked and downplayed, and Tec's book about the largest armed rescue operation of Jews by Jews during the Holocaust helps to correct this gap in Holocaust history. She also disproves the myth that all Jews were passive victims of the Nazis, and gives concrete instances of how Jewish resistance was able to save Jewish lives. David Hirsh writes that *Defiance* is an exciting adventure story as well as an important contribution to knowledge. Professor Tec knows not only how to tell a story, . . . she is brilliant in letting her subjects tell their own stories, inspiring enough confidence so that they reveal even the most intimate details of their lives in the forest. . . . That is not to say that she has not shaped the material and mediated it with scholarly research. She has. But what is more important, she has allowed her subjects to emerge in all their vitality. . . ."

Forthcoming Book on Gender

Tec's research for *Defiance: The Bielski Partisans* alerted her to the need to begin a new work on gender and the Holocaust, to be published by Yale University Press in 2003 as *Resilience and Courage*: *Women, Men and the Holocaust*. "I realized through *Defiance* that women in the forest had a special role and situation," she explained, "so I looked at women in different contexts, and realized that I also had to look at men as well as women" (remarks at Yad Vashem, Jerusalem, 18 December 2000). The result is her forthcoming book, which is a comparative analysis of men and women in the ghetto, in the forest, in resistance, and in a variety of other settings. According to Tec, her new book on gender has "whispered" to her that she is still to write three more books, going in different directions.

Tec's works, combining the analytical skills of a trained sociologist and her personal experience of living through the Holocaust, as well as her clear writing style, are important contributions to the field of Holocaust literature. Her four books on the Holocaust have won critical acclaim and awards. Among the awards Tec has received are the 1994 International Anne Frank Special Recognition Prize, the 1995 Prize for Holocaust Literature by the World Federation of Fighters, Partisans, and Concentration Camp Survivors in Israel, and the Christopher Award. From her personal search in *Dry Tears* to her forthcoming book on gender and the Holocaust, all of the books have evolved from her own experience but have been thoroughly researched to present various aspects of the Holocaust.

Bibliography

Primary Sources

Books

Gambling in Sweden. 1964.

Grass Is Green in Suburbia: A Sociological Study of Adolescent Use of Illicit Drugs. 1974.

Dry Tears: The Story of a Lost Childhood. 1982, 1984.

When Light Pierced the Darkness: Christian Rescue of Jews in Nazi-Occupied Poland. 1986.

In The Lion's Den: The Life of Oswald Rufeisen. 1990.

Defiance: The Bielski Partisans. 1993.

Resilience and Courage: The Puzzle of Gender and the Holocaust. Forthcoming, 2003.

Articles (Partial List)

"Righteous Christians—Who Are They?" Book of Proceedings, Eighth World Congress of Jewish Studies, 1982, 167–172.

"Sex Distinctions and Passing as Christians During the Holocaust." *East European Quarterly* 18, no. 1 (March 1984): 113–123.

"Rescuer-Rescued Relationship: How Did It Begin?" *Dimensions: A Journal of Holocaust Studies* 2 (1985): 4–7.

"Polish Anti-Semitism and Christian Protectors." *East European Quarterly* XX, no. 3 (1986): 299–315.

"Polish Anti-Semites and Jewish Rescue during the Holocaust." *Proceedings of the Ninth Congress of Jewish Studies*, vol. III, 1986, 181–188.

"Altruism during World War II." In *Remembering for the Future*. Oxford: Pergamon Press, 1988, pp. 542–549.

"Of Help, Understanding and Hope." *POLIN: A Journal of Polish-Jewish Studies* 4 (1989): 296–310.

"Helping Behavior and Rescue during the Holocaust." In *Lessons and Legacies: The Meaning of the Holocaust in a Changing World*. Edited by Peter Hayes. 1991, pp. 210–224.

"Reflections on Teaching the Holocaust." In *The Holocaust in University Teaching*. Edited by Gideon Shimoni. 1991, pp. 223–228.

"Altruism and Rescuing Jews." In *Bearing Witness to the Holocaust: 1939–1989*. Edited by Alan Berger. 1991, pp. 33–42.

"How Did They Survive?" In *Burning Memory: Times of Testing and Reckoning*. Edited by Alice Eckardt. 1993, pp. 109–116.

"The Historical Overview of the Hidden Child." In *The Hidden Child: The Secret Survivors of the Holocaust*. Edited by Jane Marks. 1993, pp. 273–291.

"Reflections on Edith Stein." In *The Unnecessary Problem of Edith Stein*. Edited by Harry James Cargas. 1994, pp. 51–61.

"Reflections on Rescuers of Jews." In *What Have We Learned: Telling the Story and Teaching the Lessons of the Holocaust*. Edited by Franklin Littell, Alan Berger, and Hubert Locke. 1995, pp. 71–88.

"Altruism during the Holocaust." *Social Education* 59, no. 6 (1995): 348–353.

"Women in the Forests." *Contemporary Jewry* 17 (1996): 34–47.

"Theoretical Analysis of Altruistic Rescue during the Holocaust." In *The Resister, the Rescuer and the Refugee*. Edited by John Michalczyk. 1997, pp. 155–167.

"Partisan Interconnections in Belorussian Forests and the Rescue of Jews by Jews." In *The Resister, the Rescuer and the Refugee*. Edited by John Michalczyk. 1997, pp. 116–133.

"On Forgiveness." In The Symposium of *The Sunflower* by Simon Wiesenthal. Edited by Harry James Cargas and Bonny Fetterman. 1997, pp. 241–247.

"A Historical Injustice: The Case of Masha Bruskina," with Daniel Weiss. *Journal of Holocaust and Genocide Studies* 7, no. 3 (1997): 366–377.

"On Auschwitz." *POLIN* 10 (1998): 339–343.

"Another Time Another Place." In *Peace Indeed: Essays in Honor of Harry James Cargas*. Edited by Zev Garber and Richard Libowitz. 1998.

"The Vatican, the Catholic Religion, the Jews." In *Holocaust Scholars Write to the Vatican*. Edited by Harry James Cargas. 1998.

"Partisans in the Belorussian Forests—Their Culture and Class Structure." In *Resisting the Holocaust*. Edited by Ruby Rohrlich. 1998.

"Women among the Partisans." In *Women in the Holocaust*. Edited by Dalia Ofer and Lenore Weitzman. 1998.

"Reflections on Rescuers." In *The Holocaust and History*. Edited by Michael Berenbaum and Abraham Peck. 1998, pp. 651–662.

"Diaries and Oral History: Some Methodological Considerations." *Religion and the Arts* 4–1 (2000): 87–95.

"Jewish Resistance in Eastern Europe" and "Righteous Among Nations." *Holocaust Encyclopedia*. Edited by Walter Laqueur. 2001.

"Reflections on Resistance and Gender." In *Remembering for the Future: The Holocaust in an Age of Genocide*, vol. 1. Edited by John Roth and Elisabeth Maxwell. London: Palgrave, 2001, pp. 552–569.

Secondary Sources

Ash, Timothy Garton. Review of *When Light Pierced the Darkness: Christian Rescue of Jews in Nazi-Occupied Poland* by Nechama Tec. *New York Review of Books*, 32 (19 December 1985): 26–28+.

Baumgarten, Murray. "Nechama Tec's *Dry Tears*, and the Sociological Imagination." In *Expectations and Endings: Observations on Holocaust Literature, Working Papers in Holocaust Studies III*. Holocaust Studies Program, Yeshiva University, September, 1989.

Gross, Jan Tomasz. Review of *When Light Pierced the Darkness: Christian Rescue of Jews in Nazi-Occupied Poland* by Nechama Tec. *New York Times Book Review* 91 (12 January 1986): 37.

Hirsh, David. Review of *Defiance: The Bielski Partisans*. *Shofar* 13, no. 4 (summer, 1995): 91–94.

Sheramy, Rona. "Tec, Nechama." In *Jewish Women in America: An Historical Encyclopedia*. Edited by Deborah Dash Moore and Paula Hyman. New York: Routledge, 1998, pp. 1387–1388.

Giuliana Tedeschi

(1914–)

JUDITH KELLY

Born in April 1914 into a Jewish family in Milan, Giuliana Tedeschi spent her early years in Naples, where the family was completely assimilated into local society, and where she was regarded simply as the school friend who was of another religion to that of her Christian schoolfellows. She returned to Milan where she passed her undergraduate years studying linguistics under Benvenuto Terracini, and where she married and started a family. The imposition of the Fascist Racial Laws in Italy in 1938 meant that she could no longer continue to teach in state schools, and during the occupation of northern Italy by Nazi troops in 1943, members of her family were rounded up by the Fascists. In her interview with Nicola Caracciolo, Tedeschi describes how her two little daughters were saved by the housemaid, Annetta Barale. Taking advantage of the family's false identity documents, Barale was able to hide the girls, and they, in fact, spent some months in the care of nuns in Turin. Tedeschi and her husband were sent to Auschwitz, but only she returned following the liberation of the camp by the Russian forces in January 1945.

Giuliana Tedeschi was sent from Fossoli di Carpi internment camp to Auschwitz in convoy number nine, which departed on 5 April and arrived on 10 April 1944 (Picciotto Fargion, pp. 47–48). During the journey she passed her thirtieth birthday. Out of this convoy, which numbered over six hundred people, only 154 men and eighty women were put to work in the camp; included among these were Tedeschi and her husband. The remaining members of the convoy, many of whom were elderly, were sent directly to the gas chamber. Picciotto Fargion's account of the convoy concludes with a note stating that Giuliana Tedeschi's testimony about the conditions endured was given in deposition to the Berlin Public Prosecutor's Office on 20 November 1970.

In the final days of Auschwitz-Birkenau, Tedeschi, together with the other female prisoners, was moved to Ravensbrück in Mecklenburg in northeastern Germany. This was a *Straflager*, or punishment camp, built to house women prisoners. Upon arrival they found the camp to be seriously overcrowded; so many prisoners had been taken on forced marches to Ravensbrück by the Nazis, who were fleeing from the approaching Russian forces, and they wished to leave nobody behind to tell the story of their atrocities. From Ravensbrück the women were moved to Malchow, and from Malchow to Lipsia, where they were finally liberated by the Red Army after ten days of marching and starvation.

Upon her return to Italy, Tedeschi took up the teaching post in Turin she had won through competition during the Fascist period, but from which she had been excluded because of her religion. In her interview with Nicola Caracciolo, Tedeschi recalls that upon her return home after the war most people wanted to put the past behind them, and so for some time she did not talk about her experience in Auschwitz. She goes on to recount that "*poi nella scuola sono stati i ragazzi che mi hanno chiesto e volevano sapere. Così si è aperto questo colloquio e io ho spiegato, e loro erano molto affettuosi con me*" (then at school it was the children who asked me and they wanted to know. This conversation opened up in that way and I explained, and they were very affectionate towards me) (Caracciolo, p. 197). Following her retirement from the teaching profession, Giuliana Tedeschi began to write and speak publicly about her experiences in Auschwitz.

Literary Output

Giuliana Tedeschi is best known in Italy for her narrative *C'è un punto della terra . . .* (*There Is a Place on Earth*, 1989), in which she bears testimony to the conditions suffered by women inmates of Auschwitz-

Birkenau. In Italy this text appears in a school edition, with an introduction written by Tedeschi giving details of the Nazi racial policy and Auschwitz concentration camp, and which includes a brief discussion of historical revisionism. There are also notes for guided reading, comprehension questions, and suggestions for further reading and research. The text is intended to be used as a tool for initiating serious classroom discussion about Holocaust experience among older pupils.

Tedeschi's account begins with a reference to the desolate landscape seen by the new arrivals upon entry into Auschwitz. She describes the existence of the new arrivals who are put into quarantine in Camp A of Auschwitz, awaiting the order to move to Camp B and the consequent assignment to a work detail. As with most other accounts of concentration camp experience, Tedeschi records the shock of the degradations and humiliations of the daily routine. She recalls the shower that all underwent upon entry into the camp, and the tattooing of a number on her left arm: 76847. She tells of the filthy conditions in the barracks, the disgusting and inadequate food rations, and the brutality of the *kapos*. However, perhaps the most poignant moments of her account are those in which she describes her own particular anxieties, which reflect those of the other women around her. Upon entering the camp she finds herself with those few women who were allowed to bring their children because they were baptized and of mixed parentage. Tedeschi is filled with anguish at the memory of her two little daughters whom she has left in hiding. She understands the desolation of one of her companions who is no longer able to glimpse her husband when his work detail has been sent elsewhere, and the incident reflects her own yearning to see her husband once more. When she is chosen to be one of fifteen out of the eighty women from the Italian convoy who will be sent to the block where medical experiments take place, she is filled with fear that she may never again experience the joy of giving birth to another child. Rumors abound among her fellow inmates about the horrific nature of the procedures, such as operations to remove women's reproductive organs, and mysterious injections designed to produce sterility. However, following a selection in the women's infirmary, witnessed by a fellow inmate and reported to have been presided over by Dr. Josef Mengele, Tedeschi is assigned to a work detail repairing shoes destined for use by a German firm, and is thus saved from the experiment block.

Tedeschi's account of her experience is of interest because she tells of the bonds of female companionship that were forged, despite the terrible brutality of the camp and the exhausting nature of the work. She describes the appallingly long hours spent taking apart the shoes confiscated from newly arrived convoys, the companionship of some groups of women and the hostility of others, and the ever-present knowledge of the ultimate purpose of the camp, which was borne down upon her by the close proximity of the crematorium chimney. In this sense her account can be compared to that of Liana Millu. Tedeschi's narrative is more chronological in structure, but like that of Millu it highlights the particular sufferings of women prisoners and the small tokens of solidarity that helped her to survive from moment to moment.

One of the finest examples of this solidarity, which momentarily helps lift the spirits of the women, is the incident described in chapter XVI of *C'è un punto della terra* in which Tedeschi and her French workmates are sent to dig the sand quarry. While one of them keeps watch, the women break into an impromptu concert, whistling and singing extracts from Beethoven, Mozart, and Bach. Tedeschi writes: "*il freddo era stato domato dalle risorse del nostro spirito, e . . . ciascuna sentiva in se stessa con commozione la certezza di resistere*" (the cold had been mastered by the resourcefulness of our spirit, and . . . each of us felt deep within herself that she was sure to hold out) (p. 116). This fleeting experience of musical companionship provides a moment of transcendence within the concentration camp, similar to that described by Primo Levi in *Se questo è un uomo* (*If This Is a Man*) when Levi is able to take a brief break from the filthy task of scraping out a tank to help Pikolo collect the soup ration, recalling along the way sublime verses from Dante's *Inferno*.

The final chapter of *C'è un punto della terra* . . . details the journey forced on the women prisoners by the Nazis who evacuate Auschwitz in the face of the oncoming Russian troops. There is a brief description of Ravensbrück where the women are taken, but which is so overcrowded that they cannot find a place to rest or food to eat. Marched to a state of near collapse, from Ravensbrück to Malchow, and from there to Lipsia, without food or water, the women's hope of liberation and survival is constantly dashed, until finally some Russian soldiers greet them as they pass. But it is the sight of French uniforms that allows them to give vent to their emotions as they weep and hug each other. In Tedeschi's account, unlike some others, the author is one of a close group of people who have survived to greet the moment of liberation, and she is not an isolated individual. However, in common with the testimony of both Primo Levi and Liana Millu, Tedeschi's account finishes at the moment of liberation. The experience of Auschwitz does not form part of the predeportation or postreturn flow of her life.

It is only since the 1990s that Giuliana Tedeschi's writings have come to public attention in Italy, mainly due to the publication of the school edition of *C'è un punto della terra* . . . This work has received warm acclaim because of its insight into the particular suffering of women in the Nazi concentration camps, but it is fair to state that Giuliana Tedeschi's testimony has not yet received the wider review that it deserves.

Bibliography

Primary Sources

Questo povero corpo (This Poor Body). 1946.
C'è un punto della terra. . . . Una donna nel Lager di Birkenau (*There Is a Place on Earth: A Woman in Birkenau*). 1989.
Memoria di donne e bambini nei lager nazisti (Recollection of Women and Children in the Nazi Camps). 1995.
"Ancora sul film di Benigni" (More on Benigni's Film). *Triangolo rosso* (Red Triangle), no. 4 (December 1998): 50–52.

Secondary Sources

Picciotto Fargion, Liliana. *Il libro della memoria: Gli Ebrei deportati dall'Italia (1943–1945)*. Milan: Mursia, 1991, pp. 47–48.
Rittner, Carol, and John K. Roth (eds). *Different Voices: Women and the Holocaust*. New York: Paragon House, 1993.
Sodi, Risa. "The Rhetoric of the Univers Concentrationnaire." In *Primo Levi as Writer and Witness*. Edited by Roberta S. Kremer. Albany: State University of New York Press, 2001, pp. 35–55.
Tedeschi, Giuliana. Interview by Nicola Caracciolo. In *Gli ebrei e l'Italia durante la guerra 1940–45*. Rome: Bonacci, 1986. pp. 193–197.

D. M. THOMAS
(1935–)

GARY WEISSMAN

DONALD MICHAEL THOMAS, the son of Harold and Amy Moyle Redvers, was born on 27 January 1935, in Redruth, Cornwall, England. He studied English at Oxford University, where he was awarded a B.A. degree in 1958 and an M.A. in 1961. Thomas was the head of the English department at the Hereford College of Education and had published several collections of poetry, his first translation of Russian verse, and a novel by 1979, when the college closed. He then returned to Oxford University to write a thesis on translating Pushkin. He published a second novel but, like the first, it sold poorly. His third novel, *The White Hotel*, published in Britain in late 1980, looked similarly fated for obscurity when, in the spring of 1981, it was hailed by critics in the United States and became a best-seller, turning Thomas into a literary celebrity.

Following the success of *The White Hotel*—which won the *Los Angeles Times* Fiction Prize, the PEN Fiction Prize, and the Cheltenham Prize and was nominated for the Booker Prize—Thomas returned to Cornwall, where he still resides. He has published numerous works, including novels, collections of poetry, translations of Russian poetry and drama, a memoir, and a biography, but he remains best known for *The White Hotel*. This novel, about a woman who undergoes analysis with Sigmund Freud and is later killed at Babi Yar, addresses themes to which Thomas returned in the 1990s. *Eating Pavlova* (1994) revisits Freud during his final days; *Pictures at an Exhibition* (1993) reunites psychoanalysis and the Holocaust. These and other writings by Thomas have not achieved the success of *The White Hotel*; nor have they received the critical attention that novel continues to elicit from scholars who interpret and contest the book's treatment of the Holocaust, as well as its portrayals of female sexuality and Freudian psychoanalysis.

Pictures at an Exhibition

Like *The White Hotel*, *Pictures at an Exhibition* combines Freudian analysis, sadomasochistic sexuality, and the Holocaust. And like the earlier novel, Thomas's tenth novel is composed of disparate sections that defy easy synthesis. Its first section is set at Auschwitz, where the SS officer Dr. Lorenz is psychoanalyzed by a Jewish Czech prisoner named Galewski. In one session Lorenz tells of a Jewish girl named Judith who, in order to save her life, had sex with her father while Nazis looked on; in another he and Galewski discuss an experiment in which sixty prisoners will be forced to have sex with this girl, knowing they will be shot if they cannot perform for ten minutes without ejaculating. Galewski takes comfort in knowing the Jewish prisoners will have "the chance to sleep with a girl of immense erotic power" before being killed (London: Bloomsbury, 1993, p. 58).

Following this section, the novel jumps ahead some fifty years to present-day London. Thomas introduces a circle of friends orbiting around the elderly psychoanalyst Oscar Jacobson and his wife, Myra, an Auschwitz survivor, leaving readers to question how these characters relate to the Auschwitz of Dr. Lorenz, Galewski, and Judith. While *Pictures at an Exhibition* has been described as a powerful if unpleasant reminder of "how deeply the world has been scarred by the evil and tragedy of the Holocaust" (Donna Seaman, *Booklist*, 1 October 1993, p. 255), scholars disturbed by the use of the Holocaust in *The White Hotel* have found confirmation of Thomas's bad faith in the later novel. Thus Bryan Cheyette's review of the 1993 novel concludes: "After *The White Hotel*, Thomas seems to believe that the right formula of Freud for beginners, Nazism, sadistic sex and historical revisionism will sell anything" (New York: Penguin, 1981, p. 20).

The White Hotel

The White Hotel consists of a prologue and six chapters, each written in a markedly different narrative mode and literary style. The prologue consists of fictional letters written by Freud and his fellow analysts. In one letter Freud writes that he is enclosing the writings of one of his patients, a young woman suffering from severe hysteria, whose case supports his belief in "a death instinct, as powerful in its own way (though more hidden) than the libido" (p. 8). Her writings consist of "verses" originally written between the staves of a score of Mozart's *Don Giovanni* and a "journal" originally written in a child's exercise book. In another letter Freud announces that he is prepared to publish the case history of his former patient along with her two compositions, hoping the reader "will not be alarmed by the obscene expressions scattered through her poor verses, nor by the somewhat less offensive, but still pornographic, material in the expansion of her phantasy" (p. 11).

The book's first three chapters present each of these writings in turn—the poem, the journal, and the case history. Chapter 1, "Don Giovanni," describes its narrator's stay at a white lakeside hotel where she has an affair with Freud's son. The novel's thematic conjoining of sexuality and catastrophic death is introduced in verse describing their lovemaking on a yacht as the white hotel burns and guests leap from the upper stories: "I jerked and jerked until his prick released / its cool soft flood. Charred bodies hung from trees, / he grew erect again" (pp. 19–20). Chapter 2, "The Gastein Journal," is a third-person prose elaboration of the poem, relating further incidents of sex (vaginal and anal penetration, fellatio, breast sucking) and death (by flood, fire, landslide, falling) at the white hotel. Chapter 3, "Frau Anna G.," the case history written by Thomas's Freud, identifies and analyzes the protagonist-author of the preceding accounts. We learn that "Anna" wrote the poem when Freud asked her to describe her stay at the Gastein health resort in the Austrian Alps and that the journal followed when Freud asked her to produce a sober analysis of her poem. Examination of these writings and Anna's dreams leads Freud to conclude that her hysterical symptoms, severe pains in her left breast and pelvic region, result from "her unconscious hatred of her distorted femininity" (p. 140)—that is, her repressed homosexuality.

The last three chapters, written in a third-person omniscient narrative mode, describe the fate of Lisa Erdman—Freud's "Anna"—following her analysis. Chapter 4, "The Health Resort," covers events from 1929 to 1936, when Lisa moves to Kiev to marry a Russian Jew. Chapter 5, "The Sleeping Carriage," describes Lisa's death at Babi Yar. Here we learn that Freud misinterpreted her pains, believing them to be hysterical symptoms rooted in childhood rather than prophetic signs of future events; for at Babi Yar, an SS man would stomp on Lisa's left breast and pelvis and rape her with a bayonet. The last chapter, "The Camp," follows Lisa into the afterlife, to a setting reminiscent of Palestine.

Critical Reception

Most every aspect of *The White Hotel* has generated sharply conflicting interpretations from scholars and critics. Some feminist critiques of the novel denounce it as a sexist work of pornography, in which Lisa functions as the eroticized, passive object of sexual violence (Kappeler); others contend that Thomas's novel, far from objectifying women, affirms Lisa's selfhood by undermining the authority of patriarchal discourse—particularly Freudian psychoanalysis—in a manner consistent with poststructuralist feminist theory (Bartkowski and Stearns, Hutcheon).

Freud's misdiagnosis of Lisa's symptoms has been read as a discrediting of psychoanalysis (Robertson), though scholars also note the absurdity of faulting Thomas's Freud for neglecting to connect Lisa's symptoms to unimaginable events that had not yet occurred (Vice). Scholars have suggested that Thomas draws some connection between Freud and the German soldiers at Babi Yar—both assert "patriarchal power over woman as object" (Hutcheon, p. 89)—though Thomas himself contrasts Freud with Hitler, saying that whereas Freud devoted himself to recognizing the uniqueness of each human soul, Hitler thought nothing of destroying millions of souls (Lewis, pp. 80–81). Thomas's fictionalized case history has been judged a masterful imitation (Lehmann-Haupt), as well as a failed attempt that does little to make the death instinct truly applicable to the narrative (Epstein).

Assessment of Thomas's treatment of the Holocaust has been equally divided. Some scholars regard his novel as an innovative work of Holocaust literature that raises complex questions concerning the relation of the individual psyche to history (Wirth-Nesher, Vice). Others denounce Thomas for exploiting the Holocaust in order to eroticize death and sexual violence (Rosenfeld, Cheyette). But the most discussed aspect of Thomas's representation of the Holocaust involves his effort to lend authenticity to Lisa's experiences at Babi Yar by incorporating witness testimony in his fiction.

The Plagiarism Controversy

In March 1982, a letter to the *Times Literary Supplement* set off a controversy concerning Thomas's use of *Babi Yar*, Anatoli Kuznetsov's novelistic account of the Nazi occupation of Kiev, based on his boyhood memories, interviews with witnesses, and use of historical documents. D. A. Kenrick, a London antiques dealer, wrote that Thomas's description of what Lisa saw and suffered at Babi Yar was "a superficially reworked version of the historical accounts in *Babi Yar*," particularly Dina Pronicheva's story of surviving the mass killings ([London] *Times*, 9 April 1982, p. 412). To illustrate this point, Kendrick juxtaposed lengthy passages from the two works. The passage quoted from *Babi Yar* concludes:

> On their left was the side of the quarry, to the right a deep drop; the ledge had apparently been specially cut out for the purposes of the execution, and it was so narrow that as they went along it people instinctively leaned towards the wall of sandstone, so as not to fall in.
>
> Dina looked down and her head swam, she seemed to be so high up. Beneath her was a sea of bodies covered in blood. On the other side of the quarry she could just distinguish the machine-guns which had been set up there and a few German soldiers. They had lit a bonfire and it looked as though they were making coffee on it.

The passage Kendrick quotes from *The White Hotel* concludes:

> On their left was the side of the quarry, to the right a deep drop; the ledge had apparently been specially cut out for the purposes of the execution, and it was so narrow that as they went along it people instinctively leaned towards the wall of sandstone, so as not to fall in . . .
>
> . . . Lisa looked down and her head swam, she seemed so high up. Beneath her was a sea of bodies covered in blood. On the other side of the quarry she could just see the machine guns and a few soldiers. The German soldiers had lit a bonfire and it looked as though they were making coffee on it.

Based on a comparison of the two texts, numerous critics and scholars have accused Thomas of plagiarism, or of some related but harder to define wrongdoing. In his defense, Thomas claims that when Lisa arrives at Babi Yar his novel moves from the realm of narrative fiction to "a world in which fiction is not only severely constrained but irrelevant"; at this point "the only appropriate voice becomes that voice which is like a recording camera: the voice of one who was there" (Letter, *Times Literary Supplement*, 2 April 1982, p. 383). His justification for adapting passages from *Babi Yar* raises the question of whether it is morally acceptable for anyone who was not there to imagine the Holocaust. Thomas claims to avoid "some spurious imaginative 're-creation' " by adhering to the words of the witness, Dina Pronicheva (Letter, p. 383); he would not even change the order of her words, as "that would have been untruthful" ("Author Defends His Best-Selling Novel," *Times*, 30 March 1982, p. 3).

Scholars have observed that while Thomas invokes the authority of witness testimony, the words he borrows are not those of the witness. Rather, they are taken from Kuznetsov's novelistic re-creation of Dina's story as it appears in the 1970 edition of *Babi Yar*, translated from Russian into English by David Floyd. A 1967 edition features Jacob Guralsky's notably different English translation of *Babi Yar*, as well as another version of Dina's story; for whereas Guralsky translated the heavily censored version of *Babi Yar* published in the Soviet Union, Floyd translated the revised and expanded text Kuznetsov assembled after defecting to England. Noting how Dina's testimony has been written and rewritten by Kuznetsov, his censors, and his translators, scholars have argued that Thomas does not turn from fiction to testimony in the Babi Yar section of *The White Hotel*, but uses *Babi Yar* to endow his fiction with the illusion of testimonial authority (Young).

Scholars have also noted that even as Thomas invokes the sanctity of witness testimony he fictionalizes this testimony in order to make it fit the needs of his novel, most clearly by substituting Lisa for Dina Pronicheva. Throughout most of the Babi Yar section Lisa takes Dina's place, although Dina does appear twice: first as someone Lisa knows slightly and recognizes among the Jews at Babi Yar, and then as someone who climbs out of the quarry after night falls. "Dina survived to be the only witness, the sole authority for what Lisa saw and felt," Thomas writes (p. 251)—both to acknowledge his debt to Dina's story within the novel and, as he writes in his 1988 memoir *Memories and Hallucinations*, "to suggest the symbiosis of Dina and Lisa" (London: Victer Gollancz Ltd., 1988, p. 48). In fact, *The White Hotel* developed out of Thomas's curious conviction that the anonymous heroine in one of his own poems, "The Woman to Sigmund Freud," was actually Dina Pronicheva, whose story he encountered when reading *Babi Yar*. Thomas united these two women in the character of Lisa, in a novel that incorporates the poem as its first chapter and Dina's story as the basis for the climactic chapter set at Babi Yar.

Thomas has stated (and some scholars have argued) that his intimate portrayal of Lisa's fantasies and experiences enables the Holocaust to have a more "personal effect" on readers than it has "in an historical context" (quoted in Lewis, p. 71). By utilizing fiction to portray the life story and inner life of a single victim, Thomas hopes to offer his readers a greater sense of the loss of a "quarter of a million white hotels in Babi Yar" (p. 251), if not six million white hotels in the Holocaust. Yet, as critical response to *The White Hotel* attests, the value of "the white hotel" as a metaphor applied to the Holocaust remains open to debate.

Bibliography

Primary Sources

Modern Poets 11. With Peter Redgrove and D. M. Black. 1968.
Two Voices. 1968.
Logan Stone. 1971.
The Shaft. 1973.
Love and Other Deaths. 1975.
Requiem and Poem Without a Hero. By Anna Akhmatova. Translation by Thomas. 1976.
Birthstone. 1980.
The White Hotel. 1980.
Dreaming in Bronze. 1981.
Invisible Threads. By Yevgeny Yevtushenko. Translation by Thomas. 1981.
The Bronze Horseman. By Alexander Pushkin. Translation by Thomas. 1982.
Ararat. 1983.
A Dove in Santiago. By Yevgeny Yevtushenko. Translation by Thomas. 1983.
News from the Front. With Sylvia Kantaris. 1983.
Selected Poems. By Anna Akhmatova. Translation by Thomas. 1983.
Swallow. 1984.
Boris Godunov. By Alexander Pushkin. Translation by Thomas. 1985.
You Will Hear Thunder. By Anna Akhmatova. Translation by Thomas. 1985.
Sphinx. 1986.
Summit. 1987.
Memories and Hallucinations: A Memoir. 1988.
Lying Together. 1990.
Flying in to Love. 1992.
The Puberty Tree: New and Selected Poems. 1992.
Pictures at an Exhibition. 1993.
Eating Pavlova. 1994.
Lady with a Laptop. 1996.
Alexander Solzhenitsyn: A Century in His Life. 1998.
Charlotte Brontë Revelations: The Final Journey of Jane Eyre. 2001.

Secondary Sources

Bartkowski, Frances, and Catherine Stearns. "The Lost Icon in *The White Hotel*." *Journal of the History of Sexuality* 1, no. 21 (1990): 283–295.
Cheyette, Bryan. "A Pornographic Universe." *Times Literary Supplement*, 29 January 1993, p. 20.
Dorn, Karen, and David Leon Higdon. "D(onald) M(ichael) Thomas." In *Dictionary of Literary Biography*, vol. 40. *Poets of Great Britain and Ireland Since 1960, Updated Entry*. Edited by Vincent B. Sherry, Jr. Detroit: Gale, 1985. Pp. 566–571.
Epstein, Leslie. "A Novel of Neurosis and History." *New York Times Book Review*, 15 March 1981, pp. 1, 26–27.
Hutcheon, Linda. "Subject in/of/to History and His Story." *diacritics* 16, no. 1 (Spring 1986): 78–91.
Kappeler, Susanne. *The Pornography of Representation*. Minneapolis: University of Minnesota Press, 1986.
Kuznetsov, Anatoly. *Babi Yar: A Documentary Novel*. Translated by Jacob Guralsky. New York: Dial Press, 1967.
———. *Babi Yar: A Document in the Form of a Novel*. Translated by David Floyd. London: Jonathan Cape, 1970.
Lehmann-Haupt, Christopher. "Books of the Times." *New York Times*, 13 March 1981, sec. 3, p. 29.
Levine, George. "No Reservations." *New York Review of Books*, 28 May 1981, pp. 20–23.
Robertson, Mary F. "Hystery, Herstory, History: 'Imaging the Real' in Thomas's *The White Hotel*." *Contemporary Literature* 25, no. 4 (1984): 452–477.
Rosenfeld, Alvin H. *Imagining Hitler*. Bloomington: Indiana University Press, 1985.
Vice, Sue. *Holocaust Fiction*. New York: Routledge, 2000.
Wirth-Nesher, Hana. "The Ethics of Narration in D. M. Thomas's *The White Hotel*." *Journal of Narrative Technique* 15, no. 1 (winter 1985): 15–28.
Young, James E. *Writing and Rewriting the Holocaust: Narrative and the Consequences of Interpretation*. Bloomington: Indiana University Press, 1988.

Interview

Interview by Stephen Lewis. In *Art Out of Agony: The Holocaust Theme in Literature, Sculpture, and Film*. Toronto: CBC Enterprises, 1984.

BEN ZION TOMER
(1928–1998)

MICHAEL TAUB

BEN ZION TOMER was born in Bilgoray, Poland in 1928. His father was a tailor and his mother was a homemaker. Both survived the concentration camps. At the outbreak of World War II in 1939, he fled with his family to Siberia in Russia. In 1943 Tomer was brought Palestine with a group of Jewish children known as 'the "Teheran children," for the name of the last stop in their long journey from Eastern Europe through Russia and Iran. From 1943 to 1948 Tomer lived on a kibbutz, Mishmar Haemek. During the 1947–1948 Israeli War of Independence, he served as an officer of the Palmach, the Jewish armed forces that preceded the present-day Israeli Defense Forces (IDF). He was taken prisoner by the Jordanians in the battle of Gush Etzion, a Jewish stronghold near Jerusalem, and spent a year in a Jordanian prison. After his release he served as education officer in the IDF.

Career

Tomer studied literature and philosophy at the Hebrew University in Jerusalem. While at the university he began publishing translations from Russian and Polish literature as well as writing his own material. His poetry collections are titled *Nahar Chozer* (*The River Returns*, 1959) and *Al Kay Ha-Mashve* (*On the Equator*, 1969). His prose work is titled *Derekh Hamelach* (*Salt Road*, 1978). His play, *Yaldei Ha-Izel* (*Children of the Shadows*, 1963), is his best known work and a milestone in the history of Israeli literary responses to the Holocaust. The play, and its subsequent Habima production, received many honors, including the 1963 Baratz Award. It has been translated into English, French, German, and Spanish.

Tomer worked as editor for several literary periodicals and lectured at the Teachers' College as well as at a number of institutions associated with the kibbutz movement. From 1966 until 1968 he served as cultural attaché at the Israeli embassy in Brazil. Tomer married, had one child, a son, and moved to Tel Aviv in 1948. He died in 1998.

Children of the Shadows

Yoram, a twenty-eight-year-old Israeli man, the protagonist of *Children of the Shadows* (1962), is in many regards a young Tomer: He was born in Poland, journeyed eastward to escape the Germans as part of the "Teheran children" transport, and was a member of a kibbutz and fighter in the war of independence. Yoram's parents fell into German hands and were deported to an unnamed concentration camp. When the action begins they are presumed dead. However, later on they appear in Israel with a group of other camp survivors. Yoram's brother Yanek also survives; he was a fighter in the Warsaw Ghetto Uprising. Their sister Esther died in a camp. The whereabouts of her husband, Dr. Sigmund Rabinowitz, however, are not known at the beginning of the play. A Heidelberg graduate and professor of philosophy in Lvov, he was a member of the ghetto Judenrat and as such enjoyed special privileges while in camp. In yet another surprising turn of events, the former professor and expert on Renaissance art turns out to be none other than the eccentric vagabond seen wandering about the Tel Aviv boardwalk.

Set in Tel Aviv in 1956, Tomer's play deals with two survivors who, after some period of evasive behavior, must face their past and come to terms with it. Yoram, the "new Jew," an Israeli hero of the war, a kibbutznik, has been trying very hard to blend in with the reality in Israel. While outwardly successful, he is torn apart inside by a great deal of guilt. "His crime," as Glenda Abramson points out, "lies in wanting only to be a sabra (native), to forget the past, to pretend that he had no role in the dreadful story of his sister's murder by the Nazis or in his parents' anguish—as indeed he had not" (Abramson, p. 127). This metamorphosis from Jew living in exile to free Jew means a change of name (from Yosl to Yoram) and language (from Polish/Yiddish to Hebrew), and, in general, the adoption of a mentality that is predicated on discarding the world of Eastern European *galut* (exile), life with all its negative associations, for a life full of promise and personal fulfillment in a new and free country on the shores of the Mediterranean Sea.

This guilt-ridden process of identity formation in Yoram is seen by most critics as a metaphor for the larger nation-formation process experienced by Israelis in the 1950s and early 1960s. Gideon Ofrat writes that "Tomer introduces national problems of the early 1960s while focusing on Yoram's personal issues. The play as such moves along personal and national lines. One of the work's main concerns is how memory prevents people from being themselves, which is a national issue as well—the nation is torn by memories of the past" (Ofrat, p. 62). Yoram's exchanges with his brother Yanek, the Warsaw ghetto fighter, best illustrate this point. In one of the play's most stirring scenes, Yoram recounts his activities in Tel Aviv while his brother was fighting for his life in Warsaw:

> I was sitting here. In this cafe. They brought us to demonstrate. That was my contribution. It was a lovely day. After the demonstration I went to the movies. The economy was booming. The war effort. Yes, things were good. Like now. Only no German reparations. Concerts. Culture. Like now, only on the news broadcasts they played different background music. (*Children of the Shadows*, in *Israeli Holocaust Drama*, Michael Taub, ed., p. 178).

Yoram's personal anguish over his place in the overall response by Palestine's Jewish population to the atrocities going on in Europe draws this comment by Ben Ami Feingold, the author of the only comprehensive study of the Holocaust on the Israeli stage:

> Yoram's meetings with Yanek indirectly bring up another theme found in most Holocaust drama of this time, namely the argument that the Jewish community in Palestine was passive, practically ignored its European brethren, basically did almost nothing to save them. However, after the *Shoah*, the same people were pointing fingers demanding to know why Jews went to their death like "sheep to slaughter" (Feingold, p. 37).

Sigmund's anguish, while equally deep as Yoram's, is of a very different kind. Like Yoram, he suffers from "survivor guilt," the guilt of being alive when so many others, including family and close friends, have perished. But, while Yoram was in Palestine during the Holocaust, Sigmund was actually "there," a witness to the slaughter, a man who had personally seen the murders and experienced the humiliation and suffering of both ghetto and camp life. However, since he was a member of the Judenrat, survival, in his case, meant collaborating with the Nazis. Therefore, he feels like an accomplice, a traitor who must pay the price by inflicting on himself a sort of eternal self-flagellation. In Yoram's case, the damaging emotional costs of repressing memory are seen in his conflicting attitude toward his parents, his brother, and his childhood in Poland, as well as his relationship with Nurit, a guilt-free sabra who prods him into a confrontation with his demons and finally getting on with his life. To compensate for the fact that he was not "there," that he did not suffer and, worse yet, did not do anything to alleviate the suffering of others, Yoram identifies with the strong, with sabras like Duby, an army friend also in love with Nurit.

In Sigmund's case, the opposite is true: He keeps memory alive all the time so as to suffer constantly from crimes real and imagined. Sigmund, a sensitive humanist, is incapable of running away from his sins. Acting as his own judge, he is unforgiving and cares little about external judgment. In fact, after Yanek and Yoram discover his real identity, he dares them to turn him in for collaborating with the Nazis: "Call the police. Why don't you call them? Are you afraid? So that you can remain the immaculate virgin that you are" (*Children of the Shadows*, p. 183). They do not, and Sigmund continues on his way as before. He too decided to become a new man—a penitent sinner without a name, without family and friends. In his new life as a vagabond on the Tel Aviv boardwalk, he walks around mumbling incoherent sentences about being a *medusa*, a jelly fish without a backbone, and speaking of Hamlet and the Prince's dilemma of "To be or not to be," only instead of "that is the question," Sigmund offers a slight variation—"some question" (p. 176).

In very different ways, both Yoram and Sigmund resort to extremes in their attempt to blend into the new reality of Israel—Yoram wanting to be the carefree, guilt-free sabra, Sigmund wanting to be a nobody, free to flagellate and pity himself forever. Yoram seems to be on his way to emotional peace by accepting and returning Nurit's love and by learning to live with his East European family, a constant reminder of his troubled and troubling past. Sigmund, on the other hand, shows no signs of changing; even after the crucial confrontation with Yoram in the play's final scene, he remains as unforgiving and self-pitying as before.

Ironically, Yanek and his wife Helenka, survivors who, physically, suffered the most from the *Shoah*, seem the least conflicted about their new situation in Israel. They speak freely about their camp and ghetto experiences, but they are prepared to put it all behind them and become totally acclimated in the new land. Like most new refugees they have little or no time to dwell on the past—painful as that might have been—and focus almost completely on the process of rebuilding a new life. While coping with the pain, their immediate tasks are learning a new language and finding work and a place to live. A majority of survivors who came to Palestine and Israel in the late 1940s and early 1950s and helped build the new Jewish state fall into that category, and each one has a story more heart-wrenching than the next.

Tomer, however, found drama in those who either escaped cleanly like Yoram, or those who stayed alive by being involved in some form of controversial activity, either as members of the Judenrat in ghettos or as kapos in concentration camps. For these survivors peace does not come easily, or, in some cases, at all. Most emigrants, like Yoram, eventually resolved their inner conflicts, made easier by the fact that there was no public castigation of their actions. However, Jews suspected of even a hint of cooperation with the enemy had to either change or conceal their identity (like Sigmund) or face public shame, or, in some extreme cases, even worse. In the early years of statehood, the country's leadership felt that educational and overall cultural media should mourn the innocent while praising those who carried arms and stood up to the tyrants. While partisans and resistance movement heroes received all the attention, with streets and buildings named after them, figures like Sigmund, characters who occupied those difficult, gray areas of morality, were either shunned or roundly demonized. It was not until the 1980s, thanks in large part to such groundbreaking plays as Joshua Sobol's *Ghetto* and Motti Lerner's *Kastner*, that the various "collaborators" finally had their actions properly reexamined, and, thanks to a new set of political realities in Israel, became rehabilitated (Taub, *Israeli Holocaust Drama*, pp. 14–15; quoted by Abramson in *Drama and Ideology in Israel*, p. 167).

When *Children of the Shadows* premiered in 1962 the critics hailed it as a milestone in Israeli theater for daring to tackle such difficult and controversial issues as collaboration, national guilt, survivors' guilt, and the overall conduct of Palestinian Jewry while Europe's Jews were being slaughtered by the Nazis. Feingold best sums up the sentiments of the majority of critics and viewing public: "The play is written with great care and theatrical skill. . . . It [the play] is perhaps a little too crowded with literary allusions, poetic language, and symbols; still, this work is one of the most important works in Israeli theater" (Feingold, p. 44).

Bibliography

Primary Sources

Children of the Shadows. 1962.
Yaldei HaTzel. 1962.

Secondary Sources

Abramson, Glenda. *Modern Hebrew Drama*. New York: St. Martin's Press, 1979.

———. *Drama and Ideology in Israel*. Cambridge: Cambridge University Press, 1998.

Feingold, Ben Ami. *Hashoa BaDrama HaIsraelit* (The Holocaust in Israeli Drama). Tel Aviv: 1989. Translations by Michael Taub.

Ofrat, Gideon. *Hadrama HaIsraelit* (Israeli Drama). Jerusalem: Tcherikover, 1975. Translations by Michael Taub.

Taub, Michael. "Israeli Theater and the Holocaust." Introduction to *Israeli Holocaust Drama*. Edited by Michael Taub. Syracuse, N.Y.: Syracuse University Press, 1996.

———. "The Challenge to Popular Myth and Conventions in Recent Israeli Drama." *Modern Judaism* 17 (1997): 139.

Michel Tournier

(1924–)

SARA R. HOROWITZ

In his 1977 literary autobiography, *Le Vent Paraclet* (translated in 1988 as *The Wind Spirit*), novelist Michel Tournier recalls: "my earliest memories date from the time when Nazism was engulfing Germany" (*Wind Spirit*, p. 55). Tournier was born in 1924 in Paris, a city he came to revile for its bloody history (Petkanas, p. 54). By the time he was eight, his family had moved into the suburbs of the French capital. His parents were Germanophiles who met at the Sorbonne when both were doing graduate work in German. His mother's family had strong connections to Germany, and she took him there for frequent visits. In the late 1920s and 1930s the family summered in Germany. Although the family's closest German friends were anti-Nazi, Tournier remembers seeing many political and military rallies and pageants in the streets.

The Wind Spirit

In *The Wind Spirit*, Tournier explains that these intimate ties with Germany left him impervious to the seductions of Nazism. He contrasts himself with most of his French contemporaries who, as German troops marched into Paris, "had only the most abstract idea" of Germany, seen through the "smoked lenses provided by France's inept and ignorant propaganda machine" (Boston: Beacon Press, 1988, p. 58). By contrast, he explains, his family "knew better. Having witnessed the birth of Nazism, we had been vaccinated against its blandishments. We knew what it whispered in private and mistrusted its intentions" (p. 58). At the same time, Tournier was profoundly unsettled by the implication of a culture he loved in the perpetration of atrocity.

During the German occupation of Paris, more than twenty German soldiers at a time were billeted in the Tournier's large suburban home, forcing the family into a small area on the ground floor. Tournier recollects feeling some delight at the interruption of the rigors and routines of school during the war years. In 1941 his parents abandoned their house and rented an apartment. During this era, Tournier notes, few of his countrymen joined the Resistance; after the war, however, many claimed to have taken part in its activities. Tournier worked on the farm of a French family deported to Buchenwald for anti-Nazi activity; only one member of the family survived. Tournier completed his undergraduate studies and began graduate work in philosophy and law at the Sorbonne.

After the war, Tournier's fascination with such thinkers as Fichte, Schelling, Hegel, Husserl, and Heidegger brought him to the University of Tübingen, Germany, where he studied German philosophy from 1946 until 1950. He developed a friendship with Claude Lanzmann (who would later film the celebrated documentary, *Shoah*), who was also studying philosophy at Tübingen. In addition, Tournier came to know Thomas Harlan, son of the film director Veit Harlan, who had been indicted as a war criminal and was on trial during Tournier's years in Tübingen. During the Third Reich, Harlan had been the most important director at UFA, Germany's leading film studio and essentially an arm of Nazi propaganda. UFA had issued such antisemitic films as the infamous *Jud Süss*. From the elder Harlan, Tournier heard personal anecdotes about Hitler, as well as protestations of innocence, based on the "immunity of the artist," who remains somehow outside politics and ideology (p. 80).

While in Germany, Tournier began writing for French radio and television. This work continued when Tournier returned to France and began to contribute to literary magazines as well. Over time, Tournier developed ideas about fictional narratives that would use myths to deal seriously with philosophical ideas. His first published book, *Vendredi* (*Friday*, 1969), retells Daniel Defoe's novel *Robinson Crusoe*, giving the story a philosophical and psychological complexity absent in the original. The novel was awarded the 1967 Grand Prix de Roman. His second novel, *Le Roi des Aulnes* (*The Ogre*, 1970), won the Priz Goncourt. Tournier's oeuvre to date has won him high accolades from many critics, who consider him the finest living French writer.

The Ogre

Set in Nazi era, *The Ogre* uses the myths of St. Christopher and the man-eating giant or ogre, along with Goethe's poem "The Elder King" or "Der Erlkönig," as the fulcrum by which to explore issues of collaboration and fascist ideology. For Tournier, Nazi Germany was personified in the figure of the ogre, devouring children who had been his own age during the war. For example, on April 19—the day before Hitler's birthday—all children who had turned ten during the past year were inducted into service for the Reich, an event covered both in his autobiography and in *The Ogre*. The author saw this as resembling the sacrifice of virgins to the Minotaur. Tournier connected this with what he saw as the essential childishness of fascism, with its focus on parades, youth groups, and shiny weapons (*Wind Spirit*, pp. 85–86).

The novel follows the life of Abel Tiffauges, a Frenchman and self-described gentle ogre who simultaneously inhabits the realms of myth and history. Tiffauges evolves an eccentric ideology to explain both personal events and the events of history. Something of a social misfit, he thrives as a French prisoner of war in Nazi Germany, where he gradually penetrates the Nazi elite. Serving first as a forester in Göring's private hunting estate, and then as a kidnapper of young German boys for an elite paramilitary training school, or Napola, Tiffauges abets the Nazi effort while remaining willfully oblivious to its actions.

The narrative interweaves Tiffauges's private journal entries—termed "sinister writings" and penned with the left hand—with third-person narrative. Tiffauges discerns or invents an intricate symbolic network and the concept of benign and malign "inversions," that is, reversals of meaning and moral valence. Based on this elaborate system, Tiffauges becomes an unwitting participant in the concentration camp universe, whose symbolic order, he discovers late in the narrative, corresponds perversely to his own. Tournier utilizes Tiffauges to examine the stance of the collaborator or the bystander who remains willfully unaware of the nature of his ally yet continues to benefit from the alliance.

The narrative seizes upon the ogreish aspect of Nazi Germany, portraying the regime as a monster that cannibalizes its own youth. Tiffauges links the mythological flesh-eating giant (such as the one who menaces Jack atop the beanstalk) with Göring, "the ogre of Rominten" (Göring's hunting lodge), and Hitler, "the ogre of Rastenburg" (Hitler's country retreat). Repeatedly satisfying Hitler's carnivorous demands transforms Germany into a self-consuming monster, a cannibal who ultimately eats his own flesh. Tiffauges, too, becomes a monster—"the ogre of Kaltenborn" (the estate appropriated for the Napola). He roams the countryside kidnapping prepubescent Aryans, literally sniffing them out, in an ogre-like fashion. Tiffauges remains oblivious to the boys' anguish at being torn from home and family, convinced he is reconstituting a pure and organic society.

Tournier's novel is a tour de force, a brilliant and intricate layering of symbolic elements, encompassing the concept of "phoria" — that is, bearing or carrying as St. Christopher bore Christ—dazzling word plays, an obsession with defecation. The elaborate symbolic order Tiffauges constructs helps him to ignore Nazi atrocity. Surrounded by evidence of genocidal practice, Tiffauges translates his observations into abstract terminology laden with symbolic (but never literal) meaning. Undergirded with an oversaturation of research into the Reich, the Prussian landscape, racial thinking, biology, history, and mythology, the novel develops in a mode of what the author terms "hyperrealism" (*Wind Spirit*, p. 93) that both links it to and loosens it from historical events.

Ultimately, one can see in Tournier's novel a critique of Nazi rhetoric and German romanticism, the misuse of the symbolic imagination to obfuscate, manipulate, and murder. By the novel's end, Tiffauges witnesses the brutal death of the boys he kidnapped and professed to love, and comes upon a young Jewish boy, whose presence reveals what the man had refused to see. As history finally punctures Tiffauges's linguistic shield, it exposes the horrors hidden by language and interpretative practices. Ultimately Tiffauges recognizes in Auschwitz "an infernal city . . . which corresponded stone by stone to the phoric city he himself had dreamed of . . . inverted and raised to hellish incandescence" (*The Ogre*, New York: Doubleday, 1972, p. 357). Only then does Tiffauges acknowledge and bear responsibility for his own complicity.

Readers have struggled over how to interpret the novel. In *The Wind Spirit* Tournier laments the wrongheadedness of Nazi ideology, which cost Germany its preeminence in the modern world. Despite the "miracle" of Germany's economic recovery after the war,

Tournier saw German culture as radically and profoundly impoverished by its antisemitic madness:

> the German Jew . . . those two elements combined to form such a happy marriage, yielding among other things the three pillars of modern Western civilization: Marx, Freud, and Einstein . . . Consummated by a murderous wave of antisemitism, that divorce was the beginning of the end for Germany . . . For Germans the disaster was of incalculable proportions (pp. 120–121).

This quotation encapsulates the complicated relationship to the Nazi genocide that has led some readers to praise *The Ogre* as a profound grappling with the European past, and others to criticize it as a dangerous fascination with fascist aesthetics. In the quotation from his autobiography, Tournier condemns Nazi antisemitism, both for its horrible action against the Jews, and for its undermining of German ideals and cultures. The author's focus—an unusual one in literature about the Holocaust—is on perpetrators and collaborators, rather than on the Jewish victims. The metaphor of a divorce domesticates Nazi horror, and carries the suggestion that what occurred—while painful, perhaps, and costly—implicates both parties in blame and damage.

Critical Reception

Ironically, it is precisely the literary brilliance of Tournier's narrative that has given rise to its admirers as well as its detractors. Almost universally, reviewers praised the novel's richness and complexity, comparing Tournier's accomplishment to those of Proust and Melville. They see Tiffauges as an ironic figure, whose self-delusion and opportunism are exposed and repudiated by the novel. Critics such as George Steiner, Roger Shattuck, and Janet Flanner point to Tournier's perceptive rendering of wartime France and Germany, as well as his unusual way of probing issues of collaboration and complicity. William Cloonan notes the strong parodic element that renders *The Ogre* a powerful debunking of Nazi ideology and an insightful exploration of power.

Many readers, however, see troubling ethical implications in Tournier's treatment of Nazism. Some criticize *The Ogre* for mirroring and excusing the appeal of Nazism in an aesthetically mesmerizing narrative. Jean Améry, for example, was disturbed by the novel's aestheticization of Nazi atrocity. Perhaps the strongest voice, historiographer Saul Friedländer worries that Tournier's novel mystifies and mythicizes Nazism, generating "the kitsch of death." For Friedländer, the profusion of mysterious symbols and the monstrous but clever protagonist prevent any meaningful grappling with the central moral issue raised by the Holocaust, that of human responsibility: "as Michel Tournier explains it, the entire chain of Nazi crimes is only the manifest expression of hidden forces, and the book proposes to decipher the signs that would indicate something about these mysterious impulses—something that directly puts the crime outside the human condition" (p. 102). Moreover, Friedlander sees in novels like Tournier's a dangerous fascination with fascism.

Similarly, Karl Miller finds the "dubious" concept of "malign inversions" in Tournier's novel an unsatisfactory device by which to expose the inner workings of Nazism and collaboration. He faults Tournier for presenting Nazi Germany as "a country of the mind, a country without politics, tenanted by evil magicians poring over pints of blood and suint and measuring skulls and noses in the interest of purity." In addition, although he notes Tournier's repeated reference to material obtained as evidence for the Nuremberg trials, Miller finds the depiction of Nazi leadership as mere "cranks and pedants" to be inadequate. In Tournier's novel, according to Miller, the actions taken by these cranks hardly seem "central to the history of the Reich. . . . [Tournier] has misrepresented that history while using it as a setting for an account of a fairly exotic psychological state" (pp. 42–43). Pearl K. Bell criticizes the very literariness of the novel for obscuring the real human suffering. Tournier, she observes, "is fascinated by the abstractly intellectual and formal ingenuity of his fictional house of mirrors [more than] . . . by the human implications of the characters and events so cleverly reflected here. . . . Tournier deals with . . . victims as operatic metaphors only, not as the actualities of evil and slaughter that we know them to be." For this reason, Bell judges the novel "a profoundly unforgivable work" (p. 77).

In *The Wind Spirit*, Tournier takes pains to separate himself as author from the protagonist he created in Abel Tiffauges. The reader encounters all the events of *The Ogre* from the perspective of Tiffauges, the better, Tournier explains, to comprehend the "systematic, logical madness" (p. 94) that characterizes him and the regime he comes to embody. Tournier's novel is both engaging and demanding. As one of the few works of Holocaust literature to focus on the position of the perpetrator or collaborator rather than the victim, it offers a complexity of vision that both admirers and detractors take seriously, even while disagreeing on how to interpret it.

Bibliography

Primary Sources

Friday. 1969.
Le Roi des Aulnes (*The Ogre*). 1970, 1972.
Les Météores (*Gemini*). 1975, 1981.
Le Vent Paraclet (*The Wind Spirit: An Autobiography*). 1977.
Le Coq de bruyère (*The Fetishist*). 1978, 1984.
Gaspard, Melchior, et Balthazar (*The Four Wise Men*). 1980, 1982.
Gilles & Jeanne. 1983, 1987.
La Gouette d'or (*The Golden Droplet*). 1985, 1987.
Le Tabor et le Sinaï : essais sur l'art contemporain. 1988.
La Médianoche amoureux (*The Midnight Love Feast*). 1989, 1991.
Le Miroir des idées (*The Mirror of Ideas*). 1994, 1998.
Eléazar, ou, la source et le buisson. 1996.

Secondary Sources

Améry, Jean. "Asthetizismus der Barbarei: Über Michel Tourniers Roman 'Der Erlkönig.' " *Merkur* 297 (1993): 73–79.
Bell, Pearl K. "Sterile Diversion." Review of *The Ogre* by Michel Tournier. *New Leader*, 19 February 1973: 13ff.
Cloonan, William J. *Michel Tournier*. Boston: Twayne Publishers, 1985.
Friedländer, Saul. *Reflections of Nazism: An Essay on Kitsch and Death*. New York: Harper and Row, 1984.
Horowitz, Sara R. "Refused Memory." *Voicing the Void: Muteness and Memory in Holocaust Fiction*. Albany: SUNY Press, 1997, pp. 181–216.
Miller, Karl. "The Cyclopean Eye of the European Phallus." Review of *The Ogre* by Michel Tournier. *New York Review of Books*, 30 November 1972: 40–43.
Petkanas, Christopher. "Michel Tournier: Compassionate Philosopher-Writer." *W* (1–8 January 1982): 54.
Shattuck, Roger. "Why Not the Best?" Review of fiction of Michel Tournier. *New York Review of Books*, 28 April 1983: 8–15.
Sissman, L. E. "Obversities." Review of *The Ogre* by Michel Tournier. *New Yorker*, 30 December 1972: 68–71.
Worton, Michael, ed. *Michel Tournier*. New York: Longman, 1995.

Interview

Hueston, Penny. "An Interview with Michel Tournier." *Meanjin* 38 (1979): 400–405.

JULIAN TUWIM
(1894–1953)

MONIKA ADAMCZYK-GARBOWSKA

JULIAN TUWIM WAS born in Lodz, Poland, and belonged to a group of assimilated Jewish writers who entered the mainstream of Polish literature in the 1920s. Before World War II he devoted very little attention to Jewish topics and even distanced himself from Jewishness. That is why he was often castigated by Yiddish writers or Polish Jewish writers (those who used Polish as their primary medium of expression but identified themselves as Jews).

In the years 1916 through 1918 Tuwim studied law and philosophy in Warsaw. There he made his debut in a student periodical and met four other poets, some of them also assimilated Jews, who established the Skamander group, the most significant poetic group in Poland between the wars. Tuwim was considered the most talented and original in the group. He published his first collection of poems, *Czyhanie na Boga* (Stalking God) in 1918. A number of other collections soon followed. Tuwim's poetry is characterized with vitality and glorification of life; he used colloquial language, sensual imagery, and made an enormous impact on modern Polish poetry. He was sometimes attacked by Polish nationalists who would accuse him of "Semitic sensuality" and stated that Tuwim wrote in the Polish language and not in the Polish spirit. This was an absurd claim, sometimes raised in reference to other authors as well, and based on a belief in supposed "alien elements" present in the literature created by assimilated Jews. Toward the end of the 1920s and in the 1930s Tuwim's youthful optimism subsided and his poetry became more pessimistic, which is especially visible in his long poem "Bal w Operze" ("Ball at the Opera"), written in 1936 but only published ten years later. It is a political satire composed in a black grotesque mode permeated with a strong sense of imminent catastrophe.

At the outbreak of the war, Tuwim managed to escape to the West and traveled via France and Brazil to the United States, where he stayed from 1942 to 1946. Deluded by the prospect of a democratic Poland under Communist rule, he returned and was greeted with a plethora of honors and privileges, but suffered from writer's block and produced very little. His major work, published in 1949 and titled *Kwiaty polskie* (Polish Flowers, 1949), was actually written during the war in Brazil and New York. It was never completed and is very uneven, with some brilliant parts and some weaker ones.

We, Polish Jews

It was the news of the Holocaust (reaching Tuwim in exile in the United States) that made him revise a number of his earlier views concerning his Jewishness, which he had tried to ignore or neutralize earlier. In 1944, on the first anniversary of the Warsaw ghetto uprising, he wrote his famous manifesto in which he addressed the question of his own identity, including the status of his assimilation, and commemorated the Jews who had perished at the hands of the Nazis. From a generic point of view, the piece is a combination of lamentation, eulogy, litany, public confession, and discursive essay. The work titled *My, Żydzi polscy . . .* (*We, Polish Jews . . .*), consisting of five unequal parts, was dedicated to his "Mother in Poland or to her beloved Shadow" (p. 17). At the beginning he addresses the very title, stating that he can foresee the question "What do you mean—WE?" (p. 17). Such a question might be asked both by Poles and by Jews because the former consider him Jewish while the latter consider him Polish. He answers his potential interrogators and adversaries by giving a clear declaration that he is a Pole because he wants to be one and he does not feel a need to justify this to anyone:

> I do not divide Poles into pure-stock Poles and alien-stock Poles. I leave such classification to pure and alien-stock

> advocates of racialism, to domestic and foreign Nazis. I divide Poles just as I divide Jews and all other nations into the intelligent and the fools, the honest and the dishonest, the brilliant and the dull-witted, the exploited and the exploiters, gentlemen and cads (*We, Polish Jews . . .* p. 17).

And Tuwim goes on to explain that he is a Pole because that is where he was born and raised and where he experienced both happiness and anxiety, because he feels deep attachment to the Polish language, culture, and landscape. This way he indirectly responds to his prewar critics who accused him of being "alien." However, he also feels a strong bond with the Jews whose blood flows "in widest and deepest streams. Already its blackening rivulets are flowing together into a tempestuous river" (p. 19). His tone becomes loftier with every sentence and he ends the third part of the manifesto with an appeal to his "brethren" to accept him into "that glorious bond of Innocently Shed Blood" (p. 19). He clearly uses Christian terminology when he states that he wants to belong from now on to "that church" (the Jewish church of "Shed Blood") and asks that "the rank of the Jew Doloris Causa—be bestowed upon" him, a Polish poet produced by the Jewish nation (p. 19).

Part five is the most directly connected with the Holocaust and reveals Tuwim's great empathy for those who perished and deep admiration and respect for the fighters in the Warsaw ghetto upon whose armbands the Star of David was painted. He expresses his belief in "a future Poland in which that star of [their] armbands will become the highest order bestowed upon the bravest among Polish officers and soldiers [who] will wear it proudly upon their breasts next to the old Virtuti Militari" (p. 19). He also expresses his strong hope that "there shall be in Warsaw and in every other Polish city some fragment of the ghetto left standing and preserved in its present form in all its horror of ruin and destruction" (p. 19). Such monuments will be treated with special respect and care "so that the memory of the massacred people shall remain forever fresh in the minds of the generation to come, and also as a sign of our undying sorrow for them" (p. 19).

The Jews and the Poles

These words show Tuwim's idealism and lack of realistic thinking, to a great extent caused by his longing for the homeland intensified by exile, and his belief that the unprecedented tragedy of the Jews and the suffering of the Poles would unite them and erase earlier clashes and antagonisms. Tuwim's dreams were not realized as the Holocaust in some respects worsened relations between the two groups and, what is more, the four-and-a-half-decade-long postwar Communist rule resulted in the falsification and partial erasure of the memory of Jewish losses and suffering in the country.

In his manifesto Tuwim also pays tribute to the simple unassimilated Jews, speaking on their behalf and symbolically identifying with them:

> We Abies, we Kikes, we Sheenies [in the Polish original three proper names—"Shlomos, Sruls, Mosieks"—are used, as well as three derogatory nicknames often used in reference to Jews, especially the unassimilated ones—Monika Adamczyk-Garbowska] and others whose names and nick-names will some day exceed in dignity those of Achilles, Boleslaus the Brave, and Richard Coeur-de-Lion (p. 20).

This passage recalls his early poem "Żydek" ("Jewboy") written in 1925, a rare case of Tuwim's concern for Jewish identity during his young years. In that poem a poet's alter ego, "the gentleman from the second floor" watches a Jewish beggar boy singing in the courtyard. Although there is a deep gap between the two, the last two lines contain the idea expressed by the first-person plural that "*we* (contributor's underline) singing and possessed Jews" will never find peace and haven.

Four years after composing *We, Polish Jews*, on the fifth anniversary of the Warsaw ghetto uprising, Tuwim wrote an essay titled "Pomnik i mogila" ("The Memorial and the Grave"), which is a kind of supplement to the former. It is written in a similar lofty style and includes some earlier ideas. The poet states that he has come to the site of the former ghetto, "Anonymous and Faceless—so as to light the flame of humanity at this grave and in front of this memorial. Above your ashes, my beloved Jews my brothers, I light the flame of wrath." He concludes in a universalist tone by saying that "these are not just the bones of murdered Jews lying in this grave. The conscience of humankind lies buried here as well ("We Polish Jews" and "The Memorial and the Grave," *My, Żydzi polscy . . . / We, Polish Jews . . .* , ed. Chone Shmerk, Jerusalem: Magness Press 1984, p. 24).

Apart from those texts he did not really address the *Shoah* in his poetry, which might have been for various reasons: his absence from Europe at the time of destruction, inability to express his pain in the poetic form, and the fact that after the war he generally lost much of his talent, as his late works testify.

For many years Tuwim's Jewishness was downplayed in Communist Poland. He was cherished as the most important poet of the twentieth century, but his texts concerning the Holocaust and the question of his mixed identity were practically unavailable. In Israel he had a very mixed reception because of his attachment to Polish culture, which some critics considered as a form of betrayal. In the United States he is almost unknown largely because of the untranslatability of his poetry characterized by complex rhymes, musicality, and lexical experiments.

Bibliography

Primary Sources

Czyhanie na Boga (Stalking God). 1918.
Sokrates tańczący (Dancing Socrates). 1920. English edition: *Dancing Socrates and Other Poems.* 1968. Selected and transl. by Adam Gillon, New York: Twayne Publishers.
Siódma jesień (The Seventh Autumn). 1922.
Czary i czarty polskie, oraz Wypisy czarnoksięskie (Polish Imps and Charms and Magical Stanzas). 1923.
Wierszy tom czwarty (The Fourth Volume of Poems). 1923.
Słowa we krwi (Words in Blood). 1926.
Rzecz czarnoleska (The Czarnolas Speech). 1929.
Biblia cygańska (The Gypsy Bible). 1933.
Jarmark rymów (The Fair of Rhymes). 1934.
Treść gorejąca (Fiery Essence). 1936.
Kwiaty polskie (Polish Flowers) 1949.
Pegaz dęba czyli Panopticum poetyckie (Flabbergasted Pegasus, or Poetic Panopticum). 1950.
Dzieła (Collected Works), 5 volumes. 1955–1964.
Cicer cum caule, czyli groch z kapustą: panopticum i archiwum kultury (Cicer cum Caule, or Mish-Mash: Panopticum and the Archives of Culture), 3 volumes. 1958–1963.
My, Żydzi polscy (*We, Polish Jews*). 1984.

Secondary Sources

Gross, Natan. *Poeci i Szoa.* Sosnowiec: Offmax, 1993.
Miłosz, Czesław. *A History of Polish Literature.* New York, 1969.
Ozick, Cynthia. *The Shawl.* New York: Vintage Books, 1990.

Ana Vásquez-Bronfman

(1947–)

MAGDALENA MAIZ-PEÑA

ANA VÁSQUEZ-BRONFMAN was born on 18 December 1947 in Santiago, Chile, into a family of two. She graduated from the University of Chile in Santiago, majoring in psychology and minoring in French, and was a professor there from 1967 to 1973. Since her exile from Chile in 1974 after the coup d'état undertaken by General Augusto Pinochet on 11 September 1973, she has lived in France. She earned her Ph.D. in psychology from the Sorbonne, and she has since been a researcher at the National Center for Scientific Research.

In her writings, Ana Vásquez-Bronfman represents the crude reality of daily life under a military dictatorship that governs through the systematic violation of human rights disguised under the rubric of a "war against subversion." She draws on both of her cultural heritages, Jewish and Latin American, to produce narratives that have significantly contributed to forging a Latin American Jewish discourse.

The Holocaust as Metanarrative

Although her writings bring into play mainly Latin American sociopolitical realities, the Nazi Holocaust is always a frame of reference and a significant underlying subtext of her stories, regardless of names, places, dates, events, or specific contexts. Her socially marginalized characters struggle for survival, fiercely resist tyranny, reaffirm their beliefs and pride in themselves, and undertake a collective spiritual fight for dignity, freedom, and social justice.

Ana Vásquez-Bronfman's short story "The Sign of the Star" (1999) is the strongest example of a narrative that is set in a Latin American context but is translated and filtered through analogies to and images of the Holocaust. The story is narrated from the perspective of seven-year-old Elias, who is terrorized by his second-grade classmates. They threaten and abuse him during his waking hours, haunt him in his sleep and eventually invade his feverish delirium. Vásquez-Bronfman goes beyond the depiction of Christian antisemitism in the South American cultural context as she foregrounds the religious basis of anti-Jewish discrimination in a predominantly Catholic society, although the author stages the subsequent drama in Holocaust terms, patterning the antagonists' behavior and the victim's response in ways that clearly reference the Nazi program of racially based subjugation and genocide.

Thus, upon discovering a Jewish boy in their midst, the story's predominantly Catholic Chilean children and their English Protestant classmate devise and institute a program of intimidation and abuse against seven-year-old Elias. Their remarks reveal that their cruelty is based in Christian rejection of the nonbeliever: "Only dogs are Jewish. Because, of course, in the song about who killed Jesus, you have to answer, 'the Jewish dog' " ("The Sign of the Star," in *The House of Memory: Stories by Jewish Women Writers of Latin America*, edited by Majorie Agosín, translated by Elizabeth Horan, New York: Feminist Press, 1999, p. 113). Similarly when the tormentors announce to Elias that they have decided not to speak to him anymore—"From now on, no one will be able to talk to you"—the group leader explains, "My father says you belong to the race that killed Christ" (p. 117).

Just as European Jewry was subjected to an incremental program of discrimination and violence prior to ghettoization, deportation, and annihilation, so Elias is isolated for insult and condemnation as a Jew: "they all took pains to respect his exile, and if someone accidentally spoke to him, another would give him a shove, to say, 'It's forbidden.' At recess they turned on him deliberately. They walked faster in the street so that he couldn't catch up with them. Their glances slid over his as if he didn't exist" (p. 118). As hostilities escalate, the group passes Elias a note: "JEWS TO THE CREMATORIUM" (p. 122). Vásquez-Bronfman introduces the word "crematorium" four times; it is uttered by the boys as a threat and as an accompaniment to violence, and Elias also hears it in his terror-filled imagination. Elias imagines "they were sending him to the crematorium . . . asphyxiating him with smoke" (p. 126). When the boys finally drag Elias off to a concealed corner of the school grounds to beat him, their warning—"We're going to burn you, . . . you'll die in sin. Heretic" (p. 126)—evokes the history of anti-Jewish persecution from the church-instituted pyres of the Inquisition to the twentieth-century technological advances of the Nazi crematoria. "First," the terrified child is told, "We're going to brand you with a J so you'll know why" (p. 126), a reference that directly recalls European identity cards marked with a J to distinguish Jewish citizens from other nationals. The boy alternately loses and regains consciousness, at times suffering delirium, "smell[ing] the smoke, escaping from the crematorium" (p. 127).

Just as Vásquez-Bronfman carefully plots the boys' aggression in ways evocative of the Holocaust, so too, Elias's response is mapped in a form reminiscent of the *Shoah.* Like some victims of antisemitism, he fantasizes about being part of the majority culture, denying his own heritage. Like the assimilated Jews of Germany, Elias is bewildered that his ancestral connection is grounds for abuse. Like the Jews of eastern European countries who felt the ire of their neighbors and initially welcomed ghettoization as a safe haven from neighborly violence, Elias maintains his distance from the group, avoiding eye contact "as if hiding his eyes would prevent them from identifying him and he would become truly transparent, invisible" (p. 120). He stills his voice, refusing to give correct answers in class for fear of antagonizing his jealous classmates. The tension is manifested in daily terror during the confrontations he endures, and it follows him into sleep as nightmares of assault. Nightmares of defeat ultimately become dreams of resistance, however, and the boy—like the Diaspora Jews of Europe, who "learned it was always best to keep silent"—"continues fighting in his dreams" (p. 124), until he finally does fight back and refuses the innocent teacher's request to shake the hand of his opponent, "like a gentleman."

The title of the story signifies the six-pointed Star of David, which Jews were required to wear by Nazi decree as a means of identifying them as targets, as well as the star of volition, worn by the post-Holocaust generation as a sign of pride in cultural identity and in solidarity with those who suffered under the star. Elias's aunt explains that she wears the star "because your grandparents died over there . . . It's my history, what ties me to them" (p. 125). The story concludes with the Chilean-Jewish boy's decision to wear his dead mother's star proudly, for "that way they'll all know what I am" (p. 128).

In a brief fast-forward, Vásquez-Bronfman departs from the present time of the narrative to incorporate another theme common to Holocaust literature, the survivor syndrome. She projects Elias as an adult, "a doctor and successful in life"; yet, like a Holocaust survivor, "he would still feel that ache in his chest, that anguish. As though at any moment they could again turn their backs on him, exclude him because of what he was" (p. 123). Vásquez-Bronfman recognizes in this reflection the permanent open wound that is antisemitism, whether in its religious or racial manifestation. Yet the next generation's acceptance of the legacy, of "the sign of the star"—for Elias a way of honoring his mother and his identity—is a persistent theme in post-Holocaust Jewish consciousness.

The Politics of Latin America

While the Holocaust of the European continent provides a frame of reference for her fiction, Vásquez-Bronfman contextualizes her work in her personal experience of the South American genocide of the 1970s and 1980s. She writes of the torture, suffering, and persecution of the disappeared, the mourning of those in exile, the identity crisis of the refugees, and the constant challenges brought on to the second generation by the dislocation and displacement of the Diaspora. Her memories from the political assault on Salvador Allende's socialist regime (1970–1973) elected by popular majority in Chile, her asylum at the embassy at the verge of the coup, and her relationship with the political refugees with whom she worked on a professional level in France weave through her writings and form the lifeline of her stories.

Les bisons, les bonzes, et le depotoir (The Bison, the Leaders, and the Rubbish, 1977) is a sociopolitical, gendered, and cultural microcosm that captures different facets of the ideological and political landscape in Chile after the coup d'état by Pinochet. It represents the ideologies of those in favor and against the coup and of those who had worked for Allende's political agenda. Based on the two months Vásquez-Bronfman spent at an embassy while waiting for a safe pass to leave her country, the novel portrays the distance, frictions, and fragmentations of the refugees inside the embassy. As conditions deteriorate both inside and outside, the refugees express their distrust, resentment, class hate, ideological disagreement, and mutual accusations. The bison represent the left, and many of them belonged to the Communist Party; the leaders represent the petite bourgeoisie, and many of them supported the Socialist Party and Allende's political agenda; the rubbish are those considered the trash of society. The story line and the dialogue capture the mood as the totalitarian regime settles in. The uncertain future of refugees, with their anguished questions about the fate of their loved ones; the anticipation of further oppressive tactics of the Pinochet dictatorship; the image of Chile as a grand prison; the disillusion and dismay imprinted on people's faces; the naïvité and incredulity of the faithful supporters of the populist regime; the general sense of hopelessness and demoralization among Chileans, masked by the dictatorship and the news media who insistently portray Chile as an idyllic nation are all filtered through in this microcosm.

Subsequent novels continue Vásquez-Bronfman's political themes. *Abel Rodríguez y sus hermanos* (Abel Rodriguez and His Brothers, 1981) captures the fragmentation of a family under the dictatorship. The three Rodriguez sons embrace different ideological positions reflecting the state of the nation as the Allende populist government reaches its end. *Sebasto's Angel* (1987), which Ana Vásquez-Bronfman coauthored with her son Cacho Vásquez, centers on the experience of the next generation in a new culture. This bi-generational novel, like many second-generation Holocaust novels, explores the different aspects of the identity crisis faced by the offspring of refugees, of learning to live in a foreign culture and being a product of multiple cultures. Her experimental novel *Mi amiga Chantal* (*My Friend Chantal*, 1991) revolves around the problematic of a double exile. Vivid scenes convey the details of life in Santiago during the dictatorship: books in flames, newspaper lists of the decreased, photos of "subversives" posted around the city, rumors of kidnappings and torture, and the sense always of being under the vigilant and policing gaze of the military.

Ana Vásquez-Bronfman's writings beckon the reader to new forms of knowledge and shared worlds of experience. Her translation of the Holocaust macronarrative to Chilean political upheaval provides a critical referential frame for understanding the Latin American situation, demonstrating the significance of the Holocaust beyond the borders and national boundaries of World War II.

Bibliography

Primary Sources

Les bisons, les bonzes, et le depotoir (*The Bison, the Leaders, and the Rubbish*). 1977.

Algunos problemas psicológicos de la situación de exilio (Some Psychological Problems of the Experience of Exile). 1979.

Abel Rodríguez y sus hermanos (Abel Rodríguez and His Brothers). 1981.

Adolescents from the Southern Cone of Latin American Exile: Some Psychological Problems. 1981.

Analicemos los problemas de los que no hablamos nunca: Algunas ideas para iniciar la discusión (Initiatives for the Analysis of Problems of Those Who Never Talk: Fundamentals to Initiate Discussion). 1981.

"Mujer fácil" (Easy Woman). 1983.

"El Hotel de la ballena verde" (The Green Whale Hotel). 1984.

"Pequeñas revoluciones sin importancia" (Little Revolutions Without Importance). 1984.

Sebasto's Angel. With Cacho Vásquez. 1985.

"The Doubts of a Bigamist." 1986.

"Eloísa o los tiempos del exilio" (Eloise or the Time of Exile). 1987.

"Elegancia" (Elegance). 1989.

"Le bilinguisme chez les enfants d'exiles: Affectivité et stratégies d'identité" (Bilingualism and the Children of Those in Exile: Affectivity and Identity Strategies). 1991.

Mi amiga Chantal (My Friend Chantal). 1991.

"Ritos funerarios" (Funerary Rites). 1992.

La maldición de Ulises: Repercusiones psicológicas del exilio (Ulysses's Curse: The Psychological Impact of the Experience of Exile). With Ana María Araujo. 1995.

La socialización en la escuela y la integración de los niños (Childhood Socialization and Integration to School). 1995.

"The Sign of the Star." 1999.

Secondary Sources

Alegría, Fernando. "La novela chilena del exilio interior." *Revista chilena de literatura* 42 (August 1993): 13–17.

Araujo, Helena. "Las huellas del 'propio camino' en los relatos de Ana Vásquez." *Escritura* 16, nos. 31–32 (January–December 1991): 9–16.

Blanco, Guillermo. "Novela rock a cuatro manos." *Hoy*, 16 March 1987, pp. 47–49.

Calderón, Alfonso. "*Los búfalos, los jerarcas, y la huesera.*" *Apsi*, 16 May 1988, pp. 52–53.

Cunningham, Lucía-Guerra. "Vigilancia y confesión en *Abel Rodríguez y sus hermanos*." *Literatura chilena* 8, no. 3 (July–Sept 1984): 7–8.

Díaz, Carolina. "Ana Vásquez escritora." *Análisis* 17 March 1987, p. 41.

Donoso, Claudia. "Los enjambres de una chilena en el exilio." *Apsi*, 8 June 1987, pp. 49–50.

Gebhardt, Sara. "Constructing the Self: Child Narrative in Jewish–Latin American Literature." Honors thesis, Davidson College, 1998.

Gligo, Agata. "Los búfalos, los jerarcas, y la huesera." *Mensaje*, May 1988, pp. 177–178.

Kaminsky, Amy K. *After Exile: Writing the Latin American Diaspora*. Minneapolis: University of Minnesota Press, 1999.

Loach, Barbara Lee. "Power and Women's Writing in Chile: 1973–1988." Ph.D. diss., Ohio State University, 1991.

Martin, Leona. "Ana Vásquez." In *Escritoras chilenas: Novela y cuento*. Edited by Patricia Rubio. Santiago: Editorial Cuarto Propio, 1999: 423–434.

Morganroth Schneider, Judith. "Ana Vásquez: Interrogantes sobre el exilio y la identidad." *Alba de América* 6, nos. 10–11 (July 1988): 225–234.

Ríos, Patricio. "¿Historias de la novela o novelas de la historia?" *Cauce*, 4 May 1987, p. 30.

Vidal, Virginia. "*El exilio* y *La maldición de los Ulises*." *Punto final*, 10 September 1990, p. 22.

Interview

Interview by Erna Pfeiffer. In her *Exiliadas, emigrantes, viajeras: Encuentros con diez escritoras latinoamericanas*. Madrid: Iberoamericana, 1995, pp. 177–195.

BERNARDO VERBITSKY
(1907–1979)

DARRELL B. LOCKHART

BERNARDO VERBITSKY WAS BORN on 22 November 1907 in Buenos Aires, Argentina, to parents who had come to Argentina from Russia as part of the wave of immigrants (Jewish and otherwise) who flocked there between 1880 and 1920. In his autobiographical novel *Hermana y sombra* (Sister and Shadow, 1977), Verbitsky describes poverty as the sister and shadow of his early family life and the general immigrant experience. Verbitsky's upbringing in a lower-class working family made him sensitive to the plight of the poor and working classes. Through his parents' sacrifice he was able to attend the university where he studied journalism, medicine, law, as well as the humanities.

Working for twenty years as a journalist and as editor for journals such as the Jewish publication *Davar*, Verbitsky also wrote some twenty works of fiction and three volumes of literary criticism. He established himself as a central figure in Argentine literature, particularly known for his works of social realism. He belonged to the Boedo group of writers, a politically motivated group of authors who cultivated the idea of literature as means of political protest. This stood in direct opposition to the Florida group—headed by Jorge Luis Borges—which preferred to view literature in strictly aesthetic terms. Verbitsky received numerous literary awards and prizes throughout his career, which include the Ricardo Güiraldes Award (1941), the Alberto Gerchunoff Award (1965), and the Faja de Honor (Sash of Honor) twice from the SADE (Argentine Writers Association). He died on 15 March 1979.

En esos años

While Verbitsky embraced his Jewish identity and was active in the Jewish community of Buenos Aires, relatively few of his works deal with specifically Jewish themes, and even fewer with specific Holocaust-related issues. Nevertheless, having determined this, one cannot overlook two significant texts that make valuable contributions to Holocaust literature. *En esos años* (In Those Years, 1947), although like Verbitsky's other novels in its social realism, uniquely surpasses the borders of Buenos Aires to address the problem of the war(s) in Europe. A *cronica cuasiperiodistica*, or pseudojournalistic chronicle (Senkman, p. 375), beginning in 1936 with the Spanish Civil War and continuing through the defense of Stalingrad and the end of World War II, *En esos años* examines the war and interpretations of it, specifically with regard to Jewish issues. The crux of the novel is the dilemma of Enrique Goldberg, the journalist protagonist who covers the events in Europe as they unfold and seeks to reconcile his Jewishness with a universalist view of the Holocaust. He struggles greatly with the idea that Jewish persecution at the hands of the Third Reich should be viewed as a strictly Jewish problem or event, for he sees this type of labeling as playing back into the very tenets of Nazi ideology. While denying the Christian notion of the "Jewish victim" and rejecting the social dichotomy that such a term suggests, he will not (cannot?) allow himself to feel more sympathetic toward atrocities committed against Jews than the many other atrocities of the war. In a passage compressing the complexity of issues, Goldberg's struggle with the tactics of the Anti Antisemitic Committee, who by using the label "Jews" as they decry Hitler's atrocities incite Hitler to kill all the more Jews, leads to a questioning of the meaning of Jewish identity:

> I can't avoid it, that Anti Antisemitic Committee makes me laugh: they give lectures, print pamphlets, and try to stir up the world because Hitler has killed millions and millions of Jews. I have one question. Why do they adopt Hitler's own terminology. At least they could say that they killed ten thousand men under the pretext of being Jewish. That label: the Jews. It's horrible. It's criminal. You can't modify vocabulary, but it's not just a matter of words. As long as they say that in such and such place they have murdered so many Jews, they are only inciting them to

> kill more. If it is a grave offense that the Jew in those individuals should die, then after all, at the very least, that the human being in them, which is as unquestionably true as the Jew, should die is equally as offensive (*Futuro,* 1947, p. 358, translation mine).

Senkman sees this attitude as a manifestation of Goldberg's "denial of his specific and particular difference" in relation to the rest of the population (p. 377). Verbitsky's character struggles with internalized antisemitism, as he attempts to distance himself from being labeled as a Jew and is typical of the completely assimilated and secularized Buenos Aires Jewish population concerned with fitting in as *porteños* (inhabitants of Buenos Aires). Likewise, Goldberg is a member of the Argentine political left, which demanded the erasure of expressions of Jewish identity, as these were viewed as a threat to party loyalty. A foil character to Goldberg is Pedro Lascano, another Argentine journalist who chronicles the events of the Holocaust as a Jewish tragedy. He decries the Latin American indifference to the Jewish situation in Europe, citing, for example, the Cuban refusal to grant refuge to the nine hundred aboard the ocean liner *Saint Louis* who were then forced to return to Nazi Europe.

Because of its presentation of such identity issues and competing Argentine sympathies during World War II—although officially neutral, Argentina's sympathy with the Axis powers has been well documented—*En esos años* serves forcefully as a sociocultural document of the time. As David William Foster points out.

> Verbitsky's novel is based on the representation of the tremendous preoccupation with the war in Argentina, particularly in Buenos Aires, with its millions of immigrants and sons and daughters of immigrants, its extensive commercial ties to Europe, and the fundamental conviction that the Argentine metropolis is a far-flung European capital (p. 74).

In the short story "La Culpa" ("The Flaw," found in *A pesar de todo*, 1978, and *The Silver Candelabra and Other Stories*), Verbitsky invents an allegory of the Holocaust to communicate the idea that the Holocaust should not be viewed as a uniquely Jewish event. Again we see in this story what Senkman calls Verbitsky's *ecumenismo humanista* (humanist ecumenicism, p. 382). Anchoring this tale historically with a single allusion to Treblinka, Verbitsky places it in an unnamed country ruled by the authoritarian power of *El Absoluto*. When a physical defect (a fused metatarsal bone) is discovered (quite by accident) to be common among a certain group of citizens, they are singled out for separation from the rest of society, lose their rights, and are eventually targeted for extermination. The story details how the controversy over this defect grows to become a popular movement that sweeps the fictional nation and results in the establishment of a Them/Us dichotomy that defines political boundaries. Although Verbitsky avoids making his story specific to Jewish experience, the allegory is obvious, and is even signaled by Verbitsky's use of a semiotic marker such as the choice of a physical defect paralleling the Nazis' identification of flat feet as a sign of Jewish physical-biological inferiority (Gilman). Thus, while it is an allegory for a broader interpretation, the text is clearly founded in the Jewish experience under Hitler's regime. It also alludes to other instances of mass destruction during World War II, namely the bombing of Hiroshima. This is an issue of concern for Verbitsky and one he expressed in his only volume of poetry, *Megatón* (Megaton, 1959).

The majority of Verbitsky's writing focuses on themes germane to Argentine social reality, and this has been the focus of the majority of criticism as well. Nevertheless, Verbitsky is considered to be one of the major Jewish authors of Latin America and there does exist a critical appraisal of his work in this regard. Senkman and Foster are the two critics who have specifically addressed the texts discussed here in relation to Holocaust literature. Verbitsky is unique in his outlook with regard to the Holocaust, most evident in *En esos años*, which is the main reason his works on this topic merit a broader reading public.

Bibliography

Primary Sources

En esos años. (In those years). 1947.

Megatón (Megaton). 1959.

Hermana y sombra (Sister and shadow). 1977, 1992.

"La culpa." In *A pesar de todo*. Caracas: Monte Avila, 1978, pp. 137–166.

"The Flaw." In *The Silver Candelabra and Other Stories: A Century of Jewish Argentine Literature*. Edited by Rita Gardiol. Pittsburgh: Latin American Literary Review Press, 1997, pp. 31–48.

Secondary Sources

Foster, David William. "The Formation of a Critical Argentine Consciousness in Bernardo Verbitsky's *En esos años*." In *Social Realism in the Argentine Narrative*. Chapel Hill: North Carolina Studies in the Romance Languages and Literatures/ UNC Department of Romance Languages, 1986, pp. 73–89.

Gardiol, Rita. "Bernardo Verbitsky." In *Jewish Writers of Latin America: A Dictionary*. Edited by Darrell B. Lockhart. New York: Garland, 1997, pp. 553–565.

Gilman, Sander. "The Jewish Foot: A Foot-Note to the Jewish Body." In *The Jew's Body*. New York: Routledge, 1991, pp. 38–59.

Senkman, Leonardo. *La identidad judía en la literatura argentina*. Buenos Aires: Pardés, 1983, pp. 365–382.

Ana Vinocur

(1926–)

DARRELL B. LOCKHART

Born 25 September 1926 in Lodz, Poland, Ana Benkel was the middle child and only daughter of Henoch and Rifka Benkel. Her family managed to remain together for a time in the Lodz ghetto, but they were eventually separated. Ana worked in a carpet factory, once a school, where she received a bowl of soup per day for her labor. Her father died in Auschwitz (1944) and her mother in Stutthof (1945). Her younger brother, deemed too young to be useful to the workforce, was sent to Chelmno; she never saw him again. She was also separated from her older brother, Herschek, but after the war the two were miraculously reunited in Uruguay where he took the name Enrique. Ana herself had been taken to Auschwitz, Stutthof, and aboard a ship in the Baltic Sea to be used as a human shield against Allied bombardment. After liberation, Ana Benkel immigrated to Uruguay, via Italy, where she met her husband, Alberto Vinocur. As a Holocaust survivor, Vinocur has been active not only through her writing but also by speaking. Her first book, *Un libro sin título* (A Book Without a Title, 1972) is held in the Yad Vashem archives in Israel. She was also asked by Steven Spielberg to testify as a Holocaust survivor in his project, Survivors of the *Shoah* Visual History Foundation. She has recorded Holocaust-related music albums, such as *Songs of the Ghetto and Jewish Folklore* composed by her brother Enrique, in Argentina and the United States. In Uruguay she is a member and secretary of the Victims of the Holocaust Association.

Author's Works

Vinocur's *Un libro sin título* (A Book Without a Title), a novelized autobiographical narrative of events lived by the author, has become a classic. Excerpts are used today in Uruguayan schools to instruct students about the Holocaust. The title of the book is explained with the question: Does there exist a title capable of containing and expressing a story about mass murder and the extermination of a people? (Ediciones Juventa: Montevideo, 1972, p. 5). The novel begins shortly before the German invasion of Poland with the narrator reminiscing about life in Lodz before the Nazi terror began. It describes the rise of the Nazi threat, the establishment of the Lodz ghetto, and the details of life there and their emotional toll on families. Sardonically describing ghetto elder Chaim Rumkowski as *"nuestro rey"* (our king), Vinocur provides insight into the factory system, explaining her work at the carpet factory and her brother's work at a chocolate factory and later in a metallurgy shop. In addition, she narrates the arrival of five thousand gypsies to the ghetto and how they were unable to adapt, many falling ill and the remainder being shipped off to be killed in a concentration camp when the Germans realized they were not productive as a workforce. She also details her experiences in Auschwitz and Stutthof, concentrating mainly on the difficult dealings with the notoriously cruel camp *kapos*. In the following excerpt the author compares the two camps just after her arrival to Stutthof.

> The number I received is 74.451. . . .
>
> I am observing the camp and I see that it is somewhat different from Auschwitz. Here each barrack is separated by wire, while at the other camp they were fenced off in groups of ten or more. At any rate, it makes no difference to us. When we entered the block there were already women there, some from Lithuania and Hungary.
>
> They tell us that the *blokova*, that's what they call the capo in Polish, is very cruel and that it's best to steer clear of her. I cannot believe that someone who appears to be so delicate could be so cruel. But I suppose I should listen to the advice of my captive sisters. They have no cause to lie to me (pp. 163–164, translation mine).

The book essentially spans the years 1939 to 1945 with Vinocur taking the reader on a terrifying journey of her lived nightmare. Scenes in the ghetto and concentration camps are described with the simple realism of one who was there and witnessed what she is recounting. Unencumbered by extensive use of metaphor and other literary tropes, her text voices a sense of sincerity that outweighs preoccupation with style. She ends her story with her hospitalization after being liberated. *Sin título* is not a literary masterpiece, but it is an honest and at times heart-wrenching testimony.

Her second book, *Luces y sombras después de Auschwitz* (Lights and Shadows After Auschwitz, 1991), begins where *Sin título* ended. This book, a collection of four interrelated short stories describing her experiences immediately following the war, begins with her hospitalization and ends with the story of her journey to Uruguay, where she is reunited with her brother. One of the underlying themes of the volume is the state of chaos in Europe following the war and the uncertainty of the future. The narrator struggles to make sense of what she has been through and how to proceed with any sense of normalcy following so many years of suffering and anguish. Specifically she struggles to regain her health, at least enough to begin life anew as best she can, wherever she can. Although Vinocur's tone is one of emotional detachment, her texts do not seem fictional because the author's voice is always present to explain details, add information, and clarify that the experiences narrated are her own. This is done either intratextually or through the use of footnotes. *Luces y sombras* also contains several photographs of Vinocur as a young girl with her family prior to the war as well as archival photos of concentration camps, the Lodz ghetto, and documents. Vinocur's writing testifies to the suffering and loss occasioned by Hitler as she discusses the ideology of Nazism, the numerous medical experiments carried out on Jews under Hitler's regime, and the nature of life for Jews in concentration camps. Furthermore, Vinocur explores the psychological ramifications of surviving the *Shoah* beginning with the reunion with her brother:

> I couldn't believe it when I saw Herschek, my brother. I could scarcely speak from the emotion. We hugged and kissed each other, and I thought I was dreaming. Destiny had marked us with so much suffering, but it also chose us to survive the Holocaust and be witnesses to this story (pp. 116–117, translation mine).

These are some of the shadows to which the title refers. The lights, she explains at the end of the book, are her husband, children, and grandchildren.

In 1999 the Uruguayan Ministry of Education and Culture published an expanded version of *Luces y sombras* under the title *Volver a vivir después de Auschwitz* (Living Again After Auschwitz). To the original text are appended three testimonial essays, family and archival photos, and copies of documents. In "Nuevos horizontes" (New Horizons), the author explains how she adjusted to life in Uruguay, how she met her husband, and how she has been active in Holocaust education and testimony. In "La marcha por la vida 1996" (The March for Life 1996), Vinocur describes her return trip to Poland with Enrique after fifty years of absence to participate in the March for Life. This section contains many photographs of her brother and her at Auschwitz, where they both had been held and their father killed. Vinocur speaks openly and passionately about her emotions during this trip. Finally, in "El increíble encuentro" (The Incredible Encounter), she tells how she was able to reestablish contact with a Christian Polish family who had been close to her own when they were young children in Lodz.

Ana Vinocur must be considered one of the most important survivor voices from Latin America. Her contribution to Holocaust literature in Spanish is second only to that of Simja Sneh and is an invaluable resource. She clearly feels responsible for providing testimony about the Holocaust so that future generations will be aware of this tragic period in history, that it not be repeated. Critical appraisal of her work, unfortunately, has not yet been undertaken in any serious manner. Although her works have received favorable reviews, gone through several editions, and are graced with enthusiastic prefaces, there remains to date no analysis of her work either as literature or testimonial writing.

Bibliography

Primary Sources

Un libro sin título. (A Book without a Title). 1972, 1976.

Songs of the Ghetto and Jewish Folklore. Brooklyn: Greater Recording Co., 1976. Yiddish sound recording.

Luces y sombras después de Auschwitz. (Lights and Shadows After Auschwitz). 1991.

Volver a vivir después de Auschwitz (Living Again After Auschwitz). 1999.

EDWARD LEWIS WALLANT
(1926–1962)

S. LILLIAN KREMER

BORN IN NEW Haven to Sol Ellis and Ann Mendel Wallant on 19 October 1926, Wallant followed military service in the U.S. Navy during World War II in Europe with work as a commercial artist until he received critical acclaim for his early publications. *The Human Season* (1960) was honored with the Jewish Book Council Fiction Award and later, the Danoff Memorial Fiction Prize. A Breadloaf Writer's Conference Fellowship offered further confirmation of his budding talent. Publication of his second novel, *The Pawnbroker* (1961), brought immediate critical recognition and a Guggenheim Fellowship. He resigned from his position as art director at McCann, Erickson to travel in Europe and rewrite drafts for two additional novels. He returned in 1962 with the completed manuscript for his third novel, *The Tenants of Moonbloom* (1963), and drafts for his fourth novel. Published after his death, *The Children at the Gate* (1964) was extensively edited by Dan Wickendon of Harcourt, Brace. Posthumous honors include a citation by the New Haven Festival of Arts for outstanding literary contributions and establishment of the Edward Lewis Wallant Memorial Book Award, for Wallant who died, at the height of his brief career, on 5 December 1962, of a stroke.

The Holocaust

The Pawnbroker established methods that have since become standard devices of American Holocaust fiction. The Holocaust is a major component of theme, narrative, and character constructs; the central focus of a survivor-protagonist's consciousness. The main character is surrounded by a survivor chorus and the Holocaust era is evoked through involuntary and spontaneous recollection and dreams. In Nazerman's portrait, Wallant created a figure whose sensibility and behavior constitute the components isolated by later theorists as central to posttraumatic stress disorder as "a response sometimes delayed to an overwhelming event or events, which takes the form of repeated, intrusive hallucinations, dreams, thoughts or behaviors stemming from the event, along with numbing that may have begun during or after the experience, and possibly arousal to (and avoidance of) stimuli recalling the event" (Caruth, p. 2).

The Pawnbroker's structural unity evolves from a series of dramatic dichotomies: Holocaust-era Europe and America of the late 1950s; Sol Nazerman's pre and post-*Shoah* experience; juxtaposition of Holocaust survivors with prewar immigrants and native-born Americans; and juxtaposition of the Holocaust landscape with that of an African-American ghetto neighborhood. These contrapuntal elements offer readers bridges to the concentration camp universe.

The novel is set during the summer of 1958, in ghetto Harlem and suburban Westchester, remote in time and place from Buchenwald and Bergen-Belsen. The survivor, forty-five-year-old Sol Nazerman, still bears physical and psychological wounds suffered in a Nazi medical experiment: "A piece of his pelvic bone missing, two of his ribs gone, and his collarbone slanted in weird misdirection" (*The Pawnbroker*, New York: Harcourt Brace Jovanovich, 1961, p. 37). Psychically scarred by Holocaust loss of all he held dear, he maintains an emotional barrier to keep contemporaries at a safe distance, reluctantly engaging in meaningful dialogue only when an antagonist provokes him. Holocaust experience has taught Nazerman that an external force may arbitrarily sunder the human bond and he, therefore, passionately resists intimate personal relationships. The *Shoah* accounts for Nazerman's ironic occupational metamorphosis from cultured professor to pawnbroker, a grotesque adoption of the "much maligned calling," the hateful money-lender role long and ardently assigned the Jew by Christian Europe in its religion, art, and politics. Although he still reads Chekhov and Tolstoy, he generally denigrates his pre-Holocaust values and interests, insisting: "I do not trust God or politics or newspapers or music or art. . . . But most of all, I do not trust people and their talk, for they have created hell with that talk" (pp. 114–115).

Juxtaposing pre- and post-Holocaust immigrants, those who sought economic opportunity with those who sought refuge from the hell of concentration and death camps, is the method whereby Wallant astutely underscores the survivor's alienation. Sol Nazerman is philosophically and psychologically estranged from his bourgeois sister who escaped the European catastrophe by prewar migration in search of economic advancement and assimilation to the good life. Whereas she rejects postwar perpetuation of Holocaust trauma, urging her brother to enjoy life, Sol cannot dismiss the past as past because it is his present and will be his future.

Cameo appearances of three additional survivors whose *Shoah* responses and sensibilities echo and contrast with Nazerman's postwar attitudes enlarge the novel's Holocaust canvas. The survivor community acts as a Greek chorus whose comments and behavior provide a gauge by which to measure the protagonist. Instead of love, Sol and his mistress share a common Holocaust legacy of loss, each bereft of marriage partner and children; each harboring memories and visions of the murder of their loved ones. Complementing Sol's Holocaust-wrought bitter assertiveness, Tessie is docile and easily bullied by another survivor playing on her guilt. Haunted by Bergen-Belsen memories, her only respite is rationalization that the dead are better off than the living. While the passionless union confirms Sol's emotional desolation, it reveals him as a charitable human being, the financial benefactor of Tessie and her ailing father, whose gallows humor echoes Sol's caustic wit. Another survivor, whose postwar charitable work is motivated by apparent merited guilt for betraying his family, is distinguished from Sol's guiltless shame at his inability to save his family.

Among the moving contrapuntal character constructs underscoring the survivor's contemporary alienation is that of social worker Marilyn Birchfield, who persistently reaches out to Nazerman in genuine, albeit naive, friendship. Reared in New England Protestant security, Birchfield is, as her name implies, safely rooted in her native land and culture. Conversely, the uprooted European Jew came to America to live among strangers in physical security and emotional solitude. Birchfield grants the survivor "A great deal of sadness and grief" (p. 145), yet, in her American innocence, demands he reject bitterness. Nazerman warns that she will encounter the unbearable should she probe Holocaust reality: "There is a world so different in scale," he argues, "that its emotions bear no resemblance to yours; it has emotions so different in degree that they have become a different species!" (p. 146). This relationship is emblematic of the immediate postwar conspiracy of silence adhered to by American would-be auditors and survivors, one not entirely wanting to know and the other assuming the innocent cannot enter his universe through mere empathetic imagination.

As the anniversary of the Nazerman family deaths nears, the survivor's precarious armor of self-conscious emotional control fails. Poignantly correlating the traditional month of lamentation in the Hebrew calendar with Nazerman's time of personal grief, Wallant traces Sol's bereavement from mid-month to its culmination on 28 August. His general feelings of discomfort become concretized in the novel's urban environment.

Writing at a time and for an audience that had not yet taken the Holocaust into its consciousness as late-twentieth-century Americans have, Wallant introduces the familiar black urban ghetto as a bridge to the unfamiliar Holocaust universe. Harlem is the objective correlative of Nazerman's fractured post-Holocaust existence. Wallant's ghetto is realistic and metaphoric; evoking the tormented mental state of a man remembering his brutalized family, a man in mourning for his slaughtered innocents. Dark images of filth, disease, and pollution objectify the survivor's weariness with life and his own sense of impending collapse. Paralleling the city's physical deterioration are Nazerman's physical manifestations of psychic malaise, "pressure in him, a feeling of something underneath, which caused the growing tremors on the surface of him" (p. 155). As the pawnbroker waits on the subway platform, his train approaches in a yellow beam of blinding light and thunderous roar, assaulting the passenger, "like a projectile . . . rushing to swallow him up" (p. 155). The yellow light evokes yellow stars embossed with the word "JUDE" that Jews had to affix to their outer clothing; the crowded city train recalls the congested deportation cattle cars. By setting the novel in the midst of American ghetto degradation, Wallant enables his readers to follow the survivor's free association, nightmare, and spontaneous recollection of Holocaust horrors.

Representative of Wallant's use of contemporary events as a gateway to the more traumatic past is Sol's encounter with a Harlem prostitute. As he gives the woman the money she seeks, while declining her invitation to exploit her, memories of his wife's violation in a Nazi brothel barrack flood the survivor's consciousness. He is "lost in some nameless graveyard of thought" (p. 113). In a failed effort to redirect his thinking from "burial with things he had left behind forever," his face reveals "graveyard horror, as at something exhumed" (p. 113). That Nazerman's efforts to repress his memories of Ruth's trauma are futile is foreshadowed as he drinks a nightcap from a ritual memorial glass. The oblivion he hopes sleep will bring proves illusive as he dreams of being forced to watch a black uniformed SS officer compel Ruth to commit fellatio, an expression similar to the traumatic "deep memory" as opposed to "ordinary memory" that French survivor, author Charlotte Delbo describes. As the grieved, shamed husband tries to turn away from the sordid spectacle, he is repeatedly struck and made to endure his wife's humiliation. In another sequence of the rape nightmare, Sol's anguish for his wife is supplanted by his own impotent anger and misplaced judgment of the victim, "*Why did she do this to him? He felt like tearing at her horrid nakedness*" (p. 224). In a world corrupted by Nazi values, the victim is denounced, the villain untouched.

Nightmare and involuntary recollection of his family's suffering bring the concentration camp universe to the forefront of the postwar setting. Nazerman's conscious will to repress the Holocaust is consistently overwhelmed by the subconscious will or need to confront the horror. In contrast to "ordinary memory" of the sort evoked by the approaching train, Nazerman's "deep memory," that which Lawrence Langer describes as memory that "tries to recall the Auschwitz self as it was then" (Langer, p. 6), emerges in a dream. Because Nazerman is unwilling, at this stage, to speak of his Holocaust history and because there is no listening audience, he nevertheless testifies, bearing witness through the dream.

In addition to serving as a barometer of the survivor's posttraumatic stress and a vehicle for transmitting *Shoah* history, the dream sequence also charts Holocaust chronology from the early stages of deportation in the cattle car transports, through the concentrationary experience, and the final crematoria destination. Dreaming of his family's transport to Buchenwald, Sol is incensed by his inability to aid his children during the long train journey through Poland, unable to rescue his son from drowning in excrement into which he has fallen. Other nightmares including the brutal murder of a crazed father whose son had recently been gassed—he was first mauled by guard dogs and then driven against a temporarily defused electrified fence—and Nazerman's own subjection to experimental surgery, convey the violence of the concentration camp universe. Vocal and thematic echoes unite and reverberate between these two scenes. Tension from the approaching anniversary of his family's slaughter, psychic revulsion at the memory of his job of loading corpses in the crematorium, and recent underworld threats on his life erupt in a dream of "A mountain of emaciated bodies, hands and legs tossed in nightmare abandon" (p. 197). Unlike earlier nightmares, this one moves from graphic description and registration of the protagonist's anger and humiliation for his own suffering at the prospect of finding his own family among the corpses, to compassion for all the victims and from a bitter to an elegiac tone, progressing Hebraically from expression of personal loss to collective bereavement. This dream ends in recognition—instead of averting his eyes he must look and bear witness.

Contemporary Harlem provides not only a bridge to Nazerman's *Shoah* past, but a plotline that yokes historic religious antisemitism with Nazi racism. In the novel's two crucifixion scenes, Nazerman's assistant, Jesus Ortiz, plots the robbery of the pawnshop in revenge for Nazerman's rejection of his pleas for business tutoring, the field he regards as a special talent of Jews. Facing his church, the Tabernacle of Jesus Our Lord, the assistant rationalizes his betrayal of Nazerman in classic antisemitic rhetoric: "I don't owe that Sheeny nothin' really. What is he to me?" (p. 202). The impoverished black Hispanic echoes the historic European envy of the propertied Jew, and exaggeration of Jewish economic power to justify anti-Jewish aggression. During his prerobbery meditation, Ortiz moves from sympathetic contemplation of the crucified Jesus to sadistic contemplation of the twentieth-century Jew: "Wouldn't everybody be shocked to see Sol Nazerman up there, his arm with the blue numbers stretched out to the transfixed hand?" (p. 238). The image is underscored in a second vision of "The figure of a heavy man, awkwardly transfixed on a cross, a man with blue cryptic numbers on his arm" (p. 247). These repeated visual parallels of Holocaust victim as agonized Christ in the context of the robbery meditation imply Christian Holocaust culpability, a theology and culture that systematically taught contempt for Jews as enemies of Christendom.

The metaphoric parallel established in the crucifixion scenes is dramatically substantiated in the pawnshop robbery. On 28 August Jesus Ortiz and his friends appear to execute the robbery. The new violence, coming as it does on the anniversary of the old, echoes the past and heralds a new beginning. Because Jesus, who intends no physical harm to Nazerman, instinctively steps in the path of the bullet his associate meant for the pawnbroker, Sol mourns the "one irreplaceable Negro who had been his assistant and who tried to kill him but who ended up by saving him" (p. 279). Sol's purgative tears for Ortiz free him to express the grief he had hitherto repressed; free him to weep for all his dead. This new ability to express emotion is a significant emotional release. Having wept for those he lost, Nazerman is now able to console Tessie Rubin for the recent loss of her father and to become more involved with his sister's family as foreshadowed by his invitation to his nephew to become his new assistant. The novel's conclusion, salvation of the spirit via return to human community, is central to Judaic values and teaching.

Critical Reception

Wallant's significance in the realm of postwar Jewish American literature is judged by David Mesher to be twofold: because his first novel, dealing with the Pale of Settlement history and immigrant experience in America, "displays a higher degree of Jewish content and a greater depth of involvement in Jewish life than are to be found in work from the same period by more celebrated authors" (Mesher, "Edward Lewis Wallant," p. 313), and for his overt treatment of the Holocaust, which precedes by nearly a decade the Holocaust writing by American Jews in the late 1960s and 1970s. Of the critics who focus their attention on Wallant's Holocaust writing, Alan Berger reads *The Pawnbroker* in the context of particularizing or universalizing the *Shoah*; S. Lillian Kremer analyzes the work as an early American fiction mapping survivor syndrome. Berger charges Wallant with trivializing and wrongly universalizing the *Shoah*, "while paying scarce attention to historic detail" and is offended by Wallant's mediating Jewish suffering "through Christian symbolism" (Berger, pp. 165, 166). Kremer posits an alternate ironic interpretation distancing Wallant from the Christological redemptive message and situating him closer to the position of Rolf Hochhuth and André Schwarz-Bart in his metaphoric exposé of Christian Holocaust culpability and historic European antisemitism as prologue to the Holocaust.

Bibliography

Primary Sources

Books

The Human Season. 1960.
The Pawnbroker. 1961.
The Tenants of Moonbloom. 1963.
The Children at the Gate. 1964.
The Artist's Eyesight. 1963.

Articles and Essays

"I Held Back My Hand." In *New Voices 2: American Writing Today*. Edited by Don M. Wolfe. New York: Hendricks, 1955, pp. 192–201.

"The Man Who Made a Nice Appearance." In *New Voices 3: American Writing Today*. Edited by Charles I. Glicksberg. New York: Hendricks, 1958, pp. 336–353.

"When Ben Awakened." In *American Scene: New Voices*. Edited by Don M. Wolfe. New York: Stuart, 1963, pp. 94–100.

Archives

Wallant's papers and unpublished manuscripts are in the American Literature Collection at the Beinecke Rare Book and Manuscript Library, Yale University.

Secondary Sources

Bibliographies

Ayo, Nicholas. "Edward Lewis Wallant, 1926–1962." *Bulletin of Bibliography* 28, no. 4 (1971): 119.

Cronin, Gloria L., Blaine H. Hall, and Connie Lamb. "Edward Lewis Wallant." *Jewish American Fiction Writers: An Annotated Bibliography*. New York & London: Garland, 1991, pp. 1121–1140.

Articles and Essays

Angle, James. "Edward Lewis Wallant's 'Trinity of Survival.' " *Kansas Quarterly* 7, no. 4 (1975): 106–118.

Ayo, Nicholas. "The Secular Heart: The Achievement of Edward Lewis Wallant." *Critique* 12, no. 2 (1970): 86–94.

Baumbach, Jonathan. "The Illusion of Indifference." In *The Landscape of Nightmare: Studies in the Contemporary American Novel*. New York: New York University Press, 1965, pp. 138–151.

Becker, Ernest. "*The Pawnbroker*: A Study in Basic Psychology." In *Angel in Armor: A Post-Freudian Perspective on the Nature of Man*. New York: Braziller, 1969, pp. 73–99.

Benson, Nancy A. "When This World Is Enough: The Vision of Edward Lewis Wallant." *Cross Current* 34, no. 3 (1984): 337–342.

Berger, Alan L. "Symbolic Judaism: Edward Lewis Wallant." In *Crisis and Covenant: The Holocaust in American Jewish Fiction*. Edited by Sarah Blacher Cohen. Albany: New York State University Press, 1985, pp. 164–172.

Bilik, Dorothy Seidman. "Wallant's Reborn Immigrant and Redeemed Survivor." In *Immigrant Survivors: Post-Holocaust Consciousness in Recent Jewish American Fiction*. Middletown: Wesleyan University Press, 1985, pp. 81–100.

Bitoun, Lazare. "Edward Lewis Wallant." *Caliban* 25 (1988): 103–109.

Caruth, Cathy. *Trauma: Explorations in Memory*. Baltimore: The Johns Hopkins University Press, 1995.

———. "The Sound of Silence: Edward Lewis Wallant's *The Children at the Gate*." *Cithara* 8, no. 1 (1968): 3–25.

———. "The Renewal of Dialogical Immediacy in Edward Lewis Wallant." *Renascence* 24, no. 2 (1972): 56–69.

———. "Learning to Walk on Water: Edward Lewis Wallant's *The Pawnbroker*." *Literary Review* 17, no. 2 (1973–1974): 149–165.

———. "The Impossible Possibility: Edward Lewis Wallant's *The Tenants of Moonbloom*." *Studies in American Jewish Literature* 2 (1982): 98–114.

Davis, William V. "Images of Central Europe in the Fiction of Edward Lewis Wallant." In *Images of Central Europe in Travelogues and Fiction by North American Writers*. Edited by Waldemar Zacharasiewicz. Tubingen: Stauffenberg, 1995, pp. 268–282.

Dembo, L. M. "The Tenants of Moonbloooo-ooo." *The Monological Jew: A Literary Study*. Madison: University of Wisconsin Press, 1988, pp. 44–53.

Galloway, David. *Edward Lewis Wallant*. Boston: Twayne, 1979.

Gurko, Leo. "Edward Lewis Wallant as Urban Novelist." *Twentieth Century Literature* 20, no. 4 (1974): 252–261.

Hoyt, Charles Alva. "The Sudden Hunger: An Essay on the Novels of Edward Lewis Wallant." In *Minor American Novelists*. Carbondale: Southern Illinois University Press, 1970, pp. 118–137.

Karpowitz, Stephen. "Conscience and Cannibals: An Essay in Two Exemplary Tales—*Soul of Wood* and *The Pawnbroker*." *Psychoanalytic Review* 64 (1977): 41–62.

Klein, Marcus. "Further Notes on the Dereliction of Culture: Edward Lewis Wallant and Bruce Jay Friedman." *Contemporary American-Jewish Literature: Critical Essays*. London: Indiana University Press, 1973, pp. 229–247.

Kremer, S. Lillian. "From Buchenwald to Harlem: The Holocaust Universe of *The Pawnbroker*." In *Witness through the Imagination: Jewish American Holocaust Literature*. Detroit: Wayne State University Press, 1989, pp. 63–80.

Langer, Lawrence. *Holocaust Testimonies: The Ruins of Memory*. New Haven: Yale University Press, 1991.

Leff, Leonard J. "Hollywood and the Holocaust: Remembering *The Pawnbroker*." *American Jewish History* 84 (1996): 4, 353–376.

Lewis, Robert W. "The Hung-Up Heroes of Edward Lewis Wallant." *Renascence* 24, no. 2 (1972): 70–84.

Lorch, Thomas M. "The Novels of Edward Lewis Wallant." *Chicago Review* 19, no. 2 (1967): 78–91.

Lyons, Bonnie. "Seeing and Suffering in *The Pawnbroker* and *Mr. Sammler's Planet*." *Yiddish* 6, no. 4 (1987): 114–121.

Lyons, Joseph. "*The Pawnbroker*: Flashback in the Novel and Film." *Western Humanities Review* 20 (1966): 243–248.

Marovitz, Sanford E. "A Prophet in the Labyrinth: The Urban Romanticism of Edward Lewis Wallant." *Modern Language Studies* 15, no. 4 (1985): 172–183.

Mesher, David R. "Con Artist and Middleman: The Archetypes of Wallant's Published and Unpublished Fiction." *Yale University Library Gazette* 56, nos. 1–2 (1981): 40–49.

———. "Edward Lewis Wallant." In *Dictionary of Literary Biography: Twentieth-Century American-Jewish Fiction Writers*. Edited by Daniel Walden. Detroit: Bruccoli Clark, 1984, pp. 310–316.

Miller, Gabriel. "Those Who Walk in Darkness." In *Screening the Novel: Rediscovered American Fiction in Film*. New York: Ungar, 1980, pp. 167–191.

Parks, John G. "The Grace of Suffering: The Fiction of Edward Lewis Wallant." *Studies in American Jewish Literature* 5 (1986): 11–18.

Ribalow, Harold U. "The Legacy of Edward L. Wallant." *Chicago Jewish Forum* 22 (1964): 325–327.

Rovit, Earl. "A Miracle of Moral Animation." *Shenandoah Review* 16 (1965): 60–68.

Ruland, Richard, and Malcolm Bradbury. *From Puritanism to Postmodernism*. New York: Viking, 1991.

Stanford, Raney. "The Novels of Edward Wallant." *Colorado Quarterly* 17 (1969): 393–465.

Zaitchik, Mark, and Lisa Jucknath. "Edward Lewis Wallant." Edited by Joel Shatzky and Michael Taub. *Contemporary Jewish American Novelists: A Bio-Critical Sourcebook*. Westport: Greenwood, 1997, pp. 448–456.

CLARA WEIL
(1924–1985)

DARRELL B. LOCKHART

CLARA WEIL WAS born in 1924 in Monfalcone, Italy, a town in the northern extreme of the country. She was the oldest of three sisters born into a traditional Jewish family. Her father arrived in Italy from Poland in 1920, but the family was not to stay for long. The rise of fascism under Mussolini marked clear boundaries for Italian Jews. On 2 September 1938 Mussolini promulgated the law in defense of racial purity, which demanded that all foreign Jews leave Italy within six months. Weil's family immigrated to Argentina at the beginning of 1939. Once in Argentina, the family formed part of a growing group of Italian Jews who stood out among the rest of the Jewish population, which was comprised mostly of eastern European and Russian Jews. Clara Weil's circle of friends included Vera Jarach and Eleonora Smolensky, authors of the book *Tantas voces, una historia: Italianos judíos en la Argentina, 1938–1948* (So Many Voices, One Story: Italian Jews in Argentina), as well as the journalist Arrigo Levi, Aldo Ottolenghi, Margherita Sarfatti, and others. Another important literary figure to come out of this relatively small community of Italian Jews was Humberto Costantini.

Shortly after marrying, Weil fell ill with tuberculosis at the age of twenty-two. She was bedridden for a year, but completely regained her health. She established herself in the world of fashion and worked for thirty years in *prêt-à-porter* (ready-to-wear) clothing, traveling to Europe twice a year for fashion shows and opening three boutiques in Buenos Aires. Before leaving her career in the clothing industry, she began to write by participating in literary workshops where she wrote first under the guidance of Syria Poletti and later that of Juan Carlos Merlo. She published two collections of short stories shortly before her death in 1985.

Weil's Works

One of hundreds of Jewish authors in Argentina, Weil is unique for her poignant tales dealing with the Holocaust. Most Jewish authors in Argentina write about the immigrant experience, the process of assimilation, and the realities of being Jewish in Argentina. Weil's books *Una cruz para el judío* (A Cross for the Jew; 1982) and *Del amor y la condena* (Of Love and Conviction; 1984) reflect her experience of having spent her youth in Europe and seeing firsthand the rapid political and social change sweeping the continent. This experience must have made a lasting impression. She witnessed and lived through her family's uprooting and forced exile. Clearly, as her stories so meticulously detail, the suffering and tribulations brought on by German Nazism and Italian fascism greatly influenced her well into adulthood. She was apparently driven, at least in part, to give voice not only to Jewish suffering during the Holocaust, but to Jewish courage and determination as well.

Weil's Holocaust stories are characterized by her adherence to a somewhat stark realism, which reflects the gravity of the circumstances they describe. She is adept at describing the physical surroundings, places, and people that populate her stories, but perhaps more significant is her subtle manner of presenting the painful emotions and psychology of the characters. Unsentimental, her stories often present a situation of bitter irony. In general, her Jewish characters endure (or perish in) a variety of physical trials, which lead them to struggle with issues of hope, futility, loss of faith, desperation, and the sense that one has no control over one's own fate. Weil also presents the severe cruelty of the German soldiers, the indifference and contempt of the majority of the civilian population, the abhorrent misery of concentration camps, and the ambience of hatred to which Jews were subjected. Her stories span the duration of the war, describing the climate of the rise of Nazism in Germany and fascism in Italy, to those who suffered and perished in Treblinka, Dachau, Bergen-Belsen, Auschwitz, and Buchenwald, and finally those who survived and/or escaped. Weil does not provide detailed information or in-depth descriptions of life in concentration camps. She tends to focus more on characters in various stages of flight, migration, or other forms of wandering, underscoring the instability of Jewish life during the Holocaust and early post-Holocaust years.

The title story of Weil's first book, "Una cruz para el judío" (A Cross for the Jew), is an excellent example of the author's realism, subtlety of expression, and irony. It narrates the story of a young man who is able to escape Germany with the help of his father, who bribes a German official to omit the "J" from his son's passport, believing he will be able to travel more freely. He boards a ship that docks in Marrakesh where he disembarks, but is not allowed back on to continue the voyage. The French officials believe he is a German who is trying to escape and they hold him in a prison until he is finally able to convince them that he is Jewish and they release him. He attempts to board another ship that is heading for Buenos Aires, but again the officials do not allow him to board because his passport is not stamped with the telltale "J" identifying him as a Jewish refugee. Again they accuse him of being a German who is trying to escape. The story ends with his death from cholera one year later in Marrakesh, where he is buried with only a wooden cross to mark his grave. The story sets the mood for much of the rest of the collection in that it presents the chaos, the desperation, and the randomness of events that define the war for most of the characters.

In the story "Dios me ha castigado" (God Has Punished Me, in *Una cruz para el judío*), a young Jewish woman falls in love with and marries her childhood sweetheart—who is not Jewish—just as Hitler is gaining popularity in Germany. Her husband eventually becomes enthralled with Nazism and rejects his now-pregnant wife, who first manages to escape to France but is later imprisoned in Treblinka. She survives the war and after being liberated returns to France and marries a Jewish man, but she is haunted by images of her dead son who seems to inquire about his identity. Is he Jewish or Aryan? This story is a good example of how Weil concentrates on the psychological consequences and ramifications of interpersonal relationships (the Jewish woman with the Nazi husband, and her Jewish second husband, as well as her perception of her son) against the backdrop of specific Holocaust references such as concentration camps and descriptions of the war in general.

Other stories in *Una cruz para el judío*, such as "La culpa del otro" (The Other's Fault) and "¿ Por qué el Dios de los judíos?" (Why the God of the Jews?), seem to be much more closely related to the author's own experience. They narrate the influence of Hitler in Italy, the rise of Mussolini, and emigration to Argentina. In both cases the refugees are relieved to be out of Europe just as the war is exploding.

In *Del amor y la condena*, Weil focuses even more on the specifically Jewish Italian experience. The stories "Ventanas ciegas" (Blind Windows), "Los latidos del miedo" (The Pulses of Fear), and "El juicio va a empezar" (The Trial Is About to Begin) all take place in Italy and paint a vivid portrait of life under *Il Duce*. Her story "A cada instante me muero" (I Die Every Moment) is unique among her collection. It deals with a situation after the war in which a man on a train recognizes a Nazi tormentor and goes through a series of painful memories as he tries to subdue his feelings of panic.

Clara Weil's literary works are not extensive and have made no significant impact on Argentine literature as a whole. This is evidenced by the fact that there is virtually no critical appraisal of her writing outside of brief reviews. Unfortunately, even within the field of Latin American Jewish literature her works are not well known; a serious oversight that needs to be addressed. Nevertheless, her work does make a valuable contribution to that body of world literature that seeks to give expression to the horrendous experience of the Holocaust. Likewise, she provides important literary testimony of the sociohistoric events that unfolded in Italy in relation to Holocaust studies. Clara Weil is remembered through her literature, which speaks not only to the painful Jewish past, but more broadly to the survival and continuance of the human spirit in the face of adversity.

Bibliography

Primary Sources

Una cruz para el judío. (A Cross for the Jew). 1982.
Del amor y la condena. (Of Love and Conviction). 1984.

Secondary Sources

Spens, Susan Roman. "Weil, Clara." In *Jewish Writers of Latin America: A Dictionary*. Edited by Darrell B. Lockhart. New York: Garland, 1997, pp. 577–579.

GRETE WEIL

(1906–)

STEPHAN BRAESE

GRETE WEIL SURVIVED Nazi persecution in the occupied Netherlands. The presence of the past and the price of survival in West German postwar society were the core issues of her literary work. It took quite some time before the German Jewish writer's books received any attention among the German reading public. The "literature industry" of Weil's native country abstained altogether from granting her works the recognition they deserved. One reason for this may have been and may continue to be the incompatibility of Weil's work with a widespread desire for reconciliation.

Early Years in Germany

Grete Weil was born on 18 July 1906 in Egern, upper Bavaria. She was the daughter of Siegfried Dispeker, a lawyer, and Isabella Goldschmidt. Weil and her brother, Fritz, who was twelve years older than she, were raised in an assimilated household: "I wanted to be German, not Jewish. I sat in Jewish religion class and dreamed about Egmont, the Prince of Homburg, Don Carlos. We learned to crank out Hebrew poems by heart, without knowing Hebrew.—I learned virtually nothing about Judaism, neither at home nor in school" (*Der Brautpreis*, p. 9). The children were shielded as much as possible from the antisemitic developments of the time. Under these sheltered conditions, and raised by parents who felt more German than Jewish, Grete Weil developed a deep sense of connectedness to her home. In her memoirs, *Leb ich denn, wenn andere leben* (Do I live, when others live), she recalled: "A place where one is at home, really at home, even then, when a transparency hangs above the town's sign with the inscription: 'Jews enter this place at their own risk.' " (p. 50).

Between 1929 and 1933 Grete Weil studied German language and literature in Frankfurt am Main, Berlin, and Munich. During these years she met the writer Klaus Mann and the literary academic Oskar Seidlin. In 1932 she began writing a dissertation on Friedrich Justin Bertuch's *Journal des Luxus und der Moden* (1786–1827; Journal of luxury and fashion) in Frankfurt under the supervision of Martin Sommerfeld, a professor of German literature at Frankfurt University. On 26 July of the same year, she married Edgar Weil, who was working as a producer for Munich's Münchner Kammerspiele, a well-known theater. Political reality violently affected Grete Weil's life for the first time when Edgar was abducted in March 1933. "In those days I began to understand what fascism really meant. I grasped that if you can hold a person without a reason for fourteen days without charges, without hearings, it could also be fourteen weeks, fourteen months, or fourteen years" (*Leb ich denn*, p. 108). Weil discontinued her studies and prepared to emigrate with her husband. Preparation involved learning the trade of photography while Edgar's parents moved their pharmaceutical factory to the Netherlands. Grete Weil acutely felt the intensification of Nazi persecution when her father was arrested at the turn of the year 1934–1935. In January 1935 Edgar went to Amsterdam, and Grete followed him there on 18 December 1935. Her parents remained in Munich.

Exile in the Netherlands

In Amsterdam, Grete Weil worked as a photographer. Unlike most émigrés, particularly the writers, she had no illusions about the rupture that the expulsion from Germany represented. This sensibility prompted Weil to keep her distance from the exile circuit: "We avoid any contact with artists and intellectuals. Don't get weak, don't cling to things once hoped for, accept reality. Recognize that one is granted no voice, is an outcast, a no one, unimportant to the surroundings" (*Leb ich denn*, p. 136).

Just after the German invasion of the Netherlands, Grete and Edgar Weil attempted to escape and failed. The systematic registration of Jews in the Netherlands began. Assets were seized; people were hounded down, persecuted, and deported. On 11 July 1941 Edgar Weil was arrested in a street raid, and he and 230 other Jews were deported to the concentration camp Mauthausen. Grete Weil received the notice of his death at the end of September. Edgar's death in Mauthausen is the Archimedean point of her writings—the source of her own unspeakable pain and at the same time a symbol of the devastation brought about by National Socialism.

After her husband's death Weil cooperated with the Dutch resistance. In July 1942, when the systematic deportation of Dutch Jews to the German death camps began, she sought employment with the Jewish Council of Amsterdam to avoid being apprehended. The ethical implications of working for the Jewish Counsel were later to mark the self-reflections of Weil's first-person narrators. The literary "I" of her writings is haunted by the question whether it was permissible to participate—as a means of survival—in the organization of destruction carried out by the National Socialists: "Think no longer about the Jewish Council. But the more I wish that, the more intensively I think about it, the deeper I dive into the forgotten. . . . And the event is there again, the last degradation. . . . Just as I sit here, . . . I know again what filth I went through, through what icy cold, placed in front of decisions that made me guilty no matter how they turned out" (*Meine Schwester Antigone*, pp. 97, 99).

Just prior to the planned deportation of the last members of Amsterdam's Jewish Council in September 1943, Weil went into hiding. She received the news of Germany's capitulation on 8 May 1945 in her second hiding place, in Amsterdamer Prinsengracht 257, an address to which she had moved only a few weeks earlier and one that is only a few houses away from the apartment in which Anne Frank wrote her diary.

Return to Germany

Weil wrote her short novel *Ans Ende der Welt* (To the end of the world) while still in Amsterdam. Terse and detached in tone, it tells of the Waterdrager family's deportation to Amsterdam's Schouwburg, a former theater used by the Nazis as an assembly camp for the Jews of Amsterdam. The father cannot fathom why well-known lawyers such as he are not exempt from the transports heading east but "proletarian" diamond cutters are. His daughter, Annabeth, meets and falls in love with Ben, a young man also held in the Schouwburg. Weil depicts the social surroundings in the Schouwburg with realistic precision, not failing to cast a light on the precarious role of the Jewish Council. The detached tone does not recede until Annabeth's inner monologue takes over in the last chapter, where she and Ben are being taken to a death camp. The horrendous place is referred to with few words: "It was technology, factory; it was film. End of the world 1943." The novel ends with Annabeth's final separation from Ben and her hope for the "hour of freedom that is growing more and more distant and more and more pale and that is ultimately nothing more than a rarely dreamed dream" (p. 86).

In spite of the acute awareness of Germany's crimes expressed in this first book, Weil's determination to return to Germany seems to have been unwavering. "I want to write, write German, it is impossible in a different language, and in order to do that I need surroundings in which people speak German," she wrote in *Leb ich denn* (p. 236). After a first, illegal visit to Germany in 1946, Weil wrote to the Jewish philosopher and writer Margarete Susman that she had encountered people in Germany "who understand . . . and can listen with understanding" (*Leb ich denn*, p. 254). Among these people was the opera director Walter Jockisch, whom Weil had known in her youth. Weil and Jockisch, who had lived under Adolf Hitler in passive resistance, stayed together and married in 1960. But the hope that Weil harbored for Germany and the Germans did not blind her to the far-reaching damage that twelve years of Nazi rule had inflicted. "Everyone I visit really is glad and entertains me generously, although they have nothing to eat themselves," she wrote in *Leb ich denn*. "Whether they know what happened, I don't find out, have the funny feeling that for most, one living Jew compensates for six million dead Jews" (p. 244). When Weil visited her hometown for the first time since having been forced to flee Germany, the burgomaster greeted her with the words: "Ah, there you are again, Gretel!" (Exner, p. 73). Through experiences such as this, Weil got to know the Germans' strong desire to minimize the Nazi crimes and to suppress remembrances of the extermination policy. These experiences and the great difficulties she had finding a German publisher for her book *Ans Ende der Welt* were indications of the problems Weil would confront as a Jewish woman and as a German-speaking author whose books deal with Nazi annihilation politics.

During the 1950s Weil wrote opera librettos for the composers Hans Werner Henze and Wolfgang Fortner. She worked for various publishers as a translator and wrote reviews for the broadcasting corporation Hessischen Rundfunk. It was not until 1963, with *Tramhalte Beethovenstraat* (*Last Trolley from Beethovenstraat*), that Weil published a book that struck the primary theme of her literary work: the immediacy of the past, that is, the afterlife of National Socialist annihilation politics in everyday life and in the survivors' present.

The Price of Survival

In *Tramhalte Beethovenstraat*, Weil developed the artistic melding of present-tense and past-tense narration that was to characterize her later books. The novel tells the tale of Andreas, a German author who has a vague sense of being in "inner exile." He plans to hibernate in a quiet position as an editor of light literature. But his job takes him to Amsterdam, where he experiences something that changes the course of his life. Disturbances announce themselves in nightly states of semi-slumber: "Dreamed sounds. Short fast orders, dog barking, muffled humming of many voices, the violent weeping of a woman, an extended scream that consisted of a single tone and changed to whimpering in the end, the arrival of trams, their bumpy, receding rolling" (p. 23). In a city street, the Beethovenstraat, Andreas witnesses four hundred Jews being taken every week by tram to the train station, from there to a transfer camp, and afterward "toward the East." "East," a Jewish doctor explains to him soon thereafter, "you can associate anything, Hannover is east, Berlin, Breslau, or Poland. 'East,' that is a term that says nothing, or rather, it says the Nothing, last stop, death" (p. 37).

This experience of witnessing the atrocious is a shock to Andreas's system. He laboriously tries to figure out what is going on and not to dismiss it as a fantasy or a rumor. Andreas joins the Dutch resistance and provides a hiding place in his apartment for Daniel, a young Jew to whom he feels sexually attracted. When Daniel fails to return home one evening from his work as a courier for the underground movement, the catastrophe of Nazi politics breaks into Andreas's inner life. Traumatization evinces itself in his losing the ability to write: "Four hundred wandered, a black shadow, across the paper, when he wanted to write, and broke the form. . . . He had the ambition, stressed to the extreme, to be true, a fanatic of precision. Yet he recognized no truth that didn't begin with four hundred people deported in tram trains. It wasn't possible to write about a different topic. But for this one there was no word, no sign, no metaphor that covered" (pp. 47, 50).

Andreas returns to Germany after its liberation, hoping that by living among Germans he might "get behind the secret of how it had been possible" (p. 149). This project fails—a writer's block persists. A visit with a former publisher reveals just how much this paralysis is due not only to the traumatization already suffered but also to its continuation in the "renewed" German cultural industry. The publisher, who has financially survived the Nazi years by being unscrupulously opportunistic, celebrates "youth, thoughtless youth, that doesn't give a damn about the past. That which you cried about is not even worth a kick to them. They are right. The future belongs to them. . . . You are too sentimental. Sentiment is passé" (p. 158). In a desperate attempt to reclaim his voice, Andreas decides to drive to Mauthausen, where Daniel died. But here also nothing can remove or draw "productively" from the rupture of having witnessed the deportation of Amsterdam's Jewish population.

Weil's *Tramhalte Beethovenstraat* is a political-memory project that is characterized by two striking features. On one hand, Weil transfers a specifically Jewish experience of persecution, which she herself suffered, onto a non-Jewish German figure. A close analysis of the text reveals that not only particular memories but also the particular language of recollection are passed on to the German figure. With this move Weil suggests that even in the aftermath of the Germans' having committed irreparable crimes against the European Jews a potential for accessing a common language persisted. On the other hand, Weil links this notion to a story that was bound to provoke the postwar German literature industry: that of a German author driven into writer's paralysis by his confrontation with Nazi annihilation politics. Entirely different types of stories were in demand in Germany after the war. Those writers who were most capable of verbalizing their experiences during the Hitler regime and who styled themselves as victims were considered representative of German postwar literature. An analysis of Gruppe 47, the most important literary association of postwar Germany, for instance, discloses striking correlations between historical circumstances in Germany after the war and the cultural and political relationships depicted in Weil's novel. In *Tramhalte Beethovenstraat*, Weil holds on to the idea of a common language across the abyss between German and Jew after the Holocaust and to a potential for mutual understanding; simultaneously, however, she remains aware of how the literature industry addressed the topic of Nazi persecution and the effect of that presecution on contemporary culture.

Tramhalte Beethovenstraat demonstrates the importance of memory in Weil's work with particular clarity. The tale revolves around characters for whom the present is deeply marked by individual traumatic experiences or by Nazi annihilation politics. These characters are subject to the past in the present. Weil allows her readers to participate in this temporal mode with great immediacy through the inner monologues carried on by Andreas in *Tramhalte Beethovenstraat* and by first-person narrators in later novels. These monologues often reflect on the process of writing itself, casting a light on the problems that arise from the conjoining of past and present. In all her works Weil remained committed to establishing a language that might enable dialogue between Jews and Germans about the Holocaust. The emphasis she placed on remembrance was set toward this aim. But she never fooled herself into thinking that she could communicate the core of her experience of persecution to her readers.

It was not until 1968 that Weil's third book, *Happy, Sagte der Onkel* (Happy, said the uncle), appeared on the market for German-speaking readers. In the book's three stories first-person narrators marked by details from Weil's life speak as Jewish survivors of the Holocaust. All Weil's subsequent novels work with such figures. The stories in *Happy, sagte der Onkel* deal with the protagonists' memories of persecution under the Nazis in the context of the Vietnam War and the anti-authoritarian movement. Weil's journey to North America in 1964–1965 may have determined the settings of the stories in Los Angeles, New York, and Mexico. But it becomes increasingly apparent in the texts that the protagonist has sought out these locations that are so far removed from her German home in order to comprehend her Jewish identity in entirely unfamiliar surroundings. In the title story the first-person narrator visits distant relatives in Los Angeles, Jews of German descent who survived the Holocaust and now suppress all memories of it. This everyday mode of suppression is accompanied by a wholly unreflective glorification of the "American way of life," as well as by hatred of the African American population. In the second tale, "Gloria Halleluja," the narrator journeys [illegible] against the insistent advice of her New York friends. Her determination is based on the notion that she, as a German Jew, has a background similar to that of most of Harlem's occupants: the experience of racial persecution. But in a series of at first small, and then escalating events, the narrator discovers that this supposed commonality appears utterly abstract in the direct confrontation with the socially degraded inhabitants of Harlem. She is ultimately thrown out of a bar by members of a militant African American emancipation movement, who shout slogans envisioning a country without whites. The bitterness the narrator encounters casts her into a confusing apocalyptic vision. Intermingling with the militant African Americans' frightening political utopia, her experience of being hounded and persecuted turns into a horrendous vision of renewed, reverse racism. The feeling of solidarity that had been anchored in the narrator's attempt to universalize her own history of persecution shatters under social dynamics that toss her back into the vortex of her own trauma. The trauma of having been persecuted by the Nazis is represented not through the protagonist's immediate recollections but through her involuntary discoveries of similarities, parallels, and correspondences between present events and past experiences.

"B sagen," the book's final story, describes a Holocaust survivor's self-critical assessment of her loyalties to the anti-authoritarian movement of the 1960s. As a citizen of West Germany, she identifies with the German branch of the movement, which tried to break the silence about the crimes of the Nazis. While visiting Chichén Itzá, ancient temple grounds in Mexico, the narrator meets a tour guide whom she believes to recognize as an SS officer who was in Amsterdam during the Nazis' occupation of the city. It remains unclear until the end of the tale whether or not she is mistaken. Without actually speaking to the guide, the narrator imagines a trial in which she compels him to admit to and justify his participation in the crimes of destruction. At first the "defendant" comes up with excuses similar to those put forth in trials of Nazi war criminals during the mid-1960s, such as references to inalterable duty. But the fantasized trial takes an unexpected turn: the tour guide asserts that he is not the same person who served on the ramp at Auschwitz, and he points out that she has also undergone many changes since then. He hits on an appropriate image of her adaptation to circumstances that have changed her. Nothing remains of her once-furious opposition to murder and suffering in the world:

> Either-or: You said "or," then you must also say B. Study the stock market, think about what kind of car you drive, which vacation you take, buy clothes, buy books, swim in the Mediterranean, ski the Diavolezza, mow the grass of your lawn, play out the flirts that grow more melancholy with each year, hold yourself up on the friendships that are becoming more and more rare. Say B, say B. . . . [H]ave opinions, state opinions, talk about the trial of Socrates and against all the Bogers and Kaduks, write like a cat slinking around the hot porridge, because it's not possible to write about nothing, soup stains on the paper and burned paws. . . . Say B, say B. Always implemented,

> worked on, but never brought to mastery. And the racing fear that at some point in a hospital bed or a gutter the difficult regret about not having decided for the "either" might rise up. The moment of truth, and the truth further removed than ever. Who could tell you the truth? What is your truth? (p. 106).

The narrator realizes that she has been cowardly and that she is now used to a level of comfort that she finds incompatible with full participation in the fight. In recognizing her own failure in the eyes of an imagined Nazi perpetrator, she realizes that the idea of drawing any form of strength from her experience of persecution that might be actively used in a protest movement of the 1960s is pointless. Weil's self-critical tale of 1968 measures out the burdens that marked Holocaust survivors' attempts to achieve solidarity with the anti-authoritarian movement. The anti-authoritarians themselves were not capable of questioning their own endeavors with comparable radicality and intensity.

Survivors' self-questioning when confronted with political opposition in the present is further radicalized in Weil's novel *Meine Schwester Antigone* (*My Sister, My Antigone*), which appeared in 1980. The German Jewish first-person narrator survived the Nazi period working for the resistance in Amsterdam. She is leading a reclusive life as an author in Frankfurt when her goddaughter asks her to take in a woman who is being sought by the police because she is suspected of being a sympathizer of the Red Army faction. She agrees to do this: "A refugee doesn't show another refugee the door" (p. 118). The encounter with the young woman comes at a time when the author is reflecting on her own persecution by reconstructing Antigone as a figure who resists the state authority's demands while refusing to hate that authority as the enemy. Through this construction the narrator attempts to calm the self-accusation—not to have shown enough resistance in the past, to have been too passive—by drawing parallels to Antigone's position: "Not to hate with but to love with am I there" (p. 15). But her insights into a continuum of violence—"My Lai. Lidice. Oradour. . . . Schouwburg of Amsterdam. Soccer stadium of Santiago" (pp. 75f., 94f.)—and her disquiet about the moral radicality that she perceives being lived out by people like Gudrun Ensslin, a leading member of the militant underground in West Germany at the end of the 1970s, force all her constructions to break down: "My superficial life, my amusing life, twelve years wiped away, always act as if Mauthausen never was, how could I breathe if it had been. Don't hate, love; counterfeit Antigone's ambiguous sentence that brought her death, abuse it to live. Excuses, excuses" (p. 126).

Weil sets authentic reports of a Wehrmacht soldier into the text of the novel to make the presence of the past that determines the course of the narrator's life immediate for the reader. This man witnessed the liquidation of a Polish village. The narrator's rereading of this text, and her confrontation with armed resistance in the present, lead her to construct a new Antigone tale in which the protagonist pulls out a pistol and shoots at the SS battalion leader in Amsterdam's Schouwburg. But all the stability in recalling the past that the classical Antigone had formerly provided is erased. At the end of the novel the narrator stands in the immediacy of her own past, unprotected by fiction or myth. And this immediacy seems intolerable.

This experience of the past in the everyday life of a survivor also characterizes the protagonist of Weil's 1983 novel, *Generationen* (Generations). In the novel the first-person narrator attempts to live with two younger women, Hanna and Moni. As in Weil's earlier books, the problems associated with being a Holocaust survivor figure centrally but this time against the backdrop of shorter and very diverse biographies. The narrator must recognize that an ultimately unbridgeable gap separates her experience of persecution from Hanna's and Moni's daily worries and emergencies. In the book's closing scenes Weil reflects on the broadcasting of the American television series *Holocaust* in Germany as well as on the success of her book *Meine Schwester Antigone*. Although the narrator can now determine that "one talks about it," she notes that "something strange is happening. . . . Since they talk so much about it, instead of coming closer to you, they've distanced themselves more. For them, you are now a case. They demand you to report your thoughts as death was in front of your eyes. As if that could be communicated" (p. 140).

In *Der Brautpreis* (*The Bride Price*), published in 1988, Weil attempts to clarify contemporary Jewish identity by confronting modern Jewish destiny (that is, the experience of Nazi annihilation politics) with the world of biblical Israel. In monologues that alternate between first-person voices—"I, Grete," a survivor, and "I, Michal," the first wife of King David—the story of Israel appears not as a tradition with which Grete identifies herself but as evidence of a long-standing continuum of violence, oppression, war, and destruction that also determines the present. Grete cannot sense a particular connection to Israel: "Strangeness very deep in the heart" (p. 225). In this novel, as in Weil's other works, the Jewishness of the first-person narrator is clearly dominated by the experience of destruction.

Weil's relentless probing of the self achieved a final radicalization in "Und ich? Zeugin des Schmerzes"

(And why? witness of pain), which Weil published in 1992 in the volume *Spätfolgen* (Aftereffects). Weil wrote under the influence of Bruno Bettelheim's suicide and of Primo Levi's last text (*The Drowned and the Saved*, 1986). In this autobiographical, confessional text, she revised her former notion of being a witness: "I am not a witness anymore. I didn't know anything. . . . I was not . . . with Edgar in Mauthausen" (p. 102). Simultaneously, she recognizes that this "delusion" has enabled her "to live like I have" (p. 102). This late revision stands paradigmatically for the manner in which Weil pursued her art as a Holocaust survivor and as a Jewish author residing in Germany. For Weil, writing about the Holocaust and its presence in the everyday lives of survivors was inseparably linked to a permanent search for self-awareness of her own subjective position within the scope of devastating objective history.

The German Literature Industry

Weil's work never received high-profile reviews and awards. The great difficulty her agent had getting her novel *Ans Ende der Welt* accepted by a German publisher was a sign of what lay ahead. Weil's first book did not appear until 1949 in East Berlin, and it was not published in West Germany until 1962. *Tramhalte Beethovenstraat* did receive some notice, but its consistent critique of postwar German literature was disregarded. Instead, the novel was read primarily as the impressive account of a witness. What was hardly recognized was the specific artistic quality of Weil's work. For the few reviewers who addressed it, *Happy, sagte der Onkel* remained almost entirely incomprehensible. At the end of 1968 Weil expressed to the author and critic Martin Gregor-Dellin her "deep skepticism about the book industry as it is today" (Exner, p. 87). The search for a publisher for her *Meine Schwester Antigone* lasted two full years, and at one point Weil abandoned hope of getting it published at all. The short novel ultimately hit the market during a phase of intensified reflection about Germany's Nazi past. The 1979 broadcasting of the American television series *Holocaust* had provided an important impetus toward critical retrospection, and it was within this climate that Weil's book achieved recognition. But almost all reviews avoided mentioning the Wehrmacht soldier's eyewitness accounts, an indication of just how timidly the past was being questioned. That the book received an award for its representation of old age seems to indicate further displacement tendencies in Germany. But in 1988 Weil received the renowned Geschwister-Scholl Prize for her novel *Der Brautpreis*. In his tribute, the writer and literary critic Armin Eichholz brought Weil's achievements on the subject of remembrance in West German literature to the attention of a large public for the first time. He pointed out an increasingly problematic assimilation of Grete Weil: "The German statement comes from YOU: 'I know that it is possible to live among murderers!' And you must experience how that is taken as a gesture of reconciliation" ("Wenn Sie an meinem Herzen lecken könnten, wären Sie vergiftet," *Börsenblatt für den deutschen Buchhandel* 79 [1988]. 3458). In these words, Eichholz underlines the strong tendency of Germany's literature industry to misuse Weil's work as an indicator of "normalization." Although Weil was recognized for her achievements in political remembrance during this period, she was taken only moderately seriously. But the fact is she worked intensively throughout her professional life to map out the role of remembrance in the tension between a survivor's experience and postwar German culture. And this work remained unrecognized. It is up to future readers of Weil's texts to recognize this achievement, which defines her incomparable position in the history of German literature.

Bibliography

Primary Sources

Ans Ende der Welt (To the end's world). 1949.
Tramhalte Beethovenstraat (*Last Trolley from Beethovenstraat*). 1963.
Happy, sagte der Onkel (Happy, said the uncle). 1968.
Meine Schwester Antigone (*My Sister, My Antigone*). 1980.
Generationen (Generations). 1983.
Der Brautpreis (*The Bride Price*). 1988.
Spätfolgen (Aftereffects). 1992.
Leb ich denn, wenn andere leben (Do I live when others live). 1998.

Secondary Sources

Braese, Stephan. *Die andere Erinnerung: Jüdische Autoren in der westdeutschen Nachkriegsliteratur*. Berlin: PHILO, 2001.

Exner, Lisbeth. *Land meiner Mörder, Land meiner Sprache*. Munich: A1-Verlag, 1998.

[illegible] *Das Werk der Schriftstellerin Grete Weil*. Frankfurt am Main: Peter Lang, 1996.

Interview

Interview by Liz Wieskerstrauch. "Ich habe Auschwitz, wie andere Tb oder Krebs." *Anschläge: Zeitschrift für Kunst und Literatur* 14 (1988): 22–26.

JIŘÍ WEIL
(1900–1959)

DAVID MESHER

WEIL WAS BORN in 1910 in Praskolesy, a Bohemian town then part of the Austro-Hungarian Empire—seventeen years after his more illustrious countryman, Franz Kafka, was born in nearby Prague. However, the impact of having almost all of Kafka's works published in a few short years after his death in 1924 must have made him seem more of a contemporary to an entire generation of Czech writers, Jews and Gentiles alike. One of the outstanding members of that generation, Jiří Weil, was still a student when such novels as *The Trial* (1925) and *The Castle* (1926) first appeared. In 1928 Weil received his doctorate from Prague's Charles University for a thesis that focused in part on Nikolai Gogol, whose stories, including "The Nose" and "The Overcoat," are often cited as early examples of the sort of surrealism that Kafka himself later practiced.

Initially Weil's interests were more political than literary. In the early 1930s, Weil went to work in Moscow for the Czech publishing section of the Comintern, but grew disenchanted with his Soviet comrades either before or after party reviewers attacked his 1937 novel *Moskva-hranice* (Moscow-Border, 1937) for its bleak presentation of Stalinism. In short order, Weil was thrown out of both the Communist Party and the writers' union. Back in Czechoslovakia, however, such personal reverses meant little once the Munich pact of September 1938 paved the way for German annexation of much of Bohemia and Moravia. With the Germans in control, former party allegiances meant little for a Jew trying to survive annihilation. After transportations to the death camps began, Weil spent the rest of the war hiding in Prague. Once the war was over, Weil made the most of the liberal but short-lived provisional government of Eduard Beneš, publishing his masterpiece *Life with a Star* in 1949, shortly before the Soviet takeover. Once Czechoslovakia was behind the Iron Curtain, Weil found himself ostracized by the Communist faithful in Prague for his betrayal of their cause, and under suspicion by many others for his earlier support of that cause. Largely ignored as a result in his own country, and essentially unknown outside it, Weil labored in obscurity. Only the brief post-Stalin relaxation of tensions throughout the Soviet bloc brought Weil any measure of recognition: before his death from cancer in 1959, he was readmitted to the writers' union and appointed director of the Jewish State Museum. *Mendelssohn Is on the Roof* (1960), Weil's last major work, was published posthumously in 1960.

The general wretchedness of his life under Communism notwithstanding, Weil's experiences under Nazism were the focus of his most significant works, especially *Life with a Star*. Unlike the narrator of that novel, however, who is saved from deportation purely by chance, Weil himself took a more active role in ensuring his personal survival by faking his own death early in the German occupation, and then successfully hiding from his persecutors for the duration, including a period concealed in the house of Franz Kafka's niece.

Life with a Star

Though the author was both wise enough and brave enough from the beginning to take extraordinary measures to save himself, the narrator of his novel *Life with a Star*, Josef Roubicek, is much less optimistic in the early days of German occupation. In the opening pages of the work it is clear that Josef has already given up. The only victory he can anticipate is predicated upon his own death:

> I had burned everything I could because I had no coal and because I didn't want to give them anything. They would not get anything from me. . . . When they came to confiscate the furniture they would find nothing but

> cracked walls, an empty garret, the broken-down stove, and, in the middle of the room, the coffee table; this useless piece of furniture would reign over the room (New York: Farrar, Straus & Giroux, p. 4).

This would be a small victory indeed; the irony is that in destroying almost everything of any value, including the house itself, Josef has participated in his own victimization.

"They," as mentioned in the passage above, are of course the Germans, but Weil never uses such terms as "German," "Nazi," or "Gestapo" in the novel, and the translator's note to that effect at the beginning of the English edition of *Life with a Star* tells only half the story. It would be one thing if Weil avoided identifying the perpetrators of the Holocaust in order to keep the focus fully on its victims, but Weil never identifies Jews as such, either, and this heightens the absurd dimension of the novel, as when signs proclaim "ADMITTED" (p. 17), without identifying Jews as the ones excluded. As a result, the word on Josef's yellow star is said to be in "a foreign language written in black scraggly letters" (p. 64), while the Hebrew characters on Jewish tombstones are similarly described as "foreign letters" (p. 72). Possible reasons for this technique include the parochial as well as the existential. On one hand, under the dual monarchy the German language was associated as much with Jews and other prosperous sections of Prague society as with Germans. However, since independence after World War I, nationalism established supremacy of the Czech language, so that Josef's apparent inability even to recognize German or Hebrew, if a little far-fetched by 1942, makes him all the more a Czech hero. On the other hand, the peculiar language that results, with its emphasis on "them" and "us," heightens the sense of Josef's paranoia and confusion, and makes his an existentialist narrative with his own existence in the balance.

The existential nature of Josef's narrative is clear from the opening words of the novel, with which he addresses Ruzena, a woman who, he admits, "was not in the room, she was not with me at all. . . . Perhaps she was not on earth anymore, perhaps she had never even lived" (p. 3). And yet Ruzena and Tomas the cat are Josef's two closest confidants in the novel—a woman who is not there, and an animal that cannot speak. With them Josef can afford to be affirmative, as when he says, "But happiness does exist, Tomas. It's only now that they're trying to convince us that it doesn't and that it never did" (p. 38). In the best sense of the word, these are absurd relationships, fine for a defeated Josef at the beginning of the novel, but inadequate once the narrator chooses life. So, first Tomas and then Ruzena must be removed, if not from Josef's imagination, then from the reader's. Tomas's disappearance—he is probably eaten by neighbors—creates a level of ironic melodrama in the midst of the Holocaust. As Josef himself says, "It was silly to mourn Tomas when so many people were dying. I told myself as much, but it didn't do any good" (p. 182). Later, Josef hears an announcement that Ruzena and her husband have been "shot to death" as partisans (p. 190), and he realizes that he can't cry for Ruzena as he has for Tomas (p. 193). Only then, seemingly deprived of all hope of happiness, can Josef openly rebel.

Prior to that, however, Josef like all Holocaust victims, lived with a desperate hope—a hope that seems fulfilled when he appears, as commanded, for his transportation orders and his name is never called: "Many Roubiceks were read and many Josefs; then the letter of the alphabet changed, and they read Salus, Starnic, Stein, and Steiner, and no other Roubicek appeared in the rustle of the pages" (p. 123). This seeming reprieve, however, carries a terrible burden of guilt, for Josef realizes that someone else will be transported in his place: "And so it became clear to me that a person who killed himself or didn't go bore the guilt of pulling someone else down. Of course that other person wanted to live too; it wasn't right to take someone's life, but you could always say that person would have had to go anyway. If only one word did not exist" (p. 135).

That word is "hope"—next to life itself, the one thing that victims of the Holocaust held most precious. Saving oneself by causing others to be transported, even a day or an hour early, seems to Josef an enormity because it deprives them of hope. But as Josef understands by the end of the novel, that hope works in the favor of the victimizers, preventing their targets from organizing themselves into an effective opposition. Without Ruzena, without hope, Josef's choices are much clearer to him: he can "accept extinction without fear or shame," or he can choose life. Life is the more difficult option because "the freedom" he has to bear is "a heavy load" (p. 208), but in the closing lines of the novel Josef chooses life and the responsibilities that come with such freedom: "I understood that the Josef Roubicek who wanted to make excuses, to evade, and to dodge, only to avoid freedom, no longer existed and would never exist again" (p. 208).

Mendelssohn Is on the Roof

Mendelssohn Is on the Roof, Weil's only other Holocaust novel as well as the only other one to be translated into English, was also his last work, and one with which he struggled, by some accounts, from the end of the war onward. Published posthumously in 1960, the novel was left complete but in some ways unpolished by its author; though interesting in its own right and as a companion piece to *Life with a Star, Mendelssohn* does not approach the achievement of that earlier work. Perhaps the most significant difference in Weil's two Holocaust novels is in their treatment of the absurd or grotesque. In *Life* the absurd is entirely located within either the historical reality or the consciousness of the narrator. Thus ridiculous and often contradictory pronouncements by the occupying forces create a sense of the surreal in the world Josef must inhabit, while his relationships with Ruzena, absent or dead, and Tomas, a cat, establish an internal level of absurdity in the narrator's own consciousness. Though ridiculous rules and orders are to be found in *Mendelssohn* as well—indeed, the plot of the novel is based on a plausible enough scenario in which a high-ranking German official commands that the likeness of Felix Mendelssohn, who was born of Jewish parents, be removed from among the statues of great composers installed on the roof of the concert hall in Prague—Weil also introduces a level of magical realism absent from *Life with a Star*, in the supernatural powers of Mendelssohn's statue.

The statue operates in the novel like a latter-day golem—the clay figure of a man from Jewish folklore, into whose inanimate body the spark of life can be breathed by mystical means. The novel itself suggests a different parallel: the ancient Greek flood story, presented by Weil as an epigraph in which the only survivors, Deukalion and Pyrrha, repopulate the world by throwing stones that turn into human beings. There are other animated statues in the novel, including that of the Commendatore in Mozart's *Don Giovanni*, and that of Weil's fictionalized characterization of Reinhard Heydrich, the ranking Nazi official in the German "Protectorate" of Bohemia and Moravia. In the novel, Heydrich believes his knowledge of the planned "final solution" gives him "invisible power. It means standing high above all people and looking down on them in scornful safety, like a statue. It means being made of stone or bronze" (p. 46).

As in *Life with a Star*, Weil touches on the issue of hope, but as a tool to be manipulated. Heydrich, for example, thinks, "It was also important to give the victims temporary hope, so that they wouldn't be inclined to resist" (p. 47), but despite the comic tone of much of the work, there is little hope for the characters in *Mendelssohn Is on the Roof*, and even less optimism for the world generally. Josef Roubicek, at the end of *Life with a Star*, comes to the conclusion that without hope there is at least the possibility of action, but at the end of *Mendelssohn*, Adela and Greta Roubicek—infant sisters whose repeated appearances throughout the novel help to unify its almost pastiche-like presentation of recurring characters—are savagely beaten to death by a Gestapo agent, even as the ultimate defeat of the Third Reich is described. Despite its power, the hopelessness of that final scene is less successful than in the earlier novel, in large part because the Germans, cleverly unnamed and ignored as characters in *Life with a Star*, operate here less as human beings than as figures of absolute evil, powerful as symbols but limited as fiction.

The Rehabilitation of Jiří Weil

In the mid-1970s, Philip Roth, the American novelist, served as general editor for a Penguin series titled "Writers from the Other Europe," which made available in English translation the work of a number of Eastern European writers, including Jerzy Andrzejewski, Tadeusz Borowski, Danilo Kiš, Tadeusz Konwicki, Milan Kundera, and Bruno Schulz, with introductions by authors such as Heinrich Böll, Joseph Brodsky, and John Updike. Jiří Weil was not among those selected at that time, but Roth's continuing interest eventually led to the 1989 publication of *Life with a Star* in English, accompanied by Roth's own preface. In it, Roth sums up the official party reaction to *Life with a Star*, which "was considered by the Communists a 'decadent' example of 'pernicious existentialism' " (p. vi), as well as the results of that most internal of exiles on the ostracized author. Roth describes Weil in "his lonely years as a writer and a man, unpublished, unread, withdrawn, and silent—and, by party stricture, unmentionable in literary circles and classrooms" (p. v). Together with the appearance in English of *Mendelssohn is on the Roof* two years later, this resurrection of *Life with a Star* forty years after its first printing in 1949 has helped to establish Weil as the most important Czech novelist of the Holocaust.

Bibliography

Primary Sources

Moskva-hranice (Moscow-Border). 1937.
Makanna—otec divů (Makanna, the Father of Miracles). 1945.
Barvy (Colors). 1946.
Vzpominky na Julia Fucika (Memories of Julia Fucika). 1947.
Vezen chillonský (The Prisoner of Chillon). 1949.

Zivot s hvezdou (*Life with a Star*). 1949, 1989.
Zalozpev za 77,297 obetí (Elegy for 77,297 Victims). 1958.
Na strese je Mendelssohn (Mendelssohn Is on the Roof). 1960, 1991.
Hodina pravdy, hodina zkousky (Hour of Truth, Hour of Trial). 1966.
Drevena lzíce (Wooden Spoon). 1992.

Secondary Sources

Hostovsky, Egon. "Participation in Modern Czech Literature." In *The Jews of Czechoslovakia*. Philadelphia: Jewish Publication Society, 1968, vol. 1, pp. 439–453.
Roth, Philip. Preface to *Life with a Star*, by Jiří Weil. New York: Farrar, Straus & Giroux, 1989.

Immanuel James Weißglas

(1920–1979)

AMY COLIN

At the time Immanuel James Weißglas was born (14 March 1920), Czernowitz, his multiethnic hometown and capital of the Bukovina, belonged to the Romanian kingdom but still preserved its Austro-Hungarian tradition. German-speaking Jewish poets, who were the foremost representatives of the Austro-German culture in the Bukovina, became increasingly isolated in a Romanian-speaking environment. Paradoxically, the German-Jewish literature of the Bukovina reached its culmination point precisely in this period. It is characteristic of Bukovina's flowering Austro-Jewish culture that three of its later major poets Paul Celan (1920–1970), Alfred Gong (1920–1981), and Immanuel Weißglas were classmates; Celan and Weißglas were good friends. All three poets shared the same background and later interests: all three were born into assimilated Jewish families that still preserved a link to Jewish tradition; all three had a strong interest in heterogeneous literary traditions; and they were fascinated by problems of language and translation. Weißglas and Celan became close friends with other Bukovinian Jewish poets, in particular the older writer Alfred Margul-Sperber (1898–1967), who was a mentor of many Bukovinian authors and encouraged their work as well. All three poets experienced the rise of nationalism, antisemitism, and fascism in the Bukovina, and the later historical turmoil that destroyed the cultural flowering of their homeland. During the Soviet occupation of Czernowitz (1940–1941), Weißglas, along with Alfred Kittner, worked in the town's library. In the summer of 1942, on the same day as Kittner, Weißglas and his parents were deported to death camps in Transnistria, Eastern Ukraine. They miraculously survived and returned to Soviet-occupied Czernowitz in 1944. In this period of time Weißglas worked in an insane asylum. In April 1945 he moved to Bucharest where he made a living as a piano player in an orchestra and as an editor working for a Jewish news agency. Later he worked as technical assistant and editor for the publishing house Europolis (1946–1947), and thereafter as editor and archivist of the newspaper *Romănia Liberă*. With one exception, a tourist visit to East Berlin, Weißglas never left Romania. He died on 28 April 1979 in Bucharest.

Works

Weißglas and Celan shared an interest in William Shakespeare, William Butler Yeats, Rupert Brooke, A. E. Housman, Roy Campbell, Alexander Blok, Sergej Jessenin, and Guillaume Apollinaire, whose text "Schinderhannes" they both translated into German independent of one another. As a teenager, Weißglas made a name for himself as a translator of lyric poetry, in particular Eminescu's poem "Luceafărul" ("The Evening Star") published by the Romanian journal *Viata Romănească* (Roumanian Life) in 1937. After the war, in Bucharest, Weißglas translated into Romanian Stifter's *Nachsommer* (Late Summer), Grillparzer's *Der arme Spielmann* (The Poor Musician), and Feuchtwanger's *Erfolg* (Success), publishing these translations under the pseudonym Iordan. His Romanian adaptations of Goethe's *Faust*, first and second part, are particularly remarkable because Weißglas's mother tongue was German; translation into a foreign language was a particular achievement. The Romanian Writers' Union awarded Weißglas its literary prize, for it considered his translation to be as good as the *Faust* adaptations by the Romanian poet Lucian Blaga.

In an early, prophetic poem "Europolis," Weißglas warned his contemporaries of the looming destruction of European Jewry. Although he sensed the danger, he could not flee the Bukovina. He was deported along with his parents and hundreds of other Bukovinian Jews to Transnistria. His roots in German language and literature were still so deep that among the few belongings he was allowed to take to the extermination camps, he brought a German *Sprachbrockhaus*. "A German poet cannot exist . . . without a *Sprachbrockhaus*," Weißglas remarked. Like Kittner, he continued to write German verses in the death camp. Poetry gave him the strength to go on living. The epigraph of his unpublished volume of poems, "Gottes Mühlen in Berlin" ("God's Mill in Berlin," 1947; collection of Alfred Kittner), which includes poems he wrote during his deportation to a quarry in Transnistria, states:

> The author of this book has never seen Germany face to face
> But has lived and suffered long. The German lament that we've harvested here
> of love and death instilled by centuries past and by generations sung into the grave
> is as old as language: It needed only an urgent poet. During the years of clash of arms 1940–47, not without play on God's mills
> which grind slowly, but certainly; it was written down in a German-speaking foreign land.

Although Weißglas never lived in Germany, he considered himself not just an heir of German culture and literature, but its indispensable instrument. Weißglas's poetry and poetological reflections testify to his belief in the legitimacy and validity of German language as a means of artistic expression.

Time and again, many of Weißglas's poems identify the fate of Jews during the *Shoah* with their sufferings throughout history from their captivity in Babylon to Auschwitz. "Is not our people, steppe-foreign, lost in nowwhere and never? / Misery stands in a snowy shirt, / In courtyards falling cattle groan," he writes in the poem "Die verlorene Schar" ("The Lost people"). Other of his texts place the *Shoah* in a broad historical context of different genocides occurring in the course of history. Jewish fate often stands for the fate of all victims of violence and wars. In *Der Nobiskrug* (1972, Nobis-Jar), for instance, Weißglas associates the Jews with the troops of mercenaries in the Thirty Years' War who wandered until their death—"The Lost People." So they were called the doomed masses that stormed in during the devastation of lives and countries that was the Thirty Years' War—often guiltless, often burdening themselves with guilt. Their victory was the grave, their testament that 'a speck of peace is worth more than a ton of war.' Just such a people we were, too, from 1942 to 1944" (*Nobiskrug*, p. 23; translated by J. Sheldon). Throughout their history, Jews have associated major catastrophes with God's punishment for their sins. In a desperate attempt to understand the incomprehensible, Weißglas, like many other Jewish writers and poets, clings to this ancient Jewish idea. Weißglas's allusion to Jewish self-condemnation and his identification with Ahasuerus, to whom he dedicated several poems, show that the poet ultimately internalized prejudices underlying modern antisemitism. In some of his poems, Weißglas interprets both the persecuted and the persecutors as instruments of history.

Themes

Like one of his literary models, Konrad Ferdinand Meyer, Weißglas created many themes at an early stage in his poetic development and later continuously revised these poems; his early biblical motifs, metaphors of love, and allusions to the fate of the Jews remained, but his style became decidedly tighter. Weißglas did not break traditional syntactic and semantic structures, as did Celan, but disclosed a dichotomy inherent in poetic language, its vulnerability as well as its strength and power to confront the "thousand darknesses of murderous speech" (Paul Celan, *Collected Prose*, translated by Rosemarie Waldrop. Manchester: Carcanet Press, 1985, p. 34). In contrast to hermetic poetry, Weißglas insisted upon legibility; though his poems often use enigmatic metaphors, they are ultimately intended to be clear. Although Weißglas collected his *Shoah* poetry in a first volume, "Gottes Mühlen in Berlin" ("God's Mill in Berlin") in 1947 (which remains unpublished), he succeeded in publishing another volume of his poems, titled *Kariera am Bug* (Stone Quarry at the Bug), in that same year. A few poems appeared in anthologies such as *Aufbau und Friede* (*Reconstruction and Peace*, 1950), *Das Herz ist Deine Heimat* (*The Heart Is Your Homeland*, 1955), *Welch Wort in die Kälte gerufen. Die Judenverfolgungen des Dritten Reiches im deutschen Gedicht* (*What Word Called Out in Darkness. The Third Reich's Jewish Persecution in German Poems*, 1968), and *Die Bibel in deutschen Gedichten* (1968). Some of his poems appeared in the literary journal *Neue Literatur* (1970, 1971), and the 1972 volume (*Der Nobiskrug*), including new versions of early poems, which appeared under the title *Der Nobiskrug*, and received a poetry award from the Romanian Writers' Union. The Rimbaud Verlag in Germany reprinted Weißglas's poems in the volume *Aschenzeit* (1994). A year later, the *Literaturhaus* Berlin published a typescript titled "Steinbruch am Bug" (Stone Quarry on the Bug, 1995) by Isak Weißglas, the poet's father, who documented the deportation to and life in Transnistria, covering a period in his son's life from July 1941 to spring 1943.

Critical Reception

The reception of Weißglas's work in secondary literature places the author in the broader context of Romanian-German literary development and emphasizes the role of his brilliant translations as his major contribution to Romanian-German cultural interrelations—his brilliant translations. The publication of his poem "Er" (1970), which was written in the 1940s, triggered a debate over affinities and even similarities to Celan's poems, in particular his "Todesfuge." Although Weißglas never accused Celan of plagiarism, evil-minded journalists and literary critics used these similarities as another alleged proof of Celan's so-called culpability and plagiarism. There were other explanations, however, for the affinities between these two friends: they shared a similar cultural background, spent a lot of time together exchanging ideas and reading poems, loved the same authors, and had similar experiences from Jewish persecution to emigration to Romania.

Literary criticism addresses other topics as well. Among them is Weißglas's tendency to rework his own themes, which have led some critics (Stănescu) to establish a hierarchy among the poems, arguing that the first versions were less accomplished than the later ones. By contrast, other critics (Wiedemann-Wolf) read them as variations on the same theme. Weißglas's preference for classic poetic forms was held against him and interpreted as a lack of innovative power rather than a conscious political and poetological statement. At a time when the Nazis abused classicist forms in order to propagate their ideology, Weißglas consciously used the classicist poetic tradition in order to prove that he, a persecuted Jew, was the true heir of German culture. After the war Weißglas defiantly continued to use this style of writing because he considered it an atemporal style.

Bibliography

Primary Sources

Kariera am Bug (Stone Quarry at the Bug). 1947.

Der Nobiskrug. Bucharest: Kriterion, 1972.

Aschenzeit (Time of Ashes). 1994.

Secondary Sources

Baumann, Gerhart. "Dank an die Sprache: Erinnerungen an J. Weißglas Jr." *Umwege und Erinnerungen*. In München: W. Fink Verlag, 1984, pp. 49–62.

Buck, Theo. "Eine leise Stimme: Zum Leben und Werk von Immanuel Weißglas." *Aschenzeit*. Aachen: Rimbaud, 1994, pp. 128–152.

Colin, Amy, and Alfred Kittner, eds. *Versunkene Dichtung der Bukowina: Eine Anthologie deutschsprachiger Dichtung*. München: W. Fink Verlag, 1994 pp. 304–313; 403–404.

Corbea, Andrei, and Michael Astner, eds. *Kulturlandschaft Bukowina. Studien zur deutschsprachigen Literatur der Bukowina nach 1918*. Jassy: Editural Universitatii Al I. Cuza, 1990, pp. 174–178.

Forster, Leonard. "Todesfuge: Paul Celan, Immanuel Weißglas and the Psalmist." *German Life and Letters* 39, no. 1 (October 1985): 1–20.

Kittner, Alfred. "Abschied von Immanuel Weißglas." *Neue Literatur* (Bucharest) 7, no. 28 (1979): 33–36.

Kolf, Bernd. "Stygisches: Zu Immanuel Weißglas *Der Nobiskrug*." *Neue Literatur* (Bucharest) 1, no. 24 (1973): 96–102.

Marcu, Grigore. "Mondsymbolik in 'Der Nobiskrug.' " In *Kulturlandschaft Bukowina Studienzur deutschsprachigen Literatur der Bukowina nach 1918*. Edited by Andrei Corbea and Michael Astner. Jassy: Editura Universităţii Al. I. Cuza, 1990, pp. 174–178.

Motzan, Petre. *Die rumäniendeutsche Lyrik nach 1944. Problemaufriß und historischer Überblick*. Cluj: Dacia, 1980, pp. 126–127.

Stanescu, Heinz. "Der Dichter des Nobiskruges: Immanuel Weißglas." *German Life and Letters* 39, no. 1 (October 1985): 21–47.

Weißglas, Isak. *Ghetto und Deportation in Steinbruch am Bug. Bericht einer Deportation nach Transnistiren*. With a commentary by Wolfgang Benz. Edited by Ernest Wichner and Herbert Wiesner. Berlin: Literaturhaus Berlin, 1995.

Wiedemann, Barbara. " 'Altneutränene.' Überlegungen zu Immanuel Weißglas zweiten Gedichtband.'' In *Kulturlandschaft Bukowina. Stadienzur dentschsprachigen Literatur der Bukowina nach 1918*. Edited by Andrei Corbea and Michael Astner. Jassy: Editura Univeristăţii Al. I. Cuza, 1990, pp. 155–173.

PETER WEISS
(1916–1982)

ROBERT C. HOLUB

PETER WEISS WAS a prominent author and playwright whose major works appeared in German. Although his play *Marat/Sade* (1964) and his socially engaged writings on colonialism and capitalist exploitation are his best-known works, Weiss's documentary drama *Die Ermittlung* (*The Investigation*, 1965) was a major event in postwar literature concerning the Holocaust.

Biography

Weiss was born near Berlin on 8 November 1916. His father, Janö Weiss, was a Jewish textile manufacturer and a Czech citizen; his mother, Frieda Franziska Hummel, was a German Christian who had grown up in Basel and the Alsace region. Although Weiss's parents were wed in a Jewish ceremony, his father converted to Protestantism, and Weiss was brought up as a Lutheran. For the first decade after World War I, the Weiss family lived in Bremen, and in 1929 they moved to Berlin. After the National Socialists assumed power, Weiss ceased his preparations for the university and entered a trade school. In 1935 he and his family were forced into exile. They settled first in London, moved to Czechoslovakia in 1936, and then fled to Sweden in 1938, when Hitler occupied the Sudetenland. Weiss became a Swedish citizen in 1945, and although he acquired considerable fame in Germany, he maintained his residence in Sweden throughout the rest of his life.

In his early artistic career Weiss directed his creative talents toward graphic art and film. In these endeavors he achieved moderate success. His initial literary endeavors in the postwar era were in Swedish, but he eventually settled on German as his language for literature. His early work belongs to an existentialist, autobiographical mode (*Abschied von den Eltern* [*Leavetaking*, 1961], *Fluchtpunkt* [*Vanishing Point*, 1962]); it is influenced to a degree by Franz Kafka and relates primarily to his experiences in exile. By the mid-1960s, however, Weiss, like many contemporaries, had turned to more political concerns. His breakthrough work was *Marat/Sade* (1964), an extended reflection on revolution and sensuality. The play achieved renown in the Anglophone world because of a theatrical production and subsequent film by Peter Brook. *Die Ermittlung* premiered a year after *Marat/Sade*, and it too was well received, although controversial. Thereafter, Weiss continued with documentary works that revealed his political commitment: a play against colonialist politics in Angola, *Gesang vom lusitanischen Popanz* (1967), was followed in 1968 by the documentary drama *Vietnam Discourse*, which explored the history of the anticolonialist struggle in Southeast Asia as well as the imperialism of U.S. foreign policy. Subsequent stage productions dealt with the German poet Friedrich Hölderlin, the exile and assassination of the Russian revolutionary Leon Trotski, and Kafka's main character in *Der Prozeß* (*The Trial*). Weiss's greatest work of prose was his three-volume *Ästhetik des Widerstands* (Aesthetics of Resistance, 1975, 1978, 1981), a lengthy and complex novel about working-class resistance to fascism and participation in the Spanish Civil War and World War II. Weiss died on 10 May 1982.

Contribution to Holocaust Literature

Die Ermittlung. Oratorium in 11 Gesängen is Weiss's only significant work about the Holocaust. It appeared at the onset of a movement toward politicized literature in Germany and in much of the Western world, and it marks a decisive turn on the author's part toward political engagement. Its subject is the trial of twenty-two Germans active in the concentration camp at Auschwitz-Birkenau. Beginning on 20 December 1963, the trial lasted over a year and a half; the court heard testimony from 409 witnesses relating to the twenty-two defendants and their alleged actions. On 19 August 1965 the court convicted seventeen of the defendants and gave them prison sentences ranging from three years and three months to life imprisonment. Three defendants were acquitted; one died before he could be brought to trial; another was excused because of illness. The most important proceedings against war criminals to take place in Germany since the initial Nuremburg trials in 1946, the Auschwitz trials were the first major action taken by Germans against former concentration camp guards and the first result of inquiries by the Central Office for Investigation of National Socialist Crimes, established in Ludwigsburg in 1958. They were rivaled in notoriety only by the Eichmann proceedings in Israel in 1961.

In attendance at the Auschwitz trial on 13 March 1964 was Weiss, whose play *Marat/Sade*, then in the midst of rehearsals, was to become a German, and then an international, success. Attracted to the drama of the court proceedings and fascinated by the possibility of condensing the masses of material into a structure suitable for the stage, Weiss determined shortly thereafter to compose a play based on the testimony from the Frankfurt trial. His play was meant simultaneously to disseminate information and to provoke public response. But unlike Rolf Hochhuth's sensational play from 1963, *Der Stellvertreter* (*The Deputy*), which exposed Pope Pius XII's insensitivity to the Holocaust, Weiss's play does not force his documentation into a conventional dramatic form. Instead, he abandons traditional patterns and structures his drama around a creative citation and adaptation of the documents themselves. He does not aim to represent or to invent a narrative of events, but instead seeks to recount in systematic form various aspects of the concentration camp. His eleven "acts," called "songs" or "cantos," start with testimony on the ramp and the physical structure of the camps; proceed through accounts of various persons, procedures, and instruments of death; and end with the crematorium. Instead of re-creating a possible historical occurrence during the war, Weiss allows the reports taken from the Auschwitz trial to reflect on the past, and his drama consists almost entirely of the speeches of the accused and of witnesses, prosecutors, defense attorneys, and judges. There are almost no stage directions, and Weiss provides only a short authorial note at the beginning of the play.

Structural Techniques and Significance

The method Weiss employs is condensation, a "concentration" (*Konzentrat*) of statements, as he himself writes in *The Investigation* (1965; translated by Jon Swan and Ulu Grosbard, New York: Atheneum, 1975, p. 1), playing eerily on the term "concentration camp" (*Konzentrationslager*). The 409 witnesses are reduced to an anonymous 9; eighteen of the original twenty-two defendants appear in the play; the year and a half of testimony totaling thousands of pages is presented in unrhymed, unpunctuated, and largely arrhythmic verse on fewer than two hundred pages. Weiss often takes testimony from different parts of the trial, sometimes relating to different historical persons or occurrences, and adapts it for a more coherent event involving a single individual. Weiss justifies the condensation and simplification with his belief that the experiences of the concentration camp inmates were largely interchangeable. In the brief introductory note he writes: "Personal experience and confrontations must be steeped in anonymity. Inasmuch as the witnesses in the play lose their names, they become mere speaking tubes. The nine witnesses sum up what hundreds expressed" (p. 1). Although the defendants retain their identities, they, too, are more important as vehicles for establishing facts than as illustrations of the moral depravity or gross disregard for human life in Auschwitz: the accused have merely "lent their names which, within the drama, exist as symbols of a system that implicated in its guilt many others who never appeared in court" (p. 1). Weiss is uninterested in the individuals, in individual psychology, and in personal histories; his use of three legal officials (a prosecutor, a defense attorney, and a judge), nine witnesses, and eighteen accused is arbitrary and related only to the multiples of three that abound in *Die Ermittlung*. What Weiss emphasizes is the function of these people as part of a system and as means for conveying the nature of the system to which individuals belong.

There is thus a tension present in Weiss's play between empirical reality, as recorded in documents and supra-individual structures, and ideologies, as they are constructed in Weiss's creative use of documents. This tension is manifested in the play on several levels. The title, for example, conveys very strongly the sense of facts and documented occurrences. The German word *Ermittlung* is the term used for police investigations to ascertain whether or not a crime has been committed. His title thus distances his work from the trial itself. Indeed, Weiss steers his production away from a re-creation not only of the extermination camp but also of the Auschwitz trial. There are no opening statements or lists of alleged violations of law. At the close of the play there are no verdicts or sentencing of the convicted, no legal justifications for the findings of the court. Weiss's goal is not to accuse the perpetrators once again onstage; he is relatively unconcerned with the guilt and innocence of these men as individuals. Moreover, he does not want his play to simulate closure, as a trial does. Although he sets up a rough narrative of experience starting with the arrival in Auschwitz and ending with the crematories, the investigatory aspect of the play does not bring us to any conclusions. We are left instead with documented facts.

The subtitle, however, points to the other facet of Weiss's play, his creative employment of documents. The notion that the documents can be arranged into an "Oratorio in Eleven Cantos" makes the reader aware of the constructed nature of the drama and perhaps, by extension, of the constructed nature of the camps and the events that occurred there. Weiss's play conforms to the outer structure of an oratorio in that the various witnesses and defendants simply recite their speeches. The oratorio form also suggests a degree of seriousness that is appropriate for Weiss's theme. Like works in a religious tradition, Weiss's play deals with events and persons that should have a profound effect on the audience. But Weiss's oratorio is obviously a modern and a secular variant. There are no heroes or saints populating the pages of *Die Ermittlung*; there is no redemption or salvation. The cast of characters is largely anonymous, and their actions are far removed from anything sacred or holy. Nonetheless, the suggestion that the play is an oratorio contrasts sharply with the juridical notion of the main title. Together title and subtitle reflect the dual use of the raw materials for the play: to document the facts of history and to construct a new and non-mimetic reality different from that history.

The play itself continues this tension between documentary evidence and the construction of an artistic work. On the most basic level Weiss seeks to emphasize Auschwitz life through the play's historical facticity. In "The Song of the Platform," for example, Weiss reproduces for us through testimony details about the length of the platform (850 yards long), the length of the trains that stopped there ("They usually took up about two thirds / of the platform"), the site of the selections ("In the middle of the platform"), and the width of the platform ("about 30 feet wide") (p. 26). Similarly, in "The Song of the Swing," we receive a rather graphic description of this instrument of torture and how the prisoners were bound to it:

First the prisoner had
to sit down on the floor
and draw up his knees
His hands were tied in front
and then pushed down over his knees
Then they shoved the pipe in the space
between the arms and knees
Then the pipe was raised and set into the wood frame (p. 85).

But this almost obsessive focus on the factual description of Auschwitz is situated within a structure that suggests the unreality of the documented occurrences.

Weiss himself and numerous commentators have noted that *Die Ermittlung* is modeled on Dante's *Inferno*. Weiss writes a work consisting of eleven cantos, each subdivided into three parts. As in the *Divine Comedy*, the number three and its multiples recur throughout *Die Ermittlung*, determining the number of witnesses, accused, and court personnel. But the *Inferno* is merely a structural device to assist Weiss in his work of condensation. The symmetry in Dante's poem, the intricate *terza rima* scheme, refers the reader to the harmonious universe maintained and ordained by the deity. Weiss does not attempt to follow Dante here: his "songs" are unrhymed and unmetered; lines and "songs" have varying lengths. In the modern drama the exterior structure is not matched by a harmonious interior. The secularized hell of Auschwitz may be cast in the form borrowed from a sacred model, but there is neither peace nor salvation as content or telos in the universe Weiss portrays.

Thematic Implications

The tension between document and construction in the title and the structure is found on the level of message as well. Although the documents tell the story of Auschwitz, Weiss does not assemble them into a drama primarily to admonish Germany, to publicize the crimes committed against the Jews, or to condemn the Nazi regime. The very fact that the words "Jew" and "Jewish" never occur in the play, and that there is no discussion of German antisemitism, is a good indication that Weiss's point lies in another realm. Weiss's true intention is revealed in his frequent reference to the current activities of the accused, most of whom are well integrated into postwar German society. The people who ran the extermination machinery seem to have had little trouble adjusting to civilian life in the Federal Republic. Their unproblematic integration into postwar society indicates a fundamental similarity between the factories of death and those of the postwar economic miracle. Weiss is thematizing more than the banality of evil about which Hannah Arendt wrote after the Eichmann trial. He is connecting the logic of fascism with an underlying inhumanity in the capitalist order of Germany and the industrialized world. For Weiss the extermination camps were an extreme manifestation of an order based on oppressed and oppressors, an extreme but logical extension of what occurs on an everyday basis in our own world.

The tension between documentation and construction that permeates Weiss's drama has consequences for his message as well. Although Weiss carefully arranges the testimony, questions, and remarks from his sources to support his main thesis, and even invents witness number 3 as his own mouthpiece, the documented testimony of the Nazi genocide winds up overwhelming the thesis connecting past crimes with present society and thus indicting capitalist logic as the root cause of the Holocaust. The graphic descriptions of the torture, mutilation, and death of countless individuals; the sadistic brutality and inhumanity of the camp personnel; and the squalid, depraved circumstances in which the prisoners were compelled to live ultimately vitiate the ideological premise on which the drama is based. The ideological message articulated by the third witness is drowned out by the din of the others who testify and by the silence of the millions unavailable for testimony. Composed on a contrast between documentary facticity and constructed representation, *Die Ermittlung* is itself a testimony to the power of the documentary form in dealing with the Holocaust and, simultaneously, to the impotence of documentation to convey an intelligible, cohesive story. Like prior and subsequent endeavors to harness this unique event as evidence for a political or ideological conviction, Weiss's play demonstrates again the impossibility of such an appropriation. With regard to the Holocaust, the very nature of the documented reality removes us temporarily from our historical situatedness, exploding time, place, and the prospect of coherent representation.

Bibliography

Primary Sources

Der Schatten des Körpers des Kutschers (*The Shadow of the Coachman's Body*). 1960.
Abschied von den Eltern (*Leavetaking*). 1961.
Fluchtpunkt (*Vanishing Point*). 1962.
Das Gespräche der drei Gehenden (*The Conversation of the Three Walkers*). 1963.
Die Verfolgung und Ermordung Jean Paul Marats dargestellet durch die Schaspielgruppe des Hospizes zu Charenton unter Anletiung des Herrn de Sade (*The Persecution and Assassination of Marat as Performed by the Inmates of the Asylum of Charenton Under the Direction of the Marquis de Sade*). 1964.
Die Ermittlung. Oratorium in 11 Gesängen (*The Investigation. Oratorio in 11 Cantos*). 1965.
Gesang vom lusitanischen Popanz (Song of the Lusitanian Bogey). 1967.
Diskurs über die Vorgeschichte und den Verlauf des lang andauernden Befreiungskrieges in Viet Nam als Beispiel für die Notwendigkeit des bewaffneten Kampfes der Unterdrückten gegen ihre Unterdrücker sowie über die Versuche der Vereinigten Staaten von Amerika die Grundlagen der Revolution zu vernichten (*Discourse on the Progress of the Prolonged War of Liberation in Viet Nam and the Events Leading Up to It as Illustration of the Necessity for Armed Resistance Against Oppression and on the Attempts of the United States of America to Destroy the Foundations of Revolution*). 1967.
Der Turm (*The Tower*). 1968.
Nacht mit Gästen. Wie dem Herrn Mockinpott das Leiden ausgetrieben wird (*Night with Guests: How Mr. Mockinpott Was Cured of His Sufferings*). 1969.
Trotski im Exil (*Trotsky in Exile*). 1970.
Hölderlin. 1971.
Das Duell (Original Swedish title *Duellen* [1953]; The Duel). 1972.
Der Prozess (The Trial). 1975.
Ästhetik des Widerstandes (Aesthetics of Resistance). 3 vols. 1975, 1978, 1981.
Der Fremde (*Der Vogelfreie*, 1947–1948; Swedish version titled *Dokument I* [1949]; The Stranger). 1980.
Notizbücher 1971–1980 (Notebooks 1971–1980). 1981.
Notizbücher 1960–1971 (Notebooks 1960–1971). 1982.
Der neue Prozess (The New Trial). 1984.
Von Insel zu Insel (original Swedish *Från ö till ö* [1947]; From Island to Island). 1984.
Die Besiegten (original Swedish *De Besegrade* [1948]; The Conquered). 1985.
Rekonvaleszenz (Convalescence). 1991.

Secondary Sources

Canaris, Volker, ed. *Über Peter Weiss*. Frankfurt: Suhrkamp, 1976.
Cohen, Robert. *Understanding Peter Weiss*. Columbia: University of South Carolina Press, 1993.
Falkenstein, Henning. *Peter Weiss*. Berlin: Morgenbuch, 1996.
Hermand, Jost, and Marc Silberman, eds. *Rethinking Peter Weiss*. Frankfurt: Lang, 2000.
Howald, Stefan. *Peter Weiss zur Einführung*. Hamburg: Junius, 1994.
Krause, Rolf. *Faschismus als Theorie und Erfahrung: "Die Ermittlung" und ihr Autor Peter Weiss*. Frankfurt: Lang, 1982.
Lindner, Burkhardt. *Im Inferno. "Die Ermittlung" von Peter Weiss*. Badenweiler: Oase-Verlag, 1988.
Rector, Martin, and Christoph Weiss, eds. *Peter Weiss' Dramen: Neue Interpretationen*. Opladen: Westdeutscher Verlag, 1999.
Vogt, Jochen. *Peter Weiss*. Reinbek: Rowohlt, 1987.
Weiss, Christoph. *Auschwitz in der geteilten Welt: Peter Weiss und "Die Ermittlung" im kalten Krieg*. St. Ingberg: Röhrig Universitätsverlag, 2000.

Interviews

Gerlach, Rainer, and Matthias Richeter, eds. *Peter Weiss im Gespräch*. Frankfurt: Suhrkamp, 1986.

FRANZ WERFEL

(1890–1945)

EHRHARD BAHR

FRANZ WERFEL WAS born on 10 September 1890 in Prague, the capital of Bohemia in the Austro-Hungarian Empire (until 1918; then of Czechoslovakia). His father, Rudolf Werfel, and his mother, Albine Kussi, both belonged to the German-speaking Jewish minority in Prague. After graduating from a German high school, Werfel was sent to Hamburg as a business apprentice. Showing no promise in business, he returned to Prague and made his debut as a writer with a collection of poems entitled *Der Weltfreund* (The World Friend, 1911). This title, associated with German Expressionism, made Werfel one of the young leaders of this avant-garde literary movement.

Werfel was drafted into the Austrian army during World War I but spent most of his service in the War Press Office in Vienna. At this time he met the Catholic and Pan-Germanist Alma Mahler Gropius, wife of the architect Walter Gropius and widow of Gustav Mahler, and they began a love affair.

When the state of Czechoslovakia was founded after World War I, Werfel opted for Austria and moved to Vienna in 1918. Alma insisted on Werfel's official withdrawal from Judaism as a precondition to the marriage (Walter Gropius and Alma were officially divorced in 1920); he complied and they were married in 1929, but he never converted to Christianity. After 1919, his literary production showed at times a close affinity to Catholic topics. This predilection, however, did not protect Werfel from attacks by the Nazis in 1933, when he was expelled as a corresponding member from the Prussian Academy of Arts in Berlin. Werfel happened to be on vacation in Italy when German troops invaded Austria in 1938, and never returned to his adopted country.

Revolutionary in his poetry and his politics at the end of World War I, Werfel became conservative under the influence of his wife. Her influence, however, did not always prevail, especially when he was dealing with Jewish persecution and the Holocaust. Werfel's fame rests to a degree on the fact that he wrote, in 1933, the first genocide novel, *Die vierzig Tage des Musa Dagh* (*The Forty Days of Musa Dagh*), the topic of which was the mass killing of the Armenians during the Ottoman military campaign to drive them from eastern Turkey between 1915 and 1923.

From 1938 until 1940 Werfel and his wife lived in exile on the French Riviera. After the defeat of France by Germany they were saved from extradition to the Nazis by the American Emergency Rescue Committee, which provided safe-conduct for anti-Fascist intellectuals and artists from Vichy France. The couple stayed for a short time in Lourdes, where Werfel pledged to write a novel on the life of Bernadette Soubirous, the saint of this place of pilgrimage, if they should be saved. Soon after, the Werfels were able to flee via Spain and Portugal to the United States, where they settled in Beverly Hills, California. Here Werfel wrote *Das Lied von Bernadette* (*The Song of Bernadette*, 1941), a bestseller that provided the story for *The Song of Bernadette*, a film that won five Oscars in 1943. Werfel died in his home in Beverly Hills on 26 August 1945.

Works

Werfel completed *Die vierzig Tage des Musa Dagh* in March 1933, two months after the Nazis had come to power in Germany. When he read from his novel during a lecture tour in Germany in November 1932, he had become aware of the parallels between political persecution in Turkey and in Germany. In a letter to his parents, Werfel wrote later that his novel had become "symbolically topical: suppression and extermination of minorities because of nationalism" (Abels, p. 98). This novel presented the emergence of a new kind of nationalism that combined militarism and modern technology with a biological ideology. For the historical character of General Enver Pasha, as presented in the novel, the Armenians are like bacteria, and their removal from Turkey is an issue of national health; he declares that "there can be no peace between human beings and plague germs" (New York: Viking, 1934, p. 139). A disease on the body of the Turkish people, the Armenians must be extirpated. Johannes Lepsius, also a historical figure who tried to intervene on behalf of the Armenians without success, in his encounter with Enver Pasha concludes that this new type of mass murderer does not have a face, only the "mask of a human mind which has gone beyond guilt" (p. 142). Within a few years this type of mass murder would become commonplace in Central Europe.

The rest of the novel deals with the fate of Gabriel Bagradian, who saves his people from extermination by taking them on the Musa Dagh, the "Moses Mountain," where they are able to defend themselves against the Turkish forces for forty days, until they are rescued by a French battleship. Seeing his people saved, the protagonist is killed by a Turkish bullet. *Die vierzig Tage des Musa Dagh* is a well-researched historical novel, but its special strength is the fact that it exposes the ideology of biological nationalism and presents genocide as a phenomenon that will be repeated or imitated if not stopped by international intervention. Whether Werfel superimposed Nazi rhetoric on an earlier genocide has not been decided, but critics agree that the parallels between the nationalism of the Young Turks and that of the Nazis were intentional.

Werfel's biblical drama *Der Weg der Verheißung* (*The Eternal Road*, 1935) and his biblical novel *Höret die Stimme* (*Hearken unto the Voice*, 1937) constituted political statements because they showed his renewed commitment to Judaism and to Jewish themes that he had avoided during the late 1920s and early 1930s. *The Eternal Road*, produced in New York in 1937 by Max Reinhardt, was considered a major tribute to the Jewish history of persecution and survival. The play is a reenactment of biblical history, from the patriarchs and Moses to the kings and prophets, on a multilevel stage. The lowest level is reserved for a congregation of persecuted Jews, who serve as audience. At the end of the play they are forced by armed men to leave the city by nightfall or face death. The historical time of their persecution is left open.

The best of Werfel's work during his exile in France remained, however, fragmentary and unpublished for a long time: a projected novel, *Cella, oder, Die Überwinder* (*Cella, or, The Survivors*), and the dramatic sketches *Der Arzt von Wien* (The Doctor of Vienna) and *Die Schauspielerin* (The Actress). Begun in 1938, these dealt with the Nazi annexation of Austria. The two sketches are similar to scenes from Bertolt Brecht's *Furcht und Elend im Dritten Reich* (*The Private Life of the Master Race*), produced in 1938 in Paris. Werfel's sketches were similarly designed to be parts of a cycle, entitled *Abschied von Wien* (Adieu from Vienna). In *Der Arzt von Wien*, a seventy-year-old Jewish doctor commits suicide by injection to escape deportation to a concentration camp, while in *Die Schauspielerin* an actress is forced to leave the country because of threats by a Nazi colleague. Although she is not Jewish, she has been a star of the theater of the First Republic of Austria. The actress leaves with her daughter, pretending that the forced emigration is a vacation trip, although she knows better, like the protagonist of Brecht's *Die jüdische Frau* (*The Jewish Woman*).

The eventual posthumous novel, *Cella, oder, Die Überwinder* (1982), is the best account in German literature of the *Anschluss* (German annexation of Austria) and the Nazi pogrom in Vienna. The Austrian Nazis are called the *Weißstrümpfe* (white stockings), while the members of the SS are characterized as *Motormänner* (engine men). With this latter term Werfel identified the reactionary modernism of German Fascism, which employed new technology to achieve the goals of an irrational ideology. The *Motormänner* are driven by the same biological racism as the Young Turks in *Die vierzig Tage des Musa Dagh*. A target of this racism, the protagonist, Hans Bodenheim, is forced to remove anti-Nazi slogans from the sidewalk with a nailbrush, a public humiliation historically documented. When Bodenheim protests the cruel treatment of an old Jewish woman, he is arrested and thrown into jail without trial. Finally, Bodenheim is put on a train to the Dachau concentration camp, where he is saved only by the intervention of an old army friend who has made a successful career with the Nazis. Bodenheim escapes into Switzerland without any news about his family, including his daughter Cella, an aspiring concert pianist. The novel ends with the question, Will he ever see his family again? This open ending was not planned, but is more realistic than the outline Werfel provided for the rest of the novel. He had planned a reunion of the family in Paris and a musical triumph for the daughter in a concert at New York's Carnegie Hall, but he never finished the novel that is one of his best works.

The interpolated novella, *Die wahre Geschichte vom wiederhergestellten Kreuz* (The True Story of the Restored Crucifix), exemplifies Werfel's belief in the dual mission of Judaism and the Catholic Church. The Austrian rabbi of a village near the Hungarian border restores a crucifix, desecrated by local Nazi storm troopers, and returns it to the village priest. While the rabbi is murdered by the enraged Nazi mob, the members of the Jewish community are able to escape to Hungary.

The last work completed by Werfel in Europe (but published in Buenos Aires in 1941) was *Ein blaßblaue Frauenhandschrift* (A Woman's Pale Blue Handwriting). Although sentimental in its plot, this novella effectively deals with the antisemitism and persecution of Jews in Germany and with the fact that similar attitudes were already prevalent in Austrian society in 1936. An Austrian government official is asked by his former lover, a Jew, to admit a Jewish student from Germany to an Austrian high school. He is afraid that the young student may be his own illegitimate son. Learning that his own son died seventeen years before, the official is relieved; he can continue his self-deception regarding his own antisemitism, while his former lover is forced to immigrate to South America. Traditional in form, this novella cannot compare in intensity with either *Cella, oder, Die Überwinder* or *Die wahre Geschichte vom wiederhergestellten Kreuz*, because it deals with conditions before the *Anschluss*.

Only in his last two works—a play, *Jacobowsky und der Oberst* (*Jacobowsky and the Colonel*, 1944), and a novel, *Stern der Ungeborenen* (*Star of the Unborn*, 1946)—did Werfel return to the persecution of the Jews in Central Europe. The play, which he called a "comedy of a tragedy," verges on the theater of the absurd. Despite the threat of capture by the Germans, the Polish colonel does not hesitate to display the antisemitism of his caste toward Jacobowsky, a Polish Jew who comes to his rescue again and again. Although Colonel Stjerbinsky and Jacobowsky have a common enemy, they are engaged in an eternal antagonism. Only when no other escape is possible does the colonel relinquish his prejudice in order to save himself and his despised countryman. But it is not his grand gesture that saves Jacobowsky; rather, it is the latter's will to live coupled with British pragmatism. Impressed by Jacobowsky's courage, a British naval officer declares him eligible for rescue because he is considered useful to the Allied war effort. Oversimplification mars this tragicomedy. Although Jacobowsky and the colonel are presented in the context of historical reality, they are, in fact, stereotypes. The comedy intended in the contrast between self-destructive prejudice and the tragedy of persecution fails, for the sense for the tragedy sometimes gets lost and the antagonism between the protagonists is often trivialized. The allegorical figures who appear in the play—the Eternal Jew and St. Francis of Assisi—do not add a metaphysical dimension, but are a gross simplification of the relationship between Judaism and Catholicism.

Werfel's last work, *Stern der Ungeborenen*, is a utopian novel that has the author as its narrator and protagonist. This autobiographical figure refers to the horrors of World War II that he has witnessed. He is transported from his house at 610 North Bedford Drive, Werfel's Beverly Hills address, into the same region some hundred thousand years later. A twentieth-century Dante, he explores the utopian Panopolis, a subterranean urban civilization that has abolished labor, technology, and money and has raised life expectancy up to 200 years. Death is a voluntary process of "retrogenesis" to plantlike existence in a region called the Wintergarden. But there are also failures in the "retrogenetic" process that result in idiotic turnip-men and in so-called Catabolites, who remind the narrator of the victims of concentration and extermination camps like Buchenwald and Maidanek, while the attendants remind him of the SS doctors with their murderous injections. The only institutions of the past that have survived without change are the Catholic Church and Judaism, witnesses of transcendence; but their influence is marginal.

The intersecting time levels—that of Werfel's biography from his childhood in Prague to his exile in Los Angeles and that of the narrator's jump in time—contribute to the complex structure of the novel, providing the opportunity for a review of twentieth-century European history as ancient history. According to a utopian informant, the Germans took the lead in humanitarianism and goodwill between World Wars II and III. In this sarcastic review, the Germans were then divided into the good *Heinzelmännchen* (the brownies) and the unregenerate *Wichtelmännchen* (the imps), who were indistinguishable from the brownies and worshiped an idol called Heiltier or Hiltier, an obvious allusion to Hitler. Although the novel does not deal with the Holocaust as a central topic, it includes explicit references to Buchenwald and Maidanek.

Conclusion

Franz Werfel is not a writer of Holocaust literature, but some of his works include explicit references that deserve critical attention. His treatment of the Armenian holocaust in *Die vierzig Tage des Musa Dagh* is relevant because of its parallels with the German genocide of the Jews, based on biological racism and the reasoning involved in the mass extermination of people. His works in exile dealing with the annexation of Austria and the antisemitic policies introduced by the Nazis are among the most powerful literary representations of this period of persecution. His play *Jacobowsky und der Oberst* addresses racial prejudice and persecution during the defeat of France in 1940, while his last novel, *Stern der Ungeborenen*, contains a review of twentieth-century European history that includes some references to the Holocaust; more important, though, it deals with the mentality that produced the Holocaust.

Bibliography

Primary Sources

Der Weltfreund (The World Friend, poems). 1911.
Die Geschwister von Neapel (*The Pascarella Family*, novel). 1931.
Die vierzig Tage des Musa Dagh (*The Forty Days of Musa Dagh*, novel). 1933.
Der Weg der Verheißung (*The Eternal Road: A Drama in Four Parts*). 1935.
Höret die Stimme (*Hearken unto the Voice*, novel). 1937.
Das Lied von Bernadette (*The Song of Bernadette*, novel). 1941.
Eine blaßblaue Frauenhandschrift (A Woman's Pale Blue Handwriting, novella). 1941.
Die wahre Geschichte vom wiederhergestellten Kreuz (The True History of the Restored Crucifix, novella). 1942.
Jacobowsky und der Oberst (*Jacobowsky and the Colonel*, tragicomedy). 1944.
Stern der Ungeborenen (*Star of the Unborn*, a "travel novel"). 1946.
Zwischen Oben und Unten (*Between Heaven and Earth*). 1946.
Cella, oder, Die Überwinder (*Cella, or, The Survivors*, novel). 1982.
Gesammelte Werke in Einzelbänden, collected works. 1990.

Secondary Sources

Abels, Norbert. *Franz Werfel*. Reinbek: Rowohlt, 1990.
Foltin, Lore B. *Franz Werfel, 1890–1945*. Pittsburgh: University of Pittsburgh Press, 1961.
Huber, Lothar, ed. *Franz Werfel: An Austrian Writer Reassessed*. Oxford: Berg, 1990.
Jungk, Peter Stephan. *Franz Werfel: A Life in Prague, Vienna, and Hollywood*. Translated by Anselm Hollo. New York: Weidenfeld, 1990.
Michaels, Jennifer E. *Franz Werfel and the Critics*. Columbia, S.C.: Camden House, 1994.
Robertson, Ritchie. "Leadership and Community in Werfel's *Die vierzig Tage des Musa Dagh*." In *Unser Fahrplan geht von Stern zu Stern: Franz Werfels Stellung und Werk*. Edited by Joseph Strelka. Bern: Lang, 1992, pp. 249–269.
Sokel, Walter H. *The Writer in Extremis: Expressionism in Twentieth-Century German Literature*. Stanford, Calif.: Stanford University Press, 1959.
Steimann, Lionel B. *Franz Werfel: The Faith of an Exile: From Prague to Beverly Hills*. Waterloo, Ont.: Laurier University Press, 1985.
Strelka, Joseph, ed. *Unser Fahrplan geht von Stern zu Stern: Zu Franz Werfels Stellung und Werk*. Bern: Lang, 1992.
Wagener, Hans. *Understanding Franz Werfel*. Columbia, S.C.: University of South Carolina Press, 1993.

Ruth Whitman
(1922–1999)

SHARON LEDER

Ruth Whitman is an American poet, translator, and educator whose major, original contribution to Holocaust literature is the imagined poetic diary *The Testing of Hanna Senesh* (1986). In this work, comprised of eighty-two poems, Whitman creates a compelling, intimate portrait of poet Hanna Senesh, World War II hero and Israeli parachutist, who attempted to rescue Jews from behind Nazi lines during the last months of her life. Whitman's interest in the Holocaust is also reflected in her translations from Yiddish Holocaust literature, *The Selected Poems of Jacob Glatstein* (1972) and *The Fiddle Rose: Poems 1970–1972: Abraham Sutzkever* (1990). In addition, Ruth Whitman edited and translated *An Anthology of Modern Yiddish Poetry* (1966, 1995) that includes many poets who survived the Nazi genocide. Her other writings include eight volumes of original poetry, essays on the poetic process and the teaching of poetry, and additional translations.

A distinguished poet, Whitman has won many awards, fellowships, grants, and competitions for her writing. These include grants from the National Foundation for Jewish Culture (1968) and the National Endowment for the Arts (1974–1975) and fellowships from the MacDowell Colony (1962, 1964, 1972–1974, 1979, 1982) and the senior Fulbright Writer-in-Residence Program, Jerusalem (1984–1985).

Whitman began her poetic career writing personal lyrics in her first two books—*Blood and Milk Poems* (1963) and the award-winning *The Marriage Wig and Other Poems* (1968). She then moved beyond the personal lyric "to use a more extensive narrative line" in order to speak in "the voices of others" whose lives could "expand" her own experience and teach her "something about courage and the ability to survive" (*Laughing Gas*: *Poems New and Selected 1963–1990*, Detroit: Wayne State University Press, 1991, p. 17). Among the women's lives she has taken as poetic subject and voice are pioneer Tamsen Donner; Hatshepsut, the only Egyptian female pharaoh; and Holocaust resistance fighter Hanna Senesh.

Although Whitman's comment about courage refers directly to heroic individuals like Hanna Senesh, whose lives Whitman studied and from whose perspectives she composed volumes of original verse, the comment can easily apply as well to remarkable writers like Jacob Glatstein and Abraham Sutzkever whose poetry Whitman translated. By speaking imaginatively through the voice of Senesh, and by translating the writing of Glatstein, Sutzkever, and other major Yiddish poets who survived the Holocaust, Whitman found a way to inhabit the psyches and enter into the visions of several giants in the field of Holocaust literature.

Ruth Whitman and Hanna Senesh

Ruth Whitman was born on 28 May 1922 in New York to Martha Sherman Bashein and Meyer D. Bashein. Whitman sold her first poem when she was eleven. She continued publishing volumes of poetry into her seventies, including the revised and expanded edition of *An Anthology of Modern Yiddish Poetry* (1995). Understandably, an American Jew who lived during the rise of Nazism and World War II might ask herself what her life would have been like had she lived in Eastern Europe during the Holocaust. In an interview with Sylvia Rothchild, Ruth Whitman said: " 'Ever since the Holocaust, I've asked myself what I would have done, how I would have behaved, whether I would have been a victim or a survivor' " (p. 13). It is no surprise, therefore, that Whitman identified with the young poet Hanna Senesh who was born in Budapest, Hungary, just one year earlier than herself.

Whitman's life in some ways parallels the life of the legendary Senesh, who became the subject of Whitman's original work. Both were raised in assimilated Jewish, cosmopolitan environments and began early to receive encouragement from teachers and public recognition for their poetry (Rothkirchen, pp. 14–15; Rothchild, p. 13). It was during Ruth Whitman's seventeen-year marriage to classicist poet Cedric Whitman that she became more strongly identified with her Jewishness. Whitman grew up hearing her grandfather's Yiddish and Russian lullabies, according to Miriyam Glazer (p. 458), but she did not develop her own love affair with Yiddish until late in life (Rothchild, interview, p. 13). In contrast, Senesh became attached to Zionism during high school in Budapest where the atmosphere of increasing antisemitism drove her to emigrate to Palestine at age eighteen (Rothkirchen, pp. 15–16).

As Whitman continued to develop her career, Senesh contributed to the development of Palestine until her life took its tragic turn. In 1944, when Hanna Senesh was tortured and murdered by Hungarian Nazis, Ruth Whitman received her Bachelor of Arts from Radcliffe College, graduating magna cum laude. Whitman attained a masters from Harvard University in 1947. She worked first as educational editor for Houghton Mifflin, then as freelance editor for Harvard University Press and poetry editor for *Audience* magazine in Cambridge, Massachusetts (1941–1963). She moved on to become a poetry teacher and the Director of the Poetry in the Schools Program for the Massachusetts Council on the Arts (1965–1973). Finally, Whitman became a lecturer in poetry and poet-in-residence for several arts associations across the United States, in Israel, and at various colleges and universities, including Brandeis, Brown, Harvard, Massachusetts Institute of Technology, and Tel Aviv University. Whitman wrote that she was repressed and vulnerable until she was in her thirties, rebellious in her forties, and self-empowered only in her fifties, after she had transformed her perceptions by writing poems in the voices of others (*Laughing Gas*, p. 17). Whitman's search for strong, heroic female models led her to Hanna Senesh, a woman with a poet's sensibilities, who lived to be a kibbutz pioneer and died fighting for the Allied underground.

The Testing of Hanna Senesh

The Testing of Hanna Senesh is Whitman's poetic tribute to the twenty-three-year-old woman who was ultimately murdered by the Nazis in November 1944 after a military tribunal in Budapest found her guilty of treason. Senesh's own diary documents her emotional life from age thirteen to age twenty-three. However, the diary does not extend to the months before her death, when she trained with the British as a volunteer parachutist and secret agent in order to accomplish several goals: to liberate Allied pilots shot down behind Nazi lines in the Balkans; to organize resistance; and to rescue Jews from Romania, Hungary, and Czechoslovakia by guiding them through escape routes charted by the partisan underground. Ruth Whitman takes the reader into Senesh's internal experience during the time not covered in her diary, the last nine months of her life.

Whitman's "imagined diary" of Hanna Senesh resembles an actual diary in that it is written in the perspective of the ever-moving present. However, unlike Senesh's own diary, *The Testing of Hanna Senesh* is written entirely in poetry. Whitman had the advantage of post-Holocaust knowledge and was therefore able to write about events in Senesh's life in retrospect, like a memoirist. Whitman gained knowledge about Hanna Senesh and acquired a sense of Senesh's voice by immersing herself in research. The research began in Jerusalem in 1977 and continued until 1981, when she began her writing. As well as reading Senesh's diary and poetry, Whitman studied at the Hanna Senesh Archives at Kibbutz Sdot Yam and conducted interviews with Senesh's mother and brother and with her fellow Israeli parachutists, Joel Palgi and Reuven Dafni.

The Testing of Hanna Senesh is divided into three segments. In the first section, "Budapest, June 1944," Senesh is being tortured by the Nazis for refusing to disclose the transmitter code she has been using to communicate with the underground. Whitman does not shrink from describing the physical torture Hanna Senesh endured: her pain resulting from three days of beating, her ribs aching, her wrist probably broken, her jaw throbbing where the police knocked out a tooth (*The Testing of Hanna Senesh*, Detroit: Wayne State University Press, 1986, p. 27).

It is immediately apparent from the way Senesh bears up under the pressure, letting her mind wander out of her body, that Whitman's interest is to deepen our understanding of Senesh's psychology, to move us beyond former images of Senesh as patriot or plaster saint:

> After the first shock
> it's like letting a wave of flame singe your hand:
> first a sharp sensation, then no feeling.
> I watch myself like a person in a dream
> while they invent devices to break me down (p. 28).

Section two, "Yugoslavia, March 1944 to June 1944," is set three months earlier, when Senesh is landing by parachute over Slovenia to join Tito's partisans.

This longer section treats the conflict that emerges between Senesh and the partisan authorities over their decision not to cross the border into Hungary. The decision angers Senesh, causing her to grow increasingly impatient, not only because it means she will not be able to make contact with her mother and brother still in Budapest, but also because it foils the attempt to save Hungarian Jewry.

In this section, Whitman considers the anguish of the resistance fighter who knows her mission to gather the survivors and shepherd an exodus to Palestine has failed. Whitman's Senesh cannot accept the partisans' decision to abandon the Hungarian refugees and argues, "It's better to take the risk now / than never to try at all. How can you / sit back and do nothing?" (p. 42). Senesh wants to "find a new escape route" and gains courage by thinking of the Jewish martyrs of ancient days trapped by the Romans at Masada: "I sit here in the mountains of Yugoslavia, / breathing the hot dry air of Masada" (p. 56). Senesh's own decision to expose herself to even further risk by defying authority and crossing the border without trained assistance leads to her almost immediate capture.

This section of Whitman's book also addresses Senesh's political intelligence by raising a dominant theme of Holocaust writing: moral outrage with Allied indifference to saving Jews. Senesh remembers the British blockade of Palestine, when a shipload of Jewish refugees were prevented from landing and held outside of Istanbul without food because

> Jews are enemy aliens,
> said the British.
> Tow them out to the Black Sea,
> send them to Crete, Mauritius,
> to Rumania, Germany, Jamaica,
> but don't let them come to Palestine.
> That was December 1941 (p. 44).

Another theme Whitman shares with other Holocaust writers is the peril of the hunted Jew. Her description of the downed parachutists behind enemy lines captures Senesh's terror at being discovered, "Surrounded by Nazi patrols hunting for us, / we crouch in the forest for ten hours, / not daring to speak or breathe" (p. 50).

The section culminates with Whitman's translation of Senesh's landmark poem of heroism "Blessed Is the Match":

> Blessed is the match that burns and kindles fire,
> blessed is the fire that burns in the secret heart.
> Blessed are the hearts that know how to stop with
> honor . . .
> blessed is the match that burns and kindles fire (p. 77).

Only two poems in the entire volume are translations. The other translation is Whitman's version of the letter Senesh wrote to her mother before she was executed.

The letter appears in section three, "Budapest, July 1944 to November 1944," the period when Senesh waits in jail for sentencing. Whitman imagines Senesh employing this time, as any sensitive young woman might, reflecting on those aspects of life denied to her—dashed hopes for romantic love and the inability to fulfill her mother's expectations:

> Mother dearest
> I can only say this to you: a million thanks.
> And forgive me if possible.
> You alone will understand
> why there is no longer any need for words.
> With endless love—your daughter
> Truly, there is no need for words, and there are none
> (p. 111).

The translation is immediately followed by a poem of Whitman's that combines the use of imagination and postwar knowledge. Whitman has Senesh imagine her mother first in a deportation line of Hungarian Jews bound for Auschwitz, then as an escapee who is ultimately rescued (p. 112).

General Reception

The Testing of Hanna Senesh has been well received for its stirring narrative and for Whitman's ability to convey Senesh the woman. The success of Whitman's imagined diary is reflected in these comments by reviewer Elaine Starkman: "Whitman's voice is as authentic as Hanna's own" and "Whitman's poems offer us a kind of emotional clarity and present-day hindsight that we sometimes cannot get from Hanna's original diaries" (p. 4). Whitman's engagement with Senesh and with other writers on the Holocaust demonstrates her own belief that good poetry reveals "the importance of human experience" and teaches those who write and read poetry "how to live" (Rothchild, interview, p. 13).

Bibliography

Primary Sources

Blood and Milk Poems. 1963.

(Translator with Samuel Beckett and others) Alain Bosquet, *Selected Poems*. 1963.

"Four Modern Yiddish Poets." *Antioch Review* (summer 1966): 205–212.

(Co-translator) Isaac Bashevis Singer, *Short Friday*. 1966.

(Editor and translator) *An Anthology of Modern Yiddish Poetry*. 1966, 1995.

(Translator with others) Isaac Bashevis Singer, *The Seance*. 1968.
The Marriage Wig, and Other Poems. 1968.
(Editor and translator) *The Selected Poems of Jacob Glatstein*. 1972.
The Passion of Lizzie Borden: New and Selected Poems. 1973.
(Editor) *Poemmaking: Poets in Classrooms*. 1975.
Tamsen Donner: A Woman's Journey. 1975.
Sachusest Point (Television documentary). 1977.
"The Translator as Juggler." *Jewish Quarterly* (spring–summer 1978): n.p.
"Finding Tamsen Donner." *Radcliffe Quarterly* (spring 1978): 40–41.
Permanent Address: New Poems, 1973–1980. 1980.
"The Divided Heart." In *In Her Own Image: Women Working in the Arts*. Edited by Elaine Hedges and Ingrid Wendt, 1980, pp. 151–155.
"Motor Car, Bomb, God: Israeli Poetry in Translation." *The Massachusetts Review* (spring 1982): 309–328.
Becoming a Poet: Source, Process, and Practice. 1982.
The Testing of Hanna Senesh. 1986.
"History, Myth, and Poetry: Writing the Historical Persona Poem." *Iowa English Bulletin* 35, no. 1 (1987): 65–73.
"The Last Dark Violet Plum on the Tree: Modern Yiddish Poetry." *Associated Writing Programs Chronicle* (September 1990): 2–5.
The Fiddle Rose: Poems 1970–1972: Abraham Sutzkever. 1990.
Laughing Gas: Poems New and Selected 1963–1990. 1991.
Hatshepsut: Speak to Me. 1992.

Secondary Sources

Glazer, Miriyam. "Ruth Whitman." *Jewish-American Women Writers: A Bio-Bibliographical and Critical Sourcebook*. Edited by Ann R. Shapiro. Westport, Conn.: Greenwood, 1994, pp. 458–464.
Rothchild, Sylvia. "Book Captures Glory of Yiddish Poetry." *The Jewish Advocate* (September 1–7, 1995): 23.
Rothkirchen, Livia. "The Historical Background." In *The Testing of Hanna Senesh* by Ruth Whitman. Detroit: Wayne State University Press, 1986.
Starkman, Elaine. "The Testing of Hanna Senesh." *Belles Lettres* (September/October 1987): 4.
"Whitman, Ruth (Bashein)." In *Contemporary Authors*. New Revision Series, vol. 31. Edited by James G. Leskiak. Detroit: Gale Research Inc., 1990.
Wisse, Ruth. "Introduction." In *The Fiddle Rose: Poems 1970–1972: Abraham Sutzkever*. Selected and translated by Ruth Whitman. Detroit: Wayne State University Press, 1990.

Interviews

Interview by Sylvia Rothchild. *The Jewish Advocate* (24–30 January 1992): 13.

ELIE WIESEL

(1928–)

ALAN ROSEN

ELIE WIESEL, A survivor of Auschwitz and Buchenwald, has written and lectured on the Holocaust since the mid-1950s. Born in 1928 in the Transylvanian town of Sighet, Wiesel was sixteen when the war ended. He thereafter studied in Paris and worked for many years as a journalist. In 1956 Wiesel published his first memoir, *Un di velt hot geshvign* in Yiddish (And the World Remained Silent), a memoir chronicling the fate of his town and his family during the Holocaust. In 1958 he adapted the memoir into French and retitled it *La Nuit* (*Night*). Since 1960 he was written (primarily in French, but also in Yiddish and Hebrew) and published numerous novels and collections of essays, several plays, and many books of commentary on traditional Jewish subjects and sources. Having resided primarily in New York since the late 1950s, as a naturalized United States citizen since 1963, Wiesel has nevertheless continued to play a formidable role in French cultural and Jewish life.

Life

Wiesel was born to Shlomo and Sara Wiesel on 30 September 1928. He was the third of four children, the only boy. His father's mother, Nissel, resided near his family. Wiesel was named after her husband—Eliezer—and was a regular visitor at her house. His mother's father, Dodye Feig, owned and worked a farm a short distance away. He was a Viznitzer Hasid; Wiesel speaks repeatedly throughout his writing of this grandfather's influence, and especially of his legacy of Hasidic devotion and storytelling. Wiesel's mother embodied a synthesis of this Hasidic legacy and the modern world; she hoped her son would also follow these two paths; that he would be both "a Ph.D. and a Rabbi" (Harry James Cargas, p. 73).

Wiesel's father was a shopkeeper and was active in community affairs. He devoted most of his time to these activities and, according to the author, had little time for his own household. Wiesel writes of how, as a child, he admired his father's sacrifice on behalf of those in need in the community (an ideal to which Wiesel as an adult would dedicate himself). Yet he also yearned for his father to be close and available. He notes, however, that this closeness came when, after deportation and separation from the rest of the family, they had only each other.

The Wiesels lived in Sighet, a town of 25,000 residents in northwest Romania. Jews had resided in Sighet since the seventeenth century and had developed a rich infrastructure of synagogues, schools, organizations, presses, and libraries. By the 1940s, when the town came under Hungarian rule, the Jewish population numbered approximately 10,000—the largest in the area. Both under its own name and under aliases, the town of Sighet, along with its inhabitants, has played a major role in Wiesel's writings, symbolizing a world destroyed by the Holocaust but still alive in the author's memory.

Wiesel enjoyed the traditional *cheder* education of an eastern European Jewish boy, featuring lessons in the Bible and its commentary as well as classical rabbinic texts. He pursued these studies assiduously and, as a young teenager, opened with friends a special center of learning. (Indeed, Wiesel's study of classical Jewish texts continued even after deportation. In Auschwitz, on a work detail with the head of a rabbinical academy, they passed the time studying the Talmud by memory.) In addition to his religious education, he had a regular regimen of secular studies, learned modern Hebrew, and studied violin.

Wiesel was fifteen years old when he and his family were deported to Auschwitz in the spring of 1944. His mother and younger sister, Tzipora, were murdered soon after arrival. Evacuated from Auschwitz in January 1945, Wiesel and his father were marched with other prisoners into Germany. They were transported to Buchenwald where, on January 28 and 29 (18 Shevat), Wiesel's father was murdered. Wiesel and his two older sisters survived the camps.

At the end of the war Wiesel and a group of orphaned children from concentration camps were taken to France. These children included two prominent figures in the postwar rabbinical world: Yisrael Meir Lau, who was to become a chief rabbi of Israel, and Menashe Klein, a great scholar of rabbinical law. After a time of rehabilitation, Wiesel came to Paris where he was tutored in French by philosopher François Wahl. Wahl also introduced Wiesel to classics of world literature and philosophy. Both the French language and world literature became crucial media and inspirations for Wiesel's own literary career. Soon after mastering French, Wiesel attended classes in psychology, philosophy, and literature at the Sorbonne. He focused his interest on a comparative study of asceticism, for which he traveled to India to obtain further material. Although he wrote at considerable length on the subject, he never published his findings.

It was also during this period in Paris that Wiesel first encountered Mordechai Shushani, a Lithuanian Jew of vast erudition in Jewish and non-Jewish literature. A figure whose past was shrouded in mystery, Shushani became Wiesel's mentor for several years.

In Paris, Wiesel began to write professionally, working as a journalist for French, Israeli, and later American newspapers. He continued in journalism until the mid-1960s. In addition to giving him a knowledge of current events and contacts with major political and cultural figures, the discipline of journalism taught Wiesel to write wherever he was, under whatever conditions.

In 1954 Wiesel turned to a different form of writing: a memoir of his experience during the war. The original notes were in Hebrew, the manuscript in Yiddish. The memoir was first published in 1956 in Yiddish as *Un di velt hot geshvign* (And the World Remained Silent). During an interview Wiesel conducted with the French writer Francois Mauriac, the latter became aware of the memoir and urged Wiesel to render it into French. Wiesel titled the adaptation *La Nuit* (*Night*). Mauriac thereafter played a key role in helping Wiesel find a publisher and in bringing it to the attention of the French public. In 1956 Wiesel also moved to New York, where he lived and worked as a journalist and where he wrote his first novel, *L'Aube* (*Dawn*); even while living in America, Wiesel continued to write mainly in French.

During the 1960s Wiesel, as author of five novels and two books of essays, established his international reputation. Toward the end of this period, major changes in his personal life occurred as well. In 1969 Wiesel married Marion Rose, an Austrian survivor who served as the main translator of Wiesel's writings. Their son, Shlomo Elisha, was born in 1972. Wiesel's novelistic explorations of the predicament of the children of Holocaust survivors came in the wake of his son's birth. During these years, Wiesel also developed pivotal friendships, including those with Abraham Joshua Heschel and Saul Lieberman, both of whom were on the faculty of the Jewish Theological Seminary. Heschel and Lieberman helped to nurture Wiesel's writings on Jewish tradition—Biblical, Talmudic, and Hasidic—that have played an essential role in his work since the 1970s. While these writings stand on their own, they also have been read as being shaped by Wiesel's experience during the Holocaust.

Over the past three decades, Wiesel has continued to publish fiction and essays comprising over forty books. In addition to his writing, Wiesel has addressed issues of the Holocaust by lecturing worldwide, including ongoing lecture series in New York and Boston. He has held full-time teaching positions at City College of New York (1972–1976) and at Boston University (1976–) as well as visiting positions at many other universities, including Yale University (1982). He has also chaired many committees dedicated to Holocaust remembrance. Most importantly, he served as chairman of the President's Commission on the Holocaust (1979–1980) and of the United States Holocaust Memorial Council (1980–1986), the groups that orchestrated the design and building of the Holocaust Museum in Washington, D.C. In 1986 Wiesel resigned from the commission.

One of the most publicized events of this period was Wiesel's confrontation with President Ronald Reagan in what became know as "the Bitburg Affair." In 1985, Wiesel attempted to persuade President Reagan to cancel a forthcoming trip to the Bitburg military cemetery in Germany, arguing that because members of the Nazi Waffen SS were buried in the cemetery, it was "not your place, Mr. President" (*And the Sea Is Never Full: Memoirs, 1969–*, translated by Marion Wiesel, New York: Knopf, 1999, p. 238). In the end, Reagan made the visit, but Wiesel's protest, delivered at the White House on the occasion of receiving a Congressional Medal, articulated for the nation and the world a view of the significance of the Holocaust that transcends political expedience.

While insisting on addressing the Holocaust in its specifically Jewish dimensions, Wiesel has argued that the legacy of the Holocaust compels one to intervene on behalf of victims worldwide, particularly those threatened by state-sponsored persecution. Wiesel thus visited Soviet Jewry in 1965 and chronicled their oppression in a series of articles, material later adapted into a book, *The Jews of Silence*; the cause of Soviet Jewry has continued to remain at the forefront of Wiesel's lecturing and activism to the present day. He also has written on behalf of the oppressed native peoples of Central and South America, the blacks of South Africa, and victims of the Cambodian genocide.

Wiesel's human rights activism, inspired by what he witnessed during the Holocaust, has been honored with numerous awards, including the Nobel prize for peace in 1986. Wiesel used the money awarded in conjunction with the prize to establish the Elie Wiesel Foundation for Humanity. Based in New York, the foundation has primarily sponsored interdisciplinary conferences focused on the theme of hatred.

Having devoted his writing to fiction and essay for forty years, Wiesel returned to the genre of memoir in the mid-1990s, chronicling and commenting on the events and issues, private as well as public, that have shaped his career. The first volume, ending with his 1969 Jerusalem wedding, includes Wiesel's reassessment of the war experiences he initially described in *Night*; the second volume, emphasizing the period from 1969 to 1996, details the contentious negotiations that attended the formation of the Holocaust Commission. A third volume of the memoirs, devoted to Wiesel's relations with teachers and friends, is in preparation.

Memoirs

Wiesel's first book, *Un di velt hot geshvign* (And the World Remained Silent, 1956), recounts the annihilation of his family and town in the period 1944 to 1945. The narrative proceeds step-by-step: the Nazi entry into Sighet in the spring, the gradual stages of confinement, the march from ghetto to trains, the deportation, the arrival in Auschwitz and consequent separation from his mother and sisters, forced labor at the Buna satellite camp, the marches to Germany in the dead of winter, the death of his father, and, finally and briefly, the days following liberation.

The memoir was originally published by the *Tzentral Varband fun Polishe Yidn in Argentina* (Central Union of Polish Jews in Argentina). *Un di velt* was number 117 in a series of books devoted to preserving the culture of Eastern European Jewry and commemorating those who were lost. Many, but not all, of the volumes dealt with the plight of Jews during the Holocaust. As Wiesel indicates in later memoir, he wrote the manuscript while on a voyage to South America nearly ten years after the end of the war. Soon after its publication, Wiesel adapted the memoir into French and it was published in 1958 as *La Nuit*. The English translation, *Night*, based on the French version, appeared in 1960.

The Yiddish and French versions of the memoir are similar in almost every respect. *Un di velt* contains a prologue and epilogue that are not found in *La Nuit*; both were later translated and published in the collection of Wiesel's writings, *Against Silence* (1985), and in Wiesel's later memoir, *Tous les fleuves à la mer* (All Rivers Run to the Sea, 1994). In terms of stylistic variations, readers of English can compare with *Night* the translation of chapter seven of *Un di velt*, which appears as "The Death Train" in the collection *Anthology of Holocaust Literature*, by Glatstein, Knoy, and Margshes.

Wiesel has commented that all survivor testimony seems to be written by a single person "always the same" (*A Jew Today*, trans. by Marion Wiesel, New York: Vintage, 1979, p. 237). Yet *Un di velt* has a number of distinguishing elements: (1) the role of Jewish religious and cultural life, (2) a focus on the bond between father and son, (3) the pivotal role of "illusion," and (4) the tragic predicament of the witness.

Un di velt is notable among Holocaust memoirs because it foregrounds religious life and issues of theodicy. The opening paragraph sets out the implications of the events in religious language and concepts:

> In the beginning was faith, the foolish faith; and trust, the simple trust; and illusion, the dangerous illusion.
>
> We believed in God, had trust in human kind and lived with the illusion, that in each one of us, glowed a holy spark of fire from the shechina, that each one of us carried within, in their eyes and in their soul, the image of God.
>
> That was the source—if not the reason—of all our misfortune ("The Polish Jews," no. 117, edited by Mark Turkow, Buenos Aires: Central Union of Polish Jews in Argentina, trans. by Alan Rosen).

To be sure, this passage can be read as an elegy to traditional religious belief as much as a statement of its continuing importance. The narrative that follows is nevertheless imbued with an inventory of religious objects, people, and events. Sacred books are studied, transported, discarded; prayers are recited, interrupted, anguished over; blessings are said, inverted, or withheld; rabbis lead, are humiliated, and submit. The presence and emerging impotence of these traditional media mark the destruction of a culture as well as the people who inhabit it. The festivals of the Jewish calendar, moreover, loom constantly over Wiesel's narration: the family prepares for the Sabbath; imminent deportation is viewed through the prism of Passover; prisoners run the risk of convening New Year's prayer groups; father and son debate hunger and survival in prospect of a Yom Kippur fast. Although the Jews are powerless to prevent eviction from their homes, they can and do refuse to surrender their lives according to Jewish time.

Many Holocaust memoirs emphasize the plight of the individual as he or she attempts, against tremendous adversity, to survive. In contrast, Wiesel focuses not mainly on himself but on the bond between himself and his father. Indeed, from the first page, Wiesel refracts the events through this relationship. Movingly, we see that relations between father and son were, until deportation, distant and even contentious. But as the persecution grows ever more intense, the bond between them becomes increasingly more intimate.

But this intimacy, too, has deadly ramifications. For as Wiesel's narrative implies, the rigor of Auschwitz and death marches compel even the best of sons to abandon the holiest of fathers. Ultimately, as one of the grimmest scenes in the memoir relates, sons and fathers are driven by hunger to a madness where they fight to the death over a crumb of bread. Wiesel himself only submits to this urge for self-preservation (or believes that he does) at the very end. By narrating the events to show that the logic of events nurtured intimacy but scripted inevitable destruction, Wiesel brings out the sense of loss all the more forcefully.

The deportation of this Transylvanian community took place in spring 1944; by this time most of European Jewry had been murdered. It is only in this context that one can fully understand the irony that underlies the fact that the Jews of Sighet had never heard of Auschwitz until they arrived there.

Wiesel layers onto this backdrop the dialectic of optimism and deception that he calls "illusion": the source, as the memoir's opening lines put it, of "all our misfortune." The Jews of Sighet believe, until the last minute, that disaster will be held at bay. Hence, when one of the foreign Jews who is deported from Hungary in 1942 returns and tries to alert the Jews as to the actual rather than illusory plans of the Nazis, no one is willing to believe him, even the narrator. This refusal, or inability—it is never clear which one predominates—to listen to "prophets of destruction" sets a pattern for what is to come. Tellingly, although Wiesel writes with a sense of hindsight of what might have been had Sighet's Jews been able to overcome the "dangerous illusion," he describes himself and his family as typical in their inability to do so and in their tragic quest to maintain optimism.

The focus on illusion suggests that the Holocaust is a tragedy on two levels: first, on a social level, it permitted a kind of manipulation, of being duped; second, on a religious/ethical level, it promoted a way of understanding human beings—as sacred—because formed in the divine image—that no longer corresponded to the atrocious behavior that Wiesel had witnessed.

At least three attempts are made, nevertheless, to puncture this illusion. The first is by way of testimony. The synagogue beadle, Moshe, returns to Sighet to recount the terrible massacre visited upon the Jews who were deported. The second is by way of madness: as the train transports Sighet's Jews to an unknown destination, a woman driven mad by separation from her family reports scenes of fire. Neither report is credited. The third is Wiesel's own effort as set forth in the memoir. Just as the witnesses at the time of persecution faced a unreceptive audience, so did he in its aftermath. Indeed, *Un di velt* (as opposed to *Night*) concludes with a denunciation of the world's indifference to the plight of the victims and implications of the Holocaust a mere ten years after the end of the war.

In a later full-length memoir published in 1994, in a chapter titled "Darkness," Wiesel again chronicles the devastating events of 1944 and 1945: the Nazi entry, confinement, deportation, Auschwitz, forced marches, the death of his father, and liberation. Hence, the account parallels that of *Night*. But it also differs in several ways: it adds new material, expands on previous references, addresses what has been misinterpreted, and sometimes connects incidents of the war to later postwar developments, either personal or public. Whereas *Night* maintained a childhood view, the perspective of "Darkness" is explicitly that of an adult. Finally, in a few instances, Wiesel sets off, in italicized print, short dream sequences in which he meditates on the fate of his father.

Novels

In addition to memoirs that narrate events of the Holocaust directly, Wiesel has also written a significant corpus of fictional work that addresses the Holocaust obliquely. These include short stories, plays, dialogues, two cantati, and eleven novels. It is a review of the novels that can perhaps best illustrate Wiesel's refracted approach to the Holocaust.

Most often, Wiesel's novels represent the plight of the Holocaust survivor in the aftermath of the events. They thus take up where *Night* ends, probing how the survivor can fashion a meaningful life in the wake of monumental loss, radical displacement, and perhaps most invidious, the trauma caused by having been compelled to witness unspeakable atrocities. More generally, Wiesel's protagonists question to what degree the cultural premises of the prewar world may continue to serve the post-Holocaust world the survivor encounters. Given Wiesel's religious training and convictions, he frequently directs these questions to the role of God as well. That Wiesel's narrative strategies also adapt traditional forms of biblical, rabbinic, and Hasidic storytelling make the religious nature of these questions seem of a piece with his conception of the novel.

Wiesel's later novels focus on the plight of children of survivors as well as that of the survivor (as Wiesel has himself noted, his protagonists are invariably men). The emphasis then shifts from dramatizing the predicament of the survivor—how he lives with what he has seen—to the predicament of his son—how he lives with what he hasn't seen or what he eventually comes to know about.

Having frequently commented on the difficulty (if not impossibility) of writing novels about the Holocaust, Wiesel has met this challenge by continuously experimenting with novelistic form. The earliest narratives (particularly *Dawn*, and *The Accident*) were slim volumes (reminiscent in this respect, among others, of Albert Camus's *The Stranger*) and dramatized in a single episode or situation a life-and-death struggle. The middle and later novels expand (*The Testament* is almost 350 pages), include more characters, use diverse modes of storytelling, and weave in multiple narratives. More important, beginning with *The Town Beyond the Wall* and culminating in *A Beggar in Jerusalem* and *The Oath*, the narrative becomes more oblique, fragmented, and layered, with multiple characters vying with the narrator to tell their versions of the story. The multitude of storytellers and endless threads of narrative convey how the secret of the Holocaust, from whatever angle the assault, resists being told.

Charting the evolution of the novels shows how Wiesel has set forth, reworked, and modified many of the issues he believes central to the legacy of the Holocaust. The first novel, *Dawn* (1960), tells of a young survivor compelled to become a killer. Recruited after the war by the Jewish underground in Palestine, Elisha is chosen to execute a British soldier, John Dawson, in order to avenge the slated execution of a Jewish fighter by the British. Wiesel shows the victim driven by the events of his past to fight for a state for the Jews. Yet the legacy of the Holocaust also makes the act of killing, even or especially for a just cause, something repugnant. Caught in an intolerable moral situation, Wiesel's protagonist carries out the execution only at a devastating personal price; "That's it, I said to myself. It's done. I've killed. I've killed Elisha" (Translated by Frances Frenaye, New York: Bard, 1970, p. 126).

In *The Accident* (1961), the victim turns victimizer against himself. Eliezer, a journalist who resides in New York, is struck by a taxi and badly injured. As he attempts to recover in the hospital, it is not clear that he actually wishes to live. The "accident," moreover, may have been an attempt at suicide. Wiesel again shows how the Holocaust, years after, continues to claim its victims. Lacking the just cause that motivates the hero of *Dawn*, the protagonist of *The Accident* seems even more at the mercy of the traumatic past. In the physician, Paul Russel, who tries to persuade the protagonist to choose life, and in the artist, Gyula, who paints pictures only to burn them, Wiesel also introduces the redeeming possibility of friendship—a dimension of hope that becomes crucial to virtually all the works that follow.

Wiesel's third novel, *A Town Beyond the Wall* (1962), transforms the friend into a mentor who both guides the survivor and ultimately is protected by him. A survivor in postwar France, Michael is persuaded by his friend/mentor Pedro to pay a return visit to his hometown, and in consequence discovers that he came to confront those non-Jews who silently watched the round-up and deportation of their fellow townspeople. Confrontation with the past thus becomes confrontation with the dehumanizing force of indifference. Arrested during the visit by the police, Michael refuses to speak so as not to betray Pedro. Just as Michael protects Pedro, Pedro provides Michael with the strength to endure torture and imprisonment. Wiesel thus extends the power of friendship, having it not only sustain the victim in times of crisis but reach out to those who are imprisoned.

In *The Gates of the Forest* (1964), the force of friendship is so strong that the boundaries of character become permeable; it is not clear where the character of Gregor leaves off and that of Gavriel begins. During the time of the Holocaust, the father of the protagonist, Gregor, hides him in a cave to escape round-up and deportation. Visited by a nameless figure, who recounts terrible scenes of Jewish affliction, Gregor gives this witness his own Jewish name, Gavriel. In order to continue to hide among Christians, Gregor chooses to play the part of a mute. He maintains the ruse until, cast as Judas in a community passion play, he turns the tables and accuses the Christians of betrayal of the Jews.

In complement to the previous novel, Wiesel here dramatizes not only the corrosive indifference of the bystanders but the Christian hatred of Jews. Both elements, he suggests, played a crucial supporting role in the Holocaust. In the closing section, Gregor survives and emigrates to New York, where he finds succor in a community of Hasidim. Friendship as a sustaining dimension was first suggested in the relationship of Gregor and Gavriel; Wiesel further layers onto this dimension of friendship that of the relationship between rebbe and Hasid, master and disciple—a dimension of Jewish life and storytelling that becomes increasingly important for Wiesel over the next decade.

Hasidic storytelling serves a crucial model for *A Beggar in Jerusalem* (1968), which draws its inspiration from Rebbe Nachman of Breslov's story, "The Seven Beggars." In the aftermath of the Six-Day War in June 1967, David waits with the beggars at the Western Wall in Jerusalem for his friend Katriel, who never returned from the war. Gathered at the site that symbolizes Jewish life and yearning, they relate the story of Katriel, of the war, of pivotal episodes in Jewish history, and of the Holocaust.

As with Gregor and Gavriel, Wiesel fashions David and Katriel as two sides of a mysterious whole. By means of this intimacy, Wiesel intensifies the questions around the role of the survivor: "People will ask in astonishment: 'Still no trace of Katriel?' I shall answer: 'His trace? I am his trace' " (Translated by Lily Eclelman, New York: Avon, 1971, pp. 14–15). Wiesel suggests that even with the advent of the new era in Jewish history marked by reclaiming the Western Wall, the survivor continues to live under the shadow of those who did not return.

In his seventh novel *The Oath* (1973), Wiesel uses yet a different window of Jewish history—a twentieth-century pogrom that occurred before the Holocaust—to air many of the issues the Holocaust brings to the foreground. The sole survivor of the massacre, Azriel, encounters a child of Holocaust survivors who is tempted by suicide. In order to save the child, Azriel breaks a vow of silence taken by all the town's inhabitants and tells the story of the town's destruction. In so doing, he follows the path of his father, Shmuel, who, as the town scribe, added the story of the town's last days to its thousand years of recorded history.

But Wiesel implies that Azriel's mission also marks a new stage in response to Jewish catastrophe. In contrast to his father, he tells the story without recording it, he narrates it with a specific ethical purpose, and he confesses that the story as told doesn't reflect the true story, which remains a secret. Setting the novel in a period before the Holocaust thus enables Wiesel to articulate the new dimensions of Jewish storytelling in the wake of the Holocaust. He also begins to explore the special predicament of the child of Holocaust survivors, an exploration that receives greater attention in several later novels.

Indeed, *The Testament* (1980) is the story written by a martyred father to the child who survives him. Wiesel narrates the life and death of Paltiel Kossover, a Russian-Jewish poet modeled on the writers Peretz Markish and Der Nister, who were murdered by Stalin in 1952. Wiesel's focus on a Russian Jew who is never apprehended by the Nazis appears to veer from his usual focus on the Holocaust survivor, but this, too, presents another vantage point: Kossover himself only narrowly escaped from Germany and France; he returned to his Russian home to find that his family has been murdered by the Nazis; he is among the Russian troops who visit the concentration camp of Majdanek in the aftermath. "No," says Kossover, "I shall not tell the story of Majdanek; others have done it before me; let the words of the survivors live and resound; I have no wish to cover them with mine." Having opted for restraint, Kossover nevertheless does come to write "what [he] had seen" (Translated by Marion Wiesel, New York: Summit, 1981, p. 315).

Kossover's "testament," moreover, serves as a model of victim testimony. Ordered by the "Citizen's Magistrate" to write a confession of his "treason," Kossover turns the tactics of the persecutors against them, using the confession to detail the story of his life, which they wish to obliterate. Ultimately, Wiesel makes the poet's mute son, Grisha, the testament's primary reader. Whereas in previous novels the friend or mentor symbolized the counterforce to tyranny, in *The Testament* the transmission of the story from father to son assumes that role.

The Fifth Son (1983) brings the predicament of the child of survivors fully into the limelight. Born after the war, Ariel Tamiroff has never been told by his parents the details of their ordeal in the Davarowsk ghetto, an ordeal that has caused his mother to go mad and his father to become a recluse. For Ariel, there is no testament. Eventually, he learns why: his parents had had a prior son, who was apprehended, tortured, and murdered by the ghetto's Nazi commandant.

Ariel travels to Germany, ostensibly to complete the revenge that his father had attempted to carry out against the murderer. Once he has found his brother's assassin, however, Ariel chooses not to kill but to confront him with the specter of his crimes. Patterned on the Passover Haggadah—Wiesel adds a "fifth son" to the Haggadah's four—the novel serves as an elegy for those children lost in the Holocaust, as well as an examination of the difficult necessity of narrating their loss for those who come after.

Wiesel's characters often court madness as a technique for coming to terms with a world gone mad or, as in the case of Ariel's mother, as a commensurate response to witnessing unspeakable atrocities. The protagonist of *Twilight* (1987), Raphael Lipkin, turns to the mad to help him find a way to understand the losses of the Holocaust. Child survivor of the Warsaw ghetto, Lipkin conducts research in a "mountain clinic," ostensibly for professional reasons, but his interviews with the clientele, all of whom believe they are Biblical personages, become a strategy by which to try to symbolically understand the fragmentation and destruction during the period of the Holocaust. Significantly, Wiesel juxtaposes the surreal interviews of the clinic with a realistic depiction of the wartime decimation of Lipkin's large Polish-Jewish family. Chronicling the attempts of the family to disperse and hide, Wiesel suggests that no matter how ingenious and proactive the efforts to elude the Nazis, such exertions most often ended in capture, torture, and death.

As with many of the later novels, *The Forgotten* (1989) again examines the transmission of testimony to the succeeding generation and the obligations such transmission confers. In this case, however, Wiesel shapes the plot to make the task of transmission especially urgent and necessary. A terrible disease is soon to erode the memory of survivor and distinguished academic, Elhanan Rosenbaum. To preserve it, he proposes to transmit all that he remembers to his son, Malkiel. As with Albert Camus's *The Plague* or Thomas Mann's *The Magic Mountain*, Wiesel uses the premise of disease to sharpen the sense of what is at stake in normal circumstances. By envisioning memory as susceptible to complete obliteration, Wiesel emphasizes its fragility, both in terms of the testimony of the survivor and in terms of religious and cultural traditions.

As in *The Fifth Son*, the son travels to Europe to vivify the transmitted memory. And here, too, his journey climaxes in an encounter with the persecutor, but Wiesel complicates the terms of this encounter: Malkiel meets not the persecutor but his wife, who was herself violated. Faced with a symbol of the persecutor who is herself a victim, this son faces a more ambiguous task of establishing accountability.

Critical Responses

Several critics have responded to Wiesel's work (and either explicitly or by implication, to writing by victims of the Holocaust generally) by questioning normal critical practices. George Steiner, for example, believed that the most appropriate response to *Night* was to "re-copy the book, line by line, pausing at the names of the dead and the names of the children as an orthodox scribe pauses, when re-copying the Bible, at the hallowed name of God" (*Language and Silence*, p. 168).

Irving Halperin, too, sees criticism that invokes normal literary standards as missing the mark: "Should a book like, say, *Night* be subjected to the same kinds of critical standards one would employ for a Hemingway or Fitzgerald novel?" (Halperin, p. 66). Basing his assessment on remarks of David Daiches, Halperin believes that Wiesel's books should be read "not so much as *literary* works but rather as important documents of modern consciousness" (p. 67). Reading such documents also challenges certain aesthetic biases—for example, aesthetic distancing and obliqueness—that encourage one to ask misguided questions and make insensitive judgments. These considerations did not, however, keep Halperin from pursuing a largely new critical reading of Wiesel's works.

Ted Estes begins his study by voicing similar reservations: "One is reluctant to apply the usual conventions of literary analysis to the book [*Night*], for by doing so one runs the risk of blunting the impact of its testimony by too quickly speaking of secondary matters." But, again, Estes concludes by justifying a literary (thematic and form-critical) approach: "Yet [Wiesel] did make authorial decisions that contribute to making *Night* the witness that it is" (Elie Wiesel, p. 17). In most cases, then, this rhetoric of caution is followed by more or less conventional thematic analysis. Wiesel's writing—particularly but not only *Night*—has disarmed conventional approaches to works of narrative prose even as its self-conscious style has solicited commentary. Critics have been forced to reflect on the task of criticism—its limitations and evasions—and have integrated such reflections into the act of criticism itself.

Robert MacAfee Brown has taken this reevaluation of the critical task that Wiesel's writing compels further than others: "This is not a 'critical' appraisal of Wiesel, and I make no apologies for the fact. My concern has been to expound him clearly enough and sympathetically enough so that readers can go on to confront him at first hand. Then they can, if they wish, engage in critique. The critique, for me, has been the other way around. Elie Wiesel has forced me to reevaluate a whole lifetime of assumptions" (Brown, p. xii). This reformulation of the critic's task mirrors trends in postmodern criticism that have challenged conventional critical stances—particularly as a master analyzing an inert object.

A less radical form of critical response argues that Wiesel addresses the Holocaust by inverting generic conventions. Here the critics do not question critical strategies, but rather use an overarching framework of genre criticism (most likely gleaned from Northrup Frye) to read Wiesel as going against the grain. Lawrence Langer, for instance, believes that it is through the near identity of form that *Night* acquires its power: *Night* "yields the effect of an authentic *Bildungsroman*—except that the youthful protagonist becomes an initiate into death rather than life" (Cargas, *Responses*, p. 30). The focus on reversal, or in Langer's terms, the "principle of negation," also becomes the way to invent a critical parlance to write about the Holocaust. Wiesel's writing about the Holocaust can thus be pointedly contrasted with James Joyce's *Portrait of the Artist as a Young Man*: For Stephen Dedalus, words "inspired him to affirm his spirit before a hostile or indifferent world and trust his powers of creation to shape the future." For Wiesel, "a diametrically opposite principle of negation prevails, whereby events silence the creative spirit, destroy the longings of youth, and cast over reality an all-embracing shadow of death" (p. 39).

More aggressively, Lawrence Cunningham views the inversionary force of *Night* as creating a need for a new nomenclature: "*Night* does not tell of the growth of a person even in the sense that Joyce does in *A Portrait of the Artist as a Young Man*. Whatever else *Night* might be, it is not a *Bildungsroman*. In fact, what one comes to see is that *Night* is not a story of someone's life (i.e., *bios graphe*), nor of the unfolding of the consciousness of life and growth, but rather of someone's death: the death of God, of history, of one's father and of meaning. Wiesel has written, not a biography, but a thanatography" (Cargas, *Responses*, p. 23). Cunningham invokes etymology not to convince the reader that Wiesel invents a new genre, but rather to emphasize how *Night* reverses common assumptions. Indeed, Cunningham argues that night also inverts these assumptions by means of a "near parody" of a key biblical text: "What has been largely overlooked is that Wiesel, writing some years after these events, frames the story of that inversion [from life to death] in terms of the oldest 'biography' of his own people: the story of the Exodus. The life-giving biblical myth of election, liberation, covenant, and promise becomes the vehicle for telling the story of the unnatural order of the death-domination" (p. 24).

Most commentators believe the Jewish dimension important to Wiesel's work; some see it as central. Further, the discussion turns around both content and form—Wiesel's use of figures, themes, and symbols associated with Jewish tradition on the one hand, and the Jewish modes of writing that Wiesel has adopted on the other. Again, some critics believe Wiesel has employed Jewish tradition to challenge its premises. Others share the belief that protest is crucial for Wiesel, but argue that this response does not so much challenge the premises of tradition as it links Wiesel with a certain line of Jewish tradition: a distinguished group that, throughout the history of Jewish life and letters, advocates on behalf of suffering Jews.

One of the earliest critics who located Wiesel squarely in a Jewish context was André Neher. Commenting on Wiesel's contribution in relation to a Jewish tradition of silence and language, Neher views Wiesel as a master of silence. But Neher particularly emphasizes Wiesel's role as a radical interpreter of the Bible: "Has it yet been pointed out that this first story of Wiesel's [*Night*] is from end to end [sic] a rewriting of the *Akedah* [the binding of Isaac narrated in Genesis 22] in the obscure light of the Night of Auschwitz?" (Neher, p. 216). Neher rereads the *Akedah* through the prism of *Night*: Wiesel's first memoir is "an Akedah in reverse: not a father leading his son to the sacrifice, but a son conducting, dragging, carrying to the sacrifice an old, exhausted father." The ending of the story would also be reversed: "Above all, the sacrifice would really have taken place, and one of the two protagonists would have been dead: Isaac, no doubt, because he was preordained to be the victim, but also perhaps Abraham, like the father in *Night*, because so much adversity could only have extinguished whatever life the helpless Abraham still possessed" (p. 27). Neher then goes on to interpret the *midrash* on the Akedah through this prism as well (p. 218). For Neher, Wiesel's fiction, essays, and commentary all collaborate to challenge the human and divine with the "reality of Auschwitz;" all of Wiesel's writing draws on, and then in turn "rewrites," foundational texts and personages of Jewish tradition.

In contrast, Byron Sherwin, basing his view on writings up to and including *The Gates of the Forest*, sees Wiesel's work as fully consonant with responses to catastrophe in Jewish tradition: "it can easily be shown that [Wiesel] is firmly within a tradition which finds its sources in Biblical theology and which develops throughout Jewish literature, notably Kabbalistic writings" (Cargas, *Responses*, p. 134). Wiesel uses these sources to formulate a traditional, if questioning, response to Jewish catastrophe: "Wiesel holds membership in the fellowship of those reconstructionists of faith who have arisen amongst traditional Jewish blasphemers after each major tragedy in Jewish history" (p. 134). According to Sherwin, Wiesel follows in the footsteps of Honi the Circle Maker, a talmudic sage who refused to move until God did his bidding, and Levi Yitzhak of Berdichev, a Hasidic master known for his pleas to God on behalf of suffering Jews. It should be noted, nevertheless, that while Sherwin takes pains to show Wiesel's protest as proceeding from within tradition, Sherwin's own language—"blasphemers," "reconstructionist," "writing a new Bible" (p. 134)—points outside tradition. And although Sherwin uses mainly Wiesel's literary texts, he says little regarding the influence of traditional Jewish writing on Wiesel's aesthetic strategies. He does note briefly, however, that Wiesel's emphasis on paradox links him to the strategies of paradox found in kabbalah.

Whereas Neher and Sherwin locate Wiesel in relation to traditional writing, Sidra Ezrahi, discussing "The Holocaust as a Jewish Tragedy," assesses his contribution in terms of those who write on the Holocaust "in European languages":

> Wiesel's almost unique position in the history of Holocaust literature in European languages lies in his attempt to convey in secular fiction the manner of thought and the literary modes practiced by believing Jews who perished; to apply, that is, to the most cataclysmic event of all, the internal methods by which the Jews of Eastern Europe traditionally grappled with and assimilated collective events and tragedies (Ezrahi, p. 120).

According to Ezrahi, Wiesel's attempt to adopt "internal methods" of traditional Jewry to "secular fiction" is itself an unusual response to the Holocaust—a hybrid between the Europe of modernity and classical Jewish responses. Indeed, Wiesel's use of these forms and methods—*midrash* and legend, culled from both the writings of classical Judaism and of Hasidic storytelling—serves as an elegy to "believing Jews who perished." Wiesel writes as they would have written.

Yet Wiesel also makes these methods serve other purposes: "In Wiesel's fiction the forms are preserved even if the content has been inverted" (p. 122). Ezrahi offers as an example an often-cited passage in *Night*, where Wiesel, relieved that he was able to hide his shoes, improvises a blessing that thanks God for "having created mud in His infinite and wonderful universe" (Ezrahi, p. 122). Ezrahi's point is that while Wiesel uses the traditional form of a blessing, he makes it over a substance that, in normal life, would never be so elevated. Although Ezrahi's commentary stops here, it can be noted that the inverted role of mud plays a central role in a number of Hasidic tales and may have influenced Wiesel's own formulation. And indeed, David Roskies, giving such a method of inversion the name "sacred parody," argues persuasively that this method has played a pivotal role in Jewish responses to catastrophe, an observation implying that Wiesel's inverted blessings are as traditional as straightforward ones.

While Neher, Sherwin, and Ezrahi comment on Wiesel's Jewish contribution in the context of classical European Jewish traditions, Alan Berger examines Wiesel's work in relation to American Jewish literature and the Holocaust. Accordingly, Berger focuses on two of Wiesel's novels set in the United States—*The Accident* (1962) and *The Fifth Son* (1985)—and emphasizes the ethical claims set forth by Wiesel's Jewish storytelling. In *The Accident* are sown "the seeds of Wiesel's neohasidic, post-Holocaust Judaism, which require man to assume the awesome burden of covenant by contending with God and by being responsible for one's fellow human beings" (Berger, p. 68). Berger, too, views Wiesel's contribution under the rubric of protest—here referred to as "contending." He also notes the universal range of Wiesel's concern—not only Jews but "one's fellow human beings" are essential in this ethical framework. Finally, Wiesel's path is "neo-Hasidic." The inspiration for Wiesel's approach comes out of Hasidic Jewry; its ethical rather than *halachic* (religious law) emphasis defines it as *neo*-Hasidic.

Berger goes on to suggest that, in a later novel, Wiesel makes the Jewish framework more explicit and extends its claim to the succeeding generation: "In a move characterized by both its boldness and subtleness," writes Berger,

> *The Fifth Son* reverses the theme of Wiesel's long held view that it is impossible for a nonwitness to imagine Auschwitz. Here, Wiesel the witness attempts to imagine how it is to be a nonwitness. Theologically, Wiesel advocates guidelines by which the second generation can remain within the midrashic framework while simultaneously advancing criteria for post-Holocaust Jewish authenticity (pp. 68–69).

In analyzing Wiesel's approach to silence and muteness in relation to the Holocaust, Sara Horowitz situates Wiesel firmly in a traditional rabbinic response to suffering: "Despite the impulse to absorb traumatic events into the continuum of Jewish history, classical rabbinic Judaism sees extreme suffering as characterized by the impossibility of communication, of relationship, of narration, of explanation" (Horowitz, p. 122–123). According to Horowitz, Wiesel shares the impulse to absorb but also supports the view that extreme suffering—the paradigm of which is the *Shoah*—"undercuts" the ability to do so. The "impossibility of communication" that Horowitz understands as marking rabbinic approaches thus finds its echo in Wiesel: "For Wiesel, the essence of the *Shoah* is a multifarious breakdown in communication, which his narratives paradoxically seek to communicate" (p. 124).

Bibliography

Primary Sources

Memoirs

Und die velt hot geschviegn (And the World Remained Silent). 1956.
La Nuit (*Night*). 1958.
Tous les fleuves vont à la mer: mémoires (*All Rivers Run to the Sea: Memoirs*). (1994).
Et la mer n'est pas remplie: mémoires 2 (*And the Sea Is Never Full: Memoirs*). 1969. (1996)

Novels

L'Aube (*Dawn*). 1960.
Le Jour (*The Accident*). 1961.
La Ville de la chance (*The Town Beyond the Wall*). 1962.
Les Portes de la forêt (*The Gates of the Forest*). 1964.
Les Juifs du silence: térmoignage (The Jews & Silence: A Personal Report & Soviet Jewry). 1966.
Le Mendiant de Jérusalem (*A Beggar in Jerusalem*). 1968.
Le Serment de Kovillàg (*The Oath*). 1973.
Le Testament d'un poète juif assassiné (*The Testament*). 1980.
Le Cinquième Fils (*The Fifth Son*). 1983.
Le Crépuscule, au loin (*Twilight*). 1987.
L'Oublié (*The Forgotten*). 1989.
Les Juges (*The Judges*). 1999.

Plays

Black Canopy, Black Sky. 1968.
Zalmen ou las follie de Dieu (*Zalmen, or the Madness of God*). 1968.
Le Procès de Shamgorod tel qu'il se déroula le 25 février 1649 (*The Trial of God*). 1979.

Lyrics

Ani Maamin: Un chant perdu et retrouvé (*I Believe*). 1973.
A Song for Hope. 1987.

Collections of Essays

Le Chant des morts (*Legends of Our Time*). 1966.
Entre deux soleils (*One Generation After*). 1970.
Célébration hassidique (*Souls on Fire*). 1972.
Célébration biblique (*Messengers of God*). 1975.
Un Juif aujourd'hui (*A Jew Today*). 1977.
Five Biblical Postraits. 1981.
Contre la mélancholie (*Four Hasidic Masters and Their Struggle Against Melancholy*). 1982.
Somewhere a Master: Further Hasidic Portraits and Legends. 1982.
Paroles d'étranger (*Words of a Stranger*). 1982.
The Golem: The Story of a Legend. 1983.
Against Silence: The Voice and Vision of Elie Wiesel. Edited by Irving Abrahamson. 1985.
Signes d'exode (*Signs of Exodus*). 1985.
Discours d'Oslo (*Addresses from Oslo*). 1987.
Silences et mémoire d'hommes (*Silences and Human Memory*). 1989.
From the Kingdom of Memory: Reminiscences. 1990.
Célébration talmudique: Portraits et légendes. 1991.
Sages and Dreamers: Biblical, Talmudic, and Hasidic Portraits and Legends. 1991.
A Passover Haggadah. With commentaries by Elie Wiesel, illustrations by Mark Podwal. 1993.
Célébration prophétique, Portraits et légendes. 1998.
D'où viens-tu? (*From Where Do You Come?*) 2001.
After the Darkness: Reflections on the Holocaust. 2002.

Collaborative Works

Job ou Dieu dans la tempete (*Job, or God in the Tempest*). With Josy Eisenberg. 1986.
Le Mal et L'Exil/Dix ans après (*Evil and Exile*). Dialogues with Michaël de Saint Cheron. 1988.
The Six Days of Destruction: *Meditations Toward Hope*. With Albert Friedlander. 1988.
A Journey of Faith. With John Cardinal O'Connor. 1990.
Images from the Bible, with Shalom of Safed In *Dialogue and Dilemma*. With Elie Wiesel, with David Patterson 1991.
Se taire est impossible (*To Be Silent Is Impossible*). With Jorge Semprun. 1995.
Mémoire à deux voix (*Memoir in Two Voices*). With François Mitterrand. 1996.
Conversations with Elic Wiesel. With Richard Heffner, edited by Thomas J. Vinciguerra. 2001.

Children

King Solomon and His Magic Ring. 1999.

Archives

A portion of Wiesel's personal papers and manuscripts are deposited with Special Collections, Mugar Memorial Library, Boston University.

Secondary Sources

Abramowitz, Molly, ed. *Elie Wiesel: A Bibliography*. Metuchen: Scarecrow, 1974.
Berenbaum, Michael. *The Vision of the Void: Theological Reflections on the Works of Elie Wiesel*. Middleton, Conn.: Wesleyan University Press, 1979.
Berger, Alan. *Crisis and Covenant: The Holocaust in American Jewish Fiction*. Albany: State University of New York Press, 1985.
Bloom, Harold, ed. *Modern Critical Interpretations: Elie Wiesel's* Night. Philadelphia: Chelsea House, 2001.
Boone, Susan Livingston. "The Appearance of Shame in Holocaust Witness: Elie Wiesel and Primo Levi." Ph.D. diss., Syracuse University, 1999.
Boschki, Reinhold, and Dagmar Mensink. *Kultur allein ist nicht genug, das Wérk von Elie Wiesel—Herausforderung für Religion und Gesellschaft*. Münster: LIT Verlag, 1998.
Brown, Robert MacAfee. *Elie Wiesel: Messenger to All Humanity*. Rev. ed. Notre Dame: University of Notre Dame Press, 1989.
Cargas, Harry, ed. *Responses to Elie Wiesel: Critical Essays by Major Jewish and Christian Scholars*. New York: Persea, 1978.
———. *Harry James Cargas in Conversation with Elie Wiesel*. New York: Paulist, 1976.
Davis, Colin. *Elie Wiesel's Secretive Texts*. Gainesville: University Press of Florida, 1994.
de Saint Cheron, Michaël, ed. *Le Colloque de Cerisy: Autour d'Elie Wiesel*. Paris: Editions Odile Jacob, 1997.
Engel, Vincent. *Au nom du père, de Dieu et d'Auschwitz: Regards littéraires sur des questions contemporaines au travers de l'œuvre d'Élie Wiesel*. Bern: Lang, 1997.

Estes, Ted. *Elie Wiesel*. New York: Frederick Ungar, 1980.

Ezrahi, Sidra DeKoven. *By Words Alone: The Holocaust in Literature*. Chicago: University of Chicago Press, 1980.

Felman, Shoshana, and Dori Laub. *Testimony: Crises of Witnessing in Literature, Psychoanalysis, and History*. New York: Routledge, 1992.

Fine, Ellen. *Legacy of Night: The Literary Universe of Elie Wiesel*. With a foreword by Terrence Des Pres. Albany: State University of New York Press, 1982.

Friedemann, Joë. *Le Rire dans l'univers tragique d'Elie Wiesel*. Paris: Librarie A.G. Nizet, 1987.

Friedman, Maurice. *Abraham Joshua Heschel and Elie Wiesel: You Are My Witnesses*. New York: Farrar, Strauss, Giroux, 1987.

Glatstein, Jacob, Israel Knox, and Samuel Margshes. *Anthology of Holocaust Literature*. Philadelphia: Jewish Publication Society, 1968.

Greenberg, Irving, and Alvin Rosenfeld, eds. *Confronting the Holocaust: The Impact of Elie Wiesel*. Bloomington: Indiana University Press, 1978.

Halperin, Irving. *Messengers from the Dead: Literature of the Holocaust*. Philadelphia: Westminster, 1970.

Horowitz, Sara. *Voicing the Void: Muteness and Memory in Holocaust Fiction*. Albany: State University of New York Press, 1997.

Kolbert, Jack. *The Worlds of Elie Wiesel: An Overview of His Career and His Major Themes*. Selinsgrove: Susquehanna University Press, 2001.

Langer, Lawrence. *The Holocaust and the Literary Imagination*. New Haven: Yale University Press, 1975.

Neher, André. *The Exile of the Word: From the Silence of the Bible to the Silence of Auschwitz*. Translated by David Maisel. Philadelphia: Jewish Publication Society, 1981.

Rittner, Carol, ed. *Elie Wiesel: Between Memory and Hope*. New York and London: New York University Press, 1990.

Roskies, David. *Against the Apocalypse: Responses to Catastrophe in Modern Jewish Culture*. Cambridge, Mass.: Harvard University Press, 1984.

Roth, John. *A Consuming Fire: Encounters with Elie Wiesel and the Holocaust*. Atlanta: John Knox, 1979.

Sibelman, Simon. *Silence in the Novels of Elie Wiesel*. New York: St. Martin's, 1995.

Steiner, George. *Language and Silence: Essays on Language, Literature and the Inhuman*. 1967. New York: Atheneum, 1977.

SIMON WIESENTHAL

(1908–)

HARRIET L. PARMET

SIMON WIESENTHAL WAS born on 31 December 1908 in Buchach (in Polish, Buczacz), Galicia, the son of Asher (a businessman) and Rosa (Rapp) Wiesenthal. He married Cyla Muller and had two children, Pauline Rose and Kreisberg Gerard. He attended the University of Prague (1929–1933) and the University of Lemberg, Poland, completing the course of study as an engineer-architect in 1939. Wiesenthal practiced architecture in Lemberg from 1939 to 1941, when he was arrested by Ukrainian police. He spent the World War II years in the concentration and forced-labor camps of Janowska (Lvov), Plaszow, Gross-Rosen, and Buchenwald. The United States Army liberated him from Mauthausen, where he had been imprisoned on 5 May 1945. Upon his release, Wiesenthal vowed to abandon his former career and devote his life to the investigation of Nazi war criminals.

Initially he worked for the United States Commission in Austria, the United States Office of Strategic Services, and the Counter Intelligence Corps from 1945 to 1947. In 1947 he established the Jewish Historical Documentation Center in Linz, building a vast network of documents and informants to bring Nazi war criminals to justice. When public interest in Nazi war criminals waned, he closed the Linz center (1954). Wiesenthal directed a number of Jewish welfare agencies in Linz between 1954 and 1961, and resumed his work in investigating Nazi war criminals in Vienna, establishing the Jewish Documentation Center in the wake of the Eichmann trial, which generated renewed interest in the prosecution of Nazi war criminals. The Simon Wiesenthal Center of Los Angeles was established in 1978 to honor his life's work, to investigate World War II criminals, and to fight antisemitism and intolerance (*Encyclopedia of the Holocaust*, p. 1651).

Max and Helen

Max and Helen (1982) brings the enormity of the Holocaust into humanly comprehensible dimensions. This book reads like a simple novel rather than the unusual factual account it is. Simon Wiesenthal is informed about a Nazi officer who, as head of a road-building detail in Eastern Europe beat, tortured, and killed Jews. This man was living in the 1960s as a company executive in Germany. Carefully researching events and persons, Wiesenthal finds only two surviving victims who witnessed the atrocities: Max, a doctor, and Helen, who were lovers prior to incarceration but delayed marriage. Both were put into a work gang and saw their families taken away to die. Max escaped, survived, and later learned that Helen also survived, and they married. Wiesenthal's purpose is thwarted, however, because they decline to testify against the person responsible for their personal tragedies.

Wiesenthal is not a great storyteller and does not use professional literary devices to outline and dramatize the dimensions of the catastrophe or the story of the two witnesses. Some of the writing is pedagogic, and the tale is told in a series of the author's conversations with the victims. The narrative is genuine and moving, the style notwithstanding, providing the reader with an understanding of Wiesenthal's mission.

Ich jagte Eichmann (I Hunted Eichmann)

Ich jagte Eichmann (1961), translated into Hebrew as *Ha-redifah ahat Aikman* (The Pursuit of Eichmann), is Wiesenthal's story of his sixteen-year search for Adolf Eichmann. The account covers the time from his liberation from Mauthausen concentration camp and details every stray report of the elusive Eichmann. Wiesenthal investigated accounts of his "client's" survival in the final days of the war, how he escaped from an American internment camp, stayed in Germany and Austria over four years, then fled to Italy, where he hid in a

Catholic monastery. From an undercover agent, Wiesenthal got one of the few existing photographs of Eichmann, and later took pictures of Eichmann's lookalike brothers. From letters, newspaper obituaries, and on-the-spot investigations, he traced Eichmann's wife and then his sons to Buenos Aires, eventually establishing that the killer was living there under the name Ricardo Klement. Ultimately, with all of this information in place, Israeli agents had little trouble finding the man who was in charge of the transportation of the Jews to the extermination camps.

The Murderers Among Us: The Simon Wiesenthal Memoirs (1967)

Wiesenthal's narrative begins with a discussion of his career as a Nazi hunter shortly after his liberation. He describes in detail the background and his role in the capture of Eichmann reported in *Ich jagte Eichmann*. The story continues with the locating of the Viennese police inspector Karl Silberbauer, the Gestapo man who arrested Anne Frank; Franz Murer, the Vilna Gestapo chief responsible for the deaths of 80,000 Jews; and the arrest of the notorious murderer Franz Stangl, the former commandant of Treblinka and Sobibor death camps, where at least 700,000 Jews were annihilated. In addition to recounting these famous cases, Wiesenthal describes his unsuccessful search for Josef Mengele, the murderous Auschwitz doctor. He relates the stories of Alex, the half-Jew who became one of Wiesenthal's closest collaborators after the war; Frau Keller, the German housewife who suddenly discovered that her husband had been a cold-blooded mass murderer; and Ruth, the Jewish bride-to-be of the half-crazed Doctor Babor, who conducted the selections; and Frau G., the Jewish wife of a former Nazi general.

One chapter is devoted to the organization of SS members, a secret escape structure of the SS underground railway after 1945 with huge amounts of money at its disposal. The group set up a thorough and efficient network of hotels, hideouts, and professional document forgers that channeled fleeing Nazis to the secure havens of Italy, Spain, South America, and the Near East. Among the most prominent clients were the Führer's deputy Martin Bormann and Adolf Eichmann.

Austria, by Wiesenthal's appraisal, was the most vicious of all German lands. Every tenth Austrian was a member of the Nazi party. Of the five thousand names on the list of war criminals active in Yugoslavia, where two million people were killed, half were Austrians. One person after another is delineated as a war criminal as Wiesenthal tries to make the postwar generation who find Hitler's genocide hard to believe realize that there were, and are, at large former Nazi SS members guilty of murderous war crimes. Says Wiesenthal with mock resignation: "No country will want to attempt a second Eichmann case. Deputy Fuhrer Martin Bormann (still free in Brazil) will come to his end some day and the reward of 100,000 marks ($25,000) will never be paid" (*The Murderers Among Us: The Simon Wiesenthal Memoirs*, New York: McGraw-Hill, 1967, p. 345).

The Murderers Among Us reads like a detective thriller—sickening yet fascinating.

The Sunflower: On the Possibilities and Limits of Forgiveness

In 1970 the first edition of *The Sunflower: On the Possibilities and Limits of Forgiveness* related an autobiographical incident in Wiesenthal's life and elicited responses from a number of prominent thinkers, including Primo Levi, Saul Friedländer, Abraham J. Heschel, Herbert Marcuse, Jacques Maritain, and Martin Niemoller. Twenty-seven years later it was reissued in an expanded version with thirty-two new responses from intellectuals, writers, theologians, political dissidents and religious leaders from all parts of the globe. Among the respondents are the Dalai Lama, the novelist Cynthia Ozick, and the historian and academic Deborah Lipstadt. Three contributions—by the Viennese author and Auschwitz survivor Jean Améry, Cardinal Franz König, and the German author Albert Speer, who recanted his role in the Nazi Third Reich—were translated from the 1981 German edition and appear in this text for the first time in English (Bonny V. Fetterman, preface to the Schocken edition, 1997, pp. ix, x).

Wiesenthal probes questions of ethics, responsibility, guilt, repentance, and forgiveness. He discusses the problems of living and maintaining one's humanity in Janowska (Lvov), a Nazi concentration camp where he was imprisoned in 1942—the impossibly overcrowded living conditions, the hunger and depravation, the ever-present humiliation, sadism, and brutality, the exhaustion from forced physical labor, and the ever-imminent threat of deportation to certain death.

The gripping story recounts how Wiesenthal was a concentration camp prisoner in a forced-labor detail. He was selected at random by a nurse to attend the bedside of Karl, a dying SS soldier. The terminally wounded young man had requested a Jew to hear his final confession because he felt remorse for the vicious crimes he had committed against Jewish civilians and wanted absolution from a Jew as representative of the people he had so grievously wronged, in order to die in peace. The SS man claimed he was not antisemitic and had only followed the orders and lead of his officers and peers. In a brief period of time, the soldier retold the story of his life without rationalizations or excuses. Now repentant, he asked for forgiveness.

Wiesenthal listened intently to the man's story, repelled to be physically near someone who had participated in cramming Jewish men, women, and children into a home and burning them to death; a person, unmoved by frantic cries, who shot those who tried to escape, including a dark-eyed child who, for Wiesenthal, becomes Eli, a little boy he knew and loved in the ghetto, with large, soulful, unforgettable, questioning eyes. Though all of his instincts counsel against continuing to listen, Wiesenthal remains and allows the soldier to hold his hand. As he listens, he chases a fly away from the dying man, but at the end of the confession the narrator, consumed with disgust, ambivalent fascination, and pity, walks away in silence.

Later, troubled about whether he has done the right thing, Wiesenthal recounts the incident to several close fellow inmates, who assure him that his silence was the right response. If he had granted forgiveness, his fellow inmates assure him, those murdered would haunt him as long as he lived with "What right have you to forgive our murderer?"

Shortly after the war—with most of his fellow inmates dead and after witnessing many more piles of corpses—a sunflower impels Wiesenthal to remember the dying SS man and his confession. He undertakes a visit through the ruins of postwar Germany to visit Karl's mother. He is moved to do so not only out of a vague sense of duty but also to exorcize "one of the most unpleasant experiences in his life" (p. 85). Once there he engages in a different kind of silence, for he does not tell the mother of her son's heinous deeds. It is the first silence that persistently gnaws at him, however: "Was my silence at the bedside of the dying Nazi right or wrong?" Recognizing that the crux of the matter is, of course, the question of forgiveness, he closes his account by asking the reader to change places with him, and poses the question, "What would I have done?" (p. 98).

Many of the respondents voice the dilemma that while it might be appropriate to forgive a crime directed against one's self, it would never be right for one person to forgive a crime perpetrated against another person. There is wide agreement that silence was the only suitable response for Wiesenthal.

The present edition challenges a new generation to confront the moral questions of justice and forgiveness in light of recent developments relating to German-Jewish reconciliation, Jewish-Christian dialogue, increased knowledge about the Holocaust, and recent genocides and crimes against humanity. Wiesenthal's narrative and the selected responses to it also address the perennial questions of the sins of complicity, omission, and denial that permit evil to exist and flourish—raising the issues of collective guilt and responsibility. Wiesenthal, who had every reason to be bitter or revengeful—eighty-nine of his relatives were victims of the Final Solution—displays a moral sensitivity. He retains what Friedrich Torkey calls an " intact morality." While he could not offer forgiveness, he did not hate; his visit to Karl's mother constituted an act of compassion, as is his perpetual wrestling over his behavior (Brown, p. 37).

Literary Perspective

From a literary perspective Wiesenthal integrates in *The Sunflower* psychological details as well as evocative symbols and leitmotifs, providing openings around which to generate discussion on a wide range of ethical, social, and political issues concerning the decimation of European Jewry. That there is a direct link between inciting hatred of a targeted group and subsequent genocide is underscored by the place where the encounter with the SS man took place—a hospital created in a former Polish technical high school. In this place, in his student days, Wiesenthal had been tormented by antisemitic hoodlums. These students had, with the full cognizance of the school authorities, instituted "a day without Jews" celebration, during which Jewish students would be obstructed and prevented from taking their examinations (*Sunflower*, p. 19). The image of sunflowers in a military cemetery spellbinds the narrator. One sunflower alongside each grave symbolically connects the dead buried there with the living world, with sunlight and butterflies (reminiscent of the poignant poem of Theriesenstadt, "I Never Saw Another Butterfly"). The image is contrasted to the piles of dehumanized corpses in mass graves; a fate that Weisenthal imagined could be his at any time.

Paraphrasing Cynthia Ozick and the sentiments of others in *The Sunflower*: Even fifty plus years later, it is the sins of complicity, omission, and denial that allow evil to thrive. We must make certain not to condone or even appear to condone such crimes so that other such criminals—contemporary and future ones—not think they can act without fear of punishment, that time will wash away their crimes, that they will find a safe haven anywhere.

Wiesenthal's dilemma has contemporary reverberations. Jews are often asked: Isn't it about time you forgive and forget? The historian Deborah Lipstadt responds that the world is still waiting to encounter perpetrators who are actually sincerely seeking such forgiveness.

The Sunflower is a rich text paralleling the Bible in its parable structure. It bears reading not only for the power of its evocation of the Holocaust but for its power to illuminate our own moral and ethical lives.

Bibliography

Primary Sources

K2 Mauthausen (Concentration Camp Mauthausen). 1946.
Grossmufti-Grossagent der Achse (Head-Mufti, Head-Agent of the Axis). 1947.
Ha-redifah ahat Aikman (*The Pursuit of Eichmann*). 1961.
Ich jagte Eichmann (I Hunted Eichmann). 1961.
Verjaehhrung? (Limitation). 1965.
The Murderers Among Us: The Simon Wiesenthal Memoirs. 1967.
Die Sonneblume (*The Sunflower*). 1970, 1997.
Segel der Hoffnung: Die geheine Mission des Christof Columbus (*Sails of Hope: The Secret Mission of Christopher Columbus*). 1972, 1973.
The Case of Krystyna Jaworska. 1975.
Recht, nicht Rache (Justice not Vengeance). 1989.
Max and Helen. 1982.

Secondary Sources

Brown, Robert McAfee. Review of *The Sunflower* by Simon Wiesenthal. *New York Times Book Review*, 12 September 1976.
Cooper, A. "Simon Wiesenthal: The Man, the Mission, His Message." *Encyclopedia of the Holocaust*. Vol. 4. New York: Macmillan, 1990.
Epstein, Eric Joseph, and Philip Rosen. *Dictionary of the Holocaust*. Westport, Conn.: Greenwood Press, 1997.
Grobman, Alex, and D. Landes, eds. *Simon Wiesenthal Center Annual: Critical Issues of the Holocaust*. Los Angeles: Simon Wiesenthal Center, 1983.
Levy, Alan. *The Wiesenthal File*. London: Constable & Co., 1993.

Binjamin Wilkomirski

(1941–)

DOROTA GLOWACKA

Binjamin Wilkomirski's *Bruchstücke* (*Fragments: Memories of a Wartime Childhood*, 1995), the author's first and only literary attempt, is a stunning account of the wartime ordeal of a little Jewish boy from Riga, Latvia. In loosely connected episodes, Wilkomirski describes the boy's family's flight from Latvia, during which he probably witnesses the murder of his father; a brief period of hiding on a Polish farm, ending in separation from his mother and brothers and deportation to a concentration camp, most likely Majdanek; and finally, a transport to another camp, presumably Auschwitz-Birkenau. Tossed from barracks to barracks, the boy miraculously survives the camps and, upon liberation, finds himself in an orphanage in Kraków. Under the threat of antisemitic pogroms in postwar Poland, he is smuggled (allegedly by Swiss Red Cross) into a rural orphanage in Switzerland and then placed in foster care with an affluent Swiss family. The memoir is told from the perspective of a child disoriented by the incomprehensible events he experiences and constantly thwarted in his attempts to find a sense of belonging and security. As a result, he confounds the reality of the camp barracks and his life in postwar Switzerland: in the child's eyes, his Swiss rescuers, who impose the rule of silence on his Holocaust experience, match if not exceed the cruelty of his German torturers.

A Child of the Camps

Fragments is unsparing in graphic details of the torture inflicted on the child: Binjamin survives being flung against a concrete wall, kicked on the head, incarcerated overnight in a dog kennel crawling with insects, and thrown into a ditch full of dead bodies. The reader is witness to scenes of infants chewing off their frozen fingers, rats crawling out of the stomach of a dead woman, and other unspeakable horrors. The gruesome episodes are rendered in vivid, photographic images suffused with intense physical sensations. As the narrative oscillates between the camps and the equally disastrous postwar period, Binjamin's universe is a clutter of inchoate fragments that float to the surface of memory yet resist incorporation into language: "the shards of memory with hard knife-sharp edges, which still cut flesh if touched today. Mostly a chaotic jumble, with very little chronological fit; shards that keep surfacing against the orderly grain of grown-up life and escaping the laws of logic" (*Fragments*, translated by Carol Brown Janeway, New York: Schocken, 1996, p. 4). An emblematic child without an identity, the boy has "no mother tongue, nor a father tongue either" (p. 3); deracinated from any identifiable culture and alienated from language, his dismembered narrative does not cohere into a life story but swirls in the vortex of primal sensory impressions and intense feelings. Binjamin's visual disorientation and pervasive muteness, as well as his warped sense of time, reveal the abyssal structure of memory, and the narrator's discombobulated words palpate that void. Although the story is narrated from the innocent-eye perspective of a child, the voice of a recollecting adult occasionally cuts through, tapping into these precognitive sources and struggling to string them together into a meaningful whole.

An Instant Holocaust Classic

Bruchstücke exploded onto the literary scene in 1995 (followed by an English translation as *Fragments* in 1996) to universal critical acclaim. Reputable scholars lavished praise on what was largely seen as an exemplar of Holocaust testimony; Daniel Goldhagen, quoted on the book jacket of the 1996 Schocken edition, called it a "small masterpiece that conveys the shattering effects of the Holocaust upon one child's life, human relations, and capacity to use language." It quickly ascended to the ranks of such Holocaust classics as Elie Wiesel's *Night* (1958), Anne Frank's *Diary of a Young Girl* (1947), Primo Levi's *Survival in Auschwitz* (1947), and Paul Célan's poetry, with which it was frequently and favorably compared. Highly recommended as a source of insight into the immensity of Holocaust suffering, the book in which "all children—most importantly Holocaust children—are finally vindicated" (Maurice Sendak, on the jacket of the 1996 Schocken edition), *Fragments* was promptly translated into nine languages and garnered many awards, including the Prix Mémoir de la *Shoah* in France, the Jewish Quarterly Literary Prize in Britain, and a National Jewish Book Award in Britain. It was endorsed by the United States Holocaust Memorial Museum, which sent Wilkomirski on a fund-raising tour. Wilkomirski's testimony has been filed at Yad Vashem, the national Holocaust memorial in Jerusalem, Israel; he also gave long interviews for the Holocaust Memorial Museum video collection and for Stephen Spielberg's Survivors of *Shoah* Foundation. Wilkomirski was embraced by an international community of Holocaust rememberers, including many survivors who believed that he had given voice to their collective trauma and articulated their own predicament of having to come to terms with their Holocaust experience. *Fragments* became mandatory reading in a number of university courses, and it was recommended by pedagogical journals as a reading in school.

Wilkomirski was invited to give lectures, school presentations, and seminars on the *Shoah*, in which he always underscored the plight of the children of the Holocaust—deprived of family history, often lacking basic knowledge about their identity, disbelieved and therefore neglected by historians. Wilkomirski became a resource for child survivors researching their history. Together with his friend Eli Bernstein, he devised an interdisciplinary therapy for "reactivating lost memories" to recover lost identity (Maechler, p. 247), presenting the results at prestigious conferences, including the World Congress of Psychotherapy in Vienna in June 1996.

The Wilkomirski Affair

In 1998, this harrowing Holocaust memoir came under fire following an investigation by a Swiss reporter, Daniel Ganzfried, himself a son of a Holocaust survivor. In an article for the weekly *Die Weltwoche* (27 August 1998), Granzfried charged that Wilkomirski was a fraud and "knows Auschwitz and Majdanek only as a tourist" (quoted in Maechler, p. 130). Even before the book's publication, in February 1995, a reporter named Hanno Helbling had sent a letter to the publisher discrediting *Fragments* as a fictional account; yet, on the whole, the doubters were few, compared to wholesale belief in the work's authenticity. Ganzfried's disclosures therefore caused a public uproar and received extensive media coverage. Further inquiry conducted by Stefan Maechler on behalf of Wilkomirski's literary agent, Eva Koralnik, confirmed Ganzfried's allegations, and in October 1999 the German publisher of *Fragments*, Jüdischer Verlag (a division of Suhrkamp), withdrew from stores all hardcover copies of the book. Schocken Books swiftly followed suit.

According to official documents, "Binjamin Wilkomirski" is actually Bruno Dössekker, a musician, teacher of music, and clarinet maker who lives in the small town of Amlikon, Switzerland. He is the adopted son of a Protestant couple, Kurt and Martha Dössekker, and he was born on 12 February 1941 (three years later than the boy from Riga) in the district hospital at Biel, Switzerland, to an unwed Protestant woman named Yvonne Berthe Grosjean. His birth mother's attempts to keep him were unsuccessful, and the child was placed in various foster homes before being ultimately placed in a children's home in Adelboden. Thus, although the circumstances of his childhood were horrific in their own right, Bruno Dössekker spent the war years in relative security. From 1945, he lived with his adoptive parents (according to Wilkomirski's contradictory accounts, he arrived in Switzerland in 1947), although the adoption was only formalized in 1957. He spent his adolescence in a privileged middle-class environment, went to the best schools, and studied medicine, music, and history. He married in 1964 and had three children, although the couple later separated. After Yvonne Grosjean's death in 1981, Wilkomirski accepted one-third of her inheritance, a fact seen by his detractors as incriminating evidence.

The attacks on the integrity of his biography crushed Wilkomirski, and he withdrew from the spotlight. A spatter of support and continuing sympathy failed to halt the outpouring of disdain for a man who was now considered a pathological liar, and the organizations that had endorsed him enthusiastically promptly withdrew their awards. A notable exception was the American Orthopsychiatric Association, which in April 1999 presented him with an award in recognition of his contribution to "further[ing] the understanding of genocide and the Holocaust" (quoted in Maechler, p. 156). Reiterating Ganzfried's accusations and spurred by a CBS television documentary on the Wilkomirski affair on *60 Minutes* (broadcast in February 1999), a chorus of hostile voices condemned him for deliberately perpetrating a scandalous hoax that played into the hands of Holocaust deniers. To make matters worse, Wilkomirski's crown witness and staunch defender, Laura Grabowski, whom he had previously recognized as a fellow child sufferer from the camps, was identified as Laurel Willson, alias Lauren Stratford, the author of several "autobiographies," also exposed as fictional, in which she described her abuse at the hands of the members of satanic cults.

A more sympathetic view, espoused by Elena Lappin (who dubbed Wilkomirski "the man with two heads"), Philip Gourevitch, and Stefan Maechler, among others, has been to read *Fragments* as an inscription of fictional memories of a man who, even if he was not the victim of the Holocaust, as he claimed, was the victim of a childhood trauma that pushed him into believing a compelling fictional identity of his own construction. Wilkomirski embellished his mythical account of childhood victimization by drawing on the results of his 1960s research into the fate of Jewish refugees in Eastern Europe under Nazi rule; he also relied on his later extensive studies of various archival collections. He traveled to Poland several times and made a trip to Riga, with the purpose of identifying the sites whose contours had etched themselves, as he says, in his memory. On these trips he enlisted the help of sympathetic local historians.

Elena Lappin's and Stefan Maechler's research, involving interviews with Wilkomirski's informants (mostly historians and Holocaust survivors), as well as workers at children's homes, relief agencies, state archives, and others, confirms that Wilkomirski interpreted the historical data provided to him rather loosely, altering it to corroborate his version of events. Based on historical facts, furthermore, the stories of his family's escape from Riga, of his being smuggled into Switzerland after the war, and of his being exchanged for another child, are entirely implausible. A number of people who knew Bruno Dössekker as a child (such as his teachers and caretakers or their relatives) have since positively confirmed his identity. It now appears that Wilkomirski may have appropriated elements of the biographies of survivors who confided in him in order to assemble his own identity as a Holocaust child victim. He certainly drew on the life of Karola (Mila in *Fragments*), a survivor who entrusted him with her memories in 1971 and who is now indignant that he has used–and falsified—her biography (see Maechler, pp. 196–204). People who knew him in his youth recalled that Wilkomirski had begun circulating rumors of being a Jewish boy from the Baltic region by the time he was in high school, and in the 1960s he began to claim a Jewish heritage and observe Jewish customs. By the early 1980s, his biography had gestated into an account of a child Holocaust survivor. Maechler surmises that the name Wilkomirski may have been appropriated in the early 1970s, when it was suggested to him that he bore a resemblance to the Polish pianist Wanda Wilkomirska. Other sources that may have inspired Wilkomirski were existing Holocaust literature (*The Painted Bird* in particular; he often mentions the impact Jerzy Kosinski's book had on him), documentaries from the camps and the Nazi trials, and films such as Claude Lanzmann's *Shoah* (1985).

Wilkomirski's most loyal companions in his search for the past were Verena Piller, who became his partner in 1982, and the Israeli psychologist Elitsur Bernstein, both of whom encouraged him to engage in active recollection and to write down his memories. Another crucial influence was his psychotherapist Monika Matta, who specialized in infancy and childhood trauma. Once Wilkomirski "outed" himself as a Holocaust survivor, he befriended a number of survivors, among them Lea Balint, herself a former hidden child, now helping other "children without identity" to recover their roots. Balint served as a consultant for an Israeli documentary film on child survivors, *Wanda's Lists*, which was broadcast in November 1994 and featured cameo appearances by Wilkomirski. Even after the scandal erupted, Balint swore to Wilkomirski's authenticity: "Wilkomirski's real. I'm a hundred percent convinced he is real" (quoted in Maechler, p. 105). Another pillar of Wilkomirski's unshakable belief in his identity as a Jewish victim was Yakov Maroko, an Israeli Jew who had become convinced that Wilkomirski was his long-lost son, despite the evidence to the contrary of negative DNA tests. In his book *A Life in Pieces: The Making and Unmaking of Binjamin Wilkomirski*, Blake Eskin, a member of the Wilbur family (once Wilkomirskis), describes the efforts his family made to assist Dössekker in finding relatives in Latvia—as well as their disillusionment when the impostor's story began to unravel.

In the face of what seems to be indisputable evidence, Wilkomirski continued to insist that Bruno Dössekker is a legal identity imposed on him after the war. He accuses the Swiss authorities of repeated attempts to erase his true identity as a young Jewish victim of the Holocaust, the identity which he has so painstakingly reconstructed. To explain the discrepancies between his narrative and official documentation, Wilkomirski has supplemented the story of his childhood as told in *Fragments* with a story of the Dössekkers' having secretly exchanged him for a Christian boy, who later emigrated to the United States, and he added a story of having been a victim of medical experiments to substantiate the account of his improbable survival in Auschwitz. At the same time, he refused to take a DNA test that would prove that he has no connection to Yvonne Grosjean's surviving brother, Max Grosjean, or to his birth father, Rudolf Z., whose identity has been established in the meantime.

Fabricated Memory? Outcomes and Assessments

In a way, *Fragments* is a truthful account of childhood trauma and of Wilkomirski's quest for identity, albeit cloaked in the narrative of the greatest historical disaster of the twentieth century. Indeed, many of the events he described actually did happen and people he mentioned did exist, although they were imaginatively transformed and grafted upon the landscape of the war-torn Latvia and Poland. Referring to Wilkomirski's ordeal as "tragic aberration," Maechler concludes that the author certainly did not write *Fragments* with a fraudulent intent, although it is impossible to ascertain to what extent he believed his own story. Wilkomirski insists, sententiously, in an afterword to *Fragments:* "Legally accredited truth is one thing—the truth of a life another" (p. 154). The closest the author has come to acknowledging any truth in the charges that he fabricated his story is his statement that "it was always the free choice of the reader to read my book as literature or to take it as a personal document" (Gourevitch, p. 51).

Even if the status of *Fragments* as a quintessential Holocaust testimony is disputable, the discussion it precipitated drew attention, importantly, to the poorly documented plight of a number of child survivors of the Holocaust, the so-called "children without identity." Displaced and robbed of childhood, the origins of these young victims, like that of Wilkomirski's protagonist, have been engulfed first by their war ordeal and then by the botched attempts of the postwar states to deal with this legacy of the Holocaust. Further, *Fragments* generated tempestuous debates about the status of childhood memories as related to the phenomenon of recovered memory, the function of preverbal "body memory" in the constitution of identity, the role of psychotherapy in the production of memory (repressed traumatic memory in particular), and the theories of trauma in general. The notoriety of the book and the responses to it exemplified Dori Laub's theories (in Shoshana Felman and Dori Laub, *Testimony: Crisis of Witnessing in Literature, Psychology, and History*, New York: Routledge, 1992) about the complexity and tentativeness of memory and the way individual recollection is always narratively emplotted and woven into the texture of national remembrance and collective myths. At the same time, the success of Wilkomirski's ingenious format, that is, the account of a very young child, conveys perhaps better than any clichés about the "unspeakability of the Holocaust" our inability to come to terms with the full dimension of its horror. The Wilkomirski affair alerted us to the fact that, although we hold survivors in awe, we treat them as repositories of collective memory and may appropriate their pain to confirm our own sense of belonging in the continuum of history. The debate also served as a magnifying glass under which the struggle over who owns the Holocaust memory played itself out, leaving us to conclude that perhaps no one ultimately has the monopoly on the truth about the Holocaust and, just as important, that no one has the authority to judge the substance of someone else's memory.

Behind the various efforts to get to the bottom of the Wilkomirski affair is the desire to reconcile the claims of personal memory, with its tenuous, affective grip on the past, with the genre of history, which privileges indisputable fact. Maechler's attempt to definitively unravel the veracity of *Fragments* is rightly staked on the truth of historical documentation; as the author insists, "Every detail included here has its connection to historical reality" (pp. viii–ix). At the same time, the insistence on historical reality serves as an act of censorship, since Wilkomirski's text is now available as couched in the indisputable framework of the report, which safeguards the reader against mistaking it for "the real thing." The *Fragments* conundrum, with the text's blurring of the boundaries between fact and fiction, raised further questions about the status of Holocaust literature and drew attention to it as a nexus of linguistic practices where established genres and distinctions become untenable. Last but not least, considering the sensationalist dimension of the scandal, it intensified concerns about the commodification of the Holocaust.

The Wilkomirski phenomenon merits scrupulous attention in two respects: first, in terms of the astounding success of *Fragments*, its reception as a literary masterpiece, and the fact that it was widely believed despite the hyperbolic manner of the account and the early warnings about its inauthenticity; and then in the vehemence of the attacks on Wilkomirski once his memoir was demoted to the ranks of fiction. The upheaval over Wilkomirski's claim to truth is a symptom of the terror, experienced by the second and third generation in particular, of the potential vanishing of the Holocaust memory; will the truth of the Holocaust dissolve into vicarious constructs with the death of the last witness? The recent proliferation of research into the Holocaust, accompanied by a vast array of Holocaustiana of often dubious historical and aesthetic merit, seems evidence that the Holocaust has become a litmus test of our ability to ground ourselves in the solid facts of history. The concerted, often sanctimonious, efforts to uncover the truth of Wilkomirski's story perhaps illustrate a need to uphold the reality principle in the face of the reading public's failure to distinguish the authentic voice of the victim from a fabrication.

If there is a moral to the Wilkomirski affair, it is that the onus of responsible remembering is ultimately placed on the reader, on each of us. The Holocaust story must be carefully transmitted and preserved lest "anomaly displaces history" (Ozick, p. 119). Wilkomirski's spurious theft of the survivors' memories needs to be denounced and guarded against. Yet, while Maechler contends that *Fragments*, once exposed as fabulation, deteriorates into kitsch, many readers continue to succumb to its emotional power, despite the knowledge of its historical inauthenticity. The French philosopher Emmanuel Lévinas's description of another text that has been caught up in controversy perhaps rings true for Wilkomirski's book as well: it is "a text that is both beautiful and true, true as only fiction can be" (in Zvi Kolitz, *Yosl Rakover Talks to God*, translated by Carol Brown Janeway, New York: Pantheon Books, 1999, p. 80).

Bibliography

Primary Source

Bruchstücke. 1995. Translated as *Fragments: Memories of a Wartime Childhood*. 1996.

Secondary Sources

Alter, Robert. "Arbeit Macht Fraud." *New Republic*, 30 April 2001, pp. 35–38.

Bernard-Donals, Michael. "Beyond the Question of Authenticity: Witness and Testimony in the *Fragments* Controversy." *PMLA* 116, no. 5 (2001): 1302–1315.

Daly, Martin, "An Impossible but True Story of the Holocaust." *Sunday Age*, 8 November 1998.

Eskin, Blake. *A Life in Pieces: The Making and Unmaking of Binjamin Wilkomirski*. New York: Norton, 2002.

Ganzfried, Daniel. "Die geliehene Holocaust-Biographie" (The Purloined Holocaust Biography). *Die Welwoche*, 27 August 1998.

Gourevitch, Philip. "The Memory Thief." *New Yorker*, 14 June 1999, pp. 48–68.

Glowacka, Dorota. "The Shattered Word: Writing of the Fragment and Holocaust Testimony." In *The Holocaust's Ghost: Writing on Art, Politics, Law, and Education*. Edited by F. C. DeCoste and Bernard Schwartz. Edmonton: University of Alberta Press, 2000, pp. 37–54.

Hanks, Robert. "Where Naughty Children Get Murdered." *Independent on Sunday*, 8 December 1996, p. 31. Review of *Fragments*.

Kozol, Jonathan. "Children of the Camps." *Nation*, 28 October 1996. Review of *Fragments*.

Maechler, Stefan. *The Wilkomirski Affair: A Study in Biographical Truth*. Translated by John E. Woods. New York: Schocken, 2001. Includes the text of *Fragments*.

Lappin, Elena. "The Man with Two Heads." *Granta* 66 (summer 1999): 7–65.

Ozick, Cynthia. "The Rights of History and the Rights of Imagination." In *Quarrel and Quandary*. New York: Knopf, 2000, pp. 103–119.

Pendergrast, Mark. "Recovered Memories and the Holocaust." 14 January 1999. http://www.stopbadtherapy.com/experts/fragments/fragments.html.

Salecl, Renata. "Why One Would Pretend to Be a Victim of the Holocaust." *Other Voices* 2, no. 1 (February 2000).

Silverstone, Jennifer. "*Fragments* by Binjamin Wilkomirski." *British Journal of Psychotherapy* 17, no. 1 (2000): 112–121.

SHIMON WINCELBERG

(1924–)

NORMAN J. FEDDER

SHIMON WINCELBERG WAS born 26 September 1924 in Kiel, Germany, to David and Helen Wincelberg, and emigrated to the United States in 1938. From 1946 to 1947 he studied at the Veteran's Art Center of the Museum of Modern Art and Manhattan Technical Institute in New York City; he also attended Providence College in Providence, Rhode Island. Wincelberg resides in Beverly Hills, California.

Resort 76

Doubtless Wincelberg's background as a refugee from the Nazis influenced the writing of his Holocaust drama, *Resort 76* (1981, a revised version of *The Windows of Heaven*, 1962). The play is based on *A Cat in the Ghetto*, a novella by Rachmil Bryks, a survivor of the Lodz Ghetto and Auschwitz. Though Wincelberg derives the setting, central action, and some of the characters from his source, he makes the material fully his own, turning Bryks's naturalistic and discursive tale into a deftly constructed and fully developed drama. An examination of how Wincelberg transforms Bryks's work should prove useful in assessing the playwright's achievement.

Like Bryks's novella, the play takes place in a Polish ghetto during the German occupation of World War II. While Bryks ranges widely in his depiction of the ghetto, Wincelberg confines himself to the factory, or "resort," where the starved, sickly workers live and labor—trying to avoid deportation to the death camps by turning the bloodied clothes of the murdered into replicas of fine rugs. *A Cat in the Ghetto* is rich in descriptions of the squalid environment and misery of its many denizens, but little is done in the way of dramatic and psychological development. The play, in contrast, centers on the plight of only a *few* of the characters and structures their actions in a manner both suspenseful and revelatory.

The structure of *Resort 76* has been described as consisting of five interweaving stories (Skloot, 1982, pp. 22–23). Three of these focus on Blaustain, director of the factory: first and foremost, his involvement with a cat, purportedly of great value to the authorities; second, his conflict with his sister, Anya, who urges him to desert his sickly wife, Esther, and escape with Anya and her fellow partisans; third, his dilemma as to whether or not the pregnant Esther should have an abortion. There is no Anya or Esther in the novella, and although the play's protagonist, Blaustain, is based on the novella's Zabludovich, a factory watchman, Blaustain is hardly Zabludovich's counterpart: Blaustain is beset with a multitude of problems, Zabludovich with only one, and Zabludovich's concern for the cat is throughout on a visceral level, while Blaustain's grows in moral dimension.

The fourth story is that of the antisemitic German druggist, Krause, who is humiliatingly consigned to a factory cubicle when it is discovered that his maternal grandfather was Jewish. Finally, there is the story of the teacher, Schnur, who, in the face of the senseless brutality surrounding them, attempts to impart traditional Jewish values to his student, Beryl. Krause appears briefly in the novella as a similarly named German in like circumstances, while Schnur and Beryl have their antecedents in equally unimportant characters with different names. But all three play major roles in the drama.

These stories are unified through the central story of the cat, which unfolds when the widow Hershkovitch takes possession of the coveted creature. Wincelberg's Hershkovitch comes close to the original character in name and action: In both works she wants the protagonist to keep the cat safe for her until such time that it can be exchanged with the authorities for a supply of bread and a good job at the Ration Board.

She is convinced that this outcome is assured, with cats in short supply and the food stores infested with rats and mice.

In the play, no sooner does Blaustain agree to the widow's deal and have the cat in his safekeeping than he is besieged by three workers who want him to share the cat with one of *them* instead of with Hershkovitch. Each extravagantly and ludicrously tries to offer the director a better opportunity to obtain goods for the cat and a higher percentage of the profits, while one entertains the notion, to Blaustain's disgust, that the animal might best serve them all by being *eaten*. Zabludovich is similarly badgered in the novella and the creature's edible worth is suggested and rejected.

In the play, Anya then bursts in and entreats her brother to abandon his wife and give her, Anya, the cat, for which she can procure documents to get him out of the country, or, at least, if he won't leave Esther, to arrange an abortion for her. But Blaustain won't hear of it. This scene has no parallel in the novella.

When all but the helpless Esther leave for the soup wagon, the cat is stolen by an unseen intruder. At the news, Hershkovitch is furious with Blaustain. At this point a worker enters with the cat and readily admits it was *he* who stole the animal; its supposed value has been merely a rumor, and the authorities would give him next to nothing for it. The cat is also stolen in the novella and the widow is equally furious; but there is no surprise in the thief's revelation because the author has already told us that Zabludovich had the same experience with the authorities.

Beryl now enters and displays his bloodied fingers, the result of his being tortured to reveal that Schnur has been teaching him the laws of the Talmud, a forbidden act. This so affects Krause that, in a gesture of compassion, he provides the boy with pain medicine. The druggist has just learned that his mother's delivery has been declared "illegitimate," that she no longer is to be considered the offspring of her Jewish father, so Krause can now leave the ghetto as a "pure Aryan." Nevertheless, he returns to his cubicle and poisons himself. This has no analogue in the original: Krause's moral growth and suicide are of Wincelberg's making.

Schnur has been teaching Beryl the Talmudic laws of the ritual slaughtering of animals—particularly that all "may slaughter" except "a deaf mute, an imbecile, and a child" because "a knife handled in ignorance can cause pain" (Skloot, 1982, p. 50). This Jewish concern for the animal's suffering is in ironic contrast with the "imbecilic" butchery of human beings by the Germans, who will soon arrive to take Schnur to his death. Beryl's reaction to this is to denounce God and to desire to become a killer "like *them*." The contrasting sentiments of Schnur and Beryl both derive from the speech of one of Bryks's characters, who quotes from the Talmud, "Anyone may slaughter," but who reads this quote as God's approval of the Nazi butchery—an interpretation that leads him to lose faith in the Deity.

Blaustain echoes Beryl's despair, recalling Anya's creed that "if you want the world to respect you, first become an animal" and, when attacked, defend yourself. Yet Schnur refutes both for forsaking their Maker, for wanting to be a "beast of prey without shame" (p. 106). Schnur also derives from Old Silberberg in the novella, who regards the Holocaust as yet another test of Jewish faith and endurance. But there is nothing in Bryks's tale like the nobility of Schnur's character and the complex relationship between teacher and student.

Schnur's remarks have a telling effect on Blaustain and Beryl: as the Germans arrive to take the teacher away, Beryl returns to his studies, while Blaustain accedes to Schnur's plea not to exchange the cat for Esther's abortion (the hospital nurse still thinks the cat has value). Here Wincelberg strains our credulity, because it is unlikely that the ailing woman will survive the birth, that the baby will be healthy, or that either will escape the death camps.

Nothing as dramatic and uplifting occurs at the end of the novella, where the widow releases the cat, as Zabludovich can only hope she will do; where he is given credit for his honesty, and concludes by saying something about not losing faith. In the play, however, Blaustain makes the decision to free the cat, while the worker he appoints to do so movingly exclaims: "Go . . . in peace. . . . Enjoy the sunshine . . . and tell the other animals . . . tell them . . . tell them what it was like to be a Jew" (p. 112).

Thus, along with making stageworthy Bryks's sprawling narrative, Wincelberg gives the Holocaust material a religious dimension. As compared with the novella, he raises the behavior of his major characters to the level of moral heroism: how Blaustain, Schnur, Beryl, and Krause react to their sufferings is portrayed as a test of their faith and humanity—a test which they pass with distinction.

Critical Reception

In reviewing the anthology in which *Resort 76* is published, Alvin Goldfarb dismissed the play as a conventional, "well-made" melodrama employing a central dramatic device, coincidental arrivals, and an "optimistic" resolution (p. 567), while Edward Isser demeaned it as one of quite a few American plays that simplify and sanitize the horrific events by turning them into dramatically gripping and morally edifying sagas of heroic sacrifice and religious affirmation (p. 14).

On the contrary, Eric Sterling had high regard for Wincelberg's work, particularly his portrayal of Krause. Sterling wrote at length of Krause's coming to terms with the bankruptcy of his Nazi convictions (pp. 71–80), disagreeing with Skloot that the druggist takes his life "because he cannot face the shame he will encounter when his release is finally obtained" (Skloot, *The Darkness We Carry*, p. 15). Sterling insisted, rather, that Krause was ennobled by his suicide—affirming the "new essential identity he has developed" (pp. 79–80).

Skloot acknowledged the play's "weakness" in mitigating the horrid reality of the "imminent and complete destruction" of the ghetto residents by presenting a "deliberately positive picture of victims under something slightly less than a maximum penalty." Nevertheless, he admired *Resort 76* as having achieved "a worthy mixture of sadness and hopefulness, secured by human tenacity" in confronting the ultimate in human malevolence (*The Darkness We Carry*, p. 35).

Bibliography

Primary Sources

Plays

The Conqueror. 1955.
Kataki. 1959.
The Windows of Heaven. 1962; revised and retitled *Resort 76*. 1981.

Teleplays

The Sea Is Boiling Hot. 1957.
The Crimson Halo. 1972.
Wincelberg has written close to a hundred scripts for network television, including *Naked City, Have Gun Will Travel, Eternal Night, Route 66, G. E. Theatre, Mannix, Gunsmoke*, and *Police Woman*.

Screenplay

On the Threshold of Space. 1956.

Biography

The Samurai of Vishogrod (with Anita M. Wincelberg). 1976.
The Siberian Bachelor: The Notebooks of Jacob Marateck, Outlaw (with Anita M. Wincelberg). 1995.

Reportage

The Utopian Chronicles. 1982.

Stories

"The Conqueror." 1953.

Secondary Sources

Antler, Joyce. " 'Three Thousand Miles Away': The Holocaust in Recent Works for the American Theater." In *The Americanization of the Holocaust*. Edited by Helene Flanzbaum. Baltimore: Johns Hopkins University Press, 1999, pp. 125–141.

Bryks, Rachmil. *A Cat in the Ghetto*. New York: Bloch, 1959.

Goldfarb, Alvin. "Review of *The Theatre of the Holocaust, Vol. 1*." *Theatre Journal* 35, no. 4 (1983): 567–568.

Isser, Edward R. *Stages of Annihilation: Theatrical Representations of the Holocaust*. Madison, N.J.: Fairleigh Dickinson University Press, 1997.

Langer, Lawrence. "The Americanization of the Holocaust on Stage and Screen." In *From Hester Street to Hollywood*, edited by Sarah Blacher Cohen. Bloomington: Indiana University Press, 1983, pp. 213–230.

Skloot, Robert. "Introduction." *The Theatre of the Holocaust, Vol. 1*. Edited by Robert Skloot. Madison: University of Wisconsin Press, 1982, pp. 3–37.

———. *The Darkness We Carry. The Drama of the Holocaust*. Madison: University of Wisconsin Press, 1988.

Sterling, Eric. "Loss and Growth of Identity in Shimon Wincelberg's *Resort 76*." In *Literature and Ethnic Discrimination*. Edited by Michael J. Meyer. Amsterdam: Rodopi, 1997, pp. 71–81.

"Wincelberg, Shimon." *Contemporary Authors, New Revision Series, Vol. 46*. Detroit: Gale Research, 1995.

BOGDAN WOJDOWSKI

(1930–1994)

MONIKA ADAMCZYK-GARBOWSKA

BOGDAN WOJDOWSKI BELONGS to the generation of Polish Jewish writers who were children during the war. Born in Warsaw, he spent three years of his childhood in the Warsaw ghetto and later in hiding on the "Aryan" side. In 1954 he graduated from the Department of Polish at the University of Warsaw. He published essays, reviews (a number of them on theater), stories, and journalistic pieces in various journals.

Bread for the Departed

Most of Wojdowski's prose is directly or indirectly devoted to his wartime experiences. His most outstanding achievement is his novel *Chleb rzucony umarłym* (1971, *Bread for the Departed*), perhaps the best fictionalized account of the Warsaw ghetto ever written. The novel's English title is somewhat euphemistic and less powerful than the original one, which literally means "bread thrown to the dead." The novel covers the period from the establishment of the ghetto in 1940 until January 1943, the time of the "little action." It includes a number of crucial events, like the "great action" of summer 1942, when thousands of the inhabitants, including the Polish Jewish doctor and educator Janusz Korczak, were transported to the death camps. The gradual annihilation of the ghetto is seen through a young boy's eyes, which makes the effect even stronger. The young narrator, David, perceives the world of the ghetto as it is; the most abnormal situations are a part of his reality. He never comments but gives us all the details, which together form a nightmarish image; however, there is much commentary, often quite ironic, in dialogues among the inhabitants or between Jews in the ghetto and the Nazis, as well as scraps of German orders quoted in the original. Wojdowski does not glorify the ghetto; on the contrary, he shows it in all its misery, ugliness, and corruption. The "bread" in the title is a leading motif, becoming a symbol of survival. It is the main concern of all inhabitants of the ghetto, but especially of the young boy, who, like other children, becomes a breadwinner for his family, and of the noble doctor Obuchowski, who, examining the incrementally perishing population, provides detailed observations on the symptoms of starvation, one of the main killers in the ghetto. At the center of the novel is the group of boy smugglers to which the central character belongs. They all have nicknames, like Henio the Herring, Yosele Egg Yolk, or Chaim the Orphan, and are prepared to take any risk in order to bring back food from the "Aryan" side. The events and characters are presented in a naturalistic way, bordering on the grotesque. In one of the scenes the juvenile smugglers raid corpses in the Jewish cemetery to extract gold from their teeth. In another powerful scene a janitor, driven to despair by the death of his daughter, kills a coachman's horse with an ax. The dead horse is immediately stripped to the bones by starving people.

The action of the novel rarely takes place outside the wall, focusing on the situation inside the ghetto and emphasizing the isolation of its inhabitants. The writer attempts to penetrate the core of human cruelty and degradation by creating sharp and clear visions of the apocalypse and by restrained, nonjudgmental analyses of people's behavior in extreme conditions. Chapter II presents in detail the very erection of the wall, listing all the major streets the designated area encompassed. With every passing day, as the dollar "climbs" in value and bread becomes more and more expensive, we witness the process of human life growing cheaper and cheaper.

Wojdowski's technique resembles that of Tadeusz Borowski in the latter's camp stories, as the most gruesome events are described in a matter-of-fact way, with a conscious detachment:

> Rosh Hashanah, the New Year, passed without hope or the sound of the *shofar;* Yom Kippur, the Day of Atonement, was celebrated without repentance; Sukkoth, the Feast of Tabernacles and the Harvest, dragged on without bread. Faces grew black from hunger. During those autumn days the sun hung over the city like a typhus-carrying louse threatening everyone. Those who were supposed to die had died already. Those who were going to die later were still alive, waiting their turn. Driven out by hunger from their dark, unheated dens, they ran around freely at night through the emptied streets, crowds of them crying out, making a racket, jangling their empty metal jugs. They dropped clumps of rags and lice in the streets. Dried-up skeletons, staggering weakly inside loose scraps of clothing, collapsed on the ground, whimpering pitifully. Their cries and helpless lamentations beat against the windows. In the morning the janitors covered the corpses with paper (*Bread for the Departed,* Evanston, Ill.: Northwestern University Press, 1997, p. 157).

The structure of the novel is loose and fragmentary and the language often consciously incorrect to render the Polish Jewish idiom and stress the fact that most characters speak Yiddish as their native tongue.

As in a number of other works on the Holocaust, David's mother is the real heroine as she keeps the family functioning. It is she who manages to create a meal out of nothing or devotes herself to the necessary task of delousing her son while the men engage in idle intellectual arguments.

The question of maintaining Jewish identity is also an issue in the novel. For instance, on the verge of death and driven by despair, David's grandfather tells him to abandon his Jewishness, run away, and remain silent when people say bad things about Jews. The boy should even drive his family from his memory in order to live, he proclaims. Grandfather's desperate speech sounds like an ominous prayer as he ends it with "Amen" (p. 232).

After his grandfather's death, the narrator is left with words he cannot erase from his memory, words that he treats as a curse, especially when he remembers the old man's earlier teachings as "the noble confusion or verses from Genesis about the joyous creation of the world"(p. 232).

The deportation of summer 1942, characterized as "Doomsday," is described in chapter XIII: the cruelty of the gendarmes, the vain efforts to save oneself and one's closest relatives, the Nazi propaganda promising work and bread in the east. Some people avoid deportation for a while, managing to escape or bribe the police, but such attempts are usually short-lived or futile.

In his preface to the novel (absent from the English translation) Wojdowski makes a statement that encapsulates the whole satanic idea behind the creation of the Warsaw ghetto and other ghettos less imprinted in collective memory and literary imagination: "The wall divided people and that's why it was erected; I cannot express it more briefly." He concludes his preface talking about the mission of the writer, which is to see the world sharply and clearly because "each look can be the last one" (p. 7 [translation by Monika Adamczyk-Garbowska]). These two quotations capture the essence of Wojdowski's writing, as most of his later works are related to the idea of the wall, in either a physical or a metaphorical sense. The traumatic insecurity of the writer's existence was concluded with his suicidal death on the fifty-first anniversary of the Warsaw ghetto uprising.

Other Works

Wojdowski's other works include collections of stories—*Wakacje Hioba* (1962, Job's Holidays), *Mały człowieczek, nieme ptaszę, klatka i świat* (1975, A Little Person, a Silent Bird, a Cage, and the World), and *Maniuś Bany* (1980)—as well as the novel *Konotop* (1966) and the posthumously published, unfinished novel *Tamta strona* (1997, The Other Side). *Tamta Strona* takes place after the war in a resort near Warsaw in a run-down hostel owned by the remnants of the Jewish community. The title is reminiscent of the ghetto wall but is used in a metaphorical sense in reference to death. Originally, *Bread for the Departed* was going to bear this title.

One of Wojdowski's best stories is the titular one from *Mały człowieczek, nieme ptaszę, klatka i świat,* in which the narrator recalls Belcia, a teenage girl who did not survive the Warsaw ghetto, a very plain, "gray and ordinary" girl with "a wide and flat face with red pimples, brown eyes, a fat, potato like nose" (Polonsky and Adamczyk-Garbowska, p. 241). Her family tries to escape to the east to the Soviet-occupied territories but is captured while crossing the border and must return to ghetto captivity. In the terrible conditions of the ghetto Belcia takes care of one of the birds given away by a bird collector because he could no longer feed them. Everyone laughs at Belcia, calling her "the maiden with the bird" and treating her behavior as ridiculous in the face of starvation and imminent destruction, but Belcia persists in her effort to keep the bird alive and even encourages it to sing. The bird never sings, and Belcia sets it free when she no longer can take care of it. The bird probably perishes among wild sparrows as Belcia does, but the memory remains:

> They wanted to dig out of the earth the bones that were there, burn and grind them, and sink them in the river, scatter them on the field. And that was also done. They

> wanted to tear the memory out of the brain. And this they just weren't able to do. (Polonsky and Adamczyk-Garbowska, pp. 243–244)

Wojdowski concludes metaphorically by declaring that on the large canvas depicting the Jewish experience during the Holocaust "there has to be a small dark place for that cage and the gray bird, who never cheered up anyone with her song" (p. 244).

Bibliography

Primary Sources

Wakacje Hioba (Job's Holidays). 1962.
Konotop. 1966.
Próba bez kostiumu (Rehearsal Without Costumes). 1966.
Chleb rzucony umarłym (*Bread for the Departed*). 1971. English edition, 1998.
Mały człowieczek, nieme ptaszę, klatka i świat (A Little Person, a Silent Bird, a Cage, and the World). 1975.
Maniuś Bany. 1980.
Wybór opowiadań (Selected Stories). 1982.
Mit Szagalewa. Szkice (The Myth of Szagalewo [Chagall-like shtetl]). 1982.
Tamta strona (The Other Side). 1997.

Secondary Sources

Adamczyk-Garbowska, Monika. "A New Generation of Voices in Polish Holocaust Literature." *Prooftexts* 3 (1989): 273–287.
Grynberg, Henryk. *Prawda nieartystyczna*. Berlin: Biblioteka Archipelagu, 1984.
Polonsky, Antony, and Monika Adamczyk-Garbowska, eds. *Contemporary Jewish Writing in Poland: An Anthology*. Lincoln and London: University of Nebraska Press, 2001.

Stanisław Wygodzki

(1907–1991)

MONIKA ADAMCZYK-GARBOWSKA

Stanisław Wygodzki belongs to the generation of Polish Jewish writers who survived the Holocaust as adults and who, after the war, devoted a substantial part of their work to this seminal experience. Born in Będzin in Silesia into a traditional Jewish family, he attended a Hebrew gymnasium, from which he was expelled for Communist activities shortly before graduation. Later he joined the Communist Party of Poland and was briefly imprisoned for his activities.

Wygodzki made his literary debut with *Apel* (A Roll Call), a volume of poetry, in 1933. During the Nazi occupation he spent the first years of the war in the Będzin ghetto and from 1943 was imprisoned in the camps at Auschwitz, Dachau, Sachsenhausen, and Oranienburg. After the war he remained in convalescent homes in Germany for two years to regain his health, which had greatly deteriorated from his imprisonment in camps. He returned to Poland in 1947. Enthusiastic for the new social order, which seemed to promise a fulfillment of his prewar ideals, he launched a successful career as a writer and published numerous collections of stories and poems describing the war and postwar period. The most notable among them was *Pamiętnik miłości* (Memoir of Love) of 1948, a collection of poems devoted to, among others, his murdered relatives. The tone and form of the poems are very different from his rather bombastic ideological prewar poetry. He was also an accomplished translator of Yiddish writers, including Sholem Aleichem, Efraim Kaganowski, Dovid Bergelson, and Sholem Asch.

Disillusioned by the failed promise of Communist society and additionally dismayed by the antisemitic campaign instigated by the Communist Party in 1968, Wygodzki settled in Israel, where he continued to write in Polish and published one novel and three collections of poetry. In his poems from that period, the Israeli landscape is seen as alien and unlike what he knew and loved in Poland.

Prose Works

Wygodzki's prose is often marked by didacticism and Communist ideology. Some of his stories have intricate plots, but the schematic, moralizing or overstated presentation diminishes their impact. Many of them are supposedly based on real events. Often the characters are children who rapidly mature during the terrible conditions of the Holocaust. In the story "W samo południe" (At High Noon) a young Jewish boy who no longer has strength to hide goes to a policeman and asks for death. In "Odwiedziny" (A Visit) an eight-year-old boy comes to his sick mother in the camp. He brings her bread as an expression of love but simultaneously blames her for giving him birth as a Jew and declares that when he grows up, he will give up being Jewish. The boy persists in questioning his mother and refutes her bashful responses with barely controlled anger, claiming that he is grown up enough to decide about his identity. The story is composed as a conversation consisting of laconic utterances, which is characteristic of Wygodzki's style in general, as he often uses dialogue to dramatize situations. Another of his preferred forms is the dramatic monologue, a style used in one of his best-known stories, "Koncert Życzeń" (Request Concert), in which a Jewish survivor, who was helped during the war by a Catholic priest, later helps when his rescuer is persecuted by the Stalinist authorities. The novel juxtaposes paradoxical turns of human fate. In Wygodzki's exploration of the dramatic monologue form, one can also trace his indebtedness to the Yiddish oral tradition.

One sometimes regrets that Wygodzki did not choose a different form of expression, such as the essay or memoir, to record his traumatic experiences. Fortunately, in a number of works he restrains his moralizing. Among those is one of his best-crafted stories, "Człowiek z wózkiem" (A Man with a Cart). Written in a partly naturalistic, partly surrealistic mode, it focuses on a middle-aged Jew tortured both morally and physically by two sadistic SS men who brutalize him as a form of entertainment in their boring daily routine. Having first used him for slave labor, they tell him to go home and come back the next day, but before they let him go they ask how far away he lives. When they find out that he needs approximately half an hour to reach home while pushing his cart, they keep him until it is too late for him to get home before the designated time. Then they make him follow them, pretending they want to escort him in case other patrols decide to shoot him. Finally, when they have reached the building where he lives with his old mother, they shoot at him, claiming they had to because he had broken the law. Then they force his mother to push him in the cart to a hospital:

> In silence she pulled the cart through dark streets. The SS-men followed her and each time they met another patrol they sent away the armed men, laughing.
> "Why are you escorting them?" a soldier asked.
> "Why? So that no one stops them," the SS-man explained. And he asked the woman:
> "Is the hospital far away from here?"
> "No, it's close." (Maciejewska, p. 190 [translation by Monika Adamczyk-Garbowska])

When she arrives, barely alive from enormous effort, it turns out that this is a Polish hospital, and according to the Nazi regulations the doctor is not allowed to take care of a Jew. Consequently, the mother must push her dying son to a Jewish hospital, where he dies because it is too late to save him since the bullet fatally damaged his intestines. Before leaving her there, the SS man tells the woman: "Remember, you are not allowed to return home. It's curfew!" (p. 192).

As in a number of other stories, the characters have no specific names; they are referred to in generic terms as "man," "woman," "mother," and "son," which makes them look like figures in a morality play.

Communist literary doctrine is notable in Wygodzki's proletarian stories in which, although a number of his characters are Jewish, their identity is not mentioned in accordance with the Communist belief in internationalism. In his earlier poetry Wygodzki stressed the common sufferings of all Hitler's victims regardless of nationality, stating, for instance, that his "heart is made of ashes / Of Jews, Poles, Russians and Greeks / So that in it the Future could hear the sob / of my age" (Polonsky and Adamczyk-Garbowska, p. 80). In spite of its flaws, Wygodzki's prose is an important contribution to Polish Holocaust literature and can be compared because of its scope, albeit not its literary merits, to Adolf Rudnicki's cycle of stories.

Poetry

Unlike his prose, Wygodzki's poetry is usually restrained, sparingly using words and metaphors, drawing from the Polish poetic tradition to describe enormous pain, especially the death of his young daughter. In those poems he refers to the most famous Polish Renaissance poet, Jan Kochanowski, who devoted a series of *Treny* (Laments) to his daughter Urszula, who died very young. Wygodzki himself states that his daughter Sarah is for him like Urszula for Kochanowski, and the association is so clear that it made Natan Gross entitle his essay on Wygodzki "Wygodzki's Jewish *Treny*" (Gross, pp. 70–77). As Kochanowski's *Laments* are rooted in the biblical tradition, Wygodzki's works reflect echoes of the Hebrew lamentations he knew from his traditional upbringing. What is more, one could claim Wygodzki's poems are much simpler than their prototypes, more straightforward, and in a sense more dramatic.

In a number of Wygodzki's poems, survival guilt is expressed, as in "Farewell," where he asks why he did not share the fate of "his dead":

> Why did I leave you then,
> My dead? (Polonsky and Adamczyk-Garbowska, p. 83)

He asks and recalls the circumstances of their death as well as his sense of desperation at not having shared their fate. These poems, as well as a number of others, refer to the most tragic episode from his biography when, while in Auschwitz, Wygodzki took cyanide, which he also gave to his wife and daughter. They both died as a result (his parents also perished, but in other circumstances) while Wygodzki himself survived. The awareness that indirectly he had contributed to the death of those dearest to him intensified his survivor's guilt and reverberated in different ways throughout his whole literary oeuvre.

Bibliography

Primary Sources

Apel (A Roll Call). 1933.
Chleb powszedni (Daily Bread). 1934.
Żywioł liścia (The Leaf Environment). 1936.
Pamiętnik miłości (Memoir of Love). 1948.
W kotlinie (In a Valley). 1949.
Nad Engelsem (Reading Engels). 1950.
Widzenie. Opowiadania (A Vision: Stories). 1950.
Wiersze (Poems). 1950.
Jelonek i syn. Powieść (A Fawn and a Son: A Novel). 1951.
Opowiadanie buchaltera (An Accountant's Story). 1951.
Wzgórza (Hills). 1952.
Powrót do domu (Homecoming). 1954.
Wybór wierszy (Selected Poems). 1954.
Pusty plac. Opowiadania (An Empty Square: Stories). 1955.

Opowiadania wybrane (Selected Stories). 1955–1962.
Przy szosie. Opowiadania (By the Highway: Stories). 1957.
6 opowiadań (Six Stories). 1958.
Milczenie (Silence). 1958.
O świcie (At Dawn). 1959.
Upalny dzień (A Hot Day). 1960.
Człowiek z wózkiem (A Man with a Cart). 1961.
Koncert życzeń (Request Concert). 1961.
Serca mego rodzeństwa (The Hearts of My Siblings). 1961.
W deszczu (In the Rain). 1962.
Nauczyciel tańca. Opowiadania (The Dance Master: Stories). 1963.
Opowiadania (Stories). 1964.
Basy (The Double Bass). 1965.
Boczna uliczka (A Side Street). 1966.
Powrót na ziemię. Opowiadania (Return to Earth: Stories). 1967.
Zatrzymany do wyjaśnienia. Powieść (Detained Pending Explanation: A Novel). 1968.
Drzewo ciemności (Tree of Darkness). 1971.
Pieskin został pisarzem. Powieść (Pieskin Has Become a Writer). 1973.
Podróż zimowa (Winter Journey). 1975.
Pożegnanie (Farewell). 1979.

Secondary Sources

Gross, Natan. *Poeci i Szoa* (Polish Poets and the *Shoah*). Sosnowiec: Offmax, 1993.
Maciejewska, Irena. *Męczeństwo i zagłada Żydów w zapisach literatury polskiej* (The Holocaust as Depicted in Polish Literature). Warsaw: KAW, 1988.
Polonsky, Antony, and Adamczyk-Garbowska, Monika, eds. *Contemporary Jewish Writing in Poland: An Anthology*. Lincoln and London: University of Nebraska Press, 2001.

ITAMAR YAOZ-KEST

(1934–)

GILA RAMRAS-RAUCH

ITAMAR YAOZ-KEST was born in Szarvas, Hungary, on 3 August 1934. At the age of ten, he was deported, along with his family, and interned at the Bergen-Belsen concentration camp from October 1944 to April 1945. Following liberation, the family returned to their hometown in Hungary. His father returned to his practice as a physician, while his mother searched for her parents, ultimately locating them in a mass grave in Austria. After the war, Yaoz-Kest continued his studies in Hebrew at Hungarian schools. The family ultimately settled in Budapest, but the general atmosphere of antisemitism they encountered prompted them to leave Hungary. His sister left for Israel with her husband, and in February 1951 Yaoz-Kest and his parents followed, arriving on the ship *Galilah*. In 1953 he joined the Israeli army and served for two and one-half years. He studied literature, the Bible, and Hebrew language at Tel-Aviv University, and in 1959, with his sister Mariza Rossman, he established the "Ekked" publishing house and served as its editor-in-chief for many years.

Yaoz-Kest recounted the family journey to Bergen-Belsen in stark, imagistic terms in his poem "Ordeal by Fire" (from the Bergen-Belsen Chapters, 1961). This poem, like many Holocaust poems, is an attempt to capture, in a metonymic way, the impact of the horror.

> Railway car.
>
> The landscape is startled. Embarrassed.
> It turns its page: trees, sky, tunnels – (Memory =
>   Distance + Time)
> In the dark the childhood years gallop.
>
> And in the car the laughter of the guardians collects,
>   The head of a beast sprouted on the neck.
> * * *
> Suddenly a squeal.
> The car has stopped
> In memory's compartment all is trapped. (p. 139,
>   Ekked, translation by B. Frank)

The experience of the railway car is by now a Holocaust marker. It appears in the poetry of Dan Pagis and the fiction of Aharon Appelfeld and Elie Wiesel, among others. Yaoz-Kest's poem combines two points of view; added to the childhood experience is the adult recollection of the passing images—trees, sky, tunnels. It is the combination of distance, time, and memory that informs the poem.

Career Overview

In a diverse literary career, Yaoz-Kest has published numerous collections of poetry, novels, plays, and essays. Further, he has translated numerous works of Hungarian literature into Hebrew and received several literary prizes, including the Talpir, Kugel, and Leah Goldberg Prizes, and was made laureate by the Hungarian government for his translation of Hungarian poetry. Yaoz-Kest changed his first name to Itamar and added the name Yaoz to his last, a Hebrew name that was based on his mother's maiden name. In light of the centrality of the role of assimilation and connection to roots, it is interesting that Yaoz-Kest opted to update his first name while simultaneously clinging to his past.

Primary Themes

Throughout his literary career, Yaoz-Kest has been very conscious of his role as a survivor. He ultimately does not believe in poetry that is disconnected from reality. Indeed, underlying the writing of Yaoz-Kest is the concept of the cycle: the dispersion from the homeland and the return to it; the Diaspora and the return to Israel. He has never forgotten that Israel represents his return to his source, his roots. Most of his writing contains strong autobiographical elements. The theme of return in his fiction is the return to his place of birth, to the death camps, and in a deeper sense his return to Israel. The very intense immersion into a new language required the ceding of past forms of speech and ways of thinking, and thus an inherent break with one's past. Indeed paradoxically, the process of acquiring a new identity is at the same time the "regaining" of an identity. And yet, personally and poetically, Yaoz-Kest resents the tacit pressure that requires the negation of his former self, the desertion of the language he was born to, even though he will acquire a language and an identity that are all closer to his inner self. Yaoz-Kest resists a total conversion in his call for a "double root," which will at once affirm the past and the present equally. In his fourth, and most autobiographical novel, *Ahizah Shel Hol* (Grasping the Sand, 1977), the protagonist is a young man in his early twenties who has come to Israel only a few years earlier. He is a poet who refuses to divide his life between the past and the present and see them as diametric opposites. The protagonist comes from an assimilated background, one in which ties to Judaism are scant. His counterpart is an older poet who, like the protagonist, changed his name.

The old man strikes up a conversation with the young man who happens to be carrying a book that belonged to his father: a multilingual edition of Horace. Years earlier the old poet translated Horace into Estonian; he now works as an upholsterer. He claims that in being isolated from people who speak his language, he gains a certain artistic freedom. In his writing he reconstructs a city that vanished in the Holocaust. This division between his actual existence and all that is meaningful to him, stands in stark contrast to the aspiration of the young protagonist with his search for two roots and the continuation of the past in the present. One of the major issues facing the young man is what meaning to give one's survival. The survival psychology involves a tacit dialogue with those who did not survive the Holocaust, as well as a tacit confrontation with those who did. The young man searches for a world in which the denial of one's past is not a precondition of present existence. He does not want to reach out his hand and find that he has grasped only sand.

At the same time he mocks those for whom ties with the past dominate the present. This raises the question: Is double-rootedness possible in life? Can one live in Israel and maintain a deep connection to one's past, or is that connection at once mutually exclusive with one's new identity as an Israeli?

The protagonist's search for roots parallels the author's dilemma. In terms of tone, the protagonist's experience nears the surreal or the fantastic. Simultaneously in what may be seen as one of the more autobiographical notes in his canon, we are confronted with more prosaic, traditionally descriptive scenes. His attendance at a religious observance fails to evoke ancient voices within him, once again drawing to the fore the conflict within the character. His new existence, along with the adoption of a new language for his writing and his life, are all quite remote from his identification as a Jew.

Yaoz-Kest's aesthetic search and the formation of his identity led him to create a terminology that facilitates his road to self-definition. Unlike many young men who came from the Holocaust to Israel, he did not discard his past nor did he try to eradicate it. We see, instead, attempts to bridge the two selves; on the one hand a young man who was hardly aware of Judaism and an adult who attempts to endow his life with meaning. He has said: "I was thrown toward Judaism by the Holocaust" (Interview with Hebziban Lifshitz. "Ma'ariv," 9 June 1965). At the age of fifty-five he took the final step into his conversion into Orthodox Judaism. Yaoz-Kest's poetry depicts his search for self-definition and involves personal experiences coupled with a modernistic, imagistic view. Holocaust poetry partakes of the tradition of Hebrew and Jewish Destruction Literature combining the process of witnessing and commemoration. At its core, Destruction Literature involves the justification of God's judgment.

From the early 1940s, modern Hebrew poetry has addressed the destruction of European Jewry, but uses canonical allusion and metaphors in an inverted manner, and in so doing indirectly challenges God's presence or absence during the Holocaust. Unlike classical Destruction Literature, modern Hebrew poetry (with the exception of Uri Zvi Greenberg) does not center on lamentation and rage. Yaoz-Kest is a lyric poet with secular modernistic beginnings, whose poetry grew to embrace God as a presence. This does not mean a naive acceptance or a total affirmation. In the style of biblical characters, rabbinic martyrs, and Hasidic masters, Yaoz-Kest creates a dialogue with a divine entity. His writing from its very beginning is colored by the Holocaust, it allows for a complex, tormented, and meaningful experience. Like other writers, the Holocaust is occasionally an implicit rather than an explicit presence in his poetry, but its presence is implied.

In the 1970s his narratives became highly impressionistic, often consisting of scenes that carry the burden of past memories. Despite the realistic details, the atmosphere is suffused with changing tones. The turbulent mood corresponds to the protagonist's uprooted state of mind. A sense of estrangement accompanies the young newcomer—he feels like a stranger, almost the "other" in the burgeoning Israeli society. Dream-like hallucinations emphasize the desire to belong. The search for roots for an existence that transcends mundane reality is but another way to impose meaning on a life saved. The lyrical atmosphere of much of his work parallels a state of mind afflicted by the desire to express and at the same time to experience.

In his 1972 novella, *The Phosphorus Line*, the protagonist's "return" to the death camps is motivated by his mother, who believes that her husband's death in Israel was brought about by their acceptance of German reparations, as though she and her husband were helping the Germans expiate their sins. She wishes to return to the camp where her parents perished, to ask for their forgiveness. The camp and its surroundings make up a phantasmagoric world, a sterilized inferno eroded by creeping fungi. The protagonist is tempted and detained by a child/woman who infests him with fear and desire. She appears as a challenging factor; when he searches for help after his mother has fainted in the snow, the child/woman lures him into abandoning his obligation to his past and to his mother. The camp and the desertion of his mother all suggest an inferno of dread and hesitation, a state of being into which he is thrown. The protagonist's mother seeks death in the infinite domain of the snow, but is snatched up by the son and taken on a train that will lead them not to death but to the sunlight.

In 1974 Yaoz-Kest published a pamphlet entitled "The New Judaic Outlook in Literature and Art." In it, he related the issue of the non-native population in Israel, especially those who arrived after the Holocaust, to the art created in Israel. He observed that although native writers were outnumbered by non-natives, they nonetheless dictated the tone of the Israeli narrative and Israeli cultural life. The background of the non-natives varied, many not coming to Israel out of ideological conviction but by dint of sheer necessity. For some, their relation to Judaism was dialectic: both affinity and distance. In Israel they entered the new cultural and social reality of the Jewish state, which ultimately opened a gap between demographic and cultural realities.

Search for Identity

To Yaoz-Kest, the search for a new or renewed sense of identity is paramount. For him, neo-Judaism allows the multitude of people who came to Israel to find a new voice in the new reality. In his own desire to simultaneously preserve the past and merge into the present, we see the conflict that accompanies so many wandering people—a search for roots and history coupled with a desire for a new home. Yaoz-Kest's poetry depicts his struggle with orthodoxy, religious belief, and his own sense of identity. His poem "Reveal and Conceal" ("Giluy ve Kisui," 1989) begins with the statement that with an uncovered head he feels like a sinner, but with it covered he feels like a deceiver. He continues to relate to the intermediary stage between doubt and belief, wondering how faith emerges from his being. Fear and trembling accompany him—in the past, with the wind blowing through his hair (without a *kippah*, a cap or yarmulke) he felt that the giant, empty, darkened sky was his head cover. Yaoz-Kest's poetry is a post-Holocaust spiritual quest for home and certainty. In comparison, his earlier writing possesses less of an emphasis on the spiritual and focuses more on the experience of the Holocaust. In "The Funeral," from Bergen-Belsen Chapters, the experience of the Holocaust in near-visceral terms is expressed:

> The frost lashed out.
> The four winds pulled
> At the hearse.
> Above the barracks sat
> the magician,
> His legs folded in an X,
> Staring into the searchlight circles.
> A treacherous wind
> Halted the cart of the spirits. Wearied being
> bearing.
> They sat down in the hearse.
> The silence of ashes
> Stopped the world's mouth. (p. 140, translation by B. Frank)

Certainty accompanies his later poetry—for example, in his 1990 poem "Dweller in Your House." (The title is based on verse 5 in Psalm 84: "Happy are they that dwell in Thy house, they are ever praising Thee. Selah." The verse is incorporated in daily, Shabbat, and holiday services.) Yaoz-Kest's opening verse is:

> I wished to dwell in Your house but Your house dwells within me/And yet a question emerges now: What shall I ask for?

In his development—his movement from a literary oeuvre focused on the harsh external realities of the Holocaust to the inward examination of the role of faith, belief, and the nature of Judaism, Yaoz-Kest has completed the cycle: his quest for a meaningful homeland has been accomplished.

Bibliography

Primary Sources

Books Published in Hebrew (Poetry)

Malach Lelo Knafayim (Angel without Wings). 1958.
Nof Be-Ashan/Pirkei Bergen-Belsen (Bergen-Belsen Chapters). 1961.
Yerushat Einayim (Eyes' Legacy). 1965.
Le-Morad Beitah (Down to Her House). 1969.
Kayitz Shel Viola (Viola's Summer). 1973.
13 Shirim Min Ha-Oref (13 Poems from the Back). 1974.
Du-Shoresh (Double Routed). 1976.
Metich Ha-Zehuyot (Identity Melting Pot). 1980.
Leshon Ha-Nahar, Leshon Ha-Yam (Tongue of the River, Tongue of the Sea). 1983.
Tzinorot Molichey Esh (Fire Pipes). 1986.
Yechudi'im Alei Adamot (Unique on Earth). 1990.
Zimun (Summons). 1992.
Shiv'ah Simanei Keshirah (Seven Binding Marks). 1994.
Ole Ba-Har (Up the Mountain). 1998.
Shirim Nivharim (Selected Poems). 1998.

Prose

Ha-Mehager Ha-Bayta (Emigrating Home [autobiographical trilogy]).
Ba-Halon Ha-Bayt Ha-Nosea (From the Window of the Traveling House). 1970.
Tzel Ha-Tzipor (A Bird's Shadow). 1971.
Ha-Kav Ha-Zarhani (The Phosphorescent Line). 1972.
Merkavah Leylit (Night Charist). 1973.
Ahizah Shel Hol (Grasping Sand). 1977.
"Jewish Identity and the Holocaust in New Hungarian Poetry." *Shvut: Studies in Russian and East European Jewish History and Culture* 2 (1974): 159–163.

Books in Translation

Selected Poems. Hungarian: Budapest: Europa, 1989; Budapest: Mult es Jovo, 1998.
Individual poems have been published in Arabic, English, French, German, Hungarian, Italian, Polish, Romanian, Russian, Spanish, Turkish, and Vietnamese.

Secondary Sources

Ramras-Rauch, Gila. "Yaoz-Kest: Ahizah Shel Hol." *World Literature Today* 53, no. 1 (winter 1979).
———. "A Voyage to the Death Camp." *Yediot Aharonot* 9 (June 1977).
Rubin, Riva. "The Doppelganger as Identity." *News View*, 26 (May 1980).
Tanai, Shlomo. "Between the Possible and the Expected." *Iton* 77, no. 28 (1981).

YEVGENII YEVTUSHENKO

(1933–)

ALICE NAKHIMOVSKY

YEVTUSHENKO, A RUSSIAN poet with no connection to Jews beyond friendship and moral empathy, published a poem called "Babii Yar" in 1961. The poem was conceived as a memorial to the 34,000 Jews murdered in 1941 at Babii Yar, a ravine outside Kiev. Because of the Soviet context, the writing of the poem was a political as well as a poetic act, and its appearance in print was nothing short of sensational. Among the many readers who took the poem to heart was the great composer Dmitri Shostakovich who, like Yevtushenko, had close friendships with Jews, and who, because of his own more-than-precarious position, understood and identified with them. Shostakovich used the "Babii Yar" poem as the cornerstone of his Thirteenth Symphony (1962). Like the poem, not reprinted in the Soviet Union for twenty-two years, the symphony was a short-lived triumph with long-lasting consequences.

Stalin's Death, Khrushchev, and the Arts

Yevtushenko was born in Zima (Winter) Junction, Siberia, in 1933. His paternal grandfather, a Ukrainian soldier exiled to Siberia before the revolution, was arrested during the Terror in 1938; a similar fate befell his maternal grandfather, a mathematician. His parents, Alexander and Zinaida, were educated as geologists, though after their separation, his mother sang and held minor jobs in theater. Yevtushenko and his mother moved to Moscow in the late 1930s. He was sent back to Siberia for the duration of the war, and thereafter spent a slightly vagabond but not atypical youth. His years of adolescent rebellion ended when he enrolled in Moscow's prestigious Gorky Literature Institute. He began to publish poetry in the 1950s.

With his talent, youth, and boldness, Yevtushenko was well positioned to take advantage of the "Thaw," the period of comparative creative freedom that unfolded after Stalin's death in March 1953. The young writers who comprised the "generation of the sixties" restored to literature a lyricism and individuality that had been missing in published works for decades. Poets were extremely popular, and poetry readings in large cities attracted huge crowds. Yevtushenko, as the most important of the group, became the spokesman for this era and its sentiment. His poems, like those of his compatriots, were vehicles for protest—though the Soviet context meant that the protest was measurable in small increments, to which both readers and politicians were closely attuned. Khrushchev, then engaged in a program of de-Stalinization, used Yevtushenko's voice as a means to his political end. This accounts for both the appearance of "Babii Yar" and the poem "Heirs of Stalin" one year later. Khrushchev's policies were not single-minded, however, and signs of liberalization were isolated events, often countered or suppressed by cultural bureaucrats.

If one context for the "Babii Yar" poem is Khrushchev's Thaw, another is the situation of Russian Jewry in the early post-Stalinist years. The Holocaust was unmentionable. *The Black Book*, a compilation of eyewitness reports collected by the war reporters Ilya Ehrenburg and Vasilii Grossman, was canceled and the type broken up. The Holocaust was not the singular and unfathomable event that it was in the West. The victory over the Nazis, and the liberation of many death camps by the Red Army, were followed in the Soviet Union by a series of strident antisemitic campaigns initiated by the government and halted only because of Stalin's death. The "anti-cosmopolitan" campaign, targeting Jews in the arts, journalism, and almost every visible arena, was only a decade in the past. Even closer in time was the Doctors' Plot (January–April

1953), in which a group of prominent doctors, most of them Jews, had been accused of murdering two highly placed government officials. It was not then known that the appointed end of the Doctors' Plot was to be the public hanging of the doctors themselves followed by mass deportation of all other Jews to Siberia, accompanied by "spontaneous" pogroms. But in that atmosphere of antisemitic hysteria, such an end was far from inconceivable.

Yevtushenko visited Babii Yar in 1961 on a trip to Kiev. He was taken to the site by Anatolii Kuznetsov, a Russian who had witnessed the massacre as a child and would later write a novel about it. The mass grave was by then a local dump. Anguished by the disrespect for the dead and the whole conspiracy of silence, Yevtushenko was also, he wrote much later, motivated by the memory of his own credulity during the Doctors' Plot. Not quite twenty at the time, he wrote a poem about the doctor-murderers and read it to a Jewish family. In place of the enthusiasm he expected, he was greeted with silence and the comment that if he published the poem he would never wash himself clean of it.

"Babii Yar"

"Babii Yar" is a poem of simplicity and power whose sound structure, perfectly suited for declamation, cannot be conveyed in translation. It begins with several defiant assertions: that Babii Yar exists, that silence is unconscionable, and that the Russian poet Yevtushenko, by an act of metaphoric identification, is himself a Jew:

> No monuments stand over Babii Yar.
> A sheer drop, like a crude gravestone
> I am afraid.
> Today I am as old
> As the Jewish people.
> It seems to me now
> I am a Hebrew
> Here I am wandering through ancient Egypt
> And here I am, perishing on the cross
> On my body even now are traces of nails (Translated by George Reavy, p. 471).

The continuation of the poem stresses the ancientness of Jews and the persistence of Jewish martyrdom. Yevtushenko brings up Dreyfus and Anne Frank, highlighting Dreyfus's hounding and isolation, and Anne Frank's innocence, fragility, and capacity for love. The gentleness of nature and the tenderness of love are opposed—traditionally and effectively—to the horror of anti-Jewish violence.

The experience of a Dreyfus or an Anne Frank is presented so that any reader can identify with it, becoming, like the poet himself, a Jew. But if Jews are "us," the perpetrators of violence are not "them." The word Nazi is not used. Instead, Yevtushenko recalls the actions of "pogromists" (a word from tsarist times) and inserts in the text the old slogan "Beat the Yids, save Russia" and the name of a prerevolutionary Russian-nationalist organization.

The source of faith in the poem is in the principle of internationalism, once a tenet of Communism (the fact that the Soviet government repudiated internationalism in practice is not, of course, mentioned, but a careful reader would be aware of it). Yevtushenko had been an internationalist from his earliest poems. In this poem, he equates internationalism with the best manifestation of Russianness, ending with a powerful declaration of Russian-Jewish commonality:

> I am
> every old man
> shot dead here.
> I am
> every child
> shot dead here.
> Nothing within me
> will forget this!
> Let the "International"
> thunder
> When the last antisemite on earth
> Is buried for all eternity.
> In my blood there is no Jewish blood.
> But I am hated as Jew
> by crude and angry antisemites.
> And for that reason
> I am a genuine Russian! (p. 148).

Yevtushenko's assertion of the Russian poet as Jew was not the first of its kind in Russian literature. Marina Tsvetaeva wrote in her 1924 "Poem of the End": In this most Christian of worlds / Poets are Yids (*Iz brannye proizvedeniia*, Moscow-Leningrad: Biblioteka Poeta, 1965, p. 471).

But Tsvetaeva, who died in 1941, is a complex poet; her *Selected Works*, which came out only in 1961, were never intended for a mass readership. Yevtushenko, by contrast, was read by millions.

Controversy surrounded the poem from its inception. Word that he had written about Babii Yar spread around Kiev, and Yevtushenko's reading was nearly canceled, a fate avoided, he says, by his clever insistence to authorities that such cancelation would constitute an insult (by Ukrainians) to Russian poetry. The publication of the poem in the prestigious *Literaturnaia gazeta* was an act of courage by its editor, Valerii Kosolapov, who was later fired. Yevtushenko himself became the focal point of both liberal adulation—thousands of people came to his readings—and the undisguised antisemitism he had predicted. Thus, a poetic response in the newspaper *Literaturnaia Rossiia:*

What kind of genuine Russian are you
When you have forgotten your own people?
Your soul is narrow as a stylish pair of pants
Empty as a staircase (Everaii Evtushenko, p. 440).

Shostakovich and "Babii Yar"

Yevtushenko has written of the tormented Shostakovich, "I never saw a man who so resembled his own fate." Shostakovich (1906–1975), born nearly thirty years before Yevtushenko, was the product of a different era; he was trapped in a way that Yevtushenko would never experience firsthand. Jewish themes figure unmistakably in Shostakovich's haunting and tragic Second Piano Trio (1944). In January, 1948, Shostakovich's friend, the Yiddish actor Shlomo Mikhoels, was run over by a truck. The announcement of Mikhoels's death (widely, and correctly, assumed to be the work of Stalin) initiated the virulent "anticosmopolitan campaign" that would run concurrently with a campaign against "formalist" artists, Shostakovich in particular.

That summer, Shostakovich wrote his song cycle "From Jewish Folk Poetry." The private premiere (the cycle was not played in public until after Stalin's death) took place in Shostakovich's apartment on the occasion of his forty-third birthday; he himself played the piano. A year later, with the attacks on "rootless cosmopolitans" in full swing, he wrote his Fourth Quartet with its plaintive, klezmer-like final movement.

Given this background, it is not surprising that Shostakovich seized on "Babii Yar," whose appearance in print gave the poem, however tentatively, an official seal of approval. According to Yevtushenko, Shostakovich set the poem to music before even telephoning the young poet, whom he did not know. Shostakovich asked him to write an additional poem on fears, and wrote musical settings for three other poems from Yevtushenko's already published work. The subjects of these poems (in addition to "Fears," the titles are "Humor" "In the Shop," and "Career") show the close connection between discourse about Jews and criticism of the existing order.

It was, however, "Babii Yar" that made the Thirteenth Symphony dangerous. Reacting to pressure, both the initial conductor, Yevgenii Mravinskii, and the initial bass soloist (the symphony was scored for bass soloist, chorus, and orchestra) dropped out of the project. A second bass soloist was engaged, and fortunately a third as well, because on the day of the performance the singer scheduled to perform was suddenly called upon to understudy a role at the Bolshoi. In the hours before the premiere, Yevtushenko had to talk the chorus into staying, and the conductor, Kirill Kondrashin, was asked if the symphony could go ahead without its first movement, the setting of "Babii Yar." According to Yevtushenko—Kondrashin says the change took place some weeks later—the text of the poem was altered at this penultimate moment. The verse beginning "It seems to me I am a Hebrew" (quoted previously) was replaced by one memorializing the Ukrainians and Russians who also died in Babii Yar, and the verse including the lines "I am every old man shot dead here / I am every child shot dead here" (quoted previously) was replaced by a reference to Russian heroism in fighting the Nazis.

Those ticket holders who braved KGB photographers on the first night were not likely to find the censorship surprising. Yevtushenko and the older, more embattled Shostakovich were engaged in a game of truth and compromise whose dimensions were well understood by their audience. Yevtushenko changed or added text when pressured, yet he wrote "Babii Yar" and confronted Khrushchev over abstract art. Shostakovich, by the time of the Thirteenth Symphony, was a full member of the Communist Party who famously signed anything handed to him, yet whenever possible, in the elusive language of music broadly understood by listeners, he tapped forbidden feelings. In the private, dissident side of this equation, Jewish themes played an important role. Both the audience for the symphony and the cultural bureaucrats who were partly successful in suppressing it shared the assumption that sympathetic references to Jews—and any references whatsoever to the Holocaust—were potential threats to Soviet order.

Bibliography

Primary Sources
Collections That Include the Works of Yevgeny Yevtushenko

A Precocious Autobiography. Trans. by Andrew R. MacAndrew. New York: E. P. Dutton, 1963.

Reavy, George. *The Poetry of Yevgeny Yevtushenko, 1955 to 1965, with 51 Poems in the Original Russian and Translated into English.* New York: October House, 1965.

The Collected Poems 1953–1990. 1991.

Evtushenko, Evgenii. *Volchii pasport.* Moscow: Vagrius, 1993.

Secondary Sources

Dubinsky, Rostislav. *Making Music in a Worker's State.* New York: Hill and Wang, 1989.

Fay, Laurel. *Shostakovich: A Life.* Oxford, New York: Oxford University Press, 2000.

Ho, Allan, and Dmitry Feofanov, with an overture by Vladimir Ashkenazy. *Shostakovich reconsidere.* London: Toccata Press, 1998.

Macdonald, Ian. *The New Shostakovich.* Boston: Northeastern University Press, 1990.

Volkov, Solomon. *Testimony: The Memoirs of Dmitri Shostakovich as Related to and Edited by Solomon Volkov.* New York: Limelight Editions, 1990.

Wilson, Elizabeth. *Shostakovich: A Life Remembered.* Princeton, N.J.: Princeton University Press, 1994.

AARON ZEITLIN

(1898–1973)

EMANUEL S. GOLDSMITH

AMONG THE MOST moving documents of the Holocaust are the poetry and fiction of the victims and survivors. Yiddish and Hebrew letters, in particular, abound in a large body of important works dealing with this tragic event and its aftermath. Aaron Zeitlin, one of the leading Yiddish and Hebrew authors of the twentieth century, made major contributions to this genre in both languages. His large number of Yiddish poems on the Holocaust are contained in the two volumes *Lider fun Khurbn un Lider fun Gloybn* (Poems of the Holocaust and Poems of Faith, 1967), and the smaller number of Hebrew poems in the volume *Ruah Mimetsulah* (A Spirit from the Deep, 1975). In addition, Zeitlin produced a long dramatic poem on the Holocaust in Hebrew entitled *Beyn Ha'esh Vehayesha* (Between Fire and Salvation), which may be regarded both as his major poetic statement on the Holocaust and as one of the most important works on the subject to appear in any language and in any literary form.

Zeitlin achieved recognition as an outstanding Yiddish and Hebrew poet, playwright, philosopher, essayist, editor, and journalist. Isaac Bashevis Singer often referred to him as the greatest of Yiddish poets. Although relatively few of his writings have been translated into other languages, his reputation continues to grow because of his role in the history of Yiddish literature and theater before the Holocaust, and because of his profound contribution to Holocaust literature.

Early Life and Work

Zeitlin was born in the White Russian town of Uvarovitsh on 22 May 1898. His childhood years were spent in Gomels and Vilna until his family moved to Warsaw in 1907. Zeitlin was raised in a highly cultured household. He was a son of the Yiddish and Hebrew poet, philosopher, and mystic Hillel Zeitlin, one of the leading spiritual personalities of twentieth-century Polish Jewry. Aaron studied with his father, attended a modern Jewish elementary school, completed the Polish gymnasium, and took university courses without completing a degree.

From his father, Zeitlin inherited a unique approach to Judaism and Jewish life. Deeply rooted in Jewish religion and mysticism and strongly nationalistic in spirit, this approach stressed personal religious experience as well as individualized and original interpretations of traditional texts and ideas. Though strongly opposed to atheism and secularism, the Zeitlins could never completely identify with any organized religious group, traditionalist or modernist. Even their interpretations of Kabbalah and Hasidism were highly personal and even radically individualistic. While strongly identified with Hebrew and Yiddish literature and their political expressions in Zionism and Jewish socialism, the Zeitlins constantly attacked the secularism and spiritual rootlessness of most of their fellow Yiddish and Hebrew writers.

Jewish Realism

In 1921, Zeitlin's apocalyptic Kabbalistic poem, "Metatron," was widely hailed as marking the poet's coming of age, as well as a distinct modernistic, anti-romantic and anti-expressionistic shift in his work. In 1926 he issued a poetic manifesto decrying the realistic and naturalistic trends in Yiddish literature and affirming his wholehearted embrace of the antirationalism and religious existentialism of the Russian-Jewish philosopher Lev Shestov. By the 1930s his poems were overwhelmingly grounded in personal religious experience and its expression in mythological and apocalyptic images.

Zeitlin characterized his new approach in a poem entitled "The Realism of a Jew." His aesthetics seek to distinguish the illusory from those fundamental aspects of existence in which he perceives ultimate reality. He affirms the existence of God and the soul on the one hand, and Satan and sin on the other. He forswears the kind of poetry in which these realities are merely figures of speech. He aims at the kind of writing that will encompass both the inner world of the individual and the cosmos as well as the world beyond earthly existence. He calls himself a metaphysician and journalist seeking the sight usually granted only to "the third eye of a blind man" (*Lider fun Khurbn un Lider fun Gloybn*, vol. 2 [New York: Bergen Belsen Memorial Press, 1967], p. 483).

Despite its metaphysical and abstract character, Zeitlin's poetry, like his drama, avoids the abstruse by its utilization of humor, satire, and the grotesque and by its frequent preoccupation with ethics. His "Jewish realism" abjures art for art's sake and literature for literature's sake while embracing the ethical deed, which alone endures and reverberates throughout the cosmos.

Zeitlin is unique among Yiddish writers in the frequency, profundity, and originality of his use of Jewish mysticism (Kabbalah) in his work. His appropriation of kabbalistic elements can be found both in poems on kabbalistic and Hasidic personalities and motifs and in poems in which the kabbalistic worldview illuminates personal and collective experience. In addition to poems containing visions, meditation, prayers, and credos, many of Zeitlin's poems are based on personal interpretations of biblical, Talmudic, kabbalistic, or Hasidic verses, phrases, ideas, or customs. Zeitlin also introduces these hermeneutical elements into other poems. This aspect of Zeitlin's poetry is often reminiscent of the traditional functioning of Yiddish as the interpretive language of Jewish study and worship.

The Holocaust

Zeitlin's poems of the late 1920s and early 1930s are rife with premonitions of the Holocaust. His trip to the United States in 1929 in connection with the production one of his dramas by Maurice Schwartz at New York's Yiddish Art Theatre, saved him from the destruction of his family and his civilization, but left him with guilt and anguish for the rest of his life for having survived, as expressed in the poem "KL' hob Nisht Gehat Di Khiye (I Didn't Have the Privilege)":

I left in time and
God hid the terrors from me—
Why? Why did I leave Poland?
I did not have the privilege together with my people
To walk the path of flames
And I suffer, as for an unpardonable sin—
The guilt of remaining alive,
Remaining alive and making rhymes.
This guilt will poison me
Until I heed one of the three figures
Who stand ready to hide my guilt,
Who wait and call to me passionately:
One figure is sanctity, the second is insanity,
Suicide is the third.
But suicide is too strong for a weakling like me,
My smallness makes sanctity no option,
And I can't even go out of my mind (*Lider fun Khurbn*, vol. I, p. 62).

For a survivor like Zeitlin who lost wife, child, father, brother, and other members of his family, the transformation of pain and horror into verse is not accomplished without pangs of shame and guilt. "Be silent and shudder when I scream!" ("Gornisht Oyser Verter." In *Lider fun Khurbn un Lider fun Gloybn*, vol. 1 [New York: Bergen Belsen Memorial Press, 1967], p. 58) commands the image of a survivor who castigates the poet for trivializing this newest of Israel's devastations. Out of the bitterness and anguish of his soul, the poet responds:

If we, the last Jews,
Are left with naught save words,
How can you have the heart
To want to remove our last shirt,
Our little miserable words? (p. 59).

Zeitlin concludes this brief confessional poem by turning to his readers as if they share the poet's guilt for deriving aesthetic satisfaction from the reading of poems about the Holocaust.

So again,
Last Jews, Jews of words, my weak brethren,
Again I bring you naught save words,
Naught save poems (p. 59).

It is no accident that the poet applies the appellations and phrases usually reserved for the Almighty alone to slaughtered Jewry: "Magnified and sanctified be the great name of Israel" (p. 59). In Zeitlin's works, the Holocaust renders God, even in the company of the celestial hosts, a lonely God returning home to His heavens at night, after each day of defeat on the battlefield. God has become a Job, but a Job without a Creator to dispute and contend with. When a Jew rises in the transport, en route to the gas chamber, to kindle memorial lights, others add their voices to his in reciting the kaddish (mourning prayer) in their own memory. But God also rises in order to recite the kaddish for the world. The Holocaust leaves the world "without God and without a Jew" ("Kadish in Toyt-Vagon." [Kaddish in a Death Train] in *Lider fun Khurbn*, vol. 1, p. 36). Even the Angel of Death, who in one of Peretz's dramas conjured the spirits of the dead for the playwright, is unable to do so again. The angel's wings have been destroyed together with the playwright's people. "I am no angel," he says, "but the last groan of a Jew exterminated in Treblinka" ("Nokhklang, tsu 'Baynakht Afn Altn Mark.'" ["Echo of 'Night in the Old Marketplace'"]. In *Lider fun Khurbn*, vol. 1, p. 42).

In a survey of the themes of Israeli poetry on the Holocaust, Zevi Dror subsumes the poems under ten categories: premonition and protest; descriptions of Jewish life before the Holocaust; portrayals of the Holocaust; the call for revenge; castigation of the apathetic world; utilization of symbols and heroes of the Jewish tradition; the turning to God as supreme power; songs of resistance, rebellion, and revolt; the Jewish war against the enemy and the aliyah (emigration to Israel) movement; and conclusions drawn from the Holocaust (Dror, p. 14). Zeitlin has written poems in Hebrew and Yiddish that could be included in all of these categories, but Dror's analysis misses the theme that dominates Zeitlin's Holocaust poetry—the struggle for faith, the quest for spiritual meaning, and the problem of maintaining belief despite the overwhelming tragedy.

The poetry of the Holocaust may be viewed generally as an attempt to mitigate suffering by giving intense but controlled expression to the tragedy. It represents an effort to preserve sanity by conferring a minimum of order and form on chaos and horror. Zeitlin's poems, however, go beyond this because their overriding concern is the quest for meaning and transcendent faith. Zeitlin affirms the reality of God, the efficacy of prayer, the Messiah, the millennium, immortality, and the world beyond in his poems. For him there must be a meaning to the gruesome events of our time. In his poetry one hears both the voice of utter and uncompromising despair and the voice of confidence, hope, and faith in God.

Poetry of Despair

The poems of despair are grounded in the awareness of the finality of the Holocaust. Standing on a street in Montreal in midwinter, the poet imagines for a moment that he is in Warsaw again and that his wife is about to turn a corner to meet him. But he knows that she will never ever come again. A sentimental tune that he and his wife were wont to sing in Warsaw hounds him on the streets of New York. "What do you want of me?" he says to the tune. "Everything is over, everything has been gassed. She, too, is no longer mine. She has been betrothed to blazing fire" (*Lider fun Khurbn*, vol. 1, p. 64). The poet yearns to hear his wife's voice call his name. How dark and how poor the earth has become since her voice has been silenced! "Send me your voice, call me! and I will carry myself to you as birds carry themselves south in winter" (p. 69). He recalls his wife's tears as he left Poland for the United States, expecting to return in a few months, but in reality never to return. "Everything has vanished. As a nest is dark in wintertime, so my world is empty. Those final tears knew everything. They knew all" (p. 64).

He hears his martyred son in the ghetto relate a dream to his weeping mother:

I had a dream, mama.
Father stands in a yellow hat.
Above him the sun as red as wine.
He opens America for us
And we enter.
So will it be
If the Germans don't murder us.

Mama, tell me. Why did God
Make Germans?
Don't cry. I just wanted to know.
Do we have a pencil?
I'll draw the sun for you.
I'll draw father
In the yellow hat.
We shall both look
At my dream (*Lider fun Khurbn*, vol. 1, p. 70).

When the war ends, streets are filled with flags and trucks, with shouts of joy and victory. From the gas chambers and crematoria, however, there is only silence. "The war is over and the Jews are over. No, not over. Now begins their silence, the war of the six million" (*Lider fun Khurbn*, vol. 1, p. 75).

Zeitlin reaches the lowest depths of personal despair with the thought that perhaps the game is not worth the candle, that even the end of Messianic redemption fails to justify the means of catastrophic Holocaust. What if, asks the poet, there are Hitlers in the world beyond too? What if there, too, Israel's prince is devored by cannibals? What if, even in eternity, blood spurts from a knife?

To the little child and the peaceful animals in the biblical vision of the End of Days, the poet poses the question: Was it for your sake that God needed Israel's pain and the horror of two thousand years? Buchenwald and Maidanek? Was it for your sake that the devil had a free hand while Israel was compelled to be burned? Must the poor always be humiliated? Insanity is the answer! "Be destroyed, oh End of Days, as my millions were destroyed!" (*Lider fun Khurbn*, vol. 1, p. 121).

Because life is impossible in such a profane world and death is only a passage to new life, the poet prays that God invent for him an existence between life and death. In the words of Moses, he pleads to be erased from God's book. He compares himself to the sun's afterglow at sunset. "I am such an afterglow suspended over the abyss, an afterglow of my nation's sun that set in the sea of blood of Maidanek" (p. 46). Ridden with memories of a world gone up in flames, the poet lives a dual life—as a person in New York and as a shadow in a house in Warsaw that no longer exists. "Souls of the martyred, recite the kaddish for me, a corpse who walks about on the earth!" (p. 46).

Zeitlin moves between two poles represented by the references in his poems to Bialik's "In the City of Slaughter" ("The sun shone, the almond tree blossomed, and the slaughterer slew") and the verse from Maimonides with which the martyrs went to their deaths ("I believe with perfect faith in the coming of the Messiah and even though he tarries still do I await his coming daily"). Examples of this are the two poems, written in utter despair during the war years, each of which the poet later modified—in one case with a new stanza and in the other with a new poem.

In the first, written in 1939, God marches forth to destroy the world (vol. 1, p. 53). The language of vengeance and bloodshed is that of Isaiah 63 ("I trod them in my anger and trampled them in my wrath; their life blood is sprinkled upon my garments and I have stained all my raiment"). But by 1946, when the second part of the poem was written, the poet knew that only "Jacob has been burned to death and Esau has remained." His faith, which formerly bore wings, is battered and bruised, but he cannot abandon his hope for revenge and his belief in divine justice. He dreams that the souls of the dead will be brought down to earth as children, one of whom will be the Messiah.

The second poem, "We Jews Are Not of This World" (*Lider fun Khurbn*, vol. 1, written in 1944), takes its title from a statement in which the Hasidic leader, Rabbi Nahman of Bratzlav, sought to explain the world's persecution of Israel. "There may still be Jews below, but Israel is no longer" (p. 55). On this planet Esau alone will praise God with instruments of destruction. The fires of Treblinka have destroyed the prayers of Israel, and God, too, is being punished. Yet after the war, with the birth of the State of Israel, the poet experiences a rebirth of faith. He now realizes that the last prayers had not been uttered. "Everything depends on prayer and Jew. There are no last Jews and no final prayers" (pp. 53–56).

Faith and Meaning

The essence and strength of Zeitlin's faith derive from the fact that it feeds and grows on the very edges of desperation. Zeitlin's poems of complete despair are few. His most powerful evocations of hopelessness are his most convincing demonstrations of faith. In "Post-Maidanek Dream" (*Lider fun Khurbn*, vol. 1), the poet imagines that he is an atomic scientist standing beside a massive cyclotron. In revenge for the murdered six million, he plots to destroy the earth. An angel, who himself bears a concentration camp number on his arm, appears to him, soothes him, and tells him to recall the names of Jewish children. "A child will heal you," he is told. As the poet brings the names of the martyred children to mind, the figure of a little boy, Koppele, emerges. The angel has commanded the child to be reborn, to build his life anew. The poet warns the child to return from whence he came, not to seek a new life in a wicked world that will soon have to be destroyed. The angel proclaims that Koppele must be born again. "Cease from revenge," he calls to the poet. "Leave the earth alone. Restrain the atoms. Koppele must return to hallow God's name for such is God's will" (89–97).

The poet often confronts his own mood of futility and pessimism:

I defy death with all my might.
Death is nothing but a name.
Are the six million really dead?
They are an ever present flame.
. . .
I am but a thread in the weave.
I began to rot as though dead
When martyrs' voices from Poland said
To me: Live!
. . .
"Jew" and "stop" can't unite, never will.
The meaning of Jew is anti-end (p. 150f.).

In the unfathomable pain inflicted on his people, Zeitlin hears the cry that God exists. If tortures such as Israel experienced were impossible, there might not be a God. With such afflictions, however, God's reality is a necessity. Without it, Israel's sufferings would be so hideous and senseless that the earth would reel in drunken madness and disintegrate.

Zeitlin's faith is sustained by the deep conviction that there is a world beyond. In his hopes and dreams it almost seems as though he might reach his wife. Voices reach him from that other world to tell him that "vanished does not mean dead." Though his dear ones dwell in fire now, one day he will meet them on a flaming star.

Together with faith in God and in the world beyond, faith in man wells up from the depths of despair. When he thinks of the Holocaust, the poet is ashamed to belong to the human species. He would curse the divine command to increase and multiply. Yet the recollection of his wife, an angel become woman, makes it impossible for him to forget that man is created in the divine likeness.

Tell me not man is a beast.
Compared to man, beast is—angel.
Do beasts build crematoria?
Do they hurl children to fire?
Do they take pleasure in death?
Tell me not man is a beast.

Tell me not man is a beast.
He is even more than angel.
He is word of an Isaiah.
He is outcry of a Job.
He yearns for new worlds.
Tell me not man is a beast (p. 140).

Two major Yiddish prose poems by Zeitlin deal directly with the Holocaust: "Poland: The Vision of Abraham Prokhovnik" and "The Last Walk of Janusz Korczak" (both from *Lider fun Khurbn*, vol. 1). The first reviews the tragic history of Polish Jewry within the framework of a traditional legend about the first Jew to come to Poland. Abraham Prokhovnik refuses the invitation of the ancestors of the Poles to become their king because in a vision he is permitted to see the future of the Jews in Poland.

> It is not I who should be the ruler of the Polans. The nation of the Jews is fated to tarry in this land only for the night. Generation after generation we will dwell here, but it will be as a single night. We Children of Israel wait for him whose coming is delayed. He will come when all the gods have fallen. He will gather us from among the nations and we will all go back to Zion. The day of Jerusalem will come only when our night in the land of the Polans is ended in the most dreadful of terrors (p. 149).

In the second poem, the Jewish educator, who voluntarily went to his death rather than abandon the children in the Warsaw orphanage he directed, is portrayed both spiritually and psychologically. The portrayal of his struggle with his Jewish identity and his challenge of the Divine Will in defense of his wards transformed this historical figure into a legendary Job-like hero.

Between Fire and Salvation

Aaron Zeitlin was one of the last representatives of the tradition of Yiddish-Hebrew bilingualism, which embraced some of the greatest Jewish authors of the nineteenth and twentieth centuries. Zeitlin did not exaggerate when he spoke of having done all his work in one language—"the language of the Jewish soul" (Tabachnick, "Fun a Shmues Mit Aaron Zeitlin," *Di Goldene Keyt* 65, pp. 24–25). His Yiddish and Hebrew were equally rooted in the spiritual soil of countless Jewish generations and included echoes of the great Jewish literary masterpieces of all times. Zeitlin turned to Hebrew in order to compose his magnum opus, *Beyn Ha'esh Vehayesha* (Between Fire and Salvation). Zeitlin clearly had the younger generation of Israeli readers in mind in this drama which contains several dialogues between the hero, Shealtiel (Zeitlin's alter ego), and the Sabra who represents modern Israeli youth.

Beyn Ha'esh Vehayesha is a multilayered, complex work embracing historical, metaphysical, and surrealistic elements. Written in a style reminiscent of the classical Hebrew style of the *Haskalah*, it frequently slips into a satirical and grotesque journalistic mode. Although several critics have viewed the work as structurally and stylistically deficient, Joseph Dan aptly observes that "Aaron Zeitlin's poetry in the main is written according to patterns of Hebrew poetry that were well-established at the beginning of the twentieth century. . . . The reader can only investigate and judge the work according to its own principles and objectives" (p. 149). Dan also writes that

> it is not very difficult to complain that Zeitlin's characters are stereotypes without individuality, that in some of the dialogues the rhetoric overpowers the lyrical element, that his metaphysical musings belong in an essay and not in a poem, etc. Zeitlin is fully aware of what he is doing and it would seem that posing the question [of the connection between the Holocaust and the rebirth of Israel in its land] sharply and clearly, even if it be the only contribution of *Beyn Ha'esh Vehayesha* to Hebrew literature, is enough (p. 152).

The drama opens with a poem in which the *payyetan* or bard, who narrates the plot, reacts to the events and translates the speech of the protagonists into the language of poetry, linking the Holocaust to the destruction of Jerusalem by the Romans two thousand years ago. This foreshadows one of the major themes of the work—the joining of the Holocaust to the rebuilding of Jerusalem and the rebirth of Israel on its own soil. The work deals with many of the issues we have already confronted in Zeitlin's shorter poems on the Holocaust. Here, however, they take on a new intensity and significance because they are related to Israel's struggle for independence.

In his introduction to the drama, Zeitlin warns the reader not to underestimate those elements that may appear purely literary and contrived. These, he contends, are the very same elements that constitute the essence of the experience he seeks to convey. Zeitlin is referring to the confrontations he stages between the living and the dead of many generations, to his concretization of surrealistic and kabbalistic entities, and to a variety of hermeneutical devices utilized in the poem. The intense suffering and tragedy with which the work deals make the reader open to all attempts at catharsis and render even the most remote efforts at recovery plausible and effective. Of Zeitlin's approach, Isaiah Rabinovich writes that "it is a tradition of Israel that out of the abysses of despair and nothingness man harkens anew to his own existential depths and the voice of God then penetrates from the eclipse in the void" (p. 234).

The Vision on the Rock

On the ruins of the Warsaw ghetto, Shealtiel (a biblical name that may be interpreted to mean "I asked or enquired of God"), a partisan who has lost his wife and young son in the crematoria, tries to commit suicide but is thwarted in the attempt by the "invisible hands" of past generations. With the aid of *oznayin*, a visionary concretization of the higher functions of eye and ear, Shealtiel witnesses his own trial, during which he discovers that death is an illusion and that justice and retribution do exist in the ultimate scheme of the universe. Awakened to life by this vision, Shealtiel goes to Israel and becomes a commander in the struggle of the *yishuv* (pre-state Jewish community) against the British. Later he disappears in order to assume the role of a recluse in the synagogue of the medieval mystic Rabbi Isaac Luria in Safed. When the War of Independence erupts, Shealtiel joins those defending Safed from its Arab attackers and helps liberate the city.

Zeitlin fills the poem with numerous other characters, both realistic and imaginary, who embody the problems and hopes of contemporary Jewry in Israel and the Diaspora as well as the longings and dreams of Jews throughout history. In the course of his visionary trial, Shealtiel's murdered wife and child appear to assure him that death is nonexistent and to encourage him to rebuild his life because "everything noble and desirable depends on choosing life" (Tel Aviv: Yavneh, 1957, p. 131). In this vision on the ruins of the Warsaw ghetto ("the vision on the rock of Israel's mourning"), Shealtiel also sees the martyrs of the ghetto, the Jewish commander of Masada during the war against the Romans (Eliezer ben Yair), Queen Sabbath, and King David. He witnesses the trial of Doctor Von Tod, the embodiment of the Nazi lust for genocide, at which Satan and the spirits of a dog and a cat testify that

> this brown one
> Did not murder members of his kind alone,
> He destroyed the hope of all of nature's children:
> The forest is bowed and the clod groans,
> The mountain sighs and the grass cries.
> He attempted to restrain the vibrancy
> Of eternally vibrant forces, of mighty powers (p. 163).

Numerous other characters appear during scenes depicting Shealtiel's dreams. In the Israeli scenes, the historical figure of Menahem Begin and the Sabra, Shealtiel's fighting companion, make their appearance.

Beyn Ha'esh Vehayesha captivates the reader with the magic of its poetic, dramatic, and philosophical dimensions. In terms of aesthetic structure and poetic originality, it is a tour de force encompassing a variety of poetic forms and rhyme schemes. Dramatically, it may be viewed as a motion picture script or as a play for a theater-in-the round with a revolving stage. Philosophically, it deals cogently with problems such as the meaning of faith, death, and immortality after the Holocaust, with the purpose of art, and with the spiritual meaning of Israel reborn.

Aaron Zeitlin developed a unique worldview born of his own sufferings and those of his people in modern times. The most important contribution of *Beyn Ha'esh Vehayesha* lies in the dramatic and poetic exposition of that *weltanschauung*. Zeitlin has been described as a philosophical poet with a unique point of view on both Jewish and universal matters. Zeitlin saw the essence of Jewish existence in the war against paganism and the longing for redemption.

> To be a Jew means:
> To bring a true redeemer and smash idols (p. 186).

These two concerns dominate *Beyn Ha'esh Vehayesha*. Zeitlin sets out to smash the idols of cynicism, doubt, and despair and to replace them with faith in the God of justice, immortality, and deliverance. For Zeitlin the rebirth of Israel in our time contains within it the seeds of the "Dawn of Redemption" (*athalta digeulah*) in which the spirit of martyred Israel will be linked forever to the soul of living Israel. This redemption also contains the beginnings of a new approach to life and art that will bring redemption to all humanity. As Isaiah Rabinovich writes:

> The aesthetic aspect is a very important judicial element in the "trial" which Shealtiel prepares for himself on the rock in the ghetto. It is clear that this trial in fact involves Zeitlin's self-understanding as a poet, criticism of his own artistic direction before the Holocaust . . . in the empty

vacuum of modern art which has also captured the Jewish artist, he holds on to the altar of life which is the Messianic idea (p. 241).

The principal problems of humanity in the post-Holocaust era, an era in which *eyn netsah Yisrael, yesh retsah Yisrael* ("there is no eternity of Israel, only the murdering of Israel"), the problem of God's existence and the problem of divine goodness, are among the issues Shealtiel confronts throughout the poem. Gradually Shealtiel begins to understand the secret of *lahamam* (an acronym of the words *lo haya mavet me-olam* or "death has never existed"). *Lahamam* is the opposite of the well-known acronym *lahadam* (*lo hayu devarim me-olam*) meaning "these things have never existed." It is also the secret of eternal survival in the Image or Likeness.

Every situation has its Likeness, both above and below,
Every reality and every being have their Likeness,
Your individuality or the individuality of a group or nation,
Each has its Likeness and the Likeness never ends (p. 114).

Shealtiel learns the true meaning of the verse in Psalms (30:5). He is assured that "*Adonay* has said: I shall restore from smoke, I shall restore from the depths of the sea." (This verse is based on an emended version of Isaiah 68:23.) Most important, he hears the voice of his dead wife in the ghetto praying the "prayer of perhaps":

The truth, alas,
Is clear . . . And yet . . . perhaps . . .
The Germans will discover
The bunker
And no almighty God
Will come to help . . .
It's clear . . . it's certain . . .
But the beautiful face
Of my lad as he sleeps . . . perhaps . . .
If there be a God,
There must be a continuation
Of my child's life . . . and of mine
For what will he do without me? I ask only that
In whichever world he exists
Let not my child be separated
From me . . . let us be together . . . together . . . (p. 195).

From Nihilism to Immortality

In the course of his vision, Shealtiel is taught that all wrongs are set right in eternity which holds the mysterious key to all existence and in which reward and punishment are realized. The purpose of immortality is the repair and improvement of all things; its ultimate goal is the annihilation of all evil. In Zeitlin's work, the Holocaust, in its spiritual dimensions, was a conflict between the principles of nihilism and immortality. His concept of Image or Likeness seeks to deny the very existence of death as a reality. For Zeitlin, as Hillel Barzel points out, the mystery of *lahamam* is not an aesthetic abstraction without concrete meaning. "There is a firm faith here in the eternal existence of all creatures. Zeitlin actually gives expression to the law of the preservation of phenomena" (p. 165).

The revenge Shealtiel seeks will be realized through the establishment of a country on earth that will be the opposite of the kingdom of evildoers.

a country which will not be
Animal-like, devouring all:
It will be a new kingdom inspired by the Divine Presence,
A model-land, the dwelling place of Messiah-men (p. 219).

Shealtiel must marry, bring a child into the world, and struggle for the establishment of the new country. He must become a partisan of the Messiah and of the future kingdom. One must struggle for Messiah's coming by combining prayer and deed in the way God did when He created the world.

The poem reaches its dramatic climax in the battle for Safed and its ideological climax in the final dialogue between Shealtiel and "the Sabra." Shealtiel has come to believe that the redemption will be delayed until the establishment in Israel of a new community of seekers of salvation: the community of *shin-mem-lamed-tav*. These four Hebrew letters stand for "two verses which are in truth one": "I keep Maidanek before me always" and "I keep Messiah before me always." (These phrases are Zeitlin's variations on the biblical verse, "I keep the Lord before me always," [Psalms 16:8], which was traditionally engraved or painted above the holy arks in synagogues the world over.)

One might say that in *Beyn ha'esh Vehayesha* Zeitlin's art has itself become "an art of witness, uniting past and present" (p. 378). At the conclusion of the poem, the "Bard" parts from Shealtiel with these words:

In the fire of my pain, my soul brought you forth.
I escorted you from the ruins hence.
I'm sorry we must part. I know
You are but a partial creation
But in you I implanted
My pain, my caring faith,

My life's misfortune—a personal misfortune,
A drop that contains the sea in the sea of
A nation's catastrophe (p. 388).

Bibliography

Primary Sources

Beyn Ha'esh Vehayesha (Between Fire and Salvation). 1957.

Min Ha'adam Vama'alah (Of Man and Beyond). 1964.

Medinah Vehazon Medinah (A State and the Vision of a State). 1965

Hametsiut Ha'aheret (The Other Reality). 1967.

Lider fun Khurbn un Lider fun Gloybn (Poems of the Holocaust and Poems of Faith). Vol. 1, 1967; vol. 2, 1970.

Ruah Mimetsulah (A Spirit from the Deep). 1975.

"Poland: The Vision of Abraham Prokhovnik." Translated by Emanuel S. Goldsmith. *Jewish Heritage* 12, no. 4 (summer-fall 1970): 55–61.

Gezamlte Drames (Collected Dramas). Vol. I, 1974; vol. II, 1980.

Parapsikhologyah Murhevet (An Expanded Parapsychology). 1973.

"The Last Walk of Janusz Korczak." Translated by Hadassah Rosensaft and Gertrude Hirschler. In *Ghetto Diary* by Janusz Korczak. 1978.

Brenendike Erd (Burning Earth). 1979.

Literarishe un Filosofishe Eseyen (Literary and Philosophical Essays). 1980.

Beyn Emunah L'omanut (Between Faith and Art). Two volumes. 1980.

Secondary Sources

Barzel, Hillel. *Shirah Umorashah*. Tel Aviv: Eked, 1971.

Bertini, K. A. *Sedeh Re'iyah*. Jerusalem: Mosad Bialik, 1977.

Bikl, Shlomo. *Shrayber Fun Mayn Dor*. New York: Matones, 1958, pp. 121–132.

Dan, Joseph. *Hanokhri Vehamandarin*. Ramat-Gan: Massada, 1975.

Dror, Zevi. *Nosey Hashoah Bashirah Ha-ivrit*. Tel Aviv: Seminar Hakibutsim, 1964.

Goldkorn, Yitskhok. *Heymishe un Fremde*. Buenos Aires: Svive, 1973, pp. 59–72.

Niger, Shmuel. *Yidishe Shrayber fun Tsvantsikstn Yorhurdert*. New York: Kultur-Kongres, 1972, pp. 370–404.

Rabinovich, Isaiah. *Behavley Doram*. Tel Aviv: Om Oved, 1959, 234.

Ribalow, Menachem. *Me'olam Le'olam*. New York: Ogen, 1955, 178–212.

Shpigl, Yishayohu. *Geshtaltn un Profiln*. II. Tel Aviv: Yisroel Bukh, 1980, pp. 31–41.

Shulman, Eliyohu. *Portretn un Etyudn*. New York, 1979, 348–357.

Szeintuch, Yehiel. "Beyn Sifrut Lehazon." In *Kovets Mehkarim al Yehudey Polin*. Edited by E. Mendelssohn and C. Shmeruk. 1987, pp. 117–142.

Zeitlin, Aaron. "Aaron Zeitlin Vehateatron Beyidish." In *Brener, Esterke, Vaitsman Hasheni*. Edited by Yehiel Szeintuch. Jerusalem: Magnes Press, 1993, pp. 11–56.

Yanasovitsh, Yitskhok. *Penemer un Neman*. Vol. I. Buenos Aires: Kiyem, 1971, pp. 294–305.

Yanasovitsh, Yitskhok. "Aaron Zeitlin." In *Pinkes far der Forshung fun der Yidisher Literatur un Prese*. Edited by I. Knox and E. Shulman. Vol. 3. 1975, pp. 117–136.

Interview, Letters, and Archive

Interview by A. Tabatshnik in *Di Goldene Keyt*, no. 65 (1969): 17–33.

Letters in Y. Lifshitz. *Pinkes far der Forshung fun der Yidisher Literatur un Prese*. Vol. 3. 1975, 419–484; and Y. Szeintuch, *Birshut Harabim Uvishut Hayahid*. 2000. 374pp.

Louis Zukofsky

(1904–1978)

MARK SCROGGINS

LOUIS ZUKOFSKY WAS born on 23 January 1904 in New York City, the youngest son of Pinchos and Chana Pruss Zukofsky, Lithuanian immigrant Jews. He spoke only Yiddish before attending public school, but proved talented enough to attend Columbia University, where he received a master's degree in English in 1924. Zukofsky's literary career began with great promise. In the early 1930s, under the sponsorship of the expatriate American poet Ezra Pound, Zukofsky rose to some prominence as the leader of the "Objectivist" movement—a group of mostly Jewish, left-wing writers that included George Oppen, Carl Rakosi, and Charles Reznikoff. This movement, however, soon drifted apart, and Zukofsky fell out of public view; while he continued to write and publish poetry throughout his middle years, he did not achieve any widespread fame until the 1960s, when he was rediscovered by a younger generation of American poets, among them Allen Ginsberg, Robert Creeley, and Robert Duncan. While Zukofsky wrote many short lyrics and lyric sequences, a large body of criticism, a play, a novel, and a few short stories, his major achievement is the long poem "*A*," which he wrote between 1928 and 1974. This poem is a monument on the scale of James Joyce's *Ulysses*, Marcel Proust's *A la recherche du temps perdu*, or Walter Benjamin's unfinished *Arcades Project*. "*A*" was first published as a whole in 1978, the year of Zukofsky's death (on 12 May, in Port Jefferson, Long Island). Since then he has become recognized as one of the major American poets of the century, and his work has been increasingly seen as a crucial bridge between modernist and postmodernist poetic modes.

Prewar Era

From early on, Zukofsky viewed his own Jewishness ambiguously. In "Poem Beginning 'The' " (1926), Zukofsky portrays himself as torn between an overwhelmingly Gentile literary tradition and his parents' Orthodox community. He responds by both embracing the poetics of modernism and rejecting the cultural pessimism evident in T. S. Eliot's *The Waste Land*, his poem's immediate model. Where Eliot could find only "fragments" to shore against the ruins of the post–Great War West, Zukofsky finds political hope in the Soviet Revolution and a vibrant new literature being created by "Yehoash" (Solomon Bloomgarden), translated passages of whose Yiddish poetry Zukofsky incorporates into his own poem. Zukofsky also quotes Yehoash in an early movement of "*A*," "A"-4 (1928), where the Yiddish poet's lovely orientalist verses are set in contrast to the aged, pessimistic, and disapproving voices of the Orthodox community: "We had a speech, our children have evolved a jargon" (Baltimore: Johns Hopkins University Press, 1993, p. 12).

Much of "*A*" is written in a high modernist mode similar to that of Pound's *Cantos*, which Pound had begun some ten years before Zukofsky began "*A*." Zukofsky and Pound shared a decades-long epistolatory friendship; Zukofsky admired Pound's writing extravagantly, and Pound in turn recognized his young admirer's talent and promoted his work. Pound's increasing antisemitism, however, and his support of European fascism would strain their relationship to the breaking point. Pound's scorn for "Jewish" modes of thinking sometimes sparked remarkable displays of Jewish self-hatred in Zukofsky, and at other times drove him to defend his people; when the two men disagreed, however, it was usually over politics or economics rather than antisemitism—Pound was an advocate of the eccentric economic theories known as Social Credit, Zukofsky a Marxist. (Zukofsky's period of committed Marxism lasted through the end of the 1930s; the Hitler-Stalin pact of 1939, to which he refers scornfully in "A"-10 [1940], probably contributed to his political disengagement thereafter.) Pound's steadfast admiration for Benito Mussolini, even after the downfall of the fascist regime, and his failure to recognize the enormity of the Nazi death camps, brought home to Zukofsky precisely the extent to which his guide and poetic mentor had—despite his abundant talents—been blind to human evil. The Holocaust did not touch Zukofsky directly—he seems not to have lost any near relatives in the *Shoah*—but this great rupture in Western history led him to rethink his relationship with Pound and, more important, led him to a new examination and appreciation of his own Jewish heritage.

War Years

In the spring of 1945, as evidence of the death camps was being disseminated in the United States, Zukofsky drafted the second section of "A Song for the Year's End," which centers on a visit to his mother's grave. After the war is over, Zukofsky says, he will go to his mother's grave and tell her of his marriage and his new son. He'll do this as a gesture of "loyalty," a riposte to the antisemitic inhabitants of suburban Baltimore ("wherever Jews are not the right sort of people"). When he wrote these lines, Zukofsky—a lifelong New Yorker—was working for a technical writing firm in Towson, Maryland; he lived in Baltimore, because no one in Towson would rent to Jews. Significantly, this concrete example of American antisemitism prompts one of Zukofsky's few explicit references to the fate of European Jewry, a laconic statement to his mother: "There are less Jews left in the world" (*Complete Short Poetry*, Baltimore: Johns Hopkins University Press, 1991, pp. 111–112).

Zukofsky had ceased correspondence with Pound during the war years; when he was called on to write on Pound again, it was to be in a far different key from the admiring essays he had written on *The Cantos* back in the 1920s. During the war, Pound had made antiwar broadcasts to Allied forces over Italian radio. He had been brought back to the United States to face treason charges and, having been declared mentally unfit to stand trial, had been incarcerated in St. Elizabeth's mental hospital in Washington, D.C. When Zukofsky was asked in 1948 to contribute to a symposium on Pound, he wrote an extremely brief note whose most quoted sentence is, "I never felt the least trace of antisemitism in his presence." The phrase "in his presence" shows Zukofsky's usual scrupulosity: antisemitism was certainly evident in Pound's *Letters* to Zukofsky, but Zukofsky's loyalty to the man who first sponsored his work was steadfast. Nonetheless, he noted, Pound's "finest work" would be "overshadowed in his lifetime by the hell of Belsen which he overlooked" (*Prepositions +: The Collected Critical Essays*, Hanover, N.H.: Wesleyan University Press, 2000, pp. 165–166).

Response to the Holocaust

Pound may have foolishly "overlooked" it, but the Holocaust could not be ignored. Zukofsky chose not to treat it directly, as his friend Reznikoff would in *Holocaust* (1975). Instead, in long stretches of "A"-12, the first movement of his long poem to be written after the war, Zukofsky remembers his father, who immigrated to the United States in 1898, worked multiple jobs in New York's garment district to support his family, and held fast to the Orthodox religion of his forebears and the culture of his Eastern European youth. Pinchos Zukofsky died in 1950, and "A"-12 (1950–1951) is in part an elegy for Zukofsky's father; but it is also the point at which Jewish themes and material become most prominent in "*A*." As several critics have argued, it is in "A"-12 that Zukofsky really discovers himself as a specifically Jewish poet. And "A"-12 is a poem that, for whatever reasons in his makeup, Zukofsky could not have composed before the Holocaust. More than an elegy for Zukofsky's father, it is an elegy for Pinchos Zukofsky and for the whole of Eastern European *Yiddishkayt*, a culture destroyed by the Holocaust. For Zukofsky, the *Yiddishkayt* evoked in "A"-12—often through passages quoted from Martin Buber's accounts of Eastern European Hasidism: "What is the worth of their / expounding the Torah: / All a man's actions / Should make him a Torah"—is not an alien culture, the culture of his distant forebears (p. 159). It is the culture into which he was born on the Lower East Side, his father's and mother's culture, a culture that Pinchos Zukofsky would recall with intense nostalgia ("I loved to hear them sing," he says of the songs of his youth), and a culture on which Zukofsky himself had turned his back at sixteen ("*A*," p. 151). In "A"-12, with his father dead, and his father's culture largely erased in Hitler's ovens, he turns his face to it, remembers, and mourns.

Zukofsky is rarely simple, either in his poetic modes or in his thought. But one can see a subtle shift in his attitudes toward his own Jewishness and toward Judaism in general in his post-Holocaust writing. In his early work, whether he wrote from the position of an angry, alienated young man, a political theorist, or a fierce innovator, he seemed at home in his New York setting. In his postwar writing, more and more often the Jew's position is one of exile, of "Babylon" or "Egypt"; a gift of flowers from a Gentile friend, in part

2 of "Chloride of Lime and Charcoal," is the "lancet leaves, tubular stems . . . of Egypt" (*Complete Short Poetry*, p. 125). He is no longer at home, even when he is at home. Perhaps Zukofsky's most memorable meditation on post-Holocaust themes is a brief but intensely complex poem, part 3 of "Songs of Degrees," "Nor Did the prophet" (*Complete Short Poetry*, pp. 146–147). The poem revolves around Zukofsky's 1954 visit to St. Elizabeth's and alludes to Pound's *Pisan Cantos* and to an array of passages from the Hebrew Bible. It is a poem about rebuilding the Temple in the wake of catastrophe and exile and the bitter, rueful—and ultimately hopeless—wish that one could exchange one's exilic status for some homeland or other. (Unlike the Objectivists Reznikoff, married to the noted Zionist Marie Syrkin, and Rakosi and Oppen, each of whom visited Israel, Zukofsky showed little interest in the actual Jewish state.) The poem is a recognition that in Pound's case, moral blindness has become aesthetic failure. Zukofsky contrasts the poem 2 Samuel calls "the last words of David . . . the sweet psalmist of Israel"—"The God of Israel said . . . He that ruleth over men must be just, ruling in the fear of God. And *he shall be* as the light of the morning, when the sun riseth, even a morning without clouds; as the tender grass springing out of the earth by clear shining after rain" (23.3–4)—with Pound, and finds his friend wanting. It is Pound, surely, who "does not stop from drinking water / As blood is shed." He "Does not see morning without a cloud / Upon tender grass after rain." Pound has seen "blood shed," and thereby cannot see the natural beauty that David—"the prime s.o.b.," according to *The Pisan Cantos*—so beautifully captured in his own poetry.

There are other scattered references to the Holocaust in Zukofsky's work: In section 10 of "The Old Poet Moves to a New Apartment 14 Times" (1962), there is a horrifying recollection of Josef Mengele, "Auschwitz crematories' . . . Angel Head Doctor," "whipping children" and "whistling Mozart" (*Complete Short Poetry*, p. 227). The *Shoah*, however, is not a theme on which Zukofsky cared to dwell. As he puts it in "A"-23 (1973–1974), "Histories dye the streets" (p. 563). His is a poetry of memory, but above all else it is a poetry of remembering and bringing to light "loved things." Nonetheless, the Holocaust deeply affected Zukofsky, as it affected every sensitive Jew of his generation. It reminded him that evil, or the capacity to overlook evil, could coexist with the highest aesthetic sensibilities and that those sensibilities would eventually be corroded by the evil in which they acquiesced; it galvanized him to the riches of the Eastern European culture that the Nazis had so successfully sought to exterminate; and it made him more aware of his own heritage as a Jew.

Bibliography

Primary Sources

A Test of Poetry. 1948.
Bottom: On Shakespeare. 1963.
Autobiography. 1970.
Little: for careenagers. 1970.
Arise, arise. 1973.
"*A*." 1978.
Pound/Zukofsky: Selected Letters of Ezra Pound and Louis Zukofsky. Edited by Barry Ahearn. 1987.
Collected Fiction. 1990.
Complete Short Poetry. 1991.
Prepositions +: The Collected Critical Essays of Louis Zukofsky. 2000.

Secondary Sources

Ahearn, Barry. *Zukofsky's "A": An Introduction*. Berkeley: University of California Press, 1983.
Quartermain, Peter. *Disjunctive Poetics: From Gertrude Stein and Louis Zukofsky to Susan Howe*. Cambridge: Cambridge University Press, 1992.
Scroggins, Mark. *Louis Zukofsky and the Poetry of Knowledge*. Tuscaloosa: University of Alabama Press, 1998.
———, ed. *Upper Limit Music: The Writing of Louis Zukofsky*. Tuscaloosa: University of Alabama Press, 1997.
Stanley, Sandra Kumamoto. *Louis Zukofsky and the Transformation of a Modern American Poetics*. Berkeley: University of California Press, 1994.
Terrell, Carroll F., ed. *Louis Zukofsky: Man and Poet*. Orono, Me: National Poetry Foundation, 1979.
Tomas, John. "Portrait of the Artist as a Young Jew: Zukofsky's 'Poem beginning "The" ' in Context." *Sagetrieb* 9, nos. 1–2 (spring–fall 1990): 43–64.

Archive

Most of Zukofsky's manuscripts and papers are held at the Harry Ransom Humanities Research Center, University of Texas, Austin.

Rajzel Zychlinsky

(1910–2001)

EMANUEL S. GOLDSMITH

THE YIDDISH POET Rajzel Zychlinsky had her first poem published in 1928, when she was only eighteen years of age. The distinguished poet and memoirist Melekh Ravitch later wistfully recalled that Zychlinsky's earliest poems were "extremely tender, romantic, unclear, scarcely melodic and absolutely illogical." Nevertheless, when her first book of poems appeared in 1936, the celebrated poet Itsik Manger wrote a foreword in which he hailed Zychlinsky's work as "a new authentic revelation of the feminine poetic countenance in Jewish Poland."

It was clear from Zychlinsky's first volume that she was the true heiress to generations of Yiddish female poets in Central and Eastern Europe. Most remarkable was the strong individuality in both her poetic persona and poetic gift. Her unique voice elevated her to a position of prominence among the very best writers in Yiddish.

What Zychlinsky was able to do in her first book of poems, she managed to do in all of her work. She continually demonstrated the indispensability of poetry—and especially of the short, short poem—in capturing and conveying the flavor, aroma, and impact of the interior, the hidden, and the transcendent aspects of human experiences, and in situating them in the cosmos. She also excelled in plumbing the depths of human loneliness on the one hand, and in charting its redemption in ethical sensitivity and moral responsibility on the other.

A Poet's Life

Rajzel Zychlinsky was born in Gombin, Poland on 27 July 1910. Her father, a tanner by trade, made several trips to America before settling in Chicago, where he died in 1928. Her mother was a religious woman who feared that the secular blandishments of the Golden Land would entice her children to abandon their piety, and therefore refused to emigrate. She met her death, together with her remaining children, in the gas chambers of Chelmno.

Zychlinsky, a genuinely distinctive voice in the literature of the Holocaust, received her education in a Polish public school and from private tutors. She ran an orphans' home in 1935. From 1936 to 1939 she lived in Warsaw, until, together with her husband, the psychiatrist and author Dr. Isaac Kanter, she managed to escape to Russia, where their son, Marek, was born. After the war she lived in Poland and France until she moved to America in 1951. In the United States, she continued writing Yiddish poetry while working in a factory, obtaining a high school diploma, studying at the City College of New York, and raising her son.

Zychlinsky published seven volumes of Yiddish poems between 1936 and 1993, in Poland, the United States, France, and Israel. Two volumes have appeared in German and English translation, and translations of individual poems have appeared in various anthologies. In 1975, she was awarded the Itsik Manger Prize for Yiddish literature. For many years, she lived in Brooklyn, New York, near Brighton Beach. She died in Los Angeles in 2001.

From Simplicity to Morality

In his foreword to Zychlinsky's *Lider* (Poems) of 1936, Itsik Manger noted that the things the poet wrote about could be counted on one's fingers: "mother, cat, willow, wolf, poplar, beggar, child, and well . . . It is, however, not the external poetic inventory that counts, but rather the nuancing, always illuminating the object with a different light, evoking a different mood . . . in brief, the ability to vary the [same] material to infinity, always repeating basic motifs in ever new ways." Manger also drew attention to the fact that the central figures of almost all of her early poems were mother and child, and that everything in her mother's house was deemed worthy of a poem (Reprinted in *Shriftn in Proze*. Tel Aviv: Farlag Y. L., 1980, p. 254).

As the horizons of Zychlinsky's world broadened, the intensity of her poetry deepened both technically and existentially. From the intimacy of her parental home, the poet went on to extend a warm hand of friendship to her sorely tried people, to human beings everywhere, to the animate and inanimate worlds, to nature and the cosmos. She empathized simultaneously with the loneliness of all that is and extended the caring of her own warm motherly heart to all of existence. Her poetry, which had excelled in discovering the all in the small, now commiserated with the small in the all, the micro in the macro, the perishable in the eternal.

In a fragment of red paper lying in the snow, the poet could see "the bleeding of someone's interrupted scream." Noticing a shoe lost on the pavement of a city, she would be troubled by the fact that no one was looking for its pair. The racing of police cars, the wailing of sirens would appear to her to be "waking up distant places amid the stars" (Rajzel Zychlinsky, "A Royt Shtik Papir" [A Red Piece of Paper]. *Harbstike Skvern* [Autumn Squares]. New York: Cyco Farlag, 1969, p. 60).

Zychlinsky abandoned her occasional reliance on rhyme to adorn and buttress the power of her poems, and committed herself to the more difficult but more rewarding paths of free verse, to the fires of poetic imagery, dream, and hallucination. The moral stance of her poetry became clearer and the purity of her voice among the poets unmistakable.

The poet praised the good hand that fed pigeons in New York City ("where such feeding is strictly forbidden in big letters on signs prominently displayed"), that led a heavy and dark blind man across a street, and that petted "the lonely, bowed head of a homeless dog." She was certain that that good hand would one day rescue the earth from destruction and chaos ("Di Gute Hant" [The Kind Hand]. *Harbstike Skvern*, p. 61). This poem is characteristic of the powerful ethical convictions of the poet's work.

Intimacy and Femininity

As her voice matured, Yiddish literary critics began to pay greater attention to Zychlinsky's poetry. The widely respected Shmuel Niger praised her poems on Jewish and biblical themes. Shlomo Bickel characterized her as a unique and original poet who was simultaneously related to every other Yiddish poet and distinct from all of them. He also found a sensuous intensity in her lines. Jacob Glatstein was similarly taken with her concealed eroticism, original imagery, and sparse diction. He admired the profound intimacy of her verse as well as her ability to hide her emotion behind images and her longings behind surprising lines.

"To wander within you, / as in a black, green forest: to become night within your trunk / to become day within your branches / to rest on the sunspots of your hands / to die in the voice of a bird / somewhere far off / to die in your voice" ("Blondzhen in Dir" [To Wander Within You]. *Shvaygndike Tirn* [Silent Doors], New York, 1962, p. 81).

For Yitskhok Yanasovitsh, Zychlinsky was the most original and authentic of Yiddish female poets and the poet of "associations and images that take intellectual leaps and lead us from reality to illusion and from illusion to a higher, more essential reality" (*Penemer un Nemen*, vol. 1. Buenos Aires: Kiem, 1971, p. 116). Yitskhok Goldkorn characterized her as a medium through whom the spirit of poetry, premonition, and vision speaks, bringing nature to life and identifying herself with it. Gitl Mayzil saw her work as embodying the essence of women's poetry: moral indignation at the injustices perpetrated against women, intimate association with the phenomena of nature, and impressive female tenderness, which great poets view as one of the most powerful forces in the world.

"Empty Space Awaits Me"

In addition to her remarkable poems of womanhood, motherhood, the world of the lonely individual, identification with the "other" of a society, and the world of nature, Zychlinsky has been most widely commended for the profound and proud Jewishness of her poems in general and of her poems related to the Holocaust in particular. These poems are her most emotional, most profound, and most universal, even as they constitute her most elegant work:

Yellow leaves fall, fall.
A tale wanders about on the roads,
A tale of people driven to a field—
A spring rain poured.

Three thousand Jews without bread or water
Four long spring days.
Little children cried to the stars—
They wanted to eat. ("Ikh Vil Do Amol Geyn Ibern Groz" [I Want to Walk through the Grass Here One Day]. *Shvaygndike Tirn*, p. 115).

The poet's lament encompasses the testimonial account of a mass killing scene as well as the impact of such loss on an individual alone and bereft:

> Evening will no longer lead me back
> To my mother's door.
> Even if all the stars stand in a circle about me,
> Wherever my steps turn
> Empty space awaits me.
> The wind will no longer bring
> A familiar voice to my ear–
> Cradle me, cradle me, sadness. ("Leydiker Shetakh" [Empty Space]. *Shvaygndike Tirn*, p. 126).

Since those horrible days, Zychlinsky has lived with the Holocaust in her house and in her heart. Her empathy with the members of her family, the 3,030 Jewish residents of her community who perished in the conflagration, and, indeed, for Jewry as a whole, is overwhelming in its poetic impact. Her Holocaust poems, as Yitskhok Goldkorn observes, lack the expressionistic dimension of a mourner's weeping and wailing over loss. They do, however, possess the impressionistic dimension of vision that recalls the biblical prophecy that one day "the very stone will protest from the wall" (Habakkuk 2:11).

The Poetry of Severed Lives

From Zychlinsky's apartment on New York's West Side, the heavens seem ablaze at dusk, the Hudson River runs blood as the sun sets, and the first star is, for the poet, the frozen tear of her people ("Ikh Voyn af der Vest-Zayt" [I Live on the West Side]. *Harbstike Skvern*, p. 70). What became of one of the suitors who courted her when she was a young girl? she asks, as she gazes on the black smoke across from her window: "Is he too gone with the smoke?" ("Vos iz Gevorn"). [Whatever Became of?]. *Di November-Zun* [The November Sun], Paris, 1977, p. 31). Natural phenomena such as clouds, leaves, and water recall her dead relatives and friends; as she strolls with her son, arms linked amid the shadows, she greets them: "So many severed lives cling to me . . . so many severed lives sob in May, in the spring wind" ("Fun a Volkn Kukt af Mir di Mame" [Mother Looks at Me from a Cloud]. *Shvaygndike Tirn*, p. 114). She cannot help wondering about the blonde girl and her lover in a Yiddish folk song: Was her hair used to stuff mattresses in Germany? From which smokestack did he ascend in smoke to heaven? Only the sun knows the answer, but it remains silent, preoccupied with its own flames ("Vider Voyn Ikh" [Again I Dwell]. *Naye Lider*, Tel-Aviv: Farlag, 1993, p. 12). Despite her conviction that God hid His face during the Holocaust and that He no longer calls even on those who seek Him, the poet confesses that she studies a passage of the Torah daily in order to anchor herself to her people and her God. She draws truth and sustenance for her poetry from the Bible, from Jewish history, from her childhood memories, and from the Holocaust itself.

Rajzel Zychlinsky's Holocaust poems, like all of her work, resound with the spirit of modesty, piety, and compassion of generations of Jewish women. Indeed, the two terms for compassion in both Yiddish and Hebrew, *rachmones* and *rachamim*, are both derived from the Hebrew word for "womb." Zychlinsky's poetic legacy bears testimony to the possibility of human redemption through ethical indignation and tenderness, moral responsibility and compassion. Characteristic of the mood and method of her Holocaust poetry is the following:

> Three meters wide
> Six meters deep
> And fifteen meters long—
> These are the measurements of one of the graves
> In Poland,
> To which the Germans drove Jews,
> Shot them
> And buried them.
> Three meters wide
> Six meters deep
> And fifteen meters long—
> The three dimensions.
> And the fourth dimension,
> The one in which all the murdered Jews
> Can neither die
> Nor live—
> Is the silent partner
> Of all the days of my life. ("Der Shtumer Shutef" [The Silent Partner]. *Di November-Zun*, p. 31).

Bibliography

Primary Sources

Lider (Poems). 1936.

Der Regn Zingt (The Rain Sings). 1939.

Tsu Loytere Bregn (To Clear Shores). 1948.

Shvaygndike Tirn (Silent Doors). 1962.

Harbstike Skvern (Autumn Squares). 1969.

Di November-Zun (The November Sun). 1977.

Vogelbrot–Gedichte Aus Funf Jahrzehntn. (Bread for the Birds—Five Decades of Poetry; translated into German by Hubert Witt). 1981.

Naye Lider (New Poems). 1993.

God Hid His Face (English translation, ed. B. Zumoff). 1997.
Gottes Blinde Augen (God's Blind Eyes; German translation, ed. K. Kranhold). 1997.

Secondary Sources

Bickel, Shlomo. *Shrayber fun Mayn Dor*. Vol. 2. Tel Aviv: Farlag Y. L. Peretz, 1965.

Glatstein, Jacob. *In Tokh Genumen: Eseyen 1948–1956*. New York: Yidish Natsyonalen Arbeter Farband, 1956.

Goldkorn, Yitskhok. *Heymishe un Fremde*. Buenos Aires: Farlag Svive, 1973.

Manger, Itsik. *Shriftn in Proze*. Tel Aviv: Farlag Y. L. Peretz, 1980.

Mayzil, Gitl. *Eseyen*. Tel Aviv: Farlag Y. L. Peretz, 1974.

Niger, Shmuel. *Yidishe Shrayber Fun Tsvantsikstn Yorhundert*. New York: Alveltlekher Yidisher Kultur-Kongres, 1973.

Rav, Melekh. *Mayn Leksikon*. Vol. 1. Montreal: Kiyem Farlag, 1945.

Yanasovitsh, Yitskhok. *Penemer un Nemen*. Vol. 1. Buenos Aires: Kiyem Farlag, 1971.

CONTRIBUTORS' BIOGRAPHICAL NOTES

Victoria Aarons, professor of English at Trinity University, received her Ph.D. from the University of California, Berkeley. She is the author of *A Measure of Memory: Storytelling and Identity in American Jewish Fiction,* which received the CHOICE Award for an outstanding academic book, 1996. Aarons has written numerous essays in scholarly journals and books on American Jewish literature, including a recent piece on Philip Roth, in the special issue of *Shofar* (2000). She is currently working on the literature of second-generation Holocaust writers.
Articles contributed to *Holocaust Literature*: CAROL ASCHER; BARBARA FINKELSTEIN; WILLIAM HEYEN; HUGH NISSENSON; LEV RAPHAEL.

Dvir Abramovich, the Jan Randa lecturer in Hebrew and Jewish studies, has bachelor degrees in arts and law from Monash University, a master of arts and a Ph.D. from the University of Melbourne. He lectures in modern Hebrew literature, language, and Judaic studies at the Hebrew and Jewish studies program at the University of Melbourne, in particular the subjects introduction to modern Jewish culture, the modern Jewish world and Israel, reading the Holocaust, exploring the world of Jewish literature, and Jerusalem in Jewish literature. He has also edited a book on Jewish literature to be published in 2003 and is the editor of the *Australian Journal of Jewish Studies,* and has published widely in professional and non-professional publications. Dr. Abramovich is the chairperson of the Hebrew culture department at the state Zionist council and vice president of the Australian Association of Jewish Studies.
Articles contributed to *Holocaust Literature*: HANOCH BARTOV; HAIM GOURI; SHULAMITH HAREVEN; ITAMAR LEVY; DORIT PELEG; NAVA SEMEL.

Monika Adamczyk-Garbowska is a professor of American and comparative literature and head of the Center for Jewish Studies at Maria Curie-Sklodowska University in Lublin, Poland. She is a translator from English and Yiddish and held visiting fellowships at YIVO Institute for Jewish Research, Columbia University, and Brandeis University. Her major publications include *Isaac Bashevis Singer's Poland: Exile and Return* [in Polish] (1994) and (together with Antony Polonsky) *Contemporary Jewish Writing in Poland: An Anthology* (2001). She is on the editorial board of *Polin: Studies in Polish Jewry.*
Articles contributed to *Holocaust Literature*: JERZY ANDRZEJEWSKI; JANINA BAUMAN; STANISŁAW BENSKI; HALINA BIRENBAUM; KAZIMIERZ BRANDYS; HENRYK GRYNBERG; HANNA KRALL; CZESŁAW MIŁOSZ; ZOFIA NAŁKOWSKA; ADOLF RUDNICKI; ANDRZEJ SZCZYPIORSKI; JULIAN TUWIM; BOGDAN WOJDOWSKI; STANISŁAW WYGODZKI.

Ehrhard Bahr is a professor of German at the University of California, Los Angeles. He is author of a book on Nelly Sachs and articles on Jewish emancipation, exile literature and Holocaust literature.
Articles contributed to *Holocaust Literature*: BERTOLT BRECHT; FRANZ WERFEL.

Lee Behlman is an assistant professor of English at Kansas State University. His research interests and upcoming publications are in the fields of Victorian studies and literature and religion.
Articles contributed to *Holocaust Literature*: MICHAEL CHABON.

Pascale Bos is an assistant professor of Netherlandic and Germanic Studies at the University of Texas at Austin. She has published articles on Holocaust literature and gender and the Holocaust, and is currently working on a monograph on German Jewish survivor authors and on a study on Dutch second-generation authors.
Articles contributed to *Holocaust Literature*: ANDREAS BURNIER; ARNON GRUNBERG; JUDITH HERZBERG; ETTY HILLESUM; ISCHA MEIJER.

Kathrin Bower is an associate professor of German and coordinator of Jewish studies at the University of Richmond, Virginia, and the author of *Ethics and Remembrance in the Poetry of Nelly Sachs and Rose Ausländer* (2000). She was a post-doctoral fellow at the Franz Rosenzweig Institute for German-Jewish Studies at the Hebrew University of Jerusalem. She has written and published on German Holocaust poetry and

reception, contemporary German-Jewish literature, and gender and identity politics in German film.
Articles contributed to *Holocaust Literature*: NELLY SACHS; RAFAEL SELIGMANN.

Stephan Braese teaches German literature at the University of Bremen. Among his recent books are *Die Andere Erinnerung* (2001): *Jüdische Autoren In Der Westdeutschen Nachkriegsliteratur, Bestandsaufnahme: Studien Zur Gruppe 47* (1999), and *Deutsche Nachkriegsliteratur Und Der Holocaust* (1998).
Articles contributed to *Holocaust Literature*: HEINRICH BÖLL; GRETE WEIL.

David Brauner is a lecturer in English/director of American studies at the University of Reading (UK). He is author of *Post-war Jewish Fiction: Ambivalence, Self-explanation and Transatlantic Connections* (2000), and of articles on Saul Bellow, Philip Roth, Jane Smiley and many contemporary American-Jewish and British-Jewish writers.
Articles contributed to *Holocaust Literature*: LISA APPIGNANESI; LOUISE KEHOE.

Steven Dedalus Burch, actor, director, playwright (recipient of playwriting fellowship from the New York Foundation for the Arts), teaches theatre history at Allegheny College as a visiting assistant professor of communication arts/theatre.
Articles contributed to *Holocaust Literature*: JON ROBIN BAITZ; DONALD MARGULIES; JOSHUA SOBOL.

Holly Burmeister is a Ph.D. candidate at the University of Michigan.
Articles contributed to *Holocaust Literature*: FANIA FENELON; BERTHA FERDERBER-SALZ.

Janet Handler Burstein is a professor of English literature at Drew University. She has written numerous articles on Victorian literature, women's literature, American Jewish literature; published a book—*Writing Mother, Writing Daughters: Tracing the Maternal in Stories by American Jewish Women*; and is working on a book about the last two decades of American Jewish writers.
Articles contributed to *Holocaust Literature*: HELEN EPSTEIN.

Ezra Cappell is a Ph.D. from New York University where he currently holds the American literature fellowship. Cappell has taught literature and nonfiction writing at New York University, and creative writing at the City College. He has published widely on American and Jewish American fiction. His critical study *American Talmud: The Cultural Work of Jewish American Fiction* is forthcoming. Cappell is completing a memoir *Hide and Seek in Rego Park.*
Articles contributed to *Holocaust Literature*: REBECCA GOLDSTEIN; ALLEGRA GOODMAN.

Joshua Charlson has been a lecturer and visiting assistant professor at Northwestern University, where he received his Ph.D. He is working on a study, based on his dissertation, exploring American cultural representations of the Holocaust. He has published articles on Art Spiegelman's *Maus* in *Arizona Quarterly* and Saul Bellow's *Mr. Sammler's Planet* in *Centennial Review.*
Articles contributed to *Holocaust Literature*: IRVING FELDMAN; ARNOST LUSTIG.

Richard Chess is an associate professor of literature and language at the University of Northern Carolina at Asheville where he directs UNCA's Center for Jewish Studies. He has published two books of poetry, *Chair in the Desert* (2000) and *Tekian* (1994). His poems have been anthologized in *Telling and Remembering: A Century of American-Jewish Poetry* (1997) and elsewhere.
Articles contributed to *Holocaust Literature*: YOEL HOFFMANN; JÁNOS PILINSZKY; ALAN SHAPIRO.

Amy Colin, who has personal ties to Paul Celan and the Bukovina, is the author of the monograph *Paul Celan: Holograms of Darkness* (1991) as well as essays on Bukovina's multifaceted literature, *Shoah* poetry written in German, and German-Jewish literature, in particular women's writing. She is also editor of *Argumentum e Silentio: International Paul Celan Symposium* (1987) and co-editor of *Bridging the Abyss: Reflections on Jewish Suffering, Anti-Semitism, and Exile* (1994) and *Versunkene Dichtung der Bukowina: Eine Anthologie deutschsprachiger Lyrik* (1994). After obtaining her Ph.D. from Yale, she taught and pursued her research projects at the universities of Washington, Cambridge, Cornell, Pittsburgh, Harvard, FU Berlin, Denis Diderot-Paris 7, and the Maison des Science de l'Homme (Paris, France).
Articles contributed to *Holocaust Literature*: PAUL CELAN; ALFRED KITTNER; IMMANUEL JAMES WEIßGLAS.

Colin Davis is a professor of French studies at the University of Warwick, UK. His research is principally concerned with postwar French fiction and thought. He is the author of *Michel Tournier: Philosophy and Fiction* (1988), *Elie Wiesel's Secretive Texts* (1994), *Levinas: An Introduction* (1996), *Ethical Issues in Twentieth-Century French Fiction: Killing the Other* (2000), and (with Elizabeth Fallaize) *French Fiction*

in the Mitterrand Years: Memory, Narrative, Desire (2000).
Articles contributed to *Holocaust Literature*: ROBERT ANTELME; DAVID ROUSSET; JORGE SEMPRUN.

Juliette Dickstein received her Ph.D. in Romance languages and literatures from Harvard University. She has taught at Harvard and at Intercollege, Cyprus, where she was assistant professor of foreign languages. Her research interests concern questions of nationalism and identity and the consequences of traumatic history for literature, film, and historiography. She has published articles on postwar French Jewish writing. Currently she is working as an education consultant for the United Nations Development Program in Cyprus.
Articles contributed to *Holocaust Literature*: SERGE DOUBROVSKY; SAUL FRIEDLÄNDER; ALBERT MEMMI; ANNE RABINOVITCH; HENRI RACZYMOW.

Norbert Otto Eke is professor of German and comparative literature at the University of Paderborn. His main areas of expertise are theater and literary theory, contemporary German literature and German Jewish literature; and literature of the early nineteenth century. He has numerous publications on German literature from the eighteenth century to the present day, including German-Jewish relations. Recent books include: *Heiner Müller* (1999), *Literatur und Demokratie* (ed., 2000), *Deutsche Dramatiker des 20. Jahrhunderts* (ed., 2000), *Vormärz - Nachmärz. Bruch oder Kontinuität* (ed., 2000).
Articles contributed to *Holocaust Literature*: MAXIM BILLER; EDGAR HILSENRATH.

Norman Fedder is distinguished professor emeritus of theater at Kansas State University, and was formerly director of graduate studies and founder/director of the K.S.U. drama therapy program. A member of the Kansas Theatre Hall of Fame, he is the author of a book on Tennessee Williams, articles on dramatic literature, and more than thirty produced plays. He is also a registered drama therapist/board-certified trainer. He founded the drama network of the Coalition for the Advancement of Jewish Theater.
Articles contributed to *Holocaust Literature*: ARTHUR MILLER; SHIMON WINCELBERG.

Anat Feinberg, studied English literature and theater in Tel Aviv and London (Ph.D. University of London, 1979). She lectured at Tel Aviv University and is professor for Hebrew and Jewish literature at the Hochschule für Jüdische Studien in Heidelberg. She has published articles on Elizabethan and Jacobean drama, on German theater, and on Israeli literature and culture. Among her publications are *Wiedergutmachung im Programm. Jüdisches Schicksal im deutschen Nachkriegsdrama.* (1988), and (editor) *Kultur in Israel* (1993). Her study *Embodied Memory: The Theatre of George Tabori,* (1999) and her German biography of Tabori will appear in 2003 in the series ''Portrait'' with Deutscher Taschenbuch Verlag.
Articles contributed to *Holocaust Literature*: FRITZ HOCHWÄLDER; HEINER KIPPHARDT; ERWIN SYLVANUS; GEORGE TABORI.

Shoshana Felman is Thomas E. Donnelley professor of French and comparative literature at Yale University. She is the author of *The Literary Speech Act* (1984), *Writing and Madness* (1985), *Jacques Lacan and the Adventure of Insight* (1987), and *What Does a Woman Want? Reading and Sexual Difference* (1993). She is also the editor of *Literature and Psychoanalysis: The Question of Reading—Otherwise* (1982), the co-author, with Dori Laub, of *Testimony: Crises of Witnessing in Literature, Psychoanalysis, and History* (1992), and the author of *The Juridical Unconscious: Trials and Traumas in the Twentieth Century* (forthcoming, Harvard University Press).
Articles contributed to *Holocaust Literature*: ALBERT CAMUS.

Hilene Flanzbaum is an associate professor of English at Butler University, where she also directs the creative writing program and teaches literature of the Holocaust. She is the editor of *The Americanization of the Holocaust* (1999) and the managing editor of *Jewish American Literature: A Norton Anthology.* She has been a fellow at the Center for Advanced Research at the United States Holocaust Memorial Museum and leads seminars on teaching the Holocaust at the high school and university level.
Articles contributed to *Holocaust Literature*: GERALD GREEN; JEROME ROTHENBERG.

Kristie Foell held a Fulbright research fellowship in Vienna, where she researched her dissertation on Elias Canetti (1992). Her study of gender in Canetti's novel was published by Ariadne Press in 1994. She is an assistant professor of German at Bowling Green State University (Ohio). Other research interests include German film and music and post-unification German literature, which she studied with a second Fulbright to Berlin in 1995. A co-edited volume, *Textual Responses to German Unification,* is forthcoming from de Gruyter.
Articles contributed to *Holocaust Literature*: ELIAS CANETTI; ERICH FRIED.

Eva Fogelman is a psychologist in private practice in New York City. She is a senior research fellow at the Graduate Center CUNY. Dr. Fogelman is co-director of the Psychotherapy with Generations of the Holocaust and Related Traumas, Training Institute for Mental Health. She co-directs an international study of organized persecution of children, Child Development Research.
Articles contributed to *Holocaust Literature*: JOSEPH BERGER; JONATHAN ROSEN; JULIE SALAMON.

Robert Franciosi is an associate professor of English at Grand Valley State University. His work on Holocaust literature includes papers and articles on such writers as John Hersey, William Styron, Art Spiegelman, Charlottle Delbo, and Charles Reznikoff. He is the editor of *Elie Wiesel: Conversations* (2002).
Articles contributed to *Holocaust Literature*: JOHN HERSEY; ART SPIEGELMAN.

Esther Frank is a faculty lecturer in the department of Jewish studies, McGill University. She teaches Jewish and Yiddish literatures and Yiddish language.
Articles contributed to *Holocaust Literature*: YEHUDA ELBERG.

Lea Wernick Fridman is an associate professor of English at the City University of New York and has written extensively on the issue of catastrophe and representational limit. She is the author of *Words and Witness: Narrative and Aesthetic Strategies in the Representation of the Holocaust* (2000).
Articles contributed to *Holocaust Literature*: PIOTR RAWICZ.

Roger Friedmann is an instructor in the English department at Kansas State University, where he teaches technical writing and literature. His short story ''Sabras,'' was published in *The Cimarron Review* in 1984.
Articles contributed to *Holocaust Literature*: AMOS ELON; YORAM KANIUK.

Marianne Friedrich received her Ph.D. in English and American language and literature from the University of Heidelberg. She studied and taught at Washington University in St. Louis, Missouri (Fulbright). She taught at Kent State University, Ohio, and at Webster University, St. Louis. Her publications include a book: *Character and Narration in the Short Fiction of Saul Bellow,* and articles in journals and book chapters in *Saul Bellow: A Mosaic, Saul Bellow at Seventy-Five, A Collection of Critical Essays.* Her translations include contributions to Simon Wiesenthal's new edition of *The Sunflower.*
Articles contributed to *Holocaust Literature*: EVA HOFFMAN; BERNHARD SCHLINK.

Andrew Furman, associate professor of English at Florida Atlantic University, is the author of *Israel Through the Jewish-American Imagination* (1997) and *Contemporary Jewish-American Writers and the Multicultural Dilemma* (2000). His work has appeared in a variety of periodicals including *Forward, MELUS, Contemporary Literature, Midstream, Response, Studies in American Jewish Literature, Modern Jewish Studies, Jewish Currents,* and the *Miami Herald.* He is a contributing editor of *Tikkun.*
Articles contributed to *Holocaust Literature*: MELVIN JULES BUKIET; THANE ROSENBAUM.

Ben Furnish is managing editor, BkMk Press, at the University of Missouri-Kansas City, where he teaches. He has contributed to *Contemporary Jewish-American Dramatists and Poets: A Bio-Critical Sourcebook, The Encyclopedia of Novels into Film, The Sixties in America,* and other publications. He holds a doctorate from the University of Kansas.
Articles contributed to *Holocaust Literature*: JACOB GLATSTEIN; CHAIM GRADE; ISAIAH SPIEGEL.

Dick van Galen Last is a librarian and researcher at the Nederlands Instituut voor Oorlogsdocumentatie. He is the author, with Rolf Wolfswinkel, of *Anne Frank and After* (1996), and has written and reviewed extensively for the national press of the Netherlands. He published three bibliographies in *The Bulletin of the International Committee for the History of the Second World War* (nrs. 26, 29, 30/31). More recently, he has written the chapter on the Netherlands for the book edited by Bob Moore, *The Resistance in Western Europe* (Oxford, 2000).
Articles contributed to *Holocaust Literature*: ELIE COHEN; GERHARD DURLACHER; MOSHE FLINKER; ABEL HERZBERG; PHILIP MECHANICUS; HARRY KURT VICTOR MULISCH; JONA OBERSKI.

Mark Gelber holds a Ph.D. from Yale University. He is professor of German and comparative literature at Ben-Gurion University, Beer Sheva, Israel. He was elected to membership in the German Academy of Language and Literature (Darmstadt) and has held visiting professorships at the University of Pennsylvania and the University of Graz. Alexander von Humboldt research fellow at the Free University in Berlin, his major areas of research and publication include literary

antisemitism, cultural Zionism, exile literature, and the literary and cultural legacy of central European Jewry.
Articles contributed to *Holocaust Literature*: Max Brod; Thomas Mann.

Simone Gigliotti taught modern European and Holocaust history in the department of history at University of Melbourne, Australia. She is now a fellow of that department and held a postdoctoral fellowship at the United States Holocaust Memorial Museum. She will be at the University of West Indies in Jamaica during 2002–2003. Her book *Travel and Trauma in the Holocaust*, War and Genocide Series, is forthcoming.
Articles contributed to *Holocaust Literature*: Mark Raphael Baker; Abraham Biderman; Lily Brett.

Dorota Glowacka is an associate professor of humanities and social sciences in the contemporary studies program at the University of King's College in Halifax, Canada. She teaches critical theory, feminist theory and literature, and Holocaust literature. Glowacka has published numerous articles and reviews in the area of critical theory; American, Polish, and French literature; as well as Holocaust literature and art. She has edited *Between Ethics and Aesthetics: Crossing the Boundaries* (2001). Her work focuses on representations of the Holocaust in literature and art in the context of contemporary philosophical debates. She is working on a book *The Shattered Word: Writing of the Fragment and the Holocaust Testimony.*
Articles contributed to *Holocaust Literature*: Tadeusz Różewicz; Binjamin Wilkomirski.

Myrna Goldenberg, director of the Paul Peck Humanities Institute at Montgomery College, teaches Holocaust literature and film at the college, at the University of Maryland, and at the Johns Hopkins University. She is an active Holocaust scholar, working primarily in two areas: women's experiences and the teaching of the Holocaust. A member of the Goldner Symposium on the Holocaust, a frequent speaker at national and international Holocaust conferences, Goldenberg has contributed many articles and chapters to the field.
Articles contributed to *Holocaust Literature*: Isabella Leitner; Olga Lengyel; Gisella Perl.

Emanuel S. Goldsmith is a professor of Yiddish and Hebrew language and literature, Queens College of the City University of New York. Author of *Modern Yiddish Culture: The Story of the Yiddish Language Movement,* he is editor of the two-volume anthology *Yiddish Literature in America: 1870–2000* (in Yiddish); co-editor of *The American Judaism of Mordecai M. Kaplan, Teachers and Thinkers of Modern Judaism,* and *Events and Movements of Modern Judaism.*
Articles contributed to *Holocaust Literature*: H. Leivick; Joseph Papiernikov; Aaron Zeitlin; Rajzel Zychlinsky.

Robert Gordon is a senior lecturer in Italian at the University of Cambridge and fellow of Gonville and Caius College. He previously taught at the University of Oxford. His research interests lie within modern Italian culture. He translated and co-edited (with Marco Belpoliti) *Primo Levi, The Voice of Memory. Interviews 1961–1981* (2000); and is the author of *Pasolini. Forms of Subjectivity* (1997) and *Primo Levi's Ordinary Virtues. From Testimony to Ethics* (2002).
Articles contributed to *Holocaust Literature*: Primo Levi.

Claudia Hoffer Gosselin, lecturer in French at California State University, Long Beach, teaches all levels of French language and literature, with a focus on translation. She serves as well as literary and technical editor of *The Translators' French Quarter,* sponsored by the department of Romance, German, Russian languages and literatures. A specialist on the contemporary French author, Claude Simon, she will be contributing an article on his World War II novel *La Route des Flandres* to a volume of essays to be published in 2003.
Articles contributed to *Holocaust Literature*: Pierre Gascar.

Tresa Grauer is a lecturer in the department of foreign literatures and linguistics at Ben-Gurion University of the Negev. Her recent publications include " 'The Changing Same': Narratives of Contemporary Jewish American Identity," in *Mapping Jewish Identities,* ed. Larry Silberstein, and " 'A Drastically Bifurcated Legacy:' Homeland and Jewish Identity in Contemporary Jewish American Literature," in *Divergent Jewish Cultures: Israel and America,* Deborah Dash Moore and S. Ilan Troen, eds.
Articles contributed to *Holocaust Literature*: Jerome Badanes.

Michael Greenstein is an adjunct professor of Jewish studies, McGill University. Author of *Third Solitudes: Tradition and Discontinuity in Canadian-Jewish Literature* (1989), he has published seventy articles on Jewish literature and is currently editing *Contemporary Jewish Writing in Canada.*
Articles contributed to *Holocaust Literature*: Leonard Cohen; A. M. Klein; Henry Kreisel; Irving Layton; Elias Wolf Mandel; Mordecai Richler; J. J. Steinfeld.

Charles Grimes is an assistant professor of English and theater at Saint Leo University. He has published articles on Harold Pinter's *Ashes to Ashes* and *The Dumb Waiter.* His essay "Bernard Shaw's Theory of Political Theatre: Difficulties from the Vantages of Postmodern and Modern Types of the Self" appeared in *Shaw: The Annual of Bernard Shaw Studies* (2002).
Articles contributed to *Holocaust Literature*: PETER BARNES; HAROLD PINTER.

Hanoch Guy was awarded a Ph.D. in modern Hebrew poetry by Dropsie College and an Ed.D. by Temple University, where he teaches. His specialty is Yiddish and Hebrew poetry of the *Shoah.* He has published articles and presented papers in U.S. conferences and in Oxford and Israel. Guy is preparing for publication a volume of poetry entitled: *Terra Treblinka.*
Articles contributed to *Holocaust Literature*: YEHUDAH AMICHAI; AMIR GILBOA; URI ZVI GREENBERG.

Marlene Heinemann is an instructor of English at Edmonds Community College. She is the author of *Gender and Destiny: Women Writers and the Holocaust* (1986). Heinemann, who holds a Ph.D. in comparative literature from Indiana University, has taught all levels of German to American college students at five universities.
Articles contributed to *Holocaust Literature*: LIVIA BITTON-JACKSON; GERDA WEISSMANN KLEIN.

Kathryn Hellerstein is a senior fellow in Yiddish and Jewish studies at the University of Pennsylvania. Educated at Wellesley, Brandeis, and Stanford, she is known as a poet and a translator, as well as a scholar of Yiddish poetry. Hellerstein's books include her translation and study of Moyshe-Leyb Halpern's poems, *In New York: A Selection,* (1982), *Paper Bridges: Selected Poems of Kadya Molodowsky* (1999), and *Jewish American Literature: A Norton Anthology,* of which she is co-editor (2000). Her current projects include *Anthology of Women Yiddish Poets* and a critical book, *A Question of Tradition: Women Poets in Yiddish,* supported in 1999–2000 by a fellowship from the Guggenheim Foundation.
Articles contributed to *Holocaust Literature*: KADYA MOLODOWSKY.

Donna Krolik Hollenberg is an associate professor of English at the University of Connecticut. She has published two books about H. D. (Hilda Doolittle) as well as essays about other twentieth-century writers in the U.S. and in Canada. Most recently, she has edited a collection of essays, *H. D. and Poets After* (2000). She has also published on Canadian Jewish history, "At the Western Development Museum: Ethnic Identity and the Memory of the Holocaust in the Jewish Community of Saskatoon, Sakatchewan," in *The Oral History Review.*
Articles contributed to *Holocaust Literature*: ALICIA OSTRIKER; ADRIENNE RICH.

Robert Holub teaches German literary, cultural, and intellectual history at the University of California at Berkeley. He is the author or editor of a dozen books and seventy-five essays. Among his publications are *Reception Theory* (1984), *Reflections of Realism* (1991), *Jürgen Habermas* (1991), *Crossing Borders* (1992), and *Friedrich Nietzsche* (1995). He is currently working on a study of Nietzsche and the discourses of the nineteenth century.
Articles contributed to *Holocaust Literature*: JUREK BECKER; PETER WEISS.

Sara Horowitz is the associate director of the Center for Jewish Studies at York University. Author of *Voicing the Void: Muteness and Memory in Holocaust Fiction,* which received the CHOICE Award for outstanding academic book, she has published extensively on Holocaust literature, women's studies, and contemporary Jewish writing. She is completing *Gender, Genocide, and Jewish Memory.* Co-editor of the journal *KEREM: Creative Explorations in Judaism,* she served as associate editor for fiction of *Jewish American Women Writers: A Bio-Bibliographical and Critical Sourcebook*, which received the Association of Jewish Libraries Award for outstanding Judaica reference book.
Articles contributed to *Holocaust Literature*: LOUIS BEGLEY; IDA FINK; MICHAEL TOURNIER.

Brooke Horvath, professor of English at Kent State University, served for several years as an editor with the *Review of Contemporary Fiction.* He has published articles and reviews in numerous journals and periodicals including *American Literature, Modern Fiction Studies, American Poetry Review, Southern Quarterly.* He is the editor (along with Irving Malin) of *Pynchon and Mason & Dixon* and *George Garrett's Elizabethan Trilogy*; with Joseph Dewey: *The Finer Thread, the Tighter Weave: Essays on the Short Fiction of Henry James.*
Articles contributed to *Holocaust Literature*: DANILO KIŠ.

Rita Horváth holds the M.A. in English, M.A. in archaeology, and M.A. in history from Eötvös Loránd University, Budapest, Hungary. Her Ph.D. studies were in the English literature department at Bar-Ilan

University, Israel. Her dissertation on confessional poetry was supported by a doctoral fellowship of excellence. Her major fields of interest are Holocaust literature and autobiographical writing.
Articles contributed to *Holocaust Literature*: ÁGNES GERGELY; IMRE KERTÉSZ; MIKLÓS RADNÓTI.

Edward Isser is an associate professor of theater at Holy Cross, Worchester, MA. Isser is the author of *Stages of Annihilation* (1997), and has published articles in journals such as *Modern Drama, Essays in Theatre, The Shaw Annual, The Shakespeare Bulletin.* He is the director of the Interactive Shakespeare Project and has directed productions at Stanford, University of Pennsylvania, Providence College, Brown University, and Holy Cross. He has worked on Broadway, off Broadway, and regional theatres as an actor, production manager, and stage manager.
Articles contributed to *Holocaust Literature*: JEAN-CLAUDE GRUMBERG; ROLF HOCHHUTH; BARBARA LEBOW; EMILY MANN.

Jonathan Judaken is an assistant professor of modern European cultural and intellectual history at the University of Memphis. After completing his degree at the University of California, Irvine, was a postdoctoral fellow at Hebrew University of Jerusalem. He is preparing his dissertation, ''Jean-Paul Sartre and 'the Jewish Question,' '' for publication. Judaken has published articles on Sartre in *Patterns of Prejudice, Historical Reflections/Réflexions historiques, Tympanum,* and in *Le voyage de l'intelligence* forthcoming in France. He also has published in *History Workshop Journal, Studies in Contemporary Jewry, Journal of Modern Jewish Studies* and in two forthcoming books discussing Jean-Francois Lyotard, the developing field of Jewish cultural studies and reflections on ''the Jewish Question'' in France after World War II.
Articles contributed to *Holocaust Literature*: ALAIN FINKIELKRAUT; JEAN-FRANÇOIS LYOTARD; JEAN-PAUL SARTRE.

Samuel Kassow is Northam professor of history at Trinity College. In addition to numerous articles on Russian and Jewish history, he is the author of *Students, Professors, and the State in Tsarist Russia: 1884–1917* (1989) and a co-editor of *Between Tsar and People* (1993). Kassow is working on a book, to be published by Indiana University Press, about Emanuel Ringelblum and the underground archives of the Warsaw ghetto.
Articles contributed to *Holocaust Literature*: RACHEL AUERBACH.

Judith Kauffmann is an associate professor of French at Bar-Ilan University and former head of the French department. Among her recent publications are a book on *Grotesque et Marginalité. Variations sur Albert Cohen et l'effet-Mangeclous* (2000), and the co-edition of a collection of essays on literature and World War II, LITTERATURE ET RESISTANCE (2000). She has written articles on Francophone contemporary literature, with a main focus on humor (visual and verbal, black, Jewish, and feminine), on marginality and minorities, on war, resistance and *Shoah* (in fiction and poetry).
Articles contributed to *Holocaust Literature*: ALBERT COHEN; ROMAIN GARY; ANNA LANGFUS.

Judith Kelly studied Italian at the University of Leeds, and then Hull, where she completed her doctoral dissertation on the writings of Primo Levi. She has held the post of lecturer in Italian at the universities of Leeds and Leicester, that of senior lecturer in Italian at the University of Central Lancashire, and is currently visiting lecturer in Italian at the University of Lancaster and associate lecturer with the Open University. Her publications include *Primo Levi: Recording and Reconstruction in the Testimonial Literature* (2000), an essay on translations of Primo Levi's works in the *Encyclopedia of Literary Translation* (2000), and ''Communication Holocaust Experience. Primo Levi: Source Texts and Translations'' in *Scenes of Change: Studies in Cultural Transition* (1997).
Articles contributed to *Holocaust Literature*: GIORGIO BASSANI; NATALIA GINZBURG; LIANA MILLU; GIULIANA TEDESCHI.

Samuel Khalifa is completing his Ph.D. on Patrick Modiano in the department of French literature at the Sorbonne Nouvelle. He also teaches at the Institut d'Etudes Politiques (Paris), and in business schools. His principal research concerns memory and the representation of urban space. His interests include contemporary European cinema and life writing.
Articles contributed to *Holocaust Literature*: PATRICK MODIANO; JEAN-FRANÇOIS STEINER.

Julia Klimek is an assistant professor of English at Coker College. Her research interests are autobiography, minority writing, and contemporary fiction. Her article on the use of film and photography in Edgar Reitz's film *Heimat* appeared in *Women in German Yearbook 2000,* and another, on trauma in Art Spiegelman's *Maus,* is in *Mit den Augen eines Kindes.* A book on twentieth-century immigrant autobiographies is being prepared for publication.
Articles contributed to *Holocaust Literature*: GÜNTER GRASS.

Wulf Koepke is distinguished professor of German, Texas A & M University, retired. He has written and edited books and articles on German exile literature including texts on L. Feuchtwanger, Alfred Döblin, Heinrich Mann; on German eighteenth-century literature of J. G. Herder and Jean Paul Richter. He is an active MLA member, having served as president of the German Studies Association and founding president of the International J. G. Herder Society.
Articles contributed to *Holocaust Literature*: ALFRED ANDERSCH; LION FEUCHTWANGER; EUGEN KOGON.

S. Lillian Kremer teaches courses in American literature, ethnic and women's writing, and Holocaust literature and film in the department of English at Kansas State University where she is a university distinguished professor. Holder of several NEH Fellowships and the Jewish Memorial Foundation Fellowship, she is the author of *Witness Through the Imagination: The Holocaust in Jewish American Literature* and *Women's Holocaust Writing: Memory and Imagination.* Kremer's articles have appeared in *Modern Language Studies, Contemporary Literature, Modern Jewish Studies, Saul Bellow Journal,* and *Studies in American Jewish Literature* and numerous essay collections. She is past president of the Jewish American Literature MLA Discussion Group, and serves as a juror for the Edward Lewis Wallant Prize in Jewish American literature and on the editorial board of several journals.
Articles contributed to *Holocaust Literature*: SAUL BELLOW; ARTHUR A. COHEN; HANA DEMETZ; RICHARD ELMAN; LESLIE EPSTEIN; ELŻBIETA ETTINGER; ILONA KARMEL; CYNTHIA OZICK; MARGE PIERCY; CHAIM POTOK; NORMA ROSEN; PHILIP ROTH; SUSAN FROMBERG SCHAEFFER; ISAAC BASHEVIS SINGER; GEORGE STEINER; EDWARD LEWIS WALLANT.

Phyllis B. Lassner is a senior lecturer at Northwestern University in Jewish studies, gender studies, and the writing program. She is author of two books on Anglo-Irish writer Elizabeth Bowen, many articles on interwar and World War II women writers, and most recently, *Battlegrounds of Their Own: British Women Writers of World War II.*
Articles contributed to *Holocaust Literature*: ERICA FISCHER; ANNE KARPF.

Peter Lawson has recently completed his doctoral dissertation on twentieth-century Anglo Jewish poetry at the University of Southampton, England. He is the editor of *Passionate Renewal* (2001), an anthology of Jewish poetry in Britain since 1945, published by Five Leaves. His poems, and essays on Jewish poets, have appeared in several journals, including *The Jerusalem Review, The Jewish Quarterly* and *New Voices in Jewish Thought.*
Articles contributed to *Holocaust Literature*: KAREN GERSHON; MICHAEL HAMBURGER; LOTTE KRAMER; GERDA MAYER.

Andrew Leak is a senior lecturer in French at University College, London. He is the author of books on Sartre and Barthes and editor of a volume of essays on literary representations of the Holocaust. He has written extensively on Georges Perec, and is one of Perec's English translators. Leak is currently president of the UK Society for Sartrean Studies and co-executive editor of *Sartre Studies International.*
Articles contributed to *Holocaust Literature*: GEORGES PEREC.

Sharon Leder is an associate professor of English, coordinator of the Jewish studies project at Nassau Community College, Garden City, New York. She is also coordinator of the Holocaust, Genocide, and Human Rights Institute. She is co-editor with Milton Teichman of *Truth and Lamentation: Stories and Poems of the Holocaust* (1994) and *The Burdens of History: Post-Holocaust Generations in Dialogue* (2000).
Articles contributed to *Holocaust Literature*: SARA NOMBERG-PRZYTYK; RUTH WHITMAN.

Joseph Abraham Levi holds a Ph.D. in Romance philology, (concentration: Portuguese, medieval Spanish, and Italian) from the University of Wisconsin, Madison. He has taught Portuguese at the University of Georgia and Portuguese, medieval Spanish, medieval Islam, Islam in Africa, and history of Africa at the University of Iowa. He now teaches at Rhode Island College. His publications focus on the medieval periods of the Iberian Peninsula, colonial Brazilian literature, the Sephardic Diaspora in the Americas from the sixteenth to the eighteenth centuries, history of the Portuguese expansion, the Lusophone world, as well as Portuguese philology and pedagogy.
Articles contributed to *Holocaust Literature*: CARLOS HEITOR CONY; ROBERTO DRUMMOND; MOACYR SCLIAR.

Tobe Levin is a collegiate professor at the University of Maryland in Europe. She teaches women's Holocaust memoirs published in the USA at the University of Frankfurt and reviews books on gender and the Holocaust for the *European Journal of Women's Studies.* Editor of *Feminist Europa. Review of Books* (in gender studies published in European languages other than

English) she also writes about German, Austrian, African American and Jewish women writers.
Articles contributed to *Holocaust Literature*: ALICIA APPLEMAN-JURMAN; CECILIE KLEIN; BLANCA ROSENBERG; ARANKA SIEGAL.

Madeline G. Levine is Kenan professor of Slavic literatures at the University of North Carolina, Chapel Hill. She is the author of a critical study of twentieth-century Polish poetry, *Contemporary Polish Poetry: 1925–1975* (1984), and essays on Polish literary representations of the Holocaust. Her most recent translations are *Miłosz's ABC's* by Czesław Miłosz (2001), *Lost Landscapes: In Search of Isaac Bashevis Singer and the Jews of Poland* by Agata Tuszyńska (1998), and *Bread for the Departed,* a novel of the Warsaw ghetto by Bogdan Wojdowski (1997).
Articles contributed to *Holocaust Literature*: ARTUR SANDAUER; WŁADYSŁAW SZLENGEL.

Darrell B. Lockhart is an assistant professor of Spanish at the University of Nevada, Reno. He is a specialist in Latin American Jewish literature and culture. He has published numerous articles in this area and he is the editor of *Latin American Jewish Writers: A Dictionary* (1997).
Articles contributed to *Holocaust Literature*: MARJORIE AGOSÍN; SONIA GURALNIK; SIMJA SNEH; BERNARDO VERBITSKY; ANA VINOCUR; CLARA WEIL.

Dagmar C. G. Lorenz, professor of German at the University of Illinois, Chicago, focuses her research on Austrian and German Jewish literary and cultural issues and Holocaust studies with an emphasis on history and social thought, aesthetics, and minority discourses. Recent book publications include *Keepers of the Motherland: German Texts by Jewish Women Writers* (1997), and *Verfolgung bis zu Massenmord. Duskurse zum Holocaust in deutscher Sprache* (1992). Edited volumes include *Contemporary Jewish Writing in Austria* (1999), *Transforming the Center, Eroding the Margins: Essays on Ethnic and Cultural Boundaries in German-Speaking Countries,* co-editor: Renate S. Posthofen (1998), *Insiders and Outsiders. Jewish and Gentile Culture in Germany and Austria* (1994).
Articles contributed to *Holocaust Literature*: ILSE AICHINGER; ELFRIEDE JELINEK.

Magdalena Maiz-Peña is an associate professor at Davidson College, North Carolina. Born and raised in Mexico, she holds a Ph.D. from Arizona State University. She is the author of *Identidad, nación y gesto autobiográfico* (1998), and co-author of *Modalidades de representación del sujeto auto/biográfico femenino* (Universidad Autónoma de Nuevo Léon, 1997). Her research is centered around gender, auto/biography, and biographical studies in Latin America. She is co-editing ''Género, discurso y resistencia: Elena Poniatowska ante la crítica,'' to be published in Mexico, and working on a monographic project, *Gender, Proper Names, & Auto/Biographical Signatures: Mexico 1920–1950.* She serves on several MLA and other academic committees.
Articles contributed to *Holocaust Literature*: ANA VÁSQUEZ-BRONFMAN.

Paul Marcus is a psychoanalyst in private practice. He is the author of *Autonomy in the Extreme Situation: Bruno Bettelheim, the Nazi Concentration Camps and the Mass Society.*
Articles contributed to *Holocaust Literature*: BRUNO BETTELHEIM.

Diane Matza is a professor of English at Utica College. She has written widely on the immigrant experience of Sephardi Jews in America and about Sephardi American writers. Her work has appeared in *Midstream, Shofar, American Jewish Archives,* and *American Jewish History.* She is the editor of *Sephardic American Voices: 200 Years of a Literary Legacy.*
Articles contributed to *Holocaust Literature*: GINI ALHADEFF; REBECCA CAMHI FROMER.

Steve McCullough is a doctoral candidate at Dalhousie University and editor of the journal *Henry Street: A Graduate Review of Literary Studies.* He is pursuing dissertation research into deconstruction, feminism, and women's Holocaust memoirs.
Articles contributed to *Holocaust Literature*: SARAH KOFMAN; ANNE MICHAELS.

David Mesher is a professor of English and humanities and coordinator of Jewish studies at San Jose State University. He has published articles on such Jewish writers as Hannah Arendt, Saul Bellow, Bernard Malamud, Arthur Miller, and I. B. Singer.
Articles contributed to *Holocaust Literature*: CHARLOTTE DELBO; LADISLAV FUKS; ANDRÉ SCHWARZ-BART; JIŘÍ WEIL.

Joan Michelson is an associate senior lecturer in English: creative writing and Holocaust studies at the University of Wolverhampton, England. Her essays, reviews, fiction, and poetry have been published in periodicals and anthologies including *The Jewish Quarterly, The Dybbuk of Delight: An Anthology of Jewish Women's Poetry, The British Journal of Holocaust Education,* the British Council's annual antholo-

gies of new writing from England and *Remembering the Future: The Holocaust in an Age of Genocide* (2001). She has received writing awards from the Poetry Society of England, the Virginia Center for the Arts (USA) and been a writer-in-residence at the Kunstlerhaus, Schwandorf, Germany.
Articles contributed to *Holocaust Literature*: IRENA KLEPFISZ.

Goldie Morgentaler is an associate professor of English at the University of Lethbridge. She is author of *Dickens and Heredity* (2000) and of several scholarly articles on Dickens. She has also published numerous translations from Yiddish to English, including the novels and short fiction of Chava Rosenfarb and the stories of I. L. Peretz.
Articles contributed to *Holocaust Literature*: RACHEL KORN; CHAVA ROSENFARB; SIMKHA-BUNIM SHAYEVITCH.

David Myers is an associate professor of English and religious studies at Texas A&M University. Author of *The Elephants Teach: Creative Writing Since 1880* (1996), his Holocaust publications include ''Responsible for Every Single Pain'' in *Comparative Literature* and ''Jews Without Memory'' in *American Literary History.* He is now completing a book-length study, *Canonizing the Holocaust.*
Articles contributed to *Holocaust Literature*: JEAN AMÉRY.

Alice S. Nakhimovsky is a professor of Russian and chair of the department of Russian at Colgate University, and an active member in Colgate's program in Jewish studies. Her research interests are in Russian Jewish literature, culture, and behavior. Among her books are *Russian Jewish Literature and Identity* (1992) and, together with Alexander Nakhimovsky, *Witness To History: The Photographs of Yevgeny Khaldei* (1997). Most recently, she has written on the Russian writers Il'ya Il'f and Mikhail Zhvanetsky, and translated the autobiography of the artist Grisha Bruskin. Her teaching at Colgate includes courses in Russian literature, Russian language, and Jewish literature.
Articles contributed to *Holocaust Literature*: VASILII GROSSMAN; YEVGENII YEVTUSHENKO.

Stanley Nash is a professor of Hebrew literature at Hebrew Union College-Jewish Institute of Religion in New York City. He is the author of *In Search of Hebraism: Shai Hurwitz and His Polemics in the Hebrew Press*; editor of *Migvan: Studies in Honor of Jacob Kabakoff*; and *Ben Historiyyah le-Sifrut: Studies in Honor of Isaac Barzila*; and has written numerous articles on Hebrew literary figures, novels, themes and trends. Nash holds a Ph.D. from Columbia University and Rabbinic Ordination from Jewish Theological Seminary. He has lectured and written widely in both English and Hebrew and is the author of numerous articles in *Prooftexts* and *Hadoar.* He is working on a book on the Hebrew novelist Aharon Megged. Nash has also taught at Cornell University, University of Pennsylvania, Columbia University, Jewish Theological Seminary, New York University, Drew University, and campuses of the City University of New York.
Articles contributed to *Holocaust Literature*: AHARON MEGGED.

Anita Norich is an associate professor of English and Judaic studies at the University of Michigan. She is the author of *The Homeless Imagination in the Fiction of Israel Joshua Singer* (1991), and co-editor of *Gender and Text in Modern Hebrew and Yiddish Literatures* (1992). She teaches, lectures, and publishes on a range of topics concerning Yiddish language and literature, modern Jewish culture, Jewish American literature, and Holocaust literature.
Articles contributed to *Holocaust Literature*: ISRAEL JOSHUA SINGER.

Ranen Omer-Sherman is an assistant professor at the University of Miami where he teaches courses in English and Jewish studies. His essays on Jewish writers have appeared in journals such as *Texas Studies in Literature and Language, Religion and Literature, MELUS, Shofar,* and *Modernism/Modernity.* His recent book is *Diaspora and Zionism in the Jewish-American Imagination* (2002).
Articles contributed to *Holocaust Literature*: DAVID GROSSMAN; DAN PAGIS; CHARLES REZNIKOFF.

Michael Ossar is a professor at Kansas State University where he has served as head of the department of modern languages. He holds a Ph.D. from the University of Pennsylvania and studied at the Freie Universität, Berlin. He has taught at Swarthmore College, the University of Freiburg, the University of Giessen, and Sweet Briar College. He is the author of *Anarchism in the Dramas of Ernst Toller.* He has published essays on Franz Kafka, Paul Celan, Arthur Schnitzler, Barbara Frischmuth, Adolf Muschg, Heinrich von Kleist, Goethe, Ernst Toller, Christoph Hein, and others.
Articles contributed to *Holocaust Literature*: VICTOR KLEMPERER; RUTH KLÜGER; ANNA MITGUTSCH; ROBERT SCHINDEL.

Harriet L. Parmet is a professor emerita in the department of modern foreign languages and literature, Le-

high University, where she taught Hebrew. She specializes in modern Israeli literature in translation, particularly the work of women writers. She was the co-author of a study of feminist religious views on reproductive technologies and a major article on Haviva Reik, a heroine of the Holocaust. Co-founder of Lehigh University's Jewish studies program, she has published in *Midstream, Feminist Teacher, Journal of Feminist Studies in Religion, Jewish Spectator,* NEMLA *Modern Language Studies, Studies in American Jewish Literature, Shofar, Visions International, Hakol, Literary Review and Jewish Women in America—An Historical Encyclopedia.* Parmet is the author of *The Terror of Our Days: Four American Poets Respond to the Holocaust* (2001).
Articles contributed to *Holocaust Literature*: LEA GOLDBERG; SIMON WIESENTHAL.

Susan Pentlin is a professor of modern languages at Central Missouri State University. She was a Fulbright exchange teacher in West Germany, attended a Fulbright summer seminar in Bonn and has also received a grant from the American Council of Learned Societies. She received her M.A. in German from the University of Missouri and her Ph.D. from the University of Kansas. She is preparing a new edition of *Warsaw Ghetto: A Diary* and serves as a commissioner on the Missouri Commission on Human Rights.
Articles contributed to *Holocaust Literature*: MARY BERG; JUDITH STRICK DRIBBEN.

Sanford Pinsker, Shadek professor of humanities at Franklin and Marshall College, writes about American literature and culture for such journals as *The Georgia Review, Partisan Review,* and *The Virginia Quarterly.* His books include: *Jewish American Fiction: 1917–1987* (1992), *Understanding Joseph Heller* (1991), and *The Uncompromising Fictions of Cynthia Ozick* (1987), *The Schlemiel as Metaphor* (1971). For many years he was the co-editor of *Holocaust Studies Annual.*
Articles contributed to *Holocaust Literature*: JACQUELINE OSHEROW; JOSEPH SKIBELL; GERALD STERN.

Timothy E. Pytell, visiting assistant professor, Colorado College, is author of numerous articles on Viktor Frankl and currently working on a book for Cornell University Press: *Paradoxical Intention: Viktor Frankl's Struggle for Meaning.*
Articles contributed to *Holocaust Literature*: VIKTOR FRANKL.

Gila Ramras-Rauch, is Lewis H. and Selma Weinstein professor of Jewish literature at Hebrew College, Boston. Her research has focused on Hebrew literature, modern Israeli literature, the Bible as literature, comparative literature, and Holocaust literature. In addition to many articles, she published *The Protagonist in Transition* (1982) and co-edited and wrote the introduction to an anthology *Facing the Holocaust* (1985). She has published two books, *The Arab in Israeli Literature* (1989), and *Aharon Appelfeld: The Holocaust and Beyond* (1994) Ramras-Rauch was awarded a fellowship grant by the National Endowment for the Humanities.
Articles contributed to *Holocaust Literature*: AHARON APPELFELD; ITAMAR YAOZ-KEST.

Martha Ravits is an assistant professor and acting director of women's studies at the University of Oregon and an educational consultant. She has published in the fields of American and European literature in both literary and interdisciplinary journals. Her specialty is twentieth-century women's literature.
Articles contributed to *Holocaust Literature*: ANNE FRANK; JUDITH MAGYAR ISAACSON.

Karen Remmler teaches German studies, critical social thought, women's studies and Jewish studies at Mount Holyoke College and co-directs the Weissman Center for Leadership. Her recent scholarship includes a co-edited anthology of Jewish writing in Germany (with Leslie Morris), a special issue of *German Quarterly* on "Sites of Memory" (with Amir Eshel), a lead article, "Encounters across the Void," in a collection on the unlikely history of German Jewish symbiosis edited by Jack Zipes and Leslie Morris, and articles on the German Jewish writer Barbara Honigmann, teaching the Holocaust, and issues of memory in contemporary Germany.
Articles contributed to *Holocaust Literature*: BARBARA HONIGMANN.

Jennifer Ring is professor of political science and director of women's studies at the University of Nevada, Reno. She is the author of *Modern Political Theory and Contemporary Feminism: A Dialectical Analysis*, and *The Political Consequences of Thinking: Gender and Judaism in the Work of Hannah Arendt*, as well as scholarly articles and chapters for volumes in political theory, feminist theory, and multicultural theory.
Articles contributed to *Holocaust Literature*: HANNAH ARENDT.

Theodosia Robertson is an associate professor in history at University of Michigan-Flint. She is the translator of *The Eternal Moment* by Aleksander Fiut (study of poetry of Czesław Miłosz), *Regions of the Great*

Heresy by Jerzy Ficowski (study of life and works of Bruno Schulz), and author of several articles and book chapters on Bruno Schulz.
Articles contributed to *Holocaust Literature*: JERZY FICOWSKI; JADWIGA MAURER.

Alan Rosen is a lecturer in English literature, Bar-Ilan University. He is author of a book on typology and catastrophe, *Dislocating the End,* editor of *Celebrating Elie Wiesel,* and author of articles on Holocaust literature and film, including Eliach, Spiegelman, Wallant, and Wiesel. He is at work on a book tentatively entitled *Sounds of Defiance: The Holocaust, Multilingualism, and the Problem of English.*
Articles contributed to *Holocaust Literature*: YAFFA ELIACH; ELIE WIESEL.

Thane Rosenbaum is the author of *The Golems of Gotham* (2002), *Second Hand Smoke,* which was a finalist for the National Jewish Book Award in 1999, and *Elijah Visible,* which received the Edward Lewis Wallant Book Award in 1996. His articles, reviews and essays appear frequently in *The New York Times, Los Angeles Times, The Wall Street Journal,* among other national publications. He is also the literary editor of *Tikkun.* He teaches human rights, legal humanities, and law and literature at Fordham Law School. His forthcoming nonfiction book is *Immoral Justice: Cultural Obsession and Popular Discontent in American Law.*
Articles contributed to *Holocaust Literature*: MARCIE HERSHMAN.

Michael Rothberg is an associate professor of English and comparative literature at the University of Illinois at Urbana-Champaign. He is the author of *Traumatic Realism: The Demands of Holocaust Representation* (2000) and the co-editor, with Neil Levi, of *The Holocaust: Theoretical Readings in History, Memory, and Criticism* (forthcoming in 2003). He is working on a book concerning intersections between post-Holocaust and postcolonial writings; one essay from that project on W. E. B. Du Bois has been published in *The Yale Journal of Criticism.*
Articles contributed to *Holocaust Literature*: GEOFFREY HARTMAN.

Rochelle G. Saidel is the founder and director of the Remember the Women Institute, based in New York, which carries out academic research and cultural projects that integrate women into history. Her book on Jewish women at Ravensbrück concentration camp will be published by University of Wisconsin Press in 2003. A political scientist, she is also a senior researcher at NEMGE–The Center for the Study of Women and Gender, University of São Paulo, Brazil. She is the author of *Never Too Late to Remember: The Politics Behind New York City's Holocaust Museum* (1996), and *The Outraged Conscience: Seekers of Justice for Nazi War Criminals in America* (1984).
Articles contributed to *Holocaust Literature*: VLADKA MEED; NECHAMA TEC.

Ellen Schiff is a professor emerita of French and comparative literature at Massachusetts College of Liberal Arts. She is the author of *From Stereotype to Metaphor: The Jew in Contemporary Drama,* the editor of the first two-volume anthology of American Jewish plays: *Awake and Singing and Fruitful and Multiplying,* and advisory editor of *Jewish American Women Writers.* Her essays and articles are published widely. A frequent lecturer, she serves as a consultant on drama to the National Foundation of Jewish Culture and a juror in its new Jewish plays commission.
Articles contributed to *Holocaust Literature*: LILIANE ATLAN; LEENY SACK.

Ernestine Schlant is a professor of German and comparative literature at Montclair State University. She is author of two studies on the Austrian refugee Hermann Brock, numerous articles on twentieth-century German and Austrian literature, co-editor of *Legacies and Ambiguities: Postwar Fiction and Culture in West Germany and Japan* (1991) and author of *The Language of Silence: West German Literature and the Holocaust* (1999).
Articles contributed to *Holocaust Literature*: GERT HOFMANN; W. G. SEBALD.

Daniel R. Schwarz is a professor of English and Stephen H. Weiss presidential fellow at Cornell University. He has received Cornell's College of arts and sciences Russell Award for distinguished teaching. He is the author of the widely read *Imagining the Holocaust* (1999). His most recent book is *Rereading Conrad* (2001). His prior books include *Reconfiguring Modernism: Explorations in the Relationship Between Modern Art and Modern Literature* (1997), *Narrative and Representation in Wallace Stevens* (1993), *The Case for a Humanistic Poetics* (1991), *The Transformation of the English Novel, 1890–1930* (1989; revised 1995), *Reading Joyce's "Ulysses"* (1987), *The Humanistic Heritage: Critical Theories of the English Novel from James to Hillis Miller* (1986), *Conrad: The Later Fiction* (1982), *Conrad: "Almayer's Folly" through "Under Western Eyes"* (1980), and *Disraeli's Fiction* (1979). He has directed nine NEH seminars,

and has lectured widely in the United States and abroad.
Articles contributed to *Holocaust Literature*: TADEUSZ BOROWSKI; JERZY KOSINSKI; WILLIAM STYRON.

Mark Scroggins is an associate professor of English at Florida Atlantic University. He is the author of *Louis Zukofsky and the Poetry of Knowledge* (1998) and editor of the collection *Upper Limit Music: The Writing of Louis Zukofsky* (1998). He has edited a selection of uncollected prose for *Prepositions + The Collected Critical Essays of Louis Zukofsky* (2000). He has published essays on and reviews of a wide variety of contemporary poets, and is writing a critical biography of Louis Zukofsky.
Articles contributed to *Holocaust Literature*: GEOFFREY HILL; LOUIS ZUKOFSKY.

Monika Shafi is a professor of German in the department of foreign languages and literatures at the University of Delaware. She is the author of "Utopische Entwürfe in der Literatur von Frauen" (1989), "Gertrud Kolmar: Eine Einführung in das Werk" (1995), and of "Multiple Movements: Intercultural Encounters in Contemporary German and Austrian Literature" (forthcoming). She has published on nineteenth- and twentieth-century German authors, among them Annette von Droste-Hülshoff, Theodor Fontane, Irmgard Keun, Christa Wolf, Ingeborg Drewitz, and Günter Grass.
Articles contributed to *Holocaust Literature*: GERTRUD KOLMAR.

Susan Shapiro is an associate professor of Judaic & Near Eastern studies at the University of Massachusetts, Amherst. She is the author of *Recovering the Sacred: Ethics, Hermeneutics, and Theology after the Holocaust* (forthcoming). Her articles and reviews have appeared in *Judaism, Journal of the American Academy of Religion, Religious Studies Review, Semeia, Concilium, Harvard Divinity Bulletin,* among many other journals and collected volumes. Shapiro has also been awarded a number of prestigious fellowships and grants, including a Harvard University Divinity School fellowship in women and religion, a Yad Hanadiv fellowship at the Hebrew University in Jerusalem, a Stroum teaching fellowship at the University of Washington, and an ACLS grant, among others.
Articles contributed to *Holocaust Literature*: EMIL FACKENHEIM; EMMANUEL LEVINAS.

Ziva Shavitsky is an associate professor and head of the Hebrew and Jewish studies department at the University of Melbourne. She is past president of the Australian Association for Jewish Studies in Australia and also co-editor of the *Australian Journal of Jewish Studies.* She has published many articles on Hebrew literature as well as *The People of Israel in Exile, in Syria, Mesopotamia, and Persia up to the Time of Alexander the Great,* and *The Representation of German Jewry in 20th Century Hebrew Literature.*
Articles contributed to *Holocaust Literature*: KA. TZETNIK 135633; YITZHAK KATZENELSON.

Efraim Sicher teaches British and comparative literature at Ben-Gurion University of the Negev. A graduate of London University, he did his doctoral work at Oxford, and held a junior research fellowship at Wolfson College. His publications include books and essays on a wide range of topics in modern Jewish culture, as well as English and comparative literature. His collection of essays on Holocaust memory, *Breaking Crystal: Writing and Memory after Auschwitz,* appeared in 1998.
Articles contributed to *Holocaust Literature*: CARL FRIEDMAN; MICHAL GOVRIN; ARYEH LEV STOLLMAN.

Johan P. Snapper is the Queen Beatrix professor of Dutch language, literature, and culture at the University of California at Berkeley. He has published fourteen books, the most recent is a monograph on Marga Minco (1999), that is scheduled to appear in English in 2003. The majority of his publications deal with postwar Dutch literature, especially the *Shoah.*
Articles contributed to *Holocaust Literature*: MARGA MINCO.

Naomi Sokoloff is a professor of Hebrew language and literature at the University of Washington, where she has served as chair of the Jewish studies program and as chair of the department of Near Eastern languages and civilization. She completed her Ph.D. in comparative literature at Princeton University. Her publications include *Imagining the Child in Modern Jewish Fiction*, and a number of edited volumes: *Gender and Text in Modern Hebrew and Yiddish Literature, Infant Tongues: The Voice of the Child in Literature, Israel and America: Cross Cultural Encounters and the Literary Imagination* (a special issue of the journal *Shofar*), and *Books on Israel, Vol. VI* (forthcoming). Her essays on literary responses to the Holocaust have examined the writing of David Grossman, Aharon Appelfeld, Dan Pagis, Jerzy Kosinski, Louis Begley, Gila Almagor, Aharon Megged, and Uri Orlev. She serves on the editorial boards of *Prooftexts, Shofar,* and *Hebrew Studies.* Sokoloff has been the recipient of a Fulbright-Hays faculty research grant and of grants from NEH and ACLS.
Articles contributed to *Holocaust Literature*: GILA ALMAGOR.

Ruth Starkman is a visiting assistant professor of German at UCLA. She has taught in the department of modern languages and literatures at the University of Utah and the departments of rhetoric and Scandinavian at Berkeley. Her areas of specialization are twentieth-century German literature and film, the Holocaust and postwar German culture. Recent articles have appeared in *Seminar, Film Quarterly, The Historical Journal of Film, Radio and Television.* She wrote her dissertation on Austrian author Thomas Bernhard and is currently finishing a book-length project on Jewish and non-Jewish writers in Austria after World War II.
Articles contributed to *Holocaust Literature*: THOMAS BERNHARD; PETER GAY.

Ilan Stavans is the Lewis-Sebring professor of Latin American and Latino culture at Amherst College. His books include *The Hispanic Condition* (1995), *The Oxford Book of Jewish Stories* (1998), and *On Borrowed Words* (2001). His work has been translated into half a dozen languages.
Articles contributed to *Holocaust Literature*: JORGE LUIS BORGES; ALCINA LUBITCH DOMECQ.

Hartmut Steinecke is a professor of German literature at the University of Paderborn. He studied German literature, philosophy, and history and completed the Dr. Phil. at the University of Bonn. He has been a visiting professor at the Chicago, Cornell, Dartmouth, Michigan, Kansas, Washington (St. Louis) and in several European universities. His books include volumes on theory of the novel, Hoffmann and Heine, contemporary German literature, and Austrian literature from Lenau to Broch. He has published more than 100 articles and has two books (Hermann Broch, Jenny Aloni) and many articles about Jewish authors. His most recent work is: *Deutsch-jüdische Literatur der neunziger Jahre. Die Generation nach der Shoah* (co-ed., 2002).
Articles contributed to *Holocaust Literature*: JENNY ALONI; ANNE DUDEN.

Peter Stenberg is head of the department of German studies, University of British Columbia. He earned his B.A. at Wesleyan, and his M.A. and Ph.D. at the University of California, Berkeley. Awarded Humboldt Foundation fellowships in 1980 and 1985, he was selected for a Swedish Institute fellowship in 1990. He has published many essays on Austrian, German, and Swedish literature and a book on literary presentation of Yiddish and German in Eastern Europe, *Journey to Oblivion* (1991). His current project is *Contemporary Jewish Writing in Sweden,* an anthology to be published in 2003.
Articles contributed to *Holocaust Literature*: JAKOV LIND; MANES SPERBER.

Michael Taub is an associate professor in the department of Judaic studies at the State University of New York at Binghamton. He has also been a visiting professor at Vassar College. Taub has written many books on Jewish studies and translated Israeli drama into English. He is editor of *Modern Israeli Drama in Translation* (1996), also co-editor with Joel Shatzky of *Contemporary Jewish-American Fiction: A Bio-Bibliographical and Critical Sourcebook* (1997), and *Contemporary Jewish-American Dramatists and Poets: A Bio-Critical Sourcebook* (1999).
Articles contributed to *Holocaust Literature*: MOTTI LERNER; BEN ZION TOMER.

Nechama Tec is a professor of sociology at the University of Connecticut at Stamford. She is also a senior research fellow for the study of Jewish resistance at the U.S. Holocaust Memorial Museum, and was appointed by President George W. Bush to the museum's council. Author of numerous articles, she has published book-length works, including *Defiance: The Bielski Partisans* (1993), *In the Lion's Den: The Life of Oswald Rufeisen* (1990), *When Light Pierced the Darkness: Christian Rescue of Jews in Nazi-Occupied Poland* (1986), *Dry Tears: The Story of a Lost Childhood* (1984), and *Resilience and Courage: Women, Men, and the Holocaust* (2003).
Articles contributed to *Holocaust Literature*: JAN KARSKI; EMANUEL RINGELBLUM.

Claire Tylee is a senior lecturer in English literature at Brunel University. She previously lectured at Leicester University, UK, and Málaga University, Spain. Her publications include *The Great War and Women's Consciousness* (1990), and articles on twentieth-century women's writing. She recently edited an international anthology, *War Plays by Women* (1999), and a collection of essays, *Women, World War I, and the Dramatic Imagination* (2000).
Articles contributed to *Holocaust Literature*: ELAINE FEINSTEIN; DIANE SAMUEL; LORE SEGAL.

Sue Vice is a reader in English literature at the University of Sheffield. Her recent publications include *Introducing Bakhtin* (1997), and *Holocaust Fiction* (2000).
Articles contributed to *Holocaust Literature*: MARTIN AMIS; THOMAS KENNEALLY.

Daniel Walden, professor emeritus of American studies, English, and comparative literature at Penn State

University, has published some thirty books, including *On Being Black: African American Literature* (1970), *On Being Jewish: American Jewish Literature from Abraham Cahan to Saul Bellow* (1974), *Twentieth-Century American Jewish Fiction Writers* (1984), and *Conversations with Chaim Potok* (2001). Editor of *Studies in American Jewish Literature* since 1975, Walden has taught courses in literature and the Holocaust, women writing the Holocaust, and Jewish literature: the international perspective.
Articles contributed to *Holocaust Literature*: HARVEY GROSSINGER.

Eileen H. Watts has published articles on Bernard Malamud in *MELUS* (Multi-Ethnic Literature of the United States), *Prospects for the Study of American Literature, Studies in American Jewish Literature,* and on Malamud and Kafka in *Modern Jewish Studies Annual* for 2002. Her work has also appeared in *American Imago, Modern Language Studies*, and *The Journal of Psychology and Judaism.* She has written on Malamud's use of the Holocaust in *The Magic Worlds of Bernard Malamud*, and has served as bibliographer for the Bernard Malamud Society since 1993.
Articles contributed to *Holocaust Literature*: BERNARD MALAMUD.

Gary Weissman is a visiting assistant professor of English at East Carolina University. His essays have appeared in *Confronting the Holocaust: A Mandate for the 21st Century, Part Two,* and *Media, Culture and Society.* A Fulbright grant and a Jacob K. Javits fellowship have supported his work. His teaching interests include Holocaust studies, media studies, literary theory, and the visual arts.
Articles contributed to *Holocaust Literature*: ROBERT HARRIS; FRANCINE PROSE; HELEN SCHULMAN; D. M. THOMAS.

Ruth Wisse is the Martin Peretz professor of Yiddish literature and professor of comparative literature at Harvard University. She is the author of *The Modern Jewish Canon: A Journey through Language and Culture* (2000), *If I Am Not For Myself: The Liberal Betrayal of the Jews* (1992), *I.L. Peretz and the Making of Modern Jewish Culture* (1991), *A Little Love in Big Manhattan* (1988), and *The Schlemiel as Modern Hero* (1971). She is the editor of several volumes of translated Yiddish literature and a frequent writer on cultural and political affairs.
Articles contributed to *Holocaust Literature*: ABRAHAM SUTZKEVER.

Hanna Yaoz is an associate professor and the director of the Sal Van Gelder Center for teaching and research of Holocaust literature at Bar Ilan University. Her research interests include Holocaust literature, modern Hebrew poetry, empathy of high-school students with Holocaust survivors, values in education, and pedagogical methods. She has written or edited four volumes on Holocaust literature: *Holocaust in Hebrew literature as Historical and Trans-historical Fiction* (1980), *The Holocaust in Modern Hebrew Poetry* (1984), *The Scream and the Melody* (1995), *Three Generations of Holocaust Poets* (forthcoming); and sixty essays and articles.
Articles contributed to *Holocaust Literature*: TANYA HADAR.

Leon Yudkin teaches Hebrew and comparative literature at University College, London and has lectured in the United States, France, and Australia. He is the author of *Isaac Lamdan: A Study in Twentieth-Century Hebrew Poetry* (1971), *Escape into Siege: A Survey of Israeli Literature Today* (1974), *Jewish Writing and Identity in the Twentieth Century* (1982), *1948 and After: Aspects of Israeli Fiction* (1984), *On the Poetry of Uri Zvi Greenberg* (in Hebrew, 1987), *Else Lasker-Schüler: A Study in German Jewish Literature* (1991), *Beyond Sequence: Current Israeli Fiction and Its Context* (1992), *A Home Within: Varieties of Jewish Expression in Modern Fiction* (1996), and *Public Crisis and Literary Response: The Adjustment of Modern Jewish Literature* (2001). He has edited five books and has published articles in the UK, USA, Israel, and Europe.
Articles contributed to *Holocaust Literature*: ABBA KOVNER; SAVYON LIEBRECHT.

Eric Zakim is an assistant professor at Duke University where he teaches modern Hebrew literature and Israeli culture in the department of Asian and African languages and literature. His M.A. and Ph.D. were received from the University of California, Berkeley, in comparative literature. Among his publications are "Palimsests of Identity: Israel at the End of the American Century," in *Shofar,* and "Between Fragment and Authority in David Fogel's (Re)Presention of Subjectivity," in the special issue of *Prooftexts* he co-edited on "David Fogel and the Emergence of Modernist Hebrew Poetry." He is now working on the relationship between landscape aesthetics and Zionist ideology.
Articles contributed to *Holocaust Literature*: RONIT LENTIN; RIVKA MIRIAM; AMOS OZ.

Katarzyna Zechenter teaches Polish literature and culture at the school of Slavonic and East European studies, University College, London. She has written on contemporary Polish literature and has a special inter-

est in Polish Jewish writers. She has written on Jadwiga Maurer for *Polin: Studies in Polish Jewry (2002).* Her other publications include nine articles on Polish literature for *The Encyclopedia of Modern East Europe 1815–1989. From the Congress of Vienna to the Fall of Communism.* (2000); ''Homeland without a Home—Tadeusz Konwicki's Experience of Home'' for *Home/Less: The Polish Experience* (2002), articles on Feliks Gawdzicki, Gracjan Piotrowski, and Wincenty Reklewski for *Pisarze regionu świetokrzyskiego* (1990) and an article on Hipacy Pociej and the Brest' Union for *Analecta Cracoviensia* (1988). Her book *Curse or Glory: Polish History and Politics in Tadeusz Konwicki's Fiction* is forthcoming.
Articles contributed to *Holocaust Literature*: MAREK EDELMAN; MICHAŁ GLOWIŃSKI; MAREK RYMKIEWICZ.

Wendy Zierler received her M.A. and Ph.D. degrees in comparative literature from Princeton University. A former Fulbright scholar and Whiting fellow, she served as research fellow in the department of English at the University of Hong Kong where she taught ethnic American literature and American studies. She is an assistant professor of modern Jewish literature and feminist studies at Hebrew Union College–Jewish Institute of Religion, New York. Her book, *And Rachel Stole the Idols: The Emergence of Modern Hebrew Women's Writing*, is forthcoming from Wayne State University Press.
Articles contributed to *Holocaust Literature*: ANDA AMIR-PINKERFELD; CARYL PHILIPS.

Joshua D. Zimmerman is an assistant professor of East European Jewish history and Holocaust studies at Yeshiva University. His Ph.D. was completed at Brandeis University. He is author of *Contested Memories: Poles and Jews during the Holocaust and Its Aftermath* (forthcoming).
Articles contributed to *Holocaust Literature*: ADAM CZERNIAKOW; CHAIM A. KAPLAN.

APPENDIX: AUTHOR BIRTHPLACE AND LANGUAGE OF COMPOSITION

Author	Birthplace	Language of Composition
Agosín, Marjorie	USA	Spanish
Aichinger, Ilse	Austria	German
Alhadeff, Gini	Egypt	English
Almagor, Gila	Israel	Hebrew
Aloni, Jenny	Germany	German, Hebrew
Améry, Jean	Austria	German
Amichai, Yehudah	Germany	Hebrew
Amir-Pinkerfeld, Anda	Austria-Hungary (Poland)	Polish, Hebrew
Amis, Martin	England	English
Andersch, Alfred	Germany	German
Andrzejewski, Jerzy	Poland	Polish
Antelme, Robert	Corsica	French
Appelfeld, Aharon	Romania	Hebrew
Appignanesi, Lisa	Poland	English
Appleman-Jurman, Alicia	Poland	English
Arendt, Hannah	Germany	German, English
Ascher, Carol	USA	English
Atlan, Liliane	France	French
Auerbach, Rachel	Poland	Yiddish, Polish
Badanes, Jerome	USA	English
Baitz, Jon Robin	USA	English
Baker, Mark Raphael	Australia	English
Barnes, Peter	England	English
Bartov, Hanoch	Palestine (Israel)	Hebrew
Bassani, Giorgio	Italy	Italian
Bauman, Janina	Poland	Polish, English
Becker, Jurek	Poland	German
Begley, Louis	Poland	English
Bellow, Saul	Canada	English
Benski, Stanisław	Poland	Polish
Berg, Mary	Poland	Yiddish, Polish
Berger, Joseph	Russia	English
Bernhard, Thomas	Netherlands	German
Bettelheim, Bruno	Austria	English
Biderman, Abraham	Poland	English
Biller, Maxim	Czechoslovakia (Czech Republic)	German
Birenbaum, Halina	Poland	Polish
Bitton-Jackson, Livia	Czechoslovakia (Czech Republic)	English
Böll, Heinrich	Germany	German
Borges, Jorge Luis	Argentina	Spanish
Borowski, Tadeusz	Ukraine	Polish
Brandys, Kazimierz	Poland	Polish
Brecht, Bertolt	Germany	German
Brett, Lily	Germany	English
Brod, Max	Czechoslovakia (Czech Republic)	German

Author	Birthplace	Language of Composition
Bukiet, Melvin Jules	USA	English
Burnier, Andreas	Netherlands	Dutch
Camus, Albert	Algeria	French
Canetti, Elias	Bulgaria	German
Celan, Paul	Romania	German
Chabon, Michael	USA	English
Cohen, Albert	Corfu	French
Cohen, Arthur	USA	English
Cohen, Elie	Netherlands	Dutch
Cohen, Leonard	Canada	English
Cony, Carlos Heitor	Brazil	Portuguese
Czerniakow, Adam	Poland	Polish
Delbo, Charlotte	France	French
Demetz, Hana	Czechoslovakia (Czech Republic)	German, English
Domecq, Alcina Lubitch	Guatemala	Spanish
Doubrovsky, Serge	France	French
Dribben, Judith Strick	Poland (Ukraine)	Hebrew
Drummond, Roberto	Brazil	Portuguese
Duden, Anne	Germany	German
Durlacher, Gerhard	Germany	Dutch
Edelman, Marek	Poland	Polish
Elberg, Yehuda	Poland	Yiddish
Eliach, Yaffa	Lithuania	Hebrew, English
Elman, Richard	USA	English
Elon, Amos	Austria	English
Epstein, Helen	Czechoslovakia (Czech Republic)	English
Epstein, Leslie	USA	English
Ettinger, Elżbieta	Poland	English
Fackenheim, Emil	Germany	English
Feinstein, Elaine	England	English
Feldman, Irving	USA	English
Fenelon, Fania	France	French
Ferderber-Salz, Bertha	Poland	English
Feuchtwanger, Lion	Germany	German
Ficowski, Jerzy	Poland	Polish
Fink, Ida	Poland	Polish
Finkelstein, Barbara	USA	English
Finkielkraut, Alain	France	French
Fischer, Erica	England	German
Flinker, Moshe	Netherlands	Hebrew
Frank, Anne	Germany	Dutch
Frankl, Viktor	Austria	German
Fried, Erich	Austria	German
Friedländer, Saul	Czechoslovakia (Czech Republic)	French, English
Friedman, Carl	Netherlands	Dutch
Fromer, Rebecca Camhi	USA	English
Fuks, Ladislav	Czechoslovakia (Czech Republic)	Czech
Gary, Romain	Russia	French
Gascar, Pierre	France	French
Gay, Peter	Germany	English
Gergely, Ágnes	Hungary	Hungarian
Gershon, Karen	Germany	English
Gilboa, Amir	Russia (Ukraine)	Hebrew
Ginzburg, Natalia	Italy	Italian
Glatstein, Jacob	Russia (Poland)	Yiddish

Author	Birthplace	Language of Composition
Głowiński, Michał	Poland	Polish
Goldberg, Lea	Lithuania	Hebrew
Goldstein, Rebecca	USA	English
Goodman, Allegra	USA	English
Gouri, Haim	Palestine (Israel)	Hebrew
Govrin, Michal	Israel	Hebrew
Grade, Chaim	Russia (Lithuania)	Yiddish
Grass, Günter	Germany	German
Green, Gerald	USA	English
Greenberg, Uri Zvi	Austria-Hungary (Poland)	Hebrew, Yiddish
Grossinger, Harvey	USA	English
Grossman, David	Israel	Hebrew
Grossman, Vasilii	Russia (Ukraine)	Russian
Grumberg, Jean-Claude	France	French
Grunberg, Arnon	Netherlands	Dutch
Grynberg, Henryk	Poland	Polish
Guralnik, Sonia	Russia	Spanish
Hadar, Tanya	Germany	Hebrew
Hamburger, Michael	Germany	German, English
Hareven, Shulamit	Poland	Hebrew
Harris, Robert	England	English
Hartman, Geoffrey	Germany	English
Hersey, John	China	English
Hershman, Marcie	USA	English
Herzberg, Abel	Netherlands	Dutch
Herzberg, Judith	Netherlands	Dutch
Heyen, William	USA	English
Hill, Geoffrey	England	English
Hillesum, Etty	Netherlands	Dutch
Hilsenrath, Edgar	Germany	German
Hochhuth, Rolf	Germany	German
Hochwälder, Fritz	Austria	German
Hoffman, Eva	Poland	English
Hoffmann, Yoel	Hungary	Hebrew
Hofmann, Gert	Germany	German
Honigmann, Barbara	Germany	German
Isaacson, Judith Magyar	Hungary	English
Jelinek, Elfriede	Austria	German
Ka. Tzetnik 135633 (Yehiel Dinur)	Poland	Hebrew
Kaniuk, Yoram	Palestine (Israel)	Hebrew
Kaplan, Chaim	Russia (Belarus)	Hebrew
Karmel, Ilona	Poland	English
Karpf, Anne	England	English
Karski, Jan	Poland	English
Katzenelson, Yitzhak	Russia	Hebrew, Yiddish
Kehoe, Louise	England	English
Keneally, Thomas	Australia	English
Kertész, Imre	Hungary	Hungarian
Kipphardt, Heiner	Germany	German
Kiš, Danilo	Yugoslavia	Serbian
Kittner, Alfred	Romania	German
Klein, A.M. (Abraham Moses)	Ukraine	English
Klein, Cecilie	Czechoslovakia (Czech Republic)	English
Klein, Gerda	Poland	English

Author	Birthplace	Language of Composition
Klemperer, Victor	Germany	German
Klepfisz, Irena	Poland	English, Yiddish
Klüger, Ruth	Austria	German
Kofman, Sarah	France	French
Kogon, Eugen	Germany	German
Kolmar, Gertrud	Germany	German
Korn, Rachel	Poland	Yiddish
Kosinski, Jerzy	Poland	Polish, English
Kovner, Abba	Russia (Ukraine)	Hebrew
Krall, Hanna	Poland	Polish
Kramer, Lotte	Germany	English
Kreisel, Henry	Austria	English
Langfus, Anna	Poland	French
Layton, Irving	Romania	English
Lebow, Barbara	USA	English
Leitner, Isabella	Hungary	English
Leivick, H. (Leivick Halpern)	Russia (Belarus)	Yiddish
Lengyel, Olga	Hungary	Hungarian
Lentin, Ronit	Israel	English
Lerner, Motti	Israel	Hebrew
Levi, Primo	Italy	Italian
Levinas, Emmanuel	Lithuania	French
Levy, Itamar	Israel	Hebrew
Liebrecht, Savyon	Germany	Hebrew
Lind, Jakov	Austria	German, English
Lustig, Arnost	Czechoslovakia (Czech Republic)	Czech
Lyotard, Jean-François	France	French
Malamud, Bernard	USA	English
Mandel, Elias	Canada	English
Mann, Emily	USA	English
Mann, Thomas	Germany	German
Margulies, Donald	USA	English
Maurer, Jadwiga	Poland	Polish
Mayer, Gerda	Czechoslovakia (Czech Republic)	English
Mechanicus, Philip	Netherlands	Dutch
Meed, Vladka	Poland	Yiddish
Megged, Aharon	Poland	Hebrew
Meijer, Ischa	Netherlands	Dutch
Memmi, Albert	Tunisia	French
Michaels, Anne	Canada	English
Miller, Arthur	USA	English
Millu, Liana	Italy	Italian
Miłosz, Czesław	Poland	Polish
Minco, Marga	Netherlands	Dutch
Miriam, Rivka	Israel	Hebrew
Mitgutsch, Anna	Austria	German
Modiano, Patrick	France	French
Molodowsky, Kadya	Russia (Belarus)	Yiddish
Mulisch, Harry	Netherlands	Dutch
Nałkowska, Zofia	Poland	Polish
Nissenson, Hugh	USA	English
Nomberg-Przytyk, Sara	Poland	Polish
Oberski, Jona	Netherlands	Dutch
Osherow, Jacqueline	USA	English
Ostriker, Alicia	USA	English

APPENDIX: AUTHOR BIRTHPLACE AND LANGUAGE OF COMPOSITION

Author	Birthplace	Language of Composition
Oz, Amos	Palestine (Israel)	Hebrew
Ozick, Cynthia	USA	English
Pagis, Dan	Romania	Hebrew
Papiernikov, Joseph	Poland	Yiddish
Peleg, Dorit	Israel	Hebrew
Perec, Georges	France	French
Perl, Gisella	Hungary	English
Phillips, Caryl	West Indies	English
Piercy, Marge	USA	English
Pilinszky, János	Hungary	Hungarian
Pinter, Harold	England	English
Potok, Chaim	USA	English
Prose, Francine	USA	English
Rabinovitch, Anne	France	French
Raczymow, Henri	France	French
Radnóti, Miklós	Hungary	Hungarian
Raphael, Lev	USA	English
Rawicz, Piotr	Poland (Ukraine)	Polish, French
Reznikoff, Charles	USA	English
Rich, Adrienne	USA	English
Richler, Mordecai	Canada	English
Ringelblum, Emanuel	Poland	Polish
Rosen, Jonathan	USA	English
Rosen, Norma	USA	English
Rosenbaum, Thane	USA	English
Rosenberg, Blanca	Poland	Polish, English
Rosenfarb, Chava	Poland	Yiddish
Roth, Philip	USA	English
Rothenberg, Jerome	USA	English
Rousset, David	France	French
Różewicz, Tadeusz	Poland	Polish
Rudnicki, Adolf	Poland	Polish
Rymkiewicz, Marek	Poland	Polish
Sachs, Nelly	Germany	German
Sack, Leeny	USA	English
Salamon, Julie	USA	English
Samuels, Diane	England	English
Sandauer, Artur	Austria-Hungary (Ukraine)	Polish
Sartre, Jean-Paul	France	French
Schaeffer, Susan Fromberg	USA	English
Schindel, Robert	Austria	German
Schlink, Bernhard	Germany	German
Schulman, Helen	USA	English
Schwarz-Bart, André	France	French
Scliar, Moacyr	Brazil	Portuguese
Sebald, W.G.	Germany	German
Segal, Lore	Austria	English
Seligmann, Rafael	Israel	German
Semel, Nava	Israel	Hebrew
Semprun, Jorge	Spain	French
Shapiro, Alan	USA	English
Shayevitch, Simkha-Bunim	Poland	Yiddish
Siegal, Aranka	Hungary	English
Singer, I. B.	Poland	Yiddish
Singer, I. J.	Poland	Yiddish

Author	Birthplace	Language of Composition
Skibell, Joseph	USA	English
Sneh, Simja	Poland	Yiddish, Hebrew, Spanish
Sobol, Joshua	Palestine (Israel)	Hebrew
Sperber, Manes	Austria-Hungary (Ukraine)	German
Spiegel, Isaiah	Poland	Yiddish
Spiegelman, Art	Sweden	English
Steiner, George	France	English
Steiner, Jean-François	France	French
Steinfeld, J. J.	Germany	English
Stern, Gerald	USA	English
Stollman, Aryeh Lev	Canada	English
Styron, William	USA	English
Sutzkever, Abraham	Russia (Lithuania)	Yiddish
Sylvanus, Erwin	Germany	German
Szczypiorski, Andrzej	Poland	Polish
Szlengel, Władysław	Poland	Polish
Tabori, George	Hungary	English
Tec, Nechama	Poland	English
Tedeschi, Giuliana	Italy	Italian
Thomas, D. M.	England	English
Tomer, Ben Zion	Poland	Hebrew
Tournier, Michel	France	French
Tuwim, Julian	Poland	Polish
Vásquez-Bronfman, Ana	Chile	Spanish
Verbitsky, Bernardo	Argentina	Spanish
Vinocur, Ana	Poland	Spanish
Wallant, Edward Lewis	USA	English
Weil, Clara	Italy	Spanish
Weil, Grete	Germany	German
Weil, Jiří	Austria-Hungary (Czech Republic)	Czech
Weißglas, Immanuel James	Romania	German
Weiss, Peter	Germany	German, Swedish
Werfel, Franz	Austria-Hungary (Czech Republic)	German
Whitman, Ruth	USA	English
Wiesel, Elie	Hungary (Romania)	French, Yiddish, Hebrew
Wiesenthal, Simon	Austria-Hungary (Ukraine)	German
Wilkomirski, Binjamin	Switzerland	German
Wincelberg, Shimon	Germany	English
Wojdowski, Bogdan	Poland	Polish
Wygodzki, Stanisław	Poland	Polish
Yaoz-Kest, Itamar	Hungary	Hebrew
Yevtushenko, Yevgenii	Russia	Russian
Zeitlin, Aaron	Russia (Belarus)	Hebrew, Yiddish
Zukofsky, Louis	USA	English
Zychlinski, Rajzel	Poland	Yiddish

APPENDIX: LANGUAGE OF COMPOSITION

Czech

Fuks, Ladislav
Lustig, Arnost
Weil, Jiří

Dutch

Burnier, Andreas
Cohen, Elie
Durlacher, Gerhard
Frank, Anne
Friedman, Carl
Grunberg, Arnon
Herzberg, Abel
Herzberg, Judith
Hillesum, Etty
Mechanicus, Philip
Meijer, Ischa
Minco, Marga
Mulisch, Harry
Oberski, Jona

English

Alhadeff, Gini
Amis, Martin
Appignanesi, Lisa
Appleman-Jurman, Alicia
Arendt, Hannah
Ascher, Carol
Badanes, Jerome
Baitz, Jon Robin
Baker, Mark Raphael
Barnes, Peter
Bauman, Janina
Begley, Louis
Bellow, Saul
Berger, Joseph
Bettelheim, Bruno
Biderman, Abraham
Bitton-Jackson, Livia
Brett, Lily
Bukiet, Melvin Jules
Chabon, Michael
Cohen, Arthur
Cohen, Leonard
Demetz, Hana
Eliach, Yaffa
Elman, Richard
Elon, Amos
Epstein, Helen
Epstein, Leslie
Ettinger, Elżbieta
Fackenheim, Emil
Feinstein, Elaine
Feldman, Irving
Ferderber-Salz, Bertha
Finkelstein, Barbaras
Frankl, Victor
Friedländer, Saul
Fromer, Rebecca Camhi
Gay, Peter
Gershon, Karen
Goldstein, Rebecca
Goodman, Allegra
Green, Gerald
Grossinger, Harvey
Hamburger, Michael
Harris, Robert
Hartman, Geoffrey
Hersey, John
Hershman, Marcie
Heyen, William
Hill, Geoffrey
Hoffman, Eva
Isaacson, Judith Magyar
Karmel, Ilona
Karpf, Anne
Karski, Jan
Kehoe, Louise
Keneally, Thomas
Klein, A.M.
Klein, Cecilie
Klein, Gerda
Klepfisz, Irena
Kosinski, Jerzy
Kramer, Lotte
Kreisel, Henry
Layton, Irving
Lebow, Barbara
Leitner, Isabella
Lentin, Ronit
Lind, Jakov
Lustig, Arnost
Malamud, Bernard
Mandel, Elias
Mann, Emily
Margulies, Donald
Mayer, Gerda
Michaels, Anne
Miller, Arthur
Nissenson, Hugh
Osherow, Jacqueline
Ostriker, Alicia
Ozick, Cynthia
Perl, Gisella
Phillips, Caryl
Piercy, Marge
Pinter, Harold
Potok, Chaim
Prose, Francine
Raphael, Lev
Reznikoff, Charles
Rich, Adrienne
Richler, Mordechai
Rosen, Jonathan
Rosen, Norma
Rosenbaum, Thane
Rosenberg, Blanca
Roth, Philip
Rothenberg, Jerome
Sack, Leeny
Salamon, Julie
Samuels, Diane
Schaeffer, Susan Fromberg
Schulman, Helen
Segal, Lore
Shapiro, Alan
Siegal, Aranka
Skibell, Joseph
Spiegelman, Art
Steiner, George
Steinfeld, J. J.
Stern, Gerald
Stollman, Aryeh Lev
Styron, William

Tabori, George
Tec, Nechama
Thomas, D. M.
Wallant, Edward Lewis
Whitman, Ruth
Wincelberg, Shimon
Zukofsky, Louis

French

Antelme, Robert
Atlan, Liliane
Camus, Albert
Cohen, Albert
Delbo, Charlotte
Doubrovsky, Serge
Fenelon, Fania
Finkielkraut, Alain
Friedländer, Saul
Gary, Romain
Gascar, Pierre
Grumberg, Jean-Claude
Kofman, Sarah
Langfus, Anna
Levinas, Emmanuel
Lyotard, Jean-François
Memmi, Albert
Modiano, Patrick
Perec, Georges
Rabinovitch, Anne
Raczymow, Henri
Rawicz, Piotr
Rousset, David
Sartre, Jean Paul
Schwarz-Bart, André
Semprun, Jorge
Steiner, Jean-François
Tournier, Michel
Wiesel, Elie

German

Aichinger, Ilse
Aloni, Jenny
Améry, Jean
Andersch, Alfred
Arendt, Hannah
Becker, Jurek
Bernhard, Thomas
Biller, Maxim
Böll, Heinrich
Brecht, Bertolt
Brod, Max
Canetti, Elias
Celan, Paul
Demetz, Hana
Duden, Anne
Feuchtwanger, Lion
Fischer, Erica
Frankl, Viktor
Fried, Erich
Grass, Günter
Hamburger, Michael
Hilsenrath, Edgar
Hochhuth, Rolf
Hochwälder, Fritz
Hofmann, Gert
Honigmann, Barbara
Jelinek, Elfriede
Kipphardt, Heiner
Kittner, Alfred
Klemperer, Victor
Klüger, Ruth
Kogon, Eugen
Kolmar, Gertrud
Lind, Jakov
Mann, Thomas
Mitgutsch, Anna
Sachs, Nelly
Schindel, Robert
Schlink, Bernhard
Sebald, W. G. (Winfried Georg)
Seligmann, Rafael
Sperber, Manes
Sylvanus, Erwin
Weil, Grete
Weißglas, Immanuel James
Weiss, Peter
Werfel, Franz
Wiesenthal, Simon
Wilkomirski, Binjamin

Hebrew

Almagor, Gila
Aloni, Jenny
Amichai, Yehudah
Amir-Pinkerfeld, Anda
Appelfeld, Aharon
Bartov, Hanoch
Dribben, Judith Strick
Eliach, Yaffa
Flinker, Moshe
Gilboa, Amir
Goldberg, Lea(h)
Gouri, Haim
Govrin, Michal
Greenberg, Uri Zvi
Grossman, David
Hadar, Tanya
Hareven, Shulamith
Hoffmann, Yoel
Ka. Tzetnik 135633 (Yehiel Dinur)
Kaniuk, Yoram
Kaplan, Chaim
Katzenelson, Yitzhak
Kovner, Abba
Lerner, Motti
Levy, Itamar
Liebrecht, Savyon
Megged, Aharon
Miriam, Rivka
Oz, Amos
Pagis, Dan
Peleg, Dorit
Semel, Nava
Sneh, Simja
Sobol, Joshua
Tomer, Ben Zion
Wiesel, Elie
Yaoz-Kest, Itamar
Zeitlin, Aaron

Hungarian

Gergely, Ágnes
Kertész, Imre
Lengyel, Olga
Pilinszky, János
Radnóti, Miklós

Italian

Bassani, Giorgio
Ginzburg, Natalia
Levi, Primo
Millu, Liana
Tedeschi, Giuliana

Polish

Amir-Pinkerfeld, Anda
Andrzejewski, Jerzy
Auerbach, Rachel
Bauman, Janina
Benski, Stanisław
Birenbaum, Halina
Borowski, Tadeusz
Brandys, Kazimierz
Czerniakow, Adam
Edelman, Marek
Ficowski, Jerzy
Fink, Ida
Głowiński, Michał

Grynberg, Henryk
Kosinski, Jerzy
Krall, Hanna
Maurer, Jadwiga
Miłosz, Czesław
Nałkowska, Zofia
Nomberg-Przytyk, Sara
Rawicz, Piotr
Ringelblum, Emanuel
Rosenberg, Blanca
Różewicz, Tadeusz
Rudnicki, Adolf
Rymkiewicz, Jarosław
Sandauer, Arthur
Szczypiorski, Andrzej
Szlengel, Władysław
Tuwim, Julian
Wojdowski, Bogdan
Wygodzki, Stanisław

Portuguese

Cony, Carlos Heiter
Drummond, Roberto
Scliar, Moacyr

Russian

Grossman, Vasilii
Yevtushenko, Yevgenii

Serbian

Kiš, Danilo

Spanish

Agosín, Marjorie
Borges, Jorge Luis
Domecq, Alcina Lubitch
Guralnik, Sonia
Sneh, Simja
Vásquez-Bronfman, Ana
Verbitsky, Bernardo
Vinocur, Ana
Weil, Clara

Yiddish

Auerbach, Rachel
Berg, Mary
Elberg, Yehuda
Glatstein, Jacob
Grade, Chaim
Greenberg, Uri Zvi
Katzenelson, Yitzhak
Klepfisz, Irena
Korn, Rachel
Leivick, H.
Meed, Vladka
Molodowsky, Kadya
Papiernikov, Joseph
Rosenfarb, Chava
Shayevitch, Simkha Bunim
Singer, I. B.
Singer, I. J.
Sneh, Simja
Spiegel, Isaiah
Sutzkever, Abraham
Wiesel, Elie
Zeitlin, Aaron
Zychlinski, Rajzel

APPENDIX: GENRE

Archive

Ringelblum, Emanuel

Autobiography

Gershon, Karen (collective)
Kehoe, Louise
Klüger, Ruth
Lentin, Ronit
Lind, Jakov
Sandauer, Artur
Segal, Lore
Sperber, Manes

Autobiographical Narrative

Andersch, Alfred
Ginzburg, Natalia
Langfus, Anna

Biography

Delbo, Charlotte
Epstein, Helen
Feinstein, Elaine
Fromer, Rebecca Camhi

Blended Genre

Spiegelman, Art

Diary

Berg, Mary
Czerniakow, Adam
Flinker, Moshe
Frank, Anne
Herzberg, Abel
Hillesum, Etty
Kaplan, Chaim
Katzenelson, Yitzhak
Klemperer, Victor
Mechanicus, Philip

Drama/Performance

Aichinger, Ilse
Atlan, Liliane
Barnes, Peter
Bernhard, Thomas
Brecht, Bertolt
Delbo, Charlotte
Eliach, Yaffa
Feinstein, Elaine
Fink, Ida
Grumberg, Jean-Claude
Grynberg, Henryk
Herzberg, Abel
Herzberg, Judith
Hochhuth, Rolf
Hochwälder, Fritz
Jelinek, Elfriede
Kipphardt, Heiner
Kolmar, Gertrud
Lebow, Barbara
Leivick, H.
Lerner, Motti
Mann, Emily
Megged, Aharon
Miller, Arthur
Nałkowska, Zofia
Ozick, Cynthia
Różewicz, Tadeusz
Sachs, Nelly
Sack, Leeny
Samuels, Diane
Sartre, Jean-Paul
Sobol, Joshua
Sylvanus, Erwin
Tabori, George
Tomer, Ben Zion
Weiss, Peter
Werfel, Franz
Wiesel, Elie
Wincelberg, Shimon
Zeitlin, Aaron

Fiction

Agosín, Marjorie
Aichinger, Ilse
Almagor, Gila
Aloni, Jenny
Amichai, Yehudah
Amis, Martin
Andersch, Alfred
Andrzejewski, Jerzy
Appelfeld, Aharon
Ascher, Carol
Badanes, Jerome
Bartov, Hanoch
Bassani, Giorgio
Bauman, Janina
Becker, Jurek
Begley, Louis
Bellow, Saul
Benski, Stanisław
Bernhard, Thomas
Biller, Maxim
Böll, Heinrich
Borges, Jorges Luis
Borowski, Tadeusz
Brandys, Kazimierz
Brett, Lily
Brod, Max
Bukiet, Melvin
Burnier, Andreas
Camus, Albert
Canetti, Elias
Chabon, Michael
Cohen, Albert
Cony, Carlos Heitor
Delbo, Charlotte
Demetz, Hana
Domecq, Alcina Lubitch
Doubrovsky, Serge
Drummond, Robert
Duden, Anne
Elberg, Yehuda
Elman, Richard
Elon, Amos
Epstein, Leslie
Ettinger, Elżbieta
Feinstein, Elaine
Feuchtwanger, Lion
Fink, Ida
Finkelstein, Barbara
Friedman, Carl
Fuks, Ladislav

Gary, Romain
Gascar, Pierre
Glatstein, Jacob
Głowiński, Michał
Goldstein, Rebecca
Goodman, Allegra
Gouri, Haim
Govrin, Michal
Grade, Chaim
Grass, Günter
Green, Gerald
Grossinger, Harvey
Grossman, David
Grossman, Vasilii
Grunberg, Arnon
Grynberg, Henryk
Guralnik, Sonia
Hareven, Shulamith
Harris, Robert
Hersey, John
Hershman, Marcie
Hilsenrath, Edgar
Hoffman, Eva
Hoffman, Yoel
Hofmann, Gert
Honigmann, Barbara
Ka. Tzetnik 135633 (Yehiel Dinur)
Kaniuk, Yoram
Karmel, Ilona
Keneally, Thomas
Kertész, Imre
Kiš, Danilo
Klein, A.M.
Kolmar, Gertrud
Korn, Rachel
Kosinski, Jerzy
Kovner, Abba
Krall, Hanna
Kreisel, Henry
Lentin, Ronit
Levi, Primo
Levy, Itamar
Liebrecht, Savyon
Lind, Jakov
Lustig, Arnost
Malamud, Bernard
Mann, Thomas
Maurer, Jadwiga
Megged, Aharon
Memmi, Albert
Michaels, Anne
Minco, Marga
Modiano, Patrick
Mulisch, Harry
Nałkowska, Zofia
Nissenson, Hugh
Oberski, Jona
Oz, Amos
Ozick, Cynthia
Peleg, Dorit
Perec, Georges
Piercy, Marge
Potok, Chaim
Prose, Francine
Rabinovitch, Anne
Raczymow, Henri
Raphael, Lev
Rawicz, Piotr
Rosen, Jonathan
Rosen, Norma
Rosenbaum, Thane
Rosenfarb, Chava
Roth, Philip
Rousset, David
Różewicz, Tadeusz
Rudnicki, Adolf
Rymkiewicz, Jarosław Marek
Schaeffer, Susan Fromberg
Schindel, Robert
Schlink, Bernhard
Schulman, Helen
Schwarz-Bart, André
Scliar, Moacyr
Sebald, W. G.
Seligmann, Rafael
Semel, Nava
Semprun, Jorge
Singer, I. B.
Singer, I. J.
Skibell, Joseph
Sneh, Simja
Sperber, Manes
Spiegel, Isaiah
Steiner, George
Steiner, Jean-François
Steinfeld, J. J.
Stollman, Aryeh Lev
Styron, William
Szczypiorski, Andrzej
Thomas, D. M.
Tournier, Michel
Vásquez-Bronfman, Ana
Verbitsky, Bernardo
Vinocur, Ana
Wallant, Edward Lewis
Weil, Clara
Weil, Grete
Weil, Jiří
Werfel, Franz
Wiesel, Elie
Wilkomirski, Binjamin
Wojdowski, Bogdan
Wygodzki, Stanisław
Yaoz-Kest, Itamar

History

Friedländer, Saul
Herzberg, Abel
Ringelblum, Emanuel
Tec, Nechama

Letters

Hillesum, Etty
Kolmar, Gertrud

Memoir/Testimony

Alhadeff, Gini
Améry, Jean (testimony)
Antelme, Robert (testimony)
Appignanesi, Lisa
Appleman-Jurman, Alicia
Auerbach, Rachel
Baker, Mark Raphael
Bauman, Janina
Berger, Joseph
Biderman, Abraham
Bitton-Jackson, Livia
Cohen, Elie
Delbo, Charlotte
Dribben, Judith Strick
Durlacher, Gerhard
Edelman, Marek (testimony)
Eliach, Yaffa (testimony, interviews)
Epstein, Helen
Fenelon, Fania
Ferderber-Salz, Bertha
Frankl, Viktor
Friedländer, Saul
Ginzburg, Natalia
Grade, Chaim
Hartman, Geoffrey
Herzberg, Abel
Heyen, William
Hoffman, Eva
Isaacson, Judith Magyar
Karpf, Anne
Karski, Jan (testimony)
Klein, Cecilie

Klein, Gerda
Kofman, Sarah
Leitner, Isabella
Lengyel, Olga
Levi, Primo
Meed, Vladka (testimony)
Meijer, Ischa
Millu, Liana
Nechama, Tec
Nomberg-Przytyk, Sara
Oberski, Jona
Perl, Gisella
Rosenberg, Blanca
Rousset, David (testimony)
Salamon, Julie
Sandauer, Artur
Semprun, Jorge
Siegal, Aranka
Sneh, Simja
Spiegelman, Art
Tedeschi, Giuliana (testimony)
Wiesel, Elie

Nonfiction Prose

Améry, Jean
Andersch, Alfred
Arendt, Hannah
Auerbach, Rachel
Bellow, Saul
Bettelheim, Bruno
Birenbaum, Halina
Borges, Jorge Luis
Brod, Max
Burnier, Andreas
Canetti, Elias
Cohen, Arthur
Doubrovsky, Serge
Duden, Anne
Elon, Amos
Epstein, Helen
Ettinger, Elżbieta
Fackenheim, Emil
Finkielkraut, Alain
Frankl, Viktor
Głowiński, Michał
Grossman, Vasilii
Hamburger, Michael
Hartman, Geoffrey
Herzberg, Abel
Hoffman, Eva
Jelinek, Elfriede
Kaniuk, Yoram
Kertész, Imre
Kofman, Sarah
Kogon, Eugen
Lentin, Ronit
Levinas, Emmanuel
Lyotard, Jean-François
Mandel, Elias
Molodowsky, Kadya
Nałkowska, Zofia
Ozick, Cynthia
Ringelblum, Emanuel
Rosen, Jonathan
Rosen, Norma
Roth, Philip
Sachs, Nelly
Sartre, Jean-Paul
Seligmann, Rafael
Steiner, George
Verbitsky, Bernardo
Wiesel, Elie

Poetry

Agosín, Marjorie
Aichinger, Ilse
Amichai, Yehudah
Amir Pinkerfeld, Anda
Atlan, Liliane
Birenbaum, Halina
Brecht, Bertolt
Brett, Lily
Bukiet, Melvin Jules
Celan, Paul
Cohen, Leonard
Duden, Anne
Feinstein, Elaine
Feldman, Irving
Ficowski, Jerzy
Fried, Erich
Gergely, Ágnes
Gershon, Karen
Gilboa, Amir
Glatstein, Jacob
Gouri, Haim
Govrin, Michal
Grade, Chaim
Greenberg, Uri Zvi
Grynberg, Henryk
Hadar, Tanya
Hamburger, Michael
Herzberg, Judith
Heyen, William
Hilsenrath, Edgar
Hoffman, Yoel
Ka. Tzetnik 135633 (Yehiel Dinur)
Katzenelson, Yitzhak
Kiš, Danilo
Kittner, Alfred
Klein, A.M.
Klepfisz, Irena
Kolmar, Gertrud
Korn, Rachel
Kovner, Abba
Kramer, Lotte
Layton, Irving
Leivick, H.
Levi, Primo
Mandel, Elias
Mayer, Gerda
Michaels, Anne
Miłosz, Czesław
Miriam, Rivka
Ostriker, Alicia
Pagis, Dan
Papiernikov, Joseph
Piercy, Marge
Pilinszky, János
Radnóti, Miklós
Rich, Adrienne
Rothenberg, Jerome
Różewicz, Tadeusz
Schindel, Robert
Shapiro, Alan
Shayevitch, Simkha-Bunim
Spiegel, Isaiah
Stern, Gerald
Sutzkever, Abraham
Szlengel, Władysław
Tuwim, Julian
Weißglas, Immanuel James
Whitman, Ruth
Wygodzki, Stanisław
Yaoz-Kest, Itamar
Yevtushenko, Yevgenii
Zeitlin, Aaron
Zukofsky, Louis

APPENDIX: LITERARY THEMES

Antisemitism

Relation of Christian antisemitism and the Holocaust
Demetz, Hana
Elman, Richard
Ozick, Cynthia
Piercy, Marge
Potok, Chaim
Rudnicki, Adolf
Schaeffer, Susan Fromberg
Schwarz-Bart, André
Singer, I. B.
Wallant, Edward Lewis
Wiesel, Elie

Antisemitism (pre-*Shoah*)
Aloni, Jenny
Améry, Jean
Appelfeld, Aharon
Arendt, Hannah
Biderman, Abraham
Borges, Jorge Luis
Cohen, Albert
Cohen, Arthur
Finkielkraut, Alain
Fuks, Ladislav
Ginzburg, Natalia
Glatstein, Jacob
Greenberg, Uri Zvi
Grumberg, Jean-Claude
Herzberg, Abel
Kiš, Danilo
Kolmar, Gertrud
Korn, Rachel
Lind, Jakov
Memmi, Albert
Minco, Marga
Nomberg-Przytyk, Sara
Ozick, Cynthia
Papiernikov, Joseph
Phillips, Caryl
Piercy, Marge
Potok, Chaim
Rich, Adrienne
Rothenberg, Jerome
Sartre, Jean-Paul
Schaeffer, Susan Fromberg
Schwarz-Bart, André
Singer, I. B.
Singer, I. J.
Sperber, Manes
Steiner, George
Styron, William
Tabori, George
Tuwim, Julian
Wallant, Edward Lewis
Werfel, Franz
Wiesel, Elie
Yevtushenko, Yevgenii

Antisemitism (*Shoah* era)
Améry, Jean
Andrzejewski, Jerzy
Appignancsi, Lisa
Appleman-Jurman, Alicia
Arendt, Hannah
Bassani, Giorgio
Bellow, Saul
Biderman, Abraham
Borges, Jorge Luis
Borowski, Tadeusz
Brandys, Kazimierz
Burnier, Andreas
Chabon, Michael
Cohen, Albert
Cohen, Arthur
Doubrovsky, Serge
Elman, Richard
Ettinger, Elżbieta
Fink, Ida
Grossman, Vasilii
Grumberg, Jean-Claude
Hershman, Marcie
Herzberg, Abel
Karpf, Anne
Kosinski, Jerzy
Maurer, Jadwiga
Memmi, Albert
Minco, Marga
Modiano, Patrick
Nałkowska, Zofia
Nomberg-Przytyk, Sara
Piercy, Marge
Potok, Chaim
Rymkiewicz, Jarosław Marek
Schaeffer, Susan Fromberg
Szczypiorski, Andrzej
Shapiro, Alan
Sperber, Manes
Sneh, Simja
Styron, William
Tabori, George
Weil, Clara
Weißglas, Immanuel James
Wiesel, Elie
Wincelberg, Shimon
Yevtushenko, Yevgenii
Zukofsky, Louis

Antisemitism (post-*Shoah*)
Alhadeff, Gini
Appleman-Jurman, Alicia
Bassani, Giorgio
Bauman, Janina
Begley, Louis
Bernhard, Thomas
Borges, Jorge Luis
Cohen, Arthur
Ettinger, Elżbieta
Finkielkraut, Alain
Grossman, Vasilii
Hill, Geoffrey
Hilsenrath, Edgar
Hochwälder, Fritz
Hofmann, Gert
Honigmann, Barbara
Karpf, Anne
Meijer, Ischa
Minco, Marga
Richler, Mordechai
Roth, Philip
Różewicz, Tadeusz
Rudnicki, Adolf
Sachs, Nelly
Schaeffer, Susan Fromberg
Schindel, Robert
Sneh, Simja
Steinfeld, J. J.

Vásquez-Bronfman, Ana
Wallant, Edward Lewis
Werfel, Franz

Antisemitism—Jewish response

Bellow, Saul
Bernhard, Thomas
Ettinger, Elżbieta
Grumberg, Jean-Claude
Ozick, Cynthia
Potok, Chaim
Schindel, Robert
Shapiro, Alan

Aryanization

Demetz, Hana
Elman, Richard
Epstein, Leslie
Feuchtwanger, Lion
Piercy, Marge
Schaeffer, Susan Fromberg
Spiegelman, Art
Szlengel, Władysław

Birth/abortion

Epstein, Leslie
Karmel, Ilona
Millu, Liana
Nomberg-Przytyk, Sara
Perl, Gisella
Piercy, Marge
Rosen, Norma

Bystanders

Aloni, Jenny
Fink, Ida
Flinker, Moshe
Grossinger, Harvey
Hershman, Marcie
Karmel, Ilona
Krall, Hanna
Lustig, Arnost
Miłosz, Czesław
Ozick, Cynthia
Piercy, Marge
Sachs, Nelly
Singer, I. B.
Steiner, George
Szengel, Władysław
Tournier, Michel
Verbitsky, Bernardo
Wiesel, Elie

Children

Amir-Pinkerfeld, Anda
Atlan, Liliane
Begley, Louis
Burnier, Andreas
Demetz, Hana
Doubrovsky, Serge
Epstein, Leslie
Ettinger, Elżbieta
Feinstein, Elaine
Ferderber-Salz, Bertha
Ficowski, Jerzy
Fink, Ida
Flinker, Moshe
Friedländer, Saul
Głowiński, Michał
Grynberg, Henryk
Hareven, Shulamith
Klepfisz, Irena
Kofman, Sarah
Kramer, Lotte
Lind, Jakov
Lustig, Arnost
Maurer, Jadwiga
Michaels, Anne
Nomberg-Przytyk, Sara
Oberski, Jona
Rawicz, Piotr
Ringelblum, Emanuel
Rosen, Norma
Samuels, Diane
Schaeffer, Susan Fromberg
Sebald, W. G.
Wiesel, Elie
Wilkomirski, Binjamin

Collaboration—government and individual

Appleman-Jurman, Alicia
Bassani, Giorgio (Italian)
Bernhard, Thomas
Borowski, Tadeusz (Poland)
Camus, Albert
Cohen, Elie (Netherlands)
Delbo, Charlotte (French)
Eliach, Yaffa
Elman, Richard (Hungarian)
Ferderber-Salz, Bertha (Polish)
Finkielkraut, Alain (French)
Ginzburg, Natalia (Italian)
Grossman, Vasilii (Ukrainian)
Grumberg, Jean-Claude (French)
Hershman, Marcie
Kramer, Lotte
Lerner, Motti
Lustig, Arnost
Modiano, Patrick (French)
Mulisch, Harry (Netherlands)
Nomberg-Przytyk, Sara (Poland)
Ozick, Cynthia (French)
Perec, Georges (French)
Piercy, Marge (French)
Raczymow, Henri (French)
Rosenberg, Blanca (Polish and Ukrainian)
Rudnicki, Adolf
Sobol, Joshua
Steiner, George
Steiner, Jean-François (Judenrat)
Tomer, Ben Zion
Tournier, Michel (French)

Commemoration/memorialization of Holocaust victims

Bassani, Giorgio
Birenbaum, Halina
Eliach, Yaffa
Ficowski, Jerzy
Glatstein, Jacob
Goodman, Allegra
Gouri, Haim
Guralnik, Sonia
Honigmann, Barbara
Karmel, Ilona
Katzenelson, Yitzhak
Kertész, Imre
Kovner, Abba
Molodowsky, Kadya
Ozick, Cynthia
Papiernikov, Joseph
Rabinovitch, Anne
Rosen, Jonathan
Różewicz, Tadeusz
Tuwim, Julian
Schwarz-Bart, André
Seligmann, Rafael
Singer, I. B.
Sutzkever, Abraham
Zukofsky, Louis
Zychlinski, Rajzel

Confrontation of Holocaust past: evasion and acknowledgment

Austrian response

Austria needing to face Nazi past
Schindel, Robert

Postwar Austrian-Jewish relations
Mitgutsch, Anna
Schindel, Robert

German response

Germany needing to face Nazi past

Duden, Anne
Grass, Günter
Hamburger, Michael
Kogon, Eugen
Mann, Thomas
Pinter, Harold
Schindel, Robert
Schlink, Bernhard
Sebald, W. G.

Postwar German-Jewish relations

Biller, Maxim
Gouri, Haim
Hilsenrath, Edgar
Honigmann, Barbara
Kipphardt, Heiner
Megged, Aharon
Rosen, Norma
Schindel, Robert
Sebald, W. G.
Seligmann, Rafael
Tabori, George
Tournier, Michel

Critique of Western culture/ civilization

Glatstein, Jacob
Megged, Aharon
Pilinszky, János
Różewicz, Tadeusz

Death marches

Alhadeff, Gini
Antelme, Robert
Atlan, Liliane
Cohen, Arthur
Cohen, Elie
Greenberg, Uri Zvi
Lengyel, Olga
Karmel, Ilona
Klein, Gerda
Piercy, Marge
Radnóti, Miklós
Tedeschi, Guiliana
Wiesel, Elie

Deportations

Aloni, Jenny
Appelfeld, Aharon
Atlan, Liliane
Bassani, Giorgio
Becker, Jurek
Biderman, Abraham
Bitton-Jackson, Livia
Böll, Heinrich
Czerniakow, Adam
Elman, Richard
Epstein, Leslie
Ettinger, Elżbieta
Ficowski, Jerzy
Fuks, Ladislav
Hareven, Shulamith
Hersey, John
Herzberg, Abel
Hillesum, Etty
Hoffman, Eva
Isaacson, Judith Magyar
Kaplan, Chaim
Karmel, Ilona
Katzenelson, Yitzhak
Kertész, Imre
Kittner, Alfred
Langfus, Anna
Leitner, Isabella
Lengyel, Olga
Lind, Jakov
Mechanicus, Philip
Meed, Vladka
Millu, Liana
Minco, Marga
Mitgutsch, Anna
Modiano, Patrick
Nomberg-Przytyk, Sara
Oberski, Jona
Ozick, Cynthia
Pagis, Dan
Piercy, Marge
Ringelblum, Emanuel
Rosenberg, Blanca
Rymkiewicz, Jarosław Marek
Schaeffer, Susan Fromberg
Schwarz-Bart, André
Shayevitch, Simkha-Bunim
Siegal, Aranka
Spiegelman, Art
Wallant, Edward Lewis
Weil, Grete
Wiesel, Elie
Wojdowski, Bogdan

Displaced persons

Berger, Joseph
Cohen, Arthur
Maurer, Jadwiga
Schaeffer, Susan Fromberg

European Jewish life

Pre-Holocaust, real and imagined

Bukiet, Melvin Jules
Demetz, Hana
Feldman, Irving
Goldstein, Rebecca
Grade, Chaim
Hilsenrath, Edgar
Hoffman, Eva
Raczymow, Henri
Rudnicki, Adolf
Schaeffer, Susan Fromberg
Singer, I. B.
Sperber, Manes
Tuwim, Julian
Wiesel, Elie

Precarious condition of diaspora Jews

Feuchtwanger, Lion
Kaniuk, Yoram

Commemoration of *shtetl* life

Badanes, Jerome
Elberg, Yehuda
Ficowski, Jerzy
Gilboa, Amir
Goldstein, Rebecca
Krall, Hanna
Raczymow, Henri
Rothenberg, Jerome
Singer, I. B.
Yaoz-Kest, Itamar

Exile

Gay, Peter
Ginzburg, Natalia
Guralnik, Sonia
Sachs, Nelly
Weil, Clara

Failure of Jews to recognize and cope with the Nazi threat

European

Amir-Pinkerfeld, Anda
Elman, Richard
Ginzburg, Natalia
Glatstein, Jacob
Greenberg, Uri Zvi
Grumberg, Jean-Claude
Karski, Jan
Kolmar, Gertrud
Minco, Marga
Modiano, Patrick
Raczymow, Henri

Sperber, Manes
Steiner, Jean-François
Wallant, Edward Lewis
Wiesel, Elie

Yishuv (pre-state Israeli)
Amichai, Yehudah
Amir-Pinkerfeld, Anda
Elon, Amos
Hareven, Shulamith
Megged, Aharon
Tomer, Ben Zion

Forced labor

Demetz, Hana
Elman, Richard
Epstein, Richard
Klemperer, Victor
Langfus, Anna
Piercy, Marge
Radnóti, Miklós

Gender

Agosín, Marjorie
Amir-Pinkerfeld, Anda
Berg, Mary
Brett, Lily
Demetz, Hana
Dribben, Judith Strick
Ettinger, Elżbieta
Fenelon, Fania
Fink, Ida
Isaacson, Judith Magyar
Ka. Tzetnik 135633 (Yehiel Dinur)
Karmel, Ilona
Klein, Cecilie
Klein, Gerda
Leitner, Isabella
Lengyel, Olga
Lustig, Arnost
Millu, Liana
Miriam, Rivka
Nomberg-Przytyk, Sara
Ozick, Cynthia
Perl, Gisella
Piercy, Marge
Ringelblum, Emanuel
Rosenberg, Blanca
Samuels, Diane
Schaeffer, Susan Fromberg
Tedeschi, Giuliana
Wallant, Edward Lewis

Generational perceptions/ contentions regarding the Shoah during its course

Demetz, Hana
Elman, Richard
Karmel, Ilona
Klüger, Ruth

Ghettos

Establishment
Becker, Jurek
Czerniakow, Adam
Epstein, Leslie
Grade, Chaim
Hoffman, Eva
Karmel, Ilona
Kovner, Abba
Nomberg-Przytyk, Sara
Pagis, Dan
Rosenberg, Blanca
Rudnicki, Adolf
Schaeffer, Susan Fromberg
Siegal, Aranka
Sobol, Joshua
Szlengel, Władysław

Administration and conditions
Bauman, Janina
Berg, Mary
Biderman, Abraham
Birenbaum, Halina
Czerniakow, Adam
Edelman, Marek
Eliach, Yaffa
Epstein, Leslie
Ettinger, Elżbieta
Ficowski, Jerzy
Głowiński, Michał
Hersey, John
Hilsenrath, Edgar
Kaplan, Chaim
Karmel, Ilona
Langfus, Anna
Lustig, Arnost
Meed, Vladka
Minco, Marga
Nałkowska, Zofia
Nomberg-Przytyk, Sara
Ringelblum, Emanuel
Rosenberg, Blanca
Rosenfarb, Chava
Rudnicki, Adolf
Schaeffer, Susan Fromberg
Shayevitch, Simkha-Bunim
Sobol, Joshua
Spiegelman, Art
Steiner, Jean-François
Sutzkever, Abraham
Vinocur, Ana
Wiesel, Elie
Wincelberg, Shimon
Wojdowski, Bogdan

Liquidation
Epstein, Leslie
Green, Gerald
Kaplan, Chaim
Karmel, Ilona
Katzenelson, Yitzhak
Keneally, Thomas
Nałkowska, Zofia
Rawicz, Piotr
Rosenfarb, Chava
Rothenberg, Jerome
Schaeffer, Susan Fromberg

Guilt (non-survivor)

Amichai, Yehudah
Feldman, Irving
Flinker, Moshe
Langfus, Anna
Lebow, Barbara
Lengyel, Olga
Megged, Aharon
Mulisch, Harry
Nałkowska, Zofia
Piercy, Marge
Raphael, Lev
Rosenbaum, Thane
Różewicz, Tadeusz
Sartre, Jean-Paul
Spiegelman, Art
Sylvanus, Erwin

Healing: religious and secular

Religious: Tikkun (repair)
Almagor, Gila
Appelfeld, Aharon
Ascher, Carol
Cohen, Arthur
Elberg, Yehuda
Fackenheim, Emil
Finkelstein, Barbara
Govrin, Michal
Grossman, David
Kaniuk, Yoram

Klepfisz, Irena
Kriesel, Henry
Levi, Primo
Ozick, Cynthia
Peleg, Dorit
Piercy, Marge
Potok, Chaim
Raczymow, Henri
Schaeffer, Susan Fromberg
Singer, I. B.
Stollman, Aryeh Lev
Wiesel, Elie
Wincelberg, Shimon
Zeitlin, Aaron

Secular
Ettinger, Elżbieta
Piercy, Marge
Schaeffer, Susan Fromberg
Wiesel, Elie

Hiding (concealed and open)

Amir-Pinkerfeld, Anda
Appleman-Jurman, Alicia
Baitz, Jon Robin
Bauman, Janina
Begley, Louis
Bellow, Saul
Böll, Heinrich
Brandys, Kazimierz
Burnier, Andreas
Doubrovsky, Serge
Epstein, Leslie
Ettinger, Elżbieta
Feinstein, Elaine
Ferderber-Salz, Bertha
Fink, Ida
Frank, Anne
Friedländer, Saul
Ginzburg, Natalia
Głowiński, Michał
Grumberg, Jean-Claude
Grynberg, Henryk
Herzberg, Abel
Herzberg, Judith
Karmel, Ilona
Klepfisz, Irena
Kofman, Sarah
Langfus, Anna
Maurer, Jadwiga
Michaels, Anne
Minco, Marga
Ozick, Cynthia
Pagis, Dan
Piercy, Marge
Rawicz, Piotr
Rosenberg, Blanca
Rudnicki, Adolf
Samuels, Diane
Schaeffer, Susan Fromberg
Singer, I. B.
Spiegelman, Art
Tec, Nechama
Whitman, Ruth
Wiesel, Elie
Wilkomirski, Binjamin

Identification with victims of Holocaust

Agosín, Marjorie
Aichinger, Ilse
Amichai, Yehudah
Auerbach, Rachel
Borges, Jorge Luis
Feldman, Irving
Ficowski, Jerzy
Finkielkraut, Alain
Fried, Erich
Gilboa, Amir
Gouri, Haim
Hadar, Tanya
Hareven, Shulamith
Kaniuk, Yoram
Karpf, Anne
Korn, Rachel
Kramer, Lotte
Layton, Irving
Lebow, Barbara
Leivick, H.
Malamud, Bernard
Michaels, Anne
Miriam, Rivka
Papiernikov, Joseph
Phillips, Caryl
Pilinszky, János
Raczymow, Henri
Raphael, Lev
Rich, Adrienne
Rosen, Jonathan
Rosen, Norma
Sachs, Nelly
Sack, Leeny
Samuels, Diane
Scliar, Moacyr
Shapiro, Alan
Steiner, George
Stern, Gerald
Tuwim, Julian
Vásquez-Bronfman, Ana
Verbitsky, Bernardo
Yevtushenko, Yevgenii
Zychlinski, Rajzel

Identity formation and re-evaluation

Jewish identity and assimilation—postwar
Alhadeff, Gina
Becker, Jurek
Gergely, Ágnes
Hoffman, Eva
Rich, Adrienne
Schindel, Robert

Jewish/French
Atlan, Liliane
Doubrovsky, Serge
Finkielkraut, Alain
Kofman, Sarah
Memmi, Albert
Modiano, Patrick
Piercy, Marge
Raczymow, Henri

Jewish/German
Biller, Maxim
Gay, Peter
Hilsenrath, Edgar
Honigmann, Barbara
Klemperer, Victor
Kolmar, Gertrud
Seligmann, Rafael

Jewish/Polish
Bellow, Saul
Ettinger, Elżbieta
Grynberg, Henryk
Tuwim, Julian

Diaspora/Israeli
Grossman, David
Megged, Aharon
Mitgutsch, Anna
Semel, Nava
Tomer, Ben Zion
Yaoz-Kest, Itamar

Holocaust trauma and Jewish identity
Améry, Jean
Appignanesi, Lisa
Baker, Mark Raphael
Bartov, Hanoch
Brett, Lily

Feinstein, Elaine
Feldman, Irving
Finkielkraut, Alain
Glatstein, Jacob
Grossman, David
Grossman, Vasilii
Hareven, Shulamith
Malamud, Bernard
Memmi, Albert
Ozick, Cynthia
Radnóti, Miklós
Raphael, Lev
Rawicz, Piotr
Rich, Adrienne
Rosen, Jonathan
Rosen, Norma
Roth, Philip
Salamon, Julie
Schindel, Robert
Scliar, Moacyr
Schulman, Helen
Sperber, Manes
Spiegelman, Art
Steiner, Jean-François
Steinfeld, J. J.
Tomer, Ben Zion
Vásquez-Bronfman, Ana

Jewish/Christian
Alhadeff, Gini
Begley, Louis
Bellow, Saul
Burnier, Andreas
Demetz, Hana
Ettinger, Elżbieta
Fink, Ida
Friedländer, Saul
Radnóti, Miklós
Schaeffer, Susan Fromberg

Lost/abandoned Jewish identity in response to hostile antisemitic society
Finkielkraut, Alain
Kehoe, Louise
Kriesel, Henry
Wilkomirski, Binjamin

Post-Holocaust Jewish identity
Alhadeff, Gini
Grossman, David
Jelinek, Elfriede
Kehoe, Louise
Malamud, Bernard
Ozick, Cynthia
Piercy, Marge
Rich, Adrienne
Rosen, Norma
Schindel, Robert
Shapiro, Alan
Singer, I. B.
Verbitsky, Bernardo

Post-Holocaust awakening of Jewish identity
Alhadeff, Gini
Becker, Jurek
Cony, Carlos Heitor
Elberg, Yehuda
Herzberg, Judith
Honigmann, Barbara
Jelinek, Elfriede
Ozick, Cynthia
Piercy, Marge
Raphael, Lev
Rich, Adrienne
Roth, Philip
Schindel, Robert
Shapiro, Alan
Singer, I. B.
Yaoz-Kest, Itamar
Zeitlin, Aaron
Zukofsky, Louis

Jewish self-hatred
Appignanesi, Lisa
Ozick, Cynthia

Indifference to saving Jews

Amir-Pinkerfeld, Anda
Berg, Mary
Biderman, Abraham
Burnier, Andreas
Cohen, Arthur
Durlacher, Gerhard
Elon, Amos
Grass, Günter
Hershman, Marcie
Hill, Geoffrey
Hofmann, Gert
Kaniuk, Yoram
Karpf, Anne
Katzenelson, Yitzhak
Ozick, Cynthia
Piercy, Marge
Potok, Chaim
Rich, Adrienne
Scliar, Moacyr
Steiner, George
Verbitsky, Bernardo
Weil, Clara
Whitman, Ruth
Wiesel, Elie

Israeli attitudes toward and reception of survivors

Israel as refuge from *Shoah*
Almagor, Gila
Amichai, Yehudah
Amir-Pinkerfeld, Anda
Bartov, Hanoch
Elberg, Yehuda
Kaniuk, Yoram
Kovner, Abba
Nissenson, Hugh
Piercy, Marge
Potok, Chaim
Sutzkever, Abraham
Tomer, Ben Zion
Yaoz-Kest, Itamar
Zeitlin, Aaron

Response to contact with survivors
Bartov, Hanoch
Gouri, Haim

Shame felt by Israeli *sabras* (Israeli-born) toward diaspora Jewry
Almagor, Gila
Bartov, Hanoch
Grossman, David
Hareven, Shulamith
Megged, Aharon

Jewish cultural/national continuity

Brett, Lily
Bukiet, Melvin Jules
Cohen, Arthur
Eliach, Yaffa
Friedländer, Saul
Grade, Chaim
Honigmann, Barbara
Kaniuk, Yoram
Kehoe, Louise
Leivick, H.
Miriam, Rivka
Molodowsky, Kadya
Oz, Amos
Ozick, Cynthia
Piercy, Marge
Potok, Chaim

Raphael, Lev
Reznikoff, Charles
Rosen, Jonathan
Rosen, Norma
Rosenbaum, Thane
Roth, Philip
Rothenberg, Jerome
Singer, I. B.
Sutzkever, Abraham
Wiesel, Elie
Wojdowski, Bogdan
Yaoz-Kest, Itamar
Zeitlin, Aaron

Jewish-Nazi confrontation (postwar)

Guralnik, Sonia
Layton, Irving
Ozick, Cynthia
Richler, Mordechai
Rosen, Norma
Steinfeld, J. J.
Wiesel, Elie

Judenrat

Arendt, Hannah
Biderman, Abraham
Birenbaum, Halina
Czerniakow, Adam
Edelman, Marek
Elman, Richard
Epstein, Leslie
Ettinger, Elżbieta
Green, Gerald
Kaplan, Chaim
Lustig, Arnost
Ringelblum, Emanuel
Roth, Philip
Rudnicki, Adolf
Schaeffer, Susan Fromberg
Steiner, Jean-François
Tomer, Ben Zion
Weil, Grete

Kindertransport

Gershon, Karen
Kramer, Lotte
Mayer, Gerda
Samuels, Diane
Sebald, W. G.
Segal, Lore

Language

Destruction of Yiddish
Molodowsky, Kadya

Implications of Holocaust for language

Corruption of language
Celan, Paul
Levi, Primo
Mandel, Elias Wolf
Sachs, Nelly
Steiner, George
Steiner, Jean-François
Tournier, Michel

Futility of language—post-Holocaust
Lustig, Arnost
Mandel, Elias Wolf

Language/cultural resistance
Doubrovsky, Serge

Post-Holocaust language/culture
Fackenheim, Emil
Kertész, Imre
Wiesel, Elie

Limitation of language for Holocaust representation
Antelme, Robert
Auerbach, Rachel
Celan, Paul
Durlacher, Gerhard
Fromer, Rebecca Camhi
Goldstein, Rebecca
Grass, Günter
Hareven, Shulamith
Hoffman, Eva
Hoffmann, Yoel
Karmel, Ilona
Kertész, Imre
Kofman, Sarah
Mandel, Elias Wolf
Michaels, Anne
Levi, Primo
Lyotard, Jean-François
Pilinszky, János
Sachs, Nelly
Semprun, Jorge

Power of language to restore and heal
Levi, Primo
Michaels, Anne

Misappropriation of language
Goodman, Allegra
Phillips, Caryl

Revival of Yiddish
Sutzkever, Abraham

Legislation (anti-Jewish)

Bassani, Giorgio
Chabon, Michael
Demetz, Hana
Feuchtwanger, Lion
Gay, Peter
Ginzburg, Natalia
Klemperer, Victor
Kogon, Eugen
Minco, Marga
Siegal, Aranka

Literary transmission of Holocaust

Antelme, Robert
Appelfeld, Aharon
Appignanesi, Lisa
Auerbach, Rachel
Chabon, Michael
Cohen, Albert
Delbo, Charlotte
Doubrovsky, Serge
Fink, Ida
Friedländer, Saul
Glatstein, Jacob
Goldstein, Rebecca
Grossman, David
Hartman, Geoffrey
Hoffman, Eva
Kofman, Sarah
Mandel, Elias Wolf
Miłosz, Czesław
Miriam, Rivka
Peleg, Dorit
Prose, Francine
Raczymow, Henri
Rawicz, Piotr
Rosen, Norma
Rosenbaum, Thane
Roth, Philip
Rothenberg, Jerome
Różewicz, Tadeusz
Schindel, Robert
Spiegelman, Art
Steiner, George
Thomas, D. M.

Wiesel, Elie

Alternate history—counter factuality

Harris, Robert

Mass killings—Einsatzgruppen, "actions"

Bellow, Saul
Epstein, Leslie
Kaplan, Chaim
Reznikoff, Charles
Schaeffer, Susan Fromberg
Thomas, D. M.
Wiesel, Elie
Yevtushenko, Yevgenii

Medical abuses

Amir-Pinkerfeld, Anda
Karmel, Ilona
Klein, Gerda
Lengyel, Olga
Nałkowska, Zofia
Nomberg-Przytyk, Sara
Perl, Gisella
Potok, Chaim
Reznikoff, Charles
Schaeffer, Susan Fromberg
Steinfeld, J. J.
Tedeschi, Giuliana
Vinocur, Ana
Wallant, Edward Lewis

Memory

Dynamics
Almagor, Gila
Améry, Jean
Bellow, Saul
Delbo, Charlotte
Eliach, Yaffa
Feinstein, Elaine
Grossinger, Harvey
Hareven, Shulamith
Hilsenrath, Edgar
Hoffman, Eva
Ka. Tzetnik 135633 (Yehiel Dinur)
Klein, Cecilie
Klüger, Ruth
Lengyel, Olga
Liebrecht, Savyon
Mann, Emily
Michaels, Anne
Ozick, Cynthia
Potok, Chaim
Rich, Adrienne
Roth, Philip
Salamon, Julie
Schaeffer, Susan Fromberg
Seligmann, Rafael
Tabori, George
Wilkomirski, Binjamin

As validation
Baker, Mark Raphael
Michaels, Anne

Moral imperative to remember
Agosín, Marjorie
Amichai, Yehudah
Auerbach, Rachel
Badanes, Jerome
Bassani, Giorgio
Bellow, Saul
Biderman, Abraham
Cohen, Albert
Drummond, Roberto
Finkielkraut, Alain
Fromer, Rebecca Camhi
Gilboa, Amir
Gouri, Haim
Guralnik, Sonia
Heyen, William
Kertész, Imre
Langfus, Anna
Levi, Primo
Michaels, Anne
Rich, Adrienne
Rosen, Norma
Roth, Philip
Rothenberg, Jerome
Różewicz, Tadeusz
Rudnicki, Adolf
Schaeffer, Susan Fromberg
Schindel, Robert
Steinfeld, J. J.

Identity and self-definition
Brett, Lily
Fried, Erich
Gergely, Ágnes
Grade, Chaim
Grossman, David
Levi, Primo
Modiano, Patrick
Rabinovitch, Anne
Raczymow, Henri
Rosen, Norma
Sack, Leeny
Schindel, Robert
Schlink, Bernhard
Sobol, Joshua
Steinfeld, J. J.
Tomer, Ben Zion
Wilkomirski, Binjamin

Misappropriation of Holocaust memory
Finkielkraut, Alain
Ozick, Cynthia
Prose, Francine

Excising memory
Ficowski, Jerzy
Finkielkraut, Alain

Transmission
Bauman, Janina
Brett, Lily
Fink, Ida
Friedländer, Saul
Heyen, William
Hilsenrath, Edgar
Kofman, Sarah
Ozick, Cynthia
Peleg, Dorit
Perec, Georges
Rosen, Norma
Różewicz, Tadeusz
Sack, Leeny
Sperber, Manes
Styron, William
Wiesel, Elie

Suppression of personal Holocaust history
Amichai, Yehudah
Appelfeld, Aharon
Bellow, Saul
Ettinger, Elżbieta
Ficowski, Jerzy
Grossman, David
Grossman, Vasilii
Hamburger, Michael
Herzberg, Judith
Hill, Geoffrey
Hochwälder, Fritz
Hofmann, Gert
Kogon, Eugen
Krall, Hanna
Kramer, Lotte
Layton, Irving
Liebrecht, Savyon

Meijer, Ischa
Modiano, Patrick
Ozick, Cynthia
Peleg, Dorit
Perec, Georges
Potok, Chaim
Rosen, Norma
Różewicz, Tadeusz
Rymkiewicz, Jarosław Marek
Schaeffer, Susan Fromberg
Schindel, Robert
Steiner, George
Sylvanus, Erwin
Tabori, George
Tomer, Ben Zion
Weil, Grete
Yevtushenko, Yevgenii

Memory vs. willed forgetfulness
Agosín, Marjorie
Bellow, Saul
Guralnik, Sonia
Schindel, Robert

Post-memory: second generation
Berger, Joseph
Epstein, Helen
Feinstein, Elaine
Govrin, Michal
Grossman, David
Hareven, Shulamith
Karpf, Anne
Lentin, Ronit
Liebrecht, Savyon
Miriam, Rivka
Modiano, Patrick
Rabinovitch, Anne
Raczymow, Henri
Semel, Nava
Spiegelman, Art
Steinfeld, J. J.

Problematics of recovered memory
Appignanesi, Lisa
Baker, Mark Raphael
Biderman, Abraham
Levi, Primo
Modiano, Patrick
Perec, Georges
Rich, Adrienne
Różewicz, Tadeusz
Seligmann, Rafael
Styron, William
Wilkomirski, Binjamin

Immersion in memory
Tabori, George

Recovery of memory
Almagor, Gila

Mischling status

Aichinger, Ilse
Demetz, Hana

Moral dilemmas of survival in the Nazi universe

Elberg, Yehuda
Elman, Richard
Epstein, Leslie
Fenelon, Fania
Fromer, Rebecca Camhi
Goldstein, Rebecca
Karmel, Ilona
Kogon, Eugen
Levi, Primo
Lind, Jakov
Lustig, Arnost
Mann, Emily
Modiano, Patrick
Ringelblum, Emanuel
Różewicz, Tadeusz
Sobol, Joshua
Styron, William
Wiesel, Elie

Moral indictments of perpetrators, collaborators, bystanders, Holocaust deniers

Elman, Richard
Epstein, Leslie
Feuchtwanger, Lion
Grass, Günter
Heyen, William
Hochwälder, Fritz
Karski, Jan
Kogon, Eugen
Layton, Irving
Ozick, Cynthia
Piercy, Marge
Pilinszky, János
Sartre, Jean-Paul
Sobol, Joshua
Steiner, Jean-François

"Muselmänner" ("Muslims")

Leitner, Isabella
Levi, Primo
Semprun, Jorge
Wiesel, Elie

Myths: perpetuation, refutation

Austrian myth of victimhood (first victim of Hitler)
Schindel, Robert

Dutch myth of anti-Nazi solidarity
Burnier, Andreas
Meijer, Ischa

French myth of unified resistance
Modiano, Patrick
Steiner, George

Polish myth of heroic martyrdom
Różewicz, Tadeusz

Myth of Jewish failure to resist ("sheep to the slaughter")
Piercy, Marge

Nazi bureaucracy

Barnes, Peter
Epstein, Leslie
Weiss, Peter
Wiesenthal, Simon

Nazi camp universe

Labor camp
Karmel, Ilona
Klein, Gerda
Klemperer, Victor
Memmi, Albert
Schaeffer, Susan Fromberg
Wiesel, Elie

Transit camp
Cohen, Elie
Hillesum, Etty
Mechanicus, Philip

Concentration and death camp (administration, hierarchies, punishments, living conditions, work)
Alhadeff, Gini
Aloni, Jenny
Antelme, Robert
Arendt, Hannah
Atlan, Liliane
Bitton-Jackson, Livia
Borowski, Tadeusz
Brett, Lily
Celan, Paul

Cohen, Elie
Delbo, Charlotte
Domecq, Alcina Lubitch
Dribben, Judith Strick
Duden, Anne
Durlacher, Gerhard
Eliach, Yaffa
Fenelon, Fania
Ferderber-Salz, Bertha
Frankl, Viktor
Fromer, Rebecca Camhi
Gascar, Pierre
Grossman, David
Grossman, Vasilii
Herzberg, Abel
Isaacson, Judith Magyar
Ka. Tzetnik 135633 (Yehiel Dinur)
Karmel, Ilona
Kertész, Imre
Kiš, Danilo
Kittner, Alfred
Klein, Gerda
Layton, Irving
Leitner, Isabella
Lengyel, Olga
Levi, Primo
Lustig, Arnost
Mechanicus, Philip
Millu, Liana
Nomberg-Przytyk, Sara
Oberski, Jona
Osherow, Jacqueline
Ozick, Cynthia
Pagis, Dan
Perec, Georges
Perl, Gisella
Piercy, Marge
Pilinszky, János
Reznikoff, Charles
Rousset, David
Schaeffer, Susan Fromberg
Semprun, Jorge
Spiegelman, Art
Styron, William
Tabori, George
Tedeschi, Giuliana
Wallant, Edward Lewis
Weil, Clara
Weiss, Peter
Wiesel, Elie
Wilkomirski, Binjamin

Punishments
Klein, Gerda
Leitner, Isabella

Jobs

Sonderkommando
Ka. Tzetnik 135633 (Yehiel Dinur)
Karmel, Ilona
Schaeffer, Susan Fromberg
Wallant, Edward Lewis
Wiesel, Elie

Canada
Borowski, Tadeusz

Hospital
Lengyel, Olga
Perl, Gisella

Nazi legacy

Aichinger, Ilse
Bernhard, Thomas
Camus, Albert
Fackenheim, Emil
Feinstein, Elaine
Fried, Erich
Gouri, Haim
Guralnik, Sonia
Hartman, Geoffrey
Jelinek, Elfriede
Karpf, Anne
Kiš, Danilo
Liebrecht, Savyon
Minco, Marga
Nissenson, Hugh
Ozick, Cynthia
Pagis, Dan
Roth, Philip
Scliar, Moacyr
Shapiro, Alan
Singer, I. B.
Tournier, Michel

Nazi occupation of Europe

Bitton-Jackson, Livia
Böll, Heinrich
Chabon, Michael (Czechoslovakia)
Czerniakow, Adam (Poland)
Doubrovsky, Serge (France)
Epstein, Leslie (Poland)
Fuks, Ladislav (Czechoslovakia)
Gary, Romain (France)
Ginzburg, Natalia (Italy)
Grumberg, Jean-Claude (France)
Grynberg, Henryk (Poland)
Herzberg, Abel (Netherlands)
Herzberg, Judith (Netherlands)
Hillesum, Etty (Netherlands)
Kaplan, Chaim (Poland)
Karski, Jan (Poland)
Maurer, Jadwiga (Poland)
Memmi, Albert
Millu, Liana (Italy)
Minco, Marga (Netherlands)
Modiano, Patrick (France)
Oberski, Jona (Netherlands)
Piercy, Marge (France)
Rosenberg, Blanca
Rudnicki, Adolf
Sartre, Jean-Paul (France)
Siegal, Aranka
Sneh, Simja (Poland)
Spiegelman, Art (Poland)
Weil, Jiří (Romania)
Wiesel, Elie (Romania)

Nazi racist ideology

Feuchtwanger, Lion
Kogon, Eugen
Kolmar, Gertrud
Memmi, Albert
Tedeschi, Giuliana
Tournier, Michel
Verbitsky, Bernardo

"Otherness"

Jews perceived as "Other" in host countries
Alhadeff, Gini
Appelfeld, Aharon
Bassani, Giorgio
Finkielkraut, Alain
Gershon, Karen
Lustig, Arnost
Memmi, Albert
Ozick, Cynthia
Piercy, Marge
Rawicz, Piotr
Sartre, Jean-Paul
Schindel, Robert
Singer, I. J.
Verbitsky, Bernardo

Consciousness of Jewish self as "Other"
Alhadeff, Gini
Bassani, Giorgio
Brett, Lily
Canetti, Elias

Demetz, Hana
Durlacher, Gerhard
Gay, Peter
Gershon, Karen
Grynberg, Henryk
Klüger, Ruth
Kolmar, Gertrud
Kosinski, Jerzy
Margulies, Donald
Ozick, Cynthia
Samuels, Diane
Sartre, Jean-Paul

Passing as Gentile

Appignanesi, Lisa
Appleman-Jurman, Alicia
Auerbach, Rachel
Begley, Louis
Elberg, Yehuda
Ettinger, Elżbieta
Fink, Ida
Friedländer, Saul
Herzberg, Judith
Karmel, Ilona
Klepfisz, Irena
Langfus, Anna
Lind, Jakov
Lustig, Arnost
Mann, Emily
Meed, Vladka
Piercy, Marge
Rawicz, Piotr
Schaeffer, Susan Fromberg
Siegal, Aranka
Tec, Nechama

Perpetrators

Aloni, Jenny
Amis, Martin
Appleman-Jurman, Alicia
Baitz, Jon Robin
Barnes, Peter
Bernhard, Thomas
Borges, Jorge Luis
Brett, Lily
Celan, Paul
Cohen, Albert
Domecq, Alcina Lubitch
Epstein, Leslie
Fried, Erich
Glatstein, Jacob
Gouri, Haim
Grossman, Vasilii
Hamburger, Michael
Hershman, Marcie
Herzberg, Abel
Heyen, William
Hilsenrath, Edgar
Hofmann, Gert
Jelinek, Elfriede
Karmel, Ilona
Kipphardt, Heiner
Kittner, Alfred
Kogon, Eugen
Krall, Hanna
Lind, Jakov
Layton, Irving
Lustig, Arnost
Millu, Liana
Mulisch, Harry
Nałkowska, Zofia
Perl, Gisella
Piercy, Marge
Pinter, Harold
Nomberg-Przytyk, Sara
Reznikoff, Charles
Richler, Mordechai
Rousset, David
Sachs, Nelly
Sartre, Jean-Paul
Schlink, Bernhard
Singer, I. J.
Steiner, George
Styron, William
Tournier, Michel
Tuwim, Julian
Verbitsky, Bernardo
Weil, Jiří
Weiss, Peter
Wiesel, Elie
Wiesenthal, Simon
Wygodzki, Stanisław

Poles

Betrayers/denouncers of unincarcerated Jews
Andrzejewski, Jerzy
Ettinger, Elżbieta
Głowiński, Michał
Hoffman, Eva
Schaeffer, Susan Fromberg
Szczypiorski, Andrzej
Szlengel, Władysław

Blackmailers/extortionists of Jews in hiding
Ettinger, Elżbieta
Głowiński, Michał
Ringelblum, Emanuel
Rosenberg, Blanca
Szczypiorski, Andrzej

Protectors/rescuers
Ettinger, Elżbieta
Ferderber-Salz, Bertha
Głowiński, Michał
Hoffman, Eva
Karski, Jan
Ringelblum, Emanuel
Rosenberg, Blanca
Tec, Nechama

Polish-Jewish relations (pre-*Shoah*, *Shoah* era, post-*Shoah*)
Andrzejewski, Jerzy
Appignanesi, Lisa
Biderman, Abraham
Ettinger, Elżbieta
Ferderber-Salz, Bertha
Hoffman, Eva
Karski, Jan
Ringelblum, Emanuel
Rudnicki, Adolf
Rymkiewicz, Jarosław Marek
Tuwim, Julian

Post-Holocaust universe

Jewish perspective: consciousness and implications
Badanes, Jerome
Bettelheim, Bruno
Böll, Heinrich
Brecht, Bertolt
Bukiet, Melvin Jules
Camus, Albert
Fackenheim, Emil
Feinstein, Elaine
Finkielkraut, Alain
Fried, Erich
Glatstein, Jacob
Goldstein, Rebecca
Goodman, Allegra
Gouri, Haim
Hareven, Shulamith
Hartman, Geoffrey
Honigmann, Barbara
Kiš, Danilo
Kramer, Lotte
Levinas, Emmanuel
Liebrecht, Savyon
Minco, Marga
Ozick, Cynthia

Prose, Francine
Rabinovitch, Anne
Rich, Adrienne
Roth, Philip
Różewicz, Tadeusz
Schaeffer, Susan Fromberg
Scliar, Moacyr
Singer, I. B.

Postwar lives of survivors

Aichinger, Ilse
Améry, Jean
Baitz, Jon Robin
Bauman, Janina
Becker, Jurek
Bukiet, Melvin Jules
Delbo, Charlotte
Doubrovsky, Serge
Grade, Chaim
Guralnik, Sonia
Herzberg, Judith
Honigmann, Barbara
Kaniuk, Yoram
Levi, Primo
Liebrecht, Savyon
Mann, Emily
Różewicz, Tadeusz
Samuels, Diane
Schindel, Robert
Schlink, Bernhard
Seligmann, Rafael
Semel, Nava
Singer, I. B.
Tomer, Ben Zion
Wiesel, Elie
Wilkomirski, Binjamin
Yaoz-Kest, Itamar

Presaging of Holocaust

Glatstein, Jacob
Zeitlin, Aaron

Presence of past

Ascher, Carol
Bellow, Saul
Birenbaum, Halina
Brod, Max
Cohen, Albert
Eliach, Yaffa
Feinstein, Elaine
Finkielkraut, Alain
Finkelstein, Barbara
Friedländer, Saul
Gershon, Karen
Goldstein, Rebecca
Goodman, Allegra
Hadar, Tanya
Hamburger, Michael
Herzberg, Judith
Honigmann, Barbara
Kiš, Danilo
Kovner, Abba
Langfus, Anna
Liebrecht, Savyon
Maurer, Jadwiga
Minco, Marga
Oz, Amos
Ozick, Cynthia
Peleg, Dorit
Phillips, Caryl
Pilinszky, János
Rabinovitch, Anne
Raczymow, Henri
Richler, Mordechai
Rosen, Jonathan
Rosenbaum, Thane
Salamon, Julie
Schaeffer, Susan Fromberg
Schindel, Robert
Semel, Nava
Shapiro, Alan
Spiegelman, Art
Steinfeld, J. J.
Wallant, Edward Lewis
Weil, Grete
Yaoz-Kest, Itamar

Refugees

Gershon, Karen
Karpf, Anne
Malamud, Bernard
Mayer, Gerda
Ozick, Cynthia
Piercy, Marge
Samuels, Diane
Segal, Lore
Singer, I. B.

Representation and limits of Holocaust representation

Antelme, Robert
Appelfeld, Aharon
Appignanesi, Lisa
Auerbach, Rachel
Chabon, Michael
Cohen, Albert
Delbo, Charlotte
Doubrovsky, Serge
Durlacher, Gerhard
Fink, Ida
Finkielkraut, Alain
Friedländer, Saul
Fromer, Rebecca Camhi
Glatstein, Jacob
Goldstein, Rebecca
Grossman, David
Hareven, Shulamith
Hartman, Geoffrey
Hoffman, Eva
Kertész, Imre
Kofman, Sarah
Lyotard, Jean-François
Mandel, Elias Wolf
Michaels, Anne
Miłosz, Czesław
Miriam, Rivka
Peleg, Dorit
Pilinszky, János
Prose, Francine
Raczymow, Henri
Rawicz, Piotr
Rosen, Norma
Rosenbaum, Thane
Roth, Philip
Rothenberg, Jerome
Różewicz, Tadeusz
Sachs, Nelly
Schindel, Robert
Seligmann, Rafael
Semprun, Jorge
Spiegelman, Art
Steiner, George
Steinfeld, J. J.
Thomas, D. M.
Wiesel, Elie

Rescue

Attempts
Elon, Amos
Goldberg, Lea
Kaniuk, Yoram
Keneally, Thomas
Kramer, Lotte
Lerner, Motti
Piercy, Marge
Samuels, Diane
Schaeffer, Susan Fromberg
Tec, Nechama

Christian assistance/individuals
Appignanesi, Lisa
Auerbach, Rachel
Ettinger, Elżbieta
Fink, Ida
Fromer, Rebecca Camhi
Głowiński, Michał
Grumberg, Jean-Claude
Karski, Jan
Krall, Hanna
Levi, Primo
Reznikoff, Charles
Schaeffer, Susan Fromberg
Tec, Nechama

Deception
Gouri, Haim
Lind, Jakov

Obstruction (government)
Cohen, Arthur
Elon, Amos
Hershman, Marcie
Piercy, Marge
Potok, Chaim

Resistance

Militant response of victims
Améry, Jean
Amir-Pinkerfeld, Anda
Appleman-Jurman, Alicia
Auerbach, Rachel
Bartov, Hanoch
Böll, Heinrich
Brandys, Kazimierz
Chabon, Michael
Cohen, Albert
Delbo, Charlotte
Dribben, Judith Strick
Edelman, Marek
Elberg, Yehuda
Epstein, Leslie
Ettinger, Elżbieta
Feinstein, Elaine
Fenelon, Fania
Fromer, Rebecca Camhi
Gary, Romain
Grossman, Vasilii
Hersey, John
Karmel, Ilona
Karski, Jan
Keneally, Thomas
Kovner, Abba
Krall, Hanna
Langfus, Anna
Lengyel, Olga
Levi, Primo
Lustig, Arnost
Meed, Vladka
Memmi, Albert
Millu, Liana
Mulisch, Harry
Nomberg-Przytyk, Sara
Papiernikov, Joseph
Piercy, Marge
Rosenberg, Blanca
Rousset, David
Samuels, Diane
Schaeffer, Susan Fromberg
Semprun, Jorge
Siegal, Aranka
Sneh, Simja
Sperber, Manes
Steiner, Jean-François
Styron, William
Sutzkever, Abraham
Szlengel, Władysław
Tec, Nechama
Weil, Grete
Whitman, Ruth

German anti-Nazi resistance
Birenbaum, Halina
Kogon, Eugen
Leivick, H.
Minco, Marga
Ringelblum, Emanuel
Sperber, Manes
Zeitlin, Aaron

Spiritual
Atlan, Liliane
Becker, Jurek
Bettelheim, Bruno
Bitton-Jackson, Livia
Chabon, Michael
Cohen, Arthur
Elberg, Yehuda
Eliach, Yaffa
Fackenheim, Emil
Fenelon, Fania
Hillesum, Etty
Klein, Gerda
Klüger, Ruth
Kolmar, Gertrud
Leivick, H.
Piercy, Marge
Rousset, David
Spiegelman, Art
Weil, Jiří
Whitman, Ruth
Zeitlin, Aaron

Theological implications of spiritual resistance
Fackenheim, Emil

Revenge

Amir-Pinkerfeld, Anda
Bartov, Hanoch
Domecq, Alcina Lubitch
Eliach, Yaffa
Gilboa, Amir
Greenberg, Uri Zvi
Katzenelson, Yitzhak
Leivick, H.
Steinfeld, J. J.

Second generation: discovery of Shoah; response

Jewish second generation: post-memory and inherited trauma
Almagor, Gila
Appignanesi, Lisa
Ascher, Carol
Baker, Mark Raphael
Becker, Jurek
Berger, Joseph
Brett, Lily
Bukiet, Melvin Jules
Domecq, Alcina Lubitch
Eliach, Yaffa
Epstein, Helen
Finkelstein, Barbara
Friedman, Carl
Goodman, Allegra
Govrin, Michal
Grossinger, Harvey
Grossman, David
Grunberg, Arnon
Hadar, Tanya
Hareven, Shulamith
Herzberg, Judith
Hoffman, Eva
Honigmann, Barbara
Jelinek, Elfriede
Karpf, Anne
Kehoe, Louise
Layton, Irving
Lentin, Ronit
Levy, Itamar
Liebrecht, Savyon

Meijer, Ischa
Michaels, Anne
Miriam, Rivka
Modiano, Patrick
Oberski, Jona
Pagis, Dan
Peleg, Dorit
Rabinovitch, Anne
Raczymow, Henri
Raphael, Lev
Rosen, Jonathan
Rosen, Norma
Rosenbaum, Thane
Sack, Leeny
Salamon, Julie
Samuels, Diane
Schindel, Robert
Schulman, Helen
Seligmann, Rafael
Semel, Nava
Skibell, Joseph
Spiegelman, Art
Steinfeld, J. J.
Stollman, Aryeh Lev
Wiesel, Elie

German second generation: confronting the perpetrator generation
Biller, Maxim
Duden, Anne
Goldstein, Rebecca
Heyen, William
Hofmann, Gert
Schlink, Bernhard
Sebald, W. G.

Silence/denial and marginalization of Holocaust reality/history/collaboration

Multinational
Epstein, Leslie
Feinstein, Elaine
Rich, Adrienne
Rosenbaum, Thane
Wallant, Edward Lewis

American
Roth, Philip

British
Feinstein, Elaine
Samuels, Diane

German/Austrian
Bernhard, Thomas
Elon, Amos
Hochwälder, Fritz
Hofmann, Gert
Kogon, Eugen
Mitgutsch, Anna
Schindel, Robert
Schlink, Bernhard
Sylvanus, Erwin
Weil, Grete

Israeli
Grossman, David
Hareven, Shulamith
Peleg, Dorit
Semel, Nava

Polish
Ettinger, Elżbieta
Hoffman, Eva
Krall, Hanna
Tuwim, Julian
Rymkiewicz, Jarosław Marek

Russian
Grossman, Vasilii
Yevtushenko, Yevgenii

Challenge to silencing and marginalizing Holocaust acknowledgment
Camus, Albert
Elon, Amos
Fromer, Rebecca Camhi
Grossman, David
Hill, Geoffrey
Layton, Irving
Liebrecht, Savyon
Modiano, Patrick
Peleg, Dorit
Pinter, Harold
Raczymow, Henri
Salamon, Julie
Samuels, Diane
Skibell, Joseph
Sylvanus, Erwin

Denial/revisionism
Aichinger, Ilse
Bassani, Giorgio
Benski, Stanisław
Cohen, Arthur
Ettinger, Elżbieta
Finkielkraut, Alain
Goldstein, Rebecca
Grossman, David
Harris, Robert
Herzberg, Judith
Hoffman, Eva
Lentin, Ronit
Liebrecht, Savyon
Meijer, Ischa
Oz, Amos
Ozick, Cynthia
Piercy, Marge
Raphael, Lev
Schindel, Robert
Schlink, Bernhard
Schulman, Helen
Steiner, Jean-François
Sylvanus, Erwin

Survivor silence
Berger, Joseph
Hoffman, Eva
Liebrecht, Savyon
Meijer, Ischa
Michaels, Anne
Ozick, Cynthia
Perec, Georges
Raphael, Lev
Rosenbaum, Thane

Survival strategies and struggles within the ghetto/camp universe

Escape
Elman, Richard
Grumberg, Jean-Claude
Karmel, Ilona
Schaeffer, Susan Fromberg
Steiner, Jean-François

Mutual assistance
Appignanesi, Lisa
Bettelheim, Bruno
Cohen, Elie
Fenelon, Fania
Karmel, Ilona
Klein, Cecilie
Klein, Gerda
Langfus, Anna
Leitner, Isabella
Levi, Primo
Perec, Georges
Piercy, Marge
Radnóti, Miklós
Schaeffer, Susan Fromberg
Wiesel, Elie

Organization of food and clothing
Alhadeff, Gini
Auerbach, Rachel
Cohen, Arthur
Elberg, Yehuda
Fink, Ida
Fuks, Ladislav
Hilsenrath, Edgar
Isaacson, Judith Magyar
Karmel, Ilona
Keneally, Thomas
Klein, Cecilie
Klein, Gerda
Klepfisz, Irena
Langfus, Anna
Leitner, Isabella
Lengyel, Olga
Levi, Primo
Rousset, David
Różewicz, Tadeusz
Spiegelman, Art

Political organization and cooperation with underground
Antelme, Robert
Rousset, David

Psychology of survival
Frankl, Viktor
Vinocur, Ana

Surrogate family formation
Karmel, Ilona
Klein, Gerda
Leitner, Isabella
Piercy, Marge
Schaeffer, Susan Fromberg

Survivor guilt

Appignanesi, Lisa
Appleman-Jurman, Alicia
Atlan, Liliane
Brandys, Kazimierz
Drummond, Roberto
Elman, Richard
Fink, Ida
Fried, Erich
Fromer, Rebecca Camhi
Gershon, Karen
Gilboa, Amir
Gouri, Haim
Grumberg, Jean-Claude
Grunberg, Arnon
Grynberg, Henryk
Herzberg, Judith
Ka. Tzetnik 135633 (Yehiel Dinur)
Kehoe, Louise
Klein, Cecilie
Kramer, Lotte
Kriesel, Henry
Leivick, H.
Lengyel, Olga
Levi, Primo
Mann, Emily
Minco, Marga
Molodowsky, Kadya
Piercy, Marge
Raczymow, Henri
Rosenberg, Blanca
Schaeffer, Susan Fromberg
Singer, I. B.
Sneh, Simja
Spiegelman, Art
Tomer, Ben Zion
Wallant, Edward Lewis
Weil, Jiří
Wiesel, Elie
Wygodzki, Stanisław
Yaoz-Kest, Itamar
Zeitlin, Aaron

Survivor mission in postwar era

Berger, Joseph
Biderman, Abraham
Birenbaum, Halina
Gouri, Haim
Grumberg, Jean-Claude
Grynberg, Henryk
Kaniuk, Yoram
Kertész, Imre
Klepfisz, Irena
Layton, Irving
Meed, Vladka
Ozick, Cynthia
Pagis, Dan
Potok, Chaim
Rudnicki, Adolf
Salamon, Julie
Schaeffer, Susan Fromberg
Spiegelman, Art
Steiner, George
Vinocur, Ana
Wiesel, Elie
Zeitlin, Aaron

Survivor psychology

Bettelheim, Bruno
Chabon, Michael
Gouri, Haim
Piercy, Marge
Shapiro, Alan
Singer, I. B.
Yaoz-Kest, Itamar

Survivor syndrome (post-traumatic stress stemming from Holocaust trauma manifested in depression, guilt feelings, emotional numbing, recurrent nightmares and painful memories, social alienation and isolation)

Almagor, Gila
Aloni, Jenny
Appelfeld, Aharon
Ascher, Carol
Badanes, Jerome
Becker, Jurek
Begley, Louis
Bellow, Saul
Benski, Stanisław
Birenbaum, Halina
Brett, Lily
Delbo, Charlotte
Drummond, Roberto
Ettinger, Elżbieta
Epstein, Helen
Finkelstein, Barbara
Gouri, Haim
Grossman, David
Hareven, Shulamith
Herzberg, Judith
Kaniuk, Yoram
Karpf, Anne
Klein, Cecilie
Kramer, Lotte
Langfus, Anna
Lebow, Barbara
Levi, Primo
Liebrecht, Savyon
Lustig, Arnost
Mann, Emily
Meijer, Ischa
Minco, Marga
Miriam, Rivka
Oz, Amos
Ozick, Cynthia
Pagis, Dan
Phillips, Caryl
Potok, Chaim
Raphael, Lev
Richler, Mordechai

Rosen, Norma
Rosenbaum, Thane
Rosenfarb, Chava
Samuels, Diane
Schindel, Robert
Schulman, Helen
Semel, Nava
Semprun, Jorge
Singer, I. B.
Steiner, George
Tomer, Ben Zion
Wallant, Edward Lewis

Theology

Theology after Auschwitz
Amichai, Yehudah
Cohen, Arthur
Elman, Richard
Finkielkraut, Alain
Govrin, Michal
Grade, Chaim
Greenberg, Uri Zvi
Nissenson, Hugh
Ostriker, Alicia
Potok, Chaim
Rosen, Norma
Singer, I. B.
Stollman, Aryeh Lev
Wiesel, Elie

Protesting God's failure to intervene
Elman, Richard
Glatstein, Jacob
Gouri, Haim
Grade, Chaim
Leitner, Isabella
Leivick, H.
Molodowsky, Kadya
Ostriker, Alicia
Papiernikov, Joseph
Potok, Chaim
Richler, Mordechai
Rosen, Norma
Shapiro, Alan
Singer, I. B.
Wiesel, Elie

Implications of the Holocaust
Ascher, Carol
Brod, Max
Bukiet, Melvin Jules
Eliach, Yaffa
Elman, Richard
Fackenheim, Emil
Finkelstein, Barbara
Flinker, Moshe
Frankl, Viktor
Gergely, Ágnes
Glatstein, Jacob
Goodman, Allegra
Grade, Chaim
Katzenelson, Yitzhak
Kovner, Abba
Leivick, H.
Levinas, Emmanuel
Molodowsky, Kadya
Nissenson, Hugh
Ostriker, Alicia
Ozick, Cynthia
Papiernikov, Joseph
Pilinszky, János
Potok, Chaim
Raphael, Lev
Rosen, Norma
Rosenbaum, Thane
Schindel, Robert
Schwarz-Bart, André
Seligmann, Rafael
Shapiro, Alan
Shayevitch, Simkha-Bunim
Singer, I. B.
Stollman, Aryeh Lev
Wiesel, Elie
Wincelberg, Shimon
Zeitlin, Aaron

Torture

Améry, Jean
Demetz, Hana
Guralnik, Sonia
Kolmar, Gertrud
Modiano, Patrick
Perec, Georges
Piercy, Marge
Sneh, Simja
Whitman, Ruth

Universalizing the Holocaust

Böll, Heinrich
Brecht, Bertolt
Ettinger, Elżbieta
Grossman, Vasilii
Hilsenrath, Edgar
Jelinek, Elfriede
Phillips, Caryl
Pinter, Harold
Raphael, Lev
Verbitsky, Bernardo
Yevtushenko, Yevgenii

Warsaw ghetto uprising

Ettinger, Elżbieta
Hersey, John
Katzenelson, Yitzhak

Witnessing—bearing witness

Imperative
Alhadeff, Gini
Amichai, Yehudah
Auerbach, Rachel
Badanes, Jerome
Bellow, Saul
Berg, Mary
Biderman, Abraham
Birenbaum, Halina
Brett, Lily
Bukiet, Melvin Jules
Camus, Albert
Cohen, Albert
Cohen, Arthur
Demetz, Hana
Doubrovsky, Serge
Drummond, Roberto
Elman, Richard
Epstein, Leslie
Ettinger, Elżbieta
Fromer, Rebecca Camhi
Gascar, Pierre
Gergely, Ágnes
Gershon, Karen
Goodman, Allegra
Grossman, David
Grossman, Vasilii
Hareven, Shulamith
Heyen, William
Hill, Geoffrey
Ka. Tzetnik 135633 (Yehiel Dinur)
Karmel, Ilona
Katzenelson, Yitzhak
Klein, Cecilie
Klein, Gerda
Klemperer, Victor
Kofman, Sarah
Kogon, Eugen
Kolmar, Gertrud
Kovner, Abba
Layton, Irving
Lyotard, Jean-François
Mandel, Elias Wolf

Miłosz, Czesław
Nałkowska, Zofia
Osherow, Jacqueline
Ozick, Cynthia
Pagis, Dan
Peleg, Dorit
Piercy, Marge
Pilinszky, János
Reznikoff, Charles
Rabinovitch, Anne
Raczymow, Henri
Rawicz, Piotr
Rosen, Jonathan
Rosen, Norma
Roth, Philip
Różewicz, Tadeusz
Rudnicki, Adolf
Sachs, Nelly
Salamon, Julie
Samuels, Diane
Schaeffer, Susan Fromberg
Semel, Nava
Spiegelman, Art
Steiner, George
Vinocur, Ana
Wallant, Edward Lewis
Wiesel, Elie
Yevtushenko, Yevgenii

Problematics

Michaels, Anne

Zionism

Almagor, Gila
Bellow, Saul
Brod, Max
Elman, Richard
Fackenheim, Emil
Flinker, Moshe
Friedländer, Saul
Hareven, Shulamith
Herzberg, Abel
Kovner, Abba
Nissenson, Hugh
Phillips, Caryl
Piercy, Marge
Potok, Chaim
Roth, Philip
Schaeffer, Susan Fromberg
Singer, I. B.
Singer, I. J.
Tomer, Ben Zion
Yaoz-Kest, Itamar
Zeitlin, Aaron

APPENDIX: GHETTOS NOTED IN THE LITERATURE

Authors' names preceded by an asterisk (*) were incarcerated in the ghettos that are the subject of their writing.

Except for those entries identified in parentheses as derived from other sources, all data in this appendix is compiled from the following sources.

Gutman, Israel. *Encyclopedia of the Holocaust*. 4 vols. New York: Macmillan, 1990.

Mogilansky, Roman. *The Ghetto Anthology*. Los Angeles: American Congress of Jews, 1985.

Niewyck, Donald L., and Francis Nicosia's *Columbia Guide to the Holocaust*. New York: Columbia University Press, 2000.

Beregszász (Berehovo)

Location: Berehovo, a city in Czechoslovakia (now in Ukraine). *Established:* 1941. *Administrative Responsibility:* SS and Hungarian police (1941 until liquidation). *Prisoner Work and Use:* Most of the Jewish men were sent to labor battalions. *Rate and Manner of Death:* Out of the estimated 6,000 Jews in the city, 500 were either deported or killed, while 300 Jewish families survived the war. *Resistance:* The Jewish community continued to hold services in a synagogue even during the war.

*Siegal, Aranka

Białystok

Location: Białystok, northeastern Poland. *Occupation*: 15 September 1939, but a week later handed over to the Soviet Union, which held the city for twenty-one months until the Germans reoccupied the city on 27 June 1941. At that time 2,000 Jews were burned alive, shot, or tortured to death. During the following two weeks an additional 4,000 Jews were murdered, particularly members of the intelligentsia, Communists, and other political figures. The chief rabbi was summoned and ordered to form a *Judenrat*. *Ghetto Established:* 1 August 1941 and 50,000 Białystok Jews were confined there. *Administrative Responsibility:* Jewish Council was responsible for administering the soup kitchens and two hospitals, pharmacies, and schools and other community institutions (1 August 1941–November 1942); SS and Gestapo (November 1942–August 1943). *Prisoner Work and Use:* The 50,000 Jews kept in the ghetto were forced to work in various factories. The ghetto became a center of industry, manufacturing essential items required by the economic arm of the occupation authorities. Most Jews worked in the ghetto factories and workshops and some in German establishments outside the ghetto. They also performed illegal work for their own needs in clothing and textile products. *Rate and Manner of Death:* In addition to the routine of executions and starvation, deportations to other ghettos and extermination camps account for major losses. In September and October of 1941 4,500 ill and unskilled inhabitants were sent to Pruzhany where most were killed during that liquidation in January 1943. From 5–12 February 1943 an *Aktion* was conducted in the ghetto in the course of which 2,000 Jews were shot and 10,000 deported to Treblinka. Ghetto fighters took many losses in this event. In August heavily armed SS men and Ukrainian auxiliaries surrounded the ghetto intent on its liquidation. Deportations began on 18 August and went on for three days, in the course of which most of the Jews were deported to Treblinka, Majdanek, Poniatowa, Blizyn, Auschwitz, and Theresienstadt. *Resistance:* Several youth movements existed in the ghetto forming a united underground by July 1943, including Communists, Zionists, and the Bund, whose goal was armed struggle against the Germans and engaged in armed resistance for five days upon the ghetto's liquidation. *Ghetto Liquidated:* August 1943.

*Nomberg-Pryztyk, Sara

Bochnia

Location: The town of Bochnia in Tarnow region, Poland. *Established:* 15 March 1941. *Type:* A ghetto, considered a "remnant ghetto" after November 1942. *Administrative Responsibility:* SS (15 March 1941–September 1943). *Prisoner Work and Use:* The ghetto population was primarily forced to work in road construction, while some worked as tailors or shoemakers. *Rate and Manner of Death:* Out of the estimated 15,000 Jews in the ghetto, over 6,000 were deported for extermination, while close to sixty were killed on site. *Resistance:* An underground movement, Jewish Warring Organization, which had been established before the formation of the ghetto, and which smuggled arms and false ID documents, as well as building a camouflaged bunker and making plans for armed resistance. *Ghetto Liquidated:* September 1943.

Eliach, Yaffe

Bransk

Location: The town of Bransk in the Białystok region, Poland. *Established:* fall 1941. *Administrative Responsibility:* SS (fall 1941–November 1942). *Prisoner Work and Use:* The ghetto population was forced to work in road construction, as well as sanitary jobs in the town. *Rate and Manner of Death:* Out of approximately 3,000 people in the ghetto, most were sent for extermination, while about sixty were shot in the ghetto itself. *Resistance:* Between 600 and 800 people from the ghetto managed to escape. *Ghetto Liquidated:* November 1942.

Hoffman, Eva

Buczacz (Buchach)

Location: Buczacz, a city in Tarnopol region, Ukraine. *Established:* 5 July 1941. *Administrative Responsibility:* SS with Ukrainian collaboration (5 July 1941–June 1943). *Prisoner Work and Use:* The ghetto population provided slave labor in workshops for skilled craftsmen. *Rate and Manner of Death:* Out of the 10,000 Jews from the city, less than 100 survived. About 4,000 of the ghetto population were deported to Belżec, while another 5,000 were shot. *Resistance:* At the end of 1942, organized resistance was set up, and they fought the ghetto guards upon its liquidation, as well as managing several escapes. Also, the Jewish Council provided much help to the ghetto community. *Ghetto Liquidated:* June 1943.

Appleman-Jurman, Alicia

Kaposvár

Location: Kaposvár, southwestern Hungary. *Established:* May 1944. *Administrative Responsibility: Judenrat* and SS (May 1944–4 July 1944). *Prisoner Work and Use:* The Jewish population of the area was forced into a limited space and toward the end of June transferred to an artillery barracks near a rail line. *Rate and Manner of Death:* There is a record of 5,159 Jews being deported to Auschwitz upon the ghetto's liquidation, but exact records of deaths in the ghetto are not available. *Resistance:* Jewish Council, which organized cultural activities. *Ghetto Liquidated:* 4 July 1944.

*Isaacson, Judith Magyar

Kolomyja (Kolomea)

Location: Kolomyja, a city on the Prut river, western Ukraine. *Established:* 25 March 1942. *Administrative Responsibility:* SS, with the help of the Jewish Council (25 March 1942–29 March 1944). *Prisoner Work and Use:* The ghetto population was not only subjected to intolerable living conditions, but provided slave labor as well. *Rate and Manner of Death:* Out of the 15,000 Jews from the city and the many others from the region, about 16,000 were deported to Bełżec, about 3,500 were shot in the nearby forest, and many others died of starvation and disease. *Resistance:* The Jewish community continued to organize educational and cultural activities during the ghetto's existence.

*Rosenberg, Blanca

Kraków (Cracow)

Location: City in southern Poland, third largest city in the nation and one of the oldest. *Nazi Occupation*: 6 September 1939 and persecution of Jews was launched immediately by the *Einsatzkommando* 2 of *Einsatzgruppe* I. On 26 October, Kraków was declared the capital of the *Generalgouvernement* (interior of occupied Poland) and it was from this site that the anti-Jewish decrees were announced. The first *Judenrat* was organized early in the occupation, but its leaders were soon imprisoned and a terror operation conducted in the Jewish quarters of the city. Jews were prohibited from the major squares and boulevards, and soon many were expelled to neighboring small towns. By March 1941, 40,000 were expelled (their property stolen) and no more than 11,000 left in the city. *Ghetto Established:* 3 March 1941 and sealed on 20 March within a wall and barbed wire fence. Several thousand Jews from neighboring villages were also crammed into the crowded ghetto, bringing the number to 18,000. *Administrative Responsibility:* Waffen-SS, Gestapo, and Schutzpolizei (3 March 1941–13 March 1943), as well as a Jewish Council. *Prisoner Work and Use:* The ghetto population was subjected to poor sanitary conditions, very limited living space, and forced labor in factories. *Rate and Manner of Death:* An estimated 15,000 Jews were deported to extermination camps including fifty to Auschwitz following a brutal *Aktion*, and 6,000 to Bełżec from 28 May to 7 June 1942, and 300 were murdered, followed by an October assault of 7, 000 deported and 600 shot, the home for the aged and the orphanage liquidated. In March 1943, 2,000 were transferred to Plaszow, 2,300 to Auschwitz and a part of the camp liquidated and 700 killed. Only 4,000 from the ghetto population survived. *Resistance:* Several organizations (Jewish Social Self-Help Society, Federation for the Care of Orphans) actively tried to bring relief to the suffering and in the early days tried to maintain education and cultural life. The underground organizations, including youth movements and the Jewish Fighting Organization, organized escapes and armed attacks outside the ghetto and tried to participate in partisan operations, which was difficult because of their isolation and the hostility of the local units of the Polish Home Army to Jews. In 1944 they crossed the border to Slovakia and from there to Hungary and continued their operations in Budapest. On the Aryan side of Kraków, a branch of Zegota (Council for Aid to Jews) aided several hundred of the Kraków Jews who escaped. *Ghetto Liquidated:* 13 March 1943.

*Ferderber-Salz, Bertha
*Karmel, Ilona
Keneally, Thomas

Łódż

Location: Northern part of Łódż, about 75 miles southwest of Warsaw, Poland, a large industrial city with a population of 665,000, one-third of it Jewish. *Occupation*: On 8 September 1939 the Germans occupied the city that had been a vital center of Jewish culture and industry, annexed it to the Reich, and soon renamed it Litzmannstadt. *Einsatzkommando* 2 and the local large ethnic German population immediately began to persecute the Jews, abducting many for forced labor, liquidating Jewish cultural institutions, and confiscating Jewish industries and businesses. Decrees were issued that effectively expelled Jews from industry and blocked their access to their bank accounts, restricted their cash holdings, forbade their use of public transportation, ownership of cars, radios, and other items in their possession. Synagogue services were outlawed and then synagogues destroyed. Jews were ordered to wear yellow armbands and later yellow badges on the right side of their clothing front and back, in the form of a Star of David. Jews and Poles were terrorized, several thousand in each group were arrested and either killed or deported to concentration camps. A series of expulsions from apartments was followed by mass deportations affecting 30,000 Jews and Poles. By March 1940, 70,000 Jews had left the city, among them those who fled to Warsaw believing it was safer and to Soviet controlled areas. In mid-October the Germans appointed a *Judenrat*, and a month later jailed all its members save Chaim Rumkowski, released eight from prison, and killed the remainder. Rumkowski was ordered to form another Jewish Council, which was to function under supervision of the Gestapo. *Ghetto Established:* 8 February 1940 in the Baluty slum quarter of the city, and blocked off on 30 April 1940, the second largest ghetto in Poland with a population of 164,000. In 1941 and 1942, 38,500 Jews from other countries were moved into the already densely overcrowded ghetto. The total number of people who passed through the ghetto was 204,800. The ghetto functioned as a labor camp until its liquidation in May 1944. *Administrative Responsibility:* SS and criminal police unit, with Rumkowski in charge of the ghetto's internal life (housing, food distribution, school system, health services) and organization of the factories (8 February 1940–19 January 1945). *Prisoner Work and Use:* The ghetto population was forced to work in ninety-six factories, primarily in the textile industry, a source of easy profits and exploitation accounting for the ghetto's relative longevity. *Rate and Manner of Death:* Although exact figures are not available, an estimated 80,000 Jews from the ghetto were deported to Chelmno and Auschwitz extermination camps and about 77,000 to labor camps in addition to the 43,000 Jews who died in the ghetto of disease, starvation, and murders. *Resistance:* The Jewish Council organized cultural and welfare activities, trying to prolong the ghetto's existence. Throughout its existence there was active resistance in the ghetto by many political groups that had been active prior to the war ranging from the Bund and Communists to Zionist organizations that tended to the welfare of the ghetto and sabotaged its industries and organized strikes to influence *Judenrate* administration, and manned clandestine radios to keep in touch with the outside world. *Liquidation*: Spring-summer, 1944. *Liberation*: The Soviet Army liberated several hundred prisoners who had been spared deportation to prepare shipment of ghetto property to Germany and went into hiding in the ghetto area 19 January 1945.

*Becker, Jurek
*Biderman, Abraham
Brett, Lily
Epstein, Leslie
Hersey, John
*Rosenfarb, Chava
Rudnicki, Adolf
*Shayevitch, Simkha-Bunim
*Spiegel, Isaiah
*Vinocur, Ana
Wincelberg, Shimon

L'vov

Location: Galicia province, Poland (now in Ukraine), an industrial and cultural center. Lvov was the third largest Jewish community (110,000) in the country. Occupation: The Soviets annexed Lvov to the USSR three weeks after the outbreak of war, disbanded the community institutions, outlawed political parties, nationalized factories and businesses, and and organized artisans into cooperative groups. Some 100,000 Jewish refugees from German-occupied Poland crowded into the city. Following the German invasion of the Soviet Union about 10,000 Jews escaped from Lvov with the Red Army. On 30 June 1941 the Germans occupied Lvov. *Einsatzgruppe* C and Ukrainian nationalists undertook the terrorization of the Jews. In four days of rioting 4,000 Jews were slaughtered. Jews over age fourteen were ordered to wear white armbands with blue Star of David. Ukrainians started a second rampage, murdering an additional 2,000 Jews. A *Judenrat* was established the end of July 1941. During the summer of 1941, Jewish property was plundered, Jews were put in forced labor; synagogues were burned; and cemeteries destroyed. In September 1941 a Jewish police force was formed to keep order, confiscate valuables for the Germans, and escort the Jews to forced labor. *Ghetto Established:* December 1941, following mass murders of 5,000 elderly and sick Jews in the city. The ghetto became a labor camp. *Administrative Responsibility:* SS, German and Ukrainian police (December 1941–2 June 1943) with Jewish Council responsible to the Germans. *Prisoner Work and Use:* the ghetto population was forced to work in factories and in January 1943 the ghetto officially became a labor camp. *Rate and Manner of Death:* Of about 100,000 Jews, almost all were deported to extermination camps Bełżec, Janówska, and Auschwitz and the rest were executed in Lvov. *Resistance:* A poorly consolidated underground, which published a news sheet and offered armed resistance upon the liquidation of the ghetto, killing nine Germans and Ukrainians and wounding twenty and making it impossible for the Germans to enter the ghetto buildings by attacking them with Molotov cocktails and hand grenades. The Germans set fire to or blew up the buildings. *Ghetto Liquidated:* 2 June 1943.

Eliach, Yaffe

Mir

Location: Mir, Belorussian SSR. *Occupation*: The Red Army occupied the city in September 1939 and incorporated it into the Soviet Union. Four days after the German invasion of the Soviet Union, German troops entered Mir. *Ghetto Established:* Following an *Aktion* in which 1,500 Jews and the *Judenrat* were killed, the ghetto for 850 Jews was established in November 1941. A new *Judenrat* was appointed. *Administrative Responsibility:* SS (November 1941–13 August 1942). *Resistance:* An underground group of about eighty Jews who organized escapes to the nearby forest and smuggled arms and ammunitions into the ghetto. Acting on information of an impending liquidation, 180 Jews, including members of the underground, escaped the ghetto during a raid by partisans that occupied the German forces. *Ghetto Liquidated:* 13 August 1942.

Tec, Nechama

Nagymagyer

Location: Near Samorin and Dunaszerdahely, Slovakia. *Ghetto Established:* 18 April 1944. *Administrative Responsibility:* Hungarian soldiers and military police (18 April 1944–21 May 1944). Five hundred Jewish families were crowded in a very limited area. *Ghetto Liquidated:* 21 May 1944

*Bitton-Jackson, Livia

Radom

Location: Radom, south of Warsaw, Poland. On the eve of WWII there were 30,000 Jews in Radom, constituting 33 percent of the population. *Occupation*: The Germans occupied the city on 8 September 1939 and immediately subjected the Jews to persecution, expelling 1,840 to smaller towns in the vicinity and bringing in several thousand from outlying districts. A *Judenrat* was appointed in December 1939. A wave of deportations to forced labor camps was instituted in August 1940. *Ghetto Established:* March 1941 and by 7 April the entire Jewish population was concentrated in two ghettos where they suffered from hunger and Gestapo-led terror actions, and deportations of thousands to forced labor camps and extermination camps, Auschwitz and Treblinka. *Administrative Responsibility:* SS and Gestapo with occasional Ukrainian collaboration (March 1941–August 1942). *Rate and Manner of Death:* Of over 30,000 Jews in the ghetto, almost all were deported to extermination camps or killed in ghetto actions and liquidation, with only 5,000 being deported to labor camps and having a chance to survive. *Resistance:* No consolidated underground, but different groups, which attempted escapes and organized resistance activities culminating in fleeing to the forests where they organized partisan units. While most died in combat with the Germans, a few dozen reached Warsaw and participated in the Warsaw Polish uprising of August and September 1944. *Ghettos Liquidated:* August 1942.

Baker, Mark Raphael
Karmel, Ilona

Sighet Marmatiei

Location: Two sections in northern Transylvania that were under Hungarian rule from 1940 to 1944. *Ghettos Established:* April 1944. The ghettos contained 13,000 Jews including those brought in from nearby rural communities. *Administrative Responsibility:* Local police and a Jewish Council (April 1944–May 1944). All of the 13,000 Jews were deported to Auschwitz, where most were murdered. *Ghetto Liquidated:* May 1944.

*Perl, Gisella
*Wiesel, Elie

Theresienstadt (Terezin)

Location: Theresienstadt, a fortress town in northwestern Czechoslovakia. *Ghetto Established:* November 1941 for 140,000 Jews from central and western Europe including the Jews of the Protectorate of Bohemia and Moravia and prominent Jews from western Europe. The German intent was to camouflage the true nature of the ghetto and present this as a "model" autonomous Jewish city. The International Red Cross "inspected" Terezin on 23 July 1944 and was duped by the Nazi physical disguise of dummy stores, café, bank, flower gardens, and schools. Ghetto overcrowding had been taken care of by pre-visit deportations to Auschwitz. The Nazis made a propaganda film showing ideal Jewish life in the Third Reich. When the filming was completed the "cast" was deported to Auschwitz. In reality, Terezin inhabitants suffered the same reality of hunger, epidemics, severe overcrowding, numerous deportations to Polish ghettos and to Auschwitz, Majdanek, and Treblinka extermination camps, and on-site murder that Jews of other ghettos experienced. *Administrative Responsibility:* SS and Central Office for the Solution of the Jewish Question in Bohemia and Moravia, Czech gendarmes served as guards (November 1941–8 May 1945) with the Council of Elders being responsible for making up the deportation lists. *Resistance:* Council of Elders, organizing extensive cultural and educational activities given the large number of artists, writers, and scholars in the ghetto community and efforts were made to reduce the deportation lists. *Rate and Manner of Death:* Although exact records are not available, an estimated 140,000 Jews were incarcerated in the ghetto; about 88,000 were deported to extermination camps either directly or via other ghettos and at least 33,000 died of starvation or disease within the ghetto. *Ghetto Liberated:* The Germans turned over the ghetto to the Red Cross on 3 May 1945 and it was liberated on 8 May 1945 by the Soviet army.

Atlan, Liliane
Chabon, Michael
Demetz, Hana
*Durlacher, Gerhard
*Frankl, Viktor
Fried, Erich
Green, Gerald
Hillesum, Etty
*Klüger, Ruth
*Lustig, Arnost
Samuels, Diane

Vilna

Location: Vilna, Lithuania. By 1939 more than 55,000 Jews comprised one-third of the city's population. The city was a center of Jewish education and culture and known as "the Jerusalem of Lithuania." *Occupation*: Vilna reverted to Lithuania, which reverted to Soviet control under the Nazi-Soviet agreement of 17 September 1939. With the arrival of German-Jewish refugees the Jewish population grew to 70,000 from 1939-1941. Although the Soviets outlawed the activities of Jewish organizations and political activity, and took control of Jewish schools and cultural institutions, and prohibited Jewish religious practice, Jews were at least free of German persecution. Soviet economic nationalization was a severe blow to Jewish livelihood and 6,500 emigrated. Two days after invading the Soviet Union, the Nazis occupied Vilna and issued a series of anti-Jewish decrees. Jews were ordered to wear the yellow badge, prohibited from walking on the sidewalks and certain streets, restricted to designated and limited shopping hours and locations, and put under strict curfew. On 4 July a *Judenrat* was appointed. *Ghettos Established:* 6 September 1941, after massive killings of 13,000 Jews in Ponary *Aktions* by *Eizsatzkommando* 9 assisted by Lithuanian volunteers, two ghettos were established, one for 30,000 and the second for from nine to eleven thousand, each with a Jewish Council. Following several more extensive Ponary killings, more than 12,000 "legal" Jews remained to work in one ghetto through 1942 and 1943 as well as several thousand "illegal" Jews in hiding. *Administrative Responsibility:* Two SS-appointed Jewish Councils (6 September 1941–13 July 1944). Jacob Gens, the Jewish police commander became the dominant leader of ghetto in July 1942 and instituted a policy of making Jewish workers indispensable to German needs as a means of survival. *Prisoner Work and Use:* The Jewish population worked in factories outside the ghetto and internal workshops. *Rate and Manner of Death:* Out of the 57,000 Jews in the town when the Germans occupied Vilna, the *Einsatzgruppen* killed 33,500 by the end of 1941. The Jews of Vilna were systematically removed en masse to nearby Ponary where thousands more were executed. During the ghetto liquidation in August and September of 1943 most of the survivors were deported to concentration camps in Estonia and Latvia. Over 4,000 children, women, and old men were sent to Sobibor extermination camp where they were murdered. Less than 3,000 Jews survived, 2,500 of whom had been left to work for the German military and others in hiding in the ghetto or having escaped during the September *Aktions*. *Resistance:* Cultural institutions and schools operated, as did social welfare institutions such as soup kitchens and a medical care system. The United Partisan Organization (FPO) functioned with the knowledge of the *Judenrate* from its inception in the beginning of 1942 until the spring of 1943, when Gens feared that their practice of smuggling weapons into the ghetto and maintaining contact with outside partisans was a threat to the ghetto's survival. He sent some of the leaders to external labor camps and urged the surrender of Yitzhak Wittenberg, the commander, in response to the Nazi threat to liquidate the ghetto if Wittenberg was not returned to custody following his release by the underground. The FPO convinced inhabitants to avoid scheduled deportations and fought the Germans during the ghetto liquidation actions and some escaped to form two partisan units. The final liquidation took place in September 1943 with 3,700 sent to concentration camps in Estonia and Latvia, over 4,000 children, women, and old men sent to Sobibór extermination camp, and about 2,500 left in Vilna to provide labor for the German military and burn the bodies that had been buried in Ponary. *Liberated:* 13 July 1944.

Schaeffer, Susan Fromberg
Sobol, Joshua
*Sutzkever, Abraham

Warsaw

Location: Warsaw, Poland. The city's prewar population was almost 30 percent Jewish and the largest Jewish community in Europe. One of the four Polish district centers in the *Generalgouvernement*, Polish territories not annexed by Germany or occupied by the USSR. *Occupation*: Following heavy aerial bombing of the city, the German occupation was characterized by immediate attacks on and discrimination against Jews: decrees banning travel, ordering Jews to wear white armbands with a blue Star of David, surrender radios, deposit all money in blocked bank accounts with a weekly allowance of approximately $2.50 permitted to the holder of the account, requiring registration of all assets; to be followed by plunder of shops, property confiscation, loss of positions by craftsmen and professionals, closure of Jewish schools and other institutions, frequent arrests, secret and public executions, and indiscriminate seizure for forced labor in Germany. A *Judenrat*, under Adam Czerniakow, was appointed in October 1940. *Ghetto Established:* October 1940 and sealed off by a high wall from the rest of Warsaw a month later. Jews from surrounding districts, from Germany, and several thousand Gypsies were also crammed into the crowded ghetto, bringing the population to 400,000 and monthly mortality rates of 4,000 to 5,000 from starvation and disease. *Administrative Responsibility:* SS-appointed Jewish Council, headed by Adam Czerniakow, until his suicide in July

1942 (October 1940–January 1945). *Prisoner Work and Use*: The ghetto population was a source of slave labor in the factories established within the ghetto. *Rate and Manner of Death:* Almost the entire 370,000 Jewish population. The Jews succumbed to starvation, executions, or massive deportations to the concentration and extermination camps, primarily Treblinka. Between July and October 1942 about 300,000 (83 percent of the entire ghetto population) were deported to extermination camps, most to Treblinka. About 55,000 remained in the ghetto. *Resistance:* From the beginning of the German occupation, resistance groups functioned. Many welfare organizations provided soup kitchens and medical assistance. A ghetto underground movement, including many Jewish political and Zionist groups and the Jewish Fighting Organization (ŻOB), kept a secret archive (code name *Oneg Shabbat*), and press organized and fought the Warsaw Ghetto uprising in April–May 1943. About 700 poorly equipped ghetto fighters engaged in street battles with several thousand well-equipped German soldiers, who finally resorted to burning the ghetto to flush out the fighters. About 13,000 Jews were killed in the uprising and most of the rest were sent to death in Treblinka and Majdanek. *Ghetto Liquidation and Revolt*: started 19 April 1943 (Passover eve) and continued to 16 May 1943.

Andrejewski, Jerzy
*Auerbach, Rachel
*Bauman, Janina
*Berg, Mary
*Birenbaum, Halina
Brandys, Kazimierz
*Czerniakow, Adam
*Edelman, Marek
*Elberg, Yehuda
*Ettinger, Elżbieta
Ficowski, Jerzy
*Głowiński, Michał
Green, Gerald
Grynberg, Henryk
Hersey, John
*Kaplan, Chaim
Karski, Jan
*Katzenelson, Yitzhak
*Klepfisz, Irena
Krall, Hannah
Leivick, H.
*Meed, Vladka
Nałkowska, Zofia
Raczymow, Henri
*Ringelblum, Emanuel
Rymkiewicz, Jarosław Marek
Szlengel, Władysław
Tomer, Ben Zion
*Wojdowski, Bogdan
Zeitlin, Aaron

APPENDIX: LABOR, TRANSIT, CONCENTRATION, AND EXTERMINATION CAMPS

Authors names preceded by an asterisk (*) were incarcerated in the camps treated in their writing

Except for those entries identified in parentheses as derived from other sources, all data in this appendix is compiled from the following sources:

Gutman, Israel. *Encyclopedia of the Holocaust.* 4 vols. New York: Macmillan, 1990.

Niewyck, Donald L., and Francis Nicosia's *Columbia Guide to the Holocaust.* New York: Columbia University Press, 2000.

Weinmann, Martin. *Das nationalsozialistische Lagersystem.* Frankfurt am Main: Zweitausendeins, 1990.

Amersfoort

Location: On the Leusden moor in Utrecht province, Holland. *Established:* 18 August 1941, although the barracks were built in 1939 for military use. *Liberated:* 19 April 1945. *Type:* A concentration camp, considered a police camp by the German administration. *Administrative Responsibility:* SS (18 August 1941–19 April 1945). *Prisoner Work and Use:* During the first stage of the camp's existence (18 August 1941–March 1943), Dutch and Belgian prominent citizens were held there and forced to work in various workshops, while Jews from the region were confined until deported, first to Camp Vught, another notorious camp in the Netherlands, then to Westerbork transit camp for deportation to the extermination camps in Poland. During the second stage (June 1943–19 April 1945), more than 28,000 inmates passed through the camp on their way to concentration camps within the Reich. The prisoner population consisted of Jews, Gypsies, Jehovah's Witnesses, homosexuals, Russian POWs, those who committed economic crimes, resistance fighters, and political prisoners. *Rate and Manner of Death:* Most of the prisoners were deported or executed by a firing squad, while others died of starvation and disease. Only 475 survived to witness the camp's liberation. *Resistance:* Active resistance groups, the most prominent of which was Resistance Fighters. (Hans Vanderwerff, "*Poiziliches Durgangslager Amersfoort,*" 1997 http://www.us-israel.org/source/Holocaust/cclist.html)

*Cohen, Elie

Auchhausen

Location: Dachau, northwest of Munich, Germany. *Established:* 14 April 1942. *Liquidated:* 28 July 1942. *Type:* A part of Dachau concentration camp. *Administrative Responsibility:* SS (14 April 1942–28 July 1942).

Kaniuk, Yoram

Augsburg

Location: Augsburg, southeastern Germany. *Established:* Exact date unknown. *Liquidated:* April 1945. *Type:* A labor camp. *Administrative Responsibility:* SS and German army (from establishment until April 1945). *Prisoner Work and Use:* The inmates were forced to work in a "Michelwerke" factory, manufacturing airplane parts. *Rate and Manner of Death:* Although precise figures are not available, prisoners died of exposure to cold and lack of sufficient food.

*Bitton-Jackson, Livia

Auschwitz and Auschwitz II or Auschwitz-Birkenau

Location: West of Kraków, Poland. *Established:* 27 April 1940. In March 1941, Himmler ordered the erection of a second, much larger section of the camp, called Auschwitz II or Birkenau (with nine sub-units). In March 1942 a women's section was established in the main camp, but moved to Birkenau in August 1942. Later Auschwitz III (Buna-Monowitz) was established with more than forty-five sub-units. *Liberated:* 27 January 1945 by the Soviet army. *Type:* The Auschwitz camps constituted the largest Nazi concentration and extermination camp, with a network of forty satellites, Birkenau being the largest of them. The gas chambers and crematoria operated in Birkenau; Auschwitz III and its forty-five sub-camps were forced labor operations. *Administrative Responsibility:* SS (27 April 1940–27 January 1945. *Prisoner Work and Use:* Three hundred Jews from the region were forced to work on construction of the original camp. During the first period, most inmates were Polish political prisoners. About 405,000 prisoners were registered in the system and forced into various kinds of labor. Of these, only about 65,000 survived. Not included in the registration was the vast majority who were gassed upon arrival, those destined for execution after a short stay in the camp (hostages, Soviet army officers, and partisans), and those sent to work in other camps outside the Auschwitz complex. *Rate and Manner of Death:* The system of torturing prisoners was implemented here. Currently, it is estimated that 1.5 million people found their death in the Auschwitz gas chambers, in addition to the hundreds of thousands who died of torture, executions, death marches, or the pseudo-medical experiments conducted in the camp. *Resistance:* A "multinational resistance organization," (Auschwitz Fighting Group), which prepared a rebellion, kept records, helped in numerous escapes, helping prisoners with medicine and food. Sabotage and other instances of physical rebellion, including shooting two SS men, occurred and mutual help among prisoners was widespread. *Sonderkommando* prisoners organized an uprising that took place on 7 October 1944 and destroyed one of the gas chambers. Three hundred ninety-seven prisoners escaped successfully.

Agosín, Marjorie
*Améry, Jean
Amis, Martin
Atlan, Lilane
Baker, Mark Raphael
Barnes, Peter
*Biderman, Abraham
*Birenbaum, Halina
*Bitton-Jackson, Livia
*Borowski, Tadeusz
Brett, Lily
Cohen, Arthur
*Cohen, Elie
*Delbo, Charlotte
Domecq, Alcina Lubitch
*Dribben, Judith Strick
Drummond, Roberto
*Durlacher, Gerhard
Eliach, Yaffe
*Fenelon, Fania
*Ferderber-Salz, Bertha
Ficowski, Jerzy
*Frankl, Viktor
Friedländer, Saul
Fromer, Rebecca Camhi
Green, Gerald
Grumberg, Jean-Claude
Harris, Robert
Heyen, William
*Hillesum, Etty
Hilsenrath, Edgar
Hochhuth, Rolf
*Isaacson, Judith Magyar
*Ka. Tzetnik 135633 (Yehiel Dinur)
*Kertész, Imre
Kiš, Danilo
*Klein, Cecilie
Klemperer, Victor
*Klüger, Ruth
Kogon, Eugen
*Leitner, Isabella
Leivick, H.
*Lengyel, Olga
*Levi, Primo
*Lustig, Arnost
Mandel, Elias
*Millu, Liana
*Nomberg-Pryztyk, Sara
*Perl, Gisella
Piercy, Marge
*Rawicz, Piotr
Rousset, David
Różewicz, Tadeusz
Schlink, Bernhard
Schwarz-Bart, André
*Semel, Nava (Birkenau)
*Siegal, Aranka (Birkenau)
Sperber, Manes
Spiegelman, Art
Styron, William
*Tedeschi, Guiliana
*Vinocur, Ana
Weiss, Peter
*Wiesel, Elie
Wilkomirski, Binjamin

Barneveld

Location: In a castle in the town of Barneveld, Gelderland province, Netherlands. *Established:* Late 1942. *Liquidated:* Early 1943. *Type:* A holding camp for "valuable" Dutch Jews exempt from deportation to eastern Europe. *Administrative Responsibility:* SS (late 1942–early 1943). *Prisoner Work and Use:* The prisoners were interned at the castle but not used for any kind of slave labor. *Rate and Manner of Death:* Out of the about 700 Jews in Barneveld, only some of the elderly died. However, the rest of them were deported to Theresienstadt upon the camp's liquidation.

Herzberg, Abel

Bełżec

Location: Between Lublin and L'vov, southeastern Poland. *Established:* Early 1940. *Liquidated:* December 1942. *Type:* A labor camp for Jews, then an extermination camp from 17 March 1942 onwards. *Administrative Responsibility:* SS and Ukrainian Hiwis (early 1940–December 1942). *Work and Use:* Seven hundred "work Jews" were kept to help in the extermination process mainly by cleaning the trains, removing the corpses from the gas chambers, extracting gold teeth from the mouths of the dead, preparing their belongings for shipment to Germany, and burying the dead. *Rate and Manner of Death:* At least 600,000 prisoners, mostly Jews, are believed to have found their death in the camp's gas chambers. *Resistance:* Only one successful escape.

Baker, Mark Raphael

Bergen-Belsen

Location: Near Hanover, Germany. *Established:* April 1943. *Liberated:* 15 April 1945 by the British army. *Type:* A detention camp (for holding persons to be exchanged for German nationals held by the Allies—of the 4,100 prisoners so classified, 2,041 were allowed to leave) with satellites. In March 1944, it became a "regular" concentration camp where prisoners "unfit for work" from other camps were sent to die as were the thousands sent on death marches from liquidated camps; and a Displaced Persons' Camp after liberation and until 1951. *Administrative Responsibility:* SS (April 1943–2 December 1944); (2 December 1944–15 April 1945). *Prisoner Work and Use:* Five hundred Jewish prisoners from Buchenwald and Natweiler camps worked on the construction of Bergen-Belsen. The prisoners were forced to work primarily in construction. *Rate and Manner of Death:* No precise figures are available, but at least 35,000 inmates died from January to mid-April 1945 alone. There were 60,000 prisoners in the camp when the British liberated it, most in critical condition. Another 14,000 died during the first five days following liberation and another 14,000 in the following weeks.

*Améry, Jean
*Biderman, Abraham
Eliach, Yaffe
*Fenelon, Fania
*Ferderber-Salz, Bertha
Guralnik, Sonia
*Herzberg, Abel
Heyen, William
Layton, Irving
*Leitner, Isabella
Margulies, Donald
*Oberski, Jona
*Perl, Gisella
Piercy, Marge
Potok, Chaim
*Siegal, Aranka
*Yaoz-Kest, Itamar

Bolkenhain

Location: Bolkenhain, Austria. *Established:* 2 July 1942. *Liquidated:* 8 May 1944, when all the inmates were transferred to Grünberg. *Type:* A small labor subcamp of Gross-Rosen for German-speaking Jewish women, half of whom came from Bielitz camp. *Administrative Responsibility:* SS (2 July 1942–8 May 1944). *Prisoner Work and Use:* The inmates were forced to work in textile factories. *Rate and Manner of Death:* Out of the 100 prisoners, some were sent by employers to be killed, but none died of maltreatment or starvation in the camp.

*Klein, Gerda

Bor

Location: Near Nisch, Serbia. *Established:* June 1942. *Liquidated:* 28 October 1944, when all the prisoners were evacuated to Flossenbürg. *Type:* A labor camp. *Administrative Responsibility:* SS (June 1942–28 October 1944). *Prisoner Work and Use:* The prisoners were primarily forced to construct tunnels in a copper mine. *Rate and Manner of Death:* It is not known how many of the estimated 20,000 prisoners died in the camp.

*Radnóti, Miklós

Buchenwald

Location: Thüringen, near Weimar. *Established:* 16 July 1937. *Liquidated:* 11 April 1945 and after most of the SS fled, prisoners took control of the camp. *Type:* A concentration camp with 130 subsidiary camps, one of the largest on German soil. The first group of prisoners consisted of political detainees and criminals. Large groups began to arrive by the end of 1937, mostly "politicals." By July 1938 there were 7,723 prisoners, most designated as "asocial." Jews from Austria (2,200) also arrived. After *Kristallnacht,* 10,000 Jews were added to the list of internees, with the camp population exceeding 18,000 by the end of November. Of the *Kristallnacht* prisoners, 600 were killed, committed suicide, or died from other causes. Most of the Jewish prisoners were released as the purpose of their arrest and subjection to hard labor of fourteen to fifteen hours daily in the infamous Buchenwald quarries was to encourage them to emigrate from Germany. With the outbreak of war, thousands more arrived, political prisoners and Poles (housed in the tent camp). On 17 October 1942 all Jewish prisoners except for 204 essential workers were sent to Auschwitz. As of 1943, with the completion of armament factories in the vicinity of the camp, the numbers grew steadily to 63,048 by the end of 1944, and 86,232 in February 1945. Hungarian Jews were sent to Buchenwald in 1944 to work in the armament factories. In 1945, when other camps were being evacuated, thousands of Jewish prisoners were sent to Buchenwald. In the eight years of its existence, a total of 238,980 prisoners from thirty countries passed through Buchenwald. *Administrative Responsibility:* SS (16 July 1937–April 1945) with political prisoners participating in the administration during 1938. *Prisoner Work and Use:* The inmates were forced to work in armament factories, while work in a quarry was reserved only for Jewish prisoners, who were also subjects in various medical experiments and denied the "privileges" other prisoners had. *Rate and Manner of Death:* Out of the nearly 239,000 prisoners who passed through the camp, more than 56,000 are believed to have died. *Resistance:* Resistance groups were formed on the basis of political affiliation and nationality. In 1943 an International Underground Committee, including Jewish inmates, was formed that was successful in sabotage and smuggling arms.

Aloni, Jenny
*Antelme, Robert
Baker, Mark Raphael
Bukiet, Melvin
Cohen, Arthur
Drummond, Roberto
Heyen, William
*Kertész, Imre
Klemperer, Victor
*Kogon, Eugen
*Rousset, David
*Semprun, Jorge
*Wiesel, Elie
Zeitlin, Aaron

Chełmno

Location: Chełmno, western Poland. *Established:* 8 December 1941. *Liquidated:* March 1943, but reopened April 1944 until September 1944 to process the gassing of the survivors of the Łódż ghetto. The Nazis abandoned Chelmno when the Red Army was approaching. *Type:* An extermination camp, the first Nazi camp in which mass executions were carried out by means of gas, and the first site for mass killings within the framework of the "final solution" outside the USSR. *Administrative Responsibility:* SS and German security police (8 December 1941–March 1943; April 1944–September 1944). *Prisoner Work and Use:* A small group of prisoners were kept and used as gravediggers, while the transports were initially killed in mobile gas vans upon arrival and later in 1944 in two new crematoria built specifically to handle the large number from the Łódż ghetto. *Rate and Manner of Death:* Although precise records are not available, it is estimated that up to 370,000 people, including 340,000 Jews, died in the gas vans and crematoria and their bodies were either buried in the nearby forest or cremated. *Resistance:* No record of organized resistance, but many individual attempts at escape by those inmates who were forced to bury the dead bodies.

Epstein, Leslie
Nałkowska, Zofia

Dachau

Location: Dachau, northwest of Munich, Germany. *Established:* 20 March 1933. *Liberated:* 29 April 1945 by United States Seventh Army. *Type:* Initially for "protective custody" of political opponents of National Socialism, then a concentration camp with thirty-six large subsidiary work camps. The terror system of instilling fear in opponents began in Dachau, which was a training center for the SS. After *Kristallnacht,* over 10,000 Jewish German citizens were interned in Dachau. Most were released after several months and being able to prove their intention to emigrate from Germany. When the systematic extermination of Jews began in 1942, Jewish prisoners were deported from Dachau and other German camps to the mass extermination camps in Poland. In the summer and fall of 1944 Jewish prisoners were brought to Dachau's subsidiary camps to increase armament production. *Administrative Responsibility:* Bavarian state police (22 March 1933–11 April 1933); SS (11 April 1933–29 April 1945); political and criminal prisoners appointed by SS to serve in "prisoners' internal government." *Prisoner Work and Use:* Primarily ammunitions production; built roads, drained marshes, also subjects for medical experimentation in areas of decompression, high altitude and freezing conditions, malaria and tuberculosis artificially induced to test treatments. *Rate and Manner of Death:* Not all prisoners were registered. Of 206,206 who were, 31,591 deaths were recorded, but this figure does not include victims of mass executions, typhus losses, or death marches. *Resistance:* Underground committee.

Aloni, Jenny
*Antelme, Robert
*Bitton-Jackson, Livia
Burnier, Andreas
*Frankl, Viktor
Levy, Itamar
Rousset, David

Drancy

Location: Drancy, a northeastern Paris suburb, France. *Established:* 21 August 1941. *Liquidated:* 17 August 1944. *Type:* An assembly and detention camp for the Jews of France from which they were sent to forced labor and extermination camps. Four satellite camps were added to serve as depositories for valuable art, furniture, and household goods and other property confiscated from the homes of Jews who had been arrested, imprisoned, and deported. *Administrative responsibility:* French gendarmes armed with machine guns (21 August 1941–2 July 1943); SS (2 July 1943–17 August 1944). Its organization and structure were modeled along the lines of the Nazi concentration camps. *Prisoner Work and Use:* The prisoners were subject to harsh living conditions and much cruelty. *Rate and Manner of Death:* Little is known other than the deportations to Auschwitz, which sent many victims of the July 1942 roundups to their death. A total of sixty-four transports left Drancy, with 64,759 Jews aboard; of these, sixty-one transports with 61,000 persons went to Auschwitz extermination camp, and three transports with 3,753 persons were sent to Sobibór. Among the Jews deported from Drancy were 4,051 children. *Resistance:* An underground, which organized forty-one successful escapes and the building of a tunnel, discovered shortly before completion.

Doubrovsky, Serge
*Fenelon, Fania
Grumberg, Jean-Claude
Ozick, Cynthia
Piercy, Marge
Schwarz-Bart, André

Dora Nordhausen

Location: Outskirts of Nordhausen, east Germany. *Established:* Late 1943. *Liberated:* 12 April 1945 by 104th U.S. Infantry Division. *Type:* An extermination subcamp of Dora-Mittelbau for weak and sick prisoners. Dora, on the outskirts of Nordhausen, was a top-secret satellite camp of Buchenwald where prisoners worked in subterranean caverns on rocket production. *Administrative Responsibility:* SS (late 1943–12 April 1945). *Prisoner Work and Use:* The sick and weak prisoners of Dora-Mittelbau were transferred to this camp and placed in concrete hangars without any sanitation or food to die of starvation. *Rate and Manner of Death:* Almost everybody from the camp died. Just a few survivors and about 3,000 corpses were discovered in the hangars upon liberation. *Resistance:* No data of resistance, or even of individual escapes, is available.

*Biderman, Abraham
Piercy, Marge

Ebensee

Location: Ebensee, Salzkammergut area, Austria. *Established:* 18 November 1943. *Liberated:* 6 May 1945 by American troops. *Type:* A labor sub-camp of Mauthausen. *Administrative Responsibility:* SS (18 November 1943–6 May 1945). *Prisoner Work and Use:* The camp inmates worked mainly on the construction of tunnels to house a rocket factory. *Rate and Manner of Death:* There is no precise record available. It is estimated that about 11,000 inmates died of the unbearable living and working conditions, and of cruel murders.

*Cohen, Elie

Gross-Rosen

Location: Near the Gross-Rosen quarry, Lower Silesia. *Established:* Summer of 1940 (Sachsenhausen satellite); 1 May 1941 (independent camp). *Liquidated:* Mid-February 1945 (main camp); 8 and 9 May 1945 (satellites) and liberated by Soviet troops. *Prisoner Work and Use:* Mainly quarry and construction work, but also concentration camp with satellite labor camps. Jews, mostly from Poland and Hungary, but also from Belgium, France, Greece, Yugoslavia, Slovakia, and Italy represented the largest group among the victims. They were distributed among over fifty satellite camps, designated as *Arbeitslager* (labor camps). *Administrative Responsibility:* SS (1 May 1941 work in armament, textile, and aircraft factories. *Rate and Manner of Death:* Of the 125,000 who passed through the camp, 40,000 from the main camp died in evacuation transports, and those from the satellite camps in death marches on foot in the cold of winter without food. During the evacuation Jews were moved to Bergen-Belsen, Buchenwald, Dachau, Flossenbürg, Mauthausen, Mittelbau, and Neuengamme.

*Siegal, Aranka
*Durlacher, Gerhard
*Klüger, Ruth

Grünberg

Location: Grünberg, Austria. *Established:* February 1942. *Liberated:* February 1945 by the Russian army. *Type:* a labor sub-camp of Gross-Rosen for Jewish women. *Administrative Responsibility:* SS (February 1942–February 1945). *Prisoner Work and Use:* Forced labor in the textile and viniculture factories of "Deusche Wollenwaren Manufaktur." *Rate and Manner of Death:* No precise figures are available. Hundreds of prisoners were massacred or sent to their death when they were classified as "unfit for work." Many died during the death marches upon the camp's evacuation to Bergen-Belsen. *Resistance:* A major resistance activity was a massive escape of at least twenty-five inmates, who cut through Christianstadt's fence wire while on a death march.

*Klein, Gerda

Gurs

Location: Close to the French-Spanish border. *Established:* April 1939. *Liberated:* Summer of 1944. *Type:* A camp for Spanish republican soldiers and Jewish volunteers of the International Brigade who fled to France upon Franco's victory, then a detention camp. In 1940 approximately 4,000 German and Austrian nationals (mostly Jews) and leaders of the French communist party were sent to Gurs, as was the entire Jewish population of Baden and Palatinate. *Administrative Responsibility:* SS (April 1939–summer of 1944). *Prisoner Work and Use:* The prisoners were subjected to very harsh living conditions, poor sanitation, and shortage of water. *Rate and Manner of Death:* Many died in typhus and dysentery epidemics. About 6,000 Jews were deported to Auschwitz-Birkenau and Sobibór extermination camps by way of Drancy. By December 1943, no more than forty-eight Jews were left. *Resistance:* The prisoners organized cultural and educational activities, as well as religious services.

Arendt, Hannah
Piercy, Marge

Janówska

Location: Suburb of L'vov, Ukranian SSR. *Established:* September 1941. *Liquidated:* November 1943. *Type:* A labor camp, then a concentration and an extermination camp. *Administrative Responsibility:* SS (September 1941–November 1943). Initially a network of factories was established as part of the German Armament Works, a division of the SS, which used the Jews of L'vov as forced labor. In October 1941 the factories became a restricted camp, enclosed by barbed wire, which the Jews were not permitted to leave. Following a March 1942 *Aktion* against the Jews of the city, several hundred more were put into the camp. With the deportation of Jews from eastern Galicia to Belzec extermination camp in March 1942, the role of Janówska changed. By spring it took on the character of a concentration camp and by mid-1943 it was being turned into an extermination camp. *Prisoner Work and Use:* Labor in factories supplying the SS army, mainly metalwork and carpentry. *Rate and Manner of Death:* No precise figure is available, but it is estimated that tens of thousands of Jews died due to executions, starvation, and disease and 6,000 are known to have been executed on the outskirts of town. *Resistance:* Underground resistance groups smuggled arms into the camp with the help of prisoners who worked outside the camp and killed several German guards, leading to the camp's liquidation due to fear of an uprising.

Eliach, Yaffe
*Wiesenthal, Simon

Kaiserwald

Location: Near Riga, Latvia. *Established:* March 1943. *Liquidated:* September 1944. *Type:* a concentration camp with satellites. The first inmates were several hundred German convicts. From June 1943 the majority of Jews expelled from Riga were sent to Kaiserwald. In November of that year the Latvian Jews were taken to Kaiserwald from liquidated ghettos as were the survivors of the Vilna ghetto. In 1944 thousands of Hungarian Jewish women were brought there, as was a group from Łódż. Of the camp population of 11,878 in March 1944, only ninety-five were non-Jews. *Administrative Responsibility:* SS (March 1943–September 1944). *Prisoner Work and Use:* Labor in railway and military factories, the German industrial electric corporation, mines, and farms. *Rate and Manner of Death:* The Germans started evacuation in July 1944 as the Soviet army was approaching the Latvian border. Of the 11,878 registered inmates in March 1944, thousands of sick prisoners were put to death and all Jews under eighteen and above thirty were executed. Evacuees were sent by ship and rail to Stutthof and dispersed to other camps inside Germany.

Schaeffer, Susan Fromberg

Kaufering

Location: Around the village of Kaufering, southwest of Munich, Germany. *Established:* June to October 1944. *Liberated:* 27 April 1945 by American troops. *Type:* A network of fifteen Dachau subsidiary camps, only two of which, Kaufering III and Kaufering VI, are identifiable. The first prisoners were Lithuanian Jews who arrived in June 1944. They were followed in October by large contingents of Hungarian, Polish, Czechoslovak, and Romanian Jews, most of whom came from Auschwitz. *Administrative Responsibility:* SS (June 1944–27 April 1945). *Prisoner Work and Use:* The prisoners were forced to work in armaments factories and construction firms, as well as building underground aircraft factories. *Rate and Manner of Death:* Out of the estimated 28,000 prisoners who passed through the Kaufering camps, an unknown number died of hard work, starvation, maltreatment, and diseases. *Resistance:* A few inmates managed to escape by hiding in the nearby woods during evacuation of the camps.

*Frankl, Viktor

Landeshut

Location: Near Dresden, eastern Germany. *Established:* November 1943. *Liquidated:* April 1944. *Type:* A labor camp, consisting of a Jewish and a Polish camp. *Administrative Responsibility:* SS (November 1943–April 1944). *Prisoner Work and Use:* The prisoners were forced to work in quarries, as well as in a Kramsta-Mathner-Frahne factory, weaving silk for parachutes. *Rate and Manner of Death:* An unknown number of the estimated 800 prisoners died of typhus or executions.

*Klein, Gerda

Leitmeritz

Location: Near Bayreuth, Germany. *Established:* Unknown. *Liberated:* 23 April 1945 by the 2nd U.S. Cavalry. *Type:* One of the ninety-three sub-camps of Flossenbürg. *Administrative Responsibility:* SS (from establishment until 23 April 1945). *Prisoner Work and Use:* The prisoners were forced to work in stone quarries under exceptionally hard working conditions. *Rate and Manner of Death:* Out of the estimated 111,000 prisoners who passed through the Flossenbürg system of camps, about 73,000 died of disease, malnutrition, execution, and overwork.

*Rawitz, Piotr

Majdanek

Location: Suburb of Lublin, Poland. *Established:* October 1941. *Liquidated:* July 1944. *Type:* A concentration and extermination camp with satellites, among them a POW camp and a children's camp. Until 1943 it was designated as a prisoner of war camp. Its function was to destroy Reich enemies, take part in the extermination of Jews and the deportation of people of the Zamość region. In May 1942 the method of murder changed from mass shootings to gas. The camp had seven gas chambers and a crematorium. By September 1943 a large crematorium containing five furnaces was added. *Administrative Responsibility:* Waffen-SS (October 1941–July 1944). *Prisoner Work and Use:* The prisoners were forced to work in munitions workshops and the Steyr-Daimler-Puch weapons factory. Also, they were subject to extreme cruelty on the part of Karl Koch, the camp commandant. *Rate and*

Manner of Death: Of the 500,000 prisoners (mostly Jews) who passed through the camp, about 360,000 fell victim of either gas chambers and executions, or starvation and disease. *Resistance:* A movement, including "Orzel" organization. Polish aid organizations (Polish Red Cross and Central Welfare Council) extended help to the Polish prisoners. As the Red Army advanced in July 1944, the camp was evacuated. Several escapes were arranged.

Amir-Pinkerfeld, Anda
*Birenbaum, Halina
Wiesel, Elie
Wilkomirski, Binjamin
Zeitlin, Aaron

Märzdorf

Location: Near Dresden, eastern Germany. *Established:* Unknown. *Liquidated:* 9 May 1945. *Type:* A labor sub-camp of Gross-Rosen. *Administrative Responsibility:* SS (from establishment until 9 May 1945). *Prisoner Work and Use:* The prisoners were forced to work in bricklaying, shoveling coal, and machinery maintenance. *Rate and Manner of Death:* An unknown number of the prisoners died in deportations and death marches.

*Klein, Gerda

Mauthausen

Location: A quarry near Linz, Austria. *Established:* 8 August 1938, shortly after the *Anschluss* of Austria. *Liberated:* 5 May 1945 by the American army. *Type:* A concentration camp with over thirty satellites and a "liquidation center." The first prisoners were criminals and "asocials" and most were transferred from Dachau. The first political prisoners, also from Dachau, arrived in May 1939 and soon thereafter from Czechoslovakia. In 1940 an additional 11,000 prisoners arrived from Sachsenhausen and Buchenwald. In 1941 an additional 18,000 prisoners arrived including Spanish republican prisoners who fled to France, Jews from the Netherlands, and Soviet POWs. Many other nationals arrived in 1942 and over 21,000 in 1943. A record 65,645 new prisoners arrived in 1944 with a maximum population or 114,524 in 1944. Beginning in May, more than 13,300 Jews from Auschwitz and Plaszow arrived and in 1945, 24,793 newcomers from Auschwitz, Sachenhausen, Gross-Rosen, and other camps were absorbed by the Mauthausen sub-camps as were a huge Hungarian contingent bringing the total two days before liberation to 139,157 registered prisoners. In Mauthausen, as in other camps, Jews were treated more harshly than other groups, being employed digging tunnels for the munitions factories in the subcamps and having the worst living conditions. *Administrative Responsibility:* SS (8 August 1938–5 May 1945). *Prisoner Work and Use:* Primarily hard labor in the Wiener Graben stone quarry, but also in the military industry: construction of tunnels and production of plane parts. *Rate and Manner of Death:* Of the estimated 199,000 prisoners 102,000 died, of these 38,120 were Jews, who died of epidemics, starvation, and in the gas chamber.

*Cohen, Elie
*Dribben, Judith Strick

Mechelen

Location: Mechelen, Belgium. *Established:* Summer of 1942. *Liquidated:* Early 1944. *Type:* An assembly camp for the Jews of Belgium, from which they would be deported to the east, a transit camp. The Jews in the camp were divided into several groups: those designated for deportation at the first opportunity; nationals of neutral countries or of Germany's allies, some of whom were not deported; borderline cases (people of mixed parentage or Jews married to non-Jews), who were later sent to Drancy; and the politically "dangerous," sent to prisons or punitive camps. *Administrative Responsibility:* SS and a few Flemish Belgians (summer 1942-early 1944). *Rate and Manner of Death:* Between 4 August 1942 and 31 July 1944, a total of twenty-eight trains with 25,257 Jewish prisoners left Melchelen, for camps in the east, primarily to Auschwitz. *Resistance:* An underground movement that smuggled in tools that were useful for recurring escapes from the transport trains.

*Flinker, Moshe

Melk

Location: Within a Wehrmacht garrison in Melk, Lower Austria. *Established:* 11 January 1944. *Liberated:* 5 May 1945 by U.S. troops. *Type:* A labor satellite of Mauthausen. Among the prisoners were Russians, Yugoslavs, and Poles. After June 1944, most of the arrivals were Jews from Hungary and Poland following selections at Auschwitz. Because it was located within the bounds of a Wehrmacht garrison, it was visible to soldiers and civilians. *Administrative Responsibility:* SS (11 January 1944–5 May 1945). *Prisoner Work and Use:* The prisoners were forced to work in the construction of tunnels. *Rate and Manner of Death:* Estimated 10,000 prisoners died of starvation, disease, and phenol injections, with 5,000 of those deaths recorded. In addition, an unknown number died in the tunnels. In the second week of April 1945, as Russian troops were approaching, the camp was evacuated with a small number of prisoners sent to Mauthausen and the remainder to Ebensee camp. *Resistance:* A number of successful individual escapes.

*Cohen, Elie

Neuengamme

Location: Outskirts of Hamburg, Germany. *Established:* 4 June 1940, although the building had started on 13 December 1938. *Liberated:* May 1945 by the British army, although the evacuation of both main camp and satellites had started in April. *Type:* A concentration camp with seventy satellites, which had initially been a sub-camp of Sachsenhausen (December 1938–4 June 1940). *Administrative Responsibility:* SS (June 1940–April 1945). *Prisoner Work and Use:* The prisoners were forced to work primarily in brick and weapons factories, as well as in shipbuilding. In 1944, the main camp had a prisoner population of 12,000 and about twice that number were in the satellite camps. Beginning in 1944, large numbers of Jewish prisoners (13,000) were brought in from Hungary and Poland. *Rate and Manner of Death:* Out of the estimated 106,000 prisoners who passed through the camp, at least 55,000 died of the unbearable working and living conditions.

*Rousset, David

Płaszów

Location: Suburb of Kraków, built on the site of two Jewish cemeteries. *Established:* 1942. *Liquidated:* 14 January 1945. *Type:* A forced labor camp, then a concentration camp. *Administrative Responsibility:* Until 1944 most of the camp guards were Ukrainians. When it became a concentration camp 600 SS men took over. *Prisoner Work and Use:* The prisoners were subjected to harsh living and working conditions. Following the liquidation of the Kraków ghetto the prisoner population increased from 12,000 to 24,000. *Rate and Manner of Death:* Of the 25,000 "permanent" prisoners and the unknown number of "temporary" ones, 8,000 are estimated to have been murdered, in addition to all who died due to overwork. In the summer of 1944 liquidation began as the Russian army was approaching and prisoners were transferred to other camps or deported to extermination camps. Two thousand Jewish prisoners were sent to Auschwitz where they were gassed.

*Bitton-Jackson, Livia
*Ferderber-Salz, Bertha
*Karmel, Ilona
Keneally, Thomas

Ravensbrück

Location: Ravensbrück, north of Berlin, Germany. *Established:* May 1939. *Liberated:* 30 April 1945 by the Russian army. *Type:* A concentration camp primarily for women with thirty-one subsidiaries. *Administrative Responsibility:* One hundred fifty female SS volunteer supervisors added to men who served as guards (May 1939–30 April 1945). *Prisoner Work and Use:* The inmates were subjected to inhuman living conditions and brutality, and forced to work in several SS companies, located around the camp. In late 1939 the camp had 2,000 prisoners, and by the end of 1942 the population was 10,800. In 1944 an additional 70,000 were sent to one of the thirty-four satellite camps, most of which were attached to military industrial plants. In 1944 the main camp had 26,700 female prisoners and several thousand girls in detention for minors. In April 1941 a concentration camp for men was established near the Ravensbrück camp. Of the women at Ravensbrück camp, 25 percent were Polish, 20 percent German, 19 percent Russian and Ukrainian, 15 percent Jewish, 7 percent French, 5.5 percent Gypsy, and 8.5 percent others. *Rate and Manner of Death:* Of the estimated 132,000 women and 20,000 men who passed through the camp, about 92,000 died of starvation, disease, medical experimentation, torture, murder by shooting, hanging, or phenol injections, and about 2,300 of them in the gas chambers that were constructed in late January or early February 1945. Hundreds of children incarcerated at Ravensbrück were also subjected to medical experiments and killed in front of their mothers, either by being thrown alive into the crematory, buried alive, poisoned, or drowned. (http//jewishgen.org/camps/Ravensbrück/html). In late March 1945 the order was given to evacuate Ravensbrück and 24,500 men and women were sent on a forced march to Mecklenburg. Early in April 500 women were handed over to the Swedish and Danish Red Cross and 2,500 German women were set free. Soviet liberators found 3,500 sick women being cared for by other prisoners when they liberated the camp at the end of April.

Drummond, Roberto
*Millu, Liana
Piercy, Marge

Rawa-Ruska

Location: The town of Rawa-Ruska on the Polish/ Ukrainian border. *Established:* June 1941. *Liquidated:* June 1944, after a long period of gradual evacuation and abandoning of the camp. *Type:* A disciplinary camp for French and Belgian prisoners of war. *Administrative Responsibility:* SS (June 1841–June 1944). *Prisoner Work and Use:* The inmates were forced to do excavation work along railroad lines and in stone quarries, as well as build airfields. *Rate and Manner of Death:* About seventy-five prisoners are believed to have died of disease or attempting to escape. *Resistance:* A few successful escapes, as well as association groups among prisoners coming from the same area.

Gascar, Pierre

Sachsenhausen

Location: Outskirts of Oranienburg, north of Berlin, Germany. *Established:* July 1936. *Liberated:* 27 April 1945 by Soviet troops. *Type:* Initially a camp for war prisoners, later, from November 1938, a concentration camp. *Administrative Responsibility:* SS (November 1938–27 April 1945). *Prisoner Work and Use:* The inmates were forced to work in the armaments industry near Berlin, as well as brickyard work. They manufactured grenades, and worked in the production of engines for aircraft and tanks. Following *Kristallnacht* 1,800 Jews were imprisoned in Sachsenhausen and approximately 450 were murdered shortly after their arrival. Soviet POWs, Jews, Poles, Gypsies, and others were imprisoned there. *Rate and Manner of Death:* Mass executions by shooting began in 1941 and a gas chamber was installed in 1943. Out of the estimated 200,000 prisoners who passed through the camp, 30,000 were killed in executions, the gas chamber, or during death marches with only 3,000 surviving to witness the camp's liberation.

Rousset, David

Skarżysko-Kamienna

Location: Kielce area, Poland. *Established:* August 1942. *Liquidated:* 1 August 1944. *Type:* A labor camp. *Administrative Responsibility:* SS and Radom district police leader (August 1942–1 August 1944). Each department had a German manager, with Poles acting as his deputies and as supervisors. Ukrainian factory police handled security. *Prisoner Work and Use:* Primarily work in three separate ammunition factory camps (Werke A,B,C), as well as production of underwater mines. Workers in A and B produced ammunition for the army and those in C produced the underwater mines, filling them with picric acid, which caused the skin to turn yellow and death within three months. Most of the prisoners were from Poland, and the rest from Austria, Czechoslovakia, Germany, the Netherlands, and France. *Rate and Manner of Death:* Of the 30,000 Jewish inmates, 23,000 died in mass executions or dysentery and typhus epidemics, and from picric acid work. Six thousand prisoners were transferred to Buchenwald and other camps. *Resistance:* Underground groups. Two days before liquidation a massive escape of several hundred prisoners from Werke C was attempted, but most were killed while fleeing or in the surrounding forests.

*Karmel, Ilona

Sobibór

Location: The Lublin region of eastern Poland. *Established:* May 1942. *Liquidated:* October 1943. *Type:* An extermination camp. *Administrative Responsibility:* SS officers and Ukrainian guards (May 1942–October 1943). *Prisoner Work and Use:* A small camp group of 200 to 300 Jewish prisoners was kept mainly to prepare the transports for the gas chambers, clean the trains, remove bodies from the gas chambers, clean the chambers, and bury the dead bodies. A special team nicknamed "the dentists" extracted the gold teeth from the corpses. A small number were also kept to serve the needs of the camp staff and worked as tailors, carpenters, and cobblers. Prisoners came from Poland, the Soviet Union, Austria, Czechoslovakia, France, and the Netherlands. When the decision was taken to cremate all the dead, prisoners exhumed and cremated the bodies. *Rate and Manner of Death:* Estimated 250,000 Polish Jews were killed in the camp's gas chambers. *Resistance:* Underground groups, which fought the guards and attempted numerous escapes, over fifty of them successful. On 14 October 1943 the inmates rebelled and destroyed the camp.

*Cohen, Elie
Hillesum, Etty
Mulisch, Harry

Stutthof

Location: Near Danzig, Poland. *Established:* 2 September 1939. *Liberated:* 9 May 1945 by Soviet and Polish troops. *Type:* First designated as a "camp for civilian war prisoners," and officially became a concentration camp with several dozen satellite camps 8 January 1942. *Administrative Responsibility:* SS and Ukrainian auxiliary police (2 September 1939–9 May 1945). *Prisoner Work and Use:* The inmates were subject to hard labor, primarily in the military industry. Initially the prisoners were Poles from Danzig and Pomerania; later from all parts of northern Poland and from Warsaw. Soviet prisoners, Norwegians, Danes, and other completed the population. In 1944 large transports of Jews, mostly women, were brought from the Baltic countries and Auschwitz. Of the 50,000 Jews brought there, nearly all died, thousands in the gas chambers and in the winter death marches. *Rate and Manner of Death:* Exact records are not available. Out of the 115,000 prisoners who passed through the camp, about 22,000 were moved to other camps and 65,000 died of lethal injections and executions, or in the gas chambers and the death marches. *Resistance:* Underground movement, whose activists were the main victims of frequent executions.

Grass, Günter
*Nomberg-Pryztyk, Sara
*Vinocur, Ana

Transnistria

Location: A region in the Ukraine between the Bug River in the east and the Dneister in the west, the Black Sea in the south, and a line beyond Mogilev in the north. The region was conquered by German and Romanian forces and given to Romania for its participation in the war against the Soviet Union. *Established:* Following the slaughter of tens of thousands of Jews from Bessarabia, Bukovina, and northern Moldavia by *Einsatzgruppe* D and the Romanian forces, a non-contiguous group of ghettos and camps were established in Transnistria to hold the survivors who were deported to this region, which was envisioned as a gigantic penal colony for Jews. Deportations, which included forced marches, began in mid-September 1941 and continued through the fall of 1942. *Liberated*: On 13 October 1942, Romanians stopped deportations to Transnistria. The Soviet army launched the liberation of the region on 15 March 1943 and by 15 April, the Soviets overran all of Transnistria. *Types*: Ghettos and concentration camps. *Administration:* Gendarmerie and Romanian army officers. *Rate and Manner of Death*: Romanian and German army units murdered 185,000 Ukrainian Jews. Tens of thousands perished in the camps from starvation, cold, typhus, and dysentery. Of the 145,000–150,000 deported to Transnistria, some 90,000 perished. *Resistance*: Zionist and Jewish self-help groups organized aid shipments to the region as did the American Joint Distribution Committee, the Rescue Committee of the Jewish Agency of Turkey and the World Jewish Congress, which were, in the main, delayed and obstructed by Romanian authorities.

*Kittner, Alfred
*Weißglas, Immanuel James

Treblinka

Location: Northeast of the *Generalgouvernement. Established:* 23 July 1942. *Liquidated:* August 1943. *Type:* A penal camp for Poles and Jews in 1941 and an extermination camp in 1942. *Administrative Responsibility:* SS and Ukrainian guards (23 July 1942–August 1943). *Prisoner Work and Use:* In the penal camp, known as Treblinka I, set up in 1941 for Poles and Jews, prisoners worked in the quarries and helped construct the extermination camp, including digging huge pits to be used later as mass graves. When Treblinka became as extermination camp, Jewish inmates who helped with the extermination process (removing corpses from the gas chambers and cleaning the rooms, extracting the victims' gold teeth, and burying their bodies) were kept separate from the rest of the prisoners. Cremation was introduced in 1943 and the same group of prisoners carried out this task designed to remove all traces of the mass murder. The others worked primarily in construction, as well as serving the German staff. *Rate and Manner of Death:* An estimated 870,000 Jews died in the camp's gas chambers, while the "permanent" inmates were frequently victims of epidemics or committed suicide. *Resistance:* Several individual and group resistance efforts were made at Treblinka in which SS and Ukrainian guards were killed. Prisoners from the main camp and the extermination area belonged to the underground movement planning an uprising and a massive escape on 2 August 1943, to consist of taking weapons from the SS armory and then seizing control of the camp, destroying it and joining partisans in the local forests. Originally the uprising went according to plan but when the resisters shot an SS man, guards were alerted and ended the removal and distribution of weapons. The few who had weapons fired on the SS and set some buildings of the camp on fire, but as masses of prisoners tried to escape they were mowed down from the watchtowers. Those who managed to escape were hunted down. Of approximately 750 who tried to escape, seventy survived to liberation. Most of the wooden camp buildings burned.

Agosín, Marjorie
Elberg, Yehuda
Ficowski, Jerzy
Friedländer, Saul
Grass, Günter
Grossman, Vasilii
Grynberg, Henryk
Layton, Irving
Leivick, H.
Meed, Vladka
Steiner, Jean-François
Zeitlin, Aaron

Türkheim

Location: Türkheim, Germany. *Established:* October 1944. *Liberated:* April 1945 by the U.S. army. *Type:* a sub-camp of Dachau. *Administrative Responsibility:* SS (October 1944–April 1945). *Prisoner Work and Use:* The camp prisoners, who were housed in thirty underground shelters, were forced to work primarily in construction, in the woods, or on farms. *Rate and Manner of Death:* There is no data on how many of over 3,000 prisoners found their death in the camp. *Resistance:* An underground committee.

*Frankl, Viktor

Vittel

Location: Near Nancy, northeastern France. *Established:* 1940. *Liberated:* 12 September 1944 by Allied forces. *Type:* A detention camp with hotel housing for British subjects and American citizens and a small group of Polish, Belgian, and Dutch Jews in possession of Latin American passports or other documents certifying emigration. The Germans wanted to exchange these nationals of enemy and neutral nations for Germans held by the Allies. *Administrative Responsibility:* SS (1940–12 September 1944). *Prisoner Work and Use:* The inmates were subjected to harsh living conditions. *Rate and Manner of Death:* About 300 of the camp's prisoners were sent to death camps. When the Latin American passports were declared invalid, Jewish organizations tried to help but it was too late for the Jewish internees and 173 were sent to Drancy and from there deported to Auschwitz-Birkenau and their deaths.

*Katzenelson, Yitzhak

Westerbork

Location: Northeastern Netherlands. *Established:* 1 July 1942. *Liquidated:* 12 April 1945. *Type:* A camp for illegal Jewish refugees (October 1939–1 July 1942); then a transit camp (1 July 1942–12 April 1945). Jews from all parts of the Netherlands were systematically sent to Westerbork and then transported to Auschwitz. The Jewish leadership were assigned the task of compiling lists of deportees and Adolf Eichmann's office determined the timetable for the trains, the size of the transports, and destination. Some Jews of foreign nationality had been given special status before the deportations were started and they were exempt from the deportation selections. Trains left every Tuesday as of 2 February 1943. *Administrative Responsibility:* German security police and Dutch guards (1 July 1942–1 September 1942); SS (1 September 1942–12 April 1945). *Prisoner Work and Use:* Forced labor for the "permanent" inmates mainly in metalwork and health services. *Rate and Manner of Death:* Almost 100,000 Jews passed through the camp on the their way to death camps. *Resistance:* Resistance fighters were active in the camp.

Burnier, Andreas
*Cohen, Elie
*Durlacher, Gerhard
*Herzberg, Abel
*Hillesum, Etty
*Mechanicus, Philip

APPENDIX: HISTORIC EVENTS

* Writers whose names are preceded by an asterisk participated in or witnessed the event.

Except for those entries identified in parentheses as derived from other sources, all data in this appendix is compiled from the following sources:

Gutman, Israel. *Encyclopedia of the Holocaust*. 4 vols. New York: Macmillan, 1990.

Niewyck, Donald L. and Francis Nicosia's *Columbia Guide to the Holocaust*. New York: Columbia University Press, 2000.

Anschluss

Annexation of Austria by Germany. Austria peacefully yielded when Hitler's army invaded in March 1938 and most Austrians welcomed the union.

Aichinger, Ilse
Améry, Jean

Babi Yar

A wooded ravine outside Kiev, the Ukrainian capital conquered by the Germans in September 1941, where the Nazis murdered an estimated 100,000 Jews, Gypsies, and Soviet prisoners of war.

Green, Gerald
Thomas, D. M.
Yevtushenko, Yevgenii

British Blockades to Palestine

Naval blockade carried out by the British to prevent immigration to Palestine. In 1939, the British Mandatory power issued a White Paper restricting Jewish immigration to Palestine to a total of 75,000 for the following five years, thus diminishing the capacity of the Yishuv (pre-state Israel) from saving substantial numbers of threatened European Jewry. As a result, illegal immigration became one of the principal means the Yishuv used to help European Jews during and immediately following the Holocaust as British ships attacked the ships carrying the survivors. The British intensified their position against illegal immigration during the war, including such events as sinking the the *Patria* and *Struma* and interning the immigrants in Cyprus.

Whitman, Ruth

Eichmann Trial

The trial of Adolf Eichmann held in Jerusalem in 1961 and 1962 consisting of fifteen counts of "crimes against the Jewish people," "crimes against humanity," "war crimes," and membership in a hostile organization," which had been declared a criminal organization by the International Military Tribunal at the Nuremburg Trial.

Birenbaum, Halina
Rosen, Norma

Kindertransport

The Refugee Children's Movement was established in Britain to rescue Jewish and non-Aryan Christian children from Germany, Austria, and Czechoslovakia. The first trainloads arrived on 10 December 1938 and continued for nine months. By August 1939, 9,354 children, aged from a few months to seventeen years, had been rescued.

*Gershon, Karen
*Kramer, Lotte
*Mayer, Gerda
Samuels, Diane
*Segal, Lore

Kristallnacht ("Crystal Night"; Night of Broken Glass)

A government-sanctioned pogrom occurring throughout Germany and Austria on the night of November

9-10, 1938. Storm troopers and rioters, unrestrained by police and firefighters under Nazi command, attacked and looted Jewish businesses, homes, and synagogues, littering the streets with broken glass. Ninety-one Jews were murdered and 267 synagogues vandalized and torched. Approximately 20,000 Jews were imprisoned in concentration camps until they promised to emigrate. The Jews were fined one billion marks to pay for damages.

Aichinger, Ilse
*Gay, Peter (witnessed)
Grass, Günter
Green, Gerald
Hoffmann, Yoel
Klemperer, Victor
Millu, Liana
Schwarz-Bart, André

Nuremberg Laws

On 15 September 1935, the Nazis announced at Nuremberg two laws: the "Law for the Protection of German Blood and Honor" and the "Reich Citizenship Law" designed to exclude Jews from German life. These laws banned marriages between Jews and Germans and declared sexual relations between Jews and Germans a criminal offense. *Rassenschande* (racial defilement) prohibited Jewish hiring of German maids under the age of forty-five, disallowed Jews from raising flags with traditional German colors, and rescinded exemptions granted Jewish World War I veterans and state officials. The "Reich Citizenship Law" elevated Aryans as "Reich Citizens" above Jews or others with "impure blood."

Aichinger, Ilse
Améry, Jean

Nuremberg Trial

International Military Tribunal to judge the men and women accused of crimes against humanity, by planning, organizing, and executing such crimes, or by ordering others to do so during World War II. Twenty-two of Nazi Germany's political, military, and economic leaders were tried. Judges appointed to the tribunal were from the United States, the Soviet Union, Britain, and France. Poland, Norway, and Belgium, and friends of the court such as the World Jewish Congress, cooperated with the prosecutors.

Grossman, Vasilii

Paris Roundup of Jews, 1942

Throughout the summer and fall of 1942 the French authorities rounded up Jews in the occupied and unoccupied zones of France. On 16 and 17 July, one of the largest such roundups took place in Paris capturing 12,884 previously indexed Jews, including 4,051 children. Men without families were sent directly to Drancy. Families and all women and children were crowded into and held, whence they were dispatched to Auschwitz and other camps. The deportations of the summer and fall of 1942 totaled approximately 42,500.

Gary, Romain
Grumberg, Jean-Claude
Ozick, Cynthia
Piercy, Marge

Saint Louis Refugee Ship

The German liner *Saint Louis* left Hamburg on 14 May 1939, bound for Havana, Cuba. There were 937 Jewish passengers aboard who had American quota permits and special permits to stay temporarily in Cuba until American visas were processed. On 30 May thirty passengers were allowed to disembark at Havana. The others were told their landing permits were worthless and the ship was ordered to leave Havana, accompanied by twenty-six Cuban police boats. After nearly forty days of cruising in search of asylum, England, France, Belgium, and Holland divided the human cargo.

Cohen, Arthur

Wansee Conference

A luncheon meeting of top Nazi officials held at a villa in Wansee, Berlin, on 20 January 1942, to discuss and coordinate the implementation of the "Final Solution." Eleven million European Jews, including those from England and Ireland, were to be transported to eastern Europe, first utilized for labor and then those surviving would be killed. The genocide plan was clear. This meeting involved broad participation of all the major ministries of the Reich in the systematic annihilation of the Jewish people.

Duden, Anne
Harris, Robert

Warsaw Ghetto Uprising

The first urban revolt in German occupied Europe, lasting from 19 April to 16 May 1943. As preparations for what Warsaw Ghetto Jews believed to be the final phase of the 1942 ghetto deportations were being undertaken, a meeting was called by underground leaders and those close to the underground and discussion ensued to organize resistance to the deportation by force. Some objected, fearing armed resistance would put the entire ghetto in jeopardy. Representatives of several key ghetto organizations decided to form the ŻOB (Żydowska Organizacja Bojowa), the Jewish fighting organization. They published pamphlets to inform the ghetto of the fate of the deportees and what Treblinka meant based on reports of a Bund member who managed to get close to Treblinka and return to the ghetto. Their efforts to secure weapons from the Polish Home Army failed, but they did get a small number of arms from the Communists. By October the organization was enlarged with the addition of several youth movements and splinter political groups. Other resistance groups that did not join the ŻOB coordinated activities with them. There was resistance to the January 1943 deportation order. Jews ordered to assemble for deportation did not appear. A group of fighters led by Mordecai Anielewicz and armed with pistols infiltrated the column that was en route to the *Umschlag* and engaged the Germans in direct combat. The crowd was able to disperse. The fact that the Germans were able only to seize 10 percent of the intended number for deportation was considered a victory in the ghetto. The *Judenrate* and Jewish police lost control of the population. Expecting the next deportation to be the final one, the ghetto population concentrated from January to April on preparing subterranean bunkers that would sustain life underground. The twenty-two fighting ŻOB units (totalling 700-750 fighters), positioned in strategic ghetto buildings and roof attics, engaged the Germans in combat while the masses were to hide in the bunkers, in joint resistance. The fighters were under no delusions of rescue or escape, but expected the revolt to be a protest message for the world. The final liquidation of the ghetto began on 19 April 1943, the eve of Passover. Although the Germans had a military presence for this deportation, they did not expect the direct confrontation of street battles. According to General Jürgen Stroop's report the Germans entered the ghetto with 850 men and eighteen officers and when met with armed resistance were forced to retreat. The magnitude of the hiding operation of 30,000 Jews surprised the Germans as much as the armed resistance and the trains remained empty. The Germans systematically burned the ghetto, house by house, forcing the fighters into the bunkers that eventually became infernos. After two weeks of this resistance, the Germans threw hand grenades, tear gas, and poison gas into the bunkers, forcing the victims out. Some still remained in the bunkers and joined the Warsaw Polish uprising in August 1944.

Andrejewski, Jerzy
*Edelman, Marek
*Ettinger, Elżbieta
Hersey, John
Meed, Vladka
*Rudnicki, Adolf
Rymkiewicz, Jarosław Marek
Shapiro, Alan

Warsaw Polish Uprising

This uprising took place in August 1944, carried out by the Armia Krajowa, the largest Polish resistance organization (23,000 ill-equipped forces) on the orders of the Polish government in exile in London in an effort to take control of Warsaw before the Red Army entered. The civilian population gave strong support to the uprising. The besieged city fell on 2 October, with a huge number of Polish and German dead and wounded. The Germans expelled the surviving civilians to forced labor in the Reich and concentration camps. Following the Polish surrender, the Germans burned and razed the remaining parts of the city.

*Edelman, Marek
Ettinger, Elżbieta
Green, Gerald
*Meed, Vladka
*Rudnicki, Adolf
Rymkiewicz, Jarosław Marek
Shapiro, Alan

APPENDIX: HISTORIC FIGURES TREATED OR MENTIONED IN THE LITERATURE

Except for those entries identified in parantheses as derived from other sources, all data in this appendix is compiled from the following sources:

Gutman, Israel. *Encyclopedia of the Holocaust.* 4 vols. New York: Macmillan, 1990.

Niewyck, Donald L. and Francis Nicosia's *Columbia Guide to the Holocaust.* New York: Columbia University Press, 2000.

Barbie, Klaus (1913–) joined the Nazi Party in 1932 and the SS in 1935. He began working for the Gestapo in 1942 and that year was posted to Lyons, France, where he served as Gestapo chief for the next twenty-one months and directly committed or was responsible for many atrocities, including the torture of Jean Moulin, a hero of the French Resistance, which earned him the nickname "the butcher of Lyons." He was tried *in absentia* in France in 1952 and 1954 and sentenced to death. He was discovered in La Paz, Bolivia, by Nazi hunter Beate Klarsfeld in 1971, but it was not until 1983 that the Bolivians finally expelled him and he was brought to France to stand trial. In 1987 Barbie was found guilty of crimes against humanity and sentenced to life imprisonment, the maximum penalty under French law at the time.

Finkielkraut, Alain
Piercy, Marge

Brand, Joel (1907–1964) a Budapest businessman and active Zionist, was selected by Adolf Eichmann to convey the "blood for trucks" offer to the Allies in May 1944. He took the German offer to release 1,000,000 Jews in return for 10,000 trucks very seriously, and he was shattered when the Allies turned it down and refused to negotiate with the Germans.

Cohen, Arthur
Elon, Amos
Kipphardt, Heiner

Coughlin, Charles Edward (1891–1979) a Roman Catholic priest, pastor of the Shrine of the Little Flower at Royal Oak, Michigan, broadcast radio addresses critical of trade unionists, bankers, Communists, and Jews from 1930–1940. In 1934 he organized the National Union for Social Justice critical of President Roosevelt and the New Deal. Coughlin also published a magazine, *Social Justice*, in which he expressed pro-Nazi opinions and made increasingly antisemitic remarks directed especially at Jewish members of Wall Street. The U.S. government barred the magazine from the mail for violation of the Espionage Act and publication ceased in 1942. (*New Columbia Encyclopedia* edited by William H. Harris and Judith S. Levy, New York: Columbia University Press, 1975, p. 668).

Ozick, Cynthia
Piercy, Marge

Czerniakow, Adam (1880–1942) headed the Warsaw Jewish Council (*Judenrat*) until his suicide on July 23, 1942. Under his leadership the council vastly expanded its work force and activities, taking responsibility for all areas of Jewish life from health and nutrition to work and housing. Although badly treated by the German authorities, he long believed that most of the Jews of the ghetto would be spared as long as they provided a steady work force for the German factories located in the city. Czerniakow's sense of duty held fast when the Germans began to deport ghetto residents in 1942. At first he accepted German assurances that the Jews were being resettled in order to alleviate overcrowding in the ghetto. But in July, finding that the Germans had lied to him about the extent of the deportations, and suspecting that rumors about Treblinka were true, Czerniakow swallowed poison. His diary survived the war and provides invaluable information about the functioning of the ghetto.

Edelman, Marek
Raczymow, Henri

De Gaulle, Charles (1890–1970) French general and statesman; first president of the Fifth Republic (1959–1969). During World War II, he opposed the Franco-German armistice and fled to London (June 1940) where he organized the Free French Forces.

Modiano, Patrick

Eichmann, Adolf (1906–1962) was the SS officer responsible for deporting Jews to ghettos and extermination and forced labor camps. In March 1938, sent to Vienna to organize the emigration of Austrian Jews, he established the first Central Office for Jewish Emigration (Zentralstelle für jüdische Auswanderung), which engaged the cooperation of Jewish officials in forcing the Jews to leave. Thereafter he distinguished himself in organizing expulsions of Jews from Germany and western Poland to the general government. In 1941 Eichmann was rewarded by being made head of the Jewish section of the Reich Security Main Office. He participated in the Wannsee Conference and was assigned the task of coordinating the transport of all the European Jews to camps in Poland. Members of his staff operated virtually everywhere in German-dominated regions, and Eichmann himself supervised the deportations from Hungary in 1944. After Germany's defeat, Eichmann managed to slip away to Argentina with the help of sympathetic Vatican officials. He was discovered and kidnapped by Israeli agents in 1960. His trial in Jerusalem created a sensation and introduced the Holocaust to members of the postwar generation. He was executed in 1962.

Arendt, Hannah
Cohen, Arthur
Elon, Amos
Grossman, Vasilii
Hamburger, Michael
Hochhuth, Rolf
Kipphardt, Heiner
Lerner, Motti
Mulisch, Harry
Rosen, Norma
Wiesenthal, Simon

Frank, Anne (1929–1945) is the author of the *The Diary of Anne Frank*, which has made her the best-known victim of the Holocaust. Although she was born in Frankfurt am Main, Germany, her family moved to Amsterdam to escape Hitler's persecution of German Jewry. When the Germans began to deport the Dutch Jews in 1942, the Franks were hidden with the help of Dutch friends in an unused attic. The Germans arrested them all following an anonymous telephone tip in August 1944. The Franks were sent to Auschwitz. Anne and her older sister Margot were brought from Auschwitz to Bergen-Belsen in October 1944 where they died of typhus in March 1945.

Agosín, Marjorie
Roth, Philip

Gens, Jacob (1905–1943) attempted to save the Vilna Jewish community by placating the Germans in his role as head of the Vilna ghetto Jewish Council (*Judenrat*). Following the creation of the Vilna ghetto he was named head of the Jewish police. Gens's military background enabled him to build an efficient and disciplined ghetto police force that participated in the roundups of Jews in the ghetto in the last months of 1941. The Germans came to view him as the ablest ghetto leader, and in July 1942 they appointed him chairman of the Vilna Jewish Council and also put him in charge of several smaller ghettos in the area. Gens ruled with an iron hand in order to keep the Vilna ghetto working and hence productive for the Germans. He could not avoid delivering Jews for deportations, but whenever possible he sent the old and sick rather than young women and children, hoping to preserve the biological stock. Gens was in constant contact with the ghetto underground, always urging it to avoid a premature revolt. He was shot on September 14, 1943, only days before the ghetto was liquidated.

Schaeffer, Susan Fromberg
Sobol, Joshua

Gerstein, Kurt (1905–1945) was an SS officer and head of the *Waffen*-SS Institute of Hygiene who tried to make known the reality of the "Final Solution." He joined the Nazi Party in 1933 while adhering to the Confessing Church, for which he was dismissed in 1936. After a period of imprisonment in a concentration camp, he was expelled from the party in 1938. He studied medicine and following the death of a family member in the euthenasia program, resolved to learn the truth about the program. He volunteered for the *Waffen*-SS and in 1941 was assigned to its hygiene institute. He worked with Zyklon B and was sent on an inspection tour of Bełżec, Treblinka, and Sobibór. He shared the information with several church officials and a Swedish diplomat, and some contacts in the Dutch underground to no avail. After the war, he was arrested by the French as a suspected war criminal. He either committed suicide in his cell or was murdered by fellow SS prisoners.

Hochhouth, Rolf

Goeth, Amon (1908–1946) was a sadistic SS officer. He joined the Nazi Party in 1932 and joined the SS in 1940. He was assigned to the Lublin police and subsequently was transferred to Kraków, where he was in charge of liquidating the ghettos and labor camps. From February 1943 to September 1944, he commanded the Płaszów concentration camp outside of Kraków. After the war, he was tried before the Polish Supreme Court, on a charge of committing mass murder during the liquidations, sentenced to death, and executed in Kraków.

Karmel, Ilona
Ferderber Salz, Bertha
Keneally, Thomas

Griese, (Grese) Irma (1923–1945) was a sadistic camp guard who served in Ravensbrück in 1942–March 1943, in Auschwitz from March 1943–1945 where she was promoted and put in charge of all female prisoners, and in Bergen-Belsen until liberation. She was tried by the British in the Bergen-Belsen trial, charged with torturing and assaulting prisoners, and was hanged 13 December 1945.

Lengyel, Olga
Perl, Gisella

Heydrich, Reinhard (1904–1942) was, after Heinrich Himmler, the most powerful SS leader in Germany. He was responsible for planning and executing genocide. In 1931 Himmler recruited him to set up an SS intelligence office within the Nazi Party called the *Sicherheitsdienst* (Security Service, or SD). As Himmler's faithful servant Heydrich assisted in bringing all the police forces in Germany under SS control. When Göring turned most anti-Jewish policies over to the SS in late 1938 and 1939, Heydrich took these, too, in hand, including direction of the Reich Central Office for Jewish Emigration (Reichszentrale für jüdische Auswanderung) in January 1939. Heydrich drew up plans to implement the Final Solution that were unveiled to other party and state officials at the Wannsee Conference in January 1942. Heydrich was also named deputy Reich Protector of the Protectorate of Bohemia and Moravia in 1941. He was assassinated by Czech agents in May 1942.

Green, Gerald

Himmler, Heinrich (1900–1945) responsible for clearing Europe of "racially undesirable" elements during World War II. Loyal to Hitler, who in 1929 made him chief of the SS, Himmler became head of the political police in Bavaria after the Nazi victory in 1933 and began a three-year struggle to assemble all the police forces in Germany under his own personal control. He took a giant step forward in 1934 when Hitler ordered him to purge the SA (the Nazi storm troopers), which made the SS the chief agency of terror in the Third Reich. By 1936 Himmler ran both the SS and the police, combining in his person both party and state offices with the power of life and death over everyone in Germany. This included control of the growing network of German concentration camps. During the war, his powers increased further with the creation of the *Waffen* SS, which rivaled the army as Germany's chief military force, and with his appointment as Reich commissar for the strengthening of German nationality, which gave him authority to cleanse eastern Europe of Slavs and Jews. Hence Himmler had overall responsibility for carrying out the "Final Solution," including the actions of the *Einsatzgruppen* (action squads) and the operation of the labor and extermination camps.

Duden, Anne
Fenelon, Fania
Kogon, Eugen
Sobol, Joshua

Hitler, Adolf (1889–1945) interested himself in right-wing and pan-German politics. In 1913 Hitler moved to Munich, Germany, and a year later volunteered to fight for Germany in World War I. Wounded and highly decorated, Hitler returned to Munich after the war. In his first political document in 1919, he had already identified his goal of "total removal of the Jews" and joined a small antisemitic party that took the name National Socialist Workers' Party in 1920. The party's 1920 platform called for German Jews to be deprived of their civil rights and for some to be expelled from the country. He became leader of the Nazi Party in 1921, with unlimited power. He dedicated himself to destroying the liberal and democratic Weimar Republic, and after failing to overturn it by force in the 1923 Munich (Beer Hall) Putsch, for which he was sentenced to five years in prison, but released after nine months, he worked to build his party and attain power legally. In 1925 he reestablished the Nazi Party and created the SS protection squad to serve as the party's fighting force. His intent now was to destroy the government by constitutional means by gaining a parliamentary majority, which was accomplished during the Depression. In 1933 he was appointed German chancellor, after which Germany's demoralized parliament, the Reichstag, granted him dictatorial powers. Following the Reichstag fire, basic civil rights were suspended on 27 February and on 5 March parliamentary rule abolished by the Enabling Law, which transferred power from the Reichstag to the cabinet, where the conservatives were the majority. As dictator of Germany, Hitler embarked upon racial policies aimed at removing "racially undesirable" groups such as handicapped people and Jews and preparing Germany for war to conquer *Lebensraum* (living space) for an expanding German population. Anti-Semitic riots took place in March, culminating in the boycott of 1 April 1933 and the 7 April law that was the beginning of eliminating Jews from civic life. On 14 July all political parties except Hitler's were outlawed. After Hindenburg's death in 1934, Hitler became head of state and chief of the Wehrmacht and assumed the title of *Führer* and Reich chancellor. Rearmament and antisemitic persecutions were accelerated and the Nuremberg Laws of 1935 were issued to exclude Jews from German society. By 1937, approximately one-third of German Jewry had left the country. After the *Anschluss* with Austria, 200,000 Jews were added to the Reich (although a quarter left within six months). In October 1938, 17,000 Jews of Polish origin were expelled from Germany. This would lead to the destruction of European Jewry. When the war began in Poland, the Germans began their systematic destruction of the Jews. The "Final Solution" began after the German invasion of the Soviet Union in 1941, with the mass murders carried out by the *Einsatzgruppen*, to be followed by the operation of concentration and extermination camps. Debate has arisen between "functionalist" historians who hold that the anti-Jewish persecution was largely the work of the Nazi system with Hitler as the legitimizer of the process, and the "intentionalists" who argue that the anti-Jewish policy was a long-term Nazi goal, a clearly conceived plan.

Gay, Peter
Harris, Robert
Kogon, Eugen
Pinter, Harold

Höss, Rudolf (1900–1947) was the first commandant of Auschwitz as well as its architect and builder. After Hitler came to power, Höss joined the SS and learned the skills of concentration camp administration at Dachau and Sachsenhausen. In May 1940, he was promoted and sent east to establish a concentration camp at Auschwitz. Höss introduced Zyklon B gassing techniques in 1941 and began a vast expansion of the camp and its facilities that made it into the largest concentration and extermination camp. Höss was relieved of his duties in November 1943 for large-scale corruption by the Auschwitz staff, but he arranged to return to Auschwitz in March 1944 to supervise the gassing of large numbers of Hungarian Jews. At the end of the war Höss was arrested and sent to Poland to be tried. Before being hanged on the gallows at Auschwitz, Höss wrote his memoirs, in which he portrayed himself as an officer who was duty-bound to follow orders and hence another victim of Hitler.

Brett, Lilly
Duden, Anne
Styron, William

Karski, Jan (1914–2002) was a Polish civil servant before World War II. He joined the anti-German underground during World War II and acted as one of its couriers to the Polish government in exile in London. Karski took great risks in order to familiarize himself with the "Final Solution," twice sneaking into the Warsaw ghetto and later disguising himself as a Ukrainian Hiwi to inspect Jews being readied for extermination at Bełżec. Karski made it to London in November 1942 and spoke with Winston Churchill and other English and Polish leaders. Later Karski met with President Roosevelt to inform him of the persecutions.

Piercy, Marge
Tec, Nechama

Kasztner, Rezső (1906–1957) was a journalist, lawyer, and Zionist leader, vice-chairman of the Relief and Rescue Committee of Budapest. Kasztner negotiated with the Germans in an effort to rescue Hungarian Jews from deportations. As an active Zionist and leader of Va'da, which operated an underground railroad for Jews fleeing the Nazis, he was among those Budapest Jews approached by Eichmann with the "blood for trucks" offer that was conveyed to the Western Allies in July 1944 by Joel Brand. Exploiting SS hopes for a separate peace with the Western powers, Kasztner convinced the Germans to release 1,684 Hungarian Jews to Switzerland as a good faith gesture. After the war, he was called to the Nuremburg Trials and testified on behalf of SS officer Kurt Becher with whom he negotiated to save Jews. Kasztner settled in Israel, where in 1954 he brought a suit against Malkiel Grünwald, who accused him of being a traitor, responsible for the death of many Jews while saving his family and friends. The trial turned into a trial of Kasztner and the court found against him for negotiating with Nazis. While awaiting the results of his appeal to the Israeli Supreme Court, he was murdered by extremists. Eventually the court exonerated Kasztner of all charges except the charge that he helped Nazis escape justice.

Kipphardt, Heiner
Richler, Mordecai

Korczak, Janusz (1878–1942) was a physician and educator who directed the Warsaw ghetto orphanage. He had established an international reputation as an educational reformer and child psychologist. Korczak put his theories to work in running Jewish and Polish orphanages before World War II. He declined offers to escape to the Polish side of Warsaw. On 5 August 1942, the German order came, and Korczak himself led his orphans to the rail siding. He perished with them at Treblinka.

Atlan, Liliane
Meed, Vladka
Raczymow, Henri
Zeitlin, Aaron

Mengele, Josef (1911–1979) is the best known Auschwitz physician. He was responsible along with other SS doctors for selections and medical experiments that used prisoners as guinea pigs. Mengele's medical experiments at Auschwitz reflected the Nazi preoccupation with race. He deliberately infected prisoners with contagious diseases such as tuberculosis and typhus to compare the reactions of various races to disease. His research on Gypsy and Jewish twins sought means of increasing multiple births among Germans to increase the Aryan population. When finished with his human guinea pigs, many of them children, he usually gave them fatal injections.

Durlacher, Gerhard
Fenelon, Fania
Nomberg-Przytyk, Sara
Richler, Mordecai
Schwarz-Bart, André
Tedeschi, Giuliana

Pius XII (Eugenio Pacelli, 1876–1958) was preoccupied with protecting the church and signed a concordat with Hitler's Reich. Under Pacelli's leadership, the Catholic Church did not protest the increasingly severe measures against European Jewry, although in March 1937 Pius XI denounced Nazi racism. During World War II, Pius XII pursued a policy of neutrality, although he learned of the "Final Solution" early in 1942. He made no public statement condemning Nazi atrocities, nor did he call upon Catholics to help the victims of genocide. Rather he employed traditional diplomacy, to intervene on behalf of baptized Jews, with minor success in Slovakia and Hungary.

Hochhuth, Rolf

Rumkowski, Mordechai Chaim (1877–1944) was the controversial chairman of the Jewish Council (*Judenrat*) in the Łódż ghetto from 1939 to 1944. Between 1939 and 1944 he helped establish more than one hundred factories employing Jews for the German administration in Łódż. In late 1941 the Germans forced Rumkowski to begin organizing deportations to the Chelmno extermination camp. He believed that working for the Germans and maintaining peace within the ghetto was the best way to save Jewish lives. He managed to extend the life of the Łódż ghetto longer than other ghettos in Poland, resulting in a relatively large number of survivors. With the advance of the Soviets, the Germans liquidated the ghetto, closed the factories, and dissolved the Jewish Council in August 1944. Rumkowski and his family were deported to Auschwitz, where they were killed.

Biderman, Abraham
Bellow, Saul
Epstein, Leslie
Kosinski, Jerzy
Levi, Primo
Rosenfarb, Chava
Vinocur, Ana

Schindler, Oskar (1908–1974) was a German industrialist and Nazi Party member who saved more than 1,100 Jews during the war. Schindler came to German-occupied Kraków in late 1939 and purchased a former Jewish-owned factory that produced enamel kitchenware. His firm, employing Jewish workers from the Kraków ghetto, produced pots and pans for the German army. When the ghetto was liquidated in early 1943, those not murdered were sent to nearby Płaszów labor camp. Schindler's Jewish workers continued to work for him. He protected them from the brutality at Płaszów and deportation to Auschwitz. Most of Schindler's Jewish workers survived the Holocaust, and Schindler was declared a "Righteous Gentile" after the war by Yad Vashem.

Keneally, Thomas

Senesh, Hannah (1921–1944) was a Hungarian girl who immigrated to Palestine and joined the Jewish Brigade of the British forces. She was one of thirty-two Palestinian Jews who parachuted behind enemy lines in the Balkans in 1944 to help downed Allied airmen escape and only secondarily were they allowed to aid European Jewry. The twenty-three-year-old woman, who had come to Palestine at age eighteen, together with two others, was dropped into Yugoslavia in March 1944, smuggled into Hungary, where she made contact with Hungarian partisans. Upon learning that the parachutists were Jews, the partisans turned them over to the Hungarian police, who surrendered them to the Gestapo. Senesh did not reveal British codes despite severe torture. The Gestapo returned her to the Arrow Cross government, put her on trial for espionage and executed her on 6 November 1944. (Sacher, Howard Morley. *The Course of Modern Jewish History*. New York, Dell Publishing Co., 1958, p. 454).

Rich, Adrienne
Whitman, Ruth

Speer, Albert (1905–1981), an architect and wartime minister of armaments, joined the Nazi Party in 1931 and developed a personal relationship with Hitler. He was in charge of designing the large Nazi Party rallies and major monumental buildings. As minister of armaments and war production (1942 appointment), Speer was responsible for exploiting slave labor. At his Nuremberg trial he admitted use of slave labor, was found guilty of crimes against humanity and sentenced to twenty years in prison.

Harris, Robert

Waldheim, Kurt (1918–) scrvcd as an Austrain soldier and diplomat. Following the *Anschluss,* he joined the Nazi Students' Association and an SA cavalry unit. After being drafted into the Wehrmacht, he took part in the invasion of the Sudetenland, in the campaign in France, and against the Soviet Union. From 1942 to 1945, he served in the Balkans, in the offensive against Yugoslav partisans and resultant massacre, and in Greece as an intelligence officer. In 1947, the Yugoslav government put Waldheim on the War Criminal List of the United Nations, but no further action was taken. He joined the diplomatic service of the new Austrian republic in 1945, served as foreign minister from 1968–1970, failed in his election bid for Austria's presidency in 1971, but that same year was elected United Nations secretary-general, and reelected for a second term. In 1986, he was elected president of Austria. In 1987, the United States Justice Department put Waldheim on the watch list as a suspected war criminal. In 1988 an international body of historians appointed by Austria concluded he was not personally responsible for unlawful activities during the war, but knew of them and was close to persons who carried out the atrocities and did nothing to disrupt them, and by his passivity facilitated the atrocities.

Bernhard, Thomas
Schindel, Robert

Wittenberg, Yitzhak (1907–1943) was the first commander of the United Partisan Organization and leader of the Communist underground in the Vilna ghetto. When the Nazis threatened destruction of the Vilna ghetto if Wittenberg was not surrendered, Jacob Gens, the chairman of the ghetto *Judenrat*, appealed to the ghetto population to surrender Wittenberg and the decision was taken to do so in order to save the ghetto population. Wittenberg surrendered to the Jewish police and committed suicide in prison.

Kovner, Abba
Steiner, Jean-François

GLOSSARY

Except for those entries identified in parentheses as derived from other sources, all entries are based on the following sources:

Gutman, Israel. *Encyclopedia of the Holocaust*. 4 vols. New York: Macmillan, 1990.
Niewyck, Donald L. and Francis Nicosia's *Columbia Guide to the Holocaust*. New York: Columbia University Press, 2000.
Polikov, Léon. "Jewish Resistance in France," *YIOV*. (1953).

***Aktion*:** A raid against Jews (often in ghettos); the primary purpose was to round up Jews for deportation to the concentration and extermination camps

***Appell*:** Roll call in the camps

Aryanization: An ideological, governmentally condoned "purification" of Germany initiated by Hitler in 1933. As part of the process of isolation of the Jewish population, the Nazis soon mandated the exclusion of Jews from German civic and cultural life, barring Jews from participation in government, the military, and the professions. Jews were excluded from all the arts and media and Jewish children were expelled from schools. Jewish businesses, homes, and property were transferred to Aryans.

***Blockälteste*:** (f); *Blockältester* (m): the barracks supervisor; a prisoner functionary responsible for fellow prisoners during roll call, food distribution, and for order in the barracks.

Canada: The storage center for stolen property of concentration camp prisoners. Prisoners called it "Canada" because it represented unlimited abundance.

Concentration Camps: Shortly after Hitler took power in 1933, the Nazis created camps, including Dachau, Buchenwald, Flossenbürg, Gross-Rosen, Mauthausen, Neuengamme, Ravensbrück, and Sachsenhausen, to incarcerate Hitler's political enemies—Communists, Social Democrats, and labor union leaders. By 1934 they were administered by the SS. New categories of prisoners were added including criminals, religious dissenters (Jehovah's Witnesses), Gypsies, homosexuals, prostitutes, and others defined as "asocial elements." Following *Kristallnacht* thousands of Jews were sent to concentration camps for a short duration to encourage emigration. During World War II the Nazis expanded the system greatly all over German-controlled Europe, sometimes converting east European labor camps to concentration camps and holding select groups such as Jews, resistance fighters, and prisoners of war in addition to the other categories. In some instances, concentration camps were developed into extermination camps.

Death Marches: Massive forced marches of concentration camp inmates (mostly Jews) on foot, (sometimes by train, or by ship), during the last nine months of World War II, from German camps in danger of liberation by the approaching Allies. The prisoners who survived the evacuations on foot termed them "death marches" because the enormous death rates from harsh weather conditions, lack of food and water, the already severely weakened condition of the inmates, and the brutality of the guards (anyone who fell was shot).

Deportation: The transportation or "resettlement" of Jews from Nazi-occupied countries to labor, concentration, and death camps.

Displaced Persons (DPs): Persons uprooted or displaced as a result of the war, either unable or unwilling to return to their countries of origin. The Allies, attempting to meet needs but without staff and resources, relocated these persons to DP camps, sometimes to unimproved former concentration camps.

***Einsatzgruppen*:** Elite among Hitler's hierarchy of murderers, these 3,000 men from the Security Service of the SS and the SD German Security Police, attached to the *Wehrmacht*, were divided into mobile units also known as "operational" or "action" groups, or "special strike forces." From 1941 to 1945, these forces, operating largely in Poland and the USSR, aided by German order police, the *Waffen* SS, and east European Hiwis, murdered over a million people (mostly Jews, but also Gypsies, the handicapped, Soviet prisoners of war, and Communists) primarily by shooting them.

Extermination Camps: Industrialized mass murder between 1941 and 1944, carried out in six Nazi camps designed as death factories in occupied Poland. Three and a half million Jews and tens of thousands of Gypsies and Soviet prisoners of war were murdered in the extermination camps. In December 1941, Chelmno began poisoning people in gas vans. In 1942, Auschwitz (also a concentration camp) and Majdanek began gassing victims with Zyklon B, while "Operation Reinhard" camps Bełżec, Sobibór, and Treblinka (exclusively extermination camps) used carbon monoxide. These camps were under the jurisdiction of the SS.

"Final Solution" (*Endlösung*): On January 24, 1939, SS Major General Heydrich, the chief of the Security Police and the SD, was assigned the task of "solv[ing] the Jewish problem in Europe" by emigration and evacuation. This mandate was revised, however, on July 31, 1941, when Reich Marshal Göring commissioned Heydrich to carry out all necessary preparations for a "final solution of the Jewish question in the German sphere of influence in Europe": the genocide of European Jewry.

Gas Chambers: Designed for efficiency and secrecy, these "showers," or large rooms inside the crematoria buildings, trapped prisoners as they inhaled Zyklon B or carbon monoxide gas.

Gas Vans: Piping exhaust fumes into sealed trailers, these vans were early mobile gas chambers.

***Generalgouvernement*:** German name for the administrative unit comprising those parts of occupied Poland that were not incorporated into the Reich (Galicia, Kraków, Lublin, Radom, and Warsaw).

***Gestapo*:** Secret state police of Nazi Germany, a branch of the SS that dealt with political opponents through the use of terror and torture, under the command of Heinrich Himmler.

Ghettos: Temporary geographic centers where Jews were isolated prior to deportation to the concentration and extermination camps. These ghettos were generally located in the worst sections of cities, generally walled and sealed off from the Aryan side of a city. They became death traps of overcrowding, starvation, and disease, as the Nazis interned increasing numbers of Jews from rural areas and western countries. More than 350 ghettos were established in German-occupied eastern Europe. Nazi control of the ghetto population included the *Judenräte*, or Jewish Councils, who were allowed slight autonomy if they followed Nazi orders and provided forced labor and deportation quotas. In 1943, most of the ghettos were liquidated.

***Haftling*:** Concentration camp prisoner.

Jewish Councils: (*Judenräte*) To control Jewish communities throughout German-occupied territories, the Nazis either appointed Jewish councils or ordered the Jews to choose councils that, under Nazi command and threat, enforced Jewish cooperation with Nazi goals. The Judenräte, or Judenältestenrat (Councils of Jewish Elders), governed single ghettos, groups of ghettos, or all Jews in a country, as in Belgium, France, Germany, the Netherlands, and Slovakia. The Judenräte had to oversee food distribution, removal of corpses daily found upon the streets, aid to refugees and orphans, and public institutions such as hospitals and soup kitchens. They were responsible for supplying the Nazis with Jewish forced labor and goods. Under great duress, they also were responsible for selecting Jews for deportation.

***Judenrein*:** A German term meaning "clean" of Jews.

***Kapo*:** Concentration camp prisoner trustee or overseer in charge of a work detail, usually drawn from among German criminals.

KL, KZ: *Konzentrationslager* (concentration camp).

***Kommando*:** Work crew; labor battalion in the concentration camp.

***Kennkarte*:** Official identification card.

Labor Camps: Similar to concentration camps, these east European camps, including separate camps for women, held prisoners who provided slave labor for the SS and private enterprises contributing to the Nazi military machine. Prisoners were frequently forced to build the camps and the factories where they labored. German allies Slovakia, Hungary, and Romania, also operated labor camps.

***Lager*:** Camp.

***Lebensborn*:** SS association established in 1935 for the purpose of facilitating the adoption of "racially appropriate" children by childless SS couples and to encourage the birth of "racially sound" children.

***Lebensraum*:** (Living space) A principle of Nazi ideology and foreign policy involving the conquest of territory in eastern Europe.

Madagascar Plan: A German proposal to deport European Jews to the French-controlled island of Madagascar in June 1940.

Medical Experiments: With the support of universities and institutes for research and development, medical doctors conducted unusually cruel and frequently fatal experiments on prisoners in concentration and extermination camps, to advance Nazi ideology and victory. Some experiments had military applications; others had medical applications. Dachau prisoners were subjected to high altitude and freezing temperatures and to drinking salt water. At Neuengamme and Sachsenhausen prisoners were exposed to poison chemicals. Others were exposed to malaria, typhus, and hepatitis to test experimental treatments. Women in Ravensbrück were deliberately wounded and then infected to test medical treatments. Auschwitz and Buckenwald inmates were burned to test burn treatments. Sterilization experiments using x-rays were performed on men and women. Thousands of inmates died in these criminal medical procedures.

***Mischlinge*: (Mixed Breeds)** Of mixed German and Jewish or German and Gypsy descent, *mischlinge* were thus classified legally and experienced social and civic restrictions, but were generally not incarcerated.

***Muselmänner*:** Totally impassive because of exhaustion, starvation, and despair, these prisoners, called "*muselmänner*" by fellow inmates, were close to death.

National Socialism: (Nazism) A racist, antisemitic, and xenophobic, anti-Communist ideology developed under Hitler, who became *Führer* in 1921. Its political agenda included the end of the Weimar Republic, the establishment of Hitler as dictator, the expansion of the Third Reich, and the legitimization of Aryanism. Aryan Europe would be "cleansed" of the disabled, homosexuals, Gypsies, and Jews; the Slavs, who had impure blood, would become forced labor until rendered unnecessary.

***Oneg Shabes*: (Sabbath Delight) Historian** Emanuel Ringelblum and others organized this secret archive of the daily workings of the Warsaw ghetto that has provided important documentation of the plight of Polish Jewry.

Organization: (To organize) a camp term meaning to steal, buy, exchange food or other articles like medicine or clothing needed for survival, without harming another inmate.

Partisans: Jews fought in partisan units throughout Europe. In 1942, approximately 30,000 Jewish partisans in non-Jewish or Jewish units fought in the forests of the Soviet Union and Baltic states. From 1942 to 1944, approximately 2,000 Polish Jews fought in non-Jewish partisan, Communist, or Jewish units. Between 12,000 and 15,000 Jewish partisans were active in Belarus. Often, Jewish partisans had to conceal their Jewish identities for they were shunned or betrayed by hostile fellow partisans and local populations. Jewish partisans also fought in western Europe and the Balkans, where they were generally accepted into non-Jewish units as equals. French Jews of the *Union Générale des Israélites de France* (UGIF) combined efforts with the Communists in Occupied France; in Vichy France, the *Eclairieurs Israélites de France* (EIF) (Jewish Boy Scouts) not only clandestinely worked with underground fighters, networking escape routes and transmitting information, but also evacuated threatened children to the provinces and provided help for refugees. Jewish women acted as couriers and worked in the M19 networks instrumental in rescuing thousands of British and American airmen. An unusually strong and well-organized unit was the *Armée Juive* (Jewish Army), formed in 1942 by the Jewish underground in France.

Ponar: Annihilation center on the outskirts of Vilna. Began operations in July 1941, and claimed the lives of 60,000 Jews of Vilna and environs.

Prisoner Functionaries: Using starving prisoners to effect the functioning of the camp, the SS set up an administrative hierarchy. The camp senior, appointed by the SS commandant and answerable to him, supervised the barracks chiefs (also called "block" or "barracks" seniors), who supervised room chiefs monitoring the prisoners. Other functionaries included the *capos*, or *kapos*, who directed work crews, and clerks, who kept records and managed supplies. These functionaries were rewarded with slightly more food and slightly easier jobs; some tried to use their positions to lessen the severity of task or punishment inflicted on the weakest prisoners, others performed their tasks cruelly. Any effort detected to help the inmates was punished severely by the SS.

***Rassenschände*:** Nazi term for sexual contact between an "Aryan" and a Jew; racial defilement.

"Righteous Among the Nations": In 1953, the Israeli parliament (Knesset) passed the "Martyrs' and Heroes' Remembrance Law" charging Yad Vashem, Israel's national institution for Holocaust commemoration, to establish a memorial for "Righteous Gentiles" who risked their lives to save Jews. Approximately 16,000 men and women have been declared "Righteous Among the Nations."

SA (Storm Troopers): (*Sturmabteilung*) (The Brownshirts): The SA was Hitler's military unit of the Nazi Party from 1921 to 1934. Initially under the command of Hermann Göring, the SA was dissolved in 1923 following Hitler's Beer Hall Putsch, but was reinstated in 1924 with the rest of the Nazi Party. Its activities were largely devoted to intimidation of Hitler's political opponents. Hitler turned against the SA and ordered the murder of its leader, Ernst Röhm and approximately fifty other SA leaders on June 30–July 1, 1934, the "Night of the Long Knives." Following the SS slaughter of the SA leadership and the neutralization of the force, it diminished from four million to about one million in 1938, and then supported SS endeavors in such activities as training of army conscripts, auxiliary units attached to the army and SS, and ghetto and labor camp administration.

SS (*Schutzstaffel*): (Protective Detachment): A "racially elite" group of storm troopers, selected in 1923 to be Hitler's personal bodyguard and expanded to a vast police, military, and economic power dedicated to the destruction of Hitler's enemies. Hitler appointed Heinrich Himmler as *Reichsführer*-SS (Reich leader of the SS) and Himmler oversaw the establishment of the *Sicherheitsdienst* or SD (Security Service) and the *Rasse- and Siedlungshauptamt* (Race and Settlement Main Office) to ensure racial education and purity of SS members and the resettlement of Germans in the east. Himmler and the SS were rewarded for their murders of SA leaders in the "Night of the Long Knives" by receiving control of all police offices. After *Kristallnacht*, the SS controlled Jewish emigration. In 1939, the SS created an elite military force, the *Waffen* SS, from the SS-*Verfügungstruppen* (Special Purpose Troops) and *Totenkopf* (Death's Head) units. The *Waffen* SS became the military arm of the SS. As the duties of the SS expanded they included the murder of Jews and Gypsies, administration of ghettos and camps and forced labor supply to serve its military industrial complex.

Selections: (*Selektionen*): The process of separating those prisoners to be granted temporary survival for forced labor and those to be killed directly in the gas chambers. The term also referred to ghetto selection for deportation.

***Shoah*:** Hebrew term for the Nazi murder of six million Jews. Preferred to "Holocaust," with its sacrificial connotation.

***Shtetl*:** Yiddish word signifying a small, predominantly Jewish village in eastern Europe. Thousands were destroyed in the course of the Holocaust.

***Sonderkommando*: (Special Commandos):** These "Special Commandos" at extermination camps were assigned to remove bodies from gas chambers, extract gold teeth from the corpses, transfer them from gas chamber to crematoria, burn the bodies, and dispose of the remains.

Special Treatment: (*Sonderbehandlung*): Nazi-Deutsch deceptive term to conceal the genocide from those not directly involved in its implementation.

***Szmalcownicy*:** Polish word for extortionists and blackmailers of Jews in hiding.

***Umschlagplatz*:** A collection point in the ghettos for deportation, usually near a railroad siding.

UNRRA: United Nations Relief and Rehabilitation Administration, an organization established in 1943 to help displaced persons in postwar Europe.

Vichy: In June 1940, when Germany took Paris and the northern and western regions of France, Marshal Henri Philippe Pétain established the Vichy regime, an authoritarian and collaborationist French state in unoccupied France. In a series of laws adopted during the war, the Vichy regime intensified the Aryanization of France. In 1941, Jewish assets were confiscated. In the summer of 1942, Jews were rounded up and deported to the east. Occupied by the Axis powers when the Allies invaded North Africa in November 1942, Vichy France was controlled by Germany alone after the surrender of Italy to the Allies in the fall of 1943. Jews were deported until the liberation of France in 1944.

***Volksdeutsche*:** (Ethnic Germans) living outside the Reich as minority populations, largely in eastern Europe (including non-ethnic Germans who were related to Germans). These people were allowed to seize property of ghettoized and deported Jews from annexed and occupied territories.

Wannsee Conference: In the Wannsee district of Berlin, this January 20, 1942, meeting of fourteen top Nazi officials was called by Reinhard Heydrich, the head of the Reich Security Main Office, to discuss the implementation of the "Final Solution" (*Endlösung*), a policy accepted in late 1941. Heydrich presented the plan to deport all European Jews to the east, where they would be used as forced labor and exterminated.

***Wehrmacht*:** The German army (as distinguished from the SS).

Yellow Badge: As early as 1939 in occupied Poland, and then throughout occupied Europe, Jews were forced to wear star-shaped patches sewn on their clothes, or armbands marked with the Star of David.

***Yishuv*: (Jewish Community of Palestine):** Jews of pre-state Israel, the *Yishuv* worked to save the lives of European Jews: approximately 30,000 enlisted in the British army during the war, and in January 1943 the Jewish Agency for Palestine, with offices in Geneva and Istanbul, established the Joint Rescue Committee. The agency offered money to ransom Jews in ghettos and camps, provided immigration papers for Jews to enter Palestine, encouraged the Allies to bomb Auschwitz, and supported Jewish commandos who, eager to rescue Jews, were willing to parachute into German territories. Because it had no army of its own, limited resources, and its efforts were thwarted by the Allies, the *Yishuv* was unable to save large numbers of Jews.

***Zugang*:** A newcomer to camp, or a group of newly arrived prisoners, prior to loss of the attributes of free men and women and who did not understand the Nazi system into which they had been delivered.

ŻOB: the Jewish Fighting Organization established in the Warsaw ghetto on 28 July 1942.

Zyklon B: The pesticide hydrogen cyanide used to asphyxiate Jews and other prisoners of Auschwitz-Birkenau, and Majdanek.

ACKNOWLEDGEMENTS

We are grateful to the following publishers and individuals who granted permission to reprint copyrighted material.

Marjorie Agosín

Agosín, Marjorie, pp. 17, 23 from *Dear Anne Frank: Poems.* Copyright © 1998 by Brandeis University Press, reprinted by permission of University Press of New England.

Yehudah Amichai

Excerpts from OPEN CLOSED OPEN. Copyright © 2000 by Yehuda Amichai. English translation copyright © 2000 by Chana Bloch and Chana Kronfeld. Reprinted by permission of Harcourt, Inc.

''Jews in the Land of Israel'' and ''The Jews'' from YEHUDA AMICHAI: A LIFE OF POETRY 1948–1994 by YEHUDA AMICHAI. Copyright © 1994 by HarperCollins Publishers, Inc. Hebrew-language version copyright © 1994 by Yehuda Amichai. Reprinted by permission of HarperCollins Publishers, Inc.

''For ever and ever, sweet distortions'' from GREAT TRANQUILITY: QUESTIONS AND ANSWERS by YEHUDA AMICHAI. Translated by Glenda Abramson and Tudor Parfitt. Copyright © 1983 by Yehuda Amichai. Reprinted by permission of HarperCollins Publishers, Inc.

From *Open Closed Open.* Copyright © 2000 by Yehuda Amichai. English translation copyright © 2000 by Chana Bloch and Chana Kronfeld.

Amichai, Yehuda, p. 165 from *The Selected Poetry of Yehuda Amichai.* Translated and edited by Chana Bloch and Stephen Mitchell. Copyright © 1996. Reprinted by permission of University of California Press.

Albert Camus

Copyright © 1991 From *Testimony: Crises of Witnessing in Literature, Psychoanalysis, and History* by Shoshana Felman and Dori Laub. Reproduced by permission of Routledge, Inc., part of the Taylor & Francis Group.

Anne Duden

Permission granted by copyright holder.

Irving Feldman

By permission of Irving Feldman, passages from *New and Selected Poems.* Viking Penguin, 1979.

Passages from *The Life and Letters.* University of Chicago Press, 1994. By permission of Irving Feldman.

Karen Gershon

Excerpts from the following unpublished prose and poetry: ''A Tempered Wind''; ''The Historical and Legendary Esther''; ''Notes of a Heart-Patient.''

Excerpts from the following published poems: ''The Children's Exodus''; ''Monologue''; ''In the Park''; ''My Father''; ''To My Children''; ''Married Love''; ''Samson in Gaza''; ''Esther''; ''Cheder Boy.'' By permission of copyright holder.

Amir Gilboa

Permission for songs granted by composer ACUM, Israel.

Haim Gouri

Excerpts from *Words in My Lovesick Blood.* Permission granted by copyright holder.

Uri Zvi Greenberg

Excerpts from the works of Uri Zvi Grinberg. By permission of copyright holder.

Michael Hamburger

Collected Poems 1941–1994, Anvil Press, London. Published 1995.

Judith Herzberg

The Wedding Party. Copyright © 1997 by Judith Herzberg. Published by Nick Hern Books.

Judith Herzberg, *But What: Selected Poems,* translated by Shirley Kaufman with Judith Herzberg, Field Translation Series 13. Copyright © 1988 by Oberlin College. Reprinted by permission of Oberlin College Press.

Geoffrey Hill

From NEW AND COLLECTED POEMS 1952–1992 by Geoffrey Hill. Copyright © 1994 by Geoffrey Hill. Reprinted by permission of Houghton Mifflin Company. All rights reserved.

From THE TRIUMPH OF LOVE by Geoffrey Hill. Copyright © 1998 by Geoffrey Hill. Reprinted by permission of Houghton Mifflin Company. All rights reserved.

Yoel Hoffmann

Various excerpts by Yoel Hoffmann, translated by Eddie Levenston, David Kriss and Alan Treister, from KATSCHEN & THE BOOK OF JOSEPH. Copyright © 1987, 1988, by Yoel Hoffmann. Reprinted by permission of New Directions Publishing Corp.

Yitzhak Katzenelson

Excerpts reprinted from *Literature of Destruction: Jewish Responses to Catastrophe,* by David Raskies. Copyright © 1989, by The Jewish Publication Society. Used by permission.

Gertrud Kolmar

Gertrud Kolmar, *Weibliches Bildnis, Sämtliche Gedichte*. Copyright © Jüdischer Verlag im Suhrkamp Verlag. Alle Rechte vorbehalten.

Excerpts from DARK SOLILOQUY by Gertrud Kolmar. Copyright © 1975 by Gertrud Kolmar. Reprinted by permission of Continuum Books.

Rachel Korn

Seymour Levitan is a translator of Yiddish stories and poetry living in Vancouver, British Columbia. *PAPER ROSES,* his selection and translation of Rachel Korn's poetry, was 1988 winner of The Robert Payne Award of the Translation Center at Columbia University.

Olga Lengyel

Olga, L., 1948, interview by Survivors of the *Shoah* Visual History Foundation. New York, New York, United States, 28 August. Timecodes 1 through 11.

Anne Michaels

From *The Weight of Oranges/Miner's Pond* by Anne Michaels. Used by permission, McClelland & Stewart Ltd. *The Canadian Publishers.*

From *Skin Divers* by Anne Michael. Used by permission, McClelland & Stewart Ltd. *The Canadian Publishers.*

From *Fugitive Pieces* by Anne Michaels. Used by permission, McClelland & Stewart Ltd. *The Canadian Publishers.*

Kadya Molodowsky

All translations of Kadya Molodowsky in Kathryn Hellerstein's article are by Kathryn Hellerstein, from *Paper Bridges: Selected Poems of Kadya Molodowsky.* Translated, edited, and introduced by Kathryn Hellerstein (Detroit; Wayne State University Press, 1999). All rights reserved.

Jona Oberski

Permission granted by the Literary Agency Liepman AG Zürich.

Alicia Ostriker

Excerpt from "A Meditation in Seven Days" from THE LITTLE SPACE: POEMS SELECTED AND NEW, 1968–1998, by Alicia Ostriker. Copyright © 1998. Reprinted by permission of the University of Pittsburgh Press.

Excerpt from "Holocaust" from THE LITTLE SPACE: POEMS SELECTED AND NEW, 1968–1998, by Alicia Ostriker. Copyright © 1998. Reprinted by permission of the University of Pittsburgh Press.

Dan Pagis

Excerpts from *The Selected Poetry of Dan Pagis* by Dan Pagis. Translated and edited by Stephen Mitchell. Copyright © 1996 by The Regents of the University of California. Reprinted by permission of University of California Press.

János Pilinszky

Material by and on János Pilinszky quoted from: *Metropolitan Icons: Selected Poems of János Pilinsky in Hungarian and in English.* Edited and translated by Emery George (Lewiston, Queen, Lampeter: The Edwin Mellen Press, 1995). Copyright © 1995 by Emery George. All rights reserved.

Adrienne Rich

The lines from "Eastern War Time" from AN ATLAS OF THE DIFFICULT WORLD: Poems 1988–1991 by Adrienne Rich. Copyright © 1991 by Adrienne Rich. Used by permission of the author and W. W. Norton & Company, Inc.

The lines from "1941" from MIDNIGHT SALVAGE: Poems 1995–1998 by Adrienne Rich. Copyright © 1999 by Adrienne Rich. Used by permission of the author and W. W. Norton and Company, Inc.

Tadeusz Różewicz

Różewicz, Tadeusz; "The Survivor" and Other Poems. Copyright © 1977 by Princeton University Press. Reprinted by permission of Princeton University Press.

Taken from "Tadeusz Różewicz: They Came to See a Poet." Translations copyright © Adam Czerniawski. Published by Anvil Press Poetry in 1991.

From Różewicz, Tadeusz, *Recycling*. Translated Plebanek and Howard (Todmorden, England: Arc Publications, 2001).

Alan Shapiro

Alan Shapiro is the author of several books of poetry, most recently *Song and Dance* from Houghton Mifflin and *The Dead Alive and Busy*, winner of the 2001 Kingsley Tufts Award.

ACKNOWLEDGEMENTS

Art Spiegelman

From MAUS I: A SURVIVOR'S TALE/MY FATHER BLEEDS HISTORY by Art Spiegelman. Copyright © 1973, 1980, 1981, 1982, 1984, 1985, 1986 by Art Spiegelman. Used by permission of Pantheon Books, a division of Random House, Inc.

From MAUS II: A SURVIVOR'S TALE/AND HERE MY TROUBLE BEGAN by Art Spiegelman. Copyright © 1986, 1989, 1990, 1991 by Art Spiegelman. Used by permission of Pantheon Books, a division of Random House, Inc.

Ruth Whitman

Reprinted from *The Testing of Hannah Senesh* by Ruth Whitman, by permission of the Wayne State University Press.

Reprint of material in *The Testing of Hanna Senesh* by Ruth Whitman, by permission of the Wayne State University Press.

Itamar Yaoz-Kest

Reprinted from *Modern Hebrew Poetry*, University of Iowa Press (1980), Bernhard Frank, translator.

INDEX

Note: Page numbers in **bold** refer to the main entries.

C

E

F

G

H

I

N

O

P

Q

R

T

U

V

X

Y

Z